January 14-16, 2016
Cambridge, MA, USA

I0131885

Association for Computing Machinery

Advancing Computing as a Science & Profession

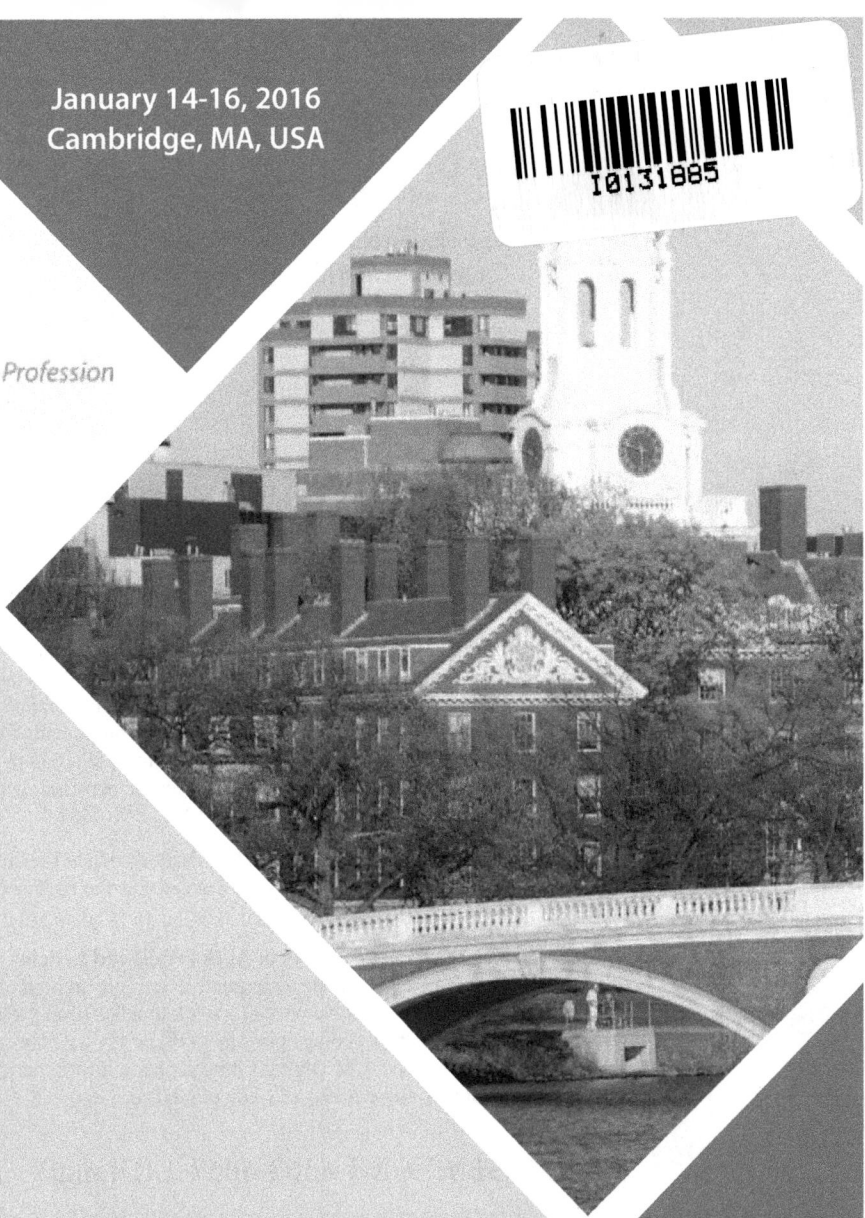

ITCS'16

Proceedings of the 2016 ACM Conference on
Innovations in Theoretical Computer Science

Sponsored by:
ACM SIGACT

Association for Computing Machinery

Advancing Computing as a Science & Profession

The Association for Computing Machinery
2 Penn Plaza, Suite 701
New York, New York 10121-0701

Copyright © 2015 by the Association for Computing Machinery, Inc. (ACM). Permission to make digital or hard copies of portions of this work for personal or classroom use is granted without fee provided that copies are not made or distributed for profit or commercial advantage and that copies bear this notice and the full citation on the first page. Copyright for components of this work owned by others than ACM must be honored. Abstracting with credit is permitted. To copy otherwise, to republish, to post on servers or to redistribute to lists, requires prior specific permission and/or a fee. Request permission to republish from: permissions@acm.org or Fax +1 (212) 869-0481.

For other copying of articles that carry a code at the bottom of the first or last page, copying is permitted provided that the per-copy fee indicated in the code is paid through www.copyright.com.

Notice to Past Authors of ACM-Published Articles
ACM intends to create a complete electronic archive of all articles and/or other material previously published by ACM. If you have written a work that has been previously published by ACM in any journal or conference proceedings prior to 1978, or any SIG Newsletter at any time, and you do NOT want this work to appear in the ACM Digital Library, please inform permissions@acm.org, stating the title of the work, the author(s), and where and when published.

ISBN: 978-1-4503-4057-1 (Digital)

ISBN: 978-1-4503-4415-9 (Print)

Additional copies may be ordered prepaid from:

ACM Order Department
PO Box 30777
New York, NY 10087-0777, USA

Phone: 1-800-342-6626 (USA and Canada)
+1-212-626-0500 (Global)
Fax: +1-212-944-1318
E-mail: acmhelp@acm.org
Hours of Operation: 8:30 am – 4:30 pm ET

Printed in the USA

Preface

The papers in this volume were presented at the 7th Innovations in Theoretical Computer Science (ITCS 2016) conference, sponsored by the ACM Special Interest Group on Algorithms and Computation Theory (SIGACT). The conference was held at the Massachusetts Institute of Technology in Cambridge, MA, USA, January 14–16, 2016. ITCS (previously known as ICS) seeks to promote research that carries a strong conceptual message, for instance, introducing a new concept or model, opening a new line of inquiry within traditional or cross-interdisciplinary areas, introducing new techniques, or making novel connections between existing areas and ideas. The conference format is single-session with ample time for discussion, to promote the exchange of ideas between different areas of theoretical computer science and with other disciplines.

The call for papers welcomed all submissions, whether aligned with current theory of computation research directions or deviating from them. 145 submissions were received. Of these, the program committee selected 40 papers. I would like to thank authors of all submissions for their interest in ITCS.

The program committee consisted of 23 members (plus the chair): Nikhil Bansal, Eindhoven; Eli Ben-Sasson, Technion; Bernard Chazelle, Princeton; Moritz Hardt, Google; Yuval Ishai, Technion; Brendan Juba, Washington U., St. Louis; Adam Kalai, MSR; Anna Karlin, U. Washington; Sanjeev Khanna, U. Penn.; Valerie King, U. Victoria; Katrina Ligett, Caltech; Ruta Mehta, Georgia Tech. ; Rotem Oshman, Tel Aviv; Rafael Pass, Cornell; Anup Rao, U. Washington; Omer Reingold, Samsung Research America; Aaron Roth, U. Penn.; Rocco Servedio, Columbia; Yaron Singer, Harvard; Adam Smith, Penn. State; Greg Valiant, Stanford; Thomas Vidick, Caltech; and Nisheeth Vishnoi, EPFL. I wish to express my sincere thanks to them for agreeing to join the committee and then for investing time and effort the merits of the submissions. The many subreviewers who assisted the reviewing process deserve acknowledgment as well.

The local organizations were undertaken by Shafi Goldwasser (MIT & Weizmann). I'd like to thank Shafi, for this service as also for her service as steering committee chair of ITCS while ITCS remains in its early stages! The submissions and program committee deliberations were conducted using the platform generated by Shai Halevi. I would like to thank Shai for generously contributing his time to the running of the system and helping me work with it! I would additionally like to thank IACR for hosting the server. I also thank Tim Roughgarden (Program Chair of ITCS 2015) for his help. Finally, I would like to thank all the presenters and the audience at ITCS and hope it continues to be a unique experience.

Madhu Sudan
ITCS 2016 Program Chair
Harvard University
Cambridge, MA USA

Preface

Table of Contents

Session 5

Session 6

Session 7

Session 8

Session 9

Session 10

Session 11

Author Index

ITCS 2016 Conference Organization

Program Chair: Madhu Sudan *(Harvard University)*

Local Organization: Shafi Goldwasser *(MIT & Weizmann Institute of Science)*

Steering Committee Chair: Shafi Goldwasser *(MIT & Weizmann Institute of Science)*

Steering Committee:
Sanjeev Arora, Princeton
Manuel Blum, Carnegie Mellon
Bernard Chazelle, Princeton
Oded Goldreich, Weizmann
Richard Karp, Berkeley
Ueli Maurer, ETH
Silvio Micali, MIT
Peter Bro Miltersen, Aarhus
Christos Papadimitriou, Berkeley
Michael Rabin, Harvard
Madhu Sudan, Harvard
Leslie Valiant, Harvard
Umesh Vazirani, Berkeley
Avi Wigderson, IAS
Andy Yao, Tsinghua

Program Committee:
Nikhil Bansal, Eindhoven
Eli Ben-Sasson, Technion
Bernard Chazelle, Princeton
Moritz Hardt, Google
Yuval Ishai, Technion
Brendan Juba, Washington U., St. Louis
Adam Kalai, MSR
Anna Karlin, U. Washington
Sanjeev Khanna, U. Penn.
Valerie King, U. Victoria
Katrina Ligett, Caltech
Ruta Mehta, Georgia Tech.
Rotem Oshman, Tel Aviv
Rafael Pass, Cornell
Anup Rao, U. Washington
Omer Reingold, Samsung Research America
Aaron Roth, U. Penn.

Program Committee (continued):
Rocco Servedio, Columbia
Yaron Singer, Harvard
Adam Smith, Penn. State
Greg Valiant, Stanford
Thomas Vidick, Caltech
Nisheeth Vishnoi, EPFL

Additional reviewers:

Nir Ailon
Andris Ambainis
Pablo Azar
Siddharth Barman
Paul Beame
Luca Becchetti
Iddo Ben-Tov
Vincenzo Bonifaci
Elette Boyle
Simina Branzei
Michael Brautbar
David Cash
Georgios Christodoulou
Kai-min Chung
Gil Cohen
Syamantak Das
Holger Dell
Stefan Dziembowski
Marc Fischlin
Parikshit Gopalan
Josh Grochow
Anupam Gupta
Iftach Haitner
Shai Halevi
Aram Harrow
Pavel Hrubes
Pavel Hubacek
Stephen Jordan
Valentine Kabanets
David Kempe
Arindam Khan
Bobby Kleinberg
Gillat Kol
Antonina Kolokolova
Ilan Komargodski

Swastik Kopparty
Amit Kumar
Troy Lee
Daniel Lokshtanov
Shachar Lovett
Mohammad Mahmoody
Guillaume Malod
Antonio Marcedone
Raghu Meka
Eric Miles
Shay Moran
Omer Paneth
Ariel Procaccia
Oded Regev
Dana Ron
Noga Ron-Zewi
Guy Rothblum
Ron Rothblum
Aviad Rubinstein
Atri Rudra
Sushant Sachdeva
Chandan Saha
Lior Seeman
Karn Seth
Abhi Shelat
Sasha Sherstov
Amir Shpilka
Nikhil Srivastava
Frank Stephan
Sebastien Tavenas
Sidharth Telang
Madhur Tulsiani
Nithin Varma
Matt Weinberg
Amir Yehudayoff

Can Almost Everybody be Almost Happy?
PCP for PPAD and the Inapproximability of Nash

Yakov Babichenko*
Technion
yakovbab@tx.technion.ac.il

Christos Papadimitriou†
UC Berkeley
christos@cs.berkeley.edu

Aviad Rubinstein‡
UC Berkeley
aviad@cs.berkeley.edu

ABSTRACT

We conjecture that PPAD has a PCP-like complete problem, seeking a near equilibrium in which all but very few players have very little incentive to deviate. We show that, if one assumes that this problem requires exponential time, several open problems in this area are settled. The most important implication, proved via a "birthday repetition" reduction, is that the $n^{O(\log n)}$ approximation scheme of Lipton et al. [23] for the Nash equilibrium of two-player games *is essentially optimum*. Two other open problems in the area are resolved once one assumes this conjecture, establishing that certain approximate equilibria are PPAD-complete: Finding a *relative* approximation of two-player Nash equilibria (without the well-supported restriction of [14]), and an approximate competitive equilibrium with equal incomes [10] with small clearing error and near-optimal Gini coefficient.

1. INTRODUCTION

It is known that finding an ϵ-approximate Nash equilibrium in a two-person game:

1. is PPAD-complete if ϵ is inversely polynomial [12];

2. but can be solved in quasipolynomial time for any fixed $\epsilon > 0$ [23]; and

3. the smallest known polynomially attainable approximation ratio is still over $\frac{3}{10}$ [28].

These three facts articulate rather dramatically the mystery, by now almost a decade old, of the problem's approximability.

Can the inversely polynomial inapproximability bound of [12] be improved to constant? Unlikely, because by [23] this would imply a quasipolynomial algorithm for the iconic problem in PPAD:

---

*Research supported by ISF grant 2021296.
†Part of the work was done at Simons Institute for the Theory of Computing. Research supported by NSF grant CCF1408635 and by Templeton Foundation grant 3966

Permission to make digital or hard copies of all or part of this work for personal or classroom use is granted without fee provided that copies are not made or distributed for profit or commercial advantage and that copies bear this notice and the full citation on the first page. Copyrights for components of this work owned by others than ACM must be honored. Abstracting with credit is permitted. To copy otherwise, or republish, to post on servers or to redistribute to lists, requires prior specific permission and/or a fee. Request permissions from Permissions@acm.org.

ITCS'16, January 14–16, 2016, Cambridge, MA, USA.
© 2016 ACM. ISBN 978-1-4503-4057-1/16/01 ...$15.00.
http://dx.doi.org/10.1145/2840728.2840731.

Definition 1. END OF THE LINE: ([15]) Let S and P be two circuits with (at most) $\tilde{O}(n)$ gates each (computing the predecessor and successor correspondences) with n input bits and n output bits each, such that $P(0^n) = 0^n \neq S(0^n)$, find an input $x \in \{0,1\}^n$ such that $P(S(x)) \neq x$ or $S(P(x)) \neq x \neq 0^n$.

Conventional wisdom, supported by black-box lower bounds [21, 5], is that this problem requires exponential time to solve. In direct analogy with the exponential time hypothesis [22], we state the following:

CONJECTURE 1. END OF THE LINE *requires* $2^{\tilde{\Omega}(n)}$ *time.*

It was recently shown that this conjecture implies an identical lower bound for the GCIRCUIT problem [12, 15]: Recall that a standard arithmetic circuit has inputs, outputs, and gates that define arithmetic operations on its lines. In a generalized circuit there are no outputs, and the dependencies between values become cyclical, thereby inducing a constraint satisfaction problem: the variables correspond to the values on the lines, and each gate induces a constraint on the incoming and outgoing lines. The ϵ-GCIRCUIT is defined to be the problem of finding values on the lines that ϵ-approximately satisfy all the constraints induced by the arithmetic gates. It was recently shown [26] that ϵ-GCIRCUIT is PPAD-complete for some small constant ϵ, via $\tilde{O}(n)$ reductions. Therefore, Conjecture 1 implies that, for some small $\epsilon > 0$, roughly exponential time is required to find a solution to this problem. There are several known ways to further reduce the ϵ-GCIRCUIT problem to the two-player Nash equilibrium problem; however, all of these reductions fail to preserve the quality of approximation, and, as we pointed out above, it is likely that no approximation-preserving reductions are possible, as this would imply a quasipolynomial-time algorithm for END OF THE LINE through the algorithm in [23], contradicting Conjecture 1.

In this paper, we identify a plausible new conjecture, a strengthening of Conjecture 1 in a natural and novel direction, which implies that the quasipolynomial approximation algorithm of [23] is optimum. In particular, we define the (ε, δ)-GCIRCUIT *to be the problem of finding values for the variables (lines) that* ε-*approximately satisfy a fraction of at least* $(1 - \delta)$ *of the constraints (gates).*

CONJECTURE 2. *There exist constants* $\epsilon, \delta > 0$ *such that there is a quasilinear reduction from* END OF THE LINE *to the problem* (ϵ, δ)-GCIRCUIT. *Therefore, also assuming Conjecture 1,* (ϵ, δ)-GCIRCUIT *requires* $2^{\tilde{\Omega}(n)}$ *time.*

As we have mentioned, this latter statement, albeit with $\delta = 0$, is known to follow from only Conjecture 1, for some $\epsilon > 0$ [26].

The Connection to PCP

The (ϵ, δ)-GCIRCUIT problem is a constraint satisfaction problem: each line/mixed strategy is a real variable, and each gate/player defines a constraint. Since we are considering ϵ-approximate satisfaction of the constraints, each variable need be represented using only a constant (depending on ϵ) number of bits. Therefore, a satisfying assignment (truncations of a Nash equilibrium) can be distinguished from an unsatisfying one (one violating the $(\epsilon - \delta)$-relaxation) by querying a constant (proportional to $1/\delta$) number of bits of the input, determined at random (but of course not uniformly so). This suggests that Conjecture 2 can be interpreted as a probabilistically checkable proof formulation of GCIRCUIT: informally, it states that "PPAD has a PCP" (that is, a complete problem whose witnesses can be verified by examining, at random, a finite number of bits).

The main result of this paper, explained next, reveals another similarity between the PCP formulation of NP and the (ϵ, δ)-GCIRCUIT problem: The intractability of the latter problem implies, among several other inapproximability theorems, the strongest possible inapproximability result for the 2-player Nash equilibrium problem, arguably the central open question in the area.

The Main Result

We denote by ε-2NASH the problem of finding an ϵ-Nash equilibrium in a bimatrix game. Our main result is the following:

THEOREM 1. *There is an $\varepsilon > 0$ such that, assuming Conjecture 2, solving ε-2NASH for two-player games with n strategies requires $n^{\tilde{\Omega}(\log n)}$ time.*

Our proof, given in Section 3, employs the technique of "birthday repetition," pioneered by [1] and used in different contexts by [8], and in particular by [9] to show intractability of a Nash equilibrium-related problem. Starting from a polymatrix game with two strategies per player and in which the player interactions form a cubic bipartite graph with n nodes on each side, the players on both sides are broken into blocks of size $\sqrt{n}$. The game is simulated by a two-player game, in which each player simulates the nodes in one of the sides of the bipartite graph by choosing a block and a strategy for each node in it; that is, the total number of actions of each of the two players is about $2^{\sqrt{n}}$, and such is the complexity of the reduction (this is necessary if one wishes to rule out better than quasipolynomial algorithms). The interactions between blocks, plus certain particular side games played by the two players, ensure a faithful enough simulation of the original multimatrix game.

Remark 1. It is not hard to see that a quasipolynomial lower bound follows from a weaker assumption than Conjecture 2, namely that the (ϵ, δ)-GCIRCUIT problem requires $2^{\tilde{\Omega}(n^{\alpha})}$ time, *for some $\alpha > \frac{1}{2}$.*

In addition to Theorem 1, we prove two other complexity consequences of Conjecture 2, solving certain open problems in the area: An improved inapproximability result for

the problem of relative (multiplicative) approximation of the Nash equilibrium first established by Dskalakis [14], and an inapproximability result for the problem of finding a competitive equilibrium with equal incomes and indivisible goods [10, 25] when one seeks to minimize the Gini index of the income distribution.

2. (ϵ, δ)-GCIRCUIT AND WEAK APPROXIMATE NASH

Generalized circuits are similar to the standard algebraic circuits, the main difference being that generalized circuits contain cycles, which allow them to verify fixed points of continuous functions. We restrict the class of generalized circuits to include only a particular list of gates described below. Formally,

Definition 2. [Generalized circuits, [12]] A *generalized circuit* $\mathcal{S}$ is a pair $(V, \mathcal{T})$, where V is a set of nodes and $\mathcal{T}$ is a collection of gates. Every gate $T \in \mathcal{T}$ is a 5-tuple $T = G(\zeta \mid v_1, v_2 \mid v)$, in which

$$G \in \{G_\zeta, G_{\times\zeta}, G_=, G_+, G_-, G_<, G_\vee, G_\wedge, G_\neg\}$$

is the type of the gate; $\zeta \in \mathbb{R} \cup \{nil\}$ is a (optional) real parameter; $v_1, v_2 \in V \cup \{nil\}$ are the first and second input nodes of the gate (one or both of them may be missing); and $v \in V$ is the output node; no two distinct gates have the same output.

Alternatively, we can think of each gate as a constraint on the values on the incoming and outgoing wires. We are interested in the following constraint satisfaction problem: given a generalized circuit, find an assignment to all the wires that simultaneously satisfies all the gates. When every gate computes a continuous function of the incoming wires, a solution must exist by Brouwer's fixed point theorem.

In particular, we are interested in the approximate version of this CSP, where we must approximately satisfy most of the constraints.

Definition 3. Given a generalized circuit $\mathcal{S} = (V, \mathcal{T})$, we say that an assignment $\mathbf{x}: V \to [0, 1]$ (ϵ, δ)-*approximately satisfies* $\mathcal{S}$ if for all but a δ-fraction of the gates, $\mathbf{x}$ satisfies the corresponding constraints.

Gate	Constraint
$G_\zeta(\alpha \parallel a)$	$\mathbf{x}[a] = \alpha \pm \epsilon$
$G_{\times\zeta}(\alpha \mid a \mid b)$	$\mathbf{x}[b] = \alpha \cdot \mathbf{x}[a] \pm \epsilon$
$G_=(\mid a \mid b)$	$\mathbf{x}[b] = \mathbf{x}[a] \pm \epsilon$
$G_+(\mid a, b \mid c)$	$\mathbf{x}[c] = \min(\mathbf{x}[a] + \mathbf{x}[b], 1) \pm \epsilon$
$G_-(\mid a, b \mid c)$	$\mathbf{x}[c] = \max(\mathbf{x}[a] - \mathbf{x}[b], 0) \pm \epsilon$
$G_<(\mid a, b \mid c)$	$\mathbf{x}[c] = \begin{cases} 1 \pm \epsilon & \mathbf{x}[a] < \mathbf{x}[b] - \epsilon \\ 0 \pm \epsilon & \mathbf{x}[a] > \mathbf{x}[b] + \epsilon \end{cases}$
$G_\vee(\mid a, b \mid c)$	$\mathbf{x}[c] = \begin{cases} 1 \pm \epsilon & \mathbf{x}[a] = 1 \pm \epsilon \text{ or } \mathbf{x}[b] = 1 \pm \epsilon \\ 0 \pm \epsilon & \mathbf{x}[a] = 0 \pm \epsilon \text{ and } \mathbf{x}[b] = 0 \pm \epsilon \end{cases}$
$G_\wedge(\mid a, b \mid c)$	$\mathbf{x}[c] = \begin{cases} 1 \pm \epsilon & \mathbf{x}[a] = 1 \pm \epsilon \text{ and } \mathbf{x}[b] = 1 \pm \epsilon \\ 0 \pm \epsilon & \mathbf{x}[a] = 0 \pm \epsilon \text{ or } \mathbf{x}[b] = 0 \pm \epsilon \end{cases}$
$G_\neg(\mid a \mid b)$	$\mathbf{x}[b] = \begin{cases} 1 \pm \epsilon & \mathbf{x}[a] = 0 \pm \epsilon \\ 0 \pm \epsilon & \mathbf{x}[a] = 1 \pm \epsilon \end{cases}$

Given a generalized circuit $\mathcal{S} = (V, \mathcal{T})$, (ϵ, δ)-GCIRCUIT is the problem of finding an assignment that (ϵ, δ)-approximately satisfies it.

Definition 4. In an (ϵ,δ)-*weak approximate Nash equilibrium at most a δ-fraction of the players can gain more than ϵ by deviating.*

THEOREM 2. *Conjecture 2 is equivalent to the following statement: There exist constants $\epsilon',\delta' > 0$, such that finding an (ϵ',δ')-weak approximate Nash equilibrium in a polymatrix graphical game with degree 3 and 2 actions per player requires $2^{\tilde{\Omega}(n)}$ time.*

PROOF. The reduction from (ϵ,δ)-GCIRCUIT to (ϵ',δ')-weak approximate Nash equilibrium follows analogously to the reduction in [26] from ϵ-GCIRCUIT to ϵ'-approximate Nash equilibrium.

The first step is to reduce (ϵ,δ)-GCIRCUIT to $(\Theta(\epsilon^2),\Theta(\epsilon\cdot\delta))$-GCIRCUIT with fan-out 2. The naive way to do this is to replace larger fan-outs with a binary tree of $G_=$ gates. Daskalakis et al. [15] successfully use this method for exponentially small ϵ, but for constant ϵ the iterative application of $G_=$ gates accumulates too much noise ($\Theta(\epsilon\cdot\log n)$). Instead, we follow [26] and focus on logical gates whose noise does not accumulate. Given an output of a logical gate ($G_<, G_\vee, G_\wedge, G_\neg$), we can introduce a binary tree (with even depth) of $G_\neg$ gates that copy the original output instead of having a single gate with a large fan-out. When we begin with an output of an arithmetic gate ($G_\zeta, G_{\times\zeta}, G_=, G_+, G_-$), we first use $\Theta(1/\epsilon)$ gates of types $G_=$ and $G_<$ to parse it into an ϵ-precision unary representation. Then, we copy each bit in the unary representation using a tree of $G_\neg$ gates. Finally, we (approximately) recover the original value from each copy of the unary representation using $\Theta(1/\epsilon)$ gates of types $G_{\times\zeta}$ and G_+. Notice that the number of new gates introduced for each gate at the leaves of the binary tree is $\Theta(1/\epsilon)$. Therefore, if the solution to the new (fan-out 2) instance violates an $O(\delta\cdot\epsilon)$-fraction of the gate-constraints, then it induces a solution to the original (arbitrary fan-out) instance that violates at most a δ-fraction of the constraints. (See the full version of [26] for more details.)

We now reduce (ϵ,δ)-GCIRCUIT with fan-out 2 to (ϵ',δ')-weak approximate Nash equilibrium. Daskalakis et al. construct, for each gate in the generalized circuit, a game gadget with a few players whose mixed strategies at approximate equilibrium simulate the computation carried by the gate. In other words, every approximate equilibrium of the gate gadget induces an approximately satisfying assignment to the corresponding input and output lines in the generalized circuit. See Lemma 1 for an example of such a gadget. The gadgets are concatenated by identifying the "output player" of one gadget with the "input player(s)" of the next gadget(s) in the generalized circuit. Since each gadget is composed of only a constant number of players, if all but a δ'-fraction of the players play approximately at equilibrium, all but a $\delta = \Theta(\delta')$-fraction of the gates are violated by the induced assignment to the generalized circuit.

The above construction suffices to show hardness for an $(\hat{\epsilon},\delta')$-weak well-supported Nash equilibrium, i.e. one for where all but a δ'-fraction of the players, every action in the support is $\hat{\epsilon}$-approximately best response. Finally, for constant degree graphical games, it is not hard to derive an $(\hat{\epsilon},\delta')$-weak well-supported Nash equilibrium from any (ϵ',δ')-weak approximate Nash equilibrium for $\epsilon' = \Theta(\hat{\epsilon}^2)$ [26, Lemma 4].

In the other direction, from (ϵ',δ')-weak approximate Nash equilibrium to (ϵ,δ)-GCIRCUIT, it suffices to construct a generalized circuit that computes an ϵ'-approximate best response of each player (except a δ'-fraction). Notice that in a graphical game with a constant number of actions per player, given a profile of mixed strategies, one only needs a constant number of arithmetic gates to compute a best response of any player. In particular, to compute an ϵ-approximate best response it suffices to use gates of finite precision $\epsilon' = \Theta(\epsilon)$. Finally, since the number of gates per player is constant, if at most a δ-fraction of the gates are ϵ-unsatisfied, they can appear in the best-response computation for at most a $\delta' = \Theta(\delta)$-fraction of the players. $\square$

LEMMA 1. *($G_{\times\zeta}$ gadget, [15])*
Let v_1, v_2, and w be players in a graphical game, and suppose that the payoffs of v_2 and w are as follows.

Payoff for v_2:

		w plays 0	w plays 1
	v_2 plays 0	0	1
	v_2 plays 1	1	0

Payoffs for w:

game with v_1:

		v_1 plays 0	v_1 plays 1
	w plays 0	0	ζ
	w plays 1	0	0

game with v_2:

		v_2 plays 0	v_2 plays 1
	w plays 0	0	0
	w plays 1	0	1

Then, in every ϵ-NE $\mathbf{p}[v_2] = \min(\zeta\mathbf{p}[v_1],1) \pm \epsilon$, where $\mathbf{p}[u]$ denotes the probability that u assigns to strategy 1.

PROOF. (Sketch) If $\mathbf{p}[v_2] > \zeta\mathbf{p}[v_1] + \epsilon$, then in every ϵ-NE $\mathbf{p}[w] = 1$, which contradicts $\mathbf{p}[v_2] > \epsilon$. Similarly, if $\mathbf{p}[v_2] < \min(\zeta\mathbf{p}[v_1],1) - \epsilon$, then $\mathbf{p}[w] = 0$, which yields a contradiction when $\mathbf{p}[v_2] < 1 - \epsilon$. $\square$

3. PROOF OF MAIN THEOREM

3.1 Overview

The proof is a reduction from weak approximation of Nash equilibrium in a polymatrix game (recall Theorem 2) to the two-player problem. The two players simultaneously play three games: the main game, which is the heart of the reduction; and two games based on a construction due to Althofer [2], which impose structural properties of any approximate Nash equilibrium (interestingly, the oblivious lower bound of [16] uses the same game). The final payoff of a player is the sum of payoffs in all three games. For convenience of notation, the payoffs in each game will be in $[0,1]$; in order to normalize the payoffs in the final game to $[0,1]$ one should multiply by $1/3$ the payoffs in all three games.

Main game

We let each of the two players "control" the vertices on one side of the bipartite graphical game (we henceforth use *players* only for the players in the bimatrix game, and refer to the players in the graphical polymatrix game as *vertices*). For ease of notation, we assume wlog that each player controls an equal number of vertices, n.

We partition the vertices of each player into n/k disjoint subsets of size at most $2k = 2\sqrt{n}$, such that every two subsets share at most 18 edges. By Lemma 6, we can efficiently find such a partition. Let $(S_1, \ldots, S_{n/k})$ and $(T_1, \ldots, T_{n/k})$ denote the partitions of the respective players. Each action of the players corresponds to a choice of a subset (out of n/k subsets in the partition), and a choice of an action for each vertex in the subset (out of at most 2^{2k} vectors of actions). Together, the main game has $\left(\frac{n}{k} \cdot 2^{2k}\right) \times \left(\frac{n}{k} \cdot 2^{2k}\right)$ action profiles. When players choose actions $(S_i, \vec{\alpha}_{S_i})$ and $\left(T_j, \vec{\beta}_{T_j}\right)$, the payoff of the row player is the sum of the payoffs over all shared edges of S_i and T_j, when they play the respective strategies from $\vec{\alpha}_{S_i}$ and $\vec{\beta}_{T_j}$ (here we use the polymatrix structure of the payoffs in the graphical game; the payoffs are defined over edges and therefore payoffs of a certain vertex can be defined even though not necessarily all its neighbours are playing). Finally, we normalize by $\lambda/18$, where $\lambda = \Theta(\delta^2)$ is a small constant that satisfies $\lambda > \epsilon'$. Similarly the payoff of the second player is derived from the payoffs of the vertices in T_j.

Althofer's games

Althofer's game [2] is an asymmetric hide-and-seek win-lose game over l locations. The hider chooses a location $i \in [l]$, the seeker chooses a subset $B \subset [l]$ of size $|B| = l/2$. The hider wins if $i \notin B$, the seeker wins if $i \in B$. Namely, the payoff function is given by

$$u_1(i, B) = 1 - u_2(i, B) = \begin{cases} 1 & \text{if } i \notin B \\ 0 & \text{if } i \in B. \end{cases}$$

In Althofer's game each player can guarantee $\frac{1}{2}$ by uniform play, therefore the value of the game is $\frac{1}{2}$. Althofer's game enjoys the following strong property: in every ε-approximate Nash equilibrium, the hider must play a mixed strategy that is $O(\varepsilon)$-close to the uniform distribution in total variation distance; see [16].

In our game each player plays two (unrelated) Althofer's games, one game as a hider, and one as a seeker. When player 1 is a hider, the locations are the sets $S_1, \ldots, S_{n/k}$ (i.e., $l = n/k$). The action from the main game $(S_i, \vec{\alpha}_{S_i})$ determines the location, where for the purposes of Althofer's game we ignore $\vec{\alpha}_{S_i}$. When player 1 is a seeker, the locations are the sets $T_1, \ldots, T_{n/k}$, and player 1 chooses an action to play in this game, independent of $(S_i, \vec{\alpha}_{S_i})$. The total number of actions for player 1 is $\left(\frac{n}{k} \cdot 2^{2k}\right) \cdot \binom{n/k}{n/(2k)} = 2^{\tilde{O}(\sqrt{n})}$. Similarly, for player 2, who is playing as a hider over $T_1, \ldots, T_{n/k}$, and as a seeker over $S_1, \ldots, S_{n/k}$.

3.2 Structure of an equilibrium

For a mixed action x of player 1 we denote by $x(S_i)$ the total probability that the player chooses to control the vertices S_i; i.e.,

$$x(S_i) = \sum_{\vec{\alpha} \in 2^{[k]}, B \subset \{T_1, \ldots, T_{n/k}\}, |B| = \frac{n}{2k}} x(((S_i, \vec{\alpha}), B)).$$

LEMMA 2. *If (x, y) is an ϵ'-Nash equilibrium, then*

$$\sum_{i \in [n/k]} \left| x(S_i) - \frac{k}{n} \right| = O(\lambda).$$

In the proof we use the following lemma from the full version of [16]:

LEMMA 3 ([16]). *Let $\{a_i\}_{i \in [l]}$ be real numbers satisfying the following properties for some $\theta > 0$: (1) $a_1 \geqslant a_2 \geqslant \ldots \geqslant a_l$; (2) $\sum_{i \in [l]} a_i = 0$; and (3) $\sum_{i \in [l/2]} a_i \leqslant \theta$. Then $\sum_{i \in [l]} |a_i| \leqslant 4\theta$.*

PROOF PROOF OF LEMMA 2. In order apply Lemma 3, we denote $a_i = x(S_i) - \frac{k}{n}$ and we assume wlog that $x(S_1) \geqslant x(S_2) \geqslant \ldots \geqslant x(S_{n/k})$. Then the first two conditions hold. Regarding the third condition, we argue that $\sum_{i \in [l/2]} x(S_i) \leqslant 3\lambda$ this will complete the proof.

Player 1 can guarantee a payoff of $1/2$ in the sum of Althofer's games as a hider and the main game, by playing uniformly and choosing an arbitrary actions for the controlled vertices (for instance, $\vec{\alpha}_{S_i} = \vec{0}$). Assume by contradiction that $\sum_{i \in [l/2]} x(S_i) > 3\lambda$. Since Player 2 is ϵ'-best replying, his payoff in the Althofer game (as a seeker) is at least $\frac{1}{2} + 3\lambda - \epsilon'$ (because he can get $1/2 + 3\lambda$ by choosing the set $[l/2]$). Therefore, Player 1's payoff in the Althofer game (as a hider) is at most $\frac{1}{2} - 3\lambda + \epsilon'$. If we add to it his payoffs in the main game, then his payoff is at most $\frac{1}{2} - 2\lambda + \epsilon'$. Therefore, player 1 can increase his payoff by $2\lambda - \epsilon' > \epsilon'$ by deviating to the uniform distribution over the locations (as a hider), and maintaining his mixed action as a seeker. $\square$

3.3 Completing the proof

Any mixed strategy x of player 1 in the bimatrix game induces a mixed strategy of all the vertices in $\cup_i S_i$ in the obvious way. Vertex $s \in S_i$ plays the action 1 with probability p where p is the conditional probability

$$Pr_x(\vec{\alpha}_{S_i}(s) = 1 | \text{Player 1 controls } S_i).$$

If the event "Player 1 controls S_i" occurs with probability 0, then we define (arbitrarily) that $p = 1$. Similarly, any mixed strategy y of player 2 induces a mixed strategy of all the vertices in $\cup_i T_i$.

We claim that if (x, y) is an ϵ'-approximate Nash equilibrium of the bimatrix game, then the induced mixed-strategies profile is an (ϵ, δ)-approximate Nash equilibrium of the original graphical game.

By Lemma 2 and Markov's inequality, for a $\left(1 - O\left(\sqrt{\lambda}\right)\right)$-fraction of the subsets, the row player distributes within a $\left(1 \pm O\left(\sqrt{\lambda}\right)\right)$-factor of the correct weight (k/n); i.e. $x(S_i) \in \frac{k}{n} \cdot \left[1 - O\left(\sqrt{\lambda}\right), 1 + O\left(\sqrt{\lambda}\right)\right]$. Let us restrict our attention only to those subsets, and call them *good*. We say that a vertex is *good* if it and all of its neighbors belong to good subsets. Since the game graph is of bounded degree, we again have that a $\left(1 - O\left(\sqrt{\lambda}\right)\right)$-fraction of the vertices is good.

Consider any good vertex whose induced mixed strategy is not ϵ-optimal in the original game given that the rest of the vertices also play according to their induced strategies. Then, changing its strategy in the bimatrix game (while leaving all other marginals the same), would increase the payoff of its player by at least

$$\left(1 - O\left(\sqrt{\lambda}\right)\right)^2 \cdot \left(\frac{k}{n}\right)^2 \cdot \left(1 - O\left(\sqrt{\lambda}\right)\right) \cdot \epsilon \cdot \frac{\lambda}{18} = \Omega\left(\epsilon\lambda/n\right),$$

where the $\left(1 - O\left(\sqrt{\lambda}\right)\right)^2 \cdot \left(\frac{k}{n}\right)^2$ term corresponds to the probabilities that the subsets corresponding to both the vertex and any of its neighbors are played; the $\left(1 - O\left(\sqrt{\lambda}\right)\right) \cdot \epsilon$ term corresponds to the improvement of the vertex in the bimatrix game, where instead of summing the payoff in all three edges (as in the graphical game) these three edges have weights $\{1 + \gamma_j\}_{j=1,2,3}$ for $|\gamma_j| = O(\sqrt{\lambda})$; finally $\lambda/18$ is the normalization. The right side follows by plugging in $k = \sqrt{n}$.

If (by a contradiction) a δ-fraction of the vertices have ϵ-improvement strategies; then one of the players has $\left(\delta/2 - O\left(\sqrt{\lambda}\right)\right) \cdot n$ good vertices with an ϵ-improvement[1]. This player can benefit $\Omega\left(\epsilon \cdot \lambda/n\right)$ from a deviation of each vertex. So his total improvement from all deviations simultaneously is $\Omega\left(\epsilon \cdot \delta \cdot \lambda\right)$ - which is impossible when (x, y) is an ϵ'-approximate Nash equilibrium for $\epsilon' = \Theta(\epsilon \cdot \delta \cdot \lambda)$.

4. IMPLICATIONS FOR RELATIVE ϵ-APPROXIMATE NASH

Daskalakis [14] defines a notion of relative (sometimes also called *multiplicative* [20], as opposed to the more standard additive) ϵ-Nash equilibrium, and proves that in two-player games with payoffs in $[-1, 1]$, finding a relative ϵ-well supported Nash equilibrium is PPAD-complete. In particular, he concludes that the quasi-polynomial algorithm of Lipton et al. [23] cannot achieve this notion of approximate equilibrium.

This result has two caveats: (1) Through the use of positive and negative payoffs, the gain from deviation is large compared to the expected payoff, only because the latter is small due to cancellation of positive and negative payoffs. Namely, the gain from deviation may be very small compared to the expected magnitude of the payoff. (2) It only applies to the more restrictive notion (thus rendering the hardness result weaker) of *well-supported* approximate equilibrium; i.e. an equilibrium where every action in the support has to be approximately optimal. Showing PPAD-hardness for both positive payoffs and general (non well-supported) approximate equilibrium were left as open questions in [14]. Recently, the first question was settled in [26] where it was shown that finding a relative ϵ-well-supported Nash equilibrium with positive payoffs is indeed PPAD-complete.

Here, assuming Conjecture 2, we settle the second question: we show that finding any relative ϵ-approximate Nash equilibrium is PPAD-complete. Furthermore, in our hard instance the row player has only positive payoffs and the column player has only negative payoffs, and so there is no cancellation of payoffs as in the construction of [14].

THEOREM 3. *Assuming Conjecture 2 there exists a constant $\epsilon' = \Theta\left(\epsilon \cdot \delta^3\right) > 0$ such that finding a relative ϵ'-approximate Nash equilibrium (ANE) in a bimatrix game where the row player's payoffs are non-negative and the column player's payoffs are non-positive is PPAD-complete.*

Proving a similar theorem when both players have positive payoffs remains an interesting open question. In fact, we do not know of any instances with positive payoffs where all ϵ-approximate Nash equilibria must have large (e.g., linear, or even super-logarithmic) support.

---

[1] Here we use our choice of $\lambda = \Theta(\delta^2)$, which guarantees that $\delta/2 - O\left(\sqrt{\lambda}\right) = \Omega(\delta)$

PROOF. We reduce from the problem of finding an (additive) (ϵ, δ)-Nash in a bipartite, degree 3, polymatrix game with two actions per player. We construct a main game where the bimatrix game players (henceforth just *players*) control the nodes of the polymatrix game, and two side games that guarantee that each player randomizes (approximately) uniformly over all her nodes.

Main game We let the row player "control" the nodes on one side of the bipartite game graph, and let the column player control the nodes on the other side. Namely, let n be the number of nodes on each side of the graph; each player has $2n$ actions, each corresponding to a choice of node and an action for that node. When the players play strategies that correspond to adjacent nodes in the graphs, they receive the payoffs of the corresponding nodes, scaled (by a small positive constant $\eta = O\left(\delta^2\right)$) and shifted to fit in the intervals: $[1, 1 + \eta]$ for the row player, and $[-(1 + \eta), -1]$ for the column player. If the nodes played do not share an edge in the bipartite game graph, the utility for both players is zero. Notice that if either player chooses her node uniformly at random (and chooses the action for that node arbitrarily), then the expected payoff is in $\frac{3}{n} \cdot [1, 1 + \eta]$ for the row player, and in $\frac{3}{n} \cdot [-(1 + \eta), -1]$ for the column player.

Side games We also let the players play two hide-and-seek win-lose zero-sum games over a space of n actions. In both games, the row player is chasing the column player. In each game, if they pick the same strategy, the row player receives payoff 1 (and the column player receives -1); otherwise the payoffs are 0. Finally, in the first side game we identify the row player's strategies with her choice of nodes in the main game. Namely, if she plays node i in the main game and the column player chose i in the first side game, then her payoff from this side game is 1. Similarly, we identify the column player's strategies in the second game with her choice of nodes in the main game.

We proceed by showing that in every relative ϵ'-ANE, the row player's utility is approximately $5/n$, and the column player's utility is approximately $-5/n$ (Lemma 4); then we show that in every relative ϵ'-ANE, both players randomize approximately uniformly over their nodes (Lemma 5); finally we use these two observations to complete the proof (Subsection 4.2). □

4.1 Value and structure of a relative ϵ'-ANE

Given mixed strategies (x, y), we let $x(i)$ denote the total probability that the row player assigns to node i, and analogously for $y(j)$. We also let $x^*(y)$ and $y^*(x)$ denote the corresponding best responses of each player. Finally, let $U_R(x; y)$ and $U_C(y; x)$ denote the expected payoffs for the row and column players, respectively.

LEMMA 4. *If (x, y) is a relative ϵ'-ANE, then*

$$\left(1 - \epsilon'\right) \cdot \frac{5}{n} \leqslant U_R\left(x; y\right) \leqslant \left(1 + \eta\right)\left(1 + \epsilon'\right) \cdot \frac{5 + 3\eta}{n} \quad (1)$$

and

$$-\left(1 - \epsilon'\right)\left(1 - \eta\right) \cdot \frac{5}{n} \geqslant U_C\left(y; x\right) \geqslant -\left(1 + \epsilon'\right) \cdot \frac{5 + 3\eta}{n} \quad (2)$$

5

PROOF. Observe that the main game is relative η-approximately zero-sum; i.e. for any pure strategy profile (x', y') the expected utilities $U_R^{\text{main}}(x'; y')$, $U_C^{\text{main}}(y'; x')$ of the row and column player, respectively, satisfy:

$$\left| U_R^{\text{main}}(x'; y') + U_C^{\text{main}}(y'; x') \right| \leq$$
$$\eta \cdot \min \left\{ U_R^{\text{main}}(x'; y'), -U_C^{\text{main}}(y'; x') \right\} \quad (3)$$

By linearity of expectation and convexity of the absolute value function, this continues to hold when (x', y') are mixed strategies. Furthermore, since the side games are exactly zero-sum and have the same signs as the main game, the same follows for the payoffs from the entire game:

$$\left| U_R(x'; y') + U_C(y'; x') \right| \leq \eta \cdot \min \left\{ U_R(x'; y'), -U_C(y'; x') \right\} \quad (4)$$

In particular, the above inequality holds for (x, y). Thus, the upper bounds in (1) and (2) follow from the lower bounds in (2) and (1), respectively.

Finally, $(1 - \epsilon') \cdot \frac{5}{n} \leq U_R(x; y)$ in every relative ϵ'-ANE, because the row player can guarantee an expected payoff of at least $\frac{5}{n}$ by randomizing uniformly over all her strategies. Similarly, $U_C(y; x) \geq -(1 + \epsilon') \left(\frac{3(1+\eta)+2}{n} \right)$ because the column player can guarantee a payoff of at least $-\frac{3(1+\eta)+2}{n}$ by randomizing uniformly over all her strategies. $\square$

LEMMA 5. *There exists a constant $\lambda = \Theta(\delta^2)$ such that for every (x, y) relative ϵ'-ANE, $\sum \left| x(i) - \frac{1}{n} \right| \leq \lambda$ and $\sum \left| y(j) - \frac{1}{n} \right| \leq \lambda$.*

PROOF. *Assume by contradiction that $\sum \left| x(i) - \frac{1}{n} \right| > \lambda$, then in particular there must exist an $i \in [n]$ such that $x(i) < (1 - \lambda/2)/n$. When the column player chooses her strategy uniformly at random in the main game and in the second side game and plays strategy i in the first side game, her expected payoff is at least*

$$U_C(y^*(x); x) \geq -\frac{3}{n}(1 + \eta) - \frac{1}{n} - x(i).$$

Therefore, in any relative ϵ'-ANE her expected utility is at least

$$U_C(y; x) \geq (1 + \epsilon') \cdot \left(\frac{-5 - 3\eta + \lambda/2}{n} \right),$$

Which contradicts the upper bound in (2) when we take λ sufficiently large, e.g. $\lambda = 10\eta$.

Similarly, if $\sum \left| y(j) - \frac{1}{n} \right| > \lambda$, there must exist an $j \in [n]$ such that $y(j) > (1 + \lambda/2)/n$. Therefore, the row player can guarantee a payoff of at least

$$U_R(x^*(y); y) \geq \frac{4}{n} + y(j).$$

Thus by relative ϵ'-ANE,

$$U_R(x; y) \geq (1 - \epsilon') \cdot \left(\frac{5 + \lambda/2}{n} \right),$$

which contradicts the upper bound in (1). $\square$

4.2 Completing the proof of Theorem 3

Now, given a relative ϵ'-ANE (x, y), we can take, for each node i, the mixed strategy induced by the probabilities

$x(i:1)/x(i)$ and $x(i:2)/x(i)$ that the row player assigns to each action (respectively, $y(j:1)/y(j)$ and $y(j:2)/y(j)$ assigned by the column player). We claim that this strategy profile is an (ϵ, δ)-approximate equilibrium for the polymatrix game. Assume by contradiction that this is not the case.

By Lemma 5 and Markov's inequality, a $\left(1 - O\left(\sqrt{\lambda}\right)\right)$-fraction of the nodes are played within $\frac{\sqrt{\lambda}}{n}$ of the correct probability $1/n$. For a node i controlled by the row player, we say that it is *good* if $|x(i) - 1/n| \leq \frac{\sqrt{\lambda}}{n}$ and $|y(j) - 1/n| \leq \frac{\sqrt{\lambda}}{n}$ $\forall j \in \mathcal{N}(i)$, and analogously for column player's nodes. Since the graph has bounded degree, a $\left(1 - O\left(\sqrt{\lambda}\right)\right)$-fraction of the nodes are good.

Let i be any good node who has an ϵ-improving deviation from her induced strategy in the polymatrix game. If the player who controls i makes the corresponding deviation in the two-player game, she increases her expected payoff by at least $\epsilon \cdot \eta \cdot \frac{1}{n^2} \cdot \left(1 - O\left(\sqrt{\lambda}\right)\right)$. (We multiply by η to account for the scaling; by $1/n^2$ for the probability that this player plays node i and the other player plays a neighbor of i; and by $\left(1 - O\left(\sqrt{\lambda}\right)\right)$ to correct for the deviation from $1/n$ in the latter probabilities.) By our assumption that the induced strategy profile is not an (ϵ, δ)-approximate equilibrium for the polymatrix game, at least one of the players has at least $\left(\delta - O\left(\sqrt{\lambda}\right)\right) n$ good nodes with ϵ-improving deviations. Summing her gains from those deviations, we get that this player has can improve her expected payoff by at least $\left[\epsilon \cdot \eta \cdot \left(1 - O\left(\sqrt{\lambda}\right)\right)\right] \left(\delta - O\left(\sqrt{\lambda}\right)\right) / n$.

However, this is a contradiction since it follows from Lemma 4, that (x, y) is also an (additive) $\epsilon' \cdot \left(\frac{6}{n}\right)$-ANE. $\square$

5. IMPLICATIONS FOR FAIRNESS MECHANISMS

Competitive equilibrium from equal incomes (CEEI) is a well-known fair allocation mechanism [18, 29, 27]: We give all agents a unit of money, and price the goods in such a way that the market clears. It is also well-known that when goods are indivisible or utilities are non-linear, an equilibrium may not exist. However, Budish [10] proves that an approximate CEEI still exists. This concept of approximate equilibrium is used in practical system for allocating seats in courses to business school students [11].

Budish [10] measures the proximity to a perfect CEEI via two parameters: a solution is an (α, β)-CEEI if the clearing error of the competitive equilibrium is less than α, and all the incomes are between 1 and $1 + \beta$. Budish shows that an (α, β) always exists for some favorable $\alpha = \alpha^*$, and any $\beta > 0$. Recently, [25] showed a reduction from ϵ-GCIRCUIT with fan-out 2, to the problem of finding an $(\alpha^*, \Theta(\epsilon/\log(1/\epsilon)))$-CEEI. In particular, when combined with the results of [26], this implies that it is PPAD-complete to find an (α^*, β)-CEEI for some constant $\beta > 0$.

The β parameter used in Budish's formulation is an imperfect way of measuring income inequalities, as it may be set by a single outlier. Perhaps the best known, and most widely used, measure of income inequality is the *Gini index* (e.g. [19, 13]) (see the Appendix for the definition). In fact, the Gini index is used to assess the performance of the class seat assignment system used in practice [11].

THEOREM 4 (INFORMAL). *Assuming Conjecture 2, finding an income assignment and prices with low market clearing error and near-optimal Gini index is PPAD-complete.*

See the appendix for the precise definitions and statement of the result.

6. DISCUSSION

The purpose of this paper is to showcase an important open problem:

reduce END OF THE LINE **to** (ϵ, δ)-GCIRCUIT

— i.e., show that Conjecture 1 implies Conjecture 2. As we mentioned, such a reduction would imply a "PCP for PPAD"; i.e. it would imply that there exists a probabilistically checkable proof for a PPAD-complete problem.

The equivalent statement for the class of NP-complete problem, is the celebrated PCP Theorem [4, 3]. What can we learn from our experience with constructing PCP's for NP? First of all, we have many different constructions of PCPs for NP, and this may be seen as circumstantial evidence that constructing a PCP for PPAD is possible. Equally important, there are several constructions of PCPs for NP that are near-linear (e.g. [6, 7, 17, 24]); notice that for the application to ϵ-Nash in bimatrix games we need the proof length to be sub-quadratic.

The next question one should ask is, whether we can adapt the techniques used in the proofs of the PCP Theorem to the class of PPAD-complete problems. We briefly and informally sketch some of our thoughts on the matter. All the proofs of the PCP Theorems that we are aware of (including [4, 3, 17]) compose an *inner verifier* with an *outer verifier*. The outer verifier in Dinur's proof [17] is combinatorial in nature, and it seems plausible that the same or similar techniques could be modified to fit the generalized circuit graph. Unfortunately, all inner verifiers that we know are discrete in nature, whereas our characterization of PPAD with GCIRCUIT (or Nash) is inherently based on continuous constraints. Thus the following interesting (and somewhat open-ended) questions arise: Can we find a characterization of PPAD via a constraint satisfaction problem whose constraints are discrete in nature? Alternatively, can one construct an inner (non-efficient) verifier using the constraints specified in the definition of the GCIRCUIT problem?

Acknowledgments

Many thanks to Boaz Barak, Paul Cristiano, Muli Safra, and Madhu Sudan for inspiring discussions about probabilistic checkable proofs.

7. REFERENCES

[1] S. Aaronson, R. Impagliazzo, and D. Moshkovitz. Am with multiple merlins. In *Computational Complexity (CCC), 2014 IEEE 29th Conference on*, pages 44–55. IEEE, 2014.

[2] I. Althofer. On sparse approximations to randomized strategies and convex combinations. 1993.

[3] S. Arora, C. Lund, R. Motwani, M. Sudan, and M. Szegedy. Proof verification and the hardness of approximation problems. *J. ACM*, 45(3):501–555, 1998.

[4] S. Arora and S. Safra. Probabilistic checking of proofs: A new characterization of NP. *J. ACM*, 45(1):70–122, 1998.

[5] P. Beame, S. A. Cook, J. Edmonds, R. Impagliazzo, and T. Pitassi. The relative complexity of NP search problems. *J. Comput. Syst. Sci.*, 57(1):3–19, 1998.

[6] E. Ben-Sasson, O. Goldreich, P. Harsha, M. Sudan, and S. P. Vadhan. Robust pcps of proximity, shorter pcps, and applications to coding. *SIAM J. Comput.*, 36(4):889–974, 2006.

[7] E. Ben-Sasson and M. Sudan. Robust locally testable codes and products of codes. *Random Struct. Algorithms*, 28(4):387–402, 2006.

[8] M. Braverman, Y. Kun-Ko, A. Rubinstein, and O. Weinstein. ETH Hardness for Densest-k-Subgraph with Perfect Completeness. In submission.

[9] M. Braverman, Y. Kun-Ko, and O. Weinstein. Approximating the best nash equilibrium in $n^{o(\log n)}$-time breaks the exponential time hypothesis. In *Proceedings of the Twenty-Sixth Annual ACM-SIAM Symposium on Discrete Algorithms, SODA 2015, San Diego, CA, USA, January 4-6, 2015*, pages 970–982, 2015.

[10] E. Budish. The combinatorial assignment problem: Approximate competitive equilibrium from equal incomes. *Journal of Political Economy*, 119(6):1061 – 1103, 2011.

[11] E. Budish, G. P. Cachon, J. Kessler, and A. Othman. Course match: A large-scale implementation of approximate competitive equilibrium from equal incomes for combinatorial allocation. Working paper, 2014.

[12] X. Chen, X. Deng, and S.-H. Teng. Settling the complexity of computing two-player nash equilibria. *J. ACM*, 56(3), 2009.

[13] F. Cowell. *Measuring inequality*. Oxford University Press, 2011.

[14] C. Daskalakis. On the complexity of approximating a nash equilibrium. *ACM Transactions on Algorithms*, 9(3):23, 2013.

[15] C. Daskalakis, P. W. Goldberg, and C. H. Papadimitriou. The complexity of computing a nash equilibrium. *Commun. ACM*, 52(2):89–97, 2009.

[16] C. Daskalakis and C. H. Papadimitriou. On oblivious ptas's for nash equilibrium. In *Proceedings of the 41st Annual ACM Symposium on Theory of Computing, STOC 2009, Bethesda, MD, USA, May 31 - June 2, 2009*, pages 75–84, 2009. Full version available at http://arxiv.org/abs/1102.2280.

[17] I. Dinur. The PCP theorem by gap amplification. *J. ACM*, 54(3):12, 2007.

[18] D. Foley. Resource Allocation and the Public Sector. *Yale Economic Essays*, 7(1):45–98, 1967.

[19] C. Gini. Variabilità e mutabilità. *Reprinted in Memorie di metodologica statistica (Ed. Pizetti E, Salvemini, T). Rome: Libreria Eredi Virgilio Veschi*, 1, 1912.

[20] S. Hémon, M. de Rougemont, and M. Santha. Approximate Nash Equilibria for Multi-player Games. In *SAGT*, pages 267–278, 2008.

[21] M. D. Hirsch, C. H. Papadimitriou, and S. A. Vavasis.

Exponential lower bounds for finding brouwer fix points. *J. Complexity*, 5(4):379–416, 1989.

[22] R. Impagliazzo and R. Paturi. On the complexity of k-sat. *J. Comput. Syst. Sci.*, 62(2):367–375, 2001.

[23] R. J. Lipton, E. Markakis, and A. Mehta. Playing large games using simple strategies. In *EC*, pages 36–41, 2003.

[24] D. Moshkovitz and R. Raz. Sub-constant error probabilistically checkable proof of almost-linear size. *Computational Complexity*, 19(3):367–422, 2010.

[25] A. Othman, C. H. Papadimitriou, and A. Rubinstein. The complexity of fairness through equilibrium. In *EC*, pages 209–226, 2014.

[26] A. Rubinstein. Inapproximability of nash equilibrium. In *STOC*, 2015. To appear.

[27] W. Thomson and H. Varian. Theories of justice based on symmetry. *Social Goals and Social Organizations: Essays in Memory of Elisha Pazner*, 1985.

[28] H. Tsaknakis and P. G. Spirakis. An optimization approach for approximate nash equilibria. *Internet Mathematics*, 5(4):365–382, 2008.

[29] H. Varian. Equity, envy, and efficiency. *Journal of Economic Theory*, 9(1):63–91, 1974.

APPENDIX

A. FINDING A GOOD PARTITION

LEMMA 6. *Let $G = (U, V, E)$ be a bipartite d-regular graph with $n = |U| = |V|$. Then we can efficiently find partitions $S_1, \ldots, S_{n/k}$ and $T_1, \ldots, T_{n/k}$ of U and V, respectively, to disjoint subsets, such that each subset has size at most $2k$, and:*

$$\forall i, j \in [n/k] \quad |(S_i \times T_j) \cap E| \leqslant 2d^2 k^2/n.$$

PROOF. Let $S_1, \ldots, S_{n/k}$ be an arbitrary partition of U into disjoint subsets of size exactly k. We inductively place the vertices of V into subsets $T_1, \ldots, T_{n/k}$, while maintaining the desiderata that each subset T_j is of size at most $2k$, and for every i, j the number of edges from S_i to T_j is at most $2d^2 k^2/n$.

It is left to show that for any partial partition of V, there is a subset T_J into which we can place the next vertex v. In expectation, every subset T_j has less than k vertices. Therefore by Markov's inequality, less than half of the subsets have $2k$ vertices or more. v has neighbors in at most d subsets S_i. Recall that the S_i's are of size exactly k. Thus each S_i with a neighbor of v has, in expectation over j, less than dk^2/n neighbors in T_j. Using Markov's inequality again, less than a $1/(2d)$-fraction of the subsets T_j contain $2d^2 k^2/n$ neighbors of S_i. In total, we lose less than half the subsets for the size desideratum, and less than $1/(2d)$-fraction of the subsets for each S_i containing a neighbor of v. Therefore there always remains at least one subset T_j to which we can add v. □

B. THE COURSE ALLOCATION PROBLEM

Even though the approximate CEEI and the existence theorem in [10] are applicable to a broad range of allocation problems, we shall describe our results in the language of the course allocation problem.

We are given a set of M courses with integer capacities (the supply) $(q_j)_{j=1}^M$, and a set of N students, where each student i has a set $\Psi_i \subseteq 2^M$ of permissible course bundles, with each bundle containing at most $k \leqslant M$ courses. The set Ψ_i encodes both scheduling constraints (e.g., courses that meet at the same time) and any constraints specific to student i (e.g. prerequisites).

Each student i has a strict ordering over her permissible schedules, denoted by $\preccurlyeq_i$. We allow arbitrarily complex preferences — in particular, students may regard courses as substitutes or complements. More formally:

Definition 5. **Course Allocation Problem** The input to a course allocation problem consists of:

- For each student i a set of course bundles $(\Psi_i)_{i=1}^N$.
- The students' reported preferences, $(\preccurlyeq_i)_{i=1}^N$,
- The course capacities, $(q_j)_{j=1}^M$, and

The output to a course allocation problem consists of:

- Prices for each course $(p_j^*)_{j=1}^M$,
- Allocations for each student $(x_i^*)_{i=1}^N$, and
- Budgets for each student $(b_i^*)_{i=1}^N$.

The quality of an allocation is evaluated based on its proximity to market clearing and income equality. As for the definition of market clearing error, it suffices for our purposes to require that no course is over-subscribed or under-subscribed by more than α^* students (we refer the curious reader to [10] for the precise definition). The Gini coefficient, which measures income inequality, is discussed in the following subsection.

B.1 The Gini coefficient

Definition 6. Gini index. Given a distribution of incomes D, the *Lorenz curve* plots, for each $x \in [0, 1]$, the cumulative wealth owned by the bottom x-fraction of the population. Let $F_D^{-1}(x) = \sup \{y : \Pr_{z \sim D}[z \leqslant y] \leqslant x\}$, and define $L_D(x) = \left(\int_0^x F_D^{-1}(x)\right) / \left(\int_0^1 F_D^{-1}(x)\right)$. Then the Lorenz curve is the graph $(x, L_D(x))$, for $x \in [0, 1]$. Notice that $F_D^{-1}(x)$ is monotonically non-decreasing, so the Lorenz curve is convex.

The *Gini index* is defined as the ratio of the area between the (x, x) line and the Lorenz curve (by the convexity, $x \geqslant L_D(x) \forall x \in [0, 1]$), divided by the entire area under the (x, x) line (the latter is always 1/2): $G_D = 2\int_0^1 (x - L_D(x))dx = 1 - 2\int_0^1 L_D(x)dx$

In general, a smaller Gini index corresponds to a more equal distribution of wealth. For example, when all incomes are exactly equal, the Lorenz curve is exactly equal to the (x, x) line, and the Gini index is 0. On the other extreme, when one person has all the wealth, the area under the Lorenz curve goes to 0 as the population size increases, and the Gini index approaches 1.

B.2 Intractability of approximate CEEI with near-optimal Gini index

THEOREM 5 (THEOREM 4, FORMAL). *Assuming Conjecture 2, there exists some constant $\gamma > 0$ such that finding an allocation with market clearing error α^* and Gini coefficient γ is* PPAD-*complete.*

The rest of this section is devoted to sketching a proof of Theorem 4. In the next subsection, we briefly outline the reduction of [25] from generalized circuits with fan-out 2 to approximate CEEI. (Recall that in Section 2 we show how to convert any generalized circuit to one with fan-out 2.) Then, we show that after normalizing the median budget to $1 + \epsilon'/2$, in any allocation which does not correspond to a valid solution to the (ϵ, δ)-GCIRCUIT instance, a δ'-fraction of the students have budgets either at most 1 or at least $1 + \epsilon'$, (for some constants $\epsilon' = \Theta(\epsilon/\log(1/\epsilon))$ and $\delta' = \Theta(\delta/\log(1/\epsilon))$). Then, the proof is complete with the following lemma:

LEMMA 7. *Let the median income be $1 + \epsilon'/2$, and suppose that a δ'-fraction of the population has income at most 1 (resp. at least $1 + \epsilon'$). Then the Gini index is at least $\gamma = \Theta(\delta' \cdot \epsilon') = \Theta(\delta \cdot \epsilon/\log^2(1/\epsilon))$.*

PROOF. The total income of the poorer half of the population is at most $(1/2 - \delta')(1 + \epsilon'/2) + \delta' = (1/2)(1 + \epsilon'/2) - \delta' \cdot \epsilon'/2$, whereas the richer half of the population has a total income of at least $(1/2)(1 + \epsilon'/2)$. Therefore, the Lorenz curve's value at $1/2$ is bounded by

$$L(1/2) \leqslant \frac{(1/2)(1 + \epsilon'/2) - \delta' \cdot \epsilon'/2}{(1 + \epsilon'/2) - \delta' \cdot \epsilon'/2} = 1/2 - \Theta(\delta' \cdot \epsilon').$$

We can now use elementary geometry to bound the area under the Lorenz curve:

$$\int_0^1 L(x)dx = \int_0^{1/2} L(x)dx + \int_{1/2}^1 L(x)dx$$
$$\leqslant \frac{1}{4}\left[0 + (1/2 - \Theta(\delta' \cdot \epsilon'))\right] + \frac{1}{4}\left[(1/2 - \Theta(\delta' \cdot \epsilon')) + 1\right]$$
$$= 1/2 - \Theta(\delta' \cdot \epsilon').$$

Therefore the Gini index is at least $\Theta(\delta' \cdot \epsilon')$. A similar argument works when a δ'-fraction of the population has income at least $1 + \epsilon'$.

□

B.3 From generalized circuits to Course Allocation

[25] reduce generalized circuits to Course Allocation, by constructing a gadget for each gate of the generalized circuit. (In fact, a few gadgets per gate are required to handle a subtle issue that [25] call "course-size amplification".) We provide the gadget for the NOT gate as an example, and then describe the properties of the [25]'s reduction that we need to complete the proof.

We henceforth normalize the prices and budgets in every assignment to the Course Allocation instance such that the median budget is $1 + \epsilon'/2$.

LEMMA 8 (ESSENTIALLY [25]). *Let $n_x > 6\alpha^*$ and suppose that the economy contains the following courses:*

- *c_x (the "input course") ;*
- *c_{1-x} with capacity $q_{1-x} = 2n_x/3$ (the "output course");*

and the following set of students:

- *n_x students interested only in the schedule $\{c_x, c_{1-x}\}$;*

and suppose further that at most $n_{1-x} = n_x/6$ other students are interested in course c_{1-x}.

Then in any normalized approximate CEEI with market clearing error at most α^*, at least one of the following must hold:

The gate is ϵ'-satisfied

$$p^*_{1-x} \in \left[1 - p^*_x, 1 - p^*_x + \epsilon'\right]$$

The gadget contributes to income inequality *A constant fraction of the n_x students have budgets either less than 1 or greater than $1 + \epsilon'$.*

PROOF. Observe that:

- If $p^*_{1-x} > 1 - p^*_x + \epsilon'$, then none of the n_x students can afford the bundle $\{c_x, c_{1-x}\}$ - except those whose budget is greater than $1 + \epsilon'$. Other than them, there are at most $n_{1-x} = n_x/6$ students enrolled in the c_{1-x} - much less than the capacity $2n_x/3$. Therefore for the market clearing error to be less than $\alpha^* = n_x/6$, $n_x/3$ of the students must have budget greater than $1 + \epsilon'$

- On the other hand, if $p^*_{1-x} < 1 - p^*_x$, then all n_x students can afford the bundle $\{c_x, c_{1-x}\}$ - except for those whose budget is less than 1. Therefore in order to satisfy the market clearing requirement, at least $n_x/6$ students must have budget less than 1.

□

Similarly, [25] provide gadgets for all the gates in the definition of the GCIRCUIT problem, and show that they can be concatenated to simulate the computation on the generalized circuit. For each gate of the generalized circuit, [25]'s reduction uses at most $\Theta(1/\log(1/\epsilon))$ (in particular, a constant) number of gadgets. Furthermore, the number of students that participate in each of those gadgets is approximately the same ($\Theta(\alpha^*)$). Therefore, for every gate which is not ϵ-satisfied, there are at least $\Theta(\alpha^*)$ students whose budgets are either at most 1 or at least $1 + \epsilon'$. Thus if the assignment to the Course Allocation problem does not correspond to an (ϵ, δ)-approximate solution to GCIRCUIT, then a $\delta' = \Theta(\delta/\log(1/\epsilon))$-fraction of the students must have budgets at most 1 or at least $1 + \epsilon'$. Applying Lemma 7 completes the proof of Theorem 4. □

Mechanisms With Costly Knowledge*

Atalay M. Ileri
MIT
atalay@mit.edu

Silvio Micali
MIT
silvio@csail.mit.edu

ABSTRACT

We propose investigating the design and analysis of game theoretic mechanisms when the players have very unstructured initial knowledge about themselves, but can refine their own knowledge at a cost.

We consider several set-theoretic models of "costly knowledge". Specifically, we consider auctions of a single good in which a player i's only knowledge about his own valuation, θ_i, is that it lies in a given interval $[a,b]$. However, the player can pay a cost, depending on a and b (in several ways), and learn a possibly arbitrary but shorter (in several metrics) sub-interval, which is guaranteed to contain θ_i.

In light of the set-theoretic uncertainty they face, it is natural for the players to act so as to minimize their regret. As a first step, we analyze the performance of the second-price mechanism in regret-minimizing strategies, and show that, in all our models, it always returns an outcome of very high social welfare.

1. INTRODUCTION

It is a traditional tenet of mechanism design that each player i knows himself *perfectly*. This assumption strikes us as an oversimplification of our daily experience. Except for whatever innate knowledge we may have, most of us incur a considerable personal cost for the knowledge we acquire. Moreover, we seldom reach "perfect knowledge". Whether on an individual basis or a collective basis (e.g., in Science) we simply *refine* our knowledge.

Accordingly, we believe it is important to investigate mechanism design when the players are very self uncertain, but have the ability of reducing their own uncertainty at a *cost*. In this paper, we put forward a first class of "costly knowledge models" and use it to analyze the efficiency guarantees of second-price mechanism.

*Funding for this research was provided by the Division of Computer and Network Systems, a core program of the NSF, under award number CNS-1519135.

Permission to make digital or hard copies of part or all of this work for personal or classroom use is granted without fee provided that copies are not made or distributed for profit or commercial advantage and that copies bear this notice and the full citation on the first page. Copyrights for third-party components of this work must be honored. For all other uses, contact the owner/author(s).

ITCS'16 January 14-16, 2016, Cambridge, MA, USA

ⓒ 2016 Copyright held by the owner/author(s).

ACM ISBN 978-1-4503-4057-1/16/01.

DOI: http://dx.doi.org/10.1145/2840728.2840742

Our Goals

Distributional approaches naturally come to mind to model costly knowledge. Indeed, the traditional way to model uncertainty is via probability distributions. Although we encourage others to work on distributional models of costly knowledge, and we may choose to do so ourselves in the future, in this paper, to explore a less-travelled road, and start investigating *set-theoretic* models of costly knowledge.

Our first such model is purposely very basic; essentially, it is a costly version of binary search. More complex models are discussed in section 5.

Our first result analyzes the efficiency guarantees of the second price mechanism in all of our models. We believe and hope that the viability of these models can be also established for more complex mechanisms, new or old.

Our First Model

A player i has no information about the true valuations of his opponents. Moreover, at each point in time, the only information he has about his own true valuation, θ_i, consists of a "knowledge" interval $[a,b]$ guaranteed to contain θ_i.

If $[a,b] \neq [0,0]$, i may "refine" such knowledge interval by paying a cost inversely proportional to $\delta = \frac{b-a}{b}$ and learn whether θ_i lies in the first or the second half of $[a,b]$.

We respectively refer to $b-a$ and δ as the (absolute) *uncertainty* and the (relative) *inaccuracy* of i's knowledge.

Remarks.

- *Incomplete Preferences.* Having set-theoretic uncertainty about his true valuation θ_i, a player i may not be able to 'compare' all possible outcomes. If his current knowledge about θ_i consists of an interval $[a,b]$, then he is only sure that he prefers an outcome ω to another outcome ω' if his utility for ω is greater than or equal to his utility for ω', no matter which element of $[a,b]$ may be his true valuation.

  Of course, one might always and more simply assume that our players have complete preferences (e.g., that they maxmin preferences [22]), or that they behave as if —say— $\theta_i = \frac{a+b}{2}$). However,
  our players have incomplete preferences.

- *Enlarged Mechanisms.* Explicitly or not, our model *de facto* turns every given normal-form mechanism into one of extensive form. To be sure, all players continue to submit their reports "simultaneously". However, prior to submitting his report, based on his current knowledge, each player can choose whether or not to refine it. Formally, therefore, he chooses his own report by executing a single-player extensive-form (sub)mechanism.

- *Defining Accuracy.* Another natural choice for defining the inaccuracy of a knowledge interval $[a, b]$ of a player i is $\delta' = \frac{b-a}{a+b}$. In this case, δ represents the percentage with which i knows his own true valuation. Indeed, letting $x = \frac{a+b}{2}$, $\theta_i \in [a, b]$ is equivalent to say that

$$"\theta_i = x \pm \delta' x".$$

These two (and other) ways of defining inaccuracy are essentially semantically equivalent. However, choosing $\delta = \frac{b-a}{b}$ enables us to express the efficiency guarantees of the second-price mechanism more easily in *all* our models of costly knowledge.

- *Inaccuracy-Based Cost.* Of course, a player i's cost for refining a knowledge interval $[a, b]$ could be defined as a function of the interval's uncertainty, rather than its inaccuracy, but we find the latter choice more meaningful. For instance, consider two possible knowledge intervals for i: $[100, 200]$ and $[10^6, 10^6 + 100]$. In both cases, the uncertainty is 100. Intuitively, however, the effort required from i to determine whether θ_i is in the first half of the interval (or not) is much smaller in the first case than in the second.

- *Simplicity vs. Robustness.* In general, given a short interval $[a, b]$, a player i may rarely be sure that his true valuation θ_i belongs to $[a, b]$. The situation, however, is very different if $[a, b]$ is an interval that i obtains after investing a lot of effort in learning θ_i.[1] In any case, in the classical model, i is assumed to know θ_i exactly. Accordingly, even perfect self knowledge could be achievable (although without cost, or via a process preceding the execution of a given mechanism).

  Still, when θ_i lies very very close to the middle, m, of i's current knowledge interval, it may be unlikely that, by means of a single (and possibly low-cost) step, i can disambiguate whether $\theta_i \leq m$ or not. Indeed, our main reason to analyze first the basic knowledge model is conceptual and calculation simplicity, not robustness.

  As we shall see in section 5, however, the social-welfare guarantee of the second-price mechanism remains the same when the refinement of a given knowledge interval yields an arbitrary interval, of half the size, that continues to include θ_i. That is, our analysis continues to hold in a model that is more robust (in that no point of a knowledge interval constitutes a "point of discontinuity"), but more complex (indeed, non-deterministic).

- *Individualized Costs.* As we shall see, two players whose knowledge interval is the same, may have different costs for refining it.

---

[1]Indeed, for most goods, i can be confident, without investing any effort, that his valuation lies between 0 and one quadrillion dollars. And his subsequent confidence in smaller and smaller uncertainty about θ_i proceeds from the investments he makes to clarify the actual value of θ_i.

Rationality.

It is continuously debated whether players should be modeled as utility maximizers or as regret minimizers. When all players have available dominant strategies, the debate is mute, because a dominant strategy is both the only undominated strategy and the only regret-minimizing one. But when this is not the case, or when dominant-strategy mechanisms are essentially useless, it becomes important to take into consideration mechanisms implementing a given social-choice function, both in undominated strategies and in regret-minimizing ones. After all, utility maximizers will only play weakly undominated strategies, and regret-minimizers will only play regret-minimizing strategies, and both sets of strategies are are guaranteed to be non-empty, at least in every mechanism in which every player has finitely many pure strategies (hardly a restriction in practice).

In light of our model, of course, the classical notions of an undominated strategy and a regret-minimizing strategy are naturally extended so as also to take into account the set-theoretic knowledge the players have about themselves.

A First Result

Our main aim is to put forward a new model, more precisely, a new class of models. But when proposing new models, it is also important to prove that they are amenable to rational analysis.

Our only theorem, for now, proves that the second-price mechanism can be analyzed in all our costly knowledge models, and, in fact, continues to guarantee high social welfare in regret minimizing strategies.

In light of the set-theoretic self uncertainty a player faces in our model, it is natural for him to act so as to minimize his regret. Nonetheless, we find it important to point out that no mechanism can hope to deliver significant social welfare in dominant strategies or in undominated strategies. For notational simplicity, let us point out both facts, assuming that there are just two players.

Denote by I_i the initial knowledge of a player i. Then,

> *For all two-player dominant-strategy mechanism M (in which each player has a strategy guaranteeing him utility at least 0, all refinement costs are incurred by the players, and all payments are made by the players) and for all possible I_1 and I_2, there exist true valuations $\theta_1 \in I_1$ and $\theta_2 \in I_2$ for which M misses the maximum social welfare at least by the length of $I_1 \cap I_2$.*

The above statement implies that the performance of any dominant-strategy mechanism is quite poor in what we consider the typical case: namely, when the players have essentially the same initial knowledge $[a, b]$, so that the length of the intersection of their initial knowledge is approximately $b - a$. In fact, when this is the case, the above statement implies that no dominant-strategy mechanism can do better than assign the good to a random player. The above statement is not hard to prove: indeed, its proof is sketched in this footnote.[2]

---

[2]First, it is easy to show that the revelation principle holds in our model. Accordingly, we might focus our attention to direct dominant-strategy truthful mechanisms (i.e., mechanisms in which each player i is allowed to report an interval, and reporting truthfully I_i is i's best strategy). Second, it is trivial to show that a dominant-strategy truthful mechanism that does not inject money into the system and providing each player with a strategy guaranteeing him a non-negative

Unfortunately, the impossibility of guaranteeing significant social welfare also applies in practice to undominated-strategies mechanisms. In fact, as long as they are *finite* (i.e., assigning finitely many pure strategies to each player[3]), such mechanisms cannot guarantee a social welfare higher than that obtainable by assigning the good to a random player. More precisely,

> *For all finite mechanism M (probabilistic or not), all $\ell > 0$, all $\varepsilon \in (0, \ell)$, and all initial knowledge such that I_i and I_{-i} whose self uncertainty is ℓ and whose intersection has length ε, there exist a profile of true valuation θ and a profile s of undominated strategies for which M misses the maximum social welfare by $\ell - \varepsilon/2$.*

The proof of this second statement easily follows from the Undominated Intersection Lemma (i.e., lemma E.1) of [12].[4]

Since dominant- and undominated-strategy mechanisms are not very useful, we now consider regret and show that it is possible to guarantee excellent social welfare in regret-minimizing strategies. In fact, without having to look very far, we prove that it suffices to consider the second-price mechanism!

Theorem 1 (Informal): *For all initial knowledge intervals $[a_i, b_i]$, if the players are regret minimizers, then the second-price mechanism misses the actual maximum social welfare by at most $O(\sqrt{b_{\max}})$, that is, the square root of the maximum possible initial valuation.*

A precise statement of Theorem 1 and a sketch of its proof, relative to our first costly knowledge model, can be found in section 4. Extensions of Theorem 1 to our other costly knowledge models are discussed in section 5.

Remark

We note that, due to a lemma of [10], our main result also continues to hold when the players are utility maximizers who resort to regret minimization solely to refine further their set of undominated strategies (if it indeed contains multiple strategies).

2. RELATED WORK

Our model of self-uncertainty can be considered a special case of the one put forward a century ago by Knight [27], and later on refined by Bewley [3]. In their model, the only knowledge of a player i consists of a set of distributions, from one of which θ_i has been drawn. (Indeed, since our utility functions are convex, a risk-neutral player i may *de facto* shrink each such distribution to its expected value, so that his knowledge about himself consists of a set, that is, the mentioned generalization of our self-uncertainty model.)

Knightian uncertainty, however, does not envisage the possibility of decreasing uncertainty at a cost.

Knightian uncertainty has been extensively studied in decision theory, see for example [1, 18, 35, 34, 16, 39, 22, 31, 5, 4]. There is also a quite rich literature on equilibrium with incomplete preferences (e.g., [32, 21, 41, 20, 37]) and on ambiguous mechanisms (e.g., [17, 6]). All this literature, however, is not directly relevant to our work.

A mechanism for rent extraction with Knightian uncertainty has been studied by Lopomo, Rigotti and Shannon [29], but in a model quite different from ours, and without considering any notion of knowledge refinement. (See also [30].)

Kiekintveld et al. [26] study a two-player Stakelberg game in which a *defender* needs to allocate his resources when he has uncertainty, also modeled as an interval, about the *attacker*'s payoffs. However, the authors do not envision any self uncertainty for the defender or the attacker, nor any way to reduce this uncertainty, with or without cost.

Our model of self-uncertainty (generalized from intervals to sets) actually coincides with that used by Chiesa, Micali, and Zhou to analyze single-good auctions [9] and multi-unit auctions [12] in undominated strategies, as well as unrestricted combinatorial auctions, both in undominated strategies and in regret-minimizing ones [11]. They too, however, do not consider any type of knowledge refinement.

In a distributional model, uncertainty reduction, with or without cost, has been studied by Thompson and Leyton-Brown for a variety of auctions [43]. The same authors prove, in a separate paper [44], that, when the players can refine their own valuations, dominant strategy single-good auctions coincide with sequential posted-price auctions. Celis et al.[8] study revenue auctions in which the players can (non-adaptively) pay an upfront cost and reduce their own uncertainty to a predetermined desired level. Celis et al. [7] investigate revenue maximization in auctions in which a buyer (1) knows a distribution from which his own true valuation has been drawn, and (2) can, at a cost, privately refine his distribution. However, these works' uncertainty is not Knightian like ours. Indeed, they assume that every player knows the distribution from which his true valuation has been drawn, and can elicit a signal allows him to further constrain this distribution.

The the notion of regret minimization was introduced by Savage [38] (reinterpreting Wald [45]) and refined by Milnor [33] and recently Stoye [42]. Many empirical works provide evidence of regret minimization, for instance [2, 14, 13, 25]. Coricelli et al. [15] actually argue that neurological evidence exists for human propensity for regret minimization.

Regret minimization has been used to analyze mechanisms, for instance in [28, 19, 40, 24, 36]. Halpern and Pass [23] put forward the solution concept of *iterated regret minimization*, and argue that it is indeed a compelling one. Our solution concept lies between traditional and iterated regret minimization. In the latter concept, the players assume that their opponents are regret minimizers. In ours, the players assume nothing about their opponents's rationality.

3. PRELIMINARIES

Below we define our refinable knowledge model as a costly version of the basic binary search process. (More general models are considered in Section 5.)

---

[3]utility will *never* (i.e., no matter what the players' reports may be) refine the knowledge of any player. Third, and finally, it is trivial to check that our result statement holds when the mechanism does not refine the player's knowledge.

This technical restriction is very mild in practice, since de facto players have finitely many strategies. Certainly this is the case for all mechanisms played via computers.

[4]In our setting, this powerful lemma can be informally simplified as follows. If I_i and I_i' are two intervals, representing the knowledge of a player i about himself, containing at least two valuations in common, then i's corresponding set of undominated strategies contain at least one strategy in common.

3.1 The Basic Costly Knowledge Model

For each player $i \in N$,

- The *true valuation* of i, θ_i, is a non-negative real.

  A *knowledge interval* for i is an interval of non-negative reals containing θ_i.

  If $[a, b]$ is such an interval, then its *uncertainty* is $b - a$, and its *inaccuracy* is $\frac{b-a}{b}$.

- R_i is the *refining* function that, given a knowledge interval I, of i, $I = [a, b]$, returns $\left[a, \frac{a+b}{2}\right]$ if $\theta_i \leq \frac{a+b}{2}$, and $\left[\frac{a+b}{2}, b\right]$ otherwise.[5]

  We refer to each evaluation of R_i as a *refinement*, to the interval $R_i(I)$ as a *refinement* of I, and to evaluating R_i on I as *refining* I. When the player i is clear, we may write R instead of R_i.

- Player i starts with an *initial knowledge interval*, denoted by $I_i^0 = [a_i^0, b_i^0]$ or more simply by $I_i = [a_i, b_i]$.

  The *knowledge of i after t refinements*, $I_i^t = [a_i^t, b_i^t]$, is the interval obtained from I_i by iterating t times the function R. (I.e., $I_i^1 = R(I_i)$, $I_i^2 = R(R(I_i))$, ...)

- i's cost for refining an interval I of inaccuracy δ, $C_i(I)$, is $\frac{c_i}{\delta}$, where c_i is a positive constant known to i.

- *Self Uncertainty.* In our model, a player i has no information about the true valuations of his opponents. Moreover, at each point in time, the only information he has about his own true valuation of the good, θ_i, consists of an interval $[a, b]$ guaranteed to contain θ_i. We refer to such an interval $[a, b]$ as i's (current) "knowledge interval", or more simply as i's (self) "knowledge", to $b - a$ as i's current (self) uncertainty, and to the ratio $\delta = \frac{b-a}{b}$, if $[a, b] \neq [0, 0]$, as the inaccuracy of i's knowledge, or the interval $[a, b]$.

- *Refinements.* A player i has always the option of refining his current knowledge, $[a, b]$, at a cost $C_i(a, b)$. By exercising this option, i's new knowledge becomes $\left[a, \frac{a+b}{2}\right]$ if $\theta_i \leq \frac{a+b}{2}$, and $\left[\frac{a+b}{2}, b\right]$ otherwise.

  (Of course, $\left[\frac{a+b}{2}, b\right]$ implies that $\theta_i \in \left(\frac{a+b}{2}, b\right]$, but for uniformity sake all knowledge intervals are closed.)

- *Costs.* A player's refinement cost is proportional to the inaccuracy of his knowledge. If the inaccuracy of $[a, b]$ is δ, then $C_i(a, b) = \frac{c_i}{\delta}$, where c_i is a player-dependent positive constant.

3.2 Single-Good Auctions in Our Model

As usual, an auction consists of (1) a context, specifying the set of possible outcomes, the players (including their initial knowledge), and their preferences over outcomes, and (2) a mechanism, specifying the players' strategies and how strategies lead to outcomes.

Our Contexts

- An outcome consists of
  - an *allocation*, a profile of bits a, $\sum_i a_i \leq 1$, where for each player i, $a_1 = i$ if and only if the good is allocated to i;
  - a profile of *prices*, $p \in \mathbb{R}^n$; and

- a profile of *total refinements*, r, where r_i is the number of times player i has refined his knowledge.

- The utility of a player i, with valuation v_i and initial knowledge I_i^0, for an outcome $\omega = (a, p, r)$, is

$$u_i(\omega) \triangleq a_i \cdot v_i - p_i - \sum_{t=0}^{r_i-1} C_i(I^t).$$

Our Mechanisms

We consider mechanisms in which (like in the second-price mechanism), each player i reports a bid $\beta_i \geq 0$ simultaneously with his opponents. However, i's set of pure strategies, S_i, does not coincide with the set of possible bids, $\mathbb{R}_{\geq 0}$, but with the set of strategies in the single-player extensive-form (sub)mechanism pictorially described below

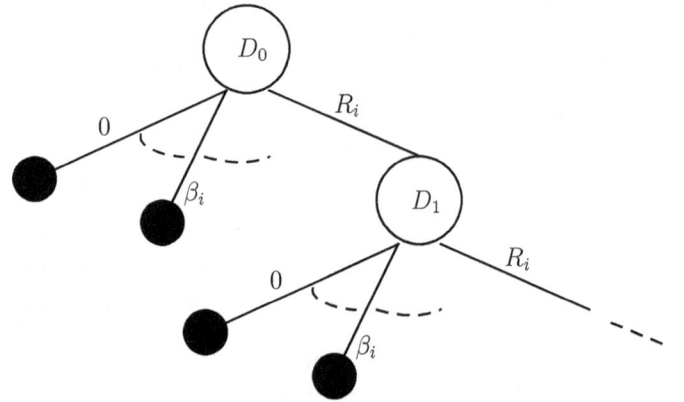

Figure 1: The Bidding Submechanism of Player i

That is, in the bidding submechanism of player i, the decision nodes, $D_0, D_1, \ldots$, are pictorially represented by "empty circles" and correspond to the number of times i has refined his knowledge interval. The terminal nodes are represented by "full circles", and correspond to i's actual bids.

A bit more precisely,

- Player i starts executing his bidding submechanism at the decision node D_0, the "root", where the information available to him consists of his initial knowledge, I_i^0.

- At every decision node D_t, the information available to i consists of the knowledge interval I_i^t, and i's action set is $\{R_i\} \cup \mathbb{R}_{\geq 0}$.

- At a decision node D_t, if he chooses an action $\beta_i \in \mathbb{R}_{\geq 0}$, then i terminates executing his bidding submechanism and reports only the bid β_i to the mechanism. Else (if i chooses the refining action R_i), the decision node D_{t+1} is reached and the bidding submechanism continues.

In every auction mechanism we consider, the underlying bidding mechanism for each player i is as above. Accordingly, the set of all pure strategies of i, S_i, always coincides with the set of all functions from $\{D_0, D_1, \ldots\}$ to $\{R_i\} \cup \mathbb{R}_{\geq 0}$.

The outcome of a mechanism M under a strategy profile s (i.e., the outcome produced by M relative to the bid profile β corresponding to s) is $M(s)$.

---

[5]More precisely, but "less uniformly", if $R([a, b]) = \left[\frac{a+b}{2}, b\right]$, then $\theta_i \in \left(\frac{a+b}{2}, b\right]$.

3.3 Regret

In a mechanism M, relative to i's initial knowledge I_i,

- i's *regret for a strategy* $s_i \in S_i$ is

$$reg_i(I_i, s_i) \triangleq \max_{v_i \in I_i} \max_{s_{-i} \in S_{-i}} \max_{s'_i \in S_i}$$

$$u_i(v_i, M(s'_i, s_{-i})) - u_i(v_i, M(s_i, s_{-i})).$$

- i's *set of regret-minimizing strategies* is

$$REG_i(I_i) \triangleq \{ s_i : s_i = \operatorname*{argmin}_{s'_i \in S_i} reg_i(I_i, s'_i) \}.$$

The set of all profiles of regret-minimizing strategies of M, relative to an initial knowledge profile I, is

$$REG(I) \triangleq REG_1(I_1) \times \cdots \times REG_n(I_n).$$

3.4 Social Welfare

As usual, social welfare and maximum social welfare are defined relative to the true valuation profile θ (independent of the fact that in our model each player i may have inaccurate knowledge about his own θ_i.) Indeed, The social welfare of an outcome $\omega = (a, p, r)$ is

$$SW(\omega) \triangleq \theta_i \text{ if } a_i = 1.$$

The maximum social welfare is

$$MSW \triangleq \max_\omega SW(\omega) = \max_i \theta_i.$$

4. A FIRST THEOREM

The (Non-Deterministic) Second Price Mechanism[6]

The second price mechanism is the normal form mechanism non-deterministically allocating the good to a player reporting the highest valuation, and choosing the price of a player i to be the second highest reported valuation, if the good has been allocated to i, and 0 otherwise.

Notation

We denote the second-price mechanism by $\mathbb{SP}$, the set of players by N, the number of players by n, and let $-i \triangleq N \setminus \{i\}$ for every player i.

Relative to an initial knowledge profile $I = ([a_1, b_1], \ldots, [a_n, b_n])$, lexicographically breaking ties if needed, let

$$\phi \triangleq \operatorname*{argmax}_{i \in N} c_i b_i.$$

(As we shall see, ϕ is the player with the highest final uncertainty. That is, the player which, at the decision node in which he finally decides to bid rather than refining his own knowledge, has the longest knowledge interval. The length of that interval will actually be $2\sqrt{c_\phi b_\phi}$.)

THEOREM 1. *In the basic costly knowledge model, for all initial knowledge profiles* $I = ([a_1, b_1], \ldots, [a_n, b_n])$, *all true*

---

[6]Should the second-price mechanism break ties deterministically, or at random, regret may not be well defined. (In particular, there may not be a strategy subprofile for a player i's opponents which maximizes i's regret. Even relying on suprema, rather than maxima, is problematic.)

valuation profiles $\theta \in [a_1, b_1] \times \cdots \times [a_n, b_n]$, *and all strategy profiles* $s \in REG(I)$,

$$SW(\mathbb{SP}(s)) \geq MSW - 2\sqrt{c_\phi b_\phi}.$$

Proof Sketch

We begin by proving that the set of regret-minimizing strategies of each player i, $REG_i(I_i)$, consists of a single strategy, s_i^*, and actually explicitly computing such s_i^*.

To this end, assume for a moment that knowledge refinement is no longer an option, and consider a regret minimizing player i, whose (current) knowledge interval is $I'_i = [a'_i, b'_i]$. Then, i must, for each possible bid β'_i, $reg_i(I'_i, \beta'_i)$, and report a bid

$$\beta_i^* \in \operatorname*{argmin}_{\beta_i} reg_i(I'_i, \beta_i).$$

LEMMA 1. $\beta_i^* = \frac{a'_i + b'_i}{2}$.

Proof of Lemma 1.

We prove Lemma 1 by considering the function $reg_i(I'_i, \cdot)$ and showing the following two properties:

(a) $reg_i(I'_i, \cdot)$ is strictly decreasing in the domain $\left[0, \frac{a'_i + b'_i}{2}\right]$; and

(b) $reg_i(I'_i, \cdot)$ is strictly increasing in the domain $\left[\frac{a'_i + b'_i}{2}, \infty\right)$.

Proof Sketch of Property (a).

Consider a generic bid α_i, $0 \leq \alpha_i \leq \frac{a'_i + b'_i}{2}$.

Let $\overline{\alpha}_i$, $\overline{\alpha}_{-i}$, and $\overline{\theta}_i$ respectively be a bid of i, a bid subprofile of the opponents of i, and a valuation of i in $[a'_i, b'_i]$ "achieving the regret of α_i". That is,

$$(\overline{\alpha}_i, \overline{\alpha}_{-i}, \overline{\theta}_i) \in \operatorname*{argmax}_{(\alpha'_i, \alpha'_{-i}, \theta'_i)} u_i((\alpha'_i, \alpha'_{-i}), \theta'_i) - u_i((\alpha_i, \alpha'_{-i}), \theta'_i).$$

It can also be seen (by a tedious case analysis) that for any such $\overline{\alpha}_i$, $\overline{\alpha}_{-i}$, and $\overline{\theta}_i$,

$$\max_{j \in -i} \overline{\alpha}_j = \alpha_i, \quad \overline{\alpha}_i = \alpha_i + 1, \quad \text{and} \quad \overline{\theta}_i = b'_i.$$

Thus, the second price mechanism

- under the strategy profile $(\alpha_i, \overline{\alpha}_{-i})$, may assign the good to an opponent of i, so that i's (worst case) utility is 0, and

- under the strategy profile $(\overline{\alpha}_i, \overline{\alpha}_{-i})$, assigns the good to i, so that i's utility is $b'_i - \alpha_i$.

Accordingly,

$$reg_i(I'_i, \alpha_i) =$$

$$u_i((\overline{\alpha}_i, \overline{\alpha}_{-i}), \overline{\theta}_i) - u_i((\alpha_i, \overline{\alpha}_{-i}), \overline{\theta}_i) =$$

$$b'_i - \alpha_i.$$

The above equality indeed shows that $reg_i(I'_i, \alpha_i)$ decreases with α_i.

$\square$

Since the bid α_i could coincide with $\beta_i^* = \frac{a_i' + b_i'}{2}$, our last equality also shows that the regret of β_i^* is

$$reg_i(I_i', \beta_i^*) = \frac{b_i' - a_i'}{2}. \qquad (1)$$

Proof Sketch of Property (b).

The proof of property (b) is essentially symmetric to that of property (a).[7]

□

Since properties (a) and (b) hold, so does Lemma 1.

∎

Consider now the following two options for a regret-minimizing player whose current knowledge interval is $[a_i', b_i']$.

- *Option 1: i bids immediately without any refinement.*

  Accordingly, lemma 1 tells us that i's bid is β_i^*. Thus, equation (1) implies that i's regret in this option is $\frac{b_i' - a_i'}{2}$, that is, half of his current uncertainty.

- *Option 2: i refines his knowledge once, and then bids.*

  By so doing, his total regret would be the sum of (1) the cost of the refinement and (2) the regret of bidding after he learns his new knowledge interval $[a_i'', b_i'']$. By definition, the above cost is $\frac{c_i b_i'}{b_i' - a_i'}$. And again by Lemma 1 and equation 1 the above regret is $\frac{b_i' - a_i'}{4}$ (because the refinement halves i's original uncertainty).

Accordingly, i will choose option 2 if and only if

$$\frac{c_i b_i'}{b_i' - a_i'} + \frac{b_i' - a_i'}{4} < \frac{b_i' - a_i'}{2}.$$

That is, after some manipulations, if and only if

$$2\sqrt{c_i b_i'} < b_i' - a_i'.$$

Applying this principle from the very beginning of i sub-mechanism, when i's knowledge is (in our notation) $[a_i, b_i]$, we see that i has a single regret-minimizing strategy, s_i^*, so defined: For all decision node D_t,

$$s_i^*(D_t) = \begin{cases} R_i & \text{if } b_i^t - a_i^t > 2\sqrt{c_i b_i^t} \\ \frac{a_i^t + b_i^t}{2} & \text{otherwise.} \end{cases}$$

Having understood the unique regret minimizing strategy s_i^* of each player i, we are ready to finish sketching the proof of our theorem. The best way to do so is pictorially.

It is easy to see that the worst scenario for the realized social welfare of the second-price mechanism is that illustrated in the figure below.

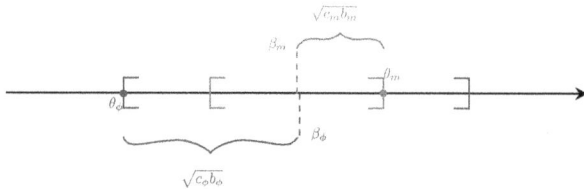

Figure 2:

In the above picture, red is the color associated to the player with the maximum true valuation, player m. The red interval represents m's *"final knowledge"*, $[a_m^*, b_m^*]$, that is the knowledge interval of m when, executing the strategy s_m^*, he decides to place the bid β_m^*. (Indeed notice that β_m^* lies in the middle of m's final knowledge.) The red dot indicates the actual value of his true valuation within this interval. The corresponding "situation" for the player with the highest final uncertainty, player ϕ, is instead depicted in blue. Our analysis of the regret-minimizing strategies s_i^*'s guarantees to upper-bound the length of the red interval in terms of m's initial knowledge interval: that is,

$$b_m^* - a_m^* \le 2\sqrt{c_m b_m}.$$

Analogously, the length of the blue interval is upper-bounded in terms of ϕ's initial knowledge interval as follows:

$$b_\phi^* - a_\phi^* \le 2\sqrt{c_\phi b_\phi}.$$

The fact that the blue dotted line is slightly on the right of the red dotted line wants to indicate that $\beta_\phi^* > \beta_m^*$. Accordingly, the good is allocated to ϕ, so that the social welfare actually realized by second-price mechanism in this case is $\sqrt{c_\phi b_\phi} + \sqrt{c_m b_m}$ smaller than the maximum one. Since, by definition, $c_\phi b_\phi \ge c_m b_m$, we conclude that, as we wanted to show,

$$SW(\mathbb{SP}(s^*)) \ge MSW - 2\sqrt{c_\phi b_\phi}.$$

∎

5. GENERALIZATIONS

Alternative Choices of Inaccuracy

As already mentioned, another natural choice for the inaccuracy of a knowledge interval $[a, b]$ is $\delta' = \frac{b - a}{a + b}$.

A slightly more general choice is

$$\delta'' = \frac{b - a}{g_i([a, b])}.$$

For such δ'',[8] the social-welfare guarantee of the second-price mechanism of course continues to be expressed in terms of the players' longest "final knowledge interval": namely,

$$SW(\mathbb{SP}(s^*)) \ge MSW - \max_{i \in N} 2\sqrt{c_i \cdot g_i([a_i^*, b_i^*])}.[9]$$

A General Notion of Inaccuracy

At the highest level, we believe that a function f provides a suitable definition of inaccuracy if it satisfies the following three conditions: for all knowledge intervals $[a, b]$, $[a', b]$, and $[a, a']$ such that $0 \le a < a' < b$,

  1. $f([a, b]) \in (0, 1]$;

---

[7]In particular, $\max_{j \in -i} \overline{\alpha}_j = \alpha_i$, $\overline{\alpha}_i = \alpha_i - 1$, and $\overline{\theta}_i = a_i'$.

[8]And continuining to assume that the cost of refinement is proportional to the inaccuracy, that is, $C_i([a, b]) = \frac{c_i}{\delta''}$.

[9]That is, in the above inequality, as in our proof sketch of Theorem 1, $[a_i^*, b_i^*]$ continues to denote the knowledge interval of player i when, executing his regret-minimizing strategy s_i^*, he decides to bid rather than refining his knowledge. In other words, $[a_i^*, b_i^*]$ is the longest knowledge interval $[a, b]$ of i such that

- $[a, b]$ is contained in i's initial knowledge interval, and

- $2\sqrt{c_i \cdot g_i([a, b])} \ge (b - a)$.

2. $f([a,b]) > f([a',b])$; and

3. $f([a,a']) < f([a,b])$.

Inaccuracy-Lowering Refinements

In one-dimensional problems, the solution space consists of an interval, and binary search proceeds by shortening the solution space (by a fixed amount).

The problem is also one-dimensional in our setting: indeed, every player seeks to figure out his own true valuation in his current knowledge interval. To mimic binary search as close as possible, we have considered refinements that yield knowledge intervals of shorter lengths. Of course decreasing the length of a knowledge interval by a precise amount also implies decreasing its inaccuracy, but not by a predictably precise amount. Thus, still in the spirit of binary search, one may consider refinements explicitly aimed at decreasing the inaccuracy of a knowledge interval by a given amount. After all, inaccuracy may be a more meaningful dimension to consider in general, not just for meaningfully defining refinement cost.

Accordingly, still within a set-theoretic framework, letting $[a,b]$ be a knowledge interval for a player i and δ be its inaccuracy, let us discuss the following two costly knowledge models that focus on decreasing inaccuracy.

1. *The Accuracy-Bisecting Model.* In this model, at a cost of $C_i(a,b) = \frac{c_i}{\delta}$, $R_i([a,b])$ returns an *arbitrary* knowledge interval of i of inaccuracy $\frac{\delta}{2}$.

   Fortunately, essentially the same proof of Theorem 1 shows that, once again, the social welfare guarantee of the second-price mechanism is
   $$SW(\mathbb{SP}(s^*)) \geq MSW - 2\sqrt{c_\phi b_\phi}.$$

2. *The Chosen-Accuracy Model.* In this model, for every chosen $\delta' < \delta$, i can, in a single step, refine $[a,b]$ to obtain an arbitrary knowledge interval whose inaccuracy is δ'.

   A reasonably natural choice for the cost of such a refinement is to be proportional to the difference of the new and the old inaccuracy: that is, to be equal to
   $$c_i \cdot \left(\frac{1}{\delta'} - \frac{1}{\delta} \right).$$

   In this model and cost function, essentially the same proof of Theorem 1 (with only a different algebraic manipulation) shows that the social welfare guarantee of the second-price mechanism again is
   $$SW(\mathbb{SP}(s^*)) \geq MSW - \sqrt{2c_\phi b_\phi}.$$

General Cost Functions

Abstractly, we believe that every cost function in the chosen-accuracy model should satisfy the following conditions: let $1 \geq \delta > \delta' > \delta'' > 0$, then

1. *Cost is always positive.*
   $$C(\delta, \delta') > 0.$$

2. *Cost function must satisfy triangle inequality.*
   $$C(\delta, \delta') + C(\delta', \delta'') \geq C(\delta, \delta'').$$

3. *Cost increases with initial inaccuracy.*
   $$C(\delta, \delta'') > C(\delta', \delta'').^{10}$$

4. *Cost decreases with desired inaccuracy*
   $$C(\delta, \delta'') > C(\delta, \delta').^{11}$$

and, preferably only,

5. *Totally erasing uncertainty has infinite cost.*
   $$C(\delta, 0) = \infty.$$

General Inaccuracy and General Cost

Finally, let us consider the chosen-accuracy model, with general inaccuracy and general cost function, and denote by by $R_i^{\delta'}$ the non-deterministic function that, given a knowledge interval of i of inaccuracy $\delta > \delta'$, returns an arbitrary knowledge (sub)interval of i of inaccuracy δ'.

In this general model, a player i may have multiple regret-minimizing strategies. Let s_i^* be one such strategy, $[a_i^t, b_i^t]$ the knowledge interval of i at a decision node D^t, δ the inaccuracy of $[a_i^t, b_i^t]$. Then an argument similar to that used in our proof sketch of Theorem 1 shows that

- $s_i^*(D^t) = R_i^{\delta'}$
  if there exists $\delta' \in (0, \delta)$ such that
  $$b_i^t - a_i^t > \max_{[a,b] \in \mathcal{I}} (2C_i(\delta, \delta') + (b-a))$$
  where $\mathcal{I}$ is the set of all subintervals of $[a_i^t, b_i^t]$ which contain θ_i and whose inaccuracy is δ'.

- $s_i^*(D^t) = \frac{a_i^t + b_i^t}{2}$ otherwise.

It is then clear that the social-welfare guarantee of the second-price mechanism continues to have the following form
$$SW(\mathbb{SP}(s^*)) \geq MSW - \max_i (b_i^* - a_i^*).$$

Above, once again, $[a_i^*, b_i^*]$ is player i's final knowledge interval, relative to the strategies s_i^*, in the current model.

Refining Our Knowledge About Our Opponents

In general, a player i may also have some knowledge about the valuations of his opponents. Initially, such knowledge of i may be very coarse, but again i may be able to refine it, although at a cost potentially much higher than that he needs to refine his knowledge about his own valuation.

(For instance, i may hire some employees of his opponents, and analyze the data they report. Alternatively, he may collect financial data about his opponents from the public domain, an operation that may be very expensive, since i does not know exactly where to look for the relevant data).

---

[10]Equivalently, for differentiable cost functions,
$$\frac{\partial C(\delta, \delta')}{\partial \delta} > 0$$

[11]Equivalently, for differentiable cost functions,
$$\frac{\partial C(\delta, \delta')}{\partial \delta'} < 0$$

In principle, for the second-price mechanism, by refining a little his knowledge about the valuations of his opponents, i may save the money necessary to refine a lot his knowledge about himself. For instance, by incurring a modest cost, i may learn than the minimum valuation of one of his opponent is larger than any valuation he may have, in which case, i should not invest a penny in improving his knowledge about his own valuation. Yet, even if i has the ability to refine his knowledge about his opponents at a cost, it can be seen that i's regret-minimizing strategy never takes advantage of this ability.

We believe, however, that a sufficiently general costly knowledge model should include a player's ability to refine his knowledge about his opponents, and that such an ability will in fact be crucial when properly analyzing some complex mechanisms.

6. CONCLUSIONS

In general, knowledge has a cost. Accordingly, we cannot always count on the players having already paid the cost necessary to exactly learn their valuations prior to playing the mechanisms we design.

Including the players' cost of knowledge acquisition in the analysis of a mechanism may thus make our predictions about the outcomes the mechanism produces more realistic and accurate.

Distilling costly knowledge models that are more realistic than the ones considered in this paper may be challenging. And so may be the analysis of new and old mechanisms in such models. We welcome both challenges.

7. REFERENCES

[1] AUMANN, R. J. Utility theory without the completeness axiom. *Econometrica 30*, 3 (July 1962), 445–462.

[2] BECK, M. J., CHORUS, C. G., ROSE, J. M., AND HENSHER, D. A. Vehicle purchasing behaviour of individuals and groups: regret or reward? *Journal of Transport Economics and Policy (JTEP) 47*, 3 (2013), 475–492.

[3] BEWLEY, T. F. Knightian decision theory. Part I. *Decisions in Economics and Finance 25*, 2 (2002), 79–110. Earlier version appeared as a discussion paper no. 807 of the Cowles Foundation at Yale University, November 1986.

[4] BODOH-CREED, A. L. Ambiguous beliefs and mechanism design. *Games and Economic Behavior 75*, 2 (2012), 518–537.

[5] BOSE, S., OZDENOREN, E., AND PAPE, A. Optimal auctions with ambiguity. *Theoretical Economics 1*, 4 (December 2006), 411–438.

[6] BOSE, S., AND RENOU, L. Mechanism design with ambiguous communication devices. *Econometrica 82*, 5 (2014), 1853–1872.

[7] CELIS, L. E., GKLEZAKOS, D. C., AND KARLIN, A. R. On revenue maximization for agents with costly information acquisition. In *Automata, Languages, and Programming*. Springer, 2013, pp. 484–495.

[8] CELIS, L. E., KARLIN, A. R., LEYTON-BROWN, K., NGUYEN, C. T., AND THOMPSON, D. R. M. Approximately revenue-maximizing auctions for deliberative agents. In *AAAI* (2012).

[9] CHIESA, A., MICALI, S., AND ZHU, Z. A. Mechanism design with approximate valuations. In *Proceedings of the 3rd Innovations in Theoretical Computer Science conference* (2012), ACM, pp. 34–38.

[10] CHIESA, A., MICALI, S., AND ZHU, Z. A. Bridging Utility Maximization and Regret Minimization. *ArXiv e-prints* (Mar. 2014).

[11] CHIESA, A., MICALI, S., AND ZHU, Z. A. Knightian self uncertainty in the vcg mechanism for unrestricted combinatorial auctions. In *Proceedings of the fifteenth ACM conference on Economics and Computation* (2014), ACM, pp. 619–620. For a full version of the paper, see http://people.csail.mit.edu/zeyuan/paper/2014-EC.pdf.

[12] CHIESA, A., MICALI, S., AND ZHU, Z. A. Knightian analysis of the vickrey mechanism. *Will appear in Econometrica* (2015).

[13] CHORUS, C. Random regret minimization: an overview of model properties and empirical evidence. *Transport Reviews 32*, 1 (2012), 75–92.

[14] CHORUS, C. G., ARENTZE, T. A., AND TIMMERMANS, H. J. Spatial choice: a matter of utility or regret. *Environment and Planning Part B 36*, 3 (2009), 538–551.

[15] CORICELLI, G., CRITCHLEY, H. D., JOFFILY, M., O'DOHERTY, J. P., SIRIGU, A., AND DOLAN, R. J. Regret and its avoidance: a neuroimaging study of choice behavior. *Nature neuroscience 8*, 9 (2005), 1255–1262.

[16] DANAN, E. Randomization vs. selection: How to choose in the absence of preference? *Management Science 56* (March 2010), 503–518.

[17] DI TILLIO, A., KOS, N., AND MESSNER, M. The design of ambiguous mechanisms. Tech. rep., 2012.

[18] DUBRA, J., MACCHERONI, F., AND OK, E. A. Expected utility theory without the completeness axiom. *Journal of Economic Theory 115*, 1 (March 2004), 118–133.

[19] ENGELBRECHT-WIGGANS, R. The effect of regret on optimal bidding in auctions. *Management Science 35*, 6 (1989), 685–692.

[20] FON, V., AND OTANI, Y. Classical welfare theorems with non-transitive and non-complete preferences. *Journal of Economic Theory 20*, 3 (June 1979), 409–418.

[21] GALE, D., AND MAS-COLELL, A. An equilibrium existence theorem for a general model without ordered preferences. *Journal of Mathematical Economics 2*, 1 (March 1975), 9–15.

[22] GILBOA, I., AND SCHMEIDLER, D. Maxmin expected utility with non-unique prior. *Journal of Mathematical Economics 18*, 2 (April 1989), 141–153.

[23] HALPERN, J. Y., AND PASS, R. Iterated regret minimization: A new solution concept. *Games and Economic Behavior 74*, 1 (2012), 184–207.

[24] HYAFIL, N., AND BOUTILIER, C. Regret Minimizing Equilibria and Mechanisms for Games with Strict Type Uncertainty. In *Proceedings of the 20th conference on Uncertainty in artificial intelligence* (July 2004), pp. 268–277.

[25] JOSEPHS, R. A., LARRICK, R. P., STEELE, C. M., AND NISBETT, R. E. Protecting the self from the negative consequences of risky decisions. *Journal of personality and social psychology 62*, 1 (1992), 26.

[26] KIEKINTVELD, C., ISLAM, T., AND KREINOVICH, V. Security games with interval uncertainty. In *Proceedings of the 2013 international conference on Autonomous agents and multi-agent systems* (2013), International Foundation for Autonomous Agents and Multiagent Systems, pp. 231–238.

[27] KNIGHT, F. H. *Risk, Uncertainty and Profit.* Houghton Mifflin, 1921.

[28] LINHART, P. B., AND RADNER, R. Minimax-regret strategies for bargaining over several variables. *Journal of Economic Theory 48*, 1 (1989), 152–178.

[29] LOPOMO, G., RIGOTTI, L., AND SHANNON, C. Uncertainty in mechanism design, 2009. http://www.pitt.edu/~luca/Papers/mechanismdesign.pdf.

[30] LOPOMO, G., RIGOTTI, L., AND SHANNON, C. Knightian uncertainty and moral hazard. *Journal of Economic Theory 146*, 3 (2011), 1148 – 1172. Incompleteness and Uncertainty in Economics.

[31] MACCHERONI, F., MARINACCI, M., AND RUSTICHINI, A. Ambiguity aversion, robustness, and the variational representation of preferences. *Econometrica 74*, 6 (2006), 1447–1498.

[32] MAS-COLELL, A. An equilibrium existence theorem without complete or transitive preferences. *Journal of Mathematical Economics 1*, 3 (December 1974), 237–246.

[33] MILNOR, J. W. Games against nature. In *Decision processes*, R. M. Thrall, C. H. Coombs, and R. L. Davis, Eds. John Wiley & Sons, Inc., 1954.

[34] NASCIMENTO, L. Remarks on the consumer problem under incomplete preferences. *Theory and Decision 70*, 1 (January 2011), 95–110.

[35] OK, E. A. Utility representation of an incomplete preference relation. *Journal of Economic Theory 104* (2002), 429–449.

[36] RENOU, L., AND SCHLAG, K. H. Minimax regret and strategic uncertainty. *Journal of Economic Theory 145*, 1 (Jan. 2010), 264–286.

[37] RIGOTTI, L., AND SHANNON, C. Uncertainty and risk in financial markets. *Econometrica 73*, 1 (01 2005), 203–243.

[38] SAVAGE, L. J. The theory of statistical decision. *Journal of the American Statistical association 46*, 253 (1951), 55–67.

[39] SCHMEIDLER, D. Subjective probability and expected utility without additivity. *Econometrica 57*, 3 (May 1989), 571–87.

[40] SELTEN, R. Blame avoidance as motivating force in the first price sealed bid private value auction. In *Economics Essays in Honor of Werner Hildenbrand*. Springer, 1989, pp. 333–344.

[41] SHAFER, W., AND SONNENSCHEIN, H. Equilibrium in abstract economies without ordered preferences. *Journal of Mathematical Economics 2*, 3 (December 1975), 345–348.

[42] STOYE, J. Axioms for minimax regret choice correspondences. *Journal of Economic Theory 146*, 6 (2011), 2226–2251.

[43] THOMPSON, D. R. M., AND LEYTON-BROWN, K. Valuation uncertainty and imperfect introspection in second-price auctions. In *PROCEEDINGS OF THE NATIONAL CONFERENCE ON ARTIFICIAL INTELLIGENCE* (2007), vol. 22, Menlo Park, CA; Cambridge, MA; London; AAAI Press; MIT Press; 1999, p. 148.

[44] THOMPSON, D. R. M., AND LEYTON-BROWN, K. Dominant-strategy auction design for agents with uncertain, private values. In *AAAI* (2011).

[45] WALD, A. Statistical decision functions. *The Annals of Mathematical Statistics 20*, 2 (1949), pp. 165–205.

On the Computational Complexity of Optimal Simple Mechanisms

Aviad Rubinstein*
UC Berkeley
aviad@eecs.berkeley.edu

ABSTRACT

We consider a monopolist seller facing a single buyer with additive valuations over n heterogeneous, independent items. It is known that in this important setting optimal mechanisms may require randomization [12], use menus of infinite size [9], and may be computationally intractable [8]. This has sparked recent interest in finding simple mechanisms that obtain reasonable approximations to the optimal revenue [10, 15, 3]. In this work we attempt to find the *optimal simple mechanism*.

There are many ways to define simple mechanisms. Here we restrict our search to *partition mechanisms*, where the seller partitions the items into disjoint bundles and posts a price for each bundle; the buyer is allowed to buy any number of bundles.

We give a PTAS for the problem of finding a revenue-maximizing partition mechanism, and prove that the problem is strongly NP-hard. En route, we prove structural properties of near-optimal partition mechanisms which may be of independent interest: for example, there always exists a near-optimal partition mechanism that uses only a constant number of non-trivial bundles (i.e. bundles with more than one item).

1. INTRODUCTION

Designing revenue-maximizing mechanisms for a seller who faces a single buyer with additive valuations over n heterogeneous, independent items is a fundamental problem in auction theory. It is known that even in this simple setting, the optimum mechanism requires randomization [12], uses a menu of infinite size [9], and may be computationally intractable [8]. Such mechanisms are often considered "impractical": buyers and sellers may be reluctant to participate in mechanisms that are too complicated; random-

*Most of this research was done while the author was an intern at Microsoft Research New England. Part of this research was supported by NSF grant CCF1408635 and Templeton Foundation grant 3966.

Permission to make digital or hard copies of all or part of this work for personal or classroom use is granted without fee provided that copies are not made or distributed for profit or commercial advantage and that copies bear this notice and the full citation on the first page. Copyrights for components of this work owned by others than ACM must be honored. Abstracting with credit is permitted. To copy otherwise, or republish, to post on servers or to redistribute to lists, requires prior specific permission and/or a fee. Request permissions from Permissions@acm.org.

ITCS'16, January 14–16, 2016, Cambridge, MA, USA.
© 2016 ACM. ISBN 978-1-4503-4057-1/16/01 ...$15.00.
DOI: http://dx.doi.org/10.1145/2840728.2840736

ization may be restricted by legal requirements (and by our poor understanding of risk aversion); describing and choosing among infinite menus raises obvious issues of communication and computational complexity, etc. Put in computer science jargon, **simplicity is a constraint**: just like the auctioneer cannot obtain the entire social welfare because of incentive compatibility constraints, the optimum mechanism's revenue is infeasible because of the simplicity constraint.

In recent years there have been many works comparing simple mechanisms to optimal mechanisms (including [13, 1, 18, 17, 4, 2]). In particular, a line of works [10, 15, 3] in our setting (a single buyer with additive valuations over independent items) culminated with a celebrated 1/6-approximation of the optimal revenue by the better of the following two mechanisms: (a) sell each item separately; and (b) auction all the items together as one grand bundle. Here, rather than comparing to the benchmark of the globally optimal (but infeasible) auction, we want to find the best feasible mechanism. Clearly, the above mechanism also obtains a 1/6-approximation of the optimal simple mechanism; but can we do better?

Can we find the optimal simple mechanism?

Alas, it is not clear how to formalize "simple". In this work we propose *partition mechanisms* as a standard for simplicity. (In a partition mechanisms the seller partitions the set of items into disjoint bundles, and posts a price for each bundle; the buyer is allowed to select any number of bundles.) In Section 2 we discuss some of the reasons that made us choose this definition, as well as some of its imperfections. We want to emphasize that the same question could be asked with respect to any definition of "simple". (For example: what is the computational complexity of finding the optimal deterministic mechanism with polynomial (additive)-menu-size?)

Our technical contributions include a PTAS, i.e. for any constant $\delta > 0$, we give a polynomial time algorithm that finds a partition mechanism that obtains $(1 - \delta)$-approximation to the optimal revenue among all partition mechanisms. Rather than developing novel algorithmic techniques, our main tool is exploring the structural properties of near-optimal partitions. For example, we prove that there exists a near-optimal partition mechanism with only a constant number of non-trivial bundles. We also prove that this problem is strongly NP-hard, i.e. there is no FPTAS (assuming $P \neq NP$).

Organization.

In Section 2 we discuss some of the merits of partition mechanisms. In Section 4 we give a few interesting examples and provide some intuition for the technical part. The NP-hardness result appears in Section 5 and the PTAS in Section 6.

1.1 Related work

We briefly discuss a few related works on computational complexity of designing simple, revenue-(near)-optimal mechanisms in settings with independent item valuations. For a constant number (or many i.i.d.) additive buyers with monotone hazard rate (MHR) valuation distributions, Cai and Huang [6] give a PTAS to the optimal mechanism. (Note that we make no assumption on the distributions except independence.) Cai and Huang's mechanism is simple in the sense that most items are sold as a single bundle, but for the remaining few items an arbitrary (potentially randomized) mechanism is used. Our restriction to partition mechanisms for an additive buyer has an analog of item-pricing mechanisms for a unit-demand buyer. For the latter, Cai and Daskalakis [5] give a PTAS for monotone hazard rate valuations and a Quasi-PTAS for regular valuations, and finding the exact optimum for general valuations is NP-hard by Chen et al. [7].

2. PARTITION MECHANISMS AS SIMPLE MECHANISMS

While there have been notable attempts to quantify complexity of different mechanisms (e.g. by Hart and Nisan [11] and recently by Morgenstern and Roughgarden [16]), it is fair to say that we have not seen an indisputable, universal definition of simple mechanisms. Most likely, because "simple" *can and should* mean different things in different settings; for example, compare the simplicity desiderata in the following scenarios: selling produce in a grocery store (buyers are limited in time and computational capacity); spectrum auctions (buyers may be limited by legal constraints); and ad-auctions in an online marketplace (decisions are often made by automated algorithms).

In this work we define simple mechanisms as partition mechanisms. Certainly, there are issues with this definition. One immediate problem with restricting to partition mechanisms is that they don't really capture all simple mechanisms. In particular, see Example 3 for a distribution where a simple, deterministic mechanism that is not a partition mechanism obtains a strictly greater revenue. More importantly, some of the advantages of partition mechanisms listed in this section are restricted to a single buyer, with additive valuations, over independent items; this issue is illustrated in Example 4 which shows that for many buyers with additive valuations over independent items, partition mechanisms achieve a revenue much lower than the optimum. Coming up with a canonical definition for simple mechanisms remains one of the most important open problems in this line of work. Nevertheless, in this section we argue that partition mechanisms have many advantages as the standard for simple mechanisms in this particular setting.

Expressiveness.

We argue that despite their simplicity, partition mechanisms can be used to express important auctions of interest. For example, they generalize both selling items separately and bundling all the items together; thus by [3] they guarantee at least a 1/6-approximation to the optimal revenue achievable with any mechanism. Furthermore, this is a strong generalization: as we show in Example 1, partition mechanisms can obtain as much as double the revenue obtained by the better of selling items separately or bundling all the items together. Also, we note that partition mechanisms can exhibit rich structure, as is evident by our NP-hardness result.

Menu complexity and false-name-proofness.

Hart and Nisan [11] discuss a measure of menu-size complexity: every truthful mechanism can be represented as a menu of (potentially randomized) outcomes and prices, where the buyer is allowed to choose one of those outcomes. As noted by Hart and Nisan, the mechanism which auctions each item separately has exponential menu-size complexity under this definition. To overcome this problem, they also introduce a measure *additive-menu-size*, where the buyer is allowed to buy an arbitrary number of outcomes from the menu. Under this definition, partition auctions have linear additive-menu-size complexity.

A related issue is that of false-name-proofness, i.e. can a buyer gain from participating in the mechanism several times? Partition mechanisms (and additive-menu mechanisms in general) have the advantage that they are always false-name-proof.

Locality and buyer-side computational complexity.

Partition mechanisms also have the advantage that the buyer's decisions are "local", i.e. the decision to buy one bundle is independent of the decision to buy other bundles. This greatly simplifies tasks such as analyzing and reasoning about such mechanisms, learning or predicting the effects of changes to the environment or the mechanism, etc. In particular, this makes the buyer's decisions very easy.

Revenue monotonicity.

Hart and Reny [12] observed an interesting phenomenon they call *revenue non-monotonicity*, where increasing the buyer's valuations (in the sense of stochastic dominance), may strictly decrease the optimal obtainable revenue. Hart and Reny showed a constant factor gap between the revenue obtainable with the higher and lower valuations, even when selling two i.i.d. items. Furthermore, [17] recently observed that for two items with correlated valuations, this gap may be infinite. Another nice property of partition mechanisms is that the maximum revenue obtainable by auctions in this class is revenue-monotone.

3. PRELIMINARIES

For any distribution $\vec{D}$ of valuations, we use the following notation, mostly due to [10, 3], to denote the optimum revenue for each class of mechanisms:

- REV $\left(\vec{D}\right)$ - the maximum revenue among all truthful mechanisms;

- DREV $\left(\vec{D}\right)$ - the maximum revenue among all truthful *deterministic* mechanisms;

- PREV $\left(\vec{D}\right)$ - the maximum revenue among all truthful *partition* mechanisms;

- BREV $\left(\vec{D} \right)$ - the maximum revenue obtainable by auctioning the grand bundle; and

- SREV $\left(\vec{D} \right)$ - the maximum revenue obtainable by pricing each item separately.

When $\vec{D}$ is clear from the context, we simply write REV, DREV, etc.

4. TECHNIQUES, INTUITION, EXAMPLES

We begin our technical exposition with the following example which separates the revenue obtainable with a partition mechanism from the better of pricing each item separately or auctioning the grand bundle.

Example 1. (**PRev** $= (2 - o(1)) \max\{$**SRev, BRev**$\}$)
Consider $2n$ items:

- *A:* n items with equal-revenue valuations. $v_a \in S \triangleq \{1, \ldots, \sqrt{n}\}$, with distribution $\Pr[v_a \geq k] = 1/k \; \forall k \in S$; and

- *B:* n items with rare-event valuations. $v_b \in \{0, \alpha n^b\}$, with distribution $\Pr[v_b = \alpha n^b] = n^{-b}$, where we set $\alpha = \mathsf{E}[v_a]$.

With a partition mechanism, we can obtain expected revenue $(1 - o(1)) n\alpha$ from the items in A by bundling them together, and also $n\alpha$ from B by selling each item i separately for price αn^i. However, selling all the items separately achieves negligible revenue on A, whereas the items in B will have negligible contribution to the revenue from selling the grand bundle.

Remark 1. We remark that the Example 1 shows, in particular, a $(2 - o(1))$-gap between $\max\{$SREV, BREV$\}$ and REV. Previously Babaioff et al. [3] cited an example due to [8] that gave a 1.05-gap.

The example above builds on the key intuition from [15, 3] that there is an interesting tradeoff between bundling and selling separately: when most revenue is distributed among many low-impact, high probability events (as in subset A), their sum concentrates and bundling is preferable; when most revenue comes from rare events (as in subset B), we want to sell the items separately. [15, 3] call this the *core-tail* decomposition.

A nice question suggested to us by Amos Fiat is whether this is the "only way" that PREV can beat $\max\{$SREV, BREV$\}$. In particular, is there always a revenue-maximizing partition mechanism with at most one non-trivial bundle? The following example shows that the answer is no.

Example 2. (**Two non-trivial bundles**)
Consider the following valuations:

- for $i \in \{1, 2\}$, let $\Pr[v_i = 1] = \Pr[v_i = 2] = 1/2$;

- for $i = \{3, 4\}$, let $(1/9) \cdot \Pr[v_i = 1] = \Pr[v_i = 10] = 1/10$.

The unique optimal partition mechanism offers bundle $\{1, 2\}$ for price 3 and bundle $\{3, 4\}$ for price 11. The revenue obtained is

$$3 \cdot \Pr\left[\sum_{i \in \{1,2\}} v_i \geq 3 \right] + 11 \cdot \Pr\left[\sum_{i \in \{3,4\}} v_i \geq 11 \right]$$
$$= 3 \cdot \frac{3}{4} + 11 \cdot \frac{19}{100} = 4.34.$$

The core-tail intuition from [15, 3] cannot explain the success of the optimal partition in Example 2. For this distribution, the optimal partition exploits the fact that the values of the bundles are slightly more likely to come out 3 and 11, respectively, than other values on the equal-revenue curve. But they are still far from concentration around 3 and 11. Our NP-hardness result constructs gadgets that generalize Example 2 to create instances where the optimal partition exhibits an arbitrarily complex structure.

Our PTAS is more intricate. Let us informally sketch the main idea. In Example 2, something interesting happens at 3, and something interesting happens at 11. In general, many interesting events can happen in different locations on the (positive) real numbers line, but one of the following two always holds:

- The interesting events are far apart on the real line - in this case we don't lose much by ignoring the events that pertain to lower values. In terms of Example 2, we exploit the asymmetry between the bundle $\{1, 2\}$ and the bundle $\{3, 4\}$.

- Most of the action is restricted to a small interval - this is a redundancy we can exploit. For example, because the sum of many independent random variables in the same range should concentrate.

More concretely, we prove (Lemmata 1 and 2) that there exists a near-optimal partition mechanism that uses only a constant number of non-trivial bundles. In some sense this is a bicriteria-approximation variant of Fiat's conjecture that Example 1 is the only reason we would want to use a partition other $\max\{$SREV, BREV$\}$. We then build on the same intuition to construct modified valuations that approximate the original distributions. Finally, we show that the new distributions admit a succinct representation, so we can find a near-optimal partition mechanism by brute-force search.

For completeness, let us conclude this technical exposition with two examples that separate DREV from PREV; they serve to remind us that there are many interesting mechanisms beyond the scope of partition mechanisms considered in this paper. The first example shows a constant separation in our setting of a single additive buyer.

Example 3. (**Hart and Nisan [10]; PRev** $= (1 - \Omega(1))$**DRev**)

Consider two i.i.d. items with valuations sampled uniformly from $\{0, 1, 2\}$. The expected revenue for selling the bundle with both items (for any price) is at most 1; and selling each item separately (for any price) yields total revenue at most 4/3. Going beyond partition mechanisms, we can offer either item for price 2, or the grand bundle for price 3.

The revenue obtained from this auction is

$$3 \cdot \Pr\left[\sum_{i \in \{1,2\}} v_i \geqslant 3\right] + 2 \cdot \Pr\left[\{v_1, v_2\} = \{2, 0\}\right]$$

$$= 3 \cdot \frac{3}{9} + 2 \cdot \frac{2}{9} = 13/9 > 4/3.$$

The second example shows that with many buyers, partition mechanisms cannot achieve any constant fraction of the optimum revenue. See also the recent paper by Yao [18] on constructing different simple mechanisms in this setting.

Example 4. (e.g. [3]; **Many buyers: PRev** = $o(1)$**DRev**)

We consider n items and $m = n^{1/4}$ buyers; we let v_i^j denote buyer j's value for item i. All v_i^j are drawn i.i.d. from the following distribution: with probability $1 - n^{-3/4}$, $v_i^j = 0$; otherwise, v_j^i is drawn from an equal-revenue distribution with support $\{1, \ldots, n^{1/10}\}$, i.e. $\Pr\left[v_i^j \geqslant k\right] = n^{-3/4}/k$.

For any one buyer, selling item i for price k yields revenue $n^{-3/4}$, which is only an $O(1/\log n)$-fraction of the expected value; but the total expected value for the grand bundle concentrates, so that revenue can easily be obtained. With m buyers, the auctioneer can guarantee almost the entire social welfare with the following mechanism: approach buyers in any order; for each buyer charge slightly lower than her expected value for the remaining items, and let her choose her favorite $n^{1/4}$ items. With a partition mechanism, on the other hand, we must fix the partition without knowing which items each buyer wants. Thus partition mechanisms can guarantee at most an $O(1/\log n)$-fraction of the optimum revenue.

5. NP-HARDNESS

THEOREM 1. *Given an explicit description of a product distribution of item valuations, computing a revenue maximizing partition is strongly NP-hard.*

PROOF. We reduce from 3D-Matching: Given sets X, Y, Z and a set of hyperedges $H \subseteq X \times Y \times Z$, find a maximum 3-dimensional matching, i.e. maximum non-intersecting subset $M \subseteq H$. Karp [14] proved that it is NP-complete to decide whether there exists a perfect matching (i.e. $|M| = |X| = |Y| = |Z|$).

Construction.

Identify the set of items with the set of vertices $I \triangleq X \cup Y \cup Z$. Identify the set of hyperedges with their indices; for each $h \in H$, let $\pi_h \triangleq |H|^6 + |H|^3 \cdot h$. Let $\pi_{\min} \triangleq \min_{h \in H} \pi_h = |H^6|$ and $\pi_{\max} \triangleq \max_{h \in H} \pi_h = \left(1 + O\left(1/|H|^2\right)\right)|H^6|$, For each item i, the distribution of valuations D_i is defined by the π_h's of its hyperedges. Specifically, we let

$$\text{supp}\left(D_i\right) = \{1\} \cup \{\pi_h : h \ni i\} \quad \text{and} \quad \Pr_{v_i \sim D_i}\left[v_i \geqslant \pi_h\right] = 1/\pi_h.$$

Observe that selling each item separately, for any price in its support, yields expected revenue of 1 per item.

Completeness.

If there exists a perfect matching M, we partition according to this matching, and set the price for bundle h at $\pi_h + 2$. For each bundle, we have

$$\Pr\left[\sum_{i \in h} v_i \geqslant \pi_h + 2\right] = 1 - (1 - 1/\pi_h)^3 = 3/\pi_h - 3/\pi_h^2 + 1/\pi_h^3.$$

The expected revenue for each bundle is therefore

$$(\pi_h + 2)\left(3/\pi_h - 3/\pi_h^2 + 1/\pi_h^3\right) = 3 + 3/\pi_h - O\left(1/\pi_h^2\right)$$

Summing over $|M|$ hyperedges (i.e. $|M|$ bundles), we guarantee a total revenue of $OPT \triangleq |M|\left(3 + 3/\pi_{\max} - O\left(1/\pi_{\max}^2\right)\right)$.

Soundness.

We first claim that there exists an optimum partition where every bundle is contained in a hyperedge. Let B be a bundle sold for some price $\pi \geqslant \pi_{\min}$. Clearly $\pi \leqslant |B| \pi_{\max}$, otherwise it never sells. Similarly, we have $\pi \leqslant |B| + \pi_{\max}$, otherwise it sells with probability at most $|B|/\pi_{\min}^2$, yielding revenue $|B| \pi/\pi_{\min}^2 \ll 1$.

Let $i \in B$ be such that $\pi \notin \left[\pi_h - |H|^2, \pi_h + |H|^2\right]$ for all $h \ni i$. We compare the revenue from selling B for price π to the revenue from selling $B \setminus \{i\}$ for price $\pi - 1$. If B sells for price π but $B \setminus \{i\}$ does not sell for price $\pi - 1$, then at least one of the following must be true: (1) $v_i \geqslant \pi - |B|$, which by our assumption on i implies $v_i \geqslant \pi + |H|^2$; or (2) $v_i > 1$ and there is some other $j \in B$ such that $v_j > 1$. We bound the probability of the union as follows:

1. $\Pr\left[v_i \geqslant \pi + |H|^2\right] \leqslant \frac{1}{\pi + |H|^2}$; the revenue loss is bounded by $\frac{\pi}{\pi + |H|^2} \leqslant \frac{\pi - |H|^2/2}{\pi}$;

2. $\Pr\left[(v_i > 1) \wedge (\exists j \in B \ v_j > 1)\right] < \frac{|B|}{\pi_{\min}^2}$; the revenue loss is bounded by $\frac{\pi|B|}{\pi_{\min}^2} \leqslant \frac{2|B|}{\pi}$.

There is also some revenue loss from the decrease in price: the original bundle sells with probability at most $\frac{|B|}{\pi - |B|} \leqslant \frac{2|B|}{\pi}$; since we decrease the price by 1, $\frac{2|B|}{\pi}$ also bounds the expected loss in revenue. The total expected loss in revenue is therefore at most $\frac{\pi - |H|^2/2}{\pi} + \frac{4|B|}{\pi} < 1$, so selling B as a bundle cannot be optimal.

There is an optimum partition that bundles items according to hyperedges in some partial matching M', and the rest of the items are in bundles of size at most two. The optimal price for a bundle of two items from hyperedge h is $\pi_h + 1$; the probability of selling for this price is $1 - (1 - 1/\pi_h)^2 = 2/\pi_h - \pi_h^2$. Multiplying by $\pi_h + 1$, we get an expected revenue of $2 + 1/\pi_h$. In particular, this is only $(1 + 1/2\pi_h)$ per item, as opposed to $(1 + 1/\pi_h)$ per item with a full hyperedge. □

6. PTAS

THEOREM 2. *For any constant $\delta > 0$, there exists a deterministic polynomial time algorithm that, given an explicit description of a product distribution of item valuations, computes a partition and prices that generate a $(1 - \delta)$-approximation to the maximum revenue obtainable by partition mechanisms.*

Proof outline.

In the next two subsections we prove a structural characterization of near optimal auctions: Lemmata 1 and 2 imply that there exists a near-optimal partition mechanism that uses only a constant number of non-trivial bundles (i.e. bundles with more than one item). Furthermore, the prices to these bundles are all within a constant factor, and all these bundles sell for these prices with constant probability.

In Subsection 6.3 we use our insight about the structure of near-optimal auctions to show that for optimizing over this restricted class of partitions, most of the information in the distribution is redundant. In particular we can place every item in one of $O(\log n)$ buckets, where the items within each bucket are indistinguishable for the algorithm. For each bucket, there are constantly-many options to approximately partition the identical items among constantly many bundles (or to be sold separately). We can enumerate over all approximate partitions for all buckets in polynomial time.

See also description of the algorithm in Subsection 6.4.

6.1 Singletons

Given the following lemma, we can assume wlog that every non-trivial bundle sells with probability at least ϵ.

LEMMA 1. *For any* $\delta > 0$*, let* $\epsilon \leq \delta^3/4$*. Let* $B \subseteq [n]$ *be a bundle of items, and let* $\pi_B \in \mathbb{R}_+$ *be an optimal price for* B*. Suppose that the revenue from auctioning* B *for price* π_B *is* $\epsilon \cdot \pi_B$*, i.e.* $\Pr\left[\sum_{i \in B} v_i \geq \pi_B\right] = \epsilon$*. Then the revenue from selling the items in* B *separately is at least* $(1-\delta) \cdot \epsilon \cdot \pi_B$*.*

PROOF. For the proof of this lemma, we simplify notation by normalizing to $\pi_B = 1$.

Below we prove that most of the revenue comes from the item with the highest value (this may be a different item in each realization). In particular, if the total value of the bundle is at least 1, then it is likely that there is a single item whose value is almost 1,

$$\Pr\left[\max_{i \in B} v_i \geq 1 - \delta/2 \mid \sum_{i \in B} v_i \geq 1\right] \geq 1 - \delta/2. \quad (1)$$

This means in particular that $\Pr\left[\max_{i \in B} v_i \geq 1 - \delta/2\right] \geq (1 - \delta/2)\epsilon$, and therefore selling each item separately for price $(1 - \delta/2)$ guarantees a $(1 - \delta/2)^2 \geq (1 - \delta)$-fraction of the revenue from selling B as a bundle.

We now prove (1). Since 1 is an optimal price for B, we have that the $\Pr\left[\sum_{i \in B} v_i \geq \delta/4\right] \leq \epsilon/(\delta/4)$, otherwise $\delta/4$ would have been a better price. What is the probability that there exist a partition $B = S \cup T$ such that $\sum_{i \in S} v_i \geq \delta/2$ and $\sum_{i \in T} v_i \geq \delta/2$? If we were to fix any partition $B = U \cup V$ before observing the realizations, or to pick one uniformly at random, we would have

$$\Pr\left[\left(\sum_{i \in U} v_i \geq \delta/4\right) \wedge \left(\sum_{i \in V} v_i \geq \delta/4\right)\right] \leq (\epsilon/(\delta/4))^2.$$

Now assume that there exist some partition (S, T) as above, and pick (U, V) uniformly at random. With probability at least $1/4$ we have that $\sum_{i \in (S \cap V)} v_i \geq \sum_{i \in (S \cap U)} v_i$ and $\sum_{i \in (T \cap V)} v_i \leq \sum_{i \in (T \cap U)} v_i$; and the same for the event that $\sum_{i \in (S \cap V)} v_i \geq \sum_{i \in (S \cap U)} v_i$ and $\sum_{i \in (T \cap V)} v_i \leq \sum_{i \in (T \cap U)} v_i$. Thus with probability at least $1/2$,

$$\min\left\{\sum_{i \in U} v_i, \sum_{i \in V} v_i\right\} \geq \min\left\{\sum_{i \in S} v_i, \sum_{i \in T} v_i\right\}/2.$$

Therefore the probability that there exist such (S, T) is at most $2(\epsilon/(\delta/4))^2$.

Observe that whenever $\sum_{i \in B} v_i \geq 1$ and $\max_{i \in B} v_i < 1 - \delta/2$, there exists a partition (S, T) as above: Let $S = \{\arg\max_{i \in B} v_i\}$ and $T = B \backslash S$; if $\max_{i \in B} v_i \geq \delta/2$, we're done. Otherwise, move items from T to S until $\sum_{i \in S} v_i \geq \delta/2$; since the last item we moved from S to T had value at most $\max_{i \in B} v_i < \delta/2$, we have $\sum_{i \in T} v_i \geq 1 - \delta > \delta/2$. Therefore,

$$\Pr\left[\max_{i \in B} v_i < 1 - \delta/2 \mid \sum_{i \in B} v_i \geq 1\right]$$
$$\leq \frac{\Pr\left[(\max_{i \in B} v_i < 1 - \delta/2) \wedge (\sum_{i \in B} v_i \geq 1)\right]}{\Pr\left[\sum_{i \in B} v_i \geq 1\right]} \leq \frac{32\epsilon}{\delta^2}.$$

Plugging in $\delta = 4\epsilon^{1/3}$ yields (1). □

6.2 Bundles

LEMMA 2. *For any constants* $0 < \epsilon \leq 1/2$ *and* $\delta > 0$ *we can replace all the bundles that sell with probability at least* ϵ *with* $\ell = \mathsf{poly}(1/\epsilon, 1/\delta)$ *bundles, while maintaining a* $(1 - 2\delta)$*-fraction of the expected revenue.*

PROOF. In Claim 1 we show that we can recursively combine bundles until in any interval of multiplicative-constant-length $[\epsilon \cdot \pi, \pi]$, there is at most a constant ($k = 8\epsilon^{-4}\delta^{-3}$) number of bundles. Then, in Claim 2 we show that we can ignore all bundles except those in some slightly larger interval $[\eta \cdot \pi, \pi]$ (for $\eta = \delta^4\epsilon^5(1 - \epsilon)$). This is a union of $\log_\epsilon \eta \leq \frac{\log \delta^4\epsilon^4(1-\epsilon)}{\log \epsilon}$ smaller intervals $[\epsilon \cdot \pi, \pi]$; together with the sparsity we obtained in Claim 1, this implies that we are left with at most $\ell = k \log_\epsilon \eta$ bundles. □

CLAIM 1. *For any* $\epsilon, \delta > 0$*, let* $k = 8\epsilon^{-4}\delta^{-3}$*. Consider only bundles* B_i *that sell for price* π_i *with probability at least* ϵ*. Partition the positive reals into multiplicative intervals* $[\epsilon \cdot \pi, \pi]$*. Consider* k *separate bundles* $B_1, \ldots, B_k$ *with prices* $\pi_1, \ldots, \pi_k$ *in the same interval* $[\epsilon \cdot \pi, \pi]$*, and associated probabilities of selling* $p_1, \ldots, p_k$*. Whenever we encounter such a* k*-tuple, we combine them into one bundle* B' *with price* $\pi' = \sum_i p_i \cdot \pi_i$ *and probability* $p' = 1$*. Recurse until every interval has at most* k *bundles. (The number of bundles decreases at each step, so this process is guaranteed to terminate.) Finally, discount all newly formed bundles by a factor of* $(1 - \delta/2)$*.*

Then every newly formed bundle sells with probability at least $1 - \delta/2$*. In particular, this guarantees an* $(1 - \delta)$ *approximation to the original revenue.*

PROOF. Let $B' = \bigcup B_i$ be any newly formed bundle, where B_i's, π_i's, and p_i's are the original bundles, prices and probabilities (i.e. B' may denote a union of union of bundles). Let v_{B_i} denote the random variable $v_{B_i} \triangleq \sum_{j \in B_i} v_j$; let also $\hat{v}_{B_i} \triangleq \min\{v_{B_i}, \pi_i\}$. Then we have

$$\mathsf{E}\left[\sum_i \hat{v}_{B_i}\right] \geq \sum_i p_i \cdot \pi_i \quad \text{and} \quad \mathsf{Var}\left[\sum_i \hat{v}_{B_i}\right] \leq \sum_i \pi_i^2.$$

Applying Chebyshev's inequality,

$$\Pr\left[\sum_i \hat{v}_{B_i} \leq (1 - \delta/2)\sum_i p_i \cdot \pi_i\right] \leq \frac{\sum \pi_i^2}{\left(\frac{\delta}{2} \cdot \sum_i p_i \cdot \pi_i\right)^2}.$$

In the last union that formed B', we combined at least k bundles, each with $p_i \pi_i \in \left[\epsilon^2 \pi, \pi\right]$. Therefore,

$$\frac{\sum_{i \in [k]} \pi_i^2}{\left(\frac{\delta}{2} \cdot \sum_{i \in [k]} p_i \cdot \pi_i\right)^2} \leqslant \frac{\sum_{i \in [k]} \pi^2}{\left(\frac{\delta}{2} \cdot \sum_{i \in [k]} \epsilon^2 \pi\right)^2} \leqslant \frac{4}{\delta^2 k \epsilon^4}.$$

Plugging in $k = 8\epsilon^{-4}\delta^{-3} \geqslant -\ln(\delta/2) \cdot (4\epsilon^{-4}\delta^{-2})$ guarantees that we sell the grand bundle with probability at least $1 - \delta/2$. $\square$

CLAIM 2. *For any $\epsilon, \delta > 0$, and let $\eta = \delta^4 \epsilon^5 (1 - \epsilon)$. Let bundles $B_1, \ldots, B_m$, have optimal prices $\pi_1, \ldots, \pi_m$, and denote $\pi^* = \max_{i \in [m]} \pi_i$. Suppose that bundle B_i sells for price π_i with probability $p_i \geqslant \epsilon$, for every $i \in [m]$. Suppose further that in each range $[\epsilon\pi, \pi]$ of prices we have at most $k = \epsilon^{-4}\delta^{-3}$ bundles (this is wlog by the previous claim). Then a $(1 - \delta)$-fraction of the revenue can be obtained by selling only the bundles with with price $\pi_i \geqslant \eta\pi^*$.*

PROOF. k bundles with prices in interval $[\epsilon\pi, \pi]$ can yield at most $k\pi$ revenue. Summing over $\pi \in \{\epsilon^0 \cdot \eta\pi^*, \epsilon^1 \cdot \eta\pi^*, \ldots\}$, we have that all those bundles together yield revenue at most $k\eta\pi^*/(1 - \epsilon)$. Plugging in $\eta = \delta^4\epsilon^5(1 - \epsilon)$ completes the proof of the claim. $\square$

6.3 Discretization

In this section we consider a sequence of manipulations on the distribution of each item's valuations. At the end of the manipulation, every item will fit in one of $O(\log n)$ buckets, with all the items in each bucket having indistinguishable distributions. The first step is to discretize the valuation distributions:

Definition 1. Let $\vec{D} \triangleq \times D_i$ be a valuation distribution over non-negative reals $(\mathbb{R}_+)$. Let

$$\mathcal{N}_\epsilon \triangleq \{0\} \cup \left\{\ldots, (1 + \epsilon)^{-1}, 1, (1 + \epsilon), (1 + \epsilon)^2, \ldots\right\}$$

be a multiplicative-$(1 + \epsilon)$-net over $\mathbb{R}_+$. For each i, we construct the *rounded valuation distribution* $D_i^{(1)}$ as follows: (a) round down every valuation in the support to the nearest smaller (or equal) element in $\mathcal{N}_\epsilon$; then (b) round down every probability of valuation in the new support to the nearest smaller (or equal) element in $\mathcal{N}_\epsilon$. Finally, we let $\vec{D}^{(1)} \triangleq \times D_i^{(1)}$.

The following lemma implies that for sufficiently small $\epsilon > 0$, the loss in revenue from rounding the valuations is negligible.

LEMMA 3. *For any constant $\epsilon > 0$, non-negative product distribution $\vec{D}$, and price π, we have*

$$\Pr_{\vec{v}^{(1)} \sim \vec{D}^{(1)}}\left[\sum v_i^{(1)} \geqslant (1 - \delta)\pi\right] \geqslant (1 - \delta)\Pr_{\vec{v} \sim \vec{D}}\left[\sum v_i \geqslant \pi\right],$$
$$(2)$$

where $\delta \triangleq 2\epsilon^{1/3}$.

PROOF. Rounding the valuations to $\mathcal{N}_\epsilon$ can decrease the sum by a factor of at most $(1 + \epsilon)$. Rounding the probabilities is slightly trickier. An equivalent way of formulating the rounded valuation distribution is to sample $\vec{v} \sim \vec{D}$, round down the valuation of each item to $\mathcal{N}_\epsilon$, and then zero the valuation of each item independently with probability at most ϵ. Inequality (2) now follows from

$$\Pr_{\vec{v} \sim \vec{D}}\left[\sum v_i^{(1)} \geqslant (1 - \delta)\pi \;\Big|\; \sum v_i \geqslant \pi\right] \geqslant 1 - \delta.$$

In particular, it suffices to show that for every $\vec{v}$ such that $\sum v_i \geqslant \pi$,

$$\Pr_{\vec{v}^{(1)}}\left[\sum v_i^{(1)} \geqslant (1 - \delta)\pi \;\Big|\; \vec{v}\right] \geqslant 1 - \delta, \qquad (3)$$

where the randomness is only over the independent zeroing of each valuation.

Fix any such $\vec{v}$ and let $\pi_{\vec{v}} \triangleq \sum v_i \geqslant \pi$. The expectation of the sum is at least $\mathsf{E}\left[\sum v_i^{(1)}\right] \geqslant (1 - \epsilon)^2 \pi_{\vec{v}}$, and the variance is at most $\epsilon \cdot (1 - \epsilon)^2 \pi_{\vec{v}}^2$. Therefore by Chebyshev's inequality,

$$\Pr\left[\sum v_i^{(1)} \leqslant (1 - \delta)\pi_{\vec{v}}\right] \leqslant \frac{\epsilon}{(\delta/2)^2}.$$

Plugging in $\delta = 2\epsilon^{1/3}$ completes yields (3). $\square$

Recall that we can assume wlog that all our bundles sell with constant probability for prices in $[\epsilon\pi, \pi]$ (Lemma 2). Thus, for the purpose of (approximately) evaluating an item's contribution to any bundle it suffices to consider only its valuations in $[\pi/n^2, \pi]$, rounding down larger valuations to π and ignoring smaller. Notice that the new support has size at most logarithmic: $\left|\mathcal{N}_\epsilon \cap [\pi/n^2, \pi]\right| = O(\log n)$. Similarly, for the purpose of bundling, we can assume wlog that every valuation in the support has probability at least $1/n^2$. Now each value in the support is associated with one of $\left|\mathcal{N}_\epsilon \cap [1/n^2, 1]\right| = O(\log n)$ potential probabilities.

In order to represent each item we need to know one more number - the revenue it can generate when sold separately. Here again we can assume wlog that this revenue is in $[\pi/n^2, \pi]$: if it is less than π/n^2, its revenue is negligible and we never want to sell this item separately; if it is greater than π, we always want to sell this item separately. The revenue from selling an item separately is a product of two numbers (price and probability) in $\mathcal{N}_\epsilon$, and therefore also belongs to $\mathcal{N}_\epsilon$. As before, this means that we can assume wlog that the expected revenue takes one of $\left|\mathcal{N}_\epsilon \cap [\pi/n^2, \pi]\right| = O(\log n)$ values.

So far for each item we need $O(\log n)$ numbers, each from a set of size $O(\log n)$. While this is much more succinct than the naive representation, it is still not good enough for our algorithmic application (at this point we still need $(\log n)^{O(\log n)} \gg n$ buckets). In the next two steps we reduce to only three numbers from sets of size $O(\log n)$: first, we show that in the lower end of the support it suffices to keep the aggregate expectation rather than probability of each value; second, we argue that we can assume wlog that all the high values in the support have approximately the same probability; and the third number is the expected revenue from selling separately.

Low values

Fix any $\epsilon > 0$, distribution $D_i^{(1)}$ over $\mathbb{R}_+$, and $\pi \in \mathbb{R}_+$. Define

$$v_i^{(2)} \triangleq \begin{cases} v_i^{(1)} & v_i^{(1)} \geqslant \epsilon\pi \\ \mathsf{E}_{u \sim D_i^{(1)}}\left[u \mid u < \epsilon\pi\right] & v_i^{(1)} < \epsilon\pi \end{cases};$$

round down the new value and probability to the nearest smaller elements in $\mathcal{N}_\epsilon$, and let $\vec{D}_i^{(2)}$ denote the resulting new distribution.

Intuitively, it may be helpful to think of $\vec{D}^{(2)}$ as "erasing" or "blurring" the information about $\vec{D}^{(1)}$ below $\epsilon\pi$. Notice that for any $\epsilon > 0$, $\mathsf{E}_{v_i^{(2)} \sim D_i^{(2)}} \left[v_i^{(2)} \right] = \mathsf{E}_{v_i^{(1)} \sim D_i^{(1)}} \left[v_i^{(1)} \right]$. The next lemma shows that $\vec{D}^{(2)}$ also generates approximately the same revenue.

LEMMA 4. *Let* $\epsilon > 0$, *let* $\delta = 2\epsilon^{1/3}$, *and let* $\vec{D}^{(1)}$ *be a product distribution. Then,*

$$\Pr_{\vec{v}^{(1)} \sim \vec{D}^{(1)}} \left[\sum v_i^{(1)} \geqslant \pi \right] - 2\delta \leqslant \Pr_{\vec{v}^{(2)} \sim \vec{D}^{(2)}} \left[\sum v_i^{(2)} \geqslant (1-\delta) \pi \right] - \delta$$

$$\leqslant \Pr_{\vec{v}^{(1)} \sim \vec{D}^{(1)}} \left[\sum v_i^{(1)} \geqslant (1-2\delta) \pi \right].$$

Recall that by Lemma 1, we can assume wlog that all bundles sell with probability $\Omega(1)$; thus we can tolerate the above additive loss in probability.

PROOF. By Chebyshev's inequality, the sum of valuations less than $\epsilon\pi$ is within an additive $\pm\delta\pi$ of its expectation with probability at least $1-\delta$ (and the rest of the valuations don't change at all). $\square$

High values

For any $\epsilon > 0$, a rounded distribution $D_i^{(2)}$ (in the sense of Definition 1), and $\pi \in \mathbb{R}_+$, let $p_i^* \triangleq \max_{v \in [\epsilon\pi, \pi]} \Pr_{u \sim D_i^{(2)}} [u = v]$ denote the most likely valuation in $[\epsilon\pi, \pi]$. Let $L_{D_i^{(2)}}^\epsilon$ denote the set of unlikely high valuations:

$$L_{D_i^{(2)}}^\epsilon \triangleq \left\{ v : \Pr_{u \sim D_i^{(2)}} [u = v] < \epsilon^4 p_i^* \right\} \cap [\epsilon\pi, \pi]$$

Let $D_i^{(3)}$ denote the restriction of $D_i^{(2)}$ to $\text{supp}\left\{ D_i^{(2)} \right\} \setminus L_{D_i^{(2)}}^\epsilon$:

$$v_i^{(3)} \triangleq \begin{cases} v_i^{(2)} & v_i^{(2)} \notin L_{D_i^{(2)}}^\epsilon \\ 0 & v_i^{(2)} \in L_{D_i^{(2)}}^\epsilon \end{cases}.$$

The following lemma implies that for each i it suffices to maintain p_i^* (which always takes one of $\left| \mathcal{N}_\epsilon \cap [1/n^2, 1] \right| = O(\log n)$ values), and a constant number of bits for each of the (constantly many) values in $\text{supp}\left\{ D_i^{(3)} \right\} \cap [\epsilon\pi, \pi]$.

LEMMA 5. *Let* $\vec{D}^{(2)}$ *be a rounded product distribution of valuations of items in* B. *Assume that selling bundle* B *for price* π *yields higher expected revenue than selling all the items in* B *separately. Then,*

$$\Pr_{\vec{v}^{(3)} \sim \vec{D}^{(3)}} \left[\sum_{i \in B} v_i^{(3)} \geqslant \pi \right] \geqslant (1-\delta) \Pr_{\vec{v}^{(2)} \sim \vec{D}^{(2)}} \left[\sum_{i \in B} v_i^{(2)} \geqslant \pi \right].$$

PROOF. We compare, for each item i, the potential revenue loss from switching from $D_i^{(2)}$ to $D_i^{(3)}$ to the expected revenue from selling i separately. We argue that for each i, the latter is much larger. Summing over all items, we have that the total loss is much smaller than the total revenue from selling every item separately. By the premise, the latter is less than the original revenue from selling the bundle.

By definition, item i has probability at least p_i^* of having value $\epsilon\pi$. Thus we can obtain revenue at least $p_i^* \cdot \epsilon\pi$ from selling it for price $\epsilon\pi$. In contrast, every time we zero a valuation, we could potentially lose revenue π. The total probability over items in $L_{D_i^{(2)}}^\epsilon$ is $\left| L_{D_i^{(2)}}^\epsilon \right| \epsilon^4 p_i^*$. Between $\epsilon\pi$ and π, there are at most $-\log\epsilon/\log(1+\epsilon) < 1/\epsilon^2$ elements

in $\mathcal{N}_\epsilon$; in particular, $\left| L_{D_i^{(2)}}^\epsilon \right| < 1/\epsilon^2$. Therefore, the revenue lost is at most an ϵ-fraction of the revenue from selling i separately. $\square$

From QPTAS to PTAS

We have reduced the representation of each item to three numbers in $\mathcal{N}_\epsilon \cap [\pi/n^2, \pi]$: the expectation over lower values, $\mathsf{E}_{u \sim D_i^{(3)}} [u \mid u < \epsilon\pi]$ (rounded down to $\mathcal{N}_\epsilon$); the quantity $p_i^* \cdot \pi$, where $p_i^* \triangleq \max_{v \in [\epsilon\pi, \pi]} \Pr_{u \sim D_i^{(3)}} [u = v]$ is the maximum probabilities over higher values; and the maximum revenue from selling i separately, $\text{SREV}(D_i)$. (For the higher values we also need a constant number of bits to specify which values have probabilities close to p_i^*, and how close.) At this point we need $O(\log^3 n)$ buckets, which would suffice for obtaining a Quasi-PTAS.

Our final step is to observe that if any of those three numbers is much lower than the maximum of the three, it might as well be zero. If $\mathsf{E}_{u \sim D_i} [u \mid u < \epsilon\pi]$ is much higher than $p_i^* \cdot \pi$, then it's contribution to revenue for any bundle outweighs the contribution from any of the higher values appearing with very low probability; similarly if $\mathsf{E}_{u \sim D_i} [u \mid u < \epsilon\pi] \gg \text{SREV}(D_i)$ we would always sell item i as part of one of the bundles. If $\text{SREV}(D_i^\epsilon)$ is much higher than either of the other two, then the contribution from selling item i separately outweighs the contribution (from the lower values, higher values, or both) to the revenue from any bundle. Finally, since $\text{SREV}(D_i) \geqslant p_i^* \epsilon\pi$, the revenue from selling separately is never much lower than the higher values' contribution.

6.4 Algorithm

We achieve a $(1-\delta)$-approximation of the optimal partition revenue for some constant $\delta > 0$; let $\epsilon = \epsilon(\delta) > 0$ be a sufficiently small constant, and let

$$\mathcal{N}_\epsilon \triangleq \{0\} \cup \left\{ \dots, (1+\epsilon)^{-1}, 1, (1+\epsilon), (1+\epsilon)^2, \dots \right\}.$$

For each item i, compute the optimum expected revenue from selling i separately, $\text{SREV}(D_i)$.

Before we analyze bundles, we first want to guess a range $[\epsilon\pi, \pi]$ in which all the bundle prices will lie. Let $v^{\min}$ denote the minimum over all nonzero values in the support of all items, and let $v^{\max}$ denote the sum, over all items, of the maximal values in their supports. An optimal π must belong to $[v^{\min}, v^{\max}]$. Enumerate over all potential π's in $\mathcal{N}_\epsilon$. By Lemma 2 for some choice of π, it suffices to optimize only over partitions with a constant number of non-trivial bundles, and each of those bundles sells for prices in $[\epsilon\pi, \pi]$ with probability at least ϵ. For the rest of the algorithm assume we have such an optimal choice of π.

For each i, round D_i as in Definition 1, and let $\vec{D}^{(1)}$ denote the resulting product distribution. ($\vec{D}^{(1)}$ is stochastically dominated by $\vec{D}$, thus the revenue obtained from a partition mechanism with valuations drawn from $\vec{D}^{(1)}$ is at most the revenue obtained with the same partition and pricing with valuations drawn from $\vec{D}$. In the other direction, Lemma 3 guarantees that the revenue lost is at most a small constant fraction.)

For each i, replace all values in $\left[0, \epsilon^2 \pi\right]$ with their expectation, and let $\vec{D}^{(2)}$ denote the resulting product distribution. (By Lemma 4, optimizing over bundles with prices in $[\epsilon\pi, \pi]$ with valuations drawn from $\vec{D}^{(2)}$ is the same up to a small constant factor as with valuations drawn from $\vec{D}^{(1)}$.)

For each i, let p_i^* denote the maximal probability $D_i^{(2)}$ gives to any value in $\left[\epsilon^2 \pi, \pi\right]$. Remove values with probabilities much smaller than p_i^* from the support of $D_i^{(2)}$, and let $\vec{D}^{(3)}$ denote the resulting product distribution. ($\vec{D}^{(3)}$ is stochastically dominated by $\vec{D}^{(2)}$, thus the revenue obtained from a partition mechanism with valuations drawn from $\vec{D}^{(3)}$ is at most the revenue obtained with the same partition and pricing with valuations drawn from $\vec{D}^{(2)}$. In the other direction, Lemma 5 guarantees that the revenue lost is at most a small constant fraction.)

For each i, we now have three variables which may be of different scale: $\text{SREV}(D_i)$, $\mathsf{E}_{u \sim D_i^{(3)}}\left[u \mid u < \epsilon^2 \pi\right]$, and $p_i^* \cdot \pi$; we also have the full description of $D_i^{(3)}$ restricted to $\left[\epsilon^2 \pi, \pi\right]$, which given p_i^* requires only a constant number of bits. If any of the three variables is much smaller than any of the others, set the smaller variable to zero.

We now represent each item with a constant number of variables, which are all either zero or within constant factors. In total, we have at most $O(\log n)$ distinct representations, which we henceforth call *buckets*.

Enumerate over the number of bundles (by Lemma 2 it suffices to consider only numbers up to some constant ℓ). For each bucket, we must decide how many items to allocate to each of the ℓ bundles, and which to sell separately. I.e. we must pick some vector in $[0,1]^{\ell+1}$, and up to $\pm\epsilon$, there are at most $\epsilon^{-(\ell+1)}$ different vectors; in particular, only a constant number of choices for each bucket. Enumerate (in polynomial time) over all choices for all $O(\log n)$ buckets.

Acknowledgments

I am grateful to Alon Eden, Amos Fiat, and Muli Safra for inspiring discussions. I also thank Jason Hartline, Christos Papadimitriou, Paul Tylkin, and anonymous reviewers for helpful comments on previous versions of this manuscript.

7. REFERENCES

[1] S. Alaei, H. Fu, N. Haghpanah, and J. Hartline. The Simple Economics of Approximately Optimal Auctions. In *the 54th Annual IEEE Symposium on Foundations of Computer Science (FOCS)*, 2013.

[2] S. Alaei, J. D. Hartline, R. Niazadeh, E. Pountourakis, and Y. Yuan. Optimal auctions vs. anonymous pricing. In *FOCS*, 2015.

[3] M. Babaioff, N. Immorlica, B. Lucier, and S. M. Weinberg. A simple and approximately optimal mechanism for an additive buyer. *FOCS*, 2014.

[4] M. Bateni, S. Dehghani, M. Hajiaghayi, and S. Seddighin. Revenue Maximization for Selling Multiple Correlated Items. *arxiv report*, 2015. http://arxiv.org/abs/1412.3187.

[5] Y. Cai and C. Daskalakis. Extreme-Value Theorems for Optimal Multidimensional Pricing. In *IEEE 52nd Annual Symposium on Foundations of Computer Science, FOCS 2011, Palm Springs, CA, USA, October 22-25, 2011*, pages 522–531, 2011.

[6] Y. Cai and Z. Huang. Simple and Nearly Optimal Multi-Item Auctions. In *the Twenty-Fourth Annual ACM-SIAM Symposium on Discrete Algorithms (SODA)*, 2013.

[7] X. Chen, I. Diakonikolas, D. Paparas, X. Sun, and M. Yannakakis. The complexity of optimal multidimensional pricing. In *the Twenty-Fifth Annual ACM-SIAM Symposium on Discrete Algorithms (SODA)*, 2014.

[8] C. Daskalakis, A. Deckelbaum, and C. Tzamos. The Complexity of Optimal Mechanism Design. In *the Twenty-Fifth Annual ACM-SIAM Symposium on Discrete Algorithms (SODA)*, 2014.

[9] C. Daskalakis, A. Deckelbaum, and C. Tzamos. Strong duality for a multiple-good monopolist. In *Proceedings of the Sixteenth ACM Conference on Economics and Computation, EC '15, Portland, OR, USA, June 15-19, 2015*, pages 449–450, 2015.

[10] S. Hart and N. Nisan. Approximate revenue maximization with multiple items. In *Proceedings of the 13th ACM Conference on Electronic Commerce, EC '12*, pages 656–656, 2012.

[11] S. Hart and N. Nisan. The menu-size complexity of auctions. In *Proceedings of the Fourteenth ACM Conference on Electronic Commerce, EC '13*, pages 565–566, 2013.

[12] S. Hart and P. J. Reny. Maximal Revenue with Multiple Goods: Nonmonotonicity and Other Observations. Discussion Paper Series dp630, The Center for the Study of Rationality, Hebrew University, Jerusalem, Nov. 2012.

[13] J. Hartline and T. Roughgarden. Simple versus optimal mechanisms. In *EC'09*, pages 225–234, 2009.

[14] R. M. Karp. Reducibility among combinatorial problems. In *Proceedings of a symposium on the Complexity of Computer Computations, held March 20-22, 1972, at the IBM Thomas J. Watson Research Center, Yorktown Heights, New York.*, pages 85–103, 1972.

[15] X. Li and A. C.-C. Yao. On revenue maximization for selling multiple independently distributed items. *Proceedings of the National Academy of Sciences*, 110(28):11232–11237, 2013.

[16] J. Morgenstern and T. Roughgarden. The pseudo-dimension of near-optimal auctions. *CoRR*, abs/1506.03684, 2015.

[17] A. Rubinstein and S. M. Weinberg. Simple mechanisms for a subadditive buyer and applications to revenue monotonicity. In *Proceedings of the Sixteenth ACM Conference on Economics and Computation, EC '15, Portland, OR, USA, June 15-19, 2015*, pages 377–394, 2015.

[18] A. C.-C. Yao. An n-to-1 Bidder Reduction for Multi-Item Auctions and its Applications. In *Proceedings of the Twenty-Sixth Annual ACM-SIAM Symposium on Discrete Algorithms, SODA 2015, San Diego, CA, USA, January 4-6, 2015*, pages 92–109, 2015.

Permanent V. Determinant: An Exponential Lower Bound Assuming Symmetry*

[Extended Abstract]

Joseph M. Landsberg
Department of Mathematics
Mailstop 3368, Texas A&M University
College Station, TX 77843-3368, USA
jml@math.tamu.edu

Nicolas Ressayre
Département de Mathématiques
Institut Camille Jordan (ICJ)
UMR CNRS 5208
Université Claude Bernard Lyon I
43 boulevard du 11 novembre 1918
69622 Villeurbanne cedex, France
ressayre@math.univ-lyon1.fr

ABSTRACT
Grenet's determinantal representation for the permanent is optimal among determinantal representations that are equivariant with respect to left multiplication by permutation and diagonal matrices (roughly half the symmetry group of the permanent). In particular, if any optimal determinantal representation of the permanent must be polynomially related to one with such symmetry, then Valiant's conjecture on permanent v. determinant is true.

Categories and Subject Descriptors
F.1.m [**Theory**]: Miscellaneous

Keywords
Geometric Complexity Theory, determinant, permanent, MSC 68Q15 (20G05)

1. INTRODUCTION
The determinant

$$\det_n(x) := \sum_{\sigma \in \mathfrak{S}_n} \mathrm{sgn}(\sigma) x^1_{\sigma(1)} x^2_{\sigma(2)} \cdots x^n_{\sigma(n)} \qquad (1)$$

is a homogeneous polynomial of degree n on the space of $n \times n$ matrices $\mathrm{Mat}_n(\mathbb{C})$. Here $\mathfrak{S}_n$ denotes the group of permutations on n elements and $\mathrm{sgn}(\sigma)$ denotes the sign of the permutation σ.

Despite its formula with $n!$ terms, $\det_n$ can be evaluated quickly, e.g., using Gaussian elimination, which exploits the large symmetry group of the determinant, e.g., $\det_n(x) = \det_n(AxB^{-1})$ for any $n \times n$ matrices A, B with determinant equal to one.

*A full version of this paper is available as [14].

Permission to make digital or hard copies of all or part of this work for personal or classroom use is granted without fee provided that copies are not made or distributed for profit or commercial advantage and that copies bear this notice and the full citation on the first page. Copyrights for components of this work owned by others than the author(s) must be honored. Abstracting with credit is permitted. To copy otherwise, or republish, to post on servers or to redistribute to lists, requires prior specific permission and/or a fee. Request permissions from Permissions@acm.org.

ITCS'16, January 14 - 16, 2016, Cambridge, MA, USA
ACM 978-1-4503-4057-1/16/01 ...$15.00.
DOI: http://dx.doi.org/10.1145/2840728.2840735

We will work exclusively over the complex numbers and with homogeneous polynomials, the latter restriction only for convenience. L. Valiant showed that given a homogeneous polynomial $P(y)$ in M variables, there exists an n and an affine linear map

$$\tilde{A} : \mathbb{C}^M \to \mathrm{Mat}_n(\mathbb{C})$$
$$y \mapsto \Lambda + A(y)$$

where Λ is a constant matrix and $y \mapsto A(y)$ is a linear map such that $P = \det_n \circ \tilde{A}$. Such $\tilde{A}$ is called a *determinantal representation* of P. When $M = m^2$ and P is the permanent polynomial

$$\mathrm{perm}_m(y) := \sum_{\sigma \in \mathfrak{S}_m} y^1_{\sigma(1)} y^2_{\sigma(2)} \cdots y^m_{\sigma(m)}, \qquad (2)$$

L. Valiant showed that one can take $n = O(2^m)$. As an algebraic analog of the $\mathbf{P} \neq \mathbf{NP}$ conjecture, he also conjectured that one cannot do much better:

CONJECTURE 1 (VALIANT [21]). *Let $n(m)$ be a function of m such that there exist affine linear maps*

$$\tilde{A}_m : \mathbb{C}^{m^2} \to \mathrm{Mat}_{n(m)}(\mathbb{C})$$

satisfying

$$\mathrm{perm}_m = \det_{n(m)} \circ \tilde{A}_m. \qquad (3)$$

Then $n(m)$ grows faster than any polynomial.

To measure progress towards Conjecture 1, define the determinantal complexity of the permanent $\mathrm{dc}(\mathrm{perm}_m)$ to be the smallest $n(m)$ such that there exists $\tilde{A}_m$ satisfying (3). The conjecture is that $\mathrm{dc}(\mathrm{perm}_m)$ grows faster than any polynomial in m. Lower bounds on $\mathrm{dc}(\mathrm{perm}_m)$ are: $\mathrm{dc}(\mathrm{perm}_m) > m$ (Marcus and Minc [15]), $\mathrm{dc}(\mathrm{perm}_m) > 1.06m$ (Von zur Gathen [23]), $\mathrm{dc}(\mathrm{perm}_m) > \sqrt{2}m - O(\sqrt{m})$ (Meshulam, reported in [23], and Cai [4]), with the current world record $\mathrm{dc}(\mathrm{perm}_m) \geq \frac{m^2}{2}$ [16] by Mignon and the second author. (Over $\mathbb{R}$, Yabe recently showed that $\mathrm{dc}_{\mathbb{R}}(\mathrm{perm}_m) \geq m^2 - 2m + 2$ [24], and in [5] Cai, Chen and Li extended the $\frac{m^2}{2}$ bound to arbitrary fields other than characteristic two.)

Inspired by *Geometric Complexity Theory* (GCT) [18], we focus on the *symmetries* of $\det_n$ and perm_m. Let $\text{GL}(\mathbb{C}^M) = \text{GL}_M$ denote the group of invertible linear maps $\mathbb{C}^M \to \mathbb{C}^M$. For $P \in S^m\mathbb{C}^{M*}$, a homogeneous polynomial of degree m on $\mathbb{C}^M$, let

$$G_P := \{g \in \text{GL}_M \mid P(g^{-1}y) = P(y) \quad \forall y \in \mathbb{C}^M\}$$

denote the *symmetry group* of P. For example $G_{\det_n} \simeq \text{S}(\text{GL}_n \times \text{GL}_n)/\mu_n \rtimes \mathbb{Z}_2$ [9], where $\text{S}(\text{GL}_n \times \text{GL}_n) = \{(A,B) \in \text{GL}_n \times \text{GL}_n \mid \det(A) = \det(B)\}$ and μ_n denotes the n-th roots of unity. The $\text{S}(\text{GL}_n \times \text{GL}_n)$ invariance comes from $\det(AxB^{-1}) = (\det A \det B^{-1})\det(x)$ and the $\mathbb{Z}_2$ is because $\det_n(x) = \det_n(x^T)$ where x^T is the transpose of the matrix x.

As observed in [18], the permanent (resp. determinant) is *characterized by its symmetries* in the sense that any polynomial $P \in S^m\mathbb{C}^{m^2*}$ with a symmetry group G_P such that $G_P \supseteq G_{\text{perm}_m}$ (resp. $G_P \supseteq G_{\det_m}$) is a scalar multiple of the permanent (resp. determinant). This property is the cornerstone of GCT. The program outlined in [18, 19] is an approach to Valiant's conjecture based on the functions on GL_{n^2} that respect the symmetry group $G_{\det_n}$, i.e., are invariant under the action of $G_{\det_n}$.

Guided by the principles of GCT, we ask:

What are the $\tilde{A}$ that respect the symmetry group of the permanent?

To make this question precise:

Definition 1. Let $\tilde{A} : \mathbb{C}^M \longrightarrow \text{Mat}_n(\mathbb{C})$ be a determinantal representation of $P \in S^m\mathbb{C}^{M*}$. Define

$$G_A = \{g \in G_{\det_n} \mid g \cdot \Lambda = \Lambda \text{ and } g \cdot A(\mathbb{C}^M) = A(\mathbb{C}^M)\},$$

the *symmetry group of the determinantal representation* $\tilde{A}$ of P.

The group G_A comes with a representation $\rho_A : G_A \longrightarrow \text{GL}(A(\mathbb{C}^M))$ obtained by restricting the action to $A(\mathbb{C}^M)$. We assume that P cannot be expressed using $M-1$ variables, i.e., that $P \notin S^m\mathbb{C}^{M-1}$ for any hyperplane $\mathbb{C}^{M-1} \subset \mathbb{C}^{M*}$. Then $A : \mathbb{C}^M \longrightarrow A(\mathbb{C}^M)$ is bijective. Let $A^{-1} : A(\mathbb{C}^M) \longrightarrow \mathbb{C}^M$ denote its inverse. Set

$$\bar{\rho}_A : G_A \longrightarrow \text{GL}_M \tag{4}$$
$$g \longmapsto A^{-1} \circ \rho_A(g) \circ A.$$

Then $\bar{\rho}_A(G_A) \subseteq G_P$.

Definition 2. We say $\tilde{A}$ is an *equivariant representation* of P if (4) surjects onto G_P.

If G is a subgroup of G_P, we say that $\tilde{A}$ *is G-equivariant* if G is contained in the image of $\bar{\rho}_A$.

In particular, in an equivariant presentation for the permanent there exists a subgroup of $\text{S}(\text{GL}_n \times \text{GL}_n)/\mu_n \rtimes \mathbb{Z}_2$ that surjects onto $[(\mathfrak{S}_m \ltimes T_m) \times (\mathfrak{S}_m \ltimes T_m)] \rtimes \mathbb{Z}_2$.

Example 1. Let $Q = \sum_{j=1}^M z_j^2 \in S^2\mathbb{C}^{M*}$ be a nondegenerate quadric. Then $G_Q = O(M)$ where $O(M) = \{B \in \text{GL}_M \mid B^{-1} = B^T\}$ is the orthogonal group, as for such B, $B \cdot Q = \sum_{i,j,k} B_{i,j}B_{k,j}z_iz_k = \sum_{ij}\delta_{ij}z_iz_j = Q$. Consider the determinantal representation

$$Q = \det_{M+1}\begin{pmatrix} 0 & -z_1 & \cdots & -z_M \\ z_1 & 1 & & \\ \vdots & & \ddots & \\ z_M & & & 1 \end{pmatrix}. \tag{5}$$

For $(\lambda, B) \in G_Q$, define an action on $Z \in \text{Mat}_{M+1}(\mathbb{C})$ by

$$Z \mapsto \begin{pmatrix} \lambda & 0 \\ 0 & B \end{pmatrix} Z \begin{pmatrix} \lambda^{-1} & 0 \\ 0 & B \end{pmatrix}^{-1}.$$

Write

$$X = \begin{pmatrix} x_1 \\ \vdots \\ x_M \end{pmatrix} \qquad \text{so} \qquad \tilde{A} = \begin{pmatrix} 0 & -X^T \\ X & \text{Id}_M \end{pmatrix}.$$

The relation $B^{-1} = B^T$ implies

$$\begin{pmatrix} \lambda & 0 \\ 0 & B \end{pmatrix} \cdot \begin{pmatrix} 0 & -X^T \\ X & \text{Id}_M \end{pmatrix} \cdot \begin{pmatrix} \lambda^{-1} & 0 \\ 0 & B \end{pmatrix}^{-1} = \begin{pmatrix} 0 & -(\lambda BX)^T \\ \lambda BX & \text{Id}_M \end{pmatrix}.$$

Taking $\det_{M+1}$ on both sides gives

$$\lambda^2 Q(X) = (\lambda, B) \cdot Q(X).$$

Thus $\tilde{A}$ is an equivariant representation of Q.

Definition 3. For $P \in S^m\mathbb{C}^{M*}$, define the *equivariant determinantal complexity* of P, denoted $\text{edc}(P)$, to be the smallest n such that there is an equivariant determinantal representation of P.

Of course $\text{edc}(P) \geq \text{dc}(P)$. We do not know if $\text{edc}(P)$ is finite in general. Our main result is that $\text{edc}(\text{perm}_m)$ is exponential in m.

2. RESULTS

2.1 Main Theorem

THEOREM 1. *Let $m \geq 3$. Then $\text{edc}(\text{perm}_m) = \binom{2m}{m} - 1 \sim 4^m$.*

There are several instances in complexity theory where an optimal algorithm partially respects symmetry, e.g. Strassen's algorithm for 2×2 matrix multiplication respects the $\mathbb{Z}_3$-symmetry of the matrix multiplication operator (see [13, §4.2]), but not the $GL_2^{\times 3}$ symmetry.

For the purposes of Valiant's conjecture, we ask the weaker question:

QUESTION 1. *Does there exist a polynomial $e(d)$ such that $\text{edc}(\text{perm}_m) \leq e(\text{dc}(\text{perm}_m))$?*

Theorem 1 implies:

COROLLARY 1. *If the answer to Question 1 is affirmative, then Conjecture 1 is true.*

We have no opinion as to what the answer to Question 1 should be, but as it provides a new potential path to proving Valiant's conjecture, it merits further investigation. Note that Question 1 is a *flip* in the terminology of [17], since a positive answer is an existence result. It fits into the more general question: *When an object has symmetry, does it admit an optimal expression that preserves its symmetry?*

Example 2. Let $T \in W^{\otimes d}$ be a symmetric tensor, i.e. $T \in S^d W \subset W^{\otimes d}$. Say T can be written as a sum of r rank one tensors, then P. Comon conjectures [6] that it can be written as a sum of r rank one symmetric tensors.

Example 3. The optimal Waring decomposition of $x_1 \cdots x_n$, dating back at least to [8] and proved to be optimal in [20] is

$$x_1 \cdots x_n = \frac{1}{2^{n-1}n!} \sum_{\substack{\epsilon \in \{-1,1\}^n \\ \epsilon_1 = 1}} \left(\sum_{j=1}^n \epsilon_j x_j \right)^n \Pi_{i=1}^n \epsilon_i, \quad (6)$$

a sum with 2^{n-1} terms. This decomposition has an $\mathfrak{S}_{n-1}$-symmetry but not an $\mathfrak{S}_n$-symmetry, nor does it preserve the action of the torus T^{SL_n} of diagonal matrices with determinant one. One can obtain an $\mathfrak{S}_n$-invariant expression by doubling the size:

$$x_1 \cdots x_n = \frac{1}{2^n n!} \sum_{\epsilon \in \{-1,1\}^n} \left(\sum_{j=1}^n \epsilon_j x_j \right)^n \Pi_{i=1}^n \epsilon_i,, \quad (7)$$

because

$$(-x_1 + \epsilon_2 x_2 + \cdots + \epsilon_n x_n)^n (-1)\epsilon_2 \cdots \epsilon_n$$
$$= (-1)^n (x_1 + (-\epsilon_2)x_2 + \cdots + (-\epsilon_n)x_n)^n (-1)\epsilon_2 \cdots \epsilon_n$$
$$= (x_1 + (-\epsilon_2)x_2 + \cdots + (-\epsilon_n)x_n)^n (-\epsilon_2) \cdots (-\epsilon_n).$$

The optimal Waring decomposition of the permanent is not known, but it is known to be of size greater than $\binom{n}{\lfloor n/2 \rfloor}^2 \sim 4^n/\sqrt{n}$. The Ryser-Glynn formula [10] is

$$\text{perm}_n(x) = 2^{-n+1} \sum_{\substack{\epsilon \in \{-1,1\}^n \\ \epsilon_1 = 1}} \prod_{1 \le i \le n} \sum_{1 \le j \le n} \epsilon_i \epsilon_j x_{i,j}, \quad (8)$$

the outer sum taken over n-tuples $(\epsilon_1 = 1, \epsilon_2, \cdots, \epsilon_n)$. This $\mathfrak{S}_{n-1} \times \mathfrak{S}_{n-1}$-invariant formula can also be made $\mathfrak{S}_n \times \mathfrak{S}_n$-invariant by enlarging it by a factor of 4, to get a $\mathfrak{S}_n \times \mathfrak{S}_n$ homogeneous depth three formula that is within a factor of four of the best known. Then expanding each monomial above, using Equation (7), one gets a $\mathfrak{S}_n \times \mathfrak{S}_n$-Waring expression within a factor of $O(\sqrt{n})$ of the lower bound.

Example 4. Examples regarding equivariant representations of $\mathfrak{S}_N$-invariant functions from the Boolean world give inconclusive indications regarding Question 1.

The MOD_m-degree of a Boolean function $f(x_1, \ldots, x_N)$ is the smallest degree of any polynomial $P \in \mathbb{Z}[x_1, \ldots, x_N]$

such that $f(x) = 0$ if and only if $P(x) = 0$ for all $x \in \{0,1\}^N$. The known upper bound for the MOD_m-degree of the Boolean OR function ($OR(x_1, \ldots, x_N) = 1$ if any $x_j = 1$ and is zero if all $x_j = 0$) is attained by symmetric polynomials [3]. Moreover in [3] it is also shown that this bound cannot be improved with symmetric polynomials, and it is far from the known lower bound.

The boolean majority function $MAJ(x_1, \ldots, x_N)$ takes on 1 if at least half the $x_j = 1$ and zero otherwise. The best monotone Boolean formula for MAJ [22] is polynomial in N and attained using random functions, and it is expected that the only symmetric monotone formula for majority is the trivial one, disjunction of all $\frac{n}{2}$-size subsets (or its dual), which is of exponential size.

QUESTION 2. *Does every P that is determined by its symmetry group admit an equivariant determinantal representation? For those P that do, how much larger must such a determinantal representation be from the size of a minimal one?*

2.2 Grenet's formulas

The starting point of our investigations was the result in [2] that $dc(\text{perm}_3) = 7$, in particular Grenet's representation [11] for perm_3:

$$\text{perm}_3(y) = \det_7 \begin{pmatrix} 0 & 0 & 0 & 0 & y_3^3 & y_2^3 & y_1^3 \\ y_1^1 & 1 & & & & & \\ y_2^1 & & 1 & & & & \\ y_3^1 & & & 1 & & & \\ & y_2^2 & y_1^2 & 0 & 1 & & \\ & y_3^2 & 0 & y_1^2 & & 1 & \\ & 0 & y_3^2 & y_2^2 & & & 1 \end{pmatrix}, \quad (9)$$

is optimal. We sought to understand (9) from a geometric perspective. A first observation is that it, and more generally Grenet's representation for perm_m as a determinant of size $2^m - 1$ is equivariant with respect to about half the symmetries of the permanent. In particular, the optimal expression for perm_3 is equivariant with respect to about half its symmetries.

For example, the action of $T_3 \subset SL_3$ on $\text{Mat}_3(\mathbb{C})$ given by

$$\begin{pmatrix} y_1^1 & y_2^1 & y_3^1 \\ y_1^2 & y_2^2 & y_3^2 \\ y_1^3 & y_2^3 & y_3^3 \end{pmatrix} \mapsto \begin{pmatrix} t_1 & & \\ & t_2 & \\ & & t_3 \end{pmatrix} \begin{pmatrix} y_1^1 & y_2^1 & y_3^1 \\ y_1^2 & y_2^2 & y_3^2 \\ y_1^3 & y_2^3 & y_3^3 \end{pmatrix}$$

with $t_1 t_2 t_3 = 1$, appears in $S(GL_7 \times GL_7)$ as

$$A \mapsto \rho(t) A \rho(t)^{-1}$$

where

$$\rho(t) = \begin{pmatrix} t_3 & & & & & \\ & t_1 t_3 & & & & \\ & & t_1 t_3 & & & \\ & & & t_1 t_3 & & \\ & & & & 1 & \\ & & & & & 1 \\ & & & & & & 1 \end{pmatrix}$$

and there is a similar inclusion of $\mathfrak{S}_3$ into $SL_7 \times SL_7$.

To explain this observation, introduce the following notation. Write $\mathrm{Mat}_m(\mathbb{C}) = \mathrm{Hom}(F, E) = F^* \otimes E$, where $E, F = \mathbb{C}^m$. This distinction of the two copies of $\mathbb{C}^m$ clarifies the action of the group $\mathrm{SL}(E) \times \mathrm{SL}(F)$ on $\mathrm{Hom}(F, E)$. This action is $(A, B).x = AxB^{-1}$, for any $x \in \mathrm{Hom}(F, E)$ and $(A, B) \in \mathrm{SL}(E) \times \mathrm{SL}(F)$. Let $T^{\mathrm{SL}(E)} \subset \mathrm{SL}(E)$ consist of the diagonal matrices and let $N(T^{\mathrm{SL}(E)}) = T^{\mathrm{SL}(E)} \rtimes \mathfrak{S}_m \subset \mathrm{GL}(E)$ be its normalizer, where $\mathfrak{S}_m$ denotes the group of permutations on m elements. Similarly for $T^{\mathrm{SL}(F)}$ and $N(T^{\mathrm{SL}(F)})$. Then $G_{\mathrm{perm}_m} \simeq [(N(T^{\mathrm{SL}(E)}) \times N(T^{\mathrm{SL}(F)}))/\mathbb{C}^*] \rtimes \mathbb{Z}_2$, where the embedding of $(N(T^{\mathrm{SL}(E)}) \times N(T^{\mathrm{SL}(F)}))/\mathbb{C}^*$ in $\mathrm{GL}(\mathrm{Hom}(F, E))$ is given by the action above and the term $\mathbb{Z}_2$ corresponds to transposition.

The following refinement of Theorem 1 asserts that to get an exponential lower bound it is sufficient to be equivariant with respect about half the symmetries of the permanent.

THEOREM 2. *Let $m \geq 3$. Let $\tilde{A}_m : \mathrm{Mat}_m(\mathbb{C}) \longrightarrow \mathrm{Mat}_n(\mathbb{C})$ be a determinantal representation of perm_m that is equivariant with respect to $N(T^{\mathrm{SL}(E)})$. Then $n \geq 2^m - 1$.*

Moreover, Grenet's determinantal representation of perm_m is equivariant with respect to $N(T^{\mathrm{SL}(E)})$ and has size $2^m - 1$.

We now explain Grenet's expressions from a representation-theoretic perspective. Let $[m] := \{1, \ldots, m\}$ and let $k \in [m]$. Note that $S^k E$ is an irreducible $\mathrm{SL}(E)$-module but it is is not irreducible as an $N(T^{\mathrm{SL}(E)})$-module. For example, let $e_1, \ldots, e_m$ be a basis of E, and let $(S^k E)_{reg}$ denote the span of $\prod_{i \in I} e_i$, for $I \subset [m]$ of cardinality k (the space spanned by the square-free monomials, also known as the space of *regular weights*): $(S^k E)_{reg}$ is an irreducible $N(T^{\mathrm{SL}(E)})$-submodule of $S^k E$. Moreover, there exists a unique $N(T^{\mathrm{SL}(E)})$-equivariant projection π_k from $S^k E$ to $(S^k E)_{reg}$.

For $v \in E$, define $s_k(v) : (S^k E)_{reg} \to (S^{k+1} E)_{reg}$ to be multiplication by v followed by π_{k+1}. Alternatively, $(S^{k+1} E)_{reg}$ is an $N(T^{\mathrm{SL}(E)})$-submodule of $E \otimes (S^k E)_{reg}$, and $s_k : E \to (S^k E)_{reg}^* \otimes (S^{k+1} E)_{reg}$ is the unique $N(T^{\mathrm{SL}(E)})$-equivariant inclusion. Let $\mathrm{Id}_W : W \to W$ denote the identity map on the vector space W. Fix a basis $f_1, \ldots, f_m$ of F^*.

PROPOSITION 1. *The following is Grenet's determinantal representation of perm_m. Let $\mathbb{C}^n = \bigoplus_{k=0}^{m-1} (S^k E)_{reg}$, so $n = 2^m - 1$, and identify $S^0 E \simeq (S^m E)_{reg}$. Set*

$$\Lambda_0 = \sum_{k=1}^{m-1} \mathrm{Id}_{(S^k E)_{reg}}$$

and define

$$\tilde{A} = \Lambda_0 + \sum_{k=0}^{m-1} s_k \otimes f_{k+1}. \tag{10}$$

Then $(-1)^{m+1} \mathrm{perm}_m = \det_n \circ \tilde{A}$. To obtain the permanent exactly, replace $\mathrm{Id}_{(S^1 E)_{reg}}$ by $(-1)^{m+1} \mathrm{Id}_{(S^1 E)_{reg}}$ in the formula for Λ_0.

In bases respecting the block decomposition induced from the direct sum, the linear part, other than the last term which lies in the upper right block, lies just below the diagonal blocks, and all blocks other than the upper right block and the diagonal and sub-diagonal blocks, are zero.

Moreover $N(T^{\mathrm{SL}(E)}) \subseteq \bar{\rho}_A(G_A)$.

Remark 1. In the spirit of the GCT program, Proposition 1 gives an essentially calculation free proof of Grenet's formulas, as the permanent is the unique polynomial up to scale invariant under $N(T^{\mathrm{SL}(E)})$. One need only check the value e.g. at the identity matrix.

2.3 An equivariant representation of the permanent

We now give a minimal equivariant determinantal representation of perm_m. By Theorem 1, its size is $\binom{2m}{m} - 1$. For $e \otimes f \in E \otimes F^*$, let $S_k(e \otimes f) : (S^k E)_{reg} \otimes (S^k F^*)_{reg} \to (S^{k+1} E)_{reg} \otimes (S^{k+1} F^*)_{reg}$ be multiplication by e on the first factor and f on the second followed by projection into

$$(S^{k+1} E)_{reg} \otimes (S^{k+1} F^*)_{reg}.$$

Equivalently,

$$S_k : (E \otimes F^*) \to$$
$$((S^k E)_{reg} \otimes (S^k F^*)_{reg})^* \otimes (S^{k+1} E)_{reg} \otimes (S^{k+1} F^*)_{reg}$$

is the unique $N(T^{\mathrm{SL}(E)}) \times N(T^{\mathrm{SL}(F)})$ equivariant inclusion.

PROPOSITION 2. *The following is an equivariant determinantal representation of perm_m: Let*

$$\mathbb{C}^n = \oplus_{k=0}^{m-1} (S^k E)_{reg} \otimes (S^k F^*)_{reg},$$

so $n = \binom{2m}{m} - 1 \sim 4^m$. Fix a linear isomorphism $S^0 E \otimes S^0 F^* \simeq (S^m E)_{reg} \otimes (S^m F^*)_{reg}$. Set

$$\Lambda_0 = \sum_{k=1}^{m-1} \mathrm{Id}_{(S^k E)_{reg} \otimes (S^k F^*)_{reg}}$$

and define

$$\tilde{A} = (m!)^{\frac{-1}{n-m}} \Lambda_0 + \sum_{k=0}^{m-1} S_k. \tag{11}$$

Then $(-1)^{m+1} \mathrm{perm}_m = \det_n \circ \tilde{A}$. In bases respecting the block structure induced by the direct sum, except for S_{m-1}, which lies in the upper right hand block, the linear part lies just below the diagonal block.

2.4 Determinantal representations of quadrics

It will be instructive to examine other polynomials determined by their symmetry groups. Perhaps the simplest such is a nondegenerate quadratic form.

Let $Q = \sum_{j=1}^{s} x_j y_j \in S^2 \mathbb{C}^{2s*}$ be a non-degenerate quadratic form in $2s$ variables (such is equivalent to $\sum_{u=1}^{2s} z_u^2$ under a change of basis). The polynomial Q is characterized by its symmetries. By [16], if $s \geq 3$, the smallest determinantal representation of Q is of size $s + 1$:

$$\tilde{A} = \begin{pmatrix} 0 & -x_1 & \cdots & -x_s \\ y^1 & 1 & & \\ \vdots & & \ddots & \\ y^s & & & 1 \end{pmatrix}. \tag{12}$$

This representation is equivariant with respect to $O(s) \subset G_Q = O(2s)$ (where the inclusion of $O(s)$ in $GL_{(s+1)^2}$ is first into GL_{s+1} acting on the last s basis vectors and then into $GL_{(s+1)^2}$ acting by conjugation) and there is no size $s+1$ determinantal representation equivariant with respect to G_Q. However, Example 1 shows there is a size $2s+1$ determinantal representation equivariant with respect to G_Q.

PROPOSITION 3. *Let $Q \in S^2\mathbb{C}^{M^*}$ be a nondegenerate quadratic form, that is, a homogeneous polynomial of degree 2. Then*

$$\mathrm{edc}(Q) = M + 1.$$

2.5 Determinantal representations of the determinant

Although it may appear strange at first, one can ask for determinantal representations of $\det_m$. In this case, to get an interesting lower bound, we add a regularity condition:

Definition 4. Let $P \in S^m\mathbb{C}^{M^*}$. A determinantal representation $\tilde{A} : \mathbb{C}^M \longrightarrow \mathrm{Mat}_n(\mathbb{C})$ is said to be *regular* if $\tilde{A}(0)$ has rank $n - 1$.

Call the minimal size of a regular determinantal representation of P the *regular determinantal complexity of P* and denote it by $\mathrm{rdc}(P)$. Let $\mathrm{erdc}(P)$ denote the minimal size of a regular equivariant determinantal representation of P.

In [23], von zur Gathen showed that any determinantal representation of perm_m or a smooth quadric is regular. In contrast, the trivial determinantal representation of $\det_m$ is not regular; but this representation is equivariant so $\mathrm{edc}(\det_m) = m$.

THEOREM 3. $\mathrm{erdc}(\det_m) = \binom{2m}{m} - 1 \sim 4^m$.

As in the case of the permanent, we can get an exponential lower bound using only about half the symmetries of the determinant.

THEOREM 4. *Let $\tilde{A}_m : \mathrm{Mat}_m(\mathbb{C}) \longrightarrow \mathrm{Mat}_n(\mathbb{C})$ be a regular determinantal representation of $\det_m$ that is equivariant with respect to $\mathrm{SL}(E)$. Then $n \geq 2^m - 1$.*

Moreover, there exists a regular determinantal representation of $\det_m$ that is equivariant with respect to $\mathrm{SL}(E)$ of size $2^m - 1$.

Remark 2. Normally when one obtains the same lower bound for the determinant as the permanent in some model it is discouraging for the model. However here there is an important difference due to the imposition of regularity for the determinant. We discuss this further below Question 3.

We now introduce notation to describe the regular determinantal representation of $\det_m$ that is equivariant with respect to $\mathrm{SL}(E)$ of size $2^m - 1$ mentioned in Theorem 4.

Observe that $(S^k E)_{reg} \subset E^{\otimes k}$ is isomorphic to the skew-symmetric tensors $\Lambda^k E \subset E^{\otimes k}$ as a $T^{\mathrm{SL}(E)}$-module but not as an $\mathfrak{S}_m$-module.

Write $\mathrm{Mat}_m(\mathbb{C}) = E \otimes F^*$. Let $f_1, \ldots, f_m$ be a basis of F^*. Let ex_k denote exterior multiplication in E:

$$ex_k : E \longrightarrow (\Lambda^k E)^* \otimes (\Lambda^{k+1} E)$$
$$v \mapsto \{\omega \mapsto v \wedge \omega\}.$$

PROPOSITION 4. *The following is a regular determinantal representation of $\det_m$ that is equivariant with respect to $\mathrm{SL}(E)$. Let*

$$\mathbb{C}^n = \bigoplus_{j=0}^{m-1} \Lambda^j E,$$

so $n = 2^m - 1$ and

$$\mathrm{End}(\mathbb{C}^n) = \oplus_{0 \leq i, j \leq m-1} \mathrm{Hom}(\Lambda^j E, \Lambda^i E).$$

Fix an identification $\Lambda^m E \simeq \Lambda^0 E$. Set

$$\Lambda_0 = \sum_{k=1}^{m-1} \mathrm{Id}_{\Lambda^k E},$$

and

$$\tilde{A} = \Lambda_0 + \sum_{k=0}^{m-1} ex_k \otimes f_{k+1}. \tag{13}$$

Then $\det_m = \det_n \circ \tilde{A}$ if $m \equiv 1, 2 \bmod 4$ and $\det_m = -\det_n \circ \tilde{A}$ if $m \equiv 0, 3 \bmod 4$. In bases respecting the direct sum, the linear part, other than the last term which lies in the upper right block, lies just below the diagonal blocks, and all blocks other than the upper right, the diagonal and sub-diagonal are zero.

Note the similarity with the expression (10). This guided the proofs in the permanent case. There is a functor, called the the Howe-Young duality functor [1], which enables one to transport arguments in the determinant case (which is more familiar) to the permanent cases. (This functor also enabled the computation of the linear strand of the minimal free resolution of the ideal generated by subpermanents in [7].)

When $m = 2$ this is

$$\begin{pmatrix} 0 & -y_2^2 & y_1^2 \\ y_1^1 & 1 & 0 \\ y_2^1 & 0 & 1 \end{pmatrix}$$

agreeing with our earlier calculation of a rank four quadric. Note the minus sign in front of y_2^2 because $ex(e_2)(e_1) = -e_1 \wedge e_2$.

For example, ordering the bases of $\Lambda^2 \mathbb{C}^3$ by $e_1 \wedge e_2, e_1 \wedge e_3, e_2 \wedge e_3$, the matrix for $\det_3$ is

$$\begin{pmatrix} 0 & 0 & 0 & 0 & y_3^3 & -y_2^3 & y_1^3 \\ y_1^1 & 1 & & & & & \\ y_2^1 & & 1 & & & & \\ y_3^1 & & & 1 & & & \\ & -y_2^2 & y_1^2 & 0 & 1 & & \\ & -y_3^2 & 0 & y_1^2 & & 1 & \\ & 0 & -y_3^2 & y_2^2 & & & 1 \end{pmatrix}.$$

We now give a regular equivariant determinantal representation of $\det_m$. Let EX_k denote the exterior multiplication

$$EX_k : E \otimes F^* \longrightarrow (\Lambda^k E \otimes \Lambda^k F^*)^* \otimes (\Lambda^{k+1} E \otimes \Lambda^{k+1} F^*)$$
$$e \otimes f \mapsto \{\omega \otimes \eta \mapsto e \wedge \omega \otimes f \wedge \eta\},$$

PROPOSITION 5. *The following is an equivariant regular determinantal representation of* $\det_m$. *Let*

$$\mathbb{C}^n = \bigoplus_{j=0}^{m-1} \Lambda^j E \otimes \Lambda^j F^*,$$

so $n = \binom{2m}{m} - 1 \sim 4^m$ *and*

$$\text{End}(\mathbb{C}^n) = \oplus_{0 \le i,j \le m} \text{Hom}(\Lambda^j E \otimes \Lambda^j F^*, \Lambda^i E \otimes \Lambda^i F^*).$$

Fix an identification $\Lambda^m E \otimes \Lambda^m F^* \simeq \Lambda^0 E \otimes \Lambda^0 F^*$. *Set*

$$\Lambda_0 = \sum_{k=1}^{m-1} \text{Id}_{\Lambda^k E \otimes \Lambda^k F^*}$$

and define

$$\tilde{A} = (m!)^{\frac{-1}{n-m}} \Lambda_0 + \sum_{k=0}^{m-1} EX_k. \qquad (14)$$

Then $(-1)^{m+1} \det_m = \det_n \circ \tilde{A}$.

Comparing Theorems 1 and 3, Theorems 2 and 4, Propositions 1 and 4 and Propositions 2 and 5, one can see that $\det_m$ and perm_m have the same behavior relatively to equivariant regular determinantal representations. This prompts the question: What is the regular determinantal complexity of the determinant? In particular:

QUESTION 3. *Let* $\text{rdc}(\det_m)$ *be the smallest value of* n *such that there exist affine linear maps* $\tilde{A}_m : \mathbb{C}^{m^2} \to \mathbb{C}^{n^2}$ *such that*

$$\det_m = \det_n \circ \tilde{A}_m \text{ and } \text{rank} \tilde{A}(0) = n-1. \qquad (15)$$

What is the growth of $\text{rdc}(\det_m)$?

In [12] it is shown that $\text{rdc}(\det_m)$ grows at most like $O(m^4)$. If one could prove a lower bound on $\text{rdc}(\det_m)$ of $m^2 \log(m)$

or better, and transfer it to the permanent via the Howe-Young duality functor this would be a significant improvement of the state of the art for $\text{dc}(\text{perm}_m)$. Because of the symmetries of $\det_n$, such a bound might be easier than determining the growth of $\text{dc}(\text{perm}_m)$. However to prove unrestricted exponential lower bounds, one must deal directly with the permanent.

3. OVERVIEW OF THE PROOFS

Let $\Lambda_{n-1} \in \text{Mat}_n(\mathbb{C})$ be the matrix with 1 in the $n-1$ last diagonal entries and 0 elsewhere. Any determinantal representation $\tilde{A}$ of P of size n with $\text{rank}(\tilde{A}(0)) = n-1$ can be transformed (by multiplying on the left and right by constant invertible matrices) to a determinantal representation of P satisfying $\tilde{A}(0) = \Lambda_{n-1}$.

The following group plays a central role in the study of regular equivariant determinantal representations:

$$G_{\det_n, \Lambda_{n-1}} = \{g \in G_{\det_n} \mid g \cdot \Lambda_{n-1} = \Lambda_{n-1}\}.$$

Let $\mathbb{H} = \mathbb{C}^{n-1} \subset \mathbb{C}^n$ denote the image of Λ_{n-1} and $\ell_1 \in \mathbb{C}^n$ its kernel. Write ℓ_2 for ℓ_1 in the target $\mathbb{C}^n$. Then $\text{Mat}_n(\mathbb{C}) = (\ell_1 \oplus \mathbb{H})^* \otimes (\ell_2 \oplus \mathbb{H})$. Let $\text{transp} \in \text{GL}(\text{Mat}_n(\mathbb{C}))$ denote the transpose, and let w^T the row vector obtained by transposing the column vector w.

LEMMA 1. *The group* $G_{\det_n, \Lambda_{n-1}}$ *is*

$$\left\{ M \mapsto \begin{pmatrix} \lambda & 0 \\ v & g \end{pmatrix} M \begin{pmatrix} \lambda^{-1} & w^T \\ 0 & g^{-1} \end{pmatrix} \right.$$
$$\left. \mid g \in \text{GL}(\mathbb{H}), v, w \in \mathbb{H}, \lambda^{-1} = \det(g) \right\} \cdot \langle \text{transp} \rangle.$$

Let $P \in S^m \mathbb{C}^{M^*}$ be either a quadric, a permanent or a determinant. Say a regular representation $\tilde{A}$ is equivariant with respect to some $G \subseteq G_P$. We may assume that $\tilde{A}(0) = \Lambda_{n-1}$.

The first step consists in lifting G to G_A. More precisely, in each case we construct a reductive subgroup $\tilde{G}$ of G_A such that $\bar{\rho}_A : \tilde{G} \longrightarrow G$ is finite and surjective. In a first reading, it is relatively harmless to assume that $\tilde{G} \simeq G$. Then, using Malcev's theorem (see, e.g. [14]), after possibly conjugating $\tilde{A}$, we may assume that $\tilde{G}$ is contained in $(\text{GL}(\ell_2) \times \text{GL}(\mathbb{H})) \rtimes \mathbb{Z}_2$. Up to considering an index two subgroup of $\tilde{G}$ if necessary, we assume that $\tilde{G}$ is contained in $\text{GL}(\ell_2) \times \text{GL}(\mathbb{H})$.

The starting point is Schur's lemma, which restricts nonzero G-module maps between irreducible G-modules to isomorphic modules. In the case $G = G_P$ (respectively $G \subset G_P$), then $\mathbb{C}^M$ is an irreducible G-module (resp. we decompose it into a direct sum of irreducible G-modules). Write $\text{Mat}_n(\mathbb{C}) = (\ell_1 \oplus \mathbb{H})^* \otimes (\ell_2 \oplus \mathbb{H})$, where $\mathbb{H} \subset \mathbb{C}^n$ is a hyperplane and the ℓ_j are lines.

In the two permanent cases $\mathbb{C}^M$ is respectively $E^{\oplus m}$ as a $\text{GL}(E)$-module and $E \otimes F$ as a $GL(E) \times GL(F)$-module

Write

$$\text{Mat}_n(\mathbb{C}) = \begin{pmatrix} \ell_1^* \otimes \ell_2 & \mathbb{H}^* \otimes \ell_2 \\ \ell_1^* \otimes \mathbb{H} & \mathbb{H}^* \otimes \mathbb{H} \end{pmatrix}, \quad \Lambda_{n-1} = \begin{pmatrix} 0 & 0 \\ 0 & \text{Id}_{\mathbb{H}} \end{pmatrix}.$$

If $m \geq 2$ the $\ell_1^* \otimes \ell_2$ coefficient of $\tilde{A}$ has to be zero. Then, since $P \neq 0$, the projection of $A(\mathbb{C}^M)$ on the first column $\ell_1^* \otimes \mathbb{H} \simeq \mathbb{H}$ has to be non-zero. We thus have a G-submodule $\mathbb{H}_1 \subset \mathbb{H}$ isomorphic to an irreducible submodule of $\mathbb{C}^M$ (in the permanent cases, respectively $E = \mathbb{C}^m$ or $E \otimes F = \mathbb{C}^{m^2}$). A similar argument shows that there must be another irreducible G-submodule $\mathbb{H}_2 \subset \mathbb{H}$ such that an irreducible submodule of $\mathbb{C}^M$ appears in $\mathbb{H}_1^* \otimes \mathbb{H}_2$.

For example, in the $SL(E)$-equivariant determinant case, $\mathbb{H}_1$ must be isomorphic to E, so $\mathbb{H}_2$ must be such that $E \subset E^* \otimes \mathbb{H}_1$. The only two $SL(E)$-modules which work are $\mathbb{H}_1 = S^2 E$ or $\mathbb{H}_1 = \Lambda^2 E$. In either case, as long as $m > 3$, we must have $E \subset \mathbb{H}_1^* \otimes \mathbb{H}_3$ which implies $\mathbb{H}_3$ is an irreducible submodule of $E^{\otimes 3}$, the smallest of which is $\Lambda^3 E$. Continuing along the minimal path, one gets the sum of exterior powers as in Proposition 4.

In each case, we construct a sequence of irreducible sub-$\tilde{G}$-modules $\mathbb{H}_k$ of $\mathbb{H}$ satisfying very restrictive conditions. This allows us to get our lower bounds.

To prove the representations A actually compute the polynomials we want, in the case $G = G_P$, we first check that G_P is contained in the image of $\bar{\rho}_A$. Since P is characterized by its symmetries, we deduce that $\det_n \circ \tilde{A}$ is a scalar multiple of P. We then specialize to evaluating on the diagonal matrices in $\mathrm{Mat}_m(\mathbb{C})$ to determine this constant, proving in particular that it is non-zero.

4. ACKNOWLEDGMENTS

The seed for this article was planted during the Fall 2014 semester program *Algorithms and Complexity in Algebraic Geometry* at the Simons Institute for the Theory of Computing, UC Berkeley. Most of the work was done when the Landsberg was a guest of Ressayre and Pascal Koiran. Landsberg thanks his hosts as well as U. Lyon and ENS Lyon for their hospitality and support. We thank: Christian Ikenmeyer for useful discussions about equivariant determinantal presentations of the permanent and Grenet's algorithm, Josh Grochow, Christian Ikenmeyer and Shrawan Kumar for useful suggestions for improving the exposition, Jérôme Germoni for mentioning the existence of the spin symmetric group, Michael Forbes for suggesting Example 3, and Avi Wigderson for suggesting Example 4. Landsberg supported by NSF grant DMS-1405348. Ressayre supported by ANR Project (ANR-13-BS02-0001-01) and by Institut Universitaire de France.

5. REFERENCES

[1] K. Akin and J. Weyman. Primary ideals associated to the linear strands of Lascoux's resolution and syzygies of the corresponding irreducible representations of the Lie superalgebra $\mathbf{gl}(m|n)$. *J. Algebra*, 310(2):461–490, 2007.

[2] J. Alper, T. Bogart, and M. Velasco. A lower bound for the determinantal complexity of a hypersurface. *ArXiv e-prints*, May 2015.

[3] D. A. M. Barrington, R. Beigel, and S. Rudich. Representing Boolean functions as polynomials modulo composite numbers. *Comput. Complexity*, 4(4):367–382, 1994. Special issue on circuit complexity (Barbados, 1992).

[4] J.-Y. Cai. A note on the determinant and permanent problem. *Inform. and Comput.*, 84(1):119–127, 1990.

[5] J. y. Cai, X. Chen, and D. Li. Quadratic lower bound for permanent vs. determinant in any characteristic. *Computational Complexity*, 19(1):37–56, 2010.

[6] P. Comon. Tensor decompositions, state of the art and applications. In J. G. McWhirter and I. K. Proudler, editors, *Mathematics in Signal Processing V*, pages 1–24. Clarendon Press, Oxford, UK, 2002. arXiv:0905.0454v1.

[7] K. Efremenko, J. M. Landsberg, H. Schenck, and J. Weyman. On minimal free resolutions and the method of shifted partial derivatives in complexity theory. *ArXiv e-prints*, Apr. 2015.

[8] I. Fischer. Sums of Like Powers of Multivariate Linear Forms. *Math. Mag.*, 67(1):59–61, 1994.

[9] G. Frobenius. Über die Darstellung der endlichen Gruppen durch lineare Substitutionen. *Sitzungsber Deutsch. Akad. Wiss. Berlin*, pages 994–1015, 1897.

[10] D. G. Glynn. The permanent of a square matrix. *European J. Combin.*, 31(7):1887–1891, 2010.

[11] B. Grenet. An Upper Bound for the Permanent versus Determinant Problem. *Theory of Computing*, 2014. Accepted.

[12] C. Ikenmeyer and J. Landsberg. Ranks of determinantal representations. *preprint*.

[13] J. Landsberg. Geometry and complexity theory. *preprint available at http://www.math.tamu.edu/~jml/simonsclass.pdf*.

[14] J. Landsberg and N. Ressayre. Permanent v. determinant: an exponential lower bound assuming symmetry and a potential path towards valiant's conjecture. *arXiv:1508.05788*, 2015.

[15] M. Marcus and H. Minc. On the relation between the determinant and the permanent. *Illinois J. Math.*, 5:376–381, 1961.

[16] T. Mignon and N. Ressayre. A quadratic bound for the determinant and permanent problem. *Int. Math. Res. Not.*, (79):4241–4253, 2004.

[17] K. D. Mulmuley. On P vs NP, geometric complexity theory, and the flip I: a high level view. *Technical Report TRâ 2007â 09, Computer Science Department, The University of Chicago, july 2007. Also available as arXiv:0709.0748*.

[18] K. D. Mulmuley and M. Sohoni. Geometric complexity theory. I. An approach to the P vs. NP and related problems. *SIAM J. Comput.*, 31(2):496–526 (electronic), 2001.

[19] K. D. Mulmuley and M. Sohoni. Geometric complexity theory. II. Towards explicit obstructions for embeddings among class varieties. *SIAM J. Comput.*, 38(3):1175–1206, 2008.

[20] K. Ranestad and F.-O. Schreyer. On the rank of a symmetric form. *J. Algebra*, 346:340–342, 2011.

[21] L. G. Valiant. Completeness classes in algebra. In *Proc. 11th ACM STOC*, pages 249–261, 1979.

[22] L. G. Valiant. Short monotone formulae for the majority function. *J. Algorithms*, 5(3):363–366, 1984.

[23] J. von zur Gathen. Permanent and determinant. *Linear Algebra Appl.*, 96:87–100, 1987.

[24] A. Yabe. Bi-polynomial rank and determinantal complexity. *CoRR*, abs/1504.00151, 2015.

On Hardness of Approximating
the Parameterized Clique Problem

Subhash Khot
khot@cims.nyu.edu

Igor Shinkar
ishinkar@cims.nyu.edu

Courant Institute of Mathematical Sciences
New York University

ABSTRACT

In the GAP-CLIQUE$(k, \frac{k}{2})$ problem, the input is an n-vertex graph G, and the goal is to decide whether G contains a clique of size k or contains no clique of size $\frac{k}{2}$. It is an open question in the study of fixed parameterized tractability whether the GAP-CLIQUE$(k, \frac{k}{2})$ problem is fixed parameter tractable, i.e., whether it has an algorithm that runs in time $f(k) \cdot n^\alpha$, where $f(k)$ is an arbitrary function of the parameter k and the exponent α is a constant independent of k.

In this paper, we give some evidence that the problem GAP-CLIQUE$(k, \frac{k}{2})$ is not fixed parameter tractable. Specifically, we define a constraint satisfaction problem, which we call DEG-2-SAT, where the input is a system of k' quadratic equations in k' variables over a finite field $\mathbb{F}$ of size n', and the goal is to decide whether there is a solution in $\mathbb{F}$ that satisfies all the equations simultaneously. The main result in this paper is an "FPT-reduction" from DEG-2-SAT to the GAP-CLIQUE$(k, \frac{k}{2})$ problem. If one were to hypothesize that the DEG-2-SAT problem is not fixed parameter tractable, then our reduction would imply that the GAP-CLIQUE$(k, \frac{k}{2})$ problem is not fixed parameter tractable either. The reduction relies on the algebraic techniques used in proof of the PCP theorem.

Categories and Subject Descriptors

F.2 [**Analysis of Algorithms and Problem Complexity**]: General

Keywords

clique, fixed parameter tractability, hardness of approximation, parameterized complexity

1. INTRODUCTION

Parameterized complexity is a promising approach to cope with $\mathcal{NP}$-hard problems [DF99, FG06]. For many $\mathcal{NP}$-hard problems, the input consists of a pair (x, k) where k is an

Permission to make digital or hard copies of all or part of this work for personal or classroom use is granted without fee provided that copies are not made or distributed for profit or commercial advantage and that copies bear this notice and the full citation on the first page. Copyrights for components of this work owned by others than the author(s) must be honored. Abstracting with credit is permitted. To copy otherwise, or republish, to post on servers or to redistribute to lists, requires prior specific permission and/or a fee. Request permissions from Permissions@acm.org.

ITCS'16, January 14 - 16, 2016, Cambridge, MA, USA

© 2016 Copyright held by the owner/author(s). Publication rights licensed to ACM.
ISBN 978-1-4503-4057-1/16/01...$15.00

DOI: http://dx.doi.org/10.1145/2840728.2840733

integer parameter and x is the "actual" input with size $|x| = n$. For instance, the input for the VERTEX-COVER problem is a pair (G, k) where G is an n-vertex graph, and the goal is to decide whether G has a vertex cover of size at most k. This is a well-known $\mathcal{NP}$-hard problem and a brute-force algorithm that tries out all vertex subsets of size k runs in time $O(n^k)$. It is not difficult to see that there is another algorithm that runs in time $O(2^k \cdot n^2)$: pick an edge of the graph, choose one of its endpoints to include in the vertex cover, remove all edges incident on the chosen endpoint, and repeat this step until at most k vertices are chosen. The algorithm accepts if no edges are left in the graph. The factor 2^k in the running time corresponds to trying out each of the two choices in the (at most) k steps. Thus the VERTEX-COVER problem is tractable for "fixed" values of the parameter k.

More generally, a problem parameterized by k is said to be *fixed-parameter tractable* (FPT) if it can be solved in time $f(k) \cdot n^\alpha$, where f is an arbitrary function depending only on k and α is a constant independent of k. For some $\mathcal{NP}$-hard problems, e.g. VERTEX-COVER as mentioned above and LONGEST PATH as another example, such an algorithm exists, while for some problems, e.g. CLIQUE, such an algorithm is not known. Downey and Fellows [DF95a, DF95b] define a hierarchy of classes of parameterized problems

$$\text{FPT} \subseteq W[1] \subseteq W[2] \subseteq \ldots \subseteq W[SAT] \subseteq W[P],$$

and identify complete problems for these classes. Each class inclusion above is believed to be strict. In particular, classes FPT and $W[1]$ are thought of as analogues of the classes $\mathcal{P}$ and $\mathcal{NP}$ respectively, and are believed to be distinct. It has been shown in [DF95b] that the CLIQUE problem is $W[1]$-complete under "FPT-reductions" defined below.

DEFINITION 1.1. *For two parameterized problems A and B, an FPT-reduction from A to B is an algorithm that gets as input an instance (x, k) of A and outputs an instance (x', k') of B such that:*

1. *$(x, k) \in A$ if and only if $(x', k') \in B$.*

2. *k' depends only on k, in an arbitrary manner, but not on x.*

3. *The running time of the reduction is $f(k) \cdot |x|^\beta$ where f is an arbitrary function depending only on k and β is a constant independent of k.*

If such a reduction exists, then we write $A \leqslant_{\text{FPT}} B$.

It is easily seen that the class FPT of fixed parameterized tractable problems is closed under FPT-reductions, that is, if $B \in \text{FPT}$ and $A \leqslant_{\text{FPT}} B$, then $A \in \text{FPT}$. Since CLIQUE is $W[1]$-complete, it is considered unlikely that CLIQUE has a FPT-algorithm. It is, therefore, natural to ask whether CLIQUE has a good "FPT approximation algorithm", i.e. given a graph G that is guaranteed to contain a clique of size k, the goal would be to find a clique of size $\rho(k)$ for some monotone function $\rho(k)$, e.g. $\frac{k}{2}$, $\sqrt{k}$ or even $\log k$. However, the fixed parameter complexity of the approximation problem, for CLIQUE as well as most other natural problems, is poorly understood. In particular, no FPT approximation algorithm is known for CLIQUE for any unbounded function $\rho(k)$ and on the other hand, there is no evidence that the approximation problem is hard either [Mar08, CGG06].

1.1 Our result

In this paper, we give some evidence that the CLIQUE problem is hard to approximate in the parameterized setting. Specifically, we show that there is an FPT-reduction from a problem that we call DEG-2-SAT to the "gap version" of the CLIQUE problem. We first define both these problems and then remark on the plausible hardness of the DEG-2-SAT problem.

DEFINITION 1.2. *For a constant $0 < \varepsilon < 1$, the problem* GAP-CLIQUE$(k, \varepsilon k)$ *is the following: given a k-partite graph G with n-vertices in each part, the goal is to decide whether G has a clique of size k (the YES instance) or has no clique of size εk (the NO instance).*

Clearly, GAP-CLIQUE$(k, \varepsilon k)$ can be solved in time $O(n^k)$ (or even $O(n^{\varepsilon k})$). Next, we define the DEG-2-SAT problem that is central to this paper.

DEFINITION 1.3. DEG-2-SAT$(\mathbb{F}, k)$ *is the following problem: given a finite field $\mathbb{F}$ of size n and a system of k quadratic equations*

$$p_1(x_1, \ldots, x_k) = 0, \quad \ldots \quad p_k(x_1, \ldots, x_k) = 0,$$

in k variables $x_1, \ldots, x_k$, the goal is to decide whether there is a solution $x = (x_1, \ldots, x_k) \in \mathbb{F}^k$ that satisfies all the equations simultaneously.

Note that the problem DEG-2-SAT, and also DEG-d-SAT where the equations have degree d, has a trivial algorithm with running time $O(n^k)$. The algorithm simply tries every possible assignments to $x_1, \ldots, x_k \in \mathbb{F}$, and checks whether it satisfies all the equations. Solving systems of polynomial equations is a classical and well studied problem. For a comprehensive study of the topic, we refer to the book of von zur Gathen and Gerhard [vzGG03], and quote a few of the known results here. Given a system of degree d equations over m variables, an algorithm of Buchberger uses Gröbner bases to find a solution to the DEG-d-SAT problem in an *extension field* of $\mathbb{F}$, if a solution exists, in time $d^{\exp(m)} \cdot \text{poly} \log(|\mathbb{F}|)$. However, note that the algorithm does not necessarily find a solution *in the field* $\mathbb{F}$. We also note that if the number of solutions is finite in the closure of $\mathbb{F}$ (known as the "zero-dimensional" case), then there are algorithms that find all the solutions in time $f(d, m) \cdot \text{poly} \log(|\mathbb{F}|)$, see e.g., [Laz79]. Still, we are not aware of an FPT-algorithm for DEG-2-SAT that finds a solution in the field $\mathbb{F}$, and it might be the case that no FPT-algorithm exists.

Note also that for a field $\mathbb{F}$ of size $|\mathbb{F}| = n$ and the parameter k, there are only $n^{O(k^3)}$ instances of the DEG-2-SAT

problem. This is because each of the k equations contains $O(k^2)$ monomials and the instance is completely specified by $O(k^3)$ coefficients of all these monomials. In this respect, the problem differs from the standard problems in $W[1]$, e.g. CLIQUE, where there are exponentially many instances of size n. Nonetheless, we do not know whether the fact that there are only $n^{O(k^3)}$ instances necessarily rules out the possibility that DEG-2-SAT is hard, or even $W[1]$-hard. Indeed, a complexity class known as MINI[1] defined in [DECF$^+$03] has the property that the languages in MINI[1] contain only n^k instances of size n. It has been shown in [DECF$^+$03] that FPT $\subseteq$ MINI[1] $\subseteq W[1]$, and to the best of our knowledge, it is plausible that the containments above are strict. The main result in this paper is an FPT-reduction from DEG-2-SAT to GAP-CLIQUE.

THEOREM 1.4 (MAIN THEOREM). *Let k be a parameter and let $\mathbb{F}$ be a finite field. There is an FPT-reduction*

$$\text{DEG-2-SAT}(\mathbb{F}, k) \leqslant_{\text{FPT}} \text{GAP-CLIQUE}\left(k', \frac{k'}{2}\right).$$

We note that, by definition of an FPT-reduction, k' depends only on k but not on $\mathbb{F}$.

Thus, if[1] there is no FPT-algorithm for DEG-2-SAT$(\mathbb{F}, k)$, then one may conclude that there is no FPT-algorithm for GAP-CLIQUE$\left(k', \frac{k'}{2}\right)$ either. For the GAP-CLIQUE problem, the "gap" can be amplified by a standard graph product operation, so for any constant C, one may conclude that there is no FPT-approximation for CLIQUE with approximation factor C. It is likely that hardness of approximating CLIQUE implies hardness of approximating other problems in the parameterized setting, but we leave out this aspect from the current paper.

2. PROOF OF THE MAIN THEOREM

Towards proving Theorem 1.4, we work with a more general version of the DEG-2-SAT problem than the version specified in Definition 1.3. The general version allows the number of variables, the number of equations, and the arity of equations to be separate parameters. Also, the instance is supposed to be a "gap instance", i.e. it is promised to be either fully satisfiable or far from satisfiable, and the "gap" itself is an additional parameter.

DEFINITION 2.1. *An instance Φ of* DEG-2-SAT$(\mathbb{F}, k, e, q, \varepsilon)$ *consists of a system of quadratic equations in k variables over the field $\mathbb{F}$. The number of equations is e and each equation depends on only q out of the k variables.*

Let $\text{val}(\Phi)$ denote the maximum fraction of equations that can be satisfied by any assignment (over the field $\mathbb{F}$) to the variables. The instance is a promise instance where either $\text{val}(\Phi) = 1$ (the YES instance) or else $\text{val}(\Phi) \leqslant \varepsilon$ (the NO instance).

With this definition the problem DEG-2-SAT$(\mathbb{F}, k)$ from Definition 1.3 is now denoted as

$$\text{DEG-2-SAT}\left(\mathbb{F}, k, e = k, q = k, \varepsilon = 1 - \frac{1}{k}\right),$$

i.e., the number of variables and equations in the system is both k, each equation may depend on all $q = k$ variables,

---

[1]We stress that we are not proposing this as conjecture.

and the instance is either satisfiable or not satisfiable, with $\mathrm{val}(\Phi) \leqslant 1 - \frac{1}{k}$ in the latter case. Note that there is really no "gap" here.

2.1 Overview of the overall reduction

Our reduction starts with an instance Φ of the problem DEG-2-SAT $\left(\mathbb{F}, k, e = k, q = k, \varepsilon = 1 - \frac{1}{k}\right)$, and transforms it, through a sequence of steps, to an instance Φ' that has a constant gap and each equation has a constant arity. From the instance Φ', it is easy to construct a GAP-CLIQUE instance by the well-known "FGLSS reduction". We give a quick overview of the steps involved before presenting the actual reductions.

Creating gap: In the first step, we give a FPT-reduction that "creates" a constant gap:

$$\text{DEG-2-SAT}\left(\mathbb{F}, k, e = k, q = k, \varepsilon = 1 - \frac{1}{k}\right)$$
$$\leqslant_{\text{FPT}}$$
$$\text{DEG-2-SAT}(\mathbb{F}, k, e' = 2k, q' = k, \varepsilon' = 0.5).$$

The number of variables stays the same, the number of equations doubles, each equation may still depend on all the variables, but now, in the NO case, the instance is only 0.5-satisfiable. The field $\mathbb{F}$ stays the same in this step as well as all the subsequent steps.

Simplifying equations: In the second step, we construct an instance where the equations have a certain simplified form (we refer to this problem as SIMPLE-DEG-2-SAT):

$$\text{DEG-2-SAT}(\mathbb{F}, k, e, q = k, \varepsilon = 0.5)$$
$$\leqslant_{\text{FPT}}$$
$$\text{SIMPLE-DEG-2-SAT}(\mathbb{F}, k', e', q' = k', \varepsilon' = 0.95).$$

The number of variables k' and the number of equations e' depend only on their initial number k and e respectively, each equation may still depend on all the variables, and the gap suffers (which is not much of an issue; it is still bounded away from 1). The main feature of this reduction is that in the new instance, each equation is of the form

$$\ell_1(x) = a \cdot \ell_2(x) \cdot \ell_3(x) + b \cdot \ell_4(x) + c,$$

where $a, b, c \in \mathbb{F}$ and $\ell_1, \ell_2, \ell_3, \ell_4$ are linear forms over the set of variables. Moreover, the coefficients of these linear forms are from a subset $L \subseteq \mathbb{F}$ such that $|L|$ is "small", depending only on k.

Reducing arity to constant: In the third step, starting with the "simple instance" as above, we construct an instance where each equation depends only on a constant number of variables:

$$\text{SIMPLE-DEG-2-SAT}(\mathbb{F}, k, e, q = k, \varepsilon = 0.95)$$
$$\leqslant_{\text{FPT}}$$
$$\text{DEG-2-SAT}(\mathbb{F}, k', e', q' = O(1), \varepsilon' = 0.999).$$

The soundness suffers, but is still a constant bounded away from 1. The number of variables k' and the number of equations e' depend only on their initial number k and e respectively and on $|L|$ where $L \subseteq \mathbb{F}$ is the set of coefficients of the linear forms in the simple instance.

FGLSS reduction: Given a gap instance with equations of constant arity, it is straightforward to construct a gap instance of the CLIQUE problem, with the same gap.

$$\text{DEG-2-SAT}(\mathbb{F}, k, e, q = O(1), \varepsilon = 0.999)$$
$$\leqslant_{\text{FPT}}$$
$$\text{GAP-CLIQUE}(k', 0.999k').$$

The graph is k'-partite and either has a clique of size k' or has no clique of size $0.999k'$. Here $k' = e$ and the number of vertices in each of the k' groups of the k'-partite graph is at most $n^{O(1)}$ where $n = |\mathbb{F}|$.

Combining the sequence of four reductions above, we get the desired reduction

$$\text{DEG-2-SAT}(\mathbb{F}, k)$$
$$\leqslant_{\text{FPT}}$$
$$\text{GAP-CLIQUE}(k', 0.999k') \leqslant_{\text{FPT}} \text{GAP-CLIQUE}(k'', 0.5k''),$$

where, at the end, the gap in the GAP-CLIQUE problem is boosted from 0.999 to 0.5 by the standard operation of graph products.

The reductions are based on standard techniques used in the algebraic proof of the PCP Theorem [FGL+96, ALM+98, AS98], though there are some new variations and ingredients. Of the four reductions, the first and the fourth are straightforward, so we present them first.

2.1.1 Creating gap

We present a FPT-reduction that creates a constant gap to begin with:

$$\text{DEG-2-SAT}\left(\mathbb{F}, k, e = k, q = k, \varepsilon = 1 - \frac{1}{k}\right)$$
$$\leqslant_{\text{FPT}}$$
$$\text{DEG-2-SAT}(\mathbb{F}, k, e' = 2k, q' = k, \varepsilon = 0.5).$$

Let Φ be the instance of DEG-2-SAT $(\mathbb{F}, k, e, q, \varepsilon)$ with equations $p_1 = 0, \dots, p_k = 0$ in k variables over the field $\mathbb{F}$, where $e = q = k$ and $\varepsilon = 1 - \frac{1}{k}$. We may assume that $|\mathbb{F}| = n \gg 2k$. We take a $2k \times k$ matrix M over the field $\mathbb{F}$ such that for every $v \in \mathbb{F}^k, v \neq 0$, it holds that at least half of the co-ordinates of Mv are non-zero. Such matrix can be constructed, e.g., by taking the generator matrix of the degree-k Reed-Solomon code over the field $\mathbb{F}$ restricted to $2k$ elements in the field. More specifically, we can define M by taking $2k$ distinct elements $a_1, \dots a_{2k} \in \mathbb{F}$, and letting $M_{i,j} = a_i^{j-1}$.

Now construct an instance Φ' of DEG-2-SAT with the same set of variables as Φ, but whose equations are linear combinations of equations of Φ using the rows of the matrix M as coefficients. Specifically, for every $i \in \{1, \dots, 2k\}$, the instance Φ' contains an equation $p'_i = 0$ where

$$p'_i = \sum_{j=1}^{k} M_{ij} p_j.$$

Clearly, if Φ has a satisfying assignment, the same assignment also satisfies all the equations of Φ'. On the other hand, if Φ has no satisfying assignment, any assignment $x \in \mathbb{F}^k$ satisfies at most half of the equations in Φ'. This is because,

$$(p'_1(x), \dots, p'_k(x))^{\top} = M \cdot (p_1(x), \dots, p_k(x))^{\top},$$

and since the vector $v = (p_1(x), \ldots, p_k(x))^\mathsf{T}$ is non-zero, at least half of the co-ordinates of Mv are non-zero, meaning at least half of the equations $p'_1(x) = 0, \ldots, p'_k(x) = 0$ fail.

2.1.2 FGLSS reduction

We describe a FPT-reduction (known as the FGLSS reduction [FGL+96]) from DEG-2-SAT with constant gap and constant arity to the GAP-CLIQUE problem:

$$\text{DEG-2-SAT}(\mathbb{F}, k, e, q = O(1), \varepsilon = 0.999)$$
$$\leqslant_{\text{FPT}}$$
$$\text{GAP-CLIQUE}(k', 0.999k'),$$

where $k' = e$ and the GAP-CLIQUE instance is a k'-partite graph with at most $|\mathbb{F}|^q = n^q$ vertices in each group. Since $q = O(1)$, the exponent of n is independent of the parameters k and e.

Given an instance Φ of DEG-2-SAT($\mathbb{F}, k, e, q = O(1), \varepsilon = 0.999$), construct an e-partite graph $G = (V, E)$ with vertex partition $V = (V_1, \ldots, V_e)$ as follows. For each equation $p_i = 0$ of Φ, $i \in \{1, \ldots, e\}$, the group of vertices V_i contains at most $|\mathbb{F}|^q$ vertices, where each vertex corresponds to a satisfying assignment to the variables of the equation $p_i = 0$. We note here that p_i depends only on q variables. There is an edge between two vertices in the graph G if the corresponding assignments to the variables are consistent, i.e., if the assignments agree on the shared variables. It is easily seen that there is a one-to-one correspondence between assignments that satisfy ℓ equations of Φ and cliques of size ℓ in G.

2.2 Simplifying equations

In this section, we describe the reduction that leads to quadratic equations with a very simple structure:

LEMMA 2.2. *There is an* FPT-*reduction*

$$\text{DEG-2-SAT}(\mathbb{F}, k, e, q = k, \varepsilon = 0.5)$$
$$\leqslant_{\text{FPT}}$$
$$\text{SIMPLE-DEG-2-SAT}(\mathbb{F}, k', e', q' = k', \varepsilon' = 0.95),$$

mapping an instance Φ of DEG-2-SAT *to an instance Φ' of* SIMPLE-DEG-2-SAT *such that:*

- *k', e' depend only on k, e.*
- *Each equation may still depend on all the variables.*
- *Each equation is of the form:*

$$\ell_1 = a \cdot \ell_2 \cdot \ell_3 + b \cdot \ell_4 + c,$$

where $a, b, c \in \mathbb{F}$ and $\ell_1, \ell_2, \ell_3, \ell_4$ are linear forms over the set of variables. Moreover, the coefficients of these linear forms are from a subset $L \subseteq \mathbb{F}$ such that $|L|$ depends only on k.

PROOF. The reduction uses algebraic ingredients used to prove the PCP Theorem, in particular the *polynomial encoding method* and the *sum check protocol* [LFKN92, Sha92]. However, we use these ingredients in a somewhat different and restricted manner. For convenience of the reader, the reduction below is presented directly, without using the language of probabilistic verifiers.

Let $S = \{s_1, \ldots, s_k\} \subseteq \mathbb{F}$ be a subset of k field elements and H be a subset of $10k^2$ field elements such that $S \subseteq H \subseteq$

$\mathbb{F}$. Denote a typical (quadratic) equation of Φ as $p = 0$ over the variables $x_1, \ldots, x_k$. We first define the variables of Φ'. There are two kinds of variables:

1. Let $\sigma : \{x_1, \ldots, x_k\} \to \mathbb{F}$ be a supposed satisfying assignment to Φ. Thus there exists a (unique) univariate polynomial $Q(z)$ of degree at most $k - 1$ such that $Q(s_i) = \sigma(x_i)$ for all $i = 1, \ldots, k$. The instance Φ' has variables $q_0, \ldots, q_{k-1}$ representing the coefficients of the polynomial $Q(z)$, i.e. $Q(z) = \sum_{i=0}^{k-1} q_i z^i$. To state differently, the instance Φ' has variables $q_0, \ldots, q_{k-1}$ and the intention is that defining a polynomial $Q(z) = \sum_{i=0}^{k-1} q_i z^i$, the values $Q(s_1), \ldots, Q(s_k)$ serve as a supposed satisfying assignment to Φ.

2. Suppose a typical equation in Φ is $p = 0$ where

$$p(x_1, \ldots, x_k) = \sum_{1 \leqslant i, j \leqslant k} c_{i,j} x_i x_j + \sum_{1 \leqslant i \leqslant k} c_i x_i + c_0.$$

Let $C_2(u, v)$ be a bi-variate polynomial of degree $k - 1$ in each variable such that $C_2(s_i, s_j) = c_{i,j}$ for all $i, j = 1, \ldots, k$. Similarly, let $C_1(u)$ be a univariate polynomial of degree $k - 1$ such that $C_1(s_i) = c_i$ for all $i = 1, \ldots, k$. Note that the polynomials C_1 and C_2 depend only on the coefficients of p, and hence can be computed explicitly.

The instance Φ' will have variables that represent the coefficients of a bi-variate polynomial Ψ_2^p and the intention is that

$$\Psi_2^p(u, v) = C_2(u, v) Q(u) Q(v).$$

Note that Ψ_2^p is intended to have degree at most $2k - 2$ in each variable. Denote its coefficients by $\{\psi_{i,j}^p : i, j = 0, \ldots, 2k-2\}$ so that these are variables of the instance Φ' and $\Psi_2^p(u, v) = \sum_{i,j=0}^{2k-2} \psi_{i,j}^p u^i v^j$.

Similarly the instance Φ' will have variables that represent the coefficients of a univariate polynomial Ψ_1^p and the intention is that

$$\Psi_1^p(u) = C_1(u) Q(u).$$

Note that Ψ_1^p is intended to have degree at most $2k - 2$. Denote its coefficients by $\{\psi_i^p : i = 0, \ldots, 2k - 2\}$ so that these are variables of the instance Φ' and $\Psi_1^p(u) = \sum_{i=0}^{2k-2} \psi_i^p u^i$.

We describe the equations of Φ' by describing how to pick one equation at random from the set of its equations. To pick an equation of Φ' at random, first pick an equation $p = 0$ of Φ at random and then, with probability $\frac{1}{3}$ each, write one of the three equations below:

- Write the equation

$$\sum_{u,v \in S} \Psi_2^p(u, v) + \sum_{u \in S} \Psi_1^p(u) = -c_0.$$

More concretely, the equation, in terms of variables $\psi_{i,j}^p$ and ψ_i^p is

$$\sum_{i,j=0}^{2k-2} \psi_{i,j}^p \left(\sum_{u,v \in S} u^i v^j \right) + \sum_{i=0}^{2k-2} \psi_i^p \left(\sum_{u \in S} u^i \right) = -c_0.$$

- Pick $u, v \in H$ at random and write the equation

$$\Psi_2^p(u,v) = C_2(u,v)Q(u)Q(v).$$

More concretely, the equation, in terms of variables $\psi_{i,j}^p$ and $q_0, \ldots, q_{k-1}$ is

$$\sum_{i,j=0}^{2k-2} \psi_{i,j}^p \cdot u^i v^j = C_2(u,v) \cdot \left(\sum_{i=0}^{k-1} q_i \cdot u^i\right) \cdot \left(\sum_{j=0}^{k-1} q_j \cdot v^j\right),$$

where $C_2(u,v) \in \mathbb{F}$ is explicitly computed.

- Pick $u \in H$ at random and write the equation

$$\Psi_1^p(u) = C_1(u)Q(u).$$

More concretely, the equation, in terms of variables ψ_i^p and $q_0, \ldots, q_{k-1}$ is

$$\sum_{i=0}^{2k-2} \psi_i^p \cdot u^i = C_1(u) \cdot \left(\sum_{i=0}^{k-1} q_i \cdot u^i\right),$$

where $C_1(u) \in \mathbb{F}$ is explicitly computed.

This completes the description of the instance Φ' and now we proceed to show the stated properties of the instance Φ' and correctness of the reduction. Clearly, the number of variables and equations in Φ' depends only on their numbers in the instance Φ (strictly speaking, the equations in Φ' have weights, but making copies of equations proportional to their weights, Φ' can easily be turned into an un-weighted instance). Also, each equation is of the form

$$\ell_1 = a \cdot \ell_2 \cdot \ell_3 + b \cdot \ell_4 + c,$$

with $a, b, c \in \mathbb{F}$ and $\ell_1, \ell_2, \ell_3, \ell_4$ are linear forms (possibly zero) in the variables of Φ'. Finally, the coefficients of these linear forms are of the type

$$\sum_{u,v \in S} u^i v^j, \quad \sum_{u \in S} u^i, \quad u^i v^j, \quad u^i, \quad 0,$$

with $u, v \in H$ and $0 \leqslant i, j \leqslant 2k-2$. There are at most $O(k^6)$ possibilities for these coefficients. Now we prove the correctness of the reduction.

2.2.1 YES Case

We show that if $\mathrm{val}(\Phi) = 1$, then $\mathrm{val}(\Phi') = 1$. This is simply by design, but we present the details for the convenience of the reader. Let $\sigma : \{x_1, \ldots, x_k\} \to \mathbb{F}$ be an assignment that satisfies every equation $p = 0$ in Φ. Define the assignment to variables of Φ', i.e. to the variables $q_0, \ldots, q_{k-1}, \psi_{i,j}^p, \psi_i^p$ so that (the polynomials C_1, C_2 depend on the equation p though our notation suppresses this):

$$\begin{aligned} Q(z) &= \sum_{i=0}^{k-1} q_i z^i, \ Q(s_i) \\ &= \sigma(x_i), \ \Psi_2^p(u,v) \\ &= C_2(u,v)Q(u)Q(v), \ \Psi_1^p(u) = C_1(u)Q(u). \end{aligned}$$

Now, we verify that this assignment satisfies each of the three kinds of equations in Φ'. The second and the third kind of equations are satisfied by definition of $\Psi_2^p(u,v)$ and

$\Psi_1^p(u)$ as above. For the equations of the first kind, we have

$$\begin{aligned} &\sum_{u,v \in S} \Psi_2^p(u,v) + \sum_{u \in S} \Psi_1^p(u) \\ &= \sum_{u,v \in S} C_2(u,v)Q(u)Q(v) + \sum_{u \in S} C_1(u)Q(u) \\ &= \sum_{i,j=1}^{k} C_2(s_i, s_j)Q(s_i)Q(s_j) + \sum_{i=1}^{k} C_1(s_i)Q(s_i) \\ &= \sum_{i,j=1}^{k} c_{i,j} \cdot \sigma(x_i)\sigma(x_j) + \sum_{i=1}^{k} c_i \cdot \sigma(x_i) \\ &= -c_0, \end{aligned}$$

where in the last step, we used the fact that σ satisfies the equation $p = 0$.

2.2.2 NO Case

Now we show that if $\mathrm{val}(\Phi) \leqslant 0.5$, then $\mathrm{val}(\Phi') \leqslant 0.95$. Suppose on the contrary that $\mathrm{val}(\Phi') \geqslant 0.95$ and fix a corresponding "highly satisfying" assignment to Φ', i.e. it is an assignment to the variables $q_0, \ldots, q_{k-1}, \psi_{i,j}^p, \psi_i^p$. As before, $p = 0$ denotes a typical equation in Φ. We may define formal polynomials

$$Q(z) = \sum_{i=0}^{k-1} q_i z^i,$$

and

$$\Psi_2^p(u,v) = \sum_{i,j=0}^{2k-2} \psi_{i,j}^p u^i v^j, \quad \Psi_1^p(u) = \sum_{i=0}^{2k-2} \psi_i^p u^i.$$

Since the assignment to Φ' satisfies at least 0.95 fraction of its equations, by an averaging argument, it must be the case that for at least 0.55 fraction of the equations $p = 0$ in Φ, after picking the equation $p = 0$, for each of the three kinds of equations in Φ', at least 0.5 fraction of the equations of that kind are satisfied. Fix any such "good" equation $p = 0$ in Φ. Note that there is only one equation of the first kind, so that equation is satisfied. Since at least 0.5 fraction of the equations of the second and the third kind are satisfied, we conclude that

$$\Pr_{u,v \in H}[\Psi_2^p(u,v) = C_2(u,v)Q(u)Q(v)] \geqslant 0.5, \quad (1)$$

and

$$\Pr_{u \in H}[\Psi_1^p(u) = C_1(u)Q(u)] \geqslant 0.5. \quad (2)$$

Since the polynomials $\Psi_2^p(u,v), \Psi_1^p(u), C_2(u,v), C_1(u), Q(u)$ all have degree at most $2k-2$ in each variable, and $|H| = 10k^2$, by the Schwartz-Zippel lemma, we must have a formal identity

$$\Psi_2^p(u,v) = C_2(u,v)Q(u)Q(v), \quad \Psi_1^p(u) = C_1(u)Q(u).$$

Now, since the equation of the first kind is satisfied, we conclude

$$-c_0 = \sum_{u,v \in S} \Psi_2^p(u,v) + \sum_{u \in S} \Psi_1^p(u)$$

$$= \sum_{u,v \in S} C_2(u,v)Q(u)Q(v) + \sum_{u \in S} C_1(u)Q(u)$$

$$= \sum_{i,j=1}^{k} C_2(s_i,s_j)Q(s_i)Q(s_j) + \sum_{i=1}^{k} C_1(s_i)Q(s_i)$$

$$= \sum_{i,j=1}^{k} c_{i,j} \cdot Q(s_i)Q(s_j) + \sum_{i=1}^{k} c_i \cdot Q(s_i).$$

Therefore, the assignment $\sigma : \{x_1,\ldots,x_k\} \to \mathbb{F}$ defined as $\sigma(x_i) = Q(s_i)$ satisfies the equation $p = 0$ in Φ. Since at least 0.55 fraction of the equations $p = 0$ in Φ are "good", it follows that $\mathrm{val}(\Phi) \geqslant 0.55$, a contradiction. $\square$

2.2.3 The choice of the set L in Lemma 2.2

Note that we have some degree of freedom in the choice of the set L, which we discuss below. The choices of the sets $S \subseteq H$ were completely arbitrary as long as $|S| = k$ and $|H| = 10k^2$. The set L contains the elements

$$\sum_{u,v \in S} u^i v^j, \quad \sum_{u \in S} u^i, \quad u^i v^j, \quad u^i, \quad 0, \tag{3}$$

with $u, v \in H$ and $0 \leqslant i, j \leqslant 2k - 2$. Depending on whether the characteristic of the field $\mathbb{F}$ is large or small, we choose the set L as below. Let C be a large enough constant chosen as below.

- **Large characteristic:** If $p = \mathrm{char}(\mathbb{F}) \geqslant k^{Ck}$, then we choose $S = \{0,\ldots,k-1\}$, $H = \{0,\ldots,10k^2-1\}$, and let $L = \{0,\ldots,D\} \subseteq \mathbb{F}_p$, where $D = k^{O(k)}$ is large enough so that all the coefficients in (3) are contained in L. Our choice of the constant C will be such that $3k^2 D \leqslant p$.

- **Small characteristic:** If $p = \mathrm{char}(\mathbb{F}) \leqslant k^{Ck}$, then we choose S and $S \subseteq H$ to be arbitrary subsets of $\mathbb{F}$ of size k and $10k^2$ respectively. Then, we choose L to be the linear span, over $\mathbb{F}_p$, of all the, at most $O(k^6)$, elements in (3). Note that in this case, L is closed under addition and $|L| \leqslant k^{O(k^7)}$.

2.3 Reducing arity to constant

In this section, we describe the reduction that starts with an instance of SIMPLE-DEG-2-SAT as in Lemma 2.2 and constructs an instance where the (quadratic) equations have constant arity and the gap is bounded away from 1.

LEMMA 2.3. *There is an* FPT-*reduction*

SIMPLE-DEG-2-SAT$(\mathbb{F}, k, e, q = k, \varepsilon = 0.95)$

$\leqslant_{\mathrm{FPT}}$

DEG-2-SAT$(\mathbb{F}, k', e', q' = O(1), \varepsilon' = 0.999)$,

mapping an instance Φ of SIMPLE-DEG-2-SAT *to an instance Φ' of* DEG-2-SAT *such that:*

- *k', e' depend only on k, e.*

- *Each equation depends only on a constant number of variables.*

We sketch the main idea first. Consider the instance Φ of SIMPLE-DEG-2-SAT such that each equation is of the form

$$\ell_1(x) = a \cdot \ell_2(x) \cdot \ell_3(x) + b \cdot \ell_4(x) + c, \tag{4}$$

where $a, b, c \in \mathbb{F}$ and the coefficients of the linear forms $\ell_i(x)$ are in $L \subseteq \mathbb{F}$ as in Lemma 2.2. Note that the linear forms are of the type $\ell(x) = \sum_{i=1}^{k} u_i x_i$ where $u_i \in L$ and $x_1,\ldots,x_k$ are the variables of the instance Φ. Our reduction constructs a new instance Φ' whose variables are intended to be the values of *all* linear forms $\ell(x) = \sum_{i=1}^{k} u_i x_i$ over *all* choices of $u_1,\ldots,u_k \in L$. Alternately, we may think of the variables of Φ' as the entries in the table of values of a function $f : L^k \to \mathbb{F}$, where the intention is that f is a linear function defined as

$$f(u_1,\ldots,u_k) = \sum_{i=1}^{k} u_i \cdot \sigma(x_i),$$

and $\sigma : \{x_1,\ldots,x_k\} \to \mathbb{F}$ is a supposed satisfying assignment to Φ. Now consider a typical equation (4) in Φ. Since the values of the linear forms $\ell_i(x)$ are supposed to appear as variables $f(u^{(i)})$ in Φ', the equation (4) is now a quadratic equation that depends only on 4 variables of Φ', i.e. the new equations have constant arity! However, to ensure the correctness of this reduction, one needs to ensure that the assignment to Φ' (given by an adversary) is indeed a linear function $f : L^k \to \mathbb{F}$, or "close" to being a linear function as we see next.

To ensure that $f : L^k \to \mathbb{F}$ is close to a linear function, we perform a "linearity test" that makes a constant number of queries to the table of f (three queries are enough). The test itself is linear in the queries made by the tester. The tests are then thought of as equations in the values of table f, i.e. the variables of Φ'. Such linearity tests are well-studied. In particular, a three query test is known so that if the test passes with probability close to 1, then the function f agrees with a (unique) linear function g, say on 0.99 fraction of the inputs in L^k. Having ensured that f is close to a linear function g, we are then faced with another issue. Equation (4) involves values of f at *specific* inputs $u \in L^k$ and even though f is close to a linear function g, it might be the case that $f(u) \neq g(u)$ at these specific inputs that we are interested in. It turns out that there is a "self-correction" procedure, that given a query access to a function f that is close to a linear function g, makes a constant number of queries to f (two queries suffice) and outputs the "correct value" $g(u)$ with high probability. The linearity testing and self-correction procedures were first considered in the paper of Blum, Luby, and Rubinfeld [BLR93].

This describes the main idea behind our reduction. We recall, from Section 2.2.3, that if the field $\mathbb{F}$ has small characteristic, then $L \subseteq \mathbb{F}$ can be taken as an additive subgroup of $\mathbb{F}$. In this case, the linearity testing and the self-correction procedures are already known, e.g. [BLR93, BOCLR08], and can be used directly. However, if the field $\mathbb{F}$ has large characteristic $p \geqslant 3k^2 D$, then $L = \{0,1,\ldots,D\} \subseteq \mathbb{F}_p$ is not closed under addition. In this case, we design new procedures for linearity testing and self-correction that might be of independent interest. These procedures closely mimic the corresponding procedures when L does have an additive group structure, but one main difference is that in addition to the table of $f : L^k \to \mathbb{F}$, the "tester" needs access to an additional, auxiliary table $\pi : \Gamma^k \to \mathbb{F}$, where

$L \subseteq \Gamma = \{0, 1, \ldots, 3k^2 D\} \subseteq \mathbb{F}_p$. The table π is supposed to be the *same* linear function as f, but evaluated over a larger domain Γ^k. We summarize the linearity testing and the self-correction procedures below in Lemma 2.4, prove Lemma 2.3, and then present a proof of Lemma 2.4.

LEMMA 2.4. *Let $\mathbb{F}$ be a finite field. Let $L \subseteq \mathbb{F}$ and $L \subseteq \Gamma \subseteq \mathbb{F}$ be such that*

- *Either, L is an additive subgroup of $\mathbb{F}$ and $\Gamma = L$,*

- *Or else, $p = \mathrm{char}(\mathbb{F}) \geqslant 3k^2 D$, $L = \{0, 1, \ldots, D\}$, $\Gamma = \{0, 1, \ldots, 3k^2 D\}$.*

There is a randomized 3-query test T that gets as input a query access to a function $f : L^k \to \mathbb{F}$ as well as an additional function $\pi : \Gamma^k \to \mathbb{F}$ such that $\pi|_{L^k} = f$, makes 3 queries to (f, π) and has the following guarantee:

- *The test is linear in the 3 queries.*

- *If f is linear, then there exists π such that T accepts with probability 1.*

- *For any $\varepsilon > 0$, if the test T accepts (f, π) with probability at least $1 - \varepsilon$, then f is $(1 - 4\varepsilon)$-close to some linear function $g : L^k \to \mathbb{F}$. Furthermore, there is a self-correcting procedure C that for any input $u \in L^k$ makes 2 queries to (f, π) and outputs $C(u)$ such that*

$$\Pr[C(u) = g(u)] \geqslant 1 - (4\varepsilon + 2/k),$$

where the probability is over the randomness of C. The output $C(u)$ is linear in the 2 queries.

If L has a group structure, the additional function π is not really needed, i.e. all queries are made to f and then the role of π is redundant. Lemma 2.4 is stated so that it conveniently applies to both the cases, when L has a group structure as well as when it doesn't. We now show how Lemma 2.4 implies Lemma 2.3.

PROOF PROOF OF LEMMA 2.3. Given an instance Φ of SIMPLE-DEG-2-SAT with variables $x_1, \ldots, x_k$ and equations of the form

$$\ell_1(x) = a \cdot \ell_2(x) \cdot \ell_3(x) + b \cdot \ell_4(x) + c,$$

we construct an instance Φ' as follows. The variables of Φ' will be the table of values of $f : L^k \to \mathbb{F}$ and the table of values of $\pi : \Gamma^k \to \mathbb{F}$ as in Lemma 2.4. In order to describe the equations of Φ', we describe a tester that uses the linearity testing, self-correction primitives as well as the equations of Φ. The equations of Φ' then correspond to the tests on the queries made by the tester. The tester works as follows:

1. With probability 0.5, perform linearity test T on (f, π) as in Lemma 2.4.

2. With probability 0.5, perform the following steps:

   (a) Pick a random equation of Φ of the form
   $$\ell_1(x) = a \cdot \ell_2(x) \cdot \ell_3(x) + b \cdot \ell_4(x) + c.$$

   (b) For each $\ell_j(x)$ let $u^{(j)} \in L^k$ be such that $\ell_j(x) = \sum_{i=1}^k u_i^{(j)} x_i$. Apply the self correcting procedure C in Lemma 2.4 to obtain the value $C(u^{(j)})$.

   (c) Accept if and only if
   $$C(u^{(1)}) = a \cdot C(u^{(2)}) \cdot C(u^{(3)}) + b \cdot C(u^{(4)}) + c.$$

That is, the equations of Φ' of the first type are independent of Φ. The second type of equations do depend on Φ. Specifically, each equation of Φ chosen in step (a) induces a collection of equations of Φ' that come from the self-correcting procedure for each $u^{(j)}$. The equation in step (c) depends on 8 variables of Φ', since each $C(u^{(j)})$ depends linearly on two values of f and π. We now prove the correctness of the reduction.

Yes Case: If $\mathrm{val}(\Phi) = 1$, it is clear that $\mathrm{val}(\Phi') = 1$. Indeed, $\mathrm{val}(\Phi) = 1$ implies that there exists an assignment $\sigma(x_1), \ldots, \sigma(x_k) \in \mathbb{F}$ to the variables of Φ that satisfies all the equations, and the corresponding assignment $\sum_{i=1}^k u_i \cdot \sigma(x_i)$ for both $f(u), u \in L^k$ and $\pi(u), u \in \Gamma^k$, will satisfy all equations of Φ'.

NO Case: Now suppose that $\mathrm{val}(\Phi') \geqslant 1 - \varepsilon$ for $\varepsilon = 0.001$. Let $f : L^k \to \mathbb{F}$ and $\pi : \Gamma^k \to \mathbb{F}$ be the assignment to the variables that satisfies $1 - \varepsilon$ of the equations of Φ'. Then, the linearity test accepts (f, π) with probability at least $1 - 2\varepsilon$, and so by Lemma 2.4, there exists a linear function $g : L^k \to \mathbb{F}$ that agrees with f on at least $1 - 8\varepsilon$ fraction of the inputs.

Similarly, (f, π) satisfies at least $1 - 2\varepsilon$ fraction of the equations of the second type. Consider now an equation of Φ and a collection of tests of Φ' of the second type defined by this equation. By an averaging argument, it follows that for $1 - 20\varepsilon$ fraction of the equations of Φ chosen in step (a), the induced tests in step (c) accept with probability at least 0.9. Call such an equation of Φ good. We show that values of $g : L^k \to \mathbb{F}$ (at specific, relevant inputs), when viewed as assignment to Φ, satisfy every good equation of Φ. Since $1 - 20\varepsilon$ fraction of the equations of Φ are good, but $\mathrm{val}(\Phi) \leqslant 0.95$, this would be a contradiction.

Indeed, fix a good equation of Φ so that the induced test in step (c) accepts with probability at least 0.9. Let $\mathcal{E}$ denote the event that the test accepts. By the "furthermore" part of Lemma 2.4 and using a union bound for $u^{(1)}, \ldots, u^{(4)}$ appearing in the equation in step (c), we get that

$$\Pr\left[C(u^{(i)}) = g(u^{(i)}) \text{ for all } i = 1, \ldots, 4 \right]$$
$$\geqslant 1 - (32\varepsilon + 8/k) \geqslant 0.5.$$

Let $\mathcal{E}'$ denote the event that $C(u^{(i)}) = g(u^{(i)})$ for all $i = 1, \ldots, 4$ so that $\Pr[\mathcal{E}'] \geqslant 0.5$. Thus, with probability at least 0.4, both events $\mathcal{E}$ and $\mathcal{E}'$ occur, which is same as saying that the values $g(u^{(i)})$ satisfy the (good) equation. This completes the proof of Lemma 2.3. □

2.4 Proof of Lemma 2.4 - Linearity-Testing and Self-Correcting

In this section, we prove Lemma 2.4. As we mentioned, when L has a group structure, the lemma is well-known, e.g. in [BLR93, BOCLR08]. Therefore, we prove the lemma only for the case when $p = \mathrm{char}(\mathbb{F})$ is large and the set L is of the form $\{0, 1 \ldots, D\}$ for some $D \ll p$. The proof follows the outline from [BOCLR08] with appropriate modifications to our setting. After presenting the proof, we also point out, for the benefit of non-expert readers, how the proof works when L does have a group structure.

We recall that $p = \mathrm{char}(\mathbb{F}) \geqslant 3k^2D$, $L = \{0, 1, \ldots, D\}$, and $\Gamma = \{0, 1, \ldots, 3k^2D\}$. The tester is given query access to function $f : L^k \to \mathbb{F}$ and to $\pi : \Gamma^k \to \mathbb{F}$ such that $\pi|_{L^k} = f$. Since the restriction of π to L^k coincides with f, in the following, we denote both f and π by the same function f, keeping in mind that the "actual" function f is the restriction to L^k. The tester T works as follows:

1. With probability 0.5, perform the following test T_1.

   (a) Pick $x \in \{0, 1, \ldots, D\}^k$, $y \in \{0, 1, \ldots, k^2D\}^k$ independently, uniformly at random.

   (b) Accept if and only if $f(x) + f(y) = f(x + y)$.

2. With probability 0.5, perform the following test T_2.

   (a) Pick $x, y \in \{0, 1, \ldots, k^2D\}^k$ independently, uniformly at random.

   (b) Accept if and only if $f(x) + f(y) = f(x + y)$.

That is, we apply the standard linearity test as in [BLR93]. However, since the domain of f does not have a group structure, we need to choose the distribution from which we choose x and y carefully.

Clearly, if f is linear, i.e. $f(u_1, \ldots, u_k) = \sum_{i=1}^{k} \sigma_i u_i$, $\sigma_i \in \mathbb{F}$, then T always accepts. Towards proving the soundness property, suppose now that T accepts f with probability $1 - \varepsilon$. Note that this implies that both T_1 and T_2 accept with probability at least $1 - 2\varepsilon$ each. Our goal is to prove that the restriction of f to $\{0, 1, \ldots, D\}^k$ is close to a linear function. Towards this goal, we define the following function $g : \{0, 1, \ldots, D\}^k \to \mathbb{F}$,

$$g(x) = \mathsf{Plurality}_y(f(x + y) - f(y)),$$

where the plurality is taken over a uniformly random $y \in \{0, 1, \ldots, k^2D\}^k$. To clarify, the plurality refers to the element in $\mathbb{F}$ that occurs most frequently as the value $f(x + y) - f(y)$. A tie is broken arbitrarily, but we show next, that the plurality is in fact always an overwhelming majority.

CLAIM 2.5. *For each* $x \in \{0, 1, \ldots, D\}^k$, *let*

$$P_x = \Pr_y[g(x) = f(x + y) - f(y)],$$

where y *is chosen from* $\{0, 1, \ldots, k^2D\}^k$ *uniformly at random. Then,* $P_x \geqslant 1 - (4\varepsilon + 2/k)$ *for every* $x \in \{0, 1, \ldots, D\}^k$.

PROOF. Let $A_x = \Pr_{y,z}[f(x + y) - f(y) = f(x + z) - f(z)]$, where y, z are chosen independently and uniformly from $\{0, 1, \ldots, k^2D\}^k$. Note first that

$$A_x \leqslant P_x. \tag{5}$$

Indeed,

$$
\begin{aligned}
A_x &= \sum_{u \in \mathbb{F}} \Pr_{y,z}[f(x + y) - f(y) = u = f(x + z) - f(z)] \\
&= \sum_{u \in \mathbb{F}} \Pr_y[f(x + y) - f(y) = u]^2 \\
&\leqslant \max_{u \in \mathbb{F}}\left(\Pr_y[f(x + y) - f(y) = u] \right) \\
&= P_x,
\end{aligned}
$$

which proves (5). On the other hand, we have

$$
\begin{aligned}
1 - A_x &= \Pr_{y,z}[f(x + y) + f(z) \neq f(x + z) + f(y)] \\
&\leqslant \Pr_{y,z}[f(x + y) + f(z) \neq f(x + y + z)] \\
&\quad + \Pr_{y,z}[f(x + z) + f(y) \neq f(x + y + z)] \\
&= 2 \cdot \Pr_{y,z}[f(x + y) + f(z) \neq f(x + y + z)].
\end{aligned}
$$

Note that the quantity $\Pr_{y,z}[f(x+y)+f(z) \neq f(x+y+z)]$ is equal to $\Pr_{y',z}[f(y') + f(z) \neq f(y' + z)]$, where y' is chosen in the domain $\{0, 1, \ldots, k^2D\}^k$ "shifted by x". For this distribution on y' we have $\Pr_{y'}[y' \in \{0, 1, \ldots, k^2D\}^k] \geqslant (1 - 1/k^2)^k \geqslant 1 - 1/k$. That is, the distribution of y' is close to the distribution of a query in T_2 and the distribution of z is the same as in T_2. Thus, since T_2 accepts f with probability at least $1 - 2\varepsilon$, it follows that

$$
\begin{aligned}
&\Pr_{y,z}[f(x + y) + f(z) \neq f(x + y + z)] \\
&= \Pr_{y',z}[f(y') + f(z) \neq f(y' + z)] \leqslant 2\varepsilon + 1/k,
\end{aligned}
$$

and hence

$$A_x \geqslant 1 - (4\varepsilon + 2/k). \tag{6}$$

Combining (5) with (6) we get that

$$P_x \geqslant 1 - (4\varepsilon + 2/k),$$

as required. $\square$

CLAIM 2.6. *Suppose that* $k \geqslant 20$ *and* $\varepsilon \leqslant 0.02$. *Then* $\Pr_{x \in \{0,1,\ldots,D\}^k}[f(x) \neq g(x)] \leqslant 4\varepsilon$.

PROOF. Note that if we choose $x \in \{0, 1, \ldots, D\}^k$ and $y \in \{0, 1, \ldots, k^2D\}^k$ according to the distribution of T_1 then

$$
\begin{aligned}
2\varepsilon &\geqslant \Pr_{x,y}[T_1 \text{ rejects}] \\
&\geqslant \Pr_{x,y}[f(x) \neq f(x + y) - f(y) | f(x) \neq g(x)] \\
&\quad \times \Pr[f(x) \neq g(x)] \\
&\geqslant \Pr_{x,y}[g(x) = f(x + y) - f(y) | f(x) \neq g(x)] \\
&\quad \times \Pr[f(x) \neq g(x)] \\
&\geqslant \min_{x \in \{0,1,\ldots,D\}^k}(P_x) \cdot \Pr[f(x) \neq g(x)] \\
&\geqslant (1 - (4\varepsilon + 2/k)) \cdot \Pr[f(x) \neq g(x)].
\end{aligned}
$$

Therefore, if k is sufficiently large and ε is sufficiently small, then $\Pr_{x \in \{0,1,\ldots,D\}^k}[f(x) \neq g(x)] \leqslant 4\varepsilon$ and the claim follows. $\square$

CLAIM 2.7. *Suppose that* $k \geqslant 20$ *and* $\varepsilon \leqslant 0.02$. *Then, the restriction of* g *to* $\{0, 1, \ldots, D\}^k$ *is a linear function.*

PROOF. In order to prove that g is linear, it is enough to show that for every $x \in \{0, \ldots, D\}^k$ and for every $i \in [k]$ it holds that $g(x) + g(e_i) = g(x + e_i)$, where $e_i \in \mathbb{F}^k$ is the vector with 1 in the ith coordinate and 0 everywhere else. By Claim 2.5, we can write down the following three inequalities. In the first inequality, $e_i + y$ is just a proxy for y and when $y \in \{0, 1, \ldots, k^2D\}$ is uniformly chosen, the distribution of $e_i + y$ is $\frac{1}{k^2}$-close to that of y. The extra $\frac{1}{k^2}$

on the R.H.S. of the first inequality accounts for this small difference.

$$\Pr_y[g(x) = f(x + (e_i + y)) - f(e_i + y)]$$
$$\geqslant 1 - (4\varepsilon + 2/k + 1/k^2)$$

$$\Pr_y[g(e_i) = f(e_i + y) - f(y)]$$
$$\geqslant 1 - (4\varepsilon + 2/k)$$

$$\Pr_y[g(x + e_i) = f(x + e_i + y) - f(y)]$$
$$\geqslant 1 - (4\varepsilon + 2/k)$$

Therefore, for ε sufficiently small and k sufficiently large, by the union bound, all three events hold for the same $y \in \{0, 1, \ldots, k^2 D\}^k$, and thus

$$\begin{aligned} g(x) + g(e_i) &= \left(f(x + e_i + y) - f(e_i + y) \right) \\ &\quad + \left(f(e_i + y) - f(y) \right) \\ &= f(x + e_i + y) - f(y) = g(x + e_i). \end{aligned}$$

Therefore, the restriction of g to $\{0, 1, \ldots, D\}^k$ is a linear function, as required. $\square$

By combining Claim 2.6 with Claim 2.7 we conclude that if T accepts f with probability $1 - \varepsilon$, then the restriction of f to $\{0, 1, \ldots, D\}^k$ is 4ε-close to a linear function $g(x) = \sum_{i=1}^{k} g(e_i)x_i$. The self-correcting procedure is straightforward: on input $x \in \{0, 1, \ldots, D\}^k$,

- Pick $y \in \{0, 1, \ldots, k^2 D\}^k$ uniformly at random.

- Output $C(x) = f(x + y) - f(y)$.

Clearly, the procedure makes 2 queries to f and by Claim 2.5, it follows that $\Pr[C(x) = g(x)] \geqslant 1 - (4\varepsilon + 2/k)$. This completes the "furthermore" part of Lemma 2.4.

Finally, we comment on how the testing and self-correction works when L has a group structure. In this case, the tester is given query access to $f : L^k \to \mathbb{F}$ and there is no additional function π. The tester tests whether $f(x) + f(y) = f(x + y)$ for uniformly random x and y. A similar proof as above shows that if the tester accepts with probability $1 - \varepsilon$, then f is $(1 - O(\varepsilon))$-close to a linear function g. Moreover, for every fixed $x \in L^k$, $g(x) = f(x + y) - f(y)$ for $(1 - O(\varepsilon))$ fraction of $y \in L^k$ and this serves as the self-correction procedure.

3. REFERENCES

[ALM+98] S. Arora, C. Lund, R. Motwani, M. Sudan, and M. Szegedy. Proof verification and the hardness of approximation problems. *Journal of the ACM*, 45(3):501–555, 1998.

[AS98] S. Arora and S. Safra. Probabilistic Checking of Proofs: A New Characterization of NP. *Journal of the ACM*, 45(1):70–122, 1998.

[BLR93] M. Blum, M. Luby, and R. Rubinfeld. Self-testing/correcting with applications to numerical problems. *J. Comput. Syst. Sci.*, 47(3):549–595, 1993.

[BOCLR08] M. Ben-Or, D. Coppersmith, M. Luby, and R. Rubinfeld. Non-abelian homomorphism testing, and distributions close to their self-convolutions. *Random Struct. Algorithms*, 32(1):49–70, 2008.

[CGG06] Y. Chen, M. Grohe, and M. GrÃijber. On parameterized approximability. In *Parameterized and Exact Computation*, volume 4169 of *Lecture Notes in Computer Science*, pages 109–120. Springer Berlin Heidelberg, 2006.

[DECF+03] R. G. Downey, V. Estivill-Castro, M. Fellows, E. Prieto, and F.A. Rosamund. Cutting up is hard to do: The parameterised complexity of k-cut and related problems. *Electronic Notes in Theoretical Computer Science*, 78:209 – 222, 2003.

[DF95a] R. G. Downey and M. R. Fellows. Fixed-parameter tractability and completeness I: basic results. *SIAM J. Comput.*, 24(4):873–921, 1995.

[DF95b] R. G. Downey and M. R. Fellows. Fixed-parameter tractability and completeness II: on completeness for W[1]. *Theor. Comput. Sci.*, 141(1&2):109–131, 1995.

[DF99] R. G. Downey and M. R. Fellows. *Parameterized Complexity*. Springer-Verlag, 1999.

[FG06] J. Flum and M. Grohe. *Parameterized Complexity Theory*. Springer-Verlag, 2006.

[FGL+96] U. Feige, S. Goldwasser, L. LovÂt'asz, S. Safra, and M. Szegedy. Approximating Clique is almost NP-complete. *Journal of the ACM*, 43:268–292, 1996.

[Laz79] D. Lazard. Systems of algebraic equations. *Symbolic and Algebraic Computation*, 72:88–94, 1979.

[LFKN92] C. Lund, L. Fortnow, H. Karloff, and N. Nisan. Algebraic methods for interactive proof systems. *J. ACM*, 39(4):859–868, October 1992.

[Mar08] D. Marx. Parameterized complexity and approximation algorithms. *The Computer Journal*, 51:60–78, 2008.

[Sha92] A. Shamir. IP = PSPACE. *J. ACM*, 39(4):869–877, 1992.

[vzGG03] J. von zur Gathen and J. Gerhard. *Modern Computer Algebra*. Cambridge University Press, New York, NY, USA, 2 edition, 2003.

The Complexity of DNF of Parities

Gil Cohen
Computing and Mathematical Sciences
Department, Caltech
coheng@gmail.com

Igor Shinkar
Courant Institute of Mathematical Sciences,
New York University
ishinkar@cims.nyu.edu

ABSTRACT

We study depth 3 circuits of the form $\mathsf{OR} \circ \mathsf{AND} \circ \mathsf{XOR}$, or equivalently – DNF of parities. This model was first explicitly studied by Jukna (CPC'06) who obtained a $2^{\Omega(n)}$ lower bound for explicit functions in this model. Several related models have gained attention in the last few years, such as parity decision trees, the parity kill number and $\mathsf{AC}^0 \circ \mathsf{XOR}$ circuits.

For a function $f : \{0,1\}^n \to \{0,1\}$, we denote by $\mathsf{DNF}_\oplus(f)$ the least integer s for which there exists an $\mathsf{OR} \circ \mathsf{AND} \circ \mathsf{XOR}$ circuit, with OR gate of fan-in s, that computes f. We summarize some of our results:

- For any affine disperser $f : \{0,1\}^n \to \{0,1\}$ for dimension k, it holds that $\mathsf{DNF}_\oplus(f) \geq 2^{n-2k}$. By plugging Shaltiel's affine disperser (FOCS'11) we obtain an explicit $2^{n-n^{o(1)}}$ lower bound.

- We give a non-trivial general upper bound by showing that $\mathsf{DNF}_\oplus(f) \leq O(2^n/n)$ for any function f on n bits. This bound is shown to be tight up to an $O(\log n)$ factor.

- We show that for any symmetric function f it holds that $\mathsf{DNF}_\oplus(f) \leq 1.5^n \cdot \mathrm{poly}(n)$. Furthermore, there exists a symmetric function f for which this bound is tight up to a polynomial factor.

- We show tighter bounds for symmetric threshold functions. For example, we show that the majority function has $\mathsf{DNF}_\oplus$ complexity of $2^{n/2} \cdot \mathrm{poly}(n)$. This is also tight up to a polynomial factor.

- For the inner product function IP on n inputs we show that $\mathsf{DNF}_\oplus(\mathrm{IP}) = 2^{n/2} - 1$. Previously, Jukna gave a lower bound of $\Omega(2^{n/4})$ for the $\mathsf{DNF}_\oplus$ complexity of this function. We further give bounds for any low degree polynomial.

- Finally, we obtain a $2^{n-o(n)}$ average case lower bound for the parity decision tree model using affine extractors.

Categories and Subject Descriptors

F.1 [**Theory of Computation**]: Unbounded-action devices

Keywords

DNF, affine disperser, affine extractors

1. INTRODUCTION

In this paper we study depth 3 circuits of the form $\mathsf{OR} \circ \mathsf{AND} \circ \mathsf{XOR}$, where all gates have unbounded fan-in. Note that such a circuit computes a DNF applied to linear combinations of the input variables. Thus, for a function $f : \{0,1\}^n \to \{0,1\}$ we denote by $\mathsf{DNF}_\oplus(f)$ the minimum top gate fan-in over all circuits of the above form that compute f. Why not define $\mathsf{DNF}_\oplus(f)$ as the minimum number of gates required by an $\mathsf{OR} \circ \mathsf{AND} \circ \mathsf{XOR}$ circuit for computing f? There are three answers to this question, which also shed more light on this model of computation.

1. There is an equivalent, yet more combinatorial meaning, to the $\mathsf{DNF}_\oplus$ complexity of a function f the way it is defined above; $\mathsf{DNF}_\oplus(f)$ is the least number of affine subspaces required to cover exactly $f^{-1}(1)$. This is because every input to the top gate is an $\mathsf{AND} \circ \mathsf{XOR}$ circuit, and such a circuit computes the indicator of an affine subspace (we allow the use of constants).

2. Although potentially the fan-in of the AND and XOR gates can be arbitrary large, one can in fact assume it is bounded by n. Indeed, since $\mathsf{AND} \circ \mathsf{XOR}$ circuit computes the indicator function of some affine subspace, one can always replace the circuit with an equivalent circuit where the fan-in of the AND and XOR gates is at most n. Thus, the minimum number of gates required by an $\mathsf{OR} \circ \mathsf{AND} \circ \mathsf{XOR}$ circuit for computing a given function f is bounded above by $\mathsf{DNF}_\oplus(f) \cdot n^2$. In this paper we are mainly interested in functions with exponentially large $\mathsf{DNF}_\oplus(f)$ complexity and we do not mind such polynomial factors.

3. The size of a DNF is defined as the number of terms it contains, which is the top gate fan-in when represented as an $\mathsf{OR} \circ \mathsf{AND}$ circuit. So the current definition is analogous to the definition of the DNF complexity of a function.

Permission to make digital or hard copies of all or part of this work for personal or classroom use is granted without fee provided that copies are not made or distributed for profit or commercial advantage and that copies bear this notice and the full citation on the first page. Copyrights for components of this work owned by others than the author(s) must be honored. Abstracting with credit is permitted. To copy otherwise, or republish, to post on servers or to redistribute to lists, requires prior specific permission and/or a fee. Request permissions from Permissions@acm.org.

ITCS'16, January 14 - 16, 2016, Cambridge, MA, USA

© 2016 Copyright held by the owner/author(s). Publication rights licensed to ACM.
ISBN 978-1-4503-4057-1/16/01...$15.00

DOI: http://dx.doi.org/10.1145/2840728.2840734

To the best of our knowledge, the DNF$_\oplus$ complexity of a function was first explicitly considered by Jukna [Juk06] (see also Chapter 11 of [Juk12]). Jukna applies graph theoretic arguments and gives $2^{\Omega(n)}$ lower bounds on the DNF$_\oplus$ complexity for several explicit and natural functions. For example, for all even n, a lower bound of $\Omega(2^{n/4})$ is given for the DNF$_\oplus$ complexity of the inner product function IP$(x) = x_1 x_2 + x_3 x_4 + \cdots + x_{n-1} x_n$, where addition is over $\mathbb{F}_2$. [1] A similar result was obtained by Grolmusz [Gro94] based on communication complexity arguments. In [Juk06] it is also shown that the disjointness function disj: $\{0,1\}^n \to \{0,1\}$ defined by disj$(x) = 1$ if and only if $x_1 x_2 + x_3 x_4 + \cdots + x_{n-1} x_n = 0$, where addition is over $\mathbb{N}$, has DNF$_\oplus$ complexity of $\Omega(2^{0.016n})$.

More generally, Jukna characterizes the DNF$_\oplus$ complexity of functions that represent bipartite graphs in a certain way. The downside of this technique is that it cannot yield lower bounds stronger than $2^{n/2}$, whereas one can show that most functions on n inputs have DNF$_\oplus$ complexity $\Omega(2^n/(n \cdot \log n))$, as we discuss later in the introduction.

Several related models have been considered in the literature. For example, the parity decision tree model, defined by Kushilevitz and Mansour [KM93] in the context of learning theory, has received a significant attention in the last few years [MO09, ZS10, TWXZ13, OST$^+$13, STV14], with motivation coming mainly from communication complexity. We elaborate on the relation between the DNF$_\oplus$ model and parity decision tree model in Section 7, and give new results for it. Another example would be a recent work of Akavia *et al.* [ABG$^+$14], who considered AC$^0 \circ$XOR circuits, which strictly generalizes the DNF$_\oplus$ model. Their motivation comes from cryptography. Another interesting question in this direction is to prove that IP cannot be computed in AC$^0 \circ$ XOR (see [SV12]). A work of O'Donnell *et al.* [OST$^+$13] is related to the *width* of OR $\circ$ AND $\circ$ XOR circuits, whereas the DNF$_\oplus$ complexity is about understanding the *size* of such circuits. We also mention the work of Grolmusz [Gro94] who studied depth 3 circuits where the top gate is a threshold gate, the middle layer contains AND gates, and the bottom layer is composed of MOD$_m$ gates, for some integer m.

1.1 Our Results

In this paper we further study the DNF$_\oplus$ model. We also obtain results for the parity decision tree model. In the remaining of the introduction we elaborate on our contributions.

Almost Optimal Lower Bounds via Affine Dispersers

The first result of this paper states that good affine dispersers have a very high DNF$_\oplus$ complexity. An *affine disperser* for dimension k is a function $f \colon \{0,1\}^n \to \{0,1\}$ with the following property: For every affine subspace $U \subseteq \{0,1\}^n$ of dimension k, f restricted to U is not constant. Using a standard probabilistic argument one can show the existence of affine dispersers for dimension $k = \log_2(n) + \log_2 \log_2(n) + O(1)$. In terms of explicit constructions, the state of the art affine disperser is due to Shaltiel [Sha11]. Shaltiel's disperser works for dimension k as low as $2^{\log^{0.9} n}$, which, although not logarithmic, is still sub-polynomial.

Affine dispersers can be thought of as a "linear analogue" to Ramsey graphs, and are very natural pseudorandom objects which gained some attention by researchers in the past few years (e.g., [BKS$^+$05, BSK12, Sha11, Li11, CT14]). Nevertheless, the only application of them we are aware of is a lower bound of $3n - O(k)$ by Demenkov and Kulikov [DK11] for circuits over the full basis. By plugging an affine disperser for sub-linear dimension this gives $(3 - o(1)) \cdot n$ lower bound, matching and simplifying a result of Blum [Blu83], and is still the state of the art lower bound for this model. Here we give another application of affine dispersers, as captured by the following lemma.

THEOREM 1.1. *Let* $f \colon \{0,1\}^n \to \{0,1\}$ *be an affine disperser for dimension* k. *Then,*

1. DNF$_\oplus(f) \geq 2^{n-2k}$.

2. $\max\left(\text{DNF}_\oplus(f), \text{DNF}_\oplus(1 - f)\right) \geq 2^{n-k}$, *where* $1 - f$ *is the negation of* f.

A clarification regarding Theorem 1.1 is in order. The first item of the theorem tells us that if f is an affine disperser for dimension k then DNF$_\oplus(f) \geq 2^{n-2k}$. This by itself is already enough to yield almost optimal explicit lower bounds for the DNF$_\oplus$ model. Indeed, since Shaltiel's disperser is an affine disperser for dimension $k = n^{o(1)}$ one obtains a $2^{n-n^{o(1)}}$ lower bound (we remark that although Shaltiel's disperser is explicit in the computational sense, its description is not at all simple! We believe it is interesting to find an explicit function in the computational sense, that also has a simple description. We discuss this in Section 2).

Nevertheless, it is not clear whether the factor of 2 in the exponent of 2^{n-2k} is necessary. Moreover, as we exemplify next, in some cases this factor of 2 is highly undesired. So, although Theorem 1.1 does not guarantee a lower bound of 2^{n-k} for any affine disperser, the second item of the theorem (which has a "one line proof") does guarantee such a lower bound for either f or its negation. We note that if f is explicit, then so is its negation, and as a result, we have this amusing scenario where any explicit affine disperser for dimension k yields an explicit lower bound of 2^{n-k}, though we do not necessarily know whether this lower bound comes from f or its negation. [2]

One application of item 2 (in which item 1 is meaningless) is in proving that DNF$_\oplus$(IP) $\geq \Omega(2^{n/2})$, which improves the lower bound of $\Omega(2^{n/4})$ obtained by Jukna. Indeed, it is a well-known fact that IP is an affine disperser for dimension $n/2 + 1$ (see Appendix A), and so the second item of Theorem 1.1 implies that either IP or its negation have DNF$_\oplus$ complexity of $\Omega(2^{n/2})$. We further discuss the inner product later in the introduction (see also Section 6), where we show that the bound holds in fact for both functions. We also give a second proof for this fact.

Item 2 of Theorem 1.1 also implies the existence of a function f on n inputs such that DNF$_\oplus(f) \geq \Omega(2^n/(n \cdot \log n))$. This can be seen by taking an affine disperser for dimension $k = \log_2(n) + \log_2 \log_2(n) + O(1)$, which is promised to exists by the probabilistic method. It is worth mentioning that by

---

[1] Jukna's lower bound holds even if one replace the top OR gate by any threshold gate.

[2] In fact, if one knows toward which value f is biased, then one can tell which of f or $1 - f$ obtains the 2^{n-k} lower bound. Still, it is not always clear if a given construction of an affine disperser is biased towards 1, and we prefer to give a statement that could be used in a "black-box" fashion.

using a counting argument (which is the most common way of proving such lower bounds) one would get a weaker lower bound of $\Omega(2^n/n^2)$.

We remark that while a random function on n inputs has $\mathsf{DNF}_\oplus$ complexity $2^n/(n \cdot \log n)$, with high probability, Theorem 1.1 gives an *explicit property* of a random function that causes its $\mathsf{DNF}_\oplus$ complexity to be large.

An Upper Bound for All Functions

Clearly the $\mathsf{DNF}_\oplus$ complexity of any function f on n bits is upper bounded by 2^n. Indeed, one can take the union of points in $f^{-1}(1)$ as these are affine subspaces of dimension 0. The next theorem gives an upper bound of $O(2^n/n)$ for the $\mathsf{DNF}_\oplus$ complexity of all functions on n bits.

THEOREM 1.2. *For any function* $f: \{0,1\}^n \to \{0,1\}$ *it holds that* $\mathsf{DNF}_\oplus(f) \leq O(2^n/n)$.

The combinatorial meaning of Theorem 1.2 is that any set (namely, $f^{-1}(1)$) can always be covered by $O(2^n/n)$ affine subspaces, regardless of its structure. By the lower bound mentioned above, it follows that this upper bound is tight up to an $O(\log n)$ factor. Our proof for the upper bound makes use of the Gowers norm, and does not seem to be related to (or to follow from) the classical $O(2^n/n)$ upper bound of Lupanov [Lup61] for general Boolean circuits.

The $\mathsf{DNF}_\oplus$ Complexity of Symmetric and Threshold Functions

We continue to study the $\mathsf{DNF}_\oplus$ complexity of natural classes of functions. Our next result gives a non-trivial upper bound for any symmetric function.

THEOREM 1.3. *For any symmetric function* $f: \{0,1\}^n \to \{0,1\}$ *it holds that*

$$\mathsf{DNF}_\oplus(f) \leq 1.5^n \cdot \mathrm{poly}(n).$$

Moreover, there exists a symmetric function $g: \{0,1\}^n \to \{0,1\}$ *such that* $\mathsf{DNF}_\oplus(g) \geq \Omega(1.5^n/\sqrt{n})$.

Theorem 1.3 states that any symmetric function has $\mathsf{DNF}_\oplus$ complexity at most $1.5^n \cdot \mathrm{poly}(n)$, and this is tight for the class of symmetric functions. One may still ask whether a better bound can be obtained for the natural subclass of symmetric threshold functions. Consider for example the majority function $\mathsf{Maj}: \{0,1\}^n \to \{0,1\}$, where n is an odd positive integer. Is the upper bound of $1.5^n \cdot \mathrm{poly}(n)$ tight for Maj? It is not hard to show that $\mathsf{DNF}_\oplus(\mathsf{Maj}) \geq \Omega(2^{n/2}) \geq \Omega(1.414^n)$. To see this we use the fact an affine subspaces of dimension d cannot be contained in Hamming balls of radius $d-1$ (see Fact 4.2). Since $\mathsf{Maj}^{-1}(1)$ is the Hamming ball of radius $(n+1)/2$ centered at the all ones vector, any affine subspace that participates in the covering of $\mathsf{Maj}^{-1}(1)$ must have dimension at most $(n+1)/2$. Thus, $\mathsf{DNF}_\oplus(\mathsf{Maj}) \geq 2^{n-1}/2^{(n+1)/2} = \Omega(2^{n/2})$.

Which of these bounds, if any, is the right one? Our next theorem states that it is the lower bound that is tight. In fact, it gives a tight bound (up to polynomial factors) for the $\mathsf{DNF}_\oplus$ complexity of any symmetric threshold function, where the threshold is at least $1/2$. In the theorem below $\mathsf{Th}_\tau: \{0,1\}^n \to \{0,1\}$ is the function such that $\mathsf{Th}_\tau(x) = 1$ if and only if $|x| \geq \tau n$, where $\tau \in [0,1]$ is an integer multiple of $1/n$, and H is the Shannon binary entropy function defined by $H(x) = -x \log_2(x) - (1-x) \log_2(1-x)$.

THEOREM 1.4. *For any integer* n *and any* $1/2 \leq \tau \leq 1$ *that is an integer multiple of* $1/n$

$$2^{(H(\tau)-(1-\tau))\cdot n} \cdot \mathrm{poly}(n^{-1}) \leq \mathsf{DNF}_\oplus(\mathsf{Th}_\tau)$$

and

$$\mathsf{DNF}_\oplus(\mathsf{Th}_\tau) \leq 2^{(H(\tau)-(1-\tau))\cdot n} \cdot \mathrm{poly}(n).$$

By plugging $\tau = 1/2$ in Theorem 1.4 we obtain that, up to $\mathrm{poly}(n)$ factors, the $\mathsf{DNF}_\oplus$ complexity of Maj on n inputs is $2^{n/2}$. It is interesting to compare this result with the classical result of Quine [Qui53] stating that the DNF complexity of Maj is $\binom{n}{n/2} = \Theta(2^n/\sqrt{n})$.

Theorem 1.4 only applies for $\tau \geq 1/2$, and there is a reason for that. Indeed, using arguments similar to the lower bound for $\mathsf{DNF}_\oplus(\mathsf{Maj})$ sketched above, one can show that for any $\tau < 1/2$ it holds that $\mathsf{DNF}_\oplus(\mathsf{Th}_\tau) \geq 2^{\tau n}$. Roughly speaking, this asymmetry of the $\mathsf{DNF}_\oplus$ complexity between threshold functions with $\tau \geq 1/2$ and $\tau < 1/2$ follows from the fact that the set of functions with low $\mathsf{DNF}_\oplus$ complexity is not closed under negation. For that one should also consider the $\mathsf{CNF}_\oplus$ complexity, defined in the natural way. A similar phenomenon occurs in the standard DNF and CNF complexity measures. We elaborate on that in Section 7.

While the lower bound in Theorem 1.3 holds for all symmetric functions, the construction we give that matches this lower bound only uses parity gates with fan-in 2 (and the upper bound in Theorem 1.4 requires only fan-in 3). Note that one can replace each fan-in 2 parity gate with a width 2 constant size CNF. By collapsing levels one then obtains a depth 3 Boolean circuit of size $1.5^n \cdot \mathrm{poly}(n)$, with fan-in 2 bottom layer gates, that computes the given symmetric function. The latter is a result that is attributed to Paturi *et al.* [PSZ97], and Theorem 1.3 reproduces it.

The Inner Product Function and Low Degree Polynomials

As mentioned above, the second item in Theorem 1.1 implies a lower bound of $\Omega(2^{n/2})$ for $\mathsf{DNF}_\oplus(\mathrm{IP})$ (or for $\mathsf{DNF}_\oplus(1-\mathrm{IP})$). We would like to get a more precise bound. It is easy to see that $\mathsf{DNF}_\oplus(\mathrm{IP}) \leq 2^{n/2}-1$. Indeed, when fixing the variables $\{x_i : i \text{ odd}\}$ to zeros we are getting the constant zero function, while for any other fix of the variables $\{x_i : i \text{ odd}\}$ we get a linear function in the $\{x_i : i \text{ even}\}$. Therefore, for all $x \in \{0,1\}^n$ it holds that $\mathrm{IP}(x_1, \ldots, x_n)$ is equal to

$$\bigvee_{(\alpha_1,\alpha_3,\ldots,\alpha_{n-1})\neq \vec{0}} \left(\left(\bigwedge_{i \text{ odd}} x_i = \alpha_i \right) \wedge \left(\bigoplus_{i \text{ odd}} \alpha_i x_{i+1} = 1 \right) \right).$$

In the following theorem we show that this is best possible.

THEOREM 1.5. *For any even integer* n, *it holds that*

$$\mathsf{DNF}_\oplus(\mathrm{IP}) = 2^{n/2} - 1.$$

We prove Theorem 1.5 in Section 6. So one completely understands the $\mathsf{DNF}_\oplus$ complexity of IP. In fact, one can prove something more general. Namely, for any degree 2 polynomial over $\mathbb{F}_2$ we have $\mathsf{DNF}_\oplus(f) = \Theta(1/\mathrm{bias}(f))$ (see Corollary 6.3). So the $\mathsf{DNF}_\oplus$ complexity of degree 2 polynomials is also well understood. What about higher degrees? In the following theorem we give a non-trivial upper bound for the $\mathsf{DNF}_\oplus$ complexity of degree $d > 2$ polynomials. The bound is meaningful for functions with degree up to roughly $\log\log n$.

THEOREM 1.6. *Let* $f\colon \{0,1\}^n \to \{0,1\}$ *be a function that has degree* $d \geq 3$ *as a polynomial over* $\mathbb{F}_2$. *Then,*

$$\mathsf{DNF}_\oplus(f) \leq 2^{n-\Omega(n^{1/(d-1)!})}.$$

On the other hand, with high probability, a random degree d *polynomial over* $\mathbb{F}_2$ *has* $\mathsf{DNF}_\oplus$ *complexity* $2^{n-O(n^{1/(d-1)})}$.

We also prove stronger upper bounds for biased low degree polynomials (see Section 6 for more details).

The Parity Decision Tree Model

As mentioned, Kushilevitz and Mansour [KM93] introduced the notion of parity decision trees, which received a significant attention in the last few years [MO09, ZS10, TWXZ13, OST⁺13, STV14]. Roughly speaking, these are decision trees where each node contains not a variable but rather a linear function of some subset of the variables (see, e.g., [STV14] for the formal definition). The parity decision tree complexity of a function $f\colon \{0,1\}^n \to \{0,1\}$, which we denote here by $\mathsf{DT}_\oplus(f)$, is the least size (that is, number of leaves) required by a parity decision tree for computing f.

In this paper we give an average case hardness result for the $\mathsf{DT}_\oplus$ model. Namely, we give an explicit construction for a function f such that any function with not too large $\mathsf{DT}_\oplus$ complexity has a small correlation with f. For this we need to recall the definition of an affine extractor, which is a strengthening of the notion of affine dispersers.

An *affine extractor* for dimension k with bias ε is a function $f\colon \{0,1\}^n \to \{0,1\}$ with the following property. For every affine subspace $U \subseteq \mathbb{F}_2^n$ of dimension k, the bias of f restricted to U, defined as $\mathrm{bias}(f|_U) = |\mathbb{E}_{u\sim U}[(-1)^{f(u)}]|$, is at most ε. A standard probabilistic argument shows the existence of an affine extractor with bias ε for dimension $k = \log_2(n/\varepsilon^2) + \log_2\log_2(n/\varepsilon^2) + O(1)$. The state of the art explicit constructions for affine extractors [Bou07, Yeh11, Li11] works for dimension $k = O(n/\sqrt{\log\log n})$, with bias that is exponentially small in $n^{\Omega(1)}$.

In the theorem below, the distance between two functions, denoted by $\mathrm{dist}(f,g)$, is defined as the fraction of points in the hypercube on which the functions disagree.

THEOREM 1.7. *Let* $f\colon \{0,1\}^n \to \{0,1\}$ *be an affine extractor for dimension* k, *with bias* $\varepsilon \leq 1/2$. *Then, for any* $g\colon \{0,1\}^n \to \{0,1\}$ *such that* $\mathsf{DT}_\oplus(g) \leq \varepsilon \cdot 2^{n-k}$ *it holds that* $\mathrm{dist}(f,g) \geq 1/2 - 4\varepsilon$.

By plugging the efficiently constructible affine extractors mentioned above, one obtains an explicit average case lower bound of $2^{n-o(n)}$ for the $\mathsf{DT}_\oplus$ model. As in the case of lower bounds for the $\mathsf{DNF}_\oplus$ model, it is also interesting to obtain explicit lower bounds that have a succinct and simple description. One example comes from the inner product function. Indeed, the fact that IP is an affine extractor for dimension $n/2 + c$, with error exponentially small in c, is considered a folklore (see Appendix A). Thus, Theorem 1.7 implies that IP has no more than ε correlation with functions having $\mathsf{DT}_\oplus$ complexity $O(\varepsilon^2 \cdot 2^{n/2})$. To break the "$n/2$ barrier", one can consider the function $\mathrm{Tr}(x^7)$ [3], which clearly

---

[3]Tr is the trace function from $\mathbb{F}_{2^n}$ to $\mathbb{F}_2$. We also assume some underlying isomorphism between the vector space $\mathbb{F}_2^n$ and the field $\mathbb{F}_{2^n}$.

has a simple description. Ben-Sasson and Kopparty [BSK12] proved that this function is an affine extractor for dimension $2n/5 + O(\log^2(1/\varepsilon))$, when n is odd. [4] Thus for, say, a constant ε, one obtains a simple and explicit average case lower bound of $\Omega(2^{0.6n})$ for this model.

Like in the case of affine dispersers, although affine extractors are natural objects, to the best of our knowledge, so far they found only few applications in the literature [BSZ11, Vio14, ST12, ST13].

A proof for Theorem 1.7 is given in Section 7, where we also relate the $\mathsf{DNF}_\oplus$ and $\mathsf{DT}_\oplus$ complexity measures. We summarize here by saying that interesting results regarding the DNF and the decision tree complexity "goes through" in the analogous models with parity gates with hardly any change in the proofs. Still, we feel it is worthwhile to point out these relations between $\mathsf{DNF}_\oplus$ and $\mathsf{DT}_\oplus$.

1.2 Preliminaries

Throughout the paper, for the sake of readability, we suppress floor and ceiling. For integers n, k such that $0 \leq k \leq n$, we denote by L_k the k'th level of the n dimensional hypercube, namely, $L_k = \{x \in \{0,1\}^n : |x| = k\}$, where $|x|$ is the Hamming weight of x. Note that n is suppressed in this notation. This will not cause a confusion because n will always be clear from the context. The bias of a Boolean function $f\colon D \to \{0,1\}$, defined on some domain D, is given by $\mathrm{bias}(f) \triangleq |D|^{-1} \cdot |\sum_{x \in D}(-1)^{f(x)}|$.

We make some use of basic results from Fourier analysis of Boolean functions. We follow the standard notations as in O'Donnell's book [O'D14].

2. ALMOST OPTIMAL LOWER BOUNDS VIA AFFINE DISPERSERS

We start this section by proving Theorem 1.1. To this end we prove the following lemma.

LEMMA 2.1. *Let* $A \subset \{0,1\}^n$ *be a set of size* $t < 2^n$. *Then, for any integer* $\ell \geq 0$ *such that*

$$(t+1) \cdot 2^{\ell-1} < 2^n, \tag{2.1}$$

there exists an affine subspace $V_\ell \subset \{0,1\}^n$ *of dimension* ℓ *such that* $A \cap V_\ell = \emptyset$.

PROOF. We construct the affine subspaces $(V_\ell)_\ell$ by induction on ℓ. We start with the base case $\ell = 0$. As we assume that $|A| = t < 2^n$, there exists a point in $\{0,1\}^n \setminus A$, which is an affine subspace of dimension $\ell = 0$, as desired.

We now construct V_ℓ given $V_{\ell-1}$, assuming ℓ satisfies (2.1). Let $\Delta_1, \ldots, \Delta_{\ell-1}$ be linearly independent vectors such that $V_{\ell-1} = \Delta_0 + \mathrm{span}(\Delta_1, \ldots, \Delta_{\ell-1})$, for some shift vector Δ_0. We wish to find a vector Δ_ℓ, independent of $\Delta_1, \ldots, \Delta_{\ell-1}$, such that $\Delta_0 + \mathrm{span}(\Delta_1, \ldots, \Delta_\ell)$ does not intersect A. This will be our V_ℓ. To this end, consider the set of "good shifts"

$$X = \{x \in \{0,1\}^n \mid (x + \mathrm{span}(\Delta_1, \ldots, \Delta_{\ell-1})) \cap A = \emptyset\}.$$

We note that $\Delta_0 \in X$. Moreover, if x is another point in X then by setting $\Delta_\ell = x + \Delta_0$ we get that

$$\Delta_0 + \mathrm{span}(\Delta_1, \ldots, \Delta_\ell)$$
$$= (\Delta_0 + \mathrm{span}(\Delta_1, \ldots, \Delta_{\ell-1})) \cup (x + \mathrm{span}(\Delta_1, \ldots, \Delta_{\ell-1})),$$

---

[4]To get this dependency in ε, one needs to use a result by Haramaty and Shpilka [HS10]. See also Theorem 6.2 in [CT14].

and since both $x, \Delta_0 \in X$, it follows that the set above does not intersect A. So, all that is left to prove is the existence of an $x \in X$ such that $\Delta_\ell = x + \Delta_0$ is linearly independent of $\Delta_1, \ldots, \Delta_{\ell-1}$, or equivalently, that $X \setminus V_{\ell-1} \neq \emptyset$. To this end, note that $x \in X$ if and only if $x \notin A + \mathrm{span}(\Delta_1, \ldots, \Delta_{\ell-1})$. So,

$$
\begin{aligned}
|X| &= 2^n - |A + \mathrm{span}(\Delta_1, \ldots, \Delta_{\ell-1})| \\
&\geq 2^n - |A| \cdot |\mathrm{span}(\Delta_1, \ldots, \Delta_{\ell-1})| \\
&= 2^n - t \cdot 2^{\ell-1}.
\end{aligned}
$$

Thus,

$$
|X \setminus V_{\ell-1}| \geq |X| - |V_{\ell-1}| \geq 2^n - (t+1) \cdot 2^{\ell-1} > 0,
$$

where the last inequality follows by Equation (2.1). Thus, $X \setminus V_{\ell-1} \neq \emptyset$, which concludes the proof. $\square$

We now turn to the proof of Theorem 1.1.

PROOF OF THEOREM 1.1. We start with the proof of the first item. Let f be an affine disperser for dimension k and set $s = \mathsf{DNF}_\oplus(f)$. Thus, f is the union of s affine subspaces. Since f is an affine disperser for dimension k, each of these affine subspaces has dimension at most $k-1$. Thus, $|f^{-1}(1)| \leq s \cdot 2^{k-1}$. By Lemma 2.1, for every integer ℓ such that $(|f^{-1}(1)|+1) \cdot 2^{\ell-1} < 2^n$, there exists an affine subspace of dimension ℓ, restricted to which f is the constant 0. Since f is an affine disperser for dimension k, we get that

$$
(s \cdot 2^{k-1} + 1) \cdot 2^{k-1} \geq (|f^{-1}(1)| + 1) \cdot 2^{k-1} \geq 2^n.
$$

Thus, $s \geq 2^{n-2k}$ as desired.

We now turn to prove the second item, which is actually even simpler to prove. As before, if f is an affine disperser for dimension k with $\mathsf{DNF}_\oplus(f) = s$ then $|f^{-1}(1)| \leq s \cdot 2^{k-1}$. So $\mathsf{DNF}_\oplus(f) \geq |f^{-1}(1)| \cdot 2^{1-k}$. Now note that if f is an affine disperser for dimension k then so is $1 - f$, and so applying the argument above for $1 - f$ gives $\mathsf{DNF}_\oplus(1 - f) \geq |(1 - f)^{-1}(1)| \cdot 2^{1-k}$. Clearly, $\max(|f^{-1}(1)|, |(1-f)^{-1}(1)|) \geq 2^{n-1}$ and so we get that $\max(\mathsf{DNF}_\oplus(f), \mathsf{DNF}_\oplus(1 - f)) \geq 2^{n-k}$, as stated.

$\square$

A discussion regarding explicitness.

As mentioned above, by plugging Shaltiel's disperser to Theorem 1.1 it follows that there exists an efficiently computable function $f : \{0,1\}^n \to \{0,1\}$ such that $\mathsf{DNF}_\oplus(f) \geq 2^{n-n^{o(1)}}$. The affine disperser of Shaltiel mentioned above, which we denote by Sha, is explicit in the computational sense. That is, given $x \in \{0,1\}^n$, one can compute $\mathsf{Sha}(x)$ in time that is polynomial in $|x|$. However, the description of the function Sha is not at all simple. Thus, it is natural to ask for an explicit lower bound for the $\mathsf{DNF}_\oplus$ model, which also has a simple description. Ben-Sasson and Kopparty [BSK12] gave such a construction that works for dimension $\Omega(n^{4/5})$ (though we omit its description here as it would require setting some notations). Thus, there is a "simple" and explicit lower bound of $2^{n-\Omega(n^{4/5})}$ for the $\mathsf{DNF}_\oplus$ model.

We next show a very simple and explicit function that has $\mathsf{DNF}_\oplus$ complexity $\Omega(2^{2n/3})$ (just to break the "$n/2$ barrier"). In [BSK12] the authors showed that for an odd n, the function $\mathsf{Tr}(x^{15})$, which evidently has a very simple description, is an affine disperser for dimension $n/3 + 10$. By examining the proof of the second item in Theorem 1.1, one can see that for any affine disperser f for dimension k, $\mathsf{DNF}_\oplus(f) \geq |f^{-1}(1)| \cdot 2^{1-k}$. Now, $\mathsf{Tr}(x^{15})$ is a non-constant degree 4 polynomial over $\mathbb{F}_2$, and so it obtains the value 1 on at least 2^{-4} fraction of the hypercube. Thus, it follows that $\mathsf{DNF}_\oplus(\mathsf{Tr}(x^{15})) \geq \Omega(2^{2n/3})$.

3. AN UPPER BOUND FOR ALL FUNCTIONS

In this section we prove Theorem 1.2. To this end we need the following lemma.

LEMMA 3.1. *Let $A \subseteq \{0,1\}^n$ be a set of size $\varepsilon \cdot 2^n$, for any $\varepsilon > 2^{-n/4}$. Then there exists an affine subspace $V \subseteq A$ of dimension $\dim(V) \geq \log(n) - \log\log(1/\varepsilon) - 2$.*

We defer the proof of Lemma 3.1 and first prove Theorem 1.2.

PROOF OF THEOREM 1.2. In order to prove Theorem 1.2, fix a function $f : \{0,1\}^n \to \{0,1\}$, and let $A = f^{-1}(1)$. We want to show that there are $s = O(2^n/n)$ affine subspaces $V_1, \ldots, V_s$ contained in A that cover A, i.e. $A = \cup_{i=1}^s V_i$. We choose the affine subspaces greedily as follows:

1. Set $A_1 = A$.

2. Set $i = 1$.

3. Repeat

   (a) Pick an affine subspace $V_i \subseteq A_i$ of maximal dimension.

   (b) Set $A_{i+1} = A_i \setminus V_i$.

   (c) Increment i by 1.

   until $|A_i| \leq 2^n/n$.

4. Output $V_1, \ldots, V_{i-1}$ together with the singleton affine subspaces for each point in A_i.

We claim that the above procedure terminates in at most $O(2^n/n)$ iterations. For every integer $t \geq 0$ define $i_t = \min\{i : A_i \leq 2^{n-t}\}$. Note that $i_0 = 1$. By Lemma 3.1, for every $i < i_t$ we have $|V_i| \geq n/4t$. Therefore,

$$
i_t - i_{t-1} \leq \frac{|A_{i_{t-1}}|}{\min_{i \leq i_t} |V_i|} \leq \frac{2^{n-t}}{n/4t}.
$$

The algorithm terminates in the iteration $i = i_{\log n}$, which is at most

$$
\begin{aligned}
i_{\log n} &= 1 + \sum_{t=1}^{\log n} (i_t - i_{t-1}) \\
&\leq 1 + \sum_{t=1}^{\log n} \frac{2^{n-t}}{n/4t} \\
&\leq 1 + \frac{4 \cdot 2^n}{n} \cdot \sum_{t=1}^{\infty} \frac{t}{2^t} \\
&= 1 + 8 \cdot \frac{2^n}{n}.
\end{aligned}
$$

Therefore, the procedure above outputs at most $1 + 8 \cdot 2^n/n + |A_{i_{\log n}}| = 1 + 9 \cdot 2^n/n$ affine subspaces. This completes the proof of the theorem. $\square$

We now return to the proof of Lemma 3.1. We need the following definition of *degree d norm* of a function, also known as the uniformity norm or Gowers norm of a function.

DEFINITION 3.2 (DEGREE d NORM). *Let $f : \{0,1\}^n \to \mathbb{R}$ be a function. The d'th norm of f is defined as*

$$U_d(f) = \left(\mathop{\mathbf{E}}_{x,y_1,\ldots,y_d \in \{0,1\}^n} \left[\prod_{S \subseteq [d]} f\left(x + \sum_{i \in S} y_i\right) \right] \right)^{1/2^d}.$$

The following proposition (known as the Gowers-Cauchy-Schwartz inequality) is standard and can be found, e.g., in [VW07].

PROPOSITION 3.3. *Let $f : \{0,1\}^n \to \mathbb{R}$ be a function. Then, $U_1(f) = |\mathbf{E}[f(x)]|$, and for any positive integer i it holds that $U_i(f) \le U_{i+1}(f)$.*

We are now ready to prove Lemma 3.1.

PROOF OF LEMMA 3.1. Let $f : \{0,1\}^n \to \{0,1\}$ be the indicator function of the set A. Then, for any $d \in \mathbb{N}$, by Proposition 3.3 we have $U_d(f) \ge \mathbf{E}[f(x)] = \varepsilon$. Therefore, since f is Boolean, by the definition of $U_d(f)$ we have

$$\mathop{\mathbf{Pr}}_{x,y_1,\ldots,y_d \in \{0,1\}^n} [x + \mathrm{span}(y_1,\ldots,y_d) \subseteq A]$$

$$= \mathop{\mathbf{E}}_{x,y_1,\ldots,y_d \in \{0,1\}^n} \left[\prod_{S \subseteq [d]} f\left(x + \sum_{i \in S} y_i\right) \right] \ge \varepsilon^{2^d}.$$

Note that uniformly random vectors $y_1,\ldots,y_d \in \{0,1\}^n$ are linearly independent with probability $(1-2^{-n})(1-2^{1-n})(1-2^{2-n})\cdots(1-2^{d-1-n}) > 1 - 2^{d-n}$. Therefore, for uniformly random $x, y_1, \ldots, y_d \in \{0,1\}^n$, with probability at least $\varepsilon^{2^d} - 2^{d-n}$, the affine subspace $x + \mathrm{span}(y_1,\ldots,y_d)$ is contained in A, and its dimension is d. Thus, as long as $\varepsilon^{2^d} > 2^{d-n}$ the set A contains an affine subspace of dimension d. It is easy to check that for $d = \lceil \log(n) - \log\log(1/\varepsilon) - 2 \rceil$ the inequality above indeed holds . $\square$

4. THE DNF$_\oplus$ COMPLEXITY OF SYMMETRIC FUNCTIONS

In this section we prove Theorem 1.3. To this end we will need the following two facts.

FACT 4.1. *Let $n > 1$ be an integer. Let $p \in (0,1)$ be such that pn is an integer. Let $q = 1 - p$. Then,*

$$\frac{1}{\sqrt{8npq}} \le \binom{n}{pn} \cdot 2^{-H(p)n} \le \frac{1}{\sqrt{3npq}}.$$

In particular,

$$\frac{1}{\sqrt{8n}} \le \binom{n}{pn} \cdot 2^{-H(p)n} \le 1.$$

A proof for Fact 4.1 can be found in, e.g., [CT12].

FACT 4.2. *Let $u + U$ be an affine subspace of dimension d. Then $u + U$ is not contained in any ball of radius $d - 1$. In particular, there exist vectors $u_1, u_2 \in u + U$ such that $|u_1| \ge d$ and $|u_2| \le n - d$.*

PROOF OF FACT 4.2. Consider a $d \times n$ generating matrix A for the subspace U. By performing a Gaussian elimination on A and permuting the columns of the resulted matrix, we can assume that the first d columns of A form the identity matrix. This can be done because such operations have no affect on Hamming weights nor on the dimension. Now let B be a ball of radius $d - 1$ around the point u_0, that is, $B = \{x \in \{0,1\}^n : |x - u_0| \le d - 1\}$. Let v be the vector in U that disagrees with u_0 on the first d entries. Such a vector exists by the structure of A deduced above. Clearly $v \notin B$ since $|v - u_0| \ge d$. The proof follows. $\square$

We start by showing that the "moreover direction" of Theorem 1.3 holds. Consider the function $g_k \colon \{0,1\}^n \to \{0,1\}$ defined by $g_k(x) = 1$ if and only if $|x| = k$, where $0 \le k \le n$ is an integer.

CLAIM 4.3. *For any integers n and $0 \le k \le n$ it holds that $\mathsf{DNF}_\oplus(g_k) \ge \binom{n}{k} \cdot 2^{-\min(k,n-k)}$.*

PROOF OF CLAIM 4.3. Note that for all k it holds that $\mathsf{DNF}_\oplus(g_k) = \mathsf{DNF}_\oplus(g_{n-k})$. This is because any covering for g_k can be translated to a covering for g_{n-k} by adding the all ones vector to the shifts of all affine subspaces in the covering. It is therefore enough to show that for all $k \le n/2$, $\mathsf{DNF}_\oplus(g_k) \ge \binom{n}{k} \cdot 2^{-k}$. Note that $\mathsf{DNF}_\oplus(g_k)$ is the minimum number of affine subspaces such that their union equals L_k. Since $|L_k| = \binom{n}{k}$ the proof follows by Fact 4.2 which guarantees that any affine subspace in this covering has dimension at most k. $\square$

Consider now the function g_k for $k = 2n/3$. By Claim 4.3 and Fact 4.1 it follows that

$$\mathsf{DNF}_\oplus(g_k) \ge \frac{\binom{n}{2n/3}}{2^{n/3}} \ge \Omega\left(\frac{1}{\sqrt{n}} \cdot 2^{n \cdot (H(2/3) - 1/3)} \right)$$

$$= \Omega\left(\frac{1}{\sqrt{n}} \cdot 1.5^n \right),$$

which concludes the "moreover direction" of Theorem 1.3. To prove the more interesting direction, we show below that Claim 4.3 is tight up to $\mathrm{poly}(n)$ factors.

LEMMA 4.4. *For any integers n and $0 \le k \le n$ it holds that*

$$\mathsf{DNF}_\oplus(g_k) \le \binom{n}{k} \cdot 2^{-\min(k,n-k)} \cdot n.$$

PROOF OF LEMMA 4.4. We start by presenting the proof for $k = n/2$ (assuming that n is even). The proof for this special case is slightly simpler than the proof for general k, and already demonstrates the proof idea.

For every permutation $\sigma \in S_n$ we define the affine subspace $V_\sigma \subseteq \{0,1\}^n$ that contains all points subject to the following $n/2$ affine constraints:

$$\begin{cases} 1 &= x_{\sigma(1)} + x_{\sigma(2)} \\ 1 &= x_{\sigma(3)} + x_{\sigma(4)} \\ &\vdots \\ 1 &= x_{\sigma(n-1)} + x_{\sigma(n)}. \end{cases}$$

Note that for every $\sigma \in S_n$, it holds that $V_\sigma \subseteq L_{n/2}$. We show next that by choosing $m = n \cdot \binom{n}{n/2} \cdot 2^{-n/2}$ random permutations $\sigma_1, \ldots, \sigma_m$ uniformly and independently from

S_n, with high probability $L_{n/2} = \cup_{i=1}^{m} V_{\sigma_i}$. To see this fix $x \in L_{n/2}$. By symmetry, for a uniformly random $\sigma \in S_n$ we have that

$$\Pr_{\sigma}[x \in V_\sigma] = \frac{|V_\sigma|}{|L_{n/2}|} = \frac{2^{n/2}}{\binom{n}{n/2}}.$$

Therefore,

$$\Pr_{\sigma_1,\dots,\sigma_m}\left[x \notin \bigcup_{i=1}^{m} V_{\sigma_i}\right] \le \left(1 - \frac{2^{n/2}}{\binom{n}{n/2}}\right)^m \le e^{-n},$$

where the last inequality holds by the choice of m. Hence, by the union bound

$$\Pr_{\sigma_1,\dots,\sigma_m}\left[\exists x \in L_{n/2} \text{ such that } x \notin \bigcup_{i=1}^{m} V_{\sigma_i}\right] \le \binom{n}{n/2} \cdot e^{-n},$$

which is smaller than 1. Therefore, there exist m affine subspaces, of the above form, such that their union equals $L_{n/2}$, and so $\mathsf{DNF}_\oplus(g_{n/2}) \le n \cdot \binom{n}{n/2} \cdot 2^{-n/2}$.

We proceed now for general $k \le n/2$. As mentioned, this would also conclude the proof for all $k \ge n/2$. Let $t = n-2k$. For every permutation $\sigma \in S_n$ define the affine subspace V_σ as the set of points that obey the following affine constraints:

$$
\begin{cases}
\begin{cases}
0 &= x_{\sigma(1)} \\
&\vdots \\
0 &= x_{\sigma(t)}
\end{cases} \\
\begin{cases}
1 &= x_{\sigma(t+1)} + x_{\sigma(t+2)} \\
&\vdots \\
1 &= x_{\sigma(n-1)} + x_{\sigma(n)}.
\end{cases}
\end{cases}
$$

Clearly, $V_\sigma \subseteq L_k$ for every permutation $\sigma \in S_n$. Moreover, for every fixed $x \in L_k$ we have that $\Pr_\sigma[x \in V_\sigma] = |V_\sigma|/|L_k| = 2^k/\binom{n}{k}$. Therefore, if we choose $m = n \cdot \binom{n}{k} \cdot 2^{-k}$ random permutations $\sigma_1,\dots,\sigma_m$ uniformly and independently at random then

$$\Pr_{\sigma_1,\dots,\sigma_m}\left[x \notin \bigcup_{i=1}^{m} V_{\sigma_i}\right] \le \left(1 - \frac{2^k}{\binom{n}{k}}\right)^m \le e^{-n},$$

where the last inequality follows by our choice of m. By taking the union bound over all $x \in L_k$ we get

$$\Pr_{\sigma_1,\dots,\sigma_m}\left[\exists x \in L_k \text{ such that } x \notin \bigcup_{i=1}^{m} V_{\sigma_i}\right] \le \binom{n}{k} \cdot e^{-n} < 1.$$

Therefore, $\mathsf{DNF}_\oplus(g_k) \le \binom{n}{k} \cdot 2^{-k} \cdot n$. $\square$

We now deduce Theorem 1.3 from Lemma 4.4. Any symmetric function $f\colon \{0,1\}^n \to \{0,1\}$ can be written as the union of some subset of $\{g_0,\dots,g_n\}$. Thus, $\mathsf{DNF}_\oplus(f) \le \sum_{k=0}^{n} \mathsf{DNF}_\oplus(g_k)$. By Lemma 4.4 and Fact 4.1,

$$\mathsf{DNF}_\oplus(g_k) \le \binom{n}{k} \cdot 2^{-\min(k,n-k)} \cdot n \le 2^{H(k/n)\cdot n - \min(k,n-k)} \cdot n.$$

One can show that the maximum over $0 \le k \le n$ of the expression $H(k/n) \cdot n - \min(k,n-k)$ that appears in the exponent above is obtained at $k = n/3$ and $k = 2n/3$. This maximum value is $(H(1/3) - 1/3) \cdot n = \log_2(1.5) \cdot n$. Thus, for all $0 \le k \le n$, $\mathsf{DNF}_\oplus(g_k) \le 1.5^n \cdot n$ and so $\mathsf{DNF}_\oplus(f) \le O(1.5^n \cdot n^2)$. We remark that by a more careful argument one can show that $\mathsf{DNF}_\oplus(f) \le O(1.5^n \cdot n)$.

5. THE $\mathsf{DNF}_\oplus$ COMPLEXITY OF THRESHOLD FUNCTIONS

In this section we prove Theorem 1.4.

PROOF. As in the proof of Theorem 1.3, it is enough to show how to cover any level ωn for $\tau \le \omega \le 1$ in the hypercube by $2^{(H(\tau)-(1-\tau))\cdot n} \cdot \mathrm{poly}(n)$ affine subspaces. However, as apposed to the way this was done in the proof of Theorem 1.3, we may now consider affine subspaces that are not restricted to level ωn, and points may "leak" to higher levels. This is the leverage we exploit so to obtain stronger results for threshold functions.

The proof is more delicate than the proof of Theorem 1.3, and for the purpose of covering $L_{\omega n}$, for different $\tau \le \omega \le 1$, we need to consider affine subspaces with different structure. Moreover, we first handle levels ωn such that $\tau \le \omega \le (3\tau + 1)/4$. We then show how to handle the higher levels.

Given $1/2 \le \tau \le 1$ and $\tau \le \omega \le (3\tau + 1)/4$, define [5]

$$\alpha = 2\omega - 1$$
$$\beta = 3\tau - 4\omega + 1$$
$$\gamma = 2\omega - 2\tau.$$

Note that by our choice of τ, ω it holds that $0 \le \alpha, \beta, \gamma \le 1$. For a permutation $\sigma \in S_n$ let V_σ be the affine subspace of $\{0,1\}^n$ that is defined by the following set of affine constraints:

$$
\begin{cases}
\begin{cases}
1 &= x_{\sigma(1)} \\
&\vdots \\
1 &= x_{\sigma(\alpha n)}
\end{cases} \\
\begin{cases}
1 &= x_{\sigma(\alpha n+1)} + x_{\sigma(\alpha n+2)} \\
&\vdots \\
1 &= x_{\sigma((\alpha+2\beta)n-1)} + x_{\sigma((\alpha+2\beta)n)}
\end{cases} \\
\begin{cases}
1 &= x_{\sigma((\alpha+2\beta)n+1)} + x_{\sigma((\alpha+2\beta)n+2)} + x_{\sigma((\alpha+2\beta)n+3)} \\
&\vdots \\
1 &= x_{\sigma(n-2)} + x_{\sigma(n-1)} + x_{\sigma(n)}.
\end{cases}
\end{cases}
$$

Namely, we have αn constraints on 1 variable, βn constraints on two variables and γn constraints on three variables, where each variable appears in exactly one constraint as σ is a permutation. Note that $\alpha + 2\beta + 3\gamma = 1$, so this set of constraints acts on all entries of x, and is well-defined in the sense that it does not operate on invalid entries of x.

We note that if x satisfies all the constraints above then $|x| \ge \tau n$. Indeed, each entry of x appears in exactly one constraint, the number of constraints is exactly $\alpha + \beta + \gamma = \tau$ and each satisfied constraint implies that at least one of the entries of x that participate in the constraint is 1. Thus, for any permutation σ, the affine subspace V_σ is contained in $\mathsf{Th}_\tau^{-1}(1)$, and so taking union of V_σ for several permutations σ would never cover undesired points.

We now compute the number of points in level ωn covered by V_σ. Let $x \in V_\sigma \cap L_{\omega n}$. Since $x \in V_\sigma$, the first αn constraints contribute αn to the Hamming weight of x.

---
[5] For ease of notation, we treat variables such as $\tau, \omega, \alpha, \beta$ and γ as if they were some real numbers in $[0,1]$ and ignore the issue of rounding to integer multiplication of $1/n$. This does not affect any of the results.

The following βn constraints contribute βn to the Hamming weight of x (as exactly one of the variables in such a constraint on two variables is 1). Since $|x| = \omega n$ and since each of the remaining γn constraints must have either 1 or 3 variables set to 1, it holds that exactly δn of these constraints have one variable with value 1 and the rest have all 3 variables set to 1, where

$$\delta = \frac{\alpha + \beta + 3\gamma - \omega}{2} = \frac{3\omega - 3\tau}{2}.$$

Moreover, there is a one to one mapping between the points in $V_\sigma \cap L_{\omega n}$ and the number of ways to choose which of the two variables in each of the βn constraints will have value 1, which δn out of the γn constraints will have exactly one variable set to 1 and which variable out of the three would that be. Hence,

$$|V_\sigma \cap L_{\omega n}| = 2^{\beta n} \cdot \binom{\gamma n}{\delta n} \cdot 3^{\delta n}$$

$$\geq \frac{1}{\sqrt{8n}} \cdot 2^{(\beta + \gamma \cdot H(\delta/\gamma) + \delta \cdot \log_2 3) \cdot n}$$

$$= \frac{1}{8\sqrt{n}} \cdot 2^{(1-\tau) \cdot n},$$

where the inequality follows by Fact 4.1, and the last equality follows by our choice of α, β and γ. Let

$$m = \sqrt{8} \cdot n^{1.5} \cdot 2^{(H(\omega) - (1-\tau)) \cdot n} \leq \sqrt{8} \cdot n^{1.5} \cdot 2^{(H(\tau) - (1-\tau)) \cdot n}.$$

As in the proof of Theorem 1.3, it follows that if $\sigma_1, \ldots, \sigma_m$ are permutations sampled uniformly and independently at random, then for any $x \in L_{\omega n}$

$$\Pr_{\sigma_1, \ldots, \sigma_m} \left[x \notin \bigcup_{i=1}^{m} V_{\sigma_i} \right] \leq \left(1 - \frac{|V_{\sigma_1} \cap L_{\omega n}|}{|L_{\omega n}|} \right)^m \leq e^{-n}.$$

Hence, by the union bound over all $x \in L_{\omega n}$, there exist m permutations $\sigma_1, \ldots, \sigma_m$ such that $V_{\sigma_1}, \ldots V_{\sigma_m}$ are all contained in $\mathsf{Th}_\tau^{-1}(1)$ and which their union covers $L_{\omega n}$. We conclude that the union of all levels $L_{\omega n}$ for $\tau \leq \omega \leq (3\tau + 1)/4$ can be covered by $O(n^{2.5} \cdot 2^{(H(\tau) - (1-\tau)) \cdot n})$ affine subspaces, all contained in $\mathsf{Th}_\tau^{-1}(1)$.

We note that the constraint $\omega \leq (3\tau + 1)/4$ is necessary for our set of affine constraints to be well-defined. Indeed, for $\omega > (3\tau + 1)/4$, we have $\beta < 0$ which makes no sense since βn represents the number of constraints on two variables. The values of α, β and γ were obtained by some optimization which was spared from the reader. The fact that this optimization process resulted in taking a negative β for high values of ω suggests that we should do as close to it as we can, and indeed to handle the higher levels $\omega > (3\tau + 1)/4$ we take $\beta = 0$, namely sets of constraints on only one or three variables.

Let $\sigma \in S_n$ be a permutation. Consider a system of affine constraints were αn constraints are on one variable, and the rest, say γn of them, are on three variables. Namely,

$$\begin{cases} \begin{cases} 1 = x_{\sigma(1)} \\ \quad \vdots \\ 1 = x_{\sigma(\alpha n)} \end{cases} \\ \begin{cases} 1 = x_{\sigma(\alpha n + 1)} + x_{\sigma(\alpha n + 2)} + x_{\sigma(\alpha n + 3)} \\ \quad \vdots \\ 1 = x_{\sigma(n-2)} + x_{\sigma(n-1)} + x_{\sigma(n)}. \end{cases} \end{cases}$$

One must take $\alpha + 3\gamma = 1$ since each entry of x should appear in exactly one constraint. Moreover, since we want that any solution to these set of constraints will be contained in $\mathsf{Th}_\tau^{-1}(1)$, one must take $\alpha + \gamma = \tau$. Solving gives

$$\alpha = \frac{3\tau - 1}{2}, \qquad \gamma = \frac{1 - \tau}{2}.$$

Note that the affine subspaces defined by these constraints is the same for all levels, as apposed to the case $\omega \leq (3\tau + 1)/4$, where the number of constraints of each type depended on ω. By our choice of α, γ, for every permutation σ it holds that $V_\sigma \subseteq \mathsf{Th}_\tau^{-1}(1)$.

We now turn to compute $|V_\sigma \cap L_{\omega n}|$. Consider x in this intersection. Suppose δn of the constraints on three variables contain exactly one entry of x with value 1. Then, $\omega = \alpha + \delta + 3(\gamma - \delta)$ and so

$$\delta = \frac{\alpha + 3\gamma - \omega}{2} = \frac{1 - \omega}{2}.$$

Moreover, as in the previous case, there is a one to one mapping between the points in $V_\sigma \cap L_{\omega n}$ and the number of ways to choose δn constraints from the γn constraints on three variables and choosing which unique variable in a triplet is set to 1. Thus,

$$|V_\sigma \cap L_{\omega n}| = \binom{\gamma n}{\delta n} \cdot 3^{\delta n} \geq \frac{1}{\sqrt{8n}} \cdot 2^{\mu \cdot n},$$

where

$$\mu = \frac{1 - \tau}{2} \cdot H\left(\frac{1 - \omega}{1 - \tau} \right) + \log_2(3) \cdot \frac{1 - \omega}{2}.$$

It is left to show that $H(\omega) - \mu \leq H(\tau) - (1 - \tau)$ for $(3\tau + 1)/4 < \omega \leq 1$, and the proof will follow. Thus, one needs to prove that for this range of ω the function $\phi_\tau(\omega)$ defined as

$$H(\tau) + \frac{1 - \omega}{2} \cdot \log_2(3) - H(\omega) - \frac{1 - \tau}{2} \cdot \left(2 - H\left(\frac{1 - \omega}{1 - \tau} \right) \right)$$

is non-negative. One can verify that

$$\phi_\tau \left(\frac{3\tau + 1}{4} \right) = H(\tau) - H\left(\frac{3\tau + 1}{4} \right) \geq 0,$$

where the last inequality holds since $1/2 \leq \tau \leq (3\tau + 1)/4$. Thus, to complete the proof it is enough to show that $\phi_\tau(\omega)$ is monotone increasing in the interval $(1/2, 1)$. To this end we consider the derivative of $\phi_\tau(\omega)$ (note that $\phi_\tau(\omega)$ is infinitely differentiable in its domain),

$$\frac{d}{d\omega} \phi_\tau(\omega) = \log_2\left(\frac{\omega}{1 - \omega} \right) + \frac{1}{2} \log_2\left(\frac{1 - \omega}{\omega - \tau} \right) - \frac{1}{2} \log_2(3)$$

$$= \frac{1}{2} \log_2\left(\frac{\omega^2}{3(1 - \omega)(\omega - \tau)} \right)$$

$$\geq \frac{1}{2} \log_2\left(\frac{\omega^2}{3(1 - \omega)(\omega - 1/2)} \right).$$

The proof then follows as one can easily verify that the expression inside the $\log(\cdot)$ is at least 1 for any $1/2 < \omega < 1$. $\square$

6. THE INNER PRODUCT FUNCTION AND LOW DEGREE POLYNOMIALS

We start this section by proving Theorem 1.5. As mentioned in the introduction, $\mathsf{DNF}_\oplus(\mathsf{IP}) \leq 2^{n/2} - 1$, so it is enough to prove a matching lower bound. We first show two proofs that almost achieve this lower bound. We will obtain the tight bound afterwards.

The first proof uses a lemma of Akavia *et al.* [ABG+14]. To state it we move to the $\{\pm 1\}$ representation of functions. Namely, we consider functions of the form $f: \{0,1\}^n \to \{\pm 1\}$. Based on a result by Jackson [Jac97], Akavia *et al.* [ABG+14] proved the following lemma.

LEMMA 6.1 ([ABG+14]). *For any boolean function $f: \{0,1\}^n \to \{\pm 1\}$ it holds that*

$$\max_{S \subseteq [n]} |\hat{f}(S)| \geq \frac{1}{2\mathsf{DNF}_\oplus(f) + 1}.$$

Since all the Fourier coefficients of IP in the $\{\pm 1\}$ representation have absolute value $2^{-n/2}$, Lemma 6.1 immediately implies that $\mathsf{DNF}_\oplus(\mathrm{IP}) \geq (2^{n/2}-1)/2$, which is almost tight – only factor 2 away from the upper bound. (This argument has also appeared in [SV12].)

The second proof, for which we gave a rough sketch in the introduction, is based on the well-known fact that IP : $\{0,1\}^n \to \{0,1\}$ is an affine disperser for dimension $n/2 + 1$ (see Appendix A). By the proof of the second item in Theorem 1.1, we get that

$$\mathsf{DNF}_\oplus(\mathrm{IP}) \geq \frac{|\mathrm{IP}^{-1}(1)|}{2^{(n/2+1)-1}} = \frac{1}{2} \cdot (2^{n/2} - 1),$$

which is also a factor of 2 away from the upper bound. Next, by being slightly more careful, we give the proof for the exact bound of $2^{n/2} - 1$. To this end we consider again the $\{\pm 1\}$ representation of functions. We use the following result regarding small bias sets. The proof of this can be found, e.g., in [AC13] Lemma 4.5.

LEMMA 6.2 ([PR04, AS10, AC13]). *Let $S \subseteq \{0,1\}^n$ be an ε-biased set. Then, for any affine subspace U it holds that*

$$\left| \frac{|S \cap U|}{|S|} - \frac{|U|}{2^n} \right| \leq \varepsilon. \qquad (6.1)$$

PROOF OF THEOREM 1.5. Recall that a set S is ε-biased if and only if $|S|^{-1} \cdot |\sum_{s \in S} [(-1)^{\langle s, \alpha \rangle}]| \leq \varepsilon$ for all non-zero $\alpha \in \{0,1\}^n$. One can easily show that this is equivalent of saying that $|\widehat{1_S}(T)| \leq \varepsilon \cdot \frac{|S|}{2^{n-1}}$ for all $\emptyset \neq T \subseteq [n]$, where 1_S is the indicator function for the set S in the $\{\pm 1\}$ representation. Recall also that all non-zero Fourier coefficients of IP in the $\{\pm 1\}$ representation have absolute value of $2^{-n/2}$. By plugging this to Equation (6.1) and rearranging we get that

$$\left| |\mathrm{IP}^{-1}(-1) \cap U| - \frac{|\mathrm{IP}^{-1}(-1)|}{2^n} \cdot |U| \right| \leq 2^{n/2-1}. \qquad (6.2)$$

Assume now that U is an affine subspace that is contained in $\mathrm{IP}^{-1}(-1)$. Using the fact that $|\mathrm{IP}^{-1}(-1)| = 2^{n-1} - 2^{n/2-1}$, Equation (6.2) implies that $|U|/2 < (1/2 + 2^{-n/2-1}) \cdot |U| \leq 2^{n/2-1}$. It follows that $|U| < 2^{n/2}$, and hence since the size of U is a power of 2, we conclude that $|U| \leq 2^{n/2-1}$. Therefore $\mathsf{DNF}_\oplus(\mathrm{IP}) \geq \frac{|\mathrm{IP}^{-1}(-1)|}{2^{n/2-1}} = 2^{n/2} - 1$, as stated. $\square$

We now deduce a result regarding general quadratic polynomials.

COROLLARY 6.3. *Let $f: \{0,1\}^n \to \{0,1\}$ be a function that has degree 2 as a polynomial over $\mathbb{F}_2$. Let $\delta = \mathrm{bias}(f) = \left| \mathbb{E}_{x \sim \{0,1\}^n} [(-1)^{f(x)}] \right|$. Then, $\mathsf{DNF}_\oplus(f) = \Theta(1/\delta)$.*

PROOF. Dickson's theorem ([Dic01], Theorem 199) states that, up to linear transformations, all degree 2 polynomials over $\mathbb{F}_2$ are essentially the inner product function. More precisely, any degree 2 polynomial $f(x)$ over $\mathbb{F}_2$ can be written us $f(x) = \ell_0(x) + \mathrm{IP}(\ell_1(x), \ell_2(x), \ldots, \ell_r(x))$, where the ℓ_i's are independent linear functions, and $\delta = \Theta(2^{-r/2})$. Theorem 1.5 implies that the inner product function on r inputs has $\mathsf{DNF}_\oplus$ complexity of $\Theta(2^{r/2}) = \Theta(1/\delta)$. The proof follows since applying the inner product function on r independent linear functions (rather than on the input bits) does not change its $\mathsf{DNF}_\oplus$ complexity. $\square$

The $\mathsf{DNF}_\oplus$ complexity of degree $d \geq 3$ polynomials

Next we prove Theorem 1.6. The first part of the theorem readily follows from the following result by Cohen and Tal (see [CT14], Theorem 2).

THEOREM 6.4 ([CT14]). *Let $f: \{0,1\}^n \to \{0,1\}$ be a function that has degree d as a polynomial over $\mathbb{F}_2$. Then, there exists a partition of $\{0,1\}^n$ to affine subspaces, each of dimension $\Omega(n^{1/(d-1)!})$, such that f is constant on each part.*

PROOF OF THEOREM 1.6. To prove the first part of Theorem 1.6 note that by Theorem 6.4 $f^{-1}(1)$ can be covered by a union of $|f^{-1}(1)|/2^{\Omega(n^{1/(d-1)!})} \leq 2^{n-\Omega(n^{1/(d-1)!})}$ affine subspaces. As for the moreover part, a result by Ben-Eliezer *et al.* [BEHL09] implies that a random degree d polynomial is, with high probability, an affine disperser for dimension $k = O(n^{1/(d-1)})$. This together with Theorem 1.1 imply the moreover part. $\square$

As in the case of quadratic polynomials, one can obtain a stronger result for the case of biased polynomials of constant degree. We start with the case of degree 3 polynomials.

THEOREM 6.5. *Let $f: \{0,1\}^n \to \{0,1\}$ be a function that has degree 3 as a polynomial over $\mathbb{F}_2$. Assume that $\mathrm{bias}(f) = \delta$. Then,*

$$\mathsf{DNF}_\oplus(f) \leq 2^{n/2 + O(\log^4(1/\delta))}.$$

For the proof of Theorem 6.5 we need the following structural result by Haramaty and Shpilka [HS10].

THEOREM 6.6 ([HS10]). *Let $f: \{0,1\}^n \to \{0,1\}$ be a cubic polynomial with bias δ. Then, for $c = O(\log^4(1/\delta))$ the function f can be written as*

$$f(x) = \sum_{i=1}^c \ell_i(x) q_i(x) + g(\ell_1(x), \ldots, \ell_c(x)),$$

where the ℓ_i's are linear functions, the q_i's are quadratic polynomials and g is a cubic polynomial.

Theorem 6.5 readily follows from Theorem 6.6. Indeed, for any fixing of $\ell_1(x), \ldots, \ell_c(x)$ the function f is reduced to a sum of quadratic polynomials, which is by itself a quadratic polynomial, and as mentioned above, has $\mathsf{DNF}_\oplus$ complexity at most $O(2^{n/2})$. One can then take the union over all (at most 2^c) appropriate fixings of $\ell_1(x), \ldots, \ell_c(x)$.

For biased polynomials of higher degrees one can prove the following theorem.

THEOREM 6.7. *Let* $f: \{0,1\}^n \to \{0,1\}$ *be a degree* d *polynomial with bias* δ. *Then, there is some* $c = c(d, \delta)$ *(independent of* n*) such that*

$$\mathsf{DNF}_\oplus(f) \le 2^{n - \frac{n^{1/(d-2)!}}{c^e} + c}.$$

The proof of Theorem 6.7 readily follows by a structural result for biased low degree polynomials of Kaufman and Lovett [KL08] combined with Theorem 4 in [CT14]. We omit the details.

7. THE PARITY DECISION TREE MODEL

As mentioned, the parity decision tree model, defined by Kushilevitz and Mansour [KM93], has received a significant attention in the last few years [MO09, ZS10, TWXZ13, OST$^+$13, STV14]. We start this section by proving Theorem 1.7 and then discuss the relation between the $\mathsf{DT}_\oplus$ complexity of a function and its $\mathsf{DNF}_\oplus$ complexity.

PROOF OF THEOREM 1.7. Let g be a function such that $\mathsf{DT}_\oplus(g) \le \varepsilon \cdot 2^{n-k}$ such that $\mathrm{dist}(f, g) = \delta$. We want to show that $\delta \ge 1/2 - 4\varepsilon$. By definition of $\mathsf{DT}_\oplus$ the function g is an indicator function of a *disjoint* union of $s \le \varepsilon \cdot 2^{n-k}$ affine subspaces $U_1, \ldots, U_s$. Let $I \subseteq [s]$ be the set of indices i for which $\dim(U_i) \ge k$.

Let $c = |f^{-1}(1) \setminus g^{-1}(1)|$ be the number of ones obtained by f outside $\cup_i U_i$. For $i \in [s]$, let a_i be the number of ones obtained by f on U_i, and let b_i be the number of zeros obtained by f on U_i. Therefore, by the disjointness of U_i's it follows tat

$$c + \sum_{i \in [s]} b_i \le \delta \cdot 2^n. \tag{7.1}$$

Since f is an affine extractor for dimension k, with bias ε, it holds that for any $i \in I$,

$$\mathrm{bias}(f|_{U_i}) = \left| \frac{a_i - b_i}{a_i + b_i} \right| \le \varepsilon.$$

Thus, for all $i \in I$,

$$a_i \le \left(\frac{1+\varepsilon}{1-\varepsilon} \right) \cdot b_i \le (1 + 4\varepsilon) \cdot b_i,$$

and so

$$\sum_{i \in I} a_i \le (1 + 4\varepsilon) \cdot \sum_{i \in I} b_i \le (1 + 4\varepsilon) \cdot (\delta \cdot 2^n - c), \tag{7.2}$$

where the last inequality follows by (7.1). Now, by Equation (7.2) and by our assumption that $s \le \varepsilon \cdot 2^{n-k}$, we have that

$$|f^{-1}(1)| \le c + s \cdot 2^k + \sum_{i \in I} a_i$$

$$\le c + s \cdot 2^k + (1 + 4\varepsilon) \cdot (\delta \cdot 2^n - c)$$

$$\le s \cdot 2^k + (1 + 4\varepsilon) \cdot \delta \cdot 2^n$$

$$\le (\delta + \varepsilon + 4\varepsilon\delta) \cdot 2^n.$$

On the other hand, f must have bias at most ε on $\{0,1\}^n$, and so $|f^{-1}(1)| \ge (1/2 - \varepsilon/2) \cdot 2^n$. Thus,

$$\delta \ge \frac{1 - 3\varepsilon}{2(1 + 4\varepsilon)} \ge \frac{1}{2} - 4\varepsilon,$$

as desired. □

The relation between $\mathsf{DT}_\oplus$ and $\mathsf{DNF}_\oplus$

One can easily see that $\mathsf{DNF}_\oplus(f) \le \mathsf{DT}_\oplus(f)$ for any function f, and a natural question is what can be said in the other direction. Let $\mathsf{DNF}(f), \mathsf{DT}(f)$ denote the size of the smallest DNF and smallest decision tree for computing f, respectively. Jukna *et al.* [JRSW99] gave an exponential separation between the DNF and DT complexity. Their proof is based on the observation that $\mathsf{DT}(f) \ge \|\hat{f}\|_1$, while on the other hand, there is a function with very large spectral norm that is computable by a small DNF. The Tribes function is one such example, where the DNF complexity is $O(n/\log n)$ while $\|\widehat{\mathrm{Tribes}}\|_1 \ge 2^{\Omega(n/\log n)}$. We observe that the arguments of Jukna *et al.* also gives an exponential separation between $\mathsf{DNF}_\oplus$ and $\mathsf{DT}_\oplus$ (and in fact even a separation between DNF and $\mathsf{DT}_\oplus$). This is because one can show that $\mathsf{DT}_\oplus(f) \ge \Omega(\|\hat{f}\|_1)$ (see the exercises of Chapter 4 in O'Donnell book [O'D14]).

It is worth mentioning that proving lower bounds on the $\mathsf{DT}_\oplus$ complexity of a function via the spectral norm cannot give bounds better than $2^{n/2}$, whereas Theorem 1.7 (and even Theorem 1.1) yield lower bounds of the form $2^{n-o(n)}$.

Let $\mathsf{CNF}(f)$ denote the size of the smallest CNF for computing f. A result of Ehrenfeucht and Haussler [EH89] states that an exponential separation such as above cannot occur when the CNF complexity of f is also small. More precisely, it is shown that $\mathsf{DT}(f) \le n^{O(\log^2(\mathsf{DNF}(f) + \mathsf{CNF}(f)))}$ (see also a proof due to Savický in [Juk12], Theorem 14.32). By inspecting the proof, one can verify that the same relation also holds in the analog $\mathsf{DNF}_\oplus, \mathsf{CNF}_\oplus$ and $\mathsf{DT}_\oplus$ models. Namely, $\mathsf{DT}_\oplus(f) \le n^{O(\log^2(\mathsf{DNF}_\oplus(f) + \mathsf{CNF}_\oplus(f)))}$. Since the verification is straightforward, we omit the proof.

We mention one more result in the standard DNF, CNF and DT models that "goes through" in the analog models with parities. So far we only discussed the size of DNFs, CNFs and decision trees. However, one can also consider the width of DNFs and CNFs and the depth of a decision tree. For a function f, we denote by $\mathsf{C}_1(f)$ the least integer w for which there exists a width w DNF that computes f. One similarly defines $\mathsf{C}_0(f)$ as the least integer w for which there exists a width w CNF that computes f. The least integer d for which there exists a depth d decision tree that computes f is denoted by $\mathsf{D}(f)$.

Several recent papers [TWXZ13, OST$^+$13, STV14] have studied the relation between the analog models with parities and properties of the Fourier spectrum of a function. Here we only want to point out the following relation. A classical result, that was rediscovered by several researchers [BI87, Tar89, HH91], states that $\mathsf{D}(f) \le \mathsf{C}_0(f) \cdot \mathsf{C}_1(f)$ (see also Theorem 14.3 in [Juk12]). Again, by inspection one can verify that this result also holds in the analog model with parities.

Acknowledgement

We wish to thank Elazar Goldenberg for discussions at early stages of this work. We thank Johan Håstad for some helpful conversations regarding this work, in particular for a key idea which enabled us to prove Theorem 1.4.

8. REFERENCES

[ABG$^+$14] A. Akavia, A. Bogdanov, S. Guo, A. Kamath, and A. Rosen. Candidate weak pseudorandom functions in AC0 ∘ MOD2. In *Proceedings of the 5th conference on Innovations in theoretical computer science*, pages 251–260. ACM, 2014.

[AC13] N. Alon and G. Cohen. On rigid matrices and U-polynomials. In *Conference on Computational Complexity (CCC), 2013 IEEE*, pages 197–206. IEEE, 2013.

[AS10] V. Arvind and S. Srinivasan. The remote point problem, small bias space, and expanding generator sets. In *27th International Symposium on Theoretical Aspects of Computer Science-STACS 2010*, pages 59–70, 2010.

[BEHL09] I. Ben-Eliezer, R. Hod, and S. Lovett. Random low degree polynomials are hard to approximate. In *Approximation, Randomization, and Combinatorial Optimization. Algorithms and Techniques*, pages 366–377. Springer, 2009.

[BI87] M. Blum and R. Impagliazzo. Generic oracles and oracle classes. In *28th Annual Symposium on Foundations of Computer Science, 1987.*, pages 118–126. IEEE, 1987.

[BKS+05] B. Barak, G. Kindler, R. Shaltiel, B. Sudakov, and A. Wigderson. Simulating independence: New constructions of condensers, Ramsey graphs, dispersers, and extractors. In *Proceedings of the thirty-seventh annual ACM symposium on Theory of computing*, pages 1–10. ACM, 2005.

[Blu83] N. Blum. A boolean function requiring 3n network size. *Theoretical Computer Science*, 28(3):337–345, 1983.

[Bou07] J. Bourgain. On the construction of affine extractors. *GAFA Geometric And Functional Analysis*, 17(1):33–57, 2007.

[BSK12] E. Ben-Sasson and S. Kopparty. Affine dispersers from subspace polynomials. *SIAM Journal on Computing*, 41(4):880–914, 2012.

[BSZ11] E. Ben-Sasson and N. Zewi. From affine to two-source extractors via approximate duality. In *Proceedings of the 43rd annual ACM symposium on Theory of computing*, pages 177–186. ACM, 2011.

[CT12] T. M. Cover and A. J. Thomas. *Elements of information theory*. John Wiley & Sons, 2012.

[CT14] G. Cohen and A. Tal. Two structural results for low degree polynomials and applications. *arXiv preprint arXiv:1404.0654*, 2014.

[Dic01] L. E. Dickson. *Linear groups with an exposition of the Galois field theory*. B.G Teubner's Sammlung von Lehrbuchern auf dem Gebiete der mathematischen Wissenschaften mit Einschluss ihrer Anwendungen. B.G. Teubner, 1901.

[DK11] E. Demenkov and A. S. Kulikov. An elementary proof of a 3n-o(n) lower bound on the circuit complexity of affine dispersers. In *Mathematical Foundations of Computer Science 2011*, pages 256–265. Springer, 2011.

[EH89] A. Ehrenfeucht and D. Haussler. Learning decision trees from random examples.

Information and Computation, 82(3):231–246, 1989.

[Gro94] V. Grolmusz. A weight-size trade-off for circuits with MOD m gates. In *Proceedings of the twenty-sixth annual ACM symposium on Theory of computing*, pages 68–74. ACM, 1994.

[HH91] J. Hartmanis and L. A. Hemachandra. One-way functions and the nonisomorphism of NP-complete sets. *Theoretical Computer Science*, 81(1):155–163, 1991.

[HS10] E. Haramaty and A. Shpilka. On the structure of cubic and quartic polynomials. In *Proceedings of the 42nd ACM symposium on Theory of computing*, pages 331–340. ACM, 2010.

[Jac97] J. C. Jackson. An efficient membership-query algorithm for learning DNF with respect to the uniform distribution. *Journal of Computer and System Sciences*, 55(3):414–440, 1997.

[JRSW99] S. Jukna, A. Razborov, P. Savický, and I. Wegener. On P versus NP ∩ co-NP for decision trees and read-once branching programs. *Computational Complexity*, 8(4):357–370, 1999.

[Juk06] S. Jukna. On graph complexity. *Combinatorics, Probability and Computing*, 15(06):855–876, 2006.

[Juk12] S. Jukna. *Boolean function complexity: advances and frontiers*, volume 27. Springerverlag Berlin Heidelberg, 2012.

[KL08] T. Kaufman and S. Lovett. Worst case to average case reductions for polynomials. In *Foundations of Computer Science (FOCS), 2008 49th Annual IEEE Symposium on*, pages 166–175. IEEE, 2008.

[KM93] E. Kushilevitz and Y. Mansour. Learning decision trees using the fourier spectrum. *SIAM J. Comput.*, 22(6):1331–1348, 1993.

[Li11] X. Li. A new approach to affine extractors and dispersers. In *Computational Complexity (CCC), 2011 IEEE 26th Annual Conference on*, pages 137–147. IEEE, 2011.

[Lup61] O. Lupanov. On realization of functions of propositional calculus by formulas of bounded depth over the basis {&, ∨, ¬}. *Dokl. Akad. Nauk SSSR*, 136(5):1041–1042, 1961.

[MO09] A. Montanaro and T. Osborne. On the communication complexity of XOR functions. *arXiv preprint arXiv:0909.3392*, 2009.

[O'D14] R. O'Donnell. *Analysis of boolean functions*. Cambridge University Press, 2014.

[OST+13] R. O'Donnell, X. Sun, L. Y. Tan, J. Wright, and Y. Zhao. A composition theorem for parity kill number. *arXiv preprint arXiv:1312.2143*, 2013.

[PR04] P. Pudlák and V. Rödl. Pseudorandom sets and explicit constructions of Ramsey graphs. *Quad. Mat*, 13:327Ü–346, 2004.

[PSZ97] R. Paturi, M. E. Saks, and F. Zane. Exponential lower bounds for depth 3 boolean circuits. In *Proceedings of the twenty-ninth* annual ACM symposium on Theory of computing, pages 86–91. ACM, 1997.

[Qui53] W. Quine. Two theorems about truth functions. Sociedade Matematica Mexicana, 1953.

[Sha11] R. Shaltiel. Dispersers for affine sources with sub-polynomial entropy. In Foundations of Computer Science (FOCS), 2011 IEEE 52nd Annual Symposium on, pages 247–256. IEEE, 2011.

[ST12] K. Seto and S. Tamaki. A satisfiability algorithm and average-case hardness for formulas over the full binary basis. In Computational Complexity (CCC), 2012 IEEE 27th Annual Conference on, pages 107–116. IEEE, 2012.

[ST13] K. Seto and S. Tamaki. A satisfiability algorithm and average-case hardness for formulas over the full binary basis. Computational Complexity, 22(2):245–274, 2013.

[STV14] A. Shpilka, A. Tal, and B. Volk. On the structure of boolean functions with small spectral norm. In Proceedings of the 5th conference on Innovations in theoretical computer science, pages 37–48. ACM, 2014.

[SV12] R. A. Servedio and E. Viola. On a special case of rigidity. 2012. http://eccc.hpi-web.de/report/2012/144/.

[Tar89] G. Tardos. Query complexity, or why is it difficult to separate $NP^A \cap coNP^A$ from P^A by random a oracle A? Combinatorica, 9(4):385–392, 1989.

[TWXZ13] H. Y. Tsang, C. H. Wong, N. Xie, and S. Zhang. Fourier sparsity, spectral norm, and the log-rank conjecture. arXiv preprint arXiv:1304.1245, 2013.

[Vio14] E. Viola. Extractors for circuit sources. SIAM Journal on Computing, 43(2):655–672, 2014.

[VW07] E. Viola and A. Wigderson. Norms, XOR lemmas, and lower bounds for GF(2) polynomials and multiparty protocols. In Computational Complexity, 2007. CCC'07. Twenty-Second Annual IEEE Conference on, pages 141–154. IEEE, 2007.

[Yeh11] A. Yehudayoff. Affine extractors over prime fields. Combinatorica, 31(2):245–256, 2011.

[ZS10] Z. Zhang and Y. Shi. On the parity complexity measures of boolean functions. Theoretical Computer Science, 411(26):2612–2618, 2010.

APPENDIX

A. THE INNER PRODUCT FUNCTION IS AN AFFINE EXTRACTOR

In this section, for completeness, we give two proofs for the following folklore result.

THEOREM A.1. Let $n \geq 2$ be an even integer and let $c \geq 1$ be an integer. Then, the inner product function IP on n inputs is an affine extractor for dimension $k = n/2 + c$ with bias $\varepsilon \leq 2^{-c}$. In particular, IP is an affine disperser for dimension $n/2 + 1$.

PROOF PROOF 1. Let U be an affine subspace with dimension $k = n/2 + c$. In order to prove that IP is balanced on U, we make the following observation.

OBSERVATION A.2. Let $f : \{0,1\}^n \to \{\pm 1\}$ be a function, and let $g : \{0,1\}^{n-1} \to \{\pm 1\}$ be obtained by restricting f to some $n - 1$ dimensional affine subspace. Suppose for concreteness that the affine subspace is $\{x \in \{0,1\}^n : x_n = \sum_{j \in J} x_j + b\}$ for some $J \subseteq [n-1]$ and $b \in \{0,1\}$. Then, we may write g as $g(x_1, \ldots, x_{n-1}) = f(x_1, \ldots, x_{n-1}, \sum_{j \in J} x_j + b)$, and hence for any $S \subseteq [n-1]$ we have $\hat{g}(S) = \hat{f}(S) + (-1)^b \cdot \hat{f}((S \cup \{n\}) \triangle J)$.

By applying this observation repeatedly, we conclude that if g is the restriction of f to the affine subspace U, then each Fourier coefficient of g is a sum/difference of 2^{n-k} Fourier coefficient of f. In particular, for $f = $ IP, since $|\widehat{\text{IP}}(S)| = -2^{n/2}$ for all $S \subseteq [n]$, each Fourier coefficient of its restriction $\text{IP}|_U$ is at most $2^{n-k} \cdot 2^{-n/2} = 2^{-c}$ in absolute value. In particular, the bias of $\text{IP}|_U$, which is equal to the empty coefficient of the restricted function, is at most $\text{bias}(\text{IP}|_U) = \widehat{\text{IP}}(\emptyset) \leq 2^{-c}$, as required. □

Next we give an alternative proof for Theorem A.1. The proof gives a bound of $2^{-c} + 2^{-n/2}$ on the bias ε, which is slightly weaker than the bound 2^{-c} stated in Theorem A.1. Still, we find the proof interesting.

PROOF PROOF 2. Let U be an affine subspace with dimension $k = n/2 + c$. We will use the fact that in the $\{\pm 1\}$ representation, all Fourier coefficients of IP have absolute value of $2^{-n/2}$. Thus, similarly to the way it was done in the proof of Theorem 1.5, one can show that $\text{IP}^{-1}(1)$ is an ε-biased set with $\varepsilon = \frac{2^{n/2-1}}{|\text{IP}^{-1}(1)|}$. Lemma 6.2 states that for any ε-biased set S and for any affine subspace U it holds that

$$\left| \frac{|S \cap U|}{|S|} - \frac{|U|}{2^n} \right| \leq \varepsilon. \tag{A.1}$$

Thus, by plugging $|U| = 2^{n/2+c}$ and $\varepsilon = \frac{2^{n/2-1}}{|\text{IP}^{-1}(1)|}$ to Equation (A.1) and rearranging we get

$$\left| \frac{|\text{IP}^{-1}(-1) \cap U|}{|U|} - \frac{|\text{IP}^{-1}(-1)|}{2^n} \right| \leq \varepsilon \cdot \frac{|\text{IP}^{-1}(-1)|}{|U|} = 2^{-c-1}. \tag{A.2}$$

Since $|\text{IP}^{-1}(-1)|/2^n = 1/2 - 2^{-n/2-1}$ it follows that the bias of IP on U is

$$\text{bias}(\text{IP}|_U) = 2 \cdot \left| \frac{|\text{IP}^{-1}(-1) \cap U|}{|U|} - \frac{1}{2} \right| \leq 2^{-c} + 2^{-n/2}.$$

□

Smooth Boolean Functions are Easy: Efficient Algorithms for Low-Sensitivity Functions

Parikshit Gopalan
Microsoft Research
parik@microsoft.com

Noam Nisan
Microsoft Research &
The Hebrew University
noam.nisan@gmail.com

Rocco A. Servedio[*]
Columbia University
rocco@cs.columbia.edu

Kunal Talwar
Google Research
ktalwar@gmail.com

Avi Wigderson
IAS
avi@ias.edu

ABSTRACT

A natural measure of smoothness of a Boolean function is its *sensitivity* (the largest number of Hamming neighbors of a point which differ from it in function value). The structure of smooth or equivalently low-sensitivity functions is still a mystery. A well-known conjecture states that every such Boolean function can be computed by a shallow decision tree. While this conjecture implies that smooth functions are easy to compute in the *simplest* computational model, to date no non-trivial upper bounds were known for such functions in *any* computational model, including unrestricted Boolean circuits. Even a bound on the description length of such functions better than the trivial 2^n does not seem to have been known.

In this work, we establish the first computational upper bounds on smooth Boolean functions:

- We show that every sensitivity s function is uniquely specified by its values on a Hamming ball of radius $2s$. We use this to show that such functions can be computed by circuits of size $n^{O(s)}$.

- We show that sensitivity s functions satisfy a strong *pointwise* noise-stability guarantee for random noise of rate $O(1/s)$. We use this to show that these functions have formulas of depth $O(s \log n)$.

- We show that sensitivity s functions can be (locally) self-corrected from worst-case noise of rate $\exp(-O(s))$.

All our results are simple, and follow rather directly from (variants of) the basic fact that the function value at few points in small neighborhoods of a given point determine its function value via a majority vote. Our results confirm

various consequences of the conjecture. They may be viewed as providing a new form of evidence towards its validity, as well as new directions towards attacking it.

CCS Concepts

- **Theory of computation** → *Circuit complexity*; *Oracles and decision trees*;

Keywords

Boolean functions; sensitivity; noise stability; formula depth; self-correction

1. INTRODUCTION

1.1 Background and motivation

The smoothness of a continuous function captures how gradually it changes locally (according to the metric of the underlying space). For Boolean functions on the Hamming cube, a natural analog is *sensitivity*, capturing how many neighbors of a point have different function values. More formally, the *sensitivity* of a Boolean function $f : \{0,1\}^n \to \{0,1\}$ at input $x \in \{0,1\}^n$, written $s(f,x)$, is the number of neighbors y of x in the Hamming cube such that $f(y) \neq f(x)$. The *max sensitivity* of f, written $s(f)$ and often referred to simply as the "sensitivity of f", is defined as $s(f) = \max_{x \in \{0,1\}^n} s(f,x)$. So, $0 \leq s(f) \leq n$, and while not crucial, it may be good for the reader to consider this parameter as "low" when e.g. either $s(f) \leq (\log n)^{O(1)}$ or $s(f) \leq n^{o(1)}$ (note that both upper bounds are closed under taking polynomials).

To see why low-sensitivity functions might be considered smooth, let $\delta(\cdot, \cdot)$ denote the normalized Hamming metric on $\{0,1\}^n$. A simple application of the triangle inequality gives

$$\mathbf{E}_{y:\delta(x,y)=\delta_0}|f(x) - f(y)| \leq \delta_0 s(f).$$

Thus $s(f)$ might be viewed as being somewhat analogous to the Lipschitz constant of f.

A well known conjecture states that every smooth Boolean function is computed by a shallow decision tree, specifically of depth polynomial in the sensitivity. This conjecture was first posed in the form of a question by Nisan [Nis91] and Nisan and Szegedy [NS94] but is now (we feel) widely believed to be true:

[*]Supported by NSF awards CCF-1319788 and CCF-1420349.

Permission to make digital or hard copies of all or part of this work for personal or classroom use is granted without fee provided that copies are not made or distributed for profit or commercial advantage and that copies bear this notice and the full citation on the first page. Copyrights for components of this work owned by others than ACM must be honored. Abstracting with credit is permitted. To copy otherwise, or republish, to post on servers or to redistribute to lists, requires prior specific permission and/or a fee. Request permissions from permissions@acm.org.

ITCS'16, January 14 - 16, 2016, Cambridge, MA, USA

© 2016 ACM. ISBN 978-1-4503-4057-1/16/01...$15.00

DOI: http://dx.doi.org/10.1145/2840728.2840738

CONJECTURE 1. *[Nis91, NS94] There exists a constant c such that every Boolean function f has a decision tree of depth $s(f)^c$.*

The converse is trivial, since every Boolean function computable by a depth d decision tree has sensitivity at most d. However, the best known upper bound on decision tree depth in terms of sensitivity is exponential (see Section 1.3).

A remarkable series of developments, starting with Nisan's paper [Nis91], showed that decision tree depth is an extremely robust complexity parameter, in being polynomially related to many other, quite diverse complexity measures for Boolean functions, including PRAM complexity, block sensitivity, certificate complexity, randomized decision tree depth, quantum decision tree depth, real polynomial degree, and approximating polynomial degree. Arguably the one natural complexity measure that has defied inclusion in this equivalence class is sensitivity. Thus, there are many equivalent formulations of Conjecture 1; indeed, Nisan originally posed the question in terms of sensitivity versus block sensitivity [Nis91]. See the extensive survey [HKP11] for much more information about the conjecture and [BdW02] for background on various Boolean function complexity measures.

Conjecture 1 is typically viewed as a *combinatorial* statement about the Boolean hypercube. However, the conjecture also makes a strong assertion about *computation*, stating that smooth functions have very low complexity; indeed, the conjecture posits that they are easy to compute in arguably the simplest computational model — deterministic decision trees. This implies that smooth functions easy for many other "low-level" computational models via the following chain of inclusions:

DecTree-depth($\text{poly}(s)$) $\subseteq$ DNF-width($\text{poly}(s)$)

$\subseteq$ AC$_0$-size($n^{\text{poly}(s)}$)

$\subseteq$ Formula-depth($\text{poly}(s)\log(n)$)

$\subseteq$ Circuit-size($n^{\text{poly}(s)}$).

Given these inclusions, and the widespread interest that Conjecture 1 has attracted in the study of Boolean functions, it is perhaps surprising that no non-trivial upper bounds were previously known on low sensitivity functions in *any* computational model, including unrestricted Boolean circuits. Indeed, a pre-requisite for a family of functions to have small circuits is an upper bound on the number of functions in the family, or equivalently on the description length of such functions; even such bounds were not previously known for low sensitivity functions. This gap in our understanding of low sensitivity functions helped motivate the present work.

An equivalent formulation of Conjecture 1 is that every sensitivity s function is computed by a real polynomial whose degree is upper bounded by some polynomial in s. This is equivalent to saying that the *Fourier expansion* of the function has degree $\text{poly}(s)$:

CONJECTURE 2. *[Nis91, NS94] (Equivalent to Conjecture 1) For some universal constant c, every Boolean function is computed by a real polynomial of degree $s(f)^c$.*

Given the analogy between sensitivity and the Lipschitz constant, this form of the conjecture gives a natural discrete analog of continuous approximations of smooth Lipschitz

functions by low-degree polynomials, first obtained for univariate case by Weierstrass [Wei85], which has had a huge influence on the development of modern analysis. This lead to a large body of work in approximation theory, and we mention here the sharp quantitative version of the theorem [Jac30] and its extension to the multivariate case [NS64].

This formulation of the conjecture is also interesting because of the rich structure of low-degree polynomials that low sensitivity functions are believed to share. For instance, low-degree real polynomials on the Boolean cube are easy to interpolate from relatively few values (say over a Hamming ball). The interpolation procedure can be made tolerant to noise, and local (these follow from the fact that low-degree real polynomials also have low degree over $\mathbb{F}_2$). Again, our understanding of the structure of low sensitivity functions was insufficient to establish such properties for them prior to this work.

Finally, to every Boolean function f one can associate the bipartite graph G_f which has left and right vertex sets $f^{-1}(0)$ and $f^{-1}(1)$, and which has an edge (x, y) if the Hamming distance $d(x, y)$ is 1 and $f(x) \neq f(y)$. A function has max sensitivity s if and only if the graph G_f has maximum degree at most s. From this perspective one can view Conjectures 1 and 2 as a step towards understanding the graph-theoretic structure of Boolean functions and relating it to their computational and analytic structure (as captured by the Fourier expansion). In this paper, we propose proving various implications of the conjecture both as a necessary first step towards the conjecture, and as a means to better understanding low sensitivity functions from a computational perspective.

1.2 Our Results

Let $\mathcal{F}(s, n)$ denote the set of Boolean functions on n variables such that $s(f) \leq s$. We sometimes refer to this class simply as "sensitivity s functions" (n will be implicit).

The starting point for our results is an upper bound stating that low-sensitivity functions can be interpolated from Hamming balls. This parallels the fact that a degree d polynomial can be interpolated from its values on a Hamming ball of radius d.

THEOREM 3. *Every sensitivity s function on n variables is uniquely specified by its values on any Hamming ball of radius $2s$ in $\{0, 1\}^n$.*

The simple insight here is that knowing the values of f at any set of $2s + 1$ neighbors of a point x uniquely specifies the value of f at x: it is the majority value over the $2s + 1$ neighbors (else the point x would be too sensitive). This implies the following upper bound on the number of sensitivity s functions:

$$|\mathcal{F}(s, n)| \leq 2^{\binom{n}{\leq 2s}}.$$

Our proof of Theorem 3 is algorithmic (but inefficient). We build on it to give efficient algorithms that compute f at any point $x \in \{0, 1\}^n$, given the values of f on a Hamming ball as advice.

Our first algorithm takes a bottom-up approach. We know the values of f on a ball of small radius around the origin, and wish to infer its value at some arbitrary point x. Imagine moving the center of the ball from the origin to x along a shortest path. The key observation is that after shifting the ball by Hamming distance 1, we can recompute the values of f on the shift using a simple Majority vote.

Our second algorithm uses a top-down approach, reducing computing f at x to computing f at $O(s)$ neighboring points of Hamming weight one less than x. We repeat this till we reach points of weight $O(s)$ (whose values we know from the advice). By carefully choosing the set of $O(s)$ neighbors, we ensure that no more than $n^{O(s)}$ values need to be computed in total:

THEOREM 4. *Every sensitivity s function is computed by a Boolean circuit of size $O(sn^{2s+1})$ and depth $O(n^s)$.*

Simon has shown that every sensitivity s function depends on at most $2^{O(s)}$ variables [Sim82]. Thus, the circuit we construct has size at most $2^{O(s^2)}$.

A natural next step would be to parallelize this algorithm. Towards this goal, we show that low sensitivity functions satisfy a very strong noise-stability guarantee: Start at any point $x \in \{0,1\}^n$ and take a random walk of length $n/10s$ to reach a point y. Then $f(x) = f(y)$ with probability 0.9, where the probability is only over the coin tosses of the walk and not over the starting point x. Intuitively, this says that the value of f at most points in a ball of radius $n/10s$ around x equals the value at x (note that in contrast, Theorem 3 only uses the fact that most points in a ball of radius 1 agree with the center). We use this structural property to get a small depth *formula* that computes f:

THEOREM 5. *Every sensitivity s function is computed by a Boolean formula of depth $O(s \log n)$ and size $n^{O(s)}$.*

(By [Sim82], these formulas have depth at most $O(s^2)$ and size at most $2^{O(s^2)}$ as before.) At a high level, we again use the the values on a Hamming ball as advice. Starting from some arbitrary input x, we use a variant of the noise-stability guarantee (which holds for "downward" random walks that only flip 1-coordinates to 0) to reduce the computation of f at x to computing f on $O(1)$ many points whose weight is less than that of x by a factor of roughly $(1 - 1/(10s))$ (a majority vote on these serves to amplify the success probability). Repeating this for each of these new points, recursively, for $O(s \log(n))$ times, we reduce computing f at x to computing f at various points in a small Hamming ball around the origin, which we know from the advice.

We also show that low-sensitivity functions admit local self-correction. The setup here is that we are given oracle access to an unknown function $r : \{0,1\}^n \to \{0,1\}$ that is promised to be close to a low sensitivity function. Formally, there exists a sensitivity s function $f : \{0,1\}^n \to \{0,1\}$ such that

$$\delta(r, f) := \Pr_{x \in \{0,1\}^n} [r(x) \neq f(x)] \leq 2^{-ds}$$

for some constant d. We are then given an arbitrary $x \in \{0,1\}^n$ as an input, and our goal is to return $f(x)$ correctly with high probability for every x, where the probability is over the coin tosses of the (randomized) algorithm. We show that there is a self-corrector for f with the following guarantee:

THEOREM 6. *There exist a constant d such that the following holds. Let $r : \{0,1\}^n \to \{0,1\}$ be such that $\delta(r, f) \leq 2^{-ds}$ for some sensitivity s function f. There is an algorithm which, when given an oracle for r and $x \in \{0,1\}^n$ as*

input, queries the oracle for r at $(n/s)^{O(s)}$ points, runs in $(n/s)^{O(s)}$ time, and returns the correct value of $f(x)$ with probability 0.99.

Our self-corrector is similar in spirit to our formula construction: our estimate for $f(x)$ is obtained by taking the majority over a random sample of points in a ball of radius $n/10s$. Rather than querying these points directly (since they might all be incorrect for an adversarial choice of x and r), we use recursion. We show that $O(s \log(n))$ levels of recursion guarantee that we compute $f(x)$ with good probability. The analysis uses Bonami's hypercontractive inequality [O'D14].

Our results imply that low-degree functions and low sensitivity functions can each be reconstructed from their value on small Hamming balls using simple but dissimilar looking "propagation rules". We show how degree and sensitivity can be characterized by the convergence of these respective propagation rules, and use this to present a reformulation of Conjecture 1.

1.3 Related Work

The study of sensitivity originated from work on PRAMs [CDR86, Sim82]. As mentioned earlier, the question of relating sensitivity to other complexity measures such as block sensitivity was posed in [NS94]. There has been a large body of work on Conjecture 1 and its equivalent formulations, and recent years have witnessed significant interest in this problem (see the survey [HKP11] and the papers cited below). To date, the biggest gap known between sensitivity and other measures such as block-sensitivity, degree and decision tree depth is at most quadratic [Rub95, AS11]. Upper bounds on other measures such as block sensitivity and certificate complexity in terms of sensitivity are given in [KK04, ABG$^+$14, AP14, APV15] (see also [AV15]). Very recently, a novel approach to this conjecture via a communication game was proposed in the work of Gilmer *et al.* [GKS15].

1.4 Preliminaries

We define the 0-sensitivity, 1-sensitivity and the max sensitivity of an n-variable function f as

$$s_0(f) = \max_{x \in f^{-1}(0)} s(f, x), \quad s_1(f) = \max_{x \in f^{-1}(1)} s(f, x),$$

$$s(f) = \max_{x \in \{0,1\}^n} s(f, x) = \max(s_0(f), s_1(f)).$$

We denote the real polynomial degree of a function by $\deg(f)$ and its $\mathbb{F}_2$ degree by $\deg_2(f)$. We write $wt(x)$ for $x \in \{0,1\}^n$ to denote the Hamming weight of x (number of ones). We write $\delta(f, g)$ for $f, g : \{0,1\}^n \to \{0,1\}$ to denote $\Pr_{x \in \{0,1\}^n}[f(x) \neq g(x)]$.

For $x \in \{0,1\}^n$, let $\mathcal{B}(x, r) \subset \{0,1\}^n$ denote the Hamming ball consisting of all points at distance at most r from x. Let $\mathcal{S}(x, r)$ denote the Hamming sphere consisting of all points at distance exactly r from x. Let $N(x)$ denote the set of Hamming neighbors of x (so $N(x)$ is shorthand for $\mathcal{S}(x, 1)$), and let $N_r(x)$ denote the set of neighbors of Hamming weight r (points with exactly r ones).

The following upper bound on sensitivity in terms of degree is due to Nisan and Szegedy.

THEOREM 7. *[NS94] For every function $f : \{0,1\}^n \to \{0,1\}$, we have $s(f) \leq 4(\deg(f))^2$.*

We record Simon's upper bound on the number of relevant variables in a low-sensitivity function:

THEOREM 8. *[Sim82] For every function $f : \{0,1\}^n \to \{0,1\}$, the number of relevant variables is bounded by $s(f)4^{s(f)}$.*

2. STRUCTURAL PROPERTIES OF LOW SENSITIVITY FUNCTIONS

2.1 Bounding the description length

We show that functions with low sensitivity have concise descriptions, so consequently the number of such functions is small. Indeed, we show that knowing the values on a Hamming ball of radius $2s + 1$ suffices.

2.1.1 Reconstruction from Hamming balls and spheres.

The following simple but key observation will be used repeatedly:

LEMMA 9. *Let $S \subseteq N(x)$ where $|S| \geq 2s + 1$. Then $f(x) = \text{Maj}_{y \in S}(f(y))$.*

Proof: Let $b \in \{0,1\}$ denote the majority value of f over S and let $S^b \subset S$ be the subset of S over which f takes the value b. Note that $|S^b| \geq \lceil |S|/2 \rceil \geq s + 1$ since $|S| \geq 2s + 1$. If $f(x) \neq b$, then every vertex in S^b represents a sensitive neighbor of x, and thus $s(f, x) \geq s + 1$ which is a contradiction. ∎

THEOREM 10. *Every sensitivity s function is uniquely specified by its values on a ball of radius $2s$.*

Proof: Suppose that we know the values of f on $\mathcal{B}(x, 2s)$. We may assume by relabeling that $x = 0^n$ is the origin. Note that $\mathcal{B}(0^n, 2s)$ is just the set of points of Hamming weight at most $2s$.

We will prove that f is uniquely specified on points x where $wt(x) \geq 2s$ by induction on $r = wt(x)$. The base case $r = 2s$ is trivial. For the induction step, assume we know f for all points of weight up to r for some $r \geq 2s$. Consider a point x with $wt(x) = r + 1$. The set $N_r(x)$ of weight-r neighbors of x has size $r + 1 \geq 2s + 1$. Hence

$$f(x) = \underset{y \in N_r(x)}{\text{Maj}} (f(y)) \tag{1}$$

by Lemma 9. ∎

Note that by Equation 1, we only need to know f on the sphere of radius r rather than the entire ball to compute f on inputs of weight $r + 1$. This observation leads to the following sharpening for $s \leq n/4$.

COROLLARY 11. *Let $s \leq n/4$. Every sensitivity s function is uniquely specified by its values on a sphere of radius $2s$.*

Proof: As before we may assume that $x = 0^n$. By Equation 1, the values of f on $\mathcal{S}(0^n, r)$ fix the values at $\mathcal{S}(0^n, r + 1)$. Hence knowing f on $\mathcal{S}(0^n, 2s)$ suffices to compute f at points of weight $2s + 1$ and beyond. In particular, the value of f is fixed at all points of weight $n/2$ through n (since $2s \leq n/2$). Hence the value of f is fixed at all points of the ball $\mathcal{B}(1^n, 2s)$, and now Theorem 10 finishes the proof. ∎

A natural question is whether there exists a significantly smaller subset S of $\{0,1\}^n$ (smaller than the sphere of radius $2s$) such that by iteratively adding to S every vertex with at least $2s$ neighbors in S, the set S grows to eventually contain all of $\{0,1\}^n$. This problem is sometimes known as the "perfect target set selection problem" for the Boolean hypercube [ABW10], and also arises as a natural extremal problem in the study of "bootstrap percolation" on the Boolean hypercube, see e.g. [CLR79]. Confirming a conjecture of Balogh and Bollobás [BB06], Morrison and Noel [MN15] have recently shown that only a small improvement over the sphere of radius $2s$ is possible in terms of minimizing the size of the set; we refer the interested reader to [BB06, MN15] for details.

2.1.2 Upper and lower bounds on $\mathcal{F}(s, n)$.

Recall that $|\mathcal{F}(s, n)|$ denotes the number of distinct Boolean functions on n variables with sensitivity at most s. We use the notation $\binom{n}{\leq k}$ to denote $\sum_{i=0}^{k} \binom{n}{i}$, the cardinality of a Hamming ball of radius k.

As an immediate corollary of Theorem 10, we have the following upper bound:

COROLLARY 12. *For all $s \leq n$, we have $|\mathcal{F}(s, n)| \leq 2^{\binom{n}{\leq 2s}}$.*

(It is possible to slightly improve this bound (by a factor of $\Theta(s)$ in the exponent) by using a construction which is slightly different from the sphere of radius $2s$; as above we refer the interested reader to [BB06, MN15] for details.)

We have the following lower bounds:

LEMMA 13. *For all $s \leq n$, we have*

$$|\mathcal{F}(s, n)| \geq \max\left\{ \binom{n}{s} 2^{2^{s-1}}, (n - s + 1)^{2^{s-1}} \right\}.$$

Proof: The first bound comes from considering s-juntas. We claim that there are at least $2^{2^{s-1}}$ functions on s variables that depend on all s variables. For any function $f : \{0,1\}^s \to \{0,1\}$ on s variables, either f or $f' = f \oplus \prod_{i=1}^{s} x_i$ is sensitive to all s variables. This is because $f \oplus f' = \prod_{i=1}^{s} x_i$, hence one of them has full degree as a polynomial over $\mathbb{F}_2$, and hence must depend on all n variables. The bound now follows by considering all subsets of n variables.

The second bound comes from the addressing functions. Divide the variables into $s - 1$ address variables $y_1, \ldots, y_{s-1}$ and $n - s + 1$ output variables $x_1, \ldots, x_{n-s+1}$. Consider the addressing function computed by a decision tree with nodes at the first $s - 1$ levels labelled by $y_1, \ldots, y_{s-1}$ and each leaf labelled by some x_i (the same x_i can be repeated at multiple leaves). It is easy to check that this defines a family of sensitivity s functions, that all the functions in the family are distinct, and that the cardinality is as claimed. ∎

In the setting when $s = o(n)$, the gap between our upper and lower bounds is roughly 2^{n^s} versus n^{2^s}. The setting where $s = O(\log(n))$ is particularly intriguing.

PROBLEM 14. *Is $|\mathcal{F}(2\log(n), n)| = 2^{n^{\omega(1)}}$?*

2.2 Noise Stability

We start by showing that functions with small sensitivity satisfy a strong noise-stability guarantee.

For a point $x \in \{0,1\}^n$ and $\delta \in [0,1]$, let $N_{1-2\delta}(x)$ denote the δ-noisy version of x, i.e. a draw of $y \sim N_{1-2\delta}(x)$ is obtained by independently setting each bit y_i to be x_i with probability $1 - 2\delta$ and uniformly random with probability 2δ. The noise sensitivity of f at x at noise rate δ, denoted $\mathrm{NS}_\delta[f](x)$, is defined as

$$\mathrm{NS}_\delta[f](x) = \Pr_{y \sim N_{1-2\delta}(x)}[f(x) \neq f(y)].$$

The noise sensitivity of f at noise rate δ, denoted $\mathrm{NS}_\delta[f]$, is then defined as

$$\mathrm{NS}_\delta[f] = \mathbb{E}_{x \sim \{0,1\}^n}[\mathrm{NS}_\delta[f](x)]$$
$$= \Pr_{x \sim \{0,1\}^n, y \sim N_{1-2\delta}(x)}[f(x) \neq f(y)].$$

The next lemma shows that low-sensitivity functions are noise-stable at every point $x \in \{0,1\}^n$:

LEMMA 15. *Let $f : \{0,1\}^n \to \{0,1\}$ have sensitivity s. For every $x \in \{0,1\}^n$ and $0 \le \delta \le 1/2$, we have $\mathrm{NS}_\delta[f](x) < 2\delta s$.*

Proof: Let $t \in [n]$. Consider a random process that starts at x and then flips a uniformly random subset $T \subseteq [n]$ of coordinates of cardinality t, which takes it from x to $y \in \{0,1\}^n$. We claim that $\Pr_T[f(x) \neq f(y)] \le \frac{st}{n-t+1}$. To see this, we can view going from x to y as a walk where at each step, we pick the next coordinate to walk along uniformly from the set of coordinates that have not been selected so far. Let $x = x_0, x_1, \ldots, x_t = y$ denote the sequence of vertices visited by this walk. At x_i, we choose the next coordinate to flip uniformly from a set of size $n - i$. Since x_i has at most s sensitive coordinates, we have $\Pr[f(x_i) \neq f(x_{i+1})] \le \frac{s}{n-i}$. Hence by a union bound we get

$$\Pr[f(x_0) \neq f(x_t)] \le \sum_{i=0}^{t-1} \Pr[f(x_i) \neq f(x_{i+1})]$$
$$\le \sum_{i=0}^{t-1} \frac{s}{n-i} \le \frac{st}{n-t+1}$$

as claimed.

Now we turn to noise sensitivity. We can view a draw of $y \sim N_{1-2\delta}(x)$ as first choosing the number t of coordinates of x to flip according to the binomial distribution $\mathrm{Bin}(n,\delta)$, and then flipping a random set $T \subseteq [n]$ of size t. From above, we have $\Pr[f(y) \neq f(x) \mid |T| = t] \le \frac{st}{n-t+1}$. Hence

$$\Pr[f(x) \neq f(y)] \le \mathbb{E}_{t \sim \mathrm{Bin}(n,\delta)}\left[\frac{st}{n-t+1}\right]$$
$$= s \sum_{t=1}^{n} \delta^t (1-\delta)^{n-t} \binom{n}{t} \cdot \frac{t}{n-t+1}$$
$$= s \sum_{t=1}^{n} \delta^t (1-\delta)^{n-t} \binom{n}{t-1}$$
$$= \frac{s\delta}{1-\delta} \sum_{t'=0}^{n-1} \delta^{t'} (1-\delta)^{n-t'} \binom{n}{t'}$$
$$= \frac{s\delta}{1-\delta}(1-\delta^n)$$

which is less than $2\delta s$ for $\delta \le 1/2$. ∎

We can restrict the noise distribution and get similar bounds. The setting that we now describe, where we only allow walks in the lower shadow of a vertex, will be useful later when we construct shallow formulas for a low sensitivity function f.

Let $D(x,t)$ denote the points in the lower shadow of x at distance t from it (so a point in $D(x,t)$ is obtained by flipping exactly t of the bits of x from 1 to 0). We show that a random point in $D(x,t)$ is likely to agree with x (for $t \le wt(x)/2s$).

LEMMA 16. *Let $wt(x) = d \ge s$. Then if $s(f) \le s$, we have $\Pr_{y \in D(x,t)}[f(x) \neq f(y)] \le \frac{st}{d-t}$.*

Proof: We consider a family of random walks that we call *downward walks*. In such a walk, at each step we pick a random index that is currently 1 and set it to 0. Consider a downward walk of length t and let $x = x_0, x_1, \ldots, x_t = y$ denote the sequence of vertices that are visited by the walk. We claim that $\Pr[f(x_i) \neq f(x_{i+1})] \le \frac{s}{d-i}$. To see this observe that out of the $d - i$ possible 1 indices in x_i that could be flipped to 0, at most s are sensitive. Hence we have

$$\Pr[f(x_0) \neq f(x_t)] \le \sum_{i=0}^{t-1} \Pr[f(x_i) \neq f(x_{i+1})]$$
$$\le \sum_{i=0}^{t-1} \frac{s}{d-i} \le \frac{st}{d-t}.$$

Since $y = x_t$ is a random point in $D(x,t)$, the proof is complete. ∎

COROLLARY 17. *Let $wt(x) = d$ and $t \le d/(10s+1)$. Then $\Pr_{y \in D(x,t)}[f(y) \neq f(x)] \le 1/10$.*

2.3 Bias and Interpolation

It is known that low sensitivity functions cannot be highly biased. For $f : \{0,1\}^n \to \{0,1\}$, let

$$\mu_0(f) = \Pr_{x \in \{0,1\}^n}[f(x) = 0], \quad \mu_1(f) = \Pr_{x \in \{0,1\}^n}[f(x) = 1],$$
$$\mu(f) = \min(\mu_0(f), \mu_1(f))$$

LEMMA 18. *For $f : \{0,1\}^n \to \{0,1\}$ we have*

$$s_0(f) \ge \log_2\left(\frac{1}{\mu_0(f)}\right) \quad if \ \mu_0(f) > 0$$
$$s_1(f) \ge \log_2\left(\frac{1}{\mu_1(f)}\right) \quad if \ \mu_1(f) > 0.$$

Equality holds iff the set $f^{-1}(b)$ is a subcube.

We note that these bounds are implied by the classical isoperimetric inequality, which shows that $\mathbb{E}_{x \in f^{-1}(b)}[s(f,x)] \ge \log(1/\mu_b(f))$ for $b = 0, 1$. We present a simple inductive proof of the max-sensitivity bounds given by Lemma 18 in the appendix.

We say that a set $K \subseteq \{0,1\}^n$ *hits* a set of functions $\mathcal{F}$ if for every $f \in \mathcal{F}$, there exists $x \in K$ such that $f(x) \neq 0$. We say that K *interpolates* $\mathcal{F}$ if for every $f_1 \neq f_2 \in \mathcal{F}$, there exists $x \in K$ such that $f_1(x) \neq f_2(x)$.

COROLLARY 19. *Let $k \ge C2^{2s}\binom{n}{\le 4s}$, and let S be a random subset of $\{0,1\}^n$ obtained by taking k points drawn uniformly from $\{0,1\}^n$ with replacement. The set S interpolates $\mathcal{F}(s,n)$ with probability $1 - \exp(-\binom{n}{\le 4s})$ (over the choice of S).*

63

Proof: We first show that large sets hit $\mathcal{F}(t,n)$ with very high probability. Fix $f \in \mathcal{F}(t,n)$. Since we have $\mu_1(f) \geq 2^{-t}$ by Lemma 18, the probability that k random points all miss $f^{-1}(1)$ is bounded by $(1 - 2^{-t})^k \leq \exp(-k/2^t)$. By Corollary 12 we have $\mathcal{F}(t,n) \leq 2^{\binom{n}{\leq 2t}}$, so by the union bound, the probability that S does not hit every function in this set is at most $2^{\binom{n}{\leq 2t}} \exp(-k/2^t)$, which is $\exp(-\binom{n}{\leq 2t})$ for $k \geq C2^t\binom{n}{\leq 2t}$.

Next, we claim that if S hits $\mathcal{F}(2s,n)$ then it interpolates $\mathcal{F}(s,n)$. Given functions $f_1, f_2 \in \mathcal{F}(s,n)$, let $g = f_1 \oplus f_2$. It is easy to see that $g \in \mathcal{F}(2s,n)$. and that $g^{-1}(1)$ is the set of points x where $f_1(x) \neq f_2(x)$, so indeed if S hits $\mathcal{F}(2s,n)$ then it interpolates $\mathcal{F}(s,n)$. Given this, the corollary follows from our lower bound on k, taking $t = 2s$. ∎

3. EFFICIENT ALGORITHMS FOR COMPUTING LOW SENSITIVITY FUNCTIONS

3.1 Small circuits

In this subsection, we will prove Theorem 4. Recall that the proof of Theorem 10 gives an algorithm to compute the truth table of f from an advice string which tells us the values on some Hamming ball of radius $2s + 1$. In this section we present two algorithms which, given this advice, can (relatively) efficiently compute any entry of the truth table without computing the truth-table in its entirety. This is equivalent to a small circuit computing f. We first give a (non-uniform) "bottom-up" algorithm for computing f at a given input point $x \in \{0,1\}^n$. In the appendix we describe a "top-down" algorithm with a similar performance bound.

3.1.1 A Bottom-Up Algorithm

The algorithm takes as advice the values of f on $\mathcal{B}(0^n, 2s)$. It then shifts the center of the ball along a shortest path from 0^n to x, computing the values of f on the shifted ball at each step. This computation is made possible by a lemma showing that when we shift a Hamming ball $\mathcal{B}$ by a unit vector to get a new ball $\mathcal{B}'$, points in $\mathcal{B}'$ either lie in $\mathcal{B}$ or are adjacent to many points in $\mathcal{B}$, which lets us apply Lemma 9.

Let $\mathbf{1}(S)$ denote the indicator of $S \subseteq [n]$ and $S\Delta T$ denote the symmetric difference of the sets S, T. For $B \subseteq \{0,1\}^n$ we write $B \oplus e_i$ to denote the pointwise shift of B by the unit vector e_i.

LEMMA 20. For any $y \in \mathcal{B}(x \oplus e_i, r) \setminus \mathcal{B}(x, r)$, we have $|N(y) \cap \mathcal{B}(x, r)| = r + 1$.

Proof: Fix any such y. Since $\mathcal{B}(x \oplus e_i, r) = \mathcal{B}(x, r) \oplus e_i$, we have that

$$y = x' \oplus e_i \text{ for some } x' \in \mathcal{B}(x, r), \text{ where}$$
$$x' = x \oplus \mathbf{1}(S) \text{ for some } S \subseteq [n], |S| \leq r, \text{ and hence}$$
$$y = x \oplus \mathbf{1}(S\Delta\{i\}).$$

If $i \in S$ or $|S| \leq r - 1$, then $|S\Delta\{i\}| \leq r$; but this means that $y \in \mathcal{B}(x, r)$, which is in contradiction to our assumption that $y \in \mathcal{B}(x \oplus e_i, r) \setminus \mathcal{B}(x, r)$. Hence $i \notin S$ and $|S| = r$. But then we have $y \oplus e_j \in \mathcal{B}(x, r)$ for precisely those j that belong to $S \cup \{i\}$, which gives the claim. ∎

COROLLARY 21. Knowing the values of f on $\mathcal{B}(x, 2s)$ lets us compute f on $\mathcal{B}(x \oplus e_i, 2s)$.

Proof: Either $y \in \mathcal{B}(x \oplus e_i, 2s)$ lies in $\mathcal{B}(x, 2s)$ so we know $f(y)$ already, or by the previous lemma y has $2s + 1$ neighbors in $\mathcal{B}(x, 2s)$, in which case Lemma 9 gives $f(y) = \mathrm{Maj}_{y' \in N(y) \cap \mathcal{B}(x, 2s)}(f(y'))$. ∎

Now we can give our algorithm for computing $f(x)$ at an arbitrary input $x \in \{0,1\}^n$.

Bottom-Up

Advice: The value of f at all points in $\mathcal{B}(0^n, 2s)$.
Input: $x \in \{0,1\}^n$.

1. Let $0^n = x_0, x_1, \ldots, x_d = x$ be a shortest path from 0^n to x.

2. For $i \in \{1, \ldots, d\}$ compute f on $\mathcal{B}(x_i, 2s)$ using the values at points in $\mathcal{B}(x_{i-1}, 2s)$.

3. Output $f(x_d)$.

THEOREM 22. The algorithm **Bottom-Up** computes $f(x)$ for any input x in time $O(sn^{2s+1})$ using space $O(n^{2s})$.

Proof: The values at $\mathcal{B}(0^n, 2s)$ are known as advice. Corollary 21 tells us how to compute the values at $\mathcal{B}(x_i, 2s)$ using the values on $\mathcal{B}(x_{i-1}, 2s)$. If we store the values at $\mathcal{B}(x_{i-1}, 2s)$ in an array indexed by subsets of size $2s$, the value at any point $y \in \mathcal{B}(x_i, 2s)$ can be computed in time $O(s)$, by performing $2s + 1$ array lookups and then taking the majority. Thus computing the values over the entire ball takes time $O(sn^{2s})$, and we repeat this $d \leq n$ times. Finally, at stage i we only need to store the values of f on the latest shift, $\mathcal{B}(x_{i-1}, 2s)$, so the total space required is $O(n^{2s})$. ∎

3.2 Small-depth Formulas

Theorem 22 established that any n-variable sensitivity-s function f is computed by a circuit of size $O(sn^{2s+1})$, but of relatively large depth $O(n^{2s})$. In this section we improve this depth by showing that *shallow* circuits of essentially the same size (equivalently, formulas of small depth) can compute low-sensitivity functions.

For $\mu < 1/2$, let $B(c, \mu)$ denote the product distribution over $y \in \{0,1\}^c$ where $\Pr[y_i = 1] = \mu$ for each $i \in [c]$. For constants $1/2 > \mu > \delta > 0$, let $c = c(\mu, \delta) \in \mathbb{Z}$ be the smallest integer constant such that

$$\Pr_{y \sim B(c,\mu)}[\mathrm{Maj}_{i \in [c]}(y_i) = 1] \leq \delta.$$

We now present a randomized parallel algorithm for computing $f(x)$.

```
┌─────────────────────────────────────────────┐
│ Parallel-Algorithm                            │
│                                               │
│ Advice: f at all points in B(0ⁿ, 10s).        │
│ Input: x ∈ {0,1}ⁿ.                            │
│ Let d = wt(x), t = ⌊d/(10s + 1)⌋,             │
│     c = c(1/5, 1/20).                          │
│                                               │
│   1. If d ≤ 10s, return A(x) = f(x).          │
│                                               │
│   2. Else sample y₁, ..., y_c randomly from   │
│      D(x, t). Recursively run Parallel-       │
│      Algorithm to compute A(yᵢ) in parallel   │
│      for all i ∈ [c].                          │
│                                               │
│   3. Return A(x) = Maj_{i∈[c]}(A(yᵢ)).         │
└─────────────────────────────────────────────┘
```

For brevity we use A to denote the algorithm above and $A(x) \in \{0,1\}$ to denote the random variable which is its output on input x. For $d \geq 10s + 1$, the random choices of A in computing $A(x)$ are described by a c-regular tree. The tree's root is labeled by x and its children are labeled by $y_1, \ldots, y_c$; its leaves are labeled by strings that each have Hamming weight at most $10s$. Further, the various subtrees rooted at each level are independent of each other.

THEOREM 23. *The algorithm runs in parallel time $O(s \log n)$ and uses $n^{O(s)}$ processors. For any $x \in \{0,1\}^n$, we have $\Pr_A[A(x) \neq f(x)] \leq \frac{1}{20}$, where $\Pr_A$ denotes that the probability is over the random coin tosses of the algorithm.*

Proof: We first prove the correctness of the algorithm by induction on $wt(x) = d$. When $d \leq 10s$, the claim follows trivially. Assume that the claim is true for $wt(x) \leq d-1$, and consider an input x of weight d. Note that every $y \in D(x, t)$ has $wt(y) = d - t \leq d - 1$, hence the inductive hypothesis applies to it. For each $i \in [c]$, we independently have

$$\Pr_A[A(y) \neq f(x)] \leq \Pr_{A, y_i}[A(y_i) \neq f(y_i)]$$
$$+ \Pr_{y_i \in D(x, t)}[f(y_i) \neq f(x)]$$
$$\leq \frac{1}{10} + \frac{1}{20} < \frac{1}{5}.$$

where the $1/10$ bound is by Corollary 17 and the $1/20$ is by the inductive hypothesis. The algorithm samples c independent points $y_i \in D(x, t)$, computes $A(y_i)$ for each of them using independent randomness, and then returns the majority of $A(y_i)$ over those $i \in [c]$. Hence, by our choice of $c = c(1/5, 1/20)$, we have that $\Pr_A[\text{Maj}_{i \in [c]}(A(y_i)) \neq f(x)] \leq \frac{1}{20}$.

To bound the running time, we observe that for $d \geq 10s + 1$,

$$t = \left\lfloor \frac{d}{10s + 1} \right\rfloor \geq \frac{d}{25s}, \quad \text{so} \quad d - t \leq d\left(1 - \frac{1}{25s}\right).$$

But this implies that in $k = O(s \log d)$ steps, the weight reduces below $10s + 1$. The number of processors required is bounded by $c^k = n^{O(s)}$. ∎

By hardwiring the random bits and the advice bits, a standard argument allows us to conclude that functions with low sensitivity have small-depth formulas, thus proving Theorem 5.

4. SELF-CORRECTION

In this section we show that functions with low sensitivity admit self-correctors. Recall that for Boolean functions, $f, g : \{0,1\}^n \to \{0,1\}$ we write $\delta(f, g)$ to denote $\Pr_{x \in \{0,1\}^n}[f(x) \neq g(x)]$.

Our self-corrector is given a function $r : \{0,1\}^n \to \{0,1\}$ such that there exists $f \in \mathcal{F}(s, n)$ satisfying $\delta(r, f) \leq 2^{-cs}$ for some constant $c > 2$ to be specified later. By Lemma 18, it follows that any two sensitivity s functions differ in at least 2^{-2s} fraction of points, so if such a function f exists, it must be unique. We consider two settings (in analogy with coding theory): in the global setting, the self-corrector is given the truth-table of r as input and is required to produce the truth-table of f as output. In the local setting, the algorithm has black-box oracle access to r. It is given $x \in \{0,1\}^n$ as input, and the desired output is $f(x)$.

At a high level, our self-corrector relies on the fact that small-sensitivity sets are noise-stable at noise rate $\delta \approx 1/s$, by Lemma 15, whereas small sets of density $\mu \leq c^{-s}$ tend to be noise sensitive. The analysis uses the hypercontractivity of the $T_{1-2\delta}(\cdot)$ operator.

Following [O'D14], for $f : \{0,1\}^n \to \mathbb{R}$, we define

$$T_{1-2\delta} f(x) = \mathbb{E}_{y \sim N_{1-2\delta}(x)}[f(y)],$$

where recall that a draw of $y \sim N_{1-2\delta}(x)$ is obtained by independently setting each bit y_i to be x_i with probability $1 - 2\delta$ and uniformly random with probability 2δ. We can view (x, y) where $x \sim \{0,1\}^n$ and $y \sim N_{1-2\delta}(x)$ as defining a distribution on the edges of the complete graph on the vertex set $\{0,1\}^n$. We refer to this weighted graph as the δ-*noisy hypercube*. The $(2,q)$-Hypercontractivity Theorem quantifies the expansion of the noisy hypercube:

THEOREM 24. *($(2,q)$-Hypercontractivity.) Let $f : \{0,1\}^n \to \mathbb{R}$. Then*

$$\|T_{1-2\delta} f\|_q \leq \|f\|_2 \quad \text{for} \quad 2 \leq q \leq 1 + \frac{1}{(1-2\delta)^2}.$$

We need the following consequence, which says that for any small set S, most points do not have too many neighbors in the noisy hypercube that lie within S. For $S \subseteq \{0,1\}^n$, let us define the set $\Lambda_{\delta, \theta}(S)$ of those points for which a θ fraction of neighbors in the δ-noisy hypercube lie in S. Formally,

$$\Lambda_{\delta, \theta}(S) = \left\{ x \in \{0,1\}^n \text{ s.t. } \Pr_{y \sim N_{1-2\delta}(x)}[y \in S] \geq \theta \right\}.$$

Abusing the notation from Section 2.3, for $S \subseteq \{0,1\}^n$ we write $\mu(S)$ to denote $\Pr_{x \in \{0,1\}^n}[x \in S]$.

LEMMA 25. *We have*

$$\mu(\Lambda_{\delta, \theta}(S)) \leq \left(\frac{\mu(S)}{\theta^2} \right)^{1+2\delta}.$$

Proof: Let $f(x) = \mathbf{1}(x \in S)$. Then

$$T_{1-2\delta} f(x) = \Pr_{y \in N_{1-2\delta}(x)}[y \in S].$$

Hence $\Lambda_{\delta, \theta}(S)$ is the set of those x such that $T_{1-2\delta} f(x) \geq \theta$.

Let $q = 2(1 + 2\delta)$. It is easy to see that q satsfies the hypothesis of Theorem 24. Hence we can bound the qth moment of $T_{1-2\delta} f$ as

$$\mathbb{E}_{x \in \{0,1\}^n}[(T_{1-2\delta} f(x))^q] \leq \|f\|_2^q = \mu(S)^{q/2}.$$

Hence by Markov's inequality,

$$\Pr_{x \in \{0,1\}^n}[T_{1-2\delta}f(x) \geq \theta] \leq \frac{\mu(S)^{q/2}}{\theta^q}.$$

The claim follows from our choice of q. ∎

COROLLARY 26. *If $\mu(S) \leq \theta^{4+2/\delta}$, then $\mu(\Lambda_{\delta,\theta}(S)) \leq \mu(S)^{1+\delta}$.*

Proof: By Lemma 25, it suffices that $\left(\frac{\mu(S)}{\theta^2}\right)^{1+2\delta} \leq \mu(S)^{1+\delta}$, and it is easy to check that this condition holds for our choice of $\mu(S)$. ∎

4.1 Global Self-correction

Our global self-corrector is given a function $r : \{0,1\}^n \to \{0,1\}$ such that there exists $f \in \mathcal{F}(s,n)$ satisfying $\delta(r,f) \leq 2^{-c_1 s}$ for some constant $c_1 > 2$ to be specified later. By Lemma 18, it follows that any two sensitivity s functions differ in at least 2^{-2s} fraction of points, so such a function f if it exists must be unique. Our self-corrector defines a sequence of functions $f_0, \ldots, f_T$ such that $f_0 = r$ and $f_T = f$ (with high probability).

Global Self-corrector

Input: $r : \{0,1\}^n \to \{0,1\}^n$ such that $\delta(r,f) \leq 2^{-c_1 s}$ for some $f \in \mathcal{F}(s,n)$.
Output: The sensitivity-s function f.

Let $f_0 = r$, $k = c_2 s \log(n/s)$, $\delta = 1/(20s)$.
For $t = 1, \ldots, k$,
  For every $x \in \{0,1\}^n$,
    Let $f_t(x) = \text{Maj}_{y \sim \mathrm{N}_{1-2\delta}(x)}(f_{t-1}(y))$.
Return f_k.

The algorithm runs in time $2^{O(n)}$, which is polynomial in the length of its output (which is a truth table of size 2^n). To analyze the algorithm, let us define the sets S_t for $t \in \{0, \ldots, T\}$ as

$$S_t = \{x \in \{0,1\}^n \text{ such that } f_t(x) \neq f(x).\}$$

The following is the key lemma for the analysis.

LEMMA 27. *We have $S_t \subseteq \Lambda_{\delta,2/5}(S_{t-1})$.*

Proof: For $x \in S_t$,

$$f(x) \neq \text{Maj}_{y \sim \mathrm{N}_{1-2\delta}(x)}(f_{t-1}(y)),$$

hence

$$\Pr_{y \sim \mathrm{N}_{1-2\delta}(x)}[f(x) \neq f_{t-1}(y)] \geq \frac{1}{2}.$$

We can upper bound this probability by

$$\Pr_{y \sim \mathrm{N}_{1-2\delta}(x)}[f(x) \neq f_{t-1}(y)]$$
$$\leq \Pr_{y \sim \mathrm{N}_{1-2\delta}(x)}[f(x) \neq f(y)] + \Pr_{y \sim \mathrm{N}_{1-2\delta}(x)}[f(y) \neq f_{t-1}(y)].$$

Since the distributions $\text{Noise}_\delta(x)$ and $\mathrm{N}_{1-2\delta}(x)$ are identical, we can bound the first term by Lemma 15, which gives

$$\Pr_{y \sim \mathrm{N}_{1-2\delta}(x)}[f(x) \neq f(y)] \leq 2s\delta = \frac{1}{10}.$$

Hence

$$\Pr_{y \sim \mathrm{N}_{1-2\delta}(x)}[f(y) \neq f_{t-1}(y)] \geq \frac{1}{2} - \frac{1}{10} = \frac{2}{5}.$$

But $f(y) \neq f_{t-1}(y)$ implies $y \in S_{t-1}$, hence by definition of $\Lambda_{\delta,\theta}(S)$ we have $x \in \Lambda_{\delta,2/5}(S_{t-1})$. ∎

We can now analyze our global self-corrector.

THEOREM 28. *There exist constants c_1, c_2 such that if $\delta(r,f) \leq 2^{-c_1 s}$ for some $f \in \mathcal{F}(s,n)$, then for $k \geq c_2 \log(n/s)$, we have $f_k = f$.*

Proof: Let $\delta = 1/(20s)$. Assume that there exists $f \in \mathcal{F}(s,n)$ such that

$$\delta(f,s) = \mu(S_0) \leq 2^{-c_1 s} \leq (2/5)^{4+40s}.$$

By Lemma 27 and Corollary 26, we have

$$\mu(S_t) \leq \mu(\Lambda_{\delta,2/5}(S_{t-1})) \leq \mu(S_{t-1})^{1+\delta} \leq \mu(S_0)^{(1+\delta)^t}.$$

For $t \geq c_2' \ln(n/s)/\delta = c_2 s \log(n/s)$, we have

$$\mu(S_t) \leq \mu(S_0)^{(1+\delta)^t} < 2^{-n}.$$

But since $S_t \subseteq \{0,1\}^n$, it must be the empty set, and this implies that $f_t = f$. ∎

4.2 Local Self-Correction

Recall that in the local self-correction problem, the algorithm is given $x \in \{0,1\}^n$ as input and oracle access to $r : \{0,1\}^n \to \{0,1\}$ such that $\delta(r,f) \leq 2^{-d_1 s}$ for some constant $d_1 > 2$ to be specified later. The goal is to compute $f(x)$. Our local algorithm can be viewed as derived from the global algorithm, where we replace the Majority computation with sampling, and only compute the parts of the truth tables that are essential to computing $f_T(x)$.

We define a distribution $\mathcal{T}_k(x)$ over c-regular trees of depth k rooted at x, where each tree node is labelled with a point in $\{0,1\}^n$. To sample a tree $T_1(x)$ from $\mathcal{T}_1(x)$, we place x at the root, then sample c independent points from $\mathrm{N}_{1-2\delta}(x)$, and place them at the leaves. To sample a tree $T_k(x)$ from $\mathcal{T}_k(x)$, we first sample $T_{k-1}(x) \sim \mathcal{T}_{k-1}(x)$ and then for every leaf $x_i \in T_{k-1}(x)$, we sample c independent points according to $\mathrm{N}_{1-2\delta}(x_i)$, and make them the children of x_i. (Note the close similarity between these trees and the trees discussed in Section 3.2. The difference is that the trees of Section 3.2 correspond to random walks that are constructed to go downward while now the random walks corresponding to the noise process $\mathrm{N}_{1-2\delta}(\cdot)$ do not have this constraint.)

Given oracle access to $r : \{0,1\}^n \to \{0,1\}$, we use the tree $T_k(x)$ to compute a guess for the value of $f(x)$, by querying r at the leaves and then using Recursive Majority. In more detail, we define functions $\tilde{r}_0, \tilde{r}_1, \ldots, \tilde{r}_k$ which collectively assign a *guess* for every node in T_k. (In more detail, each $\tilde{r}_i$ is a function from $L(T_k(x), i)$ to $\{0,1\}$, where $L(T_k(x), i)$ is the set of points in $\{0,1\}^n$ that are at the nodes at depth $k - i$ in $T_k(x)$.) For each leaf y, we let $\tilde{r}_0(y) = r(y)$. Once $\tilde{r}_{k-t}$ has been defined for nodes at depth t in $T_k(x)$, given y at depth $t-1$ in $T_k(x)$, we set $\tilde{r}_{k-t+1}(y)$ to be the majority of $\tilde{r}_{k-t}$ at its children. We output $\tilde{r}_k(x)$ as our estimate for $f(x)$.

```
Local Self-corrector

Input: x ∈ {0,1}ⁿ, oracle for r : {0,1}ⁿ → {0,1}
such that δ(r,f) ≤ 2^{-d₁s} for some f ∈ F(s,n).
Output: b ∈ {0,1} which equals f(x) with proba-
bility 1 − ε.

Let δ = 1/(20s), c = c(1/4,ε), k ∈ ℤ.
Sample Tₖ ∼ T(k,x).
For each leaf y ∈ Tₖ, query r(y).
For i = 0 to k, compute r̃ᵢ : L(Tₖ(x),i) → {0,1} as
described above.
Output r̃ₖ(x).
```

To analyze the algorithm, for $k \in \mathbb{Z}$ define

$$S_k = \left\{ x \in \{0,1\}^n \text{ such that } \Pr_{T_k(x) \sim \mathcal{T}_k(x)}[\tilde{r}_k(x) \neq f(x)] > \epsilon \right\}.$$

The following is analogous to Lemma 27:

LEMMA 29. *For $k \geq 1$ and $\epsilon < 1/25$, we have $S_k \subseteq \Lambda_{\delta,1/10}(S_{k-1})$.*

Proof: We have $\tilde{r}_k(x) = \mathrm{Maj}_{1 \leq i \leq c}(b_i)$ where each b_i is drawn independently according to $\tilde{r}_{k-1}(N_{1-2\delta}(x))$. If $x \in S_k$, then by our choice of $c = c(1/4,\epsilon)$,

$$\Pr_{\substack{y \sim N_{1-2\delta}(x) \\ T_{k-1}(y) \sim \mathcal{T}_{k-1}(y)}}[\tilde{r}_{k-1}(y) \neq f(x)] > \frac{1}{4}.$$

On the other hand, we also have

$$\Pr_{\substack{y \sim N_{1-2\delta}(x) \\ T_{k-1}(y) \sim \mathcal{T}_{k-1}(y)}}[\tilde{r}_{k-1}(y) \neq f(x)]$$
$$\leq \Pr_{\substack{y \sim N_{1-2\delta}(x) \\ T_{k-1}(y) \sim \mathcal{T}_{k-1}(y)}}[f(y) \neq f(x)]$$
$$+ \Pr_{\substack{y \sim N_{1-2\delta}(x) \\ T_{k-1}(y) \sim \mathcal{T}_{k-1}(y)}}[\tilde{r}_{k-1}(y) \neq f(y)].$$

The first term on the LHS is bounded by $1/10$ by Lemma 15. Hence we have

$$\Pr_{\substack{y \sim N_\delta(x) \\ T_{k-1}(y) \sim \mathcal{T}_{k-1}(y)}}[\tilde{r}_{k-1}(y) \neq f(y)] \geq \frac{1}{4} - \frac{1}{10} > \frac{1}{7}.$$

But by the definition of S_{k-1},

$$\Pr_{\substack{y \sim N_{1-2\delta}(x) \\ T_{k-1}(y) \sim \mathcal{T}_{k-1}(y)}}[\tilde{r}_{k-1}(y) \neq f(y)]$$
$$\leq \epsilon \cdot \Pr_{y \sim N_{1-2\delta}(x)}[y \notin S_{k-1}] + \Pr_{y \sim N_{1-2\delta}(x)}[y \in S_{k-1}]$$
$$\leq \epsilon + \Pr_{y \sim N_{1-2\delta}(x)}[y \in S_{k-1}].$$

Hence for $\epsilon < 1/25$,

$$\Pr_{y \sim N_{1-2\delta}(x)}[y \in S_{k-1}] \geq \frac{1}{7} - \epsilon \geq \frac{1}{10},$$

so by the definition of $\Lambda_{\delta,\theta}(S)$ we have $x \in \Lambda_{\delta,1/10}(S_{k-1})$. ∎

We can now analyze our local self-corrector.

THEOREM 30. *There exist constants d_1, d_2 such that if $\delta(r,f) \leq 2^{-d_1 s}$ for some $f \in F(s,n)$, then for $k \geq d_2 s \log(n/s)$ we have that $\tilde{r}_k(x) = f(x)$ with probability 0.99. The algorithm queries the oracle for r at $(n/s)^{O(s)}$ points.*

Proof: Let $\delta = 1/(20s)$. Let $d_1 > 0$ be such that

$$2^{-d_1 s} < (0.1)^{4+60s}.$$

Assume there exists $f \in F(s,n)$ such that

$$\delta(r,f) \leq 2^{-d_1 s}.$$

Observe that $\tilde{r}_0(x) = r(x)$, so consequently $\mu(S_0) = \delta(r,f)$. By Lemma 29 and Corollary 26, we have

$$\mu(S_k) \leq \mu(\Lambda_{\delta,1/10}(S_{k-1})) \leq \mu(S_{k-1})^{1+\delta} \leq \mu(S_0)^{(1+\delta)^k}.$$

For $k \geq d_2' \ln(n/s)/\delta = d_2 s \log(n/s)$, we have $\mu(S_t) < 2^{-n}$, so S_t must be the empty set. But this implies that $\tilde{r}_k(x) = f(x)$ except with probability ϵ.

The number of queries to the oracle is bounded by the number of leaves in the tree, which is c^k. Setting $\epsilon = 1/100$, since $c(1/4, 1/100) = O(1)$, this is at most $c^k = (n/s)^{O(s)}$. We can amplify the success probability to $1-\epsilon$ using $c(1/100, \epsilon) = O(\log(1/\epsilon))$ independent repetitions. ∎

Discussion. Every real polynomial of degree d computing a Boolean function is also a degree d polynomial over $\mathbb{F}_2$. Hence, it has a natural self-corrector which queries the value at a random affine subspace of dimension $d+1$ containing x, and then outputs the XOR of those values. Conjecture 2 implies that this self-corrector also works for low sensitivity functions. The parameters one would get are incomparable to Theorem 6; we find it interesting that this natural self-corrector is very different from the algorithm of Theorem 6.

We further remark that every Boolean function with real polynomial degree $\deg(f) \leq d$ satsifies $s(f) \leq O(d^2)$ (recall Theorem 7). Thus, Theorem 6 gives a self-corrector for functions with $\deg(f) \leq d$ that has query complexity $n^{O(d^2)}$. It is interesting to note (by considering the example of parity), that this performance guarantee does not extend to all functions with $\mathbb{F}_2$ degree $\deg_2(f) \leq d$.

5. PROPAGATION RULES

We have seen that low-degree functions and low-sensitivity functions share the property that they are uniquely specified by their values on small-radius Hamming balls. In either case, we can use these values over a small Hamming ball to infer the values at other points in $\{0,1\}^n$ using simple "local propagation" rules. The propagation rules for the two types of functions are quite different, but Conjecture 2 and its converse given by Theorem 7 together imply that the two rules must converge beyond a certain radius. In this section, we discuss this as a possible approach to Conjecture 2 and some questions that arise from it.

5.1 Low sensitivity functions: the Majority Rule

If $f : \{0,1\}^n \to \{0,1\}$ has sensitivity s, Theorem 10 implies that given the values of f on a ball of radius $2s$, we can recover f at points at distance $r + 1 \geq 2s + 1$ from the center by taking the Majority value over its neighbors at distance r (see Equation (1)). It is worth noting that as r gets large, the Majority is increasingly lopsided: at most s out of r points are in the minority. We refer to the process of inferring f's values everywhere from its values on a ball via the Majority rule, increasing the distance from the center by one at a time, as "applying the Majority rule".

For concreteness, let us conder the ball centered at 0^n. If there exists a sensitivity s function $f : \{0,1\}^n \to \{0,1\}$ such that the points in $\mathcal{B}(0^n, 2s)$ are labelled according to f, then applying the Majority rule recovers f. However, not every labeling of $\mathcal{B}(0^n, 2s)$ will extend to a low sensitivity function on $\{0,1\}^n$ via the Majority Rule. It is an interesting question to characterize such labelings; progress here will likely lead to progress on Question 14. An obvious necessary condition is that every point in $\mathcal{B}(0^n, 2s)$ should have sensitivity at most s, but this is not sufficient. This can be seen by considering the DNF version of the "tribes" function, where there are n/s disjoint tribes, each tribe is of size s, and $n > s^2$. (So this function f is an (n/s)-way OR of s-way ANDs over disjoint sets of variables.) Every $x \in \mathcal{B}(0^n, 2s)$ has $s(f, x) \leq s$ — in fact, this is true for every $x \in \mathcal{B}(0^n, s(s-1))$ — but it can be verified that applying the Majority rule starting from the ball of radius $2s$ does recover the Tribes function, which has sensitivity $n/s > s$. Another natural question is whether there is a nice characterization of the class of functions that can be obtained by applying the majority rule to a labeling of $\mathcal{B}(0^n, 2s)$.

5.2 Low degree functions: the Parity Rule

It is well known that all functions $f : \{0,1\}^n \to \mathbb{R}$ with $\deg(f) \leq d$ are uniquely specified by their values on a ball of radius d. This follows from the Möbius inversion formula. Again, let us fix the center to be 0^n for concreteness. Letting $\mathbf{1}(T)$ denote the indicator vector of the set T, the formula (see e.g. Section 2.1 of [Juk12]) states that

$$f(x) = \sum_{S \subseteq [n]} c_S \prod_{i \in S} x_i \quad \text{where} \quad c_S = \sum_{T \subseteq S} (-1)^{|S|-|T|} f(\mathbf{1}(T)).$$
(2)

From this it can be inferred that if $\deg(f) \leq d$, then for $|S| \geq d+1$, we have

$$f(\mathbf{1}(S)) = \sum_{T \subset S} (-1)^{|S|-|T|+1} f(\mathbf{1}(T)).$$
(3)

We will refer to Equation (3) as the "Parity rule", since it states that f is uncorrelated with the parity of the variables in S on the subcube given by $\{\mathbf{1}(T) : T \subseteq S\}$. We refer to the process of inferring f's values everywhere from its values on a ball of radius d via the Parity rule, increasing the distance from the center by one at a time, as "applying the Parity rule".

Given a (partial) function $f : \mathcal{B}(0^n, d) \to \{0,1\}$, applying the Parity rule starting from the values of f on $\mathcal{B}(0^n, d)$ lets us extend f to all of $\{0,1\}^n$. Note that the resulting total function f is guaranteed to have degree at most d, but it is not guaranteed to be Boolean-valued everywhere on $\{0,1\}^n$. Indeed, an easy counting argument (see e.g. Lemma 31 of [MORS07]) shows that there are at most $2^{d^2 2^{2d}} \cdot \binom{n}{d2^d}$ degree-d functions over $\{0,1\}^n$, whereas the number of partial functions $f : \mathcal{B}(0^n, d) \to \{0,1\}$ is $2^{\binom{n}{\leq d}}$. It is an interesting question to characterize the set of partial functions $f : \mathcal{B}(0^n, d) \to \{0,1\}$ whose extension by the Parity rule is a Boolean function.

On the other hand, every partial function $f : \mathcal{B}(0^n, d) \to \{0,1\}$ can be uniquely extended to a total function $f : \{0,1\}^n \to \{0,1\}$ such that $\deg_2(f) = d$. This follows from the Mobius inversion formula for multilinear polynomials

over $\mathbb{F}_2$:

$$f(x) = \sum_{S \subseteq [n]} c_S \prod_{i \in S} x_i \quad \text{where} \quad c_S = \sum_{T \subseteq S} f(\mathbf{1}(T)) \quad (4)$$

where the sums are modulo 2. If $\deg_2(f) \leq d$, then $c_S = 0$ for all S where $|S| \geq d+1$. Hence by Equation (2), for $|S| \geq d+1$, we have the simple rule

$$f(\mathbf{1}(S)) = \sum_{T \subset S} f(\mathbf{1}(T)). \quad (5)$$

We can view this as a propagation rule for functions with $\deg_2(f) \leq d$, which extends a labeling of the ball $\mathcal{B}(0^n, d)$ to the entire cube $\{0,1\}^n$. If we start from a labeling of the ball which corresponds to a function $f : \{0,1\}^n \to \{0,1\}$ with $\deg(f) \leq d$, then Equation (5) above coincides with the Parity rule.

5.3 When do the rules work?

Given a partial function $g : \mathcal{B}(x_0, r) \to \{0,1\}$, we can extend it to a total function $g^{\mathrm{Maj}} : \{0,1\}^n \to \{0,1\}$ by applying the Majority rule (if there is not a clear majority among the neighbors queried, the value is underetmined). We can also extend it to a total function $g^{\mathrm{Par}} : \{0,1\}^n \to \mathbb{R}$ using the Parity rule. Given a function $f : \{0,1\}^n \to \{0,1\}$, and a center x_0, we define a series of partial functions $f|_{\mathcal{B}(x_0, r)}$ obtained by restricting f to the ball of radius r around x_0. We are interested in how large r needs to be for the Parity and Majority rules to return the function f for every choice of center x_0. Formally, we define the following quantities.

DEFINITION 31. *Let $r^{\mathrm{Par}}(f)$ be the smallest r such that for every $x_0 \in \{0,1\}^n$, the Parity rule applied to $\mathcal{B}(x_0, r)$ returns the function f. Formally,*

$$r^{\mathrm{Par}}(f) = \min\{r : \forall x_0 \in \{0,1\}^n, \, (f|_{\mathcal{B}(x_0, r)})^{\mathrm{Par}} = f\}.$$

Similarly, let $r^{\mathrm{Maj}}(f)$ be the smallest r such that for every $x_0 \in \{0,1\}^n$, the Majority rule applied to $\mathcal{B}(x_0, r)$ returns the function f. Formally,

$$r^{\mathrm{Maj}}(f) = \min\{r : \forall x_0 \in \{0,1\}^n (f|_{\mathcal{B}(x_0, r)})^{\mathrm{Maj}} = f\}.$$

It is easy to see that r^{Par} captures the real degree of f:

LEMMA 32. *For all $f : \{0,1\}^n \to \{0,1\}$, we have $r^{\mathrm{Par}}(f) = \deg(f)$.*

Proof: The inequality $r^{\mathrm{Par}}(f) \leq \deg(f)$ follows from the fact that the Parity rule correctly extends degree d functions starting from any Hamming ball of radius d.

On the other hand, for any center x_0, running the Parity rule on $f|_{\mathcal{B}(x_0, r)}$ for some $r < \deg(f)$ results in a function $(f|_{\mathcal{B}(x_0, r)})^{\mathrm{Par}}$ of degree at most r, since the Parity rule explicitly sets the coefficients of monomials of degree higher than r to 0. But then it follows that $(f|_{\mathcal{B}(x_0, r)})^{\mathrm{Par}} \neq f$, since their difference is a non-zero multilinear polynomial. ∎

The proof above shows that quantifying over x_0 is not necessary in the definition of $r^{\mathrm{Par}}(f)$, since for every $x_0 \in \{0,1\}^n$, we have

$$r^{\mathrm{Par}}(f) = \min\{r : \, (f|_{\mathcal{B}(x_0, r)})^{\mathrm{Par}} = f\}.$$

We now turn to the Majority rule.

LEMMA 33. *For all* $f : \{0,1\}^n \to \{0,1\}$, *we have* $r^{\mathrm{Maj}}(f) = \min(2s(f), n)$.

Proof: We have $r^{\mathrm{Maj}}(f) \leq n$, since $\mathcal{B}(x_0, n)$ is the entire Hamming cube. The upper bound $r^{\mathrm{Maj}}(f) \leq 2s(f)$ follows from the definiton of the Majority rule and Theorem 10.

For the second part, we show that for each $r < \min(2s(f), n)$, there exists a center x_0 such that $(f|_{\mathcal{B}(x_0, r)})^{\mathrm{Maj}} \neq f$. Let x be a point with sensitivity $s(f)$, and let $S \subset [n]$ be the set of $s(f)$ sensitive coordinates at x. We will pick x_0 so that $d(x, x_0) = r + 1$ as follows. If $r + 1 \leq s(f)$, we obtain x_0 from x by flipping some $r + 1$ coordinates from S. If $r + 1 > s(f)$, then we obtained x_0 from f by flipping all the coordinates in S, and any $r + 1 - s(f)$ other coordinates $T \subseteq [n] \setminus S$. The condition $r + 1 \leq n$ guarantees that a subset of the desired size exists, while $r + 1 \leq 2s(f)$ enures that $|T| \leq |S|$.

Since $d(x, x_0) = r + 1$, the value at x is inferred using the Majority rule applied to the neighbors of x in $\mathcal{B}(x_0, r)$. These neighbors are obtained by either flipping coordinates in S or T (where T might be empty). The former disagree with $f(x)$ while the latter agree. Since $|S| \geq |T|$, the Majority rule either labels x wrongly, or leaves it undetermined (in the case when $r = 2s(f)$). This shows that $(f|_{\mathcal{B}(x_0, r)})^{\mathrm{Maj}} \neq f(x)$, hence $r^{\mathrm{Maj}} \geq \min(2s(f), n)$. ∎

In contrast with Lemma 32, quantifying over all centers x_0 in the defintion of r^{Par} is crucial for the lower bound in Lemma 33. This is seen by considering the n-variable OR function, where the sensitivity is n. Applying the Majority rule to a ball of radius 2 around 0^n returns the right function, but if we center the ball at 1^n, then the Majority rule cannot correctly infer the value at 0^n, so it needs to be part of the advice, hence $r^{\mathrm{Maj}}(\mathrm{OR}) = n$.

5.4 Agreement of the Majority and Parity Rule

Lemmas 32 and 33 can be viewed as alternate characterizations of the degree and sensitivity of a Boolean function. The degree versus sensitivity conjecture asserts that both these rules work well (meaning that they only require the values on a small ball as advice) for the same class of functions. Given that the rules are so simple, and seem so different from each other, we find this assertion surprising.

In particular, Conjecture 2 is equivalent to the following statement:

CONJECTURE 34. *There exists constants* d_1, d_2 *such that*

$$r^{\mathrm{Par}}(f) \leq d_1 (r^{\mathrm{Maj}})^{d_2}. \quad (6)$$

Along similar lines, one can use Theorem 7, due to [NS94], to show that the Majority rule recovers low-degree Boolean functions:

$$r^{\mathrm{Maj}}(f) \leq 8(r^{\mathrm{Par}}(f))^2. \quad (7)$$

Their proof uses Markov's inequality from analysis. It might be interesting to find a different proof, which one could hope to extend to proving Equation (6) as well.

6. CONCLUSION (AND MORE OPEN PROBLEMS)

We have presented the first upper bounds on the computational complexity of low sensitivity functions. We believe this might be a promising alternative approach to Conjecture 1 as opposed to getting improved bounds on specific low

level measures like block sensitivity or decision tree depth [KK04, ABG+14, AS11].

Conjecture 1 implies much stronger upper bounds than are given by our results. We list some of the ones which might be more approachable given our results:

1. Every sensitivity s function has a TC_0 circuit of size $n^{O(s)}$.

2. Every sensitivity s function has a polynomial threshold function (PTF) of degree poly(s).

3. Every sensitivity s function f has $\deg_2(f) \leq s^c$ for some constant c.

7. REFERENCES

[ABG+14] Andris Ambainis, Mohammad Bavarian, Yihan Gao, Jieming Mao, Xiaoming Sun, and Song Zuo. Tighter relations between sensitivity and other complexity measures. In *Automata, Languages, and Programming - 41st International Colloquium, ICALP 2014*, pages 101–113, 2014.

[ABW10] Eyal Ackerman, Oren Ben-Zwi, and Guy Wolfovitz. Combinatorial model and bounds for target set selection. *Theor. Comput. Sci.*, 411(44-46):4017–4022, 2010.

[AP14] Andris Ambainis and Krisjanis Prusis. A tight lower bound on certificate complexity in terms of block sensitivity and sensitivity. In *MFCS*, pages 33–44, 2014.

[APV15] Andris Ambainis, Krisjanis Prusis, and Jevgenijs Vihrovs. Sensitivity versus certificate complexity of boolean functions. *CoRR*, abs/1503.07691, 2015.

[AS11] Andris Ambainis and Xiaoming Sun. New separation between $s(f)$ and $bs(f)$. *CoRR*, abs/1108.3494, 2011.

[AV15] Andris Ambainis and Jevgenijs Vihrovs. Size of sets with small sensitivity: a generalization of simon's lemma. In *Theory and Applications of Models of Computation - 12th Annual Conference, TAMC 2015*, pages 122–133, 2015.

[BB06] J. Balogh and B. Bollobás. Bootstrap percolation on the hypercube. *Probab. Theory Related Fields*, 134(4):624–648, 2006.

[BdW02] H. Buhrman and R. de Wolf. Complexity measures and decision tree complexity: a survey. *Theoretical Computer Science*, 288(1):21–43, 2002.

[CDR86] Stephen A. Cook, Cynthia Dwork, and Rüdiger Reischuk. Upper and lower time bounds for parallel random access machines without simultaneous writes. *SIAM J. Comput.*, 15(1):87–97, 1986.

[CLR79] J. Chalupa, P.L. Leath, and G. R. Reich. Bootstrap percolation on a Bethe lattice. *J. Phys. C*, 12:L31–L35, 1979.

[GKS15] Justin Gilmer, Michal Koucký, and Michael E. Saks. A new approach to the sensitivity conjecture. In *Proceedings of the 2015 Conference on Innovations in Theoretical*

Computer Science, ITCS 2015, pages 247–254, 2015.

[HKP11] Pooya Hatami, Raghav Kulkarni, and Denis Pankratov. *Variations on the Sensitivity Conjecture*. Number 4 in Graduate Surveys. Theory of Computing Library, 2011.

[Jac30] Dunham Jackson. The theory of approximation. *New York*, 19:30, 1930.

[Juk12] S. Jukna. *Boolean Function Complexity: Advances and Frontiers*. Springer, 2012.

[KK04] Claire Kenyon and Samuel Kutin. Sensitivity, block sensitivity, and l-block sensitivity of Boolean functions. *Information and Computation*, pages 43–53, 2004.

[MN15] Natasha Morrison and Jonathan A. Noel. Extremal bounds for bootstrap percolation in the hypercube, 2015.

[MORS07] K. Matulef, R. O'Donnell, R. Rubinfeld, and R. Servedio. Testing Halfspaces. Technical Report 128, Electronic Colloquium in Computational Complexity, 2007. Full version in FOCS 2007.

[Nis91] Noam Nisan. CREW PRAMs and decision trees. *SIAM Journal on Computing*, 20(6):999–1007, 1991.

[NS64] DJ Newman and HS Shapiro. Jackson's theorem in higher dimensions. In *On Approximation Theory/Über Approximationstheorie*, pages 208–219. Springer, 1964.

[NS94] N. Nisan and M. Szegedy. On the degree of Boolean functions as real polynomials. *Comput. Complexity*, 4:301–313, 1994.

[O'D14] Ryan O'Donnell. *Analysis of Boolean Functions*. Cambridge University Press, 2014.

[Rub95] David Rubinstein. Sensitivity vs. block sensitivity of Boolean functions. *Combinatorica*, pages 297–299, 1995.

[Sim82] Hans-Ulrich Simon. A tight omega(log log n)-bound on the time for parallel ram's to compute nondegenerated boolean functions. *Information and Control*, 55(1-3):102–106, 1982.

[Wei85] Karl Weierstrass. Über die analytische darstellbarkeit sogenannter willkürlicher functionen einer reellen veränderlichen. *Sitzungsberichte der Königlich Preußischen Akademie der Wissenschaften zu Berlin*, 2:633–639, 1885.

Local Algorithms for Block Models with Side Information

[Extended Abstract] [*]

Elchanan Mossel
Department of Statistics
University of Pennsylvania and U.C. Berkeley
mossel@wharton.upenn.edu

Jiaming Xu
Department of Statistics
University of Pennsylvania
jiamingx@wharton.upenn.edu

ABSTRACT

There has been a recent interest in understanding the power of local algorithms for optimization and inference problems on sparse graphs. Gamarnik and Sudan (2014) showed that local algorithms are weaker than global algorithms for finding large independent sets in sparse random regular graphs thus refuting a conjecture by Hatami, Lovász, and Szegedy (2012). Montanari (2015) showed that local algorithms are suboptimal for finding a community with high connectivity in the sparse Erdős-Rényi random graphs. For the symmetric planted partition problem (also named community detection for the block models) on sparse graphs, a simple observation is that local algorithms cannot have non-trivial performance.

In this work we consider the effect of *side information* on local algorithms for community detection under the binary symmetric stochastic block model. In the block model with side information each of the n vertices is labeled + or − independently and uniformly at random; each pair of vertices is connected independently with probability a/n if both of them have the same label or b/n otherwise. The goal is to estimate the underlying vertex labeling given 1) the graph structure and 2) side information in the form of a vertex labeling positively correlated with the true one. Assuming that the ratio between in and out degree a/b is $\Theta(1)$ and the average degree $(a+b)/2 = n^{o(1)}$, we show that a local algorithm, namely, belief propagation run on the local neighborhoods, maximizes the expected fraction of vertices labeled correctly in the following three regimes:

- $|a - b| < 2$ and all $0 < \alpha < 1/2$

- $(a - b)^2 > C(a + b)$ for some constant C and all $0 < \alpha < 1/2$

- For all a, b if the probability that each given vertex label is incorrect is at most α^* for some constant $\alpha^* \in (0, 1/2)$.

---

[*]A full version of this paper is available at arXiv:1508.02344.

Permission to make digital or hard copies of all or part of this work for personal or classroom use is granted without fee provided that copies are not made or distributed for profit or commercial advantage and that copies bear this notice and the full citation on the first page. Copyrights for components of this work owned by others than ACM must be honored. Abstracting with credit is permitted. To copy otherwise, or republish, to post on servers or to redistribute to lists, requires prior specific permission and/or a fee. Request permissions from Permissions@acm.org.

ITCS '16 January 14–16, 2016, Cambridge, MA, USA
2016 ACM ISBN 978-1-4503-4057-1/16/01 ...$15.00.
http://dx.doi.org/10.1145/2840728.2840749.

Thus, in contrast to the case of independent sets or a single community in random graphs and to the case of symmetric block models without side information, we show that local algorithms achieve optimal performance in the above three regimes for the block model with side information.

To complement our results, in the large degree limit $a \to \infty$, we give a formula of the expected fraction of vertices labeled correctly by the local belief propagation, in terms of a fixed point of a recursion derived from the density evolution analysis with Gaussian approximations.

Categories and Subject Descriptors

I.5.3 [**PATTERN RECOGNITION**]: Clustering—*Algorithms*; G.3 [**PROBABILITY AND STATISTICS**]: [Statistical computing]

Keywords

Local algorithms; random graphs; community detection

1. INTRODUCTION

In this work we study the performance of *local algorithms* for *community detection* in sparse graphs thus combining two lines of work which saw recent breakthroughs.

The optimality of the performance of local algorithm for optimization problems on large graphs was raised by Hatami, Lovász, and Szegedy [26] in the context of a theory of graph limits for sparse graphs. The conjecture, regarding the optimality for finding independent sets in random graphs was refuted by Gamarnik and Sudan [20]. More recently, local algorithms are shown to be strictly suboptimal comparing to the maximum likelihood estimator for finding a community of higher connectivity than the background Erdős-Rényi random graph [35, 25].

In a different direction, following a beautiful conjecture from physics [17], new efficient algorithms for the stochastic block models (i.e. planted partition) were developed and shown to detect the blocks whenever this is information theoretically possible [39, 37, 32, 9]. It is easy to (see e.g. [29]) that no local algorithm with access to neighborhoods of radius $o(\log n)$ can have non-trivial performance for this problem.

Our interest in this paper is in the application of local algorithms for community detection with side information on community structures. We show that unlike the cases of independent sets on regular graphs or the case of community detection on sparse random graphs, local algorithms do have optimal performance.

1.1 Local algorithms

Local algorithms for optimization problems on sparse graphs are algorithms that determine if each vertex belongs to the solution or not based only on a small radius neighborhood around the node. Such algorithms are allowed to have an access to independent random variables associated to each node.

A simple example for a local algorithm is the following classical algorithm for finding independent sets in graphs. Attach to each node v an independent uniform random variable U_v. Let the independent set consist of all the vertices whose U_v value is greater than that of all of their neighbors. See Definition 2 for a formal definition of a local algorithm and [31, 26, 20, 35] for more background on local algorithms.

There are many motivations for studying local algorithms. These algorithms are efficient. For example, for bounded degree graphs they run in linear time in the size of the graph n and for graphs with maximal degree polylog(n) they run in time $O(n \times \text{polylog}(n))$. Moreover, by design, these algorithms are easy to run in a distributed fashion. In addition, the optimality of local algorithms implies correlation decay properties that are of interest in statistical physics, graph limit theory and ergodic theory. Loosely speaking, correlation decay means that the solution in one part of the graph is asymptotically independent of the solution in a far away part, see [31, 26, 20] for a more formal and comprehensive discussion.

A striking conjecture of Hatami, Lovász, and Szegedy [26] stated that local algorithms are able to find independent sets of the maximal possible density in random regular graphs. This conjecture was refuted by Gamarnik and Sudan [20]. The work of Gamarnik and Sudan [20] highlights the role of long range correlation and clustering in the solution space as obstacles for the optimality of local algorithms. Refining the methods of Gamarnik and Sudan, Rahman and Virag [44] showed that local algorithms cannot find independent sets of size larger than half of the optimal density.

1.2 Community detection in sparse graphs

The stochastic block model is one of the most popular models for networks with clusters. The model has been extensively studied in statistics [27, 46, 8, 22, 10, 50, 21], computer science (where it is called the planted partition problem) [19, 28, 16, 33, 14, 15, 12, 4, 13, 48] and theoretical statistical physics [17, 51, 18]. In the simplest binary symmetric form, it assumes that n vertices are assigned into two clusters, or equivalently labeled with $+$ or $-$, independently and uniformly at random; each pair of vertices is connected independently with probability a/n if both of them are in the same cluster or b/n otherwise.

In the dense regime with $a = \Omega(\log n)$, it is possible to exactly recover the clusters from the observation of the graph. A sharp exact recovery threshold has been found in [1, 38] and it is further shown that semi-definite programming can achieve the sharp threshold in [23, 5]. More recently, exact recovery thresholds have been identified in a more general setting with a fixed number of clusters [24, 49], and with heterogeneous cluster sizes and edge probabilities [2, 43].

Real networks are often sparse with bounded average degrees. In the sparse setting with $a = \Theta(1)$, exact recovery of the clusters from the graph becomes hopeless as the resulting graph under the stochastic block model will have many isolated vertices. Moreover, it is easy to see that even vertices with constant degree cannot be labeled accurately given all the other vertices' labels are revealed. Thus the goal in the sparse regime is to find a labeling that has a non-trivial or maximal correlation with the true one (up to permutation of cluster labels). It was conjectured in [17] and proven in [39, 37, 32] that nontrivial detection is feasible if and only if $(a - b)^2 > 2(a + b)$. A spectral method based on the non-backtracking matrix is shown to achieve the sharp threshold in [9]. In contrast, a simple argument in [29] shows that no local algorithm running on neighborhoods of radius $o(\log n)$ can attain nontrivial detection.

1.3 Community detection with side information

The community detection problem under stochastic block model is an idealization of a network inference problem. In many realistic settings, in addition to network information, some partial information about vertices' labels is also available. There has been much recent work in the machine learning and applied networks communities on combining vertex and network information (see for example [11, 6, 7, 42]). In this paper, we ask the following natural but fundamental question:

With the help of partial information about vertices' labels, can local algorithms achieve the optimal detection probability?

This question has two motivations: 1) from a theoretical perspective we would like to understand how side information affects the existence of optimal local algorithms; 2) from the application perspective, it is important to develop fast community detection algorithms which exploit side information in addition to the graph structure.

There are two natural models for side information of community structures. A model where a small random fraction of the vertices' labels is given accurately. This model was considered in a number of recent works in physics and computer science [17, 47, 3, 52, 29]. The emerging conjectured picture is that in the case of the binary symmetric stochastic block model, the local application of BP is able to achieve the optimal detection probability. This is stated formally as one of the main conjectures of [29], where it is proven in an asymptotic regime where the fraction of revealed information goes to 0 *and* assuming $(a - b)^2 > C(a + b)$ for some large constant C.

The model considered in this paper is where noisy information is provided for each vertex. Specifically, for each vertex, we observe a noisy label which is the same as its true label with probability $1 - \alpha$ and different with probability α, independently at random, for some $\alpha \in [0, 1/2)$. For this model, by assuming that $a/b = \Theta(1)$ and the average degree $(a + b)/2 = n^{o(1)}$ is smaller than all powers of n, we prove that local application of belief propagation maximizes the expected fraction of vertices labelled correctly, i.e., achieving the optimal detection probability, in the following three regimes: 1) $|a - b| < 2$; 2) $(a - b)^2 > C(a + b)$ for some constant C; 3) $\alpha \leq \alpha^*$ for some constant $0 < \alpha^* < 1/2$. Note that this proves the conjectured picture in a wide range of the parameters. In particular, compared to the results of [29], we prove the conjecture in the whole regime $((a - b)^2 > C(a + b)) \times (\alpha \in (0, 1/2))$ while in [29] the result is only proven for the limiting interval of this region

$((a - b)^2 > C(a + b)) \times (\alpha' \to 0^+)$, where each vertex's true label is revealed with probability α'.

In the large degree limit $a \to \infty$ we further provide a simple formula of the expected fraction of vertices labeled correctly by BP, in terms of a fixed point of a recursion, based on the density evolution analysis. Density evolution has been used for the analysis of sparse graph codes [45, 34], and more recently for the analysis of finding a single community in a sparse graph [35].

In closing, we remark that the proofs of our main theorems are sketched in this paper. The excluded proofs can be found in the arXiv version of the paper [41].

2. MODEL AND MAIN RESULTS

We next present a formal definition of the model followed by a formal statement of the main results.

2.1 Model

We consider the binary symmetric stochastic block model with two clusters. This is a random graph model on n vertices, where we first independently assign each vertex into one of the clusters uniformly at random, and then independently draw an edge between each pair of vertices with probability a/n if two vertices are in the same clusters or b/n otherwise. Let $\sigma_i = +$ if vertex i is in the first cluster and $\sigma_i = -$ otherwise.

Let $G = G_n = (V, E)$ denote the observed graph (without the labels σ). Let $\widetilde{\sigma}$ be an α noisy version of σ: for each vertex i independently, $\widetilde{\sigma}_i = \sigma_i$ with probability $1 - \alpha$ and $\widetilde{\sigma}_i = -\sigma_i$ with probability α, where $\alpha \in [0, 1/2)$ is a fixed constant. Hence, $\widetilde{\sigma}$ can be viewed as the side information for the cluster structure.

DEFINITION 1. *The* detection problem with side information *is the inference problem of inferring σ from the observation of $(G, \widetilde{\sigma})$. The estimation accuracy for an estimator $\widehat{\sigma}$ is defined by*

$$p_{G_n}(\widehat{\sigma}) = \frac{1}{n} \sum_{i=1}^{n} \mathbb{P}\{\sigma_i = \widehat{\sigma}_i\}, \qquad (1)$$

which equals to the expected fraction of vertices labeled correctly. Let $p_{G_n}^*$ denote the optimal estimation accuracy.

The optimal estimator in maximizing the success probability $\mathbb{P}\{\sigma_i = \widehat{\sigma}_i\}$ is the maximum a posterior (MAP) estimator, which is given by $2 \times \mathbf{1}_{\{\mathbb{P}\{\sigma_i = +|G, \widetilde{\sigma}\} \geq \mathbb{P}\{\sigma_i = -|G, \widetilde{\sigma}\}\}} - 1$, and the maximum success probability is

$$\frac{1}{2} \mathbb{E}\left[|\mathbb{P}\{\sigma_i = +|G, \widetilde{\sigma}\} - \mathbb{P}\{\sigma_i = -|G, \widetilde{\sigma}\}|\right] + \frac{1}{2}.$$

Hence, the optimal estimation accuracy $p_{G_n}^*$ is given by

$$p_{G_n}^* = \frac{1}{2n} \sum_{i=1}^{n} \mathbb{E}\left[|\mathbb{P}\{\sigma_i = +|G, \widetilde{\sigma}\} - \mathbb{P}\{\sigma_i = -|G, \widetilde{\sigma}\}|\right] + \frac{1}{2}$$

$$= \frac{1}{2} \mathbb{E}\left[|\mathbb{P}\{\sigma_i = +|G, \widetilde{\sigma}\} - \mathbb{P}\{\sigma_i = -|G, \widetilde{\sigma}\}|\right] + \frac{1}{2}, \quad (2)$$

where the second equality holds due to the symmetry. However, computing the MAP estimator is computationally intractable in general, and it is unclear whether the optimal estimation accuracy $p_{G_n}^*$ can be achieved by some estimator computable in polynomial-time.

In this paper, we focus on the regime:

$$\frac{1}{c_0} \leq \frac{a}{b} \leq c_0, \quad a = n^{o(1)}, \quad \text{as } n \to \infty, \qquad (3)$$

where c_0 is a fixed positive constant. It is well known that in the regime $a = n^{o(1)}$, a local neighborhood of a vertex is with high probability a tree. Thus, it is natural to study the performance of local algorithms. We next present a formal definition of local algorithms which is a slight variant of the definition in [35].

Let $\mathcal{G}_*$ denote the space of graphs with one distinguished vertex and labels $+$ or $-$ on each vertex. For an estimator $\widehat{\sigma}$, it can be viewed as a function $\widehat{\sigma} : \mathcal{G}_* \to \{\pm\}$, which maps $(G, \widetilde{\sigma}, u)$ to $\widehat{\sigma}_u$ for every $(G, \widetilde{\sigma}, u) \in \mathcal{G}_*$.

DEFINITION 2. *Given a $t \in \mathbb{N}$, an estimator $\widehat{\sigma}$ is t-local if there exist a function $\mathcal{F} : \mathcal{G}_* \to \{\pm\}$ such that for all $(G, \widetilde{\sigma}, u) \in \mathcal{G}_*$,*

$$\widehat{\sigma}(G, \widetilde{\sigma}, u) = \mathcal{F}(G_u^t, \widetilde{\sigma}_{G_u^t}),$$

where G_u^t is the subgraph of G induced by vertices whose distance to u is at most t; the distinguished vertex is u, and each vertex i in G_u^t has label $\widetilde{\sigma}_i$; $\widetilde{\sigma}_{G_u^t}$ is the restriction of $\widetilde{\sigma}$ to vertices in G_u^t. Moreover, we call an estimator $\widehat{\sigma}$ local, if it is t-local for some fixed t, regardless of the graph size n.

We can potentially allow local algorithms to access local independent uniform random variables as defined in [26, 20]. Since our main results show that the local BP algorithm which does not need to access external randomness, is already optimal, the extra randomness is not needed in our context.

2.2 Local belief propagation algorithm

It is known that, see e.g. [35, Lemma 4.3], local belief propagation algorithm as defined in Algorithm 1 maximizes the estimation accuracy among local algorithms, provided that the graph is locally tree-like. Thus we focus on studying the local BP. Specifically, let ∂i denote the set of neighbors of i and $F(x) = \tanh^{-1}(\tanh(\beta)\tanh(x))$ with $\beta = \frac{1}{2}\log\frac{a}{b}$, and define

$$R_{i \to j}^t = h_i + \sum_{\ell \in \partial i \setminus \{j\}} F(R_{\ell \to i}^{t-1}), \qquad (4)$$

with initial conditions $R_{i \to j}^0 = \gamma$ if $\tau_i = +$ and $R_{i \to j}^0 = -\gamma$ if $\tau_i = -$, for all $i \in [n]$ and $j \in \partial i$. Then we approximate $\frac{1}{2}\log\frac{\mathbb{P}\{G, \widetilde{\sigma}|\sigma_u = +\}}{\mathbb{P}\{G, \widetilde{\sigma}|\sigma_u = -\}}$ by R_u^t given by

$$R_u^t = h_u + \sum_{\ell \in \partial u} F(\Lambda_{\ell \to u}^{t-1}). \qquad (5)$$

Algorithm 1 Local belief propagation with side information

1: Input: $n \in \mathbb{N}$, $a > b > 0$, $\alpha \in [0, 1/2)$, adjacency matrix $A \in \{0, 1\}^{n \times n}$, and $t \in \mathbb{N}$.
2: Initialize: Set $R_{i \to j}^0 = 0$ for all $i \in [n]$ and $j \in \partial i$.
3: Run $t - 1$ iterations of message passing as in (4) to compute $R_{i \to j}^{t-1}$ for all $i \in [n]$ and $j \in \partial i$.
4: Compute R_i^t for all $i \in [n]$ as per (5).
5: Return $\widehat{\sigma}_{\mathrm{BP}}^t$ with $\widehat{\sigma}_{\mathrm{BP}}^t(i) = 2 \times \mathbf{1}_{\{R_i^t \geq 0\}} - 1$.

We remark that in each BP iteration, each vertex i needs to transmit the outgoing message $R_{i \to j}^t$ to its neighbor j according to (4). To do so, vertex i can first compute R_i^t as per (5) and then subtract neighbor j's contribution from it to get the desired message $R_{i \to j}^t$. In this way, each vertex i needs $O(|\partial i|)$ basic operations and the total time complexity of one BP iteration is $O(|E|)$. As a consequence, $\widehat{\sigma}_{\mathrm{BP}}^t$ is computable in time $O(t|E|)$.

2.3 Main results

THEOREM 1. *Consider the detection problem with side information assuming that $a/b = \Theta(1)$ and that $a = n^{o(1)}$. Let $\widehat{\sigma}_{\mathrm{BP}}^t$ denote the estimator given by Belief Propagation applied for t iterations, as defined in Algorithm 1. Then*

$$\lim_{t \to \infty} \limsup_{n \to \infty} \left(p_{G_n}^* - p_{G_n}(\widehat{\sigma}_{\mathrm{BP}}^t) \right) = 0$$

in the following three regimes:

- $|a - b| < 2$,
- $(a - b)^2 > C(a + b)$ *for some constant C,*
- $\alpha \le \alpha^*$ *for some $0 < \alpha^* < 1/2$.*

In other words, in each of these regimes a local application of belief propagation provides an optimal detection probability.

The above results should be contrasted with the case with no side information available, where it is known, see e.g. [29], that BP applied for $t = o(\log n)$ iterations cannot recover a partition better than random, i.e., achieving the non-trivial detection.

In the large degree regime, we further derive an asymptotic formula for $p_{G_n}(\widehat{\sigma}_{\mathrm{BP}}^t)$ in terms of a fixed point of a recursion.

THEOREM 2. *Consider the regime (3). Assume further that as $n \to \infty$, $a \to \infty$ and $\frac{a-b}{\sqrt{b}} \to \mu$, where μ is a fixed constant. Let $h(v) = \mathbb{E}[\tanh(v + \sqrt{v}Z + U)]$, where $Z \sim \mathcal{N}(0,1)$; U is independent of Z and $U = \gamma$ with probability $1 - \alpha$ and $U = -\gamma$ with probability α, where $\gamma = \frac{1}{2}\log\frac{1-\alpha}{\alpha}$. Define $\underline{v}$ and $\overline{v}$ to be the smallest and largest fixed point of $v = \frac{\mu^2}{4}h(v)$, respectively. let $\widehat{\sigma}_{\mathrm{BP}}^t$ denote the estimator given by Belief Propagation applied for t iterations, as defined in Algorithm 1. Then,*

$$\lim_{t \to \infty} \lim_{n \to \infty} p_{G_n}(\widehat{\sigma}_{\mathrm{BP}}^t) = 1 - \mathbb{E}\left[Q\left(\frac{\underline{v} + U}{\sqrt{\underline{v}}}\right)\right],$$

$$\limsup_{n \to \infty} p_{G_n}^* \le 1 - \mathbb{E}\left[Q\left(\frac{\overline{v} + U}{\sqrt{\overline{v}}}\right)\right],$$

where $Q(x) = \int_x^\infty \frac{1}{\sqrt{2\pi}} e^{-y^2/2} dy$. Moreover, $\underline{v} = \overline{v}$ and $\lim_{t \to \infty} \lim_{n \to \infty} p_{G_n}(\widehat{\sigma}_{\mathrm{BP}}^t) = \limsup_{n \to \infty} p_{G_n}^*$ in the following three regimes:

- $|\mu| < 2$,
- $|\mu| > C$ *for some constant C,*
- $\alpha \le \alpha^*$ *for some $0 < \alpha^* < 1/2$.*

2.4 Proof ideas

The complete proofs can be found in the arXiv version of the paper [41]. The proof of Theorem 1 follows ideas from [39, 36].

- To bound from above the accuracy of an arbitrary estimator, we bound its accuracy for a specific random vertex u. Following [39], we consider an estimator, which in addition to the graph structure and the noisy labels, the exact labels of all vertices at distance exactly t from u is also given. As in [39], it is possible to show that the best estimator in this case is given by BP for t levels using the exact labels at distance t.

- The only difference between our application of BP and the BP upper bound above is the quality of information at distance exactly t from vertex u. Our goal is to now analyze the recursion of random variables defining BP in both cases and show they converge to the same value given exact or noisy information at level t.

- In the two cases where 1) $(a-b)^2 > C(a+b)$ and 2) where α is small, our proof follows the pattern of [36]. We note however that the paper [36] did not consider side information and the adaptation of the proof is far from trivial. Similar to the setup in [36], the noisy labels at the boundary, i.e., level t, play the role as an initialization of the recursion. However, the noisy labels inside the tree results in less symmetric recursions that need to be controlled. Finally in the case where α is small they play a novel role as the reason behind the contraction of the recursion.

- The case where $a - b < 2$ corresponds to the uniqueness regime. Here the recursion converges to the same value if all the vertices at level t are $+$ or all vertices at level t are $-$. This implies that it converges to the same value for all possible values at level t.

The proof of Theorem 2 instead follows the idea of density evolution [45, 34], which was recently used for analyzing the problem of finding a single community in a sparse graph [35].

- The neighborhood of a vertex u is locally tree-like and thus the incoming messages to vertex u from its neighbors in BP iterations are independent. In the large degree limit, the sum of incoming messages is distributed as Gaussian conditional on its label. Moreover, its mean and variance admit a simple recursion over t, which converge to a fixed point as $t \to \infty$.

- As we pointed out earlier, the only difference between our application of BP and the BP upper bound discussed above is the quality of information at distance exactly t from vertex u. Hence, the mean and variance for both BPs satisfy the same recursion but with different initialization. If there is a unique fixed point of the recursion for mean and variance, then the mean and variance for both BPs converge to the same values as $t \to \infty$.

- The case $|\mu| < 2$ exactly corresponds to the regime below the Kesten-Stigum bound [30]. In this case, we can show that the recursion is a contraction mapping and thus has a unique fixed point.

2.5 Conjectures and open problems

There are many interesting conjectures and open problems resulting from this work. First, we believe that local BP with side information always achieves optimal estimation accuracy.

CONJECTURE 1. *Under the binary symmetric stochastic block model with α-noisy side information, for all a, b, and α,*

$$\lim_{t \to \infty} \lim_{n \to \infty} p_{G_n}(\widehat{\sigma}_{\mathrm{BP}}^t) = \limsup_{n \to \infty} p_{G_n}^*.$$

In the large degree regime with $a \to \infty$, $a = n^{o(1)}$, and $\frac{a-b}{\sqrt{b}} \to \mu$, Theorem 2 implies that the above conjecture is true if $v = \mu^2 h(v)/4$ always has a unique fixed point. Through simulations, we find that $v = \mu^2 h(v)/4$ seems to have a unique fixed point for all μ and α, and the asymptotically optimal estimation accuracy is depicted in Fig. 1.

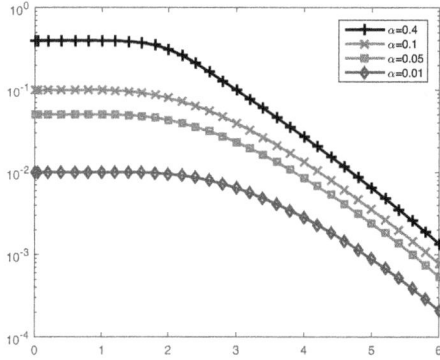

Figure 1: Numerical calculation of $\mathbb{E}\left[Q\left(\frac{v+U}{\sqrt{v}}\right)\right]$ for $v = \underline{v} = \overline{v}$ (y axis) versus μ (x axis) with different α.

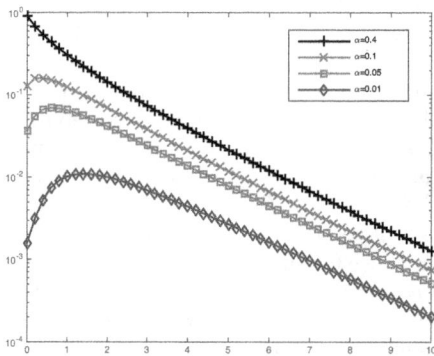

Figure 2: Numerical calculation of $h'(v)$ (y axis) versus $v \in [0, 10]$ (x axis) with different α.

We are only able to show $h(v)$ has a unique fixed point if $|\mu| < 2$, but we believe that it is true for all μ.

CONJECTURE 2. *For all $|\mu| \geq 2$ and $\alpha \in (0, 1/2)$, $v = \mu^2 h(v)/4$ has a unique fixed point.*

It is tempting to prove Conjecture 2 by showing that $h(v)$ is concave in v for all $\alpha \in (0, 1/2)$. However, through numerical experiments depicted in Fig. 2, we find that $h(v)$ is convex around $v = 0$ when $\alpha \leq 0.1$.

In this work, we assume that there is a noisy label for every vertex in the graph. Previous work [29] instead assumes that a fraction of vertices have true labels. However, in practice, it is neither easy to get noisy labels for every vertex or true labels. Thus, there arises an interesting question: are local algorithms still optimal with noisy labels available only for a small fraction of vertices?

Moreover, we only studied the binary symmetric stochastic block model as a starting point. It would be of great interest to study to what extent our results generalize to the case with multiple clusters. Finally, the local algorithms are powerless in the symmetric stochastic block model simply because the local neighborhoods are statistically uncorrelated with the cluster structure. It is intriguing to investigate whether the local algorithms are optimal when the clusters are of different sizes or connectivities; such attempt has been recently pursued in [40].

3. INFERENCE PROBLEMS ON GALTON-WATSON TREE MODEL

A key to understanding the inference problem on the graph is understanding the corresponding inference problem on Galton-Watson trees. We introduce the problem now.

DEFINITION 3. *For a vertex u, we denote by $(T_u, \tau, \widetilde{\tau})$ the following Poisson two-type branching process tree rooted at u, where τ is a $\pm$ labeling of the vertices of T. Let τ_u is chosen from $\{\pm\}$ uniformly at random. Now recursively for each vertex i in T_u, given its label τ_i, i will have $L_i \sim \mathrm{Pois}(a/2)$ children j with $\tau_j = +\tau_i$ and $M_i \sim \mathrm{Pois}(b/2)$ children j with $\tau_j = -\tau_i$. Finally for each vertex i, let $\widetilde{\tau}_i = \tau_i$ with probability $1 - \alpha$ and $\widetilde{\tau}_i = -\tau_i$ with probability α.*

It follows that the distribution of τ conditional on $\widetilde{\tau}$ and a finite T_u is given by

$$\mathbb{P}\left\{\tau | \widetilde{\tau}, T_u\right\} \propto \exp\left(\beta \sum_{i \sim j} \tau_i \tau_j + \sum_i h_i \tau_i\right),$$

where $\beta = \frac{1}{2} \log \frac{a}{b}$, $h_i = \frac{1}{2} \widetilde{\tau}_i \log \frac{1-\alpha}{\alpha}$, and $i \sim j$ means that i and j are connected in T_u. Observe that $\mathbb{P}\left\{\tau | \widetilde{\tau}, T_u\right\}$ is an Ising distribution on tree T_u with external fields given by h.

Let T_i^t denote the subtree of T_u rooted at vertex i of depth t, and ∂T_i^t denote the set of vertices at the boundary of T_i^t. With a bit abuse of notation, let τ_A denote the vector consisting of labels of vertices in A, where A could be either a set of vertices or a subgraph in T_u. Similarly we define $\widetilde{\tau}_A$. We first consider the problem of estimating τ_u given observation of T_u^t, $\tau_{\partial T_u^t}$, and $\widetilde{\tau}_{T_u^t}$. Notice that the true labels of vertices in T_u^{t-1} are not observed in this case.

DEFINITION 4. *The detection problem with side information in the tree and exact information at the boundary of the tree is the inference problem of inferring τ_u from the observation of T_u^t, $\tau_{\partial T_u^t}$, and $\widetilde{\tau}_{T_u^t}$. The success probability for an estimator $\widehat{\tau}_u(T_u^t, \tau_{\partial T_u^t}, \widetilde{\tau}_{T_u^t})$ is defined by*

$$p_{T^t}(\widehat{\tau}_u) = \frac{1}{2}\mathbb{P}\left\{\widehat{\tau}_u = + | \tau_u = +\right\} + \frac{1}{2}\mathbb{P}\left\{\widehat{\tau}_u = - | \tau_u = -\right\}.$$

Let $p_{T^t}^*$ denote the optimal success probability.

It is well-known that the optimal estimator in maximizing p_T^t, is the maximum a posterior (MAP) estimator. Since the prior distribution of τ_u is uniform over $\{\pm\}$, the MAP estimator is the same as the maximum likelihood (ML) estimator, which can be expressed in terms of log likelihood ratio:

$$\widehat{\tau}_{\mathrm{ML}} = 2 \times \mathbf{1}_{\{\Lambda_u^t \geq 0\}} - 1,$$

where

$$\Lambda_i^t \triangleq \frac{1}{2} \log \frac{\mathbb{P}\left\{T_i^t, \tau_{\partial T_i^t}, \widetilde{\tau}_{T_i^t} | \tau_i = +\right\}}{\mathbb{P}\left\{T_i^t, \tau_{\partial T_i^t}, \widetilde{\tau}_{T_i^t} | \tau_i = -\right\}},$$

for all i in T_u. Moreover, the optimal success probability $p_{T^t}^*$ is given by

$$p_{T^t}^* = \frac{1}{2}\mathbb{E}\left[|X_u^t|\right] + \frac{1}{2}, \tag{6}$$

where X_i^t is known as *magnetization* given by

$$X_i^t \triangleq \mathbb{P}\left\{\tau_i = +|T_i^t, \tau_{\partial T_i^t}, \widetilde{\tau}_{T_i^t}\right\} - \mathbb{P}\left\{\tau_i = -|T_i^t, \tau_{\partial T_i^t}, \widetilde{\tau}_{T_i^t}\right\}$$

for all i in T_u. In view of the identity $\tanh^{-1}(x) = \frac{1}{2}\log\left(\frac{1+x}{1-x}\right)$ for $x \in [-1, 1]$, we have that $\tanh^{-1}(X_i^t) = \Lambda_i^t$.

We then consider the problem of estimating τ_u given observation of T_u^t and $\widetilde{\tau}_{T_u^t}$. Notice that in this case the true labels of vertices in T_u^t are not observed.

DEFINITION 5. *The detection problem with side information in the tree is the inference problem of inferring τ_u from the observation of T_u^t and $\widetilde{\tau}_{T_u^t}$. The success probability for an estimator $\widehat{\tau}_u(T_u^t, \widetilde{\tau}_{T_u^t})$ is defined by*

$$q_{T^t}(\widehat{\tau}_u) = \frac{1}{2}\mathbb{P}\left\{\widehat{\tau}_u = +|\tau_u = +\right\} + \frac{1}{2}\mathbb{P}\left\{\widehat{\tau}_u = -|\tau_u = -\right\}.$$

Let $q_{T^t}^*$ denote the optimal success probability.

We remark that the only difference between Definition 4 and Definition 5 is that the exact labels at the boundary of the tree is revealed to estimators in the former and hidden in the latter. The optimal estimator in maximizing q_{T^t} can be also expressed in terms of log likelihood ratio:

$$\widehat{\tau}_{\mathrm{ML}} = 2 \times \mathbf{1}_{\{\Gamma_u^t \geq 0\}} - 1,$$

where

$$\Gamma_i^t \triangleq \frac{1}{2}\log \frac{\mathbb{P}\left\{T_i^t, \widetilde{\tau}_{T_i^t} | \tau_i = +\right\}}{\mathbb{P}\left\{T_i^t, \widetilde{\tau}_{T_i^t} | \tau_i = -\right\}},$$

for all i in T_u. Moreover, the optimal success probability $q_{T^t}^*$ is given by

$$q_{T^t}^* = \frac{1}{2}\mathbb{E}\left[|Y_u^t|\right] + \frac{1}{2}, \tag{7}$$

where magnetization Y_i^t is given by

$$Y_i^t \triangleq \mathbb{P}\left\{\tau_i = +|T_i^t, \widetilde{\tau}_{T_i^t}\right\} - \mathbb{P}\left\{\tau_i = -|T_i^t, \widetilde{\tau}_{T_i^t}\right\}$$

for all i in T_u. Again we have that $\tanh^{-1}(Y_i^t) = \Gamma_i^t$.

The log likelihood ratios and magnetizations can be computed via the belief propagation algorithm. The following lemma gives recursive formula to compute Λ_i^t (Γ_i^t) and X_i^t

(Y_i^t): no approximations are needed. Notice that the Λ_i^t and Γ_i^t satisfy the same recursion but with different initialization; similarly for X_i^t and Y_i^t. Let ∂i denote the set of children of vertex i.

LEMMA 1. *Define $F(x) = \tanh^{-1}\left(\tanh(\beta)\tanh(x)\right)$. Then for $t \geq 1$,*

$$\Lambda_i^t = h_i + \sum_{\ell \in \partial i} F(\Lambda_\ell^{t-1}) \tag{8}$$

$$\Gamma_i^t = h_i + \sum_{\ell \in \partial i} F(\Gamma_\ell^{t-1}), \tag{9}$$

where $\Lambda_i^0 = \infty$ if $\tau_i = +$ and $\Lambda_i^0 = -\infty$ if $\tau_i = -$; $\Gamma_i^0 = \gamma$ if $\tau_i = +$ and $\Gamma_i^0 = -\gamma$ if $\tau_i = -$. It follows that for $t \geq 1$.

$$X_i^t = \frac{e^{h_i}\prod_{\ell \in \partial i}(1 + \theta X_i^{t-1}) - e^{-h_i}\prod_{\ell \in \partial i}(1 - \theta X_i^{t-1})}{e^{h_i}\prod_{\ell \in \partial i}(1 + \theta X_i^{t-1}) + e^{-h_i}\prod_{\ell \in \partial i}(1 - \theta X_i^{t-1})} \tag{10}$$

$$Y_i^t = \frac{e^{h_i}\prod_{\ell \in \partial i}(1 + \theta Y_i^{t-1}) - e^{-h_i}\prod_{\ell \in \partial i}(1 - \theta Y_i^{t-1})}{e^{h_i}\prod_{\ell \in \partial i}(1 + \theta Y_i^{t-1}) + e^{-h_i}\prod_{\ell \in \partial i}(1 - \theta Y_i^{t-1})}, \tag{11}$$

where $X_i^0 = 1$ if $\tau_i = +$ and $X_i^0 = -1$ if $\tau_i = -$; $Y_i^0 = 1 - 2\alpha$ if $\tau_i = +$ and $Y_i^0 = 2\alpha - 1$ if $\tau_i = -$.

As a corollary of Lemma 1, Λ_u is monotone with respect to the boundary conditions. For any vertex i in T_u, let

$$\Lambda_i^t(\xi) \triangleq \frac{1}{2}\log\frac{\mathbb{P}\left\{T_i^t, \tau_{\partial T_i^t} = \xi, \widetilde{\tau}_{T_i^t} | \tau_i = +\right\}}{\mathbb{P}\left\{T_i^t, \tau_{\partial T_i^t} = \xi, \widetilde{\tau}_{T_i^t} | \tau_i = -\right\}},$$

where $\xi \in \{\pm\}^{|\partial T_i^t|}$.

COROLLARY 1. *Fix any vertex i in T_u and $t \geq 1$. If the boundary conditions ξ and $\widehat{\xi}$ are such that $\widehat{\xi}_\ell \geq \xi_\ell$ for all $\ell \in \partial T_i^t$, then $\Lambda_i^t(\widehat{\xi}) \geq \Lambda_i^t(\xi)$ for $a \geq b$ and $\Lambda_i^t(\widehat{\xi}) \leq \Lambda_i^t(\xi)$ otherwise. In particular, $\Lambda_i^t(\xi)$ is maximized for $a \geq b$ and minimized for $a \leq b$, when $\xi_\ell = +$ for all $\ell \in \partial T_i^t$.*

3.1 Connection between the graph problem and tree problems

For the detection problem on graph, recall that $p_{G_n}(\widehat{\sigma}_{\mathrm{BP}}^t)$ denote the estimation accuracy of $\widehat{\sigma}_{\mathrm{BP}}^t$ as per (1); $p_{G_n}^*$ is the optimal estimation accuracy. For the detection problems on tree, recall that $p_{T^t}^*$ is the optimal estimation accuracy of estimating τ_u based on T_u^t, $\widetilde{\tau}_{T_u^t}$, and $\tau_{\partial T_u^t}$ as per (6); $q_{T^t}^*$ is the optimal estimation accuracy of estimating τ_u based on T_u^t and $\widetilde{\tau}_{T_u^t}$ as per (7). In this section, we show that $p_{G_n}(\widehat{\sigma}_{\mathrm{BP}}^t)$ equals to $q_{T^t}^*$ asymptotically, and $p_{G_n}^*$ is bounded by $p_{T^t}^*$ from above for any $t \geq 1$. Notice that the dependency of $q_{T^t}^*$ and $p_{T^t}^*$ on n is only through the dependency of a and b on n. Hence, if a and b are fixed constants, then both $q_{T^t}^*$ and $p_{T^t}^*$ do not depend on n.

A key ingredient is to show G is locally tree-like in the regime $a = n^{o(1)}$. Let G_u^t denote the subgraph of G induced by vertices whose distance to u is at most t and let ∂G_u^t denote the set of vertices whose distance from u is precisely t. With a bit abuse of notation, let σ_A denote the vector consisting of labels of vertices in A, where A could be either a set of vertices or a subgraph in G. Similarly we define $\widetilde{\sigma}_A$. The following lemma proved in [39] shows that we can construct a coupling such that $(G^t, \sigma_{G^t}, \widetilde{\sigma}_{G^t}) = (T^t, \tau_{T^t}, \widetilde{\tau}_{T^t})$ with probability converging to 1 when $a^t = n^{o(1)}$.

LEMMA 2. *For $t = t(n)$ such that $a^t = n^{o(1)}$, there exists a coupling between $(G, \sigma, \widetilde{\sigma})$ and $(T, \tau, \widetilde{\tau})$ such that with probability converging to 1,*

$$(G^t, \sigma_{G^t}, \widetilde{\sigma}_{G^t}) = (T^t, \tau_{T^t}, \widetilde{\tau}_{T^t}).$$

In the following, for ease of notation, we write T_u^t as T^t and G_u^t as G^t when there is no ambiguity. Suppose that $(G^t, \sigma_{G^t}, \widetilde{\sigma}_{G^t}) = (T^t, \tau_{T^t}, \widetilde{\tau}_{T^t})$, then by comparing BP iterations (4) and (5) with the recursions of log likelihood ratio Γ^t (9), we find that R_u^t exactly equals to Γ_u^t. In other words, when local neighborhood of u is a tree, the BP algorithm defined in Algorithm 1 exactly computes the log likelihood ratio Γ_u^t for the tree model. Building upon this intuition, the following lemma shows that $p_{G_n}(\widehat{\sigma}_{\mathrm{BP}}^t)$ equals to $q_{T^t}^*$ asymptotically.

LEMMA 3. *For $t = t(n)$ such that $a^t = n^{o(1)}$,*

$$\lim_{n\to\infty} |p_{G_n}(\widehat{\sigma}_{\mathrm{BP}}) - q_{T^t}^*| = 0.$$

We are going to show that as $n \to \infty$, $p_{G_n}^*$ is bounded by $p_{T^t}^*$ from above for any $t \geq 1$. Before that, we need a key lemma which shows that conditional on $(G^t, \widetilde{\sigma}_{G^t}, \sigma_{\partial G^t})$, σ_u is almost independent of the graph structure and noisy labels outside of G^t.

LEMMA 4. *For $t = t(n)$ such that $a^t = n^{o(1)}$, there exists a sequence of events $\mathcal{E}_n$ such that $\mathbb{P}\{\mathcal{E}_n\} \to 1$ as $n \to \infty$, and on event $\mathcal{E}_n$, for all $x \in \{\pm\}$,*

$$\mathbb{P}\{\sigma_u = x | G^t, \widetilde{\sigma}_{G^t}, \sigma_{\partial G^t}\} = (1 + o(1))\mathbb{P}\{\sigma_u = x | G, \widetilde{\sigma}, \sigma_{\partial G^t}\}. \tag{12}$$

Moreover, on event $\mathcal{E}_n$, $(G^t, \sigma_{G^t}, \widetilde{\sigma}_{G^t}) = (T^t, \tau_{T^t}, \widetilde{\tau}_{T^t})$ holds.

LEMMA 5. *For $t = t(n)$ such that $a^t = n^{o(1)}$,*

$$\limsup_{n\to\infty}(p_{G_n}^* - p_{T^t}^*) \leq 0.$$

The following is a simple corollary of Lemma 3 and Lemma 5.

COROLLARY 2. *For $t = t(n)$ such that $a^t = n^{o(1)}$,*

$$\limsup_{n\to\infty} (p_{G_n}^* - p_{G_n}(\widehat{\sigma}_{\mathrm{BP}})) \leq \limsup_{n\to\infty} (p_{T^t}^* - q_{T^t}^*).$$

The above corollary implies that $\widehat{\sigma}_{\mathrm{BP}}^t$ achieves the optimal estimation accuracy $p_{G_n}^*$ asymptotically, provided that $p_{T^t}^* - q_{T^t}^*$ converges to 0, or equivalently, $\mathbb{E}\left[|X_u^t - Y_u^t|\right]$ converges to 0. Notice that the only difference between $p_{T^t}^*$ and $q_{T^t}^*$ is that in the former, exact label information is revealed at the boundary of T^t, while in the latter, only noisy label information at level t is available. In the next three sections, we provide three different sufficient conditions under which $\mathbb{E}\left[|X_u^t - Y_u^t|\right]$ converges to 0, yielding Theorem 1.

4. OPTIMALITY OF LOCAL BELIEF PROPAGATION

Recall that Λ_u^t is a function of $\tau_{\partial T_u^t}$, i.e., the labels of vertices at the boundary of T_u^t. Let $\Lambda_u^t(+)$ denote Λ_u^t with the labels of vertices at the boundary of T_u^t all equal to $+$. Similarly define $\Lambda_u^t(-)$. The following lemma shows that Λ_u^t is asymptotically independent of $\tau_{\partial T_u^t}$ as $t \to \infty$ if $|a-b| < 2$.

LEMMA 6. *For all $t \geq 0$, let*

$$e(t + 1) = \mathbb{E}\left[|\Lambda_u^{t+1}(+) - \Lambda_u^{t+1}(-)|\right].$$

Then

$$e(t + 1) \leq e(1)\left(|\tanh(\beta)|d\right)^t,$$

where $e(1) = 2\beta d$ and $d = (a + b)/2$.

Lemma 6 immediately implies the following theorem.

THEOREM 3. *If $|a - b| < 2$, then*

$$\lim_{t\to\infty} \limsup_{n\to\infty} \mathbb{E}\left[|X_u^t - Y_u^t|\right] = 0.$$

Recall that $d = (a + b)/2$ and $\beta = \frac{1}{2}\log\frac{a}{b}$. We introduce the notation $\theta = \tanh(\beta)$ and $\eta = (1 - \theta)/2$. Let $\mathbb{E}^+[X]$ and $\mathbb{E}^-[X]$ denote the expectation of X conditional on $\tau_u = +$ and $\tau_u = -$, respectively. The following theorem shows that if $(a - b)^2/(a + b)$ is sufficiently large, then local BP is optimal.

THEOREM 4. *There exists a constant C depending only on c_0 given in (3) such that if $(a - b)^2 \geq C(a + b)$, then*

$$\lim_{t\to\infty} \limsup_{n\to\infty} \mathbb{E}\left[|X_u^t - Y_u^t|\right] = 0.$$

The proof of Theorem 4 is divided into three steps. Firstly, we show that if $\theta^2 d = \frac{(a-b)^2}{2(a+b)}$ is large, then $\mathbb{E}^+[X_u^t]$ and $\mathbb{E}^+[Y_u^t]$ are close to 1 for all sufficiently large t. This result allows us to analyze the recursions (10) and (11) by assuming $\mathbb{E}^+[X_u^t]$ and $\mathbb{E}^+[Y_u^t]$ are close to 1. Secondly, we show that when $|\theta|$ is small, the recursion of $\mathbb{E}\left[(X_u^t - Y_u^t)^2\right]$ is a contraction:

$$\mathbb{E}\left[(X_u^{t+1} - Y_u^{t+1})^2\right] \leq \sqrt{\alpha(1-\alpha)}\mathbb{E}\left[(X_u^t - Y_u^t)^2\right].$$

Finally, we prove that when $|\theta|$ is large, the recursion of $\mathbb{E}\left[\sqrt{|X_u^t - Y_u^t|}\right]$ is also a contraction:

$$\mathbb{E}\left[\sqrt{|X_u^{t+1} - Y_u^{t+1}|}\right] \leq \sqrt{\alpha(1-\alpha)}\mathbb{E}\left[\sqrt{|X_u^t - Y_u^t|}\right].$$

The partition of analysis of recursions into small $|\theta|$ and large $|\theta|$ cases, and the study of different moments of $|X_u^t - Y_u^t|$, are related to the fact that for different values of θ we expect the distributions of X_u^t and Y_u^t correspond to different power-laws. When θ is small, we have many small contributions from neighbors and therefore it is expected that X_u^t and $Y_u^t|$ will have thin tails. When θ is large, we have a few large contributions from neighbors and we therefore expect fat tails.

The following theorem shows that local BP is optimal if the side information is very accurate. Its proof is similar to the proof of Theorem 4.

THEOREM 5. *There exists a constant $0 < \alpha^* < 1/2$ depending only on c_0 given in (3) such that if $\alpha \leq \alpha^*$, then*

$$\lim_{t\to\infty} \limsup_{n\to\infty} \mathbb{E}\left[|X_u^t - Y_u^t|\right] = 0.$$

The excluded proofs can be found in the arXiv version of the paper [41].

5. DENSITY EVOLUTION IN THE LARGE DEGREE REGIME

In this section, we consider the regime (3) and further assume that as $n \to \infty$,

$$a \to \infty \qquad \frac{a-b}{\sqrt{b}} \to \mu,$$

where μ is a fixed constant. For $t \geq 1$, define

$$\Phi_u^t = \sum_{\ell \in \partial u} F(\Phi_\ell^{t-1} + h_\ell), \qquad (13)$$

$$\Psi_u^t = \sum_{\ell \in \partial u} F(\Psi_\ell^{t-1} + h_\ell), \qquad (14)$$

where $\Phi_u^0 = \infty$ if $\tau_u = +$ and $\Phi_u^0 = -\infty$ if $\tau_u = -$; $\Psi_u^0 = 0$ for all u. Then $\Lambda_u^t = \Phi_u^t + h_u$ and $\Gamma_u^t = \Psi_u^t + h_u$ for all $t \geq 0$. Notice that subtrees $\{T_\ell^t\}_{\ell \in \partial u}$ are independent and identically distributed conditional on τ_u. Thus $\{\Phi_\ell^{t-1}\}_{\ell \in \partial u}$ ($\{\Psi_\ell^{t-1}\}_{\ell \in \partial u}$) are independent and identically distributed conditional on τ_u. As a consequence, when the expected degree of u tends to infinity, due to the central limit theorem, we expect that the distribution of Φ_u^t (Ψ_u^t) conditional on τ_u is approximately Gaussian.

Let W_+^t (Z_+^t) denote a random variable that has the same distribution as Φ_u^t (Ψ_u^t) conditional on $\tau_u = +$, and W_-^t (Z_-^t) denote a random variable that has the same distribution as Φ_u^t (Ψ_u^t) conditional on $\tau_u = -$. The following lemma shows that the distributions of W_+^t (Z_+^t) and W_-^t (Z_-^t) are asymptotically Gaussian.

LEMMA 7. *Suppose* $\alpha \in (0, 1/2]$ *is fixed. Let* $h(v) = \mathbb{E}[\tanh(v + \sqrt{v}Z + U)]$, *where* $Z \sim \mathcal{N}(0,1)$ *and* $U = \gamma$ *with probability* $1 - \alpha$ *and* $U = -\gamma$ *with probability* α, *where* $\gamma = \frac{1}{2}\log\frac{1-\alpha}{\alpha}$. *Define* $(v_t : t \geq 0)$ *recursively by* $v_0 = 0$ *and* $v_{t+1} = \frac{\mu^2}{4}h(v_t)$. *For any fixed* $t \geq 0$, *as* $n \to \infty$,

$$\sup_x \left| \mathbb{P}\left\{ \frac{Z_{\pm}^t \mp v_t}{\sqrt{v_t}} \leq x \right\} - \mathbb{P}\{Z \leq x\} \right| = O(a^{-1/2}). \quad (15)$$

Define $(w_t : t \geq 1)$ *recursively by* $w_1 = \mu^2/4$ *and* $w_{t+1} = \frac{\mu^2}{4}h(w_t)$. *For any fixed* $t \geq 1$, *as* $n \to \infty$,

$$\sup_x \left| \mathbb{P}\left\{ \frac{W_{\pm}^t \mp w_t}{\sqrt{w_t}} \leq x \right\} - \mathbb{P}\{Z \leq x\} \right| = O(a^{-1/2}). \quad (16)$$

We are about to prove Theorem 2 based on Lemma 7. Before that, we need a lemma showing that h is monotone.

LEMMA 8. $h(v)$ *is continuous on* $[0, \infty)$ *and* $0 \leq h'(v) \leq 1$ *for* $v \in (0, +\infty)$.

PROOF OF THEOREM 2. In view of Lemma 7,

$$\lim_{n \to \infty} \mathbb{P}\left\{ \Gamma_u^t \geq 0 | \tau_u = - \right\}$$

$$= \lim_{n \to \infty} \mathbb{P}\left\{ \Gamma_u^t \leq 0 | \tau_u = + \right\}$$

$$= (1 - \alpha)Q\left(\frac{v_t + \gamma}{\sqrt{v_t}}\right) + \alpha Q\left(\frac{v_t - \gamma}{\sqrt{v_t}}\right).$$

Hence, it follows from Lemma 3 that

$$\lim_{n \to \infty} p_{G_n}(\widehat{\sigma}_{\text{BP}}^t) = \lim_{n \to \infty} q_{T^t}^* = 1 - \mathbb{E}\left[Q\left(\frac{v_t + U}{\sqrt{v_t}}\right)\right].$$

We prove that $v_{t+1} \geq v_t$ for $t \geq 0$ by induction. Recall that $v_0 = 0 \leq v_1 = (1-2\alpha)^2\mu^2/4 = \mu^2 h(v_0)/4$. Suppose

$v_{t+1} \geq v_t$ holds; we shall show the claim also holds for $t+1$. In particular, since h is continuous on $[0, \infty)$ and differential on $(0, \infty)$, it follows from the mean value theorem that

$$v_{t+2} - v_{t+1} = \frac{\mu^2}{4}\left(h(v_{t+1}) - h(v_t)\right) = \frac{\mu^2}{4}h'(x),$$

for some $x \in (v_t, v_{t+1})$. Lemma 8 implies that $h'(x) \geq 0$ for $x \in (0, \infty)$, it follows that $v_{t+2} \geq v_{t+1}$. Hence, v_t is non-decreasing in t. Next we argue that $v_t \leq \underline{v}$ for all $t \geq 0$ by induction, where $\underline{v}$ is the smallest fixed point of $v = \frac{\mu^2}{4}h(v)$. For the base case, $v_0 = 0 \leq \underline{v}$. If $v_t \leq \underline{v}$, then by the monotonicity of h, $v_{t+1} = \frac{\mu^2}{4}h(v_t) \leq \frac{\mu^2}{4}h(\underline{v}) = \underline{v}$. Thus, $\lim_{t \to \infty} v_t$ exists and $\lim_{t \to \infty} v_t = \underline{v}$. Therefore,

$$\lim_{t \to \infty} \lim_{n \to \infty} p_{G_n}(\widehat{\sigma}_{\text{BP}}^t) = \lim_{t \to \infty} \lim_{n \to \infty} q_{T^t}^* = 1 - \mathbb{E}\left[Q\left(\frac{\underline{v} + U}{\sqrt{\underline{v}}}\right)\right].$$

Next, we prove the claim for $p_{G_n}^*$. In view of Lemma 7,

$$\lim_{n \to \infty} \mathbb{P}\left\{ \Lambda_u^t \geq 0 | \tau_u = - \right\}$$

$$= \lim_{n \to \infty} \mathbb{P}\left\{ \Lambda_u^t \leq 0 | \tau_u = + \right\}$$

$$= (1 - \alpha)Q\left(\frac{w_t + \gamma}{\sqrt{w_t}}\right) + \alpha Q\left(\frac{w_t - \gamma}{\sqrt{w_t}}\right).$$

Hence, it follows from Lemma 5 that

$$\limsup_{n \to \infty} p_{G_n}^* \leq \lim_{n \to \infty} p_{T^t}^* = 1 - \mathbb{E}\left[Q\left(\frac{w_t + U}{\sqrt{w_t}}\right)\right].$$

Recall that $w_1 = \mu^2/4 \geq w_t$. By the same argument of proving v_t is non-decreasing, one can show that w_t is non-increasing in t. Also, by the same argument of proving v_t is upper bounded by $\underline{v}$, one can show that w_t is lower bounded by $\overline{v}$, where $\overline{v}$ is the largest fixed point of $v = \frac{\mu^2}{4}h(v)$. Thus, $\lim_{t \to \infty} w_t$ exists and $\lim_{t \to \infty} w_t = \overline{v}$. Therefore,

$$\lim_{t \to \infty} \limsup_{n \to \infty} p_{G_n}^* \leq \lim_{t \to \infty} \lim_{n \to \infty} p_{T^t}^* = 1 - \mathbb{E}\left[Q\left(\frac{\overline{v} + U}{\sqrt{\overline{v}}}\right)\right].$$

Finally, notice that

$$w_{t+1} - v_{t+1} = \frac{\mu^2}{4}\left(h(w_t) - h(v_t)\right) \leq \frac{\mu^2}{4}(w_t - v_t),$$

where the last inequality holds because $0 \leq h'(x) \leq 1$. If $|\mu| < 2$, then $\mu^2/4 \leq 1 - \epsilon$ for some $\epsilon > 0$. Hence, $(w_{t+1} - v_{t+1}) \leq (1-\epsilon)(w_t - v_t)$. Since $w_1 - v_1 = \mu^2 \alpha(1-\alpha)$, it follows that $\lim_{t \to \infty}(w_t - v_t) = 0$ and thus $\underline{v} = \overline{v}$. If instead $|\mu| \geq C$ for some sufficiently large constant C or $\alpha \leq \alpha^*$ for some sufficiently small constant $0 < \alpha^* < 1/2$, then it follows from Theorem 4 and Theorem 5 that $\lim_{t \to \infty} \lim_{n \to \infty} p_{T^t}^* = \lim_{t \to \infty} \lim_{n \to \infty} q_{T^t}^*$. As a consequence, $\underline{v} = \overline{v}$. $\square$

6. ACKNOWLEDGMENTS

Research supported by NSF grant CCF 1320105, DOD ONR grant N00014-14-1-0823, and grant 328025 from the Simons Foundation.

7. REFERENCES

[1] E. Abbe, A. S. Bandeira, and G. Hall. Exact recovery in the stochastic block model. arXiv 1405.3267, October 2014.

[2] E. Abbe and C. Sandon. Community detection in general stochastic block models: fundamental limits and efficient recovery algorithms. *arXiv 1503.00609*, March, 2015.

[3] A. E. Allahverdyan, G. Ver Steeg, and A. Galstyan. Community detection with and without prior information. *Europhysics Letters*, 90:18002, 2010.

[4] A. Anandkumar, R. Ge, D. Hsu, and S. M. Kakade. A tensor spectral approach to learning mixed membership community models. *Journal of Machine Learning Research*, 15:2239–2312, June 2014.

[5] A. Bandeira. Random Laplacian matrices and convex relaxations. arXiv 1504.03987, April, 2015.

[6] S. Basu, A. Banerjee, and R. J. Mooney. Semi-supervised clustering by seeding. In *ICML*, volume 2, pages 27–34, 2002.

[7] S. Basu, M. Bilenko, and R. J. Mooney. A probabilistic framework for semi-supervised clustering. In *Proceedings of the tenth ACM SIGKDD international conference on Knowledge discovery and data mining*, pages 59–68. ACM, 2004.

[8] P. J. Bickel and A. Chen. A nonparametric view of network models and Newman-Girvan and other modularities. *Proceedings of the National Academy of Science*, 106(50):21068–21073, 2009.

[9] C. Bordenave, M. Lelarge, and L. Massoulié. Non-backtracking spectrum of random graphs: community detection and non-regular Ramanujan graphs. ArXiv 1501.06087, January 2015.

[10] T. Cai and X. Li. Robust and computationally feasible community detection in the presence of arbitrary outlier nodes. *arXiv preprint arXiv:1404.6000*, 2014.

[11] O. Chapelle, J. Weston, and B. Schoelkopf. Cluster kernels for semi-supervised learning. In *NIPS*, pages 585–592, 2002.

[12] Y. Chen, S. Sanghavi, and H. Xu. Improved graph clustering. *IEEE Transactions on Information Theory. An earlier version of this work appeared under the title "Clustering Sparse Graphs" at NIPS 2012*, 60(10):6440–6455, Oct 2014.

[13] Y. Chen and J. Xu. Statistical-computational tradeoffs in planted problems and submatrix localization with a growing number of clusters and submatrices. In *Proceedings of ICML 2014 (Also arXiv:1402.1267)*, Feb 2014.

[14] A. Coja-Oghlan. A spectral heuristic for bisecting random graphs. In *Proceedings of the sixteenth annual ACM-SIAM symposium on Discrete algorithms*, SODA '05, pages 850–859, Philadelphia, PA, USA, 2005. Society for Industrial and Applied Mathematics.

[15] A. Coja-Oghlan. Graph partitioning via adaptive spectral techniques. *Comb. Probab. Comput.*, 19(2):227–284, March 2010.

[16] A. Condon and R. M. Karp. Algorithms for graph partitioning on the planted partition model. *Random Structures and Algorithms*, 18(2):116–140, 2001.

[17] A. Decelle, F. Krzakala, C. Moore, and L. Zdeborová. Asymptotic analysis of the stochastic block model for modular networks and its algorithmic applications. *Phys. Rev. E*, 84:066106, Dec 2011.

[18] A. Decelle, F. Krzakala, C. Moore, and L. Zdeborová. Inference and phase transitions in the detection of modules in sparse networks. *Phys. Rev. Lett.*, 107:065701, 2011.

[19] M. E. Dyer and A. M. Frieze. The solution of some random NP-hard problems in polynomial expected time. *Journal of Algorithms*, 10(4):451–489, 1989.

[20] D. Gamarnik and M. Sudan. Limits of local algorithms over sparse random graphs. In *Proceedings of the 5th conference on Innovations in theoretical computer science*, pages 369–376. ACM, 2014.

[21] C. Gao, Z. Ma, A. Y. Zhang, and H. H. Zhou. Achieving optimal misclassification proportion in stochastic block model. *arXiv:1505.03772*, 2015.

[22] O. Guédon and R. Vershynin. Community detection in sparse networks via grothendieck's inequality. *Probability Theory and Related Fields*, pages 1–25, 2015.

[23] B. Hajek, Y. Wu, and J. Xu. Achieving exact cluster recovery threshold via semidefinite programming. arXiv1 412.6156, Nov. 2014.

[24] B. Hajek, Y. Wu, and J. Xu. Achieving exact cluster recovery threshold via semidefinite programming: Extensions. *arXiv:1502.07738*, 2015.

[25] B. Hajek, Y. Wu, and J. Xu. Recovering a hidden community beyond the spectral limit in $O(|E| \log^* |V|)$ time. arXiv 1510.02786, October 2015.

[26] H. Hatami, L. Lovász, and B. Szegedy. Limits of local-global convergent graph sequences. *arXiv preprint arXiv:1205.4356*, 2012.

[27] P. W. Holland, K. B. Laskey, and S. Leinhardt. Stochastic blockmodels: First steps. *Social Networks*, 5(2):109–137, 1983.

[28] M. Jerrum and G. B. Sorkin. The Metropolis algorithm for graph bisection. *Discrete Applied Mathematics*, 82(1–3):155–175, 1998.

[29] V. Kanade, E. Mossel, and T. Schramm. Global and local information in clustering labeled block models. *In Proceedings of Approximation, Randomization, and Combinatorial Optimization. Algorithms and Techniques*, pages 779–810, 2014.

[30] H. Kesten and B. P. Stigum. Additional limit theorems for indecomposable multidimensional Galton-Watson processes. *Ann. Math. Statist.*, 37:1463–1481, 1966.

[31] R. Lyons and F. Nazarov. Perfect matchings as iid factors on non-amenable groups. *European Journal of Combinatorics*, 32(7):1115–1125, 2011.

[32] L. Massoulié. Community detection thresholds and the weak Ramanujan property. In *Proceedings of the Symposium on the Theory of Computation (STOC)*, 2014.

[33] F. McSherry. Spectral partitioning of random graphs. In *Proceedings of IEEE Conference on the Foundations of Computer Science (FOCS)*, pages 529–537, 2001.

[34] M. Mezard and A. Montanari. *Information, Physics, and Computation*. Oxford University Press, Inc., New York, NY, USA, 2009.

[35] A. Montanari. Finding one community in a sparse random graph. arXiv 1502.05680, Feb 2015.

[36] E. Mossel, J. Neeman, and A. Sly. Belief propogation, robust reconstruction, and optimal recovery of block models. arXiv 1309.1380, 2013.

[37] E. Mossel, J. Neeman, and A. Sly. A proof of the block model threshold conjecture. arXiv 1311.4115, 2013.

[38] E. Mossel, J. Neeman, and A. Sly. Consistency thresholds for the planted bisection model. In *Proceedings of the Forty-Seventh Annual ACM on Symposium on Theory of Computing*, STOC '15, pages 69–75, New York, NY, USA, 2015. ACM.

[39] E. Mossel, J. Neeman, and A. Sly. Reconstruction and estimation in the planted partition model. To appear in Probability Theory and Related Fields. The Arxiv version of this paper is titled Stochastic Block Models and Reconstruction, 2015.

[40] E. Mossel and J. Xu. Density evolution in the degree-correlated stochastic block model. *arXiv:1509.03281*, Sept. 2015.

[41] E. Mossel and J. Xu. Local algorithms for block models with side information. In *Accepted to The 7th Innovations in Theoretical Computer Science (ITCS) conference. arXiv:1508.02344*, 2015.

[42] M. J. Newman and A. Clauset. Structure and inference in annotated networks. *arXiv:1507.04001*, July, 2015.

[43] W. Perry and A. S. Wein. A semidefinite program for unbalanced multisection in the stochastic block model. *arXiv:1507.05605v1*, 2015.

[44] M. Rahman and B. Virag. Local algorithms for independent sets are half-optimal. arXiv preprint arXiv:1402.0485, 2014.

[45] T. Richardson and R. Urbanke. *Modern Coding Theory*. Cambridge University Press, 2008. Cambridge Books Online.

[46] T. A. B. Snijders and K. Nowicki. Estimation and prediction for stochastic blockmodels for graphs with latent block structure. *Journal of Classification*, 14(1):75–100, 1997.

[47] G. Ver Steeg, C. Moore, A. Galstyan, and A. E. Allahverdyan. Phase transitions in community detection: A solvable toy model. arXiv 1312.0631, 2013.

[48] S. Yun and A. Proutiere. Community detection via random and adaptive sampling. In *Proceedings of The 27th Conference on Learning Theory*, 2014.

[49] S.-Y. Yun and A. Proutiere. Accurate community detection in the stochastic block model via spectral algorithms. arXiv 1412.7335, 2014.

[50] A. Y. Zhang and H. H. Zhou. Minimax rates of community detection in stochastic block models. *arXiv:1507.05313*, 2015.

[51] P. Zhang, F. Krzakala, J. Reichardt, and L. Zdeborová. Comparitive study for inference of hidden classes in stochastic block models. *Journal of Statistical Mechanics : Theory and Experiment*, 2012.

[52] P. Zhang, C. Moore, and L. Zdeborová. Phase transitions in semisupervised clustering of sparse networks. *Phys. Rev. E*, 90:052802, Nov 2014.

Distribution Design

Amos Beimel
Dept. of Computer Science
Ben Gurion University
amos.beimel@gmail.com

Ariel Gabizon
Dept. of Computer Science
Technion
ariel.gabizon@gmail.com

Yuval Ishai
Dept. of Computer Science
Technion and UCLA
yuvali@cs.technion.ac.il

Eyal Kushilevitz
Dept. of Computer Science
Technion
eyalk@cs.technion.ac.il

ABSTRACT

Motivated by applications in cryptography, we introduce and study the problem of *distribution design*. The goal of distribution design is to find a joint distribution on n random variables that satisfies a given set of constraints on the marginal distributions. Each constraint can either require that two sequences of variables be identically distributed or, alternatively, that the two sequences have disjoint supports. We present several positive and negative results on the existence and efficiency of solutions for a given set of constraints.

Distribution design can be seen as a strict generalization of several well-studied problems in cryptography. These include secret sharing, garbling schemes, and non-interactive protocols for secure multiparty computation. We further motivate the problem and our results by demonstrating their usefulness towards realizing non-interactive protocols for *ad-hoc* secure multiparty computation, in which any subset of the parties may choose to participate and the identity of the participants should remain hidden to the extent possible.

Keywords

Secret sharing, secure multiparty computation, obfuscation, garbling schemes, multi-input functional encryption.

1. INTRODUCTION

Several questions in cryptography, including ones related to secret sharing [13, 4] and secure multiparty computation (MPC) [16, 8], call for the design of probability spaces with special properties. Such a probability space can often be described as a joint probability distribution $(X_1, X_2, \ldots, X_n)$ that satisfies a given set of constraints on the marginal distributions. Each constraint can either be an *equality constraint* of the form $(X_{i_1}, \ldots, X_{i_d}) \equiv (X_{i'_1}, \ldots, X_{i'_d})$, in which case the two distributions should be identical, or a *disjointness constraint* of the form $(X_{i_1}, \ldots, X_{i_d}) \| (X_{i'_1}, \ldots, X_{i'_d})$, in

Permission to make digital or hard copies of all or part of this work for personal or classroom use is granted without fee provided that copies are not made or distributed for profit or commercial advantage and that copies bear this notice and the full citation on the first page. Copyrights for components of this work owned by others than the author(s) must be honored. Abstracting with credit is permitted. To copy otherwise, or republish, to post on servers or to redistribute to lists, requires prior specific permission and/or a fee. Request permissions from Permissions@acm.org.

ITCS'16, January 14–16, 2016, Cambridge, MA, USA.
Copyright is held by the owner/author(s). Publication rights licensed to ACM.
ACM 978-1-4503-4057-1/16/01 ...$15.00.
DOI: http://dx.doi.org/10.1145/2840728.2840759 .

which case the two distributions should have disjoint supports. We will later consider a computational version of the problem in which equality is relaxed to computational indistinguishability.

As an example, consider the problem of sharing a secret $s \in \{0, 1\}$ between k parties, such that every t parties learn nothing about the secret and every $t + 1$ parties can reconstruct the secret from their shares. This problem can be formulated as that of designing a joint distribution on $n = 2k$ variables X_i^b, for $1 \le i \le k$ and $b \in \{0, 1\}$, where $(X_1^0, \ldots, X_k^0)$ represent the shares of $s = 0$ and $(X_1^1, \ldots, X_k^1)$ represent the shares of $s = 1$. The secrecy requirement can be expressed by a set of equality constraints of the form $X_T^0 \equiv X_T^1$ for all $T \subseteq [k]$ of size t. The reconstruction requirement can be expressed by a set of disjointness constraints of the form $X_T^0 \| X_T^1$ for all $T \subseteq [k]$ of size $t + 1$.

Other than secret sharing, several additional cryptographic primitives can be viewed as special cases of distribution design. These include: (1) k-party private simultaneous messages (PSM) protocols [5], which correspond to the special case where the variable set is partitioned into k parts and each sequence of variables involves exactly one variable from each part; (2) information-theoretic garbling schemes [16, 10, 3], which can be viewed as a special type of PSM protocols; (3) robust protocols for non-interactive secure multiparty computation (NIMPC) [2], an information-theoretic variant of multi-input functional encryption [9] that strengthens PSM protocols by imposing additional secrecy requirements; and (4) an information-theoretic variant of the notion of functional secret sharing from [11].

The above special cases only capture a small fragment of all distribution design instances that can be specified by a set of constraints. In fact, even general "graph-based" constraints, which only involve a pair of variables in each side, are not covered by any prior work we are aware of.

1.1 Our Contribution

We initiate a systematic study of the problem of distribution design. We address the following natural questions: (1) Which sets of constraints admit a solution? (2) What is the computational complexity of deciding whether a solution exists? (3) How efficient can the solutions be?

We give a simple answer to the first question: a set of constraints can be realized if and only if a natural closure of the equality constraints does not contradict any of the disjointness constraints. For the other questions we obtain partial answers, proving both positive and negative results. We now give a more detailed overview of the results.

We consider two special cases of the general problem that are of particular interest. A *projective* set of constraints is one where the constraints are restricted to be of the form $X_S \equiv X_{S'}$ or $X_S \| X_{S'}$ for *sets* $S, S' \subset [n]$. That is, in such constraints each variable sequence is sorted according to the variable indices. For instance, $(X_1, X_2, X_3) \equiv (X_2, X_3, X_1)$ is a non-projective constraint. All of the above examples for distribution designs that arise in cryptography are projective. A *d-homogenous* set of constraints is one where all sequences have the same length d. Among the above examples, the constraints corresponding to PSM protocols and garbling schemes are homogenous, whereas those corresponding to secret sharing schemes and NIMPC protocols are not homogenous.

It will be convenient to describe the efficiency of our solutions by only referring to the *share size*, defined as the maximal bit-length of a variable (i.e., $\max_i \lceil \log_2 |\text{support}(X_i)| \rceil$), with the implicit understanding that the distribution can be sampled in time polynomial in this share size, the number of variables n, and the number of constraints m.

We obtain the following main results.

The projective case. In the case of projective constraints, we show that a solution exists if and only if the closure of the equality constraints defined by the following generation rules does not contradict any disjointness constraint. The generation rules include the natural symmetric and transitive rules (e.g., $X_A \equiv X_B$ and $X_B \equiv X_C$ generate $X_A \equiv X_C$) as well as the following projection rule: $X_A \equiv X_B$, where A and B are viewed as sequences of length d, generate $X_{A_I} \equiv X_{B_I}$ for every $I \subseteq [d]$. That is, one can remove from both sides of an equality constraint variables occurring in the same set of locations.

When the set of projective constraints is d-homogenous, this implies a simple polynomial-time algorithm for deciding whether a solution exists. In case it does exist, the share size of our construction is $O(md \log n)$ bits. Our construction enjoys two other properties that are useful for applications: it is *d-symmetric* in the sense that the joint distribution of every d variables is invariant under permutations, and it is $(d-1)$-*secret* in the sense that the joint distribution of every $d-1$ variables is the same. On the other hand, when the set of constraints is not homogenous, it is PSPACE-complete to decide whether a solution exists. In case it does exist, the share size of our construction is $O(2^t mn)$, where t is an upper bound on the number of variables appearing in a single constraint. Thus, the non-homogenous case appears to be qualitatively harder (at least from a computational point of view) than the homogenous case.

The general case. The case of non-projective sets of constraints, where the variables may appear in different orders (e.g., $(X_1, X_2, X_3) \equiv (X_3, X_1, X_2)$), is somewhat more involved. First, as in the projective case, we can characterize the existence of solutions using a natural closure of the equality constraints. In addition to the generation rules mentioned above, we add the following additional rule: if A, B are sequences of length d, then $X_A \equiv X_B$ generates $X_{\pi(A)} \equiv X_{\pi(B)}$ for every permutation $\pi : [d] \to [d]$.

If the m constraints are d-homogenous then, as in the projective case, we show a polynomial-time algorithm for deciding whether a solution exists. However, in contrast to the projective case, here the share size of our construction

is super-polynomial and is bounded by $n^{O(d^2)}$. For non-homogenous sets of general constraints, we have a $2^{O(n)}$-time algorithm to decide whether a solution exists (as in the projective case, the decision problem is PSPACE-complete), and the share size of the construction is $n^{O(n^2)}$.

Implicitly represented constraints. Up to this point, we assumed that a set of m constraints is given explicitly. However, for cryptographic applications it is often useful to consider an exponentially large number of constraints that are succinctly described by some implicit representation. More concretely, we assume that the constraints are implicitly represented by a circuit C that, given a sequence of n variable indices, either outputs a positive integer, representing an equivalence class, or 0, representing "don't care." (In the projective case, the input can be just an n-bit characteristic vector of a set.) If C has the same nonzero output on two sequences, the corresponding distributions are required to be (either perfectly or computationally) indistinguishable, whereas if C has different nonzero outputs the distributions should be efficiently distinguishable. In fact, we require the existence of an efficient decoder that recovers an identifier of the equivalence class given a sample from a distribution.

We present an efficient algorithm that, given such an implicit representation of a *projective* set of constraints, can efficiently sample from a distribution that satisfies the computational variant of the above requirements. The above is guaranteed to hold under a technical condition on C that includes two interesting cases: the case where constraints are consistent and are fully specified (i.e., $C(S)$ never outputs 0) and the case where the constraints are d-homogenous (i.e., $C(S)$ outputs 0 on all sets whose size is different from d). The algorithm is based on the assumptions that indistinguishability obfuscation (iO) [1, 7] and one-way functions exist, and builds on recent constructions of multi-input functional encryption [9]. On the negative side, we also show that there is no similar algorithm in the general (non-projective) case, even for homogenous constraints, unless RP = NP. This establishes a qualitative separation between the projective and the general case.

Application to secure ad-hoc computation. We further motivate the study of distribution design and our results by demonstrating their usefulness for realizing non-interactive protocols for *ad-hoc* secure multiparty computation, in which only a subset of the parties may choose to participate and the identity of participants should remain hidden to the extent possible. This application is an instance of distribution design which does not seem to be captured by known primitives. See Section 5 for more details.

Open questions. Many natural open questions concerning the complexity of distribution design are left open. For instance, can *every* set of constraints on n variables be realized with share size that is polynomial in n? This question is wide open even in the special cases of secret sharing schemes and PSM protocols. However, the extra generality of distribution design may give rise to stronger lower bounds, and possibly serve as a stepping stone towards improved lower bounds for secret sharing and PSM protocols. A potentially easier question is that of obtaining sharp bounds on the minimal share size required by *simple* instances of distribution design, such as a design that "singles out" one set of d variables (see Lemma 3.1).

2. PRELIMINARIES

In this section we define the problem of distribution design and some of its useful special cases.

NOTATION 2.1. *We denote by $[n]$ the set $\{1,\ldots,n\}$ and by $\langle n \rangle_d$ the set of ordered sequences of distinct elements from $[n]$ of length d; that is, an element of $\langle n \rangle_d$ has the form $(i_1,\ldots,i_d)$ where each i_j is in $[n]$ and, for all $j_1 \neq j_2$, we have $i_{j_1} \neq i_{j_2}$. Finally, let $\langle n \rangle \triangleq \cup_{d=1}^{n} \langle n \rangle_d$.*

For a random variable Y supported on a finite set $\mathrm{supp}(Y)$, denote $|Y| = \lceil \log_2 |\mathrm{supp}(Y)| \rceil$. For a sequence of jointly distributed random variables $X = (X_1,\ldots,X_n)$ and a sequence of indices $S = (i_1,\cdots,i_d) \in \langle n \rangle$, we denote $X_S \triangleq (X_{i_1},\ldots,X_{i_d})$.

For an (unordered) subset $A \subseteq [n]$, where $i_1 < i_2 < \cdots < i_d$ are the elements of A in ascending order, we identify the set A with the (ordered) sequence $(i_1,\ldots,i_d)$, and denote $X_A \triangleq (X_{i_1}\ldots,X_{i_d})$.

For two random variables Y, Z, we denote $Y \equiv Z$ if Y and Z are identically distributed, and $Y \| Z$ if the supports of Y and Z are disjoint.

DEFINITION 2.2 (DISTRIBUTION DESIGN). *A set of constraints $\mathcal{R}$ is a set of the form $\{ "T_i \circ_i Q_i" \}_{i=1}^{m}$, where $T_i, Q_i \in \langle n \rangle$, $|T_i| = |Q_i|$, and $\circ_i \in \{\equiv, \|\}$. A distribution design realizing $\mathcal{R}$ is a sequence $X = (X_1,\ldots,X_n)$ of random variables such that*

- *For every "$Q \equiv T$" $\in \mathcal{R}$, $X_Q \equiv X_T$.*

- *For every "$Q \| T$" $\in \mathcal{R}$, $X_Q \| X_T$.*

Let $X = (X_1,\ldots,X_n)$ be a distribution design. Borrowing notation from secret sharing schemes, for $(x_1,\ldots,x_n) \in \mathrm{supp}(X)$, we will call x_i the ith share. We define the share size of X to be $\max_{i \in [n]} |X_i|$.

A definition of computational distribution designs will be given in Section 6.1. Next, we consider the following special types of constraints, where the constraints are only on sets.

DEFINITION 2.3 (PROJECTIVE SET OF CONSTRAINTS). *The constraints in $\mathcal{R}$ are projective if for every "$S \circ Q$" $\in \mathcal{R}$, where $S = (i_1,\ldots,i_d)$ and $Q = (j_1,\ldots,j_d)$, it holds that $i_1 < i_2 < \cdots < i_d$ and $j_1 < j_2 < \cdots < j_d$. We refer to distribution designs for such sets of constraints as being projective.*

Note that projective constraints can be expressed by a set of constraints of the form $X_S \equiv X_T$ or $X_S \| X_T$ for sets S, T of the same size.

DEFINITION 2.4 (SYMMETRIC DISTRIBUTION DESIGNS). *A sequence of random variables $(Y_1,\ldots,Y_d)$ is symmetric if $(Y_1,\ldots,Y_d) \equiv (Y_{\pi(1)},\ldots,Y_{\pi(d)})$ for every permutation $\pi : [d] \rightarrow [d]$. A distribution design X is d-symmetric if X_S is symmetric for any $S \subseteq [n]$ with $|S| = d$.*

DEFINITION 2.5 (t-SECRET DISTRIBUTION DESIGNS). *A distribution design X is t-secret if $X_S \equiv X_Q$ for any sequences $S, Q \in \langle n \rangle$ with $|Q| = |S| \leq t$.*

DEFINITION 2.6. *A set of constraints $\mathcal{R}$ is d-homogenous if $|S| = |Q| = d$ for every constraint "$S \circ Q$" $\in \mathcal{R}$. A set of constraints $\mathcal{R}$ is t-bounded if $|S| = |Q| \leq t$ for every constraint "$S \circ Q$" $\in \mathcal{R}$.*

REMARK 2.7 (A NOTE ON EFFICIENCY). *In all our constructions of distribution designs (as described in the various theorems throughout the paper), the running time of the algorithm for generating the distribution design is polynomial in the number of variables in the distribution design and in the share size.*

Furthermore, when describing algorithms, we assume that for any integer N the algorithm can perfectly sample a uniformly random number in the range $[N]$ in time $\mathrm{poly}(\log N)$. If we insist on algorithms that can only generate random bits, some of our stated running times become expected rather than strict.

3. PROJECTIVE DISTRIBUTION DESIGNS

In this section we construct distribution designs for projective constraints. We start with homogenous projective sets of constraints, where we have a construction with polynomial share size; in the full version we deal with non-homogenous projective sets of constraints. We only consider $d > 1$ as the case $d = 1$ is trivial (e.g., can be solved with one vector of shares). We construct a distribution design for homogeneous constraints in three steps. In the first step, we present a construction of a distribution design that "singles out" one set A_0 of size d.

LEMMA 3.1. *Let $A_0 \subseteq [n]$ be a set of size $1 < d < n$ and consider the d-homogenous projective set of constraints $\mathcal{R}_{A_0} = \{ "A \| A_0" : A \subset [n], |A| = d, A \neq A_0 \} \cup \{ "A \equiv A'" : A, A' \subset [n], |A| = |A'| = d, A, A' \neq A_0 \}$. Then, there exists a $(d-1)$-secret d-symmetric distribution design for $\mathcal{R}_{A_0}$ with share size at most $\min\{2d \cdot \log n, n-1\}$.*

PROOF. For simplicity of notation, assume that $A_0 = \{1,\ldots,d\}$. We first describe, slightly informally, the solution with share size $n-1$: Choose $X_2,\ldots,X_n$ to be random linearly independent vectors in $\mathbb{F}_2^{n-1}$, set $X_1 \triangleq \sum_{i=2}^{d} X_i$ and let $X^{\mathrm{I}} = (X_1,\ldots,X_n)$. It is easy to see that any set of size d besides A_0 "sees" d random linearly independent vectors, whereas $X_{A_0}^{\mathrm{I}}$ consists of $d-1$ random linearly independent vectors followed by their sum.

We now describe the solution with share size $2d \cdot \log n$. Let $\mathbb{F}$ be a field of characteristic two of size $n \leq |\mathbb{F}| \leq 2n$. Fix vectors $v_2,\ldots,v_n \in \mathbb{F}^{2d-1}$ that are $2d-1$-wise linearly independent, i.e., for any sequence $1 < i_1 < \cdots < i_{2d-1} \leq n$, the vectors $v_{i_1},\ldots,v_{i_{2d-1}}$ are linearly independent over $\mathbb{F}$ (using Vandermonde matrices, it is well-known that such a set of vectors exists when $|\mathbb{F}| \geq n-1$). Let $v_1 \triangleq \sum_{i=2}^{d} v_i$. We have the following relations between $v_1,\ldots,v_n$.

- $\sum_{i=1}^{d} v_i = 0$.

- If $S \subsetneq \{1,\ldots,d\}$, the vectors $\{v_i\}_{i \in S}$ are linearly independent.

- If $S = \{i_1,\ldots,i_d\} \neq \{1,\ldots,d\}$ then $v_{i_1},\ldots,v_{i_d}$ are linearly independent: If $1 \notin S$, this is immediate. When $1 \in S$, if the vectors $\{v_i\}_{i \in S}$ are dependent, then the set of vectors $\{v_2,\ldots,v_d\} \cup \{v_i\}_{i \in S \setminus \{1\}}$ of size at most $2d-1$ are dependent, contradicting the choice of $v_2,\ldots,v_n$.

Denote $s \triangleq 2d - 1$. Define a sequence of random variables $X^{\mathrm{II}} = (X_1,\ldots,X_n)$ as follows. Uniformly select a random $\mathbb{F}$-linear map $T : \mathbb{F}^s \rightarrow \mathbb{F}^s$ of *full rank*, i.e., $T(\mathbb{F}^s) = \mathbb{F}^s$. Now, for $i \in [n]$, define $X_i \triangleq T(v_i)$. We claim that X^{II}

realizes $\mathcal{R}_{A_0}$: fix any subset $A \neq A_0$ of $[n]$ of size d. The set of vectors $\{v_i\}_{i \in A}$ is linearly independent. As one way to sample T is by first choosing random linearly independent vectors $\{T(v_i)\}_{i \in A}$ and then defining T on some completion of $\{v_i\}_{i \in A}$ to a basis, $X_A^{\mathrm{II}} = (T(v_i))_{i \in A}$ is uniformly distributed amongst sequences of d linearly independent vectors in $\mathbb{F}^s$. In particular, $X_A^{\mathrm{II}} \equiv X_B^{\mathrm{II}}$ for any $A, B \neq A_0$ of size d. Furthermore, X_A^{II} is a symmetric distribution, as a random permutation of d random linearly independent vectors is itself a sequence of d random linearly independent vectors.

On the other hand, any sequence $(u_1 = T(v_1), \ldots, u_d = T(v_d))$ in the support of $X_{A_0}^{\mathrm{II}}$ will satisfy $\sum_{i=1}^{d} u_i = 0$. In particular, there will not be any sequences of d linearly independent vectors in the support of $X_{A_0}^{\mathrm{II}}$ and hence, $X_{A_0}^{\mathrm{II}} \| X_A^{\mathrm{II}}$ for any $A \neq A_0$. Furthermore, any $d - 1$ vectors out of $\{u_1, \ldots, u_d\}$ are random linearly independent vectors. Thus, $X_{A_0}^{\mathrm{II}}$ is also a symmetric distribution. $\square$

Using the above lemma, we can "separate" one set $\mathcal{A}$ of subsets of size d from all other subsets of size d.

LEMMA 3.2. *Given a set $\mathcal{A}$ of subsets of $[n]$ of size d, there is a $(d-1)$-secret d-symmetric distribution design X of share size $|\mathcal{A}| \cdot \min\{2d \cdot \log n, n-1\}$ such that for any $A, B \subseteq [n]$ of size d*

- *If $A, B \in \mathcal{A}$ or $A, B \notin \mathcal{A}$, then $X_A \equiv X_B$.*

- *If $A \in \mathcal{A}$ and $B \notin \mathcal{A}$, then $X_A \| X_B$.*

PROOF. Let $s = |\mathcal{A}|$ and denote $\mathcal{A} = \{A_1, \ldots, A_s\}$. For each $i \in [s]$, we use Lemma 3.1 to generate a distribution design $X^i = (X_1^i, \ldots, X_n^i)$ of share size $\min\{2d \cdot \log n, n-1\}$, such that $X_{A_i}^i \| X_B^i$ for all $A_i \neq B \subseteq [n]$ with $|B| = d$. We next choose a random permutation π of $[s]$. Now, we define a distribution design $X = (X_1, \ldots, X_n)$ by $X_j \triangleq (X_j^{\pi(i)})_{i \in [s]}$. That is, for each set $A_0 \in A$, we generate shares according to the distribution design of Lemma 3.1, and we concatenate these shares in a random order.

We next argue that this distribution design satisfies all the constraints. First fix a set $A \in \mathcal{A}$. We view the random variable X as consisting of s rows, each row corresponding to shares generated according to one copy of the distribution design of Lemma 3.1 and consider X_A – these rows restricted to A. Of these restricted rows, $s - 1$ rows contain d random linearly independent vectors, and the remaining row, whose location is uniformly distributed because of π, contains $d - 1$ random linearly independent vectors followed by their sum. For a set $B \notin \mathcal{A}$, the random variable X_B simply consists of s rows each containing d random linearly independent vectors. The lemma follows. $\square$

Before proceeding to the main result of this subsection, we introduce the notion of *concatenation* of distribution designs: Given distribution designs $X^1 = (X_1^1, \ldots, X_n^1)$ and $X^2 = (X_1^2, \ldots, X_n^2)$, we define the distribution design $X = X^1 \circ X^2$ by $X = (X_1, \ldots, X_n)$ where $X_i \triangleq X_i^1 \circ X_i^2$. For sets $A, B \subseteq [n]$, the following hold:

- If $X_A^1 \equiv X_B^1$ and $X_A^2 \equiv X_B^2$, then $X_A \equiv X_B$.

- If $X_A^1 \| X_B^1$ or $X_A^2 \| X_B^2$, then $X_A \| X_B$.

We note that the distribution designs of Lemmas 3.1 and 3.2 can clearly be sampled in polynomial time in n and their share sizes. This will be used in the following theorem.

THEOREM 3.3. *There exists an algorithm running in time* $\mathrm{poly}(|\mathcal{R}|, n)$ *that given a projective d-homogenous set of constraints $\mathcal{R}$ on n variables*

- *determines whether $\mathcal{R}$ is realizable.*

- *If so, returns a sample $(x_1, \ldots, x_n)$ from a $(d-1)$-secret d-symmetric distribution design X realizing $\mathcal{R}$ with share size $2|\mathcal{R}| \cdot \min\{2d \cdot \log n, n-1\}$.*

PROOF. The algorithm starts by computing the set of equivalence classes of sets of size d "induced" by $\mathcal{R}$. More precisely, we create a graph of the subsets of size d appearing in one of the constraints in $\mathcal{R}$. We connect vertices A and B if and only if "$A \equiv B$" $\in \mathcal{R}$, and find the connected components $\mathcal{A}_1, \ldots, \mathcal{A}_\ell$ of this graph. Note that the total number of vertices in the graph is at most $2|\mathcal{R}|$. We now check whether for some constraint "$A \| B$" $\in \mathcal{R}$ the sets A and B are in the same component $\mathcal{A}_i$. If so, we declare that $\mathcal{R}$ is not realizable. Otherwise, "$A \equiv B$" $\in \mathcal{R}$ obviously implies that A and B are in the same connected component, and "$A \| B$" $\in \mathcal{R}$ implies that A and B are in different components. Thus, it is enough to construct a distribution design X where $X_A \equiv X_B$ whenever A and B are in the same component $\mathcal{A}_i$, and $X_A \| X_B$ whenever A and B are in different components. First, for each class $\mathcal{A}_i$ we generate a distribution design X^i separating $\mathcal{A}_i$ from all other subsets of size d using Lemma 3.2. The share size will be $|\mathcal{A}_i| \cdot \min\{2d \cdot \log n, n-1\}$. Now define the distribution design $X \triangleq X^1 \circ \cdots \circ X^\ell$. On one hand, if "$A \equiv B$" $\in \mathcal{R}$ for two sets A, B, then $A, B \in \mathcal{A}_i$ for some $i \in [\ell]$, and $X_A^j \equiv X_B^j$ for all $j \in [\ell]$, thus, $X_A \equiv X_B$. On the other hand, if "$A \| B$" $\in \mathcal{R}$ for two sets A, B, then $A \in \mathcal{A}_i, B \in \mathcal{A}_j$ for $i \neq j$, thus, $X_A^i \| X_B^i$, implying that $X_A \| X_B$. Therefore, X realizes $\mathcal{R}$. The claim regarding share size follows from the fact that $|\mathcal{A}_1| + \cdots + |\mathcal{A}_\ell| \leq 2|\mathcal{R}|$. $\square$

In the full version of this paper, we present a construction of distribution designs realizing non-homogenous projective sets of constraints. The idea of the construction is to partition the set of constraints $\mathcal{R}$ into sets $\mathcal{R}_1, \ldots, \mathcal{R}_n$, where $\mathcal{R}_d$ contains all constraints in $\mathcal{R}$ with sets of size d. We would like to realize each $\mathcal{R}_d$ independently. However, we need to add constraints to ensure the consistency. For example, if "$\{1, 2, 3\} \equiv \{4, 5, 6\}$" $\in \mathcal{R}$, then we will add the constraint "$\{1, 3\} \equiv \{4, 6\}$" (and all other constraints with sets of size 1 and 2 for the appropriate subsets). After adding these additional constraints we can realize each $\mathcal{R}_d$ and concatenate the shares; using additional properties of the distribution design we constructed (e.g., $(d-1)$-secrecy), we can prove that the resulting design realizes $\mathcal{R}$.

4. CONSTRUCTIONS OF GENERAL DISTRIBUTION DESIGNS

In this section, we characterize when a set of constraints $\mathcal{R}$ can be realized by a distribution design. For lack of space, most of the proofs in this section are deferred to the full version of the paper.

4.1 A Construction for n-Homogeneous Sets of Constraints

As a first step of the characterization, we consider an n-homogeneous set of constraints, that is, all the sequences appearing in the constraints are of length n, i.e., each sequence is a permutation. In the following, we represent a permutation $\pi \in S_n$ by a vector $(\pi(1), \ldots, \pi(n))$ (this notation should not be confused with describing a permutation as a list of cycles). The latter vector is also used as a vector of shares in a distribution design.

We next recall some background on S_n, the group of permutations over $[n]$. For two permutations $\pi_1, \pi_2 \in S_n$, let $\pi = \pi_1 \cdot \pi_2$ be the permutation defined by $\pi(a) = \pi_2(\pi_1(a))$ for every $a \in [n]$. Let G be a subgroup of S_n. A *left coset* of G is the set of permutations $\{\pi_0 \cdot \pi : \pi \in G\}$ for some $\pi_0 \in S_n$. The left cosets of G partition S_n into disjoint cosets (of equal size). Two permutations $\pi_1, \pi_2 \in S_n$ are in the same left coset of G if and only if $\pi_1^{-1} \cdot \pi_2 \in G$. Finally, let id be the identity permutation.

Clearly, if $\mathcal{R}$ contains the constraints "$S \equiv Q$", "$Q \equiv T$", "$S\|T$", then $\mathcal{R}$ cannot be realized by a distribution design. However, there are more complex reasons why a set of constraints $\mathcal{R}$ cannot be realized. The next example shows such $\mathcal{R}$ and gives a motivation for using the group of permutations.

EXAMPLE 4.1. *Consider the set of constraints $\mathcal{R}_{\mathrm{swap}}$ that contains the constraint $(1, \ldots, n) \equiv (1, \ldots, i-1, i+1, i, i+2, \ldots, n)$ for every $1 \leq i \leq n-1$. Notice that $(1, \ldots, i-1, i+1, i, i+2, \ldots, n)$ is the permutation that swaps the i-th and $(i+1)$-th elements. Assume that there is a distribution design X realizing $\mathcal{R}_{\mathrm{swap}}$ and let $(x_1, \ldots, x_n)$ be any vector of shares in the support of X. Since $(1, \ldots, n) \equiv (2, 1, 3, \ldots, n)$ we get that $(x_2, x_1, x_3, \ldots, x_n)$ is in the support of X. Since $(1, \ldots, n) \equiv (1, 3, 2, 4, \ldots, n)$ we get that also $(x_2, x_3, x_1, x_4, \ldots, x_n)$. We can apply such steps (at most $O(n^2)$ times) and conclude that every permutation of $(x_1, \ldots, x_n)$ is in the support of X, thus, $X \equiv X_S$ for every permutation S.*

We have shown that if $X_{\mathrm{id}} \equiv X_S$, for some permutation S, then $X_{\mathrm{id}} \equiv X_{S'}$, where the permutation S' is obtained from S by swapping the i-th and $(i+1)$-th elements. In other words, we consider the group of permutations generated by swaps and all of them are equivalent. As swaps generate all permutations, then in any distribution design realizing $\mathcal{R}_{\mathrm{swap}}$ all permutations are equivalent.

We characterize the n-homogeneous sets of constraints that can be realized by a distribution design (using groups terminology).

THEOREM 4.2. *Let $\mathcal{R}$ be an n-homogeneous set of constraints and let G be the subgroup of S_n generated by the permutations $\{Q^{-1} \cdot S : \text{"}S \equiv Q\text{"} \in \mathcal{R}\}$. Then, there exists a distribution design realizing $\mathcal{R}$ if and only if for every constraint "$S\|Q$" $\in \mathcal{R}$ the permutations S and Q are in different left cosets of G.*

The theorem follows from the following two lemmas.

LEMMA 4.3. *Let $\mathcal{R}$ be an n-homogeneous set of constraints and let G be the subgroup of S_n generated by the permutations $\{Q^{-1} \cdot S : \text{"}S \equiv Q\text{"} \in \mathcal{R}\}$. If for every "$S\|Q$" $\in \mathcal{R}$ the permutations S and Q are in different left cosets of G, then there exists a distribution design realizing $\mathcal{R}$.*

PROOF. Consider the following distribution design: Choose, uniformly at random, a permutation $\pi \in G$, and let $X_i = \pi(i)$ for $i \in [n]$. We claim that $X = (X_1, \ldots, X_n)$ is a distribution design for $\mathcal{R}$. Note that any vector of shares of X is,

by the construction, a permutation. Furthermore, for any sequence S of length n, a permutation τ is in $\mathrm{supp}(X_S)$ if and only if there is a permutation $\pi \in \mathrm{supp}(X)$, i.e. $\pi \in G$, such that $\tau = S \cdot \pi$.

We next prove that X satisfies each constraint in $\mathcal{R}$. First, assume that "$S \equiv Q$" $\in \mathcal{R}$, and let $\tau \in \mathrm{supp}(X_S)$. Thus, there is a permutation $\pi \in \mathrm{supp}(X) = G$ such that $\pi = S^{-1} \cdot \tau$. As $Q^{-1} \cdot S$ is a generator of G, we deduce that $(Q^{-1} \cdot S) \cdot \pi \in G$. Therefore, $(Q^{-1} \cdot S) \cdot \pi = (Q^{-1} \cdot S) \cdot (S^{-1} \cdot \tau) = Q^{-1} \cdot \tau \in G = \mathrm{supp}(X)$. We conclude that $\tau = Q \cdot (Q^{-1} \cdot \tau) \in \mathrm{supp}(X_Q)$. We have proved that $\mathrm{supp}(X_S) = \mathrm{supp}(X_Q)$. As the vectors of shares π and $Q^{-1} \cdot S \cdot \pi$ are chosen with equal probability, i.e. $1/|G|$, the variables X_S and X_Q are equally distributed.

Next, assume that "$S\|Q$" $\in \mathcal{R}$, and let $\tau \in \mathrm{supp}(X_S)$. There is a permutation $\pi \in \mathrm{supp}(X) = G$ such that $\pi = S^{-1} \cdot \tau$, which implies $S = \tau \cdot \pi^{-1}$. If τ is also in $\mathrm{supp}(X_Q)$, then there is a permutation $\pi' \in \mathrm{supp}(X) = G$ such that $\pi' = Q^{-1} \cdot \tau$, which implies $Q = \tau \cdot (\pi')^{-1}$. Thus, S and Q are in the same left coset of G (specifically, $\tau \cdot G$), contradicting the assumptions of the lemma. This implies that $\mathrm{supp}(X_S)$ and $\mathrm{supp}(X_Q)$ are disjoint, as required. $\square$

LEMMA 4.4. *Let $\mathcal{R}$ be an n-homogeneous set of constraints and let G be the subgroup of S_n generated by the permutations $\{Q^{-1} \cdot S : \text{"}S \equiv Q\text{"} \in \mathcal{R}\}$. If there exists a distribution design realizing $\mathcal{R}$, then for every "$S\|Q$" $\in \mathcal{R}$ the permutations S and Q are in different left cosets of G.*

PROOF SKETCH. Let $(x_1, \ldots, x_n)$ be a vector of shares in $\mathrm{supp}(X)$. It can be proved that $(x_{\pi(1)}, \ldots, x_{\pi(n)}) \in \mathrm{supp}(X)$, for every $\pi \in G$ (this is proved by induction on the number of steps by which π is generated). Next, assume that S and Q are in the same left coset of G and let $(x_1, \ldots, x_n)$ be a vector in the support of X. On one hand, $(x_{S(1)}, \ldots, x_{S(n)}) \in \mathrm{supp}(X_S)$. On the other hand, $Q^{-1} \cdot S \in G$ since S and Q are in the same left coset of G. Thus, by the above induction, $(x_{(Q^{-1} \cdot S)(1)}, \ldots, x_{(Q^{-1} \cdot S)(n)}) \in \mathrm{supp}(X)$ and the vector $(x_{Q \cdot (Q^{-1} \cdot S)(1)}, \ldots, x_{Q \cdot (Q^{-1} \cdot S)(n)}) = (x_{S(1)}, \ldots, x_{S(n)})$ is in $\mathrm{supp}(X_Q)$. Therefore, there is a vector of shares in both $\mathrm{supp}(X_S)$ and $\mathrm{supp}(X_Q)$ implying that "$S\|Q$" $\notin \mathcal{R}$. $\square$

We next summarize our results for n-homogeneous sets of constraints.

THEOREM 4.5. *There exists an algorithm running in time $\mathrm{poly}(n, |\mathcal{R}|)$ that given an n-homogeneous set of constraints $\mathcal{R}$ on n variables,*

- *determines whether $\mathcal{R}$ is realizable.*

- *If so, returns a sample $(x_1, \ldots, x_n)$ from a distribution design X realizing $\mathcal{R}$ with share size $\log_2 n$.*

PROOF. By Theorem 4.2, we need to check that S, Q are in different left cosets of G for every "$S\|Q$" $\in \mathcal{R}$. Checking whether two permutations S, Q are in the same left coset of G is equivalent to checking whether $S^{-1}Q$ is in G, which, when G is given as a list of generators, can be computed in polynomial time in the number of generators and in n (see, e.g., [14, 6]). If $\mathcal{R}$ is realizable, the distribution design of Lemma 4.3, which realizes $\mathcal{R}$, samples a permutation in $\pi \in G$ with uniform distribution and sets $X_i = \pi(i)$. Thus, the share size of the distribution design is $\log n$. Furthermore, there is a randomized algorithm running in time polynomial in n and the number of generators of G that, given a set of generators of a subgroup of S_n, outputs a random permutation in the group with uniform distribution (see, e.g., [12, Page 30]). □

4.2 A Construction for Homogeneous Sets of Constraints

As the next step of constructing distribution designs, we characterize when d-homogeneous sets of constraints can be realized for some $d < n$.

NOTATION 4.6. *Given a sequence $S = (i_1, \ldots, i_d) \in \langle n \rangle_d$ and a permutation $\pi \in S_d$, denote $\pi(S) = (i_{\pi(1)}, \ldots, i_{\pi(d)})$.*

Given a matrix M with n columns, and a sequence $S = (i_1, \ldots, i_d)$ we define the matrix $M\!\downarrow_S$ as the restriction of M to the columns indexed by S, that is, the j-th column of $M\!\downarrow_S$ is the i_j-th column of M.

Assume that there is a distribution design X realizing $\mathcal{R}$. For every sequence $S \in \langle n \rangle$, the distribution design X_S satisfies all constraints in $\mathcal{R}$ involving only permutations of S. This implies that if X realizes $\mathcal{R}$, then $\mathcal{R}$ restricted to S has to satisfy the conditions of Theorem 4.2. Furthermore,

OBSERVATION 4.7. *Let X be a distribution design realizing a set of constraints $\mathcal{R}$. For every two sequences $S, T \in \langle n \rangle_d$, if "$S \equiv T$" $\in \mathcal{R}$ and "$T \equiv \pi(T)$" $\in \mathcal{R}$ then $X_S \equiv X_{\pi(S)}$.*

As a warmup, we consider 2-homogeneous sets of constraints with exactly two equivalence classes (and an additional restriction described bellow). This construction contains the ideas of the construction for arbitrary d-homogenous sets of constrains.

Formally, we consider a set of constraints $\mathcal{R}$ for which there are two sequences $T_1, T_2 \in \langle n \rangle_2$ such that "$T_1 \| T_2$" $\in \mathcal{R}$ and for every $T \in \langle n \rangle_2$ it holds that "$T \equiv T_\alpha$" $\in \mathcal{R}$ for exactly one $\alpha \in \{1, 2\}$. We extend $\mathcal{R}$ to $\mathcal{R}'$ by considering the transitive closure of $\equiv$, that is, $\mathcal{R}'$ contains $\mathcal{R}$ and for every α, S_1, S_2 such that "$S_1 \equiv T_\alpha$" $\in \mathcal{R}$ and "$S_2 \equiv T_\alpha$" $\in \mathcal{R}$, we add "$S_1 \equiv S_2$" $\in \mathcal{R}'$. Clearly, if a distribution design realizes $\mathcal{R}$, then it realizes $\mathcal{R}'$. We define a function $f : \langle n \rangle_2 \to \{1, 2\}$, where $f(i_1, i_2) = \alpha$ for the α such that "$(i_1, i_2) \equiv T_\alpha$" $\in \mathcal{R}$. Assume that X realizes $\mathcal{R}$. Then, for every $S_1, S_2 \in \langle n \rangle_2$, if $f(S_1) = f(S_2)$ then $X_{S_1} \equiv X_{S_2}$, otherwise, $X_{S_1} \| X_{S_2}$.

Assume that $f(j_1, j_2) \neq f(j_2, j_1)$ for every $j_1 \neq j_2$. We next show that, in this case, $\mathcal{R}$ can be realized by a distribution design. Consider the following matrix N with n columns. For every pair $(i_1, i_2) \in [n]^2$, where $i_1 < i_2$, we have a row in the matrix, where the i_1-th entry is $f(i_1, i_2)$ and the i_2-nd entry is $f(i_2, i_1)$; all other entries in this row are 0. We next add rows to N. For every $1 \leq i \leq n$, let $\#_{i,1} = |\{(i, i_2) : i < i_2, f(i, i_2) = 1\}| + |\{(i_1, i) : i > i_1, f(i_1, i) = 1\}|$. That is, $\#_{i,1}$ is the number of entries that are 1 in the i-th column and $n - 1 - \#_{i,1}$ is the number of entries that are 2 in this column. We add $n - 1 - \#_{i,1}$ rows to the matrix, where the i-th entry is 1; all other entries in these rows are 0. Similarly, we add $\#_{i,1}$ rows to the matrix, where the i-th entry is 2; all other entries in these rows are 0. Thus, the number of 1's and 2's in each column is $n - 1$.

Now consider $N\!\downarrow_{\{i_1, i_2\}}$, the matrix N restricted to columns i_1 and i_2 for some $i_1 < i_2$. All rows in $N\!\downarrow_{\{i_1, i_2\}}$, except for one, contain at most 1 non-zero entry. In the row where there are two non-zero elements (the row labeled by (i_1, i_2)),

if $f(i_1, i_2) = 1$ then the entries are $(1, 2)$, otherwise the entries are $(2, 1)$. This implies that for every i_1, i_2 such that $f(i_1, i_2) = 1$, the matrix $N\!\downarrow_{\{i_1, i_2\}}$ is the same up to a permutation of the rows. This is also true for all matrices $N\!\downarrow_{\{i_1, i_2\}}$ for i_1, i_2 such that $f(i_1, i_2) = 2$. Thus, to construct a distribution design realizing $\mathcal{R}$, we choose with uniform distribution a permutation on the rows of the matrix, and the i-th share is the i-th permuted row.

EXAMPLE 4.8. Consider the 2–homogeneous set of requirements $\mathcal{R}$ with 3 variables and two equivalence classes, described by the constraints "$(1, 2) \| (2, 1)$", "$(1, 2) \equiv (1, 3)$", "$(1, 2) \equiv (3, 2)$", "$(2, 1) \equiv (3, 1)$", "$(2, 1) \equiv (2, 3)$". To construct a distribution design realizing $\mathcal{R}$, we first construct the following matrix.

	1	2	3
$(1,2)$	1	2	0
$(1,3)$	1	0	2
$(2,3)$	0	2	1

In this matrix $\#_{1,1} = 2$, $\#_{2,1} = 0$, and $\#_{3,1} = 1$. So we add rows to the matrix and obtain N:

	1	2	3
$(1,2)$	1	2	0
$(1,3)$	1	0	2
$(2,3)$	0	2	1
	2	0	0
	2	0	0
	0	1	0
	0	1	0
	0	0	1
	0	0	2

To construct a distribution design realizing $\mathcal{R}$, we randomly permute the rows of N and X_i is the permuted i-th column of N.

As we have seen in Theorem 4.7, constraints on a pair of sequences imply constraints on other sequences. This motivates the definition of $\mathrm{cl}(\mathcal{R})$ – the closure of the set of constraints $\mathcal{R}$ – which contains all constraints implied by $\mathcal{R}$.

DEFINITION 4.9. *Let $\mathcal{R}$ be a d-homogeneous set of constraints. The closure of $\mathcal{R}$, denoted $\mathrm{cl}(\mathcal{R})$, is the minimal set such that:*

1. *$\mathcal{R} \subseteq \mathrm{cl}(\mathcal{R})$,*

2. *If "$S \equiv Q$" $\in \mathrm{cl}(\mathcal{R})$, then "$Q \equiv S$" $\in \mathrm{cl}(\mathcal{R})$,*

3. *If "$S \circ Q$" $\in \mathrm{cl}(\mathcal{R})$ for some $\circ \in \{\equiv, \|\}$, then "$S \equiv S$" $\in \mathrm{cl}(\mathcal{R})$,*

4. *If "$S \equiv Q$" $\in \mathrm{cl}(\mathcal{R})$ and "$Q \circ T$" $\in \mathrm{cl}(\mathcal{R})$ for some $\circ \in \{\equiv, \|\}$, then "$S \circ T$" $\in \mathrm{cl}(\mathcal{R})$,*

5. *If "$S \circ Q$" $\in \mathrm{cl}(\mathcal{R})$, then "$\pi(S) \circ \pi(Q)$" $\in \mathrm{cl}(\mathcal{R})$ for every $\pi \in S_d$.*

LEMMA 4.10. *If X is a distribution design realizing $\mathcal{R}$, then X realizes $\mathrm{cl}(\mathcal{R})$.*

We next define $\mathcal{R}_S$, the projection of $\mathcal{R}$ to permutations of S.

DEFINITION 4.11. *Let $\mathcal{R}$ be a set of constraints and $S \in \langle n \rangle$. We define $\mathcal{R}_S \triangleq$*

$$\{\text{"}Q_1 \circ Q_2\text{"} : \text{"}Q_1 \circ Q_2\text{"} \in \mathcal{R} \wedge \exists_{\pi_1, \pi_2} \, Q_1 = \pi_1(S), Q_2 = \pi_2(S)\},$$

that is, $\mathcal{R}_S$ contains all constraints in $\mathcal{R}$ in which both sequences are permutations of S.

THEOREM 4.12. *A d-homogeneous set of constraints $\mathcal{R}$ is realizable if and only if for every sequence $S \in \langle n \rangle_d$ the set of constraints $\mathrm{cl}(\mathcal{R})_S$ is realizable.*

Theorem 4.12 provides a necessary and sufficient condition characterizing when a d-homogeneous set of constraints is realizable. The proof of Theorem 4.12 follows from Lemma 4.10, where we prove that the condition is necessary (since if $\mathcal{R}$ is realizable, then $\mathrm{cl}(\mathcal{R})$ and, hence, $\mathrm{cl}(\mathcal{R})_S$ are realizable), and a construction of a distribution design showing that the condition is sufficient, which is described in the full version of this paper.

The next theorem, whose proof appears in the full version of this paper, summarizes the properties of the distribution design for homogenous sets of constraints.

THEOREM 4.13. *There is an algorithm running in time $\mathrm{poly}(|\mathcal{R}|, n)$ that, given a d-homogeneous set of constraints $\mathcal{R}$ on n variables, determines if $\mathcal{R}$ is realizable. If $\mathcal{R}$ is realizable, then there is a distribution design realizing it with share size $n^{O(d^2)}$.*

The description of the construction of the distribution design for non-homogenous sets of constraints appears in the full version.

5. APPLICATION TO MPC

As discussed in the introduction, the problem of distribution design can be seen as a strict generalization of several well-studied problems in cryptography. These include secret sharing, garbling schemes, and non-interactive protocols for secure multiparty computation. We demonstrate the usefulness of more general instances of distribution design by describing an application that is not captured by any of the above primitives.

We consider an *ad-hoc* flavor of secure multiparty computation (MPC), where it is known in advance which function should be computed but the identity of the participants is not known a-priori. The output of the function may depend just on the inputs of the participants, or alternatively may also depend on their identities or even on the order in which they show up. That is, this function accepts as input a sequence of *at most* k pairs of the form (i, w_i), where the first entry is an identity of a party and the second entry is its secret input. We assume for simplicity that the parties are honest-but-curious and that each party may participate at most once. Ideally, we would like such ad-hoc MPC protocols to also guarantee *anonymity*, namely hide everything except the number of participating parties and the output of the function.

In the standard interactive model for MPC, the ad-hoc nature of the protocol does not pose a significant challenge. Indeed, if the set of participating parties can agree on pseudo-identities and communicate directly with each other, then they can simply use a standard general-purpose MPC protocol to evaluate the desired function on the inputs (i, w_i).

However, as we argue below, in the case of *non-interactive* MPC protocols, where the single message sent by each party cannot depend on the messages of the other parties, this variant of the model introduces significant new challenges.

PSM protocols. As a baseline, consider the private simultaneous messages (PSM) model of Feige et al. [5]. In this model there are k parties $P_1, \ldots, P_k$ where each party P_i holds a secret input $w_i \in W$ and all parties have access to common randomness r. The parties wish to securely evaluate a function f on their inputs by simultaneously sending messages to a referee, where the message sent by P_i may only depend on w_i and r. The referee, who does not know r, should be able to correctly recover $f(w_1, \ldots, w_k)$ from the k messages but should learn no additional information about the inputs. Stronger notions of PSM protocols, which guarantee the best possible secrecy even when the referee colludes with subsets of parties, were considered in [2]. However, here we assume that only the referee is corrupted.

Ad-hoc PSM protocols. Suppose we would like to run a PSM protocol even if only $d < k$ parties wish to participate and send messages, where the output of f may depend on the inputs of the participants and possibly also on their identities. The function f is defined over sequences of inputs of the form (i, w_i), where each i is guaranteed to appear at most once in the sequence. Given an input sequence, we would like the referee to learn the value of f on this sequence, but learn no additional information about the input sequence, including the identity of participants, except what should inevitably be leaked (namely, the value of f on all subsequences and their permutations).

We will typically be interested in symmetric f, where the output is not sensitive to the order in which the inputs (i, w_i) are given, but one may also consider non-symmetric f (e.g., for giving priority to parties who act faster). It is also useful to consider partial f that are only defined on sequences of bounded length.

As an example for a simple symmetric f, consider the following problem of "matching in the dark." There are n people whose matching preferences are represented by an undirected graph (which is known to the protocol designer). When two people would like to go out, they anonymously send messages to the referee. The referee should learn whether they have mutual interest in going out together without learning anything else about their identities. In this case, the function f depends only on the identities of the participating parties (i.e., the w_i are empty) and it is defined on sequences of length at most 2. The output of f on input (i, j) is "yes" or "no" depending on whether i and j are connected, and its output on input i (a sequence of length 1) is "no". If the matching criterion may also depend on the type of activity (e.g., "going to a movie" or "going to a restaurant") then the inputs w_i can contain this additional information.

An ad-hoc PSM protocol for f is defined as follows. Syntactically, such a protocol is very similar to a standard PSM protocol. As in standard PSM, each party P_i is defined by a message function $M_i(r, w_i)$ that determines the message it sends to the referee on input w_i and common randomness r. The referee is defined by a reconstruction function that given a sequence of messages produces an output. However, unlike standard PSM, here the sequences can contain anywhere from 1 to k messages. The correctness requirement is that on any input sequence for which the output of f is defined, the referee should reconstruct the correct output with probability 1 over the choice of r. The security requirement should take into account the inevitable attacks mentioned above, namely computing f on sub-sequences of inputs and their permutations. Concretely, for any two input sequences of the same length such that the value of f on *all* of their (permuted) sub-sequences is the same, the distributions of the corresponding two message sequences should be identical. See full version for a simulation-based variant of the definition.

An ad-hoc PSM protocol for f can be reduced to an instance of distribution design in the following natural way. Assume for simplicity that each input w_i is a single bit (an extension to the general case is straightforward). The design involves $n = 2k$ variables X_i^b, where $1 \le i \le k$ and $b \in \{0,1\}$, and where X_i^b denotes the message of P_i on input $w_i = b$. For any two sequences $I = ((i_1, w_{i_1}), \ldots, (i_d, w_{i_d}))$ and $I' = ((i'_1, w'_{i'_1}), \ldots, (i'_d, w'_{i'_d}))$ on which f has different outputs, we include a disjointness constraint between the corresponding variable sequences. If I and I' satisfy the above criterion for indistinguishability, then we include an equality constraint.

Our results provide a perfectly secure ad-hoc PSM protocol for every f, whose complexity is generally exponential in the input length. However, we do get polynomial-time solutions in cases where the input domain is finite and the length of admissible sequences is bounded by a constant. For instance, the matching in the dark problem described above reduces to a 2-homogenous, projective distribution design. We defer further details about the application to ad-hoc PSM to the full version.

6. DISTRIBUTION DESIGN WITH IMPLICIT CONSTRAINTS

In this section we define distribution designs generators, in which the constraints are given in an implicit representation and the generation of the shares and the reconstruction of the equivalence class of a set from their shares should be done in polynomial time. We consider three variants of the security for distribution designs generators, computational, statistical, and perfect. The emphasis of this section is on computationally-secure distribution designs generators, where it is only required that a *polynomial-time* adversary cannot distinguish between shares of two equivalent sequences. We then construct computational distribution designs for *projective* homogeneous sets of constraints using previous constructions for multi-input functional encryption (MIFE) [9]. Finally, we show that in the general (non-projective) case, if RP $\ne$ NP, then there is no distribution designs even for homogeneous sets of constraints.

6.1 Definition of Distribution Designs for Implicit Constraints

We first define implicit representations of a set of constraints for a distribution design by a circuit specifying the equivalence class of each sequence. This gives a much more compact representation of a set of constraints.

DEFINITION 6.1 (IMPLICIT REPRESENTATION). *An implicit representation of a set of constraints with n variables*

is a circuit[1] C with $n \log n$ inputs and $\lceil \log(t+1) \rceil$ outputs (for some integer t) computing a function $f : \langle n \rangle \to [t] \cup \{0\}$, which represents the set of constraints

$$\begin{aligned} \mathcal{R}_f \;=\; & \{S \equiv Q : f(S) = f(Q) \ne 0\} \\ & \bigcup \{S \| Q : f(S) \ne f(Q), f(S) \ne 0, f(Q) \ne 0\}. \end{aligned}$$

When we represent projective constraints, the circuit gets n bits as its input (i.e., a characteristic vector of a set) and it computes a function $f : 2^{[n]} \to [t] \cup \{0\}$.

In an implicit representation, we specify an equivalence class for each sequence, where 0 is a "don't care". Two sequences of the same length whose equivalence class is non-zero are equivalent if their equivalence class (i.e., the value of f computed on them) are the same, and they are disjoint otherwise. Clearly, every set of constraints described by an implicit representation can be explicitly represented (usually, with a much longer description). The other direction is not true. For example, for $\mathcal{R} = \{$"$(1,2) \equiv (3,4)$", "$(1,3) \equiv (2,4)$"$\}$, the sequences $(1,2)$ and $(1,3)$ are not constrained. This set of constraints cannot be implicitly represented.

We next define distribution designs generators for implicit constraints. We use the term generator since we have an encoding algorithm, which gets as an input a circuit representing the constraints, and generates the shares. This algorithm should run in time polynomial in the circuit size and in a security parameter.

The output of our generator is $n+1$ values $x_0, x_1, \ldots, x_n$. We think of x_0 as a public share. It is used to simply the presentation and to separate between public parameters and private information. Technically speaking, given a distribution design $X = (X_0, X_1, \ldots, X_n)$ with public information, we can define a a distribution design $X' = (X'_1, \ldots, X'_n)$ without public information, where $X'_i = X_0 \circ X_i$; the results is a distribution designs satisfying the same constraints.[2]

DEFINITION 6.2 (DISTRIBUTION DESIGNS GENERATOR). *A distribution design generator for a class of circuits $\mathcal{C}$ consists of two algorithms (ENC, DEC) described below.*

Encoding. ENC$(1^k, C)$ *is a probabilistic polynomial-time algorithm (abbreviated PPT algorithm) that takes as and input a security parameter 1^k and a circuit $C \in \mathcal{C}$ and outputs $n+1$ shares $(x_0, x_1, \ldots, x_n)$.*

Decoding. DEC$(x_0, x_1, \ldots, x_d)$ *is a deterministic polynomial time algorithm that takes as input d shares, for some $1 \le d \le n$, and outputs an integer in $[t]$.*

A distribution design generator for a class of circuits $\mathcal{C}$ is correct if for every n, every circuit $C \in \mathcal{C}$ representing constraints on n variables, every $d \in [n]$, and every $S =$

---

[1] We can also consider other models computing the function f, e.g., formulas. This can change the efficiency measure of the distribution design generator, since we will alow it to run in time polynomial in the size of the representation of f.

[2] Furthermore, in the information-theoretic setting we can choose a possible value x_0 for X_0 and sample $(X_0, \ldots, X_n)$ conditioned on $X_0 = x_0$. The result is a distribution design satisfying the constraints of $\mathcal{R}$ whose share size is $\max_{i \in [n]} \{|X_i|\}$. The above transformation, in general, does not preserve the efficiency of sampling from $(X_0, \ldots, X_n)$.

$(i_1, \ldots, i_d) \in \langle n \rangle_d$ such that $C(S) \neq 0$:

$$\Pr \left[\begin{array}{l} (x_0, x_1, \ldots, x_n) \leftarrow \text{Enc}(1^k, C); \\ \text{Dec}(x_0, x_{i_1}, \ldots, x_{i_d}) = C(S) \end{array} \right] \geq 1 - \text{negl}(k),\text{[3]}$$

where the probability is taken over the coins of Enc. Notice that there are no correctness requirement when $C(S) = 0$.

Next we define the security of distribution design generators.

DEFINITION 6.3. *Consider the following game between an adversary $\mathcal{A}$ and a challenger:*

1. *The adversary on input 1^k generates a circuit $C \in \mathcal{C}$. Let n be the number of variables in the constraints represented by C. The adversary also chooses two sequences $S_0 = (i_1^0, \ldots, i_d^0), S_1 = (i_1^1, \ldots, i_d^1) \in \langle n \rangle$ such that $C(S_0) = C(S_1) \neq 0$. The adversary sends 1^k, C, S_0, S_1 to the challenger.*

2. *The challenger chooses with uniform distribution a bit $b \in \{0, 1\}$ and sets $(x_0, x_1, \ldots, x_n) \leftarrow \text{Enc}(1^k, C)$. It then sends $(x_0, x_{i_1^b}, \ldots, x_{i_d^b})$ to the adversary.*

3. *The adversary outputs a bit b'.*

The adversary wins the game if $b' = b$.

We say that a distribution design generator (Enc, Dec) is computationally secure if for every non-uniform polynomial-time adversary $\mathcal{A}$, the probability that $\mathcal{A}$ wins is at most $1/2 + \text{negl}(k)$ for some negligible function negl. Similarly, we say that a distribution design generator is statistically secure if for every unbounded adversary $\mathcal{A}$, the probability that $\mathcal{A}$ wins is at most $1/2 + \text{negl}(k)$ for some negligible function negl, and it perfectly secure if for every unbounded adversary $\mathcal{A}$, the probability that $\mathcal{A}$ wins is at most $1/2$.

DEFINITION 6.4. *A distribution design generator for projective constraints is a distribution design generator for the class of circuits representing projective constraints. The correctness and security is only required for sets $S \subseteq [n]$.*

6.2 Projective Distribution Designs Generators and Non-Interactive Multi-Party Protocols

Protocols for non-interactive secure multi-party computation (NIMPC) were studied by Beimel et al. [2]. NIMPC protocols strengthen PSM protocols by additionally considering collusions between the referee and subsets of the parties. The focus of [2] was on perfectly secure NIMPC protocols. In this work we are interested in broader feasibility results, thus, we consider also computationally secure NIMPC protocols, in which all participants and the adversary run in polynomial time.

Similarly to PSM protocols, an NIMPC protocol involve n parties $P_1, \ldots, P_n$, and a referee. (For simplicity, we restrict the attention to the case of single-bit inputs.) An NIMPC protocol additionally involves a dealer that distributes correlated randomness to the parties. The dealer's inputs are a circuit C, which computes a function $f : \{0, 1\}^n \rightarrow \{0, \ldots, t\}$ for some integers n, t, and a security parameter 1^k. It computes $2n$ messages $(M_{i,\sigma})_{i \in [n], \sigma \in \{0,1\}}$ and gives to P_i the messages $M_{i,0}, M_{i,1}$ for every $i \in [n]$. Each party P_i, holding input $x_i \in \{0, 1\}$, sends the message $M_i = M_{i,x_i}$ to the

referee. The referee after getting n messages $M_1, \ldots, M_n$ should be able to efficiently compute $f(x_1, \ldots, x_n)$.

Notice that in such non-interactive protocols, a coalition $T \subseteq \{P_1, \ldots, P_n\}$ that hears all messages sent in the protocol can compute f on many points: given messages $(M_{i,x_i})_{i \notin T}$ (for unknown inputs $(x_i)_{i \notin T}$), the set T can simulate the referee with messages $(M_{i,y_i})_{i \in T}$ for every inputs $(y_i)_{i \in T}$. Informally, the protocol is said to be *robust* if every set T can only learn this information, namely, a coalition T can learn no more than the restriction of f fixing the inputs of parties not in T.

DEFINITION 6.5. *An NIMPC protocol consists of two algorithms (NimpcEnc, NimpcDec) described below.*

Encoding. NimpcEnc$(1^k, C)$ *is a PPT algorithm that takes as input a security parameter 1^k and a circuit C and outputs $2n$ messages $(M_{i,\sigma})_{i \in [n], \sigma \in \{0,1\}}$.*

Decoding. NimpcDec$(M_1, \ldots, M_n)$ *is a deterministic polynomial time algorithm that takes as input n messages $M_1, \ldots, M_n$ and outputs an integer in $[t]$.*

An NIMPC protocol is correct if for every n, every circuit C computing a function with n bit input, and every $x \in \{0, 1\}^n$:

$$\Pr \left[\begin{array}{l} (M_{i,\sigma})_{i \in [n], \sigma \in \{0,1\}} \leftarrow \text{NimpcEnc}(1^k, C); \\ \text{Dec}(M_{1,x_1}, \ldots, M_{n,x_n}) = C(x) \end{array} \right]$$

$$\geq 1 - \text{negl}(k),$$

where the probability is taken over the coins of NimpcEnc.

We next formalize the robustness requirement of NIMPC protocols.

DEFINITION 6.6. *Consider the following game between an adversary $\mathcal{A}$ and a challenger:*

1. *The adversary on input 1^k generates a circuit C. Let n be the number of inputs in C. The adversary also chooses a set T and two inputs for $\overline{T}$, namely, $(x_i^0)_{i \notin T}$ and $(x_i^1)_{i \notin T}$. The adversary sends $C, T, (x_i^0)_{i \notin T}, (x_i^1)_{i \notin T}$ to the challenger.*

2. *The challenger chooses a bit $b \in \{0, 1\}$ and computes messages $(M_{i,\sigma})_{i \in [n], \sigma \in \{0,1\}}$ for the circuit C. It then sends $(M_{i,0}, M_{i,1})_{i \in T}$ and $(M_{i,x_i^b})_{i \notin T}$ to the adversary.*

3. *The adversary outputs a bit b'.*

The adversary wins if $b' = b$ and if for every $(y_i)_{i \in T}$

$$f((y_i)_{i \in T}, (x_i^0)_{i \notin T}) = f((y_i)_{i \in T}, (x_i^1)_{i \notin T}).$$

We say that an NIMPC protocol is computationally-secure if for every non-uniform polynomial-time adversary $\mathcal{A}$, the probability that $\mathcal{A}$ wins is at most $1/2 + \text{negl}(k)$ for some negligible function negl. Similarly, we say that an NIMPC protocol is statistically-secure if for every unbounded adversary $\mathcal{A}$, the probability that $\mathcal{A}$ wins is at most $1/2 + \text{negl}(k)$ for some negligible function negl, and it is perfectly-secure if for every unbounded adversary $\mathcal{A}$, the probability that $\mathcal{A}$ wins is at most $1/2$.

In our security definition, an NIMPC protocol hides the information on $(x_i)_{i \notin T}$. The security requirement in [2] is stronger as it requires that the NIMPC protocol also hides

---

[3]By negl($\cdot$) we denote a *negligible* function, i.e., a function that vanishes faster than any (positive) inverse-polynomial.

the function. We can strengthen our definition by allowing the adversary to choose two circuits C_0, C_1 instead and the challenger computes the messages for the circuit C_b. We define the weaker notion as it suffices for constructing distribution design generators.

We next show that if there exists a secure NIMPC protocol for all circuits, then there exists a secure generator for projective homogeneous distribution designs. Our result applies to a broader class of projective distribution designs, which we define below.

DEFINITION 6.7 (SUBSET CONSISTENCY). *We say that an implicit representation f of a set of projective constraints is* subset consistent *if for every two sets $A, B \subset [n]$ such that $f(A) = f(B) \neq 0$ and for every $S \subseteq [d]$, where $d = |A| = |B|$,*

$$f(A_S) = f(B_S).^{4} \tag{1}$$

We represent a projective d-homogeneous set of constraints by a circuit computing a function $f : 2^{[n]} \to [t]$, where $f(x) = 0$ for every $x \in \{0,1\}^n$ whose weight is not d (that is, the circuit returns "Don't care" for every set whose size is not d). Thus, projective d-homogeneous sets of constraints are subset consistent. Furthermore, if C represents a fully-specified projective set of constrains (i.e., $C(S) \neq 0$ for all sets S), then subset-closure is a necessary condition for realizability of the set of constraints.

THEOREM 6.8. *Let type $\in \{$computationally, statistically, perfectly$\}$. If there is a type-secure NIMPC protocol for all circuits, then there is a type-secure generator for subset-consistent projective distribution designs, in particular, for homogeneous projective distribution designs.*

PROOF. Let $(\text{NimpcEnc}, \text{NimpcDec})$ be a secure NIMPC protocol. We would want to simply execute the NIMPC protocol with the circuit describing the constraints. However, this is not possible since an NIMPC protocol does not hide the identity of the party sending the message. To hide this identity, we first shuffle the order of the inputs and then execute the NIMPC protocol.

We construct a distribution design generator (ENC, DEC) as follows:

The ecncoding algorithm ENC.

- **Input.** A circuit C computing a function f (with inputs $x_1, \ldots, x_n$) and a security parameter 1^k,

- Construct a circuit C' computing the following function g with $n + 1$ inputs

$$g(\pi, x_1, \ldots, x_n) \triangleq f(x_{\pi(1)}, \ldots, x_{\pi(n)}),$$

  where π is a permutation in S_n.

- Choose a random permutation $\rho \in S_n$.

- Compute $\text{NimpcEnc}(1^k, C')$ – the messages for the function g; denote by M_ρ the message of the 0-th player with input ρ and, for $i \in [n]$ and $j \in \{0, 1\}$, denote by $M_{i,j}$ the message of the i-th player with input j.

---

^{4}A similar condition to subset consistency, namely, $f(A_S) = f(B_S) \lor f(A_S) = 0 \lor f(B_S) = 0$, is a necessary condition for realizability of a set of requirements.

- Define a public share x_0 by $x_0 \triangleq (M_\rho, M_{1,0}, \ldots, M_{n,0})$.

- For $i \in [n]$, define $x_i \triangleq (M_{\rho(i),1}, \rho(i))$.

- **Output.** $x_0, x_1, \ldots, x_n$.

The decoding algorithm DEC.

- **Input.** Shares $x_0 = (M_\rho, M_{1,0}, \ldots, M_{n,0})$, $(x_i = (M_{j_i,1}, j_i))_{i \in S}$, for an unknown set S.

- Let $M_{j_\ell} = M_{j_\ell,1}$ for $1 \le \ell \le |S|$ and $M_j = M_{j,0}$ for $j \notin \{j_1, \ldots, j_{|S|}\}$.

- **Output.** $\text{NimpcDec}(M_\rho, M_1, \ldots, M_n)$.

We first prove the correctness of ENC, DEC. For simplicity of notations, assume that $S = \{1, \ldots, d\}$, and let $y_1, \ldots, y_n$ be the characteristic vector of S (that is, $y_1 = \cdots = y_d = 1$ and $y_{d+1} = \cdots = y_n = 0$). First let $j = \rho(\ell)$ for some $1 \le \ell \le d$. We get that $M_j = M_{j,1} = M_{j,y_\ell} = M_{j,y_{\rho^{-1}(j)}}$. On the other hand, for all other values of j we get that $M_j = M_{j,0} = M_{j,\rho^{-1}(j)}$. Thus, NimpcDec gets the messages $M_\rho, M_{1,y_{\rho^{-1}(1)}}, \ldots, M_{n,y_{\rho^{-1}(n)}}$ and outputs

$$\text{NimpcDec}(M_\rho, M_1, \ldots, M_n) = g(\rho, y_{\rho^{-1}(1)}, \ldots, y_{\rho^{-1}(n)})$$

$$= f(y_1, \ldots, y_n)$$

as required.

We next prove robustness. Assume towards contradiction that there is an adversary $\mathcal{A}$ that violates the security of the distribution design. We construct an adversary $\mathcal{B}$ that violates the security of the NIMPC protocol. The adversary $\mathcal{B}$ behaves as follows:

- Execute $\mathcal{A}$ and get a circuit C computing a function f representing some set of constraints for a distribution design and two sets $S_0 = \{i_1^0, i_2^0, \cdots, i_d^0\}$ and $S_1 = \{i_1^1, i_2^1, \cdots, i_d^1\}$ (where $i_1^j < i_2^j < \cdots < i_d^j$ for $j \in \{0, 1\}$); let $y_1^0, \ldots, y_n^0$ and $y_1^1, \ldots, y_n^1$ be the characteristic vectors of S_0 and S_1 respectively.

- Construct a circuit C' computing the function g.

- Choose two random permutations ρ_0 and ρ_1 such that $\rho_0(i_j^0) = \rho_1(i_j^1) \triangleq a_j$ for $1 \le j \le d$; Set $T = \{a_1, \ldots, a_d\}$ and define $x_\ell^0 = x_\ell^1 = 1$ if $\ell \in T$ and $x_\ell^0 = x_\ell^1 = 0$ otherwise.

- Send $C', T, (\rho_0, (x_i^0)_{i \notin T}), (\rho_1, (x_i^1)_{i \notin T})$ to the challenger of the NIMPC game.

- The challenger returns messages $(M_{\ell,0}, M_{\ell,1})_{\ell \in T}, M_{\rho_b}, (M_{\ell,0})_{\ell \in [n] \setminus T}$ for a random b.

- Set $X_0 = (M_{\rho_b}, M_{1,0}, \ldots, M_{n,0})$ and $Y_j = (M_{j,1}, a_j)$ for $j \in [d]$.

- Give $X_0, Y_1, \ldots, Y_d$ to $\mathcal{A}$, get a bit b' from $\mathcal{A}$, and output b'.

Note that in the distribution design realizing C, the share $X_{i_j^b}$ is $(M_{\rho_b(i_j^b)}, i_j^b) = (M_{j,1}, a_j)$ as $\rho_b(i_j^b) = a_j$ (and ρ_b is chosen at random). Thus, $\mathcal{A}$ gets shares of S_b for a uniformly chosen b and it returns $b' = b$ with probability noticeably greater than $1/2$, and thus, $\mathcal{B}$ returns $b' = b$ with probability noticeably greater than $1/2$. To complete the proof that this violates the security of the NIMPC protocol, we need to show that g restricted to the two inputs is the same function. Formally, for $j \in \{0,1\}$ we define $g_j((y_i)_{i \in T}) = g(\rho_j, (x_i)_{i \notin T}, (y_i)_{i \in T})$, where $x_i = 0$ for every $j \notin T$, and prove that $g_0 = g_1$. First note that $g_0(1, \ldots, 1) = f(S_0) = f(S_1) = g_1(1, \ldots, 1)$ by the choice of ρ_0, ρ_1 and the definition of g. Furthermore, since f is subset consistent, $f((S_0)_A) = f((S_1)_A)$, thus $g_0((y_i)_{i \in T}) = g_1((y_i)_{i \in T})$.

To conclude, given an adversary $\mathcal{A}$ violating the security of the generator for distribution designs, we constructed an adversary $\mathcal{B}$ violating the security of the NIMPC protocol, where both adversaries are of the same type. Assuming that the NIMPC protocol is secure, no such $\mathcal{B}$ exists, thus, the generator for distribution designs is secure. $\square$

REMARK 6.9. *In the above proof, given a function f with n variables, we defined a function g with $n + 1$ variables $\rho, x_1, \ldots, x_n$, where ρ is a permutation and it is not binary as we defined NIMPC protocols. To fix this, we consider g as a function of $n \log n + n$ binary variables, where the first $n \log n$ variables describe ρ.*

Goldwasser et al. [9] defined and studied multi-input functional encryption schemes (MIFE). They proved that such 1-selective secure schemes exist assuming that indistinguishability obfuscation for circuits and one-way functions exist.[5] We observe that 1-selective multi-input functional encryption schemes can be used to construct robust NIMPC protocols. A formal definition of MIFE and a proof of the following theorem appears in the full version.

THEOREM 6.10. *If 1-selective multi-input functional encryption schemes for circuits exist, then computationally secure NIMPC protocols for circuits exist.*

COROLLARY 6.11. *If indistinguishability obfuscation for circuits and one-way functions exist, then computationally-secure distribution design generators for subset-consistent sets of projective designs exist.*

6.3 Hardness Results for General Distribution Design Generators

We next argue that, in the general case, there are no efficient distribution design generators even for homogenous sets of constraints unless RP = NP.

THEOREM 6.12. *If RP $\neq$ NP, then computationally-secure distribution design generators for circuits representing n-homogeneous sets of constraints over n variables do not exist.*

The idea of the proof is as follows. Let f be such that $f(S) = 0$ for every even permutation. We now plant an additional secret constraint of the form $f(S) = b$, where S is a "secret" odd permutation and b is either 1 or 2. We claim that from f it is hard to know if $b = 1$ or $b = 2$, while it would be easy to compute b from a distribution design realizing f generated by an efficient generator, contradicting the existence of the generator. Formally, we prove hardness via a reduction from the following hard problems.

The promise problem Ternary Unique SAT (TUSAT).

---

[5] In contrast, the known construction provided the stronger notion of IND-secure MIFE (where the adversary chooses its messages after seeing the keys) require indistinguishability obfuscation for circuits and one-way functions that are secure against exponential-time adversaries.

Input: A boolean circuit $C : \{0,1\}^n \to \{0,1\}^2$ with the promise that there is exactly one special input on which the output is not 00.

Output: Decide whether the output on this special input is 01.

The promise problem Unique SAT (USAT).

Input: A boolean circuit $F : \{0,1\}^n \to \{0,1\}$ with the promise that F has at most one satisfying assignment.

Output: Decide whether F is satisfiable or not.

CLAIM 6.13. *If TUSAT $\in$ BPP, then RP = NP.*

PROOF. By [15], if USAT $\in$ BPP, then RP = NP. We show that if TUSAT $\in$ BPP then USAT $\in$ BPP. Without loss of generality, we assume that there exists a probabilistic polynomial-time algorithm $\mathcal{A}$ for TUSAT, whose error is less than $1/4n$. We construct a randomized algorithm $\mathcal{A}'$ for USAT, whose (one-sided) error is less than $1/4$. Given a USAT instance F with exactly one satisfying assignment, we can extract this assignment using $\mathcal{A}$ as we next describe. For every $i \in [n]$, construct a circuit C_i, where $C_i(x) = (\overline{x_i} \wedge F(x), x_i \wedge F(x))$ (that is, $C_i(x)$ outputs 00 if $F(x) = 0$ and otherwise its output is 01 or 10 depending on the i-th bit of x) and execute $\mathcal{A}$ on C_i. If $C_i \in$ TUSAT, set $a_i = 1$; otherwise set $a_i = 0$. Finally, if $F(a_1, \ldots, a_n) = 1$, answer "YES", otherwise answer "NO". If F is unsatisfiable, then, clearly, $F(a_1, \ldots, a_n) = 0$, and $\mathcal{A}'$ answers "NO". On the other hand, assume that F has a unique satisfying assignment $(a_1, \ldots, a_n)$. If $a_i = 0$ then $C_i(a_1, \ldots, a_n) = 10$ and $C_i \notin$ TUSAT. If $a_i = 1$ then $C_i(a_1, \ldots, a_n) = 01$ and $C_i \in$ TUSAT. To conclude, the probability that $\mathcal{A}$ errs in one of its n executions is less than $1/4$, and if it does not err, $\mathcal{A}'$ returns the correct answer for the promise problem USAT. $\square$

We now argue that an efficient computationally-secure distribution design generator for non-homogenous sets of constraints implies a probabilistic polynomial-time algorithm for TUSAT (the same hardness result holds for statistically-secure and perfect distribution design generators).

LEMMA 6.14. *If there is a computationally-secure distribution design generator for n-homogeneous sets of constraints over n variables, then TUSAT $\in$ BPP.*

PROOF. Given a TUSAT instance C with input length m, define an implicit representation f of an n-homogeneous set of constraints for a distribution design with $n = 3m + 2$ variables as follows. First, if S is an even permutation then $f(S) = 2$ (note that determining if S is an even permutation can be done efficiently). Next, for every $x \in \{0,1\}^m$ we define an odd permutation S_x as follows: $S_x(1) = 2, S_x(2) = 1$ and for every $i \in [m]$ if $x_i = 1$ then $S_x(3i) = 3i+1, S_x(3i+1) = 3i+2, S_x(3i+2) = 3i$, else $S_x(3i) = 3i, S_x(3i+1) = 3i+1, S_x(3i+2) = 3i+2$. That is, S_x is composed of one transposition between 1 and 2, and from 3 cycles for every i such that $x_i = 1$; hence S_x is an odd permutation. Let $f(S_x) = 0$ if $C(x) = 00$, $f(S_x) = 2$ if $C(x) = 01$, and $f(S_x) = 1$ if $C(x) \in \{10, 11\}$. Otherwise (that is, if S is a permutation not in the above forms or if the length of S is less than n), let $f(S) = 0$. The above construction implies that the special input for C encodes an odd permutation on which the output of f is either 1 or 2 depending on the output of C on this special input. Furthermore, f can be computed by a circuit whose size is polynomial in the size of the original size of C and in m.

We now describe a probabilistic polynomial-time algorithm $\mathcal{B}$ for TUSAT(assuming a distribution design generator), whose input is a circuit C satisfying the promise of TUSAT.

- Construct a circuit F computing the constraints for the function f described above.

- Let $(x_1, \ldots, x_{3m+2}) \leftarrow \text{Enc}(1^n, F)$.

- If $\text{Dec}(x_2, x_1, x_3, \ldots, x_{3m+2}) = 2$, then output "YES", else output "NO".

Assume that $\mathcal{B}$ errs with probability at least $1/4$ on infinite number of inputs satisfying the TUSAT promise. Let $C_1, C_2, \ldots$ be an infinite sequence of inputs on which $\mathcal{B}$ errs, where the size of C_i is s_i and $s_1 < s_2 < \ldots$. Let m_i be the number of variables in C_i. Furthermore, let a^i be the special input of C_i for $i \in \mathbb{N}$. We now construct a non-uniform adversary violating the security of the distribution design generator. On input 1^k, the adversary outputs C_i for the largest i such that $s_i < k$, and the sequences $(1, 2, \ldots, 3m_i + 2)$ and S'_{a_i}, where $S'_{a_i}(j) = j$ for $j \in \{1, 2\}$ and $S'_{a_i}(j) = S_{a_i}(j)$ for $j \in \{3, \ldots, 3m_i + 2\}$ (notice that both of these permutations are even). Let $(y_1, \ldots, y_{3m_i+2})$ be the shares that the adversary gets from the challenger and $d \leftarrow \text{Dec}(y_2, y_1, y_3, \ldots, y_{3m_i+2})$. Now, if $C_i \in \text{TUSAT}$, then the adversary returns $b' = 3 - d$, otherwise it returns $b' = -d + 2$. We claim that the adversary wins with probability nearly $3/4$.

First, assume that $C_i \in \text{TUSAT}$, hence, $f(S_{a^i}) = 2$. Thus, by the correctness of the distribution design, if $b = 1$, then $d = \text{Dec}(y_2, y_1, y_3, \ldots, y_{3m_i+2}) = 2$ with probability $1 - \text{negl}(n)$. However, since $\mathcal{B}$ errs on C_i with probability at least $1/4$, if $b = 0$, then $\text{Dec}(y_2, y_1, y_3, \ldots, y_{3n_i+2}) = \text{Dec}(x_2, x_1, x_3, \ldots, x_{3m_i+2}) \neq 2$, with probability at least $1/4$. Thus, the adversary can distinguish between the two permutations by computing $\text{Dec}(y_2, y_1, y_3, \ldots, y_{3m_i+2})$, although both permutations are even, thus, should be indistinguishable. Similar arguments hold when $C_i \notin \text{TUSAT}$. This implies that (assuming the existence of a secure distribution design generator), algorithm $\mathcal{B}$ can only err with probability at least $1/4$ on a finite number of inputs. $\square$

Acknowledgements. This work was done in part while the first, third, and forth authors were visiting the Simons Institute for the Theory of Computing, supported by the Simons Foundation and by the DIMACS/Simons Collaboration in Cryptography through NSF grant #CNS-1523467. Research by the first three authors received funding from the European Union's Tenth Framework Programme (FP10/2010-2016) under grant agreement no. 259426 ERC-CaC. The first author was supported by ISF grant 544/13 and by the Frankel center for computer science. Research by the second author received funding from the European Union's Seventh Framework Programme (FP7/2007-2013) under grant agreement no. 257575. Research by the third author received funding from a DARPA/ ARL SAFEWARE award, NSF Frontier Award 1413955, NSF grants 1228984, 1136174, 1118096, and 1065276. This material is based upon work supported by the Defense Advanced Research Projects Agency through the ARL under Contract W911NF-15-C-0205. The views expressed are those of the author and do not reflect the official policy or position of the Department of Defense, the National Science Foundation, or the U.S. Government. The third and fourth authors were supported by ISF grant 1709/14 and BSF grant 2012378.

7. REFERENCES

[1] B. Barak, O. Goldreich, R. Impagliazzo, S. Rudich, A. Sahai, S. P. Vadhan, and K. Yang. On the (im)possibility of obfuscating programs. *J. of the ACM*, 59(2):6, 2012.

[2] A. Beimel, A. Gabizon, Y. Ishai, E. Kushilevitz, S. Meldgaard, and A. Paskin-Cherniavsky. Non-interactive secure multiparty computation. In *CRYPTO 2014*, vol. 8617 of *LNCS*, pp. 387–404, 2014.

[3] M. Bellare, V. T. Hoang, and P. Rogaway. Foundations of garbled circuits. In *CCS '12*, pages 784–796, 2012.

[4] G. R. Blakley. Safeguarding cryptographic keys. In *Proc. of the 1979 AFIPS National Computer Conference*, volume 48, pages 313–317, 1979.

[5] U. Feige, J. Kilian, and M. Naor. A minimal model for secure computation. In *Proc. of the 26th STOC*, pages 554–563, 1994.

[6] M. L. Furst, J. E. Hopcroft, and E. M. Luks. Polynomial-time algorithms for permutation groups. In *Proc. of the 21st FOCS*, pages 36–41, 1980.

[7] S. Garg, C. Gentry, S. Halevi, M. Raykova, A. Sahai, and B. Waters. Candidate indistinguishability obfuscation and functional encryption for all circuits. In *Proc. of the 54th FOCS*, pages 40–49, 2013.

[8] O. Goldreich, S. Micali, and A. Wigderson. How to play any mental game. In *Proc. of the 19th STOC*, pages 218–229, 1987.

[9] S. Goldwasser, S. D. Gordon, V. Goyal, A. Jain, J. Katz, F. Liu, A. Sahai, E. Shi, and H. Zhou. Multi-input functional encryption. In *EUROCRYPT 2014*, volume 8441 of *LNCS*, pages 578–602, 2014.

[10] Y. Ishai and E. Kushilevitz. Perfect constant-round secure computation via perfect randomizing polynomials. In *Proc. of the 29th ICALP*, volume 2380 of *LNCS*, pages 244–256, 2002.

[11] I. Komargodski and M. Zhandry. Cutting-edge cryptography through the lens of secret sharing. *IACR Cryptology ePrint Archive*, 2015:735, 2015. To appear in Proc. of TCC 2016A.

[12] A. Seress. *Permutation Group Algorithms*, volume 152 of *Cambridge Tracts in Mathematics*. Cambridge University Press, 2003.

[13] A. Shamir. How to share a secret. *Communications of the ACM*, 22:612–613, 1979.

[14] C. C. Sims. Computational methods in the study of permutation groups. In *Computational Problems in Abstract Algebra (Proc. Conf., Oxford, 1967)*, pages 169–183, 1970.

[15] L. G. Valiant and V. V. Vazirani. NP is as easy as detecting unique solutions. *Theoretical Computer Science*, 47:85–93, 1986.

[16] A. C. Yao. How to generate and exchange secrets. In *Proc. of the 27th FOCS*, pages 162–167, 1986.

Sampling Correctors

[Extended Abstract] [*]

Clement L. Canonne[†]
Columbia University
ccanonne@cs.columbia.edu

Themis Gouleakis[‡]
CSAIL, MIT
tgoule@mit.edu

Ronitt Rubinfeld[§]
CSAIL, MIT and the Blavatnik
School of Computer Science,
Tel Aviv University
ronitt@csail.mit.edu

ABSTRACT

In many situations, sample data is obtained from a noisy or imperfect source. In order to address such corruptions, this paper introduces the concept of a *sampling corrector*. Such algorithms use structure that the distribution is purported to have, in order to allow one to make "on-the-fly" corrections to samples drawn from probability distributions. These algorithms then act as filters between the noisy data and the end user.

We show connections between sampling correctors, distribution learning algorithms, and distribution property testing algorithms. We show that these connections can be utilized to expand the applicability of known distribution learning and property testing algorithms as well as to achieve improved algorithms for those tasks. As a first step, we show how to design sampling correctors using proper learning algorithms. We then focus on the question of whether algorithms for sampling correctors can be more efficient in terms of sample complexity than learning algorithms for the analogous families of distributions. When correcting monotonicity, we show that this is indeed the case when also granted query access to the cumulative distribution function. We also obtain sampling correctors for monotonicity without this stronger type of access, provided that the distribution be originally *very* close to monotone (namely, at a distance $O(1/\log^2 n)$). In addition to that, we consider a restricted error model that aims at capturing "missing data" corruptions. In this model, we show that distributions that are close to monotone

have sampling correctors that are significantly more efficient than achievable by the learning approach. We then consider the question of whether an additional source of independent random bits is required by sampling correctors to implement the correction process. We show that for correcting close-to-uniform distributions and close-to-monotone distributions, no additional source of random bits is required, as the samples from the input source itself can be used to produce this randomness.

Categories and Subject Descriptors

G.3 [**Probability and Statistics**]: Miscellaneous; G.2.m [**Discrete Mathematics**]: Miscellaneous

General Terms

Theory, Algorithms

Keywords

probability distributions, randomized algorithms, property testing, learning

1. INTRODUCTION

Data consisting of samples from distributions is notorious for reliability issues: Sample data can be greatly affected by noise, calibration problems or other faults in the sample recording process; portions of data may be lost; extraneous samples may be erroneously recorded. Such noise may be completely random, or may have some underlying structure. To give a sense of the range of difficulties one might have with sample data, we mention some examples: A sensor network which tracks traffic data may have dead sensors which transmit no data at all, or other sensors that are defective and transmit arbitrary numbers. Sample data from surveys may suffer from response rates that are correlated with location or socioeconomic factors. Sample data from species distribution models are prone to geographic location errors [28].

Statisticians have grappled with defining a methodology for working with distributions in the presence of noise by *correcting* the samples. If, for example, you know that the uncorrupted distribution is Gaussian, then it would be natural to correct the samples of the distribution to the nearest Gaussian. The challenge in defining this methodology is: how do you correct the samples if you do not know much about the original uncorrupted distribution? To analyze

[*]A full version of this paper is available at http://arxiv.org/abs/1504.06544

[†]Research supported in part by NSF CCF-1115703 and NSF CCF-1319788. Some of this work was done when the author was an intern at Microsoft Research New England.

[‡]Research supported by NSF grants CCF-1420692, CCF-1217423 and CCF-1065125.

[§]Research supported by ISF grant 1536/14 and NSF grants CCF-1420692, CCF-1217423 and CCF-1065125.

Permission to make digital or hard copies of all or part of this work for personal or classroom use is granted without fee provided that copies are not made or distributed for profit or commercial advantage and that copies bear this notice and the full citation on the first page. Copyrights for components of this work owned by others than the author(s) must be honored. Abstracting with credit is permitted. To copy otherwise, or republish, to post on servers or to redistribute to lists, requires prior specific permission and/or a fee. Request permissions from Permissions@acm.org.

ITCS'16, January 14–16, 2016, Cambridge, MA, USA.
Copyright is held by the owner/author(s). Publication rights licensed to ACM.
ACM 978-1-4503-4057-1/16/01 ...$15.00.
DOI: http://dx.doi.org/10.1145/2840728.2840729 .

distributions with noise in a principled way, approaches have included *imputation* [34, 41, 38] for the case of missing or incomplete data, and *outlier detection and removal* [27, 3, 29] to handle "extreme points" deviating significantly from the underlying distribution. More generally, the question of coping with the *sampling bias* inherent to many strategies (such as opportunity sampling) used in studying rare events or species, or with inaccuracies in the reported data, is a key challenge in many of the natural and social sciences (see e.g. [43, 42, 36]). While these problems are usually dealt with drawing on additional knowledge or by using specific modeling assumptions, no general procedure is known that addresses them in a systematic fashion.

In this work, we propose a methodology which is based on using *known structural properties* of the distribution to design *sampling correctors* which "correct" the sample data. While assuming these structural properties is in itself a type of modeling, it is in general much weaker than postulating a strict form of the data (e.g., that it follows a linear model perturbed by Gaussian noise). Examples of structural properties which might be used to correct samples include the property of being bimodal, a mixture of several Gaussians, or an independent joint distribution. Within this methodology, the main question is: how best can one output samples of a distribution in which on one hand, the structural properties are restored, and on the other hand, the corrected distribution is close to the original distribution? We show that this task is intimately connected to distribution learning tasks, but we also give instances in which such tasks can be performed strictly more efficiently.

1.1 Our model

We introduce two (related) notions of algorithms to correct distributions: *sampling correctors* and *sampling improvers*. Although the precise definitions are deferred to Section 2, we describe and state informally what we mean by these. In what follows, $\mathcal{X}$ is a finite domain, $\mathcal{P}$ is any fixed property of distributions, i.e., a subset of distributions, over $\mathcal{X}$ and distances between distributions are measured according to their *total variation distance*.[1]

A *sampling corrector* for $\mathcal{P}$ is a randomized algorithm which gets samples from a distribution D guaranteed to be ε-close to having property $\mathcal{P}$, and outputs a sample from a "corrected distribution" $\tilde{D}$ which, with high probability, (a) *has* the property; and (b) is still close to the original distribution D (i.e., within distance ε_1). The *sample complexity* of such a corrector is the number of samples it needs to obtain from D in order to output one from $\tilde{D}$.

To make things concrete, we give a simple example of correcting independence of distributions over a product space $[n] \times [m]$. For each pair of samples (x, y) and (x', y') from a distribution D which is ε-close to independent, output *one* sample (x, y'). As x and y' are independent, the resulting distribution clearly has the property; and it can be shown that if D was indeed ε-close to independent, then the distribution of (x, y') will indeed be 3ε-close to D [39]. (Whether this sample complexity can be reduced further to $q < 2$, even on average, is an open question.)

Note that in some settings it may be too much to ask for complete correction (or may even not be the most desirable option). For this reason, we also consider the weaker notion of *sampling improvers*, which is similar to a sampling corrector but is only required to transform the distribution into a new distribution which is *closer* to having the property $\mathcal{P}$.

One naive way to solve these problems, the "learning approach," is to approximate the probability mass function of D, and find a candidate $\tilde{D} \in \mathcal{P}$. Since we assume we have a complete description of $\tilde{D}$, we can then output samples according to $\tilde{D}$ without further access to D. In general, such an approach can be very inefficient in terms of time complexity. However, if there is an *efficient* agnostic proper learning algorithm[2] for $\mathcal{P}$, we show that this approach can lead to efficient sampling correctors. For example, we use such an approach to give sampling correctors for the class of monotone distributions.

In our model, we focus on optimizing the following two parameters of our correcting algorithms: The first parameter is the number of samples of D needed to output samples of $\tilde{D}$. The second parameter is the number of *additional* truly random bits needed for outputting samples of $\tilde{D}$. Note that in the above learning approach, the dependence on each of these parameters could be quite large. Although these parameters are not independent of each other (if D is of high enough entropy, then it can be used to simulate truly random bits), they can be thought of as complementary, as one typically will aim at a tradeoff between the two. Furthermore, a parsimonious use of extra random bits may be crucial for some applications, while in others the correction of the data itself is the key factor; for this reason, we track each of the parameters separately. For any property $\mathcal{P}$, the main question is whether one can achieve improved complexity in terms of these parameters over the use of the naive (agnostic) learning approach for $\mathcal{P}$.

1.2 Our results

In this work, we focus on two particular properties of interest, namely *uniformity* and *monotonicity*. The first one, arguably one of the most natural and illustrative properties to be considered, is nonetheless deeply challenging in the setting of randomness scarcity. As for the second, not only does it provide insight in the workings of sampling correctors as well as non-trivial connections and algorithmic results, but is also one of the most-studied classes of distributions in the statistics and probability literature, with a body of work covering several decades (see e.g. [26, 9, 7, 21], or [22] for a detailed list of references). Moreover, recent work on distribution testing [22, 13] shows strong connections between monotonicity and a wide range of other properties, such as for instance log-concavity, Monotone Hazard Risk and Poisson Binomial Distributions. This gives evidence that the study of monotone distributions may have direct implications for correction of many of these "shape-constrained properties."

---

[1] The total variation distance is defined as $d_{TV}(D_1, D_2) \overset{\text{def}}{=} \max_{S \subseteq \mathcal{X}} (D_1(S) - D_2(S)) = \frac{1}{2} \sum_{x \in \mathcal{X}} |D_1(x) - D_2(x)|$.

[2] Recall that a *learning algorithm* for a class of distributions $\mathcal{C}$ is an algorithm which gets independent samples from an unknown distribution $D \in \mathcal{C}$; and on input ε must, with high probability, output a hypothesis which is ε-close to D in total variation distance. If the hypotheses the algorithm produces are guaranteed to belong to $\mathcal{C}$ as well, we call it a *proper learning algorithm*. Finally, if the – not-necessarily proper – algorithm is able to learn distributions that are only *close* to $\mathcal{C}$, returning a hypothesis at a distance at most OPT $+ \varepsilon$ from D – where OPT is the distance from D to the class, it is said to be *agnostic*. For a formal definition of these concepts, the reader is referred to the full version.

Sampling correctors, learning algorithms and property testing algorithms.

We begin by showing implications of the existence of sampling correctors for the existence of various types of learning and property testing algorithms in other models. We first show in Theorem 3.1 that learning algorithms for a distribution class imply sampling correctors for distributions in this class (under *any* property to correct) with the same sample complexity, though not necessarily the same running time dependency. However, when efficient agnostic proper learning algorithms for a distribution class exist, we show that there are efficient sampling correctors for the same class. In [9, 18] efficient algorithms for agnostic learning of concise representations for several families of distributions are given, including distributions that are monotone, k-histograms, Poisson binomial, and sums of k independent random variables. Not all of these algorithms are proper.

Next, we show in Theorem 3.3 that the existence of (a) an efficient learning algorithm, as e.g. in [31, 17, 20, 19], and (b) an efficient sampling corrector for a class of distributions implies an efficient *agnostic* learning algorithm for the same class of distributions. It is well known that agnostic learning can be much harder than non-agnostic learning, as in the latter the algorithm is able to leverage structural properties of the class $\mathcal{C}$. Thus, by the above result we also get that any agnostic learning lower bounds can be used to obtain sampling corrector lower bounds.

Our third result in this section, Theorem 3.5, shows that an efficient property tester, an efficient distance estimator (which computes an additive estimate of the distance between two distributions) and an efficient sampling corrector for a distribution class imply a tolerant property tester with complexity equal to the complexity of correcting the number of samples required to run both the tester and estimator.[3] As tolerant property testing can be much more difficult than property testing [25, 6, 35, 46], this gives a general purpose way of getting both upper bounds on tolerant property testing and lower bounds on sampling correctors.

We describe how these results can be employed in Section 3, where we give specific applications in achieving improved property testers for various properties.

Is sampling correction easier than learning?.

We next turn to the question of whether there are natural examples of sampling correctors whose query complexity is much smaller than that of distribution learning algorithms for the same class. While the sample complexity of learning monotone distributions is known to be $\Omega(\log n)$ [9] (this lower bound on the sample and query complexity holds even when the algorithm is allowed both to make queries to the cumulative distribution function as well as to access samples of the distribution), we present an oblivious sampling corrector for monotone distributions with sample complexity $O(1)$, which corrects error smaller than $\varepsilon \leq O(1/\log^2 n)$. This is done by first implicitly approximating the distribution by a "histogram" on only a small number of intervals, using ingredients from [9]. This (very close) approximation can then be combined, still in an oblivious way, with a carefully

chosen slowly decreasing distribution, so that the resulting mixture is not only guaranteed to be monotone, but also close to the original distribution.

It is open whether there exist sampling correctors for monotone distributions with sample complexity $o\big((\log n)/\varepsilon^3\big)$ that can correct arbitrary error $\varepsilon \in (0,1)$, thus beating the sample complexity of the "learning approach." (We note however that a logarithmic dependence on n is inherent when $\varepsilon = \omega(1/\log n)$, as pointed out to us by Paul Valiant [47].)

Assuming a stronger type of access to the unknown distribution – namely, query access to its cumulative distribution function (CDF) as in [4, 15], we describe in Section 4 a sampling corrector for monotonicity with (expected) query complexity $O\big(\sqrt{\log n}\big)$ which works for arbitrary $\varepsilon \in (0,1)$. At a high-level, our algorithm combines the "succinct histogram" technique mentioned above with a two-level bucketing approach to correct the distribution first at a very coarse level only (on "superbuckets"), and defer the finer corrections (within a given superbucket) to be made on-the-go at query time. The challenge in this last part is that one must ensure that all of these disjoint local corrections are consistent with each other – and crucially, *with all future sample corrections*. To achieve this, we use a "boundary correction" subroutine which fixes potential violations between two neighboring superbuckets by evening out the boundary differences. To make it possible, we use rejection sampling to allocate adaptively an extra "budget" to each superbucket that this subroutine can use for corrections.

Restricted error models.

Since many of the sampling correction problems are difficult to solve in general, we suggest error models for which more efficient sampling correction algorithms may exist. A first class of error models, which we refer to as *missing data errors*, is introduced in the full version of this paper and defined as follows – given a distribution over $[n]$, all samples in some interval $[i,j]$ for $1 < i < j < n$ are deleted. Such errors could correspond to samples from a sensor network where one of the sensors ran out of power; emails mistakenly deleted by a spam filter; or samples from a study in which some of the paperwork got lost. Whenever the input distribution D, whose distance from monotonicity is $\varepsilon \in (0,1)$, falls under this model, we give a sampling improver that is able to find a distribution both ε_2-close to monotone and $O(\varepsilon)$-close to the original using $\tilde{O}\big(1/\varepsilon_2^3\big)$ samples. The improver works in two stages. In the "preprocessing stage," we detect the location of the missing interval (when the missing weight is sufficiently large) and then estimate its missing weight, using a "learning through testing" approach from [21] to keep the sample complexity under control. In the second stage, we give a procedure by which the algorithm can use its knowledge of the estimated missing interval to correct the distribution by rejection sampling.

Randomness Scarcity.

We then consider the case where only a limited amount of randomness (other than the input distribution) is available, and optimizing its use, possibly at the cost of worse parameters and/or sample complexity of our sampling improvers, is crucial. This captures situations where generating

---

[3]Recall that the difference between testing and tolerant testing lies in that the former asks to distinguish whether an unknown distribution *has* a property, or is far from it, while the latter requires to decide whether the distribution is *close* to the property versus far from it.

the random bits the algorithm use is either expensive[4] (as in the case of physical implementations relying on devices, such as Geiger counters or Zener diodes) or undesirable (e.g., when we want the output distribution to be a deterministic function of the input data, for the sake of reproducibility or parallelization). We focus on this setting in the second part of the full version, and provide sampling correctors and improvers for uniformity that use samples *only* from the input distribution. For example, we give a sampling improver that, given access to distribution ε-close to uniform, grants access to a distribution ε_2-close to uniform distribution and has *constant* sample complexity $O_{\varepsilon, \varepsilon_2}(1)$. We achieve this by exploiting the fact that the uniform distribution is not only an absorbing element for convolution in Abelian groups, but also an *attractive fixed point* with high convergence rate. That is, by convolving a distribution with itself (i.e., summing independent samples modulo the order of the group) one gets very quickly close to uniform. Combining this idea with a different type of improvement (based on a von Neumann-type "trick") allows us to obtain an essentially optimal tradeoff between closeness to uniform and to the original distribution.

1.3 Open problems

Correcting vs. Learning. A main direction of interest would be to obtain more examples of properties for which correcting is strictly more efficient than (agnostic or non-agnostic) learning. Such examples would be insightful even if they are more efficient only in terms of the number of samples required from the original distribution, without considering the additional randomness requirements for generating the distribution. More specifically, one may ask whether there exists a sampling corrector for monotonicity of distributions (i.e., one that beats the learning bound from Theorem 4.1) for all $\epsilon < 1$ which uses at most $o\big((\log n)/\varepsilon^3\big)$ samples from the original distribution per sample output of the corrected distribution. Other properties of interest, among many, include log-concavity of distributions, having a piecewise-constant density (i.e., being a k-histogram for some fixed value k), or being a Poisson Binomial Distribution.

The power of additional queries. Following the line of work pursued in [16, 14, 15] (in the setting of distribution testing), it is natural in many situations to consider additional types of queries to the input distribution: e.g., either *conditional queries* (getting a sample conditioned on a specific subset of the domain) or *cumulative queries* (granting query access to the cumulative distribution function, besides the usual sampling). By providing algorithms with this extended access to the underlying probability distribution, can one obtain faster sampling correctors for specific properties, as we do in the case of monotonicity?

Confidence boosting. Suppose that there exists, for some property $\mathcal{P}$, a sampling improver $\mathcal{A}$ that only guarantees a success probability[5] of 2/3. Using $\mathcal{A}$ as a black-box, can

one design a sampling improver $\mathcal{A}'$ which succeeds with probability $1 - \delta$, for any δ?

More precisely, let $\mathcal{A}$ be a batch improver for $\mathcal{P}$ which, when queried, makes $q(\varepsilon_1, \varepsilon_2)$ queries and provides $t \geq 1$ samples, with success probability at least 2/3. Having black-box access to $\mathcal{A}$, can we obtain a batch improver $\mathcal{A}'$ which on input $\delta > 0$ provides $t' \geq 1$ samples, with success probability at least $1 - \delta$? If so, what is the best t' one can achieve, and what is the minimum query complexity of $\mathcal{A}'$ one can get (as a function of $q(\cdot, \cdot)$, t' and δ)?

This is known for property testing (by running the testing algorithm independently $O(\log(1/\delta))$ times and taking the majority vote), as well as for learning (again, by running the learning algorithm many times, and then doing hypothesis testing, e.g. *à la* [23] (Theorem 19)). However, these approaches do not straightforwardly generalize to sampling improvers or correctors, respectively because the output is not a single bit, and as we only obtain a sequence of samples (instead of an actual, fully-specified hypothesis distribution).

1.4 Other previous work

Dealing with noisy or incomplete datasets has been a challenge in Statistics and data sciences, and many methods have been proposed to handle them. Such methods include *imputation* and *multiple imputation* [37], which creates new datasets from incomplete datasets by filling in the missing values randomly according to a maximum likelihood distribution computed from the observations and a modeling assumption made on the data. The parameters of this model are then updated in a manner that resembles the Expectation-Maximization (EM) algorithm [24, 41, 34].

From a Theoretical Computer Science perspective, the problem of local correction of data has received much attention (some examples include [10, 48, 2, 40, 8, 32]). To the best of our knowledge, this is the first work to address the correction of data from distributions.

It is instructive to compare the goal of our model of distribution sampling correctors to that of extractors: in spite of many similarities, the two have essential differences and the results are in many cases incomparable. We defer this discussion to the full version.

Organization.

After stating the formal definition of our model in Section 2, we draw in Section 3 some connections it yields to learning and testing. Section 4 focuses on the sample complexity of correcting monotonicity, and contains three different algorithmic results for this problem. as well as a corrector for the "missing data error" model. Due to space constraints, our results on randomness scarcity and all proofs are deferred to the full version.

2. OUR MODEL: DEFINITIONS

In this section, we state the precise definitions of sampling correctors, improvers and batch sampling improvers. To get an intuition, the reader may think for instance of the parameter ε_1 below as being 2ε, and the error probability δ as 1/3. Although all definitions are presented in terms of the total variation distance, analogous definitions in terms of other distances can also be made.

DEFINITION 2.1 (SAMPLING CORRECTOR). *Fix a given property $\mathcal{P}$ of distributions on $\mathcal{X}$. An $(\varepsilon, \varepsilon_1)$-sampling correc-*

---

[4]On this topic, see for instance the discussion in [33, 30], and references therein.

[5]We note that the case of interest here is of batch sampling improvers: indeed, in order to generate a single draw, a sampling improver acts in a non-trivial way only if the parameter ε is greater than its failure probability δ. If not, a draw from the original distribution already satisfies the requirements.

tor for $\mathcal{P}$ is a randomized algorithm which is given parameters $\varepsilon, \varepsilon_1 \in (0,1]$ such that $\varepsilon_1 \geq \varepsilon$ and $\delta \in [0,1]$, as well as sampling access to a distribution D. Under the promise that $d_{\mathrm{TV}}(D, \mathcal{P}) \leq \varepsilon$, the algorithm must provide, with probability at least $1 - \delta$ over the samples it draws and its internal randomness, sampling access to a distribution $\tilde{D}$ such that

(i) $\tilde{D}$ is close to D: $d_{\mathrm{TV}}(\tilde{D}, D) \leq \varepsilon_1$;

(ii) $\tilde{D}$ has the property: $\tilde{D} \in \mathcal{P}$.

In other terms, with high probability the algorithm will simulate exactly a sampling oracle for $\tilde{D}$. The query complexity $q = q(\varepsilon, \varepsilon_1, \delta, \mathcal{X})$ of the algorithm is the number of samples from D it takes per query in the worst case.

One can define a more general notion, which allows the algorithm to only get "closer" to the desired property, and convert some type of access ORACLE$_1$ into some other type of access ORACLE$_2$ (e.g., from sampling to evaluation access):

DEFINITION 2.2 (SAMPLING IMPROVER). *Fix a given property $\mathcal{P}$ over distributions on $\mathcal{X}$. A sampling improver for $\mathcal{P}$ (from ORACLE$_1$ to ORACLE$_2$) is a randomized algorithm which, given parameter $\varepsilon \in (0,1]$ and ORACLE$_1$ access to a distribution D with the promise that $d_{\mathrm{TV}}(D, \mathcal{P}) \leq \varepsilon$ as well as parameters $\varepsilon_1, \varepsilon_2 \in [0,1]$ satisfying $\varepsilon_1 + \varepsilon_2 \geq \varepsilon$, provides, with probability at least $1 - \delta$ over the answers from ORACLE$_1$ and its internal randomness, ORACLE$_2$ access to a distribution $\tilde{D}$ such that*

$$d_{\mathrm{TV}}(\tilde{D}, D) \leq \varepsilon_1 \qquad \text{(Close to } D\text{)}$$

$$d_{\mathrm{TV}}(\tilde{D}, \mathcal{P}) \leq \varepsilon_2 \qquad \text{(Close to } \mathcal{P}\text{)}$$

In other terms, with high probability the algorithm will simulate exactly ORACLE$_2$ access to $\tilde{D}$. The query complexity $q = q(\varepsilon, \varepsilon_1, \varepsilon_2, \delta, \mathcal{X})$ of the algorithm is the number of queries it makes to ORACLE$_1$ in the worst case.

Finally, one may ask for such an improver to provide *many* samples from the (same) improved distribution,[6] where "many" is a number committed in advance. We refer to such an algorithm as a *batch sampling improver* (or, similarly, batch sampling corrector):

DEFINITION 2.3 (BATCH SAMPLING IMPROVER). *For $\mathcal{P}$, D, ε, $\varepsilon_1, \varepsilon_2 \in [0,1]$ as above, and parameter $m \in \mathbb{N}$, a batch sampling improver for $\mathcal{P}$ (from ORACLE$_1$ to ORACLE$_2$) is a sampling improver which provides, with probability at least $1 - \delta$, ORACLE$_2$ access to $\tilde{D}$ for as many as m queries, in between which it is allowed to maintain some internal state ensuring consistency. The query complexity of the algorithm is now allowed to depend on m as well.*
Note that, in particular, when providing sampling access to $\tilde{D}$ the batch improver must guarantee independence of the m samples. When ε_2 is set to 0 in the above definition, we will refer to the algorithm as a batch sampling corrector.

REMARK 2.4 (ON PARAMETERS OF INTEREST). *We observe that the regime of interest of our correctors and improvers is when the number of corrected samples to output is*

---

[6]Indeed, observe that as sampling correctors and improvers are randomized algorithms with access to their "own" coins, there is no guarantee that fixing the input distribution D would lead to the same output distribution $\tilde{D}$.

at least of the order $\Omega(1/\varepsilon)$. Indeed, if fewer samples are required, then the assumption that the distribution D be ε-close to having the property implies that – with high probability – a small number of samples from D will be indistinguishable from the closest distribution having the property. (So that, intuitively, they are already "as good as it gets," and need not be corrected.)

REMARK 2.5 (ON TESTING LOWER BOUNDS). *A similar observation holds for properties $\mathcal{P}$ that are known to be hard to test, that is for which some lower bound of $q(n, \varepsilon)$ samples holds to decide whether a given distribution satisfies $\mathcal{P}$, or is ε-far from it. In light of such a lower bound, one may wonder whether there is something to be gained in correcting $m < q(n, \varepsilon)$ samples, instead of simply using m samples from the original distribution altogether. However, such a result only states that there exists some worst-case instance D^* that is at distance ε from the property $\mathcal{P}$, yet requires this many samples to be distinguished from it: so that any algorithm relying on samples from distributions satisfying $\mathcal{P}$ could be fed $q(n, \varepsilon) - 1$ samples from this particular D^* without complaining. Yet, for "typical" distributions that are ε-close to $\mathcal{P}$, it may be that far fewer samples are required to reveal their deviation from it: for many, as few as $O(1/\varepsilon)$ suffice. Thus, an algorithm that expects to get say $q(n, \varepsilon)^{.99}$ samples from a honest-to-goodness distribution from $\mathcal{P}$, but instead is provided with samples from one that is merely ε-close to it, may break down very quickly. Our corrector, in this very regime of $o(q(n, \varepsilon))$ samples, guarantees this will not happen.*

3. CONNECTIONS TO LEARNING AND TESTING

In this section, we draw connections between sampling improvers and other areas, namely testing and learning. These connections shed light on the relation between our model and these other lines of work, and provide a way to derive new algorithms and impossibility results for both testing or learning problems.

3.1 From learning to correcting

As a first observation, it is not difficult to see that, under the assumption that the unknown distribution D belongs to some specific class $\mathcal{C}$, correcting (or improving) a property $\mathcal{P}$ requires at most as many samples as learning the class $\mathcal{C}$; that is, *learning (a class of distributions) is at least as hard as correcting (distributions of this class)*. Here, $\mathcal{P}$ and $\mathcal{C}$ need not be related.

Indeed, assuming there exists a learning algorithm $\mathcal{L}$ for $\mathcal{C}$, it suffices to run it on the unknown distribution $D \in \mathcal{C}$ to learn a hypothesis $\hat{D}$ sufficiently close to D. In particular, $\hat{D}$ must itself still be close to $\mathcal{P}$. One can then (e.g., by exhaustive search) find $\tilde{D}$ in $\mathcal{P}$ which is closest to $\hat{D}$ (and therefore at most ε_1-far from D), and use it to produce as many "corrected samples" as wanted:

THEOREM 3.1. *Let $\mathcal{C}$ a class of probability distributions over $\mathcal{X}$. Suppose there exists a learning algorithm $\mathcal{L}$ for $\mathcal{C}$ with sample complexity $q_{\mathcal{L}}$. Then, for any property $\mathcal{P}$ of distributions, there exists a (not-necessarily computationally efficient) sampling corrector for $\mathcal{P}$ with sample complexity $q(\varepsilon, \varepsilon_1, \delta) = q_{\mathcal{L}}\left(\frac{\varepsilon_1 - \varepsilon}{2}, \delta\right)$, under the promise that $D \in \mathcal{C}$.*

Furthermore, if the (efficient) learning algorithm $\mathcal{L}$ has the additional guarantee that the hypotheses it outputs always belong to (a subset of) $\mathcal{P}$, and allow efficient generation of samples, then we immediately obtain a computationally efficient sampling corrector: indeed, in this case $\hat{D} \in \mathcal{P}$ already. Furthermore, as mentioned in the introduction, when efficient agnostic proper learning algorithms for distribution classes exist, then there are efficient sampling correctors for the same classes. Yet, it is worth pointing out that this correcting-by-learning approach is quite inefficient with regard to the amount of extra randomness needed: indeed, every sample generated from $\tilde{D}$ requires fresh new random bits.

To illustrate our theorem, we give here an easy corollary. This result follows from Chan et al., who showed in [17] that monotone hazard risk distributions can be learned to accuracy ε using $\tilde{O}\big(\log n/\varepsilon^4\big)$ samples; moreover, the hypothesis obtained is a $O\big(\log(n/\varepsilon)/\varepsilon^2\big)$-histogram.

COROLLARY 3.2. *Let $\mathcal{C}$ be the class of monotone hazard risk distributions over $[n]$, and $\mathcal{P}$ be the property of being a histogram with (at most) $\sqrt{n}$ pieces. Then, under the promise that $D \in \mathcal{C}$ and as long as $\varepsilon = \tilde{\Omega}(1/\sqrt{n})$, there is a sampling corrector for $\mathcal{P}$ with sample complexity $\tilde{O}\Big(\frac{\log n}{(\varepsilon_1 - \varepsilon)^4}\Big)$.*

3.2 From correcting to agnostic learning

Let $\mathcal{C}$ and $\mathcal{H}$ be two classes of probability distributions over $\mathcal{X}$. Recall that a *(semi-)agnostic learner for $\mathcal{C}$* (using hypothesis class $\mathcal{H}$) is a learning algorithm $\mathcal{A}$ which, given sample access to an arbitrary distribution D and parameter ε, outputs a hypothesis $\hat{D} \in \mathcal{H}$ such that, with high probability, $\hat{D}$ does "as much as well as the best approximation from $\mathcal{C}$:" $\mathrm{d_{TV}}\big(D, \hat{D}\big) \leq c \cdot \mathrm{OPT}_{\mathcal{C},D} + O(\varepsilon)$, where $\mathrm{OPT}_{\mathcal{C},D} = \inf_{D_{\mathcal{C}} \in \mathcal{C}} \mathrm{d_{TV}}(D_{\mathcal{C}}, D)$ and $c \geq 1$ is some absolute constant (if $c = 1$, the learner is said to be agnostic).

In the full version, we first describe how to combine a (non-agnostic) learning algorithm with a sampling corrector in order to obtain an agnostic learner, under the strong assumption that a (rough) estimate of OPT is known. Then, we explain how to get rid of this extra requirement, using machinery from the distribution learning literature (namely, an efficient *hypothesis selection* procedure). This leads to the following result:

THEOREM 3.3. *Let $\mathcal{C}$ be as above. Suppose there exists a learning algorithm $\mathcal{L}$ for $\mathcal{C}$ with sample complexity $q_{\mathcal{L}}$, and a batch sampling corrector $\mathcal{A}$ for $\mathcal{C}$ with sample complexity $q_{\mathcal{A}}$. Suppose further that a constant-factor estimate $\widehat{\mathrm{OPT}}$ of $\mathrm{OPT}_{\mathcal{C},D}$ is known (up to a multiplicative c).*

Then, there exists a (semi) agnostic learner for $\mathcal{C}$ with sample complexity $q(\varepsilon, \delta) = q_{\mathcal{A}}\big(\widehat{\mathrm{OPT}}, \widehat{\mathrm{OPT}} + \varepsilon, q_{\mathcal{L}}(\frac{\varepsilon}{2}), \frac{\delta}{2}\big)$ (where the constant in front of $\mathrm{OPT}_{\mathcal{C},D}$ is c). Moreover, if such $\widehat{\mathrm{OPT}}$ is not known, the result still holds at the price of a $\mathrm{polylog}(1/\varepsilon)$ blowup in the sample complexity.

It is worth noting that in the case the learning algorithm is *proper* (meaning the hypotheses it outputs belong to the target class $\mathcal{C}$: that is, $\mathcal{H} = \mathcal{C}$), then so is the agnostic learner obtained with Theorem 3.3. This turns out to be a very strong guarantee: specifically, getting (computationally efficient) proper agnostic learning algorithms remains a challenge for many classes of interest – see e.g. [20], which mentions efficient proper learning of Poisson Binomial Distributions as an open problem.

We stress that the above can be viewed as a *generic* framework to obtain efficient agnostic learning results from known efficient learning algorithms. For the sake of illustration, let us consider the simple case of Binomial distributions: it is known, for instance as a consequence of the aforementioned results on PBDs, that learning such distributions can be performed with $\tilde{O}\big(1/\varepsilon^2\big)$ samples (and that $\Omega\big(1/\varepsilon^2\big)$ are required). Our theorem then provides a simple way to obtain agnostic learning of Binomial distributions with sample complexity $\tilde{O}\big(1/\varepsilon^2\big)$: namely, by designing an efficient sampling corrector for this class with sample complexity $\mathrm{poly}(\log \frac{1}{\varepsilon}, \log \frac{1}{\varepsilon_1})$. (Since publication of our work, we have learned that [1] provides such a result unconditionally.)

COROLLARY 3.4. *Suppose there exists a batch sampling corrector $\mathcal{A}$ for the class $\mathcal{B}$ of binomial distributions over $[n]$, with sample complexity $q_{\mathcal{A}}(\varepsilon, \varepsilon_1, m, \delta) = \mathrm{polylog}(\frac{1}{\varepsilon}, \frac{1}{\varepsilon_1}, m, \frac{1}{\delta})$. Then, there exists a semi-agnostic learner for $\mathcal{B}$, which, given access to an unknown distribution D promised to be ε-close to some binomial distribution, takes $\tilde{O}\big(\frac{1}{\varepsilon^2}\big)$ samples from D and outputs a distribution $\hat{B} \in \mathcal{B}$ such that*

$$\mathrm{d_{TV}}\big(D, \hat{B}\big) \leq 3\varepsilon$$

with probability at least $2/3$.

To the best of our knowledge, an agnostic learning algorithm for the class of Binomial distributions with sample complexity $\tilde{O}\big(1/\varepsilon^2\big)$ is not explicitly known, although the results of [18] do imply a $\tilde{O}\big(1/\varepsilon^3\big)$ upper bound and a modification of [20] (to make their algorithm agnostic) seems to yield one. The above suggests an approach which would lead to the (essentially optimal) sample complexity.

3.3 From correcting to tolerant testing

We observe that the existence of sampling correctors for a given property $\mathcal{P}$, along with an efficient distance estimation procedure, allows one to convert any distribution testing algorithm into a tolerant distribution testing algorithm. This is similar to the connection between "local reconstructors" and tolerant testing of graphs described in [11] (Theorem 3.1) and [12] (Theorem 3.1). That is, if a property $\mathcal{P}$ has both a distance estimator and a sampling corrector, then one can perform *tolerant* testing of $\mathcal{P}$ in the time required to generate enough corrected samples for both the estimator and a (non-tolerant) tester.

We first state our theorem in all generality, before instantiating it in several corollaries. For the sake of clarity, the reader may wish to focus on these on a first pass.

THEOREM 3.5. *Let $\mathcal{C}$ be a class of distributions, and $\mathcal{P} \subseteq \mathcal{C}$ a property. Suppose there exists an $(\varepsilon, \varepsilon_1)$-batch sampling corrector $\mathcal{A}$ for $\mathcal{P}$ with complexity $q_{\mathcal{A}}$, and a distance estimator $\mathcal{E}$ for $\mathcal{C}$ with complexity $q_{\mathcal{E}}$ – that is, given sample access to $D_1, D_2 \in \mathcal{C}$ and parameters ε, δ, $\mathcal{E}$ draws $q_{\mathcal{E}}(\varepsilon, \delta)$ samples from D_1, D_2 and outputs a value $\hat{d}$ such that $\big|\hat{d} - \mathrm{d_{TV}}(D_1, D_2)\big| \leq \varepsilon$ with probability at least $1 - \delta$.*

Then, from any property tester $\mathcal{T}$ for $\mathcal{P}$ with sample complexity $q_{\mathcal{T}}$, one can get a tolerant tester $\mathcal{T}'$ with query complexity $q(\varepsilon', \varepsilon, \delta) = q_{\mathcal{A}}\Big(\varepsilon', \Theta(\varepsilon), q_{\mathcal{E}}(\frac{\varepsilon - \varepsilon'}{4}, \frac{\delta}{3}) + q_{\mathcal{T}}(\frac{\varepsilon - \varepsilon'}{4}, \frac{\delta}{3}), \frac{\delta}{3}\Big)$.

REMARK 3.6. *Only asking that the distance estimation procedure $\mathcal{E}$ be specific to the class $\mathcal{C}$ is not innocent; indeed,* it is known ([46]) that for general *distributions, distance estimation has sample complexity* $\Omega(n^{1-o(1)})$. *However, the task becomes significantly easier for certain classes of distributions: and for instance can be performed with only* $\tilde{O}(k \log n)$ *samples, if the distributions are guaranteed to be k-modal* [22]. *This observation can be leveraged in cases when one knows that the distribution has a specific property, but does not quite satisfy a second property: e.g. is known to be k-modal but not known to be, say, log-concave.*

The reduction above can be useful both as a black-box way to derive upper bounds for tolerant testing, as well as to prove lower bounds for either testing or distance estimation. For the first use, we give two applications of our theorem to provide tolerant monotonicity testers for k-modal distributions. The first is a conditional result, showing that the existence of good monotonicity correctors yield tolerant testers. The second, while unconditional, only guarantees a weaker form of tolerance (guaranteeing acceptance only of distributions that are very close to monotone); and relies on a corrector we describe in Section 4. As we detail shortly after stating these two results, even this weak tolerance improves upon the one provided by currently known testing algorithms.

COROLLARY 3.7. *Suppose there exists an* $(\varepsilon, \varepsilon_1)$-*batch sampling corrector for monotonicity with complexity* q. *Then, for any* $k = O(\log n / \log \log n)$, *there exists an algorithm that distinguishes whether a k-modal distribution is (a)* ε-*close to monotone or (b)* 5ε-*far from monotone with success probability* $2/3$, *and sample complexity* $q\left(\varepsilon, 2\varepsilon, C\frac{k \log n}{\varepsilon^4 \log \log n}, \frac{1}{9}\right)$ *where* C *is an absolute constant.*

Another application of this theorem, but this time taking advantage of a result from Section 4, allows us to derive an *explicit* tolerant tester for monotonicity of k-modal distributions:

COROLLARY 3.8. *For any* $k \geq 1$, *there exists an algorithm that distinguishes whether a k-modal distribution is (a)* $O(\varepsilon^3 / \log^2 n)$-*close to monotone or (b)* ε-*far from monotone with success probability* $2/3$, *and sample complexity* $O\left(\frac{1}{\varepsilon^4}\frac{k \log n}{\log(k \log n)} + \frac{k^2}{\varepsilon^4}\right)$. *In particular, for* $k = O\left(\frac{\log n}{\log \log n}\right)$ *this gives a weakly tolerant tester with sample complexity* $O\left(\frac{k \log n}{\varepsilon^4 \log \log n}\right)$.

Note that, to the best of our knowledge, no tolerant tester for monotonicity of k-modal distributions was previously known, though using the (regular) $O(k/\varepsilon^2)$-sample tester of [21] and standard arguments, one can achieve a weak tolerance on the order of $O(\varepsilon^2/k)$. While the sample complexity obtained in Corollary 3.8 is worse by a polylog(n) factor, it has better tolerance for $k = \Omega(\log^2 n/\varepsilon)$.

4. CORRECTING MONOTONICITY

In this section, we focus on the sample complexity aspect of correcting, considering the specific example of monotonicity correction. As a first result, we show in Theorem 4.1 how to design a simple batch corrector for monotonicity which, after a preprocessing step costing logarithmically many samples, is able to answer an arbitrary number of queries. This corrector follows the "learning approach" described in Section 3.1, and in particular provides a very efficient way to amortize the cost of making many queries to a corrected distribution.

THEOREM 4.1 (CORRECTING BY LEARNING). *Fix any constant* $c > 0$. *For any* ε, $\varepsilon_1 \geq (3 + c)\varepsilon$ *and* $\varepsilon_2 = 0$ *as in the definition, any type of oracle* ORACLE *and any number of queries* m, *there exists a sampling corrector for monotonicity from sampling to* ORACLE *with sample complexity* $O\left(\log n / \varepsilon^3\right)$.

A natural question is then whether one can "beat" this approach, and correct the distribution without approximating it as a whole beforehand. Theorem 4.2 answers it by the affirmative: namely, we show that one can correct distributions that are guaranteed to be $(1/\log^2 n)$-close to monotone in a completely *oblivious* fashion, with a non-adaptive approach that does not require to learn anything about the distribution.

THEOREM 4.2 (OBLIVIOUS CORRECTING OF MONOTONICITY). *For every* $\varepsilon' \in (0, 1)$, *there exists an (oblivious) sampling corrector for monotonicity, with parameters* $\varepsilon = O\left(\varepsilon'^3 / \log^2 n\right)$, $\varepsilon_1 = \varepsilon'$ *and sample complexity* $O(1)$.

Finally, we give with Theorem 4.3 a corrector for monotonicity with no restriction on the range of parameters, but assuming a stronger type of query access to the original distribution. Namely, our algorithm leverages the ability to make *cdf queries* to the distribution D, in order to generate independent samples from a corrected $\tilde{D}$. This sampling corrector also outperforms the one from Theorem 4.1 whenever the number of samples to generate is $o(\log n)$, making only $O\left(\sqrt{\log n}\right)$ queries per sample on expectation.

THEOREM 4.3. *For any* $\varepsilon \in (0, 1]$, *any number of queries* m *and* $\varepsilon_1 = O(\varepsilon)$ *as in the definition, there exists a sampling corrector for monotonicity from Cumulative Dual to* SAMP *with expected sample complexity* $O\left(\sqrt{m \log n}/\varepsilon\right)$.

High-level idea of the proofs.

Our first corrector works in a straightforward fashion: it *learns* a good approximation of the distribution to correct, which is also concisely represented. It then uses this approximation to build a sufficiently good monotone distribution M' "offline," by searching for the closest monotone distribution, which in this case can be achieved *via* linear programming. Any query made to the corrector is then answered according to the latter distribution, at no additional cost.

We next turn to our second monotonicity corrector, which achieves constant sample complexity for distributions already $(1/\log^2 n)$-close to monotone.[7] The overall idea is to treat the distribution as a k-histogram on the Birgé decomposition (for $k = O(\log n)$), thus "implicitly approximating" it; and to correct this histogram by adding a certain amount of probability weight to every interval, so that each gets slightly more than the next one. By choosing these quantities carefully, this ensures that *any* violation of monotonicity gets corrected

---

[7]Note that while this is a very strong assumption (as samples from such a distribution D are essentially indistinguishable from samples originating from its closest monotone distribution, unless $\Omega(\log^2 n)$ of them are taken already), our construction actually yields a stronger guarantee: namely, given *evaluation (query)* access to D, it can answer evaluation queries to the corrected distribution as well.

99

in the process, without ever having to find out *where* they actually occur.

Our next result shows that correcting monotonicity with $o(\log n)$ queries (on expectation) is possible when one allows CDF queries to the original distribution. The main idea of the proof is to first reduce (*via* the same "Birgé decomposition" technique as before) the problem to that of correcting a *histogram* supported of logarithmically many intervals, then group these ℓ intervals in K "superbuckets," each containing $L = \sqrt{\log n / \varepsilon}$ consecutive intervals from that histogram ("buckets") and finally use a multi-stage approach to correct all monotonicity violations:

Global violation fixing First, we obtain the weights of all superbuckets *via* K CDF queries and optimally reweight them so that average weights are non-increasing.

Budget allocation using rejection sampling, we allocate adaptively to each superbucket a "weight budget" it can use to fix *on-the-go* (at sampling time) boundary violations between adjacent superbuckets.

Local violation fixing we sample a superbucket from the coarse distribution, and use $O(L)$ CDF queries to correct monotonicity of the weights of the L buckets it contains; we also do this for the adjacent superbucket.

Boundary violation fixing to ensure monotonicity at a global scale, we then use the "allocated budget" of the superbucket to fix any possible violation at the boundary with its neighbor.

We stress that the above sweeps many details and difficulties under the rug. For the full description and proofs of the algorithms, the reader is referred to the full version of this extended abstract.

4.1 A restricted error model: missing data

In the previous sections, no assumption was made on the form of the error, only on the amount. In this section, we suggest a model of errors capturing the deletion of a whole "chunk" of the distribution. We refer to this model as the *missing data model*, where we assume that some ε probability is removed by taking out all the weight of an arbitrary interval $[i,j]$ for $1 \leq i < j \leq n$ and redistributing it on the rest of the domain as per rejection sampling (See Figure 1 for an illustration).[8] We show that one can design sampling improvers for monotone distributions with arbitrarily large amounts of error.

THEOREM 4.4. *For the class of distributions following the "missing data" error model, there exists a batch sampling improver* MISSING-DATA-IMPROVER, *that, on input* ε, q, δ *and* α, *achieves parameters* $\varepsilon_1 = O(\varepsilon)$ *and any* $\varepsilon_2 < \varepsilon$; *and has sample complexity* $\tilde{O}\left(\frac{1}{\varepsilon_2^3} \log \frac{1}{\delta}\right)$ *independent of* ε.

Our sampling improver follows what could be called the "learning-just-enough" approach: instead of attempting to approximate the *whole* unaltered original distribution, it only tries to learn the values of i, j; and then generates samples "on-the-fly." At a high level, the algorithm works

---

[8] That is, if D was the original distribution, the "faulty" one $D^{(i,j)}$ is formally defined as $(1+\varepsilon)\mathbb{1}_{[n]\setminus[i,j]} \cdot D - \varepsilon \cdot \mathcal{U}_{[i,j]}$, where $\varepsilon = D([i,j])$.

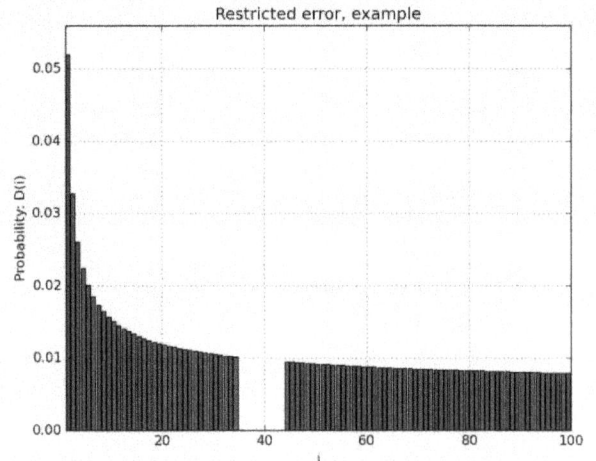

Figure 1: An example of distribution with "missing data" (here, $n = 100$ and $[i,j] = [35, 43]$).

by (i) detecting the location of the missing interval (drawing a large (but still independent of n) number of samples), then (ii) estimating the weight of this interval under the original, unaltered distribution; and finally (iii) filling this gap uniformly by moving the right amount of probability weight from the end of the domain. To perform the first stage, we follow a paradigm first appeared in [21], and utilize *testing* as a subroutine to detect "when enough learning has been done." (To efficiently implement this, we can leverage the structure of the error itself, which allows use to circumvent the prohibitive cost of testing monotonicity of general distributions.)

5. REFERENCES

[1] J. Acharya, I. Diakonikolas, J. Z. Li, and L. Schmidt. Sample-optimal density estimation in nearly-linear time. *CoRR*, abs/1506.00671, 2015. 3.2

[2] N. Ailon, B. Chazelle, S. Comandur, and D. Liu. Property-preserving data reconstruction. *Algorithmica*, 51(2):160–182, 2008. 1.4

[3] V. Barnett. The study of outliers: purpose and model. *Applied Statistics*, pages 242–250, 1978. 1

[4] T. Batu, S. Dasgupta, R. Kumar, and R. Rubinfeld. The complexity of approximating the entropy. *SIAM Journal on Computing*, 35(1):132–150, 2005. 1.2

[5] T. Batu, L. Fortnow, R. Rubinfeld, W. D. Smith, and P. White. Testing that distributions are close. In *Proceedings of FOCS*, pages 189–197, 2000. 6

[6] T. Batu, L. Fortnow, R. Rubinfeld, W. D. Smith, and P. White. Testing closeness of discrete distributions. *ArXiV*, abs/1009.5397, 2010. This is a long version of [5]. 1.2

[7] T. Batu, R. Kumar, and R. Rubinfeld. Sublinear algorithms for testing monotone and unimodal distributions. In *Proceedings of STOC*, pages 381–390, New York, NY, USA, 2004. ACM. 1.2

[8] A. Bhattacharyya, E. Grigorescu, M. Jha, K. Jung, S. Raskhodnikova, and D. P. Woodruff. Lower bounds for local monotonicity reconstruction from

transitive-closure spanners. *SIAM Journal on Discrete Mathematics*, 26(2):618–646, 2012. 1.4

[9] L. Birgé. On the risk of histograms for estimating decreasing densities. *The Annals of Statistics*, 15(3):pp. 1013–1022, 1987. 1.2, 1.2, 1.2

[10] M. Blum, M. Luby, and R. Rubinfeld. Self-testing/correcting with applications to numerical problems. In *Proceedings of the Twenty-second Annual ACM Symposium on Theory of Computing*, STOC '90, pages 73–83, New York, NY, USA, 1990. ACM. 1.4

[11] Z. Brakerski. Local property restoring. Manuscript, 2008. 3.3

[12] A. Campagna, A. Guo, and R. Rubinfeld. Local reconstructors and tolerant testers for connectivity and diameter. *CoRR*, abs/1208.2956, 2012. 3.3

[13] C. L. Canonne, I. Diakonikolas, T. Gouleakis, and R. Rubinfeld. Testing Shape Restrictions of Discrete Distributions. *ArXiV*, abs/1507.03558, July 2015. 1.2

[14] C. L. Canonne, D. Ron, and R. A. Servedio. Testing equivalence between distributions using conditional samples. In *Proceedings of SODA*, pages 1174–1192. Society for Industrial and Applied Mathematics (SIAM), 2014. 1.3

[15] C. L. Canonne and R. Rubinfeld. Testing probability distributions underlying aggregated data. In *Proceedings of ICALP*, pages 283–295, 2014. 1.2, 1.3

[16] S. Chakraborty, E. Fischer, Y. Goldhirsh, and A. Matsliah. On the power of conditional samples in distribution testing. In *Proceedings of the 4th conference on Innovations in Theoretical Computer Science*, ITCS '13, pages 561–580, New York, NY, USA, 2013. ACM. 1.3

[17] S.-O. Chan, I. Diakonikolas, R. A. Servedio, and X. Sun. *Learning mixtures of structured distributions over discrete domains*, chapter 100, pages 1380–1394. SIAM, 2013. 1.2, 3.1

[18] S.-O. Chan, I. Diakonikolas, R. A. Servedio, and X. Sun. Efficient density estimation via piecewise polynomial approximation. In *Proceedings of the 46th Annual ACM Symposium on Theory of Computing*, STOC '14, pages 604–613, New York, NY, USA, 2014. ACM. 1.2, 3.2

[19] C. Daskalakis, I. Diakonikolas, R. O'Donnell, R. A. Servedio, and L.-Y. Tan. Learning sums of independent integer random variables. In *Proceedings of the 2013 IEEE 54th Annual Symposium on Foundations of Computer Science*, FOCS '13, pages 217–226, Washington, DC, USA, 2013. IEEE Computer Society. 1.2

[20] C. Daskalakis, I. Diakonikolas, and R. A. Servedio. Learning Poisson Binomial Distributions. In *Proceedings of the Forty-fourth Annual ACM Symposium on Theory of Computing*, STOC '12, pages 709–728, New York, NY, USA, 2012. ACM. 1.2, 3.2, 3.2

[21] C. Daskalakis, I. Diakonikolas, and R. A. Servedio. Learning k-modal distributions via testing. *Theory of Computing*, 10(20):535–570, 2014. 1.2, 1.2, 3.3, 4.1

[22] C. Daskalakis, I. Diakonikolas, R. A. Servedio, G. Valiant, and P. Valiant. Testing k-modal distributions: Optimal algorithms via reductions. In *Proceedings of SODA*, pages 1833–1852. Society for Industrial and Applied Mathematics (SIAM), 2013. 1.2, 3.6

[23] C. Daskalakis and G. Kamath. Faster and sample near-optimal algorithms for proper learning mixtures of Gaussians. In *Proceedings of The 27th Conference on Learning Theory, Barcelona, Spain, June 13-15, 2014*, COLT '14, pages 1183–1213, 2014. 1.3

[24] A. P. Dempster, N. M. Laird, and D. B. Rubin. Maximum likelihood from incomplete data via the em algorithm. *JOURNAL OF THE ROYAL STATISTICAL SOCIETY, SERIES B*, 39(1):1–38, 1977. 1.4

[25] O. Goldreich and D. Ron. On testing expansion in bounded-degree graphs. Technical Report TR00-020, Electronic Colloquium on Computational Complexity (ECCC), 2000. 1.2

[26] U. Grenander. On the theory of mortality measurement. *Scandinavian Actuarial Journal*, 1956(1):70–96, 1956. 1.2

[27] D. M. Hawkins. *Identification of outliers*, volume 11. Springer, 1980. 1

[28] T. J. Hefley, D. M. Baasch, A. J. Tyre, and E. E. Blankenship. Correction of location errors for presence-only species distribution models. *Methods in Ecology and Evolution*, 5(3):207–214, 2014. 1

[29] B. Iglewicz and D. C. Hoaglin. *How to detect and handle outliers*, volume 16. Asq Press, 1993. 1

[30] R. Impagliazzo and D. Zuckerman. How to recycle random bits. In *Proceedings of the 30th Annual Symposium on Foundations of Computer Science*, SFCS '89, pages 248–253, Washington, DC, USA, 1989. IEEE Computer Society. 4

[31] P. Indyk, R. Levi, and R. Rubinfeld. Approximating and testing k-histogram distributions in sub-linear time. In *Proceedings of the 31st Symposium on Principles of Database Systems*, PODS '12, pages 15–22, New York, NY, USA, 2012. ACM. 1.2

[32] M. Jha and S. Raskhodnikova. Testing and reconstruction of Lipschitz functions with applications to data privacy. In *Proceedings of FOCS*, pages 433–442, Oct 2011. 1.4

[33] E. Kushilevitz and A. Rosén. A randomness-rounds tradeoff in private computation. In Y. Desmedt, editor, *Advances in Cryptology — CRYPTO '94*, volume 839 of *Lecture Notes in Computer Science*, pages 397–410. Springer Berlin Heidelberg, 1994. 4

[34] R. J. A. Little and D. B. Rubin. *Statistical Analysis with Missing Data*. Wiley Series in Probability and Statistics. John Wiley & Sons, 2002. Second edition. 1, 1.4

[35] L. Paninski. A coincidence-based test for uniformity given very sparsely sampled discrete data. *IEEE Transactions on Information Theory*, 54(10):4750–4755, 2008. 1.2

[36] S. Panzeri, C. Magri, and L. Carraro. Sampling bias. *Scholarpedia*, 3(9):4258, 2008. revision #91742. 1

[37] D. B. Rubin. *Multiple imputation for nonresponse in surveys*. John Wiley & Sons, 1987. 1.4

[38] M. Saar-Tsechansky and F. Provost. Handling missing values when applying classification models. *J. Mach. Learn. Res.*, 8:1623–1657, Dec. 2007. 1

[39] A. Sahai and S. Vadhan. Manipulating statistical difference. In *DIMACS Series in Discrete Mathematics and Theoretical Computer Science*, pages 251–270. American Mathematical Society, 1998. 1.1

[40] M. Saks and C. Seshadhri. Local monotonicity reconstruction. *SIAM Journal on Computing*, 39(7):2897–2926, 2010. 1.4

[41] J. L. Schafer. *Analysis of incomplete multivariate data.* CRC press, 1997. 1, 1.4

[42] P. D. Senese and J. A. Vasquez. A unified explanation of territorial conflict: Testing the impact of sampling bias, 1919–1992. *International Studies Quarterly*, 47(2):275–298, 2003. 1

[43] P. W. Signor and J. H. Lipps. Sampling bias, gradual extinction patterns and catastrophes in the fossil record. *Geological Society of America Special Papers*, 190:291–296, 1982. 1

[44] G. Valiant and P. Valiant. A CLT and tight lower bounds for estimating entropy. *Electronic Colloquium on Computational Complexity (ECCC)*, 17:179, 2010. 46

[45] G. Valiant and P. Valiant. Estimating the unseen: A sublinear-sample canonical estimator of distributions. *Electronic Colloquium on Computational Complexity (ECCC)*, 17:180, 2010. 46

[46] G. Valiant and P. Valiant. The power of linear estimators. In *Proceedings of FOCS*, pages 403–412, Oct. 2011. See also [44] and [45]. 1.2, 3.6

[47] P. Valiant. Private communication, May 2015. 1.2

[48] S. Yekhanin. *Locally decodable codes.* Now Publishers Inc., 2010. 1.4

On Being Far from Far
and on Dual Problems in Property Testing

[Extended Abstract]*

Roei Tell
Department of Computer Science and Applied Mathematics
Weizmann Institute of Science
Rehovot, Israel
roei.tell@weizmann.ac.il

ABSTRACT

This work studies a new type of problems in property testing, called *dual problems*. For a set Π in a metric space and $\delta > 0$, denote by $\mathcal{F}_\delta(\Pi)$ the set of elements that are δ-far from Π. Then, in property testing, a δ-tester for Π is required to accept inputs from Π and reject inputs from $\mathcal{F}_\delta(\Pi)$. A natural *dual problem* is the problem of δ-testing the set of "no" instances, that is $\mathcal{F}_\delta(\Pi)$: A δ-tester for $\mathcal{F}_\delta(\Pi)$ needs to accept inputs from $\mathcal{F}_\delta(\Pi)$ and reject inputs that are δ-far from $\mathcal{F}_\delta(\Pi)$; that is, it rejects inputs from $\mathcal{F}_\delta(\mathcal{F}_\delta(\Pi))$. When $\Pi = \mathcal{F}_\delta(\mathcal{F}_\delta(\Pi))$ the dual problem is essentially equivalent to the original one, but this equality does not hold in general.

Many dual problems constitute appealing testing problems that are interesting by themselves. In this work we study sets of the form $\mathcal{F}_\delta(\mathcal{F}_\delta(\Pi))$, and apply this study to investigate several natural dual problems. In particular, we derive lower bounds and upper bounds on the query complexity of several classes of natural dual problems: These include dual problems of properties of functions (e.g., testing error-correcting codes and testing monotone functions), of properties of distributions (e.g., testing equivalence to a known distribution), and of various graph properties in the dense graph model and in the bounded-degree model. We also show that testing any dual problem with *one-sided error* is either trivial or requires a linear number of queries.

Categories and Subject Descriptors

F.2.m [**Theory of Computation**]: Analysis of algorithms and problem complexity—*Miscellaneous: Property Testing*

Keywords

Metric spaces; Property testing; Dual problems; Closure operator

---

*A full version of this paper is available on ECCC [16].

Permission to make digital or hard copies of all or part of this work for personal or classroom use is granted without fee provided that copies are not made or distributed for profit or commercial advantage and that copies bear this notice and the full citation on the first page. Copyrights for components of this work owned by others than the author(s) must be honored. Abstracting with credit is permitted. To copy otherwise, or republish, to post on servers or to redistribute to lists, requires prior specific permission and/or a fee. Request permissions from Permissions@acm.org.

ITCS'16, January 14–16, 2016, Cambridge, MA, USA.

Copyright is held by the owner/author(s). Publication rights licensed to ACM.

ACM 978-1-4503-4057-1/16/01 ...$15.00.

DOI: http://dx.doi.org/10.1145/2840728.2840732 .

1. INTRODUCTION

Let (Ω, Δ) be a metric space,[1] let $\Pi \subseteq \Omega$ be a set in this space, and let $\delta > 0$ be a distance parameter. A natural object that we are frequently interested in is the set of points in Ω that are δ-far from Π, denoted $\mathcal{F}_\delta(\Pi) = \{x \in \Omega : \Delta(x, \Pi) \geq \delta\}$. Viewing $\mathcal{F}_\delta$ as an operator on the power set of Ω, a natural question is what happens when applying the operator $\mathcal{F}_\delta$ twice; that is, what is the structure of sets of the form $\mathcal{F}_\delta(\mathcal{F}_\delta(\Pi))$ for some $\Pi \subseteq \Omega$. One might mistakenly expect that for any metric space Ω, set $\Pi \subseteq \Omega$, and distance parameter $\delta > 0$ it holds that $\mathcal{F}_\delta(\mathcal{F}_\delta(\Pi)) = \Pi$. However, although it is always true that $\Pi \subseteq \mathcal{F}_\delta(\mathcal{F}_\delta(\Pi))$, it is not necessarily true that $\Pi = \mathcal{F}_\delta(\mathcal{F}_\delta(\Pi))$. Furthermore, in some spaces, most notably in the Boolean hypercube, the equality is even *typically* false (i.e., it is false for most subsets; see Section 2). In fact, the study of sets of the form $\mathcal{F}_\delta(\mathcal{F}_\delta(\Pi))$ turns out to be quite complex. To the best of our knowledge, this basic question has not been explored so far.

The study of sets of the form $\mathcal{F}_\delta(\mathcal{F}_\delta(\Pi))$ has an interesting application in theoretical computer science, specifically in the context of *property testing* (see, e.g., [6]). In property testing, an ϵ-tester for $\Pi \subseteq \{0,1\}^n$ is required to accept every input in Π, with high probability, and reject every input in $\mathcal{F}_\delta(\Pi)$, with high probability, where $\delta = \epsilon \cdot n$ refers to absolute distance, and $\epsilon > 0$ refers to the relative distance.[2] This constitutes a promise problem, in which the set of "yes" instances is Π and the set of "no" instances is $\mathcal{F}_\delta(\Pi)$. One plausible question in this context is what is the relationship between the complexity of ϵ-testing the set of "yes" instances Π and the complexity of the *dual problem* of ϵ-testing the set of "no" instances $\mathcal{F}_\delta(\Pi)$. In many cases, the "far set" (i.e., $\mathcal{F}_\delta(\Pi)$) actually constitutes a natural property, making the corresponding dual problem an interesting testing problem by itself (see elaboration in Section 3).

For any set $\Pi \subseteq \{0,1\}^n$ and $\delta = \epsilon \cdot n$, an ϵ-tester for the dual problem of Π is required to accept every input in $\mathcal{F}_\delta(\Pi)$, with high probability, and reject every input in $\mathcal{F}_\delta(\mathcal{F}_\delta(\Pi))$, with high probability. Indeed, if $\Pi = \mathcal{F}_\delta(\mathcal{F}_\delta(\Pi))$, then the

---

[1]Throughout the paper we will usually identify a metric space (Ω, Δ) with its set of elements Ω, in which case the metric is implicit and denoted by Δ.

[2]Being consistent with the property testing literature, we let $\epsilon > 0$ denote the relative (Hamming) distance. In contrast, it is more convenient to analyze the δ-far operator while referring to absolute distance (denoted by $\delta > 0$). Note that the abstract indeed used different notations, merely for simplicity of presentation.

problem of ϵ-testing Π is essentially equivalent to its dual problem. We call such sets $\mathcal{F}_\delta$-closed:

DEFINITION 1.1. *($\mathcal{F}_\delta$-closed sets). For a metric space Ω, a parameter $\delta > 0$, and a set $\Pi \subseteq \Omega$, if $\Pi = \mathcal{F}_\delta(\mathcal{F}_\delta(\Pi))$, then we say that Π is $\mathcal{F}_\delta$-closed in Ω.*

However, as mentioned above, not all sets are $\mathcal{F}_\delta$-closed, and for some spaces and δ parameters, most sets are actually *not* $\mathcal{F}_\delta$-closed. Moreover, in many cases it is unfortunately non-obvious to determine whether Π is $\mathcal{F}_\delta$-closed or not.

Key contributions.
The contributions in this work consist of two parts. First, in Section 3 we *introduce dual problems in property testing*, motivate their study, and obtain results regarding their complexity. We show that in general, testing dual problems with *one-sided error* requires a linear number of queries, unless the problem is trivial to begin with; this stands in sharp contrast to testing standard problems with one-sided error. In addition, we determine the complexity of *several specific natural dual problems*, corresponding to well-known testing problems; these dual problems include:

- Testing whether a string is **far from being a codeword** in an error-correcting code.

- Testing whether a function is **far from being monotone**.

- Testing whether a distribution is **far from being uniform**.

- Testing whether a graph is **far from being k-colorable** in the dense graph model.

- Testing whether a graph is **far from being connected** in the bounded-degree model.

- Testing whether a graph is **far from being cycle-free** in the bounded-degree model.

Some of these dual problems are essentially equivalent to their original problems (i.e., the corresponding sets $\Pi_n \subseteq \{0,1\}^n$ are $\mathcal{F}_\delta$-closed, for $\delta = \epsilon \cdot n$; see Definition 3.1), and in these cases the query complexity of the dual is the same as the query complexity of the original. However, other dual problems mentioned above are different from the original problems (i.e., $\Pi_n \neq \mathcal{F}_\delta(\mathcal{F}_\delta(\Pi_n))$), and sometimes even significantly different; in these cases we present a tester for the dual problem, which is different from known testers for the original problem, and sometimes also has higher query complexity. Beyond the immediate implications of these results (of determining the complexity of specific problems), their proofs typically also include structural results related to the relevant property.

The second topic in the paper is the generic study of *sets of the form $\mathcal{F}_\delta(\mathcal{F}_\delta(\Pi))$* in metric spaces. In Section 4 we present several necessary and/or sufficient conditions for a set to be $\mathcal{F}_\delta$-closed; some of these conditions are applicable in general metric spaces, whereas others apply only in graphical metric spaces. Two interesting general observations in this context are that (1) the condition of being $\mathcal{F}_\delta$-closed can be presented as a collection of local conditions, where each local condition depends only on a δ-neighborhood in the space (see discussion after Theorem 4.1); and (2) the

operator $\Pi \mapsto \mathcal{F}_\delta(\mathcal{F}_\delta(\Pi))$ has the structure of a *closure operator* on the power set of Ω (see Section 4.1 for details on the latter).

The two topics mentioned above appear very natural to us, and they are related to problems studied for a long time. However, even given the results in this work, very little is currently known about either of them. In particular, with regards to dual testing problems, the current work proves one general lower bound (on testing with one-sided error), and several specific upper bounds. The latter are proved mainly via reductions to *tolerant testing*; see Section 5 for an elaboration on our techniques. We thus suggest, in Section 6, several *broad questions* concerning dual testing problems that could promote the understanding of both "far-from-far" sets and dual testing problems.

Organization.
In Section 2 we set the stage for the rest of the paper, by asserting the existence, and in some sense the abundance, of sets that are not $\mathcal{F}_\delta$-closed. Section 3 presents our main results regarding dual problems in property testing as well as a generalization of the notion of dual testing problems. In Section 4 we study the generic question of identifying $\mathcal{F}_\delta$-closed sets in metric spaces. In Section 5 we describe, in high-level, the techniques used to obtain several results regarding dual problems in property testing. In Section 6 we suggest several open questions.

2. ON THE NON-TRIVIALITY OF THE NOTION OF $\mathcal{F}_\delta$-CLOSED SETS

As mentioned in the beginning of the introduction, one might mistakenly expect that for every Ω and δ, all sets will be $\mathcal{F}_\delta$-closed. Indeed, for any metric space Ω, taking a value of δ such that $\delta \leq \inf_{x \neq y \in \Omega}\{\Delta(x,y)\}$ ensures that all sets are trivially $\mathcal{F}_\delta$-closed, since for any $\Pi \subseteq \Omega$ it holds that $\mathcal{F}_\delta(\Pi) = \Omega \setminus \Pi$. In contrast, taking a value of δ such that $\delta > \sup_{x,y}\{\Delta(x,y)\}$ ensures that all non-trivial subsets are not $\mathcal{F}_\delta$-closed, since any $\Pi \neq \emptyset$ satisfies $\mathcal{F}_\delta(\Pi) = \emptyset$ and $\mathcal{F}_\delta(\mathcal{F}_\delta(\Pi)) = \Omega$. The following theorem asserts that for any δ in between these two values there exist both $\mathcal{F}_\delta$-closed sets and sets that are not $\mathcal{F}_\delta$-closed.

THEOREM 2.1. *(non-triviality of the notion of $\mathcal{F}_\delta$-closed sets; see [16, Thm 3.9]). For any Ω, if $\delta \in \left(\inf_{x \neq y}\{\Delta(x,y)\}, \sup_{x \neq y}\{\Delta(x,y)\} \right)$, then there exists a non-trivial $\Pi \subseteq \Omega$ that is $\mathcal{F}_\delta$-closed and a non-trivial $\Pi' \subseteq \Omega$ that is not $\mathcal{F}_\delta$-closed.*

In addition to the *existence* of sets that are not $\mathcal{F}_\delta$-closed, in some metric spaces such sets are actually the typical case, rather than the exception. Most notably, in the Boolean hypercube it holds that a $(1 - o(1))$-fraction of the sets are not $\mathcal{F}_\delta$-closed. (This is the case since for a random set $\Pi \subseteq \{0,1\}^n$ and $\delta \geq 3$, with high probability it holds that $\mathcal{F}_\delta(\Pi) = \emptyset$.) In addition, consider a metric space in which there exist N pairwise-disjoint δ-neighborhoods, each containing at most $\log(N)$ points; in such a space, most sets are not $\mathcal{F}_\delta$-closed (see [16, Prop. 3.11]).

Furthermore, in contrast to what one might expect, points in $\mathcal{F}_\delta(\mathcal{F}_\delta(\Pi))$ might not even be *close* to Π. In particular, there exist spaces Ω and sets $\Pi \subseteq \Omega$ such that some points in $\mathcal{F}_\delta(\mathcal{F}_\delta(\Pi)) \setminus \Pi$ are relatively far from Π (i.e., almost δ-far from Π); such sets also exist in the Boolean hypercube.

There even exist spaces Ω, parameters $\delta > 0$, and sets $\Pi \subseteq \Omega$ such that *all* points in $\mathcal{F}_\delta(\mathcal{F}_\delta(\Pi)) \setminus \Pi$ are almost δ-far from Π (see [16, Sec. 3.4]).

3. DUAL PROBLEMS IN PROPERTY TESTING

For a space $\Omega = \Sigma^n$, and a set $\Pi \subseteq \Sigma^n$, and $\epsilon > 0$, the standard property testing problem is the one of ϵ-testing Π, and the corresponding *dual problem* is the one of ϵ-testing $\mathcal{F}_{\epsilon \cdot n}(\Pi)$.

What is the meaning of dual testing problems? First, for *some* properties, the dual problem is an appealing property that is interesting by itself. Consider, for example, the set of distributions that are far from uniform, the set of functions that are far from monotone, or the set of graphs that are far from being connected. All these sets constitute natural properties, and one might be interested in testing them. Secondly, in general, for *every* property Π the dual problem is intuitively related to the original problem: It can be viewed as distinguishing between inputs that any ϵ-tester for Π must reject, and inputs that need to be significantly changed in order to be rejectetd by any ϵ-tester for Π. Thirdly, the *query complexity* of a testing problem and of its dual problem are related: Specifically, the complexity of a dual problem is lower bounded by the complexity of the original problem (see Observation 3.2).

Similar to standard testing problems, in dual problems we are also interested in the *asymptotic* complexity. That is, for a property $\Pi = \{\Pi_n\}_{n \in \mathbb{N}}$ such that $\Pi_n \subseteq \Sigma^n$, we seek either an asymptotic upper bound on the query complexity of ϵ-testing $\mathcal{F}_{\epsilon \cdot n}(\Pi_n)$ for *every* $\epsilon > 0$, or a lower bound for *some* value of $\epsilon > 0$. Accordingly, for a property $\Pi = \{\Pi_n\}_{n \in \mathbb{N}}$, we will usually refer to the *dual problem of the problem of testing* Π, or in short to *the dual problem of* Π.

DEFINITION 3.1. *(dual problems that are equivalent to the original problems).* For a set Σ, let $\Pi = \{\Pi_n\}_{n \in \mathbb{N}}$ such that $\Pi_n \subseteq \Sigma^n$. If for every sufficiently small $\epsilon > 0$ and sufficiently large n it holds that Π_n is $\mathcal{F}_{\epsilon \cdot n}$-closed, then the problem of testing Π is equivalent to its dual problem. Otherwise, the problem of testing Π is different from its dual problem.

We stress that even if a standard testing problem Π is equivalent to its dual, it does not imply that the standard problem is the "dual problem of its dual". This is since the definition of dual problems is inherently different than that of standard problems, with respect to the dependence on the proximity parameter $\epsilon > 0$. In particular, in standard problems, the sets of "yes" instances $\{\Pi_n\}_{n \in \mathbb{N}}$ are fixed, and the sets of "no" instances $\{\mathcal{F}_{\epsilon \cdot n}(\Pi_n)\}_{n \in \mathbb{N}}$ depend on the proximity parameter $\epsilon > 0$; in contrast, in dual problems, both the sets of "yes" instances $\{\mathcal{F}_{\epsilon \cdot n}(\Pi_n)\}_{n \in \mathbb{N}}$ and the sets of "no" instances $\{\mathcal{F}_{\epsilon \cdot n}(\mathcal{F}_{\epsilon \cdot n}(\Pi_n))\}_{n \in \mathbb{N}}$ depend on ϵ.

3.1 General results regarding the query complexity of dual problems

The query complexity of any dual problem is closely related to the query complexity of its original problem. First, since for every set $\Pi \subseteq \Sigma^n$ and every $\delta > 0$ it holds that $\Pi \subseteq \mathcal{F}_\delta(\mathcal{F}_\delta(\Pi))$, an ϵ-tester for $\mathcal{F}_{\epsilon \cdot n}(\Pi)$ always yields an ϵ-tester for Π, by complementing the output of the tester. (This is since the promise problem that corresponds to the

original problem is $(\Pi, \mathcal{F}_{\epsilon \cdot n}(\Pi))$, whereas the promise problem for the dual is $(\mathcal{F}_{\epsilon \cdot n}(\Pi), \mathcal{F}_{\epsilon \cdot n}(\mathcal{F}_{\epsilon \cdot n}(\Pi))) \supseteq (\mathcal{F}_{\epsilon \cdot n}(\Pi), \Pi)$.) Thus:

OBSERVATION 3.2. *(the query complexity of dual problems).* The query complexity of a dual problem is lower bounded by the query complexity of its original problem.

Needless to say, *if the dual problem is equivalent to its original problem, then their query complexities are identical.*

Building on Observation 3.2, we show a lower bound for testing dual problems with *one-sided error*, regardless of whether the dual problem is equivalent to its original. Recall that in property testing, testers with one-sided error are ones that always accept "yes" inputs; in the case of dual problems, these are testers that always accept inputs from $\mathcal{F}_{\epsilon \cdot n}(\Pi)$.

THEOREM 3.3. *(testing dual problems with one-sided error; see [16, Cor. 5.7]).* For a set Σ, let $\Pi = \{\Pi_n\}_{n \in \mathbb{N}}$ such that $\Pi_n \subseteq \Sigma^n$. Suppose that for all sufficiently large n it holds that $\Pi_n \neq \emptyset$ and that there exist inputs that are $\Omega(n)$-far from Π_n. Then, the query complexity of testing the dual problem of Π with one-sided error is $\Omega(n)$.

It follows that testing the dual problem of a (non-empty) property with one-sided error and query complexity $o(n)$ is possible only if the distance of every input from the property is $o(n)$. However, in this case both the original problem and its dual are trivial to begin with, since for any $\epsilon > 0$ and sufficiently large n it holds that $\mathcal{F}_{\epsilon \cdot n}(\Pi_n) = \emptyset$.

The fact that testing dual problems with one-sided error is either trivial or requires a linear number of queries stands in *sharp contrast to standard property testing problems*. This is since in standard property testing problems, essentially for any sub-linear function $q : \mathbb{N} \to \mathbb{N}$, there exists a property of Boolean functions such that the query complexity of testing it with one-sided error is $\Theta(q(n))$ [9].

3.2 Dual problems in testing properties of functions

When testing properties of functions, we identify each function $f : [n] \to \Sigma$ with its evaluation sequence, viewed as $f \in \Sigma^n$. The metric space is thus Σ^n, and the (absolute) distance between two functions is the Hamming distance between their string representations in Σ^n; equivalently, it is the number of inputs on which they disagree.

Many well-known properties of functions induce an error-correcting code with constant relative distance in Σ^n. The following theorem asserts that for such properties, the dual testing problem is equivalent to the original problem.

THEOREM 3.4. *(testing duals of error-correcting codes; see [16, Thm 5.8]).* For any error-correcting code with constant relative distance, *the problem of testing the code is equivalent to its dual problem.*

One fundamental problem in this field that involves testing error-correcting codes is the problem of *linearity testing* [2], which consists of testing whether a function $\varphi : G \to H$, where G and H are groups, is a group homomorphism (see [11] for sufficient conditions on G and H such that the set of homomorphisms $G \to H$ is an error-correcting code). Another fundamental problem that induces an error-correcting code is that of *low-degree testing* [15], which consists of testing the set of low-degree multivariate polynomials over a finite field.

A notable example of a property of functions that does *not* induce an error-correcting code is the property of *monotone functions*, first considered for testing in [7]. For a poset $[n]$ and an ordered set Σ, a function $f : [n] \to \Sigma$ is *monotone* if for every $x, y \in [n]$ such that $x \leq y$ it holds that $f(x) \leq f(y)$. Nevertheless, the problem of testing this property is also equivalent to its dual problem:

THEOREM 3.5. *(testing whether a function is far from monotone). The problem of testing* monotone Boolean functions over the Boolean hypercube *is equivalent to its dual problem.*

In fact, in [16, Sec. 5.3] we prove a broad generalization of Theorem 3.5, as follows. For every $n \in \mathbb{N}$, consider functions from a poset $([n], \leq)$ to a range Σ_n, and assume that the width of the poset is at most $\frac{n}{2 \cdot |\Sigma_n|}$, where the width of a poset is the size of a maximum antichain in it. In this case, the problem of testing monotone functions from $[n]$ to Σ_n is equivalent to its dual problem. Note that the width requirement is quite mild: In particular, an ℓ-dimensional hypercube has size $n = 2^\ell$ and width $O(2^\ell/\sqrt{\ell}) = o(n)$.

3.3 Dual problems in distribution testing

Turning to *distribution testing* [1], one well-known problem is as follows: Fixing a predetermined distribution $\mathbf{D}$ over $[n]$, an ϵ-tester gets independent samples from an input distribution $\mathbf{I}$, and its task is to determine whether $\mathbf{I} = \mathbf{D}$ or $\mathbf{I}$ is ϵ-far from $\mathbf{D}$ in the ℓ_1 norm. We consider the dual problem of this problem, which consists of testing whether a distribution is *far* from the predetermined distribution. When considering the worst-case, over all families of distributions, the distribution testing problem is different from its dual problem.

PROPOSITION 3.6. *(testing whether a distribution is far from a known distribution; see [16, Prop 5.12]). There exists a distribution family $\{\mathbf{D}_n\}_{n\in\mathbb{N}}$ such that the problem of testing whether an input distribution $\mathbf{I}_n$ is identical to $\mathbf{D}_n$ is different from its dual problem.*

However, for several specific classes of distribution families, this problem is equivalent to its dual problem. In particular,

THEOREM 3.7. *(testing whether a distribution is far from a predetermined distribution that has low ℓ_∞ norm; see [16, Thm. 5.16]). Let $\{\mathbf{D}_n\}_{n\in\mathbb{N}}$ be a family of distributions such that $\lim_{n\to\infty} \|\mathbf{D}_n\|_\infty = 0$ (where we denote $\|\mathbf{D}_n\|_\infty = \max_{i\in[n]} \{\Pr_{\mathbf{r}\sim\mathbf{D}_n}[\mathbf{r} = i]\}$). Then, the problem of testing whether an input distribution $\mathbf{I}_n$ is identical to $\mathbf{D}_n$ is equivalent to its dual problem.*

Theorem 3.7 implies that the problem of testing whether an input distribution is *far from being the uniform distribution* is equivalent to its original problem. Some distribution families that do not meet the condition of Theorem 3.7 also induce dual problems that are equivalent to their original problems: In particular, this applies to distribution families that assign $\Omega(1)$ probabilistic mass to *every* element in their support (see [16, Prop 5.13]).

3.4 Dual problems in testing graph properties

When testing graph properties, we are interested in metric spaces in which the points are graphs, and the absolute distance between two graphs is the size of the symmetric difference of their edge-sets. A property of graphs is a set of graphs that is closed under taking isomorphisms of the graphs. We consider dual problems in two models of testing graph properties: The dense graph model [8] and the bounded-degree model [10]. In both models, many well-known testing problems are different from their dual problems.

3.4.1 The dense graph model

In the dense graph model [8], an ϵ-tester queries the adjacency matrix of a graph over v vertices, and tries to determine whether the graph has some property or $\epsilon \cdot \binom{v}{2}$ edges need to be added and/or removed from the edge-set of the graph in order for it to have the property.

One well-known problem in this model is that of testing whether a graph is k-colorable (see [8]). We consider the dual problem, of testing whether a graph is *far from being k-colorable*. This problem is *different* from its original problem, but its query complexity is nevertheless $O(1)$, as is the case for the original problem.

THEOREM 3.8. *(testing whether a graph is far from being k-colorable; see [16, Thm. 5.22]). For any $k \geq 2$, the problem of testing whether a graph is k-colorable is different from its dual problem. Nevertheless, the query complexity of the dual problem is $O(1)$.*

However, unlike the complexity of the original problem, the constant in the $O(1)$ notation in Theorem 3.8 might be huge; in particular, our upper-bound has a tower-type dependence on the reciprocal of the proximity parameter. (This is the case since our proof relies on a result by Fischer and Newman [5], which in turn relies on Szemerédi's regularity lemma.)

The following proposition asserts that two other well-known problems in the dense graph model are different from their dual problems. The first problem is testing, for $\rho \in (0, 1)$, whether a graph on v vertices has a *clique of size $\rho \cdot v$* (see [8]). The second is the *graph isomorphism* problem (see [3, 4]): For an explicitly known graph G that is fixed in advance, the problem consists of testing whether an input graph is isomorphic to G.

PROPOSITION 3.9. *(ρ-clique and graph isomorphism; see [16, Prop. 5.23 and 5.24]).*

1. *For any $\rho \leq \frac{1}{2}$, the problem of testing whether a graph on v vertices has a clique of size $\rho \cdot v$ is different from its dual problem.*

2. *There exist graph families $\{G_n\}_{n\in\mathbb{N}}$ such that testing whether an input graph H_n is isomorphic to G_n is different from its dual problem.*

In contrast to the dual problem of k-colorability, we do not know what is the query complexity of the two dual problems mentioned in Proposition 3.9.

3.4.2 The bounded-degree model

In the bounded-degree model [10] we are interested only in graphs that are very sparse. In particular, we assume that the degree of every vertex in an input graph is at most d, where typically $d = O(1)$. A testing scenario in this model is as follows. Given an input graph over n vertices, we fix in advance an arbitrary ordering of the neighbors of each vertex in the graph. Then, an ϵ-tester may issue queries of the form "who is the ith neighbor of $u \in [n]$?", and needs to determine whether the graph has some property or $\epsilon \cdot d \cdot n$ edges need to be added and/or removed from the edge-set of the graph in order for it to have the property.

One well-known problem in this model is that of testing whether a graph is connected (see [10]). We consider the dual problem, of testing whether a graph is *far from being connected*. Interestingly, although the dual problem is "very different" from the original one (in the sense that $\mathcal{F}_\delta(\mathcal{F}_\delta(\Pi_n))$ contains graphs that are $\Omega(n)$-far from being connected), the query complexity of the dual problem is nevertheless very close to that of the original problem.

THEOREM 3.10. *(testing whether a graph is far from being connected; see [16, Thm. 5.31]). For any $d \geq 3$, the problem of testing whether a graph is connected is different from its dual problem. Nevertheless, the query complexity of the dual problem is poly$(1/\epsilon)$.*

Another well-known problem in this model is testing cycle-free graphs (see [10]). We consider the dual problem, of testing whether a graph is *far from being cycle-free*.

THEOREM 3.11. *(testing whether a graph is far from being cycle-free; see [16, Thm. 5.34]). For any $d \geq 3$, the problem of testing whether a graph is cycle-free (i.e., a forest) is different from its dual problem. Nevertheless, the query complexity of the dual problem is poly$(1/\epsilon)$.*

The well-known problem of testing bipartiteness in this model is also not equivalent to its dual problem, but we do not know what its query complexity is.

PROPOSITION 3.12. *(testing whether a graph is far from bipartite; see [16, Prop. 5.35]). The problem of testing whether a graph is bipartite is different from its dual problem.*

3.5 A generalization: On being δ'-far from δ-far

So far, the dual problem of a property $\Pi = \{\Pi_n\}_{n \in \mathbb{N}}$ was defined using a *single* proximity parameter $\epsilon > 0$. This parameter $\epsilon > 0$ determines both the "yes" inputs for testing (i.e., $\mathcal{F}_{\epsilon \cdot n}(\Pi_n)$) and the distance of the "no" inputs from the "yes" inputs (i.e., it also determines $\mathcal{F}_{\epsilon \cdot n}(\mathcal{F}_{\epsilon \cdot n}(\Pi_n))$). A more general notion of dual testing problems is obtained by considering *two* proximity parameters, $\epsilon > 0$ and $\epsilon' > 0$, such that $\epsilon > 0$ determines the "yes" inputs for testing, and $\epsilon' > 0$ is the proximity parameter that determines the distance of the "no" inputs from the "yes" inputs; that is, the generalized dual problem consists of distinguishing between $\mathcal{F}_{\epsilon \cdot n}(\Pi_n)$ and $\mathcal{F}_{\epsilon' \cdot n}(\mathcal{F}_{\epsilon \cdot n}(\Pi_n))$.

Generalized dual problems are actually more similar to standard testing problems, compared to non-generalized dual problems. This is the case since we can fix $\epsilon > 0$, and define the *generalized ϵ-dual problem* as the problem of testing the fixed property $\{\mathcal{F}_{\epsilon \cdot n}(\Pi_n)\}_{n \in \mathbb{N}}$ with an arbitrarily small

proximity parameter $\epsilon' > 0$.[3] The latter definition is just the standard definition of property testing, for the fixed property $\{\mathcal{F}_{\epsilon \cdot n}(\Pi_n)\}_{n \in \mathbb{N}}$. In [16, Sec. 5.7] we formalize this notion, and show the following (informally stated):

THEOREM 3.13. *(testers for generalized dual problems; informal). For every constant $\epsilon, \epsilon' > 0$:*

1. *The query complexity of the generalized dual problem of k-colorable graphs in the dense graphs model is $F(\epsilon, \epsilon')$, for some function F that does not depend on n.* [4]

2. *The query complexity of the generalized dual problem of connected graphs in the bounded-degree graphs model is poly$(1/\min\{\epsilon', \epsilon\})$.*

3. *The query complexity of the generalized dual problem of cycle-free graphs in the bounded-degree graphs model is poly$(1/\min\{\epsilon', \epsilon\})$.*

4. $\mathcal{F}_\delta$-CLOSED SETS AND THE OPERATOR $\Pi \mapsto \mathcal{F}_\delta(\mathcal{F}_\delta(\Pi))$

Our results in this section are intended to facilitate the analysis of sets of the form $\mathcal{F}_\delta(\mathcal{F}_\delta(\Pi))$, and in particular to simplify the identification of sets that are $\mathcal{F}_\delta$-closed.

4.1 General metric spaces

The following are several equivalent *characterizations of all $\mathcal{F}_\delta$-closed sets* in any metric space Ω and for any $\delta > 0$.

THEOREM 4.1. *(characterizations of $\mathcal{F}_\delta$-closed sets; see [16, Thm. 3.2]). For any Ω, $\delta > 0$, and $\Pi \subseteq \Omega$, the following statements are equivalent:*

1. *Π is $\mathcal{F}_\delta$-closed (i.e., $\Pi = \mathcal{F}_\delta(\mathcal{F}_\delta(\Pi))$).*

2. *For every $x \notin \Pi \cup \mathcal{F}_\delta(\Pi)$ there exists $z \in \mathcal{F}_\delta(\Pi)$ such that $\Delta(z, x) < \delta$.*

3. *There exists $\Pi' \subseteq \Omega$ such that $\Pi = \mathcal{F}_\delta(\Pi')$.*

4. *There exists $\Pi' \subseteq \Omega$ such that $\Pi = \bigcap_{x \in \Pi'} \mathcal{F}_\delta(\{x\})$.*

Condition (2) of Theorem 4.1 is the basic technical tool that we use to analyze $\mathcal{F}_\delta$-closed sets when lacking a more convenient tool for the specific case. Interestingly, this condition is actually a *collection of local conditions*, where by "local" we mean that each condition depends only on a ball of radius 2δ in Ω.[5] Thus, if Π violates one of these conditions, then it is not $\mathcal{F}_\delta$-closed, and otherwise it is $\mathcal{F}_\delta$-closed.

Condition (3) of Theorem 4.1 implies, in particular, that all sets of the form $\mathcal{F}_\delta(\Pi')$, for some $\Pi' \subseteq \Omega$, are $\mathcal{F}_\delta$-closed. Thus, it is always true that $\mathcal{F}_\delta(\mathcal{F}_\delta(\mathcal{F}_\delta(\Pi))) = \mathcal{F}_\delta(\Pi)$, which

---

[3]When fixing $\epsilon > 0$, and letting $\epsilon' > 0$ be arbitrarily small, we focus mainly on the setting of $\epsilon' \leq \epsilon$. This focus is justified by the fact that the case of $\epsilon' > \epsilon$ reduces to the case of $\epsilon' \leq \epsilon$ (see [16, Obs. 5.37]).

[4]The function F comes from the query complexity of the tolerant tester of Fischer and Newman [5], which has a tower-type dependency on the proximity parameters that is not fully specified (see [5, Sec. 7]).

[5]Each condition depends on a ball of radius 2δ, since Condition (2) requires the existence of $z \in \mathcal{F}_\delta(\Pi)$ such that $\Delta(z, x) < \delta$, which holds if z is in the open radius-δ ball around x and the open radius-δ ball around z does not intersect with Π.

implies that repeated applications of the operator $\mathcal{F}_\delta$ on a set Π yield a sequence that consists only of the sets Π, $\mathcal{F}_\delta(\Pi)$, and $\mathcal{F}_\delta(\mathcal{F}_\delta(\Pi))$. Moreover, if Π is $\mathcal{F}_\delta$-closed, then the sequence consists only of Π and $\mathcal{F}_\delta(\Pi)$.

Condition (4) of Theorem 4.1 implies that the potentially small collection $\{\mathcal{F}_\delta(\{x\})\}_{x \in \Omega}$ "generates" the collection of all $\mathcal{F}_\delta$-closed sets (i.e., a set is $\mathcal{F}_\delta$-closed if and only if it is an intersection of sets from $\{\mathcal{F}_\delta(\{x\})\}_{x \in \Omega}$).

The operator $\Pi \mapsto \mathcal{F}_\delta(\mathcal{F}_\delta(\Pi))$ is a closure operator.

For a space Ω and parameter $\delta > 0$, consider the operator $\mathcal{F}_\delta \circ \mathcal{F}_\delta$ (i.e., $\Pi \mapsto \mathcal{F}_\delta(\mathcal{F}_\delta(\Pi))$) on the power set of Ω. This operator satisfies the following:

PROPOSITION 4.2. *(structural results regarding the operator $\Pi \mapsto \mathcal{F}_\delta(\mathcal{F}_\delta(\Pi))$; see [16, Prop. 3.5]). For any Ω, $\delta > 0$, and $\Pi, \Pi' \subseteq \Omega$ it holds that:*

1. *(extensiveness) $\Pi \subseteq \mathcal{F}_\delta(\mathcal{F}_\delta(\Pi))$.*

2. *(upwards monotonicity) If $\Pi \subseteq \Pi'$ then $\mathcal{F}_\delta(\mathcal{F}_\delta(\Pi)) \subseteq \mathcal{F}_\delta(\mathcal{F}_\delta(\Pi'))$.*

3. *(idempotency) $\mathcal{F}_\delta^{(4)}(\Pi) = \mathcal{F}_\delta(\mathcal{F}_\delta(\Pi))$ (where $\mathcal{F}_\delta^{(4)}$ means four applications of $\mathcal{F}_\delta$).*

The three assertions in Proposition 4.2 suffice to deduce that the operator $\Pi \mapsto \mathcal{F}_\delta(\mathcal{F}_\delta(\Pi))$ is a *closure operator* (or *hull operator*) on the power set of Ω, a well-studied notion in many mathematical fields including algebra, topology, and matroid theory (see, e.g., [12, Chp. 2] or [18, Chp. 1]). A closure operator is characterized by a corresponding collection of closed sets, which are the sets in its image; in our case, this is exactly the collection of $\mathcal{F}_\delta$-closed sets. A general result about closure operators, which holds also in the specific case of $\Pi \mapsto \mathcal{F}_\delta(\mathcal{F}_\delta(\Pi))$, is that the closure of a set Π (i.e., the image of the set under the operator) is the unique intersection of all closed sets that contain the set Π.

4.2 Graphical metric spaces

If the metric space Ω is an undirected connected graph equipped with the shortest path metric, then we call it a *graphical* metric space. In this section we show several conditions that are either necessary or sufficient to deduce that a set in a graphical space is $\mathcal{F}_\delta$-closed. We also study these conditions in the special case of the Boolean hypercube, since the latter is important for property testing and since it belongs to several interesting graph classes.

One *necessary* condition for a set (in a graphical space) to be $\mathcal{F}_\delta$-closed is that, loosely speaking, it does not "fully enclose" some vertex $x \notin \Pi \cup \mathcal{F}_\delta(\Pi)$. More precisely, if a set Π is $\mathcal{F}_\delta$-closed, then every $x \notin \Pi \cup \mathcal{F}_\delta(\Pi)$ is connected to $\mathcal{F}_\delta(\Pi)$ via a path that does not intersect Π nor any vertex adjacent to Π. However, this necessary condition is not a sufficient one: There exist graphs, values of $\delta > 0$ and sets that satisfy this condition but are *not* $\mathcal{F}_\delta$-closed. Moreover, the condition is not a sufficient one even in the special case of the Boolean hypercube (see [16, Prop. 4.3]).

The following *sufficient* condition for a set in a graphical space to be $\mathcal{F}_\delta$-closed is a strengthening of the aforementioned necessary condition.

DEFINITION 4.3. *(strongly $\mathcal{F}_\delta$-closed). For a graphical Ω and $\delta > 0$, a set $\Pi \subseteq \Omega$ is strongly $\mathcal{F}_\delta$-closed if every $x \notin \Pi \cup \mathcal{F}_\delta(\Pi)$ lies on a shortest path (i.e., a path of length δ) from Π to $\mathcal{F}_\delta(\Pi)$.*

Indeed, as implied by its name, a set that is strongly $\mathcal{F}_\delta$-closed is $\mathcal{F}_\delta$-closed (see [16, Prop. 4.5]). An equivalent definition of being strongly $\mathcal{F}_\delta$-closed is as follows: A set Π is *strongly $\mathcal{F}_\delta$-closed* if and only if, for every $x \notin \Pi \cup \mathcal{F}_\delta(\Pi)$, there exists a neighbor x' such that $\Delta(x', \Pi) = \Delta(x, \Pi) + 1$.

The condition of being strongly $\mathcal{F}_\delta$-closed might be more convenient to evaluate in some cases, compared to the characterizations in Theorem 4.1, since it might be easier to argue about the immediate neighbors of $x \notin \Pi \cup \mathcal{F}_\delta(\Pi)$ instead of about the δ-neighborhood of x (i.e., about a vertex $z \in \mathcal{F}_\delta(\Pi)$ such that $\Delta(x, z) < \delta$) as is required in Condition (2) of Theorem 4.1. However, being strongly $\mathcal{F}_\delta$-closed is not a necessary condition for being $\mathcal{F}_\delta$-closed: There exist graphical spaces Ω, parameters $\delta > 0$ and subsets $\Pi \subseteq \Omega$ such that Π is $\mathcal{F}_\delta$-closed but not strongly $\mathcal{F}_\delta$-closed. Furthermore, such sets exist even in the special case of the Boolean hypercube.

PROPOSITION 4.4. *(strongly $\mathcal{F}_\delta$-closed is not a necessary condition for $\mathcal{F}_\delta$-closed in the Boolean hypercube; see [16, Prop. 4.7]). For $n \geq 9$ and $4 \leq \delta \leq \frac{n}{2}$ such that $\delta - 1$ divides n, there exist sets in the Boolean hypercube that are $\mathcal{F}_\delta$-closed but are not strongly $\mathcal{F}_\delta$-closed.*

Nevertheless, there exists graphs and values of $\delta > 0$ such that every $\mathcal{F}_\delta$-closed set in the graph is also strongly $\mathcal{F}_\delta$-closed. In particular, this holds for any graph when $\delta = 2$ (but not when $\delta \geq 3$). Also, there exist graph families such that for every $\delta > 0$, every $\mathcal{F}_\delta$-closed set in the graph is also strongly $\mathcal{F}_\delta$-closed; these graph families include simple paths, cycles, and all $2 \times n$ grids (see [16, Prop. C.2]).

A different direction of study is as follows: Instead of fixing δ and asking which sets are $\mathcal{F}_\delta$-closed, we ask, for a fixed set $\Pi \subseteq \Omega$, what are the values of δ for which Π is strongly $\mathcal{F}_\delta$-closed, $\mathcal{F}_\delta$-closed, or not $\mathcal{F}_\delta$-closed. Interestingly, for any set Π in a graphical space with bounded diameter, the values of δ for which Π is $\mathcal{F}_\delta$-closed constitute a single bounded interval. This interval starts at $\delta = 1$ (since every set is $\mathcal{F}_1$-closed), and for any set Π we denote the right-end of this interval by $\delta^{\mathrm{c}}(\Pi)$ (i.e., $\delta^{\mathrm{c}}(\Pi)$ is the maximal value for which Π is $\mathcal{F}_\delta$-closed). A similar claim holds for values of δ for which Π is strongly $\mathcal{F}_\delta$-closed. That is –

PROPOSITION 4.5. *(values of δ for which a set is $\mathcal{F}_\delta$-closed and strongly $\mathcal{F}_\delta$-closed; see [16, Prop. 4.12]). For a graphical Ω with bounded diameter and a non-trivial $\Pi \subseteq \Omega$, there exist two integers $\delta^{\mathrm{c}}(\Pi)$ and $\delta^{\mathrm{sc}}(\Pi)$ such that $\delta^{\mathrm{sc}}(\Pi) \leq \delta^{\mathrm{c}}(\Pi)$ and for every integer $\delta > 0$ it holds that*

1. *Π is $\mathcal{F}_\delta$-closed if and only if $\delta \in [1, \delta^{\mathrm{c}}(\Pi)]$.*

2. *Π is strongly $\mathcal{F}_\delta$-closed if and only if $\delta \in [1, \delta^{\mathrm{sc}}(\Pi)]$.*

In contrast, if the space Ω is not graphical, then a statement analogous to Item (1) in Proposition 4.5 does not necessarily hold (see [16, Prop. 4.13]), and also recall that the notion of strongly $\mathcal{F}_\delta$-closed sets was not defined for non-graphical metric spaces).

5. OUR TECHNIQUES

This section focuses on our techniques for proving claims regarding dual problems in property testing (i.e., the claims in Section 3). In comparison, the proofs for the claims of Section 4 are easier, and some are straightforward. We note, however, that some constructions for counter-examples in Section 4 are quite evasive, and it seems a-priori non-obvious that a counter-example should even exist in these cases (see, e.g., Proposition 4.4).

The lower bound regarding testing dual problems with one-sided error (i.e., Theorem 3.3) stems from a similar lower bound with respect to testing standard problems with *perfect soundness*; that is, testing a property such that "no" inputs are *always* rejected. The query complexity of testing standard problems with perfect soundness is linear, unless the problem is trivial (i.e., unless $\mathcal{F}_\delta(\Pi_n) = \emptyset$ for a sufficiently large n). The lower bound regarding dual problems follows, since the query complexity of testing a dual problem with one-sided error is lower bounded by the query complexity of testing a standard problem with perfect soundness.

In testing specific dual problems, we rely on one of two general techniques. The first, which we apply in the cases of error-correcting codes (Theorem 3.4), monotone functions (Theorem 3.5), and distribution identity testing (Theorem 3.7), is showing that the dual problem is equivalent to the original. For a property $\Pi = \{\Pi_n\}_{n\in\mathbb{N}}$, this requires showing that for every sufficiently large n and sufficiently small $\epsilon > 0$, the set Π_n is $\mathcal{F}_{\epsilon\cdot n}$-closed (as in Definition 3.1). The latter is done relying on the characterizations of $\mathcal{F}_\delta$-closed sets and on the sufficient conditions for a set to be $\mathcal{F}_\delta$-closed, described in Section 4.

The second technique is useful when the dual problem is different from the original one. Specifically, for the three dual problems that we solve in the context of graph property testing (k-colorability in the dense graph model, and connectivity and cycle-free graphs in the bounded-degree model), we reduce the dual problem to the problem of *tolerant testing*, introduced by Parnas, Ron, and Rubinfeld [14]: Given a set Π_n, a parameter $\delta > 0$ and $\alpha < 1$, the tolerant testing problem consists of distinguishing between inputs that are $(\alpha \cdot \delta)$-close to Π_n and inputs that are δ-far from Π_n. Reducing dual problems to tolerant testing problems is done by showing that, for some $\alpha < 1$, all points in $\mathcal{F}_\delta(\mathcal{F}_\delta(\Pi_n))$ are $(\alpha\cdot\delta)$-close to Π_n. These are structural results regarding the property Π_n, which are of independent interest.

Then, we need to show that the corresponding tolerant testing problem can be efficiently solved. In the case of k-colorability in the dense graph model, the tolerant testing problem was solved by Fischer and Newman [5]; in the case of connected graphs in the bounded-degree model, we solve the tolerant testing problem ourselves (see [16, Sec. 5.6.1.3]); and in the case of cycle-free graphs in the bounded-degree model, the tolerant testing problem was solved by Marko and Ron [13].

We stress several points regarding reductions of dual problems to tolerant testing. Firstly, as mentioned in Section 2, it is *not* true in general that points in $\mathcal{F}_\delta(\mathcal{F}_\delta(\Pi_n))$ are $(\alpha\cdot\delta)$-close to Π_n, for some $\alpha < 1$. In fact, we show an artificial property $\Pi = \{\Pi_n\}_{n\in\mathbb{N}}$ of strings in the Boolean hypercube such that for every small $\epsilon > 0$ (of the form $\epsilon = 2^{-k}$) and sufficiently large n there exist strings in $\mathcal{F}_{\epsilon\cdot n}(\mathcal{F}_{\epsilon\cdot n}(\Pi_n))$ that are almost $(\epsilon \cdot n)$-far from Π_n (see [16, Prop. 3.15]). Secondly, even in the cases in which we know that the property reduces to tolerant testing (i.e., for the three properties mentioned above), the proofs are not very straightforward; and we were so far unable to prove such reductions for several related natural properties (e.g., for the property of graphs containing a large clique). And thirdly, there exist cases

in which the tolerant testing problem is *significantly more difficult* than the dual problem. For example, according to Theorem 3.7, the complexity of testing whether a distribution is far from uniform is $\Theta(\sqrt{n})$; however, the results of Valiant and Valiant [17] imply that the complexity of the corresponding tolerant testing problem is $\Theta(n/\log(n))$.

The general technical question underlying both techniques outlined above is the following: *Given a metric space Σ^n, a set $\Pi_n \subseteq \Sigma^n$, a parameter $\delta > 0$, and a point x that satisfies some requirements regarding its distance from Π_n, does there exist a point z such that $\Delta(x,z) < \delta$ and $\Delta(z,\Pi_n) \geq \delta$?* In most cases, given a point x that satisfies some distance requirement from Π_n, we show how to explicitly modify x to a corresponding suitable z. Our modification of x to z capitalizes on structural features of objects in the relevant metric space that satisfy the specific distance requirement. For example, when relying on Condition (2) of Theorem 4.1 to show that a set Π_n is $\mathcal{F}_\delta$-closed, we start from a point $x \notin \Pi_n \cup \mathcal{F}_\delta(\Pi_n)$, and modify it into $z \in \mathcal{F}_\delta(\Pi_n)$ such that $\Delta(x,z) < \delta$. Similarly, to reduce a dual problem to the corresponding tolerant testing problem (i.e., to prove that $\mathcal{F}_\delta(\mathcal{F}_\delta(\Pi_n)) \subseteq \{y : \Delta(y,\Pi_n) \leq \alpha \cdot \delta\}$), we start with x such that $\Delta(x,\Pi_n) \in (\alpha \cdot \delta, \delta)$, and modify it into $z \in \mathcal{F}_\delta(\Pi_n)$ such that $\Delta(x,z) < \delta$, which implies that $x \notin \mathcal{F}_\delta(\mathcal{F}_\delta(\Pi_n))$.

6. OPEN QUESTIONS

In the current work we were able to prove one general lower bound on dual testing problems, and several specific upper bounds. However, many interesting and natural *general questions* that concern dual testing problems are left without answer. In this section we suggest a few of these questions, which we suspect might lead towards better understanding of dual testing problems and of "far-from-far" sets.

Can the query complexity of a dual problem be significantly higher than that of the original problem? Recall that the (two-sided error) query complexity of a dual problem is lower bounded by the query complexity of the original problem. A natural question is thus:

QUESTION 1. *Does there exist a property such that the query complexity of its dual problem is significantly higher than that of the original problem?*

Note that one of the upper bounds for a dual problem given in this work (testing k-colorability in the dense graph model) is significantly higher than the known upper bound for the corresponding original problem.[6]

Do all natural dual problems reduce to tolerant testing? Recall that (in Section 5) we mentioned an example of an artificial property of Boolean strings whose dual problem does not reduce to tolerant testing. However, it is not clear whether this happens for natural properties (e.g., for properties that are closed to specific types of invariances, such as graph properties or affine-invariant properties).

One specific setting that might be convenient for tackling this question is the dense graph model.

---

[6] The original problem is testable using $\mathrm{poly}(1/\epsilon)$ queries [8], whereas the upper bound for the dual problem is a function that has a tower-type dependency on ϵ (the latter is the complexity of the tolerant tester by Fischer and Newman [5], which relies on Szemerédi's regularity lemma).

QUESTION 2. Do the dual problems of all graph properties in the dense graph model reduce to tolerant testing?

Relying on the results by Fischer and Newman [5], an affirmative answer to Question 2 would imply that a property in the dense graph model is testable with $O(1)$ queries *if and only if* its dual problem is testable with $O(1)$ queries.

Upper bounds for dual problems without reductions to tolerant testing. All the testers we presented for dual problems that are different than the original problems relied on reductions to tolerant testing. Thus, these testers do not fully exploit the structure of "far-from-far" sets, but rather only use the fact that "far-from-far" inputs are sufficiently close to the property. Hence, we ask:

QUESTION 3. Does there exist a tester for a natural dual problem (that is different than the original problem) that uses significantly fewer queries than the corresponding tolerant tester?

When the dual problem is equivalent to the original problem, the dual problem might indeed be easier to test than the corresponding tolerant testing problem (e.g., in the case of testing whether a distribution is uniform; see Section 5).

7. ACKNOWLEDGMENTS

The author thanks his advisor, Oded Goldreich, for suggesting the core questions and observations leading to this work, and for his guidance and support during the research and writing process. The author is grateful to Neta Atzmon for several helpful observations and discussions regarding "far-from-far" sets and dual property testing problems, and for her valuable comments on a draft of this paper. The author thanks Gil Cohen for a helpful discussion regarding decomposition of posets to monotone chains, and Clément Canonne for useful discussions and suggestions. The author also thanks two anonymous reviewers for helpful suggestions. This research was partially supported by the Israel Science Foundation (grant No. 671/13).

8. REFERENCES

[1] Tuğkan Batu, Lance Fortnow, Ronitt Rubinfeld, Warren D. Smith, and Patrick White. Testing closeness of discrete distributions. *Journal of the ACM*, 60(1):4:1–4:25, 2013.

[2] Manuel Blum, Michael Luby, and Ronitt Rubinfeld. Self-testing/correcting with applications to numerical problems. *Journal of Computer and System Sciences*, 47:549–595, 1990.

[3] Eldar Fischer. The difficulty of testing for isomorphism against a graph that is given in advance. *SIAM Journal of Computing*, 34(5):1147–1158, 2005.

[4] Eldar Fischer and Arie Matsliah. Testing graph isomorphism. *SIAM Journal of Computing*, 38(1):207–225, 2008.

[5] Eldar Fischer and Ilan Newman. Testing versus estimation of graph properties. *SIAM Journal of Computing*, 37(2):482–501, 2007.

[6] Oded Goldreich, editor. *Property Testing - Current Research and Surveys*, volume 6390 of *Lecture Notes in Computer Science*. Springer, 2010.

[7] Oded Goldreich, Shafi Goldwasser, Eric Lehman, Dana Ron, and Alex Samorodnitsky. Testing monotonicity. *Combinatorica*, 20(3):301–337, 2000.

[8] Oded Goldreich, Shafi Goldwasser, and Dana Ron. Property testing and its connection to learning and approximation. *Journal of the ACM*, 45(4):653–750, 1998.

[9] Oded Goldreich, Michael Krivelevich, Ilan Newman, and Eyal Rozenberg. Hierarchy theorems for property testing. *Computational Complexity*, 21(1):129–192, 2012.

[10] Oded Goldreich and Dana Ron. Property testing in bounded degree graphs. *Algorithmica*, 32(2):302–343, 2002.

[11] Alan Guo. Group homomorphisms as error correcting codes. *Electronic Journal of Combinatorics*, 22(1):14, 2015.

[12] Jörg Koppitz and Klaus Denecke. *M-Solid Varieties of Algebras (Advances in Mathematics)*. Springer-Verlag New York, Inc., 2006.

[13] Sharon Marko and Dana Ron. Distance approximation in bounded-degree and general sparse graphs. In *Proc. 10th International Workshop on Randomization and Approximation Techniques in Computer Science (RANDOM)*, pages 475–486, 2006.

[14] Michal Parnas, Dana Ron, and Ronitt Rubinfeld. Tolerant property testing and distance approximation. *Journal of Computer and System Sciences*, 72(6):1012–1042, 2006.

[15] Ronitt Rubinfeld and Madhu Sudan. Robust characterizations of polynomials with applications to program testing. *SIAM Journal of Computing*, 25(2):252–271, 1996.

[16] Roei Tell. On being far from far and on dual problems in property testing. *Electronic Colloquium on Computational Complexity: ECCC*, 22:72, 2015.

[17] Gregory Valiant and Paul Valiant. Estimating the unseen: an n/log(n)-sample estimator for entropy and support size, shown optimal via new clts. In *Proc. 43rd Annual ACM Symposium on Theory of Computing (STOC)*, pages 685–694, 2011.

[18] Marcel L.J. van de Vel. *Theory of Convex Structures*. North-Holland Mathematical Library. Elsevier Science, 1993.

Strategic Classification

Moritz Hardt
Google Research
Mountain View, CA
m@mrtz.org

Nimrod Megiddo
IBM Almaden Research Center
San Jose, CA
megiddo@us.ibm.com

Christos Papadimitriou[*]
UC Berkeley
Berkeley, CA
christos@cs.berkeley.edu

Mary Wootters[†]
Carnegie Mellon University
Pittsburgh, PA
marykw@cs.cmu.edu

ABSTRACT

Machine learning relies on the assumption that unseen test instances of a classification problem follow the same distribution as observed training data. However, this principle can break down when machine learning is used to make important decisions about the welfare (employment, education, health) of strategic individuals. Knowing information about the classifier, such individuals may manipulate their attributes in order to obtain a better classification outcome. As a result of this behavior—often referred to as *gaming*—the performance of the classifier may deteriorate sharply. Indeed, gaming is a well-known obstacle for using machine learning methods in practice; in financial policy-making, the problem is widely known as Goodhart's law. In this paper, we formalize the problem, and pursue algorithms for learning classifiers that are robust to gaming.

We model classification as a sequential game between a player named "Jury" and a player named "Contestant." Jury designs a classifier, and Contestant receives an input to the classifier drawn from a distribution. Before being classified, Contestant may change his input based on Jury's classifier. However, Contestant incurs a cost for these changes according to a cost function. Jury's goal is to achieve high classification accuracy with respect to Contestant's original input and some underlying target classification function, assuming Contestant plays best response. Contestant's goal is to achieve a favorable classification outcome while taking into account the cost of achieving it.

For a natural class of *separable* cost functions, and certain generalizations, we obtain computationally efficient learning algorithms which are near optimal, achieving a classifica-tion error that is arbitrarily close to the theoretical minimum. Surprisingly, our algorithms are efficient even on concept classes that are computationally hard to learn. For general cost functions, designing an approximately optimal strategy-proof classifier, for inverse-polynomial approximation, is NP-hard.

Keywords

Classification; learning theory; game theory

1. INTRODUCTION

Studies have found that a student's success at school is highly correlated with the *number of books in the parents' household* [EKST10]. Therefore, in theory, this attribute should be of great value when using machine-learning techniques for student admission. However, this statistical pattern is obviously open to manipulation: books are relatively cheap and, knowing that their number matters, parents can easily buy an attic full of unread books in preparation for admission decisions.

This behavior is often called *gaming*: the strategic use of methods that, while not dishonest or against the rules, give the individual an unintended advantage.[1] The problem of gaming is well known and can be seen as a consequence of a classical principle in financial policy making known as *Goodhart's law*:

> "If a measure becomes the public's goal, it is no longer a good measure."

Goodhart's law is highly relevant for the practice of machine learning today. Machine learning relies on the idea that patterns observed in training data translate to accurate predictions about unseen instances of a classification problem. Machine learning is increasingly used to make decisions about individuals in areas such as employment, health, education and commerce. In each such application, an individual may try to achieve a more favorable classification outcome with little effort by exploiting information that may be available about the classifier. Goodhart's law suggests that if a classifier is exposed to public scrutiny, its prediction accuracy vanishes and it becomes useless. Indeed, concerns of gaming and manipulation are often used as a reason for keeping

[*]This research was supported by NSF grant CCF1408635, and by Templeton Foundation grant 3966.

[†]Some of this research was done at IBM Almaden. Research funded in part by NSF MSPRF grant DMS-1400558.

Permission to make digital or hard copies of all or part of this work for personal or classroom use is granted without fee provided that copies are not made or distributed for profit or commercial advantage and that copies bear this notice and the full citation on the first page. Copyrights for components of this work owned by others than the author(s) must be honored. Abstracting with credit is permitted. To copy otherwise, or republish, to post on servers or to redistribute to lists, requires prior specific permission and/or a fee. Request permissions from Permissions@acm.org.

ITCS'16, January 14–16, 2016, Cambridge, MA, USA.
Copyright is held by the owner/author(s). Publication rights licensed to ACM.
ACM 978-1-4503-4057-1/16/01 ...$15.00.
DOI: http://dx.doi.org/10.1145/2840728.2840730

---

[1]See, for instance, http://www.thefreedictionary.com/gamesmanship.

classification mechanisms secret, which is a major concern in credit scoring (cf. [CP14]). Secrecy is not a robust solution to the problem; information about a classifier may leak, and it is often possible for an outsider to learn such information from classification outcomes. Moreover, transparency is highly desirable and sometimes even mandated by regulation in applications of public interest.

Our goal in this work is to formalize gaming in classification and to develop approaches and techniques for designing classifiers that are near optimal in the presence of public scrutiny and gaming. The hope is that this analysis may lead, in certain cases, to classifiers with performance comparable to ones that rely on secrecy. In other cases, our analysis may lead to the realization that secrecy is necessary for a good classification performance.

As gaming entails strategic behavior, any attempt to formalize it must incorporate the strategic response of an individual to a classifier. We propose a general model for *strategic classification*, based on a sequential two-player game between a party that wishes to learn a classifier and a party that is being classified. This is different from the standard supervised-learning setup, which is commonly viewed as a one-shot learning process, in which an algorithm produces a classifier from labeled training examples. Our model combines the statistical elements of learning theory—namely, seeking a small generalization error given a finite number of training data—with a game-theoretic notion of equilibrium. This combination allows us to build classifiers that achieve high classification accuracy at equilibrium, when both parties respond strategically to each other.

Informal description of our model and results.

We model learning and classification as a sequential two-player game. The first player, named "Jury," has a learning task: she is given labeled examples from some true classifier h, and must publish a classifier f. The second player, named "Contestant," receives an input to the classifier, and is given a chance to "game" it. That is, Contestant may change his input based on f. However, Contestant incurs a cost for these changes according to a *cost function* known to both players. Jury's goal is to achieve high classification accuracy with respect to Contestant's *original* input and the true classifier h. Contestant's goal is to be accepted by Jury, without paying too much to change his input. The cost function plays an important role in our framework as it determines the flexibility of Contestant in changing his input. Ideally, the cost function should capture ground truth or our best approximation thereof.

Our contributions are the following:

- For certain cost functions, we give an efficient strategy for Jury which approaches the optimal payoff. Surprisingly, this result holds even for concept classes which are computationally intractable to learn. The intuitive reason is that Contestant's changes to his input "smooth out" any intractability.

- Those cost functions for which Jury has near-optimal algorithms include *separable cost functions*. This is a natural class of cost functions which generalize our introductory example of school admissions and books. We also obtain results for a broad generalization of these separable functions.

- In contrast, we show that, for general cost functions—even for cost functions which are metrics, another nice class—it is hard to approximate the optimum classification score with reasonable accuracy.

- We observe through experiments on real data that our approach leads to higher classification accuracy compared with standard classifiers in situations where even a small amount of gaming occurs. We also experimentally demonstrate the robustness of our framework to inaccuracies in our modeling assumptions and the modeling of the cost function.

1.1 Our model

We first describe an idealized version of the game, where Jury has perfect information. This will serve as a reference point for how well Jury may hope to do. We will later relax this to a version where Jury knows neither h nor $\mathcal{D}$, and only sees labeled examples.

DEFINITION 1.1 (FULL INFORMATION GAME). *The players are Jury and Contestant. Fix a* population X, *and a* probability distribution $\mathcal{D}$ over X. *Fix a* cost function $c : X \times X \to \mathbb{R}_+$ *and a target* classifier $h : X \to \{-1, 1\}$.

1. *Jury (who knows the cost function c, the distribution $\mathcal{D}$, and the true classifier h) publishes a classifier $f : X \to \{-1, 1\}$.*

2. *Contestant (who knows $c, h, \mathcal{D}$, and f), produces a function $\Delta : X \to X$.*

The payoff to Jury is $\mathrm{Pr}_{x \sim \mathcal{D}} \{h(x) = f(\Delta(x))\}$. *The payoff to Contestant is* $\mathbb{E}_{x \sim \mathcal{D}} [f(\Delta(x)) - c(x, \Delta(x))]$.

Definition 1.1 is an example of a *Stackelberg competition*, which means that the first player (Jury) has the ability to commit to her strategy (a classifier f) before the second player (Contestant) responds. We wish to find a *Stackelberg equilibrium*, that is, a highest-payoff strategy for Jury, assuming best response of Contestant; equivalently, a perfect equilibrium in the corresponding strategic-form game.

Notice that designing the optimum f, given h, $\mathcal{D}$ and c, for a finite X, is a conventional combinatorial optimization problem. We seek to label the points in X with ± 1 so that the expectation, over $\mathcal{D}$, of $h(x) \cdot f(\Delta(x))$ is maximized. Here, $\Delta(x)$ is a best move of Contestant, that is,

$$\Delta(x) = \mathrm{argmax}_{y \in X} f(y) - c(x, y). \qquad (1)$$

We note that $\Delta(x)$ may not be well-defined, if there are multiple y which attain the maximum. In the following, we assume that Contestant may move to any of them; for simplicity, we do assume that if one of the maximum-attaining y is x itself, then $\Delta(x) = x$. That is, if Contestant is indifferent between moving and not moving, he will default to not moving. We refer to the best payoff for Jury in the above full-information game at the "strategic maximum" of the game:

DEFINITION 1.2 (STRATEGIC MAXIMUM). *The strategic maximum in the full-information game is defined as*

$$\mathrm{OPT}_h(\mathcal{D}, c) = \max_{f : X \to \{-1, 1\}} \mathrm{Pr}_{x \sim \mathcal{D}} [h(x) = f(\Delta(x))],$$

where $\Delta(x)$ is defined as in (1). *Notice that $\Delta(x)$ depends on f.*

REMARK 1.3. *For intuition, notice that if $c(x,x) = 0$ (that is, it costs nothing for Contestant to stay where he is), then $\Delta(x)$ has the following characterization:*

- *if $f(x) = 1$, then $\Delta(x) = x$;*

- *if $f(x) = -1$, let $y = \operatorname{argmin}_{y \in X \,:\, f(y)=1} c(x,y)$; then*

$$\Delta(x) = \begin{cases} y & c(x,y) < 2 \\ x & c(x,y) \geqslant 2. \end{cases}$$

Indeed, since Contestant is best-responding, he only makes a move from input x to point y if $c(x,y)$ is strictly less than 2, which is the payoff he obtains by improving his outcome from "rejected" to "accepted." In this case, the quantity $f(\Delta(x))$ in the definition of the strategic maximum becomes

$$f(\Delta(x)) = \max_{y:c(x,y)<2} f(y).$$

In Section 4 we show that, for general cost functions, the strategic maximum is NP-hard to approximate. However, we will also show that for a natural class of cost functions, it is possible to to design a classifier for which Jury's payoff is arbitrarily close to the strategic maximum, even when Jury has *incomplete* information. To formalize this, we introduce a second game, which we call the *statistical classification game*. In this game, Jury does not know the target classifier h for every point in X, but instead is given a few labeled examples from an unknown distribution $\mathcal{D}$. Contestant best-responds to Jury's published classifier f.

DEFINITION 1.4 (STATISTICAL CLASSIFICATION GAME). *The players are Jury and Contestant. Fix a population X and a probability distribution $\mathcal{D}$ over X. Fix a cost function $c : X \times X \to \mathbb{R}_+$ and a target classifier $h : X \to \{-1,1\}$.*

1. *Jury (who knows only the cost function c) can request labeled examples of the form $(x, h(x))$, with x being drawn from $\mathcal{D}$. She publishes a classifier $f : X \to \{-1,1\}$.*

2. *Contestant (who knows c and f), produces a function $\Delta : X \to X$.*

The payoff to Jury is $\Pr_{x \sim \mathcal{D}} \{h(x) = f(\Delta(x))\}$. The payoff to Contestant is $\mathbb{E}_{x \sim \mathcal{D}}[f(\Delta(x)) - c(x, \Delta(x))]$.

1.2 Strategy-robust learning

A learning algorithm in our setting has to accomplish two goals. First, it needs to learn the unknown target classifier from labeled examples. Second, it needs to achieve high payoff for Jury in the statistical classification game, by anticipating Contestant's best response. Below, we give two definitions of stategy-robust learning which combine these goals; the second is a stronger requirement than the first. In our first definition, we fix an unknown target classifier h, and demand an algorithm which, with high probability over the samples, returns a classifier f guaranteeing a near-optimal payoff to Jury in the statistical classification game. In our second definition, we present a uniform notion: the learning algorithm must, with high probability, return a classifier that is guaranteed to work on *any* target classifier h in some concept class $\mathcal{H}$.

DEFINITION 1.5 (STRATEGY-ROBUST LEARNING). *Let $\mathcal{C}$ be a class of cost functions. We say that an algorithm $\mathcal{A}$ is a strategy-robust learning algorithm for $\mathcal{C}$ if the condition that follows holds. For all distributions $\mathcal{D}$, for all classifiers h, all $c \in \mathcal{C}$ and for all ε and δ, given a description of c and access to labeled examples of the form $(x, h(x))$, where $x \sim \mathcal{D}$, $\mathcal{A}$ produces a classifier $f : X \to \{-1,1\}$ so that, with probability at least $1 - \delta$ over the samples,*

$$\Pr_{x \sim \mathcal{D}}[h(x) = f(\Delta(x))] \geqslant OPT_h(\mathcal{D}, c) - \varepsilon. \qquad (2)$$

where $\Delta(x)$ is defined as in (1).

One might expect, in line with PAC-learning [Val84], that Definition 1.5 might restrict h to be in some concept class $\mathcal{H}$. However, we will show that for a natural class $\mathcal{C}$ of cost functions, in fact it is possible to achieve strategy-robust learning with no dependence on h!

However, we may want to ask a bit more. Suppose that Jury builds a classifier for some property, and later wants to re-use the data to build a classifier for a slightly different property. For example, returning to the scenario from the introduction, suppose that the school admissions board collects data on students and tries to predict academic success. Later, the board is charged with recruiting to maximize the quality of the basketball team; they would like to use the same dataset to predict who will be a good student-athlete. Later still, suppose that the this data set is made public, and many other schools try to use it to predict many things. If enough different classifiers are trained on this data, the guarantee of Definition 1.5 starts to degrade. A strategy-robust learning algorithm should succeed with high probability on a single classifier, but there are no guarantees (beyond what the union bound gives) if it is used repeatedly. This situation motivates the following definition.

DEFINITION 1.6 (UNIFORM STRATEGY-ROBUST LEARNING). *Let $\mathcal{H}$ be a concept class and $\mathcal{C}$ be a class of cost functions. We say that an algorithm $\mathcal{A}$ is a uniform strategy-robust learning algorithm for $(\mathcal{H}, \mathcal{C})$ if the condition that follows holds. For all distributions $\mathcal{D}$, for all $c \in \mathcal{C}$ and for all ε and δ, with probability at least $1 - \delta$ over draws $x \sim \mathcal{D}$, the following holds simultaneously for all $h \in \mathcal{H}$. Given a description of c and access to labels $(x, h(x))$, $\mathcal{A}$ produces a classifier $f : X \to \{-1,1\}$ so that*

$$\Pr_{x \sim \mathcal{D}}[h(x) = f(\Delta(x))] \geqslant OPT_h(\mathcal{D}, c) - \varepsilon, \qquad (3)$$

where $\Delta(x)$ is defined as in (1).

We will typically specify the number of labeled examples that the algorithm requires as a function of ε, δ and a parameter that depends on the domain size (e.g., the number of features).

1.3 Our contributions

Our main result is a strategy-robust learning algorithm, which comes with both uniform and non-uniform guarantees. Our algorithm is computationally efficient when the cost function comes from a broad class of functions that we call *separable*. In the non-uniform case, the target classifier h can be anything. In the uniform case, the algorithm is efficient as long as the concept class $\mathcal{H}$ is statistically learnable, but it notably does not require that $\mathcal{H}$ be efficiently learnable.

Separable cost functions are functions of the form $c(x, y) = \max\{0, c_2(y) - c_1(x)\}$, where c_1 and c_2 are arbitrary functions, mapping the domain X into the real numbers. We take the maximum with 0 to obtain a nonnegative cost function. We will later see and discuss a number of natural examples of separable cost functions.

Our main theorem, and our stronger result, is about uniform strategy-robust learning.

THEOREM 1.7 (INFORMAL). *Let $\mathcal{H}$ be a concept class that is learnable from m examples up to error ε and confidence $1 - \delta$, and let $\mathcal{S}$ be the class of separable cost functions. Then, there is a uniform strategy-robust learning algorithm for $(\mathcal{H}, \mathcal{S})$ with running time and sample complexity $\text{poly}(m, 1/\varepsilon, \log(1/\delta))$.*

In fact, (the formal statement of) this theorem implies a non-uniform result:

THEOREM 1.8 (INFORMAL). *Let $\mathcal{S}$ be the class of separable cost functions. There is a non-uniform strategy-robust learning algorithm for $\mathcal{S}$ with polynomial running time and sample complexity.*

Our main theorem (and the non-uniform corollary) can be extended to a more general class of cost functions, which are obtained by taking the minimum of k separable cost functions. We state only the uniform version here, the non-uniform version follows similarly.

THEOREM 1.9 (INFORMAL). *Let $\mathcal{H}$ be a concept class that is learnable from m examples up to error ε and confidence $1 - \delta$, and let $\mathcal{S}^{(k)}$ be the class of minima of k separable cost functions. Then, there is a uniform strategy-robust learning algorithm for $(\mathcal{H}, \mathcal{S}^{(k)})$ with sample complexity $\text{poly}(m, k, 1/\varepsilon, \log(1/\delta))$ and running time $\text{poly}(m, \exp(k), 1/\varepsilon, \log(1/\delta))$.*

Theorem 1.9 applies to a broad class of cost functions: it is not hard to see that any cost function on a finite domain X can be written as a minimum of separable cost functions. Of course, the sample complexity in Theorem 1.9 depends on k, the number of cost functions involved. For general cost functions, k grows with $|X|$ and might be quite large. However, many spaces admit a more efficient representation—for instance, if the cost function defines a metric that admits a small ε-net, k depends only on the size of the net. Thus, k is a parameter that interpolates nicely between tractable cases where k is small and the general case where k is unrestricted.

The fact that the sample complexity in Theorem 1.9 might be large is unavoidable: for general cost functions, we have the following negative result.

THEOREM 1.10 (INFORMAL). *There is a class of metrics $\mathcal{S}$ such that, unless $P = NP$, there is no efficient strategy-robust learning algorithm for $\mathcal{S}$ that achieves expected payoff within $\varepsilon = 1/|X|^\eta$ of the optimum, for any constant $\eta > 0$.*

Recall that a distance function is a *metric* if it is nonnegative, symmetric, and satisfies the triangle inequality. This result is an immediate corollary of the fact (which we will prove in Section 4) that approximating the strategic maximum for metrics is NP-complete.

1.3.1 *Experimental evaluation*

We experimentally evaluate our framework on real data from a Brazilian social network called Apontador. The data set deals with instances of review spam and was recently studied in the context of spam fighting [CdCMBB14]. Classification of spammers is a natural setting for our methods, because spammers will of course try to game any automated attempt to identify them. We model a cost function that roughly reflects the loss in revenue that a spammer experiences when changing certain attributes. For instance, when a spam message contains a URL pointing to malware, it is costly for the spammer to remove this URL from his message as his message loses its intended purpose. Acknowledging that the modeling of a cost function can never be perfectly realistic, we evaluate our approach while explicitly taking into account several types of modeling inaccuracies. Specifically, we only assume that our cost function is roughly correct and that the amount of gaming is possibly below or above the threshold predicted by our theoretical framework. Our empirical observations demonstrate that even in the presence of significant modeling errors and only a small amount of gaming, our algorithm already outperforms a standard SVM classifier. Complementing our robustness analysis, we explore an approach for creating hybrid classifiers that interpolate between our classifier and standard classifiers that aren't by themselves strategy-robust. We observe that such hybrids often achieve an excellent trade-off between resilience to gaming and classification accuracy.

1.4 Related work

The deterioration of prediction accuracy due to unforeseen events is often described as *concept drift* and arises in a number of contexts. A sequence of works on *adversarial learning* is motivated by the question of learning in the presence of an adversary that tampers with the examples of a learning algorithm. Typical application examples in this line of work include intrusion detection and spam fighting. Early works considered zero-sum games [DDM+04] which are not very applicable to our problem as there are almost always cases where the payoff should be high for both players (e.g, a good student being admitted to a good college). More recent work considers alternative game-theoretic notions [BS09, BS11, BKS12, GSBS13]. The most closely related is the work by Brückner and Scheffer [BS11], which considered a Stackelberg competition for adversarial learning. A notable difference with our setup is that they define the equilibrium with respect to the sample, while we define it with respect to the underlying distribution. Our definition requires us to provide generalization bounds. Beyond this difference, Brückner and Scheffer focus on learning centered linear classifiers when the Euclidean squared norm is the cost function. The Euclidean norm is not separable and so our results are incomparable. Stackelberg competitions have also been studied extensively in the context of security games [KYK+11, KCP10].

2. SEPARABLE COST FUNCTIONS

We begin by studying the class of *separable* cost functions, which arise naturally in the context of gaming. To motivate the definition, recall the example of the school board which wants to exploit the correlation between parents' books and students' performance. In this (admittedly rather stylized) example, the cost to Contestant from moving from a household $x \in X$ with 50 books to a household $y \in X$ with 100 books is simply the cost of the the additional books.

More generally, this logic applies to any situation where Contestant can assign a cost to each state $x \in X$, independently of how it was reached. If the cost of a state x is $g(x)$, then the cost to Contestant of moving from x to y is simply any additional cost: $c(x, y) = \max\{0, g(y) - g(x)\}$. For example, suppose that Jury is designing a spam filter, and Contestant wishes to send an email. Independently of the spam filter, Contestant wants his message to serve a purpose such as advertising or distributing malware. We can assign a score $g(x)$ to each message in $x \in X$ that expresses how much utility the spammer experiences when this message is delivered without being classified as spam. For example, a message is significantly less useful for the spammer after the URL pointing to malware has been removed. The expression $\max\{0, g(y) - g(x)\}$ then captures the loss in utility (or expected revenue) when moving from x to y. We will return to this example in detail in our experimental evaluation in Section 5.

With these examples in mind, we define a *separable* cost function as follows.

DEFINITION 2.1. *A cost function $c(x, y)$ is called separable if it can be written as*

$$c(x, y) = \max\{0, c_2(y) - c_1(x)\},$$

for functions $c_1, c_2 : X \to \mathbb{R}$ satsifying $c_1(X) \subset c_2(X)$.

Above, the term "separable" is a slight abuse of terminology, because the cost function cannot be negative, and because of the assumption about $c_1(X) \subset c_2(X)$; a truly "separable" function would be of the form $c_2(y) - c_1(x)$, for arbitrary c_1, c_2. However, we will stick with it for simplicity of exposition. The two extra conditions are natural for cost functions. The maximum with 0 ensures that the cost function is non-negative. The condition $c_1(X) \subset c_2(X)$ means that there is always a 0-cost option (that is, Contestant can opt not to game, and can pay nothing).

Another important special case of a separable cost functions are linear cost functions of the form

$$c(x, y) = \langle \alpha, (y - x) \rangle_+,$$

for $\alpha \in \mathbb{R}^n$. With this cost function, each attribute can be increased independently at some linear cost, and can be decreased for free. For our arguments that follow, a linear cost function is helpful for intuition.

Our main result is that for separable cost functions, there is a nearly optimal algorithm for Jury, with a uniform guarantee. The sample complexity and running time of this algorithm depend on the Rademacher complexity of the class $\mathcal{H}$ of classifiers.

DEFINITION 2.2. *For a class $\mathcal{F}$ of functions $f : X \to \mathbb{R}$, the Rademacher complexity $R_m(\mathcal{F})$ of $\mathcal{F}$ with sample size m is defined as*

$$R_m(\mathcal{F}) :=$$

$$\mathbb{E}_{x_1, \ldots, x_m \sim \mathcal{D}} \mathbb{E}_{\sigma_1, \ldots, \sigma_m} \left[\sup \left\{ \frac{1}{m} \sum_{i=1}^{m} \sigma_i f(x_i) \ : \ f \in \mathcal{F} \right\} \right],$$

where $\sigma_1, \ldots, \sigma_m$ are i.i.d. Rademacher random variables.

Our algorithm, given below as Algorithm 1, has the following uniform guarantee.

THEOREM 2.3. *Suppose the cost function c is separable, i.e., $c(x, y) = \max\{0, c_2(y) - c_1(x)\}$ and $c_1(X) \subseteq c_2(X)$. Let $\mathcal{H}$ be a concept class, and let $\mathcal{D}$ be a distribution. Let m denote the number of samples in Algorithm 1, and suppose*

$$R_m(\mathcal{H}) + 2\sqrt{\frac{\ln(m+1)}{m}} + \sqrt{\frac{\ln(2/\delta)}{8m}} \leqslant \frac{\varepsilon}{8} .$$

Under these conditions, with probability at least $1 - \delta$, (3) holds for all $h \in \mathcal{H}$.

Notice that Theorem 2.3 indeed implies the "informal" version, Theorem 1.7. This is, if $\mathcal{H}$ is statistically learnable (i.e., $R_m(\mathcal{H})$ decays inversely polynomially with m for all distributions $\mathcal{D}$, or sufficiently that the VC dimension of $\mathcal{H}$ is bounded[2]), then Algorithm 1 is a efficient, uniform strategy-robust learning algorithm for $\mathcal{H}$.

It is worth pointing out that Algorithm 1 is *computationally* efficient as long as $\mathcal{H}$ has low sample complexity—even if $\mathcal{H}$ itself is not computationally efficiently learnable! As we mentioned above, the proof of Theorem 2.3 also implies that our algorithm satisfies the following non-uniform guarantee.

COROLLARY 2.4. *Suppose the cost function c is separable. Let m denote the number of samples in Algorithm 1, and suppose that*

$$2\sqrt{\frac{\ln(m+1)}{m}} + \sqrt{\frac{\ln(2/\delta)}{8m}} \leqslant \frac{\varepsilon}{8} .$$

Then with probability at least $1 - \delta$, (3) holds for all distributions $\mathcal{D}$. In particular, Algorithm 1 is an efficient (non-uniform) strategy-robust learning algorithm.

Corollary 2.4 follows from Theorem 2.3 by setting $\mathcal{H} = \{h\}$, the singleton containing the fixed target classifier h. Indeed, in this case $R_m(\mathcal{H}) = 0$.

Before proving Theorem 2.3, we state the algorithm and discuss the intuition behind it. In Figure 1, we illustrate the idea for a linear cost function, $c(x, y) = \langle \alpha, y - x \rangle_+$. Because moving perpendicularly to α is free for Contestant, Jury may as well choose a classifier f that accepts some affine halfspace whose normal is α (see Figure 1). Thus, the only issue is finding the correct shift for this halfspace. We choose the shift that is empirically best, based on the samples; this can be calculated quickly because it is a one-dimensional problem.

For a more general separable cost function

$$c(x, y) = \max\{0, c_2(y) - c_1(x)\} ,$$

by the same argument, Jury may as well return a classifier $c_2[t]$ of the form:

$$c_2[t](x) = \begin{cases} 1 & \text{if } c_2(x) \geqslant t \\ -1 & \text{if } c_2(x) < t \end{cases} \qquad (x \in X)$$

for some t. Algorithm 1 gives the details, and we proceed with the proof below.

---

[2] Indeed, if d is the VC dimension of $\mathcal{H}$, we have

$$R_m(\mathcal{H}) \leqslant \sqrt{\frac{2d \log(em/d)}{m}}$$

for all distributions $\mathcal{D}$ (notice that $R_m(\mathcal{H})$ depends on $\mathcal{D}$).

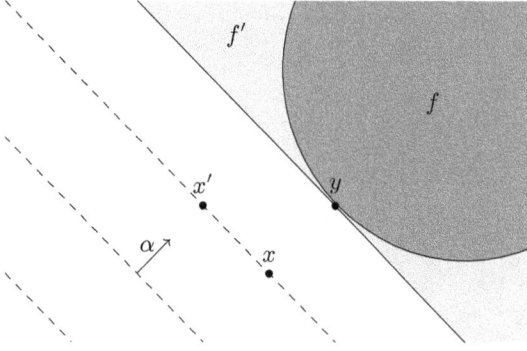

Figure 1: Suppose the optimal classifier for Jury is f (which accepts the dark gray region), and the cost function is $c(x,y) = \langle \alpha, y - x \rangle_+$. Because moving perpendicular to α is free for Contestant, then the payoff for Jury if she plays f' (shown above, which accepts the light gray region) is the same as her payoff if she plays f. Indeed, suppose that the agent x shown above would be willing to move to y to get accepted by f. Then x' would also be willing to move to y, because the cost is the same. Thus, Jury may restrict his or her search to classifiers f' that accept all points in some affine halfspace whose normal is α.

REMARK 2.5 (INPUT TO ALGORITHM 1). *Algorithm 1 takes a cost function $c(x,y) = \max\{0, c_2(y) - c_1(x)\}$ as an input, and it returns some threshold function based on c_2. We have been a little sloppy about how exactly c should be represented. A quick inspection of the algorithm shows that in order to compute the threshold, $\mathcal{A}$ needs only black-box access to c_1, and enough access to c_2 to determine $c_2(X) \cap [t_i, t_i + 2]$. In order to return the classifier f, $\mathcal{A}$ additionally needs whatever access to c_2 it is expected to return. For example, if we only ask that $\mathcal{A}$ be able to provide black-box access to f, then black-box access to c_2 suffices for this step. If we ask that $\mathcal{A}$ return a short description of f, then a short description of c_2 suffices for this step.*

PROOF OF THEOREM 2.3. Assume for simplicity that the cost function satisfies $c(x,y) \neq 2$, for all $x, y \in X$. First, for any mapping $f : X \to \{-1, 1\}$, define

$$
\begin{aligned}
\Gamma(f) &:= \left\{ x \,:\, \max\{f(y) \,:\, c(x,y) < 2\} = 1 \right\} \\
&= \left\{ x \,:\, (\exists y \in X)(f(y) = 1, \ c(x,y) < 2) \right\} \\
&= \left\{ x \,:\, c_1(x) > \min\{c_2(y) \,:\, f(y) = 1\} - 2 \right\} .
\end{aligned}
$$

CLAIM 2.6. *$\Gamma(f)$ is the set of $x \in X$ such that $f(\Delta(x)) = 1$ when Δ is a best response of Contestant.*

PROOF. Indeed, for $x \in \Gamma(f)$, there exists some y such that $f(y) = 1$, so that the payoff to Contestant when he plays $\Delta(x) = y$ is equal to $1 - c(x,y) > -1$. On the other hand, suppose that Contestant plays $\Delta(z) \in X$ for some with $f(z) \neq 1$. Then the best payoff of Contestant is equal to $-1 - c(x,z) \leqslant -1$, because $c(x,z) \geqslant 0$. So, the best response of Contestant is to choose $\Delta(x) = y$ for some y with $f(y) = 1$. This establishes that $\Gamma(f) \subseteq \{x \in X \,:\, f(\Delta(x)) = 1\}$.

For the other direction, suppose that $f(\Delta(x)) = 1$. Then there is some $y \in X$ so that

$$
1 - c(x,y) > -1 - \min_{z \in X} c(x,z) = -1,
$$

Algorithm 1: $\mathcal{A}$: gaming-robust classification algorithm for separable cost functions

1 **Inputs:** Labeled examples $(x_1, h(x_1)), \ldots, (x_m, h(x_m))$ from $x_i \sim \mathcal{D}$ i.i.d.. Also, a description of a separable cost function $c(x,y) = \max\{0, c_2(y) - c_1(x)\}$.

2 For $i = 1, \ldots, m$, let

$$
t_i := c_1(x_i)
$$

3
$$
s_i := \begin{cases} \max\left(c_2(X) \cap [t_i, t_i + 2]\right) & c_2(X) \cap [t_i, t_i + 2] \neq \emptyset \\ \infty & c_2(X) \cap [t_i, t_i + 2] = \emptyset . \end{cases}
$$

For convenience, set $s_{m+1} = \infty$.

4 Compute

$$
\widehat{\mathrm{err}}(s_i) := \frac{1}{m} \sum_{j=1}^{m} \mathbf{1}\left\{h(x_j) \neq c_1[s_i - 2](x_j)\right\} .
$$

5 Find i^*, $1 \leqslant i^* \leqslant m + 1$, that minimizes $\widehat{\mathrm{err}}(s_i)$.

6 **Return:** $f := c_2[s_{i^*}]$.

---

using from the definition of separability that $c_1(X) \subseteq c_2(X)$, and hence for all x,

$$
\min_{z \in X} c(x,z) = \min_{z \in X} \max\{0, c_2(z) - c_1(x)\} = 0.
$$

In particular, $c(x,y) < 2$, so $x \in \Gamma(x)$. Thus,

$$
\{x \in X \,:\, f(\Delta(x)) = 1\} \subseteq \Gamma(f),
$$

which proves the claim. □

Claim 2.6 is the only place in the proof where we need either of the extra conditions in Definition 2.1 (that $c(x,y) \geqslant 0$ and $c_1(X) \subseteq c_2(X)$).

Given this characterization of $\Gamma(f)$, we next argue that we may replace f by a much more structured function f' so that $\Gamma(f) = \Gamma(f')$; in particular, the payoff to Jury under f will be the same as under f', and so we can restrict our attention to these more structured functions. For any f, let

$$
f'(y) = \begin{cases} 1 & \text{if } c_2(y) \geqslant \min\{c_2(z) \,:\, f(z) = 1\} \\ -1 & \text{otherwise} . \end{cases} \tag{4}
$$

Then we have

$$
\begin{aligned}
\Gamma(f) &= \left\{ x \,:\, c_1(x) > \min\{c_2(y) \,:\, f(y) = 1\} - 2 \right\} \\
&= \left\{ x \,:\, c_1(x) > \min\{c_2(y) \,:\, f'(y) = 1\} - 2 \right\} \\
&= \Gamma(f') .
\end{aligned}
$$

In particular, for any true classifier $h \in \mathcal{H}$, the payoff to Jury if she plays f is the same as if she plays f':

$$
\begin{aligned}
&\mathbb{P}\left\{h(x) = \max\{f(y) \,:\, c(x,y) < 2\}\right\} \\
&= \mathbb{P}\left\{x \in \left(\Gamma(f) \triangle \{y \,:\, h(y) = 1\}\right)^c\right\} \\
&= \mathbb{P}\left\{x \in \left(\Gamma(f') \triangle \{y \,:\, h(y) = 1\}\right)^c\right\} \\
&= \mathbb{P}\left\{h(x) = \max\{f'(y) \,:\, c(x,y) < 2\}\right\} .
\end{aligned}
$$

Above, $\triangle$ denotes symmetric difference. Thus, it suffices to consider classifiers of the form of (4). That is, our classifier may as well be equal to $c_2[s]$, for some $s \in c_2(X) \cup \{\infty\}$, where s plays the role of $\min\{c_2(z) \,:\, f(z) = 1\}$, and $s = \infty$

means that there is no z such that $f(z) = 1$. Let

$$S := c_2(X) \cup \{\infty\}$$

be the set of these relevant values of s. Recall the definition of s_i from Algorithm 1. For $s \in S$, we have[3]

$$\Gamma(c_2[s]) = \{x : c_1(x) > s - 2\} \ .$$

The best possible payoff to Jury is obtained by finding the best threshold s, i.e.,

$$OPT_h(\mathcal{D}, c) = 1 - \inf\{\operatorname{err}(s) : s \in S\} \ ,$$

where $\operatorname{err}(s) := \mathbb{P}\{h(x) \neq c_1[s-2](x)\}$. In Algorithm 1, Jury returns $f = c_2[s_{i^*}]$, and as above the payoff to Jury from this f is equal to

$$\mathbb{P}\{h(x) \neq c_1[s_{i^*} - 2](x)\} = 1 - \operatorname{err}(s_{i^*}) \ .$$

Thus, to prove Theorem 2.3, it suffices to show that for all $h \in \mathcal{H}$,

$$\operatorname{err}(s_{i^*}) \leqslant \inf\{\operatorname{err}(s) : s \in S\} + \varepsilon \ . \tag{5}$$

To establish this, we first observe that there is no loss of generality in Algorithm 1 by considering only the s_i, $i = 1, \dots, m+1$, where as in Algorithm 1 we set $s_{m+1} = \infty$.

CLAIM 2.7.

$$\widehat{\operatorname{err}}(s_{i^*}) = \min\{\widehat{\operatorname{err}}(s_i) : i = 1, \dots, m+1\}$$
$$= \inf\{\widehat{\operatorname{err}}(s) : s \in S\} \ .$$

PROOF. The first equality is just the definition of i^*. The second equality follows from the fact that

$$\widehat{\operatorname{err}}(s) = \frac{1}{m} \sum_{j=1}^{m} \mathbf{1}\{h(x_j) \neq c_1[s-2](x_j)\}$$

only changes when $c_1[s-2](x_j)$ changes for some j. Thus, by construction, this sum takes on every possible value (as s ranges over $S = c_2(X) \cap \{\infty\}$) at the points s_i, for $i = 1, \dots, m+1$. $\square$

CLAIM 2.8. *With probability at least $1 - \delta$, for all $h \in \mathcal{H}$ and for all $s \in S$,*

$$|\widehat{\operatorname{err}}(s) - \operatorname{err}(s)| \leqslant 4R_m(\mathcal{H}) + 8\sqrt{\tfrac{\ln(m+1)}{m}} + \sqrt{\tfrac{2\ln(2/\delta)}{m}} \ .$$

In particular, under the conditions of Theorem 2.3, with probability at least $1 - \delta$,

$$\sup\{|\widehat{\operatorname{err}}(s) - \operatorname{err}(s)| : h \in \mathcal{H}, \ s \in S\} \leqslant \varepsilon/2 \ .$$

PROOF. Writing out the definition of $\widehat{\operatorname{err}}$ and err, we need to bound the absolute value of the difference

$$\widehat{\operatorname{err}}(s) - \operatorname{err}(s)$$
$$= \frac{1}{m} \sum_{j=1}^{m} \mathbf{1}\{h(x_j) \neq c_1[s-2](x_j)\}$$
$$- \mathbb{E}_{x \sim \mathcal{D}}[\mathbf{1}\{h(x) \neq c_1[s-2](x)\}]$$

simultaneously for all $h \in \mathcal{H}$, $s \in S$. By standard arguments (see, for example, Theorem 3.2 in [BBL05]), for all $h \in \mathcal{C}$ and for all $s \in S$,

$$|\widehat{\operatorname{err}}(s) - \operatorname{err}(s)| \leqslant 2R_m(\mathcal{X}) + \sqrt{\tfrac{2\ln(2/\delta)}{m}} \ , \tag{6}$$

[3] As usual, $\infty - 2 = \infty$.

where

$$\mathcal{X} = \{h \cdot c_1[s-2] : h \in \mathcal{H}, s \in S\} \ .$$

Thus, it suffices to control the Rademacher complexity of $\mathcal{X}$, which is in turn controlled by

$$R_m(\mathcal{X}) \leqslant 2\left(R_m(\mathcal{H}) + R_m(\mathcal{Y})\right), \tag{7}$$

where $\mathcal{Y} = \{c_1[s-2] : s \in S\}$. Note that, because all the functions in $\mathcal{H} \cup \mathcal{Y}$ are ± 1-valued,

$$h(x) \cdot c_1[s-2](x) = |h(x) + c_1[s-2](x)| - 1$$

for every x. Inequality (7) follows from a contraction principle (see, e.g., Theorem 4.2 in [LT91]) and the definition of the Rademacher complexity.

It remains to bound $R_m(\mathcal{Y})$. Fix $x_1, \dots, x_m \in X$ and sign flips $\sigma_i \in \{-1, 1\}$. As in the proof of Claim 2.7, all of the values that $\sum_{i=1}^{m} \sigma_i c_1[s-2](x_i)$ takes on as s ranges over S are attained at $\{s_1, \dots, s_{m+1}\}$. Thus, for fixed $x_1, \dots, x_m \in X$, using a Chernoff bound and the union bound, and integrating to bound the expectation, we obtain

$$\mathbb{E}_\sigma\left[\sup\left\{\tfrac{1}{m}\sum_{i=1}^{m}\sigma_i c_1[s-2](x_i) : s \in S\right\}\right]$$
$$= \mathbb{E}_\sigma\left[\sup\left\{\tfrac{1}{m}\sum_{i=1}^{m}\sigma_i c_1[s_j-2](x_i) : j = 1, \dots, m+1\right\}\right]$$
$$\leqslant 2\sqrt{\tfrac{\ln(m+1)}{m}} \ .$$

Thus, we have

$$R_m(\mathcal{Y}) \leqslant 2\sqrt{\tfrac{\ln(m+1)}{m}},$$

and altogether inequality (6) implies that for all $h \in \mathcal{H}$ and $s \in S$,

$$|\widehat{\operatorname{err}}(s) - \operatorname{err}(s)| \leqslant 4\left(R_m(\mathcal{H}) + 2\sqrt{\tfrac{\ln(m+1)}{m}}\right) + \sqrt{\tfrac{2\ln(2/\delta)}{m}} \ ,$$

which completes the proof of the claim. $\square$

Claims 2.7 and 2.8 establish Theorem 2.3. Indeed, we have, with probability at least $1 - \delta$, for all $h \in \mathcal{C}$,

$$\operatorname{err}(s_{i^*}) \leqslant \widehat{\operatorname{err}}(s_{i^*}) + \varepsilon/2$$
$$= \inf\{\widehat{\operatorname{err}}(s) : s \in S\} + \varepsilon/2$$
$$\leqslant \inf\{\operatorname{err}(s) : s \in S\} + \varepsilon \ ,$$

establishing inequality (5) and completing the proof.

3. GENERAL COST FUNCTIONS

While separable cost functions are quite reasonable, they do not capture everything. In this section, we consider more general cost functions. We extend Algorithm 1 to work for a cost function that is the minimum of an arbitrary set of separable cost functions. This is a much broader class. In fact, *every* cost function can be represented as the minimum of separable cost functions, although not necessarily very parsimoniously.

PROPOSITION 3.1. *Let X be any finite set and let $c : X \times X \to \mathbb{R}$ be any mapping. Suppose*

$$D \geqslant \max\{c(x, y) : x, y \in X\} \ .$$

Under these conditions, $c(x, y)$ is equal to

$$\min\{c(w, z) + D \cdot \mathbf{1}\{x \neq w\} + D \cdot \mathbf{1}\{y \neq z\} : w, z \in X\} \ .$$

Since each of the cost functions $c_{w,z}(x,y) = c(w,z) + D \cdot \mathbf{1}\{x \neq w\} + D \cdot \mathbf{1}\{y \neq z\}$ is a separable cost function, Proposition 3.1 implies that any c can be written as the minimum of $|X|^2$ cost functions. The sample complexity of our extension depends on the number of cost functions; since $|X|$ may be quite large (possibly exponential in the parameter of interest), Proposition 3.1 might not help. However, a smaller number of cost functions can be used if X has nice geometric structure.

PROPOSITION 3.2. *Let X be any finite set and let $c : X \times X \to \mathbb{R}$ be a metric. Let S be an ε-net of X: that is, for every $x \in X$, there is some $s \in S$ so that $c(x,s) \leqslant \varepsilon$. Under these conditions, for every $x, y \in X$,*

$$c(x,y) \leqslant \min\{c(x,w) + c(w,z) + c(z,y) : w, z \in S\}$$
$$\leqslant c(x,y) + 4\varepsilon .$$

Thus, when c is a metric, our problem is very close to a problem where the cost function is the minimum of separable cost functions, and the number of cost functions we need to consider depends essentially on the covering number of the metric space (X,c).

Algorithm 2 is an adaptation of Algorithm 1 for cost functions of the form

$$c(x,y) = \min\{b(x,y) : b \in \mathcal{B}\} ,$$

where each function $b \in \mathcal{B}$ is separable, i.e.,

$$b(x,y) = \max\{0, b_2(y) - b_1(x)\} .$$

Algorithm 2: $\mathcal{A}$: gaming-robust classification algorithm for minima of separable cost functions

1 **Inputs:** Labeled examples $(x_1, h(x_1)), \ldots, (x_m, h(x_m))$ from $x_i \sim \mathcal{D}$ i.i.d.. Also, a description of k separable cost functions $b(x,y) = \max\{0, b_2(y) - b_1(x)\}$ for $b \in \mathcal{B}$.
2 For $i = 1, \ldots, m$ and $b \in \mathcal{B}$, set

$$t_{i,b} = b_1(x_i)$$

$$s_{i,b} = \begin{cases} \max\{b_2(X) \cap [t_{i,b}, t_{i,b} + 2]\} \\ \qquad \text{if} \quad b_2(X) \cap [t_{i,b}, t_{i,b} + 2] \neq \emptyset \\ \infty \\ \qquad \text{if} \quad b_2(X) \cap [t_{i,b}, t_{i,b} + 2] = \emptyset \end{cases}$$

3 and set $s_{m+1,b} = \infty$ for all $b \in \mathcal{B}$.
4 For each $\boldsymbol{s} \in \bigoplus_{b \in \mathcal{B}} \{s_{i,b} : i = 1, \ldots, m+1\}$, compute

$$\widehat{\mathrm{err}}(\boldsymbol{s}) := \frac{1}{m} \sum_{j=1}^{m} \mathbf{1}\{h(x_j) \neq \min\{b_1[\boldsymbol{s}_b - 2](x_j) : b \in \mathcal{B}\}\} .$$

5 Find a $\boldsymbol{s}^*$ that minimizes $\widehat{\mathrm{err}}(\boldsymbol{s})$.
6 **Return:** $f(x) = \min\{b_2[\boldsymbol{s}_b^*](x) : b \in \mathcal{B}\}$.

THEOREM 3.3. *Suppose the cost function c is the minimum of separable functions,*

$$c(x,y) = \min\{b(x,y) : b \in \mathcal{B}\} ,$$

where each $b : X \times X \to \mathbb{R}$ is separable. Let $\mathcal{D}$ be a distribution on X and suppose that Algorithm 2 uses m samples,

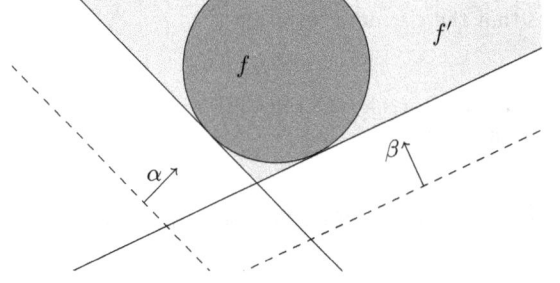

Figure 2: Suppose the the optimal classifier for Jury is f (which accepts the dark grey region), and the cost function is $c(x,y) = \min\{\langle \beta, y - x \rangle_+, \langle \alpha, y - x \rangle_+\}$. For the same reasoning as in Figure 1, the classifier f' has the same payoff to Jury as f does. Thus, Jury may restrict his/her search to classifiers f that are the intersections of two affine halfspaces.

so that m satisfies

$$R_m(\mathcal{H}) + 2\sqrt{\frac{|\mathcal{B}|\ln(m+1)}{m}} + \sqrt{\frac{\ln(2/\delta)}{8m}} \leqslant \frac{\varepsilon}{8} .$$

Under these conditions, with probability at least $1 - \delta$, (3) holds for all $h \in \mathcal{H}$ and for the distribution $\mathcal{D}$. The running time of Algorithm 2 is $O(m^{|\mathcal{B}|})$.

The intuition for Algorithm 2 is similar to that for Algorithm 1, and is illustrated in Figure 2 for the minimum of two linear cost functions. The proof of Theorem 3.3 is also similar to that of Theorem 2.3; we omit it here due to space constraints, but it can be found in the full version of this paper [HMPW15].

REMARK 3.4. *When the size of $\mathcal{B}$ is small, Theorem 3.3 gives a nice bound. However, if $\mathcal{B}$ is large (as in our extreme example of the beginning of this section), these guarantees are not so good. An inspection of the proof (available in the full version [HMPW15]) shows that the term $\sqrt{\frac{|\mathcal{B}|\ln(m+1)}{m}}$ may be replaced by $R_m(\mathcal{H})$, where*

$$\mathcal{H} = \left\{ \min_{b \in \mathcal{B}} b_1[\boldsymbol{s}_b - 2] \ : \ \boldsymbol{s} \in \bigoplus_{b \in \mathcal{B}} (b_2(X) \cup \{\infty\}) \right\} .$$

For some sets $\mathcal{B}$ of separable cost functions, this may be much smaller.

4. NP-COMPLETENESS

What happens when the cost function c is not separable? It turns out that for general cost functions, any algorithm for Jury requires more than polynomial time to obtain a near-optimum classifier, unless $P = NP$. This holds true

(a) even if the underlying distance function is a metric (another very natural class of cost function), and

(b) even if the learning algorithm were given correct labels $h(x)$ for *all* members $x \in X$ of the population,

when the desired deviation ε is inverse-polynomially small and the distribution $\mathcal{D}$ is uniform. The above statements are consequences of the following result:

THEOREM 4.1. *Given a finite population X with the uniform distribution, a metric c on X, and a target labeling $h : X \mapsto \{-1, +1\}$, it is NP-hard to compute the strategic optimum within $\varepsilon = \frac{1}{|X|^\eta}$ for any constant $\eta > 0$.*

PROOF OF THEOREM 4.1. We will reduce from 3SAT. Suppose we are given a 3SAT Boolean formula with n variables $x_1, \ldots, x_n$ and m clauses $C_1, \ldots, C_m$, where C_i has three literal occurrences L_{i1}, L_{i2}, L_{i3}. We now construct our instance of STRATEGIC OPTIMUM as follows. We need to specify X, h, and c. We begin by constructing a weighted population Y, which will consist of points y and positive integer weights $w(y)$ for each $y \in Y$. Our population X will simply consist of $w(y)$ identical copies of each $y \in Y$. Thus, $|X| = \sum_{y \in Y} w(y)$. We will also specify labels $h(y)$ for each $y \in Y$, which the points $x \in X$ will inherit. Fix a number K (polynomial in m) to be chosen later. Our weighted population Y consists of:

- $3m$ points L_{ik} for $1 \leqslant i \leqslant m$ and $k \in \{1, 2, 3\}$, corresponding to the literal occurrences in the clauses. These points each have weight $w(L_{ik}) = K(m-1-\frac{1}{m})$ and label $h(L_{ik}) = -1$.

- $\binom{m}{2}$ points P_{ij} for $1 \leqslant i < j \leqslant m$ corresponding to unordered pairs $\{C_i, C_j\}$ of clauses. These points each have weight $w(P_{ij}) = 2K$ and label $h(P_{ij}) = +1$.

- $9 \cdot \binom{m}{2}$ points $Q_{ikj\ell}$, for $1 \leqslant i < j \leqslant m$, and for $k, \ell \in \{1, 2, 3\}$ so that L_{ik} is *not* the negation of $L_{j\ell}$. These points correspond to unordered pairs of literal occurrences $\{L_{ik}, L_{j\ell}\}$ of literal occurrences in different clauses *which are not contradictory*. They have weight $w(Q_{ijk\ell}) = 1$ and label $h(Q_{ijk\ell}) = -1$. (Actually, their label does not matter).

- One other point R with a huge weight $w(R) = KM$, for a very large value M, and label $h(R) = -1$. Choose $M = 2\binom{m}{2}$.

We next define a metric $c : X \times X \to \mathbb{R}_+$. It will take only two nonzero values, 1.5 and 2.5. Notice that this guarantees c satisfies the triangle inequality. We will choose c so that $c(x, x) = 0$ and $c(x, y) = c(y, x)$, and so c will indeed be a metric. To describe c, it suffices to describe the points which are "close," that is, which have distance 1.5. Further, it suffices to define c for points in Y, and we will extend it to X in a natural way: for points $x, x' \in X$, if they come from the same $y \in Y$, they will have distance 1.5; if x, x' come from $y \neq y'$ respectively, then $c(x, x') = c(y, y')$. The close pairs of points in Y are:

- All pairs of the form $\{P_{ij}, Q_{ijkl}\}$;

- All pairs of the form $\{P_{ij}, R\}$;

- All pairs of the form $\{Q_{ijk\ell}, L_{ik}\}$ or $\{Q_{ijk\ell}, L_{j\ell}\}$.

CLAIM 4.2. *If the given formula is unsatisfiable, the number of points labeled $+1$ by the Jury's optimum f is equal to*

$$b = K\left(M + 3m\left(m - 1 - \frac{1}{m}\right)\right) + 9\binom{m}{2},$$

which we call the baseline payoff. *Otherwise, if the given formula is satisfiable, then there is a labeling f of the points with payoff at least $b + K - 9\binom{m}{2}$.*

PROOF. In the following, we will consider a graph with vertices Y. Two vertices x, y are neighbors in this graph if $c(x, y) = 1.5$. Let $\Gamma(x)$ denote the neighbors of x in this graph. Thus, the best-response Δ to a classifier f is

$$\Delta(x) = \begin{cases} x & f(x) = 1 \\ x & f(x) = -1 \text{ and } f(y) = -1 \forall y \in \Gamma(x) \, , \\ y & f(x) = -1 \text{ and } f(y) = 1, y \in \Gamma(x) \end{cases}$$

where above if y in the last case is not uniquely defined Contestant can pick any such y.

First observe that the baseline payoff is obtained by the classifier $f(x) = -1$ for all $x \in X$, and so it is certainly acheivable. We now argue that Jury can do better if and only if the original formula was satisfiable. We make a few observations about Jury's optimal classifier f.

- First, because of our choice of M, we must have $f(P_{ij}) = -1$ for all i, j. Indeed, our choice implies that $KM > |X| - KM$; thus, if $f(P_{ij}) = 1$ for some i, j, then Contestant will set $\Delta(R) = P_{ij}$, and Jury will mis-classify the point R, and get a payoff worse than the baseline.

- Next, $f(L_{ik}) = -1$ for all i, k. Indeed, since $h(L_{ik}) = -1$ and $h(x) = -1$ for all of the (Q-type) neighbors of L_{ik}, there can be no benefit to Jury for making $f(L_{ik}) = +1$.

- For each P_{ij}, at most one Q-point $Q_{ikj\ell}$ in $\Gamma(P_{ij})$ has $f(Q_{ikj\ell}) = +1$. Indeed, each Q-point is connected to exactly one P_{ij}, and once one of them is accepted by Jury, she can gain nothing by accepting additional points of $\Gamma(P_{ij})$.

Thus, the optimal f only assigns positive weights to Q points, and it does so to at most one Q-point in each $\Gamma(P_{ij})$. Suppose that $f(x) = +1$ for the set A of Q-points, and let $B = \Gamma_L(A)$ be the set of L-points adjacent to A. Now, the size of B can vary based on how the literals overlap with the clauses. It satisfies

$$\frac{2|A|}{m - 1} \leqslant |B| \leqslant 2|A|,$$

where the lower end is attained when there are complete collisions, and the upper end is attained when there are no collisions. Now consider the number of points of X that Jury classifies correctly under such an f. It is

$$K\left(M + (3m - |B|)\left(m - 1 - \frac{1}{m}\right) + 2|A|\right) + \left(9\binom{m}{2} - |A|\right),$$

which is equal to $b + \delta$, where

$$\delta = K\left(|B|\left(m - 1 - \frac{1}{m}\right) + 2|A|\right) - |A|.$$

Consider this first term, which is multiplied by K. This is only positive when $|B| = \frac{2|A|}{m-1}$ is as small as it can possibly be, which happens only if $|A| = \binom{m}{2}$ and $|B| = m$. In this case, the first term is equal to K, and we have $\delta = K - |A| \geqslant K - 9\binom{m}{2}$. But this happens if and only if we can choose m different literals L_{ik}, one from each clause, so that no pair of them contradict each other; that is, if and only if the original formula was satisfiable. $\square$

Now the theorem follows quickly from the claim. We choose K to be a large polynomial in m, say $m^{2/\eta}$ for some small constant η. Thus, $|X|$ is on the order of $m^{2/\eta+2}$. Suppose there is a polynomial-time algorithm which approximates the strategic optimum up to ε. Claim 4.2 implies a contradiction for any

$$\varepsilon < \frac{K - 9\binom{m}{2}}{|X|} = \frac{K - 9\binom{m}{2}}{K\left(3m + \binom{m}{2} + M\right) + 9\binom{m}{2}}.$$

Using our choice of K, for sufficiently large m the right hand side is at least $|X|^{-\eta}$. Thus, we have a contradiction whenever $\varepsilon < |X|^{-\eta}$.

We note that the metric constructed in the proof has "separability dimension" (the smallest number of separable functions needed to achieve it as a minimum) that grows linearly with the population. The same dimension appears in the exponent of the running time of the algorithm of the previous section. It is an interesting open problem to determine whether this exponential dependence is inherent; the other possibility is that the problem is *fixed-parameter tractable* with respect to the "separability dimension" parameter. We suspect that exponential dependence is necessary.

5. EXPERIMENTS

We conducted experiments on real data from a Brazilian social network called Apontador that provides location-based recommendations and reviews. The data set was introduced in the context of spam fighting in a recent work by Costa et al. [CdCMBB14] and is available from the authors upon request. The data set consists of 7076 instances of so-called "tips" half of which are labeled as "spam". Tips are pieces of user-provided content associated with the places listed on Apontador. The paper distinguishes between different types of spam, but the distinction does not matter for us, so we will only consider one category. There are 60 features in total, but to facilitate the modeling of a cost function we restricted our attention to the 15 most discriminative features as indicated by previous work [CdCMBB14]. We normalized all features of the data to have zero mean and unit standard deviation.

The goal of our cost function is not primarily to capture monetary cost of changing certain attributes. Apart from attributes like "number of followers", most attributes are technically easy to change. Rather the goal of a cost function is to capture the loss in expected revenue that a spammer experiences when changing certain parts of the spam message. If, for instance, it is essential for the spam message to contain a URL or contact information, then the spammer experiences lost revenue when such information is omitted. Similarly, the spammer could choose to post his messages on the pages of lower-rated places, but such pages are less frequented and hence his utility decreases. Similar reasoning applies to the modeling of the other attributes. Cheap attributes are those that can be changed without a loss in utility for the spammer. For example, the "number of words" is not robust as the spammer can freely choose to write longer or shorter messages.

With this intuition in mind, we model our cost function as a simple linear function truncated at 0 to make it nonnegative. That is we consider a cost function of the form $c(x, y) = \langle \alpha, y - x \rangle_+$. Truncation at 0 is a meaningful modeling decision, since a spammer doesn't derive any utility from,

say, decreasing the number of his followers even though it is costly to increase this attribute.

The cost vector α specifies for each attribute a coefficient quantifying the cost of changing that attribute. We do not attempt to construct as realistic a cost function as possible. We only distinguish between three types of cost: somewhat costly to increase (coefficient 1), somewhat costly to decrease (coefficient -1.0) and cheap to increase (coefficient 0.1). The concrete values of these coefficients are rather arbitrary and different choices may be more suitable. The next table details each feature with its description and its associated cost. For a more detailed explanation of these features, the reader is referred to [CdCMBB14].

	Description	Cost coefficient
1	Number of tips on the place	-1
2	Place rating	-1
3	Number of emails	-1
4	Number of contact information	-1
5	Number of URLs	-1
6	Number of phone numbers	-1
7	Number of numeric characters	-1
8	SentiStrength score	1
9	Combined-method	1
10	Number of words	0.1
11	Ratio of followers to followees	1
12	Number of distinct 1-grams	0.1
13	Number of tips posted by user	0.1
14	Number of followers	1
15	Number of capital letters	0.1

We made no attempt to arrive at a perfectly-realistic cost function. Instead our focus is on a qualitative comparison of our approach with a standard SVM classifier, which does not take gaming into account. We selected SVM as a representative classifier as it was shown in previous work [CdCMBB14] to achieve high classification accuracy on this data set compared with other standard classifiers. For simplicity and increased interpretability, we use a *linear* SVM which still achieves high accuracy.

If we were to assume that our model of gaming and choice of cost function were perfectly correct, then a standard SVM would perform very poorly when compared with our algorithm. To obtain a more balanced comparison, we take modeling inaccuracies into account in our experiments. Specifically, we account for two potential inaccuracies in our model:

1. The true cost function is not the one on which we train our algorithm.

2. The amount of gaming varies and does not necessarily correspond to the threshold predicted by our theoretical framework.

Finally, we explore a convenient way to interpolate between the classifier suggested by our approach and standard classifiers. This leads to different trade-offs which are more favorable in certain settings.

5.1 Comparison with SVM under robustness to modeling errors

We now show that our method is robust to significant modeling errors while simultaneously outperforming SVM even if only a small amount of gaming occurs.

To formalize our error model, we assume that there is a true underlying cost function which differs from the cost function we feed into Algorithm 1. We imagine that the true cost function is some mixture of the linear cost function described above, plus a squared Euclidean distance term:

$$c_{\text{true}}(x, y) = (1 - \varepsilon) \langle \alpha, y - x \rangle_+ + \varepsilon \|x - y\|_2^2. \quad (8)$$

On the other hand, we run our algorithm on a cost function which is incorrect in two ways. First, it is separable, so it necessarily ignores the squared-distance term. Second, we do not imagine that we have correctly identified α, and we replace it with some α':

$$c_{\text{assumed}}(x, y) = \langle \alpha', y - x \rangle_+ .$$

The addition of the Euclidean norm in (8) reflects the possibility that our separability assumption does not exactly hold. The difference between α and α' reflects the possibility that we may not even have accurately identified the separable part. We stress that not only does our algorithm not know the true cost function, it also does not know the parameter ε, or how much α differs from α'.

For our experiments, we considered a range of values of ε, and we generated α' from α at random by adding Gaussian noise and re-normalizing. We develop our classifier using c_{assumed}, but then for tests allow Contestant to best-respond to the classifier given the cost function c_{true}. We note that finding the best response to a linear classifier given the cost function c_{true} is a simple calculus problem.

The other parameter we varied is the amount of gaming allowed. In our theoretical framework above, the Contestant is always willing to pay a cost of up to 2, since his payoff for switching is $1 - (-1) = 2$. To relax this assumption and vary the amount of gaming allowed, we multiply both c_{true} and c_{assumed} by $2/t$; we say that this allows t units of gaming. Notice that by the definition of c_{true}, this means that the Contestant is willing to move distance t in the direction of α, and possibly more in other directions. As mentioned above, we have normalized the standard deviation of all attributes to be 1.

Within the above error model, we compare our algorithm with SVM as a representative standard classifier. Figures 3 show that our algorithm outperforms SVM, even under a small amount of gaming, and even in the presence of significant modeling errors.

5.2 A hybrid approach for higher accuracy

In practice it is convenient to start from a standard classifier and make it more robust to gaming and as opposed to adopting an entirely new classifier. Our framework gives a convenient way to incorporate a set of known classifiers into the design of a strategy-robust classifier. As we show below this can lead to more favorable trade-offs between gaming and accuracy.

The basic idea is to use each known classifier as a feature to which we assign a positive weight in the cost function. In other words, we stipulate that the classifier is by itself a somewhat reliable attribute of the data. Below we try out this hybrid approach by combining our classifier with the standard SVM classifier. Indeed, we find in our experiments that the hybrid has higher accuracy in a robust range of parameters. This is shown in Figure 4.

In the case of a linear SVM, the decision boundary is given by a vector β and we can simple add this vector to our cost

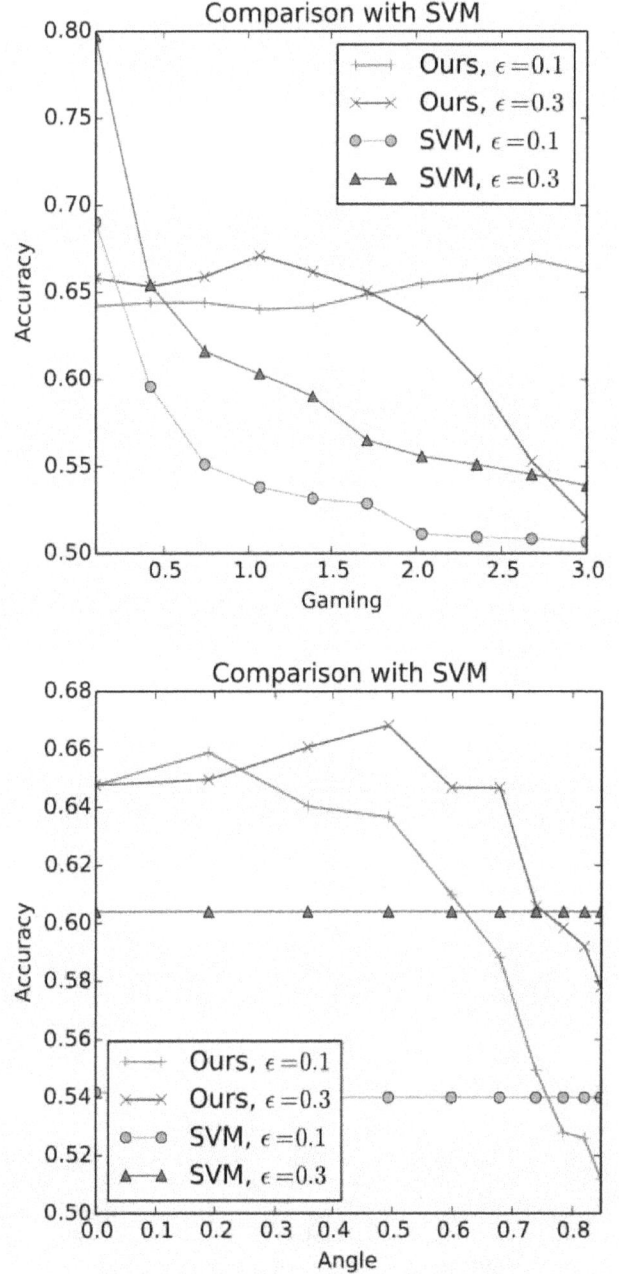

Figure 3: **Top:** Our algorithm compared with SVM as the amount of gaming is increased. The x-axis tracks the amount of gaming, which is quantified as described above. The parameter ε in c_{true} is specified in the legend. We have set $\sin\theta(\alpha, \alpha') = 0.394$ (again, α' was randomly generated from α by adding Gaussian noise and re-normalizing). **Bottom:** Our algorithm compared with SVM as the angle between α and α' increases. The x-axis measures the angle $\sin\theta(\alpha, \alpha')$. The amount of gaming was fixed at 1.0, and the parameter ε in c_{true} is specified in the legend.

function. We assume that the true cost function c_{true} is as above, but we modify c_{assumed} as:

$$c_{\text{assumed}}(x, y) = \langle (1 - \gamma)\alpha' + \gamma\beta, y - x \rangle_+ ,$$

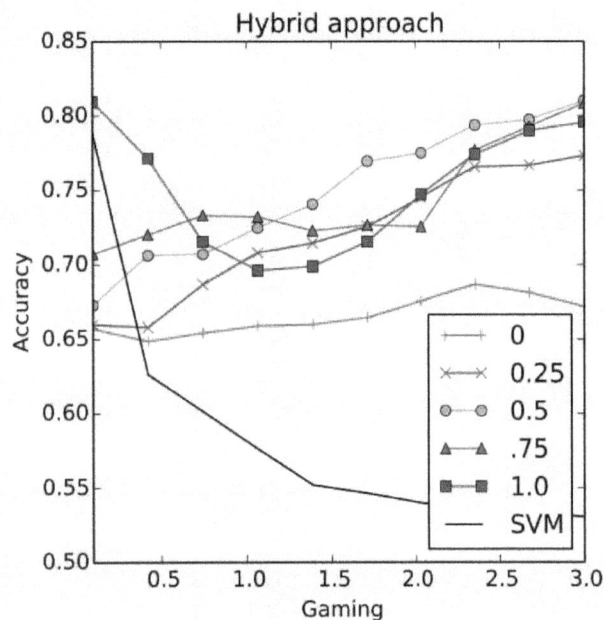

Figure 4: Interpolation between the SVM classifier and our classifier. In the model above, we begin with a cost function that has $\sin\theta(\alpha, \alpha') \approx 0.2$ and $\varepsilon = 0.2$. Then we mix the weight vector α' with the weights β obtained from SVM to arrive at $\alpha'' = (1 - \gamma)\alpha + \gamma\beta$ which defines the assumed cost function. The lines in the plot above show what happens as the amount of gaming increases when setting $\gamma = 0, 0.25, 0.5, 0.75, 1$. Notice that the difference between the SVM curve and the curve with $\gamma = 1$ is that the classifier for $\gamma = 1$ is shifted according to our algorithm.

where β are the SVM coefficients learned from the training data set.

Acknowledgments

We are grateful for stimulating discussions with Cynthia Dwork, Brendan Juba, Silvio Micali, Omer Reingold and Aaron Roth. We are also grateful to Fabricio Benevenuto for pointing us to the Apondator data set and sharing it with us, and to an anonymous reviewer for pointing out that our uniform result implied the non-uniform corollary.

6. REFERENCES

[BBL05]   Stéphane Boucheron, Olivier Bousquet, and Gábor Lugosi. Theory of classification: A survey of some recent advances. *ESAIM: probability and statistics*, 9:323–375, 2005.

[BKS12]   Michael Brückner, Christian Kanzow, and Tobias Scheffer. Static prediction games for adversarial learning problems. *Journal of Machine Learning Research*, 13:2617–2654, 2012.

[BS09]   Michael Brückner and Tobias Scheffer. Nash equilibria of static prediction games. In *Proc. 23rd NIPS 2009*, pages 171–179, 2009.

[BS11]   Michael Brückner and Tobias Scheffer. Stackelberg games for adversarial prediction problems. In *Proc 17th ACM SIGKDD*, pages 547–555, 2011.

[CdCMBB14] Helen Costa, Luiz Henrique de Campos Merschmann, Fabrício Barth, and Fabrício Benevenuto. Pollution, bad-mouthing, and local marketing: The underground of location-based social networks. *Inf. Sci.*, 279:123–137, 2014.

[CP14]   Danielle Keats Citron and Frank Pasquale. The scored society: Due process for automated predictions. *89 Washington Law Review*, 1, 2014.

[DDM+04]   Nilesh N. Dalvi, Pedro Domingos, Mausam, Sumit K. Sanghai, and Deepak Verma. Adversarial classification. In *Proc 10th ACM SIGKDD*, pages 99–108, 2004.

[EKST10]   M.D.R. Evans, J. Kelley, J. Sikora, and D. J. Treiman. Family scholarly culture and educational success: Evidence from 27 nations. *Research in Social Stratification and Mobility*, 28:171–197, 2010.

[GSBS13]   Michael Großhans, Christoph Sawade, Michael Brückner, and Tobias Scheffer. Bayesian games for adversarial regression problems. In *Proc. 30th ICML*, pages 55–63, 2013.

[HMPW15]   Moritz Hardt, Nimrod Megiddo, Christos H. Papadimitriou, and Mary Wootters. Strategic classification. *CoRR*, abs/1506.06980, 2015.

[KCP10]   Dmytro Korzhyk, Vincent Conitzer, and Ronald Parr. Complexity of computing optimal Stackelberg strategies in security resource allocation games. In *Proc. AAAI*, 2010.

[KYK+11]   Dmytro Korzhyk, Zhengyu Yin, Christopher Kiekintveld, Vincent Conitzer, and Milind Tambe. Stackelberg vs. Nash in security games: An extended investigation of interchangeability, equivalence, and uniqueness. *J. Artif. Intell. Res.(JAIR)*, 41:297–327, 2011.

[LT91]   Michel Ledoux and Michel Talagrand. *Probability in Banach Spaces: isoperimetry and processes*, volume 23. Springer, 1991.

[Val84]   Leslie Valiant. A theory of the learnable. *Communications of the ACM*, 27(11):1134–1142, 1984.

A PAC Approach to Application-Specific Algorithm Selection

[Extended Abstract] *

Rishi Gupta
Stanford University
450 Serra Mall
Stanford, CA 94305
rishig@cs.stanford.edu

Tim Roughgarden[†]
Stanford University
450 Serra Mall
Stanford, CA 94305
tim@cs.stanford.edu

ABSTRACT

The best algorithm for a computational problem generally depends on the "relevant inputs," a concept that depends on the application domain and often defies formal articulation. While there is a large literature on empirical approaches to selecting the best algorithm for a given application domain, there has been surprisingly little theoretical analysis of the problem.

This paper adapts concepts from statistical and online learning theory to reason about application-specific algorithm selection. Our models capture several state-of-the-art empirical and theoretical approaches to the problem, ranging from self-improving algorithms to empirical performance models, and our results identify conditions under which these approaches are guaranteed to perform well. We present one framework that models algorithm selection as a statistical learning problem, and our work here shows that dimension notions from statistical learning theory, historically used to measure the complexity of classes of binary- and real-valued functions, are relevant in a much broader algorithmic context. We also study the online version of the algorithm selection problem, and give possibility and impossibility results for the existence of no-regret learning algorithms.

Categories and Subject Descriptors

I.2.6 [**Artificial Intelligence**]: Learning; F.2.0 [**Analysis of Algorithms and Problem Complexity**]: General

---

*A full version of this paper is available at `http://arxiv.org/pdf/1511.07147`.

[†]This research was supported in part by NSF Awards CCF-1215965 and CCF-1524062.

Permission to make digital or hard copies of all or part of this work for personal or classroom use is granted without fee provided that copies are not made or distributed for profit or commercial advantage and that copies bear this notice and the full citation on the first page. Copyrights for components of this work owned by others than the author(s) must be honored. Abstracting with credit is permitted. To copy otherwise, or republish, to post on servers or to redistribute to lists, requires prior specific permission and/or a fee. Request permissions from Permissions@acm.org.

ITCS'16, January 14–16, 2016, Cambridge, MA, USA.
Copyright is held by the owner/author(s). Publication rights licensed to ACM.
ACM 978-1-4503-4057-1/16/01 ...$15.00.
DOI: http://dx.doi.org/10.1145/2840728.2840766

Keywords

Algorithm selection; Parameter tuning; PAC learning; Online learning; Meta-algorithms

1. INTRODUCTION

Rigorously comparing algorithms is hard. The most basic reason for this is that two different algorithms for a computational problem generally have incomparable performance: one algorithm is better on some inputs, but worse on the others. How can a theory advocate one of the algorithms over the other? The simplest and most common solution in the theoretical analysis of algorithms is to summarize the performance of an algorithm using a single number, such as its worst-case performance or its average-case performance with respect to an input distribution. This approach effectively advocates using the algorithm with the best summarizing value (e.g., the smallest worst-case running time).

Solving a problem "in practice" generally means identifying an algorithm that works well for most or all instances of interest. When the "instances of interest" are easy to specify formally in advance — say, planar graphs — the traditional analysis approaches often give accurate performance predictions and identify useful algorithms. However, instances of interest commonly possess domain-specific features that defy formal articulation. Solving a problem in practice can require selecting an algorithm that is optimized for the specific application domain, even though the special structure of its instances is not well understood. While there is a large literature, spanning numerous communities, on empirical approaches to algorithm selection (e.g. [Fin98, HXHL14, HRG+01, HJY+10, KGM12, LNS09]), there has been surprisingly little theoretical analysis of the problem. One possible explanation is that worst-case analysis, which is the dominant algorithm analysis paradigm in theoretical computer science, is deliberately application-agnostic.

This paper demonstrates that application-specific algorithm selection can be usefully modeled as a learning problem. Our models are straightforward to understand, but also expressive enough to capture several existing approaches in the theoretical computer science and AI communities, ranging from the design and analysis of self-improving algorithms [ACCL06] to the application of empirical performance models [HXHL14].

We present one framework that models algorithm selection as a statistical learning problem. We prove that many useful families of algorithms, including broad classes of greedy and local search heuristics, have small pseudo-dimension and hence low generalization error. Previously, the pseudo-dimension (and the VC dimension, fat shattering dimension, etc.) has been used almost exclusively to quantify the complexity of classes of prediction functions (e.g. [AB99]).[1] Our results demonstrate that this concept is useful and relevant in a much broader algorithmic context. It also offers a novel approach to formalizing the oft-mentioned but rarely-defined "simplicity" of a family of algorithms.

We also study regret-minimization in the online version of the algorithm selection problem. We show that the "non-Lipschitz" behavior of natural algorithm classes precludes learning algorithms that have no regret in the worst case, and prove positive results under smoothed analysis-type assumptions.

Paper Organization.

Section 2 outlines a number of concrete problems that motivate the present work, ranging from greedy heuristics to SAT solvers, and from self-improving algorithms to parameter tuning. The reader interested solely in the technical development can skip this section with little loss. Section 3 models the task of determining the best application-specific algorithm as a PAC learning problem, and brings the machinery of statistical learning theory to bear on a wide class of problems, including greedy heuristic selection, sorting, and gradient descent step size selection. A time-limited reader can glean the gist of our contributions from Sections 3.1–3.3.3. Section 4 considers the problem of learning an application-specific algorithm online, with the goal of minimizing regret, and presents negative and positive results for worst-case and smoothed instances, respectively. Section 5 concludes with a number of open research directions.

2. MOTIVATING SCENARIOS

Our learning framework sheds light on several well-known approaches, spanning disparate application domains, to the problem of learning a good algorithm from data. To motivate and provide interpretations of our results, we describe several of these in detail.

2.1 Example #1: Greedy Heuristic Selection

One of the most common and also most challenging motivations for algorithm selection is presented by computationally difficult optimization problems. When the available computing resources are inadequate to solve such a problem exactly, heuristic algorithms must be used. For most hard problems, our understanding of when different heuristics work well remains primitive. For concreteness, we describe one current and high-stakes example of this issue, which also aligns well with our model and results in Section 3.3. The computing and operations research literature has many similar examples.

---

[1]A few exceptions: [Lon01] parameterizes the performance of the randomized rounding of packing and covering linear programs by the pseudo-dimension of a set derived from the constraint matrix, and [MM14, MR15] use dimension notions from learning theory to bound the sample complexity of learning approximately revenue-maximizing truthful auctions.

In 2016 the FCC is slated to run a novel double auction to buy back licenses for spectrum from certain television broadcasters and resell them to telecommunication companies for wireless broadband use. The auction is expected to generate over \$20 billion dollars for the US government [CBO14]. The "reverse" (i.e., buyback) phase of the auction must determine which stations to buy out (and what to pay them). The auction is tasked with buying out sufficiently many stations so that the remaining stations (who keep their licenses) can be "repacked" into a small number of channels, leaving a target number of channels free to be repurposed for wireless broadband. To first order, the feasible repackings are determined by interference constraints between stations. Computing a repacking therefore resembles familiar hard combinatorial problems like the independent set and graph coloring problems. In the currently proposed auction format [MS14], the plan is to use a greedy heuristic to compute the order in which stations are removed from the reverse auction (removal means the station keeps its license). The proposed approach is to favor stations with high value, and discriminate against stations that interfere with a large number of other stations.[2] There are many ways of combining these two criteria, and no obvious reason to favor one specific implementation over another. The currently proposed implementation for the FCC auction has been justified through trial-and-error experiments using synthetic instances that are thought to be representative [MS14]. One interpretation of our results in Section 3.3 is as a post hoc justification of this exhaustive approach for sufficiently simple classes of algorithms, including the greedy heuristics proposed for this FCC auction.

2.2 Example #2: Self-Improving Algorithms

The area of *self-improving algorithms* was initiated by [ACCL06], who considered sorting and clustering problems. Subsequent work [CS08, CMS10, CMS12] studied several problems in low-dimensional geometry, including the maxima and convex hull problems. For a given problem, the goal is to design an algorithm that, given a sequence of i.i.d. samples from an unknown distribution over instances, converges to the optimal algorithm for that distribution. In addition, the algorithm should use only a small amount of auxiliary space. For example, for sorting independently distributed array entries, the algorithm in [ACCL06] solves each instance (on n numbers) in $O(n \log n)$ time, uses space $O(n^{1+c})$ (where $c > 0$ is an arbitrarily small constant), and after a polynomial number of samples has expected running time within a constant factor of that of an information-theoretically optimal algorithm for the unknown input distribution. Section 3.4 reinterprets self-improving algorithms via our general framework.

2.3 Example #3: Parameter Tuning in Optimization and Machine Learning

Many "algorithms" used in practice are really meta-algorithms, with a large number of free parameters that need to be instantiated by the user. For instance, implementing even in the most basic version of gradient descent requires choosing

---

[2]Analogously, greedy heuristics for the maximum-weight independent set problem favor vertices with higher weights and with lower degrees [STY03]. Greedy heuristics for welfare maximization in combinatorial auctions prefer bidders with higher values and smaller demanded bundles [LOS02].

a step size and error tolerance. For a more extreme version, CPLEX, a widely-used commercial linear and integer programming solver, comes with a 221-page parameter reference manual describing 135 parameters [XHHL11].

An analogous problem in machine learning is "hyperparameter optimization," where the goal is to tune the parameters of a learning algorithm so that it learns (from training data) a model with high accuracy on test data, and in particular a model that does not overfit the training data. A simple example is regularized regression, such as ridge regression, where a single parameter governs the trade-off between the accuracy of the learned model on training data and its "complexity." More sophisticated learning algorithms can have many more parameters.

Figuring out the "right" parameter values is notoriously challenging in practice. The CPLEX manual simply advises that "you may need to experiment with them." In machine learning, parameters are often set by discretizing and then applying brute-force search (a.k.a. "grid search"), perhaps with random subsampling ("random search") [BB12]. When this is computationally infeasible, variants of gradient descent are often used to explore the parameter space, with no guarantee of converging to a global optimum.

The results in Section 3.6 can be interpreted as a sample complexity analysis of grid search for the problem of choosing the step size in gradient descent to minimize the expected number of iterations needed for convergence. We view this as a first step towards reasoning more generally about the problem of learning good parameters for machine learning algorithms.

2.4 Example #4: Empirical Performance Models for SAT Algorithms

The examples above already motivate selecting an algorithm for a problem based on characteristics of the application domain. A more ambitious and refined approach is to select an algorithm on a *per-instance* (instead of a per-domain) basis. While it's impossible to memorize the best algorithm for every possible instance, one might hope to use coarse *features* of a problem instance as a guide to which algorithm is likely to work well.

For example, [XHHL08] applied this idea to the satisfiability (SAT) problem. Their algorithm portfolio consisted of a small number (precisely, 7) of state-of-the-art SAT solvers with incomparable and widely varying running times across different instances. The authors identified a number of instance features, ranging from simple features like input size and clause/variable ratio, to complex features like Knuth's estimate of search tree size [Knu75] and the rate of progress of local search probes.[3] The next step involved building an "empirical performance model" (EPM) for each of the 7 algorithms in the portfolio — a mapping from instance feature vectors to running time predictions. They then computed their EPMs using labeled training data and a suitable regression model. With the EPMs in hand, it is clear how to perform per-instance algorithm selection: given an instance, compute its features, use the EPMs to predict the running time of each algorithm in the portfolio, and run the algorithm with the smallest predicted running time. Using these ideas (and several optimizations), their "SATzilla" algorithm won numerous medals at the 2007 SAT Competi-

tion.[4] Section 3.5 outlines how to extend our PAC learning framework to reason about EPMs and feature-based algorithm selection.

3. PAC LEARNING AN APPLICATION-SPECIFIC ALGORITHM

This section casts the problem of selecting the best algorithm for a poorly understood application domain as one of learning the optimal algorithm with respect to an unknown instance distribution. Section 3.1 formally defines the basic model, Section 3.2 reviews relevant preliminaries from statistical learning theory, Section 3.3 bounds the pseudo-dimension of many classes of greedy and local search heuristics, Section 3.4 re-interprets the theory of self-improving algorithms via our framework, Section 3.5 extends the basic model to capture empirical performance models and feature-based algorithm selection, and Section 3.6 studies step size selection in gradient descent.

3.1 The Basic Model

Our basic model consists of the following ingredients.

1. A fixed computational or optimization problem Π. For example, Π could be computing a maximum-weight independent set of a graph (Section 2.1), or sorting n elements (Section 2.2).

2. An unknown distribution $\mathcal{D}$ over instances $x \in \Pi$.

3. A set $\mathcal{A}$ of algorithms for Π; see Sections 3.3 and 3.4 for concrete examples.

4. A performance measure COST : $\mathcal{A} \times \Pi \to [0, H]$ indicating the performance of a given algorithm on a given instance. Two common choices for COST are the running time of an algorithm, and, for optimization problems, the objective function value of the solution produced by an algorithm.

The "application-specific information" is encoded by the unknown input distribution $\mathcal{D}$, and the corresponding "application-specific optimal algorithm" $A_\mathcal{D}$ is the algorithm that minimizes or maximizes (as appropriate) $\mathbf{E}_{x \in \mathcal{D}}[\text{COST}(A, x)]$ over $A \in \mathcal{A}$. The *error* of an algorithm $A \in \mathcal{A}$ for a distribution $\mathcal{D}$ is

$$\left| \mathbf{E}_{x \sim \mathcal{D}}[\text{COST}(A, x)] - \mathbf{E}_{x \sim \mathcal{D}}[\text{COST}(A_\mathcal{D}, x)] \right|.$$

In our basic model, the goal is:

Learn the application-specific optimal algorithm from data (i.e., samples from $\mathcal{D}$).

More precisely, the learning algorithm is given m i.i.d. samples $x_1, \ldots, x_m \in \Pi$ from $\mathcal{D}$, and (perhaps implicitly) the corresponding performance $\text{COST}(A, x_i)$ of each algorithm $A \in \mathcal{A}$ on each input x_i. The learning algorithm uses this information to suggest an algorithm $\hat{A} \in \mathcal{A}$ to use on future inputs drawn from $\mathcal{D}$. We seek learning algorithms that almost always output an algorithm of $\mathcal{A}$ that performs almost as well as the optimal algorithm in $\mathcal{A}$ for $\mathcal{D}$.

---

[3]It is important, of course, that computing the features of an instance is an easier problem than solving it.

[4]See [XHHL12] for details on the latest generation of their solver.

Definition 3.1 A learning algorithm L (ϵ, δ)-*learns the optimal algorithm in $\mathcal{A}$ from m samples* if, for every distribution $\mathcal{D}$ over Π, with probability at least $1 - \delta$ over m samples $x_1, \ldots, x_m \sim \mathcal{D}$, L outputs an algorithm $\hat{A} \in \mathcal{A}$ with error at most ϵ.

3.2 Pseudo-Dimension and Uniform Convergence

PAC learning an optimal algorithm, in the sense of Definition 3.1, reduces to bounding the "complexity" of the class $\mathcal{A}$ of algorithms. We next review the relevant definitions from statistical learning theory.

Let $\mathcal{H}$ denote a set of real-valued functions defined on the set X. A finite subset $S = \{x_1, \ldots, x_m\}$ of X is *(pseudo-)shattered* by $\mathcal{H}$ if there exist real-valued *witnesses* $r_1, \ldots, r_m$ such that, for each of the 2^m subsets T of S, there exists a function $h \in \mathcal{H}$ such that $h(x_i) > r_i$ if and only if $i \in T$ (for $i = 1, 2, \ldots, m$). The *pseudo-dimension* of $\mathcal{H}$ is the cardinality of the largest subset shattered by $\mathcal{H}$ (or $+\infty$, if arbitrarily large finite subsets are shattered by $\mathcal{H}$). The pseudo-dimension is a natural extension of the VC dimension from binary-valued to real-valued functions.[5]

To bound the sample complexity of accurately estimating the expectation of all functions in $\mathcal{H}$, with respect to an arbitrary probability distribution $\mathcal{D}$ on X, it is enough to bound the pseudo-dimension of $\mathcal{H}$.

Theorem 3.2 (E.g. [Hau92, Corollary 2]) *Let $\mathcal{H}$ be a class of functions with domain X and range in $[0, H]$, and suppose $\mathcal{H}$ has pseudo-dimension $d_{\mathcal{H}}$. For every distribution $\mathcal{D}$ over X, every $\epsilon > 0$, and every $\delta \in (0, 1]$, if*

$$m \geq c \left(\frac{H}{\epsilon} \right)^2 \left(d_{\mathcal{H}} \ln \left(\frac{H}{\epsilon} \right) + \ln \left(\frac{1}{\delta} \right) \right) \quad (1)$$

for a suitable constant c (independent of all other parameters), then with probability at least $1 - \delta$ over m samples $x_1, \ldots, x_m \sim \mathcal{D}$,

$$\left| \left(\frac{1}{m} \sum_{i=1}^{m} h(x_i) \right) - \mathbf{E}_{x \sim \mathcal{D}}[h(x)] \right| < \epsilon$$

for every $h \in \mathcal{H}$.

We can identify each algorithm $A \in \mathcal{A}$ with the real-valued function $x \mapsto \text{COST}(A, x)$. Regarding the class $\mathcal{A}$ of algorithms as a set of real-valued functions defined on Π, we can discuss its pseudo-dimension, as defined above. We need one more definition before we can apply our machinery to learn algorithms from $\mathcal{A}$.

Definition 3.3 (Empirical Risk Minimization (ERM)) Fix an optimization problem Π, a performance measure COST, and a set of algorithms $\mathcal{A}$. An algorithm L is an *ERM algorithm* if, given any finite subset S of Π, L returns an (arbitrary) algorithm from A with the best average performance on S.

For example, for any Π, COST, and finite $\mathcal{A}$, there is a trivial ERM algorithm which simply computes the average performance of each algorithm on S by brute force, and returns the best one. The next corollary follows easily from Definition 3.1, Theorem 3.2, and Definition 3.3.

Corollary 3.4 *Fix parameters $\epsilon > 0$, $\delta \in (0, 1]$, a set of problem instances Π, and a performance measure COST. Let $\mathcal{A}$ be a set of algorithms that has pseudo-dimension d with respect to Π. Then any ERM algorithm $(2\epsilon, \delta)$-learns the optimal algorithm in $\mathcal{A}$ from m samples, where m is defined as in (1).*

Corollary 3.4 is only interesting if interesting classes of algorithms $\mathcal{A}$ have small pseudo-dimension. In the simple case where $\mathcal{A}$ is finite, as in our example of an algorithm portfolio for SAT (Sections 2.4 and 3.5.2), the pseudo-dimension of $\mathcal{A}$ is trivially at most $\log_2 |\mathcal{A}|$. The next few sections demonstrate the much less obvious fact that natural infinite classes of algorithms also have small pseudo-dimension.[6]

3.3 Application: Greedy Heuristics and Extensions

The goal of this section is to bound the pseudo-dimension of many classes of greedy heuristics including, as a special case, the family of heuristics relevant for the FCC double auction described in Section 2.1. It will be evident that analogous computations are possible for many other classes of heuristics, and we provide several extensions in Section 3.3.4 to illustrate this point. Throughout this section, the performance measure COST is the objective function value of the solution produced by a heuristic on an instance, where we assume without loss of generality a maximization objective.

3.3.1 Definitions and Examples

Our general definitions are motivated by greedy heuristics for (NP-hard) problems like the following; the reader will have no difficulty coming up with additional natural examples.

1. *Knapsack.* The input is n items with values $v_1, \ldots, v_n$, sizes $s_1, \ldots, s_n$, and a knapsack capacity C. The goal is to compute a subset of $S \subseteq \{1, 2, \ldots, n\}$ with maximum total value $\sum_{i \in S} v_i$, subject to having total size $\sum_{i \in S} s_i$ at most C. Two natural greedy heuristics are to greedily pack items (subject to feasibility) in order of nonincreasing value v_i, or in order of nonincreasing density v_i / s_i (or to take the better of the two, see Section 3.3.4).

2. *Maximum-Weight Independent Set (MWIS).* The input is an undirected graph $G = (V, E)$ and a nonnegative weight w_v for each vertex $v \in V$. The goal is to compute the independent set — a subset of mutually non-adjacent vertices — with maximum total weight. Two natural greedy heuristics are to greedily

---

[5]The *fat shattering dimension* is another common extension of VC dimension to real-valued functions. It is a weaker condition, in that the fat shattering dimension of $\mathcal{H}$ is always at most the pseudo-dimension of $\mathcal{H}$, that is still sufficient for sample complexity bounds. Most of our arguments give the same upper bounds on pseudo-dimension and fat shattering dimension, so we present the stronger statements.

[6]The present work focuses on the sample complexity rather than the computational aspects of learning, so outside of a few remarks we won't say much about the existence or efficiency of ERM in our examples. A priori, an infinite class of algorithms may not admit any ERM algorithm at all, though all of the examples in this section do have ERM algorithms under mild assumptions.

choose vertices (subject to feasibility) in order of non-increasing weight w_v, or nonincreasing density $w_v/(1 + \deg(v))$. (The intuition for the denominator is that choosing v "uses up" $1 + \deg(v)$ vertices — v and all of its neighbors.) The latter heuristic also has a (superior) adaptive variant, where the degree $\deg(v)$ is computed in the subgraph induced by the vertices not yet blocked from consideration, rather than in the original graph.[7]

3. *Machine Scheduling.* This is a family of optimization problems, where n jobs with various attributes (processing time, weight, deadline, etc.) need to be assigned to m machines, perhaps subject to some constraints (precedence constraints, deadlines, etc.), to optimize some objective (makespan, weighted sum of completion times, number of late jobs, etc.). A typical greedy heuristic for such a problem considers jobs in some order according to a score derived from the job parameters (e.g., weight divided by processing time), subject to feasibility, and always assigns the current job to the machine that currently has the lightest load (again, subject to feasibility).

In general, we consider *object assignment problems*, where the input is a set of n objects with various attributes, and the feasible solutions consist of assignments of the objects to a finite set R, subject to feasibility constraints. The attributes of an object are represented as an element ξ of an abstract set. For example, in the Knapsack problem ξ encodes the value and size of an object; in the MWIS problem, ξ encodes the weight and (original or residual) degree of a vertex. In the Knapsack and MWIS problems, $R = \{0, 1\}$, indicating whether or not a given object is selected. In machine scheduling problems, R could be $\{1, 2, \ldots, m\}$, indicating the machine to which a job is assigned, or a richer set that also keeps track of the job ordering on each machine.

By a *greedy heuristic*, we mean algorithms of the following form (cf., the "priority algorithms" of [BNR03]):

1. While there remain unassigned objects:

    (a) Use a *scoring rule* σ (see below) to compute a score $\sigma(\xi_i)$ for each unassigned object i, as a function of its current attributes ξ_i.

    (b) For the unassigned object i with the highest score, use an *assignment rule* to assign i a value from R and, if necessary, update the attributes of the other unassigned objects.[8] For concreteness, assume that ties are always resolved lexicographically.

A *scoring rule* assigns a real number to an object as a function of its attributes. Assignment rules that do not modify objects' attributes yield non-adaptive greedy heuristics, which use only the original attributes of each object (like v_i or v_i/s_i in the Knapsack problem, for instance). In this case, objects' scores can be computed in advance of the main

---

[7]An equivalent description is: whenever a vertex v is added to the independent set, delete v and its neighbors from the graph, and recurse on the remaining graph.

[8]We assume that there is always as least one choice of assignment that respects the feasibility constraints; this holds for all of our motivating examples.

loop of the greedy heuristic. Assignment rules that modify object attributes yield adaptive greedy heuristics, such as the adaptive MWIS heuristic described above.

In a *single-parameter* family of scoring rules, there is a scoring rule of the form $\sigma(\rho, \xi)$ for each parameter value ρ in some interval $I \subseteq \mathbb{R}$. Moreover, σ is assumed to be continuous in ρ for each fixed value of ξ. Natural examples include Knapsack scoring rules of the form v_i/s_i^ρ and MWIS scoring rules of the form $w_v/(1 + \deg(v))^\rho$ for $\rho \in [0, 1]$ or $\rho \in [0, \infty)$. A single-parameter family of scoring rules is κ-*crossing* if, for each distinct pair of attributes ξ, ξ', there are at most κ values of ρ for which $\sigma(\rho, \xi) = \sigma(\rho, \xi')$. For example, all of the scoring rules mentioned above are 1-crossing rules.

For an example assignment rule, in the Knapsack and MWIS problems, the rule simply assigns i to "1" if it is feasible to do so, and to "0" otherwise. A typical machine scheduling assignment rule assigns the current job to the machine with the lightest load. In the adaptive greedy heuristic for the MWIS problem, whenever the assignment rule assigns "1" to a vertex v, it updates the residual degrees of other unassigned vertices (two hops away) accordingly.

We call an assignment rule β-*bounded* if every object i is guaranteed to take on at most β distinct attribute values. For example, an assignment rule that never modifies an object's attributes is 1-bounded. The assignment rule in the adaptive MWIS algorithm is n-bounded, since it only modifies the degree of a vertex (which lies in $\{0, 1, 2 \ldots, n-1\}$).

Coupling a single-parameter family of κ-crossing scoring rules with a fixed β-bounded assignment rule yields a (κ, β)-*single-parameter family of greedy heuristics*. All of our running examples of greedy heuristics are $(1, 1)$-single-parameter families, except for the adaptive MWIS heuristic, which is a $(1, n)$-single-parameter family.

3.3.2 Upper Bound on Pseudo-Dimension

We next show that every (κ, β)-single-parameter family of greedy heuristics has small pseudo-dimension. This result applies to all of the concrete examples mentioned above, and it is easy to come up with other examples (for the problems already discussed, and for additional problems).

Theorem 3.5 (Pseudo-Dimension of Greedy Algorithms) *If $\mathcal{A}$ denotes a (κ, β)-single-parameter family of greedy heuristics for an object assignment problem with n objects, then the pseudo-dimension of $\mathcal{A}$ is $O(\log(\kappa \beta n))$.*

In particular, all of our running examples are classes of heuristics with pseudo-dimension $O(\log n)$.

PROOF. Recall from the definitions (Section 3.2) that we need to upper bound the size of every set that is shatterable using the greedy heuristics in $\mathcal{A}$. For us, a set is a fixed set of s inputs (each with n objects) $S = x_1, \ldots, x_s$. For a potential witness $r_1, \ldots, r_s \in \mathbb{R}$, every algorithm $A \in \mathcal{A}$ induces a binary labeling of each sample x_i, according to whether $\text{COST}(A, x_i)$ is strictly more than or at most r_i. We proceed to bound from above the number of distinct binary labellings of S induced by the algorithms of $\mathcal{A}$, for any potential witness.

Consider ranging over algorithms $A \in \mathcal{A}$ — equivalently, over parameter values $\rho \in I$. The trajectory of a greedy heuristic $A \in \mathcal{A}$ is uniquely determined by the outcome of the comparisons between the current scores of the unassigned objects in each iteration of the algorithm. Since the family uses a κ-crossing scoring rule, for every pair i, j of distinct objects and possible attributes ξ_i, ξ_j, there are at most κ values of ρ for which there is a tie between the score of i (with attributes ξ_i) and that of j (with attributes ξ_j). Since σ is continuous in ρ, the relative order of the score of i (with ξ_i) and j (with ξ_j) remains the same in the open interval between two successive values of ρ at which their scores are tied. The upshot is that we can partition I into at most $\kappa + 1$ intervals such that the outcome of the comparison between i (with attributes ξ_i) and j (with attributes ξ_j) is constant on each interval.[9]

Next, the s instances of S contain a total of sn objects. Each of these objects has some initial attributes. Because the assignment rule is β-bounded, there are at most $sn\beta$ object-attribute pairs (i, ξ_i) that could possibly arise in the execution of any algorithm from $\mathcal{A}$ on any instance of S. This implies that, ranging across all algorithms of $\mathcal{A}$ on all inputs in S, comparisons are only ever made between at most $(sn\beta)^2$ pairs of object-attribute pairs (i.e., between an object i with current attributes ξ_i and an object j with current attributes ξ_j). We call these the *relevant comparisons*.

For each relevant comparison, we can partition I into at most $\kappa + 1$ subintervals such that the comparison outcome is constant (in ρ) in each subinterval. Intersecting the partitions of all of the at most $(sn\beta)^2$ relevant comparisons splits I into at most $(sn\beta)^2\kappa + 1$ subintervals such that *every* relevant comparison is constant in each subinterval. That is, all of the algorithms of $\mathcal{A}$ that correspond to the parameter values ρ in such a subinterval execute identically on every input in S. The number of binary labellings of S induced by algorithms of $\mathcal{A}$ is trivially at most the number of such subintervals. Our upper bound $(sn\beta)^2\kappa + 1$ on the number of subintervals exceeds 2^s, the requisite number of labellings to shatter S, only if $s = O(\log(\kappa\beta n))$. □

Theorem 3.5 and Corollary 3.4 imply that, if κ and β are bounded above by a polynomial in n, then an ERM algorithm would (ϵ, δ)-learn the optimal algorithm in $\mathcal{A}$ from only $m = \tilde{O}(\frac{H^2}{\epsilon^2})$ samples,[10] where H is the largest objective function value of a feasible solution output by an algorithm of $\mathcal{A}$ on an instance of Π.[11]

We note that Theorem 3.5 gives a quantifiable sense in which natural greedy algorithms are indeed "simple algorithms." Not all classes of algorithms have such a small pseudo-dimension; see also the next section for further discussion.[12]

---

[9]This argument assumes that $\xi_i \neq \xi_j$. If $\xi_i = \xi_j$, then because we break ties between equal scores lexicographically, the outcome of the comparison between $\sigma(\xi_i)$ and $\sigma(\xi_j)$ is in fact constant on the entire interval I of parameter values.

[10]The notation $\tilde{O}(\cdot)$ suppresses logarithmic factors.

[11]Alternatively, the dependence of m on H can be removed if learning error ϵH (rather than ϵ) can be tolerated — for example, if the optimal objective function value is expected to be proportional to H anyways.

[12]When the performance measure COST is solution quality, as in this section, one cannot identify "simplicity" with "low pseudo-dimension" without caveats: strictly speaking, the set $\mathcal{A}$ containing only the optimal algorithm for the problem has pseudo-dimension 1. When the problem Π is NP-hard and $\mathcal{A}$ consists only of polynomial-time algorithms (and assuming $P \neq NP$), the pseudo-dimension is a potentially relevant complexity measure for the heuristics in $\mathcal{A}$.

Remark 3.6 (Non-Lipschitzness) We noted in Section 3.2 that the pseudo-dimension of a finite set $\mathcal{A}$ is always at most $\log_2 |\mathcal{A}|$. This suggests a simple discretization approach to learning the best algorithm from $\mathcal{A}$: take a finite "ϵ-net" of $\mathcal{A}$ and learn the best algorithm in the finite net. (Indeed, Section 3.6 uses precisely this approach.) The issue is that without some kind of Lipschitz condition — stating that "nearby" algorithms in $\mathcal{A}$ have approximately the same performance on all instances — there's no reason to believe that the best algorithm in the net is almost as good as the best algorithm from all of $\mathcal{A}$. Two different greedy heuristics — two MWIS greedy algorithms with arbitrarily close ρ-values, say — can have completely different executions on an instance. This lack of a Lipschitz property explains why we take care in Theorem 3.5 to bound the pseudo-dimension of the full infinite set of greedy heuristics.

3.3.3 Computational Considerations

The proof of Theorem 3.5 also demonstrates the presence of an efficient ERM algorithm: the $O((sn\beta)^2)$ relevant comparisons are easy to identify, the corresponding subintervals induced by each are easy to compute (under mild assumptions on the scoring rule), and brute-force search can be used to pick the best of the resulting $O((sn\beta)^2\kappa)$ algorithms (an arbitrary one from each subinterval). This algorithm runs in polynomial time as long as β and κ are polynomial in n, and every algorithm of $\mathcal{A}$ runs in polynomial time.

For example, for the family of Knapsack scoring rules described above, implementing this ERM algorithm reduces to comparing the outputs of $O(n^2 m)$ different greedy heuristics (on each of the m sampled inputs), with $m = O(\log n)$. For the adaptive MWIS heuristics, where $\beta = n$, it is enough to compare the sample performance of $O(n^4 m)$ different greedy algorithms, with $m = O(\log n)$.

3.3.4 Extensions: Multiple Algorithms, Multiple Parameters, and Local Search

Theorem 3.5 is robust and its proof is easily modified to accommodate various extensions. For a first example, consider algorithms than run q different members of a single-parameter greedy heuristic family and return the best of the q feasible solutions obtained.[13] Extending the proof of Theorem 3.5 yields a pseudo-dimension bound of $O(q\log(\kappa\beta n))$ for the class of all such algorithms.

For a second example, consider families of greedy heuristics parameterized by d real-valued parameters $\rho_1, \ldots, \rho_d$. Here, an analog of Theorem 3.5 holds with the crossing number κ replaced by a more complicated parameter — essentially, the number of connected components of the cozero set of the difference of two scoring functions (with ξ, ξ' fixed and variables $\rho_1, \ldots, \rho_d$). This number can often be bounded (by a function exponential in d) in natural cases, for example using Bézout's theorem.

For a final extension, we sketch how to adapt the definitions and results of this section from greedy to local search heuristics. The input is again an object assignment problem (see Section 3.3.1), along with an initial feasible solution (i.e., an assignment of objects to R, subject to feasibility constraints). By a *k-swap local search heuristic*, we mean algorithms of the following form:

---

[13]For example, the classical $\frac{1}{2}$-approximation for Knapsack has this form (with $q = 2$).

1. Start with arbitrary feasible solution.

2. While the current solution is not locally optimal:

    (a) Use a *scoring rule* σ to compute a score $\sigma(\{\xi_i : i \in K\})$ for each set of objects K of size k, where ξ_i is the current attribute of object i.

    (b) For the set K with the highest score, use an *assignment rule* to re-assign each $i \in K$ to a value from R. If necessary, update the attributes of the appropriate objects. (Again, assume that ties are resolved lexicographically.)

We assume that the assignment rule maintains feasibility, so that we have a feasible assignment at the end of each execution of the loop. We also assume that the scoring and assignment rules ensure that the algorithm terminates, e.g. via the existence of a global objective function that decreases at every iteration (or by incorporating timeouts).

A canonical example of a k-swap local search heuristic is the k-OPT heuristic for the traveling salesman problem (TSP)[14] (see e.g. [JM97]). We can view TSP as an object assignment problem, where the objects are edges and $R = \{0, 1\}$; the feasibility constraint is that the edges assigned to 1 should form a tour. Recall that a local move in k-OPT consists of swapping out k edges from the current tour and swapping in k edges to obtain a new tour. (So in our terminology, k-OPT is a $2k$-swap local search heuristic.) Another well-known example is the local search algorithms for the p-median problem studied in [AGK+04], which are parameterized by the number of medians that can be removed and added in each local move. Analogous local search algorithms make sense for the MWIS problem as well.

Scoring and assignment rules are now defined on subsets of k objects, rather than individual objects. A single-parameter family of scoring rules is now called κ-*crossing* if, for every subset K of at most k objects and each distinct pair of attribute sets ξ_K and ξ'_K, there are at most κ values of ρ for which $\sigma(\rho, \xi_K) = \sigma(\rho, \xi'_K)$. An assignment rule is now β-*bounded* if for every subset K of at most k objects, ranging over all possible trajectories of the local search heuristic, the attribute set of K takes on at most β distinct values. For example, in MWIS, suppose we allow two vertices u, v to be removed and two vertices y, z to be added in a single local move, and we use the single-parameter scoring rule family

$$\sigma_\rho(u, v, y, z) = \frac{w_u}{(1 + \deg(u))^\rho} + \frac{w_v}{(1 + \deg(v))^\rho} - \frac{w_y}{(1 + \deg(y))^\rho} - \frac{w_z}{(1 + \deg(z))^\rho}.$$

Here $\deg(v)$ could refer to the degree of vertex v in original graph, to the number of neighbors of v that do not have any neighbors other than v in the current independent set, etc. In any case, since a generalized Dirichlet polynomial with t terms has at most $t - 1$ zeroes (see e.g. [Jam06, Corollary 3.2]), this is a 3-crossing family. The natural assignment rule is n^4-bounded.[15]

---

[14]Given a complete undirected graph with a cost c_{uv} for each edge (u, v), compute a tour (visiting each vertex exactly once) that minimizes the sum of the edge costs.

[15]In general, arbitrary local search algorithms can be made β-bounded through time-outs: if such an algorithm always halts within T iterations, then the corresponding assignment rule is T-bounded.

By replacing the number n of objects by the number $O(n^k)$ of subsets of at most k objects in the proof of Theorem 3.5, we obtain the following.

Theorem 3.7 (Pseudo-Dimension of Local Search Algorithms) *If $\mathcal{A}$ denotes a (κ, β)-single-parameter family of k-swap local search heuristics for an object assignment problem with n objects, then the pseudo-dimension of $\mathcal{A}$ is $O(k \log(\kappa \beta n))$.*

3.4 Application: Self-Improving Algorithms Revisited

We next give a new interpretation of the self-improving sorting algorithm of [ACCL06]. Namely, we show that the main result in [ACCL06] effectively identifies a set of sorting algorithms that simultaneously has low representation error (for independently distributed array elements) and small pseudo-dimension (and hence low generalization error). Other constructions of self-improving algorithms [ACCL06, CS08, CMS10, CMS12] can be likewise reinterpreted. In contrast to Section 3.3, here our performance measure COST is the running time of an algorithm A on an input x, which we want to minimize.

Consider the problem of sorting n real numbers in the comparison model. By a *bucket-based sorting algorithm*, we mean an algorithm A for which there are "bucket boundaries" $b_1 < b_2 < \cdots < b_\ell$ such that A first distributes the n input elements into their rightful buckets, and then sorts each bucket separately, concatenating the results. The degrees of freedom when defining such an algorithm are: (i) the choice of the bucket boundaries; (ii) the method used to distribute input elements to the buckets; and (iii) the method used to sort each bucket.

The key steps in the analysis in [ACCL06] can be reinterpreted as proving that this set of bucket-based sorting algorithms has low representation error, in the following sense.

Theorem 3.8 ([ACCL06, Theorem 2.1]) *Suppose that each array element a_i is drawn independently from a distribution $\mathcal{D}_i$. Then there exists a bucket-based sorting algorithm with expected running time at most a constant factor times that of the optimal sorting algorithm for $\mathcal{D}_1 \times \cdots \times \mathcal{D}_n$.*

The proof in [ACCL06] establishes Theorem 3.8 even when the number ℓ of buckets is only n, each bucket is sorted using InsertionSort, and each element a_i is distributed independently to its rightful bucket using a search tree stored in $O(n^c)$ bits, where $c > 0$ is an arbitrary constant (and the running time depends on $\frac{1}{c}$).[16] Let $\mathcal{A}_c$ denote the set of all such bucket-based sorting algorithms.

Theorem 3.8 reduces the task of learning a near-optimal sorting algorithm to the problem of (ϵ, δ)-learning the optimal algorithm from $\mathcal{A}_c$. Since $\mathcal{A}_c$ is a finite set, it admits an ERM algorithm, and Corollary 3.4 reduces this learning problem to bounding the pseudo-dimension of $\mathcal{A}_c$. We next prove such a bound, which effectively says that bucket-based sorting algorithms are "relatively simple" algorithms.[17]

---

[16]For small c, each search tree T_i is so small that some searches will go unresolved; such unsuccessful searches are handled by a standard binary search over the buckets.

[17]Not all sorting algorithms are simple in the sense of having polynomial pseudo-dimension. For example, the space

Theorem 3.9 (Pseudo-Dimension of Bucket-Based Sorting Algorithms) *The pseudo-dimension of $\mathcal{A}_c$ is $O(n^{1+c})$.*

PROOF. Recall from the definitions (Section 3.2) that we need to upper bound the size of every set that is shatterable using the bucket-based sorting algorithms in $\mathcal{A}_c$. For us, a set is a fixed set of s inputs (i.e., arrays of length n), $S = x_1, \ldots, x_s$. For a potential witness $r_1, \ldots, r_s \in \mathbb{R}$, every algorithm $A \in \mathcal{A}_c$ induces a binary labeling of each sample x_i, according to whether $\text{COST}(A, x_i)$ is strictly more than or at most r_i. We proceed to bound from above the number of distinct binary labellings of S induced by the algorithms of $\mathcal{A}_c$, for any potential witness.

By definition, an algorithm from $\mathcal{A}_c$ is fully specified by: (i) a choice of n bucket boundaries $b_1 < \cdots < b_n$; and (ii) for each $i = 1, 2, \ldots, n$, a choice of a search tree T_i of size at most $O(n^c)$ for placing x_i in the correct bucket. Call two algorithms $A, A' \in \mathcal{A}_c$ *equivalent* if their sets of bucket boundaries $b_1, \ldots, b_n$ and $b'_1, \ldots, b'_n$ induce the same partition of the sn array elements of the inputs in S — that is, if $x_{ij} < b_k$ if and only if $x_{ij} < b'_k$ (for all i, j, k). The number of equivalence classes of this equivalence relation is at most $\binom{sn+n}{n} \le (sn+n)^n$. Within an equivalence class, two algorithms that use structurally identical search trees will have identical performance on all s of the samples. Since the search trees of every algorithm of $\mathcal{A}_c$ are described by at most $O(n^{1+c})$ bits, ranging over the algorithms of a single equivalence class generates at most $2^{O(n^{1+c})}$ distinct binary labellings of the s sample inputs. Ranging over all algorithms thus generates at most $(sn+n)^n 2^{O(n^{1+c})}$ labellings. This exceeds 2^s, the requisite number of labellings to shatter S, only if $s = O(n^{1+c})$. $\square$

Theorem 3.9 and Corollary 3.4 imply that $m = \tilde{O}(\frac{H^2}{\epsilon^2} n^{1+c})$ samples are enough to (ϵ, δ)-learn the optimal algorithm in $\mathcal{A}_c$, where H can be taken as the ratio between the maximum and minimum running time of any algorithm in $\mathcal{A}_c$ on any instance.[18] Since the minimum running time is $\Omega(n)$ and we can assume that the maximum running time is $O(n \log n)$ — if an algorithm exceeds this bound, we can abort it and safely run MergeSort instead — we obtain a sample complexity bound of $\tilde{O}(n^{1+c})$.[19]

Remark 3.10 (Comparison to [ACCL06]) The sample complexity bound implicit in [ACCL06] for learning a near-optimal sorting algorithm is $\tilde{O}(n^c)$, a linear factor better than the $\tilde{O}(n^{1+c})$ bound implied by Theorem 3.9. There is good reason for this: the pseudo-dimension bound of Theorem 3.9 implies that an even harder problem has sample complexity $\tilde{O}(n^{1+c})$, namely that of learning a near-optimal bucket-based sorting algorithm with respect to an *arbitrary* distribution over inputs, *even with correlated array*

---

lower bound in [ACCL06, Lemma 2.1] can be adapted to show that no class of sorting algorithms with polynomial pseudo-dimension (or fat shattering dimension) has low representation error in the sense of Theorem 3.8 for general distributions over sorting instances, where the array entries need not be independent.

[18]We again use $\tilde{O}(\cdot)$ to suppress logarithmic factors.

[19]In the notation of Theorem 3.2, we are taking $H = \Theta(n \log n)$, $\epsilon = \Theta(n)$, and using the fact that all quantities are $\Omega(n)$ to conclude that all running times are correctly estimated up to a constant factor. The results implicit in [ACCL06] are likewise for relative error.

elements.[20] The bound of $\tilde{O}(n^c)$ in [ACCL06] applies only to the problem of learning a near-optimal bucket-based sorting algorithm for an unknown input distribution with independent array entries — the savings comes from the fact that all n near-optimal search trees $T_1, \ldots, T_n$ can be learned in parallel.

3.5 Application: Feature-Based Algorithm Selection

Previous sections studied the problem of selecting a single algorithm for use in an application domain — of using training data to make an informed commitment to a single algorithm from a class $\mathcal{A}$, which is then used on all future instances. A more refined and ambitious approach is to select an algorithm based both on previous experience *and on the current instance to be solved*. This approach assumes, as in the scenario in Section 2.4, that it is feasible to quickly compute some features of an instance and then to select an algorithm as a function of these features.

Throughout this section, we augment the basic model of Section 3.1 with:

5. A set $\mathcal{F}$ of possible instance feature values, and a map $f : X \to \mathcal{F}$ that computes the features of a given instance.[21]

For instance, if X is the set of SAT instances, then $f(x)$ might encode the clause/variable ratio of the instance x, Knuth's estimate of the search tree size [Knu75], and so on.

Section 3.5.1 describes how our work on the basic model (Sections 3.1–3.4) extends to an augmented model with instance features. This extension yields good results if $\mathcal{F}$ is finite and small. Section 3.5.2 considers the case of rich feature sets, as in the SAT application described in Section 2.4. We show that the basic model can be easily augmented to capture state-of-the-art empirical approaches to feature-based algorithm selection.

3.5.1 The Case of Few Features: Estimating Selection Maps

When the set $\mathcal{F}$ of possible instance feature values is finite, the guarantees for the basic model can be extended with at most a linear (in $|\mathcal{F}|$) degradation in the pseudo-dimension.[22] To explain, we add an additional ingredient to the model.

6. A set $\mathcal{G}$ of *algorithm selection maps*, with each $g \in \mathcal{G}$ a function from $\mathcal{F}$ to $\mathcal{A}$.

An algorithm selection map recommends an algorithm as a function of the features of an instance.

We can view an algorithm selection map g as a real-valued function defined on the instance space X, with $g(x)$ defined

[20]When array elements are not independent, however, Theorem 3.8 fails and the best bucket-based sorting algorithm might be more than a constant-factor worse than the optimal sorting algorithm.

[21]Defining a good feature set is a notoriously challenging and important problem, but it is beyond the scope of our model — we take the set $\mathcal{F}$ and map f as given.

[22]For example, [XHHL08] first predicts whether or not a given SAT instance is satisfiable or not, and then uses a "conditional" empirical performance model to choose a SAT solver. This can be viewed as an example with $|\mathcal{F}| = 2$, corresponding to the feature values "looks satisfiable" and "looks unsatisfiable."

as $\text{COST}(g(f(x)), x)$. That is, $g(x)$ is the running time on x of the algorithm $g(f(x))$ advocated by g, given that x has features $f(x)$. The basic model studied earlier is the special case where $\mathcal{G}$ is the set of constant functions, which are in correspondence with the algorithms of $\mathcal{A}$.

Corollary 3.4 reduces bounding the sample complexity of (ϵ, δ)-learning the best algorithm selection map of $\mathcal{G}$ to bounding the pseudo-dimension of the set of real-valued functions induced by $\mathcal{G}$. When $\mathcal{G}$ is finite, there is a trivial upper bound of $\log_2 |\mathcal{G}|$. The pseudo-dimension is also small whenever $\mathcal{F}$ is small and the set $\mathcal{A}$ of algorithms has small pseudo-dimension.

Theorem 3.11 (Pseudo-Dimension of Algorithm Selection Maps) *If $\mathcal{G}$ is a set of algorithm selection maps from a finite set $\mathcal{F}$ to a set $\mathcal{A}$ of algorithms with pseudo-dimension d, then $\mathcal{G}$ has pseudo-dimension $O(|\mathcal{F}|d)$.*

PROOF. Fix a set $S \subseteq X$ of size s and a potential witness $r_1, \ldots, r_s$. For a value $\varphi \in \mathcal{F}$, consider the subset S_φ of instances $x \in S$ with $f(x) = \varphi$. Using the bound on the growth function given by Sauer's Lemma (see e.g. [SB14]), we see that ranging over all $A \in \mathcal{A}$ generates at most $|S_\varphi|^d$ different binary labellings (w.r.t. the r_i's) of S_φ. Thus, ranging over all $g \in \mathcal{G}$ generates at most

$$\prod_{\varphi \in \mathcal{F}} |S_\varphi|^d \leq s^{|\mathcal{F}|d}$$

binary labellings of S. This is at least 2^s, the requisite number of labellings to shatter S, only if $s = O(|\mathcal{F}|d)$. $\square$

Remark 3.12 An alternative approach is to just separately learn the best algorithm for each feature value $\varphi \in \mathcal{F}$. This straightforward idea yields sample complexity upper bounds similar to those implied by Theorem 3.11, provided two extra assumptions hold. First, that $\mathcal{G}$ is the set of all maps from $\mathcal{F}$ to $\mathcal{A}$ (otherwise, this approach might output a map not in the allowed set $\mathcal{G}$); second, that all feature values of $\mathcal{F}$ appear with approximately equal probability in the unknown distribution $\mathcal{D}$ (otherwise, there is a corresponding blow-up in sample complexity).

3.5.2 Feature-Based Performance Prediction

The bound in Theorem 3.11 is meaningless when $\mathcal{F}$ is very large (or infinite). In this case, there is no hope of observing one or more instances x with $f(x) = \varphi$ for every possible φ, and one must learn a model that predicts the performance of an algorithm as a function of the features of an instance.

We focus on the case where $\mathcal{A}$ is small enough that it is feasible to learn a separate performance prediction model for each algorithm $A \in \mathcal{A}$ (though see Remark 3.15). This is exactly the approach taken in the motivating example of empirical performance models (EPMs) for SAT described in Section 2.4. In this case, we augment the basic model to include a family of performance predictors.

6. A set $\mathcal{P}$ of *performance predictors*, with each $p \in \mathcal{P}$ a function from $\mathcal{F}$ to $\mathbb{R}$.

Performance predictors play the same role as the EPMs used in [XHHL08].

The goal is to learn, for each algorithm $A \in \mathcal{A}$, among all permitted predictors $p \in \mathcal{P}$, the one that minimizes some loss function. Like the performance measure COST, we take

this loss function as given. The most commonly used loss function is squared error; in this case, for each $A \in \mathcal{A}$ we aim to compute the function that minimizes

$$\mathbf{E}_{x \sim \mathcal{D}}\left[(\text{COST}(A, x) - p(f(x)))^2\right].$$

over $p \in \mathcal{P}$.[23] For a fixed algorithm A, this is a standard regression problem, with domain $\mathcal{F}$, real-valued labels, and a distribution on $\mathcal{F} \times \mathbb{R}$ induced by $\mathcal{D}$ via $x \mapsto (f(x), \text{COST}(A, x))$. Bounding the sample complexity of this learning problem reduces to bounding the pseudo-dimension of $\mathcal{P}$ (see e.g. [AB99]). We conclude the section by noting two choices of $\mathcal{P}$ that are common in empirical work and that have modest pseudo-dimension. For both, suppose the features are real-valued, with $\mathcal{F} \subseteq \mathbb{R}^d$.

For the first example, suppose the set $\mathcal{P}$ is the class of *linear predictors*, with each $p \in \mathcal{P}$ having the form $p(f(x)) = a^T f(x)$ for some coefficient vector $a \in \mathbb{R}^d$.[24] The following is well known (see e.g. [AB99]).

Proposition 3.13 (Pseudo-Dimension of Linear Predictors) *If $\mathcal{F}$ contains real-valued d-dimensional features and $\mathcal{P}$ is the set of linear predictors, then the pseudo-dimension of $\mathcal{P}$ is at most d.*

If all functions in $\mathcal{P}$ map all possible φ to $[0, H]$, then Proposition 3.13 and Corollary 3.4 imply a sample complexity bound of $\tilde{O}(\frac{H^4}{\epsilon^2}d)$ for (ϵ, δ)-learning the predictor with minimum expected square error. Similar results hold, with worse dependence on d, if $\mathcal{P}$ is a set of low-degree polynomials [AB99].

For another example, suppose $\mathcal{P}_\ell$ is the set of regression trees with at most ℓ nodes, where each internal node performs an inequality test on a coordinate of the feature vector φ (and leaves are labelled with performance estimates).[25] This class also has low pseudo-dimension[26], and hence the problem of learning a near-optimal predictor has correspondingly small sample complexity.

Theorem 3.14 (Pseudo-Dimension of Regression Trees) *Suppose $\mathcal{F}$ contains real-valued d-dimensional features and let $\mathcal{P}_\ell$ be the set of regression trees with at most ℓ nodes, where each node performs an inequality test on one of the features. Then, the pseudo-dimension of $\mathcal{P}_\ell$ is $O(\ell \log(\ell d))$.*

PROOF. Suppose $S = \{x_1, \ldots, x_s\} \subset \mathcal{F}$ is shattered by $\mathcal{P}_\ell$, and let $r_1, \ldots, r_s$ be its real-valued witnesses. We count the number of binary labellings $\mathcal{P}_\ell$ can induce on S. For convenience, relabel the samples so that the r_i's are nondecreasing.

---

[23] Note that the expected loss incurred by the best predictor depends on the choices of the predictor set $\mathcal{P}$, the feature set $\mathcal{F}$, and map f. Again, these choices are outside our model.

[24] A linear model might sound unreasonably simple for the task of predicting the running time of an algorithm, but significant complexity can be included in the feature map $f(x)$. For example, each coordinate of $f(x)$ could be a nonlinear combination of several "basic features" of x. Indeed, linear models often exhibit surprisingly good empirical performance, given a judicious choice of a feature set [LNS09].

[25] Regression trees, and random forests thereof, have emerged as a popular class of predictors in empirical work on application-specific algorithm selection [HXHL14].

[26] We suspect this fact is known, but have been unable to locate a suitable reference.

First, there are $O(4^\ell)$ binary trees with at most ℓ internal nodes. Fix such a binary tree. Each node can partition $x_1, \ldots, x_s$ in at most $d(s+1)$ different ways, since there are d ways to pick a coordinate, and each coordinate induces up to $s+1$ different splits of $x_1, \ldots, x_s$. At each leaf, there are at most $s+1$ equivalence classes of predictions, corresponding to the intervals $(-\infty, r_1), [r_1, r_2), \ldots, [r_s, \infty)$.

Putting it together, there are $O(4^\ell \cdot (d(s+1))^\ell \cdot (s+1)^{\ell+1})$ different binary labellings of S, where we use the fact that every tree in P_ℓ has at most ℓ nodes and $\ell+1$ leaves. This exceeds 2^s, the requisite number of labellings to shatter S, only if $s = O(\ell \log(\ell d))$. $\square$

Remark 3.15 (Extension to Large $\mathcal{A}$) We can also extend our approach to scenarios with a large or infinite set $\mathcal{A}$ of possible algorithms. This extension is relevant to state-of-the-art empirical approaches to the auto-tuning of algorithms with many parameters, such as mathematical programming solvers [HXHL14]; see also the discussion in Section 2.3. (Instantiating all of the parameters yields a fixed algorithm; ranging over all possible parameter values yields the set $\mathcal{A}$.) In parallel with our formalism for accommodating a large number of possible features, we now assume that there is a set $\mathcal{F}'$ of possible "algorithm feature values" and a mapping f' that computes the features of a given algorithm. A performance predictor is now a map from $\mathcal{F} \times \mathcal{F}'$ to $\mathbb{R}$, taking as input the features of an algorithm A and of an instance x, and returning as output an estimate of A's performance on x. If $\mathcal{P}$ is the set of linear predictors, for example, then by Proposition 3.13 its pseudo-dimension is $d + d'$, where d and d' denote the dimensions of $\mathcal{F}$ and $\mathcal{F}'$, respectively.

3.6 Application: Choosing the Step Size in Gradient Descent

For our last PAC example, we give sample complexity results for the problem of choosing the best step size in gradient descent. When gradient descent is used in practice, the step size is generally taken much larger than the upper limits suggested by theoretical guarantees, and often converges in many fewer iterations than with the step size suggested by theory. This motivates the problem of learning the step size from examples. We view this as a baby step towards reasoning more generally about the problem of learning good parameters for machine learning algorithms.

In this section, we look at a setting where the approximation quality is fixed for all algorithms, and the performance measure COST is the running time of the algorithm. Unlike the applications we've seen so far, the parameter space here will indeed satisfy a Lipschitz-like condition, and we will be able to follow the discretization approach suggested by Remark 3.6.

3.6.1 Gradient Descent Preliminaries

Recall the basic gradient descent algorithm for minimizing a function f given an initial point z_0 over $\mathbb{R}^n$:

1. Initialize $z := z_0$.
2. While $\|\nabla f(z)\|_2 > \nu$:
   (a) $z := z - \rho \cdot \nabla f(z)$.

We take the error tolerance ν as given and focus on the more interesting parameter, the step size ρ. Bigger values

of ρ have the potential to make more progress in each step, but run the risk of overshooting a minimum of f.

We instantiate the basic model (Section 3.1) to study the problem of learning the best step size. There is an unknown distribution $\mathcal{D}$ over instances, where an instance $x \in \Pi$ consists of a function f and an initial point z_0. Each algorithm A_ρ of $\mathcal{A}$ is the basic gradient descent algorithm above, with some choice ρ of a step size drawn from some fixed interval $[\rho_\ell, \rho_u] \subset (0, \infty)$. The performance measure $\text{COST}(A, x)$ is the number of iterations (i.e., steps) taken by the algorithm for the instance x.

To obtain positive results, we need to restrict the allowable functions f (see full version of the paper). First, we assume that every function f is convex and L-smooth for a known L. A function f is L-smooth if it is everywhere differentiable, and $\|\nabla f(z_1) - \nabla f(z_2)\| \le L \|z_1 - z_2\|$ for all z_1 and z_2 (all norms in this section are in ℓ_2). Since gradient descent is translation invariant, and f is convex, we can assume for convenience that the (uniquely attained) minimum value of f is 0, with $f(0) = 0$.

Second, we assume that the magnitudes of the initial points are bounded, with $\|z_0\| \le Z$ for some known constant $Z > \nu$.

Third, we assume that there is a known constant $c \in (0, 1)$ such that $\|z - \rho \nabla f(z)\| \le (1-c)\|z\|$ for all $\rho \in [\rho_\ell, \rho_u]$. In other words, the norm of any point z — equivalently, the distance to the global minimum — decreases by some minimum factor after each gradient descent step. We refer to this as the *guaranteed progress* condition. This is satisfied (for instance) by L-smooth, m-strongly convex functions[27] which is a well studied regime (see e.g. [BV04]). The standard analysis of gradient descent implies that $c \ge \rho m$ for $\rho \le 2/(m+L)$ over this class of functions.

Under these restrictions, we can compute a nearly optimal ρ given a reasonable number of samples from $\mathcal{D}$.

Theorem 3.16 (Learnability of Step Size in Gradient Descent)[28] *There is a learning algorithm that $(1.1, \delta)$-learns the optimal algorithm in $\mathcal{A}$ using $m = \tilde{O}\left(\frac{\log(Z/\nu)}{c}\right)^3$ samples from $\mathcal{D}$.*[29]

A proof appears in the full version of the paper.

4. ONLINE LEARNING OF APPLICATION-SPECIFIC ALGORITHMS

This section studies the problem of learning the best application-specific algorithm *online*, with instances arriving one-by-one.[30] The goal is choose an algorithm at each time step,

---

[27] A (continuously differentiable) function f is m-*strongly convex* if $f(y) \ge f(w) + \nabla f(w)^T (y - w) + \frac{m}{2}\|y - w\|^2$ for all $w, y \in \mathbb{R}^n$. The usual notion of convexity is the same as 0-strong convexity. Note that the definition of L-smooth implies $m \le L$.

[28] One can also directly get a pseudo-dimension-like bound as in the previous examples, using a generalization known as the γ-fat shattering dimension. In particular, $\mathcal{A}$ has 1.01-fat shattering dimension $\log|N| = \frac{\log(Z/\nu)}{c}$.

[29] We again use $\tilde{O}(\cdot)$ to suppress logarithmic factors.

[30] The online model is obviously relevant when training data arrives over time. Also, even with offline data sets that are very large, it can be computationally necessary to process training data in a one-pass, online fashion.

before seeing the next instance, so that the average performance is close to that of the best fixed algorithm in hindsight. This contrasts with the statistical (or "batch") learning setup used in Section 3, where the goal was to identify a single algorithm from a batch of training instances that generalizes well to future instances from the same distribution. For many of the motivating examples in Section 2, both the statistical and online learning approaches are relevant. The distribution-free online learning formalism of this section may be particularly appropriate when instances cannot be modeled as i.i.d. draws from an unknown distribution.

The rest of this section appears in the full version of the paper.[31]

5. CONCLUSIONS AND FUTURE DIRECTIONS

Empirical work on application-dependent algorithm selection has far outpaced theoretical analysis of the problem, and this paper has taken an initial step toward redressing this imbalance. We formulated the problem as one of learning the best algorithm or algorithm sequence from a class with respect to an unknown input distribution or input sequence. Many state-of-the-art empirical approaches to algorithm selection map naturally to instances of our learning frameworks. We demonstrated that many well-studied classes of algorithms have small pseudo-dimension, and thus it is possible to learn a near-optimal algorithm from a relatively modest amount of data. We proved that worst-case guarantees for no-regret online learning algorithms are impossible, but that good online learning algorithms exist in a natural smoothed model.

Our work suggests numerous wide-open research directions worthy of further study. For example:

1. Which computational problems admit a class of algorithms that simultaneously has low representation error and small pseudo-dimension (like in Section 3.4)?

2. When is it possible to learn a near-optimal algorithm using only a polynomial amount of computation?

3. For what settings is there is a learning algorithm better than brute-force search? Alternatively, are there (conditional) lower bounds stating that brute-force search is necessary for learning?[32]

4. Are there any non-trivial relationships between statistical learning measures of the complexity of an algorithm class and more traditional complexity measures?

5. How should instance features be chosen to minimize the representation error of the induced family of algorithm selection maps (cf., Section 3.5.1)?

Acknowledgements

We are grateful for the comments provided by anonymous reviewers.

---

[31] http://arxiv.org/pdf/1511.07147
[32] Recall the discussion in Section 2.3: even in practice, the state-of-the-art for application-specific algorithm selection often boils down to brute-force search.

6. REFERENCES

[AB99] M. Anthony and P. L. Bartlett. *Neural Network Learning: Theoretical Foundations*. Cambridge University Press, 1999.

[ACCL06] N. Ailon, B. Chazelle, S. Comandur, and D. Liu. Self-improving algorithms. In *Symposium on Discrete Algorithms (SODA)*, pages 261–270, 2006.

[AGK+04] Vijay Arya, Naveen Garg, Rohit Khandekar, Adam Meyerson, Kamesh Munagala, and Vinayaka Pandit. Local search heuristics for k-median and facility location problems. *SIAM Journal on Computing*, 33(3):544–562, 2004.

[BB12] James Bergstra and Yoshua Bengio. Random search for hyper-parameter optimization. *Journal of Machine Learning Research*, 13(1):281–305, 2012.

[BNR03] Allan Borodin, Morten N. Nielsen, and Charles Rackoff. (Incremental) priority algorithms. *Algorithmica*, 37(4):295–326, 2003.

[BV04] Stephen Boyd and Lieven Vandenberghe. *Convex optimization*. Cambridge University Press, 2004.

[CBO14] U. S. Congressional Budget Office: The budget and economic outlook: 2015 to 2025. 2014.

[CL06] Nicolo Cesa-Bianchi and Gábor Lugosi. *Prediction, learning, and games*. Cambridge University Press, 2006.

[CMS10] Kenneth L. Clarkson, Wolfgang Mulzer, and C. Seshadhri. Self-improving algorithms for convex hulls. In *Symposium on Discrete Algorithms (SODA)*, pages 1546–1565, 2010.

[CMS12] Kenneth L. Clarkson, Wolfgang Mulzer, and C. Seshadhri. Self-improving algorithms for coordinate-wise maxima. In *Symposium on Computational Geometry (SoCG)*, pages 277–286, 2012.

[CS08] K. L. Clarkson and C. Seshadhri. Self-improving algorithms for Delaunay triangulations. In *Symposium on Computational Geometry (SoCG)*, pages 148–155, 2008.

[Fin98] Eugene Fink. How to solve it automatically: Selection among problem solving methods. In *International Conference on Artificial Intelligence Planning Systems*, pages 128–136, 1998.

[Hau92] D. Haussler. Decision theoretic generalizations of the PAC model for neural net and other learning applications. *Information and Computation*, 100(1):78–150, 1992.

[HJY+10] Ling Huang, Jinzhu Jia, Bin Yu, Byung-Gon Chun, Petros Maniatis, and Mayur Naik. Predicting execution time of computer programs using sparse polynomial regression. In *Neural Information Processing Systems (NIPS)*, pages 883–891, 2010.

[HRG+01] Eric Horvitz, Yongshao Ruan, Carla P. Gomes, Henry A. Kautz, Bart Selman, and David Maxwell Chickering. A Bayesian approach to tackling hard computational problems. In *Conference in Uncertainty in*

Artificial Intelligence (UAI), pages 235–244, 2001.

[HXHL14] Frank Hutter, Lin Xu, Holger H. Hoos, and Kevin Leyton-Brown. Algorithm runtime prediction: Methods & evaluation. *Artificial Intelligence*, 206:79–111, 2014.

[Jam06] G. J. O. Jameson. Counting zeros of generalized polynomials: DescartesâĂŹ rule of signs and LaguerreâĂŹs extensions. *Mathematical Gazette*, 90(518):223–234, 2006.

[JM97] David S Johnson and Lyle A McGeoch. The traveling salesman problem: A case study in local optimization. *Local search in combinatorial optimization*, 1:215–310, 1997.

[KGM12] Lars Kotthoff, Ian P. Gent, and Ian Miguel. An evaluation of machine learning in algorithm selection for search problems. *AI Communications*, 25(3):257–270, 2012.

[Knu75] D. E. Knuth. Estimating the efficiency of backtrack programs. *Mathematics of Computation*, 29:121–136, 1975.

[LNS09] Kevin Leyton-Brown, Eugene Nudelman, and Yoav Shoham. Empirical hardness models: Methodology and a case study on combinatorial auctions. *Journal of the ACM*, 56(4), 2009.

[Lon01] Philip M. Long. Using the pseudo-dimension to analyze approximation algorithms for integer programming. In *International Workshop on Algorithms and Data Structures (WADS)*, pages 26–37, 2001.

[LOS02] Daniel Lehmann, Liadan Ita Oćallaghan, and Yoav Shoham. Truth revelation in approximately efficient combinatorial auctions. *Journal of the ACM (JACM)*, 49(5):577–602, 2002.

[LW94] Nick Littlestone and Manfred K Warmuth. The weighted majority algorithm. *Information and computation*, 108(2):212–261, 1994.

[MM14] Mehryar Mohri and Andres Munoz Medina. Learning theory and algorithms for revenue optimization in second price auctions with reserve. In *International Conference on Machine Learning (ICML)*, pages 262–270, 2014.

[MR15] Jamie Morgenstern and Tim Roughgarden. The pseudo-dimension of near-optimal auctions. *CoRR*, abs/1506.03684, 2015.

[MS14] P. Milgrom and I. Segal. Deferred-acceptance auctions and radio spectrum reallocation. 2014.

[SB14] S. Shalev-Shwartz and S. Ben-David. *Understanding Machine Learning: From Theory to Algorithms*. Cambridge, 2014.

[ST09] Daniel A Spielman and Shang-Hua Teng. Smoothed analysis: an attempt to explain the behavior of algorithms in practice. *Communications of the ACM*, 52(10):76–84, 2009.

[STY03] Shuichi Sakai, Mitsunori Togasaki, and Koichi Yamazaki. A note on greedy algorithms for the maximum weighted independent set problem. *Discrete Applied Mathematics*, 126(2):313–322, 2003.

[XHHL08] Lin Xu, Frank Hutter, Holger H. Hoos, and Kevin Leyton-Brown. SATzilla: Portfolio-based algorithm selection for SAT. *J. Artificial Intelligence Research (JAIR)*, 32:565–606, 2008.

[XHHL11] Lin Xu, Frank Hutter, Holger H Hoos, and Kevin Leyton-Brown. Hydra-mip: Automated algorithm configuration and selection for mixed integer programming. In *RCRA workshop on experimental evaluation of algorithms for solving problems with combinatorial explosion at the international joint conference on artificial intelligence (IJCAI)*, pages 16–30, 2011.

[XHHL12] Lin Xu, Frank Hutter, Holger H. Hoos, and Kevin Leyton-Brown. SATzilla2012: Improved algorithm selection based on cost-sensitive classification models. In *International Conference on Theory and Applications of Satisfiability Testing (SAT)*, 2012.

An Axiomatic Approach to Community Detection

Christian Borgs
Microsoft Research
borgs@microsoft.com

Jennifer Chayes
Microsoft Research
jchayes@microsoft.com

Adrian Marple
Stanford
adrian.marple@gmail.com

Shang-Hua Teng*
USC
shanghua@usc.edu

ABSTRACT

Inspired by social choice theory in voting and other contexts [2], we provide the first axiomatic approach to community identification in social and information networks. We start from an abstract framework, called *preference networks* [3], which, for each member, gives their ranking of all the other members of the network. This preference model enables us to focus on the fundamental conceptual question:

What constitutes a community in a social network?

Within this framework, we axiomatically study the formation and structures of communities in two different ways. First, we apply social choice theory and define communities indirectly by postulating that they are fixed points of a preference aggregation function obeying certain desirable axioms. Second, we directly postulate six desirable axioms for communities to satisfy, without reference to preference aggregation. For the second approach, we prove a taxonomy theorem that provides a *structural characterization* of the family of *axiom-conforming* community rules as a lattice. We complement this structural theorem with a *complexity result*, showing that, while for some rules in the lattice, community characterization is straightforward, it is coNP-complete to characterize subsets according to others. Our study also sheds light on the limitations of defining community rules solely based on preference aggregation, namely that many aggregation functions lead to communities which violate at least one of our community axioms. These include any aggregation function satisfying Arrow's "independence of irrelevant alternatives" axiom, as well as commonly used aggregation schemes like the Borda count or generalizations thereof. Finally, we give a polynomial-time rule consistent with five axioms and weakly satisfying the sixth axiom.

*Supported in part by a Simons Investigator Award from the Simons Foundation and by NSF grant CCF-1111270.

Permission to make digital or hard copies of all or part of this work for personal or classroom use is granted without fee provided that copies are not made or distributed for profit or commercial advantage and that copies bear this notice and the full citation on the first page. Copyrights for components of this work owned by others than the author(s) must be honored. Abstracting with credit is permitted. To copy otherwise, or republish, to post on servers or to redistribute to lists, requires prior specific permission and/or a fee. Request permissions from Permissions@acm.org.

ITCS'16, January 14–16, 2016, Cambridge, MA, USA.
Copyright is held by the owner/author(s). Publication rights licensed to ACM.
ACM 978-1-4503-4057-1/16/01 ...$15.00.
DOI: http://dx.doi.org/10.1145/2840728.2840748.

Categories and Subject Descriptors

Theory of computation [**Algorithmic game theory and mechanism design**]: Social networks; Information systems [**World Wide Web**]: Web applications—*Social networks*; Information systems [**Information systems applications**]: Data mining—*Clustering*; Human-centered computing [**Collaborative and social computing**]: Social network analysis

Keywords

Network Analysis; social choice theory; community identification; social and information networks; axiomatic framework; taxonomy of community rules; stable communities

1. INTRODUCTION

A fundamental problem in network analysis is the characterization and identification of subsets of nodes in a network that have significant structural coherence. This problem is usually studied in the context of *community identification* and *network clustering*. Like other inverse problems in data mining and machine learning, this one is conceptually challenging: There are many possible ways to measure the degree of coherence of a subset and many possible interpretations of preferences and affinities to model network data. As a result, various seemingly reasonable/desirable conditions to qualify a subset as a community have been studied in the literature [17, 14, 13, 19, 25, 9]. However, direct comparison of different community characterizations is quite difficult.

A community is formed by a group of individuals, while an information/social network is usually specified by data describing each individual's direct neighbors, or the individuals' affinities or preferences for other members in the network. Thus, in order to answer the fundamental question, *"What constitutes a community in a social network?,"* it is desirable to first answer

How do individual preferences (affinities or connectivities) result in group preferences?

In this paper, we take what we believe is a novel and principled approach to the problem of community identification. Inspired by work on clustering [12], and, more conceptually, by classic work in social choice theory [2], we propose an axiomatic approach towards understanding network communities, both providing a framework for comparison of different community characterizations, and relating community identification to well-studied problems in social choice theory.

1.1 Preference Networks and Community Identification Functions

Our axiomatic approach uses an abstract social network framework. Our framework is analogous to the clustering approach of Kleinberg [12] in which network nodes are clustered according to similarity, specified by a similarity matrix derived from a metric over nodes. In Kleinberg's view, a clustering algorithm inputs a similarity matrix, and outputs a set of *non-overlapping* subsets called *clusters*. Analogously, we view community detection as an algorithmic problem which inputs a *preference network*, and outputs a set of (overlapping) subsets identified as *communities*.

To formalize this, consider a non-empty finite set V, let $L(V)$ denote the set of all linear orders π on V, with $\pi(u)$ denoting the rank of member u, from 1 for the highest rank to $|V|$ for the lowest. For $\pi \in L(V)$ and $i, j \in V$, we use the notation $i \succ_\pi j$ if i is ranked higher than j, i.e., $\pi(i) < \pi(j)$.

DEFINITION 1.1 (PREFERENCE NETWORKS). *A preference network is a pair $A = (V, \Pi)$, where V is a non-empty finite set and Π is a preference profile on V, defined as an element $\Pi = \{\pi_i\}_{i \in V} \in L(V)^V$. Here π_i specifies the ranking of V in the order of i's preference. We denote the collection of all preference networks[1] by $\mathcal{A}$.*

The preference network framework is inspired by social choice theory [2]. This framework is already used extensively — for voting, college admissions, medical residency assignments [8, 21, 10], for studying coalition formation in collaborative games [5, 22], for specifying routing preferences in the Border Gateway Protocol between autonomous systems of the Internet [20, 6], to name just a few contexts.

Community Identification Rules

The preference framework provides a complete-information network model that enables us to focus on the fundamental conceptual question regarding how to transform individual preferences into community identification rules. Like the work of Arrow [2] and Kleinberg [12], our axiomatic theory identifies basic desirable axioms which *consistent* community characterizations should satisfy, and also specifies the structures of consistent rules and the communities that they identify. Within the framework of preference networks, we can define the community-identification rules, the main subject of our study, as set-theoretical functions.

DEFINITION 1.2 (COMMUNITY FUNCTIONS). *A community function or rule is a function $\mathcal{C}$ that maps a preference network $A = (V, \Pi)$ onto a collection of non-empty sets $S \subset V$, $A \mapsto \mathcal{C}(A) \in 2^{2^V - \{\emptyset\}}$. We say a subset $S \subseteq V$ is a community in a preference network $A = (V, \Pi)$ according to a community function $\mathcal{C}$ if and only if $S \in \mathcal{C}(A)$.*

The preference network framework offers a natural, although highly selective, community rule, which we call the *Clique Rule* ($\mathcal{C}_{clique}$). We say $S \subseteq V$ is a *clique* in preference network $A = (V, \Pi)$ if each member of S prefers every member of S over every non-member.

RULE 1. (CLIQUE RULE) *Cliques and only cliques are communities.*

---

[1] To avoid paradoxes, we assume that V is a subset of some reference set $\mathcal{V}$, say the set of natural numbers.

Another example of natural rules for community identification is the rule defined in Balcan *et al.* [3] — which we will denote by $\mathcal{C}_{democratic}$ — based on "democratic voting:" For a preference network $A = (V, \Pi)$, let $\phi_S^\Pi(i)$, for $S \subseteq V$ and $i \in V$, denote the number of votes that i would receive when each member $s \in S$ casts one vote for each of its $|S|$ most preferred members according to its preference π_s.

RULE 2 (DEMOCRATIC RULE). *S is a democratically-certified community in a preference network $A = (V, \Pi)$, if every member in S receives more votes from S than every non-member, i.e., $\min_{u \in S} \phi_S^\Pi(u) - \max_{v \notin S} \phi_S^\Pi(v) > 0$.*

The set-theoretical formulation of community rules of Definition 1.2 implies some direct comparison of community rules. For example, we say a community function $\mathcal{C}_1$ is *more selective* than another community function $\mathcal{C}_2$ if, for all preference networks $A = (V, E)$, $\mathcal{C}_1(A) \subseteq \mathcal{C}_2(A)$. Clearly, $\mathcal{C}_{clique}$ is more selective than $\mathcal{C}_{democratic}$.

1.2 Our Work

Within the framework of preference networks, we axiomatically study the formation and structures of communities in two related approaches:

1. *Axiomatization and Characterization Community Rules:* We postulate six desirable axioms for community-identification rules to satisfy as well as provide a *structural characterization* of the family of *axiom-conforming* community rules in terms of a lattice. We also complement this structural theorem with a *complexity result*.

2. *Understanding Social-Choice Aggregation-Based Community Rules:* We examine a family of natural community-identification rules inspired by the classic social-choice theory from the lens of our axiomatic framework. We present two impossibility results that illustrate the limitation of defining community rules solely based on social-choice preference aggregation.

We now present the highlight of these results.

Axiomatization

We use *axioms* to state properties, such as fairness and consistency, that a *desirable* community function should have when applied to *all* preference networks. Our framework characterizes community-identification rules using a natural set of six axioms which will be defined formally in Section 2. Below, we summarize these axioms, which can be organized into three sets:

Social-Choice Fundamentals: The first three axioms are inspired by social choice theory. They reflect the intuition that community identification in preference networks is a form of social choice within each subset in the network. The two most fundamental axioms are Anonymity (Axiom 1) and Monotonicity (Axiom 2). The former states that a community rule should be isomorphism-invariant, i.e., they should not use the individuals' labels. The latter captures that the community characterization of a subset should be monotonically consistent — if community members' preferences change in favor of its members, then the community should remain a community. The third axiom, Embedding (Axiom 3), states that, if newcomers join the population of a preference network in such way that members of the existing population all retain their orignal preferences for each other, and prefer them over any new member, then the community characterization regarding members of the original network should remain unchanged in this bigger network, independent of the preferences towards and of the newcomers.

Cliques and the Entire Population: The fouth axiom, World Community (Axiom 4), is a basic one, stating that the entire population V of any preference network $A = (V, \Pi)$ is a community of A. Note that V is a clique of $A = (V, \Pi)$. In fact, if we replace Axiom World Community by the axiom that "all cliques are communities," we obtain an equivalent axiomatic system.

Baseline Stability and Self-Respect: The next two axioms are inspired by the classical game-theoretical studies of stable marriage and coalition formation [8, 21, 10, 5, 22]. The first, Self-Approval (Axiom 5), states that a community should have the necessary "self-respect:" It is not the case that everyone in the community "unanimously prefers" an outside group of the same size over the community itself. The last, Group Stability (Axiom 6), states that a community should have the necessary stablility: No subgroup in the community is replaceable by an equal-sized group of non-members who are "unanimously" preferred by the rest of community members.

Structural Characterization Community Rules

The set-theoretical formulation of community rules also provides the following natural definiton.

DEFINITION 1.3. (OPERATIONS OVER COMMUNITY RULES) *For two community functions $\mathcal{C}_1$ and $\mathcal{C}_2$, we define their intersection and union, $\mathcal{C}_1 \cap \mathcal{C}_2$ and $\mathcal{C}_1 \cup \mathcal{C}_2$, respectively, to be the community functions which, for all preference networks $A = (V, \Pi)$ characterize subsets of V according to*

$$(\mathcal{C}_1 \cap \mathcal{C}_2)(A) := \mathcal{C}_1(A) \cap \mathcal{C}_2(A) \tag{1}$$
$$(\mathcal{C}_1 \cup \mathcal{C}_2)(A) := \mathcal{C}_1(A) \cup \mathcal{C}_2(A). \tag{2}$$

Note that $\mathcal{C}_1 \cap \mathcal{C}_2$ is more *selective* than both $\mathcal{C}_1$ and $\mathcal{C}_2$, and $\mathcal{C}_1 \cup \mathcal{C}_2$ is more *inclusive* than both $\mathcal{C}_1$ and $\mathcal{C}_2$. Our main structural result is the following taxonomy theorem and the complete characterization of the most comprehensive and the most selective community rules consistent with all our community axioms.

> *The set of axiom-conforming community rules is not empty, and forms a lattice under the operations of union and intersection defined above.*

This result provides an interesting contrast to the classic axiomatization result of Arrow [2] and the more recent result of Kleinberg on clustering [12] that inspired our work. Unlike voting or clustering where the basic axioms lead to impossiblity theorems, the preference network framework has a natural community rule, the *Clique Rule*. Indeed, the Clique Rule satisfies all our axioms. One may ask:

> *Is the Clique rule the only axiom-conforming community identification rule?*

Our initial attempt to prove the "impossibility beyond the Clique rule" conjecture in fact led us to another community rule consistent with all axioms.[2] We call this rule the *Comprehensive Rule* ($\mathcal{C}_{comprehensive}$) because our proof shows the

[2]"If we knew what we were doing it wouldn't be research", Einstein once said.

following: For any community rule $\mathcal{C}$ satisfying all axioms, for all preference network A:

$$\mathcal{C}_{clique}(A) \subseteq \mathcal{C}(A) \subseteq \mathcal{C}_{comprehensive}(A). \tag{3}$$

Thus, $\mathcal{C}_{clique}(A)$ and $\mathcal{C}_{comprehensive}(A)$ form a lower and upper bound, respectively, for the lattice of axiom-comforming community rules. We complement this structural theorem with a complexity result: We show that while identifying a community by the Clique Rule is straightforward, it is coNP-complete to determine if a subset satisfies the Comprehensive Rule.

Communities as Fixed Points of Social Choice: Schema and Limitation

Our approach of starting from preference networks to study community identification connects community formation to social choice theory [2], thus providing a theoretical framework for understanding the problem of combining individual preferences into a community preference. One way to define communities is to generalize the principle of the Clique rule by classifying a set $S \subseteq V$ to be a community if, collectively, the members of S prefer every member in S to every element outside of S — community members collectively "certify themselves." To formalize what "collectively prefer" means, we use the notion of preference aggregation functions from social choice theory [2].

A *preference aggregation function* is a function which generates a single aggregate preference from a set of individual preferences. In this context, it is useful to allow for ties in the aggregate preference. To formalize this, we introduce the set $\overline{L(V)}$ of rankings with ties (see Section 4 for the precise definition), and then define preference aggregation as a function $F : L(V)^* \to \overline{L(V)}$, where $L(V)^*$ is the union of $L(V)^S$ over all non-empty, finite subsets of a countable reference set, which here we take as the union $\mathcal{V}$ of all possible groundsets V. Given a non-empty finite set $S \subset \mathcal{V}$ and a preference profile $\Pi_S = \{\pi_s : s \in S\} \in L(V)^S$, we say the image $F(\Pi_S)$ is the *aggregated preference* of S according to Π_S.

DEFINITION 1.4. (COMMUNITIES AS FIXED POINTS OF SOCIAL CHOICE) *Let $F : L(V)^* \to \overline{L(V)}$ be a preference aggregation function. For $A = (V, \Pi)$, define f_F as the map on non-empty subsets $S \subset V$ which maps S to the subset $f_F(S) := \{v \in V \mid F(\Pi_S)(v) \leq |S|\}$. A non-empty subset $S \subset V$ is called a* community *of A with respect to F if and only if $f_F(S) = S$. The function $\mathcal{C}_F$ mapping A into the set of communities defined above is called the* fixed-point rule *with respect to F.*

The fixed-point rule captures the strongest notion of "collective self-preference" based on social-choice aggregation.

While Definition 1.2 is convenient for studying the mathematical structures of our theory, community identification is a computational problem as much as a mathematical problem. Thus, it is desirable that communities can be characterized by a constructive community function $\mathcal{C}$ that is:

- **Consistent**: $\mathcal{C}$ satisfies all (or nearly all) axioms;

- **Constructive**: Given a preference network $A = (V, \Pi)$, and a subset $S \subseteq V$, one can determine in polynomial-time (in $n = |V|$) if $S \in \mathcal{C}(A)$.

The above mentioned co-NP completeness of the Comprehensive Rule highlights the computational difficulty of community identification based on axiom-conforming rules, raising the question of whether there are natural community rules that are indeed constructive. In this context, communities defined in terms of fixed point rules provide a rich source of candidates in terms of various aggregation functions studied in social choice; indeed, any aggregation function that can be calculated in polynomial time gives rise to a constructive community rule via the fixed point Definition 1.4. Defining community rules in terms of aggregation functions also gives us another perspective on community rules, since we can examine aggregation functions themselves through the lens of social choice theory, and connect the properties of the aggregation functions with the properties of their fixed rules from the lens of our axiomatic framework.

Our studies shed light on the limitations of formulating community rules solely based on preference aggregation: We show that, although the fixed-point community rules systematically generalizes the Clique rule, many aggregation functions lead to rules which violate at least one of our community axioms. We prove two impossibility theorems.

1. For any aggregation function satisfying Arrow's Independence of Irrelevant Alternatives axiom, its fixed-point rule must violate one of our axioms.

2. Any fixed-point rule based on commonly-used weighted aggregation schemes like Borda count or generalizations thereof is inconsistent with (at least) one of our axioms.

The second impossibility result was more surprising to us than the first one: While weighted fixed-point rules are natural from a social choice viewpoint, it turns out that the fixed-point rules of several weighted aggregation functions, including $\mathcal{C}_{democratic}$, are inconsistent with the Axiom Monotonicity! We believe this violation is illustrative of the fundamental subtlety of community rules. This leads us to consider fixed-point rules, $\mathcal{C}_{harmonious}$, which are not given in terms of weighted voting schemes, such as the following.

RULE 3 (HARMONIOUS COMMUNITIES). *Let $A = (V, \Pi)$ be a preference network. A non-empty subset $S \subseteq V$ is a harmonious community of A if for all $u \in S$ and $v \in V - S$, the majority of $\{\pi_s \; : \; s \in S\}$ prefer u over v.*

This rule can be formulated as a fixed-point rule of a topologically defined aggregation function — see Proposition 4.9 — and satisfies Axioms 1-5, as well as a weaker form of Axiom Group Stability.

2. COHERENT COMMUNITIES: AXIOMS

We now define our six core axioms. Below, we fix a ground set V and a community function $\mathcal{C}$.

AXIOM 1 (Anonymity (A)). *Let $S, S' \subset V$ and Π, Π' be such $S' = \sigma(S)$ and $\Pi' = \sigma(\Pi)$ for some permutation $\sigma : V \to V$. Then $S \in \mathcal{C}(V, \Pi) \iff S' \in \mathcal{C}(V, \Pi')$.*

This is a standard axiom: labels should have no effect on a community function.

AXIOM 2 (Monotonicity (Mon)). *Let $S \subset V$. If Π and Π' are such that $\forall s \in S$, $\forall u \in S$ and $\forall v \in V$, $u \succ_{\pi'_s} v \implies u \succ_{\pi_s} v$, then $S \in \mathcal{C}(V, \Pi') \implies S \in \mathcal{C}(V, \Pi)$.*

The Axiom Monotonicity states that, if the profile changes so that the rank of a community member increases without decreasing the rank of other members, then this remains a community in the new ranking. Mon also allows non-members to change arbitrarily, as long as their positions relative to any members remains the same or worse. To state the next axiom, we define the projection $A|_{V'}$ of a preference network $A = (V, \Pi)$ onto a subset $V' \subset V$ as the preference network $A|_{V'} = (V', \Pi|_{V'})$ where $\Pi|_{V'} = \{\pi'_s\}_{s \in V'}$ is defined by setting π'_s to be the ranking on V' which maintains the relative ordering of all members of V', i.e., for all $s, u, v \in V'$, $u \succ_{\pi'_s} v \iff u \succ_{\pi_s} v$. We say that A' is EMBEDDED into A if $A' = A|_{V'}$ for some $V' \subset V$.

AXIOM 3 (Embedding (Emb)). *If $A' = (V', \Pi')$ is embedded into $A = (V, \Pi)$ and $\pi_i(j) = \pi'_i(j)$ for all $i, j \in V'$ then $\mathcal{C}(A') = \mathcal{C}(A) \cap 2^{V'}$.*

In other words, if a network is embedded into a larger network in such a way that, with respect to the preferences in the larger network, the members of the smaller network prefer each other over everyone else, then the community classification regarding members of the smaller network remains unchanged. The next axiom is self explanatory.

AXIOM 4 (World Community (WC)). *For all preference profiles Π, $V \in \mathcal{C}(V, \Pi)$.*

To state the last two axioms, we start with a few definitions to formalize the notion that a member prefers a group over another of the same size. Given $(V, \Pi) \in \mathcal{A}$ and non-empty disjoint sets $G, G' \subset V$ of equal size, we say that $s \in V$ *prefers* G' *over* G if, after reordering the elements $g_1, \ldots, g_{|G|}$ and $g'_1, \ldots, g'_{|G|}$ of G and G' according to her preferences, s prefers g'_i to g_i $\forall i = 1, \ldots, |G|$. We sometimes also refer to this preference as *lexicographical preference*. Let $(V, \Pi) \in \mathcal{A}$. A set $S \subset V$ is called *group stable* with respect to Π if for all non-empty $G \subsetneq S$ there exists no $G' \subset V - S$ that has the same size as G and is *preferred* to G by all $s \in S - G$. S is called *self-approving* with respect to Π if there exists set no $G' \subseteq V - S$ that has the same size as S and is *preferred* to S by all $s \in S$.

AXIOM 5 (Self-Approval (SA)). *If Π is a preference profile over V and $S \in \mathcal{C}(V, \Pi)$, then S is SELF-APPROVING with respect to Π.*

AXIOM 6 (Group Stability (GS)). *If Π is a preference profile over V and $S \in \mathcal{C}(V, \Pi)$, then S is GROUP STABLE with respect to Π.*

Axiom Group Stability provides a type of game-theoretic stability [16, 15, 4, 23, 24], and states that no subgroup in a community can be replaced by an equal-size group of non-members who are lexicographically preferred by the remainder of the community members, while Axiom Self-Approval provides a stability notion of minimum *self-respect*, and requires that there is no outside group of the same size as S which is lexicographically preferred to S by everyone in S. Note that the set V is trivially group stable for all Π, and that any set S with $|S| > |V|/2$ is self-approving for all Π.

It is easy to check that the Clique Rule satisfies all six axioms. However, the clique rule has a structural feature which essentially rules out any non-trivial overlap of communities, while "Real-world" communities typically have non-trivial overlaps among themselves.

PROPOSITION 2.1. $\forall A = (V, \Pi)$, if $S_1, S_2 \in \mathcal{C}_{clique}(A)$, then either $S_1 \cap S_2 = \emptyset$ or $S_1 \subset S_2$, or $S_2 \subset S_1$.

Given this property, it is desirable to answer the question whether there are other community functions that satisfy all axioms. The answer is yes, and in fact, the set of all axiom conforming rules has interesting structural properties, which we study of our next section.

3. LATTICE OF AXIOM-CONFORMING COMMUNITY RULES

Let $\mathcal{C}$ denote the family of all axiom-conforming community rules. Let $\mathcal{C}_B$ be a superset of $\mathcal{C}$ consisting of all community rules satisfying Axioms 1-4. The main result of this section is that both $\mathcal{C}$ and $\mathcal{C}_B$ are not empty, and in fact, they each form a lattice under the natural union and intersection operations given by Definition 1.3. Two community rules are special for the lattice of $\mathcal{C}$. The first one is the Clique Rule ($\mathcal{C}_{clique}$) defined in Section 1. The second one is the following Comprehensive Rule:

RULE 4 (COMPREHENSIVE RULE). *For any preference network A, let $\mathcal{C}_{SA}(A)$ and $\mathcal{C}_{GS}(A)$ denote the subsets $S \subset V$ which are self-approving and group stable, respectively. Then, $\mathcal{C}_{comprehensive} := \mathcal{C}_{SA} \cap \mathcal{C}_{GS}$.*

Finally, let $\mathcal{C}_{all}$ be the rule declaring every non-empty set S to be a community.

3.1 Taxonomy of Community Rules

THEOREM 3.1 (LATTICE OF COMMUNITY RULES).

1. *The algebraic structure,*

$$\mathcal{T} = (\mathcal{C}, \cup, \cap, \mathcal{C}_{clique}, \mathcal{C}_{comprehensive})$$

is a bounded lattice, with $\mathcal{C}_{comprehensive}$ and $\mathcal{C}_{clique}$ as the lattice's top and bottom.

2. *The algebraic structure,*

$$\mathcal{T}_B = (\mathcal{C}_B, \cup, \cap, \mathcal{C}_{clique}, \mathcal{C}_{all})$$

is a bounded lattice, with $\mathcal{C}_{all}$ and $\mathcal{C}_{clique}$ as the lattice's top and bottom.

Part 1 of the theorem implies that, for any axiom-conforming community function $\mathcal{C}$, it must be the case that, for every preference network A,

$$\mathcal{C}_{clique}(A) \subseteq \mathcal{C}(A) \subseteq \mathcal{C}_{comprehensive}(A).$$

The following basic lemma is key for establishing our Taxonomy Theorem.

LEMMA 3.2. (INTERSECTION LEMMA) *For all community rule $\mathcal{C}$, if $\mathcal{C} \in \mathcal{C}_B$ then $\mathcal{C} \cap \mathcal{C}_{GS} \cap \mathcal{C}_{SA} \in \mathcal{C}$.*

PROOF. Let $\widetilde{\mathcal{C}} := \mathcal{C} \cap \mathcal{C}_{GS} \cap \mathcal{C}_{SA}$, where $\mathcal{C} \in \mathcal{C}_B$. Because $\mathcal{C}_{GS}$ and $\mathcal{C}_{SA}$ are both consistent with Axioms A, WC, and Emb, $\widetilde{\mathcal{C}}$ remains consistent with these three axioms. To see $\widetilde{\mathcal{C}}$ satisfies Axiom Mon, choose Π, Π' such that, for all $u, s \in S$ and $v \in V$, $u \succ_{\pi'_s} v \implies u \succ_{\pi_s} v$. We need to show that if $S \in \widetilde{\mathcal{C}}((V, \Pi'))$ then $S \in \widetilde{\mathcal{C}}((V, \Pi))$. Suppose this is not the case, then either (1) $S \notin \mathcal{C}_{GS}((V, \Pi))$ or (2) $S \notin \mathcal{C}_{SA}((V, \Pi))$. In Case (1), there exists $G \subset S$, $G' \subset V - S$, $|G| = |G'|$,

and bijections $(f_s : S \to G' | s \in S - G)$ such that $\forall s \in S - G, \forall u \in G$, $u \prec_{\pi_s} f_s(u)$. By Mon, $u \prec_{\pi'_s} f_s(u)$, which shows $S \notin \mathcal{C}_{GS}(A')$. In Case (2), $\exists G' \subset V - S$, bijections $(f_s : S \to G')$ such that $\forall s, u \in S$, $u \prec_{\pi_s} f_s(u)$. By Mon, $u \prec_{\pi'_s} f_s(u)$, which implies that $S \notin \mathcal{C}_{GS}(A')$.

Finally, by definition, $\mathcal{C} \cap \mathcal{C}_{GS} \cap \mathcal{C}_{SA}$ satisfies GS and SA. Thus, $\mathcal{C} \cap \mathcal{C}_{GS} \cap \mathcal{C}_{SA} \in \mathcal{C}$. $\square$

PROOF. (Proof of Theorem 3.1) We first prove that $\mathcal{C}_{clique}$ and $\mathcal{C}_{comprehensive}$ are, respectively, the most selective and inclusive axiom-conforming community rules. On one hand it is easy to see that for any rule that satisfies WC and Emb, all cliques must be communities, showing that $\mathcal{C}_{clique}(A) \subseteq \mathcal{C}(A)$ whenever $\mathcal{C}$ satisfies WC and Emb; see also Proposition 4.2 below. On the other hand, $\mathcal{C}_{all}(A) = 2^V - \{\emptyset\}$ satisfies Axioms 1-4, and hence $\mathcal{C}_{all} \in \mathcal{C}_B$. Since $\mathcal{C}_{comprehensive} = \mathcal{C}_{all} \cap \mathcal{C}_{GS} \cap \mathcal{C}_{SA}$, by the Intersection Lemma, $\mathcal{C}_{comprehensive} \in \mathcal{C}$. Thus, for any $\mathcal{C}$ that satisfies all axioms, $\mathcal{C}_{clique}(A) \subseteq \mathcal{C}(A) \subseteq \mathcal{C}_{comprehensive}(A)$.

The two operations $\cap$ and $\cup$ over the community functions are both commutative and associative. They also satisfy the *absorption property*. In other words, $\forall \mathcal{C}_1, \mathcal{C}_2 \in \mathcal{C}$:

$$\mathcal{C}_1 \cup (\mathcal{C}_1 \cap \mathcal{C}_2) = \mathcal{C}_1 \quad \text{and} \quad \mathcal{C}_1 \cap (\mathcal{C}_1 \cup \mathcal{C}_2) = \mathcal{C}_1.$$

For example, to see the first one, for any affinity network A, we have:

$$\begin{aligned}
(\mathcal{C}_1 \cup (\mathcal{C}_1 \cap \mathcal{C}_2))(A) &= \mathcal{C}_1(A) \cup (\mathcal{C}_1 \cap \mathcal{C}_2)(A) \\
&= \mathcal{C}_1(A) \cup (\mathcal{C}_1(A) \cap \mathcal{C}_2(A)) \\
&= \mathcal{C}_1(A).
\end{aligned}$$

To complete the proof that $\mathcal{T}$ and $\mathcal{T}_B$ are lattices, we need to prove that $\mathcal{T}$ and $\mathcal{T}_B$ are closed under $\cap$ and $\cup$. We organize the arguments as following:

- A, WC: it is obvious that if $\mathcal{C}_1$ and $\mathcal{C}_2$ satisfy Axioms A and WC, then both $\mathcal{C}_1 \cup \mathcal{C}_2$ and $\mathcal{C}_1 \cap \mathcal{C}_2$ also satisfy Axioms A and WC.

- Mon: Suppose $A = (V, \Pi)$ and $A' = (V, \Pi')$ are two preference networks considered in Axiom Mon, and $S \subset V$. Then if $\mathcal{C}_1$ and $\mathcal{C}_2$ satisfy Mon, we have $S \in \mathcal{C}_i(A') \Rightarrow S \in \mathcal{C}_i(A)$ for $i \in 1, 2$. Thus, if $S \in \mathcal{C}_1(A') \cap \mathcal{C}_2(A')$ then $S \in \mathcal{C}_1(A) \cap \mathcal{C}_2(A)$, and if $S \in \mathcal{C}_1(A') \cup \mathcal{C}_2(A')$ then $S \in \mathcal{C}_1(A) \cup \mathcal{C}_2(A)$. Thus, both $\mathcal{C}_1 \cup \mathcal{C}_2$ and $\mathcal{C}_1 \cap \mathcal{C}_2$ also satisfy Axioms Mon.

- Emb: If both $\mathcal{C}_1$ and $\mathcal{C}_2$ satisfy Emb, then for any $A = (V, \Pi)$ and any "embedded world" $A' = (V', \Pi')$ such that Π, Π' satisfy the assumption of Axiom Emb, we have $\mathcal{C}_i(A') = \mathcal{C}_i(A) \cap 2^{V'}$ for $i \in \{1, 2\}$. So

$$\begin{aligned}
\mathcal{C}_1(A') \cap \mathcal{C}_2(A') &= \left(\mathcal{C}_1(A) \cap 2^{V'}\right) \cap \left(\mathcal{C}_2(A) \cap 2^{V'}\right) \\
&= (\mathcal{C}_1(A) \cap \mathcal{C}_2(A)) \cap 2^{V'} \\
\mathcal{C}_1(A') \cup \mathcal{C}_2(A') &= \left(\mathcal{C}_1(A) \cap 2^{V'}\right) \cup \left(\mathcal{C}_2(A) \cap 2^{V'}\right) \\
&= (\mathcal{C}_1(A) \cup \mathcal{C}_2(A)) \cap 2^{V'}.
\end{aligned}$$

Thus, both $\mathcal{C}_1 \cup \mathcal{C}_2$ and $\mathcal{C}_1 \cap \mathcal{C}_2$ satisfy Axioms Emb.

Together, this shows that $\forall \mathcal{C}_1, \mathcal{C}_2 \in \mathcal{C}_B, \mathcal{C}_1 \cap \mathcal{C}_2 \in \mathcal{C}_B$ and $\mathcal{C}_1 \cup \mathcal{C}_2 \in \mathcal{C}_B$. Thus, $\mathcal{T}_B = (\mathcal{C}_B, \cup, \cap, \mathcal{C}_{clique}, \mathcal{C}_{all})$ is a lattice with $\mathcal{C}_{all}$ as the lattice's top and $\mathcal{C}_{clique}$ as the lattice's bottom. (4) GS, SA: Assume $\mathcal{C}_1 \in \mathcal{C}$ and $\mathcal{C}_2 \in \mathcal{C}$ satisfy Axioms GS and SA. We can then argue as for Axiom Mon above to show that both $\mathcal{C}_1 \cup \mathcal{C}_2$ and $\mathcal{C}_1 \cap \mathcal{C}_2$ satisfy Axioms GS, SA. Thus, $\mathcal{T} = (\mathcal{C}, \cup, \cap)$ is a lattice. $\square$

3.2 Complexity of Community Rules

The first part of Theorem 3.1 shows that $\mathcal{C}_{comprehensive}$ and $\mathcal{C}_{clique}$, respectively, are the most inclusive and selective axioms-conforming rules. While it is easy to determine whether, for $A = (V, \Pi)$, a subset of V lies in $\mathcal{C}_{clique}(A)$, the rule $\mathcal{C}_{comprehensive}$ turns out to be highly "non-constructive".

THEOREM 3.3   (RICHNESS OF COMPREHENSIVE RULE). *It is* coNP-complete *to determine whether given* $A = (V, \Pi)$, $S \subset V$ *is a member of* $\mathcal{C}_{comprehensive}(A)$.

Before starting the proof, we introduce a notation which we will use throughout this section. Given a preference profile (V, Π) and a non-empty set $S \subset V$, we say that a set $G' \subset V - S$ is a *witness that S is not self-approving*, if S lexicographically prefers G' to S, and we say that a pair $(G, G') \subset S \times (V - S)$ is a *witness that S is not group-stable* if $S - G$ lexicographically prefers G' to G. We say that $G \subset S$ *threatens the stability of S* if there exists a $G' \subset V - S$ such that $S - G$ lexicographically prefers G' to G. Let's first characterize the complexity of Axiom Self-Approval.

THEOREM 3.4. (COMPLEXITY OF SA) *It is* coNP-complete *to determine whether a subset $S \subset V$ is* self-approving *in a given preference network* $A = (V, \Pi)$.

PROOF. We reduce 3-SAT to this decision problem: Suppose $\mathbf{c} = (c_1, \ldots, c_m)$ is a 3-SAT instance with Boolean variables $\mathbf{x} = (x_1, \ldots, x_n)$ (i.e., $c_j = \{u_j, v_j, w_j\} \subset \cup_{i=1}^n \{x_i, \bar{x}_i\}$). We define a preference network as follows:

- $V = A \cup B \cup D \cup X$ has $m + n + m + 2n$ members, where $A = \{a_1, \ldots, a_m\}$, $B = \{b_1, \ldots, b_n\}$, $D = \{d_1, \ldots, d_m\}$, and $X = \{x_1, \ldots, x_n, \bar{x}_1, \ldots, \bar{x}_n\}$. The distinguished subset will be $S = A \cup B$, and for convenience we will denote its complement as $U = D \cup X$.

- Since we will focus on subset S, here we only define the preferences of members in S. The preferences of U can be chosen arbitrarily.

    - Member b_i has preference $D \succ A \succ \{x_i, \bar{x}_i\} \succ \{b_i\} \succ X - \{x_i, \bar{x}_i\} \succ B - \{b_i\}$, where preferences between elements of each set can be chosen arbitrarily.
    - Member a_j has preference $c_j \succ \{a_j\} \succ D \cup X - c_j \succ B \cup A - \{a_j\}$, where again preferences between elements of each set are arbitrary.

Intuitively, members of A are used to enforce clause consistency and members of B are used to enforce variable consistency (no variable can be set to both true and false at the same time). Subsets of X naturally constitute an assignment of the variables, and D provides necessary padding in order to apply Self-Approval. We now show that S is not self-approving if and only if the 3-SAT instance is satisfiable.

In one direction, suppose $Y = \{y_1, \ldots, y_n\}$ where $y_i \in \{x_1, \bar{x}_i\}$ is a satisfying assignment for the 3-SAT instance. Let $G' = Y \cup D$. Consider the bijection, f, where $f(a_j) = d_j$ and $f(b_i) = y_i$. Then for all $s \in S$ and all i, $f(s) \succ_{\pi b_i} s$. All that is left is to find similar bijections for each a_j. First,

note that for a_j all bijections f_j trivially satisfy $f_j(s) \succ_{\pi a_j} s$ where $s \in B \cup A - \{a_j\}$, since this set is ranked at the bottom of π_{a_j}. Thus it is sufficient to show that there exists an element of G' that a_j prefers to itself. This happens so long as one of the literals from its clause is in G', which must be true by the fact that Y is a satisfying assignment. In the other direction, suppose $G' \subset U = D \cup X$ is a witness that S is not self-approving. Note the following:

- $D \subset G'$ otherwise any b_i will have a member of A that cannot be mapped to a more preferred member of G'.

- Let $Y = X \cap G'$. Then $|Y| = n$ by the above fact and the fact that $|G'| = n + m$.

- $\{x_i, \bar{x}_i\} \cap G' \neq \emptyset$ by b_i's preference, and by the pigeonhole principle the literals of Y are consistent (i.e. $\{x_i, \bar{x}_i\} \nsubseteq Y$).

- $c_j \cap Y \neq \emptyset$ by a_j's preferences.

Thus, the variable assignment implied by Y is a satisfying assignment for the 3-SAT instance. $\square$

The following lemma allows us to reduce various complexity results concerning community axioms to Theorem 3.4.

LEMMA 3.5   (PADDING). *Let* $\emptyset \neq S \subset V \subset V'$ *be such that the size of* $\tilde{S} = V' - V$ *is at least* $|S|$, *and let* $S' = S \cup \tilde{S}$. *Then each preference profile Π on V can be mapped onto a preference profile Π' on V' such that*

(i) $S' \in \mathcal{C}_{GS}(V', \Pi') \cap \mathcal{C}_{SA}(V', \Pi') \Leftrightarrow S' \in \mathcal{C}_{GS}(V', \Pi')$.

(ii) $S' \in \mathcal{C}_{GS}(V', \Pi') \Leftrightarrow S \in \mathcal{C}_{SA}(V, \Pi)$.

PROOF. Since $|\tilde{S}| \geq |S|$, we can find a surjective map $g : \tilde{S} \to S$. Given such a map, define Π' arbitrarily, except for the following two constraints:

- If $s \in S$, then π'_s ranks all of $S' = \tilde{S} \cup S$ before anyone in $V - S = V' - S'$;

- If $\tilde{s} \in \tilde{S}$, then $\pi'_{\tilde{s}}$ ranks all of $\tilde{S}$ first, and then gives the rank $\pi'_{\tilde{s}}(v) = |\tilde{S}| + \pi_{g(\tilde{s})}(v)$ to every $v \in V = V' - \tilde{S}$.

Since every $s \in S \subset S'$ ranks all of S' before $V' - S'$, no subset $G' \subset V' - S'$ can be lexicographically preferred by π'_s to a subset of S'. As a consequence, S' is trivially self-approving with respect to Π', proving statement (i). Furthermore, G cannot threaten the stability of S' if $G \subset S'$ is such that $(S' - G) \cap S \neq \emptyset$. If $G \subset S'$ threatens the stability of S', we therefore must have that $G \supset S$. On the other hand, if $G \supsetneq S$, then G contains an element $\tilde{s} \in \tilde{S}$ which means that no set G' can be lexicographically preferred G, since all elements of S' prefer all of $\tilde{S}$ to anyone in $V' - S'$.

Thus G can only threaten the stability of S' if $G = S$. In other words, $S' \notin \mathcal{C}_{GS}(\Pi')$ if and only if there exists $G' \subset V' - S'$ such that for all $\tilde{s} \in \tilde{S} = S' - G$, G' is lexicographically preferred to S with respect to $\pi'_{\tilde{s}} = \pi_{g(\tilde{s})}$. Since by assumption, the image of $\tilde{S}$ under g is all of S, this is equivalent to the statement that for all $s \in S$, G' is lexicographically preferred to S with respect to π_s, which is the condition that G' is a witness to $S \notin \mathcal{C}_{SA}(\Pi)$, proving statement (ii). $\square$

Given this lemma, both the next theorem and Theorem 3.3 are immediate consequences of Theorem 3.4.

THEOREM 3.6. (COMPLEXITY OF GS) *It is* coNP-complete *to determine whether a subset $S \subset V$ is* group-stable *in a given preference network* $A = (V, \Pi)$.

3.3 Paths up the Taxonomy Lattice

The Intersection Lemma provides us with a tool for exploring the taxonomy of community rules. Together with Theorem 3.1, it gives us the following scheme to map an arbitrary community rule, $\mathcal{C}$, to an axiom-conforming community rule: First take the unique smallest (with respect to the lattice $\mathcal{T}_B$) rule $\bar{\mathcal{C}}$ that contains $\mathcal{C}$ and satisfies all axioms besides SA and GS. Then, remove all communities which are not both self-approving and group stable. In other words, the map is: $\mathcal{C} \longmapsto \bar{\mathcal{C}} \cap \mathcal{C}_{SA} \cap \mathcal{C}_{GS}$. By moving up lattice $\mathcal{T}_B$, we can apply the Intersection Lemma to define more inclusive axiom-conforming community rules. We now give two example paths up taxonomy lattice, and state their algorthmic and complexity consequences.

RULE 5. (RELAXED CLIQUE RULE: $\mathcal{C}_{Clique(g)}$) *For a non-negative function* $g : \mathbb{N} \to \mathbb{N} \cup \{0\}$, *a non-empty subset* $S \subseteq V$ *is a community in* $A = (V, \Pi)$ *if and only if* $\forall u, s \in S$, $\pi_s(u) \in [1 : |S| + g(|S|)]$.

$\mathcal{C}_{Clique(g)} \in \mathcal{C}_B$ and hence $(\mathcal{C}_{Clique(g)} \cap \mathcal{C}_{GS} \cap \mathcal{C}_{SA})$ satisfies all axioms. As g varies from 0 to ∞, $\mathcal{C}_{Clique(g)}$ moves up the lattice $\mathcal{T}_B$ from $\mathcal{C}_{clique}$ to $\mathcal{C}_{all}$. The intersection with $\mathcal{C}_{SA} \cap \mathcal{C}_{GS}$ provides a "vertical" glimpse of the taxonomy lattice $\mathcal{T}$. In particular, as the community rules along this vertical path become more inclusive (when g increases), they become less constructive for community identification.

PROPOSITION 3.7. *Given a preference network* $A = (V, \Pi)$ *and a subset* $S \subseteq V$, *we can determine in* $O(2^g |S|^{g+3})$ *time whether or not* $S \in (\mathcal{C}_{Clique(g)} \cap \mathcal{C}_{GS} \cap \mathcal{C}_{SA})(A)$. *Particularly, if* $g = \Theta(1)$, *then this decision problem is in P. However, the decision problem is co-NP complete for* $g = |S|^\delta$ *for any constant* $\delta \in (0, 1]$.

RULE 6. (HARMONIOUS PATH: $\mathcal{C}_{harmonious(\lambda)}$) *For* $\lambda \in [0 : 1]$, *a non-empty subset* S *is a* λ-*harmonious community in* $A = (V, \Pi)$ *if* $\forall u \in S, v \in V - S$, *at least* λ-*fraction of* $\{\pi_s : s \in S\}$ *prefer* u *over* v.

$\mathcal{C}_{harmonious(\lambda)} \in \mathcal{C}_B$. Thus, $\mathcal{C}_{harmonious(\lambda)} \cap \mathcal{C}_{GS} \cap \mathcal{C}_{SA}$ satisfies all axioms, Therefore, as λ varies from 1 to 0, the community function $\mathcal{C}_{harmonious(\lambda)}$ moves up the lattice $\mathcal{T}_B$ from $\mathcal{C}_{harmonious(1)} = \mathcal{C}_{clique}$ to $\mathcal{C}_{harmonious(0)} = \mathcal{C}_{all}$.

PROPOSITION 3.8. *Given* $A = (V, \Pi)$ *and a subset* $S \subseteq V$, *we can determine whether* $S \in (\mathcal{C}_{harmonious(\lambda)} \cap \mathcal{C}_{GS} \cap \mathcal{C}_{SA})(A)$ *in polynomial time, if* $(1 - \lambda)|S| < 2$, *while it is co-NP complete to answer this question if* $(1 - \lambda)|S| \geq 16$.

3.4 Number of Potential Communities

PROPOSITION 3.9. *Assume that* $n \geq 8$. *There exists a preference network* A *such that* $\mathcal{C}_{comprehensive}(A) \geq 2^{n/2}$.

PROOF. The preference profile, $\Pi_{H\&S}$, that is about to be described has been dubbed the "hero and sidekick" example as will soon become clear. Consider a world composed of $n/2$ hero-sidekick duos. Each member of a hero-sidekick duo first prefers the hero of that duo then the sidekick of the duo, then all other heroes, followed lastly by all other sidekicks (in some fixed but arbitrary order). Now consider a subset, S, that is composed of all heroes and an arbitrary set of sidekicks. Note that because there are $2^{n/2}$ different sets of sidekicks, it is sufficient to show that S is a community in

$\mathcal{C}_{comprehensive}([n], \Pi_{H\&S})$. First, note that S clearly satisfies SA. To show that S satisfies GS, consider two sets $G \subset S$ and $G' \subset V - S$ of equal size. We first note that it will be enough to consider the case where $(S - G) \times G$ contains no hero-sidekick pair (u, v), since otherwise u would prefer v over everyone else, in particular over everyone in G'. Applying this to the sidekicks in G, we conclude that G must contain at least as many heros as sidekicks. On the other hand, G' can't be lexicographically preferred to G if G contains at least two heros, showing that only two cases are possible: G consisting of a hero-sidekick pair, or G made up of just a single hero. But neither one leads to a counterexample if $|S - G| > |G| = |G'|$, since then we can find an $s \in S - G$ which is not the partner of any sidekick in G', which means that s prefers the hero in G to everyone in G'. Since S contains all heros by assumption, we see that S is group stable as soon as $n \geq 8$. $\square$

4. FIXED-POINT RULES AND LIMITATION OF SOCIAL-CHOICE AGGREGATION

We now examine aggregation functions and their community rules through the lens of our axiomatic framework. We prove two *impossibility results* which may help to shed light on the limitations of defining community rules solely based on preference aggregation.

4.1 Social Choice Axioms and Implications for Fixed-Point Community Rules

We first review the basic axioms from the traditional social choice theory [2]. To this end, we begin by formally defining the set, $\overline{L(V)}$, of preferences with ties (or indifference) as the set of all maps $\pi : V \to \{1, \ldots, |V|\}$ such that whenever k elements $v_1, \ldots, v_k$ have the same rank $\pi(v_1) = \cdots = \pi(v_k)$, then we skip the ranks $\pi(v_k) + 1, \ldots, \pi(v_k) + k - 1$. So for example, if 3 elements are tied at rank 2, the next rank in the image of π will be 5. $\overline{L(V)}$ is also known as the *ordered partition* of V. We also need the notion of an election, which will be defined as a triple (V, F, S) where V and S are finite sets (called the set of candidates and voters, respectively), and $F : L(V)^* \to \overline{L(V)}$ is a preference aggregation function.

SOCIAL CHOICE AXIOM 1 (Unanimity (U)). *An election* (V, F, S) *satisfies* Unanimity *if, for all preference profiles,* $\Pi_S = \{\pi_s : s \in S\} \in L(V)^S$ *and all pairs of candidates,* $\{i, j\} \subseteq V$, $\pi_s(i) > \pi_s(j), \forall s \in S \implies F(\Pi_S)(i) > F(\Pi_S)(j)$.

The question then is: what properties capture the intuition behind Unanimity and how do they relate to this social choice axiom? To answer this, we define the following two properties:

PROPERTY 1 (Pareto Efficiency (PE)). *A community function,* $\mathcal{C}$, *is* Pareto Efficient *if, given* $A \in \mathcal{A}$ *and* $S \in \mathcal{C}(A)$, *for all* $u \in S$, $v \notin S$, *there is a* $s \in S$ *such that* $u \succ_{\pi_s} v$.

PROPERTY 2 (Clique (Cq)). *A community function* $\mathcal{C}$ *satisfies the* Clique *Property if for all* $A \in \mathcal{A}$, $u \succ_{\pi_s} v, \forall u, s \in S, \forall v \notin S \implies S \in \mathcal{C}(A)$.

Property Pareto Efficiency is a negative property that states that subsets in which a non-member is preferred to a member by everyone inside the subset should not be a community. In contrast, Clique is a positive property that states that a completely self-loving group (i.e., a clique) must be a community. It turns out that both of these properties are implied by Unanimity, and that the second is implied by the Axioms World Community and Embedding.

PROPOSITION 4.1. *Fix V and a preference aggregation function F, and let $\mathcal{C}_F$ be the fixed point rule with respect to F. If all elections (V, F, S) with $S \subsetneq V$ satisfies Unanimity, then $\mathcal{C}_F$ satisfies the properties Pareto Efficiency and Clique.*

PROPOSITION 4.2. *Let $\mathcal{C}$ be a community rule that satisfies the World Community and Embedding Axioms. Then $\mathcal{C}$ must also satisfy the Clique Property.*

SOCIAL CHOICE AXIOM 2 (Non-Dictatorship (ND)). *An election (V, S, F) is Non-Dictatorial if there exists no dictator, i.e., no voter $i \in S$ such that $F(\Pi_S) = \pi_i$ for all preference profiles $\Pi_S \in L(V)^S$.*

Instead of showing properties implied by ND as we did with Unanimity, we do the inverse, and show that a dictatorship violates some of our axioms.

PROPOSITION 4.3. *Fix V and a preference aggregation function F. If $\mathcal{C}_F$, the fixed point rule with respect to F, satisfies Group Stability or Anonymity, then all elections (V, F, S) with $S \subset V$ and $1 < |S| < |V|$ satisfy Non-Dictatorship.*

SOCIAL CHOICE AXIOM 3. (Independence of Irrelevant Alternatives) *An election (V, F, S) satisfies Independence of Irrelevant Alternatives (IIA) if, for all preference profiles, Π_S and $\Pi'_S \in L(V)^S$ and all candidates $a, b \in V$, we have that*

$$\left(\forall s \in S, a \succ_{\pi_s} b \Leftrightarrow a \succ_{\pi'_s} b \right) \implies \left(a \succ_{F(\Pi_S)} b \Leftrightarrow a \succ_{F(\Pi'_S)} b \right).$$

This axiom can reasonably be considered the strongest of the three, in that it says that the aggregate preference between two candidates does not depend on the preferences voters have between either of the two and some other candidate. Arrow's celebrated impossibility result immediately leads to impossibility results in our settings, showing in particular that Independence of Irrelevant Alternatives for the aggregation function is inconsistent with at least one of Axioms 3, 4, or 6.

THEOREM 4.4. (IMPOSSIBILITY OF FIXED-POINT RULE WITH IIA AGGREGATION) *Let F be an aggregation function such that the fixed point rule with respect to F satisfies the Clique Property and the Group Stability Axiom. Then no election (V, F, S) with $S \subseteq V$ and $1 < |S| < |V|$ satisfies IIA.*

PROOF. Let $S \subseteq V$ such that $1 < |S| < |V|$. Assume that the election (V, F, S) satisfies IIA, and the resulting fixed point rule $\mathcal{C}_F$ satisfies Cq and GS. We will first show that the election (V, F, S) must satisfy Unanimity. In the following preference profiles, Π, Π', $\Pi'' \in L(V)^S$, we assume that every member of S has the same preference, π, π', and π'' respectively. First, let π rank all members of S above non-members. By the Clique Property, $S \in \mathcal{C}_F(V, \Pi)$ and thus

$$\forall s \in S, v \notin S, s \succ_{F(\Pi)} v. \tag{4}$$

Thus, by IIA, if $s \in S$ is unanimously preferred to $v \notin S$, s must be strictly preferred to v in the aggregate preference. Now let π' be the same as π only with the least preferred member of S, s', and the most preferred non-member, v',

switched in rank. By the partial Unanimity property (4), in the aggregate $F(\Pi')$, all members of $S - \{s'\}$ are preferred to all $v \notin S$, and all members of S are preferred to all $v \in V - S - \{s'\}$. But, by GS, $S \notin \mathcal{C}_F(\Pi')$, which is only possible is if $v' \succeq_{F(\Pi')} s'$. Applying the partial Unanimity property once more yields the following two statements:

$$\forall s \in S - \{s'\}, s \succ_{F(\Pi')} s' \quad \text{and} \quad \forall v \notin S \cup \{v'\}, v' \succ_{F(\Pi')} v,$$

and by IIA, this in turn implies

$$\forall s \in S - \{s'\}, s \succ_{F(\Pi)} s' \quad \text{and} \quad \forall v \notin S \cup \{v'\}, v' \succ_{F(\Pi)} v. \tag{5}$$

By IIA, this means that for any two members or two non-members, if one is unanimously preferred to the other, then it must be strictly preferred in aggregate preference. Indeed, consider, e.g., $s, s' \in S$ and a profile $\tilde{\Pi}_S$ such that $s \succ_{\tilde{\pi}_i} s'$ for all $i \in S$. Choose Π in such a way that every member has the same profile, s' has rank $|S|$ and $s \succ_{\pi_i} s'$ for all $i \in S$. By IIA, $s \succ_{F(\tilde{\Pi})} s' \Longleftrightarrow s \succ_{F(\Pi)} s'$, so by (5), s is preferred to s' in aggregate.

Finally, consider π'' where v' is switched with the second lowest ranked member, s''. By the above additional partial Unanimity property, s' must be strictly preferred to s'' in the aggregation $F(\Pi'')$, and thus v' must be strictly rather than weakly preferred to s'' in the aggregate preference. Again by IIA, if a non-member, $v \notin S$, is unanimously preferred to a member $s \in S$, v must be strictly preferred to s in the aggregate preference. Taken together, these three partial Unanimity properties constitute Unanimity. Since the election (V, F, S) satisfies both IIA and Unanimity, by Arrow's Impossibility Theorem [2], it must be a dictatorship, contradicting Proposition 4.3. $\square$

4.2 Weighted-Aggregations and Limitations of Their Fixed-Point Rules

There are many preference aggregation functions satisfying the other two standard axioms of social choice theory, Unanimity and Non-Dictatorship, e.g., the well-known Borda count [27]. Moreover, there are many interesting fixed point rules generalizing Borda count, several of which can be cast as *weighted voting schemes* as follows: Let $W = (w^1, w^2, \dots)$ be a sequence of weight vectors $w^i \in \mathbb{R}^V$. For $\Pi_S \in L(V)^*$, we then define the aggregate preference $F_W(\Pi_S)$ on V by

$$i \succ_{F(\Pi_s)} j \quad \Longleftrightarrow \quad \sum_{s \in S} w^{|S|}_{\pi_s(i)} > \sum_{s \in S} w^{|S|}_{\pi_s(j)}.$$

For Borda count, $w^k = (|V|, |V| - 1, \dots, 1) \; \forall k$, and for the $\mathcal{C}_{democratic}$ rule of [3], w^k consists of k ones followed by $(|V| - k)$ zeros, implying that every voter has to choose k candidates, with all votes counting equally.

DEFINITION 4.5 (WEIGHTED FIXED POINT RULE). *For a sequence of vectors $W = (w^1, w^2, \dots)$ in $\mathbb{R}^n$, $\mathcal{C}_W$ is the fixed point rule with respect to F_W.*

PROPOSITION 4.6. *All weighted fixed-point rules satisfy Axiom Anonymity. They satisfy Property Clique iff $\forall k \in [n-1]$ the vector w^k is such that $w^k_i > w^k_j$ for $i \leq k$ and $j > k$.*

While weighted fixed-pointed rules are natural from a social choice viewpoint, it turns out that they are again incompatible with at least one of Axioms 3, 4, or 6. We first note that $\mathcal{C}_{democratic}$ violates both Axioms Mon and GS.

THEOREM 4.7. $\mathcal{C}_{democratic}$ *does not satisfy Axioms* Monotonicity *or* Group Stability. *It satisfies all other axioms, as well as Properties* Pareto Efficiency *and* Clique.

PROOF. From its voting function ϕ_S^Π, $\mathcal{C}_{democratic}$ satisfies Axioms A, WC, Emb, and Properties PE and Cq. Suppose $\mathcal{C}_{democratic}$ does not satisfy SA. Then, there exists a preference network $A = (V, \Pi)$, $S \in \mathcal{C}_{democratic}(A)$, $T \subseteq V - S$, and a tuple of bijections $(f_s : S \to T)$ that for all $s, u \in S$, $u \prec_{\pi_s} f_s(u)$. It follows that $\forall s \in S$, the numbers of votes cast by s for S according to ϕ_S^Π is less than the numbers of votes that s casts for T. Summing up the votes from S, the average votes that members of T receive is larger than the average votes that members of S receive, contradicting the assumption that everyone in S receives more votes than everyone in T. Thus, $\mathcal{C}_{democratic}$ satisfies SA.

Let $V = [1:6]$, $S = [1:3]$, let $\Pi = (\pi_1, ..., \pi_6)$ be the preference profile

$$\pi_1 = [142356], \quad \pi_2 = [253416], \quad \pi_3 = [631425]$$
$$\pi_4 = [456123], \quad \pi_5 = [156423], \quad \pi_6 = [165423]$$

and let Π' be the preference profile

$$\pi_1' = [142356], \quad \pi_2' = [234516], \pi_3' = [314625]$$
$$\pi_4' = \pi_4, \quad \pi_5' = \pi_5, \quad \pi_6' = \pi_6.$$

Then $S = [1:3] \in \mathcal{C}_{democratic}(V, \Pi)$, as each members of S receives two votes while everyone in $[4:6]$ receives only one vote. However, in violation of Axiom Mon, S is no longer a $\mathcal{C}_{democratic}$ community w.r.t Π', since 4 now receives three votes, one more than 1, 2 and 3.

Note also $T = (1, 5, 6) \in \mathcal{C}_{democratic}(V, \Pi)$. Let $G = \{5, 6\} \subset T$ and $G' = (2, 4) \subset V - T$. As member 1 prefers 2 to 5 and 4 to 6, T does not satisfy Group Stability. □

The violation of the monotonicity axiom was initially surprising and rather counterintuitive to us, and indeed motivated some of the research in this paper. This violation is illustrative of the subtlety of community rules. It leads us to the following general impossibility result, which together with Theorem 4.4, illustrates some basic limitations of fixed-point community rules.

THEOREM 4.8. (IMPOSSIBILITY OF WEIGHTED AGGREGATION SCHEMA) *Weighted Fixed Point Rules are inconsistent with either the* Group Stability *or the* Clique *Property.*

PROOF. Let $A = (V, \Pi)$ be a preference network, $S \subset V$, and $\mathcal{C}_W$ a weighted fixed point rule satisfying the the Clique Property. Throughout the the proof, we will take

$$V = \{a, b, c, d, e\} \quad \text{and} \quad S = \{a, b, c\},$$

and consider preference profiles such that S violates Group Stability. In order for $\mathcal{C}_W$ to obey the Axiom GS, we would need the weight vector $w^3 \in \mathbb{R}^5$ to be such that $S \notin \mathcal{C}(V, \Pi)$ for all Π considered in this proof. Our goal is to show that this will lead to a contradiction. We start under the assumption that the weights are decreasing, i.e., in addition to the already established fact that $w_i^3 > w_j^3$ when $i = 1, 2, 3$ and $j = 4, 5$ (since $\mathcal{C}_W$ satisfies the the Clique Property), we first assume that $w_1^3 \geq w_2^3 \geq w_3^3$ and $w_4^3 \geq w_5^3$.

Consider the following scenario: $\pi_a = [adebc]$, $\pi_b = \pi_c = [abcde]$. Since a prefers d and e over b and c, S is not group stable and cannot be a community. By our assumption that $w_1^3 \geq w_2^3 \geq w_2^3 > w_4^3 \geq w_4^3$, we have that $a \succ_{F_W(\Pi_S)}$

$b \succeq_{F_W(\Pi_s)} c \succ_{F_W(\Pi_S)} e$ and $b \succ_{F_W(\Pi_S)} d$. Thus, the only way S cannot be a community is that $d \succeq_{F_W(\Pi_S)} c$, i.e., $w_2^3 + 2w_4^3 \geq 2w_3^3 + w_5$. This implies that we cannot have both $w_2^3 = w_3^3$ and $w_4^3 = w_5^3$.

Now consider a modified preference profile: $\pi_a' = \pi_b' = [abdce]$, $\pi_c' = [caebd]$. In this profile a and b prefer d over c, so again S violates GS and hence cannot be a community. On the other hand, we now have $a \succ_{F_W(\Pi_S')} b$, $b \succeq_{F_W(\Pi_S')} d \succ_{F_W(\Pi_S')} e$. Thus we must have either $b \sim_{F_W(\Pi')} d$ or $d \succeq_{F_W(\Pi_S')} c$. The former, however, implies $w_2^3 = w_3^3$ and $w_4^3 = w_5^3$ and is hence a contradiction. Therefore the latter must be true which implies $2w_3^3 + w_5^3 \geq w_1^3 + 2w_4^3$.

This brings us to the final preference profile:

$$\pi_a'' = [abdce], \quad \pi_b'' = [dcabe], \quad \pi_c'' = [cbaed].$$

Again a and b prefer d to c, so the profile violates GS, and hence again can't be a community. Now $a \succ_{F_W(\Pi'')} c \succeq_{F_W(\Pi'')} b$ and $d \succ_{F_W(\Pi'')} e$, showing that for S not to be a community, we must have $d \succeq_{F_W(\Pi'')} b$, which gives $w_1^3 + w_3^3 + w_5^3 \geq 2w_2^3 + w_4^3$.

Defining $d_i = w_i^3 - w_{i-1}^3$, we can write the bounds obtained so far as (1) $d_4 \leq d_3 + d_5$, (2) $d_2 + d_3 + d_5 \leq d_4$, (3) $d_3 + d_4 + d_5 \leq d_2$. Chaining up these three bounds, we get

$$d_3 + d_5 \geq d_4 \geq d_2 + d_3 + d_5$$
$$\geq d_3 + d_4 + d_5 + d_3 + d_5 = 2(d_3 + d_5) + d_4,$$

contradicting our assumption $d_i \geq 0$ and the fact that Cq implies $d_4 > 0$.

To relax the constraint that the weights are ordered, we observe that all three profiles in the proof are such that, under arbitrary permutations of the first three and the last two positions, S still violates GS: for any permutation σ of $[1:5]$ that leaves $[1:3]$ and $[4:5]$ invariant, S violates GS under the profiles $\{\sigma \circ \pi_s\}_{s \in S}$, $\{\sigma' \circ \pi_s\}_{s \in S}$, and $\{\sigma'' \circ \pi_s\}_{s \in S}$. Choosing the permutation such that $\tilde{w}_i^3 = w_{\sigma(i)}^3$ are ordered, we obtain the above three inequalities for the weights $\tilde{w}_i^3$, leading again to a contradiction. □

4.3 Harmonious Communities

We will close this section with a discussion of the harmonious community rule, $\mathcal{C}_{harmonious}$, of Section 1. First, we prove $\mathcal{C}_{harmonious}$ is a fixed-point rule associated with a topologically defined aggregation function.

PROPOSITION 4.9. *There exists a preference aggregation function* $F_\mathcal{H} : L(V)^* \to \overline{L(V)}$ *such that defines* $\mathcal{C}_{harmonious}$.

PROOF. Given V, a finite set S, and a preference profile $\Pi_S \in L(V)^S$, we consider the following directed graph $G_{\Pi_S} = (V, E_{\Pi_S})$ where $(i, j) \in E_{\Pi_S}$ if at least half of S prefers i to j. Note that if $|S|$ is an odd number, then G_{Π_S} is a *tournament graph*. If $|S|$ is an even number, then E_{Π_S} contains both (i, j) and (j, i) if exactly half of Π_S prefer i to j. G_{Π_S} is *total* since for all $i, j \in V$, either $(i, j) \in E_{\Pi_S}$ or $(j, i) \in E_{\Pi_S}$. Because G_{Π_S} is total, the graph $\hat{G}_{\Pi_s}$ obtained from G_{Π_S} by contracting each strongly connected component into a single vertex is an *acyclic*, tournament graph. Thus, the graph $\hat{G}_{\Pi_s}$ has exactly one Hamiltonian path that totally orders its vertices. Let $(V_1, ..., V_t)$ be the strongly connected components of G_{Π_S}, sorted by the order determined by the Hamiltonian path. The partition $(V_1, ..., V_t)$ of V then defines an ordered partition $F_\mathcal{H}(\Pi_S)$, with $V_i \succ_{F_\mathcal{H}(\Pi_S)} V_j$ iff $i \leq j$.

Next, we consider a subset $T \subset V$. It is then easy to check that if T is of the form $T = \cup_{j \leq i} V_j$ for some $i \in [1 : t]$, then for all $u \in T, v \in V - T$, a majority of S prefers u to v, and vice versa. Specializing to $S = T$, we see that $\mathcal{C}_{harmonious}$ is defined by the preference aggregation function $F_{\mathcal{H}}$. □

THEOREM 4.10. $\mathcal{C}_{harmonious}$ satisfies Axioms 1-5. but it does not satisfy GS.

PROOF. One easily establish that $\mathcal{C}_{harmonious}$ satisfies Axioms A, Mon, Emb and WC. We will now prove that $\mathcal{C}_{harmonious}$ satisfies SA: If $S \in \mathcal{C}_{harmonious}(A)$ does not satisfy SA, then there exists a $T \subset V - S$ of the same size as S such that each $s \in S$ lexicographically prefers T over S. This implies that, for each $s \in S$, there are at least $(1 + 2 + \cdots + |S|)$ pairs $(u, v) \in S \times T$ such that s prefers v over u. Thus the number of triples (s, u, v) such that $s \in S$ prefers $v \in T$ over $u \in S$ is at least $|S|^2(|S| + 1)/2$. However, $S \in \mathcal{C}_{harmonious}(A)$ implies that this number has to be strictly smaller than $|S|^3/2$. The set T in the proof of Theorem 4.7 is also an example that $\mathcal{C}_{harmonious}$ violates Axiom GS. □

While $\mathcal{C}_{harmonious}$ does not satisfy the GS Axiom, it satisfies the following weaker property.

PROPERTY 3. Weak Group Stability   *For all preference profiles Π on V and all $S \in \mathcal{C}(V, \Pi)$, S is weakly group stable. Here a set $S \subset V$ is called weakly group stable if for all $G \subset S$, $G' \subset V - S$ s.t. $0 < |G| = |G'| \leq |S|/2$, and all bijections $(f : G \to G', i \in S - G)$ there exists $s \in S - G$, $u \in G$ such that $u \succ_{\pi_s} f(u)$.*

Note that the property is weaker than the GS Axiom in two ways: we restrict ourselves to groups G of size at most $|S|/2$, and we only allow for a global bijection f, rather than individual bijections f_s.

PROPOSITION 4.11. $\mathcal{C}_{harmonious}$ *is* weakly group stable, *while* $\mathcal{C}_{democratic}$ *and* $\mathcal{C}_{Borda}$ *are not.*

PROOF. Consider a set $S \in \mathcal{C}_{harmonious}(V, \Pi)$, subsets $G \subset S$ and $G' \subset V - S$ such that $0 < |G| = |G'| \leq |S|/2$, and a bijection $f : G \to G'$. For each $u \in G$ the majority of S prefer u to $f(u)$ (who is not a member of S), and since $|G| \leq |S|/2$, this implies that there must be at least one $s \in S - G$ such that s prefers u to $f(u)$, as required.

To give a counterexample for both $\mathcal{C}_{democratic}$ and $\mathcal{C}_{Borda}$, consider $V = [1 : 6]$, $G = [3 : 4]$ and $G' = [5 : 6]$, with preference profiles

$$\pi_1 = [125463], \pi_2 = [126354], \pi_3 = [341256], \pi_4 = [341256].$$

Then 1 and 2 prefer 5 over 4, and 6 over 3, but S is a community both with respect to $\mathcal{C}_{democratic}$ (where 1 and 2 get four votes, 3 and 4 get three votes, and 5 and 6 get only one vote), and with respect to Borda count (with counts $20, 16, 18, 16, 10, 8$ for $1, \ldots, 6$, respectively). □

We will now compare fixed-point community rules based on the three aggregation functions that we have discussed so far: Borda voting, democratic voting, and $F_{\mathcal{H}}$. While all three have their own appealing simplicity and intuition, and all satisfy Axioms A, SA, Emb, and WC, they have significant differences with respect to Axioms Mon and GS, and the Outsider Departure property. (1) Outsider Departure: A harmonious community S remains a harmonious community when any outsider $v \notin S$ leaves the system, since the

departure does not alter any pairwise preferences. However, for a $\mathcal{C}_{democratic}$ or $\mathcal{C}_{Borda}$ community S, the departure of an outsider can increase the votes for other outsiders to destabilize the community. (2) Monotonicity: The harmonious rule satisfies Axiom Mon. The other two only satisfy the weaker Outsider Respecting Monotonicity property[3]. (3) Group Stability: The subset T in the proof of Theorem 4.7 is a community according to all these three community rules. But T violates GS because 1 prefers outsiders over 5 and 6, even though 5 and 6 prefer 1 over everyone else: Element 1 is an *"arrogant"* member of its community. All aggregation functions satisfying Unanimity seem to be prone to existence of "arrogant" members. The harmonious rule satisfies the stability of majority subgroup under a global bijection f. $\mathcal{C}_{democratic}$ and $\mathcal{C}_{Borda}$ essentially have no guarantee on group stability. (4) Small World: We say a community function $\mathcal{C}$ satisfies the Small World property if

$$S \in \mathcal{C}((V, \Pi)) \text{ if and only if } S \in \mathcal{C}(S \cup U, \Pi|_{S \cup U}),$$
$$\forall U \subseteq V - S, |U| < |S|.$$

This Helly-type property [7] localizes the identification of a community. Note that the Small World property includes some form of Outsider Departure together with the property that every community is "locally" verifiable. One can easily show that $\mathcal{C}_{democratic}$ and $\mathcal{C}_{Borda}$ do not have the Small World property, while $\mathcal{C}_{harmonious}$ enjoys the following stronger variant of the small world property

$$S \in \mathcal{C}_{harmonious}((V, \Pi)) \text{ if and only if } \forall v \in V - S,$$
$$S \in \mathcal{C}_{harmonious}(S \cup \{v\}, \Pi|_{S \cup \{v\}}).$$

4.4   Stability of Communities

In real-world social interactions, some communities are more stable or durable than others, when people's interests and preferences evolve over time. For example, some music bands stay together longer than others. We consider the following stability model that is inspired by the work of Balcan *et al.* [3] and Mishra *et al.* [14].

DEFINITION 4.12. (PREFERENCE PERTURBATIONS) *Let $\mathcal{C}$ be a community rule and $A = (V, \Pi)$ be a preference network. For $\delta \in (0, 1)$, we say a community $S \in \mathcal{C}(A)$ is stable under δ-perturbations if $S \in \mathcal{C}((V, \Pi'))$ for all preference profiles Π' such that $|\{i \in S : \pi_i(v) \neq \pi_i'(v)\}| \leq \delta|S|, \forall v \in V$.*

In other words, stable communities remain communities even after some changes to their members' preferences.

Both the community rule $\mathcal{C}$ and stability parameter δ can impact community structures. The main result of Balcan *et al.* [3] can be restated as:

THEOREM 4.13. ([3]) *For $\delta \in (0, 1)$, every preference network $A = (V, \Pi)$ has $n^{O(\log(1/\delta)/\delta)}$ democratic communities, that are stable under δ-perturbations of Π.*

Definition 4.12 can be directly applied to $\mathcal{C}_{harmonious}$, which is connected with the following natural notion of robust harmonious communities: For $\delta \in [0 : 1/2]$, a nonempty subset S is a $(\delta + 1/2)$-*harmonious community* in $A = (V, \Pi)$ if $\forall u \in S, v \in V - S$, at least $(1/2 + \delta)$-fraction of $\{\pi_s : s \in S\}$ prefer u over v.

---

[3]Again, we can use the profiles from the proof of Theorem 4.7 to show that the Borda count rule does not satisfy Mon.

PROPOSITION 4.14. *For any $\delta \in [0:1/2)$, and preference network A, every $(1/2 + \delta)$-harmonious community is stable under $\delta/2$-perturbations. Conversely, any community in $\mathcal{C}_{harmonious}$ that is stable under δ perturbations is a $(1/2+\delta)$-harmonious community.*

Using a simple probabilistic argument, we can establish the following bound:

THEOREM 4.15. *For any $\delta \in [0:1/2)$, the number of δ-stable harmonious communities in any preference network is at most $n^{12 \log n/\delta^2}$.*

PROOF. Let S be a δ-stable harmonious communities. For any multi-set $T \subseteq S$, we say T *identifies* S if for all $u \in S$ and $v \in V - S$, the majority of T prefer u to v. Note that such a T determines S once the size of S is set. To see this, note that the condition implies that $u \succ_{F(\Pi_T)} v$ for all $(u,v) \in S \times (V - S)$, which in turn implies that S is of the form $V_1 \cup \cdots \cup V_i$ where $(V_1, V_2, \ldots)$ are the components of the ordered partition $F(\Pi_T)$, ordered in such a way that $V_1 \succ_{F(\Pi_T)} V_2, \ldots$ (see Proposition 4.9 and its proof). Thus once $F(\Pi_T)$ and the size of S are fixed, S is uniquely determined.

We now show that $\exists T \subset V$ of size $12 \log n/\delta^2$ that identifies S. To this end, we consider a sample $T \subset S$ of $k = 12 \log n/\delta^2$ randomly chosen elements (with replacements). We analyze the probability that T identifies S. Let $T = \{t_1, \ldots, t_k\}$, and for each $u \in S$ and $v \in V - S$, let $x_i^{(u,v)} = [u \succ_{\pi_{t_i}} v]$, where $[B]$ denotes the indicator varable of an event B. Then T identifies S iff $\sum_{i=1}^{k} x_i^{(u,v)} > k/2, \forall u \in S, v \in V - S$. We now focus on a particular (u,v) pair and bound $\Pr\left[\sum_{i=1}^{k} x_i^{(u,v)} \leq k/2\right]$. We first note that

$$\mathbf{E}\left[\sum_{i=1}^{k} x_i^{(u,v)}\right] = \sum_{i=1}^{k} \mathbf{E}\left[x_i^{(u,v)}\right] \geq \left(\frac{1}{2} + \delta\right) \cdot k.$$

By a standard use of the Chernoff-Hoeffding bound

$$\Pr\left[\sum_{i=1}^{k} x_i^{(u,v)} \leq k/2\right]$$
$$\leq \Pr\left[\sum_{i=1}^{k} x_i^{(u,v)} \leq (1+2\delta)^{-1}\mathbf{E}\left[\sum_{i=1}^{k} x_i^{(u,v)}\right]\right]$$
$$\leq \Pr\left[\sum_{i=1}^{k} x_i^{(u,v)} \leq (1-\delta)\mathbf{E}\left[\sum_{i=1}^{k} x_i^{(u,v)}\right]\right]$$
$$\leq e^{-\frac{\delta^2}{2}(1/2+\delta)k} \leq e^{-\frac{\delta^2}{4}k} \leq \frac{1}{n^3},$$

where we used that $(1+2\delta)^{-1} \leq 1-\delta$ in the third step. If T fails to identify S, then there exists $(u \in S, v \in V - S)$ such that $\sum_{i=1}^{k} x_i^{(u,v)} \leq k/2$. As there are at most $|S||V-S| \leq n^2$ such (u,v) pairs to consider, by the union bound,

$$\Pr\left[T \text{ identifies } S\right] \geq 1 - \sum_{u \in S, v \in V-S} \Pr\left[\sum_{i=1}^{k} x_i^{(u,v)} \leq k/2\right]$$
$$> 1 - 1/n > 0.$$

Thus, if S is a δ-stable harmonious communities, then there exists a multi-set $T \subset V$ of size $12 \log n/\delta^2$ that identifies S. We can thus enumerate all δ-stable harmonious communities by enumerating all (T, t) pairs, where T ranges from all multi-subsets of V of size $12 \log n/\delta^2$ and $t \in [1:n]$ and check if T can identify a set of size t. $\square$

5. REMARKS

Our work can be partially applied to other network models. With simple modifications to our axioms, we can extend results of this paper to preference networks that allow *indifferences*. In other words, each preference network $A = (V, \Pi)$ is now given by n ordered partitions $\pi_1, \ldots, \pi_n \in \overline{L(V)}$. By allowing indifference, we can partially apply our results to practical social networks, where community identification is posted as the problem of detecting communities in an observed social network, $G = (V, E)$, which is usually sparse. To apply our framework, we first define an affinity network $(V, [\mathbf{w}_1, \ldots, \mathbf{w}_n])$, where $\mathbf{w}_v$ is the personalized PageRank vector of vertex v [11]. We then obtain a preference network $A_G = (V, \Pi)$: For each $v \in V$, we extract a preference vector, $\pi_v \in \overline{L(V)}$ from $\mathbf{w}_v$, by sorting entries in $\mathbf{w}_v$ — elements with the same weight are assigned to the same partition. In other words, $\pi_v \in \overline{L(V)}$ ranks vertices in V by v's PageRank contributions [1] to them. Although this conversion may lose some valuable affinity information encoded in the numerical values, it offers a path to apply our community identification theory to network analysis.

To better model preferences in practical social networks, we can also use *multifaceted preference networks* [3], in which each node can have more than one ranking of other nodes. For example, one member may have three rankings — one based on "family/friends", one based on "academic interests", and one based on "business interests." Meanwhile, another member may have two rankings — one based on "sports" and one based on "music". Formally, in a *multifaceted preference network $A = (V, \Pi)$*, each $u \in V$ specifies d_u preferences in Π. We call d_u the *preference degree* of u. Our results extend to multifaceted preference networks.

A real-world (observed) social network may be viewed as sparse, observed social interactions induced by an underlying preference/affinity network. Thus, the conceptual question of community identification studied in this paper is a basic question in Network Sciences regarding both network formation and network structures. Our work suggests that simultaneous axiomatization of network formation and community characterization could be beneficial and essential. We expect that an axiomatization theory, for (1) personalized ranking in networks and (2) for community characterization in preference networks with partially ordered preferences, will offer us new insight for addressing the two fundamental mathematical questions, that are essential for understanding community formation in social/information networks:

- Inference of the underlying network model from observed networks.

- Community formulation from individual affinities and preferences (based on the underlying network model).

Extending our work to preference networks with partially ordered preferences will provide a concrete step to understand community formation in networks with incomplete or incomparable preferences. Like our current study, we believe that the existing literature in social choice — e.g., [18] — will be valuable to our understanding. For both fundamental problems, we can also consider other frameworks, such as the game-theory based incentive networks [26], for formulating the underlying network model from observed networks. These network models offer richer structures for capturing interactions among members in networks. As both parts of theory become sufficiently well developed, well-designed experiments with real-world social networks will be necessary to further enhance this theoretical framework.

In summary, our taxonomy theorem provides the basic structure of communities in a preference network, while the complexity (coNP-Completeness) result illustrates the algorithmic challenges for community identification in addition to community enumeration. On the other hand, our analysis of the harmonious rule and the work of [3] seem to suggest some efficient notion of communities can be defined. However, it remains an open question if there exists a natural, constructive and axiom-conforming community rule that allows overlapping communities, and has stable communities which are polynomial-time samplable and enumerable. Finally, we hope that we can further develop our axiomatic system to better connect with practical networks.

Acknowledgements

We thank Nina Balcan of CMU, Mark Braverman of Princeton, and Madhu Sudan of Microsoft Research for the insightful discussions. We also thank Gang Zeng and Xingwu Liu of Chinese Academy of Sciences for pointing out a subtle error in an earlier version of this work.

6. REFERENCES

[1] R. Andersen, C. Borgs, J. Chayes, J. Hopcraft, V. S. Mirrokni, and S.-H. Teng. Local computation of pagerank contributions. In *Proceedings of the 5th International Conference on Algorithms and Models for the Web-graph*, WAW'07, pages 150–165. Springer-Verlag, 2007.

[2] K. J. Arrow. *Social Choice and Individual Values.* Wiley, New York, 2nd edition, 1963.

[3] M. F. Balcan, C. Borgs, M. Braverman, J. T. Chayes, and S.-H. Teng. Finding endogenously formed communities. In *SODA*, pages 767–783, 2013.

[4] O. N. Bondareva. Some applications of the methods of linear programming to the theory of cooperative games. *Problemy Kibernet.*, (10):119–139, 1963.

[5] S. J. Brams, M. A. Jones, and D. M. Kilgour. Dynamic models of coalition formation: Fallback vs. build-up. In *Proceedings of the 9th Conference on Theoretical Aspects of Rationality and Knowledge*, TARK '03, pages 187–200, 2003.

[6] M. Caesar and J. Rexford. Bgp routing policies in isp networks. *Netwrk. Mag. of Global Internetwkg.*, 19(6):5–11, Nov. 2005.

[7] L. Danzer, Grünbaum, and V. Klee. Helly's theorem and its relatives. *Proc. Symp. Pure Math. 7, American Mathematical Society*, pages 101– 179, 1963.

[8] D. Gale and L. S. Shapley. College admissions and the stability of marriage. *The American Mathematical Monthly*, 69(1):9–15, 1962.

[9] R. Ghosh, S.-H. Teng, K. Lerman, and X. Yan. The interplay between dynamics and networks: Centrality, communities, and Cheeger inequality. In *KDD 2014*, pages 1406–1415. ACM, Aug. 2014.

[10] D. Gusfield and R. W. Irving. *The Stable Marriage Problem: Structure and Algorithms.* MIT Press, Cambridge, MA, USA, 1989.

[11] T. Haveliwala. Topic-sensitive pagerank: A context-sensitive ranking algorithm for web search. In *Trans. Knowl. Data Eng*, volume 15(4), pages 784 – 796, 2003.

[12] J. Kleinberg. An impossibility theorem for clustering. In *NIPS*, pages 463–470, 2002.

[13] J. Leskovec, K. Lang, A. Dasgupta, and M. Mahoney. Community structure in large networks: Natural cluster sizes and the absence of large well-defined clusters. *Internet Mathematics*, pages 29–123, 2009.

[14] N. Mishra, R. Schreiber, I. Stanton, and R. Tarjan. Finding strongly-knit clusters in social networks. *Internet Mathematics*, pages 155–174, 2009.

[15] J. Nash. Equilibrium points in n-person games. *Proceedings of the National Academy of the USA*, 36(1):48–49, 1950.

[16] J. Nash. Noncooperative games. *Annals of Mathematics*, 54:289–295, 1951.

[17] M. E. J. Newman. Modularity and community structure in networks. *PNAS*, 2006.

[18] M. S. Pini, F. Rossi, K. B. Venable, and T. Walsh. Aggregating partially ordered preferences: Impossibility and possibility results. *TARK*, 10, 2005.

[19] F. Radicchi, C. Castellano, F. Cecconi, V. Loreto, and D. Parisi. Defining and identifying communities in networks. *PNAS*, 2004.

[20] Y. Rekhter and T.Li. A border gateway protocol4. *IETF RFC 1771*, 1995.

[21] A. E. Roth. The evolution of the labor market for medical interns and residents: A case study in game theory. *Journal of Political Economy*, 92:991–1016, 1984.

[22] A. E. Roth. *Stable Coalition Formation: Aspects of a Dynamic Theory*, pages 228–234. Wuerzberg: Physica-Verlag, 1984.

[23] H. E. Scarf. The core of an N person game. *Econometrica*, 69:35–50, 1967.

[24] L. S. Shapley. On balanced sets and cores. *Naval Res. Logist. Quarter.*, 14, 1967.

[25] D. A. Spielman and S.-H. Teng. A local clustering algorithm for massive graphs and its application to nearly-linear time graph partitioning. *SIAM J. Comput.*, 42(1):1–26, 2013.

[26] S.-H. Teng. *Scalable Algorithms for Data and Network Analysis.* Foundations and Trends in Theoretical Computer Science, 2016.

[27] H. P. Young. An axiomatization of Borda's rule. *Journal of Economic Theory*, 9(1):43–52, 1974.

Obfuscating Conjunctions under Entropic Ring LWE[*]

Zvika Brakerski
Weizmann Institute

Vinod Vaikuntanathan[†]
MIT

Hoeteck Wee[‡]
ENS

Daniel Wichs[§]
Northeastern

ABSTRACT

We show how to securely obfuscate *conjunctions*, which are functions $f(x_1, \ldots, x_n) = \bigwedge_{i \in I} y_i$ where $I \subseteq [n]$ and each literal y_i is either just x_i or $\neg x_i$ e.g., $f(x_1, \ldots, x_n) = x_1 \wedge \neg x_3 \wedge \neg x_7 \cdots \wedge x_{n-1}$. Whereas prior work of Brakerski and Rothblum (CRYPTO 2013) showed how to achieve this using a non-standard object called cryptographic multilinear maps, our scheme is based on an "entropic" variant of the Ring Learning with Errors (Ring LWE) assumption. As our core tool, we prove that hardness assumptions on the recent multilinear map construction of Gentry, Gorbunov and Halevi (TCC 2015) can be established based on entropic Ring LWE. We view this as a first step towards proving the security of additional multilinear map based constructions, and in particular program obfuscators, under standard assumptions.

Our scheme satisfies virtual black box (VBB) security, meaning that the obfuscated program reveals nothing more than black-box access to f as an oracle, at least as long as (essentially) the conjunction is chosen from a distribution having sufficient entropy.

1. INTRODUCTION

Program Obfuscation [6, 24, 4, 19] is a central cryptographic primitive which enables one to "encrypt" a program in a way that preserves its input-output behavior, yet hides its inner workings. There are several definitions of what it means to "hide the inner workings" of a program, including the virtual black-box definition and the weaker indistinguishability obfuscation definition of Barak et al. [4]. Rather unfortunately, Barak et al. also showed that *general purpose* virtual black-box obfuscation is unachievable. Still, notwithstanding the bleak outlook projected by this result, several positive results for obfuscation have emerged recently.

In particular, several specific and useful classes of functions have been shown to be virtual black-box obfuscatable. This includes constructions of point function obfuscators either in the random oracle model [6, 29] or assuming exponentially strong one-way functions [34], hyperplane obfuscators assuming strong DDH [7], and very recently conjunction obfuscators and average-case evasive function obfuscators under strong assumptions on multilinear maps [5, 3]. Weakening the definition of obfuscation to an indistinguishability-based notion [4, 23] (called IO obfuscation), Garg, Gentry, Halevi, Raykova, Sahai and Waters [19] showed how to IO-obfuscate any family of polynomial-size circuits.

In this work, we address the question of whether VBB obfuscation of advanced functionalities can be based on standard assumptions. Our contribution is the construction of an average-case virtual black box obfuscator for conjunctions assuming an entropic version of the Ring learning with errors (Ring LWE) assumption. Our construction uses the techniques of [5] and the recent multilinear map candidate of Gentry, Gorbunov and Halevi [20]. Our main contribution is the *first proof technique* for a non-trivial obfuscator under an assumption related to a standard and well-studied problem (namely, a generalization of Ring LWE to entropic secrets).

Conjunctions. We define conjunctions as functions of the form $f(x_1, \ldots, x_n) = \bigwedge_{i \in I} y_i$ with literals y_i being either x_i or $\neg x_i$ and $I \subseteq [n]$. Alternatively we can think of this as checking that the values $x_i : i \in I$ match some fixed pattern while values outside of I can be arbitrary. Perhaps the simplest way to represent conjunctions, which we will use by default in this work, is as a vector $v \in \{0, 1, \star\}^n$ where we define $F_v(x_1, \ldots, x_n) = 1$ iff for all $i \in [n]$ we have $x_i = v_i$ or $v_i = \star$. We refer to $\star$ as a "wildcard".

Conjunction Obfuscation. A conjunction obfuscator takes as input a conjunction function F_v and outputs an obfuscated program Π_v such that $\Pi_v(x) = F_v(x)$ for all x. Our goal is to achieve virtual black box (VBB) security

[*]This work was done in part while the authors were visiting the Simons Institute for the Theory of Computing, supported by the Simons Foundation and by the DIMACS/Simons Collaboration in Cryptography through NSF grant CNS-1523467.

[†]Supported by NSF Grants CNS-1350619 and CNS-1414119, DARPA Safeware grant, Alfred P. Sloan Research Fellowship, Microsoft Faculty Fellowship, the NEC Corporation, and a Steven and Renee Finn Career Development Chair from MIT.

[‡]Supported in part by ERC Project aSCEND (639554) and NSF Award CNS-1445424.

[§]Supported in part by NSF grants CNS-1347350, CNS-1314722, CNS-1413964.

Permission to make digital or hard copies of all or part of this work for personal or classroom use is granted without fee provided that copies are not made or distributed for profit or commercial advantage and that copies bear this notice and the full citation on the first page. Copyrights for components of this work owned by others than ACM must be honored. Abstracting with credit is permitted. To copy otherwise, or republish, to post on servers or to redistribute to lists, requires prior specific permission and/or a fee. Request permissions from permissions@acm.org.

ITCS'16, January 14-16, 2016, Cambridge, MA, USA

© 2016 ACM. ISBN 978-1-4503-4057-1/16/01...$15.00

DOI: http://dx.doi.org/10.1145/2840728.2840745

which says that the code of the program Π_v reveals no more information than having black-box access to an oracle for the function F_v. We relax this requirement by considering a *distributional VBB security*, where we only require the above to hold when v is chosen from a distribution that has sufficient entropy, even when conditioned on the wildcard locations $\{i : v_i = \star\}$.

Our Results and Assumption. We show how to obfuscate conjunctions with distributional VBB security under a variant of the Ring LWE assumption, which we call entropic Ring LWE.

The Ring LWE assumption (for a ring $\mathcal{R}$) says that, when $s \in \mathcal{R}$ is a random secret ring element then $(\mathbf{A}, s\mathbf{A} + \mathbf{e})$ is indistinguishable from uniform, where $\mathbf{A} \in \mathcal{R}^m$ is random and $\mathbf{e} \in \mathcal{R}^m$ is a short Gaussian error. The entropic Ring LWE assumption says that, when $s_1, \ldots, s_n \in \mathcal{R}$ are random (short) *public* ring elements and $x \in \{0,1\}^n$ is a *secret* bit-vector chosen from a high entropy distribution, then the Ring LWE assumption holds with $s = \prod_i s_i^{x_i}$ as the secret. See Definition 2.7 for a precise statement.

1.1 Our Techniques

Directed Encoding. We rely on (a special case of) the construction of [20] which can be thought of as a variant of a multilinear map, that we call a directed encoding. For public keys $\mathbf{A}, \mathbf{A}' \in \mathcal{R}^m$, we define an encoding of a short ring element $s \in \mathcal{R}$ under $\mathbf{A} \to \mathbf{A}'$ as a short matrix $\mathbf{R} \in \mathcal{R}^{m \times m}$ such that

$$\mathbf{A}\mathbf{R} = s\mathbf{A}' + \mathbf{e}$$

where $\mathbf{e}$ is short Gaussian error. This allows us to multiply encodings $\mathbf{R}^\times = \mathbf{R}_1 \cdot \mathbf{R}_2$ so that, if $\mathbf{R}_1$ is an encoding of s_1 under $\mathbf{A}_0 \to \mathbf{A}_1$ and $\mathbf{R}_2$ is an encoding of s_2 under $\mathbf{A}_1 \to \mathbf{A}_2$ then $\mathbf{R}^\times$ is an encoding of $s_1 \cdot s_2$ under $\mathbf{A}_0 \to \mathbf{A}_2$.

Furthermore, we can detect if a value $\mathbf{R}$ is an encoding of 0 under $\mathbf{A} \to \mathbf{A}'$ by checking whether $\mathbf{A}\mathbf{R}$ is short. This also allows us to check for equality of encoded values.

Conjunction Obfuscator Construction. To obfuscate a conjunction F_v with $v \in \{0, 1, \star\}^\ell$ we do the following:

- Choose random short ring elements
$$\{s_{i,b}, r_{i,b} : i \in [\ell], b \in \{0,1\}\}$$
subject to $s_{i,0} = s_{i,1}$ if $v_i = \star$.

- Create encodings $R_{i,b}$ of $r_{i,b}$ and encodings $S_{i,b}$ of $r_{i,b} \cdot s_{i,b}$ under $\mathbf{A}_{i-1} \to \mathbf{A}_i$.

- Choose random short ring element $r_{\ell+1}$. Create the encodings $R_{\ell+1}$ of $r_{\ell+1}$ and $S_{\ell+1}$ of $r_{\ell+1} \cdot \prod_{i=1}^\ell s_{i,v_i}$ where we let $s_{i,\star} = s_{i,0} = s_{i,1}$ when $v_i = \star$. These encodings are under $\mathbf{A}_\ell \to \mathbf{A}_{\ell+1}$.

Set the obfuscated program to be

$$\Pi_v = (\{S_{i,b}, R_{i,b}\}_{i \in [\ell], b \in \{0,1\}}, R_{\ell+1}, S_{\ell+1})$$

To evaluate Π_v on an input $x \in \{0,1\}^\ell$ we compute

$$S^* = \left(\prod_{i=1}^\ell S_{i,x_i}\right) R_{\ell+1} \quad , \quad R^* = \left(\prod_{i=1}^\ell R_{i,x_i}\right) S_{\ell+1}$$

If $F_v(x) = 1$ then both S^* and R^* are encodings of the same value $r_{\ell+1} \prod_{i=1}^\ell s_{i,v_i}$ under $\mathbf{A}_0 \to \mathbf{A}_{\ell+1}$ and if $F_v(x) = 0$

then S^*, R^* are extremely unlikely to encode the same value. Therefore, we can compute the output of the program by testing for equality of encoded values.

To argue security, we rely on (entropic) Ring LWE to replace the components of the program Π_v by random elements independent of v. As an important step of the proof, we show that the encodings satisfy a decisional Diffie Hellman (DDH) like security property: Given the encodings of ring elements $r_0, r_0 s_0, r_1, r_1 s_1$ under $\mathbf{A} \to \mathbf{A}'$, one cannot distinguish whether $s_0 = s_1$ or whether s_0, s_1 are independent.

The Directed Encoding Abstraction. In the body of the paper, we present the construction through the abstraction of directed encoding schemes (as opposed to directly, starting from Ring LWE, as above). As Halevi recently observed [25], we still lack a commonly accepted syntax for describing the intended functionality of multi-linear maps as well as a succinct description of the underlying hardness assumptions, along with a candidate that realizes the functionality and the hardness assumptions under simple and plausible intractability assumptions. We view our abstraction of directed encodings as an important step in that direction. We adopt the syntax and the candidate for directed encodings from [20]; the novelty of this work lies in (i) putting forth concrete hardness assumptions about directed encodings, (ii) showing that the functionality and these hardness assumptions for directed encodings already suffices for the application to obfuscating conjunctions as in [5], and most importantly, (iii) demonstrating a reduction of these hardness assumptions to standard ring LWE assumptions and a simple and plausible strengthening there-of.

1.2 Discussion

All of the known approaches for obfuscation beyond point functions rely on multi-linear maps. A crucial theoretical limitation of these approaches is that they all rely on non-standard assumptions; we have few candidates for multi-linear maps [18, 12, 20, 13] and the corresponding assumptions are presently poorly understood and not extensively studied in cryptanalysis, and in many cases, broken [8, 11, 28, 9, 32, 10]. Indeed, these latter attacks highlight the importance of obtaining constructions and developing techniques that work under standard cryptographic assumptions, as is the focus of this work.

Our work may be viewed as taking a step towards basing obfuscation on standard assumptions, starting with conjunctions, which is an important special case of evasive functions, namely functions for which it is hard to find an input that evaluates to 0. As articulated by Badrinarayanan et al. [2], we *can* hope to obfuscate the class of evasive functions in a way that survives "all known attacks" on the multilinear maps, where no encodings of 0 can be created by a generic-model adversary. The reason this is meaningful is that all of the recent attacks on candidate multi-linear maps rely crucially on the ability of the adversary to create encodings of 0. We leave as an important open problem to extend our construction to the class of all evasive functions.

On the Entropic Ring LWE Assumption. A few works have studied entropic variants of the LWE assumption. Goldwasser, Kalai, Peikert and Vaikuntanathan [22] showed that, roughly speaking, LWE with n-dimensional secrets

148

over $\mathbb{Z}_q$ drawn from a distribution with min-entropy k is at least as hard as LWE with uniformly random secrets in $O(k/\log q)$ dimensions. However, such a result is not known for Ring LWE to the best of our knowledge. Another source of difficulty is that the min-entropy of our secrets is $o(\log q)$, much too small for the results in [22] to be applicable, even if they do extend to the Ring LWE setting.

We view the question of understanding the entropic ring LWE assumption, both in the [22] range of parameters (namely, $k = \omega(\log q)$) as well as our more aggressive range of parameters (namely, $k = o(\log q)$) to be very interesting questions for future research, with many potential applications.

On Coron's Attack. Coron [10] recently came up with an attack against the multiparty key exchange protocol based on the GGH15 encoding scheme [20]. This attack relies on extraneous properties of the key-agreement protocol of GGH15 (which had no security reduction) and does not seem to contain any new insights that could be leveraged to attack the Ring-LWE assumption or its entropic variant on which our scheme is based. In a bit more detail, Coron's attack relies on the adversary being able to obtain many "encodings" of 0, a "feature" that is inherent to the key exchange protocol, but not present in our scheme. Indeed, we believe the attack only strengthens the premise of our paper, which focuses on provable security under a (almost) standard assumption, namely an entropic variant of Ring-LWE.

Organization of the Paper. We present an abstract framework for the syntax of directed encodings and its underlying assumptions in Section 3, and its instantiation in Section 4. In particular, the hardness assumptions are presented in Sections 3.1 (abstract) and 4.3 (concrete). We present our conjunction obfuscator in Section 5 relying only on our abstract framework.

2. PRELIMINARIES

2.1 Average Min-Entropy

We use information theoretic tools similar to those in [5].

DEFINITION 2.1 (AVERAGE MIN-ENTROPY [15]). *Let X and Z be (possibly dependent) random variables, the average min entropy of X conditioned on Z is:*

$$\widetilde{\mathbf{H}}_\infty(X|Z) = -\log\left(\mathop{\mathbb{E}}_{z\leftarrow Z}\left[2^{-\mathbf{H}_\infty(X|Z=z)}\right]\right).$$

LEMMA 2.1 ([15]). *Let X, Y, Z be (possibly dependent) random variables, where the support of Z is of size $\leq 2^\ell$. Then $\widetilde{\mathbf{H}}_\infty(X|Y,Z) \geq \widetilde{\mathbf{H}}_\infty(X|Y) - \ell$.*

2.2 Distributional VBB Obfuscation

The notion of obfuscation discussed in this paper is distributional (or average case) VBB [16, 27, 26, 4], defined as follows.

DEFINITION 2.2 (DISTRIBUTIONAL VBB). *Consider a circuit family $\mathcal{C} = \{\mathcal{C}_n\}_{n\in\mathbb{N}}$ with input size n and let Obf be a p.p.t. algorithm, which takes as input a circuit $C \in \mathcal{C}$, a security parameter $\lambda \in \mathbb{N}$, and outputs a boolean circuit $\mathsf{Obf}(1^\lambda, C)$ (which is itself not necessarily in $\mathcal{C}$). Let $\mathcal{D}$ be*

a class of distribution ensembles $D = \{D_\lambda\}_{\lambda\in\mathbb{N}}$ that sample $(C, \mathsf{aux}) \leftarrow D_\lambda$ with $C \in \mathcal{C}$.

Obf is an obfuscator for the distribution class $\mathcal{D}$ over the circuit family $\mathcal{C}$, if it satisfies the following properties:

1. *Preserving Functionality: There is some negligible function $\nu(\lambda) = \mathsf{negl}(\lambda)$ such that for all circuits $C \in \mathcal{C}$ we have $\Pr[\forall x \in \{0,1\}^n : C(x) = \mathsf{Obf}(1^\lambda, C)(x)] \geq 1 - \nu(\lambda)$, where the probability is over the coin tosses of Obf.*

2. *Polynomial Slowdown: For every $\lambda \in \mathbb{N}$ and $C \in \mathcal{C}$, the circuit $\mathsf{Obf}(1^\lambda, C)$ is of size at most $\mathsf{poly}(|C|, \lambda)$.*

3. *Distributional Virtual Black-Box: For every (non-uniform) polynomial size adversary Adv, there exists a (non-uniform) polynomial size simulator Sim, such that for every distribution ensemble $D = \{D_\lambda\} \in \mathcal{D}$, and every (non-uniform) polynomial size predicate $P : \mathcal{C} \to \{0,1\}$:*

$$\left| \mathop{\Pr}_{(C,\mathsf{aux})\sim D_\lambda, \mathsf{Obf}, \mathsf{Adv}}[\mathsf{Adv}(\mathsf{Obf}(1^\lambda, C), \mathsf{aux}) = P(C)] \right.$$
$$\left. - \mathop{\Pr}_{(C,\mathsf{aux})\sim D_\lambda, \mathsf{Sim}}[\mathsf{Sim}^C(1^\lambda, 1^{|C|}, \mathsf{aux}) = P(C)] \right| = \mathsf{negl}(\lambda)$$

2.3 Conjunctions and Conjunction Obfuscators

The class of conjunctions $\mathcal{C}^{\mathsf{conj}} = \{\mathcal{C}_n^{\mathsf{conj}}\}_{n\in\mathbb{N}}$ is defined as $\mathcal{C}_n^{\mathsf{conj}} = \{F_v : \{0,1\}^n \to \{0,1\}\}_{v\in\{0,1,\star\}^n}$ where, for every $v = (v_1,\ldots,v_n) \in \{0,1,\star\}^n$ and input $x = (x_1,\ldots,x_n) \in \{0,1\}^n$

$F_v(x) = 1$ if and only if for all $i \in [n]$, $v_i = \star$ or $x_i = v_i$

As an abuse of notation, we also use F_v denote the canonical circuit representation of the function F_v, from which it is easy to recover the value v.

We can define the set $w = \{i : v_i = \star\}$ corresponding to the "wildcard locations". The classes of conjunctions we are able to obfuscate are those where there is sufficient entropy in v, even when w is fully known. The following definition is adapted from [5] to also handle auxiliary input.

DEFINITION 2.3 (ENTROPY GIVEN WILDCARDS). *Let $D = \{D_\lambda\}$ be a distribution ensemble that samples $(F_v, \mathsf{aux}) \leftarrow D_\lambda$ with $F_v \in \mathcal{C}_{n(\lambda)}^{\mathsf{conj}}$ for some polynomial $n(\cdot)$. We say that D has $\alpha(\lambda)$ entropy given wildcards if $\widetilde{\mathbf{H}}_\infty(v|w, \mathsf{aux}) \geq \alpha(\lambda)$ where $(F_v, \mathsf{aux}) \leftarrow D_\lambda$ and $w = \{i : v_i = \star\}$.*

We let $\mathcal{D}_\alpha$ denote the class of all efficiently samplable distribution ensembles $D = \{D_\lambda\}$ such that D has $\alpha(\lambda)$-entropy given wildcards.

DEFINITION 2.4. *We say that Obf is a $\alpha(\lambda)$-distributional VBB obfuscator for conjunctions if it is a distributional VBB obfuscator for the class $\mathcal{D}_\alpha$ consisting of all distribution ensembles D such that D has $\alpha(\lambda)$ entropy given wildcards.*

We mention an alternate definition of obfuscation security that we call $\alpha(\lambda)$-entropic security.

DEFINITION 2.5. *A conjunction obfuscator Obf satisfies $\alpha(\lambda)$-entropic security if there exists a polynomial-size simulator Sim such that for all efficiently samplable distributions $D \in \mathcal{D}_\alpha$ that have $\alpha(\lambda)$-entropy given wildcards, we have*

$$(\mathsf{Obf}(1^\lambda, F_v), \mathsf{aux}) \stackrel{c}{\approx} (\mathsf{Sim}(1^\lambda, 1^{|v|}), \mathsf{aux}).$$

where $(F_v, \text{aux}) \leftarrow D_\lambda$.

Note that, in the above definition, the simulator does not depend on the distribution D and therefore, we can think of this definition as saying that the obfuscation hides all properties of the distribution. Also note that the simulator here does not get any oracle access to F_v and therefore does not learn anything at all. As such it's clear that such a definition cannot be achieved for general circuits (where oracle access to the circuit can provide some useful information) but it does make sense for evasive functions.

2.3.1 A Lemma on Entropic Security and Distributional VBB

LEMMA 2.2. *If a conjunction obfuscator* Obf *satisfies the functionality preserving and polynomial slowdown properties and has $\alpha(\lambda)$-entropic security, then it is an $(\alpha(\lambda) + 1)$-distributional VBB obfuscator for conjunctions.*

PROOF. Let Obf be an obfuscator satisfying $\alpha(\lambda)$-entropic security with simulator Sim$'$. Let $D = \{D_\lambda\}$ be any efficiently samplable distribution having $\alpha(\lambda) + 1$ entropy given wildcards, meaning that for $(F_v, \text{aux}) \leftarrow D_\lambda$ we have $\tilde{\mathbf{H}}_\infty(v|\text{aux}, w) \geq \alpha(\lambda)$ where $w = \{i : v_i = \star\}$. Furthermore, there is some polynomial $n(\lambda)$ such that $(F_v, \text{aux}) \leftarrow D_\lambda$ has $|v| = n(\lambda)$. For polynomial size adversary Adv, define a (non-uniform) polynomial size simulator $\text{Sim}_{\text{Adv}}(1^\lambda, 1^n) = \text{Adv}(\text{Sim}'(1^\lambda, 1^n))$.

Let $P : \mathcal{C}^{\text{conj}} \to \{0, 1\}$ be any polynomial-size predicate. Define the efficiently samplable distribution $D' = \{D'_\lambda\}$ that samples $(v, \text{aux}') \leftarrow D'_\lambda$ by choosing $(F_v, \text{aux}) \leftarrow D_\lambda$ and setting $\text{aux}' = (\text{aux}, P(F_v))$. Then, by applying Lemma 2.1,

$$\tilde{\mathbf{H}}_\infty(v|\text{aux}', w) = \tilde{\mathbf{H}}_\infty(v|\text{aux}, w, P(F_v))$$
$$\geq \tilde{\mathbf{H}}_\infty(v|\text{aux}, w) - 1 \geq \alpha(\lambda).$$

Therefore, by $\alpha(\lambda)$-entropic security, we have

$$(\text{Obf}(1^\lambda, F_v), \text{aux}, P(F_v)) \overset{c}{\approx} (\text{Sim}'(1^\lambda, 1^n), \text{aux}, P(F_v))$$

when $(v, \text{aux}' = (\text{aux}, P(F_v))) \leftarrow D'_\lambda$. In particular, this means that

$$\left| \Pr_{(F_v, \text{aux}) \sim D_\lambda} [\text{Adv}(\text{Obf}(1^\lambda, F_v), \text{aux}) = P(F_v)] \right.$$
$$\left. - \Pr_{(F_v, \text{aux}) \sim D_\lambda} [\text{Adv}(\text{Sim}'(1^\lambda, 1^{|v|}), \text{aux}) = P(F_v)] \right| = \text{negl}(\lambda)$$

by recalling that $\text{Sim}_{\text{Adv}}(1^\lambda, 1^n) = \text{Adv}(\text{Sim}'(1^\lambda, 1^n))$ we get the proof of the lemma. $\square$

2.4 Lattice Preliminaries

For a vector $\mathbf{x}$, we let $\|\mathbf{x}\|$ denote its ℓ_2 norm and $\|\mathbf{x}\|_\infty$ denote its infinity norm. For a matrix $\mathbf{R} \in \mathbb{Z}^{m \times m}$ we define $\|\mathbf{R}\|$ (resp. $\|\mathbf{R}\|_\infty$) as the ℓ_2 (resp. infinity) length of the longest column of $\mathbf{R}$. Let $D_{\mathbb{Z}^m, \sigma}$ be the truncated discrete Gaussian distribution over $\mathbb{Z}^m$ with parameter σ, that is, we replace the output by $\mathbf{0}$ whenever the $\|\cdot\|_\infty$ norm exceeds $\sqrt{m} \cdot \sigma$ (this is statistically close to the discrete Gaussian distribution with parameter σ as long as $m = \omega(\log \lambda)$).

LEMMA 2.3 (LATTICE TRAPDOORS [1, 21, 31]). *There is an efficient randomized algorithm* TrapSamp$(1^n, 1^m, q)$ *that, given any integers $n \geq 1$, $q \geq 2$, and sufficiently large $m = \Omega(n \log q)$, outputs a matrix $\mathbf{A} \in \mathbb{Z}_q^{n \times m}$ and a trapdoor*

matrix $\mathbf{T} \in \mathbb{Z}^{m \times m}$ such that the distribution of $\mathbf{A}$ is $\text{negl}(n)$-close to uniform.

Moreover, there is an efficient algorithm GaussSamp *that with overwhelming probability over all random choices, does the following: For any $\mathbf{u} \in \mathbb{Z}_q^n$, and large enough $s = \Omega(\sqrt{n \log q})$, the randomized procedure* GaussSamp$(\mathbf{A}, \mathbf{T}, \mathbf{u}, s)$ *outputs a vector $\mathbf{r} \in \mathbb{Z}^m$ with norm $\|\mathbf{r}\|_\infty \leq \|\mathbf{r}\|_2 \leq s\sqrt{n}$ (with probability 1). Furthermore, the following distributions of the tuple $(\mathbf{A}, \mathbf{T}, \mathbf{U}, \mathbf{R})$ are within $\text{negl}(n)$ statistical distance of each other for any polynomial $k \in \mathbb{N}$:*

- $(\mathbf{A}, \mathbf{T}) \leftarrow$ TrapSamp$(1^n, 1^m, q)$; $\mathbf{U} \leftarrow \mathbb{Z}_q^{n \times k}$; $\mathbf{R} \leftarrow$ GaussSamp$(\mathbf{A}, \mathbf{T}, \mathbf{U}, s)$.

- $(\mathbf{A}, \mathbf{T}) \leftarrow$ TrapSamp$(1^n, 1^m, q)$; $\mathbf{R} \leftarrow (D_{\mathbb{Z}^m, s})^k$; $\mathbf{U} := \mathbf{AR} \pmod{q}$.

This also extends to the ring setting with $\mathbf{A} \in \mathcal{R}_q^m, \mathbf{T} \in \mathcal{R}^{m \times m}, \mathbf{U} \in \mathcal{R}^k, \mathbf{R} \in \mathcal{R}^{m \times k}$.

LEMMA 2.4 ("NOISE SMUDGING" [14]). *Let $\beta > 0$ and $y \in \mathbb{Z}$ be arbitrary. Then, the statistical distance between the distributions $D_{\mathbb{Z}, \beta}$ and $D_{\mathbb{Z}, \beta + y}$ is at most $|y|/\beta q$.*

The lemma below (restated from [33, Lemma 10]) states that most "small" polynomials are units in the ring $R_q = \mathbb{Z}_q[x]/(x^n + 1)$.

LEMMA 2.5. *Let $n \geq 8$ be a power of 2 such that $x^n + 1$ splits into n linear factors modulo prime $2^n \geq q \geq 5$. (In particular, setting $q = 1 \pmod{2n}$ satisfies this condition). Let $\sigma = \Omega(\sqrt{n \log q \log n})$. Then,*

$$\Pr[s \leftarrow D_{\mathbb{Z}^n, \sigma} : s \notin R_q^\times] = O(n/q)$$

2.5 The Ring Learning with Errors Problem

We start by defining a simple special case of the ring LWE problem [30]. We define the operator MakePoly such that for all rings $\mathcal{R}$, if $\mathbf{a} \in \mathcal{R}^n$, then $\text{MakePoly}(\mathbf{a}) \in \mathcal{R}[x]$ is the polynomial whose coefficients are the elements of $\mathbf{a}$. If D is a distribution over $\mathcal{R}^n$ then $\text{MakePoly}(D)$ is the respective distribution over $\mathcal{R}[x]$.

DEFINITION 2.6. *Let n be a power of 2, and let $\mathcal{R} = \mathbb{Z}[x]/\langle x^n + 1 \rangle$. Let q be such that $q \equiv 1 \pmod{2n}$ and define $\mathcal{R}_q = \mathcal{R}/q\mathcal{R}$. Let $m \in \mathbb{N}$ and let χ be a distribution over the integers. The $\text{PLWE}_{n,m,q,\chi}$ problem is the problem of distinguishing $\{(a_i, a_i \cdot s + e_i \pmod{x^n + 1, q})\}_{i \in [m]}$ from $\{(a_i, u_i)\}_{i \in [m]}$, where $s \overset{\$}{\leftarrow} \text{MakePoly}(\chi^n)$, $a_i \overset{\$}{\leftarrow} \text{MakePoly}(\mathbb{Z}_q^n)$, $e_i \overset{\$}{\leftarrow} \text{MakePoly}(\chi^n)$, $u_i \overset{\$}{\leftarrow} \text{MakePoly}(\mathbb{Z}_q^n)$.*

The following is an immediate corollary from [17], together with a standard Hermite Normal Form reduction, see e.g. [30].

COROLLARY 2.6. *Let n, m, q be as in Definition 2.6 above. Then for all $B \geq \sqrt{n} \cdot (nm/\log(nm))^{1/4} \cdot \omega(\sqrt{\log n})$, there exists a B-bounded distribution χ such that $\text{PLWE}_{n,m,q,\chi}$ is at least as hard as quantumly approximating the shortest vector in worst case ideal lattice over $\mathbb{Z}[\zeta_{2n}]$ to within $\tilde{O}\left(n \cdot (nm/\log(nm))^{1/4} \cdot (q/B)\right)$ factor.*

We also define an entropic version of the problem as follows.

DEFINITION 2.7 (α-ENTROPIC PLWE). *Let n, m, q, χ be parameters of λ and $\mathcal{R}_q$ be as in Definition 2.6, and let $D = \{D_\lambda\}$ be an efficiently samplable distribution with $(x, z) \leftarrow D_\lambda$ having $x \in \{0, 1\}^\ell$ for some $\ell = \ell(\lambda)$ and $\widetilde{\mathbf{H}}_\infty(x|z) \geq \alpha(\lambda)$. The α-entropic $\mathsf{PLWE}_{n,m,q,\chi}$ problem is to distinguish*

$$\left(\{s_j\}_{j \in [\ell]}, z, \{(a_i, a_i \cdot s + e_i)\}_{i \in [m]} \right)$$

from $\quad \left(\{s_j\}_{j \in [\ell]}, z, \{(a_i, u_i)\}_{i \in [m]} \right)$,

where $s_j \xleftarrow{\$} \mathsf{MakePoly}(\chi^n)$, *we let* $(x, z) \xleftarrow{\$} D$ *and set* $s = \prod_{j \in [\ell]} s_j^{x_j}$, *and as above* $a_i \xleftarrow{\$} \mathsf{MakePoly}(\mathbb{Z}_q^n)$, $e_i \xleftarrow{\$} \mathsf{MakePoly}(\chi^n)$, $u_i \xleftarrow{\$} \mathsf{MakePoly}(\mathbb{Z}_q^n)$. *All operations are over the ring* $\mathcal{R}_q$.

3. DIRECTED ENCODING SCHEMES

Directed encoding schemes are a special case of graph-induced multi-linear maps of Gentry, Gorbunov and Halevi [20], specialized to a line. Let R_M be a ring. In this section, we present an abstract framework for the syntax of directed encodings and its underlying assumptions, and we describe our instantiation in Section 4.

DEFINITION 3.1 (DIRECTED ENCODING SCHEME). *A directed encoding scheme associated with a message space $\mathcal{M} \subseteq R_M$ is a tuple of p.p.t. algorithms*

(Setup, Encode, REncode, Mult, EqualTest)

which work as follows.

- Setup$(1^\lambda, 1^L)$, *on input a security parameter λ and an upper-bound L on the number of levels, generates a public key PK and a private encoding key EK.*

- Encode$_{\mathsf{PK}_0 \to \mathsf{PK}_1}(\mathsf{EK}_0, s)$, *on input a "source" key-pair $(\mathsf{PK}_0, \mathsf{EK}_0)$, a "target" public key PK_1, and a message $m \in \mathcal{M}$, outputs an encoding c.*

- REncode$_{\mathsf{PK}_0 \to \mathsf{PK}_1}(1^\lambda)$, *on input a "source" public key PK_0 and a "target" public key PK_1, outputs an encoding c.*

- EqualTest$_{\mathsf{PK}_0 \to \mathsf{PK}_1}(c_0, c_1)$, *on input two public keys PK_0 and PK_1, and two encodings c_0, c_1, outputs a bit b (signifying accept or reject).*

- Mult(c_1, c_2), *on input two encodings c_1, c_2, outputs an encoding $c_\times$.*

We also extend Mult to handle multiple encodings in the natural way:

Mult$(c_1, c_2, c_3, \dots) = \mathsf{Mult}(c_1, \mathsf{Mult}(c_2, \mathsf{Mult}(c_3, \dots)))$.

Informally, correctness stipulates that the encodings uniquely determine the underlying message, and that we can multiply up to L encodings.

REMARK 3.1. *We could extend this by an "addition" operation or adding a zero test capability, but we don't need it here.*

Correctness. We write $\mathcal{M}^i = \{s_1 s_2 \cdots s_i : s_1, s_2, \dots, s_i \in \mathcal{M}\}$. We require the following correctness properties from the scheme to hold with probability $1 - \mathsf{negl}(\lambda)$ over $(\mathsf{PK}_0, \mathsf{EK}_0), (\mathsf{PK}_1, \mathsf{EK}_1), (\mathsf{PK}_2, \mathsf{EK}_2)$. For each $s \in \mathcal{M}^L$, there exists a family of sets $\mathcal{E}^{(1)}_{\mathsf{PK}_0, \mathsf{PK}_1, s}, \dots, \mathcal{E}^{(L)}_{\mathsf{PK}_0, \mathsf{PK}_1, s}$ where $\mathcal{E}^{(1)}_{\mathsf{PK}_0, \mathsf{PK}_1, s} \subseteq \cdots \subseteq \mathcal{E}^{(L)}_{\mathsf{PK}_0, \mathsf{PK}_1, s}$ such that:

- For all $s \in \mathcal{M}$, $\mathsf{Encode}_{\mathsf{PK}_0 \to \mathsf{PK}_1}(\mathsf{EK}_0, s) \in \mathcal{E}^{(1)}_{\mathsf{PK}_0, \mathsf{PK}_1, s}$.

- For all $s_1, s_2 \in \mathcal{M}^L$ and all $(c_1, c_2) \in \mathcal{E}^{(L)}_{\mathsf{PK}_0, \mathsf{PK}_1, s_1} \times \mathcal{E}^{(L)}_{\mathsf{PK}_0, \mathsf{PK}_1, s_2}$, we have $\mathsf{EqualTest}_{\mathsf{PK}_0 \to \mathsf{PK}_1}(c_1, c_2) = 1$ iff $s_1 = s_2$.

- For all i, j for which $i + j \leq L$, for all $(s_1, s_2) \in \mathcal{M}^i \times \mathcal{M}^j$ and all $(c_1, c_2) \in \mathcal{E}^{(i)}_{\mathsf{PK}_0, \mathsf{PK}_1, s_1} \times \mathcal{E}^{(j)}_{\mathsf{PK}_1, \mathsf{PK}_2, s_2}$ we have $\mathsf{Mult}(c_1, c_2) \in \mathcal{E}^{(i+j)}_{\mathsf{PK}_0, \mathsf{PK}_2, s_1 s_2}$.

Note that there is no correctness requirement for "malformed encodings" that do not belong to some $\mathcal{E}^{(L)}_{\mathsf{PK}_0, \mathsf{PK}_1, s}$.

3.1 Security Assumptions

For the security properties, we define an efficiently samplable distribution $\mathcal{D}_M$ over $\mathcal{M}$. We require the following security properties from the encoding scheme.

PROPERTY 1 (GRADED EXTERNAL DH). *For every polynomial $L = L(\lambda)$ the following experiments $\mathsf{exp}^{\mathsf{gxdh}}(1^\lambda, 1^{L(\lambda)})$ and $\mathsf{exp}^{\mathsf{rand}}(1^\lambda, 1^{L(\lambda)})$ should produce indistinguishable outputs.*

We can also define two special sub-cases of the GXDH assumption which are already useful. We define the *2-element GXDH*, denoted GXDH-2, the same way as above but modify the experiments $\mathsf{exp}^{\mathsf{gxdh}}$, $\mathsf{exp}^{\mathsf{rand}}$ to only output $(\mathsf{PK}_0, \mathsf{PK}_1, \mathsf{EK}_0, c_0, d_0)$. We also define the *1-element GXDH*, denoted GXDH-1, the same way as above but modify $\mathsf{exp}^{\mathsf{gxdh}}$ and $\mathsf{exp}^{\mathsf{rand}}$ to only output $(\mathsf{PK}_0, \mathsf{PK}_1, \mathsf{EK}_0, c_0)$. The following is clear.

PROPOSITION 3.1. *The GXDH security property implies GXDH-2 and GXDH-1.*

Our second assumption is entropic security which is similar in spirit to, but weaker than, the "GCAN" assumption from [5]. In the GCAN assumption on multilinear maps, the adversary was given access to the complete encoding parameters of the scheme (which roughly correspond to the encoding keys EK_0 and EK_1 below). However, in our setting this assumption is seems too strong and quite possibly incorrect. We thus notice that so long as the adversary is unable to obtain the encoding key EK_1 for the "target", we can establish security based on entropic RLWE (see Section 4.3) and this is in fact sufficient for our construction (see Section 5).

PROPERTY 2 (α-ENTROPIC SECURITY). *For a parameter $\alpha = \alpha(\lambda)$, we say that the encoding scheme is α-entropic secure if for all polynomial $\ell = \ell(\lambda), L = L(\lambda)$ and all efficiently samplable distributions $D = \{D_\lambda\}_{\lambda \in \mathbb{N}}$ such that $(x, z) \leftarrow D_\lambda$ contains $x \in \{0, 1\}^{\ell(\lambda)}$ and $\widetilde{\mathbf{H}}_\infty(x|z) \geq \alpha(\lambda)$ the following two distributions are computationally indistinguishable:*

$$\left(\mathsf{PK}_0, \mathsf{PK}_1, \mathsf{EK}_0, z, s_1, s_2, \dots, s_\ell, c \leftarrow \mathsf{Encode}_{\mathsf{PK}_0 \to \mathsf{PK}_1}(\mathsf{EK}_0, s_x) \right)$$

and

$$\left(\mathsf{PK}_0, \mathsf{PK}_1, \mathsf{EK}_0, z, s_1, s_2, \dots, s_\ell, c \leftarrow \mathsf{REncode}_{\mathsf{PK}_0 \to \mathsf{PK}_1}(1^\lambda) \right) ,$$

where $(\mathsf{PK}_0, \mathsf{EK}_0) \leftarrow \mathsf{Setup}(1^\lambda, 1^L)$, $(\mathsf{PK}_1, \mathsf{EK}_1) \leftarrow \mathsf{Setup}(1^\lambda, 1^L)$, $s_1, s_2, \dots, s_\ell \leftarrow \mathcal{D}_M$, $(x, z) \leftarrow D_\lambda$ *and* $s_x = \prod_{i=1}^\ell s_i^{x_i}$.

Figure 1: The experiments $\exp^{\text{gxdh}}$ and $\exp^{\text{rand}}$ in the SXDH security game. See Definition 1.

$\underline{\exp^{\text{gxdh}}(1^\lambda, 1^L)}$:	$\underline{\exp^{\text{rand}}(1^\lambda, 1^L)}$:
1: $(\text{PK}_0, \text{EK}_0) \leftarrow \text{Setup}(1^\lambda, 1^L)$;	1: $(\text{PK}_0, \text{EK}_0) \leftarrow \text{Setup}(1^\lambda, 1^L)$;
2: $(\text{PK}_1, \text{EK}_1) \leftarrow \text{Setup}(1^\lambda, 1^L)$;	2: $(\text{PK}_1, \text{EK}_1) \leftarrow \text{Setup}(1^\lambda, 1^L)$;
3: $r_0, r_1, s \leftarrow \mathcal{D}_M$;	3:
4: $c_b \leftarrow \text{Encode}_{\text{PK}_0 \rightarrow \text{PK}_1}(\text{EK}_0, r_b)$;	4: $c_b, d_b \leftarrow \text{REncode}_{\text{PK}_0 \rightarrow \text{PK}_1}(1^\lambda)$;
5: $d_b \leftarrow \text{Encode}_{\text{PK}_0 \rightarrow \text{PK}_1}(\text{EK}_0, s \cdot r_b)$;	5:
6: Output $(\text{PK}_0, \text{PK}_1, \text{EK}_0, c_0, c_1, d_0, d_1)$.	6: Output $(\text{PK}_0, \text{PK}_1, \text{EK}_0, c_0, c_1, d_0, d_1)$.

4. AN INSTANTIATION OF A DIRECTED ENCODING SCHEME

Let $\mathcal{R}$ be a degree-n number ring $\mathbb{Z}[x]/(f(x))$ for some degree-n polynomial $f(x)$. (We will be mostly agnostic of the specifics of what $f(x)$ is, but encourage the reader to think of a cyclotomic polynomial $f(x) = x^n + 1$ where n is a power of two.) Let q be a rational prime, and $\mathcal{R}_q = \mathcal{R}/q\mathcal{R}$ be the quotient ring. Let $\sigma \in \mathbb{R}^+$ be the Gaussian standard deviation parameter.

4.1 The Encoding Scheme

- Setup$(1^\lambda, 1^L)$ runs $(\mathbf{A}, \mathbf{T}) \leftarrow \text{TrapSamp}(1^\lambda)$ and outputs

$$(\text{PK}, \text{EK}) = (\mathbf{A}, \mathbf{T}) \in \mathcal{R}_q^m \times \mathcal{R}^{m \times m}.$$

Set

$$n = \Theta(L\lambda \log(L\lambda)), \quad m = \Theta(nL \log q),$$

$$q = (L\lambda)^{\Theta(L)}, \quad \sigma = \Theta(\sqrt{nL \log q})$$

- $\mathcal{M} = \{s \in \mathcal{R} : \|s\|_\infty \leq m\}$.

- Encode$_{\mathbf{A}_0 \rightarrow \mathbf{A}_1}(s; \mathbf{T}_0)$, where $(\mathbf{A}_0, \mathbf{T}_0), (\mathbf{A}_1, \mathbf{T}_1) \leftarrow \text{Setup}(1^\lambda)$ and $s \in \mathcal{R}$, works as follows.

  - Compute $\mathbf{b}_1 = s\mathbf{A}_1 + \mathbf{e}_1 \in \mathcal{R}_q^m$, where $\mathbf{e}_1 \leftarrow D_{\mathcal{R}^m, \sigma}$.

  - Output a matrix $\mathbf{R}_{0 \rightarrow 1} \leftarrow \text{GaussSamp}(\mathbf{A}_0, \mathbf{b}_1; \mathbf{T}_0; \sigma)$.

  We note that $\mathbf{R}_{0 \rightarrow 1} \in \mathcal{R}^{m \times m}$ and

$$\mathbf{A}_0 \mathbf{R}_{0 \rightarrow 1} = \mathbf{b}_1 = s\mathbf{A}_1 + \mathbf{e}_1 \quad (\text{over } \mathcal{R}_q)$$

- REncode$_{\mathbf{A}_0 \rightarrow \mathbf{A}_1}(1^\lambda)$ is the public encoding procedure that simply samples a matrix $\mathbf{R}_{0 \rightarrow 1} \leftarrow D_{\mathbb{Z}^n, \sigma}^{m \times m}$.

- Mult$(\mathbf{R}, \mathbf{R}') = \mathbf{R}\mathbf{R}'$, where multiplication is done over $\mathcal{R}_q$.

- EqualTest$_{\mathbf{A}_0 \rightarrow \mathbf{A}_1}(\mathbf{R}_0, \mathbf{R}_1)$ outputs "yes" if

$$\|\mathbf{A}_0(\mathbf{R}_0 - \mathbf{R}_1)\|_\infty \leq q/8$$

and "no" otherwise. (Note that this procedure does not depend on $\mathbf{A}_1$ at all.)

As remarked above, we never use addition or extraction, in contrast to the encoding schemes of [18, 12, 13, 20].

4.2 Correctness of the Encoding Scheme

Fix $\mathbf{A}_0, \mathbf{A}_1 \in \mathcal{R}_q^m$ throughout. We define

$$\mathcal{E}_{\mathbf{A}_0, \mathbf{A}_1, s}^{(i)} = \{\mathbf{R} : \|\mathbf{R}\|_\infty \leq 2^{i-1} m^i$$

and

$$\|\mathbf{A}_0 \mathbf{R} - s\mathbf{A}_1\|_\infty \leq 2^{i-1} m^i\}$$

First, it is easy to check that the output of $\text{Encode}_{\mathbf{A}_0 \rightarrow \mathbf{A}_1}(s; \mathbf{T}_0)$ lies in $\mathcal{E}_{\mathbf{A}_0, \mathbf{A}_1, s}^{(1)}$. We then establish correctness in the following lemmas:

LEMMA 4.1 (CORRECTNESS OF EqualTest). *Suppose $q \geq 16Lm^L$. Then, for any $\mathbf{R}_0 \in \mathcal{E}_{\mathbf{A}_0, \mathbf{A}_1, s_0}^{(L)}$, $\mathbf{R}_1 \in \mathcal{E}_{\mathbf{A}_0, \mathbf{A}_1, s_1}^{(L)}$, we have*

$$\|\mathbf{A}_0(\mathbf{R}_0 - \mathbf{R}_1)\|_\infty \leq q/8 \text{ iff } s_0 = s_1.$$

PROOF. The direction $\Leftarrow$ is straight-forward. Now, suppose $s_0 \neq s_1$. Then, we have

$$\|\mathbf{A}_0(\mathbf{R}_0 - \mathbf{R}_1)\|_\infty \geq \|(s_0 - s_1)\mathbf{A}_1\|_\infty - 2m^{2L} > q/8$$

The last line holds since, with overwhelming probability over the choice of $\mathbf{A}_1$, it holds that for all $s \neq 0$, $\|s\mathbf{A}_1\|_\infty > q/4$. □

LEMMA 4.2 (CORRECTNESS OF Mult). *For all i, j for which $i + j \leq L$, for all $(s_1, s_2) \in \mathcal{M}^i \times \mathcal{M}^j$ and all $(c_1, c_2) \in \mathcal{E}_{\text{PK}_0, \text{PK}_1, s_1}^{(i)} \times \mathcal{E}_{\text{PK}_1, \text{PK}_2, s_2}^{(j)}$ we have $\text{Mult}(c_1, c_2) \in \mathcal{E}_{\text{PK}_0, \text{PK}_2, s_1 s_2}^{(i+j)}$*

PROOF. First, observe that

$$\|\mathbf{R}_0 \mathbf{R}_1\|_\infty \leq \|\mathbf{R}_0\|_\infty \|\mathbf{R}_1\|_\infty \leq 2^{i+j-1} m^{i+j}.$$

Now, write $\mathbf{A}_0 \mathbf{R}_0 = s_0 \mathbf{A}_1 + \mathbf{e}_0$ and $\mathbf{A}_1 \mathbf{R}_1 = s_1 \mathbf{A}_1 + \mathbf{e}_1$. Let us unfold the expression $\mathbf{A}_0 \cdot \mathbf{R}_0 \mathbf{R}_1$:

$$\begin{aligned} \mathbf{A}_0 \cdot \mathbf{R}_0 \mathbf{R}_1 &= (s_0 \mathbf{A}_1 + \mathbf{e}_0) \mathbf{R}_1 & \text{rewriting } \mathbf{A}_0 \mathbf{R}_0 \\ &= s_0(s_1 \mathbf{A}_2 + \mathbf{e}_1) + \mathbf{e}_0 \mathbf{R}_1 & \text{rewriting } \mathbf{A}_1 \mathbf{R}_1 \\ &= s_0 s_1 \mathbf{A}_2 + \mathbf{e}_0 \mathbf{R}_1 + s_0 \mathbf{e}_1 \end{aligned}$$

Hence,

$$\|\mathbf{A}_0 \cdot \mathbf{R}_0 \mathbf{R}_1 - s_0 s_1 \mathbf{A}_2\|_\infty = \|\mathbf{e}_0 \mathbf{R}_1 + s_0 \mathbf{e}_1\|_\infty \leq 2^{i+j-1} m^{i+j}$$

where we used the bounds

$$\|\mathbf{e}_0\|_\infty \leq 2^{i-1} m^i, \quad \|\mathbf{R}_1\|_\infty \leq 2^{j-1} m^j,$$

$$\|s_0\|_\infty \leq m^i, \quad \|\mathbf{e}_1\|_\infty \leq 2^{j-1} m^j.$$

□

152

4.3 Security of the Encoding Scheme

We prove the security properties of our encoding scheme (see Section 3.1) under the PLWE and the entropic PLWE assumption (see Section 2.5). These security properties are essentially analogous to the GXDH and GCAN assumptions from the work of Brakerski and Rothblum [5]. However, the key novelty in this work is that we are able to establish these security properties based on the hardness of problems relating to learning with errors over rings [30].

LEMMA 4.3 (GRADED EXTERNAL DIFFIE-HELLMAN). *Let n be a power of 2, and let $\mathcal{R} = \mathbb{Z}[x]/\langle x^n + 1\rangle$. Let $q = 2^{\omega(\log \lambda)}$ be such that $q \equiv 1 \pmod{2n}$ and define $\mathcal{R}_q = \mathcal{R}/q\mathcal{R}$. Let $m \in \mathbb{N}$ and let χ be a distribution over the integers. Then, our encoding scheme satisfies the Graded external Diffie-Hellman (GXDH) property (Property 1) assuming the hardness of the $\mathsf{PLWE}_{n,m,q,\chi}$ problem (Definition 2.6).*

PROOF. We first show that the distributions

$$\Big(\mathbf{A}_1, r_0\mathbf{A}_1 + \mathbf{e}_0, r_1\mathbf{A}_1 + \mathbf{e}_1, sr_0\mathbf{A}_1 + \mathbf{e}_0', sr_1\mathbf{A}_1 + \mathbf{e}_1'\Big) \quad (1)$$

and $\Big(\mathbf{A}_1, \mathbf{U}_0, \mathbf{U}_1, \mathbf{U}_0', \mathbf{U}_1'\Big)$ $\quad (2)$

are computationally indistinguishable under PLWE, where $(\mathbf{A}_b, \mathbf{T}_b) \leftarrow \mathsf{TrapSamp}(1^\lambda)$, $\mathbf{e}_b, \mathbf{e}_b' \leftarrow D_{\mathcal{R}^m,\sigma}$, $s, r_0, r_1 \leftarrow \mathcal{R}_M$ (the message space), and $\mathbf{U}_b, \mathbf{U}_b' \leftarrow \mathcal{R}^m$ (uniformly chosen from the ring).

We show the indistinguishability of (1) and (2) through a sequence of hybrid distributions.

Hybrid 1 is distribution (1).

Hybrid 2. This is the distribution

$$\Big(\mathbf{A}_1, r_0\mathbf{A}_1 + \mathbf{e}_0, r_1\mathbf{A}_1 + \mathbf{e}_1, s \cdot (r_0\mathbf{A}_1 + \mathbf{e}_0) + \mathbf{e}_0',$$
$$s \cdot (r_1\mathbf{A}_1 + \mathbf{e}_1) + \mathbf{e}_1'\Big)$$

where $\mathbf{e}_1 \leftarrow D_{\mathcal{R}^m,\sigma}$ and $\mathbf{e}_1' \leftarrow D_{\mathcal{R}^m,\sigma'}$.

Hybrids 1 and 2 are statistically indistinguishable assuming that $\sigma' = \omega(\log \lambda) \cdot \|s\|_\infty \cdot \sigma$ (by Lemma 2.4). Roughly speaking, the only difference between hybrids 1 and 2 is in the noise distribution of the last two PLWE samples, where in the former, the noise is drawn from $D_{\mathcal{R}^m,\sigma'}$, and in the latter, they are computed as $s\mathbf{e}_b + \mathbf{e}_b'$. If the magnitude of the noise terms $\mathbf{e}_b'$ is much larger than the norm of $s\mathbf{e}_b$, by "noise smudging" (Lemma 2.4), these two distributions have statistical distance $\mathsf{negl}(\lambda)$.

Hybrid 3. This is the distribution

$$\Big(\mathbf{A}_1, \mathbf{U}_0, \mathbf{U}_1, s\mathbf{U}_0 + \mathbf{e}_0', s\mathbf{U}_1 + \mathbf{e}_1'\Big)$$

where $\mathbf{e}_1' \leftarrow D_{\mathcal{R}^m,\sigma'}$. Hybrids 2 and 3 are computationally indistinguishable under the $\mathsf{PLWE}_{n,m,q,\sigma}$ assumption.

Hybrid 4 is distribution (2). That is,

$$\Big(\mathbf{A}_1, \mathbf{U}_0, \mathbf{U}_1, \mathbf{U}_0', \mathbf{U}_1'\Big)$$

Hybrids 3 and 4 are computationally indistinguishable under the $\mathsf{PLWE}_{n,m,q,\sigma'}$ assumption.

To finish the proof, note that the indistinguishability of distributions 1 and 2 immediately imply the indistinguishability of the following two distributions

$$\Big(\mathbf{A}_0, \mathbf{T}_0, \mathbf{A}_1, \mathsf{GaussSamp}(\mathbf{A}_0, r_b\mathbf{A}_1 + \mathbf{e}_b; \mathbf{T}_0),$$
$$\mathsf{GaussSamp}(\mathbf{A}_0, sr_b\mathbf{A}_1 + \mathbf{e}_b'; \mathbf{T}_0)\Big)$$

$$\approx_c \Big(\mathbf{A}_0, \mathbf{T}_0, \mathbf{A}_1, \mathsf{GaussSamp}(\mathbf{A}_0, \mathbf{U}_b; \mathbf{T}_0),$$
$$\mathsf{GaussSamp}(\mathbf{A}_0, \mathbf{U}_b'; \mathbf{T}_0)\Big)$$

$$\approx_s \Big(\mathbf{A}_0, \mathbf{T}_0, \mathbf{A}_1, \mathbf{R}_b, \mathbf{R}_b'\Big)$$

where $\mathbf{R}_b, \mathbf{R}_b' \leftarrow D_{\mathcal{R}^m,\sigma}$. Since this is exactly the distribution generated by REncode, this establishes GXDH. $\square$

Entropic security of our encoding scheme follows directly from the entropic PLWE assumption. We state the lemma below.

LEMMA 4.4 (ENTROPIC SECURITY). *Let n be a power of 2, and let $\mathcal{R} = \mathbb{Z}[x]/\langle x^n + 1\rangle$. Let $q = 2^{\omega(\log \lambda)}$ be such that $q \equiv 1 \pmod{2n}$ and define $\mathcal{R}_q = \mathcal{R}/q\mathcal{R}$. Let $m \in \mathbb{N}$ and let χ be a distribution over the integers. Then, for every α, our encoding scheme satisfies α-entropic security (Property 2) under the α-entropic $\mathsf{PLWE}_{n,m,q,\chi}$ assumption (Definition 2.7).*

5. THE CONJUNCTION OBFUSCATOR

Let $(\mathsf{Setup}, \mathsf{Encode}, \mathsf{Mult}, \mathsf{EqualTest})$ be a directed encoding scheme with associated with a message space $\mathcal{M} \subseteq R_M$ for some ring R_M, and a distribution $\mathcal{D}_M$ over $\mathcal{M}$. Given a conjunction $F_v \in \mathcal{C}_\ell^{\mathsf{conj}}$ represented via a vector $v \in \{0, 1, \star\}^\ell$, the obfuscator $\Pi_v \leftarrow \mathsf{Obf}(1^\lambda, F_v)$ proceeds as follows.

- Choose $(\mathsf{PK}_i, \mathsf{EK}_i) \leftarrow \mathsf{Setup}(1^\lambda, 1^{\ell+1})$ for $i \in \{0, \ldots, \ell+1\}$.

- Choose uniformly random $s_{i,b}, r_{i,b} \leftarrow \mathcal{D}_M$ for every $i \in [\ell]$ and $b \in \{0, 1\}$ subject to the condition that for every i such that $v_i = \star$, we set $s_{i,0} = s_{i,1}$. For such positions i, we define $s_{i,\star} = s_{i,0} = s_{i,1}$.

- Compute $S_{i,b} = \mathsf{Encode}_{\mathsf{PK}_{i-1} \to \mathsf{PK}_i}(\mathsf{EK}_{i-1}, s_{i,b}r_{i,b})$ and $R_{i,b} = \mathsf{Encode}_{\mathsf{PK}_{i-1} \to \mathsf{PK}_i}(\mathsf{EK}_{i-1}, r_{i,b})$ for every $i \in [\ell]$ and $b \in \{0, 1\}$.

- Compute $S_{\ell+1} = \mathsf{Encode}_{\mathsf{PK}_\ell \to \mathsf{PK}_{\ell+1}}(\mathsf{EK}_\ell, r_{\ell+1} \cdot \prod_{i=1}^\ell s_{i,v_i})$ and $R_{\ell+1} = \mathsf{Encode}_{\mathsf{PK}_\ell \to \mathsf{PK}_{\ell+1}}(\mathsf{EK}_\ell, r_{\ell+1})$.

The description[1] of the obfuscated program Π_v consists of

$$\Pi_v = \Big(\{\mathsf{PK}_i\}_{i \in \{0, \ldots, \ell+1\}}, \{S_{i,b}, R_{i,b}\}_{i \in [\ell], b \in \{0, 1\}}, S_{\ell+1}, R_{\ell+1}\Big)$$

The obfuscated program Π_v, on input $x \in \{0, 1\}^\ell$, proceeds as follows.

- Compute $S^* \leftarrow \mathsf{Mult}(S_{1,x_1}, S_{2,x_2}, \ldots, S_{\ell,x_\ell}, R_{\ell+1})$ and $R^* \leftarrow \mathsf{Mult}(R_{1,x_1}, R_{2,x_2}, \ldots, R_{\ell,x_\ell}, S_{\ell+1})$

---
[1] It suffices to give out $\mathsf{PK}_0, \mathsf{PK}_{\ell+1}$ instead of $(\mathsf{PK}_0, \ldots, \mathsf{PK}_{\ell+1})$.

- Output whatever $\mathsf{EqualTest}_{\mathsf{PK}_0 \to \mathsf{PK}_{\ell+1}}(S^*, R^*)$ outputs.

THEOREM 5.1 (DISTRIBUTIONAL VIRTUAL BLACK-BOX). *Based on the GXDH and the $\alpha(\lambda)$-entropic security properties on the directed encoding scheme, our obfuscator is an $(\alpha(\lambda) + 1)$-distributional VBB obfuscator for conjunctions (Definition 2.4).*

We first prove that the obfuscator is functionality preserving. The polynomial slowdown property follows directly by inspection.

LEMMA 5.2 (FUNCTIONALITY). *There is a negligible function $\nu(\lambda)$ such that, for every $\ell \in \mathbb{N}$ and every $v \in \{0, 1, \star\}^\ell$:*

$$\Pr\left[\forall x \in \{0,1\}^\ell \ : \ \Pi_v(x) = F_v(x)\right] \geq 1 - \nu(\lambda).$$

where the probability is over $\Pi_v \leftarrow \mathsf{Obf}(1^\lambda, F_v)$.

Informally, functionality follows from the fact that with high probability,

$$F_v(x) = 1 \Leftrightarrow s_{i,v_i} = s_{i,x_i} \ \forall i \in [\ell] \Leftrightarrow \prod_{i \in [\ell]} s_{i,v_i} = \prod_{i \in [\ell]} s_{i,x_i}$$

PROOF. Fix any $\ell \in \mathbb{N}$ and $v \in \{0, 1, \star\}^\ell$ and $x \in \{0,1\}^\ell$. Let $\Pi_v \leftarrow \mathsf{Obf}(1^\lambda, F_v)$. During the evaluation of the obfuscated program Π_v on input x the values S^*, R^* that are computed satisfy $S^* \in \mathcal{E}^{(\ell+1)}_{\mathsf{PK}_0, \mathsf{PK}_{\ell+1}, s^*}$ and $R^* \in \mathcal{E}^{(\ell+1)}_{\mathsf{PK}_0, \mathsf{PK}_{\ell+1}, r^*}$ where

$$s^* = r_{\ell+1} \prod_{i=1}^{\ell} s_{i,x_i} r_{i,x_i} \quad \text{and} \quad r^* = r_{\ell+1} \prod_{i=1}^{\ell} s_{i,v_i} r_{i,x_i}$$

The program outputs 1 iff $\mathsf{EqualTest}_{\mathsf{PK}_0 \to \mathsf{PK}_{\ell+1}}(S^*, R^*) = 1$ which, by the correctness of the encoding scheme, happens iff $s^* = r^*$. This happens with probability 1 if $F_v(x) = 1$ and therefore correctness always holds in this case. On the other hand, if $F_v(x) = 0$ then let j be some index such that $v_j \neq \star$ and $x_j \neq v_j$. We have

$$\Pr[F_v(x) \neq \Pi_v(x)]$$

$$= \Pr_{\{s_{i,b}, r_{i,b}\}, r_{\ell+1}}\left[r_{\ell+1} \prod_{i=1}^{\ell} s_{i,x_i} r_{i,x_i} = r_{\ell+1} \prod_{i=1}^{\ell} s_{i,v_i} r_{i,x_i}\right]$$

$$\leq \Pr[\mathsf{NotInv}] + \Pr_{s_{j,x_j}}\left[s_{j,x_j} = z\right]$$

where NotInv is the event that one of $r_{i,b}, s_{i,b}, r_{\ell+1}$ (other than s_{j,x_j}) is non-invertible and $z = \prod_{i \neq j} s_{i,v_i} / s_{i,x_i}$. By lemma 2.5, we can bound the first probability by $\mathrm{poly}(\lambda)/q$ and the second probability is $\leq 2^{-\mathbf{H}_\infty(\mathcal{D}_M)} \leq 1/q$. By our choice of q, this is $\leq 2^{-\ell}\nu(\lambda)$ for some negligible $\nu(\lambda)$. Taking a union bound over all $x \in \{0,1\}^\ell$, we get

$$\Pr[\forall x \in \{0,1\}^\ell \ : \ \Pi_v(x) = F_v(x)] \geq 1 - \nu(\lambda)$$

which proves the lemma. $\square$

Next we prove that the obfuscator is secure. It suffices to prove that the obfuscator satisfies $\alpha(\lambda)$-entropic security (Definition 2.5), as we can then rely on Lemma 2.2 to argue that this implies $(\alpha(\lambda) + 1)$-distributional VBB security.

LEMMA 5.3 (SECURITY). *Based on the GXDH and $\alpha(\lambda)$-entropic security properties of the directed encoding scheme, our obfuscator satisfies $\alpha(\lambda)$-entropic security (Definition 2.5).*

PROOF. The simulator $\mathsf{Sim}(1^\lambda, 1^\ell)$ chooses $(\mathsf{PK}_i, \mathsf{EK}_i) \leftarrow \mathsf{Setup}(1^\lambda, 1^{\ell+1})$ for $i \in \{0, \ldots, \ell + 1\}$. It chooses $\widetilde{S}_{i,b} \leftarrow \mathsf{REncode}_{\mathsf{PK}_{i-1} \to \mathsf{PK}_i}()$, $\widetilde{R}_{i,b} \leftarrow \mathsf{REncode}_{\mathsf{PK}_{i-1} \to \mathsf{PK}_i}()$ for $i \in [\ell + 1]$. Finally it outputs the simulated program $\widetilde{\Pi} = \left(\{PK_i\}_{i \in \{0,\ldots,\ell+1\}}, \{\widetilde{S}_{i,b}, \widetilde{R}_{i,b}\}_{i \in [\ell], b \in \{0,1\}}, \widetilde{S}_{\ell+1}, \widetilde{R}_{\ell+1}\right)$.

We want to show that, for any efficiently samplable distribution $D = \{D_\lambda\} \in \mathcal{D}_\alpha$ having $\alpha(\lambda)$-entropy given wildcards, the real distribution (Π_v, aux) is indistinguishable from the simulated $(\widetilde{\Pi}, \mathsf{aux})$ where $(F_v, \mathsf{aux}) \leftarrow D_\lambda$, $\Pi_v \leftarrow \mathsf{Obf}(1^\lambda, F_v)$ and $\widetilde{\Pi} \leftarrow \mathsf{Sim}(1^\lambda, 1^\ell)$. We do so via a series of hybrids.

Hybrid 0. This is the real distribution (Π_v, aux) consisting of:

$$\left(\{\mathsf{PK}_i\}_{i \in \{0,\ldots,\ell+1\}}, \{S_{i,b}, R_{i,b}\}_{i \in [\ell], b \in \{0,1\}},\right.$$
$$\left. S_{\ell+1}, R_{\ell+1}, \mathsf{aux}\right).$$

Hybrid 1. This is the distribution:

$$\left(\{\mathsf{PK}_i\}_{i \in \{0,\ldots,\ell+1\}}, \{S_{i,b}, R_{i,b}\}_{i \in [\ell], b \in \{0,1\}},\right.$$
$$\left. \boxed{\widetilde{S}_{\ell+1}}, R_{\ell+1}, \mathsf{aux}\right).$$

where everything is the same as in Hybrid 0 except that we now choose $\widetilde{S}_{\ell+1} \leftarrow \mathsf{REncode}_{\mathsf{PK}_\ell \to \mathsf{PK}_{\ell+1}}()$.

LEMMA 5.4. *Assuming α-entropic security of the encoding scheme, Hybrid 1 is indistinguishable from Hybrid 0.*

PROOF. Assume that a PPT adversary Adv can distinguish between Hybrid 0 and 1 with probability $\varepsilon(\lambda)$. By the $\alpha(\lambda)$-entropic security of D we know that $(F_v, \mathsf{aux}) \leftarrow D_\lambda$ satisfies $\widetilde{\mathbf{H}}_\infty(v|\mathsf{aux}, w) \geq \alpha(\lambda)$ where $w = \{i \ : \ v_i = \star\}$. Then we construct an efficiently samplable distribution $D' = \{D'_\lambda\}$ such that $(x, z) \leftarrow D'_\lambda$ satisfies $\widetilde{\mathbf{H}}_\infty(x|z) \geq \alpha(\lambda)$ and a PPT adversary Adv' that breaks entropic security of the encoding with the distribution D'.

Define $(x, z) \leftarrow D'_\lambda$ where $x \in \{0,1\}^{2\ell+1}$ is chosen as follows. First, select $(v, \mathsf{aux}) \leftarrow D_\lambda$ and, for $i \in [\ell]$, set:

- $x_{2i-1} := 1, x_{2i} := 0$ if $v_i = 0$ or $v_i = \star$
- $x_{2i-1} := 0, x_{2i} := 1$ otherwise

Set $x_{2\ell+1} := 1$. The side information is going to be the $z = (\mathsf{aux}, w = \{i \ : \ v_i = \star\})$. Since v can be recovered from x, z we have $\widetilde{\mathbf{H}}_\infty(x|z) \geq \widetilde{\mathbf{H}}_\infty(v|w, \mathsf{aux}) \geq \alpha(\lambda)$.

The adversary Adv' gets $2\ell + 1$ random elements $\widetilde{s}_1, \ldots, \widetilde{s}_{2\ell+1}$, keys $\mathsf{PK}, \mathsf{PK}', \mathsf{EK}$, side information $z = (\mathsf{aux}, w)$ and an encoding c. It defines $r_{\ell+1} = \widetilde{s}_{2\ell+1}$ and:

- $s_{i,0} := \widetilde{s}_{2i-1}$ and $s_{i,1} := \widetilde{s}_{2i}$ for $i \in [\ell] \setminus w$,
- $s_{i,0} := \widetilde{s}_{2i-1}, s_{i,1} := \widetilde{s}_{2i-1}$ for $i \in w$.

154

Note that this ensures that $r_{\ell+1} \prod_{i\in[\ell]} s_{i,v_i} = \prod_{i\in[2\ell+1]} \widetilde{s}_i^{x_i}$. The adversary Adv' chooses $(\mathsf{PK}_i, \mathsf{EK}_i) \leftarrow \mathsf{Setup}(1^\lambda, 1^{\ell+1})$ for $i \in [\ell-1]$ and sets $\mathsf{PK}_\ell = \mathsf{PK}$, $\mathsf{EK}_\ell = \mathsf{EK}$ and $\mathsf{PK}_{\ell+1} = \mathsf{PK}'$. It chooses $r_{i,b} \leftarrow \mathcal{D}_M$ $i \in [\ell]$ $b \in \{0,1\}$ at random. It uses the above values to define $S_{i,b}, R_{i,b}$, and $R_{\ell+1}$ the same way as the obfuscation scheme. Finally, it sets $S_{\ell+1} := c$. It then runs:

$$\mathsf{Adv}\bigg(\{\mathsf{PK}_i\}_{i\in\{0,\ldots,\ell+1\}}, \{S_{i,b}, R_{i,b}\}_{i\in[\ell],b\in\{0,1\}},$$
$$S_{\ell+1}, R_{\ell+1}, \mathsf{aux} \bigg)$$

and outputs what it outputs.

It's easy to see that if $c \leftarrow \mathsf{Encode}_{\mathsf{PK}\to\mathsf{PK}'}(\mathsf{EK}, \prod_{i=1}^{2\ell+1} \widetilde{s}_i^{x_i})$ then this matches the distribution in Hybrid 0 while if $c \leftarrow \mathsf{REncode}_{\mathsf{PK}\to\mathsf{PK}'}()$ then this matches the distribution of Hybrid 1. Therefore the advantage of Adv' in the in the entropic security game is the same as that of Adv in distinguishing Hybrids 0 and 1. $\square$

Hybrid 2. This is the distribution

$$\bigg(\{\mathsf{PK}_i\}_{i\in\{0,\ldots,\ell+1\}}, \{S_{i,b}, R_{i,b}\}_{i\in[\ell],b\in\{0,1\}},$$
$$\widetilde{S}_{\ell+1}, \boxed{\widetilde{R}_{\ell+1}}, \mathsf{aux} \bigg).$$

where everything is the same as in Hybrid 1 except that we now choose $\widetilde{R}_{\ell+1} \leftarrow \mathsf{REncode}_{\mathsf{PK}_\ell\to\mathsf{PK}_{\ell+1}}()$.

LEMMA 5.5. *Hybrid 2 is indistinguishable from Hybrid 1 by GXDH-1 security of the encoding scheme.*

PROOF. Assume a PPT adversary Adv can distinguish Hybrids 1 and 2 with advantage ε. We construct an adversary Adv' that has advantage ε in the GXDH-1 security game.

The adversary $\mathsf{Adv}'(\mathsf{PK}, \mathsf{PK}', \mathsf{EK}, c)$ needs to distinguish between $c \leftarrow \mathsf{Encode}_{\mathsf{PK}\to\mathsf{PK}'}(\mathsf{EK}, r)$ where $r \leftarrow \mathcal{D}_M$ and $c \leftarrow \mathsf{REncode}_{\mathsf{PK}\to\mathsf{PK}'}()$. It samples the distribution of Hybrid 1 by setting $\mathsf{PK}_\ell := \mathsf{PK}$, $\mathsf{EK}_\ell := \mathsf{EK}$, $\mathsf{PK}_{\ell+1} := \mathsf{PK}'$ and $R_{\ell+1} := c$ and otherwise selects the rest of the components as in Hybrid 1. Finally it runs Adv on the sampled values and outputs what it outputs.

It's easy to see that if $c \leftarrow \mathsf{Encode}_{\mathsf{PK}\to\mathsf{PK}'}(\mathsf{EK}, r)$ where $r \leftarrow \mathcal{D}_M$ then the above matches Hybrid 1, and if $c \leftarrow \mathsf{REncode}_{\mathsf{PK}\to\mathsf{PK}'}()$ then the above matches Hybrid 2. Therefore the advantage of Adv' in the in the GXDH-1 security game is the same as that of Adv in distinguishing Hybrids 1 and 2. $\square$

Hybrid 3.j. For $j \in \{0, \ldots, \ell\}$ we define Hybrid 3.j as the distribution

$$\bigg(\{\mathsf{PK}_i\}_{i\in\{0,\ldots,\ell+1\}}, \{S_{i,b}, R_{i,b}\}_{i\in[j],b\in\{0,1\}},$$
$$\boxed{\{\widetilde{S}_{i,b}, \widetilde{R}_{i,b}\}_{i\in\{j+1,\ldots,\ell\},b\in\{0,1\}}}, \widetilde{S}_{\ell+1}, \widetilde{R}_{\ell+1} \bigg)$$

where everything is the same as in Hybrid 2 except that we now choose $\widetilde{R}_{i,b}, \widetilde{S}_{i,b} \leftarrow \mathsf{REncode}_{\mathsf{PK}_{i-1}\to\mathsf{PK}_i}()$ for $i \in \{j+1, \ldots, \ell\}, b \in \{0,1\}$.

Note that Hybrid 3.ℓ is the same as Hybrid 2 and Hybrid 3.0 is the same as $(\widetilde{\Pi}, \mathsf{aux})$ where $\widetilde{\Pi}$ is the simulated program . Therefore it suffices to prove the following.

LEMMA 5.6. *For all $j \in [\ell]$ Hybrid 3.j is indistinguishable from Hybrid 3.$(j-1)$ by the GXDH security of the encoding scheme.*

PROOF. We first define an intermediate distribution Hybrid' 3.j which is the same as Hybrid 3.j except that when $v_j \neq \star$ then the values $\{S_{j,b}, R_{j,b}\}_{b\in\{0,1\}}$ are replaced by random $\{\widetilde{S}_{j,b}, \widetilde{R}_{j,b}\}_{b\in\{0,1\}}$.

We claim that Hybrid 3.j and Hybrid' 3.j are indistinguishable. In particular, if there is a PPT adversary Adv that distinguishes Hybrid 3.j and Hybrid' 3.j with advantage ε then we construct a PPT adversary Adv' with advantage ε in the GXDH problem. The adversary $\mathsf{Adv}'(\mathsf{PK}, \mathsf{PK}', \mathsf{EK}, c_0, c_1, d_0, d_1)$ samples the distribution of Hybrid 3.j except that it sets $\mathsf{PK}_{j-1} := \mathsf{PK}, \mathsf{EK}_{j-1} := \mathsf{EK}, \mathsf{PK}_j := \mathsf{PK}'$ and, when $v_j \neq \star$, it plugs in $R_{j,0} := c_0, R_{j,1} := c_1, S_{j,0} := d_0, S_{j,1} := d_1$. It then runs Adv on the sampled distribution. It is easy to see that when Adv' gets as input a GXDH tuple then the distribution it samples matches Hybrid 3.j and else it matches Hybrid' 3.j which proves the claim.

Next we define and intermediate distribution Hybrid'' 3.j which is the same as Hybrid' 3.j except that when $v_j = \star$ then the values $\{S_{j,0}, R_{j,0}\}$ are also replaced by random $\{\widetilde{S}_{j,0}, \widetilde{R}_{j,0}\}$.

We claim that Hybrid' 3.j and Hybrid'' 3.j are indistinguishable. In particular, if there is a PPT distinguisher Adv that distinguishes Hybrid' 3.j and Hybrid'' 3.j with advantage ε then we construct a PPT distinguisher Adv' with advantage ε in the GXDH-2 problem. The adversary $\mathsf{Adv}'(\mathsf{PK}, \mathsf{PK}', \mathsf{EK}, c, d)$ samples the distribution of Hybrid' 3.j except that it sets $\mathsf{PK}_{j-1} := \mathsf{PK}, \mathsf{EK}_{j-1} := \mathsf{EK}, \mathsf{PK}_j := \mathsf{PK}'$ and, when $v_j = \star$, it plugs in $R_{j,0} := c, S_{j,0} := d$. It then runs Adv on the sampled distribution. It is easy to see that when Adv' gets as input a GXDH tuple then the distribution it samples matches Hybrid' 3.j and else it matches Hybrid'' 3.j which proves the claim.

Lastly, we claim that Hybrid'' 3.j and Hybrid 3.$(j-1)$ are indistinguishable. The proof of this is identical to that showing the indistinguishability of Hybrid' 3.j and Hybrid'' 3.j.

Combining the above, we get the proof of the lemma. $\square$

Combining the above we see that Hybrid 0 (obfuscated program) is indistinguishable from Hybrid 3.0 (simulated program) which proves the lemma.

6. REFERENCES

[1] Miklós Ajtai. Generating hard instances of the short basis problem. In *ICALP*, pages 1–9, 1999.

[2] Saikrishna Badrinarayanan, Eric Miles, Amit Sahai, and Mark Zhandry. Post-zeroizing obfuscation: The case of evasive circuits. Cryptology ePrint Archive, Report 2015/167, 2015. http://eprint.iacr.org/.

[3] Boaz Barak, Nir Bitansky, Ran Canetti, Yael Tauman Kalai, Omer Paneth, and Amit Sahai. Obfuscation for evasive functions. In *TCC*, pages 26–51, 2014.

[4] Boaz Barak, Oded Goldreich, Russell Impagliazzo, Steven Rudich, Amit Sahai, Salil P. Vadhan, and Ke Yang. On the (im)possibility of obfuscating programs. *J. ACM*, 59(2):6, 2012.

[5] Zvika Brakerski and Guy N. Rothblum. Obfuscating conjunctions. In *CRYPTO (2)*, pages 416–434, 2013.

[6] Ran Canetti. Towards realizing random oracles: Hash functions that hide all partial information. In *CRYPTO*, pages 455–469, 1997.

[7] Ran Canetti, Guy N. Rothblum, and Mayank Varia. Obfuscation of hyperplane membership. In *TCC*, pages 72–89, 2010.

[8] Jung Hee Cheon, Kyoohyung Han, Changmin Lee, Hansol Ryu, and Damien Stehlé. Cryptanalysis of the multilinear map over the integers. In *EUROCRYPT*, 2015. Also, Cryptology ePrint Archive, Report 2014/906.

[9] Jung Hee Cheon, Changmin Lee, and Hansol Ryu. Cryptanalysis of the new CLT multilinear maps. Cryptology ePrint Archive, Report 2015/934, 2015. http://eprint.iacr.org/.

[10] Jean-Sebastien Coron. Cryptanalysis of GGH15 multilinear maps. Cryptology ePrint Archive, Report 2015/1037, 2015. http://eprint.iacr.org/.

[11] Jean-Sébastien Coron, Craig Gentry, Shai Halevi, Tancrède Lepoint, Hemanta K. Maji, Eric Miles, Mariana Raykova, Amit Sahai, and Mehdi Tibouchi. Zeroizing without low-level zeroes: New MMAP attacks and their limitations. In *CRYPTO I*, pages 247–266, 2015.

[12] Jean-Sébastien Coron, Tancrède Lepoint, and Mehdi Tibouchi. Practical multilinear maps over the integers. In *CRYPTO (1)*, pages 476–493, 2013.

[13] Jean-Sébastien Coron, Tancrède Lepoint, and Mehdi Tibouchi. New multilinear maps over the integers. In *CRYPTO I*, pages 267–286, 2015.

[14] Yevgeniy Dodis, Shafi Goldwasser, Yael Tauman Kalai, Chris Peikert, and Vinod Vaikuntanathan. Public-key encryption schemes with auxiliary inputs. In *TCC*, pages 361–381, 2010.

[15] Yevgeniy Dodis, Rafail Ostrovsky, Leonid Reyzin, and Adam Smith. Fuzzy extractors: How to generate strong keys from biometrics and other noisy data. *SIAM J. Comput.*, 38(1):97–139, 2008.

[16] Yevgeniy Dodis and Adam Smith. Correcting errors without leaking partial information. In *STOC*, pages 654–663, 2005.

[17] Léo Ducas and Alain Durmus. Ring-LWE in polynomial rings. In *PKC 2012*, pages 34–51, 2012.

[18] Sanjam Garg, Craig Gentry, and Shai Halevi. Candidate multilinear maps from ideal lattices. In *EUROCRYPT*, pages 1–17, 2013.

[19] Sanjam Garg, Craig Gentry, Shai Halevi, Mariana Raykova, Amit Sahai, and Brent Waters. Candidate indistinguishability obfuscation and functional encryption for all circuits. In *FOCS*, pages 40–49, 2013. Also, Cryptology ePrint Archive, Report 2013/451.

[20] Craig Gentry, Sergey Gorbunov, and Shai Halevi. Graph-induced multilinear maps from lattices. In *TCC*, pages 498–527, 2015.

[21] Craig Gentry, Chris Peikert, and Vinod Vaikuntanathan. Trapdoors for hard lattices and new cryptographic constructions. In *STOC*, pages 197–206, 2008.

[22] Shafi Goldwasser, Yael Tauman Kalai, Chris Peikert, and Vinod Vaikuntanathan. Robustness of the learning with errors assumption. In *Innovations in Computer Science - ICS*, pages 230–240, 2010.

[23] Shafi Goldwasser and Guy N. Rothblum. On best-possible obfuscation. In *TCC*, pages 194–213, 2007.

[24] Satoshi Hada. Zero-knowledge and code obfuscation. In *ASIACRYPT*, pages 443–457, 2000.

[25] Shai Halevi. Graded encoding, variations on a scheme. Cryptology ePrint Archive, Report 2015/866, 2015. http://eprint.iacr.org/.

[26] Dennis Hofheinz, John Malone-Lee, and Martijn Stam. Obfuscation for cryptographic purposes. In *TCC*, pages 214–232, 2007.

[27] Susan Hohenberger, Guy N. Rothblum, Abhi Shelat, and Vinod Vaikuntanathan. Securely obfuscating re-encryption. In *TCC*, pages 233–252, 2007.

[28] Yupu Hu and Huiwen Jia. Cryptanalysis of GGH map. Cryptology ePrint Archive, Report 2015/301, 2015. http://eprint.iacr.org/.

[29] Ben Lynn, Manoj Prabhakaran, and Amit Sahai. Positive results and techniques for obfuscation. In *EUROCRYPT*, pages 20–39, 2004.

[30] Vadim Lyubashevsky, Chris Peikert, and Oded Regev. On ideal lattices and learning with errors over rings. *J. ACM*, 60(6):43, 2013.

[31] Daniele Micciancio and Chris Peikert. Trapdoors for lattices: Simpler, tighter, faster, smaller. In *EUROCRYPT*, pages 700–718, 2012.

[32] Brice Minaud and Pierre-Alain Fouque. Cryptanalysis of the new multilinear map over the integers. Cryptology ePrint Archive, Report 2015/941, 2015. http://eprint.iacr.org/.

[33] Damien Stehlé and Ron Steinfeld. Making NTRU as secure as worst-case problems over ideal lattices. In *EUROCRYPT*, pages 27–47, 2011.

[34] Hoeteck Wee. On obfuscating point functions. In *STOC*, pages 523–532, 2005.

Secure Multiparty Computation with General Interaction Patterns

Shai Halevi
IBM Research, USA

Yuval Ishai
Technion, Israel and UCLA

Abhishek Jain
Johns Hopkins University

Eyal Kushilevitz
Technion, Israel

Tal Rabin
IBM Research, USA

ABSTRACT

We present a unified framework for studying secure multiparty computation (MPC) with *arbitrarily restricted interaction patterns* such as a chain, a star, a directed tree, or a directed graph. Our study generalizes both standard MPC and recent models for MPC with specific restricted interaction patterns, such as those studied by Halevi et al. (Crypto 2011), Goldwasser et al. (Eurocrypt 2014), and Beimel et al. (Crypto 2014).

Since restricted interaction patterns cannot always yield full security for MPC, we start by formalizing the notion of "best possible security" for any interaction pattern. We then obtain the following main results:

- **Completeness theorem.** We prove that the star interaction pattern is *complete* for the problem of MPC with general interaction patterns.

- **Positive results.** We present both information-theoretic and computationally secure protocols for computing arbitrary functions with general interaction patterns. We also present more efficient protocols for computing *symmetric* functions, both in the computational and in the information-theoretic setting.

  Our computationally secure protocols for general functions *necessarily* rely on indistinguishability obfuscation while the ones for computing symmetric functions make simple use of multilinear maps.

- **Negative results.** We show that, in many cases, the complexity of our information-theoretic protocols is essentially the best that can be achieved.

All of our protocols rely on a correlated randomness setup, which is *necessary* in our setting (for computing general functions). In the computational case, we also present a generic procedure to make any correlated randomness setup *reusable*, in the common random string model.

Although most of our information-theoretic protocols have exponential complexity, they may be practical for functions

on small domains (e.g., $\{0,1\}^{20}$), where they are concretely faster than their computational counterparts.

1. INTRODUCTION

Secure multiparty computation (MPC) allows n mutually suspicious parties to evaluate a function on their joint inputs in such a manner that no information about their inputs, beyond the output of the computation, is revealed to each other. Since the first general feasibility results for MPC [43, 28, 5, 12], almost all prior work in this area has considered protocols that require *full interaction* between the parties. Such protocols typically proceed in rounds, where in each round each party may send messages to all other parties, thus requiring that all parties remain online throughout the execution of the protocol.

MPC with Restricted Interaction. Full interaction between the parties is often problematic, and in many scenarios, simply infeasible. For instance, physical distances between wireless devices may prevent them from directly communicating with each other, and temporal constraints may restrict their availability to send or receive messages (e.g. due to battery life). Furthermore, efficiency considerations may also motivate a leaner form of communication. Consider, for instance, the goal of computing the majority vote over the inputs of n parties. While this task can be performed using only $(n-1)$ messages if no security is needed, typical MPC protocols with full interaction involve $\Omega(n^2)$ point-to-point messages to compute the same task securely.

Such considerations have motivated the study of MPC protocols with *restricted* interaction between the parties. Halevi, Lindell, and Pinkas [33] were the first to study this problem: they consider an interaction pattern where each of the n parties, in an ordered fashion, sends a single message to a central server, who eventually computes the output of the function. A different interaction pattern, where each party independently (i.e., without any predetermined order) sends a single message to the server, was recently considered by Goldwasser et al. [29] and Beimel et al. [3]. In both cases, the security guarantee is *necessarily* weaker than the standard simulation-based security for MPC (see below for further discussion on security).

The above works constitute two specific examples of restricted interaction patterns. In general, different application scenarios may dictate different interaction patterns. For example, applications involving data aggregation typically use interaction patterns that can be represented as a directed tree. Furthermore, the topology of the communication network (used by an application) may itself limit the

Permission to make digital or hard copies of all or part of this work for personal or classroom use is granted without fee provided that copies are not made or distributed for profit or commercial advantage and that copies bear this notice and the full citation on the first page. Copyrights for components of this work owned by others than ACM must be honored. Abstracting with credit is permitted. To copy otherwise, or republish, to post on servers or to redistribute to lists, requires prior specific permission and/or a fee. Request permissions from Permissions@acm.org.

ITCS'16, January 14-16, 2016, Cambridge, MA, USA
© 2016 ACM. ISBN 978-1-4503-4057-1/16/01 ...$15.00.
DOI: http://dx.doi.org/10.1145/2840728.2840760.

choices of interaction patterns: e.g., a communication network without any node with full degree is not consistent with server-centered interaction patterns. Importantly, as we discuss below, the security guarantees that we get would typically depend on the interaction pattern at hand.

Our Goal: MPC with General Interaction Patterns. Seeking to understand the fundamental role of interaction patterns in MPC, we study the problem of MPC with arbitrarily restricted or *general* interaction patterns. We ask the following broad question:

> Given an arbitrary n-party interaction pattern $\mathcal{I}$ and an n-input function f, can f be securely realized by a protocol that complies with $\mathcal{I}$? If so, how efficiently and under what assumptions?

Before addressing this question, we should clarify how we model interaction patterns, what we mean by "securely," and what setup assumptions we are willing to make.

Modeling Interaction Patterns. A natural starting approach is to represent an interaction pattern as a directed acyclic graph (DAG), where each node represents a party who expects to receive messages from all of its parents and can then send messages to all of its children, and where the sinks of the graph compute outputs. Two simple examples of DAGs include a *chain*, a simple directed path traversing all nodes, and a *star*, a graph connecting all nodes to a single central node. The protocols from [33, 32] can be adapted to accommodate a chain-based interaction, whereas the protocols from [29, 3] were designed for the case of a star-based interaction. More general DAG-based interaction patterns naturally arise in "self-forming sensor networks," where multiple sensor nodes form an arbitrary communication graph and then collect and compute on data that is transmitted, using the smallest possible number of messages, to a central base station.

While DAGs are an important special case, general interaction patterns are not necessarily restricted to DAGs. Some other useful patterns include the server-centered interaction pattern from [33], a *two-way chain*, where messages travel along a chain from P_n to P_1 and back to P_n who computes an output, or the traditional multi-round protocols over a fully-connected point-to-point network. In the full paper we describe a unified modeling of general interaction patterns.

1.1 Formulating Achievable Security

In the traditional model of MPC, the corrupted parties are restricted to learning the outputs of f on just a *single* input $(x_1, \ldots, x_n)$. However, as observed by [33], this property cannot always be achieved in the case of restricted interaction patterns. For instance, in the server-centered interaction pattern of [33], if both the server and the last few parties $P_i, \ldots, P_n$ are corrupted, there is nothing to prevent the adversary from learning the value of f on the honest inputs $x_1, \ldots, x_{i-1}$ and *every possible choice* of corrupted inputs $x_i^*, \ldots, x_n^*$.

To define the "best possible security" for a fixed interaction pattern, we use the notions of free and fixed inputs and residual function from [33]. We call the inputs that the adversary can vary the *free inputs*, and the other inputs are the *fixed inputs*. Clearly, all the honest parties' inputs are fixed. Crucially, however, some of the inputs controlled by the adversary can be fixed as well. For example, in the protocols from [33], the only free inputs are those of corrupted

parties that send messages *after the last honest party does*; the inputs of all other corrupted parties are fixed.

Extending the model from [33] to our setting of general interaction patterns, we first consider the case where only one party computes an output and call this party the evaluator. The input of a corrupted party P_i is considered fixed if the interaction pattern includes *any message path* that leads from P_i to the evaluator and passes through *some* honest party. The input of a corrupted P_i is free if *all paths* from P_i to the evaluator consist only of other corrupted parties. For example, in a star pattern with a corrupted center, the inputs of all the corrupted parties are free [29, 3]. In contrast, traditional MPC requires the inputs of all corrupted parties to be fixed.

The "best possible security" is defined by the *residual function*, that captures everything that the adversary can learn about the honest parties' by restricting f to the values of all the fixed inputs while allowing arbitrary choices of the free inputs. Some additional subtleties arise in the malicious-adversary model when multiple parties compute outputs; in particular, security in this case generalizes goals such as Byzantine agreement. We discuss these issues further in the full paper leaving the issue of malicious-security with multiple output nodes to future work.

An important technical point relates to the achievable notion of simulation. Traditional ideal-vs-real definitions of security (cf. [31, 9, 27]) require *efficient simulation*, but it is known that efficient simulation is, in general, impossible in our setting [33, 29]. For example, protocols with efficient simulation for a star (or even chain) interaction pattern imply virtual black-box obfuscation [29], which is known to be impossible in general [2]. To get around these impossibility results, we settle for security with respect to *indistinguishability* or *unbounded simulation*.

Correlated randomness setup. It is not hard to see that without any form of setup, even very simple functions such as majority cannot always be realized with any meaningful notion of security. Consider for instance the star pattern: here, all the adversary's inputs are *free*; as such, the adversary can simply learn the residual function in the information-theoretic setting in the absence of any setup [3].[1]

Perhaps the simplest model to circumvent such impossibility results is the "minimal model" (PSM) from [21] with general *correlated randomness setup*, where the parties have access to a source $(r_1, \ldots, r_n)$ of correlated random strings. When implementing such protocols, the correlated randomness can come from a trusted dealer or generated using an offline MPC protocol that takes place before the inputs are known and before the limitations on interaction are imposed. This clean model is popular both for a theoretical study of MPC and as a platform for practical implementations that exploit the efficiency benefits of offline preprocessing. (See [6, 16, 3, 17] and references therein.)

The correlated randomness setup can either be *reusable* or *non-reusable*. Namely, it can either be akin to a one-time pad, allowing only a single run of the protocol (which is typically the case for protocols with information-theoretic security), or it can allow polynomial number of runs (which is sometimes possible in the computational setting). A key advantage of the correlated randomness setup model is that

---

[1]In the computational setting, such an attack can be applied to learnable functions.

we can hope to tolerate any number of corrupted parties even in the information-theoretic setting [37, 35, 6].

Is "Best Possible Security" Good Enough? Though weaker than the standard notion of security for MPC protocols, our notion of "best possible security" is still meaningful in many interesting cases. First, depending on the interaction pattern and the set of corrupted parties, it could be that most corrupted parties are fixed and hence the residual function is quite degenerate (or even all inputs are fixed as in standard MPC). Second, there are functions for which access even to a "large" residual function does not compromise the secrecy of uncorrupted inputs significantly. Examples include symmetric functions (such as majority) where the size of the residual truth table is not very significant (see [3] for a discussion), as well as unlearnable functions where it is computationally hard to figure out the inputs of honest parties even when given a polynomially large residual function.

1.2 Our Results

We give a variety of answers to the main question posed above. Our results come in three different flavors: (a) "low-end" protocols that offer unconditional security and are generally exponential in the input size (except for special function classes and special interaction patterns); (b) "high-end" protocols that (necessarily) use general-purpose obfuscation techniques to achieve polynomial-time solutions for general functions and interaction patterns; and (c) "mid-range" protocols that make simple use of multilinear maps to compute symmetric functions with general interaction patterns.

Our protocols tolerate an arbitrary number of corrupted parties in the static corruption model. Below, when describing our results, we use the phrase $\mathcal{I}$-compliant to denote that the interaction pattern in a protocol is consistent with $\mathcal{I}$.

I. A Completeness Theorem for Interaction Patterns. In Section 2 we show that the star interaction pattern is *complete* for secure computation with restricted interaction patterns. Specifically, we give an efficient, unconditional reduction from the problem of realizing a function f using a general interaction pattern $\mathcal{I}$ to that of realizing the same f on a star. This transformation requires its own non-reusable correlated randomness setup (in addition to the setup for the underlying star-pattern protocol).

THEOREM 1 (INFORMAL). *There exists an efficient transformation $\mathcal{T}$ that, for any n-party interaction pattern $\mathcal{I}$ and any star-compliant protocol $\Pi^\star$ for computing f, generates an $\mathcal{I}$-compliant protocol $\Pi^{\mathcal{I}}$ for computing f in the non-reusable correlated randomness setup model. If $\Pi^\star$ is statistical/computational semi-honest secure then the resulting $\Pi^{\mathcal{I}}$ is statistical/computational malicious secure. Moreover, the randomness-size (resp. communication complexity) are only a factor of $O(n\lambda)$ (resp. $O(n^2\lambda)$) above those of the underlying protocol $\Pi^\star$, where λ is a security parameter.*

We remark that the above theorem is for the case where f operates over binary inputs. When the function f computed by $\Pi^{\mathcal{I}}$ accepts larger inputs, our transformation requires $\Pi^\star$ for a different (but related) function f' that operates over binary inputs. We also remark that we only consider $\mathcal{I}$ with a single sink; in the semi-honest case, this can be trivially extended to allow for multiple sink nodes.

II. Information-Theoretic Protocols for General Functions. In the information-theoretic setting, we present in

Section 3 perfectly (resp., statistically) secure protocols for computing any deterministic function against semi-honest (resp., malicious) adversaries. For $f : \{0,1\}^n \to \{0,1\}$, our semi-honest protocols give each party 2^n bits of correlated randomness and require each party to communicate $O(n \cdot 2^n)$ bits. For malicious security, the correlated randomness and communication are of size $O(\lambda n \cdot 2^n)$, with λ the security parameter.

THEOREM 2 (INFORMAL). *For every $f : \{0,1\}^n \to \{0,1\}$ and any DAG interaction pattern $\mathcal{I}$, there is a semi-honest, perfectly-secure, $\mathcal{I}$-compliant protocol for f, in which each party gets $2^n + 1$ bits of correlated randomness and sends at most $n \cdot 2^{n-1}$ bits of communication. Also, there is a malicious, statistically-secure, $\mathcal{I}$-compliant protocol for f, in which each party gets $O(\lambda n \cdot 2^n)$ bits of correlated randomness and sends at most $O(\lambda n \cdot 2^n)$ bits of communication.*

For non-DAG patterns, we can use our protocol for star (which is a special case of the above; see Section 3.2) and then apply our reduction to obtain:

THEOREM 3 (INFORMAL). *For every $f : \{0,1\}^n \to \{0,1\}$ and any interaction pattern $\mathcal{I}$, there is a semi-honest, perfectly-secure, $\mathcal{I}$-compliant protocol for f, in which each party gets $n + (n+1) \cdot (2^n + 1)$ bits of correlated randomness and sends at most $n^2 \cdot (2^{n-1} + 2)$ bits of communication. Also, there is a malicious, statistically-secure, $\mathcal{I}$-compliant protocol for f, in which each party gets $O(\lambda n \cdot 2^n)$ bits of correlated randomness and sends at most $O(\lambda n^2 \cdot 2^n)$ bits of communication.*

We stress again that for small input domains, these protocols could be quite practical, see Table 1 for some concrete numbers for computing general functions with binary inputs, a single output and semi-honest security.

Better Communication Complexity. For the chain interaction pattern, we describe in Section 3.1 protocols for computing arbitrary functions where the total communication complexity is only polynomial in the input size, though the correlated randomness is still exponential.

THEOREM 4 (INFORMAL). *For every $f : \{0,1\}^n \to \{0,1\}$, there is a semi-honest, perfectly-secure protocol for f with a chain pattern in which each party gets at most $n \cdot 2^n$ bits of correlated randomness and sends at most n bits of communication. Also, there is a malicious, statistically-secure protocol for f with a chain pattern in which each party gets at most $O(\lambda n \cdot 2^n)$ bits of correlated randomness and sends at most $O(n^2 + \lambda n)$ bits of communication.*

In the full paper, we give evidence against the possibility of extending this result to more general interaction patterns: concretely, we show that even in a network $\mathcal{N}_n$ consisting of two chains (each of length n) that lead to a common endpoint, a similar protocol would imply a 3-server protocol for information-theoretic PIR [13] with poly-logarithmic communication, which is an unexpected result.

THEOREM 5 (INFORMAL). *Assume that, for every $f : \{0,1\}^{2n} \to \{0,1\}$, there exists a semi-honest, statistically-secure $\mathcal{N}_n$-compliant protocol that computes f with communication complexity $c(n)$. Then, there exists an (interactive, statistical) 3-server PIR protocol, with communication complexity $O(c(\log N) + \log N + \log 1/\epsilon)$, where N is the database size and ϵ is the statistical security parameter.*

	Correlated Randomness	Online Communication
Previous work: Star [3]	2.5MB	2.5MB
Star (Lemma 3.2)	128KB	128KB
Chain (Theorem 11)	2.5MB	20bits
DAG (Theorem 2)	128KB	1.25MB
Gen. Patterns (Theorem 3)	2.5MB	25MB

Table 1: Concrete complexity numbers (per party) for $n = 20$ for computing general functions with single output with information-theoretic security in the semi-honest model.

III. Efficient Information-Theoretic Protocols for Symmetric Functions. For symmetric functions, we construct in the full paper *efficient*, perfectly (resp., statistically) secure protocols over a chain against semi-honest (resp., malicious) adversaries where both the offline and online phases are polynomial in the input size.

THEOREM 6 (INFORMAL). *For every symmetric binary function $f : \{0,1\}^n \to \{0,1\}$, there is a semi-honest perfectly-secure protocol for f for the chain network in which each party gets $(n+1)^2$ bits of correlated randomness and sends at most $(n+1)^2$ bits of communication. Also, there is a malicious statistically-secure protocol for f for the chain in which each party gets $O(\lambda n^2)$ bits of correlated randomness and sends at most $O(\lambda n^2)$ bits of communication, where λ is the statistical security parameter. Moreover, both these protocols have efficient simulators.*

IV. Computational Protocols for General Functions from Obfuscation. In the computational setting, we observe in the full paper that the multi-input functional encryption scheme of [29] already yields a protocol for computing general functions with a star interaction against semi-honest adversaries based on indistinguishability obfuscation (iO) [2, 24] and one-way functions. Combining this with Theorem 1, we obtain a malicious-secure protocol for computing general functions with general interaction patterns.

THEOREM 7 (INFORMAL). *Assuming iO for general circuits and one-way functions, for every interaction pattern $\mathcal{I}$, there exists an $\mathcal{I}$-compliant protocol for computing any polynomial-time function that achieves malicious security against any number of corruptions, in the (non-reusable) correlated randomness setup model.*

Making Correlated Randomness Reusable. We also present a generic procedure to transform any non-reusable correlated randomness setup into one that is *reusable*. Our transformation works in the common random string (CRS) model where the size of the CRS grows linearly with the number of uses of the correlated randomness. We note, however, that since the CRS is "public" randomness, it can be easily compressed in the random oracle model.

Our transformation builds on the recent work of [34] and inherits their assumptions of iO and fully homomorphic encryption (FHE). Composing our transformation with Theorem 7, we obtain the following:

THEOREM 8 (INFORMAL). *Assuming iO for general circuits and FHE, for every interaction pattern $\mathcal{I}$, there exists an $\mathcal{I}$-compliant protocol for computing any polynomial-time function that achieves malicious security against any number of corruptions. The protocol uses a reusable correlated randomness setup in the CRS model where the size of the CRS grows linearly with the number of uses of the protocol.*

Necessity of iO. We note that general-purpose iO is a *necessary* assumption for the above results. Indeed, for the special case of a star pattern, it was already shown by [29] that a secure protocol for general functions implies general-purpose iO.

V. Computational Protocols for Symmetric Functions from Multilinear Maps. For the case of symmetric functions, we describe in the full paper a much simpler protocol for general interaction patterns that uses multilinear maps but does not require general-purpose obfuscation. The security of that protocol reduces to a very simple variant of the Multilinear Decisional Diffie-Hellman (MDDH) assumption over multilinear maps [8, 23], which we call the *bookend MDDH* assumption. Unfortunately, this assumption (and indeed the security of our protocol) *does not hold* for any of the current multilinear map candidates [23, 14, 26, 15].

VI. Implications to standard MPC. We note that our results for MPC with general interaction patterns also have relevance to *standard* MPC over *fully connected* networks. For instance, suppose that there is a cost $c_{i,j}$ associated with sending a message from P_i to P_j. Our results reduce the question of minimizing the total cost of an MPC protocol in this setting to a combinatorial optimization problem. For instance, for standard n-party MPC where only P_1 has an output, our results imply general protocols with only $2n - 2$ point-to-point messages (e.g., a chain from P_1 to P_n and back), which can be shown to be optimal.

1.3 Technical Overview

We now give an overview of our protocols. We only focus on some of the main results and defer the reader to the technical sections for the details on all of our results.

Reduction to Star Pattern. Recall that our goal here is to transform an n-party protocol for computing general functions with a star pattern into another protocol for general interaction patterns $\mathcal{I}$. For simplicity, here we focus only on computing functions with binary inputs and achieving semi-honest security and defer the reader to Section 2 for the general case. It is instructive to consider the naive protocol where each party just sends to the evaluator whatever message it was supposed to send in the underlying star protocol over the paths in $\mathcal{I}$. This protocol falls short of providing the "best possible security" for the pattern $\mathcal{I}$, because in the star pattern the inputs of all the corrupted parties are free while some (or all) of them can be fixed in $\mathcal{I}$.

To do better, we start with the observation that in the underlying star protocol, once all the randomness is fixed, then every party P_i sends one of two fixed messages (m_i^0, m_i^1) to the evaluator, depending upon its input bit. In our transformation, we share the two possible messages of each party using an n-out-of-n secret-sharing, giving each party one share of every message. These shares comprise the correlated randomness that each party gets under our transformation. The omission of any share will prevent the reconstruction of the original message. Thus, if only one of the two shares of party P_i's messages is sent by P_j then this in a way forces P_i's input to be fixed, even if P_i is corrupted.

The challenge is to let P_j know which of the two shares to send to the evaluator without revealing P_i's input. To that end, we distribute the shares of P_i's two messages to all the parties in a *random but consistent order*. That is, either they all get first the share of m_i^0 followed by share of m_i^1, or vice-versa. Furthermore, this random permutation bit is given to party P_i. During the protocol P_i will xor that bit with its input, sending the resulting bit to the other parties to indicate which shares they should send to the evaluator and which to omit. See Section 2 for more details of this protocol and its proof of security.

Information-Theoretic Protocols for General Functions. Our information-theoretic protocols follow a somewhat similar approach to the general reduction discussed above. Specifically, we secret-share the truth table of f, giving each party a share for each of the 2^n inputs, and then have the honest parties omit some of their shares during the protocol run. This is done so as to ensure that when the input of P_i is fixed, the adversary can obtain all the shares for inputs with $x_i = 0$ or all the shares for inputs with $x_i = 1$, *but not both*.

We remark that this is easy to implement in a star pattern: since the only fixed inputs are those of the honest parties, we can have each honest party send to the evaluator only the shares consistent with its own input bit. A protocol for a general pattern can be obtained using the transformation from above, but we can get a better communication complexity by instead tailoring the share-omission rules to the communication pattern. To obtain security in the malicious-adversary model, we add authentication information to the correlated randomness. See Sections 3.1 and 3.2 for details.

Efficient Information-Theoretic Protocols for Symmetric Functions. In the case of symmetric functions, we capitalize on the fact that there is a small representation of the truth table of the function. In particular, the residual function in this representation can be obtained from the global truth table by having each party locally drop one of the rows, depending on its input.

A similar approach was considered by [33] in the computational setting. In their case, the rows of the truth table were encrypted using an additively homomorphic scheme so that party P_{i+1} does not learn what row was dropped by party P_i. In our information-theoretic setting, however, such an additively homomorphic scheme is not available so we use a different hiding mechanism. Specifically, we view messages as matrices, letting each party in the protocol multiply its received message by a random matrix (which is given to it in its correlated randomness), then dropping one column and forwarding the result to the next party. The correlated randomness of the evaluator consists of the columns of the resulting product matrix, tagged by the function output and permuted randomly. In a run of the protocol, the evaluator will receive one of these columns and will use it to determine the corresponding function output.

Adding security against a malicious adversary is harder here than in our other information-theoretic protocols, since parties do more than just forwarding some pre-determined messages that are given to them as part of their correlated randomness. Our solution still uses authentication to force

the corrupted parties to send the right messages, but we must ensure that the added authentication information does not leak information on potential messages that are not sent in a particular run of the protocol. To ensure that, we use an authentication mechanism that doubles also as a randomness extractor, namely the "extractor-MAC" construction from [18], which is based on almost-universal hashing [42]. We also need to withhold from the evaluator the columns of the product matrix, replacing them by just the authentication information needed to recognize these columns. Details and proofs of security in the full paper.

Computational Protocols for General Functions. Here, we focus on our generic transformation from a non-reusable correlated randomness setup $\mathcal{CR}_{nr}$ into a *reusable* one $\mathcal{CR}$. As mentioned earlier, our transformation works in the CRS model.

Our starting idea is to use an MPC protocol Π to compute the function F_{cr} that takes small randomness as input and outputs $L = \text{poly}(k)$ independent instances of $\mathcal{CR}_{nr}$. Note that such a function F_{cr} is easy to define: on input a short random seed, F_{cr} first expands it into a large pseudorandom string using a PRG (of appropriate stretch) and then uses different "chunks" of the resultant string to compute L independent instances of $\mathcal{CR}_{nr}$. Now, fix an honest execution of Π and consider the view view_i of each party i in the execution consisting of its random tape and the protocol messages. Note that if each $|\text{view}_i|$ was independent of L, then we could simply set $(\text{view}_1, \ldots, \text{view}_n)$ as an instance of the *reusable* correlated randomness setup $\mathcal{CR}$. This is because given view_i, party P_i can locally compute the output of Π, which consists of L instances of $\mathcal{CR}_{nr}$.

Thus, we have effectively reduced our problem of making any correlated randomness setup reusable to the problem of constructing an MPC protocol $\Pi_{\text{out-ind}}$ that computes n-party functions with "long" outputs where the communication complexity of the protocol as well as the size of randomness of each party is *independent of the function output length*. A moments reflection, however, reveals that such a protocol is *impossible* in the standard model.[2] Instead, our solution will use a (long) common random string (CRS).

Our starting point is a recent work of Hubáček and Wichs [34], who constructs a secure two-party computation protocol where the communication complexity of the protocol is independent of the function output length. However, the size of the randomness of each party does grow with the function output length. We extend their protocol to the multiparty setting. Let $\Pi_{\text{long-rand}}$ denote the resulting protocol. Our key observation then is that the long randomness of the parties in $\Pi_{\text{long-rand}}$ can be "compressed" by using a long public CRS. In particular, we transform $\Pi_{\text{long-rand}}$ into a new protocol $\Pi_{\text{short-rand}}$ using a public random string $\text{CRS} = \text{CRS}_1, \ldots, \text{CRS}_n$ where each CRS_i is as long as the function output length. The randomness of each party P_i in $\Pi_{\text{short-rand}}$ is set to be a short seed r_i. At the start of the protocol, P_i first locally computes a large random string $R_i = \text{PRG}(r_i) \oplus \text{CRS}_i$. It then executes the strategy of the i'th party in $\Pi_{\text{long-rand}}$ using R_i for the rest of the protocol.

Combining the above steps, we obtain our desired MPC protocol. We stress that we are able to bypass the aforemen-

---

[2]Consider an execution of $\Pi_{\text{out-ind}}$ for evaluating a PRG with "long" stretch. The view of any party i in the protocol is a "compressed" representation of the long protocol output. This can be used to derive a computational incompressibility argument, similar to several recent works [1, 10, 34].

tioned impossibility result since we are working in the CRS model, where the size of the CRS grows with the function output length.

Computational Protocols for Symmetric Functions. For symmetric functions, we use multilinear maps to construct simple protocols that achieve computational security against semi-honest adversaries. Here we focus on the star pattern; a protocol for general interaction patterns can be obtained by composing the star protocol with our general reduction to star.

Consider an n-level multilinear map where $[x]_i$ denotes an encoding of x at level i. In our star protocol, as part of the correlated randomness, each party P_i is given two level-1 encodings $[a_i]_1, [a_i \times r]_1$ for random and independent elements a_i's and the same random r. Let $A = \prod_{i=1}^{n} a_i$ denote the product of the a_i's. The evaluator is given all the $n+1$ (level-n) encodings $[b_i]_n = [A \times r^i], i = 0, 1, \ldots n$ in a random order, where each b_i is tagged with the function value $f_i = f(1^i 0^{n-i})$.

In the protocol, each party P_i simply sends the encoding $[a_i]_1$ or $[a_i \times r]_1$, depending upon whether its input bit is 0 or 1, respectively. The evaluator multiplies the n encodings that it receives and then compares the resulting encoding against the b_i's to determine the function output. More details are provided in the full version. As mentioned above, this protocol is unfortunately insecure using current multilinear-map candidates.

1.4 Related Work

There is a very large body of recent work about minimizing interaction in cryptography (mostly concentrating on the number of rounds, rather than the number of messages): whereas classical MPC results show that every cryptographic task can be realized with sufficient interaction, popular recent research topics such as garbling schemes [44, 4, 30], fully homomorphic encryption [25], functional encryption [40, 7, 39], and obfuscation [2, 24], are all about minimizing interaction. Our work can be seen as taking the question of "what can we do with a given type of interaction" to its ultimate level of generality. One can view the previous notions, as well as standard interactive MPC, as special cases of this general problem.

Another large body of work, originating from [19], studies the problem of secure *communication* (or message transmission) in general networks, where only certain pairs of parties can communicate with each other. This goal is trivialized when allowing a correlated randomness set-up, as we do here, and so the challenges that arise in that setting are very different from the ones we face in our work. The same is true for a recent extension of this problem to secret sharing in general networks [41], a task whose feasibility reduces to that of secure message transmission.

Another line of work, originating from earlier works in the context of distributed computing [20], studies the possibility of realizing MPC on sparse networks [22, 11]. These works use specially designed (expander-based) networks to allow MPC in graphs of a small degree. To this end, they also need to relax the traditional goal of MPC by assuming that some honest inputs are being compromised. However, in contrast to the model considered in our work, being compromised there means "known or fixed by the adversary" as opposed to being "free" in the sense considered here. In particular, general solutions for MPC in that model have no consequences for obfuscation.

Finally, Kearns et al. [36] also study secure computation in a model with restricted communication. Their restriction is more liberal than our definition of interaction pattern: each message from P_i to P_j should be computed by a small neighborhood of P_i, P_j (in an undirected network graph). Their positive results provide computational security against a *single* corrupted party, a limitation which they show to be inherent to their model. In contrast, our protocols provide a meaningful notion of security with respect to any number of corrupted parties.

2. A REDUCTION TO STAR

In the Technical Overview (Section 1.3) we described a reduction from the problem of realizing a function f using an arbitrary interaction pattern $\mathcal{I}$ to that of realizing the same f on a star. Our transformation is information-theoretic and does not require any cryptographic assumptions, but it requires its own non-reusable correlated randomness (in addition to whatever setup is needed for the underlying star-pattern protocol). Below we prove that if the underlying star protocol is semi-honest secure then so is the resulting general-pattern protocol, achieving possibly even better security. Furthermore, in Section 2.2 we modify the transformation so that the general-pattern protocol is malicious-secure. This proof will imply that the star interaction pattern is *complete* for secure computations with restricted interaction patterns.

Our transformation assumes that the function f depends on all its inputs, that it has only a single party with output (as this is inherent in having a secure star-protocol for f), and that the interaction pattern has at least one message path from every party to the evaluator. We note that in the semi-honest model one can easily extend a solution for the one output case to multiple outputs by just running separate protocols for the different outputs (piggybacking over the same messages of $\mathcal{I}$ as needed).

2.1 The Semi-Honest Transformation

THEOREM 9. *There exists an efficient transformation $\mathcal{T}$ such that for any function $f : \{0,1\}^n \to \{0,1\}$ that depends on all inputs, any interaction pattern $\mathcal{I}$ with a single sink, and any star-compliant protocol Π^* for f, $\mathcal{T}(\Pi^*, \mathcal{I})$ generates an $\mathcal{I}$-compliant protocol $\Pi^{\mathcal{I}}$ for f (with non-reusable correlated randomness) with the following properties:*

- *If in Π^* each party gets at most R bits of correlated randomness and sends at most M bits of communication, then in $\Pi^{\mathcal{I}}$ each party gets at most $R + 2n \cdot M$ bits of correlated randomness and sends at most $n^2(M+1)$ bits of communication.*

- *If Π^* is perfect/statistical/computational semi-honest secure then so is the resulting $\Pi^{\mathcal{I}}$.*

PROOF. Let $P_1, P_2, \ldots, P_{n+1}$ be the parties, and assume without loss of generality that P_{n+1} is the evaluator. Let $\Pi^* = (\mathsf{Gen}^*, \mathsf{Msg.int}^*, \mathsf{Msg.eval}^*)$ be a protocol for computing f on the star, where Gen^* generates correlated randomness, $\mathsf{Msg.int}^*$ is the next message function of the parties, and $\mathsf{Msg.eval}^*$ is used by the evaluator to compute the output. For any communication pattern $\mathcal{I}$, we construct a protocol $\Pi^{\mathcal{I}} = (\mathsf{Gen}^{\mathcal{I}}, \mathsf{Msg.int}^{\mathcal{I}}, \mathsf{Msg.eval}^{\mathcal{I}})$ for computing f on $\mathcal{I}$ as follows.

Setup. The randomness-generation procedure $\mathsf{Gen}^{\mathcal{I}}$ begins by running Gen^* to generate correlated randomness

$r_1, \ldots, r_{n+1}$ for the underlying star protocol, and then proceeds as follows:

1. For each party $i \leq n$, and for every input bit $\sigma \in \{0,1\}$, compute a message that P_i could send in the underlying star protocol, $m_i^\sigma \leftarrow \mathsf{Msg.int}^\star(\sigma, r_i)$.

2. Compute an n-out-of-n secret sharing of each message m_i^σ. Let $m_{i,1}^\sigma, \ldots, m_{i,n}^\sigma$ denote the n shares of m_i^σ.

3. Choose random permutation bits $b_1, \ldots, b_n$, one for each party $P_i, i \leq n$.

The correlated randomness of each party P_i includes the permutation bit b_i, and all the pairs $(m_{j,i}^{b_j}, m_{j,i}^{1-b_j})$ for every $j \leq n$. Below we denote $(M_{j,i}^0, M_{j,i}^1) = (m_{j,i}^{b_j}, m_{j,i}^{1-b_j})$. The evaluator receives in addition also r_{n+1}.

Messages and Output. On input x_i, each party P_i computes $c_i = x_i \oplus b_i$, which determines which shares of P_i's messages should be used. Then it proceeds as follows:

1. P_i sends the bit c_i on every path to the evaluator in $\mathcal{I}$.

2. Then, for every P_j such that some path from P_j to the evaluator goes through P_i, party P_i waits until it receives the bit c_j and then sends $M_{j,i}^{c_j} = m_{j,i}^{x_i}$ on the path to the evaluator.

3. For every P_j such that *no path from P_j to the evaluator goes through P_i*, party P_i sends both shares on some $\mathcal{I}$-path to the evaluator.

4. In addition, P_i forwards every messages that it receives from other parties on some $\mathcal{I}$-path to the evaluator.

After receiving all the messages, the evaluator collects the set of shares $\{M_{i,1}^{c_i}, \ldots, M_{i,n}^{c_i}\}_{i \in [n]}$ and reconstructs all the messages $m_i^{x_i}$ from the corresponding n shares, for every $i \in [n]$. Finally, it runs the evaluator algorithm $\mathsf{Msg.eval}^\star$ on inputs r_{n+1} and $\{m_i^{x_i}\}_{i \in [n]}$ and returns its output.

This completes the description of $\Pi^\mathcal{I}$. The correctness of the protocol is easy to verify.

Complexity. To achieve the communication complexity stated in Theorem 9, the parties need to send their messages only once on all paths to the evaluator and forward each message that they receive only once. Specifically each P_i needs to send the bits c_j (either its own or others') toward each $P_{j'}$ downstream only in the first opportunity that it has according to $\mathcal{I}$. Similarly it needs to send shares toward the evaluator (both its own and forwarded) only in the last opportunity that it has according to $\mathcal{I}$. All other $\mathcal{I}$ messages (if any) should be empty. Done this way, the complexity of the resulting $\Pi^\mathcal{I}$ depends only on the number of parties n and NOT on the number of messages N in the communication pattern $\mathcal{I}$.

Some further optimization is possible, in that each P_i need not forward all messages from other parties, it can drop messages that it already knows are inconsistent with the c_j's that it saw. This modification changes the (worst-case) complexity stated in Theorem 9 by at most a small constant factor.

Proof of Security. We need to describe a simulator $\mathsf{Sim}^\mathcal{I}$ for the resulting protocol $\Pi^\mathcal{I}$, using the simulator $\mathsf{Sim}^\star$ of the underlying star-protocol. The simulator, $\mathsf{Sim}^\mathcal{I}$, gets the corrupted parties' input and the residual truth table, and needs to produce the correlated randomness of the corrupted parties and the messages of the honest parties. It will utilize the simulator of the star to achieve this goal. As explained above, the residual truth table that $\mathsf{Sim}^\mathcal{I}$ gets is more restricted than that of $\mathsf{Sim}^\star$, as in $\mathcal{I}$ some of the corrupt parties' inputs may be fixed. However, we show that this residual function is sufficient to simulate the communications. Let $T \subseteq [n+1]$ be the set of corrupted parties in a run of $\Pi^\mathcal{I}$, and partition it into fixed and free parties $T = T_{\mathsf{Fixed}} \cup T_{\mathsf{Free}}$. Denote the set of honest parties by $H = [n+1] \setminus T$. Let $T^* = T_{\mathsf{Free}}$ be the set of corrupted parties used for simulator $\mathsf{Sim}^\star$ and $H^* = T_{\mathsf{Fixed}} \cup H$ be the set of honest parties.

The $\mathcal{I}$-simulator $\mathsf{Sim}^\mathcal{I}$ gets the input bits x_i for all $i \in T$ and the residual function $f'(x_{T_{\mathsf{Free}}}) = f(x_{H^*}, x_{T_{\mathsf{Free}}})$. It runs the star-simulator $\mathsf{Sim}^\star$, giving it the input bits x_i for $i \in T_{\mathsf{Free}}$ and the same residual function. $\mathsf{Sim}^\star$ returns the correlated randomness r_i for $i \in T_{\mathsf{Free}}$ and messages m_i for $i \in H^*$. (Recall that $m_i = m_i^{x_i}$ for some $x_i \in \{0,1\}$, but $\mathsf{Sim}^\mathcal{I}$ does not know x_i.)

Next $\mathsf{Sim}^\mathcal{I}$ computes the corrupted-party messages of the underlying star protocol as $m_i^\sigma \leftarrow \mathsf{Msg.int}^\star(\sigma, r_i)$ for $i \in T_{\mathsf{Free}}, \sigma \in \{0,1\}$, and also chooses random bits $b_1, \ldots, b_n$. It computes n-out-of-n secret sharing of all the m's that it knows, chooses at random shares for the m's that it does not know, and orders the shares as follows:

- For all $i \in T_{\mathsf{Free}}, j \in [n]$, the simulator sets $c_i := b_i \oplus x_i$ and then for $\sigma \in \{0,1\}$ it sets $M_{i,j}^\sigma$ to be the j'th share of the message $m_i^{\sigma \oplus b_i}$.

- For all $i \in H^*, j \in [n+1]$, the simulator sets $c_i := b_i$ and then it sets $M_{i,j}^{b_i}$ to be the j'th share of the message m_i, and it chooses $M_{i,j}^{1-b_i}$ uniformly at random.

The $\mathcal{I}$-simulator $\mathsf{Sim}^\mathcal{I}$ gives every $i \in T$ the correlated randomness b_i and shares $\{(M_{j,i}^0, M_{j,i}^1) : j \in [n]\}$, and if the evaluator is corrupted then $\mathsf{Sim}^\mathcal{I}$ gives it also the correlated randomness r_{n+1} of the underlying star protocol. Finally, $\mathsf{Sim}^\mathcal{I}$ runs the actual protocol $\Pi^\mathcal{I}$ using the shares that it computed and the c_i bits to determine the honest parties' messages in the $\mathcal{I}$-protocol.

We observe that the simulated view is identical/statistically-close/computationally indistinguishable to the real view, depending on the properties of the underlying simulator $\mathsf{Sim}^\star$, Indeed, if the simulated view contains all the shares of some messages m of the underlying protocol, then either m was produced directly by $\mathsf{Sim}^\star$ or it was computed from the correlated randomness r_i produced by $\mathsf{Sim}^\star$. All other shares in the view, as well as the permutation bits b_i, are uniformly random and independent of everything else. $\square$

Handling Functions Over a Large Domain. The transformation above can handle a function with a large range without any change, but its efficiency relies crucially on the domain being small, so that once the correlated randomness is fixed each party has only a small number of messages that it can possibly send in the star protocol, depending on its input. Applying the transformation as-is to a function $f : D^n \rightarrow R$ with a large domain D, would increase the complexity of the star protocol for f roughly by a factor of $|D|$.

To do better, we can always represent each inputs to f in binary using $\ell = \log |D|$ bits and apply the above transformation to a star protocol for the modified function $f' : \{0,1\}^{n\ell} \rightarrow R$, defined as:

$$f'(x_1, \ldots, x_{\ell n}) = f\big((x_1, \ldots, x_\ell), \ldots, (x_{(n-1)\ell+1}, \ldots, x_{n\ell})\big).$$

Note that this requires that we view the n-player interaction pattern $\mathcal{I}$ as an $n\ell$-player pattern, which we can always do by introducing dummy communication flows between the virtual players that are implemented by a single real player. More importantly, though, it requires a star protocol for f' rather than a star protocol for f.

2.2 Reduction for Malicious Security

THEOREM 10. *There exists an efficient transformation $\mathcal{T}$ such that for any function $f : \{0,1\}^n \rightarrow \{0,1\}$ that depend on all its inputs, any n-party interaction pattern $\mathcal{I}$ with a single sink, and any star-compliant protocol $\Pi^\star$ for f, $\mathcal{T}(\Pi^\star, \mathcal{I})$ generates an $\mathcal{I}$-compliant protocol $\Pi^{\mathcal{I}}$ for f (with non-reusable correlated randomness) with the following properties:*

- *If in $\Pi^\star$ the evaluator gets R bits of correlated randomness and the other parties send at most M bits of communication each, then in $\Pi^{\mathcal{I}}$ each party gets at most $R + 2n \cdot M \cdot O(\lambda)$ bits of correlated randomness and sends at most $nR + n^2 M \cdot O(\lambda)$ bits of communication, with λ the statistical security parameter.*

- *If the underlying protocol $\Pi^\star$ is statistical/computational semi-honest secure, then the resulting $\Pi^{\mathcal{I}}$ is statistical/computational malicious secure.*

PROOF. (sketch) The transformation for malicious security is very similar to the semi-honest transformation from above, except that we also secret-share the evaluator randomness r_{n+1}, and we authenticate all the messages (say, using an information-theoretic two-time MAC, e.g. 3-wise independent hash functions). Specifically, the parties are given the authentication tags for the messages that they may need to send (and they attach these tags to the messages that they actually send), and the evaluator is given the keys to verify these MACs.

The complexity is easy to verify, and the security proof is quite similar to the one from above. The main difference is that before $\mathsf{Sim}^{\mathcal{I}}$ learns the inputs of the fixed corrupted parties, it needs to give all the corrupted parties their correlated randomness and the messages from honest parties (other than the last one). Moreover, $\mathsf{Sim}^{\mathcal{I}}$ needs to extract these inputs from messages that the fixed corrupted parties send.

To do this, $\mathsf{Sim}^{\mathcal{I}}$ chooses the bits b_i and the shares uniformly at random (and the authentication keys and tags are chosen as in the protocol). When a fixed corrupted party P_i sends the bit c_i towards an honest party, $\mathsf{Sim}^{\mathcal{I}}$ extracts the input bit $x_i = c_i \oplus b_i$. Once it has all the input bits x_i for the fixed corrupted parties, $\mathsf{Sim}^{\mathcal{I}}$ gets the residual function and it can then run the semi-honest simulator $\mathsf{Sim}^\star$ for the underlying star protocol (choosing arbitrary inputs for the free corrupted parties). Now $\mathsf{Sim}^{\mathcal{I}}$ learns from $\mathsf{Sim}^\star$ the correlated randomness r_i for corrupted parties and the messages m_i for the honest parties, so it can compute all the relevant m_i's and choose the shares of the last honest party to match these m_i's (and also the randomness r_{n+1} of the evaluator, if it is corrupted). Finally $\mathsf{Sim}^{\mathcal{I}}$ can compute the authentication tags using the keys that it prepared for the evaluator, so it has everything that it needs for the simulation.

Another difference from the semi-honest case is that, when the evaluator is honest, we need to use the authentication tags. Namely, if the evaluator receives a message which is not consistent with the shares that $\mathsf{Sim}^{\mathcal{I}}$ generated, then the simulator aborts, since this is what would happen whp in the protocol itself.

It is not hard to see that this simulation strategy produces a distribution which is statistically close (upto authentication error) to the real-protocol distribution if $\mathsf{Sim}^\star$ is perfect or statistical, and is computationally indistinguishable from the real-protocol distribution if $\mathsf{Sim}^\star$ is computational. □

3. INFO-THEORETIC PROTOCOLS FOR GENERAL FUNCTIONS

Below, we present information-theoretically secure protocols with one-time setup for computing arbitrary functions. We begin in Section 3.1 with a protocol for computing arbitrary functions on a chain which is communication efficient (but still requires exponential randomness). Then, in Section 3.2, we describe a protocol for computing arbitrary deterministic functions on arbitrary DAGs with exponential communication and randomness. We also describe, in Section 3.2.1, a protocol which is insecure as per our definition, but has some interesting implications for garbled circuits.

We identify an n-input function $f(x_1, \ldots, x_n)$ with a binary decision tree for f. Each input is associated with a level in the tree and the input ordering in the tree is made to respect the topological order in the DAG. That is, if there is a path from party A to B in the DAG, then we put the input of A before the input of B in the decision tree. In particular, for a chain network, the ordering in the tree agrees completely with the linear order of nodes on the chain.

In the protocols, a party associated with level-i in the tree will be given correlated randomness associated with each edge leading from level i to level $i+1$. During the computation of the function it will send some of the information which is associated with the edges that match its input (i.e. left edges if the input is 0 and right-edges if it is 1). This can be visualized as each party marking some of the edges in its layer of the tree. The markings create a single marked path from the root to a leaf. The value of the function will be computed by the evaluator based on the information in this leaf.

In the description below, we use the following notations: We have a height-n decision tree $\mathcal{T}$, with the root at level 0 and the leaves at level n. The left edge of every intermediate node is labeled with 0, and the right edge is labeled with 1. We name each node in the tree by the labels on the path leading to it, so the root is named ϵ, its left- and right-children are 0 and 1, respectively, their children are 00,01,10,11, etc. (In the protocols we will attach labels to nodes that may be different from their names, but it is convenient to have the names fixed.) Party P_i (who gets the i'th input bit x_i) is associated with level i in the tree,[3] and a special party $\mathcal{E}$ (the *evaluator*) associated with the leaves. The evaluator does not have an input, but it is the one who will learn the value of the function.

3.1 Computing Any Function on a Chain

We consider below only a chain network, and describe *communication-efficient* protocols that still require exponential randomness.

---

[3]For ease of description we start the enumeration of the parties at 0 rather than 1.

THEOREM 11. *For every function $f : \{0,1\}^n \to \{0,1\}$, there is a semi-honest, perfectly-secure protocol for f for the chain network in which each party gets at most $n \cdot 2^n$ bits of correlated randomness and sends at most n bits of communication.*

Setup and Correlated Randomness. We have parties $P_0, \ldots, P_{n-1}, P_n$ who are connected in a chain starting at P_0, where the last party P_n is the evaluator who does not have an input. Party P_i is associated with level i in the decision tree $\mathcal{T}$ for f.

The correlated randomness in the protocol is determined by a set of random permutations, one for every level in the tree. For level i (with 2^i nodes) we select a random permutation $\pi_i : \{0,1\}^i \to \{0,1\}^i$, and assign to each node with name $x \in \{0,1\}^i$ the label $a = \pi_i(x)$.[4] These node-permutations induce 1-1 mappings as follows: for a node named $x \in \{0,1\}^i$, its label $a = \pi_i(x) \in \{0,1\}^i$ and an edge labeled $b \in \{0,1\}$ that leads to its child $(x|b)$, we have the mapping $m_i : \{0,1\}^i \times \{0,1\} \to \{0,1\}^{i+1}$, defined as

$$m_i(a,b) = \pi_{i+1}\big(\pi_i^{-1}(a), b\big).$$

Party P_i is given the mapping m_i from above. That is, for the two edges $x \to (x|0), (x|1)$, from any node x at level i to its two children at level $i+1$, the party P_i is given the tuple $(\pi_i(x), \pi_{i+1}(x0), \pi_{i+1}(x1))$. These tuples are given to P_i in an order that does not reveal any extra information about the permutations π_i and π_{i+1} (e.g., in lexicographic order of the $\pi_i(x)$'s). For example, the first party P_0 is given just a single tuple, $(\epsilon, \pi_1(0), \pi_1(1))$, and the second party P_1 is given 2 tuples, $((0, \pi_2(\pi_1^{-1}(0)|0), \pi_2(\pi_1^{-1}(0)|1))$ and $(1, \pi_2(\pi_1^{-1}(1)|0), \pi_2(\pi_1^{-1}(1)|1)))$. Overall, P_i is given 2^i such tuples (which takes $(i+1) \cdot 2^{i+1}$ bits to write down).

The evaluator, $\mathcal{E}$ is given the "translation" of π_n to the function values, i.e., $\pi_n(x) \mapsto f(x)$ for all x. In other words, the evaluator is given the table $\{\langle a : f(\pi_n^{-1}(a)) \rangle | a \in \{0,1\}^n\}$, ordered lexicographically by a.

An illustration of the permutations and associated function values for a simple 2-input function is given in Figure 1.

Messages in the Chain Protocol. Party P_i with input bit b_i gets a message a_i from its predecessor in the chain P_{i-1} (initially $a_0 = \epsilon$). It applies its mapping to compute $a_{i+1} \leftarrow m_i(a_i, b_i)$ and sends a_{i+1} to the next party P_{i+1}. At the end of the chain, the evaluator $\mathcal{E}$ receives a_n and outputs the corresponding $w_n = f(\pi_n^{-1}(a_n))$ from its table.

LEMMA 3.1. *For any n-bit-input function f, the above chain-compliant protocol for computing f is semi-honest secure.*

PROOF. Correctness is obvious. For security, let the last honest party be P_t, at level t of the tree. The simulator has the inputs of all the corrupted parties, and the residual truth table of the function, i.e. for all $e_{t+1}, \ldots, e_{n-1} \in \{0,1\}^{n-t-1}$ it gets the values $f(b_0, b_1, \ldots, b_t, e_{t+1}, \ldots, e_{n-1})$ where b_i is the fixed input for $0 \le i \le t$.

The simulator chooses at random a sequence $a_1, \ldots, a_{t+1}$. For every party P_i, it fixes a mapping m_i such that $m_i(a_i, b_i) =$

---

[4]Some of our techniques have superficial similarity to [38]; in particular, the use of decision trees and permuting the nodes at each level. However, the setting and goals, as well as the technical details, are very different. In particular, they deal with two-party protocols that have unlimited interaction and they cannot provide information-theoretic security (even with correlated randomness).

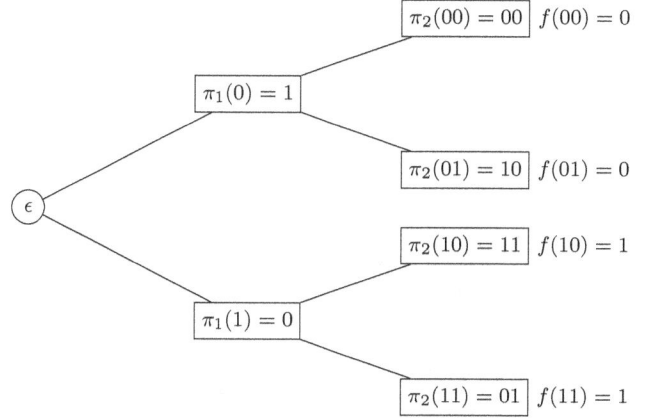

Figure 1: Correlated randomness in the chain protocol. Party i gets the edges from level i to $i+1$, in the form $\{(\pi_i(x) : \pi_{i+1}(x0), \pi_{i+1}(x1)) | x \in \{0,1\}^i\}$, ordered lexicographically by $\pi_i(x)$. The evaluator $\mathcal{E}$ gets the leaves in the form $\{(\pi_n(x) : f(x)) | x \in \{0,1\}^n\}$, ordered lexicographically by $\pi_n(x)$.

a_{i+1}, for all faulty parties, and $m_i(a_i, 0) = a_{i+1}$, for all honest parties. All other values are chosen at random. If P_0 is faulty it fixes $m_0(\epsilon, b_0) = a_1$ and if P_0 is honest $m_0(\epsilon, 0) = a_1$. Furthermore, it chooses random mappings for all faulty parties $P_{t+1}, \ldots, P_{n-1}$. The simulator creates the table for $\mathcal{E}$ in the following manner. For $e_{t+1}, \ldots, e_{n-1} \in \{0,1\}^{n-t-1}$ it computes the chain $a_{t+2} = m_{t+1}(a_{t+1}, e_{t+1})$ and continues $a_{i+1} = m_i(a_i, e_i)$ until a_n. It sets the value of the table in location a_n to be the value of the function which it received for $e_{t+1}, \ldots, e_{n-1}$. The simulator gives the adversary the mappings for the faulty parties, the table for $\mathcal{E}$ and the sequence $a_1, \ldots, a_{t+1}$.

In the real execution, if the input of the honest party is 0, then it uses the mapping created by the simulator. If the input is 1, and say that $m_i(a_i, 1) = a'_{i+1}$ then it changes the mapping by switching the two values a_{i+1} and a'_{i+1}. This results in an execution which is identical to the view of the adversary. $\square$

Malicious Security. In the full paper we convert the protocol from Section 3.1 to the malicious-adversary model, simply by authenticating the randomness, achieving the following theorem.

THEOREM 12. *For every function $f : \{0,1\}^n \to \{0,1\}$, there is a malicious, statistically-secure protocol for f for the chain network in which each party gets $O(\lambda n \cdot 2^n)$ bits of correlated randomness and sends $O(n^2 + \lambda n)$ bits of communication.*

3.2 Protocol for General DAGs

Below, we describe a protocol for computing any deterministic function on any DAG network.

THEOREM 13. *For every function $f : \{0,1\}^n \to \{0,1\}$ and any DAG interaction pattern $\mathcal{I}$, there is a semi-honest, $\mathcal{I}$-compliant, perfectly-secure protocol for f, in which each party gets $2^n + 1$ bits of correlated randomness and sends at most $n \cdot 2^{n-1}$ bits of communication.*

To simplify the presentation, we first describe the protocol for a star network where parties just send one message to the evaluator, and later explain how to generalize. The solution has both communication and randomness complexity that are exponential in the number of parties. In the full paper, we give evidence that achieving a solution with polynomial communication might be impossible.

Recall that we identify a function f with its binary decision tree, where in the case of a star network the order of inputs is arbitrary and we denote by P_i the party associated with level i in the tree, and its input is denoted b_i.

3.2.1 A First Attempt

We begin with a protocol which is *insecure* as per our definition, but will nonetheless be useful to provide some intuition. In this protocol, every party P_i is given an input-masking random bit r_i and also random output-masking bits s_e^i for every edge e leading from level i to level $i+1$ in the tree. Roughly speaking, the input-masking bits will be used to map the input string $b_0, \ldots, b_{n-1}$ to the root-to-leaf path $b_0 \oplus r_0, \ldots, b_{n-1} \oplus r_{n-1}$ in the tree, and the output-masking bits on the edges of this path will be used to mask the function value that the evaluator gets for that leaf. Namely, the evaluator $\mathcal{E}$ is given a table that holds, for each leaf with name $c_0, \ldots, c_{n-1}$, the value $f(c_0 \oplus r_0, \ldots, c_{n-1} \oplus r_{n-1}) \oplus s_{c_0}^0 \oplus s_{c_0,c_1}^1 \oplus \cdots \oplus s_{c_0,\ldots,c_{n-1}}^{n-1}$.

During the protocol execution, party P_i computes $c_i \leftarrow b_i \oplus r_i$ and sends to the evaluator the bit c_i and all the output masking bits associated with edges that are consistent with c_i. Namely, the bits $s_{e|c_i}^i$ for all $e \in \{0,1\}^i$. The bits $c_0, \ldots, c_{n-1}$ that the evaluator $\mathcal{E}$ receives define a complete root-to-leaf path in the tree. Moreover the evaluator gets the associated output-masking bits $s_{c_0,\ldots,c_i}^i$ for $i = 0, 1, \ldots, n$, so it can remove the output masking bits to get $f(c_0 \oplus r_0, \ldots, c_{n-1} \oplus r_{n-1}) = f(b_0, \ldots, b_{n-1})$.

Unfortunately, while the protocol above turns out to be secure when *only the evaluator is corrupted*, it does not satisfy our notion of security. Consider a 3-argument function $f(x_0, x_1, x_2)$, where on input $f(0, x_1, x_2)$ the outputs are split to three 0's and a single 1, and for $f(1, x_1, x_2)$ the outputs are balanced 2-2. If the evaluator corrupts P_2 (the party of the last level of the tree) and receives its output-masking bits, it immediately learns whether the right side of the tree corresponds to $f(0, x_1, x_2)$ or to $f(1, x_1, x_2)$. This is due to the fact that the output-masking bits up to that level are the same for the sub tree with the two 0's. Thus, the last output-masking bit reveals these values. When the adversary gets c_0 from P_0, it immediately knows whether its input is 0 or 1.

3.2.2 A Secure Solution

It turns out that the insecure protocol from above can be made secure by using per-leaf output-masking bits rather than per-edge. Namely, each P_i still gets one input-masking bit r_i, but now it gets 2^n output-masking bits, one for each leaf in the tree, $s_{c_0,\ldots,c_{n-1}}^i$ for all $(c_0, \ldots, c_{n-1}) \in \{0,1\}^n$. The table given to the evaluator also changes accordingly, namely for each leaf with name $c_0, \ldots, c_{n-1}$ the table holds the value $f(c_0 \oplus r_0, \ldots, c_{n-1} \oplus r_{n-1}) \oplus s_{c_0,\ldots,c_{n-1}}^0 \oplus s_{c_0,\ldots,c_{n-1}}^1 \oplus \cdots \oplus s_{c_0,\ldots,c_{n-1}}^{n-1}$.

The protocol is modified to reflect the above change as follows. On input b_i, party P_i sets $c_i \leftarrow b_i \oplus r_i$, then it assembles a subset of its output-bit masks that are consistent with c_i; namely, $S_i = \{s_{e_0,\ldots,e_{i-1},c_i,e_{i+1},\ldots,e_{n-1}}^i\}$ for all $e_0, \ldots, e_{i-1}, e_{i+1}, \ldots, e_{n-1} \in \{0,1\}^{n-1}$ (in order), and sends

(c_i, S_i) to the evaluator. As before, the bits $c_0, \ldots, c_{n-1}$ that the evaluator $\mathcal{E}$ receives define a complete root-to-leaf path in the tree, and $\mathcal{E}$ has all the associated output-masking bits $s_{c_1,\ldots,c_n}^i$, so it can remove those masks to get $f(c_0 \oplus r_0, \ldots, c_{n-1} \oplus r_{n-1}) = f(b_0, \ldots, b_{n-1})$. It is easy to see that the different masking for each leaf prevent the adversary from analyzing the tree, yielding the following lemma.

LEMMA 3.2. *For any n-bit-input function f, the above star-compliant protocol for function f, is secure in the semi-honest model. Each party gets at most $2^n + 1$ bits of correlated randomness and sends at most $2^{n-1} + 1$ bits.*

PROOF. Let $T = \{i_1, \ldots, i_l\}$ be the corrupted parties. The simulator has the corrupted-parties' input and the residual function. For the star pattern, all the corrupted parties are free, so the simulator gets all the values $f(b_0, \ldots, b_{n-1})$ where the honest parties' input is fixed and the corrupted parties' input vary over all 2^l possibilities.

To compute the table for $\mathcal{E}$, the simulator first chooses random bits $r_0, \ldots, r_{n-1}$ and also random bits $s_{c_0,\ldots,c_{n-1}}^i$ for all $i \leq n$ and $c_0, \ldots, c_{n-1} \in \{0,1\}^n$. It chooses a vector of inputs for the honest parties which is consistent with the inputs of the faulty parties and the residual function; denote by b_i the input chosen for the honest party P_i. For every value of the residual function related to $e_{i_1}, \ldots, e_{i_l}$, the simulator computes the leaf to which this value will be assigned as follows: for a fixed input, if the party is honest then it uses the value b_i it chose for it and if the party is faulty it uses the value it got from the adversary, and sets $c_i = b_i \oplus r_i$. For the free inputs, it sets $c_i = e_i \oplus r_i$. It will compute the value for the table at location $c_0, \ldots, c_{n-1}$ by taking the value d, from the residual function associated with $e_{i_1}, \ldots, e_{i_l}$ and computing $d \oplus s_{c_0,\ldots,c_{n-1}}^0 \oplus \cdots \oplus s_{c_0,\ldots,c_{n-1}}^{n-1}$.

Once all the values at the locations associated with the residual function have been entered, the simulator completes populating the table for $\mathcal{E}$ with random values.

It computes the view for the adversary by running the computation on the fixed inputs that it had chosen and all the random values. The result of this computation is given to the adversary. It includes all the randomness that relates to the faulty parties (whether their inputs are fixed or free), the table for $\mathcal{E}$ and all the values that the honest parties would transfer to $\mathcal{E}$ during the execution as computed above.

In the real execution for an honest party P_i on input b_i', the simulator fixes r_i' to be $b_i \oplus r_i \oplus b_i'$. Furthermore, it uses the paddings for the leaves that it chose above. This would result in an identical execution for any input vectors of the honest parties that are consistent with the values of the residual function. □

3.2.3 Extending the Star Protocol to General DAGs

Although we can use the reduction from Section 2 to transform the star protocol to a protocol for any other patterns, below we describe a direct approach that yields more efficient protocols for DAG patterns.

The format of the decision tree and its randomness for the case of the DAG are identical to the star, except that we require the ordering of parties to be consistent with the topological order on the DAG. (Namely each party is assigned to a level of the tree larger than that of all its predecessors in the DAG, and smaller than that of all its successors.) Again, we will call the node assigned to level i party P_i, and give it the input-masking bit r_i and the leaf-masking randomness for each leaf in the tree. Also the evaluator $\mathcal{E}$ is given exactly the same table as in the star protocol above, namely for each leaf with name $c_0, \ldots, c_{n-1}$ the table holds the value $f(c_0 \oplus r_0, \ldots, c_{n-1} \oplus r_{n-1}) \oplus s^0_{c_0,\ldots,c_{n-1}} \oplus \ldots \oplus s^{n-1}_{c_0,\ldots,c_{n-1}}$.

The Protocol. The difference between the star protocol and the general-DAG protocol is that P_i that gets sets of output-masking bits $S^{i'}$ from other parties upstream ($i' < i$) will prune them to be consistent with its input and with each other before forwarding these sets downstream toward the evaluator.[5] Party P_0 computes $c_0 = b_0 \oplus r_0$, a sequence of labeled output-masking bits

$$S_0 = \{ \langle (c_0, e_1, \ldots, e_m) : s^0_{c_0, e_1, \ldots, e_m} \rangle \mid (e_1, \ldots, e_m) \in \{0,1\}^m \}$$

where $m = n - 1$, and a pattern-vector $V_0 = (c_0, *, \ldots, *)$ that reflects the coordinates that P_0 knows to be fixed. As it is at the root of the tree it only knows its own coordinate. P_0 sends $(0, V_0, S_0)$ to all the nodes that it can reach in the DAG.

Party P_i receives a collection of tuples (i_j, V_{i_j}, S_{i_j}) belonging to parties upstream from it, $i_1, \ldots, i_l < i$. (It may get multiple tuples $(i_j, \star, \star)$ for the same i_j on several incoming edges, since this is a semi-honest execution then the corresponding V_{i_j}, S_{i_j} can only differ by having different pruning.) Each vector V_{i_j} reflects inputs that a node upstream knows to be fixed, and hence represents some pruning of previous values.

Party P_i creates the "merged vector" V_i, in which a coordinate k has $V_i[k] = *$ if and only if (a) $V_{i_j}[k] = *$ in *all the incoming vectors* V_{i_j}, and (b) $k \neq i$. It sets the i'th coordinate to be $V_i[i] = c_i$, and the value of every other non-star coordinate is taken from one of the incoming V_{i_j} where this entry is not a $*$. (Again, since this is a semi-honest execution, then if $V_{i_j}[k] \neq *$ it must be the case that $V_{i_j}[k] = c_k$, i.e., this entry contains the c_k value of the party who first set it to a non-$*$ value.)

Then, P_i prunes the sets of output-masking bits in all the S_{i_j}'s to include only those consistent with V_i. In other words, denote the set of labels in S_{i_j} by X_{i_j}, then the set of labels consistent with V_i is the intersection of all the X_{i_j}'s, further reduced to only the labels with the i'th bit equals c_i. Party P_i then drops all the bits from each S_{i_j} that are labeled by inconsistent labels. It also computes its own set of labeled output-masking bits

$$S_i = \{ \langle (e_0, \ldots, e_m) : s^i_{e_0, \ldots, e_m} \rangle \mid (e_0, \ldots, e_m) \text{ consistent with } V_i \}$$

where $m = n - 1$ and sends on all its outgoing edges all the pruned (V_{i_j}, S_{i_j})'s together with its own (V_i, S_i).

The evaluator applies exactly the same pruning procedure as before, and if all the nodes are upstream from it then this leaves a single labeled output-masking bit from every party $\langle (c_0, \ldots, c_{n-1}) : s^i_{c_0, \ldots, c_{n-1}} \rangle$. The evaluator looks up the value that it has for the leaf $(c_0, \ldots, c_{n-1})$ and unmask all the output-masking bits to get the function value $f(c_0 \oplus r_0, \ldots, c_{n-1} \oplus r_{n-1}) = f(b_0, \ldots, b_{n-1})$. This completes the description of the protocol.

LEMMA 3.3. *For any n-bit-input function f and a DAG pattern $\mathcal{I}$, the above $\mathcal{I}$-compliant protocol for computing the function f is semi-honest secure.*

PROOF. The proof for the DAG follows the exact same proof as for the case of the star with the addition that when

---

[5]This can be thought of as similar to what happens in the chain protocol, where only a single value needs to be forwarded, but the pruning in this protocol is not as efficient (even if the DAG happens to be a chain).

the simulator computes the execution of the protocol it also creates the vectors V_i and does the same pruning. These vectors can be created in a straightforward manner from all the information which the simulator holds.

A simple change of the randomness will yield an identical execution in the real and simulated worlds. $\square$

See the full version for the malicious security case.

Acknowledgments

We thank Mor Weiss for her useful comments on an earlier version of this manuscript.

This work was done in part while the authors were visiting the Simons Institute for the Theory of Computing, supported by the Simons Foundation and by the DIMACS/Simons Collaboration in Cryptography through NSF grant #CNS-1523467. First and fifth authors supported in part by the Defense Advanced Research Projects Agency (DARPA) and Army Research Office (ARO) under Contract No. W911NF-15-C-0236. Second author supported by ERC grant 259426, a DARPA/ARL SAFEWARE award, NSF Frontier Award 1413955, NSF grants 1228984, 1136174, 1118096, and 1065276, and by the DARPA through the ARL under Contract W911NF-15-C-0205. Second and fourth authors supported by ISF grant 1709/14 and BSF grant 2012378. Third author supported in part by DARPA/ARO Safeware Grant # W911NF-15-C-0213. The views expressed are those of the authors and do not reflect the official policy or position of the Department of Defense, the National Science Foundation, or the U.S. Government.

4. REFERENCES

[1] S. Agrawal, S. Gorbunov, V. Vaikuntanathan, and H. Wee. Functional encryption: New perspectives and lower bounds. In *CRYPTO*, pages 500–518, 2013.

[2] B. Barak, O. Goldreich, R. Impagliazzo, S. Rudich, A. Sahai, S. P. Vadhan, and K. Yang. On the (im)possibility of obfuscating programs. *J. ACM*, 59(2):6, 2012.

[3] A. Beimel, A. Gabizon, Y. Ishai, E. Kushilevitz, S. Meldgaard, and A. Paskin-Cherniavsky. Non-interactive secure multiparty computation. In *CRYPTO*, pages 387–404, 2014.

[4] M. Bellare, V. T. Hoang, and P. Rogaway. Foundations of garbled circuits. In *ACM CCS*, pages 784–796, 2012.

[5] M. Ben-Or, S. Goldwasser, and A. Wigderson. Completeness theorems for non-cryptographic fault-tolerant distributed computation. In *STOC*, pages 1–10, 1988.

[6] R. Bendlin, I. Damgård, C. Orlandi, and S. Zakarias. Semi-homomorphic encryption and multiparty computation. In *EUROCRYPT*, pages 169–188, 2011.

[7] D. Boneh, A. Sahai, and B. Waters. Functional encryption: Definitions and challenges. In *TCC*, pages 253–273, 2011.

[8] D. Boneh and A. Silverberg. Applications of multilinear forms to cryptography. *IACR Cryptology ePrint Archive*, 2002:80, 2002.

[9] R. Canetti. Security and composition of multiparty cryptographic protocols. *J. Cryptology*, 13(1):143–202, 2000.

[10] A. D. Caro, V. Iovino, A. Jain, A. O'Neill, O. Paneth, and G. Persiano. On the achievability of

simulation-based security for functional encryption. In *CRYPTO*, pages 519–535, 2013.

[11] N. Chandran, J. A. Garay, and R. Ostrovsky. Improved fault tolerance and secure computation on sparse networks. In *ICALP*, pages 249–260, 2010.

[12] D. Chaum, C. Crépeau, and I. Damgård. Multiparty unconditionally secure protocols. In *STOC*, pages 11–19, 1988.

[13] B. Chor, E. Kushilevitz, O. Goldreich, and M. Sudan. Private information retrieval. *J. ACM*, 45(6):965–981, 1998.

[14] J. Coron, T. Lepoint, and M. Tibouchi. Practical multilinear maps over the integers. In *CRYPTO*, pages 476–493, 2013.

[15] J. Coron, T. Lepoint, and M. Tibouchi. New multilinear maps over the integers. In *CRYPTO*, pages 267–286, 2015.

[16] I. Damgård, V. Pastro, N. P. Smart, and S. Zakarias. Multiparty computation from somewhat homomorphic encryption. In *CRYPTO*, pages 643–662, 2012.

[17] I. Damgård and S. Zakarias. Constant-overhead secure computation of boolean circuits using preprocessing. In *TCC*, pages 621–641, 2013.

[18] Y. Dodis, J. Katz, L. Reyzin, and A. Smith. Robust fuzzy extractors and authenticated key agreement from close secrets. In *CRYPTO*, pages 232–250, 2006.

[19] D. Dolev, C. Dwork, O. Waarts, and M. Yung. Perfectly secure message transmission. *J. ACM*, 40(1):17–47, 1993.

[20] C. Dwork, D. Peleg, N. Pippenger, and E. Upfal. Fault tolerance in networks of bounded degree. *SIAM J. Comput.*, 17(5):975–988, 1988.

[21] U. Feige, J. Killian, and M. Naor. A minimal model for secure computation. In *STOC*, pages 554–563, 1994.

[22] J. A. Garay and R. Ostrovsky. Almost-everywhere secure computation. In *EUROCRYPT*, pages 307–323, 2008.

[23] S. Garg, C. Gentry, and S. Halevi. Candidate multilinear maps from ideal lattices. In *EUROCRYPT*, pages 1–17, 2013.

[24] S. Garg, C. Gentry, S. Halevi, M. Raykova, A. Sahai, and B. Waters. Candidate indistinguishability obfuscation and functional encryption for all circuits. In *FOCS*, pages 40–40, 2013.

[25] C. Gentry. Fully homomorphic encryption using ideal lattices. In *STOC*, pages 169–178, 2009.

[26] C. Gentry, S. Gorbunov, and S. Halevi. Graph-induced multilinear maps from lattices. In *TCC*, pages 498–527, 2015.

[27] O. Goldreich. *The Foundations of Cryptography - Volume 2, Basic Applications*. Cambridge University Press, 2004.

[28] O. Goldreich, S. Micali, and A. Wigderson. How to play any mental game or a completeness theorem for protocols with honest majority. In *STOC*, pages 218–229, 1987.

[29] S. Goldwasser, S. D. Gordon, V. Goyal, A. Jain, J. Katz, F. Liu, A. Sahai, E. Shi, and H. Zhou. Multi-input functional encryption. In *EUROCRYPT*, pages 578–602, 2014.

[30] S. Goldwasser, Y. T. Kalai, R. A. Popa, V. Vaikuntanathan, and N. Zeldovich. Reusable garbled circuits and succinct functional encryption. In *STOC*, pages 555–564, 2013.

[31] S. Goldwasser, S. Micali, and C. Rackoff. The knowledge complexity of interactive proof systems. *SIAM J. Comput.*, 18(1):186–208, 1989.

[32] S. D. Gordon, T. Malkin, M. Rosulek, and H. Wee. Multi-party computation of polynomials and branching programs without simultaneous interaction. In *EUROCRYPT*, pages 575–591, 2013.

[33] S. Halevi, Y. Lindell, and B. Pinkas. Secure computation on the web: Computing without simultaneous interaction. In *CRYPTO*, pages 132–150, 2011.

[34] P. Hubacek and D. Wichs. On the communication complexity of secure function evaluation with long output. In *ITCS*, pages 163–172, 2015.

[35] Y. Ishai, M. Prabhakaran, and A. Sahai. Founding cryptography on oblivious transfer – efficiently. In *CRYPTO*, pages 572–591, 2008.

[36] M. Kearns, J. Tan, and J. Wortman. Network-faithful secure computation.

[37] J. Kilian. Founding cryptography on oblivious transfer. In *STOC*, pages 20–31, 1988.

[38] M. Naor and K. Nissim. Communication preserving protocols for secure function evaluation. In *STOC*, pages 590–599, 2001.

[39] A. O'Neill. Definitional issues in functional encryption. *IACR Cryptology ePrint Archive*, 2010:556, 2010.

[40] A. Sahai and B. Waters. Fuzzy identity-based encryption. In *EUROCRYPT*, pages 457–473, 2005.

[41] N. B. Shah, K. V. Rashmi, and K. Ramchandran. Secret share dissemination across a network. *CoRR*, abs/1207.0120, 2012.

[42] A. Srinivasan and D. Zuckerman. Computing with very weak random sources. *SIAM J. Comput.*, 28(4):1433–1459, 1999.

[43] A. Yao. Protocols for secure computations. In *FOCS*, pages 160–164, 1982.

[44] A. C.-C. Yao. How to generate and exchange secrets. In *FOCS*, pages 162–167, 1986.

Fully Succinct Garbled RAM

Ran Canetti
Tel-Aviv University and Boston University
canetti@bu.edu

Justin Holmgren
MIT
holmgren@csail.mit.edu

ABSTRACT

We construct the first fully succinct garbling scheme for RAM programs, assuming the existence of indistinguishability obfuscation for circuits and one-way functions. That is, the size, space requirements, and runtime of the garbled program are the same as those of the input program, up to poly-logarithmic factors and a polynomial in the security parameter. The scheme can be used to construct indistinguishability obfuscators for RAM programs with comparable efficiency, at the price of requiring sub-exponential security of the underlying primitives.

In particular, this opens the door to obfuscated computations that are *sublinear* in the length of their inputs.

The scheme builds on the recent schemes of Koppula-Lewko-Waters and Canetti-Holmgren-Jain-Vaikuntanathan [STOC 15]. A key technical challenge here is how to combine the fixed-prefix technique of KLW, which was developed for deterministic programs, with randomized Oblivious RAM techniques. To overcome that, we develop a method for arguing about the indistinguishability of two obfuscated randomized programs that use correlated randomness. Along the way, we also define and construct garbling schemes that offer only partial protection. These may be of independent interest.

Keywords

Obfuscation, Randomized Encodings, Garbling, Delegation

1. INTRODUCTION

A garbling scheme $\mathcal{G}$ converts programs and input values into "opaque" constructs that reveal nothing but the corresponding output values. That is, $\mathcal{G}$ turns a program M into a garbled program $\tilde{M}$ and, separately, turns a value x into a garbled input $\tilde{x}$, with the guarantee that $\tilde{M}(\tilde{x}) = M(x)$ and in addition the pair $(\tilde{M}, \tilde{x})$ reveals nothing but $M(x)$. Originally conceived by Yao [Yao86], garbling schemes are a pillar of cryptographic protocol design, with numerous ap-

plications such as secure two-party and multiparty computation protocols, verifiable delegation schemes, randomized encoding schemes, one time programs, and functional encryption.

A drawback of Yao's original construction is that the size and runtime of the garbled program are proportional to the circuit representation of the input program. This holds even if the plaintext program is represented more succinctly, say as a Turing machine or a RAM program. (Essentially, one has to first translate the plaintext program to a circuit, and then apply Yao's garbling method in a gate by gate manner.) This drawback becomes especially significant in situations where the input x is much larger than the program's size or runtime — as in, say, keyword search in a large-but-sorted database — or when the runtime of the plaintext program varies from input to input.

Noticing this drawback, Goldwasser Kalai et al. [GKP+13] construct a garbling scheme for *Turing machines,* namely a scheme where the size, runtime and space requirements of the garbled program are proportional to those of the Turing machine representation of the plaintext program. To do that, they make strong *extractability* assumptions. Namely, they postulate existence of an efficient algorithm for extracting secrets from a certain class of adversaries.

Noticing the same drawback, Lu and Ostrovsky, and later Gentry Halevi et al. and Garg Lu et al. [LO13, GHL+14, GLOS15], construct garbling schemes for RAM programs, where the runtime of the garbled program is proportional only to the runtime of the plaintext program on that input. In [GLOS15] this is done assuming only one way functions. Still, the *size* of the garbled program is proportional to the *runtime* of the plaintext program.

Bitansky Garg et al. and Canetti Holmgren et al. construct a *semi-succinct* garbling scheme for RAM programs, assuming non-succinct Indistinguishability Obfuscation (IO) and injective one way functions [BGL+15, CHJV15]. That is, they construct garbling schemes where the space and runtime of the garbled program are proportional to the space and runtime of the plaintext program, and where the size of the garbled program is proportional to the *space* complexity of the plaintext program. For this they assume existence of non-succinct IO schemes, i.e. schemes where the complexity of the obfuscated program is polynomial in the size of the circuit representation of the plaintext program. (Indeed, current candidate indistinguishability obfuscators are such [GGH+13, BGK+14, Zim14, AB15].) We note that, although the overall parameters of these two schemes are roughly comparable, the underlying techniques are different.

Permission to make digital or hard copies of all or part of this work for personal or classroom use is granted without fee provided that copies are not made or distributed for profit or commercial advantage and that copies bear this notice and the full citation on the first page. Copyrights for components of this work owned by others than ACM must be honored. Abstracting with credit is permitted. To copy otherwise, or republish, to post on servers or to redistribute to lists, requires prior specific permission and/or a fee. Request permissions from Permissions@acm.org.

ITCS'16, January 14–16, 2016, Cambridge, MA, USA.
© 2016 ACM. ISBN 978-1-4503-4057-1/16/01 ...$15.00.
DOI: http://dx.doi.org/10.1145/2840728.2840765

Koppula, Lewko and Waters [KLW15] devise a *fully succinct* garbling scheme for Turing machines from non-succinct IO and one way functions, using techniques that extend those of [CHJV15]. That is, in their garbling scheme the runtime, space and description size of the garbled program are proportional to those of the Turing machine representation of the plaintext program. This leaves open the following natural question:

> Do there exist fully succinct garbling schemes for RAM programs? If so, under what assumptions?

Any advancement on this question directly applies to the many applications of succinct garbling mentioned in these works, including delegation of computation, functional encryption and others.

From succinct garbling to succinct obfuscation.

In [BGL+15, CHJV15] it is also shown how to turn a garbling scheme into a full-fledged program obfuscation scheme with comparable efficiency and succinctness properties, at the price of making stronger assumptions on the underlying cryptographic building blocks. That is, given non-succinct IO (namely IO for circuits), one-way functions, and a garbling scheme $\mathcal{G}$, they construct an IO scheme $\mathcal{O}$ with similar efficiency and size overhead as that for $\mathcal{G}$. The security of $\mathcal{O}$ loses a factor of D, where D is the size of the domain of inputs to the plaintext program. Using this transformation, and assuming sub-exponential one-way functions and IO for circuits, [BGL+15, CHJV15] show a semi-succinct IO scheme for RAM machines and [KLW15] show a fully succinct IO scheme for Turing machines. However:

> Is there a fully succinct IO scheme for RAM programs? If so, under what assumptions?

We note that, due to the exponential degradation in security in that transform, the security parameter needs to grow linearly with $\log D$. The size of the obfuscated program thus grows polynomially in the length of input to the plaintext program. We only know how to get below this bound under significantly stronger assumptions on the underlying obfuscation scheme [BCP14, IPS15].

1.1   Our contribution

We answer both questions. Given an IO scheme for circuits and one way functions we construct a fully succinct garbling scheme for RAM programs. That is, the runtime, space, and size of the garbled program are the same as those of the plaintext program, up to polylogarithmic factors and a polynomial in the security parameter. The security of the scheme degrades polynomially with the runtime of the plaintext program. Assuming quasipolynomial security of the underlying primitives, the scheme guarantees full security even for programs with arbitrary polynomial runtime. Using the transformation of [BGL+15, CHJV15], and assuming subexponential security of the underlying primitives, we obtain a fully succinct IO scheme for RAM programs.

Furthermore, similarly to the schemes of [CHJV15, BGL+15, KLW15], our garbling scheme extends easily to support persistent data: Multiple machines $M_1, \ldots, M_\ell$ can be garbled, along with some (potentially very large) data, such that machine M_i acts on the data configuration left by M_{i-1}, and

such that having access to the garbled data and garbled machines gives no information other than $y_1, \ldots, y_\ell$, where y_i is the output of M_i when executed in sequence on the data after $M_1, \ldots, M_{i-1}$. Importantly, in our case of RAM machines, each machine can run in time that is *sublinear* in the entire data; for example, each machine may execute a database query, modifying the database and returning some small result. Our transformation preserves the sub-linear complexity of the machines.

The preservation of sublinear complexity is powerful also in the context of delegation of computation. Indeed, consider the task of delegating the computation of sublinear-time RAM programs over large delegated databases. Indeed, when instantiated with our scheme, the delegation of computation scheme for RAM-IO (described in [CHJV15]) is the *first* to guarantee both correctness and *privacy* of the computation, while preserving full succinctness and *sublinear* complexity for the prover.[1]

We note that in this work we achieve security only when the RAM machine M and database x are chosen ahead of time. In a follow-up work [CCHR15], it is shown how to achieve security against adaptively chosen RAM machines.

Our Techniques.

While our result may come across as natural and expected given the results of [KLW15] and [CHJV15], obtaining it does require new ideas and significant work. Indeed, naive attempts to extend the techniques of [KLW15] to RAM programs encounter the following problem: The [KLW15] technique applies when the plaintext machine is deterministic and its memory access pattern is fixed and independent of the inputs. When the plaintext program is a Turing machine, making sure that the memory access pattern is fixed incurs only small overhead in complexity. In contrast, hiding the memory access pattern in a RAM program in an efficiency-preserving way requires the memory access pattern to be randomized. Indeed, this is the case for Oblivious RAM schemes [GO96]. Furthermore, the security guarantees provided by Oblivious RAM (ORAM) schemes hold only when the internal random choices of the scheme are hidden from the adversary. However, in our case these internal random choices are encapsulated in a succinct program that is only protected by indistinguishability obfuscation.

A second look reveals the following basic discrepancy between the [CHJV15] technique (which is ORAM-friendly) and the [KLW15] technique (which is not). In both works, security of the garbled program is demonstrated by gradually moving, in a way that's indistinguishable to the adversary, from the real garbled program to a dummy garbled program, where the dummy program has just the result hardwired and is running a fake computation in all steps but the last one. In [CHJV15], the intermediate, hybrid programs start with some number, i, of dummy steps, and then continue the computation from the ith intermediate configuration all the way to the end. To make this technique work with ORAM, [CHJV15] use an ORAM scheme with a strong *forward security* property: Essentially, the addresses accessed before time i must appear independent of

---

[1]In particular, the "generic" method of guaranteeing privacy in delegation schemes by encrypting the data using fully homomorphic encryption incurs a super-linear complexity overhead. We thank Yael Kalai for this observation.

the underlying access pattern, even given the scheme's internal state at time $i + 1$.

In contrast, [KLW15] move from the real garbled program to the dummy one via intermediate programs that perform the computation from the beginning until some step, i. From then on, the intermediate program performs the dummy computation and in the end it outputs its hardwired value. This reversal of the order of steps in the intermediate programs is the key idea that allows the size of their garbled program to not depend on the space requirements of the plaintext program. However, this new structure of the hybrid programs seems incompatible with ORAM techniques: Indeed, the natural way to extend the [KLW15] argument to this case would be to argue that the program's memory access pattern at steps i and up is random even given the program's state at steps 1 through $i - 1$. But this does not hold, since all the steps of the computation up to the transition point i are executed, including the internal random choices of whatever ORAM scheme is in use.

Our first step towards getting around this difficulty is to identify the following property of ORAM schemes. Recall that an ORAM scheme translates the memory access requests made by the underlying program to randomized locations in the actual external memory. We say that an ORAM scheme has **localized randomness** if the random variable describing the physical location of the memory cell accessed by the plaintext program at a certain step of the computation depends only on a relatively small portion of the entire random input of the ORAM scheme. Furthermore, we require that the location of this portion depends only on the last step in which this memory cell was accessed, which in of itself is a deterministic function of the underlying program. To the best of our knowledge, this property of Path ORAMs has not been utilized in previous work, but we observe that the ORAM of [CP13] has localized randomness. (In fact, it seems likely that other schemes do as well, or can be slightly modified to be so.) Now, given an ORAM scheme with localized randomness, we "puncture" the scheme at exactly the points that are necessary for making the external memory access locations at step i appear random even given the punctured program state at step $i - 1$. Furthermore, we can perform this puncturing with minimal overhead in terms of the size of the obfuscated program.

More concretely, we proceed in two main steps. (The actual construction goes through a number of smaller steps, for sake of modularity and clarity.) We first build a "fixed-address" garbler which guarantees that the garbled versions of two machines M_0 and M_1 with inputs x_0 and x_1 are indistinguishable as long they access the same sequence of addresses. We believe that this property is of independent interest. In the second step we use an ORAM scheme with localized randomness to obtain full garbling. Below we provide more detail on these two steps.

1.1.1 Fixed Address Garbling

As an intermediary step towards a fully succinct garbling scheme for RAM programs, we define and obtain the following weaker security property for garbling schemes. We say that a garbling scheme is a *fixed-address garbler* if for any two same-size deterministic programs M_0 and M_1, and any same-length input values x_0 and x_1, it holds that $(\tilde{M}_0, \tilde{x}_0) \approx (\tilde{M}_1, \tilde{x}_1)$ as long as (a) $M_0(x_0) = M_1(x_1)$ and (b) The sequence of memory addresses accessed by M_0 when run on

x_0 is identical to the sequence of memory addresses accessed by M_1 when run on x_1. (Here $\tilde{M}$ and $\tilde{x}$ are the garbled versions of M and x, respectively.) Furthermore, the sequence of addresses accessed by $\tilde{M}$ on input $\tilde{x}$ is identical to the sequence of addresses accessed by M on input x.

The fact that $\tilde{M}$ preserves the access pattern of M provides potential efficiency and practical applicability gains that are not possible in the context of fully secure and succinct garbling of RAM programs, since in the latter the access pattern is inherently randomized. For instance, the garbled machine necessarily has the same fine-grain cache performance as the original one. In contract, ORAM-based techniques need to resort to coarse-grain cache or other workarounds which impact cache performance.

We construct a fully succinct fixed-address garbling scheme. As a preliminary step, we construct a garbling scheme that is fixed-address, except that $(\tilde{M}_0, \tilde{x}_0) \approx (\tilde{M}_1, \tilde{x}_1)$ only when the two computations have the exact same memory access pattern, including the *contents* of the memory cells accessed. (We call such schemes *fixed-memory* garbling schemes.) Here our technique follows the steps of the [KLW15] machine-hiding encoding scheme. In particular we use the same underlying primitives, namely positional accumulators, cryptographic iterators, and splittable signatures. (We somewhat simplify their interfaces.) We note however that the [KLW15] construction cannot be used in a "black box" way and needs to be redone in the RAM model.

We then move from fixed-memory garbling to fixed-address garbling. Similarly to the move in [KLW15] from machine-hiding encoding to garbling, this step requires encrypting the memory contents in an IO-friendly scheme. We stress however that our situation is different: In their oblivious Turing machine model the memory access pattern contains no information. In contrast, as argued in more detail below, in our case the access pattern can in of itself contain information that is hard to compress in a security-preserving manner. The way we argue about the security of the scheme must change accordingly.

Concretely, to garble M we transform it to a program M' which interleaves *two* executions of M, on two parallel tracks 'A' and 'B' of memory. Whenever M would access a memory address, M' accesses the corresponding address in both tracks 'A' and 'B'. At each point in time, tracks 'A' and 'B' both store memory contents corresponding to an execution of M. We then apply the fixed-memory garbling scheme to M'. Let $\tilde{M}'$ denote the resulting program.

To argue fixed-address security, consider two programs M_0 and M_1 and input values x_0 and x_1 that satisfy the fixed-address requirements. To show that $(\tilde{M}'_0, \tilde{x}_0) \approx (\tilde{M}'_1, \tilde{x}_1)$, we consider an intermediate hybrid in which M'_0 is replaced by a new machine M_{01} which now executes M_0 on track 'A' but M_1 on track 'B'. Indistinguishability of the intermediate hybrid from either end is shown by demonstrating how to indistinguishably switch from a machine that outputs the result of track 'A' to a machine that outputs the result of track 'B'.

1.1.2 Full Garbling

Our final and main step is a construction of a succinct fully secure garbler for RAM machines from a succinct fixed-address garbler. Our construction is fully general; it does not use any special properties of the fixed-address garbler, not even the address-preserving property which we explicitly highlighted above.

Recall that for a fully secure garbler we require that $(\tilde{M}_0, \tilde{x}_0)$ is computationally indistinguishable from $(\tilde{M}_1, \tilde{x}_1)$ whenever $M_0(x_0) = M_1(x_1)$, and in addition he runtime and space requirement of M_0 on x_0 is the same as the runtime and space requirement of M_1 on x_1.

Furthermore, recall that hiding the memory access pattern in an efficiency preseving way is done by Oblivious RAM (ORAM) techniques, which make crucial use of randomness that remains secret within the program. In contrast, our fixed-address garbler guarantees security only when the access pattern of the underlying machine is *fixed*.

Our first step towards making use of a fixed-address garbler is to "derandomize" the ORAM scheme by setting its randomness to be the result of applying a puncturable PRF to the program's input. This indeed means that, for any givn input, the access pattern is fixed. Still, it is not clear how to argue security of the scheme; in particular, the access pattern of $\tilde{M}_0$ when run on $\tilde{x}_0$ may well be different than the access pattern of $\tilde{M}_1$ when run on $\tilde{x}_1$.

For this purpose, we use the *localized randomness* property sketched above and described in more detail here. Localized randomness requires a particularly structured relationship between the random tape R of an ORAM and the addresses $\mathbf{a}_1, \ldots, \mathbf{a}_t$ that it accesses. Here each $\mathbf{a}_i$ is itself a sequence of addresses $a_{i,1}, \ldots, a_{i,\eta}$, accessed in the emulation of the underlying RAM machine's i^{th} step. Specifically, we require that (for given underlying memory operations $\mathsf{op}_1, \ldots, \mathsf{op}_t$), each $\mathbf{a}_i$ is influenced only by a small subset D_i of the bits of R, and each bit of R influences at most one of $\mathbf{a}_i$. The ORAM must also come with a p.p.t. algorithm $\mathsf{OSample}$ such that $\mathsf{OSample}(i)$ has the same distribution as $\mathbf{a}_i$, independently of $\mathsf{op}_1, \ldots, \mathsf{op}_t$. A simple analysis in the supporting materials (Appendix A) shows that the ORAM of Chung and Pass [CP13, SCSL11] satisfies this locality property.

To analyze the composition of a fixed-address garbler with a localized-randomness ORAM, we adapt the punctured programming technique of [SW14]. To simulate a garbled program whose output is y and runs in time T, apply a fixed-address garbler to the program that for each i from 1 to T, simulates addresses $\mathbf{a}_i$ to access using $\mathsf{Sim}(F(i))$ for some puncturable PRF F, and output the resulting garbled program. We need to prove that this simulation is indistinguishable from the real garbled machine M, in a sequence of hybrids which changes each $\mathbf{a}_i$ to $\mathsf{Sim}(F(i))$.

This argument is reminiscent of the proof of security for the [CLTV15] construction of a probabilistic iO (PIO) obfuscator, with the complication that $\mathbf{a}_1$ through $\mathbf{a}_t$ are generated adaptively. This complication is handled by switching the $\mathbf{a}_i$'s in reverse order – starting with $\mathbf{a}_t$ and ending with $\mathbf{a}_1$. Here it is crucial to note that, despite the adaptivity, $\mathbf{a}_1$ through $\mathbf{a}_t$ are mutually independent random variables by the localized randomness property of the ORAM scheme.

To switch $\mathbf{a}_i$ to $\mathsf{Sim}(F(i))$, we first hard-code $\mathbf{a}_i$, and then puncture the ORAM's PRF on exactly the points which determine $\mathbf{a}_i$. ORAM locality implies that this set is *small* and that the puncturing does not affect any $\mathbf{a}_j$ for $j \neq i$, so the security of the fixed access garbler is applicable. We then indistinguishably replace $\mathbf{a}_i$ with $\mathsf{Sim}(F(i))$. Finally we remove the hard-codings and unpuncture all the PRFs, relying again on security of the fixed-access garbler.

1.2 Related Work

In an independent and concurrent work, Chen et al. [CCC⁺15] also show how to garble RAM and even develop new tools to garble *parallel* RAM programs. In the RAM setting, our constructions are essentially the same. Our proof of security is significantly more modular however, while their analysis achieves a slightly better concrete security parameter.

1.3 Roadmap

As mentioned, we build up our main construction in four stages, at each stage strengthening the security properties. In the first two stages, we directly apply the techniques of [KLW15] to produce a very weak garbling scheme for RAM machines. For ease of exposition, we separate this into two parts: In Section 3, we give a garbler which only guarantees indistinguishability of the garbled programs as long as the entire execution transcripts of the two plaintext machines look identical; that is, if they specify the same sequence of internal local states, same addresses accessed, and same values written to memory. We call such schemes *fixed transcript garblers*. In Section 4, we upgrade this garbling scheme to a *fixed-memory garbler*, which no longer needs the machines to have the same internal local states.

Our main technical contributions are the construction of a *fixed-address garbler* in Section 5, and its combination with a local ORAM in Section 6 to build a full RAM garbler. Section 7 presents the application to persistent data.

2. PRELIMINARIES

2.1 Notation

- $\mathbb{N}$ denotes the set $\{0, 1, 2, \ldots\}$ For any integer $n \in \mathbb{N}$, $[n]$ denotes the set $\{0, 1, \ldots, n-1\}$.

- For a set X and a set Y, Y^X denotes the set of all functions from X to Y. When $X = \mathbb{N}$, $f \in Y^{\mathbb{N}}$ is also identified as the infinite sequence $(f(0), f(1), \ldots)$.

- For $n \in \mathbb{N}$, X^n denotes the set of n-tuples of elements of X.

- X^* denotes $\cup_{i \in \mathbb{N}} X^i$.

- For a set $S \subset [n]$, $S = \{i_1, \ldots, i_\ell\}$ with $i_1 < \cdots < i_\ell$, and a sequence $\vec{a} = (a_0, \ldots, a_{n-1}) \in X^n$, we write $\vec{a}_S$ to denote the tuple $(a_{i_1}, \ldots, a_{i_\ell})$. We use analogous notation for subsequences of infinite sequences $(X^{\mathbb{N}})$. More generally, if f is a function from X to Y, and if S is a subset of X, we write $f(S)$ to denote $\{f(x) : x \in S\}$. If S is an ordered set, $f(S)$ inherits the same ordering.

- For a finite set S, we write ℓ_S to denote the worst-case length of binary strings encoding elements of S (typically this will be $\lceil \log(|S|) \rceil$). We identify S with a subset of $\{0, 1\}^{\ell_S}$.

- For a randomized algorithm $\mathcal{A}$, we write $\mathcal{A}(x; r)$ to denote running $\mathcal{A}$ on input x with randomness r.

2.2 Indistinguishability Obfuscation

We assume the existence of an indistinguishability obfuscator [BGI⁺01, GGH⁺13].

Syntax.

An indistinguishability obfuscator for circuits is a p.p.t. algorithm $i\mathcal{O}$ which takes as input a security parameter 1^λ, a circuit C, and outputs a circuit $\tilde{C}$.

Correctness.

For all x, $\Pr[i\mathcal{O}(1^\lambda, C)(x) = C(x)] = 1$.

Security.

If $|C_0| = |C_1|$ and $C_0(x) = C_1(x)$ for every x, then

$$i\mathcal{O}(1^\lambda, C_0) \approx i\mathcal{O}(1^\lambda, C_1).$$

2.3 The RAM Model

2.3.1 RAM Machines

In this work, a RAM machine M is defined as a tuple (Σ, Q, Y, C), where:

- Σ is a finite set, which is the possible contents of a memory cell. For example, $\Sigma = \{0, 1\}$.

- Q is the set of all possible "local states" of M, containing some initial state q_0. (We think of Q as a set that grows polynomially as a function of the security parameter. That is, a state $q \in Q$ can encode cryptographic keys, as well as "local memory" of size that is bounded by some fixed polynomial in the security parameter.)

- Y is the output space of M.

- C is a circuit implementing a transition function which maps $Q \times (\Sigma \cup \{\epsilon\}) \to (Q \times O_\Sigma) \cup Y$. Here O_Σ denotes the set of memory operations with Σ as the alphabet of possible memory symbols. Precisely, $O_\Sigma = (\mathbb{N} \times \Sigma)$. That is, C takes the current state and the value returned by the memory access function, and returns a new state, a memory address, a read/write instruction, and a value to be written in case of a write.

We write $|M|$ to denote the tuple $(\ell_\Sigma, \ell_Q, \ell_Y, |C|)$, where ℓ_Σ is the length of a binary encoding of Σ, and similarly for ℓ_Q and ℓ_Y.

2.3.2 Memory Configurations

A memory configuration on alphabet Σ is a function $s : \mathbb{N} \to \Sigma \cup \{\epsilon\}$. Let $\|s\|_0$ denote $|\{a : s(a) \neq \epsilon\}|$ and, in a horrific abuse of notation, let $\|s\|_\infty$ denote $\max(\{a : s(a) \neq \epsilon\})$, which we will call the *length* of the memory configuration. A memory configuration s can be implemented (say with a balanced binary tree) by a data structure of size $O(\|s\|_0)$, supporting updates to any index in $O(\log \|s\|_\infty)$ time.

We can naturally identify a string $x = x_1 \dots x_n \in \Sigma^*$ with the memory configuration s_x, defined by

$$s_x(i) = \begin{cases} x_i & \text{if } i \leq |x| \\ \epsilon & \text{otherwise} \end{cases}$$

Looking ahead, efficient representations of sparse memory configurations (in which $\|s\|_0 < \|s\|_\infty$) are convenient for succinctly garbling computations where the space usage is larger than the input length.

2.3.3 Execution

We now define what it means to execute a RAM machine $M = (\Sigma, Q, Y, C)$ on an initial memory configuration $s_0 \in \Sigma^\mathbb{N}$ to obtain $M(s_0)$.

Define $a_0 = 0$. For $i > 0$, iteratively define $(q_i, a_i, v_i) = C(q_{i-1}, s_{i-1}(a_{i-1}))$ and define the ith memory configuration s_i as

$$s_i(a) = \begin{cases} v_i & \text{if } a = a_i \\ s_{i-1}(a) & \text{otherwise} \end{cases}$$

If $C(q_{t-1}, s_{t-1}(a_{t-1})) = y \in Y$ for some t, then we say that $M(s_0) = y$. If there is no such t, we say that $M(s_0) = \bot$. When $M(s_0) \neq \bot$, it is convenient to define the following functions:

- Define the *running time* of M on s_0 as the above t, and denote it $\mathsf{Time}(M, s_0)$.

- Define the *space usage* of M on s_0 as $\max_{i=0}^{t-1}(\|s_i\|_\infty)$, and denote it $\mathsf{Space}(M, s_0)$.

- Define the *execution transcript* of M on s_0 as

$$((q_0, a_0, v_0), \dots, (q_{t-1}, a_{t-1}, v_{t-1}), y),$$

and denote it $\mathcal{T}(M, s_0)$.

- Define the *resultant memory configuration* of M on s_0 as s_t, and denote it $\mathsf{NextMem}(M, s_0)$.

2.4 Garbling

Syntax.

A garbling scheme for RAM progams is a tuple of p.p.t. algorithms (KeyGen, GbPrg, GbMem, Exec).

- **Key Generation:** $\mathsf{KeyGen}(1^\lambda, S, T)$ takes the security parameter λ in unary, a space bound S and a time bound T in binary, and outputs a secret key SK.

- **Machine Garbling:** $\mathsf{GbPrg}(SK, M)$ takes as input a secret key SK and a RAM machine M, and outputs a RAM machine $\tilde{M}$

- **Memory Garbling:** $\mathsf{GbMem}(SK, s)$ takes as input a secret key SK and a memory configuration s, and then outputs a memory configuration $\tilde{s}$.

We are interested in garbling schemes which are *correct*, *efficient*, and *secure*.

Correctness.

A garbling scheme is said to be correct if for all RAM machines M and all memory configurations s which satisfy $\mathsf{Time}(M, s) \leq T$ and $\mathsf{Space}(M, s) \leq S$, we have

$$\Pr\left[\tilde{M}(\tilde{s}) = M(s) \,\middle|\, \begin{array}{l} SK \leftarrow \mathsf{KeyGen}(1^\lambda, S, T) \\ \tilde{M} \leftarrow \mathsf{GbPrg}(SK, M) \\ \tilde{s} \leftarrow \mathsf{GbMem}(SK, s) \end{array}\right] \geq 1 - \mathrm{negl}(\lambda).$$

Efficiency.

A garbling scheme is said to be efficient if:

1. KeyGen, GbPrg, and GbMem are all p.p.t. algorithms. In particular, we emphasize that:

- The bounds T and S are encoded in binary, so the time to garble does not significantly depend on either of these quantities.

    - The running time of GbMem is polynomial in $\|s\|_0$, the number of non-empty addresses in s. In fact in our scheme the running time is linear in $\|s\|_0$.

2. $\mathsf{Time}(\tilde{M}, \tilde{s}) = \tilde{O}(\mathsf{Time}(M, s))$ (hiding polylogarithmic factors in S), and $\mathsf{Space}(\tilde{M}, \tilde{s}) \leq S$.

Security.

A garbling scheme is said to be *secure* if there is an efficient algorithm Sim such that for all RAM machines M and memory configurations s with $\mathsf{Time}(M, s) \leq T$ and $\mathsf{Space}(M, s) \leq S$, no p.p.t. algorithm can distinguish

$$\tilde{M}, \tilde{s}$$

from

$$\mathsf{Sim}(1^\lambda, M(s), \mathsf{Time}(M, s), T, S, |M|, \|s\|_0).$$

in the probability space defined by sampling

$$SK \leftarrow \mathsf{KeyGen}(1^\lambda, S, T)$$
$$\tilde{M} \leftarrow \mathsf{GbPrg}(SK, M)$$
$$\tilde{s} \leftarrow \mathsf{GbMem}(SK, s)$$

3. FIXED-TRANSCRIPT GARBLING

We first construct a garbling scheme with a very weak security definition. Both the construction and the security proof closely follow the techniques of [KLW15], adapting them to RAM machines.

DEFINITION 1. *A garbling scheme* $(\mathsf{KeyGen}, \mathsf{GbPrg}, \mathsf{GbMem})$ *is said to be fixed-transcript secure if for all RAM machines* M_0 *and* M_1 *and all memory configurations* s *such that:*

- $|M_0| = |M_1|$

- $\mathcal{T}(M_0, s) = \mathcal{T}(M_1, s)$

for all p.p.t. algorithms $\mathcal{A}$,

$$\Pr\left[\mathcal{A}(1^\lambda, \tilde{M}_b, \tilde{s}) = b\right] \leq \frac{1}{2} + \mathsf{negl}(\lambda)$$

in the probability space defined by sampling

$$SK \leftarrow \mathsf{KeyGen}(1^\lambda, S, T)$$
$$b \leftarrow \{0, 1\}$$
$$\tilde{M}_b \leftarrow \mathsf{GbPrg}(SK, M_b)$$
$$\tilde{s} \leftarrow \mathsf{GbMem}(SK, s).$$

THEOREM 1. *If one-way functions and an indistinguishability obfuscator for circuits exist, then there is a fixed-transcript secure garbling scheme for RAM machines.*

In the full version [CH15] we include this theorem's proof, which closely follows the machine-hiding encoding construction of [KLW15].

4. FIXED MEMORY GARBLING

We now use a fixed transcript garbling scheme to satisfy a slightly stronger notion which we call fixed-memory garbling. In fixed-memory garbling, the garblings of two different machines are indistinguishable as long as the memory accesses are the same. Notably, it is possible for the two machines to have differing local states.

DEFINITION 2 (FIXED MEMORY SECURITY). *A garbling scheme* $(\mathsf{KeyGen}, \mathsf{GbPrg}, \mathsf{GbMem})$ *is said to be fixed-memory secure if for all RAM machines* M_0 *and* M_1, *memory configurations* s, *all time bounds* T *and space bounds* S *satisfying:*

- $\mathsf{Time}(M_0, s) \leq T$

- $\mathsf{Space}(M_0, s) \leq S$

- $M_0(s) = M_1(s)$

- $|M_0| = |M_1|$

- *Writing* $\mathcal{T}(M_0, s) = ((q_0, a_0, v_0), \ldots, (q_{t-1}, a_{t-1}, v_{t-1}))$ *and* $\mathcal{T}(M_1, s) = ((q'_0, a'_0, v'_0), \ldots, (q'_{t'-1}, a'_{t'-1}, v'_{t'-1}))$, *it holds that* $t = t'$ *and for each* $i \in [t]$, $a_i = a'_i$ *and* $v_i = v'_i$.

it holds that for all p.p.t. adversaries $\mathcal{A}$

$$\Pr\left[\mathcal{A}(1^\lambda, \tilde{M}_b, \tilde{s}) = b\right] \leq \frac{1}{2} + \mathsf{negl}(\lambda)$$

in the probability space defined by sampling

$$SK \leftarrow \mathsf{KeyGen}(1^\lambda, T, S)$$
$$b \leftarrow \{0, 1\}$$
$$\tilde{M}_b \leftarrow \mathsf{GbPrg}(SK, M)$$
$$\tilde{s} \leftarrow \mathsf{GbMem}(SK, s)$$

4.1 Construction

Given a garbling scheme $(\mathsf{KeyGen}', \mathsf{GbPrg}', \mathsf{GbMem}')$ satisfying fixed transcript security, we build a garbling scheme $(\mathsf{KeyGen}, \mathsf{GbPrg}, \mathsf{GbMem})$ satisfying fixed-memory security. All we need to do is mask the internal state for each timestamp with a different pseudorandom value.

CONSTRUCTION 1. *We define* $(\mathsf{KeyGen}, \mathsf{GbPrg}, \mathsf{GbMem})$:

- $\mathsf{KeyGen}(1^\lambda, T, S)$ *samples* $K' \leftarrow \mathsf{KeyGen}'(1^\lambda, T, S)$ *and a puncturable PRF* F, *and outputs* $K = (K', F, T, S)$.

- $\mathsf{GbPrg}(K, M = (\Sigma, Q, Y, C))$ *samples and outputs*

$$\tilde{M} \leftarrow \mathsf{GbPrg}'(K', M' = (\Sigma, Q', Y, C')),$$

where $Q' = [T] \times \{0, 1\}^{\ell_Q}$, *and* C' *is defined in Algorithm 1.* q'_0, *the initial state for* M', *is defined as* $(0, F(0) \oplus q_0)$,

- $\mathsf{GbMem}(K, s)$ *outputs* $\mathsf{GbMem}'(K', s)$.

4.2 Proof of Security

THEOREM 2. *If* $(\mathsf{KeyGen}', \mathsf{GbPrg}', \mathsf{GbMem}')$ *is a fixed transcript secure garbling scheme, then Construction 1 defines a fully succinct, efficient, fixed memory secure garbling scheme for RAM machines.*

A proof is given in the full version of this paper [CH15].

```
Input: state q, memory symbol σ
Data: Puncturable PRF F, underlying transition
      function C
1 Parse q as (t, c_q);
2 q_in := F(t) ⊕ c_q;
3 out := C(q_in, σ);
4 if out ∈ Y then return out;
5 else
6 │ Parse out as (q_out, op);
7 │ return ((t + 1, F(t + 1) ⊕ q_out), op);
8 end
```

Algorithm 1: Transition function C'

5. FIXED ADDRESS GARBLING

We now use a fixed memory garbling scheme to construct a slightly stronger notion of garbling. Namely, we will now hide the *data* in memory, but not yet the addresses which are accessed. As discussed in the introduction, in applications where the memory access pattern is known not to leak sensitive information, this notion of garbling may be significantly more efficient. In particular, it preserves the efficacy of cache, for which real-world RAM programs are extensively optimized.

DEFINITION 3. *A garbling scheme* (KeyGen, GbPrg, GbMem) *is said to be fixed-address secure if for all RAM machines M, memory configurations s, time bounds T, and space bounds S satisfying the following conditions:*

- Space$(M_0, s_0) \leq S$ and Time$(M_0, s_0) \leq T$.
- $\{a : s_0(a) \neq \epsilon\} = \{a : s_1(a) \neq \epsilon\}$
- *If $\mathcal{T}(M_0, s) = ((q_0, a_0, v_0), \ldots, (q_{t-1}, a_{t-1}, v_{t-1}))$ and $\mathcal{T}(M_1, s) = ((q'_0, a'_0, v'_0), \ldots, (q'_{t'-1}, a'_{t'-1}, v'_{t'-1}))$, then $t = t'$ and for each $i \in [t]$, $a_i = a'_i$.*
- $M_0(x_0) = M_1(x_1)$
- $|M_0| = |M_1|$

for all p.p.t. adversaries $\mathcal{A}$, it holds that

$$\Pr\left[\mathcal{A}(1^\lambda, \tilde{M}_b, \tilde{s}) = b\right] \leq \frac{1}{2} + \text{negl}(\lambda)$$

in the probability space defined by sampling

$$SK \leftarrow \text{KeyGen}(1^\lambda, T, S)$$
$$b \leftarrow \{0, 1\}$$
$$\tilde{M}_b \leftarrow \text{GbPrg}(SK, M)$$
$$\tilde{s} \leftarrow \text{GbMem}(SK, s)$$

5.1 Construction

Given a garbling scheme (KeyGen', GbPrg', GbMem') satisfying fixed-memory security, we build a garbling scheme (KeyGen, GbPrg, GbMem) satisfying fixed-address security.

Overview.

Our construction of Garble(M, x, T, S) applies Garble' to a transformed version of the machine M and a correspondingly transformed of the input x. The transformed machine, which we will denote by M', differs from M in three ways:

- M' executes two copies of M in parallel (thereby using twice as much memory). We think of these as an 'A' execution and a 'B' execution. We think of the external storage of M' as correspondingly consisting of an 'A' track and a 'B' track. We implement the 'A' and 'B' tracks by modifying the memory alphabet Σ to hold two symbols.

- M' writes metadata alongside each value to indicate the time and address at which it is written.

- M' authenticates each value it writes: instead of writing (t, a, v, v) to an address a, it writes $(t, a, F((t, a)) \oplus v, G((t, a)) \oplus v)$, where F and G are puncturable pseudorandom functions.

CONSTRUCTION 2. *We define* (KeyGen, GbPrg, GbMem):

- KeyGen$(1^\lambda, T, S)$ *samples* $K' \leftarrow$ KeyGen'$(1^\lambda, T, S)$, *as well as puncturable PRFs F and G and outputs*

$$K = (K', F, G, T, S).$$

- GbPrg$(K, M = (\Sigma, Q, Y, C))$ *samples and outputs*

$$\tilde{M} \leftarrow \text{GbPrg}'(K', M' = (\Sigma', Q', Y, C')),$$

where

$$\Sigma' = [T] \times [S] \times \{0,1\}^{\ell_\Sigma} \times \{0,1\}^{\ell_\Sigma},$$

$$Q' = [T] \times Q \times Q,$$

and C' is defined in Algorithm 2. The initial state $q'_0 \in Q'$ of M' is defined as $(0, q_0, q_0)$.

- GbMem$((K, F, G, T, S), s)$ *samples* $\tilde{s} \leftarrow$ GbMem(K, s'), *where s' is defined such that $s'(a) = \epsilon$ if $s(a) = \epsilon$, and otherwise*

$$s'(a) = (0, a, F((0, a)) \oplus s(a), G((0, a)) \oplus s(a))$$

```
Data: Underlying transition function C, puncturable
      PRFs F and G
Input: State q, symbol σ
1 Parse q as (t_q, q_A, q_B);
2 Parse σ as (t_σ, a_σ, σ_A, σ_B);
3 Compute out ← C(q_A, F((t_σ, a_σ)) ⊕ σ_A);
4 if out ∈ Y then return out;
5 Parse out as (q_out, (a_out, op_out, σ_out));
6 return
  ((t_q + 1, q_out, q_out), (a_out, op_out, (t_q, a_out, F((t_q, a_out)) ⊕
  σ_out, G((t_q, a_out)) ⊕ σ_out));
```

Algorithm 2: C'

THEOREM 3. *If* (KeyGen', GbPrg', GbMem') *is a fixed memory secure garbling scheme, and if one-way functions (and hence puncturable PRFs) exist, then Construction 2 defines a fully succinct, fixed address secure garbling scheme for RAM machines.*

A proof is given in the full version of this paper [CH15].

6. FULL SECURITY

This section constructs a secure garbling scheme for RAM machines, as in defined in Section 2.4, from any fixed-address garbling scheme. As sketched and motivated in the introduction, this is done by combining the fixed address garbling scheme with an oblivious RAM (ORAM) scheme that has a special property, namely localized randomness. We start by formally defining oblivious RAM schemes and localized randomness, and then present the garbling scheme.

6.1 Oblivious RAM

6.1.1 Syntax

An oblivious RAM is a tuple of probabilistic polynomial-time algorithms (Setup, OMem, OProg)

- Setup($1^\lambda, S$) takes a security parameter in unary and a space bound S, and outputs a secret key SK.

- OProg(SK, M) takes a secret key SK and a RAM machine M, and outputs a probabilistic RAM machine M'.

- OMem(SK, s) takes a secret key SK and a memory configuration s, and outputs a memory configuration s'

6.1.2 Correctness

For all RAM machines M, space bounds S, and memory configurations s such that $\mathsf{Space}(M, s) \leq S$,

$$\Pr\left[M'(s') = M(s)\right] \geq 1 - \mathsf{negl}(\lambda)$$

in the probability space defined by sampling

$$SK \leftarrow \mathsf{Setup}(1^\lambda, S)$$
$$M' \leftarrow \mathsf{OProg}(SK, M)$$
$$s' \leftarrow \mathsf{OMem}(SK, s)$$

6.1.3 Efficiency

There is a function

$$\eta : \mathbb{N} \to \mathbb{N}$$
$$\eta(S) = \Theta(\mathrm{polylog}(S))$$

such that whenever $\mathsf{Space}(M, s) \leq S$ for a RAM machine M, a memory configuration s, and a space bound S,

$$\Pr\left[\mathsf{Time}(M', s') = \eta(S) \cdot \mathsf{Time}(M, s)\right] = 1,$$

in the same probability space as above.

6.1.4 Localized Randomness

Let $T = \mathsf{Time}(M, s)$ and $\eta = \eta(S)$ for some RAM machine M, memory configuration s, and space bound S. Consider the deterministic function

$$\mathsf{addr}'_{M,s,S,\lambda} : \{0,1\}^\mathbb{N} \to \mathbb{N}^{\eta T}$$

$$\mathsf{addr}'_{M,s,S,\lambda}(\vec{r}) = \vec{a}$$

where $\vec{r}$ is used as a random tape to sequentially sample

$$SK \leftarrow \mathsf{Setup}(1^\lambda, S)$$
$$M' \leftarrow \mathsf{OProg}(SK, M)$$
$$s' \leftarrow \mathsf{OMem}(SK, s)$$
$$\vec{a} \leftarrow \mathsf{addr}(M', s')$$

DEFINITION 4. *An ORAM* (Setup, OProg, OMem) *is said to have localized randomness if there is a deterministic algorithm* Sim *such that for all RAM machines M, memory configurations s, and space bounds $S \geq \mathsf{Space}(M, s)$ and running times $t = \mathsf{Time}(M, s)$, there exist sets $R_1, \ldots, R_t \subseteq \mathbb{N}$ such that,*

- *For each i, $|R_i| \leq \mathrm{poly}(\log S, \lambda)$.*

- *For each $i \neq j$, $R_i \cap R_j = \varnothing$.*

- *For each i,*

$$\mathsf{addr}'_{M,s,S,\lambda}(\vec{r})_{\{\eta(i-1),\ldots,\eta i - 1\}} = \mathsf{Sim}(\vec{r}_{R_i})$$

with high probability over a uniformly random $\vec{r} \in \{0,1\}^\mathbb{N}$.

In the full version of this paper [CH15], we show that the Chung-Pass ORAM [CP13] satisfies these properties.

6.2 Construction

Our garbling scheme is very simple; essentially, we just compose the fixed address garbler on top of an ORAM scheme with localized randomness. That is, to garble a machine M, we first transform it via the ORAM, and then apply the fixed address garbler to that transformed machine.

CONSTRUCTION 3. *Let* (KeyGen', GbPrg', GbMem') *be a fixed-address garbling scheme, and let* (Setup, OProg, OMem) *be an ORAM scheme with localized randomness. We define a garbling scheme* (KeyGen, GbPrg, GbMem):

- KeyGen($1^\lambda, T, S$) *samples* $K_{FA} \leftarrow$ KeyGen'($1^\lambda, T, S$) *and* $K_{ORAM} \leftarrow$ Setup($1^\lambda, S$), *and a puncturable PRF F and outputs* (K_{FA}, K_{ORAM}, F).

- GbPrg((K_{FA}, K_{ORAM}, F), M) *samples and outputs*

$$\tilde{M} \leftarrow \mathsf{GbPrg}'(K_{FA}, \mathsf{OProg}(K_{ORAM}, M)^F)$$

- GbMem((K_{FA}, K_{ORAM}), s) *samples and outputs*

$$\tilde{s} \leftarrow \mathsf{GbMem}'(K_{FA}, \mathsf{OMem}(K_{ORAM}, s)).$$

THEOREM 4. *If* (KeyGen', GbPrg', GbMem') *is a fixed address secure garbling scheme for RAM machines, then Construction 3 defines a (fully secure) garbling scheme for RAM machines.*

A proof is given in the full version of this paper [CH15].

7. PERSISTENT DATA

The garbled RAM construction and security proof above can be generalized to a setting in which the garbled RAM programs act on a persistent database. That is, the updates that a garbled RAM program makes to a database D are accessible to the next garbled program to be executed on that database.

DEFINITION 5. *A RAM garbling scheme with persistent data is a tuple of p.p.t. algorithms* (KeyGen, GbPrg, GbMem):

KeyGeneration. KeyGen($1^\lambda, T, S$) *takes as input a security parameter λ in unary, as well as time and space bounds T and S, and outputs a secret key SK.*

Program Garbling. GbPrg(SK, M_i, i) *takes as input a secret key SK, a RAM machine M_i and an index i, and outputs a RAM program $\tilde{M}_i$.*

Memory Garbling. GbMem(SK, s) *takes a secret key SK and a memory configuration s, and outputs a memory configuration database $\tilde{s}$.*

DEFINITION 6. *A RAM garbling scheme with persistent data is said to be* correct *if for every memory configuration s_0, for every $\ell = \text{poly}(\lambda)$, and every tuple of RAM machines $(M_1, \ldots, M_\ell)$, it holds that the outputs of the garbled machines, when run in sequence on the garbled data, equal the outputs of the plaintext machines when run in sequene on the plaintext data. That is:*

$$\Pr\left[y_1 = y_1' \wedge \cdots \wedge y_\ell = y_\ell' \right] \geq 1 - \text{negl}(\lambda)$$

in the probability space defined by sampling

$$
\begin{aligned}
&SK \leftarrow \text{KeyGen}(1^\lambda) \\
&\tilde{s}_0 \leftarrow \text{GbMem}(SK, s_0) \\
&\textit{For } i = 1, \ldots, \ell \\
&\quad \tilde{M}_i \leftarrow \text{GbPrg}(SK, M_i, i) \\
&\quad y_i \leftarrow M_i(s_{i-1}) \\
&\quad y_i' \leftarrow \tilde{M}_i(\tilde{s}_{i-1}) \\
&\quad s_i \leftarrow \text{NextMem}(M_i, s_{i-1}) \\
&\quad \tilde{s}_i \leftarrow \text{NextMem}(\tilde{M}_i, \tilde{s}_{i-1})
\end{aligned}
$$

DEFINITION 7. *A RAM garbling scheme with persistent data is said to be* secure *if there is a p.p.t. algorithm* Sim *such that for all memory configurations s_0, all $\ell = \text{poly}(\lambda)$, and all RAM machines $M_1, \ldots, M_\ell$, no p.p.t. algorithm $\mathcal{A}$ can correctly distinguish between*

$$(\tilde{s}_0, \tilde{M}_1, \ldots, \tilde{M}_\ell)$$

and

$$\text{Sim}(y_1, \ldots, y_\ell, |s_0|, |M_0|, \ldots, |M_\ell|, 1^\lambda)$$

in the probability space defined by sampling

$$
\begin{aligned}
&SK \leftarrow \text{KeyGen}(1^\lambda) \\
&\tilde{s}_0 \leftarrow \text{GbMem}(SK, s_0) \\
&\textit{For } i = 1, \ldots, \ell \\
&\quad \tilde{M}_i \leftarrow \text{GbPrg}(SK, M_i, i)
\end{aligned}
$$

and defining

$$
\begin{aligned}
&\textit{For } i = 1, \ldots, \ell \\
&\quad y_i \leftarrow M_i(s_{i-1}) \\
&\quad s_i \leftarrow \text{NextMem}(M_i, s_{i-1})
\end{aligned}
$$

THEOREM 5. *If there is an indistinguishability obfuscator for circuits and there exist one-way functions, then there is a correct, secure RAM garbling scheme with persistent data.*

PROOF. *(Sketch.)* The scheme and the analysis are straightforward extensions of the single-machine case. That is, the memory garbling is identical to the single-machine case, except that the string "step 0" is attached to the root of the merkle tree before signing; The ith machine is garbled by applying the machine garbling algorithm of the single-machine case, with the exception that now the signed root of the Merkle tree is expected to contain also "step $i-1$", and the root of the Merkle-tree-hash of the final memory configuration is signed together with "step i". (All machines are garbled with the same accumulator, iterator, and splittable signature parameters.)

Correctness, efficiency and succinctness are straightforward. For security, recall that the single-machine simulator generates a dummy (but legal) initial memory configuration, and a dummy machine that first verifies the signature on the memory configuration and then runs a dummy computation for a fixed number of steps at the end of which a hardcoded value is output. Here we extend this simulation strategy in the natural way. That is, the simulator first generates a dummy legal initial memory configuration. The ith dummy machine first checks the signature on its initial memory configuration, and verifies that the signed string has "step $i-1$" encoded in it. Then the machine runs a dummy computation for a fixed number of steps, outputs the hardcoded value, and signs the final memory configuration along with "step i". Analysis of the simulator is extended in a natural way. In particular, it can be done in the same modular way as in the single-machine case. □

We note that, by garbling one machine per bit of an output, we can garble machines with long outputs. Full compactness with simulation security is easily seen to be impossible in this setting, and recent work strengthens this impossibility result to hold even for a weaker notion of security [LPST15]. Our work does not contradict these results, because the combined size of the garbled machines grows proportionally to the total output length.

Acknowledgements

This work was done in part while the authors were visiting the Simons Institute for the Theory of Computing, supported by the Simons Foundation and by the DIMACS/Simons Collaboration in Cryptography through NSF grant #CNS-1523467.

Ran Canetti is supported by the Check Point Institute for Information Security, ISF grant 1523/14, and NSF Frontier CNS-1413920 and 1218461 grants.

Justin Holmgren is supported by the NSF Frontier CNS-1413920 grant.

8. REFERENCES

[AB15]   Benny Applebaum and Zvika Brakerski. Obfuscating circuits via composite-order graded encoding. In *Theory of Cryptography - 12th Theory of Cryptography Conference, TCC 2015, Warsaw, Poland, March 23-25, 2015, Proceedings, Part II*, pages 528–556, 2015.

[BCP14] Elette Boyle, Kai-Min Chung, and Rafael Pass. On extractability obfuscation. In *Theory of Cryptography - 11th Theory of Cryptography Conference, TCC 2014, San Diego, CA, USA, February 24-26, 2014. Proceedings*, pages 52–73, 2014.

[BGI+01] Boaz Barak, Oded Goldreich, Russell Impagliazzo, Steven Rudich, Amit Sahai, Salil P. Vadhan, and Ke Yang. On the (im)possibility of obfuscating programs. In *CRYPTO*, pages 1–18, 2001.

[BGK+14] Boaz Barak, Sanjam Garg, Yael Tauman Kalai, Omer Paneth, and Amit Sahai. Protecting obfuscation against algebraic attacks. In

Phong Q. Nguyen and Elisabeth Oswald, editors, *Advances in Cryptology – EUROCRYPT 2014*, volume 8441 of *Lecture Notes in Computer Science*, pages 221–238. Springer Berlin Heidelberg, 2014.

[BGL+15] Nir Bitansky, Sanjam Garg, Huijia Lin, Rafael Pass, and Sidharth Telang. Succinct randomized encodings and their applications. In Ronitt Rubinfeld, editor, *Symposium on the Theory of Computing (STOC)*, 2015.

[CCC+15] Yu-Chi Chen, Sherman S. M. Chow, Kai-Min Chung, Russell W. F. Lai, Wei-Kai Lin, and Hong-Sheng Zhou. Computation-trace indistinguishability obfuscation and its applications. Cryptology ePrint Archive, Report 2015/406, 2015. http://eprint.iacr.org/.

[CCHR15] Ran Canetti, Yilei Chen, Justin Holmgren, and Mariana Raykova. Succinct adaptive garbled ram. Cryptology ePrint Archive, Report 2015/1074, 2015. http://eprint.iacr.org/.

[CH15] Ran Canetti and Justin Holmgren. Succinct garbled ram. Cryptology ePrint Archive, Report 2015/388, 2015. http://eprint.iacr.org/.

[CHJV15] Ran Canetti, Justin Holmgren, Abhishek Jain, and Vinod Vaikuntanathan. Succinct garbling and indistinguishability obfuscation for ram programs. In Ronitt Rubinfeld, editor, *Symposium on the Theory of Computing (STOC)*, 2015.

[CLTV15] Ran Canetti, Huijia Lin, Stefano Tessaro, and Vinod Vaikuntanathan. Probabilistic indistinguishability obfuscation. In *TCC*, 2015.

[CP13] Kai-Min Chung and Rafael Pass. A simple ORAM. *IACR Cryptology ePrint Archive*, 2013:243, 2013.

[GGH+13] Sanjam Garg, Craig Gentry, Shai Halevi, Mariana Raykova, Amit Sahai, and Brent Waters. Candidate indistinguishability and functional encryption for all circuits. In *FOCS*, pages 40–49, 2013.

[GHL+14] Craig Gentry, Shai Halevi, Steve Lu, Rafail Ostrovsky, Mariana Raykova, and Daniel Wichs. Garbled RAM revisited. In *EUROCRYPT*, pages 405–422, 2014.

[GKP+13] Shafi Goldwasser, Yael Tauman Kalai, Raluca A. Popa, Vinod Vaikuntanathan, and Nickolai Zeldovich. Reusable garbled circuits and succinct functional encryption. In *Symposium on Theory of Computing Conference, STOC'13, Palo Alto, CA, USA, June 1-4, 2013*, pages 555–564, 2013.

[GLOS15] Sanjam Garg, Steve Lu, Rafail Ostrovsky, and Alessandra Scafuro. Garbled ram from one-way functions. In Ronitt Rubinfeld, editor, *Symposium on the Theory of Computing (STOC)*, 2015.

[GO96] Oded Goldreich and Rafail Ostrovsky. Software protection and simulation on oblivious rams. *Journal of the ACM (JACM)*, 43(3):431–473, 1996.

[IPS15] Yuval Ishai, Omkant Pandey, and Amit Sahai. Public-coin differing-inputs obfuscation and its applications. In *Theory of Cryptography - 12th Theory of Cryptography Conference, TCC 2015, Warsaw, Poland, March 23-25, 2015, Proceedings, Part II*, pages 668–697, 2015.

[KLW15] Venkata Koppula, Allison Bishop Lewko, and Brent Waters. Indistinguishability obfuscation for turing machines with unbounded memory. In Ronitt Rubinfeld, editor, *Symposium on the Theory of Computing (STOC)*, 2015.

[LO13] Steve Lu and Rafail Ostrovsky. How to garble ram programs? In Thomas Johansson and Phong Q. Nguyen, editors, *Advances in Cryptology – EUROCRYPT 2013*, volume 7881 of *Lecture Notes in Computer Science*, pages 719–734. Springer Berlin Heidelberg, 2013.

[LPST15] Huijia Lin, Rafael Pass, Karn Seth, and Sidharth Telang. Output-compressing randomized encodings and applications. Cryptology ePrint Archive, Report 2015/720, 2015. http://eprint.iacr.org/.

[SCSL11] Elaine Shi, T.-H. Hubert Chan, Emil Stefanov, and Mingfei Li. Oblivious RAM with o((logn)3) worst-case cost. In *ASIACRYPT*, pages 197–214, 2011.

[SW14] Amit Sahai and Brent Waters. How to use indistinguishability obfuscation: deniable encryption, and more. In *STOC*, pages 475–484, 2014.

[Yao86] Andrew Chi-Chih Yao. How to generate and exchange secrets. In *Proceedings of the 27th Annual Symposium on Foundations of Computer Science*, SFCS '86, pages 162–167, Washington, DC, USA, 1986. IEEE Computer Society.

[Zim14] Joe Zimmerman. How to obfuscate programs directly. *IACR Cryptology ePrint Archive*, 2014:776, 2014.

Cryptography for Parallel RAM
from Indistinguishability Obfuscation[*]

Yu-Chi Chen
Academia Sinica, Taiwan
wycchen@iis.sinica.edu.tw

Sherman S. M. Chow[†]
Chinese University of
Hong Kong, Hong Kong
sherman@ie.cuhk.edu.hk

Kai-Min Chung[‡]
Academia Sinica, Taiwan
kmchung@iis.sinica.edu.tw

Russell W. F. Lai
Chinese University of
Hong Kong, Hong Kong
wflai@ie.cuhk.edu.hk

Wei-Kai Lin
Academia Sinica, Taiwan
wklin@iis.sinica.edu.tw

Hong-Sheng Zhou
Virginia Commonwealth
University, VA, USA
hszhou@vcu.edu

ABSTRACT

Since many cryptographic schemes are about performing computation on data, it is important to consider a computation model which captures the prominent features of modern system architecture. Parallel random access machine (PRAM) is such an abstraction which not only models multiprocessor platforms, but also new frameworks supporting massive parallel computation such as MapReduce.

In this work, we explore the feasibility of designing cryptographic solutions for the PRAM model of computation to achieve security while leveraging the power of parallelism and random data access. We demonstrate asymptotically optimal solutions for a wide-range of cryptographic tasks based on indistinguishability obfuscation. In particular, we construct the first publicly verifiable delegation scheme with privacy in the persistent database setting, which allows a client to privately delegate both computation and data to a server with optimal efficiency. Specifically, the server can perform PRAM computation on private data with parallel efficiency preserved (up to poly-logarithmic overhead). Our results also cover succinct randomized encoding, searchable encryption, functional encryption, secure multiparty computation, and indistinguishability obfuscation for PRAM.

We obtain our results in a modular way through a notion of computational-trace indistinguishability obfuscation (Ci$\mathcal{O}$), which may be of independent interests.

1. INTRODUCTION

1.1 The PRAM Model

The parallel random-access machine (PRAM) is an abstract computation or programming model of a canonical structured parallel machine. It consists of a polynomial number of synchronous processors. Each of them is similar to an individual (non-parallel) RAM with its central processing unit (CPU) performing computation locally. In addition to the local memory, CPUs in PRAM have random access of a common array of memory which is potentially unbounded. Parallel and distributed computing community suggested many algorithms which are parallelizable in the PRAM model, resulting in an exponential gap between solving the same problem in the RAM and PRAM models. Examples include parallel sorting or searching in a database, which have linear size input but run in polylogarithmic time.

Being an abstract model, PRAM not only models multiprocessor platforms, but also new frameworks in the big-data era such as MapReduce, GraphLab, Spark, etc. Running time is a critical factor, especially when data is being generated in every second worldwide which are too big to be processed by traditional information processing technique or by a single commodity computer. For individuals, or even enterprises without in-house resource/expertise, there is an emerging demand for *delegation* of both data and computation to a third-party server, often called "the cloud", a distributed computing platform with a large amount of CPUs to perform computations in *parallel*. We found PRAM a clean theoretical model to work with for these scenarios.

PRAM with Persistent Database.

With the high volume of data to process and the potentially high volume of output data, it is natural to perform multiple computations over the *"big data"* that persists in the cloud storage. Such functionality is supported by introducing the notion of *persistent database* on top of the PRAM

[*]A full version is available at http://ia.cr/2015/406.

[†]This work is supported in part by the Early Career Award and the grants from the Research Grants Council, Hong Kong (CUHK 439713 & 14201914). Part of this work was done while the author was visiting Academia Sinica.

[‡]This work is partially supported by Ministry of Science and Technology, Taiwan, under Grant no. MOST 103-2221-E-001-022-MY3. This work was done in part while the author was visiting the Simons Institute for the Theory of Computing, supported by the Simons Foundation and by the DIMACS/Simons Collaboration in Cryptography through NSF grant #CNS-1523467; and while the author was visiting the Chinese University of Hong Kong.

Permission to make digital or hard copies of all or part of this work for personal or classroom use is granted without fee provided that copies are not made or distributed for profit or commercial advantage and that copies bear this notice and the full citation on the first page. Copyrights for components of this work owned by others than ACM must be honored. Abstracting with credit is permitted. To copy otherwise, or republish, to post on servers or to redistribute to lists, requires prior specific permission and/or a fee. Request permissions from Permissions@acm.org.

ITCS'16, January 14-16, 2016, Cambridge, MA, USA
© 2016 ACM. ISBN 978-1-4503-4057-1/16/01 ...$15.00.
DOI: http://dx.doi.org/10.1145/2840728.2840769

model. A motivating example is a special kind of delegation, known as searchable symmetric encryption (SSE), which features parallel search and update algorithms.

1.2 Crypto for PRAM

Many cryptographic schemes are about performing computation on data. Traditionally, cryptographers worked on the circuit model of computations; for example, the celebrated result of Yao's garbled circuit for two-party computation [Yao82]. Many cryptographic notions can be benefited by parallelism and persistent database.

Secure Multiparty Computation (SMC).

Secure multiparty computation (SMC) generalizes two-party computation. Consider using SMC on electronic health record (EHR) for collaborative research, EHR often involves patients' medical and genetic information which are often expensive to collect and should be kept confidential as mandated by law. Such kind of large-scale SMC [BCP15] further motivates the benefits of PRAM.

Although (highly optimized) circuit-based SMC protocols and RAM-based solutions of SMC exist, they have inherent drawbacks. Circuit-based solutions are not feasible for big data since circuit representations are huge and the (worst case) runtime can be dependent on the input length. Consequently, it cannot represent sublinear time algorithm. Existing RAM-based solutions cannot exploit parallelism even when the program is parallelizable (which is often the case for processing big data). On the other hand, PRAM is an expressive model to capture the requirements in this case.

Secure and Efficient Delegation.

Security concern manifests in various forms when we consider outsourcing. For a concrete discussion, we consider the *delegation* problem, faced by an enterprise which is outsourcing a newly-developed big data analytic algorithm for uncovering market trends from the customer preferences collected. Data owners demand confidentiality. Secrecy of the algorithm is also desired, or competitors may gather the same kind of business intelligence (from their own data). The output of data analytics is also sensitive, both its confidentiality and authenticity (i.e., the correctness of the algorithm invocation) are crucial for the success of any corresponding strategic plan. It is risky to place all these strong trust in different dimensions on the cloud. Cloud client should safeguard the outsourcing process by resorting to cryptography.

The next concern is about efficiency. The client would want both storage and computation required for secure delegation to be significantly less than the actual data and computation. On the other hand, the server, who is actually storing the data and performing the computation, would like to operate on the (private) data as a PRAM program, and not to perform too much work when compared to computation on the plaintext data. There exists verifiable delegation with privacy, but the solution is based on the circuit model, and is far from suitable for outsourcing big data. Recent work provides heuristic solution for RAM delegation with persistent database [GHRW14], but the solution is only a heuristic one based on a stronger variant of differing-inputs obfuscation (diO), which is subject to implausibility result.

More formally, we consider secure delegation of PRAM program with persistent database, as follows. A (very large) database x is firstly delegated from the client to the server.

The client can make arbitrary number of PRAM program queries to the server, who performs the computation to update the database, and returns the answer with a proof. Ideally, we want the efficiency to match the "unsecured" solution. Namely, delegating database takes $O(|x|)$ cost, and for each PRAM program query, the client's runtime depends only on the description size of the PRAM program, the server's parallel runtime is linear in the parallel runtime of the program, and the client's verification time is independent of the program complexity and the database size.

We pose ourselves this question: Can we outsource both data and computation, leveraging parallelism and random data access, i.e., in the PRAM model?

Functional Encryption (FE).

Another primitive in cloud cryptography which attracts much attention recently is functional encryption (FE), a generalized notion of attribute-based encryption (ABE) originally proposed for enforcing cryptographic access control. FE enables a user with the function key for $f(\cdot)$ to learn $f(x)$ given an encryption of x. Consider x to be the encrypted cloud storage and each user can only access part of the shared storage space (for obvious security reason). FE for PRAM means that the function key can be associated to a PRAM program taking the large x as an input. The access control policy can be very general. We can even embed some sort of parallel logic into it for operating on the relevant parts of the cloud storage in parallel.

We remark that a very recent result achieved FE for Turing machines with unbounded input [AS16].

1.3 Our Goal

To summarize, current study of cryptography does not work in a model which fully leverages the important features of modern architecture to handle the computation problem nowadays; namely, massive parallel computation on big data. In this work, we address the following basic question:

> "How to do Cryptography in the PRAM model —
> How to design cryptographic solutions that achieve
> security and simultaneously leverage the power of
> parallelism and random data access?"

Our work provides general feasibility and asymptotically optimal results for various important cryptographic primitives based on indistinguishability obfuscation for circuits (iO).

1.4 Summary of Our Results

We develop techniques to obtain (asymptotically) optimal constructions for several cryptographic primitives (i.e., multiparty computation, delegation, and functional encryption) in the PRAM model. We do so in modular steps, and our results are presented below. Please also refer to Table 1 for the efficiency of our schemes.

Computation-Trace Indistinguishability Obfuscation.

First, we define a new primitive named computation-trace indistinguishability obfuscation (CiO), which obfuscates a computation instance instead of a program. A computation instance Π is defined by a program P and an input x. Evaluation of Π produces a *computation trace*; namely, all CPU states, memory content, and memory access instructions throughout the computation. A CiO obfuscator takes in a computation instance Π as an input, and outputs $\tilde{\Pi}$ as an obfuscated computation instance that can be evaluated to correctly output $P(x)$. We only require a very weak indistinguishability-based security for CiO, where two obfuscations $CiO(\Pi)$ and $CiO(\Pi')$ are required to be indistinguishable only when the evaluation of Π and Π' produce identical computation trace (which implies their inputs are the same). While the security is weak, we demand stringent efficiency that the obfuscator's runtime depends only on the instance description size, but not the evaluation runtime.

We construct CiO-RAM based on iO for circuits and one-way functions, by adopting techniques developed in a very recent result due to Koppula, Lewko, and Waters [KLW15] (hereinafter referred as KLW). We then (non-trivially, to be elaborated in the next section) extend it into CiO-PRAM. The main challenge is to avoid linear overhead on the number of CPUs in both *parallel runtime* and *obfuscation size* — note that such overhead would obliterate the gain of parallelism for a PRAM computation. To summarize, we have:

THEOREM 1.1 (INFORMAL). *Assuming the existences of indistinguishability obfuscation* (iO) *and one-way functions* (OWF), *there exists (fully succinct) computation-trace indistinguishability obfuscation for PRAM computation.*

While the notion of CiO is weak, we immediately obtain optimal publicly-verifiable delegation of PRAM computation. In particular, the program encoding has size independent of the output length.

COROLLARY 1.2 (INFORMAL). *Assuming the existences of* iO *and* OWF, *there exists a two-message publicly-verifiable delegation scheme for PRAM computation, where the delegator's runtime depends only on the program description and input size, and the server's complexity matches the PRAM complexity up to polynomial factor of program description size.*

Fully Succinct Randomized Encoding.

More importantly, we show how to use our (fully succinct) CiO-PRAM to construct the *first fully succinct* randomized encoding (RE) for PRAM computation. The notion of *randomized encoding*, proposed by Ishai and Kushilevitz [IK00], allows a "complex" function f on an input x to be represented by a "simpler to compute" randomized encoding $\hat{f}(x; r)$ whose output distribution encodes $f(x)$, such that the encoding reveals nothing else regarding f and x, and one can decode by extracting $f(x)$ from $\hat{f}(x; r)$. The original measure of simplicity [IK00] considers the circuit depth (i.e., parallel runtime) of the encoding. Very recently, Bitansky, Garg, Lin, Pass, and Telang [BGL+15] focus on encoding time. Bitansky et al. consider f as represented by a RAM program P, and construct *(space-dependent) succinct randomized encodings* where the encoding time is independent of the time complexity of $P(x)$ (as a RAM program evaluation), but depends on the space complexity of $P(x)$.[1]

We extend the RE notion further to the PRAM model. More precisely, given a PRAM computation instance Π defined by a PRAM program P and an input x, an RE-PRAM generates a randomized encoding $\tilde{\Pi} = RE.\mathsf{Encode}(\Pi)$ that can be decoded/evaluated to obtain $P(x)$, but reveals nothing else regarding both P and x (except the size/time/space

[1]Canetti et al. [CHJV15] achieved a similar result in the context of garbling.

bound of $P(x)$). *Full succinctness* means the encoder's runtime (and thus the encoding size) depends on the description size of P, the input length of x, and the output length of $P(x)$, but is essentially independent of both time and space complexities of $P(x)$. To the best of our knowledge, there was *no known fully succinct construction* of RE, even in the RAM model, before our result.

THEOREM 1.3 (INFORMAL). *Assuming the existence of* iO *and* OWF, *there exists fully succinct randomized encoding for PRAM, where the encoding time depends only on the program description and input/output size, and the server's complexity matches the PRAM complexity of the computation up to polynomial factor of program description size.*

REMARK 1.4. *In the RE construction, the output is not private. Actually, when the output is private, we can provide constructions with slightly better efficiency where the encoding time depends only on program description and input size, but* independent of the output size. *See Table 1.*

Building Cryptography for PRAM.

By plugging our RE-PRAM into various transformations in the literature [GHRW14, BGL+15, CHJV15], we obtain the first constructions of a wide range of cryptographic primitives for PRAM (with the corresponding full succinctness), including non-interactive zero-knowledge, functional encryption, garbling, secure multi-party computation, and indistinguishability obfuscation for PRAM, and we have the following two corollaries.

COROLLARY 1.5 (INFORMAL). *Assuming the existences of* iO *and* OWF, *there exist (fully) succinct non-interactive zero-knowledge, functional encryptions with succinct (PRAM) function keys, succinct reusable garbling, and secure multi-party computation for PRAM with optimal communication.*

Notably, while CiO is syntactically weaker than iO, sub-exponential CiO-PRAM still implies iO for PRAM with sub-exponential security by complexity leveraging (e.g., [BGL+15, CHJV15]).

COROLLARY 1.6 (INFORMAL). *Sub-exponentially secure CiO-PRAM implies sub-exponentially secure iO for PRAM.*

Optimal Delegation with Persistent Database.

Finally, we generalize to the persistent database setting where a computation consists of a database and multiple programs. The generalization is straightforward, and leads to optimal delegation with persistent database.

THEOREM 1.7 (INFORMAL). *Assuming the existence of* iO *and* OWF, *there exists fully succinct delegation schemes for PRAM with persistent database, where the encoding time depends on the database size and the size of each program description, and the server's complexity matches the PRAM complexity of the computation up to polynomial factor of program description size.*

We remark that this immediately gives us the feasibility of optimal symmetric searchable encryption without leakage.

Scheme	Encoding Time for Each Program P_i	Encoding Time for Database	Decoding Time	Decoding Space
PRAM unsecured delegation	$\|P_i\|$	$\|D\|$	$T_i \cdot \|P_i\|$	$\tilde{O}(m) + S_i$
CiO-PRAM / Delegation without privacy	$\tilde{O}(\mathsf{poly}(\|P_i\|) + \ell_i^{\mathrm{out}})$	$\tilde{O}(\|D\|)$	$\tilde{O}(T_i \cdot \mathsf{poly}(\|P_i\|))$	$\tilde{O}(m + S_i)$
$\mathcal{RE}$-PRAM / Delegation with program and input privacy	$\tilde{O}(\mathsf{poly}(\|P_i\|) + \ell_i^{\mathrm{out}})$	$\tilde{O}(\|D\|)$	$\tilde{O}(T_i \cdot \mathsf{poly}(\|P_i\|))$	$\tilde{O}(m + S_i)$
Delegation with full privacy	$\tilde{O}(\mathsf{poly}(\|P_i\|))$	$\tilde{O}(\|D\|)$	$\tilde{O}(T_i \cdot \mathsf{poly}(\|P_i\|))$	$\tilde{O}(m + S_i)$

Table 1: Summarizing efficiency of our schemes in PRAM with persistent database, where the computation consists of L sessions among m parallel CPUs and a shared database D. In each session $i \in [L]$, program F_i is executed with input-size ℓ_i^{in}, output-size ℓ_i^{out}, using time T_i and space S_i. We use $\tilde{O}$ to ignore logarithmic factors. We remark that the efficiency for schemes in the single-session setting can easily be derived from the table by dropping the subscript i, and by replacing $|D|$ (the encoding time for database) with ℓ^{in} (the encoding time for input). The efficiency for schemes in the RAM setting can also be derived by setting $m = 1$.

1.5 Related Works

Independent and Concurrent Work.

Canetti and Holmgren [CH15] also proposed a fully succinct garbling scheme for RAM programs, based on the same assumption of the existences of $i\mathcal{O}$ and OWF. However, our motivation is different. Specifically, we aim for developing cryptographic solutions for PRAM model of computation to capture the power of both parallelism and random data access. Achieving full succinctness in the PRAM model is a major technical novelty of our result.

On the technical level, we note that both our construction and theirs can be viewed as a natural generalization and modularization of the construction of KLW for succinct encoding for Turing machines. Both works first construct a succinct encoding that satisfies a weak indistinguishability-based security (in our case, the notion of CiO). With this encoding, both rely on encryption and oblivious RAM (ORAM) to hide the memory content and access pattern of the RAM computation respectively. At the core of both security proofs are approaches to "puncture" ORAM execution to switch the access pattern step by step. From here, Canetti and Holmgren [CH15] additionally introduce a novel dual-encryption mechanism with a security property of tree-based ORAM constructions, which makes their security analysis more modular, at the cost of slightly increasing the security loss in the hybrid. Their techniques can be generalized to provide a more modular proof of $\mathcal{RE}$-PRAM from CiO-PRAM.[2]

Other Related Works and Open Problems.

As mentioned, Boyle et al. [BCP16, BCP15] constructed the first oblivious PRAM compiler and applied it to obtain secure MPC for PRAM. Recently, Chen, Lin, and Tessaro [CLT16] showed a more efficient OPRAM compiler, as well as a generic transformation taking any generic ORAM compiler to an OPRAM compiler. However, the compilers of [CLT16] only apply to PRAM programs with a fixed number of CPUs. Boyle et al. [BCP16] also constructed the first (non-succinct) garbling PRAM schemes based on identity-based encryptions. This is subsequently improved by a very recent work of Lu and Ostrovsky [LO15], who proposed a black-box construction based on the minimal assumption of OWF.

In succinct $i\mathcal{O}$-based setting with persistent database, our construction achieves only selective security, where the database and programs are chosen by the adversary in advance. Two independent subsequent works [ACC+15, CCHR15] achieved stronger adaptive security, where the adversary can make adaptive queries based on previous database and program encodings. Both works rely on additional assumptions than $i\mathcal{O}$ and OWF.

Finally, while we demonstrated general feasibility results for several cryptographic primitives for PRAM, our constructions are based on very strong and less well-understood assumptions of indistinguishability obfuscations. A natural and important research direction is to understand the landscape of cryptography for PRAM without assuming $i\mathcal{O}$. For example, can we construct attribute-based encryptions and functional encryptions for PRAM based on LWE?

2. CONSTRUCTIONS OVERVIEW

Our starting point is the succinct primitives (message-hiding encodings and machine-hiding encodings) for Turing machines constructed by Koppula, Lewko, and Waters (KLW) [KLW15]. Our constructions are natural generalizations of their constructions to handle PRAM with persistent database, where the major challenge is to develop new techniques to handle parallel processors and random access pattern. On the conceptual level, our constructions are modular and simple. Therefore, in this section, we first focus on illustrating our constructions. We will include a brief description of the application of the techniques by KLW in our context, and discuss our new techniques in the next section. We start by describing the way we view (parallel) RAM model.

2.1 The (Parallel) RAM Model

In the RAM model, computation is done by the CPU with random access to the memory in time steps (CPU cycles). At each time step t, the CPU (represented as a *next-step circuit*) receives the read memory content, performs one step of computation to update its CPU state, and outputs a memory access (read or write) instruction for time step $t + 1$. The computation terminates when the CPU reaches a special halting state. A RAM computation instance Π is defined by a CPU next-step program P, and an input x stored in the memory as initial memory content (and a default initial CPU state). At the end of the computation, the output y is stored in the CPU state (with the special halting symbol).

---

[2] We could include the modular proof; yet, we think it would be better to keep the two works separate for the readers.

The PRAM model is similar to the RAM model, except that there are multiple CPUs executing in parallel with random access to a shared memory (and reaching the halting state at the same time). The CPUs share the same CPU program P, but have distinct CPU id's. In this overview, we assume that there is no conflict writes throughout the computation. We note that our construction can handle the general CRCW (concurrent read concurrent write) model.

2.2 High Level Ideas

Let us motivate our work through the context of delegation, where a client delegates computation of a PRAM instance $\Pi = (P, x)$ to a server. Without security consideration, the client can simply send Π in the clear to the server, who can evaluate the PRAM program and return $y = P(x)$. Our goal is to achieve *publicly verifiable* delegation with *privacy* and (asymptotically) the same client and server efficiencies. Specifically, the server learns nothing except for the output y, whose correctness can be verified publicly.[3]

At a high level, we let the client send an obfuscated program $\tilde{P}$ and encoded input $\tilde{x}$ to the server with the aim that the obfuscation and encoding hide P and x, yet allowing the server to perform PRAM evaluation on $\tilde{P}(\tilde{x})$. (Obfuscation preserves input/output behavior and thus allows PRAM evaluation). To protect the privacy of P, we must restrict $\tilde{P}$ to evaluate *only* on input x, since $P(x')$ may leak additional information about P beyond $y = P(x)$. We need some *authentication mechanism* to *authenticate* the whole evaluation of P on x but nothing else. Moreover, the evaluation of P on x produces a long computation trace in addition to y. We need some *hiding mechanism* to hide the evaluation process. We discuss these two major ingredients in turn. First, we show the design of an authentication mechanism which gives CiO for RAM and PRAM from iO for circuits. Next, we show the design of a hiding mechanism which gives $\mathcal{RE}$ for RAM and PRAM from CiO in the respective models.

2.3 CiO Construction

Our construction of CiO for (parallel) RAM computation is based on iO for circuits and the novel iO-friendly authentication techniques developed originally to build iO for Turing machines (TM) [KLW15]. Let Π be a computation instance for (parallel) RAM computation defined by (P, x), where P is represented as a next-step circuit for the CPU program and x is the input.[4] The goal is to allow $\tilde{P}$ to evaluate on x but nothing else. At a high level, our CiO construction outputs iO of a compiled version of P and a compiled input. We proceed to discuss the intuition of our construction.

Recall that if two computation instances Π and Π', defined by (P, x) and (P', x') respectively, have identical computation trace (which implies $x = x'$), the security of CiO requires that their CiO-ed computation instances should be computationally indistinguishable, i.e., $\mathsf{CiO}(\Pi) \approx \mathsf{CiO}(\Pi')$. The two programs P and P' may behave differently on other inputs $x'' \neq x$. So, to ensure $\mathsf{CiO}(\Pi) \approx \mathsf{CiO}(\Pi')$, we must restrict the obfuscation to only evaluate the program on the specific input x, but not other inputs. A natural approach is to use *authentication*. Note that computation involves updating CPU states and memory, where the later may be

large in size. We can authenticate CPU states by signatures and memory by signing on a Merkle-tree-like data structure.

More precisely, consider a compiled program P_{auth}, which at each time step expects a signed CPU state from the previous time step, and signs the output state for the next time step. To authenticate the memory, a Merkle tree root is stored in the CPU state, and each memory read/write is authenticated via *authentication path* (i.e., the path from the root to the memory location with siblings in the Merkle tree). In other words, P_{auth} expects from the evaluator signed CPU states and the authentication path for the read memory content before evaluating P (otherwise, P_{auth} outputs Reject). In this way, the input x can simply be authenticated by signing the initial CPU state with Merkle tree root of x stored. Intuitively (i.e., assuming security of all used primitives "works"), the evaluator can evaluate P_{auth} only on x.

Finally, we consider a CiO obfuscator which outputs $\tilde{\Pi}_{\mathsf{auth}}$ defined by $(\mathsf{iO}(P_{\mathsf{auth}}), x_{\mathsf{auth}})$, where x_{auth} is an authenticated input. The hope is that the authentication mechanism, together with iO security, can ensure that an adversary receiving $\tilde{\Pi}_{\mathsf{auth}}$ can only generate the honest computation trace of Π, and further imply CiO security. Authentication alone implies publicly verifiable delegation without privacy, by using a special signing key to sign the output y and publishing the corresponding verification key for public verification.

We further discuss how this can be done in finer details. We first focus on the simpler case of RAM computation, which can be viewed as an abstraction of the existing techniques for TM. To handle the full-fledged PRAM computation, we introduce several techniques to tackle the challenges in the parallel setting. In particular, we avoid the dependency on the number of CPUs to achieve full succinctness.

2.3.1 CiO-RAM Construction

The following is essentially the intuition behind the construction of message-hiding encoding (MHE) [KLW15]. Our CiO-RAM construction is heavily inspired by their work, and can be viewed as an abstraction of what is achieved by their techniques. As a result, CiO is closely related to MHE, and the former can be used to construct the later readily.

For convenience, we assume that P only writes to the memory cell it reads in the previous time step.[5] We also assume that the CPU state stores the time step t.

As mentioned, to authenticate the whole memory, we build a Merkle tree with each memory cell being a leaf node, and store the tree root as the digest in the CPU state. Our CiO construction outputs $\tilde{\Pi}$ defined by $(\mathsf{iO}(P_{\mathsf{auth}}), x_{\mathsf{auth}})$, where the compiled program P_{auth} expects as input a signed CPU state, the read memory cell ℓ, and its authentication path. If the authentication path and the signature pass verification, P_{auth} outputs a signed next CPU state and memory access instruction. Additionally, if the memory access is a write to the cell ℓ, it also updates the digest stored in the CPU state using the authentication path. The authenticated input x_{auth} consists of the initial memory content x, and a signed initial CPU state that contains the Merkle tree digest of x.

Let Π and Π' be two computation instances defined by (P, x) and (P', x) respectively with identical computation trace. To prove security, we consider a sequence of hybrids starting from $\tilde{\Pi}$ that switches the program from P to P' time step by time step. However, to switch based on iO

---

[3]We consider other settings as well, but focus on this particular setting here.

[4]For uniform programs, the circuit size is polylogarithmic.

[5]This convention can be imposed without loss of generality.

security, the programs in the hybrids need to be functionally equivalent, while P to P' only behave identically during honest execution. Note that normal signatures and Merkle tree cannot guarantee functional equivalence as forgeries exist information-theoretically. Instead, we rely on the powerful $i\mathcal{O}$-friendly authentication primitives, which are *splittable signatures* and *accumulators* [KLW15], respectively. At a very high level, they allow us to switch to a hybrid program that, at a particular time step t (i.e., input with time step t stored in the CPU state), only accepts the honest input but rejects all other inputs (and outputs Reject), which enables us to switch from P to P' at time step t using $i\mathcal{O}$ security. Additionally, a primitive called *iterators* is introduced [KLW15] to facilitate the argument about the above hybrids. Details can be found in [KLW15] and Section 3.1.1.

2.3.2 CiO-PRAM Construction

We then extend the above approach to the PRAM model with some care of the efficiency issues in the parallel setting.

Recall that a PRAM computation instance Π is also specified by a next-step circuit P for the CPU program and an input x stored in the memory. However, instead of a single CPU, there are m CPUs, specified by the same program P but with different CPU id's, performing the computation in parallel with shared random access to the memory. We assume that there are no conflict writes throughout the computation, all CPUs have synchronized read/write memory access, and all terminate at the same time step.[6]

A Naïve Attempt.

We can view the m copies of next-step circuit as a single giant next-step circuit P^m that accesses m memory locations at each CPU time step. We can then compile P^m to P_{auth}^m and output $\tilde{\Pi}$ defined by $(i\mathcal{O}(P_{\mathsf{auth}}^m), x_{\mathsf{auth}})$ in a similar way as before. This approach indeed works in terms of security and correctness. However, as P^m has description size $\Omega(m)$ (since it operates on $\Omega(m)$-size input), the obfuscated computation will have description size $\mathsf{poly}(m)$, which incurs $\mathsf{poly}(m)$ overhead in the evaluation time.[7]

Avoiding the Dependency on the Number of CPUs.

We thus observe that, to preserve the parallel run-time, we can only $i\mathcal{O}$ a single (compiled) CPU program P_{auth}, and run m copies of $i\mathcal{O}(P_{\mathsf{auth}})$ in the evaluation of obfuscated instance with different CPU id's (as in evaluating the original Π).

We use accumulator to authenticate the (shared) memory. That is a Merkle-tree-like structure with the tree root as the (shared) accumulator value w stored in the CPU state, which needs to be updated when the memory content is changed. Specifically, consider a time step where m CPUs perform parallel write to distinct memory cells. The CPUs need to update the shared accumulator value w to reflect the m writes in some way. We cannot let a single CPU perform the update in one time step, because it involves processing $\Omega(m)$-size data, which makes the size of the next-step circuit dependent on $\Omega(m)$ again. Also, we cannot afford to update sequentially (i.e., each CPU takes turns to update the digest), since this blows up the parallel run-time of the

evaluation algorithm by m and obliterates the gains of parallelism. So, we design an $O(\mathsf{poly}\log m)$-round distributed algorithm to update the digest as follows.

First, we allow the instances of the (compiled) CPU program P_{auth} to communicate with each other. Namely, each CPU can send a message to other CPUs at each time step. Such CPU-to-CPU communications can be emulated readily by storing the messages in the memory for the evaluator of the obfuscation. Recall that P_{auth} needs to authenticate the computation, so the program needs to authenticate the communication as well. Fortunately, this can be done using splittable signatures in a natural way. We can now formulate the problem of updating the accumulator value as a distributed computing problem as follows:

There are m CPUs, each holding an accumulator value w, memory cell index ℓ_i, write value val_i, and an authentication path ap_i for ℓ_i (received from the evaluation algorithm) as its inputs. Their common goal is to compute the updated accumulator value w' with respect to the write instructions $\{(\ell_i, val_i)\}_{i\in[m]}$. Our task is to design a distributed algorithm for this problem with oblivious communication pattern[8], in $\mathsf{poly}\log(m)$ rounds, and with per-CPU space complexity $\mathsf{poly}\log(m)$. If this is achieved, the blow-up in both the parallel run-time and obfuscation size can be reduced from $\Omega(m)$ to $\mathsf{poly}\log(m)$.

We construct such *oblivious update* protocol with desired complexity based on two oblivious protocols by Boyle et al. [BCP16]: an aggregation protocol that allows m CPUs to aggregate information they need in parallel, and a multicasting protocol that allows m CPUs to receive messages from other CPUs in parallel. Both protocols have run-time poly-logarithmic in m. Roughly, our oblivious update protocol updates the Merkle tree layer-by-layer from leaves to root. For each layer, the CPUs engage in the oblivious aggregation protocol to aggregate information for updating their local branches of the tree. They then distribute their results using the oblivious multi-casting protocol.

Back to our CiO construction, we output $\tilde{\Pi}$ defined by $(i\mathcal{O}(P_{\mathsf{auth}}), x_{\mathsf{auth}})$, where P_{auth} is a compiled CPU program that can communicate with other CPUs and authenticate the communication by splittable signatures. The evaluation of $\tilde{\Pi}$ runs m copies of $i\mathcal{O}(P_{\mathsf{auth}})$ and emulates the communication by routing the messages. After each memory-write time step, P_{auth} maintains the accumulator value by invoking the oblivious update protocol. Finally, for the authenticated input x_{auth}, it consists of the initial memory content x, and the accumulator value of x stored in signed CPU states as before. However, it cannot contain initial CPU states with m different signatures, as otherwise the obfuscation has size dependent on m. This can be solved by a simple trick: we let x_{auth} only consists of a single signed "seed" CPU state $\mathsf{st}_{\mathsf{seed}}$, and when P_{auth} takes $\mathsf{st}_{\mathsf{seed}}$ and a CPU id i as input, P_{auth} outputs a signed initial state of CPU i.

We stress that there is a more subtle and challenging issue arises when we try to generalize the security proof for TM/RAM model to handle PRAM while preserving parallel run-time. In short, a naïve generalization of the security proof would require hardwiring the m CPU sates at some time steps, which results in $\Omega(m)$ amount of hardwired in-

---

[6] We note that the later two conventions can be imposed with $O(\log m)$ blow up in the parallel run-time.

[7] While P^m has low depth (independent of m), its obfuscated version may not, as the security of $i\mathcal{O}$ needs to hide the circuit depth. Thus, the parallel run-time is not preserved.

[8] We mention that the oblivious communication pattern property may not be essential, but a useful feature to make the construction simple, since the CPUs do not need to decide who to send/receive messages.

formation, and causes unacceptable poly(m) overhead in size of the obfuscated program. We address this by developing a *"branch-and-combine"* technique to emulate PRAM computation, which enables us to reduce the amount of hardwired information in the hybrids to $O(\log m)$, in Section 3.1.

2.4 $\mathcal{RE}$ Construction

The next goal is to hide information through the evaluation process of $\tilde{P}$ on $\tilde{x}$. A natural approach is to use encryption schemes to hide the CPU states and the memory content. Namely, $\tilde{P}$ always outputs encrypted CPU states and memory, and on (authenticated) input of ciphertexts, performs decryption before the actual computation. Note, however, that the memory access pattern cannot be encrypted (otherwise the server cannot evaluate), which may also leak information. A natural approach is to use oblivious (parallel) RAM (OPRAM/ORAM) to hide the access pattern. Namely, we use OPRAM compiler to compile the program (and add an "encryption layer") before obfuscating it. Again, intuitively (i.e., assuming all primitives "works"), the server cannot learn information from the evaluation process.

We note that the construction of machine-hiding encoding for Turing machine [KLW15] uses public-key encryption to hide the memory content of TM evaluation, and hides the TM access pattern by oblivious Turing machine compiler [PF79], which is *deterministic*. In our case, hiding random memory access pattern for (parallel) RAM (which is necessary to capture sublinear time computation) requires new techniques, since OPRAM/ORAM compilers are *probabilistic*, and we cannot use OPRAM/ORAM security in a black-box way. We deal with this issue by developing "puncturing" technique for specific OPRAM construction.

At a high level, constructing fully succinct randomized encoding ($\mathcal{RE}$) from CiO-RAM requires hiding both the memory content and the access pattern of the computation. We first consider the simpler case where the computation has oblivious access pattern (so we only need to hide the memory content), which we can rely on techniques of using public-key encryption [KLW15]. In fact, if the access pattern is not required to be hidden, the construction of machine-hiding encoding for TM [KLW15] can be modified in a straightforward way to yield $\mathcal{RE}$-RAM. Our construction can be viewed as a modularization and simplification of their construction through our CiO notion in a black-box way (which in a sense captures security achieved by authentication).

We next discuss how to hide access pattern, which is the major challenge for the construction of fully succinct $\mathcal{RE}$-RAM. We follow a natural approach to use ORAM compiler to hide it. However, the main difficulty is that ORAM only hides the access pattern when the CPU state and the memory contents are hidden from the adversary, which is hard to argue for unless the obfuscation is virtual-black-box (VBB) secure [BGI$^+$12], while CiO (just like iO) does not hide anything explicitly. We develop a *puncturable* ORAM technique to tackle this issue. We rely on a simple ORAM construction [CP13] (referred to as CP ORAM) and show that it can be "punctured" at time step i so that the access pattern at the i-th time step of $P(x)$ can be simulated even given the punctured program. Armed with this technique, we can simulate the access pattern at time step i by puncturing the ORAM compiled program at step i (through hybrids), replacing the access pattern at this step, and then unpuncturing the program. Yet, the computation traces of a punctured program can differ from the original ones in many steps. Therefore, arguing the indistinguishability of a hybrid using a punctured program is non-trivial. We do so by defining a sequence of "partially punctured" hybrids that gradually modifies the program step by step.

Finally, we extend the above construction to handle PRAM computation, where we simply replace the ORAM compiler by the oblivious PRAM compiler [BCP16]. The security proof also generalizes in a natural way, except that we need to take care of some issues aroused in the parallel setting. The main issue is to generalize the puncturing argument to puncture OPRAM in a way that avoids dependency on the number of CPU m to maintain full succinctness. This can be done by puncturing the OPRAM CPU by CPU.

2.4.1 $\mathcal{RE}$-ORAM Construction

We first focus on the simpler case of $\mathcal{RE}$ for *oblivious* RAM computation where the given RAM computation instance $\Pi = (P, x)$ has oblivious access pattern. Namely, we assume that there is a public function $\mathsf{ap}(t)$ that predicts the memory access at each time step t, to be given to the simulator.

For this simpler case, we do not need to use ORAM to hide the access pattern. We can modify existing machine-hiding encoding for TM [KLW15] which hides the CPU state and the memory content using $\mathcal{PKE}$ in a straightforward way to yield $\mathcal{RE}$ for oblivious RAM computation. Our construction presented below can be viewed as a modularization and simplification of their construction through our CiO notion.

Consider an encoding algorithm $\mathcal{RE}.\mathsf{Encode}(\Pi)$ which outputs $\mathsf{CiO}(P_{\mathcal{PKE}}, x_{\mathcal{PKE}})$, where $P_{\mathcal{PKE}}$ is a compiled version of P, and $x_{\mathcal{PKE}}$ is an encrypted version of x. At a high level, $P_{\mathcal{PKE}}$ emulates P step by step. Instead of outputting the CPU state and the memory content in the clear, $P_{\mathcal{PKE}}$ outputs encrypted versions of them. $P_{\mathcal{PKE}}$ also expects encrypted CPU states and memory contents as input, and emulates P by first decrypting them. A key idea here (following [KLW15]) is to encrypt each message (a CPU state or a memory cell) using a different key, and generate these keys (as well as encryption randomness) using puncturable PRF (PPRF), which allows us to use a standard puncturing argument in the security proof (extended to work with CiO instead of iO) to move to a hybrid where semantic security holds for a specific message so that we can "erase" it.

To make sure that each key is used to encrypt a single message, at time step t, $P_{\mathcal{PKE}}$ encrypts the output state and memory content using the "t-th" keys, which are generated by PPRF with input t (and some additional information to distinguish between state and memory). Likewise $x_{\mathcal{PKE}}$ contains the encryption of the initial memory x with different keys for each memory cell. To decrypt the input memory, $P_{\mathcal{PKE}}$ needs to know which secret key to use. This can be addressed by simply storing the time tag t with the encrypted memory (as a single memory cell). Namely, each memory cell for $P_{\mathcal{PKE}}$ contains a ciphertext ct_{mem} and a time tag t. As authentication is taken care of by CiO as a black box, no additional authentication mechanisms are needed.

At a high level, we prove the security of the above construction by defining a sequence of hybrids that "erase" the computation *backward in time*, which leads to a simulated encoding $\mathsf{CiO}(P_{\mathsf{Sim}}, x_{\mathsf{Sim}})$ where all ciphertexts generated by P_{Sim}, as well as those in x_{Sim}, are replaced by some encrypted special dummy symbols. More precisely, P_{Sim} simulates the access pattern using the public access function ap. For each time step $t < t^*$, P_{Sim} simply ignores the input and outputs encrypted `dummy` symbols (for both CPU state and memory content), and outputs y at time step $t = t^*$.[9]

By erasing the computation backward in time, we consider the intermediate hybrids $\mathbf{Hyb}_i$ where the computations of the first i time steps are real, and those of the remaining time steps are simulated. Namely, $\mathbf{Hyb}_i$ is a hybrid encoding $\mathsf{CiO}(P_{\mathbf{Hyb}_i}, x_{\mathcal{PKE}})$, where $P_{\mathbf{Hyb}_i}$ acts as $P_{\mathcal{PKE}}$ in the first i time steps, and acts as P_{Sim} in the remaining time steps. To argue for the indistinguishability between $\mathbf{Hyb}_i$ and $\mathbf{Hyb}_{i-1}$, which corresponds to erasing the computation at the i-th time step, the key observation is that the i-th decryption key is *not* used in the honest evaluation, which allows us to replace the output of the i-th time step by an encryption of `dummy` through a puncturing argument. We can then further remove the computation at the i-th time step readily by CiO security.

In more details, to move from $\mathbf{Hyb}_i$ to $\mathbf{Hyb}_{i-1}$, we further consider an intermediate hybrid $\mathbf{Hyb}_i'$ where the output of the i-th time step is replaced by an encryption of `dummy`, but the real computation is still performed. Namely, at the i-th time step, $P_{\mathbf{Hyb}_i'}$ in $\mathbf{Hyb}_i'$ still decrypts the input and emulates P, but replaces the output by an encryption of `dummy`. Note that indistinguishability between $\mathbf{Hyb}_i'$ and $\mathbf{Hyb}_{i-1}$ follows immediately from CiO security by observing that $(P_{\mathbf{Hyb}_i'}, x_{\mathcal{PKE}})$ and $(P_{\mathbf{Hyb}_{i-1}}, x_{\mathcal{PKE}})$ have identical computation trace. To argue for the indistinguishability between $\mathbf{Hyb}_i$ and $\mathbf{Hyb}_i'$, we note that the i-th decryption key is *not* used in the honest evaluation, since the computation after time step i is erased. Thus, we can puncture the randomness and erase the decryption key from the program (which uses CiO security as well), and reach a hybrid (from $\mathbf{Hyb}_i$) where semantic security holds for the output ciphertext at time step i. We can then replace the ciphertext by an encryption of `dummy` and undo the puncturing to reach $\mathbf{Hyb}_i'$.

There remain some details to complete the proof. First, the real encoding $\mathsf{CiO}(P_{\mathcal{PKE}}, x_{\mathcal{PKE}})$ and $\mathbf{Hyb}_{t^*-1}$ have identical computation trace, so indistinguishability follows by CiO security. Second, moving from $\mathbf{Hyb}_0$ to the simulated encoding $\mathsf{CiO}(P_{\mathsf{Sim}}, x_{\mathsf{Sim}})$ requires replacing $x_{\mathcal{PKE}}$ by x_{Sim}, which can be done by a similar puncturing argument.

2.4.2 $\mathcal{RE}$-RAM Construction

We now deal with the main challenge of hiding access pattern by using ORAM. Recall that an ORAM compiler compiles a RAM program by replacing each memory access by a *probabilistic* procedure OAccess that implements memory access in a way that hides the access pattern.[10]

Given a computation instance $\Pi = (P, x)$, we first compile P using an ORAM compiler, with randomness supplied by puncturable PRF for succinctness, and initiate the ORAM memory by inserting the input x. Let $(P_{\mathsf{ORAM}}, x_{\mathsf{ORAM}})$ be the compiled program and the resulting memory. It is then compiled in the same way as in Section 2.4.1 with $\mathcal{PKE}$. Namely, we use PPRF to generate multiple keys, and use each key to encrypt a single message, including the initial memory x_{ORAM}. Let the resulting instance be $(P_{\mathsf{hide}}, x_{\mathsf{hide}})$.

Our randomized encoding of Π is $\mathsf{CiO}(P_{\mathsf{hide}}, x_{\mathsf{hide}})$. However, as we discussed earlier, it is unlikely that we can use the security of ORAM in a black-box way, since ORAM security only holds when the adversary does not learn any content of the computation. Indeed, recall in the previous section, we can only use puncturing argument to argue that semantic security holds *locally* for some encryption at a time.

We remark that the work of Canetti et al. [CHJV15] encountered a similar technical problem in their construction of one-time RAM garbling scheme. Their construction has similar high level structure as ours, but based on a quite different machinery called asymmetrically constrained encapsulation (ACE) they built from iO for circuits. Canetti et al. provided a novel solution to this problem, but their garbling incurs dependency on the space complexity of the RAM program, and thus is not fully succinct.

A natural approach to avoid such dependency in our construction is to establish indistinguishability of hybrids *backwards in time*, as in the previous section. Namely, we consider intermediate hybrids $\mathbf{Hyb}_i$ where the computations of the first i time steps are real, and those of the remaining time steps are simulated (appropriately). Yet, since the computation trace of the first $(i-1)$ time steps is real, it contains enough information to carry out the rest of the (deterministic) computation. In particular, the access pattern at time step i is determined by the first $(i-1)$ time steps, that means we cannot replace it by a simulated access pattern.

To solve this problem, we develop a puncturing ORAM technique to reason about the simulation specifically for CP ORAM [CP13][11]. At a very high level, to move from $\mathbf{Hyb}_i$ to $\mathbf{Hyb}_{i-1}$ (i.e., erase the computation at i-th time step), we "puncture" ORAM at time step i (i.e., the i-th memory access), which enables us to replace the access pattern by a simulated one at this time step. We can then move (from $\mathbf{Hyb}_i$) to $\mathbf{Hyb}_{i-1}$ by erasing the memory content and computation, and undoing the "puncturing."

Roughly speaking, "puncturing" CP ORAM at i-th time step can be viewed as injecting a piece of *"puncturing"* code in OAccess to erase the information rand_i about access pattern at time step i information-theoretically: rand_i is generated at the latest time step t' that accesses the same memory location as time step i. The puncturing code simply removes the generation of rand_i at time step t'.

However, the last access time t' can be much smaller than i, so the puncturing may cause global changes in the computation. Thus, moving to the punctured mode requires defining a sequence of hybrids that modifies the computation step by step. We do so by further introducing an auxiliary *"partially puncturing"* code that punctures rand_i from certain threshold time step $j \geq t'$. The sequence of hybrids to move to the punctured code corresponds to moving the threshold $j \leq i$ backwards from i to t'.

2.4.3 $\mathcal{RE}$-PRAM Construction

Our construction of $\mathcal{RE}$-PRAM replaces the CP ORAM compiler of our construction of $\mathcal{RE}$-RAM by the OPRAM compiler of Boyle et al. [BCP16] (referred to as BCP OPRAM hereafter), a generalization of tree-based ORAM to the parallel setting. Namely, given a PRAM computation instance Π defined by (P, x), we first compile P into P_{OPRAM} using the

---

[9]Here we only consider honest evaluation of P_{Sim} on x_{Sim}. Any "dishonest" evaluation is disallowed by CiO security.

[10]In contrast, for Turing machines (TM), one can make the access pattern oblivious by a *deterministic* oblivious TM compiler. This is why [KLW15] does not need to address the issue of hiding access pattern for TM computation.

[11]We believe that our puncturing technique works for any tree-based ORAM constructions, but we work with CP ORAM for concreteness.

BCP OPRAM compiler with randomness supplied by puncturable PRF. We also initiate the OPRAM memory by inserting the input x. Let x_{OPRAM} be the resulting memory. We then compile $(P_{\mathsf{OPRAM}}, x_{\mathsf{OPRAM}})$ using $\mathcal{PKE}$ in the same way as in Section 2.4.1. A small difference here is that we also need to include CPU id as PPRF input to ensure single usage of each key. Denote the resulting instance by $(P_{\mathsf{hide}}, x_{\mathsf{hide}})$. Our randomized encoding of Π is $\mathsf{CiO}(P_{\mathsf{hide}}, x_{\mathsf{hide}})$.

The security proof also follows identical steps, where we prove the security by a sequence of hybrids that erases the computation backward in time, and simulate access patterns by generalizing the puncturing ORAM argument to puncturing BCP OPRAM. At a high level, the arguments generalize naturally with the following two differences: First, as the OPAccess algorithm of BCP OPRAM is more complicated, we need to be slightly more careful in defining the simulated encoding $\mathsf{CiO}(P_{\mathsf{Sim}}, x_{\mathsf{Sim}})$. Second, to avoid dependency on the number m of CPUs, we need to handle a single CPU at a time in the hybrids to puncture OPRAM.

2.5 Extension for Persistent Database

Finally, we note that our construction can be generalized readily to handle delegation with persistent database. In this setting, the client additionally delegates his database to the server at beginning, and then delegates multiple computation to evaluate and *update* the database in a verifiable and private way. Recall that we authenticate every step of computation by signatures. We can "connect" two programs by letting P_i to sign its halting state using a special "termination" signing key, and letting the next program P_{i+1}, upon receiving this signed state, initiate itself by signing its initial state, and inheriting the Merkle tree root of the database from P_i (stored in the halting CPU state).

3. TECHNICAL HIGHLIGHTS

Here we highlight the technical difficulties on handling multiple parallel CPUs and random memory access in PRAM computations, and our new techniques to resolve them.

3.1 Handling Parallel Processors

Algorithmic Issue.

To preserve the gain of parallelism, we need to run m (obfuscated) CPU programs in parallel, each of which has small $\mathsf{poly} \log(n)$-sized state. When there is a parallel write to the memory, these m CPUs need to update the digest of the large memory in parallel efficiently. Note that no CPU can have global update information (since each only has $\mathsf{poly} \log(n)$-sized state), so they need to do it in a distributed fashion without incurring $\Omega(m)$ efficiency overhead. We handle this issue based on the techniques in the OPRAM construction of Boyle, Chung, and Pass [BCP16]. At a high level, we allow the CPUs to communicate with each other, and design an $O(\mathsf{poly} \log m)$-round distributed algorithm for updating the digest with *oblivious* communication pattern[12].

Security Proof Issue.

This is a more subtle and challenging issue arises when we try to generalize the security proof for TM/RAM model to handle PRAM. At a very high level, the security proof consists of a (long) sequence of hybrids in time steps, where in the intermediate hybrids, we need to hardwire the CPU state at some time steps to the obfuscated program. Generalizing the idea to PRAM in a naïve way would require us to hardwire the m CPU sates at some time steps, which results in $\Omega(m)$ amount of hardwired information. This in turn requires us to pad the program to size $\Omega(m)$ and causes $\mathsf{poly}(m)$ overhead in size of the obfuscated program. To see why, and to pave the way for discussing our idea for resolving it, we must take a closer look at the technique of KLW.

3.1.1 Proof Techniques of KLW

We now provide a very high level overview of the security proof of our CiO-RAM based on the machinery of KLW. The techniques serve as a basis for the discussion of our construction of CiO-PRAM. Recall that our construction can be viewed as $\mathsf{CiO}(\Pi) = (\mathsf{iO}(P_{\mathsf{auth}}), x_{\mathsf{auth}})$, where $(P_{\mathsf{auth}}, x_{\mathsf{auth}})$ is just (P, x) augmented with iO-friendly authentication mechanism of KLW. Let $\Pi = (P, x)$ and $\Pi' = (P', x)$ be two computation instances with identical computation trace. Our goal is to show $\tilde{\Pi} \leftarrow \mathsf{CiO}(\Pi)$ and $\tilde{\Pi}' \leftarrow \mathsf{CiO}(\Pi')$ are computationally indistinguishable. To prove security, we consider a sequence of hybrids starting from $\tilde{\Pi}$ that switches the program from P to P' time step by time step. Very roughly, those iO-friendly authentication mechanisms allow us to switch from P to P' at time step t using iO security. It can be viewed as introducing "*check-points*" to hybrid programs as follows (which is implicit in [KLW15])[13]:

- We can place a check-point at the initial step of computation, and move it from a time step t to time step $(t + 1)$ through hybrids.

- Check-point is a piece of code that at a time step t, checks if the input (or output) is the same as that in the honest computation, and forces the program to output Reject if it is different. This is an information-theoretic guarantee which enables us to switch the program at time step t based on iO security.

We can then move the check-point from the beginning to the end of the computation, and along the way switch the program from P to P'. This check-point technique is essential to illustrate our issue on PRAM model.

3.1.2 Proof Issue Illustrated as a "Pebble Game"

The Pebble Game for RAM.

We now discuss the issue of hardwiring $\Omega(m)$ amount of information in intermediate hybrids when we generalize the KLW techniques to handle PRAM with m CPUs. To illustrate, we cast the security proof as a "*pebble game*" over a graph defined by the computation, and the required amount of hardwire information in the hybrids can be captured by the "*pebble complexity*" of the game.

We first illustrate this pebble game abstraction for the case of RAM. Recall that the security proof relies on a check-point technique that allows us to place a check-point on

---

[12] The CPU to CPU communication could be done through memory access (e.g., CPU i writes to a specific memory address and CPU j reads it). However, we cannot do so in our context of OPRAM since communication through memory requires updating the digest, which leads to a circularity.

[13] The description here over-simplifies many details.

the initial time step, and move it from a time step t to its next time step $(t + 1)$. Placing a check-point at a time step requires hardwiring information proportional to the input (or output) size of the CPU program. The goal is to travel all time steps (to switch the programs on all time steps). In this example, the RAM computation can be viewed as a line graph with each time step being a node. A check-point is a pebble that can be placed on the first node, and can be moved from node t to node $(t + 1)$. The winning condition of the pebble game is to "cover" the graph, namely, to ever place a pebble on each node. The pebble complexity is the maximum number of pebbles needed to cover the graph, which is 2 for the case of RAM (since technically we need to place a pebble at $(t + 1)$ before removing the pebble at t).

The Pebble Game for PRAM.

Next, we attempt to generalize the pebble game to the PRAM setting so as to capture the direct generalization of the previous security argument (including generalization of both accumulators and iterators).

The graph is a layered (directed acyclic) graph with each layer corresponds to m CPUs' at a certain time step. Namely, each node is indexed by (t, i) where t is the time step and i is the CPU id. It also consists of a node 0 corresponding to the seed state. Node 0 has an outgoing edge to node $(t = 1, i)$ for every $i \in [m]$. Each node (t, i) has an outgoing edge to $(t + 1, i)$ indicating the (trivial) dependency of i-th CPU between time step t and $t + 1$. Recall that the CPUs have communication (to jointly update the digest of the memory). If CPU i sends a message to CPU j at time step t, we also put an outgoing edge from (t, i) to $(t + 1, j)$ to indicate the dependency.[14]

The pebbling rule is defined as follows: First, we can place a pebble on node 0. To place a pebble on a node v, all nodes of v's incoming edges need to have a pebble on it. To remove a pebble on a node v, we need to "cover" all v's outgoing nodes, i.e., ever place a pebble on each outgoing node. These capture the conditions for placing and removing a check-point to a computation step respectively, for our generalization of the $i\mathcal{O}$-friendly authentication techniques of KLW to the parallel setting.

As before, the goal is to cover the whole graph (i.e., ever places a pebble on every node) using a minimal number of pebbles. The pebble complexity of the game is the maximum number of pebbles we need to simultaneously use to cover the graph. Covering the graph corresponds to switching the programs for every computation step, and the pebble complexity captures the amount of hardwire information required in the intermediate hybrids.

Recall that our P_{auth} invokes a distributed protocol to update the digest of the memory for every (synchronized) memory-writes. To play the pebble game induced by multiple invocations of this distributed protocol, a trivial solution with $2m$ pebbles is to place pebbles on two neighboring layers. Unfortunately, it is unclear how to play this pebble game with $o(m)$ pebble complexity, and it seems likely that the pebble complexity is indeed $\Omega(m)$. Therefore, it may seem that hardwiring $\Omega(m)$ amount of information in intermediate hybrids is required. As a result, P_{auth} needs to be padded to size $\Omega(m)$, and thus $|\tilde{\Pi}|$ has $\mathsf{poly}(m)$ overhead.

---

[14] In general, the memory accesses may create dependency. We ignore it here as the pebble complexity is already high.

3.1.3 Reducing Information Hardwiring

To reduce information to be hardwired, we introduce a "branch-and-combine" approach to emulate a PRAM computation, which transforms the computation graph to one with $\mathsf{poly}\log(m)$ pebble complexity, and preserves the parallel run-time and obfuscation size with a $\mathsf{poly}\log(m)$ overhead.

At a high level, after one parallel computation step, we combine m CPU states into one "digest" state, then branch out from the digest state for another parallel computation step, which results in m CPU states to be combined again. The PRAM computation is emulated by alternating the branch and combine steps. The combine step involves $\log m$ rounds where we combine two states into one in parallel (which forms a complete binary tree). The branch step is done in one shot which branches out m CPUs in one step in parallel. Thus, the branch-and-combine emulation only incurs $O(\log m)$ overhead in parallel run-time. Note that this transforms the computation graph into a sequence of complete binary trees where each time step of the original PRAM computation corresponds to a tree, and the root of a time step connects to all leaf nodes of the next time step.

Now, we observe that only $O(\log m)$ pebbles are used to traverse the computation graph of the branch-and-combine PRAM emulation. This is because whenever we put two pebbles at a pair of sibling nodes in the complete binary tree of the combine step, we can merge them into a single one at their parent node. This means that only one pebble is necessary for each height level of the tree. More precisely, we can move pebbles from one root to the next one by simply putting pebbles at its branched out nodes one by one in order, and merging the pebbles greedily whenever it is possible. Very roughly, the combine step corresponds to constructing an accumulator tree for CPU states, and the branch step verifies an input CPU state using the accumulator and performs one computation step.

3.2 Handling Memory Access

We next discuss the difficulties in hiding memory access pattern. Recall that our construction to achieve privacy is very natural: We hide CPU states and memory content using public-key encryption ($\mathcal{PKE}$) and hide access pattern using oblivious (parallel) RAM. Note that KLW already showed how to use $\mathcal{PKE}$ to hide the memory content of Turing machine evaluation. Roughly speaking, the security proof is done by a sequence of hybrids that "erases" the computation step by step *backward* in time. However, hiding access pattern for Turing machine is simple since oblivious Turing machine compiler [PF79] is *deterministic*.

In contrast, ORAM and OPRAM compilers are probabilistic, and they only hide the access pattern statistically when the adversary learns only the access pattern, but not the CPU states and the memory content. However, since the obfuscated program contains the hardwired secret key of $\mathcal{PKE}$, we can only argue that the memory content is hidden by puncturing argument at the cost of hardwiring information. In other words, we can only afford to argue hiding holds "locally" but not "globally". This is why the proof of KLW erases the computation step by step. More importantly, this prevents using ORAM/OPRAM security in a black-box way.

We overcome this issue by a puncturing ORAM/OPRAM technique that relies on some specific ORAM/OPRAM constructions [CP13, BCP16], to be elaborated below for the case of RAM. The high level strategy is to switch the ORAM access pattern from a real one to a simulated one step by step (backward in time). To enable switching at time step i (i.e., for the i-th memory access), we "puncture" the real execution in a way that ensures that the i-th memory access is information theoretically hidden even given the memory content of the first $(i-1)$ steps execution. Since we do hybrids backward in time, the computation after i-th step is already erased, and so once the ORAM is "punctured", we can replace the real i-th step access pattern by a simulated one (both of which are random given full information of the punctured real ORAM execution). To further explain how this is done, we first review the CP ORAM construction.

3.2.1 Review of the CP ORAM Construction

In a tree-based ORAM (CP ORAM), the memory is stored in a complete binary tree (as known as ORAM tree), where each node is associated with a bucket. A bucket is a vector of K elements, where each element is either a memory block, or a unique symbol dummy stands for an empty slot. Note that a memory block is the smallest unit of operation in CP ORAM, which consists of a fixed small number of memory cells. In particular, a position map pos (stored in CPU state) records where each memory block is stored in the tree, i.e., a node somewhere along a path from the root to the leaf indexed by $pos[\ell]$. Each memory block ℓ in the ORAM tree also stores its index ℓ and position map value $pos[\ell]$ as meta data. Each memory access to block ℓ is performed by OAccess, which (i) reads the position map value $p = pos[\ell]$ and refreshes $pos[\ell]$ to a random value, (ii) fetches and removes the block ℓ (i.e., replaces it by dummy) from the path, (iii) updates the block content and puts it back to the root (i.e., replace a dummy block by the updated memory block), and (iv) performs a flush operation along another random path p' to move the blocks down along p' (subject to the condition that each block is stored in the path specified by their position map value). At a high level, the security follows by the fact that the position map values are uniformly random and hidden from the adversary, and thus the access pattern of each OAccess is simply two uniformly random paths, which is trivial to simulate.

Although the position map as described above is large, it can be recursively outsourced to lower level ORAM structures to reduce its size. For simpler illustration, we consider here a non-recursive version of the CP ORAM, where the large position map is stored in the CPU state. We note that our construction can handle full-fledged recursion.

3.2.2 Puncturing CP ORAM

Consider the execution of an CP ORAM compiled program which accesses memory block ℓ in the i-th time step (corresponds to the i-th OAccess call), the access pattern at this time step is determined by the position map value $p = pos[\ell]$ at this time.[15] So, as long as this value p is information-theoretically hidden from the adversary, we can simulate the access pattern by a random path even if everything else is leaked to the adversary. On the other hand, the value is generated at the last access time t' of this block, which can be much smaller than i, stored in both the position map and the block ℓ (as part of the meta data), and can be touched multiple times from time step t' to i. Thus, the value may appear many times in the computation trace

of the evaluation. Nevertheless, by a sequence of carefully defined hybrids (which we refer to as partially punctured ORAM hybrids), we can erase the information of p step by step with constant-size data hardwired, which allows us to carry through the puncturing ORAM argument (see our full version for detailed hybrids).

3.3 Handling Parallel Memory Access

Lastly, we discuss how the techniques above for ORAM can be extended to the OPRAM setting.

3.3.1 Review of BCP OPRAM Construction

BCP OPRAM [BCP16] is a natural generalization of tree-based ORAM. Consider that each CPU j wants to access memory block ℓ_j in a (parallel) memory access. At a high level, the CPUs first communicate with each other to resolve the conflicts, and recursively invoke OPAccess to fetch and refresh the position map values. They then fetch the memory blocks from the path, put the blocks back, and flush the tree in parallel. Since the m CPUs want to access m paths p_j of the tree in parallel, they need to communicate with each other to avoid write conflicts. In BCP OPRAM, the CPUs access the tree level by level, and in each level, they aggregate the access instructions, select representative to perform the access, and then distribute the answers via oblivious aggregation and oblivious multi-casting protocols.

3.3.2 Simulated Encoding $\text{CiO}(P_{\text{Sim}}, x_{\text{Sim}})$

As before, P_{Sim} simulates P_{hide} for each (parallel) time step of $P(x)$. At each step P_{Sim} uses the simulated access pattern and erases the computation by ignoring the input and then outputting encryption of dummy. Here, we need to simulate the parallel access pattern of OPAccess, which is more complicated and involves polylogarithmic time steps because all CPUs in OPAccess interact with each other. In particular, the access pattern of the OPAccess depends on the paths p_j's each CPU wants to access, where each CPU manipulates its path with its own state and OPAccess. If we still erase all the CPU states step by step, we would not have enough information to simulate the second half access pattern of OPAccess once the CPU states in the first half is erased. Nevertheless, the key observation here is that the access pattern is fully determined by the paths p_j's each CPU wants to access, which are *public* information revealed in the execution. So, we can view these p_j's as *public states* of OPAccess, and do not erase its content in the hybrids. In other words, we generate simulated path p_j for each CPU, and store them as public states to simulate the access pattern of OPAccess.

3.3.3 Puncturing BCP OPRAM CPU by CPU

As BCP OPRAM is a generalization of tree-based ORAM, it is not hard to see that the puncturing argument generalizes to work for BCP OPRAM as well (while maintaining full succinctness). Namely, it suffices to information-theoretically hide the values of the paths p_j's to simulate the access pattern, and this can be done by injecting a puncturing code. Additionally, we observe that this can be done CPU by CPU. Namely, for each p_j accessed by CPU j, we can (for all CPUs) inject a puncturing code at the corresponding time step t'_j that the value p_j is generated, to remove the generation of p_j. Also, we can move to this punctured hybrid by a sequence of partially punctured hybrids as before, by gradually puncturing the value of p_j backwards in

---

[15]We ignore the uniformly random path used in the flush operation here, which is trivial to simulate.

time, per time-step and per CPU. Upon reaching this punctured hybrid, we can switch p_j to a simulated one, undo the puncturing, and move to the next CPU. In this way, we switch the paths p_j's to simulated version one by one, and never need to hardwire information of size depending on m throughout the hybrids, which maintains full succinctness.

4. REFERENCES

[ACC+15] Prabhanjan Ananth, Yu-Chi Chen, Kai-Min Chung, Huijia Lin, and Wei-Kai Lin. Delegating RAM computations with adaptive soundness and privacy. Cryptology ePrint 2015/1082, 2015.

[AS16] Prabhanjan Ananth and Amit Sahai. Functional encryption for Turing machines. In *TCC 2016-A*, 2016. To appear.

[BCP15] Elette Boyle, Kai-Min Chung, and Rafael Pass. Large-scale secure computation: Multi-party computation for (parallel) RAM programs. In *CRYPTO 2015 Part-II*, pages 742–762, 2015.

[BCP16] Elette Boyle, Kai-Min Chung, and Rafael Pass. Oblivious parallel RAM and applications. In *TCC 2016-A*, 2016. To appear.

[BGI+12] Boaz Barak, Oded Goldreich, Russell Impagliazzo, Steven Rudich, Amit Sahai, Salil P. Vadhan, and Ke Yang. On the (im)possibility of obfuscating programs. *J. ACM*, 59(2):6:1–6:48, 2012.

[BGL+15] Nir Bitansky, Sanjam Garg, Huijia Lin, Rafael Pass, and Sidharth Telang. Succinct randomized encodings and their applications. In *STOC*, pages 439–448, 2015.

[CCHR15] Ran Canetti, Yilei Chen, Justin Holmgren, and Mariana Raykova. Succinct adaptive garbled RAM. Cryptology ePrint 2015/1074, 2015.

[CH15] Ran Canetti and Justin Holmgren. Fully succinct garbled RAM. Cryptology ePrint 2015/388, 2015.

[CHJV15] Ran Canetti, Justin Holmgren, Abhishek Jain, and Vinod Vaikuntanathan. Succinct garbling and indistinguishability obfuscation for RAM programs. In *STOC*, pages 429–437, 2015.

[CLT16] Binyi Chen, Huijia Lin, and Stefano Tessaro. Oblivious parallel RAM: Improved efficiency and generic constructions. In *TCC 2016-A*, 2016. To appear.

[CP13] Kai-Min Chung and Rafael Pass. A simple ORAM. Cryptology ePrint 2013/243, 2013.

[GHRW14] Craig Gentry, Shai Halevi, Mariana Raykova, and Daniel Wichs. Outsourcing private RAM computation. In *FOCS*, pages 404–413, 2014.

[IK00] Yuval Ishai and Eyal Kushilevitz. Randomizing polynomials: A new representation with applications to round-efficient secure computation. In *FOCS*, pages 294–304, 2000.

[KLW15] Venkata Koppula, Allison Bishop Lewko, and Brent Waters. Indistinguishability obfuscation for Turing machines with unbounded memory. In *STOC*, pages 419–428, 2015.

[LO15] Steve Lu and Rafail Ostrovsky. Black-box parallel garbled RAM. Cryptology ePrint Archive, Report 2015/1068, 2015. http://ia.cr/2015/1068.

[PF79] Nicholas Pippenger and Michael J. Fischer. Relations among complexity measures. *J. ACM*, 26(2):361–381, 1979.

[Yao82] Andrew Chi-Chih Yao. Protocols for secure computations. In *STOC*, pages 160–164, 1982.

Timeability of Extensive-Form Games

Sune K. Jakobsen
School of Mathematical Sciences and
School of Electronic Engineering and Computer Science
Queen Mary, University of London
Mile End Road
London E1 4NS, UK
s.k.jakobsen@qmul.ac.uk

Troels B. Sørensen
Theoretical Computer Science Section
IT-University of Copenhagen
Rued Langgaards Vej 7
2300 København S, Denmark
trbj@itu.dk

Vincent Conitzer
Department of Computer Science
Duke University
Box 90129
Durham, NC 27708, USA
conitzer@cs.duke.edu

ABSTRACT

Extensive-form games constitute the standard representation scheme for games with a temporal component. But do all extensive-form games correspond to protocols that we can implement in the real world? We often rule out games with *imperfect recall*, which prescribe that an agent forget something that she knew before. In this paper, we show that even some games with perfect recall can be problematic to implement. Specifically, we show that if the agents have a sense of time passing (say, access to a clock), then some extensive-form games can no longer be implemented; no matter how we attempt to time the game, some information will leak to the agents that they are not supposed to have. We say such a game is not *exactly timeable*. We provide easy-to-check necessary and sufficient conditions for a game to be exactly timeable. Most of the technical depth of the paper concerns how to *approximately* time games, which we show can always be done, though it may require large amounts of time. Specifically, we show that some games require time proportional to the power tower of height proportional to the number of players, which in practice would make them untimeable. We hope to convince the reader that timeability should be a standard assumption, just as perfect recall is today. Besides the conceptual contribution to game theory, we show that timeability has implications for onion routing protocols.

Categories and Subject Descriptors

I.2.11 [**Distributed Artificial Intelligence**]: Multiagent Systems; J.4 [**Computer Applications**]: Social and Behavioral Sciences–Economics

Permission to make digital or hard copies of all or part of this work for personal or classroom use is granted without fee provided that copies are not made or distributed for profit or commercial advantage and that copies bear this notice and the full citation on the first page. Copyrights for components of this work owned by others than the author(s) must be honored. Abstracting with credit is permitted. To copy otherwise, or republish, to post on servers or to redistribute to lists, requires prior specific permission and/or a fee. Request permissions from Permissions@acm.org.

WSDM'16, February 22–25, 2016, San Francisco, CA, USA.
Copyright is held by the owner/author(s). Publication rights licensed to ACM.
ACM 978-1-4503-3716-8/16/02 ...$15.00.
DOI: http://dx.doi.org/10.1145/2840728.2840737 .

Keywords

Computational Game Theory; Equilibrium Computation

1. INTRODUCTION

The *extensive form* is a powerful representation scheme for games. It allows one to naturally specify how the game unfolds over time, and what each player knows at each point of action. This allows one to model, for example, card games such as poker, but also real-world strategic situations with similar aspects.

Besides asking whether all strategic situations one might encounter in the real world can be modelled as extensive-form games, one may also ask whether all extensive-form games correspond to something one might encounter in the real world. This question is important for several reasons. One is that if the answer is "no", then there should be some well-motivated restricted subclasses of extensive-form games that may be more tractable from the perspective of algorithmic and other theoretical analysis. Another is that if we are interested in designing a protocol, extensive-form games give us a natural language in which to express the protocol—but this language may lead us astray if some of its games are not actually implementable in the real world.

Games of *imperfect recall*, in which an agent sometimes forgets something she knew before, constitute a natural example of games that may be difficult to implement in the real world.[1] Indeed, restricting attention to perfect recall is often useful for algorithmic and other theoretical purposes. From a theoretical perspective, perfect recall is required [12] for behavioral strategies to be as expressive as mixed strate-

---

[1]Computer poker provides some amusing anecdotes in this regard. When comparing two poker-playing bots by letting them play a sequence of hands, one way to reduce the role of luck and thereby improve statistical significance is to wipe clean the bots' memory and let them play the same sequence of hands again, but with the bots' roles in the hands reversed. This is not feasible for *human* players, of course. Because of this, events pitting computers against humans have generally pitted a *pair* of players against one copy of the bot each, in separate rooms. In this setup, each human-computer pair receives the same hands, though the bot's role in one room is the human's role in the other.

gies. Perfect recall also allows for the use of the sequence form [17], which allows linear optimization techniques to be used for computing equilibria of two-person extensive-form games [19]. The sequence form can also be used to compute equilibrium refinements [14, 13], again requiring perfect recall. Without perfect recall, otherwise simple single agent decision problems become complicated [16, 1, 2], and even the existence of equilibria in behavior strategies becomes NP-hard to decide [5]. Imperfect recall has proven useful for computing approximate minimax strategies for poker [21], even though the agent following the strategy does have perfect recall when playing the game.

We believe that many researchers are under the impression that, given any finite extensive-form game of perfect recall, one could in principle have agents play that game in the real world, with the actions of the game unfolding in the order suggested by the extensive form. In this paper, we prove that this is not so, at least if agents have a sense of *time*. If the players have a sense of time, we show that some games cannot be implemented in actual time in a way that respects the information sets[2] of the extensive form. The games that can be implemented in time are exactly those that have *chronologically ordered information sets*, as defined in a set of lecture notes by Weibull [23, page 91]. Weibull argues that games with this property constitute the natural domain of *sequential equilibria* [10]. The concept of sequential equilibrium is arguably the most used equilibrium refinement for extensive-form games with imperfect information. Kreps and Ramey [9] provided an example where the unique sequential equilibrium requires some level of cognitive dissonance from the players [22], forcing a player to best-respond to strategies that are not consistent with her beliefs. However, examples of this type only work because they have no ordering of the information sets, which is Weibull's point in restricting attention to games with chronologically ordered information sets. In this paper, we argue something stronger: we argue that extensive-form games without this property cannot model any real world strategic situation, since the information structure of the model cannot be enforced.

We emphasize that our paper is not intended as a criticism of extensive-form games. Rather, the goal is to point out a natural restriction – timeability – that is needed to ensure that the game can be implemented as intended in practice. Again, perfect recall is a restriction that is similar in nature. Restricting attention to those games that have perfect recall has been useful for many purposes, and the notion has also been useful to understand why certain games have odd features—namely, they have imperfect recall. We suspect the notion of timeability can be used similarly. At least one paper already implicitly assumes that all games are timeable [11], while another paper would have been much simpler if it had assumed timeability [20]. We hope that more applications of timeability will be found, and we encourage game theorists (algorithmic or otherwise) to, in contexts where they consider the restriction of perfect recall, consider that of timeability as well.

---

[2]Recall that for extensive-form games, the information available to the players is represented using *information sets*. Two nodes in a game tree belong to the same information set if they belong to the same player, and the player has the same information at those two nodes.

One place where the analogy between timeability and perfect recall perhaps breaks down is that we have shown that games that are not exactly timeable can nevertheless be approximately timed, in some cases even in a reasonable amount of time. It is not clear whether an analogous notion of approximately perfect recall could be given.

Most of our technical work concerns whether games that do not have an exact timing can nevertheless be approximately timed, and if so, how much time is required to do so. This latter contribution may have important ramifications for the design of protocols that run a risk of leaking information to participants based on the times at which they are requested to take action. While we show that all games are at least approximately timeable, we also show that some games require so much time that in practice they are untimeable.

1.1 Motivating example

Consider the following simple 2-player extensive-form game (Figure 1(a)). In it, first a coin is tossed that determines which player goes first. Then, each player, in turn, is asked to guess whether she has gone first. If the player is correct, she is paid 1 (and otherwise 0). The information sets of the game suggest that a player cannot at all distinguish the situation where she goes first from the one where she goes second, and thus, she gets expected utility 1/2 no matter her strategy.

However, now consider implementing this game in practice. Assume that the game starts at time 0. Clearly, if we toss the coin at time 0, ask one player to bet at time 1, and the other at time 2, a time-aware player will know exactly whether she is being asked first or second (assuming the timing protocol is common knowledge), and will act accordingly. This implementation blatantly violates the intended information structure of the extensive-form representation of the game; indeed, it results in an entirely different game (one that is much more beneficial to the players!). We say that this protocol is not an *exact timing* of the game in Figure 1(a).

Of course, the general protocol of taking one action per time unit is a perfectly fine timing of many games, including games where every action is public (as in, say, Texas Hold'em poker). Also, there are games where taking one action per time unit fails to exactly time the game, but nevertheless an exact timing is available. For example, consider the modified game in Figure 1(b), where player 1 only plays if the coin comes up Heads, and if so plays first. This game can be timed by letting player 1 play at time 1 and player 2 at time 2, even if player 1 does not go first.

But what about the game in Figure 1(a)? Can it not be timed at all? We will pose the constraint that there must be at least one time unit between successive actions in the extensive form. Without this constraint, we could take the normal form of the game and let players play it by declaring their entire strategy at once—but this scheme violates the natural interpretation of the extensive form, and would allow us to play games of imperfect recall just as well. (One may argue that we should just let the players play in parallel after the coin flip in the game in Figure 1(a)—however, a simple modification of the game where the second player is only offered a bet if the first player guessed correctly (Figure 1(c)) would disallow this move.) It is easy to see that no *deterministic* timing will suffice. This is because

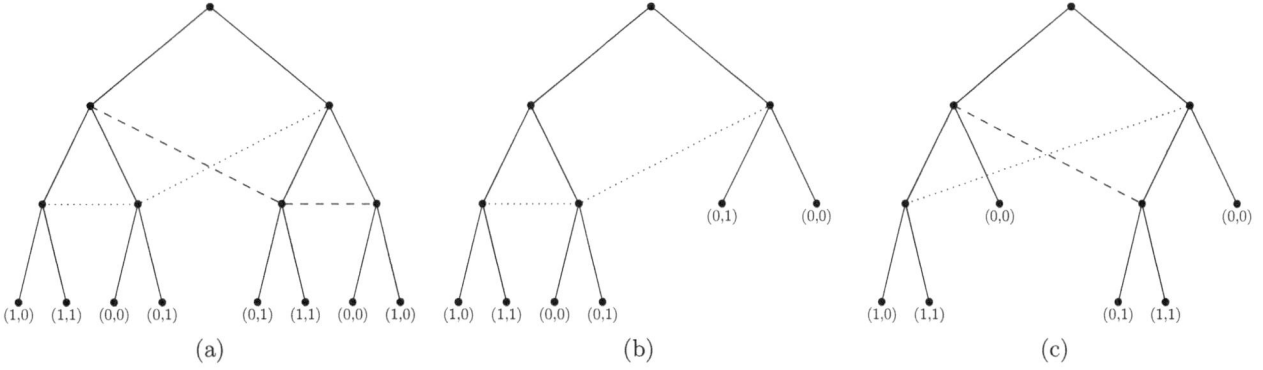

Figure 1: Three examples. The roots are Chance nodes where Chance chooses its move uniformly at random. Dashed information sets belong to player 1 and dotted ones to player 2. The node in game (b) that forms its own information set belongs to player 1. (b) has an exact deterministic timing, but (a) and (c) do not.

every node within an information set would have to have the same time associated with it; but then, the left-hand side of the tree requires that player 1's information set has a time strictly before that of player 2, but the right-hand side implies the opposite.

For games where deterministic timing cannot be done, one might turn to randomized timing when trying to implement the game. However, if the time at which a node is played is to reveal *no information whatsoever* about which node in the information set has been reached, then the *distribution* over times at which it is played must be identical for each node in the information set. But this cannot be achieved in the game in Figure 1(a), because the left-hand side of the tree ensures that the expectation of the time distribution for player 1's information set must be at least 1 lower than that for player 2's information set, but the right-hand side implies the opposite. Still, we may achieve *something* with randomization. For example, we may draw an integer i uniformly at random from $[N-1] = \{1, \ldots, N-1\}$, offer the first player to move a bet at time i and the second player a bet at time $i+1$. Then, if a player is offered a bet at time 1 or time N, the player will know exactly at which node in the extensive form she is. On the other hand, if she is offered a bet at any time $t \in \{2, \ldots, N-1\}$, she obtains no additional information at all, because the conditional probability of t being the selected time is the same whether she is the first or the second player to move. Hence, as long as $i \in \{2, \ldots, N-2\}$, which happens with probability $(N-3)/(N-1)$, neither player learns anything from the timing. We say the game is *approximately timeable*: we can come arbitrarily close to timing the game by increasing N, the number of time periods used. This immediately raises the question of whether *all* games are approximately timeable, and if so how large N needs to be for a particular approximation.

1.2 Our contribution

In the next section we define *exactly timeable games*, give a characterization of these games, and show that there is a linear-time algorithm that decides whether an extensive-form game is exactly timeable. In Section 3 we define ϵ-timeability and argue that this is the correct definition. In Section 4 we give an example of an onion routing game that is not timeable. This shows that, due to timeability issues, onion routing protocols can only approximately ob-

tain a certain desired property. In Section 5 we show that all extensive-form games are ϵ-timeable for any $\epsilon > 0$, but also that these ϵ-timings can easily become too time-consuming for this universe: for any number r, there exists a game Γ_r such that for sufficiently small ϵ, any ϵ-timing of Γ_r will take time at least $2^{2^{\cdots 2^{\frac{1}{\epsilon}}}}$ where the tower has height r. In Section 6 we ask what happens if we have some control over the players' perception of time. We assume that there exists a constant c such that any player will always perceive a time interval of length t as having length between $\frac{t}{c}$ and ct, and otherwise we have complete control over the players' perception of time. We show that even under these assumptions, the lower bound from Section 5 still holds.

2. EXACTLY TIMEABLE GAMES

DEFINITION 1. *For an extensive-form game [3] Γ, a deterministic timing is a labelling of the nodes in Γ with nonnegative real numbers such that the label of any node is at least one higher than the label of its parent. A deterministic timing is exact if any two nodes in the same information set have the same label.*

An exact deterministic timing is the same as the time function in the definition of a chronological order by Weibull [23]. Since we will also be discussing games that cannot be timed, we need this more general definition of timings that are not exact.

This definition allows times to be nonnegative real numbers rather than integers, which makes some of the proofs cleaner. However, given a deterministic timing with real values, one can always turn it into a timing with integer values by taking the floor function of each of the times.

The following theorem says that it is easy to check whether a game has an exact deterministic timing, providing multiple equivalent criteria. Criterion 2 is presumably most useful for a human being looking at small extensive-form games, while criterion 3 is easy for a computer to check.

THEOREM 1. *For an extensive-form game Γ, the following are equivalent:*

---

[3] For an introduction to the game-theoretical concepts used in this paper, see, for example, [15]

1. Γ has an exact deterministic timing.

2. The game tree Γ can be drawn in such a way that a node always has a lower y-coordinate than its parent, and two nodes belong to the same information set if and only if they have the same y-coordinate.

3. Contracting each information set in the directed graph Γ to a single node results in a graph without oriented cycles.

PROOF. "1 $\Rightarrow$ 2:" Given an exact deterministic timing (WLOG, with integer-valued times), we draw Γ such that each node has y-coordinate equal to the negative of its time. As the timing is exact, nodes in the same information set have the same y-coordinate. To ensure that any two nodes with the same y-coordinate are in the same information set, we perturb each node based on its information set. This can be done deterministically: for example, if there are q information sets in the game, then subtract i/q from the time of each node in the ith information set.

"2 $\Rightarrow$ 3:" Given such a drawing, contracting each information set results in all edges going downwards, so the resulting graph cannot have directed cycles.

"3 $\Rightarrow$ 1:" The nodes of a directed acyclic graph can be numbered such that each edge goes from a smaller to a larger number. This numbering can be used as a deterministic timing. $\square$

We can use criterion 3 of Theorem 1 to test whether the games in Figure 1(a) and 1(b) are timeable. First we draw a node for each information set: One for the root, one for player 1's information set and one for player 2's information set. (If one of the players had more than one information set, that player would have had more than one node in the contracted graph.) We ignore the leaves, as they can never form cycles. In the games in Figure 1(a) and 1(b), we can get from the root to each of the two players' information sets, so we draw a directed edge from the root to each of the two other nodes. We can also get from player 1's information set to player 2's, and in the game in Figure 1(a) we can go from player 2's information set to player 1's. When we draw these directed edges (without multiplicity) we get Figure 2(a) and Figure 2(b), respectively. We see that the graph in Figure 2(a) has a cycle, so the game in Figure 1(a) is not exactly timeable, while graph in Figure 2(b) does not have a cycle, so the game in Figure 1(b) is exactly timeable. The contracted graph can be constructed in linear time, and given this directed graph, we can in linear time test for cycles [3, Section 22.4]. Thus, we can test in linear time whether a game is exactly timeable.

3. ϵ-TIMEABILITY

We now move on to approximate timeability.

DEFINITION 2. The total variation distance (also called statistical distance) between two discrete random variables X_1 and X_2 is given by

$$\delta(X_1, X_2) = \sum_x \max(\Pr(X_1 = x) - \Pr(X_2 = x), 0)$$

where the sum is over all possible values of X_1 and X_2. This measure is symmetric in X_1 and X_2. If $\delta(X_1, X_2) \le \epsilon$ we say that X_1 and X_2 are ϵ-indistinguishable.

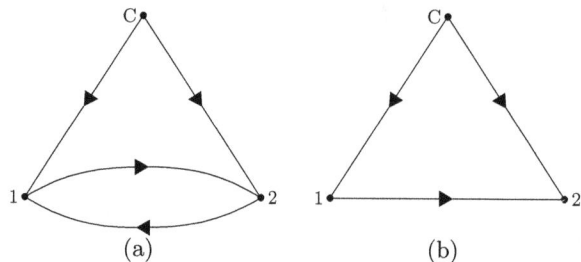

Figure 2: Example of how to use Theorem 1 to test if the extensive-form games (a) and (b) in Figure 1 have exact deterministic timings. The top node is the Chance node, the left node corresponds to player 1's information set, and the right node corresponds to player 2's information set.

A (randomized) timing is a discrete distribution over deterministic timings. For a game, a timing of the game, a player and a node v belonging to that player, the player's timing information at v denoted $X_{\preceq v}$ is the sequence of times X_u for nodes u belonging to that player on the path from the root to v (including v itself). Thus, for a fixed game, timing, player, and node, the timing information is a random variable.

The timing is an ϵ-timing if for any two nodes u and v in the same information set, $\delta(X_{\preceq u}, X_{\preceq v}) \le \epsilon$. A 0-timing is also called an exact timing.

A game is exactly timeable if it has an exact timing, ϵ-timeable if it has an ϵ-timing, and approximately timeable if it is ϵ-timeable for all $\epsilon > 0$.

The following proposition implies that Γ being exactly timeable is equivalent to each of the three criteria in Theorem 1.

PROPOSITION 2. A game is exactly timeable if and only if it has an exact deterministic timing.

PROOF. An exact deterministic timing is a special case of an exact randomized timing. Conversely, given an exact randomized timing of a game, we can label each node with its expected time to obtain an exact deterministic timing. $\square$

We will show that in fact all games are approximately timeable.

3.1 Justification of definition

As stated in [18] and [7] the total variation distance $\delta(X_1, X_2)$ can be seen as a betting advantage: Suppose you are given a random value X_I were I is uniformly distributed on $\{1, 2\}$ independently from X_1 and X_2. You then bet on whether $I = 1$ or $I = 2$. If you guess correctly you get utility 1 and otherwise you get -1. If you play this game optimally, your expected utility is $\delta(X_1, X_2)$. More generally, if a player is playing a game Γ and is in an information set with two nodes 1 and 2 which have different optimal actions, we can think of this as the player betting on which node she is in. For this reason, total variation distance is a good measure of how much a game is distorted by side information. This is captured by the following theorem.

THEOREM 3. Let Γ be an extensive-form game with perfect recall and utilities in $[0, 1]$ where player i has at most m

nodes in any history, and let X be an ϵ-timing. If σ_i' is a player i strategy that uses the timing information,[4] there is a strategy σ_i that does not use timing information, such that for any strategy for the other players σ_{-i}', which may also use the timing information, we have $u_i(\sigma_i', \sigma_{-i}') - u_i(\sigma_i, \sigma_{-i}') \leq m\epsilon$.

The proof of this theorem, as well as later theorems, can be found in the full version [8]. Conversely, an example, also in the full version, shows that the $m\epsilon$ cannot, for any m and ϵ, be improved to something better than $1 - (1-\epsilon)^m$, which for small ϵ is approximately $m\epsilon$. By using the above theorem on each player in a game we get this corollary.

COROLLARY 4. *Let Γ be a perfect recall game with utilities in $[0,1]$ where each player has at most m nodes in any history. If Γ' is the game Γ with timing information X, where X is an ϵ-timing, then any Nash-equilibrium σ of Γ is an $m\epsilon$-approximate Nash equilibrium of Γ'.*

One possible criticism of the definition of ϵ-timings is that it is only about the advantage the players get *on average*. Another definition would be to require that with probability $1 - \epsilon$ the players learn nothing at all from the timing information. We say a timing X is ϵ-*ex-post-perfect* if for any node u there is probability at least $1 - \epsilon$ that the timing information $X_{\preccurlyeq u}$ at u takes a value $x_{\preccurlyeq u}$ such that for all v in the same information set as u we have $\Pr(X_{\preccurlyeq u} = x_{\preccurlyeq u}) = \Pr(X_{\preccurlyeq v} = x_{\preccurlyeq u})$. The following theorem shows that this definition would give essentially the same results as our definition of ϵ-timeablility.

THEOREM 5. *Let Γ be an extensive-form game with perfect recall. If X is a ϵ-ex-post-perfect timing of Γ then X is an ϵ-timing of Γ. Conversely, there exists a constant c_Γ such that for all ϵ if X is an ϵ-timing of Γ using time at most N then there exists a $c_\Gamma \epsilon$-ex-post-perfect timing of Γ that uses time at most $2N + 1$.*

The first part of the theorem is obvious from the two definitions. The intuition in the second part is to modify the ϵ-timing X to get a $c_\Gamma\epsilon$-ex-post-timing X': We can assume that all times in X are integers. With high probability, the times in X' will just be twice the time in X. However, in cases where X gives away some probabilistic information (this could happen in all cases), X' will, with small probability take an odd value instead. This is done in such a way that given that the time is even, we have $\Pr(X_{\preccurlyeq u}' = x_{\preccurlyeq u}) = \Pr(X_{\preccurlyeq v}' = x_{\preccurlyeq u})$.

Another possible criticism of the concept of timeability is that you can always transform a not exactly timeable extensive-form game to its normal form, that is, you ask each player one by one to report what they would do in any possible situation. This normal-form game can be considered to be an extensive-form game where each player only has one move. This game is clearly timeable. However, there are several problems in doing this. First of all you lose the temporal information, so this transformation can

change properties of the game which depend on temporal information or on the beliefs the players have during the game. For example, transforming an extensive-form game to a normal-form game will often introduce new sequential equilibria.

A second problem in transforming to normal form, is that conceptually simple modifications of an extensive-form game might correspond to complicated modifications of the normal-form version. One example is from correlated equilibria, where the players get access to some correlated randomness during the game. For each distribution of the randomness, we get an extensive-form game which can be transformed to normal form. Thus, any question about correlated equilibria of an extensive-form game and be formulated as questions about classes of normal form games, but this would be a different and more complicated question. So although all not exactly timeable extensive-form games can be transformed to normal-form (and hence timeable) games it is possible that some theorems which hold for such modifications of timeable game, do not hold for in general for similar modifications of extensive-form games.

Finally, when transforming an extensive-form game to its normal form, there will generally be an exponential blow-up, both in the amount of communication needed to play the game, and in the description length of the game. This means that unless the game is a small toy example, it will not be feasible to play the game as a normal-form game. This also gives another example of how a theorem can hold for all timeable games, but not necessarily for all extensive-form games: Suppose you care about some function f defined on extensive-form games, and f is *not* affected when you transform a game from its extensive-form version to its normal form. Suppose further that you have a polynomial time algorithm for computing f on timeable games. Clearly, this algorithm can be used to compute f on all extensive-form games as well: You first transform your extensive-form game to a normal-form, and hence timeable, game, and then you apply the function on the transformed game. While this algorithm will correctly compute f, the algorithm will not be computable in polynomial time because of the blow-up in description size.

We have argued that there are many reasons not to transform extensive-form games to normal form, but you could argue that some not exactly timeable games have "equivalent" extensive-form games that can be timed, for some definition of equivalent. For example, in the game in Figure 1(a) one player's choice does not affect the other player's knowledge or options, so you could define an "equivalent" game where first player 1 moves and then player 2 moves. However, we do not see this as a weakness of the definition: When you define the rational numbers, you do not have to give an algorithm for checking if e.g. a fraction between two square roots is rational, even though such an algorithm may be useful. Similarly, in this paper we will not investigate which games that can somehow be "simplified" to timeable games, but we think it will be an interesting question for future research. One of the points in this paper is to argue that when proving theorems about games that have real world applications, you do not lose much by assuming timeability. This point stands: If you prove that a proposition P holds for all timeable games and you have an equivalence relation on all games which behave well with respect to P (meaning that if Γ and Γ' are equivalent then $P(\Gamma) \Leftrightarrow P(\Gamma')$)

---

[4]Formally, this is a strategy in the extensive-form game Γ' where the first move is a chance move which gives all the randomness in X, and all the next moves are as in Γ. Two nodes belong to the same information set in Γ' if they belong to the same information set in Γ and have the same timing history.

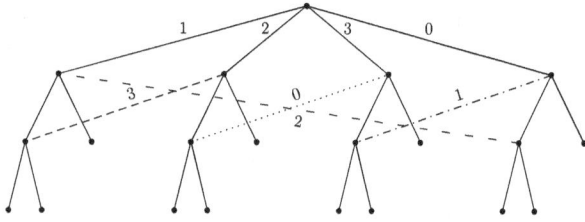

Figure 3: The extensive form of the onion routing game. The root belongs to chance who decides who is going to send a message. Each of the four players has only one information set illustrated by dashed/dotted lines. Using criterion 2 or 3 from Theorem 1 it is clear that this game is not exactly timeable.

then P clearly holds for all games that are equivalent to a timeable game.

4. AN ONION ROUTING EXAMPLE

Suppose four players, $\{0,1,2,3\}$ are sending messages to each other. Each player i can only send envelopes to the next player, player $i+1$ (modulo 4), but is only interested in sending a message to the previous player. The player sends these messages by using 3 nested envelopes. For example, if player 2 wants to send a message to player 1 she will write down the message, put it in an envelope marked "1", put that in an envelope marked "0", put that in an envelope marked "3" and hand that to player 3.

We now define a game where first chance chooses one player j. Now player j will nest three envelopes as described above and hand it to $j+1$. Each of the two players on the way, $j+1$ and $j+2$ can choose wether to follow the protocol of opening their envelope and passing on the envelope inside or to obstruct the protocol by keeping the envelope. Player i gets utility -1 if a message went from $i+2$ to $i+1$ and player i gets utility $1+\epsilon$ if a message went from $i+3$ to $i+2$. That is, each player want to obstruct the protocol if they are the second person to pass on an envelope, but wants to help if they are the first.

This defines an extensive-form game with perfect recall as shown in Figure 3, and without any timing information each player will collaborate in the protocol. However, using Theorem 1 it is easy to see that the game is not exactly timeable. One possible way to ϵ-time it is to let X_1 be uniformly distributed on $\{1,\ldots,N-1\}$ and let the sender send the first envelope at time X_1 and and let each of the two helpers make their move one time unit after receiving the envelope. This way the players will follow the protocol, unless they receive an envelope at time N. Thus, the protocol will fail with probability $\frac{1}{N-1}$.

In this example the players used envelopes because they could not send the message directly. However, in the Tor network [4] a similar protocol is instead used to provide anonymity. In this protocol the concern is not so much reliability, but how much the Tor nodes learn about your communication. Because the onion routing game is not exactly timeable, you cannot avoid giving the routers some information about how far they are from the sender of the message. In particular, one router might learn that it is communicating directly with the original sender. As long as

there are only messages going one way, the routers might not get much information if the network has been running for years, because this means that N is large.[5] However, if the recipient wants to answer the message within a few seconds, the routers will get more information: Now each router will be passing on two messages within a few seconds and the time gap between the messages will always be smallest for the router closest to the recipient of the first message.

Notice that this is *not* a problem for the Tor network, as it was never designed to hide this information from the router. However, if we wanted to design an onion routing protocol where the routers do not know how far they are from the end-points, this would be a problem. This is why the concept of timeability is important: you cannot just define an extensive-form game with perfect recall and expect that it can be implemented (even in principle), unless you check that it is timeable.

Except for onion routing related games, we have not been able to find games that are not exactly timeable but would be useful to play in real life. However this only strengthens our thesis that when you want to prove a theorem about all extensive-form games, you do not lose much from assuming timeability.

5. UPPER AND LOWER BOUNDS

From [7] we have the following definition and theorem.

DEFINITION 3. *Let $X_1,\ldots,X_n$ be random variables over $\mathbb{N}$ with some joint distribution such that we always have $X_1 < X_2 < \cdots < X_n$. We say that $(X_1,\ldots,X_n)$ has ϵ-indistinguishable m-subsets if for any two sets in indices $\{i_1,\ldots,i_m\}$, $\{j_1,\ldots j_m\} \subset [n]$ of size m, the two random sets $\{X_{i_1},\ldots,X_{i_n}\}$ and $\{X_{j_1},\ldots,X_{j_n}\}$ are ϵ-indistinguishable. We slightly abuse notation and say that $(X_1,\ldots,X_n)$ has ϵ-indistinguishable subsets if for all $m < n$ it has ϵ-indistinguishable m-subsets.*

In the following $\exp_2$ denotes the function $\exp_2(x) = 2^x$, and $\exp_2^n(x)$ denotes iteration of $\exp_2$, so $\exp_2^n(x) = 2^{2^{\cdot^{\cdot^{2^x}}}}$ where the tower contains n 2's.

THEOREM 6. *For any $n \in \mathbb{N}$ and any $\epsilon > 0$ there exists a distribution of $(X_1,\ldots,X_n)$ such that $1 \leq X_1 < X_2 < \cdots < X_n$ are all integers and X has ϵ-indistinguishable subsets. For fixed n we can ensure that X_n never take values larger than $\exp_2^{n-2}\left(O\left(\frac{1}{\epsilon}\right)\right)$. Conversely, for any such distribution, X_n must take values of at least $\exp_2^{n-2}\left(\Omega\left(\frac{1}{\epsilon}\right)\right)$ for sufficiently small ϵ. This lower bound holds even if we only require the $n-1$-subsets of $(X_1,\ldots,X_n)$ to be ϵ-indistinguishable.*

The following gives intuition for the upper bound on N. For $n = 2$ it is easy to construct (X_1, X_2) that has ϵ-indistinguishable subsets. For example, we can take X_1 to be uniformly distributed on $[N-k]$ for some constants N and k and set $X_2 = X_1 + k$. We can then use a recursive construction for higher n. If $(X_1,\ldots,X_n)$ has ϵ-indistinguishable

---

[5]If the time a user decides to send a message over the network in not uniformly distributed over the day or the week, the routers would get some information about their position in the path. However, if it takes less than a couple of seconds to send a message through the path, that will only be a very small amount of information.

subsets and consecutive X_i's are usually not too close to each other, we can construct $(Y_1, Y_2, \ldots, Y_{n+1})$ that has ϵ'-indistinguishable subsets for some ϵ'. To do this, we choose Y_1 uniformly between 1 and a sufficiently large number, and choose each gap $Y_{i+1} - Y_i$ uniformly and independently from $\{1, 2, \ldots, 2^{X_i}\}$. For a proof that this works, see [7].

The intuition about the lower bound on N is that for $n = 2$ an $n - 1$-subset contains 1 number, and the *size* of this number gives away some information about whether it is the higher or lowest. For $n = 3$ an $n - 1$ subset contains two numbers and their *distance* gives away some information about whether it is the middle number or another number that is missing from the set. For $n = 4$ an $n - 1$ subset contains 3 numbers, and now the *ratios between the two distances* gives away information about which number is missing, and so on.

We can use the construction to approximately time any game.

THEOREM 7. *All games with at most m nodes in each history can be ϵ-timed in time $\exp_2^{m-3}\left(O\left(\frac{1}{\epsilon}\right)\right)$. In particular, all games are approximately timeable.*

PROOF. Take any game and $\epsilon > 0$. We want to show that the game is ϵ-timeable. First we find some distribution of $(X_1, \ldots, X_{m-1})$ that has ϵ-indistinguishable subsets. Now we let the time of the root be 0 and the time of a node at depth d be given by X_d. As the X_d's take values in $\mathbb{N}$ and are increasing this gives a timing of the game. If two nodes v and w belong to the same information set, the player i who owns these nodes will have the same number $j - 1$ of previous nodes at v and at w. As $(X_1, \ldots, X_{m-1})$ has ϵ-indistinguishable subsets, it has ϵ-indistinguishable j-subsets, so if the root does not belong to player i there is total variation distance at most ϵ between the two nodes' timing information. Similarly, $(X_1, \ldots, X_{m-1})$ has ϵ-indistinguishable $j - 1$-subsets, so if the root belongs to player i the total variation distance between the two nodes' timing information is also at most ϵ. □

Unfortunately the above upper bound on the time needed to ϵ-time is beyond astronomical even for moderate values of m and ϵ. The following lower bounds shows that for any r there are games that take time $2^{2^{\cdots^{\frac{1}{\epsilon}}}}$ to ϵ-time, where the hight of the tower is r.

THEOREM 8. *Given $r \geq 1$ there exists $\epsilon_r > 0$ and a game with $16r + 3$ players and at most $\max(3r, 2r + 3)$ nodes per player per history such that for any ϵ-timing of the game with $\epsilon \leq \epsilon_r$ we need time at least $\exp_2^r\left(\epsilon^{-1}\right)$.*

The proof has some similarities to the lower bound part of Theorem 6, but we also need some new ideas. If extensive-form games could have nodes that belong to more than one player the theorem would follow from Theorem 6: We would define a "game" Γ where the first node was a chance node which assigned the numbers from 1 to n to the n players, and the players do *not* learn this number. Then, for each such choice, we would have a node belonging to all but the player who was assigned the number 1, followed by a node belonging to all but the player who was assigned the number 2 and so on. Let X_i denote the time of the i'th node, and suppose

that this time is independent from the assignment of numbers to the players. Then a player who was assigned number i gets timing information $(X_1, \ldots X_{i-1}, X_{i+1}, \ldots, X_n)$. If we have an ϵ-timing of this "game", the players should not be able to figure out their assigned number, so the $n - 1$-subsets of $(X_1, \ldots, X_n)$ should be ϵ-indistinguishable. Thus, by Theorem 6 this "game" would take time $\exp_2^{n-2}\left(\Omega\left(\frac{1}{\epsilon}\right)\right)$ to ϵ-time for sufficiently small ϵ.

However, in extensive-form games each node only belongs to one player. To fix this problem we could split the node belonging to many players in our "game" to many nodes each belonging to one player to get a real game. For example, if there where three players, we would first have a node belonging to player 2 then one belonging to player 3 (omitting player 1), then one belonging to player 1 and one to player 3 (omitting player 2), and finally one belonging to player 1 and one to player 2. We will denote this game by just listing the order of the nodes: 231312. This strategy does not work, as this game can be ϵ-timed in time $O(\epsilon^{-1})$ by having the three first nodes immediately after each other, then a gap of variable length and then the three last nodes immediately after each other. In this case, with just three players, this problem can be fixed by reordering the nodes to get 233112 which takes time $2^{\Omega(\epsilon^{-1})}$ to ϵ-time. A similar strategy works for four players but this strategy does not seem to work for more than four players.

Instead, the idea is to prove the claim by induction. You take a game Γ that takes time $\exp_2^r\left(O(\epsilon^{-1})\right)$ to ϵ-time and combine it with copies of the four-player game with node order given by 243314412213, where the four-player games and Γ are played by different players. The nodes from Γ and the nodes from the four-player game are ordered in a way that ensures that if the four-player games are ϵ-timed, then the gaps between certain points in Γ will either all get larger and larger or all get smaller and smaller (in both cases by at least some factor greater than 1). This means that if you take the logarithms of certain gaps between node times you get a timing of Γ. As Γ takes time $\exp_2^r\left(O(\epsilon^{-1})\right)$ to ϵ-time, this means that the new game must take $\exp_2^{r+1}\left(O(\epsilon^{-1})\right)$. This is the idea in the proof of Theorem 8, but the actual proof is more complicated because you need a stronger induction hypothesis.

Theorem 8 as stated only shows that the players can get some ϵ advantage if they have unbounded computational power. So we might hope that we could find a timing such that a player with bounded computational power cannot get an ϵ advantage. However, we will now see that this is not possible. The proof of Theorem 8 shows that for any r there exists a game Γ_r, such that for any timing X of the game using time at most N, there is a player i who will be able to earn some ϵ amount in expectation by betting on a *fair bet*. Here a *fair bet* means a bet about which branch of the game that was played, such that the player would have expectation 0 if he did not have the information from the timing, and where the player can win or lose at most 1.

Given Γ_r and N we can define a new two-player game Γ_T between a player master-mind and a scheduler. Here the player master-mind is just a useful abstraction of all the players. To play Γ_T, the player master-mind secretly chooses one player i from Γ_r who is going to make a fair bet, and a strategy which given the available timing information chooses a fair bet. At the same time the scheduler chooses the timing X of Γ_r. Now the game Γ_r is played and player i

gets some timing information from X. Then player i makes a fair bet according to the strategy chosen by the player master-mind. The player master-mind gets the utility which the player wins from the bet, and the scheduler gets minus this utility.

Now Γ_T is a two player zero-sum game, and for a fixed value of N there is only a finite number of pure strategies for each player, so we can use the Minimax Theorem. Now Theorem 8 shows that if the scheduler commits to some randomised strategy, there is a move that gives the player master-mind a utility of ϵ. By the Minimax Theorem this implies that there is a randomised strategy for the player master-mind which guarantees a utility of at least ϵ. As this strategy is fixed, the players only need a certain amount of computational power to follow it, no matter how complicated a strategy the scheduler chooses.

6. IMPERFECT TIMEKEEPING

Previously we assumed that at any time all the players knew the exact time. In practice, this is not a realistic assumption. Even our model of time—that there exists an absolute time, and that everybody's time goes at the same speed—has been proven wrong by relativity theory. If the players cannot feel acceleration, one could use the twin paradox to time games that otherwise cannot be exactly timed [6].[6] A more down-to-earth objection is that it might be possible to affect humans' or even computers' perception of time if you control their environment. The purpose of this section it to show that our lower bounds are quite robust: even if we can determine the players' perception of time within some reasonable bounds, there are games that take a long time to ϵ-time. We will assume each node occurs at some "official" time, x, and that we can also decide the players' perception y of that time. The following definition models a situation where a time interval of length t can be perceived as anything between $l(t)$ and $u(t)$ and where the players do not know when the game started.

DEFINITION 4. *Let* $l, u : \mathbb{R}^+ \to \mathbb{R}^+$ *be weakly increasing functions satisfying* $l(t) \leq t \leq u(t)$. *A deterministic* $[l, u]$-*timing of a game* Γ *is an assignment of a tuple* (x_v, y_v) *(two nonnegative real numbers) to each node* v *such that:*

1. *If we label* Γ *with just the* x_v *values we have a deterministic timing of* Γ.

2. *If* v *and* w *are two nodes belonging to the same player and* v *is on the path from the root to* w *then* $l(x_w - x_v) \leq y_w - y_v \leq u(x_w - x_v)$.

An $[l, u]$-*timing is a distribution over deterministic* $[l, u]$-*timings. The* timing information *of player* i *at a node* w *given an* $[l, u]$-*timing consists of the* perceived times, y_v, *of all nodes* v *belonging to that player between the root and* w. *Now an* $(\epsilon, [l, u])$-*timing is an* $[l, u]$-*timing such that for any two nodes belonging to the same information set, the current player's timing information at the two nodes has total variation distance at most* ϵ. *An* $[l, u]$-*timing is an* exact $[l, u]$-*timing if it is a* $(0, [l, u])$-*timing.*

---

[6]The question whether it is possible to implement a not exactly timeable game on players who are equipped with a perfect accelerometer is beyond the scope of this paper.

We now show that even if we can affect the players' clocks by some large constant factor c, there still exist games that cannot be ϵ-timed in time $\exp_2^r(\frac{1}{\epsilon})$.

THEOREM 9. *Let c be an integer and let l, u be functions as in Definition 4 and such that $l(x) \geq \frac{x}{c}$ and $u(x) \leq cx$. Then for any r there exists a game $\Gamma_{c,r}$ with $16(2c^4+r)+11$ players such that for sufficiently small ϵ any $(\epsilon, [l(x), u(x)])$-timing of $\Gamma_{c,r}$ has to use time at least $\exp_2^r\left(\frac{1}{\epsilon}\right)$.*

PROOF SKETCH. This proof follows the same idea as the induction step of the proof of Theorem 8. We start with a game Γ_r that does not have an ϵ-timing in time less than $\exp_2^r\left(\frac{1}{\epsilon}\right)$. Instead of the four-player game used in the proof of Theorem 8 we now use a $2(4c^4 + 1)$-player game. □

The next theorem shows that the above is the strongest theorem we can hope for: if we can make the players' clocks go faster or slower by more that a constant factor, we can implement all games.

THEOREM 10. *Let Γ be a game and l, u functions as in Definition 4 with $\frac{u(t)}{l(t)} \to \infty$ as $t \to \infty$. Then Γ is exactly $[l, u]$-timeable.*

7. CONCLUSION

Not every extensive-form game can be naturally implemented in the world. Games with imperfect recall constitute a well known example of this. In this paper, we have drawn attention to another feature that is likely to prevent the direct implementation of the game in the world: games that are not exactly timeable. We gave necessary and sufficient conditions for a game to be exactly timeable and showed that they are easy to check. Most of the technical contribution concerned approximately timing games; we showed that this can always be done, but can require large amounts of time.

Future research can take a number of directions. Does restricting attention to exactly timeable games allow one to prove new results about these games, or develop new algorithms for solving them—as is the case for perfect recall? It is conceivable that the possibility of games that are not exactly timeable has been an unappreciated and unnecessary roadblock to the development of certain theoretical or algorithmic results. Can our techniques be applied to the design of protocols that should not leak information to participants by means of the time at which they receive messages? Are there natural families of games for which we can obtain desirable bounds for the amount of time required to approximately time them?

We have argued that not exactly timeable games cannot be played, but you can transform such a game to a normal-form game. This normal-form game is identical to the original game in some regards, for example it has the same Nash equilibria, but different in others, for example it might have new sequential equilibria. Furthermore, the normal-form game is typically not playable in practice because it takes exponentially more communication. Is it possible to transform a general not exactly timeable game to an "equivalent" timeable game which only requires polynomially more communication that the original? Here, one possible definition of "equivalent" is that the two games give the same game when transformed to normal form, but other definitions might also be relevant. Answers to this question for different definitions of "equivalent" would tell us in what situations it could be useful to assume timeability for certain algorithmic purposes.

8. ACKNOWLEDGMENTS

We thank Jörgen Weibull for helpful feedback.

Conitzer thanks ARO and NSF for support under grants W911NF-12-1-0550, W911NF-11-1-0332, IIS-0953756, CCF-1101659, CCF-1337215, and IIS-1527434.

References

[1] AUMANN, R. J., HART, S., AND PERRY, M. 1997a. The absent-minded driver. *Games and Economic Behavior 20*, 1, 102–116.

[2] AUMANN, R. J., HART, S., AND PERRY, M. 1997b. The forgetful passenger. *Games and Economic Behavior 20*, 1, 117–120.

[3] CORMEN, T. H., STEIN, C., RIVEST, R. L., AND LEISERSON, C. E. 2001. *Introduction to Algorithms* 2nd Ed. McGraw-Hill Higher Education.

[4] DINGLEDINE, R., MATHEWSON, N., AND SYVERSON, P. 2004. Tor: The second-generation onion router. In *Proceedings of the 13th USENIX Security Symposium.*

[5] HANSEN, K. A., MILTERSEN, P. B., AND SØRENSEN, T. B. 2007. Finding equilibria in games of no chance. In *Computing and Combinatorics.* Springer Berlin Heidelberg, 274–284.

[6] HARTLE, J. B. 2002. *Gravity: An Introduction to Einstein's General Relativity.* Addison Wesley.

[7] JAKOBSEN, S. K. 2015. A numbers-on-foreheads game. arxiv:1502.02849.

[8] JAKOBSEN, S. K., SØRENSEN, T. B., AND CONITZER, V. 2015. Timeability of extensive-form games. arxiv:1502.03430.

[9] KREPS, D. M. AND RAMEY, G. 1987. Structural consistency, consistency, and sequential rationality. *Econometrica: Journal of the Econometric Society*, 1331–1348.

[10] KREPS, D. M. AND WILSON, R. 1982. Sequential equilibria. *Econometrica: Journal of the Econometric Society*, 863–894.

[11] KROER, C. AND SANDHOLM, T. 2014. Extensive-form game abstraction with bounds. In *Proceedings of the fifteenth ACM conference on Economics and computation.* ACM, 621–638.

[12] KUHN, H. W. 1953. Extensive games and the problem of information. *Contributions to the Theory of Games 2*, 28, 193–216.

[13] MILTERSEN, P. B. AND SØRENSEN, T. B. 2008. Fast algorithms for finding proper strategies in game trees. In *Proceedings of the nineteenth annual ACM-SIAM symposium on Discrete algorithms.* Society for Industrial and Applied Mathematics, 874–883.

[14] MILTERSEN, P. B. AND SØRENSEN, T. B. 2010. Computing a quasi-perfect equilibrium of a two-player game. *Economic Theory 42*, 1, 175–192.

[15] NISAN, N., ROUGHGARDEN, T., TARDOS, E., AND VAZIRANI, V. V. 2007. *Algorithmic Game Theory.* Cambridge University Press, New York, NY, USA.

[16] PICCIONE, M. AND RUBINSTEIN, A. 1997. On the interpretation of decision problems with imperfect recall. *Games and Economic Behavior 20*, 1, 3–24.

[17] ROMANOVSKY, J. 1962. Reduction of a game with perfect recall to a constrained matrix game. *Doklady Akademii Nauk SSSR 144*, 62–64.

[18] SPEYER, D. 2008. What is total variation distance? https://sbseminar.wordpress.com/2008/01/14/what-is-total-variation-distance/.

[19] VON STENGEL, B. 1996. Efficient computation of behavior strategies. *Games and Economic Behavior 14*, 2, 220–246.

[20] VON STENGEL, B. AND FORGES, F. 2008. Extensive-form correlated equilibrium: Definition and computational complexity. *Mathematics of Operations Research 33*, 4, 1002–1022.

[21] WAUGH, K., ZINKEVICH, M., JOHANSON, M., KAN, M., SCHNIZLEIN, D., AND BOWLING, M. H. 2009. A practical use of imperfect recall. In *SARA.*

[22] WEIBULL, J. W. 1992. On self-enforcement in extensive-form games. *Games and Economic Behavior 4*, 3, 450–462.

[23] WEIBULL, J. W. 2009. Lecture notes in game theory and economic analysis. Department of Economics, Ecole Polytechnique (Paris), ECO574.

Auction Revenue in the General Spiteful-Utility Model

Jing Chen
CS Department, Stony Brook University
Stony Brook, NY 11794, USA
jingchen@cs.stonybrook.edu

Silvio Micali
CSAIL, MIT
Cambridge, MA 02139, USA
silvio@csail.mit.edu

ABSTRACT

It is well accepted that, in some auctions, a player's "true utility" may depend not only on the price he pays and whether or not he wins the good, but also on various forms of *externalities*, such as the prices paid by his competitors, and the identity and true value of the actual winner.

In this work, we study revenue generation in single-good auctions under a very general model of externalities: the *General Spiteful-Utility Model*. Specifically, we

- Put forward new revenue benchmarks and solution concepts;

- Design new mechanisms when some information about the players' externalities is known; and

- Analyze the revenue of the second-price mechanism when only the players have information about each other.

Categories and Subject Descriptors

[**Theory of computation**]: Algorithmic game theory and mechanism design

Keywords

externality; spitefulness; revenue; single-good auction; undominated strategy; light Bayesian setting

1. INTRODUCTION

In single-good auctions, the famous second-price mechanism guarantees revenue equal to the second highest true value in dominant strategies. This revenue guarantee is very attractive and does not require the mechanism to have any information about the players' true values. However, it only holds for players with *classical utilities*. The classical utility of a player i is $cu_i \triangleq v_i - p_i$, if he wins the good, and $-p_i$ otherwise, where v_i and p_i respectively are i's value for the good and i's price.

Permission to make digital or hard copies of all or part of this work for personal or classroom use is granted without fee provided that copies are not made or distributed for profit or commercial advantage and that copies bear this notice and the full citation on the first page. Copyrights for components of this work owned by others than the author(s) must be honored. Abstracting with credit is permitted. To copy otherwise, or republish, to post on servers or to redistribute to lists, requires prior specific permission and/or a fee. Request permissions from Permissions@acm.org.
ITCS'16, January 14–16, 2016, Cambridge, MA, USA.
Copyright is held by the owner/author(s). Publication rights licensed to ACM.
ACM 978-1-4503-4057-1/16/01 ...$15.00.
DOI: http://dx.doi.org/10.1145/2840728.2840741.

The General Spiteful-Utility Model.

It has been widely recognized (see, e.g., [29, 7, 30, 19]) that classical utilities are only "part of the story", and a player's "true utility" may also depend on various *externalities*, such as the prices paid by his competitors or the identity of the actual winner.

In this paper, we study auction revenue under a very general externality model: the *general spiteful-utility* (GSU) model. In this model, the utility of a player i is

$$u_i = cu_i - \sum_{j \neq i} \alpha_{ij} cu_j$$

where each α_{ij} is a constant in $[0,1]$, referred to as i's *utility exchange rate* for player j. In other words, for all players i and j, a monetary gain/loss of x for j translates into a corresponding loss/gain of $\alpha_{ij}x$ for i.[1] When all exchange rates are 0, the players have classical utilities. When $\alpha_{ij} > 0$, player i is *spiteful* of player j.

(Note: Our results hold also when spitefulness is recursively defined, see Section 7.)

An important special case of the GSU model is when each player i spites his opponents equally, but possibly differently from other players. That is, for each i, there exists a value α_i such that $\alpha_{ij} = \alpha_i$ for all $j \neq i$ (but α_i and α_j may be different if $i \neq j$). We refer to this important case as the *individually uniformly spiteful model*.

The GSU model is not a mere syntactic generalization of the classical utility model, but is very natural and meaningful. In particular, it may endogenously model the players' strategic interests in their interactions after or outside the auction. For instance, let the good be a large oil field and players i and j two oil companies, which will continue to compete fiercely after the auction. Assume now that j wins the oil field for a minimal price, and i pays nothing at all. Then, although i's classical utility is 0, his 'true' utility would actually be negative, because he will 'suffer' in the future, as j will use his newly acquired resource against i. However, if j paid a very high price for the oil field, then i's suffering would be amply mitigated, as j would have less net resources to use against i in the future.

Related Work on Auctions.

Up to now, in auctions, mostly special cases of the GSU model have been studied. In particular, [35] experimen-

---

[1] Although utility exchange rates > 1 could be justified in some extreme settings, we prefer to assume that a player strictly prefers receiving one dollar himself to having a competitor lose one dollar or less.

tally studies auctions and other games in which the utility-exchange rates are severely restricted;[2] [43] studies auctions where all exchange rates are the same; and there is another work which studied auctions where each player i has the same number of non-zero utility-exchange rates and all such rates are equal, but due to an unfixable problem in the analysis the paper has been essentially retracted[3] and the authors have asked the paper not to be cited.

The economic literature contains many studies of auctions where a player's utility depends on (besides his own valuation and price) just the valuation, or the price, or the identity of the actual winner of the good. Games other than auctions have also been studied under various models of externalities. We provide a more detailed discussion about this literature in Section 2.

To the best of our knowledge, [19] is the only work in the literature studying an auction mechanism in the GSU model; yet, as pointed out by the authors themselves, their mechanism only works when the utility exchange rates are "extremely small": namely, when $\alpha_{ij} = O(1/n^3)$ for any i, j, where n is the number of players.

In sum, it is fair to say that, despite its meaningfulness, the general spiteful-utility model remains vastly understudied in auctions.

Our Goal.

We aim at starting the study of auction *revenue* in the general spiteful-utility model, without any restrictions. By contrast, the auction mechanism of [19] focuses on social welfare. Accordingly, their paper aims at *overcoming* the players' spitefulness,[4] so as to incentivize them to bid almost truthfully. We instead aim at *leveraging* the players' spitefulness, so as to incentivize them to place bids higher than their true valuations. Again, in [19], the exchange rates are assumed to be extremely small; while by contrast, our results hold for all (positive) exchange rates.

Participation.

Generating revenue is trivial when a mechanism is able to impose arbitrarily high prices to 'unwilling players'. An important principle in designing revenue mechanisms is to allow players to 'opt out' of the auction without paying anything and without receiving the good. We do follow this principle: all mechanisms studied allow a player to opt out by bidding 0. In auctions without externalities, the utility of a player opting out is 0. However, this may not be true for a spiteful player. Indeed, if a player i opts out, and the good is allocated at price 0 to a player spited by i, then, without any fault of the mechanism, i's utility will be negative.

Potential and Challenges of the GSU model.

Intuitively, an auction with spiteful players is 'more competitive than a classical one'. Thus, a properly designed mechanism may be able to translate this additional competition into additional revenue. To realize this potential, however, several challenges must be met. Most importantly, to act rationally in a mechanism, spiteful players in general need to know their own utility functions exactly, which they do only in auctions of complete information, where the true valuation profile is common knowledge among the players. Thus, analyzing classical and new mechanisms with spiteful players less informed about each other requires the adoption of new and appropriate solution concepts.

Results.

We show that the slightest information about the players' exchange rates can be extremely powerful, even when the players have no information about the valuations and exchange rates of their opponents. Informally, we prove that

1. *A mechanism knowing a positive lower bound about the exchange rate of just two players can extract arbitrarily high revenue in strictly dominant strategies.*

When the mechanism has no information about the spiteful players, they must have some information about each other, as argued above, in order to be able to act rationally. The first setting to consider is one of complete information. Indeed, this extreme case allows us to study how spiteful players behave in the GSU model when they know their utility functions exactly. For auctions of complete information we exactly characterize the players' weakly undominated strategies in the classic second-price mechanism in the GSU model and prove that

2. *The revenue obtainable by the second-price mechanism in weakly undominated strategies is at least the second-highest virtual value, and this lower bound is tight.*

Above, the second-highest *virtual value*, a new benchmark for the GSU model, is always greater than or equal to a half of the second highest true value, less than or equal to the second highest true value when there are at least three players, but can be much larger than the latter when there are two players. Furthermore, for the same setting, we prove that

3. *The revenue obtainable by the second-price mechanism in strategies surviving two levels of elimination of weakly dominated strategies is at least the highest virtual value.*

This lower bound is actually tight as well.

Settings of complete information are of course quite ideal. We thus consider the *Light Bayesian Setting*. In this setting, essentially, the true value of each player i is independently drawn from a distribution $\mathcal{D}_i$ and each player i *individually knows* $\mathcal{D}_{-i}$. (Note that the Light Bayesian Setting is much weaker and more realistic than the traditional common prior model, where the distribution profile $(\mathcal{D}_1, \ldots, \mathcal{D}_n)$ is *common knowledge* to the players, and often to the mechanism as well!) Here we prove that

4. *In the individually uniformly spiteful model, the expected revenue of the second-price mechanism, in Bayesian undominated strategies, can be smaller than the expectation of the second-highest valuation, but is never smaller than a half of it.*

---

[2] Namely, there is a common parameter λ and each player i has his own parameter a_i (positive if the player is spiteful, and negative if he is 'altruistic'), so that i's utility exchange rate for an opponent j is $\frac{a_i + \lambda a_j}{1 + \lambda}$.

[3] We thank an anonymous reviewer for pointing this out.

[4] A player i is *spiteful* towards another player j if $\alpha_{ij} > 0$, and *altruistic* if $\alpha_{ij} < 0$. Actually, [19] also wish to overcome the players' altruism. But, aiming at maximizing revenue, we focus solely on spitefulness.

Above, *implementation in Bayesian undominated strategies* is a new and very compelling solution concept put forward by us. We consider this as a conceptual contribution that will prove useful in mechanism design in the GSU model.

In Sum.

We show that spitefulness can yield very high revenue when a mechanism designer has even a small amount of information about the exchange rate of the players, or when the players have a lot of information about each other, but otherwise can lead to much less revenue than when the players have classical utilities (e.g., a half in the worst case). For an auctioneer, the latter information, although demoralizing, is useful to know. Since the auctioneer in general has no way to tell whether the players have externalities or not, he is better off knowing how much revenue he is risking losing if he decides to adopt a classical mechanism like the second-price. And he may actually be encouraged to investigate totally new mechanisms designed to take advantage of this difficult setting. One step at a time. We believe mechanism analysis and design in the GSU model to be challenging, meaningful, and fun.

2. ADDITIONAL RELATED WORKS

Generating Revenue in Auctions with Externalities.

There have been many works on *financial externalities* in auctions; see, e.g., [16, 8, 15, 17, 25, 37]. In general, they assume that the losers' utilities in an auction depend on the *payment* of the winner, but not on the true value or the identity of the winner. Moreover, the parameters for measuring externality have the same values for all players. In [36], the author studies financial externalities among players with regular i.i.d. values, where different players have different externality parameters. The author allows each player to have a non-negative gain from the winner's value—rather than a loss as in our model—and characterizes the optimal Bayesian mechanisms.

In another line of works [29, 30, 28, 44, 1, 31], the externalities in auctions come from the *identity* of the winner rather than his payment, and may not be the same among the players.

In [18] and [21] the authors consider models where the players hold "shares" in the goods, so that the losers receive positive externality from the winner's utility. Recall that in our model the players are spiteful and the loser receives negative externality from the winner's utility.

Most of the works mentioned above have focused on analyzing the revenue performance of the first-price mechanism and/or the second-price mechanism (sometimes with reserve prices), under various equilibrium-based solution concepts. In [29, 30] the authors studied mechanism design for single-good auctions to generate revenue, and characterized the optimal mechanisms in complete information as well as Bayesian settings. As mentioned above, the externality model they use is identity-based and does not depend on the players' payments.

Finally, the above models of externalities are *one sided* —only the losers have externality from the winner and not viceversa. This is without loss of generality for their studies, since in both the second-price and the first-price mechanisms the loser does not get any good and does not pay anything,

and in the identity-based model the value received by the losers is 0. By contrast, our model allows the possibility that the mechanism gives all players positive prices, and thus externalities are defined for both the winner and the loser.

Externalities in Other Contexts.

As mentioned, in [19] the externality model is the same as ours, but the major goal there is to generate social welfare, and their mechanism works when the exchange rates are extremely small. There are many other studies on games with externalities, but the contexts, models, and goals are all quite different from ours. Thus we do not elaborate on them here, and only mention several examples. In [33, 4, 13] the authors mainly focus on the computational complexity for finding/approximating desired outcomes when there are externalities. In [40, 20, 24, 32, 23, 26, 41, 14] the authors examine sponsored-search auctions and incorporate the externalities affecting the probability for an advertisement to receive a click, caused by other advertisements shown on the same webpage. In [22] and [10] the authors study externalities raised on social networks, in [2] and [42] externalities in congestion games, in [6] network formation with externalities, and in [5, 9, 45, 38] coalition formation with externalities. Finally, [34] is on experimental study, [12] on traffic routing, and a detailed review of the literature can be found in [11].

3. OUR FIRST RESULT

Given a mechanism, letting S_i be the set of available strategies of each player i, a strategy $s_i \in S_i$ is a *strictly dominant* strategy if $u_i(s_i, s_{-i}) > u_i(s_i', s_{-i})$ for all strategy subprofiles $s_{-i} \in S_{-i}$ and all strategies $s_i' \in S_i \setminus \{s_i\}$. Notice that if a strictly dominant strategy exists, then it must be unique.

Below, we construct a normal-form mechanism, M_P, that takes an arbitrarily high number P as an input and generates revenue at least P at the strictly dominant strategy profile. Surprisingly, the mechanism M_P *never sells* the good, but generates revenue solely by leveraging the players' spitefulness.

Of course, we do not consider never selling the good as an 'advantage' (particularly when the auctioneer wishes to guarantee a minimum of social welfare). But we consider it important to highlight how much revenue potential lies in knowing the players' spitefulness. Actually, a minimum amount of such knowledge suffices. Indeed, to use M_P, the auctioneer need only know ℓ, i and j, such that $0 < \ell \le \alpha_{ij}$, but nothing else about the players' values or exchange rates.

Letting, without loss of generality, $i = 1$ and $j = 2$; and recalling that the number of players is n, our mechanism M_P works as follows.

Mechanism M_P

Each player i announces $b_i \in \{0, 1\}$, where 0 means "opting out" and 1 means "participating".

The good is unsold and each player $i \notin \{1, 2\}$ receives a payment equal to b_i. The prices of players 1 and 2 are as follows:

> *If $b_2 = 0$, then player 1 receives a payment equal to b_1 and player 2 receives 0.*

If $b_1 = 0$ and $b_2 = 1$, then player 2 receives $\frac{P+n}{\ell}$ and player 1 receives 0.

If $b_1 = b_2 = 1$, then player 1 pays $P + n - 1$ and player 2 receives $\frac{1}{2}$.

We have the following theorem, whose proof is provided in the appendix.

THEOREM 1. *For any $n \geq 2$ and $P > 0$, in mechanism M_P, it is strictly dominant for each player to announce 1; and the revenue of M_P under the strategy profile $(1, 1, \ldots, 1)$ is at least P.*

Remark.

We stress that M_P making a big payment is just a *threat*: at the unique dominant-strategy equilibrium, he only receives payments from the players. Yet, as proven by the extraordinary revenue performance that it entails, such a (credible) ability cannot be taken for granted.

4. OUR SECOND RESULT

Now we consider the extreme, yet fundamental, case where the players have complete information about each other's valuation and exchange rates.

To begin with, the second-price mechanism naturally allows players to 'opt out': if a player bids 0, then he is considered non-participating and the mechanism is run on the remaining players. It is not hard to see there is no (strictly or weakly) dominant strategies for players with externalities, thus the solution concept we consider is *undominated* strategies:

A strategy $s_i \in S_i$ is *weakly dominated* by $s_i' \in S_i$ if

(a) $u_i(s_i, s_{-i}) \leq u_i(s_i', s_{-i})$ for all strategy subprofiles $s_{-i} \in S_{-i}$, and

(b) $u_i(s_i, s_{-i}) < u_i(s_i', s_{-i})$ for at least one strategy subprofile $s_{-i} \in S_{-i}$.

If s_i is not weakly dominated by any other strategy, then it is *undominated*.

In the individually uniformly spiteful model, for each player i, let $m_i = \operatorname{argmin}_{j \neq i} v_j$ and $v_i' = \frac{v_i + \alpha_i v_{m_i}}{1 + \alpha_i}$. The value v_i' is referred to as player i's *virtual value*. We have the following theorem.

THEOREM 2. *The revenue of the second-price mechanism at any undominated strategy profile is at least the second highest virtual value, and this lower bound is tight.*

To prove Theorem 2, the lemma below, proved in the appendix, characterizes the players' sets of undominated strategies.

LEMMA 1. *For each player i, a strategy b_i is undominated if and only if $b_i \geq v_i'$.*

That is, with spitefulness, a player will not bid anything lower than a convex combination of his own true value and the lowest one among all other players. This lower bound of his bid is determined by his exchange rate and may be lower than his true value.

Theorem 2 follows directly from Lemma 1.

PROOF OF THEOREM 2. For any undominated strategy profile b, the revenue is the second highest in b, which is at least the second highest in $(v_i')_{i \in [n]}$, since by Lemma 1, $b_i \geq v_i'$ for each player i. Moreover, this lower bound is tight when $b_i = v_i'$ for each i. □

We denote the lower bound in Theorem 2 by $rev(2ndP)$. Notice that when $n = 2$, $rev(2ndP)$ is at least the second highest (i.e., the smaller) true value of the players; while when $n \geq 3$, it is at most the second highest true value. To see more clearly how it compares with the mechanism's revenue when there is no externality, without loss of generality we assume $v_1 \leq v_2 \leq \cdots \leq v_n$. Accordingly, $m_1 = 2$, $m_i = 1$ for any $i \neq 1$, the second highest true value is v_{n-1}, and $rev(2ndP)$ is the second highest in $T = \{\frac{v_1 + \alpha_1 v_2}{1 + \alpha_1}\} \cup \{\frac{v_i + \alpha_i v_1}{1 + \alpha_i}\}_{i \neq 1}$. We have the following corollary.

COROLLARY 1. *As a function of the profile of exchange rates $(\alpha_1, \ldots, \alpha_n)$, $rev(2ndP)$*

1. *is continuous on $(0, 1]^n$;*

2. *is decreasing when $n \geq 3$ and increasing when $n = 2$;*

3. *goes to v_{n-1} when all α_i's go to 0, goes to $\frac{v_{n-1} + v_1}{2}$ when $n \geq 3$ and all α_i's go to 1, and goes to $\frac{v_1 + v_2}{2}$ when $n = 2$ and both α_i's go to 1; and*

4. *is also continuous at $(\alpha_1, \ldots, \alpha_n) = (0, \ldots, 0)$.*

PROOF. Property 1 is true since all the v_i''s are continuous. To see why Property 2 is true, notice that $\frac{v_i + \alpha_i v_1}{1 + \alpha_i}$ is decreasing in α_i for any $i \neq 1$, and $\frac{v_1 + \alpha_1 v_2}{1 + \alpha_1}$ is increasing in α_1. Because

$$\frac{v_1 + \alpha_1 v_2}{1 + \alpha_1} \leq \frac{v_1 + v_2}{2}, \quad \frac{v_1 + v_2}{2} \leq \frac{v_2 + \alpha_2 v_1}{1 + \alpha_2},$$

$$\text{and} \quad \frac{v_1 + v_2}{2} \leq \frac{v_1 + v_i}{2} \leq \frac{v_i + \alpha_i v_1}{1 + \alpha_i} \quad \forall i > 2,$$

we have that $\frac{v_1 + \alpha_1 v_2}{1 + \alpha_1}$ is the smallest in T. Accordingly, when $n \geq 3$, the second highest value in T is the same as the second highest value in $(\frac{v_i + \alpha_i v_1}{1 + \alpha_i})_{i \neq 1}$, which is decreasing in the profile $(\alpha_1, \ldots, \alpha_n)$. When $n = 2$, the second highest value in T is $\frac{v_1 + \alpha_1 v_2}{1 + \alpha_1}$, which is increasing in the profile (α_1, α_2).

Property 3 holds by continuity, and Property 4 holds because v_{n-1} is exactly the revenue when there is no externality (that is, when each player reports his true value). □

We say that the players have *symmetric externality* if there exists α such that $\alpha_i = \alpha$ for each player i. When this is the case, we further have the following corollary, whose proof is omitted.

COROLLARY 2. *When the players have symmetric externality, $rev(2ndP) = \frac{v_{n-1} + \alpha v_1}{1 + \alpha}$ when $n \geq 3$, and $rev(2ndP) = \frac{v_1 + \alpha v_2}{1 + \alpha}$ when $n = 2$.*

5. OUR THIRD RESULT

Now, a natural question raises: if a player knows that his opponents' bids are lower bounded as described above, can he further refine his undominated strategies? In this section, we answer this question by fully characterizing the players' strategies surviving such a 2-step elimination procedure.

More precisely, the solution concept used below is *two-step elimination of weakly dominated strategies*. That is, starting from the strategy set S_i for each player i, all players eliminate all of their weakly dominated strategies; and then, in the new game where the strategy set of each player i is his set of surviving strategies, all players again eliminate all of their weakly dominated strategies. A strategy s_i is *level-2 undominated* if it survives such a two-step elimination procedure. (For a thorough discussion about iterated elimination of dominated strategies, see, e.g., [39].)

In the individually uniformly spiteful model, assume there is a unique player i^* such that $v'_{i^*} = \max_i v'_i$: in particular, this is true when the players are in a generic position.

THEOREM 3. *The revenue of the second-price mechanism at any level-2 undominated strategy profile is at least v'_{i^*}, and this lower bound is tight.*

Theorem 3 follows directly from the following lemma, which is proved in the appendix.

LEMMA 2. *For each player i, a strategy b_i is level-2 undominated if and only if $b_i \geq v'_{i^*}$.*

We denote the lower bound in Theorem 3 by $rev^{(2)}(2ndP)$: that is, $rev^{(2)}(2ndP) = v'_{i^*}$. Again, assuming without loss of generality $v_1 \leq v_2 \leq \cdots \leq v_n$, we have the following corollary.

COROLLARY 3. *As a function of $(\alpha_1, \ldots, \alpha_n)$, $rev^{(2)}(2ndP)$*

1. *is continuous and decreasing on $(0, 1]^n$;*

2. *goes to $\frac{v_n + v_1}{2}$ when all α_i's go to 1, and goes to v_n when all α_i's go to 0; and*

3. *is discontinuous at $(\alpha_1, \ldots, \alpha_n) = (0, \ldots, 0)$.*

In particular, notice that when all α_i's become arbitrarily close to 0 but are still positive, the revenue of the second-price mechanism under level-2 undominated strategies becomes arbitrarily close to the *highest* true value. However, when there is no externality, the revenue is the *second highest* true value (as is well known). Thus, when the players further refine their strategies from their undominated strategies, the existence of externality makes a big difference for the revenue of the second-price mechanism.

What if the players continue refining their strategies based on level-2 undominated strategies? Technically, one can define k-step elimination of weakly dominated strategies and level-k undominated strategies. However, they will not make a difference here: it is not hard to verify that no strategy can be further eliminated from level-2 undominated strategies, thus the revenue guaranteed by the second-price mechanism under level-k undominated strategies with $k > 2$ is still $rev^{(2)}(2ndP)$. Finally, we have the following corollary.

COROLLARY 4. *When the players have symmetric externality, $rev^{(2)}(2ndP) = \frac{v_n + \alpha v_1}{1 + \alpha}$.*

6. OUR FOURTH RESULT

When the players have incomplete information, we consider the *Light-Bayesian Setting*:

- The true value of each player i, v_i, is independently drawn from a distribution $\mathcal{D}_i$. Without loss of generality, $\mathcal{D}_i$ has support $T_i = [\underline{a}_i, \overline{a}_i]$ with $\underline{a}_i \geq 0$, and the probability density function of $\mathcal{D}_i$ is positive on T_i. Let $\mathcal{D} = \times_i \mathcal{D}_i$ and $\mathcal{D}_{-i} \triangleq \times_{j \neq i} \mathcal{D}_j$ for each i.

- Each player i individually knows his own true value, utility-exchange rates, and $\mathcal{D}_{-i}$.

- The auctioneer has no information about $\mathcal{D}$ or the utility-exchange rates of the players.

For a player i to determine whether a strategy s_i is dominated by another strategy s'_i, he need not only know his own true value v_i, but also the others' true value subprofile v_{-i}. This is not a problem if the auction is of complete information, but some care is needed when i only knows $\mathcal{D}_{-i}$.

Revenue under non-Bayesian Undominated Strategies.

Before defining our new solution concept for Bayesian settings, let us first consider an existing notion of weak domination in auctions of incomplete information and with externality [19]. For any player i and value $v_i \in T_i$, a strategy s_i is *weakly dominated* by another strategy s'_i under v_i if, for *every* value subprofile $v_{-i} \in T_{-i}$, s_i is weakly dominated by s'_i when the true value profile is (v_i, v_{-i}).[5] Since this notion does not depend on the distribution $\mathcal{D}$, if a strategy s_i is not weakly dominated by any other strategy under v_i, we say that s_i is *non-Bayesian undominated* under v_i. In the individually uniformly spiteful model, our Proposition 1 below fully characterizes each player's non-Bayesian undominated strategies in the second-price mechanism. The proof is similar to that of Lemma 1 and thus omitted.

PROPOSITION 1. *For any player i and value $v_i \in T_i$, a strategy b_i is non-Bayesian undominated under v_i if and only if $b_i \geq \frac{v_i + \alpha_i \min_{j \neq i} \underline{a}_j}{1 + \alpha_i}$.*

For any profile of reals b, let $Second(b)$ be the second highest value in b. For any distribution $\mathcal{D}$, the expected revenue that the second-price mechanism guarantees under non-Bayesian undominated strategies, denoted by

$$rev_{nonB}(2ndP), \text{ is } \mathbb{E}_{(v_1, \ldots, v_n)} Second\left(\left(\frac{v_i + \alpha_i \min_{j \neq i} \underline{a}_j}{1 + \alpha_i}\right)_{i \in [n]}\right).$$

It is not hard to see that $rev_{nonB}(2ndP) \geq \frac{\mathbb{E} Second((v_i)_{i \in [n]})}{2}$ $\forall n \geq 2$ and $rev_{nonB}(2ndP) \leq \mathbb{E} Second((v_i)_{i \in [n]}) \, \forall n \geq 3$, where $\mathbb{E} Second((v_i)_{i \in [n]})$ is the expected revenue without externality.

Moreover, when there are two players j and j' such that $\underline{a}_j = \underline{a}_{j'} = 0$, we have

$$rev_{nonB}(2ndP) = \mathbb{E}_{(v_1, \ldots, v_n)} Second\left(\left(\frac{v_i}{1 + \alpha_i}\right)_{i \in [n]}\right).$$

That is, even if v_j and $v_{j'}$ are very high with probability close to 1, the expected revenue only depends on their smallest possible value (i.e., 0). With symmetric externality, we

---

[5]The definition in [19] is slightly different: it does not require the utility of s'_i be strictly larger than that of s_i in any case.

further have

$$rev_{nonB}(2ndP) = \frac{1}{1+\alpha} \cdot \mathop{\mathbb{E}}_{(v_1,\ldots,v_n)} Second\left((v_i)_{i\in[n]}\right).$$

Proposition 1 shows that, if the players do not know the distributions of each other and only know the lower bounds of their supports, then the revenue guaranteed by the second-price mechanism is diluted by the smallest value in the support of every player's distribution, and in the worst case it can be a half of the expected revenue when there is no externality.

When a player i does know $\mathcal{D}_{-i}$, it is natural that he will reason about his strategies based on this information. Below, we provide a new solution concept to formalize this reasoning.

Revenue under Bayesian Undominated Strategies.

Our solution concept, *implementation in Bayesian undominated strategies*, generalizes the classical notion of implementation in undominated strategies [27] to the GSU model and the light-Bayesian settings.

For any player i, let $u_i(s_i, s_{-i}; v_i, v_{-i})$ be the utility of i under strategy profile (s_i, s_{-i}) and true value profile (v_i, v_{-i}). A strategy s_i is *weakly Bayesian dominated* by another strategy s_i' under v_i if
(a) $\forall s_{-i} \in S_{-i}$,
$\mathbb{E}_{v_{-i}\sim\mathcal{D}_{-i}} u_i(s_i, s_{-i}; v_i, v_{-i}) \leq \mathbb{E}_{v_{-i}\sim\mathcal{D}_{-i}} u_i(s_i', s_{-i}; v_i, v_{-i})$; and
(b) $\exists s_{-i} \in S_{-i}$ such that
$\mathbb{E}_{v_{-i}\sim\mathcal{D}_{-i}} u_i(s_i, s_{-i}; v_i, v_{-i}) < \mathbb{E}_{v_{-i}\sim\mathcal{D}_{-i}} u_i(s_i', s_{-i}; v_i, v_{-i})$.
When the distribution $\mathcal{D}$ is clear from the context, we may write $\mathbb{E}_{v_{-i}} u_i(\cdot)$ instead of $\mathbb{E}_{v_{-i}\sim\mathcal{D}_{-i}} u_i(\cdot)$. Notice that player i can indeed make the comparisons in (a) and (b), because he knows $\mathcal{D}_{-i}$.

If $s_i \in S_i$ is not weakly Bayesian dominated by any $s_i' \in S_i$ under v_i, then s_i is *Bayesian undominated* under v_i. A *Bayesian strategy* of player i is a function mapping T_i to S_i.[6] Such a strategy $\boldsymbol{s}_i$ is *Bayesian undominated* if, for each $v_i \in T_i$, $\boldsymbol{s}_i(v_i)$ is Bayesian undominated under v_i.

The intuition behind weak Bayesian domination is that, as in any other notion of domination, a player i does not need to believe that his opponents are rational, and considers it possible for them to use arbitrary strategies no matter what their true values are. Thus, seeing a particular strategy subprofile s_{-i} being used does not give player i any posterior information about v_{-i}, and from his point of view, v_{-i} is still distributed according to $\mathcal{D}_{-i}$. Accordingly, player i's perceived utility under strategy profile (s_i, s_{-i}) is $\mathbb{E}_{v_{-i}} u_i(s_i, s_{-i}; v_i, v_{-i})$.

At the highest level, a Bayesian undominated strategy for a player i is any strategy that is 'not blatantly stupid for i to play in light of his knowledge of $\mathcal{D}_{-i}$ and his exchange rates'. Our notion of implementation is then very robust, as it ensures that a desirable outcome occurs for any possible profile of such non-stupid strategies.

---

[6]In general, a Bayesian strategy maps player i's possible *types* to strategies. Thus, strictly speaking, it should map $T_i \times [0,1]^{n-1}$ (i.e., the set of possible values and exchange rates of i) to S_i. However, since only player i's true value is drawn from a distribution, for simplicity we define Bayesian strategies over player i's possible values only. Similarly, we write player i's utility as $u_i(s_i, s_{-i}; v_i, v_{-i})$ instead of $u_i(s_i, s_{-i}; v_i, v_{-i}; \alpha_{i1}, \ldots, \alpha_{in})$.

In the individually uniformly spiteful model, for each player i and value v_i, let $m_i' = \operatorname*{argmin}_{j\neq i} \mathop{\mathbb{E}}_{v_j\sim\mathcal{D}_j} v_j$ and $g_i(v_i) = \frac{v_i + \alpha_i \mathbb{E} v_{m_i'}}{1+\alpha_i}$. We have the following.

THEOREM 4. *The expected revenue of the second-price mechanism under Bayesian undominated strategies is at least*

$$\mathop{\mathbb{E}}_{(v_1,\ldots,v_n)} Second\left((g_i(v_i))_{i\in[n]}\right),$$

and this lower bound is tight.

Theorem 4 follows directly from Lemma 3 below, whose proof is provided in the appendix.

LEMMA 3. *For any player i, a Bayesian strategy $\boldsymbol{b}_i$ is Bayesian undominated if and only if $\boldsymbol{b}_i(v_i) \geq g_i(v_i)$ for each $v_i \in T_i$.*

Notice that for a player i to compute his undominated strategies, he does not even need to know $\mathcal{D}_{-i}$: it is sufficient that he knows the expected values of his opponents.

Let $rev_B(2ndP) = \mathbb{E}_{(v_1,\ldots,v_n)} Second((g_i(v_i))_{i\in[n]})$. When the players have symmetric externality and their true values are i.i.d., we have

$$
\begin{aligned}
rev_B(2ndP) &= \mathop{\mathbb{E}}_{(v_1,\ldots,v_n)} Second\left(\left(\frac{v_i + \alpha\, \mathbb{E} v_1}{1+\alpha}\right)_{i\in[n]}\right) \\
&= \mathop{\mathbb{E}}_{(v_1,\ldots,v_n)} \frac{Second((v_i)_{i\in[n]}) + \alpha\, \mathbb{E} v_1}{1+\alpha} \\
&= \frac{\mathbb{E}_{(v_1,\ldots,v_n)} Second((v_i)_{i\in[n]}) + \alpha\, \mathbb{E} v_1}{1+\alpha}.
\end{aligned}
$$

Similar to what we have seen before, this revenue goes to the expected revenue with no externality when α goes to 0, and goes to the average of the two when α goes to 1.

Following Theorem 4, it is not hard to see that

$$rev_B(2ndP) \geq rev_{nonB}(2ndP)$$

for all $\mathcal{D}$ and α_i's. In the worst case (e.g., when all exchange rates are 1 and when there are two players whose values are 0 with probability 1), $rev_B(2ndP)$ may be as low as $\mathbb{E}\, Second((v_i)_{i\in[n]})/2$. However, different from $rev_{nonB}(2ndP)$ which is upper bounded by $\mathbb{E}\, Second((v_i)_{i\in[n]})$ when $n \geq 3$, $rev_B(2ndP)$ may actually be strictly larger than $\mathbb{E}\, Second((v_i)_{i\in[n]})$.

As an example where $rev_B(2ndP) > \mathbb{E}\, Second(\{v_i\}_{i\in[n]})$, consider the case where $n = 3$, each player's value is 0 with probability 0.99 and 100 with probability 0.01, and $\alpha_i = 1/2$ for each i. We have $\mathbb{E}\, Second(\{v_i\}_{i\in[n]}) \approx 0.03$ and $rev_B(2ndP) \approx 0.35$. Moreover, $rev_{nonB}(2ndP) \approx 0.02$.

Furthermore, as an example where

$$rev_B(2ndP) < \mathbb{E}\, Second((v_i)_{i\in[n]}),$$

consider the case where $n = 9$, all players' values are uniform from $[0, 100]$, and $\alpha_1 = \cdots = \alpha_n = 1/2$. We have $\mathbb{E}\, Second(\{v_i\}_{i\in[n]}) = 80$ and $rev_B(2ndP) = \frac{80+50/2}{3/2} = 70$. Moreover, $rev_{nonB}(2ndP) = 160/3$.

In general, the relation between $rev_B(2ndP)$ and $\mathbb{E}\, Second((v_i)_{i\in[n]})$ depends on the relation between the $(n-1)$st order statistics and the expectations of the $\mathcal{D}_i$'s, which is beyond the scope of this paper.

Remark.

We believe the characterization of Bayesian undominated strategies provided in Lemma 3 to be of interest too, in light of both the centrality of the second-price mechanism in the auction literature and the fact that so little is known about the general spiteful-utility model, whether in undominated strategies, at Bayesian Nash equilibrium, or under other solution concepts.

One might also consider two-step (or more generally, k-step) elimination of dominated strategies in Bayesian auctions with externality. However, the revenue of the second-price mechanism under this solution concept will be much harder to analyze than with complete information. Indeed, in Bayesian auctions a player only knows a distribution over possible sets of surviving strategies of the other players, and can only refine his own set of surviving strategies based on this distribution. We leave the analysis of the second-price mechanism under this solution concept as an open problem.

7. RECURSIVE EXTERNALITY

In the last secion, we briefly discuss an extension of our model, which defines the players' utilities recursively. For any player i, player $j \neq i$ and $k \geq 1$, the *level-k exchange rate* of i about j, α_{ij}^k, is such that $\alpha_{ij}^1 \in (0, 1]$ and $\alpha_{ij}^k \in (0, \alpha_{ij}^{k-1}]$ for any $k > 1$. Given an outcome ω, each player i's *level-0 utility*, $u_i^0(\omega)$, is defined to be his classical utility $cu_i(\omega)$. Recursively, for each $k \geq 1$, each player i's *level-k utility*, $u_i^k(\omega)$, is defined to be $-\sum_{j \neq i} \alpha_{ij}^k u_j^{k-1}(\omega)$. Player i's *utility* is $u_i(\omega) = \sum_{k \geq 0} u_i^k(\omega)$. That is, player i cares about not only the other players' classical utilities, but also the external utilities they get from their opponents' classical utilities (i.e., their level-1 utilities), the external utilities they get from their opponents' level-1 utilities (i.e., their level-2 utilities), etc. However, player i cares less and less about the others' level-k utilities as k increases, which is reflected by the non-increasing sequence $(\alpha_{ij}^1, \alpha_{ij}^2, \ldots)$ for each $j \neq i$.

We say the players have *persistent* externality if for each player i and $j \neq i$, there exists $\alpha_{ij} \in (0, 1]$ such that $\alpha_{ij}^k = \alpha_{ij}$ for all $k \geq 1$. With persistent externality, it is easy to see that

$$
\begin{aligned}
u_i(\omega) &= \sum_{k \geq 0} u_i^k(\omega) = u_i^0(\omega) - \sum_{k \geq 1} \sum_{j \neq i} \alpha_{ij} u_j^{k-1}(\omega) \\
&= u_i^0(\omega) - \sum_{j \neq i} \alpha_{ij} \sum_{k \geq 0} u_j^k(\omega) \\
&= u_i^0(\omega) - \sum_{j \neq i} \alpha_{ij} u_j(\omega),
\end{aligned}
$$

which coincides with the recursive interdependent utility studied in [3], except that in [3] the players are altruistic instead of spiteful.

Let A be the $n \times n$ matrix where $A_{ii} = 0$ for each i and $A_{ij} = -\alpha_{ij}$ for each i and $j \neq i$, $u^0(\omega) = (u_1^0(\omega), \ldots, u_n^0(\omega))^T$, and $u(\omega) = (u_1(\omega), \ldots, u_n(\omega))^T$. We have $u(\omega) = u^0(\omega) + Au(\omega)$. If the matrix $I - A$ is strictly diagonally dominant, namely, $\sum_{j \neq i} \alpha_{ij} < 1$ for each player i, then it is invertible and each $u_i(\omega)$ has a unique closed-form solution which is a linear combination of the players' classical utilities: that is, $u(w) = (I - A)^{-1} u^0(w)$. However, different from [3] where $(I - A)^{-1}$ has all entries non-negative and thus the closed-form utility functions are still altruistic among all players, in our model, $(I - A)^{-1}$ may have both positive and negative

entries off the diagonal, showing that *recursive spitefulness may actually lead to altruism among some players.*[7] Notice that this will never happen when $n = 2$.

We leave it as an open problem to characterize the conditions under which recursive spitefulness leads to spitefulness among all players. All of our results continue to hold in these circumstances.

References

[1] J. Aseff and H. Chade. An optimal auction with identity-dependent externalities. *RAND Journal of Economics*, 39(3):731–746, 2008.

[2] M. Babaioff, R. Kleinberg, and C. H. Papadimitriou. Congestion games with malicious players. In *Proceedings of the 8th ACM Conference on Electronic Commerce (EC '07)*, pages 103–112, 2007.

[3] T. C. Bergstrom. Systems of benevolent utility functions. *Journal of Public Economic Theory*, 1(1):71–100, 1999.

[4] S. Bhattacharya, D. Korzhyk, and V. Conitzer. Computing a profit-maximizing sequence of offers to agents in a social network. In *Proceedings of the 8th international conference on Internet and Network Economics (WINE '12)*, pages 482–488, 2012.

[5] F. Bloch. Sequential formation of coalitions in games with externalities and fixed payoff division. *Games and Economic Behavior*, 14(1):90–123, 1996.

[6] F. Bloch and M. Jackson. The formation of networks with transfers among players. *Journal of Economic Theory*, 133(1):83–110, 2007.

[7] F. Brandt, T. Sandholm, and Y. Shoham. Spiteful bidding in sealed-bid auctions. In *Proceedings of IJCAI'07*, pages 1207–1214, 2007.

[8] J. Bulow, M. Huang, and P. Klemperer. Toeholds and takeovers. *Journal of Political Economy*, 107:427–454, 1999.

[9] B. Caillaud and P. Jéhiel. Collusion in auctions with externalities. *RAND Journal of Economics*, 29(4):680–702, 1998.

[10] T. Calvo-Armengol and M. Jackson. Like father, like son: network externalities, parent-child correlation in behavior, and social mobility. *American Economic Journal: Microeconomics*, 1(1):124–150, 2009.

[11] P. Chen. *The effects of altruism and spite on games.* PhD thesis, University of Southern California, October 2011.

[12] P. Chen and D. Kempe. Altruism, selfishness, and spite in traffic routing. In *Proceedings of the 9th ACM conference on Electronic Commerce (EC '08)*, pages 140–149, 2008.

---

[7]As an example, let $n = 3$ and
$$
A = \begin{bmatrix} 0 & -1/10 & -1/2 \\ -1/100 & 0 & -1/3 \\ -1/4 & -1/10 & 0 \end{bmatrix}.
$$

[13] V. Conitzer and T. Sandholm. Computing optimal outcomes under an expressive representation of settings with externalities. *Journal of Computer and System Sciences (JCSS), Special Issue devoted to Knowledge Representation and Reasoning*, 78(1):2–14, 2012.

[14] F. Constantin, M. Rao, D. C. Parkes, and C. Huang. On expressing value externalities in position auctions. In *Sixth Workshop on Ad Auctions (at EC '10)*, 2010.

[15] G. Deltas. Determining damages from the operation of bidding rings: an analysis of the post-auction "knockout" sale. *Economic Theory*, 19:243–269, 2002.

[16] R. Engelbrecht-Wiggans. Auctions with price-proportional benefits to bidders. *Games and Economic Behavior*, 6:339–346, 1994.

[17] M. Engers and B. McManus. Charity auctions. 2004. Memo.

[18] D. Ettinger. Efficiency in auctions with crossholdings. *Economics Letters*, 80:1–7, 2003.

[19] A. Fiat, A. Karlin, E. Koutsoupias, and A. Vidali. Approaching Utopia: Strong truthfulness and externality-resistant mechanisms. In *Proceedings of the 4th Conference on Innovations in Theoretical Computer Science (ITCS '13)*, pages 221–230, 2013.

[20] S. M. G. Aggarwal, J. Feldman and M. Pál. Sponsored search auctions with Markovian users. In *Proceedings of the 4th Workshop on Internet and Network Economics (WINE '08)*, pages 621–628, 2008.

[21] S. Gasgupta and K. Tsui. Auctions with cross-shareholdings. *Economic Theory*, 24:163–194, 2004.

[22] A. Ghosh and M. Mahdian. Charity auctions on social networks. In *Proceedings of the 19th ACM-SIAM Symposium on Discrete Algorithms (SODA '08)*, pages 1019–1028, 2008.

[23] A. Ghosh and A. Sayedi. Expressive auctions for externalities in online advertising. In *5th Workshop on Ad Auctions (at EC '09)*, 2009.

[24] I. Giotis and A. R. Karlin. On the equilibria and efficiency of the GSP mechanism in keyword auctions with externalities. In *Proceedings of the 4th Workshop on Internet and Network Economics (WINE '08)*, pages 629–638, 2008.

[25] J. K. Goeree, E. Maasland, S. Onderstal, and J. L. Turner. How (not) to raise money. *Journal of Political Economy*, 113(4):897–918, 2005.

[26] R. Gomes, N. Immorlica, and V. Markakis. Externalities in keyword auctions: An empirical and theoretical assessment. In *Fifth Workshop on Ad Auctions (at EC '09)*, 2009.

[27] M. Jackson. Implementation in undominated actions: A look at bounded mechanisms. *The Review of Economic Studies*, 59(4):757–775, 1992.

[28] P. Jehiel and B. Moldovanu. Auctions with downstream interaction among buyers. *RAND Journal of Economics*, 31:768–791, 2000.

[29] P. Jehiel, B. Moldovanu, and E. Stacchetti. How (not) to sell nuclear weapons. *American Economic Review*, 86(4):814–829, 1996.

[30] P. Jehiel, B. Moldovanu, and E. Stacchetti. Multidimensional mechanism design for auctions with externalities. *Journal of Economic Theorey*, 85:258–283, 1999.

[31] S. E. Jeong. Multidimensional second-price and english auctions. Job Market Paper, 2015.

[32] D. Kempe and M. Mahdian. A cascade model for externalities in sponsored search. In *Proceedings of the 4th Workshop on Internet and Network Economics (WINE '08)*, pages 585–596, 2008.

[33] P. Krysta, T. Michalak, T. Sandholm, and M. Wooldridge. Combinatorial auctions with externalities (extended abstract). In *Proceedings of the 9th International Joint Conference on Autonomous Agents and Multi-Agent Systems (AAMAS '10)*, pages 10–14, 2010.

[34] J. O. Ledyard. Public goods: A survey of experimental research. In J. H. Kagel and A. E. Roth, editors, *The Handbook of Experimental Economics*, pages 111–193. Princeton University Press, 1997.

[35] D. K. Levine. Modeling altruism and spitefulness in experiments. *Review of Economic Dynamics*, 1(3):593–622, 1998.

[36] J. Lu. Optimal auctions with asymmetric financial externalities. *Games and Economic Behavior*, 74(2):561–575, 2012.

[37] E. Maasland and S. Onderstal. Auctions with financial externalities. *Economic Theory*, 32(3):551–574, 2007.

[38] I. Macho-Stadler, D. Pérez-Castrillo, and D. Wettstein. Sharing the surplus: An extension of the Shapley value for environments with externalities. *Journla of Economic Theory*, 135(1):339–356, 2007.

[39] M. Osborne and A. Rubinstein. *A Course in Game Theory*. MIT Press, 1994.

[40] D. Parkes and T. Sandholm. Optimize-and-dispatch architecture for expressive Ad auctions. In *First Workshop on Sponsored Search Auctions (at EC '05)*, 2005.

[41] D. H. Reiley, S. Li, and R. A. Lewis. Northern exposure: A field experiment measuring externalities between search advertisements. In *Proceedings of the ACM Conference on Electronic Commerce (EC '10)*, pages 297–304, 2010.

[42] A. Roth. The price of malice in linear congestion games. In *Proceedings of the 4th Workshop on Internet and Network Economics (WINE '08)*, pages 118–125, 2008.

[43] P. Tang and T. Sandholm. Optimal auctions for spiteful bidders. In *Proceedings of the Twenty-Sixth AAAI Conference on Artificial Intelligence (AAAI)*, 2012.

[44] G. D. Varma. Standard auctions with identity-dependent externalities. *RAND Journal of Economics*, 33:689–708, 2002.

[45] S. Yi. Stable coalition structures with externalities. *Games and Economic Behavior*, 20(2):201–237, 1997.

APPENDIX

Proofs of Theorem 1 and Lemmas 1, 2, and 3

Theorem 1. (restated) *For any $n \geq 2$ and $P > 0$, in mechanism M_P, it is strictly dominant for each player to announce 1; and the revenue of M_P under the strategy profile $(1, 1, \ldots, 1)$ is at least P.*

PROOF. For any player $i \notin \{1, 2\}$ and strategy subprofile b_{-i}, notice that the only difference between the outcomes of strategy profiles $(1, b_{-i})$ and $(0, b_{-i})$ is that, in the former player i gets a payment equal to 1, while in the latter he gets 0. Indeed, for each player $j \notin \{1, 2, i\}$, j's price only depends on b_j; and the prices of players 1 and 2 only depend on b_1 and b_2. Accordingly, $cu_i(1, b_{-i}) - cu_i(0, b_{-i}) = 1$ and, for each $j \neq i$, $cu_j(1, b_{-i}) = cu_j(0, b_{-i})$. Thus

$$
\begin{aligned}
&u_i(1, b_{-i}) - u_i(0, b_{-i}) \\
&= \left(cu_i(1, b_{-i}) - \sum_{j \neq i} \alpha_{ij} cu_j(1, b_{-i}) \right) \\
&\quad - \left(cu_i(0, b_{-i}) - \sum_{j \neq i} \alpha_{ij} cu_j(0, b_{-i}) \right) \\
&= cu_i(1, b_{-i}) - cu_i(0, b_{-i}) = 1 > 0,
\end{aligned}
$$

and it is strictly dominant for player i to announce 1.

For player 1 and any strategy subprofile b_{-1}, if $b_2 = 0$ then, similar as above, we have $cu_1(1, b_{-1}) = 1$, $cu_1(0, b_{-1}) = 0$, and for each $i \neq 1$, $cu_i(1, b_{-1}) = cu_i(0, b_{-1}) = b_i$. Thus

$$
\begin{aligned}
&u_1(1, b_{-1}) - u_1(0, b_{-1}) \\
&= cu_1(1, b_{-1}) - cu_1(0, b_{-1}) = 1 > 0. \quad (1)
\end{aligned}
$$

If $b_2 = 1$, then by announcing 0 player 1 enables player 2 to get a payment equal to $\frac{P+n}{\ell}$, while he himself gets 0. Thus

$$
\begin{aligned}
u_1(0, b_{-1}) &= cu_1(0, b_{-1}) - \sum_{i \neq 1} \alpha_{1i} cu_i(0, b_{-1}) \\
&= 0 - \alpha_{12} \cdot \frac{P+n}{\ell} - \sum_{i \neq 1, 2} \alpha_{1i} b_i \\
&\leq -P - n - \sum_{i \neq 1, 2} \alpha_{1i} b_i. \quad (2)
\end{aligned}
$$

If player 1 announces 1 instead, then he pays $P + n - 1$ and player 2 gets $\frac{1}{2}$. Thus

$$
\begin{aligned}
u_1(1, b_{-1}) &= cu_1(1, b_{-1}) - \sum_{i \neq 1} \alpha_{1i} cu_i(1, b_{-1}) \\
&= -P - n + 1 - \frac{\alpha_{12}}{2} - \sum_{i \neq 1, 2} \alpha_{1i} b_i. \quad (3)
\end{aligned}
$$

By Equations 2 and 3, when $b_2 = 1$,

$$
u_1(1, b_{-1}) - u_1(0, b_{-1}) \geq 1 - \frac{\alpha_{12}}{2} \geq \frac{1}{2} > 0. \quad (4)
$$

By Equations 1 and 4, it is strictly dominant for player 1 to announce 1.

Next, for player 2 and any strategy subprofile b_{-2}, if player 2 announces 0, then his utility is

$$
u_2(0, b_{-2}) = cu_2(0, b_{-2}) - \sum_{i \neq 2} \alpha_{2i} cu_i(0, b_{-2}) = -\sum_{i \neq 2} \alpha_{2i} b_i.
$$

If player 2 announces 1 while $b_1 = 0$, then player 2 gets $\frac{P+n}{\ell}$ and player 1 gets $0 = b_1$, thus

$$
\begin{aligned}
u_2(1, b_{-2}) &= cu_2(1, b_{-2}) - \sum_{i \neq 2} \alpha_{2i} cu_i(1, b_{-2}) \\
&= \frac{P+n}{\ell} - \sum_{i \neq 2} \alpha_{2i} b_i \\
&> -\sum_{i \neq 2} \alpha_{2i} b_i = u_2(0, b_{-2}). \quad (5)
\end{aligned}
$$

If player 2 announces 1 while $b_1 = 1$, then player 1 pays $P + n - 1$ and player 2 gets $\frac{1}{2}$, thus

$$
\begin{aligned}
u_2(1, b_{-2}) &= cu_2(1, b_{-2}) - \sum_{i \neq 2} \alpha_{2i} cu_i(1, b_{-2}) \\
&= \frac{1}{2} + \alpha_{21} \cdot (P + n - 1) - \sum_{i \neq 1, 2} \alpha_{2i} b_i \\
&> -\sum_{i \neq 1, 2} \alpha_{2i} b_i \geq -\sum_{i \neq 2} \alpha_{2i} b_i \\
&= u_2(0, b_{-2}), \quad (6)
\end{aligned}
$$

where the inequalities are because $\alpha_{21} \geq 0$. By Equations 5 and 6, it is strictly dominant for player 2 to announce 1.

In sum, the strategy profile $s = (1, 1, \ldots, 1)$ is strictly dominant. It is easy to see that the revenue of M_P at s is

$$
(P + n - 1) - \frac{1}{2} - \sum_{i \neq 1, 2} b_i = P + n - \frac{3}{2} - (n - 2) > P,
$$

and Theorem 1 holds. $\square$

Lemma 1. (restated) *For each player i, a strategy b_i is undominated if and only if $b_i \geq v_i'$.*

PROOF. We first show that

if $b_i < v_i'$ then b_i is weakly dominated by v_i'.

To do so, arbitrarily fix a strategy subprofile b_{-i}. If player i gets the good under both (b_i, b_{-i}) and (v_i', b_{-i}), then under both strategy profiles his price is $\max_{j \neq i} b_j$ and all other players' prices are 0. Thus $cu_i(b_i, b_{-i}) = cu_i(v_i', b_{-i}) = v_i - \max_{j \neq i} b_j$ and $cu_j(b_i, b_{-i}) = cu_j(v_i', b_{-i}) = 0$ for any $j \neq i$. Accordingly,

$$
\begin{aligned}
u_i(v_i', b_{-i}) &= cu_i(v_i', b_{-i}) - \alpha_i \sum_{j \neq i} cu_j(v_i', b_{-i}) \\
&= cu_i(b_i, b_{-i}) - \alpha_i \sum_{j \neq i} cu_j(b_i, b_{-i}) \\
&= u_i(b_i, b_{-i}). \quad (7)
\end{aligned}
$$

If player i gets the good in neither (b_i, b_{-i}) nor (v_i', b_{-i}), then the winner w is the same under both strategy profiles. Furthermore, if

$$
v_i' \leq \max_{j \neq w, i} b_j,
$$

then under both strategy profiles the winner's price is $\max_{j \neq w, i} b_j$ and all other players' prices are 0. Thus

$cu_w(b_i, b_{-i}) = cu_w(v'_i, b_{-i}) = v_w - \max_{j \neq w, i} b_j$ and $cu_j(b_i, b_{-i}) = cu_j(v'_i, b_{-i}) = 0$ for all $j \neq w$. Accordingly, we again have

$$u_i(v'_i, b_{-i}) = u_i(b_i, b_{-i}). \tag{8}$$

If player i gets the good in neither (b_i, b_{-i}) nor (v'_i, b_{-i}), but

$$v'_i > \max_{j \neq w, i} b_j,$$

then w's price is v'_i under (v'_i, b_{-i}) and $\max_{j \neq w} b_j$ under (b_i, b_{-i}). Since $v'_i > b_i$ by assumption, we have $v'_i > \max\{b_i, \max_{j \neq w, i} b_j\} = \max_{j \neq w} b_j$. Thus

$$cu_w(v'_i, b_{-i}) = v_w - v'_i < v_w - \max_{j \neq w} b_j = cu_w(b_i, b_{-i}).$$

Moreover, $cu_j(b_i, b_{-i}) = cu_j(v'_i, b_{-i}) = 0$ for all $j \neq w$. Accordingly,

$$\begin{aligned} u_i(v'_i, b_{-i}) &= -\alpha_i cu_w(v'_i, b_{-i}) \\ &> -\alpha_i cu_w(b_i, b_{-i}) = u_i(b_i, b_{-i}). \end{aligned} \tag{9}$$

The last case we need to consider is when player i does not get the good under (b_i, b_{-i}) but gets it under (v'_i, b_{-i}). Let w be the winner under (b_i, b_{-i}) and p_w his price. We have

$$b_i \leq \max_{j \neq w} b_j = p_w \leq b_w = \max_{j \neq i} b_j \leq v'_i,$$

where the first inequality is because $w \neq i$ and the last one is because i is the highest bidder in (v'_i, b_{-i}). Thus

$$\begin{aligned} u_i(b_i, b_{-i}) &= -\alpha_i cu_w(b_i, b_{-i}) = -\alpha_i(v_w - p_w) \\ &\leq -\alpha_i(v_{m_i} - v'_i) \\ &= -\alpha_i \left[v_{m_i} - \frac{v_i + \alpha_i v_{m_i}}{1 + \alpha_i} \right] \\ &= \frac{\alpha_i(v_i - v_{m_i})}{1 + \alpha_i}, \end{aligned} \tag{10}$$

where the first equality is because $cu_j(b_i, b_{-i}) = 0$ for any $j \neq w$, and the inequality is because $v_w \geq \min_{j \neq i} v_j = v_{m_i}$ and $p_w \leq v'_i$. Moreover,

$$\begin{aligned} u_i(v'_i, b_{-i}) &= cu_i(v'_i, b_{-i}) = v_i - b_w \geq v_i - v'_i \\ &= v_i - \frac{v_i + \alpha_i v_{m_i}}{1 + \alpha_i} = \frac{\alpha_i(v_i - v_{m_i})}{1 + \alpha_i}, \end{aligned} \tag{11}$$

where the first equality is because $cu_j(v'_i, b_{-i}) = 0$ for any $j \neq i$, the second equality is because the price of i under (v'_i, b_{-i}) is $\max_{j \neq i} b_j = b_w$, and the inequality is because $b_w \leq v'_i$. By Equations 10 and 11, we have

$$u_i(v'_i, b_{-i}) \geq u_i(b_i, b_{-i}) \tag{12}$$

in this case.

Combining Equations 7, 8, 9 and 12, we have that b_i is weakly dominated by v'_i, as we wanted to show. It remains to prove that,

for any strategy $b_i \geq v'_i$, b_i is not weakly dominated by any other strategy b'_i.

To see why this is true, arbitrarily fix a strategy b'_i. If $b'_i < b_i$, then let b_{-i} be a strategy subprofile such that (1) $b_w > b_i$ where $w = \text{argmax}_{j \neq i} b_j$, and (2) $\max_{j \neq i, w} b_j \leq b'_i$. That is, the highest bid of all the other players is larger than b_i, but the second highest is at most b'_i. Accordingly, player

w gets the good under both (b_i, b_{-i}) and (b'_i, b_{-i}), with price b_i in the former and b'_i in the latter. All other players always have price 0 and classical utility 0. Thus

$$\begin{aligned} u_i(b_i, b_{-i}) &= -\alpha_i cu_w(b_i, b_{-i}) = -\alpha_i(v_w - b_i) \\ &> -\alpha_i(v_w - b'_i) \\ &= -\alpha_i cu_w(b'_i, b_{-i}) = u_i(b'_i, b_{-i}), \end{aligned} \tag{13}$$

and b_i is not weakly dominated by b'_i.

If $b'_i > b_i$, then let b_{-i} be such that $\max_{j \neq i, m_i} b_j \leq b_i < b_{m_i} < b'_i$. By construction, player m_i gets the good at price b_i under (b_i, b_{-i}), and player i gets the good at price b_{m_i} under (b'_i, b_{-i}). Again, all players who do not get the good have classical utility 0. Thus

$$\begin{aligned} u_i(b_i, b_{-i}) &= -\alpha_i cu_{m_i}(b_i, b_{-i}) = -\alpha_i(v_{m_i} - b_i) \\ &\geq -\alpha_i(v_{m_i} - v'_i) = -\alpha_i \left[v_{m_i} - \frac{v_i + \alpha_i v_{m_i}}{1 + \alpha_i} \right] \\ &= \frac{\alpha_i(v_i - v_{m_i})}{1 + \alpha_i} \end{aligned}$$

and

$$\begin{aligned} u_i(b'_i, b_{-i}) &= cu_i(b'_i, b_{-i}) = v_i - b_{m_i} \\ &< v_i - v'_i = v_i - \frac{v_i + \alpha_i v_{m_i}}{1 + \alpha_i} \\ &= \frac{\alpha_i(v_i - v_{m_i})}{1 + \alpha_i}, \end{aligned}$$

where the inequalities are because $v'_i \leq b_i < b_{m_i}$. Combining these two inequalities, we again have

$$u_i(b_i, b_{-i}) > u_i(b'_i, b_{-i}), \tag{14}$$

and b_i is not weakly dominated by b'_i.

By Equations 13 and 14, b_i is not weakly dominated by any other strategy b'_i, as we wanted to show. In sum, b_i is undominated if and only if $b_i \geq v'_i$, and Lemma 1 holds. $\square$

Lemma 2. (restated) *For each player i, a strategy b_i is level-2 undominated if and only if $b_i \geq v'_{i^*}$.*

PROOF. For each player i, let S'_i be his set of strategies surviving the first-step elimination of weakly dominated strategies. By Lemma 1, we have $S'_i = \{b_i \mid b_i \geq v'_i\}$.

First, for any player $i \neq i^*$ and any strategy $b_i \in [v'_i, v'_{i^*})$, we show that

b_i is weakly dominated in the game with strategy space $S' = S'_1 \times S'_2 \times \cdots \times S'_n$.

To do so, let b'_i be a strategy such that

$$b'_i \in (\max_{j \neq i^*} v'_j, v'_{i^*}) \cap (b_i, v'_{i^*}).$$

Notice that, since i^* is unique, we have $\max_{j \neq i^*} v'_j < v'_{i^*}$ and such a b'_i exists. Arbitrarily fix a strategy subprofile $b_{-i} \in S'_{-i}$. Since $b_{i^*} \in S'_{i^*}$, we have $b_{i^*} \geq v'_{i^*} > b'_i > b_i$, and player i gets the good in neither (b_i, b_{-i}) nor (b'_i, b_{-i}). Thus the winner of the good under both strategy profiles is the same, denoted by player w (who may or may not be player i^*). Below, we compare $u_i(b_i, b_{-i})$ and $u_i(b'_i, b_{-i})$ by distinguishing two cases for b_{-i}.

When $b_{-i} = v'_{-i}$, we have that: (1) $w = i^*$; (2) the price of w under (b_i, b_{-i}) is

$$p_w = \max_{j \neq w} b_j = \max\{b_i, \max_{j \neq i^*, i} v'_j\} = \max\{b_i, \max_{j \neq i^*} v'_j\},$$

where the third equality is because $v_i' \leq b_i$; and (3) the price of w under (b_i', b_{-i}) is

$$p_w' = b_i',$$

since $b_i' > \max_{j \neq i^*} v_j' \geq \max_{j \neq i^*, i} v_j' = \max_{j \neq i^*, i} b_j$. Because $b_i' > b_i$ and $b_i' > \max_{j \neq i^*} v_j'$ by definition, we have $p_w < p_w'$, and thus

$$cu_{i^*}(b_i, b_{-i}) = v_{i^*} - p_w > v_{i^*} - p_w' = cu_{i^*}(b_i', b_{-i}).$$

Accordingly,

$$
\begin{aligned}
u_i(b_i, b_{-i}) &= -\alpha_i cu_{i^*}(b_i, b_{-i}) \\
&< -\alpha_i cu_{i^*}(b_i', b_{-i}) = u_i(b_i', b_{-i}). \quad (15)
\end{aligned}
$$

For any other $b_{-i} \in S_{-i}'$, we have $p_w \leq p_w'$, since $b_i' > b_i$ and all of the other players' bids remain the same under the two strategy profiles. Accordingly, $cu_w(b_i, b_{-i}) \geq cu_w(b_i', b_{-i})$ and

$$
\begin{aligned}
u_i(b_i, b_{-i}) &= -\alpha_i cu_w(b_i, b_{-i}) \\
&\leq -\alpha_i cu_w(b_i', b_{-i}) = u_i(b_i', b_{-i}). \quad (16)
\end{aligned}
$$

By Equations 15 and 16, we have that b_i is weakly dominated by b_i' in the game with strategy space S', as we wanted to show.

Next, for any player $i \neq i^*$ and any strategy $b_i \geq v_{i^*}'$, we show that

b_i is not weakly dominated in the game
with strategy space S'.

We distinguish two cases.

On the one hand, for any strategy $b_i' \in [v_i', b_i)$, consider the strategy subprofile b_{-i} such that $b_{i^*} > b_i$ and $b_j = v_j'$ for any $j \notin \{i, i^*\}$. Clearly, $b_{-i} \in S_{-i}'$. Because

$$b_{i^*} > b_i \geq v_{i^*}' > \max_{j \neq i^*, i} v_j' = \max_{j \neq i^*, i} b_j,$$

player i^* gets the good under both strategy profile (b_i, b_{-i}) and (b_i', b_{-i}). Moreover, his price under the former is

$$p_{i^*} = \max\{b_i, \max_{j \neq i^*, i} b_j\} = b_i,$$

and that under the latter is

$$p_{i^*}' = \max\{b_i', \max_{j \neq i^*, i} b_j\} = \max\{b_i', \max_{j \neq i^*, i} v_j'\} < b_i = p_{i^*}.$$

Accordingly, $cu_{i^*}(b_i, b_{-i}) = v_{i^*} - p_{i^*} < v_{i^*} - p_{i^*}' = cu_{i^*}(b_i', b_{-i})$, and

$$
\begin{aligned}
u_i(b_i, b_{-i}) &= -\alpha_i cu_{i^*}(b_i, b_{-i}) \\
&> -\alpha_i cu_{i^*}(b_i', b_{-i}) = u_i(b_i', b_{-i}). \quad (17)
\end{aligned}
$$

Thus, for any strategy $b_i' \in [v_i', b_i)$, b_i' does not weakly dominate b_i in the game with strategy space S'.

On the other hand, for any strategy $b_i' > b_i$, consider the strategy subprofile b_{-i} such that $b_{m_i} \in (b_i, b_i')$ and $b_j = v_j'$ for any $j \notin \{i, m_i\}$. Again we have $b_{-i} \in S_{-i}'$. Because

$$b_{m_i} > b_i \geq v_{i^*}' = \max_j v_j' \geq \max_{j \neq m_i, i} v_j' = \max_{j \neq m_i, i} b_j,$$

player m_i gets the good under strategy profile (b_i, b_{-i}) with price b_i. Accordingly,

$$
\begin{aligned}
u_i(b_i, b_{-i}) &= -\alpha_i cu_{m_i}(b_i, b_{-i}) = -\alpha_i(v_{m_i} - b_i) \\
&> -\alpha_i(v_{m_i} - v_i') = -\alpha_i \left[v_{m_i} - \frac{v_i + \alpha_i v_{m_i}}{1 + \alpha_i} \right] \\
&= \frac{\alpha_i(v_i - v_{m_i})}{1 + \alpha_i},
\end{aligned}
$$

where the inequality is because $b_i \geq v_{i^*}' > v_i'$. Furthermore, since $b_i' > b_{m_i}$, player i gets the good under strategy profile (b_i', b_{-i}) with price b_{m_i}. Thus

$$
\begin{aligned}
u_i(b_i', b_{-i}) &= cu_i(b_i', b_{-i}) = v_i - b_{m_i} < v_i - b_i \\
&< v_i - v_i' = v_i - \frac{v_i + \alpha_i v_{m_i}}{1 + \alpha_i} \\
&= \frac{\alpha_i(v_i - v_{m_i})}{1 + \alpha_i} < u_i(b_i, b_{-i}), \quad (18)
\end{aligned}
$$

and such a b_i' does not weakly dominate b_i in the game with strategy space S'.

By Equations 17 and 18, b_i is not weakly dominated in the game with strategy space S', as we wanted to show. Accordingly, for any player $i \neq i^*$, a strategy b_i is level-2 undominated if and only if $b_i \geq v_{i^*}'$.

Finally, it remains to show that for player i^* and any strategy $b_{i^*} \geq v_{i^*}'$,

b_{i^*} is not weakly dominated by any strategy b_{i^*}' in the game
with strategy space S'.

For any strategy $b_{i^*}' \in [v_{i^*}', b_{i^*})$, the analysis is very similar to the deduction of Inequality 17 (under the case where $i \neq i^*$, $b_i \geq v_{i^*}'$, and $b_i' \in [v_i', b_i)$). For any strategy $b_{i^*}' > b_{i^*}$, the analysis is very similar to the deduction of Inequality 18 (under the case where $i \neq i^*$, $b_i \geq v_{i^*}'$, and $b_i' > b_i$). Thus the detailed analysis for this part is omitted.

In sum, Lemma 2 holds. $\square$

Lemma 3. (restated) *For any player i, a Bayesian strategy $\mathbf{b}_i$ is Bayesian undominated if and only if $\mathbf{b}_i(v_i) \geq g_i(v_i)$ for each $v_i \in T_i$.*

PROOF. It suffices to prove that for any $v_i \in T_i$, a strategy b_i is Bayesian undominated under v_i if and only if $b_i \geq g_i(v_i)$. To see why this is true, notice that for any strategy b_i and strategy subprofile b_{-i}, the mechanism's outcome under (b_i, b_{-i}) does not depend on the true values. Let w be the winner under this strategy profile and p_w his price. We have that for any value subprofile v_{-i}, $u_i(b_i, b_{-i}; v_i, v_{-i}) = v_i - p_w$ if $w = i$, and $u_i(b_i, b_{-i}; v_i, v_{-i}) = -\alpha_i cu_w(b_i, b_{-i}; v_i, v_{-i}) = -\alpha_i(v_w - p_w)$ otherwise. Accordingly,

$$\mathbb{E}_{v_{-i}} u_i(b_i, b_{-i}; v_i, v_{-i}) = v_i - p_w$$

if $w = i$, and

$$\mathbb{E}_{v_{-i}} u_i(b_i, b_{-i}; v_i, v_{-i}) = -\alpha_i \mathbb{E}_{v_w}(v_w - p_w) = -\alpha_i(\mathbb{E} v_w - p_w)$$

otherwise. That is, player i's expected utility under strategy profile (b_i, b_{-i}) in the Bayesian auction is exactly his utility under the same strategy profile in the auction of complete information where his true value is v_i and, for any $j \neq i$, player j's true value is $\mathbb{E} v_j$. Therefore b_i is weakly Bayesian dominated under v_i in the Bayesian auction if and only if it is weakly dominated in the auction of complete information with true value profile $(v_i, (\mathbb{E} v_j)_{j \neq i})$. By Lemma 1, we immediately have that b_i is Bayesian undominated under v_i if and only if $b_i \geq g_i(v_i)$, and Lemma 3 holds. $\square$

How to Incentivize Data-Driven Collaboration Among Competing Parties

[Extended Abstract] *

Pablo Daniel Azar[†]
MIT

Shafi Goldwasser[‡]
MIT and Weizmann

Sunoo Park[‡]
MIT

32 Vassar Street
Cambridge, MA 02139, USA
{azar,shafi,sunoo}@csail.mit.edu

ABSTRACT

The availability of vast amounts of data is changing how we can make medical discoveries, predict global market trends, save energy, and develop new educational strategies. In certain settings such as Genome Wide Association Studies or deep learning, the sheer size of data (patient files or labeled examples) seems critical to making discoveries. When data is held distributedly by many parties, as often is the case, they must share it to reap its full benefits.

One obstacle is the reluctance of different entities to share their data, due to privacy concerns or loss of competitive edge. Work on cryptographic multi-party computation over the last 30 years address the privacy aspects, but sheds no light on individual parties' losses and gains when access to data carries tangible rewards. Even if it is clear that better overall conclusions can be drawn from collaboration, are individual collaborators better off by collaborating? Addressing this question is the topic of this paper.

The *order* in which collaborators receive the outputs of a collaboration will be a crucial aspect of our modeling and solutions. We believe that timing is an important and unaddressed issue in data-based collaborations.

Our contributions are as follows. We formalize a model of n-party collaboration for computing functions over private inputs in which the participants receive their outputs in sequence, and the order depends on their private inputs. Each output "improves" on all previous outputs according to a reward function. We say that a mechanism for collaboration achieves a *collaborative equilibrium* if it guarantees a higher reward for all participants when joining a collaboration compared to not joining it. We show that while in general computing a collaborative equilibrium is NP-complete, we can design polynomial-time algorithms for computing it for a range of natural model settings. When possible, we design mechanisms to compute a distribution of outputs and an ordering of output delivery, based on the n participants' private inputs, which achieves a collaborative equilibrium.

The collaboration mechanisms we develop are in the standard model, and thus require a central trusted party; however, we show that this assumption is not necessary under standard cryptographic assumptions. We show how the mechanisms can be implemented in a decentralized way by n distrustful parties using new extensions of classical secure multiparty computation that impose order and timing constraints on the delivery of outputs to different players, in addition to guaranteeing privacy and correctness.

1. INTRODUCTION

The availability of vast amounts of data is affecting how we can make medical discoveries, predict global market trends, save energy, improve our infrastructures, and develop new educational strategies. Indeed, it is is becoming clearer that *sample size* may be the most important factor in making surprising new discoveries, in areas such as *genome-wide association studies* (GWAS) in order to identify genetic variants that are associated with a given trait [7, 18, 11][1] and the success of deep learning in *machine learning*.

When large amounts of data are required, parts of the data are often held by different entities. Such entities need to share their data, or at least engage in a collaborative computation where each entity manages its own private data, in order for society to reap the benefit of large sample sizes. Referring back to the GWAS example, success is often explicitly attributed to such collaboration: "The schizophrenia study was made possible due to unusually large scale collaborations among many institutes... This level of cooperation between institutions is absolutely essential... If we are to continue elucidating the biology of psychiatric disease through genomic research, we must continue to work together." [15]

*Full version of this paper: http://eprint.iacr.org/2015/178

[†]Research supported by Robert Solow Fellowship 3310100.

[‡]Research supported by NSF Eager CNS-1347364, NSF Frontier CNS-1413920, the Simons Foundation (agreement dated June 5, 2012), Air Force Laboratory FA8750-11-2-0225, and Lincoln Lab PO7000261954. This work was done in part while these authors were visiting the Simons Institute for the Theory of Computing, supported by the Simons Foundation and by the DIMACS/Simons Collaboration in Cryptography through NSF grant CNS-1523467.

Permission to make digital or hard copies of all or part of this work for personal or classroom use is granted without fee provided that copies are not made or distributed for profit or commercial advantage and that copies bear this notice and the full citation on the first page. Copyrights for components of this work owned by others than the author(s) must be honored. Abstracting with credit is permitted. To copy otherwise, or republish, to post on servers or to redistribute to lists, requires prior specific permission and/or a fee. Request permissions from Permissions@acm.org.

ITCS'16, January 14 - 16, 2016, Cambridge, MA, USA

© 2016 Copyright held by the owner/author(s). Publication rights licensed to ACM.
ISBN 978-1-4503-4057-1/16/01...$15.00

DOI: http://dx.doi.org/10.1145/2840728.2840758

[1]This is quite striking in the success of GWAS studies with large samples for schizophrenia. "Dramatic increase in patient data size enabled the discovery of more than 100 gene loci associated with the disease up from a handful loci seen with small sets of patients. This was made possible due to an unusually large scale collaborations among many institutes."

The above example seems an exception rather than the rule. A major obstacle to the big-data revolution is so-called "data hoarding". One reason is privacy concerns, where parties refuse to collaborate in order to protect the privacy of their data. Privacy, however, is not the only obstacle.

An equally important obstacle is competition between entities holding data. When access to data carries tangible rewards (say, if the entities are companies competing for a share of the same market or research laboratories competing for scientific credit), it is unclear whether an individual collaborator is better off by collaborating, even if it is clear that better overall conclusions can be drawn from collaboration. Stated in more game-theoretic terms, the entities face the following dilemma which is the topic of this paper: *whereas the overall societal benefit of collaboration is clear, the utility for an individual collaborator may be negative, so why collaborate?*

In Section 2, we present a formal model for collaboration in which this question can be analyzed, as well as design mechanisms to enable collaboration where all collaborators are provably "better off", when possible. The *order* in which collaborators receive the outputs of a collaboration will be a crucial aspect of our model and mechanisms. For example, in the scientific research community, data sharing can translate to losing a prior publication date. In financial enterprises, the timing of investments and stock trading can translate to large financial gains or losses.

We show in Section 3 that the collaboration mechanisms we develop can be implemented in a decentralized way by n distrustful parties even in the presence of a subset of colluding polynomial time parties who may deviate in an arbitrary fashion, under standard cryptographic assumptions. To achieve this we extend the theory of multi-party computation (MPC) to impose order and time on the delivery of outputs to different players.

1.1 Detailed summary of contributions

1.1.1 A model of collaboration

We propose a model for collaboration which enables the determination of whether the utility obtained by a collaborator outweighs the utility he may obtain without collaboration. The ultimate desired outcome of a collaboration is to learn a parameter of the (unknown) joint distribution from which the participants' input data $x_1, \ldots, x_n$ is drawn. This can be expressed as $y^* = f(\mathcal{X})$ where $\mathcal{X}$ is the joint distribution of input data and f is a known function. In our model, the outcome of a collaboration is a pair $(\pi, \vec{\mathcal{Z}})$ where π is a permutation of player identities and $\vec{\mathcal{Z}} = (\mathcal{Z}_1, \ldots, \mathcal{Z}_n)$ where each $\mathcal{Z}_{\pi(i)}$ is a distribution that corresponds to player i's "estimate" of y^*. We think of $\mathcal{Z}_{\pi(i)}$ as the public output of player i: for example, in the setting of scientific collaboration, $\mathcal{Z}_{\pi(i)}$ would be player i's academic publication. Our model setup assumes an underlying score function which assigns scores to the players' outputs.

The model includes a *reward function* R_t which characterizes the gain in utility for any given party i in a collaboration. The reward that a party i gets depends on how much his score $s(\mathcal{Z}_{\pi(i)})$ *improves* on the previous state of the art $s(\mathcal{Z}_{\pi(i)-1})$, and on $\pi(i)$, namely, *when* the party makes his public output. Specifically, the reward function includes a multiplicative *discount factor* β^t where $\beta \in [0, 1]$ and t is the time of publication, meaning that the reward from a publication is "discounted" more as time goes on.

$$R_t(\pi, \vec{\mathcal{Z}}) = \beta^t \cdot (s(\mathcal{Z}_{\pi(t-1)}) - s(\mathcal{Z}_{\pi(t)}))$$

To determine whether the utility of collaboration outweighs the utility of working alone, our model uses "outside payoff" values α_i which are the score that party i would obtain *without collaborating*. α_i can be computed directly from the input x_i of party i.

1.1.2 Mechanisms and collaborative equilibrium

We define a notion of *collaborative equilibrium* in which all parties are guaranteed non-negative reward, and develop *mechanisms* for collaboration that compute such equilibria. When an equilibrium exists, our mechanism delivers a sequence of progressively improving "partial information" about y^* to the collaborating parties. More specifically, the mechanism takes as input the data of all parties, and outputs a pair $(\pi, \vec{\mathcal{Y}})$ where π is a permutation of player identities and $\vec{\mathcal{Y}} = (\mathcal{Y}_1, \ldots, \mathcal{Y}_n)$ specifies the outcomes to be delivered to the players: each $\mathcal{Y}_{\pi(i)}$ is the approximation to y^* that is given to player i at time-step $\pi(i)$, such that the score of the outputs is increasing with time. That is, $s(\mathcal{Y}_{\pi(1)}) > \cdots > s(\mathcal{Y}_{\pi(n)})$. We emphasize that both π and the outputs $\mathcal{Y}_i$ are computed based on all players' inputs.

When player i receives an output $\mathcal{Y}_{\pi(i)}$ from the central mechanism, she may combine $\mathcal{Y}_{\pi(i)}$ with the information that she learned from prior public outputs and her own input x_i, to generate a public output $\mathcal{Z}_{\pi(i)}$. We first prove that the ability of the players to learn from others' publications, in general, will make the problem of deciding whether there exists an equilibrium is NP-complete (see Theorem 13).

Next, we show that there is a polynomial-time mechanism that can output an equilibrium whenever one exists (or output NONE if one does not exist) for a variety of model settings and parameters which we characterize (see Theorem 11). An example of a setting when a polynomial-time mechanism is possible is when

- there is an upper bound μ_j on the amount of information that any player can learn from a given player j's publication, and
- it is possible to efficiently compute, for any y^* and $\delta > 0$, an "approximation" $\mathcal{Y}'$ such that $s(\mathcal{Y}') = \delta$.

In a nutshell, the bounds μ_j are used to define a weighted graph where the weight of the minimum-weight perfect matching determines the existence of a collaborative equilibrium.

1.1.3 Protocols to implement the mechanisms

We develop cryptographic protocols for implementing the mechanisms without a centralized trusted party and in the presence of a subset of colluding players who may deviate from the protocol in an arbitrary fashion, under cryptographic assumptions. The protocols compute the collaboration outcome $(\pi, \vec{\mathcal{Y}})$ via multi-party secure computation on players' private inputs. Since a crucial aspect of the mechanism's ability to yield non-negative reward to all players is the delivery of outputs in order, we need to extend the classical notion of MPC to incorporate guarantees on the order and timing of output delivery. These extensions may be of interest independent of the application of mechanisms for incentivizing collaborations.

We define *ordered MPC* as follows. Let f be an arbitrary n-ary function and p be an n-ary function that outputs permutation $[n] \to [n]$. An ordered MPC protocol is executed by n parties, where each party $i \in [n]$ has a private input $x_i \in \{0, 1\}^*$, who wish to securely compute $f(x_1, \ldots, x_n) = (y_1, \ldots, y_n)$ where y_i is the output of party i. Moreover, the parties are to receive their outputs in a particular *ordering* dictated by $p(x_1, \ldots, x_n) = \pi$ where π is a permutation of the player identities. Since the choice of π depends on private inputs, it may leak information: hence, we formulate an enhanced *privacy* requirement for ordered MPC that each player should learn his output and his *own* position in the output ordering, and nothing more (see Definition 14).

We show a simple transformation from classical MPC protocols for general functionalities f to ordered MPC protocols for general functionalities f and permutation functions p that achieve enhanced privacy, even when a minority of the n players are colluding to sabotage the protocol (Theorem 17). The assumptions required are the same as for the classical MPC constructions (e.g. [12]). When the colluding players are in majority, it is well known that output delivery to all honest parties cannot be guaranteed [10].

Next, we define *timed-delay MPC*, where explicit time delays are introduced into the output delivery schedule. Time delays between the outputs may be crucial to enable parties to reap the benefits of their position in the order. We give two constructions of timed-delay MPC in the honest majority setting[2]. First, we give a conceptually simple protocol which runs "dummy rounds" of communication in between issuing outputs to different players, in order to measure time-delays. The simple protocol has the flaw that all (honest) players must continue to interact until the last party receives his output (that is, they must stay online until all the time-delays have elapsed).

To address this issue, we present a second protocol assuming the existence of time-lock puzzles [19] in addition to the classical MPC [12] assumptions (see Theorem 23). Informally, a time-lock puzzle is a primitive which allows "locking" of data, such that it will be released after a pre-specified time delay, and no earlier. Our second timed-delay MPC protocol, instead of issuing outputs to players in the clear, gives to each party his output *locked* into a time-lock puzzle; and in order to enforce the desired ordering, the delays required to unlock the puzzles are set to be an increasing sequence. An issue that arises when giving out time-lock puzzles to many parties is that different parties may have different computing power, and hence solve their puzzles at different speeds: for example, it is clear that we cannot guarantee that players learn their outputs in the desired ordering if some players compute arbitrarily faster than others. Still, we show that our protocol is secure and achieves ordered output delivery in the case that the difference between any two players' computing power is known to be bounded by a logarithmic factor. If the assumption about computing power does not hold, then the protocol still achieves security (i.e. correctness and privacy), but the ordering of outputs is not guaranteed.

The definitions of ordered and timed-delay MPC inspire new notions unrelated to the central topic of this paper.

Time-lines. Inspired by the application of time-lock puzzles to time-delayed MPC, we propose the new concept of a *time-line*, where multiple data items can be locked so that their unlocking must be serialized in (future) time. See full version [1] for details.

Prefix-fairness. In the traditional MPC landscape, fairness is the one notion that addresses the idea that either all parties participating in an MPC should benefit, or none should. Fairness requires that either all players receive their output, or none do. It is well-known that fairness is achievable when a majority of the players are honest, but it is

---

[2] We cannot hope to achieve timed-delay MPC in the case of dishonest majority since, as mentioned in the preceding paragraph, even output delivery cannot be guaranteed in this setting.

not achievable for general functionalities when a majority of players are faulty [10]. We propose a refinement of the classical notion of fairness in the setting of ordered MPC, called *prefix-fairness*, where players are to receive their outputs one after the other according to a given ordering π, and the guarantee is that *either* no players receive an output *or* those who do strictly belong to a prefix of the mandated order π (see Definition 16). Prefix-fairness can be achieved for general functionalities and *any number* of faulty players, under the same assumptions as classical MPC (Theorem 18).

1.2 Discussion and interpretation of our work

Slowing down scientific discovery? Intuitively, the mechanisms we develop always take the following form: the mechanism computes the "best possible estimate" $\mathcal{Y}^*$ of y^* given the input data of the players, and then hands out a sequence of successively more accurate (according to the score function) outcomes, where the final party receives $\mathcal{Y}^*$.

One may ask: why slow down scientific progress and hand out inferior results when better ones are available? We argue that progress will in fact be *enhanced*, not slowed down, by this methodology, as it will be a decisive factor in parties' willingness to collaborate in the first place. This bears great similarity to the original philosophy of *differential privacy* and privacy-preserving data analysis more generally. In these fields, accuracy (so-called utility) of answers to aggregate queries over items in database is partially sacrificed in order to preserve privacy of individual data items, as a way to encourage individuals to contribute their data items to the database. In an analogous way, in order to get results based on the large data sets held by potential collaborators, we sacrifice the *speed* of discovery of the "ultimate" collaboration outcome: we are willing to pay this price to incentivize parties to collaborate and contribute their data. In contrast to differential privacy, we do not sacrifice ultimate accuracy. The last collaborator to receive an output, receives the ideal outcome $\mathcal{Y}^*$. Namely, $\mathcal{Y}_n = \mathcal{Y}^*$.

Fort Lauderdale: the importance of time. A recurring idea in our work is the importance of time and ordering of research discoveries, which is inspired in part by the following striking example from the field of genomics. In the 2003 Fort Lauderdale meeting on large-scale biological research [20], the gathering of leading researchers in the field recognized that "pre-publication data release can promote the best interests of [the field of genomics]" but "might conflict with a fundamental scientific incentive – publishing the first analysis of one's own data". Researchers at the meeting agreed to adopt a set of principles by which although data is shared upon discovery, researchers hold off publication until the original holder of the data has published a first analysis. Being a close-knit community in which reputation is key, this was a viable agreement which has led to great productivity and advancement of the field. However, more generally, their report states that "incentives should be developed by the scientific community to support the voluntary release of [all sorts of] data prior to publication". This example teaches us to focus on three key aspects of collaboration: the incentive to collaborate has to be clear to all collaborators; there must be a way to ensure adherence to the rules of collaboration; and timing is of the essence.

Privacy implies increased utility. Although the goal of our work is to design mechanisms *to incentivize collaboration* by increasing the utility of collaborations rather than focusing on the privacy of individual entities' input data, MPC protocols prove to be an important technical tool to implement the mechanisms which guarantee increased utility. As a by-product, the use of MPC provides our mechanisms with the additional guarantee of privacy.

Future directions. When collaboration is feasible, each party i in our model is guaranteed a reward from collaborating that is greater than the reward α_i they could get on their own. However, the contributions of the players' data to the computation of the final output $\mathcal{Y}^*$ may be asymmetric: some special player i^* may have some data that helps solve the "puzzle", but this player i^* may not be known a priori before the participants decide to collaborate[3] An interesting future direction would be developing mechanisms where, even without a priori knowledge of which players have higher quality data, we can still design collaborations where the players whose contribution turned out most valuable get most credit.

Another future direction of interest to design *truthful* mechanisms so that collaborating parties will be provably incentivized to submit their true and accurate data as input. In our work, we assume that, while we can incentivize the players to collaborate or not, once they decide to collaborate they are truthful about the value of their dataset x_i. From the point of view of scientific publications, this assumption is reasonable if we believe that the experiments that generate this data can be verified or replicated, and that a failure to replicate would hurt a scientific group's reputation. However, there are many settings, such as businesses pooling their data together to generate larger profits, where the parties may be incentivized to lie about their output x_i. Since we are already assuming that parties are rational, a future direction would be to develop mechanisms where, even when parties can lie about x_i (because x_i cannot be verified by others), they are still incentivized to report it truthfully. One possible direction is where x_i is the output of some long $\#P$ computation (for example, a Markov Chain Monte-Carlo simulation), where (a) replicating the computation would take a very long time and delay publication for everyone in the group and (b) player i cannot prove in a classical way that their output x_i is correct. Even in this case, player i can be incentivized to give the right answer via a rational proof [2, 3, 13].

Our setting is useful and most likely to lead to collaboration when there are increasing marginal returns from adding new data. It will be interesting to discover new settings where this is provably the case.

1.3 Other related work

Banerjee, Goel and Krishnaswamy [4] consider the problem of partial progress sharing, where a scientific task is modeled as a directed acyclic graph of subtasks. Their goal is to minimize the time for all tasks to be completed by selfish agents who may not wish to share partial progress.

Kleinberg and Oren [16] study a model where researchers have different projects, each with a different reward, to choose from. If multiple researchers solve the problem, they study how to split the reward in a socially optimal way. They show that assigning credit asymmetrically can be socially optimal when researchers seek to maximize individual reward, and they suggest implementing a "Matthew Effect", where researchers who are already credit-rich are allocated more credit than in an even-split system. Interestingly, this

is coherent with our paper, where it is socially optimal to obfuscate data so that researchers who are already "ahead" (in terms of data), end up "ahead" in terms of credit.

Cai, Daskalakis and Papadimitriou [9] study the problem of incentivizing n players to share data, in order to compute a statistical estimator. Their goal is to minimize the sum of rewards made to the players, as well as the statistical error of their estimator. In contrast, our goal is to give a decentralized mechanism through which players can pool their data, and distribute partial information to themselves in order to increase the utility of every collaborating player.

Boneh and Naor [8] construct timed commitments that can be "forced open" after a certain time delay, and discuss applications of these to achieve fair two-party contract signing (and coin-flipping) under certain timing assumptions including bounded network delay and the assumption of sequentiality of modular exponentiation from [19].

Due to space constraints, we omit all proofs in this extended abstract. Proofs are given in the full version [1].

2. DATA SHARING MODEL

In this section, we present a model for scientific collaboration and analyze mechanisms within it. Our exposition focuses primarily on the setting of scientific collaboration and publication. However, our results apply to more broad collaboration and discovery in general, in which case a "publication" should be thought of as any kind of public output.

Notation. We denote by $[n]$ the set $\{1,\ldots,n\}$ of integers between 1 and n, and by $[n] \to [n]$ the set of all permutations of $[n]$. For a set X, we write $\Delta(X)$ to denote the set of all distributions over X. The symbol $\sqcup$ denotes the disjoint union operation. An *efficient* algorithm is one which runs in probabilistic polynomial time (PPT).

2.1 The model

We propose a model of collaboration between n research groups which captures the following features: groups may pool their data, but each group will publish their own results; only results that improve on the "state of the art" may be published; more credit may be given to earlier publications; a group will learn not only from pooling their data with other groups, but also from other groups' publications.

To formalize the intuitions outlined above, we specify a model as follows.

- There is a set $[n]$ of players.
- Each player i has a dataset x_i which is sampled as follows.
  - For each $i \in [n]$, there is a set X_i of possible datasets, which is common knowledge. Let X denote $X_1 \times \cdots \times X_n$.
  - There is a distribution $\mathcal{X} \in \Delta(X)$ over X, from which the x_i are sampled: $(x_1,\ldots,x_n) \leftarrow \mathcal{X}$.
  - The distribution $\mathcal{X}$ is not known to any of the players, but comes from a commonly known distribution $\mathcal{D}$. That is, $\mathcal{X} \leftarrow \mathcal{D}$, for some $\mathcal{D} \in \Delta(\Delta(X))$.
- There is an output space Y, and a function $f : \Delta(X_1 \times \cdots \times X_n) \to Y$ such that $\hat{y} = f(\mathcal{X})$ is the value which the players wish to learn. That is, the players want to learn some property of the unknown distribution $\mathcal{X}$ from which their datasets were sampled. Y and f are common knowledge.
- $\mathcal{Y}_0$ denotes the distribution of $\hat{y}$ given f and $\mathcal{D}$.
- There is a *score function* $s : \Delta(Y) \to \mathbb{R}_+$, which varies with f and $\mathcal{D}$. The score function $s(\cdot)$ is maximized by the distribution $\hat{\mathcal{Y}}$ which puts probability 1 on the true value $\hat{y}$. The score function s is common knowledge.
  - We require a natural *monotonicity* property of the score function. Namely, let $\mathcal{Y}$ and $\mathcal{Z}$ be any distributions, and

---

[3]An example in the same vein is the following. In the medical setting, a hospital with a larger patient population will clearly have more patient data than a small facility, and yet access to data of small but homogeneous or rare communities can at times be more valuable than access to larger heterogeneous sets of data.

let z be a value in the support of $\mathcal{Z}$. Then

$$s(\mathcal{Y}) \leq s(\mathcal{Y}|z \leftarrow \mathcal{Z}),$$

where $z \leftarrow \mathcal{Z}$ denotes the event that z is sampled from the distribution $\mathcal{Z}$.

- *Remark.* Let $\{\hat{y}|x_1,\ldots,x_n\}$ denote the distribution of $\hat{y}$ given certain datasets $(x_1,\ldots,x_n) \in X$. A consequence of the monotonicity condition is that given all of the datasets $x_1,\ldots,x_n$ of all players in the model, the best achievable score is $s(\{\hat{y}|x_1,\ldots,x_n\})$.

- A *collaboration outcome* is given by a permutation $\pi : [n] \to [n]$ and a vector of output distributions $(\mathcal{Z}_1,\ldots,\mathcal{Z}_n) \in (\Delta(Y))^n$ such that $s(\mathcal{Y}_0) < s(\mathcal{Z}_{\pi(1)}) < \cdots < s(\mathcal{Z}_{\pi(n)})$.

  The intuition behind this condition is that, at time t, player $\pi(t)$ will publish $\mathcal{Z}_{\pi(t)}$. Since only results that improve on the "state of the art" can be published, we must have that the score $s(\mathcal{Z}_{\pi(t)})$ increases with the time of publication t.

- For a collaboration outcome $\omega = (\pi, \vec{\mathcal{Z}})$, the player who publishes at time t obtains a reward

$$R_t(\pi, \vec{\mathcal{Z}}) = \beta^t \cdot (s(\mathcal{Z}_{\pi(t)}) - s(\mathcal{Z}_{\pi(t-1)}))$$

where $\beta \in (0,1]$ is a *discount factor* which penalizes later publications.[4]

- For each player i, we define $\alpha_i = s(\{\hat{y}|x_i\}) - s(\mathcal{Y}_0) \in \mathbb{R}_+$, where $\{\hat{y}|x_i\}$ is the distribution of $\hat{y}$ given that the ith dataset is x_i. This models the "outside payoff" that player i could get if she does not collaborate and simply publishes on her own.

- Players may learn information not only from their own data, but also from the prior publications of others. A *learning bound vector* $\{\lambda_{\pi,i}\}_{\pi \in ([n] \to [n]), i \in [n]}$ characterizes, for any publication order π, the maximum amount that each player i can learn from prior publications. This notion is defined formally in Section 2.3.

- We define CK to be the collection of all common-knowledge parameters of the model:

$$\mathsf{CK} = (\mathcal{D}, f, s, \beta).$$

2.2 Examples

To illustrate the range of settings to which our model applies, we describe several concrete model instantiations.

Recall that our goal is to build mechanisms to enable collaborations by sharing data, in settings where such collaboration would be beneficial to all parties. Intuitively, such settings occur when the result that can be obtained based on the union of all players' datasets is "much better" than the results that can be obtained based on the individual datasets: in other words, the "size of the pie" to be split between the collaborating players is at least as large as the sum of the "slices" obtained by players working individually. This intuition is made rigorous in Lemma 10, where we discuss score functions which satisfy a superadditivity condition (Property 9).

Toy Example I: Secret-sharing. We begin with a "toy example" based on secret-sharing. This artificial first example is a dramatic illustration that the size of reward from collaboration can be much larger than the sum of individual rewards without collaborating.

Consider a stylized secret-sharing model with a secret $\hat{y}$ drawn uniformly at random from $\{0,1\}^n$. Each player's data consists of a share $x_i \in \{0,1\}^n$ such that $\hat{y} = x_1 \oplus \ldots \oplus x_n$ be the secret the players are trying to reconstruct. The shares are correlated and drawn from a distribution $\mathcal{X}$ as follows:

- For each $i \in [n-1]$, x_i is uniformly random in $\{0,1\}^n$.

- The last share is chosen such that $x_n = \hat{y} \oplus x_1 \oplus \ldots \oplus x_{n-1}$.

The players want to learn $f(\mathcal{X}) = \hat{y}$. The score from publishing a distribution $\mathcal{Y}$ is $s(\mathcal{Y}) = H(\hat{y}) - H(\hat{y}|\mathcal{Y})$ where $H(\hat{y}) = n$ is the entropy of the uniformly random string $\hat{y}$ and $H(\hat{y}|\mathcal{Y})$ is the entropy of $\hat{y}$ given the distribution $\mathcal{Y}$.

Without collaborating, each player i only knows a uniformly random string x_i. Thus, $H(\hat{y}|x_i) = H(\hat{y}) = n$ and $\alpha_i = H(\hat{y}|x_i) - H(\hat{y}) = 0$ for each player i. Consider the following collaboration mechanism:

- Each player contributes share x_i to the mechanism.

- The mechanism computes $\hat{y} = x_1 \oplus \ldots \oplus x_n$.

- The mechanism reveals i^{th} digit $\hat{y}_i$ to each player i.

When participating in this mechanism, the first player will publish a guess $\mathcal{Y}_1$ which is a distribution over $\{0,1\}^n$ where the first bit of $y \leftarrow \mathcal{Y}_1$ is always $\hat{y}_1$. All other players learn $\hat{y}_1$ from player 1's publication. Proceeding inductively, the ith player will publish a guess $\mathcal{Y}_i$ such that the first i bits are correct, that is, $(y_1,\ldots,y_i) = (\hat{y}_1,\ldots,\hat{y}_i)$ for any $y \leftarrow \mathcal{Y}_i$. Note that since $\alpha_i = 0$ for each player i, and $H(\hat{y}|\mathcal{Y}_i) - H(\hat{y}|\mathcal{Y}_{i-1}) = 1 > \alpha_i$, this mechanism incentivizes players to collaborate.

Toy Example II: Network flow. Let $G = (V, E)$ be a graph. Let $\tilde{s}, \tilde{t} \in V$ be vertices which are connected by some number of disjoint paths. Consider a model where V, $\tilde{s}$, and $\tilde{t}$ are common knowledge, and each player's data consists of a disjoint subset of edges in $x_i \subseteq E$. More precisely, $(x_1,\ldots,x_n) \leftarrow \mathcal{X}(E)$ where $\mathcal{X}$ samples a partition of E.

The players want to learn the set of paths from $\tilde{s}$ to $\tilde{t}$. That is, $f(\mathcal{X}(E))$ is the set of paths in E from $\tilde{s}$ to $\tilde{t}$. The score from publishing a distribution $\mathcal{Z}$ over edges is

$$s(\mathcal{Z}) = |\{p : p \text{ is a path in } E \text{ from } \tilde{s} \text{ to } \tilde{t}, \text{ and } \Pr_{z \leftarrow \mathcal{Z}}[p \subseteq z] = 1\}|.$$

In other words, the player's score is given by how many paths from $\tilde{s}$ to $\tilde{t}$ she knows with certainty to exist in E. In some cases, it may be that no player knows any path from $\tilde{s}$ to $\tilde{t}$ based only on her own data, as illustrated by the simple example in the diagram. Consider the following collaboration mechanism:

- Each player contributes their edges x_i to the mechanism.

- The mechanism computes $E = x_1 \cup \cdots \cup x_n$, and the set $P = \{p_1,\ldots,p_k\}$ of paths in E that start at $\tilde{s}$ and end at $\tilde{t}$.

- The mechanism reveals the ith path p_i to player i. If $k < n$, then the last $k - n$ players will get no output. If $k > n$, the "extra" paths are allocated arbitrarily to players.[5]

When participating in this mechanism, the first player will publish a guess $\mathcal{Z}_1$ which (always) samples the set $\{p_1\}$. All other players learn p_1 from player 1's publication. Then, the ith player will publish a guess $\mathcal{Z}_i$ that samples the set $\{p_1,\ldots,p_i\}$. As long as $s(\mathcal{Z}_i) - s(\mathcal{Z}_{i-1}) \geq \alpha_i$ for all $i \in [n]$ (note that this is the case in the diagram), this mechanism incentivizes players to collaborate.

Example III: Correlating gene loci with disease

This example is inspired by successful GWAS studies to identify gene loci associated with schizophrenia. Consider a model where each player holds a set of patients' medical (and in particular, genetic) data x_i which comes from some unknown patient distribution $\mathcal{X}$. The players wish to

---

[4]This is motivated by market scoring rules [14], where experts are rewarded according to how much they improve existing predictions.

[5]It may be beneficial to allocate the "extra" paths strategically in order to reward players more fairly, or in order to make collaboration possible when the outside option values α_i are nonzero. However, in this example, we allocate them arbitrarily for simplicity.

learn the set $f(\mathcal{X})$ of gene loci that are correlated with the occurrence of schizophrenia in patients.

Let Γ be the set of all gene loci. For $\gamma \in \Gamma$, define $\mathbb{I}_\gamma$ to be 1 if $\gamma \in f(\mathcal{X})$ and 0 otherwise. The score from publishing a distribution $\mathcal{Z}$ over $\mathcal{P}(\Gamma)$ (i.e. over subsets of gene loci) could be:[6]

$$s(\mathcal{Z}) = \sum_{\gamma \in f(\mathcal{X})} \Pr_{z \leftarrow \mathcal{Z}}[\gamma \in z] - \sum_{\gamma \notin f(\mathcal{X})} \Pr_{z \leftarrow \mathcal{Z}}[\gamma \in z].$$

This score function rewards players for assigning high probabilities to gene loci γ which are actually correlated with schizophrenia, and penalizes them for assigning high probabilities to those which are not. As in our previous examples, it turns out that in this setting, the reward that can be obtained based on pooling all the players' data is much greater than the sum of the rewards that could be obtained individually, as illustrated in Figure 1.

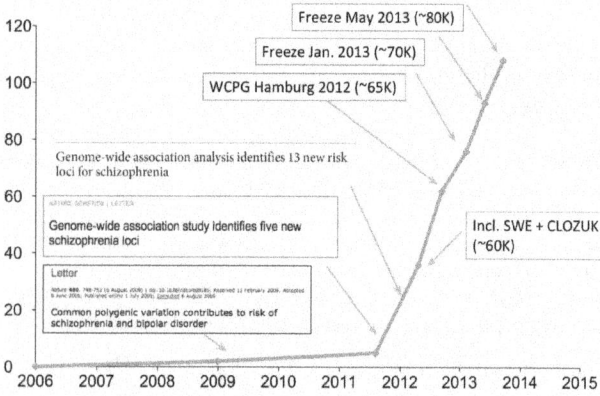

Figure 1: GWAS study success: the y-axis is the number of gene loci correlated with schizophrenia, and the x-axis is time (which corresponds to *amount of data*, since the reason for the improved findings was accumulation of data over time). Image ©Stephan Ripke

Consider the following collaboration mechanism:[7]

- Each player contributes some patient data x_i.

- The mechanism computes $\mathcal{Y}^* = \{f(\mathcal{X})|x_1, \ldots, x_n\}$, i.e. the distribution of $f(\mathcal{X})$ given all players' input data. Let $\Gamma^* = \{\gamma \in \Gamma : \Pr_{y \leftarrow \mathcal{Y}^*}[\gamma \subset y] > 0.5\}$, that is, the set of gene loci that are more likely than not to be in $f(\mathcal{X})$, according to $\mathcal{Y}^*$.

- The mechanism reveals to player i the ith gene locus γ_i in Γ^*. If $|\Gamma^*| < n$, then the last $k - n$ players will get no output. If $|\Gamma^*| > n$, the "extra" gene loci are allocated arbitrarily.[8]

---

[6] In practice, a more realistic scenario might be to model the *extent* to which particular gene loci are found to be correlated with the occurrence of schizophrenia, rather than classifying into binary categories "correlated" and "not correlated". This case could be modeled, for example, by letting $f(\mathcal{X})$ be a vector $((\gamma_1, p_1), \ldots, (\gamma_N, p_N))$ where $\Gamma = \{\gamma_1, \ldots, \gamma_N\}$ is the set of gene loci, and for each $j \in [N]$, p_j is the correlation coefficient between γ_1 and occurrence of schizophrenia. While Example IV presents the simpler "binary" model for ease of exposition, we remark that with appropriate modifications to the score function and mechanism, our model can accommodate the more complex case of estimating correlations, too.

[7] This is just one example of a reasonable mechanism for this model; we do not mean to claim that it is a canonical or optimal one. There are many variants which could make sense: for example, a simple modification would be to change the threshold 0.5 in the second step.

[8] As remarked in Footnote 5, it can be beneficial to allocate the "extra" gene loci in a way which is not arbitrary, but instead optimized for making collaboration possible. In this example, for simplicity, we allocate them arbitrarily.

When participating in this mechanism, the first player will publish a guess $\mathcal{Z}_1$ which (always) samples the set $\{\gamma_1\}$. All other players learn γ_1 from player 1's publication. Then, the ith player will publish a guess $\mathcal{Z}_i$ that samples the set $\{\gamma_1, \ldots, \gamma_i\}$. Provided that $s(\mathcal{Z}_i) - s(\mathcal{Z}_{i-1}) \geq \alpha_i$ for all $i \in [n]$ (note that Figure 1 depicts exactly such a scenario), this mechanism incentivizes players to collaborate.

Example IV: Statistical estimation

Our last example is one where – in contrast to the examples so far – there are *decreasing* marginal returns from adding new information, and thus collaboration will not be feasible.

We consider a simple Bayesian model where the distribution $\mathcal{X}$ is itself drawn from a "distribution over distributions" $\mathcal{D}$. More concretely, each player i receives a vector of k_i samples $(x_{i,1}, \ldots, x_{i,k_i})$ drawn independently from a normal distribution $N(\mu, \sigma^2)$ with unknown mean μ and known variance σ^2. The mean μ is itself drawn from a commonly known prior distribution $\mathcal{D} = N(m, 1)$ with known mean m and variance 1. In this case, the ground set X_i is $\mathbb{R}^{k_i}$. The distribution $\mathcal{X}(\mu, \sigma)$ is a product distribution over $\mathbb{R}^{\sum_{i=1}^n k_i}$, where each component of $(x_{1,1}, \ldots, x_{n,k_n})$ is drawn independently from $N(\mu, \sigma)$. The players want to learn $f(\mathcal{X}(\mu, \sigma)) = \mu$.

An estimator for μ is a random variable $\hat{\mu}$. The score of such a guess $\hat{\mu}$ is $s(\hat{\mu}) = -\mathbb{E}[(\hat{\mu} - \mu)^2]$. It is well known that if we have a vector $(x_{i,1}, \ldots, x_{i,k_i})$ of random samples drawn from $N(\mu, \sigma)$, the estimator that minimizes the expected squared error to μ is $\hat{\mu}_i = \frac{1}{k_i} \sum_{j=1}^{k_i} x_{i,j}$. Note that this is a normal random variable since each $x_{i,j}$ is sampled from normal random variable. The expectation of $\hat{\mu}_i$ is $\frac{1}{k_i} \cdot k_i \cdot \mu = \mu$ and the variance of $\hat{\mu}_i$ is $\frac{1}{k_i^2} \cdot k_i \cdot \sigma^2 = \frac{1}{k_i} \cdot \sigma^2$. Thus, $s(\hat{\mu}_i) = \frac{1}{k_i} \cdot \sigma^2$. If a player published by herself and did not collaborate, her reward would be the difference $\alpha_i = \sigma^2 - \frac{1}{k_i} \cdot \sigma^2$ between the priorly known variance σ^2 and the variance $\frac{1}{k_i} \cdot \sigma^2$ of player i's estimate.

If the players collaborate, they can obtain the estimator $\hat{\mu}^* = \frac{1}{\sum_{i=1}^n k_i} \sum_{i=1}^n \sum_{j=1}^{k_i} x_{i,j}$ which has variance $s(\hat{\mu}^*) = \frac{1}{\sum_{i=1}^n k_i} \sigma^2$. The reward for $\hat{\mu}^*$ is the reduction in variance $\sigma^2 - s(\hat{\mu}^*) = \sigma^2 \cdot (1 - \frac{1}{\sum_{i=1}^n k_i})$. Note that in this case, the reward from an estimator only depends on the number of data points N used to construct this estimator (in the above notation, $N = \sum_{i=1}^n k_i$). Furthermore, the reward $R(N) = \sigma^2(1 - \frac{1}{N})$ that one could obtain with N data points is concave in N. Intuitively, if one only has $N = 2$ data points, and gets 10 new ones, those 10 new data points are very valuable. However, if one already has $N = 2000000$ data points and gets 10 new ones, those 10 new data points do not increase the score very much.

This setting is in contrast to our Example III, where the score seemed to increase in a convex way with the number of data points. Indeed, in this Bayesian example, we will always have that

$$R(\sum_{i=1}^n k_i) = \sigma^2(1 - \frac{1}{\sum_{i=1}^n k_i}) \leq \sigma^2 \sum_{i=1}^n (1 - \frac{1}{k_i}) = \sum_{i=1}^n R(k_i).$$

In Section 2.5 we elaborate on why the above inequality is bad for collaboration. Intuitively, the left-hand side is the "size of the pie" if all players were to collaborate, and the right-hand side is the sum of the rewards that each player could receive on her own. The inequality implies there is no way to "slice the pie" so that every player has a bigger reward than the α_i they can get without collaborating, and thus collaboration is impossible.

In this simple Bayesian example, the marginal value of extra information will be decreasing. This raises the interesting question of *when* the value of information is (and is not) not convex with the amount of information available. For example, consider machine learning: learning problems whose objectives can be stated as minimizing a convex loss function (or maximizing a concave value function) seem to induce natural score functions which do not have increasing marginal returns, so our model may be more applicable to problems with non-convex objectives. We remark that such non-convex learning problems, in which our model seems more applicable, are an area of interest in machine learning as solving them is lately becoming practical – we refer to Bengio and LeCun [5] for a more thorough discussion of this situation.

2.3 Data-sharing mechanisms

We now return to the general formulation of our collaboration model, and we seek to design a general data-sharing mechanism that takes as input the data of all the parties, computes an output distribution $\mathcal{Y}_i \in \Delta(Y)$ for each $i \in [n]$, and outputs $\mathcal{Y}_i$ to each player i. The mechanism will output the $\mathcal{Y}_i$ values to players sequentially, in a particular order. Upon receiving $\mathcal{Y}_i$, player i produces a public output (i.e a publication in the research collaboration example) which we denote by $\mathcal{Z}_i \in Y$.

We note that the public output of player i will not necessarily be the same as what was delivered by the data-sharing mechanism. Since player i wants to maximize her reward, she will publish a result $\mathcal{Z}_i$ that will maximize her reward, conditional on the information she has at the time of publication. This information includes, in addition to the output $\mathcal{Y}_i$ which she receives from the mechanism (and her knowledge of how the mechanism works[9]), also her own dataset $x_i \in X_i$, and all the outputs $\mathcal{Z}_j$ of other players that published before her.

Recall that a *collaboration outcome* $(\pi, \vec{\mathcal{Z}})$ is given by a permutation $\pi : [n] \to [n]$ and a vector of output distributions $\vec{\mathcal{Z}} = (\mathcal{Z}_1, \ldots, \mathcal{Z}_n) \in (\Delta(Y))^n$ such that $s(\mathcal{Y}_0) < s(\mathcal{Z}_{\pi(1)}) < \cdots < s(\mathcal{Z}_{\pi(n)})$. We now define a *proposed collaboration outcome* $(\pi, \vec{\mathcal{Y}})$ as a permutation $\pi : [n] \to [n]$ together with a vector of *proposed outputs* $\vec{\mathcal{Y}} = (\mathcal{Y}_1, \ldots, \mathcal{Y}_n) \in (\Delta(Y))^n$ generated by a data-sharing mechanism, satisfying $s(\mathcal{Y}_0) < s(\mathcal{Y}_{\pi(1)}) < \cdots < s(\mathcal{Y}_{\pi(n)})$.

Recall also that we need to bound how much player i can learn from previous publications (and from her own dataset). We formally capture this with the notion of *learning bound vectors* $\lambda_{\pi,i}$, which give an upper bound on the amount that player i learns from all previous publications when the order of publication is determined by permutation π.

DEFINITION 1. *A learning bound vector*

$$\vec{\lambda} = (\lambda_{\pi,i})_{\pi \in ([n] \to [n]), i \in [n]}$$

is a non-negative vector such that, if $(\pi, \vec{\mathcal{Y}})$ is a collaboration outcome proposed by a data-sharing mechanism, and $\mathcal{Z}_i$ is the best (i.e. highest-scoring) distribution that player i can compute at the time $\pi^{-1}(i)$ of her publication, then $s(\mathcal{Z}_i) \leq s(\mathcal{Y}_i) + \lambda_{\pi,i}$. Let $\Lambda = \mathbb{R}_+^{n! \times n}$ denote the set of all learning bound vectors.

[9]The mechanism description is common knowledge.

DEFINITION 2. *For a learning bound vector $\vec{\lambda}$, the set of inferred output distributions derived from a proposed collaoration outcome $(\pi, \vec{\mathcal{y}})$ is given by the following expression:*

$$\mathcal{I}_{\vec{\lambda}}(\pi, \vec{\mathcal{y}}) =$$
$$\{(\mathcal{Z}_1, \ldots, \mathcal{Z}_n) : \forall t \in [n], \; s(\mathcal{Y}_{\pi(t)}) \leq s(\mathcal{Z}_{\pi(t)}) \leq s(\mathcal{Y}_{\pi(t)}) + \lambda_{\pi, \pi(t)}\}.$$

The intuition behind the above definition is that the amount of information that player $\pi(t)$ (namely, the player who publishes at time t) can learn from prior outputs is measured by how much her score increases based on these prior outputs. This increase in score is bounded by $\lambda_{\pi,\pi(t)}$. Thus, her eventual output will be some $\mathcal{Z}_{\pi(t)}$ with score between $s(\mathcal{Y}_{\pi(t)})$ and $s(\mathcal{Y}_{\pi(t)}) + \lambda_{\pi,\pi(t)}$.

REMARK 1. *In certain cases, $\lambda_{\pi,\pi(t)}$ measures exactly the amount of information that player $\pi(t)$ can learn from her data. However, in our definition $\lambda_{\pi,\pi(t)}$ is an upper bound, and we emphasize that it may be a loose upper bound on the amount of information $\pi(t)$ can learn. Our emphasis on this point comes from the following two reasons.*

- *In general, the vector $\vec{\lambda} \in \mathbb{R}^{n! \times n}$ has very high dimension, and finding such a vector is infeasible. We may want to approximate this vector via a low-dimensional encoding (as we will do below, where we encode learning bounds using n-dimensional vectors). Since this low-dimensional encoding will lose information, we will not be able to represent $\lambda_{\pi,\pi(t)}$ exactly, but may get a reasonable upper bound on its value.*

- *For some other settings, we may not be able to derive a precise expression for $\lambda_{\pi,\pi(t)}$ in terms of expectations, but we may still be able to derive an upper bound on the amount of information that player $\pi(t)$ learns.*

Now that we have established a formal definition of learning bound vectors, we define a data-sharing mechanism.

DEFINITION 3. *For model parameters CK, a data sharing mechanism is a function*

$$M : X \times \Lambda \to ([n] \to [n]) \times (\Delta(Y))^n$$

which takes as inputs a vector $\vec{x} = (x_1, \ldots, x_n)$ of datasets and $\vec{\lambda} = (\lambda_{\pi,i})_{\pi \in ([n] \to [n]), i \in [n]}$ a learning bound vector, and outputs an ordering π of the players and an output vector $(\mathcal{Y}_1, \ldots, \mathcal{Y}_n) \in (\Delta(Y))^n$.

REMARK 2. *In the definition, for the sake of generality, we assume that the $\vec{\lambda}$ values are given as input to the mechanism. We remark that in certain settings, these values can be computed directly from the inputs x_i of the parties, as discussed in the examples of Section 1.1.2. In this case, one may think of the mechanism $M : X \to ([n] \to [n]) \times (\Delta(Y))^n$ as having input domain X only.*

2.4 Collaborative equilibria

In our model, each research group $\pi(t)$ will collaborate only if the credit they obtain from doing so is greater than the "outside option" reward $\alpha_{\pi(t)}$. We want to design a mechanism that guarantees collaboration whenever possible. Accordingly, we define the following equilibrium concept.

DEFINITION 4. *Let CK be the model parameters. Let $(\vec{x}, \vec{\lambda}) \in X \times \Lambda$ and let $(\pi, (\mathcal{Y}_1, \ldots, \mathcal{Y}_n)) \in ([n] \to [n]) \times (\Delta(Y))^n$. We say that $(\pi, (\mathcal{Y}_1, \ldots, \mathcal{Y}_n))$ is a collaborative equilibrium with respect to $(\vec{x}, \vec{\lambda})$ if for all inferred output distributions $\vec{\mathcal{Z}} = (\mathcal{Z}_1, \ldots, \mathcal{Z}_n) \in \mathcal{I}(\pi, (\mathcal{Y}_1, \ldots, \mathcal{Y}_n))$ and all $t \in [n]$, it holds that $R_t(\pi, \vec{\mathcal{Z}}) \geq \alpha_{\pi(t)}$.*

Our goal is to find data-sharing mechanisms for which collaboration is an equilibrium. Intuitively, since we are searching for a feasible permutation over a very high-dimensional space ($n!$-dimensional, to be precise), the problem will be NP-complete (Theorem 13). However, there is a very natural condition on learning vectors for which we can reduce the dimension of the search space and efficiently find a collaborative equilibrium. The feasible case corresponds to the case where, for any player j, there is a bound on the amount of information that player j could *teach* any other players. We denote this bound by μ_j. Analogously, we could define μ_j to be a bound on the amount that player j can *learn* from any other player. In this work, we describe only the first case, when μ_j represents a bound on how much information player j can teach other players. The other case is analogous.

We define a learning bound vector to be n-dimensional if it satisfies the following property.

DEFINITION 5. *A learning vector* $\vec{\lambda} \in \Lambda$ *is n-dimensional if there is a non-negative vector* $(\mu_1, \ldots, \mu_n)$ *such that* $\lambda_{\pi,\pi(t)} = \sum_{\tau=1}^{t-1} \mu_{\pi(\tau)}$. *Let* $\Lambda_1 \subset \Lambda$ *denote the set of all n-dimensional learning vectors.*

When $\vec{\lambda}$ is an n-dimensional learning vector, the total amount that player $\pi(t)$ learns from all prior outputs is $\sum_{\tau=1}^{t-1} \mu_{\pi(\tau)}$. In this case, we can give necessary and sufficient conditions for an equilibrium to exist (detailed in Theorem 6 below), provided that the following Output Divisibility Condition is satisfied.

Output Divisibility Condition. Given the model parameters CK and any real $0 < \delta \le 1$,[10] there exists a distribution $\mathcal{Y} \in \Delta(Y)$ such that $s(\mathcal{Y}) = \delta$.

REMARK 3. *The above condition holds for many natural score functions. In general, score functions which reward "how close" a distribution is to the true value $\hat{y} = f(\mathcal{X})$ decrease (continuously) with the addition of random noise to a distribution. Provided that this holds, the condition can be satisfied by taking the optimal distribution $\{\hat{y}|\mathcal{X}\}$ and perturbing it with random noise: the exact amount of noise to be added depends on the desired value of δ. To give a concrete example: in Example III (Gene loci), the perturbed distribution could simply add noise to the probabilities that each gene locus is sampled. Here, "adding noise" can mean simply adding some $\eta \leftarrow N(0, \sigma^2)$ to the relevant parameters, where the magnitude of σ depends on the precise formulation of the score function and the desired value of δ.*

THEOREM 6. *Suppose that the Output Divisibility Condition holds. Let $\vec{x}$ be a vector of inputs and $\vec{\lambda}$ be an n-dimensional learning bound vector. Let $\lambda_{\pi,\pi(t)} = \sum_{\tau=1}^{t-1} \mu_{\pi(\tau)}$. Then for $(\pi, \vec{\mathcal{Y}})$ to be a collaborative equilibrium, it is necessary and sufficient that*

$$\sum_{t=1}^{n} \frac{\alpha_{\pi(t)}}{\beta^t} + \sum_{t=1}^{n} (n-t)\mu_{\pi(t)} \le s(\mathcal{Y}_{\pi(n)}) - s(\mathcal{Y}_0).$$

Recall from the definition of the score function that the best score that can be attained given datasets $x_1, \ldots, x_n$ is equal to $s(\{\hat{y}|x_1, \ldots, x_n\})$. Based on Theorem 6, we can now characterize the datasets and learning bound vectors for which a collaborative equilibrium is possible.

DEFINITION 7. *Let* CK *be the model parameters and let* $(\vec{x}, \vec{\lambda}) \in X \times \Lambda$. *We say that* $(\vec{x}, \vec{\lambda})$ *supports a collaborative equilibrium if it holds that*

$$\sum_{t=1}^{n} \frac{\alpha_{\pi(t)}}{\beta^t} + \sum_{t=1}^{n} (n-t)\mu_{\pi(t)} \le s(\{\hat{y}|x_1, \ldots, x_n\}) - s(\mathcal{Y}_0).$$

2.4.1 How do the model parameters affect feasibility of collaborative equilibria?

Consider for a moment the simple case where $\beta = 1$ and $\vec{\lambda} = \vec{0}$, that is, there is no discount factor and players do not learn from others' publications. We can show that in this case, if the score function satisfies the following Property 9, then it holds that for *all* $\vec{x} \in X$, $(\vec{x}, \vec{\lambda})$ supports a collaborative equilibrium. That is, in this simple case, the condition for $(\vec{x}, \vec{\lambda})$ to support an equilibrium reduces to the superadditivity of the auxiliary score function $\bar{s}$ given in Property 9.

DEFINITION 8. *Let S be a set. A function $f : S \to \mathbb{R}$ is superadditive if for all disjoint $S_1, S_2 \subseteq S$, it holds that $f(S_1) + f(S_2) \le f(S_1 \cup S_2)$.*

PROPERTY 9 (SUPERADDITIVE DIFFERENCES). *Let* CK *be the model parameters. We define an auxiliary score function $\bar{s} : X_1 \sqcup \cdots \sqcup X_n \to \mathbb{R}_+$ which maps a set of datasets to a real-valued score, as follows:*

$$\bar{s}(\{(i_1, x_{i_1}), \ldots, (i_k, x_{i_k})\}) = s(\{\hat{y}|x_{i_1}, \ldots, x_{i_k}\}) - s(\mathcal{Y}_0),$$

where $\{\hat{y}|x_{i_1}, \ldots, x_{i_k}\}$ denotes the distribution of $\hat{y}$ given that the datasets $x_{i_1}, \ldots, x_{i_k}$ were sampled[11] from $\mathcal{X}$. The score function s satisfies the Superadditive Differences Property if $\bar{s}$ is superadditive.

We observe that this precisely captures the intuition initially described in Section 2.2, that our model is designed to promote collaboration in situations where the reward that can be obtained from pooling all players' data is more than the sum of the individual rewards that players can get.

LEMMA 10. *Let* CK *be model parameters such that $\beta = 1$, let $\vec{x} \in X$ be arbitrary, and let $\vec{\lambda} = \vec{0} \in \Lambda$. If $\bar{s}$ is a superadditive function on the input data, then $(\vec{x}, \vec{\lambda})$ supports a collaborative equilibrium.*

Finally, we remark that either decreasing the discount factor β or increasing the learning bound vector $\vec{\lambda}$ will make it harder to support a collaborative equilibrium (i.e. a lower value of β means there will be fewer $(\vec{x}, \vec{\lambda})$ which support an equilibrium), since these cause the left-hand side of the inequality to increase. So, while superadditivity is a sufficient condition in the simplest case, we observe that determining which $(\vec{x}, \vec{\lambda})$ support a collaborative equilibrium is a more complex problem when the model parameters are varied.

2.5 The polynomial-time mechanism

We show a polynomial-time mechanism that computes a collaborative equilibrium in the case that learning bounds are given by a n-dimensional vector, provided that the following *Efficient* Output Divisibility Condition is satisfied. This condition is a natural extension of the Output Divisibility Condition, which requires not only existence but also

---

[10] Recall (from the model description) that $s(\{\hat{y}|\mathcal{X}\}) = \max_{\mathcal{Y} \in \Delta(Y)}(s(\mathcal{Y}))$. Without loss of generality, we assume in our analysis that the score function is normalized so that its maximum value $s(\{\hat{y}|\mathcal{X}\}) = 1$.

[11] More precisely: $\{\hat{y}|x_{i_1}, \ldots, x_{i_k}\}$ is the distribution of $\hat{y}$ given that each x_{i_j} was sampled in the $i_j{}^{th}$ position. (Recall that the distribution $\mathcal{X}$ is over tuples of datasets $(x_1, \ldots, x_n)$.)

efficient computability of distributions with arbitrary score, while taking into account that the best possible score for given input datasets $x_1, \ldots, x_n$ is equal to $s(\{\hat{y}|x_1, \ldots, x_n\})$.

Efficient Output Divisibility Condition. Given model parameters CK, datasets $x_1, \ldots, x_n \in X$, and any real $0 < \delta < s(\{\hat{y}|x_1, \ldots, x_n\})$, it is possible to efficiently compute a distribution $\mathcal{Y} \in \Delta(Y)$ such that $s(\mathcal{Y}) = \delta$.

REMARK 4. *The above condition holds for a wide variety of score functions, too: in particular, it holds for the class of score functions described in Remark 3. Suppose that the score function is continuous and decreases with the addition of random noise to a distribution. Then the condition can be satisfied by taking the "best computable" distribution $\{\hat{y}|x_1, \ldots, x_n\}$ and perturbing it with random noise: the amount of noise to add will depend on the desired value of δ.*

THEOREM 11. *Suppose the Efficient Output Divisibility Condition holds. Then there is a polynomial-time mechanism SHARE-DATA : $X \times \Lambda_1$ that, given inputs $(\vec{x}, \vec{\mu})$ where $\vec{\mu} = (\mu_1, \ldots, \mu_n)$ represents a n-dimensional learning vector, outputs a collaborative equilibrium $(\pi, \vec{\mathcal{Y}})$ whenever an equilibrium is supported by the inputs $(\vec{x}, \vec{\mu})$ (as defined in Definition 7), and outputs NONE otherwise.*

Algorithm 1 SHARE-DATA$((x_1, \ldots, x_n), (\mu_1, \ldots, \mu_n))$

---

1. Let $\mathcal{Y}^* = \{\hat{y}|x_1, \ldots, x_n\}$ and $\delta^* = s(\mathcal{Y}_0)$.

2. Construct a complete weighted bipartite graph $G = (L, R, E)$ where $L = [n], R = [n], E = L \times R$. For each edge (i, t), assign a weight $w(i, t) = \frac{\alpha_i}{\beta^t} + (n-t)\mu_i$.

3. Let M be the minimum-weight perfect matching on G. For each node $t \in R$, let $\pi(t) \in L$ be the node that it is matched with. If the weight of M is larger than δ^*, output NONE. Else, define $\delta_{\pi(n)} = \delta^*, \mathcal{Y}_{\pi(n)} = \mathcal{Y}^*$.

4. For t from n to 2:
   - Let $\delta_{\pi(t-1)} = \delta_{\pi(t)} - \frac{\alpha_{\pi(t)}}{\beta^t} - \sum_{\tau=1}^{t-2} \mu_{\pi(\tau)}$.
   - Let $\mathcal{Y}_{\pi(t-1)}$ be such that $s(\mathcal{Y}_{\pi(t-1)}) = \delta_{\pi(t-1)}$.

5. Output $\omega = (\pi, (\mathcal{Y}_{\pi(1)}, \ldots, \mathcal{Y}_{\pi(n)}))$.

2.6 General NP-completeness

One may wonder if we can get an efficient mechanism for learning vectors which are not n-dimensional. We show that this is unlikely, since finding a collaborative equilibrium is NP-complete even under a weak generalization of n-dimensional learning vectors.

DEFINITION 12. *We say that a learning vector $\lambda \in \Lambda$ is n^2-dimensional if there exists a non-negative matrix $(\mu_{i,j})_{(i,j)\in[n]\times[n]}$ such that $\lambda_{\pi,\pi(t)} = \sum_{\tau=1}^{t-1} \mu_{\pi(t),\pi(\tau)}$. We denote by $\Lambda_2 \subset \Lambda$ the set of all n^2-dimensional learning vectors.*

When λ is an n^2-dimensional learning vector, the amount that player $\pi(t)$ learns from $\pi(\tau)$'s output is bounded above by $\mu_{\pi(t),\pi(\tau)}$. Thus, the total amount that player $\pi(t)$ learns from all prior outputs is $\sum_{\tau=1}^{t-1} \mu_{\pi(t),\pi(\tau)}$. The corresponding necessary condition for a collaborative equilibrium to be supported by some $(\vec{x}, \vec{\lambda})$ is that there is a permutation π

such that

$$\sum_{t=1}^{n} \frac{\alpha_{\pi(t)}}{\beta^t} + \sum_{t=1}^{n} \sum_{s>t} \mu_{\pi(s),\pi(t)} \leq s(\{\hat{y}|x_1, \ldots, x_n\}) - s(\mathcal{Y}_0).$$

We show that even checking whether this condition holds is NP-complete.

THEOREM 13. *Given model parameters CK, input datasets $(x_1, \ldots, x_n) \in X$, and a n^2-dimensional learning bound vector $(\mu_{i,j})_{(i,j)\in[n]\times[n]}$, it is NP-complete to decide whether there exists π such that*

$$\sum_{t=1}^{n} \frac{\alpha_{\pi(t)}}{\beta^t} + \sum_{t=1}^{n} \sum_{s>t} \mu_{\pi(s),\pi(t)} \leq s(\{\hat{y}|x_1, \ldots, x_n\}) - s(\mathcal{Y}_0).$$

PROOF. To show that the problem is NP-hard, we reduce it to the *minimum weighted feedback arc set problem*. The proof is given in our full version [1]. $\square$

We have shown that in our model of scientific collaboration, it can indeed be very beneficial to *all parties involved* to collaborate under certain ordering functions, and such collaboration outcomes can be efficiently computed under certain realistic conditions (but probably not in general).

3. ORDERED MPC

We introduce formal definitions of ordered MPC and associated notions of fairness and ordered output delivery, and give protocols that realize these notions. Our definitions build on the standard security notion[12] for traditional MPC.

Throughout this work, we consider computationally bounded (rushing) adversaries in a synchronous complete network, and we assume the players are honest-but-curious, since any protocol secure against honest-but-curious players can be transformed into one secure against malicious players [12].

Let f be an arbitrary n-ary function and p be an n-ary function that outputs permutation $[n] \rightarrow [n]$. An ordered MPC protocol is executed by n parties, where each party $i \in [n]$ has a private input $x_i \in \{0,1\}^*$, who wish to securely compute $f(x_1, \ldots, x_n) = (y_1, \ldots, y_n) \in (\{0,1\}^*)^n$ where y_i is the output of party i. Moreover, the parties are to receive their outputs in a particular *ordering* dictated by $p(x_1, \ldots, x_n) = \pi \in ([n] \rightarrow [n])$. That is, for all $i < j$, party $\pi(i)$ must receive his output *before* party $\pi(j)$ receives her output. Note that the output ordering π is *data-dependent*, as p is a function of the parties' inputs.

Following [12], the security of ordered MPC with respect to a functionality f and permutation function p is defined by comparing the execution of a protocol to an ideal process $\mathcal{F}_{\text{Ordered-MPC}}$ where the outputs and ordering are computed by a trusted party who sees all the inputs. An ordered MPC protocol F is considered to be secure if for any real-world adversary $\mathcal{A}$ attacking the real protocol F, there exists an ideal adversary $\mathcal{S}$ in the ideal process whose outputs (views) are indistinguishable from those of $\mathcal{A}$. Note that this implies that no player learns more information about the other players' inputs than can be learned from his own input and output, *and his own position in the output delivery order*. The latter condition is important because the output ordering depends on parties' private inputs, and thus we require that the protocol reveals as little information as possible about the ordering.

---

[12] Note that throughout this work, we use "stand-alone" security notions rather than "universally composable" ones. The standard definition is given formally in our full version [1].

Many rather than one view. In the ordered MPC setting, the ideal adversary S and the real-world adversary $\mathcal{A}$ each output a view after each output phase. This is in contrast to standard MPC, where the adversaries simply output one view at the end of the protocol execution.

Ideal functionality $\mathcal{F}_{\text{Ordered-MPC}}$

In the ideal model, a trusted third party T is given the inputs, computes the functions f, p on the inputs, and outputs to each player i his output y_i in the order prescribed by the ordering function. In addition, we model an ideal process adversary S who attacks the protocol by corrupting players in the ideal setting.

Public parameters. *$\kappa \in \mathbb{N}$, the security parameter; $n \in \mathbb{N}$, the number of parties; $f : (\{0,1\}^*)^n \to (\{0,1\}^*)^n$, the function to compute; and $p : (\{0,1\}^*)^n \to ([n] \to [n])$, the ordering function.*

Private parameters. *Each player $i \in [n]$ has input $x_i \in \{0,1\}^*$.*

1. INPUT. *Each player i sends his input x_i to T.*

2. COMPUTATION. *T computes $(y_1, \ldots, y_n) = f(x_1, \ldots, x_n)$ and $\pi = p(x_1, \ldots, x_n)$.*

3. OUTPUT. *The output proceeds in n sequential output rounds. At the start of the jth round, T sends the output value $\mathsf{out}_{i,j}$ to each party i, where $\mathsf{out}_{j,j} = y_{\pi(j)}$ and $\mathsf{out}_{i,j} = \bot$ for all $i \neq j$. When party $\pi(j)$ receives his output, he responds to T with the message ack. (The players who receive $\bot$ are not expected to respond.) Upon receipt of the ack, T proceeds to the $(j+1)^{th}$ round – or, if $j = n$, then the protocol terminates.*

4. OUTPUT OF VIEWS. *At each output round, after receiving his message from T, each party produces an output, as follows. Each uncorrupted party i outputs y_i if he has already received his output, or $\bot$ if he has not. Each corrupted party outputs $\bot$. Additionally, the adversary S outputs an arbitrary function of the information that he has learned during the execution of the ideal protocol.*

Let the output of party i in the jth round be denoted by $\mathcal{V}_{i,j}$, and let the view outputted by S in the jth round be denoted by $\mathcal{V}_{S,j}$. Let $\mathcal{V}^{\text{ideal}}_{\text{Ordered-MPC}}$ denote the collection of all views for all output rounds:

$$\mathcal{V}^{\text{ideal}}_{\text{Ordered-MPC}} =$$
$$\left((\mathcal{V}_{S,1}, \mathcal{V}_{1,1}, \ldots, \mathcal{V}_{n,1}), \ldots, (\mathcal{V}_{S,n}, \mathcal{V}_{1,n}, \ldots, \mathcal{V}_{n,n}) \right).$$

(If the protocol is terminated early, then views for rounds which have not yet been started are taken to be $\bot$.)

DEFINITION 14 (SECURITY). *A multi-party protocol F is said to securely realize $\mathcal{F}_{\text{Ordered-MPC}}$, if the following conditions hold.*

1. *The protocol description specifies n check-points $C_1, \ldots, C_n$ corresponding to events during the execution of the protocol.*

2. *Take any PPT adversary $\mathcal{A}$ who corrupts a subset of players $S \subset [n]$, and let $V_{\mathcal{A},j}$ be the result of an arbitrary function A applies to his view after each check-point C_j. Let*

$$V^{\text{real}}_{\mathcal{A}} = ((V_{A,1}, V_{1,1}, \ldots, V_{n,1}), \ldots, (V_{A,n}, V_{1,n}, \ldots, V_{n,n}))$$

be the tuple consisting of the adversary $\mathcal{A}$'s outputted views along with the outputs of the real-world parties as specified in the ideal functionality description. Then there is a PPT ideal adversary S which, attacking $\mathcal{F}_{\text{Ordered-MPC}}$ by corrupting the same subset S of players, can output views $\mathcal{V}_{S,j}$ such that for each $j \in [n]$, it holds that $\mathcal{V}_{S,j} \stackrel{c}{\approx} V_{\mathcal{A},j}$, where $\stackrel{c}{\approx}$ denotes computational indistinguishability.

In the context of ordered MPC, the standard guaranteed output delivery notion is insufficient. Instead, we define *ordered output delivery*, which requires in addition that all parties receive their outputs in the order prescribed by p.

DEFINITION 15 (ORDERED OUTPUT DELIVERY). *An ordered MPC protocol satisfies* ordered output delivery *if for any inputs $x_1, \ldots, x_n$, functionality f, and ordering function p, it holds that all parties receive their outputs before protocol termination, and moreover, if $\pi(i) < \pi(j)$, then party i receives his output before party j receives hers, where $\pi = p(x_1, \ldots, x_n)$.*

We also define a natural relaxation of the fairness requirement for ordered MPC, called *prefix-fairness*. Although it is known that fairness is impossible for general functionalities in the presence of a dishonest majority, we show in the next subsection that prefix-fairness can be achieved even when a majority of parties are corrupt. We emphasize that this notion relaxes *only* the fairness requirement: that is, prefix-fair protocols satisfy full privacy (and correctness) guarantees.

DEFINITION 16 (PREFIX-FAIRNESS). *An ordered MPC protocol is* prefix-fair *if for any inputs $x_1, \ldots, x_n$, the set of parties who have received their outputs when the protocol terminates (or aborts) is a prefix of $(\pi(1), \ldots, \pi(n))$, where $\pi = p(x_1, \ldots, x_n)$ is the permutation induced by the inputs.*

Prefix-fairness can be useful, for example, in settings where it is more important for one party to receive the output than the other; or where there is some prior knowledge about the trustworthiness of each party (so that more trustworthy parties may receive their outputs first).

3.1 Construction

Ordered MPC is achievable by using standard protocols for general MPC, as described in Protocol 1 below. The protocol has n sequential output phases, so that the n outputs can be issued in order. A subtle point is that because the ordering is a function of the input data, knowledge of the ordering may reveal information about the inputs. Thus, we have to "mask" the output values such that each party only learns the minimal possible amount of information about the ordering: namely, his own position in the ordering.

Protocol 1. Ordered MPC

Public parameters. *$\kappa \in \mathbb{N}$, the security parameter; $n \in \mathbb{N}$, the number of parties; $k \in \mathbb{N}$, an upper bound on the number of corrupt parties; $f : (\{0,1\}^*)^n \to (\{0,1\}^*)^n$, the function to be computed; and $p : (\{0,1\}^*)^n \to ([n] \to [n])$, the ordering function.*

1. ***Computing shares of $(\pi, \mathbf{y})$:*** *Using any general secure MPC protocol (such as [12]) on inputs $x_1, \ldots, x_n$, jointly compute a k-out-of-n secret-sharing[13] of $(\pi, \mathbf{y})$ where $\mathbf{y} = (y_1, \ldots, y_n) = f(x_1, \ldots, x_n)$ and $\pi = p(x_1, \ldots, x_n)$ is a permutation of $[n]$. At the end of this step, each player possesses a share of the outputs $\mathbf{y} = (y_1, \ldots, y_n)$ and of the permutation π.*

2. ***Outputting $y_1, \ldots, y_n$ in n phases:*** *In the ith output phase, player $\pi^{-1}(i)$ will learn his output. In phase i the parties run a new instance of a general secure MPC protocol such that:*

   - *Player j's inputs to the protocol are: the shares of $\mathbf{y}$ and π that he got in step 1, and a random string $r_{i,j}$.*
   - *The functionality computed is:*
     ```
     for j from 1 to n: if π(j) = i then z_{i,j} :=
        y_j ⊕ r_{i,j} else z_{i,j} := ⊥ ⊕ r_{i,j}.
     output z_i := (z_{i,1}, ..., z_{i,n}).
     ```
     where $\bot$ is a special string outside f's output domain.
   - *To recover his output, each player j computes $y'_{i,j} = z_{i,j} \oplus r_{i,j}$ for all i. By construction, there is exactly one $i \in [n]$ for which $y'_{i,j} \neq \bot$, and that is equal to the output value y_j for player j.*

Check-points. *There are n check-points. For $i \in [n]$, the check-point C_i is at the end of the ith output phase, when z_i is learned by all players.*

In case of abort. *When running the protocol for the honest majority setting, the honest players continue until the end of the protocol regardless of other players' behavior. When running the protocol for dishonest majority, if any party aborts in an output phase[14], then the honest players abort before the next phase.*

THEOREM 17. *Protocol 1 securely realizes $\mathcal{F}_{\text{Ordered-MPC}}$.*

THEOREM 18. *In the case of honest majority, Protocol 1 achieves fairness. In the dishonest majority setting, prefix-fairness is achieved.*

4. TIMED-DELAY MPC

In this section, we implementing *time delays* between different players receiving their outputs. The model is exactly as before, with n players wishing to compute a function $f(x_1, \ldots, x_n)$ in an ordering prescribed by $p(x_1, \ldots, x_n)$ – except that now, there is an additional requirement of a delay after each player receives his output and before the next player receives her output. To realize the timed-delay MPC functionality, we make use of time-lock and time-line puzzles, which are introduced in Section 4.2.1.

4.1 Ideal functionality with time delays

We measure time delay in units of computation, rather than seconds of a clock: that is, rather than making any assumption about global clocks (or synchrony of local clocks)[15], we measure time by the *evaluations of a particular function* (on random inputs), which we call the *clock function*.

Ideal functionality $\mathcal{F}_{\text{Timed-MPC}}$

In the ideal model, a trusted third party T is given the inputs, computes the functions f, p on the inputs, and outputs to each player i his output y_i in the order prescribed by the ordering function. Moreover, T imposes delays between the issuance of one party's output and the next. In addition, we model an ideal process adversary $\mathcal{S}$ who attacks the protocol by corrupting players in the ideal setting.

Public parameters. *$\kappa \in \mathbb{N}$, the security parameter; $n \in \mathbb{N}$, the number of parties; $f : (\{0,1\}^*)^n \to (\{0,1\}^*)^n$, the function to be computed; $p : (\{0,1\}^*)^n \to ([n] \to [n])$, the ordering function; and $G = G(\kappa) \in \mathbb{N}$, the number of time-steps between the issuance of one party's output and the next.*

Private parameters. *Each player $i \in [n]$ has input $x_i \in \{0,1\}^*$.*

---

[13] The standard definition of a secret-sharing scheme can be found in our full version [1].

[14] Each output phase consists of an execution of the underlying general MPC protocol. If a party aborts at any time during (and before the end of) the execution of the underlying general MPC protocol, this fact will be detected by all honest parties by the end of the phase.

[15] A particular issue that arises when considering a clock-based definition is that it is not clear that we can reasonably assume or prove that clocks are in synchrony between the real and ideal world – but this seems necessary in order to prove security by simulation in the ideal functionality.
We remark that if one is happy to assume the existence of a global clock (or synchrony of local clocks), then there are other ways to implement timed-delay MPC which sidestep many of the issues inherent in the arguably more realistic model where clocks may not be perfectly synchronized between different (adversarial) parties. One example is the "Bitcoin model" where the assumption is that the Bitcoin block-chain can serve as a global clock: in this model, existing protocols such as [6] implement some time-delays in MPC, and it seems likely that such protocols can be adapted to achieve our notion of timed-delay MPC.

1. INPUT. *Each player i sends his input x_i to T. If, instead of sending his input, any player sends the message* quit, *then the computation is aborted.*

2. COMPUTATION. *T computes $(y_1, \ldots, y_n) = f(x_1, \ldots, x_n)$ and $\pi = p(x_1, \ldots, x_n)$.*

3. OUTPUT. *The output proceeds in n sequential output phases. At each phase j, T waits for G time-steps, then sends the jth output, $y_{\pi(j)}$, to party $\pi(j)$.*

4. OUTPUT OF VIEWS. *At the end of each output phase, each party produces an output as follows. Each uncorrupted party i outputs y_i as his view if he has already received his output, or $\perp$ if he has not. Each corrupted party outputs $\perp$. Additionally, the adversary $\mathcal{S}$ outputs an arbitrary function of the information that he has learned during the execution of the ideal protocol, after each check-point.*

Let the output of party i in the jth round be denoted by $\mathcal{V}_{i,j}$, and let the view outputted by $\mathcal{S}$ in the jth round be denoted by $\mathcal{V}_{\mathcal{S},j}$. Let $\mathcal{V}_{\text{Timed-MPC}}^{\text{ideal}}$ denote the collection of all views for all output phases:

$$\mathcal{V}_{\text{Timed-MPC}}^{\text{ideal}} = \\ ((\mathcal{V}_{\mathcal{S},1}, \mathcal{V}_{1,1}, \ldots, \mathcal{V}_{n,1}), \ldots, (\mathcal{V}_{\mathcal{S},n}, \mathcal{V}_{1,n}, \ldots, \mathcal{V}_{n,n})).$$

For an algorithm $\mathcal{A}$, let the run-time[16] of $\mathcal{A}$ on input inp be denoted by $\text{time}_{\mathcal{A}}(\text{inp})$. If $\mathcal{A}$ is probabilistic, the run-time will be a distribution over the random coins of $\mathcal{A}$. Note that the exact run-time of an algorithm will depend on the underlying computational model in which the algorithm is run. In this work, all algorithms are assumed to be running in the same underlying computational model, and our definitions and results hold regardless of the specific computational model employed.

DEFINITION 19 (SECURITY). *A multi-party protocol F (with parameters κ, n, f, p, G) securely realizes $\mathcal{F}_{\text{Timed-MPC}}$ if the following conditions hold.*

1. *The protocol description specifies n check-points $C_1, \ldots, C_n$ corresponding to events during protocol execution.*

2. *There exists a "clock function" g such that between any two consecutive checkpoints C_i, C_{i+1} during an execution of F, any one of the parties (in the real world) must be able to locally run $\Omega(G)$ sequential evaluations of g on random inputs. g may also be a protocol (involving $n' \le n$ parties) rather than a function, in which case we instead require that any subset consisting of n' parties must be able to run $\Omega(G)$ sequential executions of g (on random inputs) over the communication network being used for the main multi-party protocol F. Then, we say that F is "clocked by g".*

3. *Take any PPT adversary $\mathcal{A}$ attacking the protocol F by corrupting a subset of players $S \subset [n]$, which outputs an arbitrary function $V_{\mathcal{A},j}$ of the information that it has learned in the protocol execution after each check-point C_j. Let*

$$V_{\mathcal{A}}^{\text{real}} = ((V_{\mathcal{A},1}, V_{1,1}, \ldots, V_{n,1}), \ldots, (V_{\mathcal{A},n}, V_{1,n}, \ldots, V_{n,n}))$$

be the tuple consisting of the adversary $\mathcal{A}$'s outputted views along with the views of the real-world parties as specified in the ideal functionality description. Then there is a PPT ideal adversary $\mathcal{S}$ which, attacking $\mathcal{F}_{\text{Timed-MPC}}$ by corrupting the same subset S of players, can output views $\mathcal{V}_{\mathcal{S},1}, \ldots, \mathcal{V}_{\mathcal{S},n}$ (at

---

[15] The use of checkpoints is introduced to capture the views of players and the adversary at intermediate points in protocol execution.

[16] Run-time is, naturally, measured in "CPU time" (i.e. the number of instructions executed in the underlying computational model) as opposed to real-world "clock time".

check-points $C_1, \ldots, C_n$ respectively) such that for each $j \in [n]$, it holds that

$$| \Pr \left[D(\mathcal{V}_{\mathcal{S},j}, \mathcal{V}_{1,j}, \ldots, \mathcal{V}_{n,j}) = 1 \right]$$
$$- \Pr \left[D(V_{\mathcal{A},j}, V_{1,j}, \ldots, V_{n,j}) = 1 \right] |$$
$$\leq \mathsf{negl}(\kappa),$$

for any distinguisher D such that

$$\Pr_{\vec{v} \leftarrow \mathcal{V}} [\mathsf{time}_D(\vec{v}) \leq j \cdot \mathsf{time}_{\mathcal{G}}()] = 1/\mathsf{poly}(\kappa),$$

when $\mathcal{V}$ is the distribution of views outputted by $\mathcal{A}$ or $\mathcal{S}$ (that is, for $\mathcal{V} \in \{(\mathcal{V}_{\mathcal{S},j}, \mathcal{V}_{1,j}, \ldots, \mathcal{V}_{n,j}), (V_{\mathcal{A},j}, V_{1,j}, \ldots, V_{n,j})\}$), and $\mathcal{G}$ is the algorithm that computes the function g sequentially on G random inputs.

4.2 Realizing timed-delay MPC

A simple protocol for securely realizing timed-delay MPC is to implement delays by running G "dummy rounds" of communication between issuing outputs to different players. In our full version, we formally describe such a protocol and prove that it securely realizes $\mathcal{F}_{\text{Timed-MPC}}$.

However, a downside of the simple solution above is that it requires all (honest) parties to be online and communicating until the last player receives his output. To address this, we propose an alternative solution based on *timed-release cryptography*, at the cost of an additional assumption that all players have comparable computing speed (within a logarithmic factor).

Informally, a time-lock puzzle is a primitive which allows "locking" of data, such that it will be released after a pre-specified time delay, and no earlier. Our next protocol, instead of issuing outputs to players in the clear, gives to each party his output *locked* into a time-lock puzzle; and in order to enforce the desired ordering, the delays required to unlock the puzzles are set to be an increasing sequence. We first give the definition of time-lock puzzles (in Section 4.2.1) then describe and prove security of our time-lock-based protocol (in Section 4.2.2).

4.2.1 Time-lock puzzles

The delayed release of data in MPC protocols can be closely linked to the problem of "timed-release crypto" in general, which was introduced by [17] and constructed first by [19] with their proposal of *time-lock puzzles*. We assume time-lock puzzles with a particular structure (that is present in all known implementations): namely, the passage of "time" will be measured by sequential evaluations of a function (TimeStep). Unlocking a t-step time-lock puzzle can be considered analogous to following a chain of t pointers, at the end of which there is a special value x_t (e.g. a decryption key) that allows retrieval of the locked data.

DEFINITION 20 (TIME-LOCK PUZZLE SCHEME). *A time-lock puzzle scheme is a tuple of PPT algorithms:*

$$T = (\mathsf{Lock}, \mathsf{TimeStep}, \mathsf{Unlock})$$

- $\mathsf{Lock}(1^\kappa, d, t)$ takes parameters $\kappa \in \mathbb{N}$ the security parameter, $d \in \{0,1\}^\ell$ the data to be locked, and $t \in \mathbb{N}$ the number of steps needed to unlock the puzzle, and outputs a time-lock puzzle $P = (x, t, b, a) \in \{0,1\}^n \times \mathbb{N} \times \{0,1\}^{n''} \times \{0,1\}^{n'}$ where $\ell, n, n', n'' = \mathsf{poly}(\kappa)$.
- $\mathsf{TimeStep}(1^\kappa, x', a')$ takes parameters $\kappa \in \mathbb{N}$ the security parameter, a bit-string $x' \in \{0,1\}^n$, and auxiliary information a', and outputs a bit-string $x'' \in \{0,1\}^n$.
- $\mathsf{Unlock}(1^\kappa, x', b')$ takes parameters $\kappa \in \mathbb{N}$ the security parameter, a bit-string $x' \in \{0,1\}^n$, and auxiliary information $b' \in \{0,1\}^{n'}$, and outputs some data $d' \in \{0,1\}^\ell$.

To unclutter notation, we will sometimes omit the initial security parameter of these functions (writing e.g. simply $\mathsf{Lock}(d, t)$). We now define some auxiliary functions. For a time-lock puzzle scheme $T = (\mathsf{Lock}, \mathsf{TimeStep}, \mathsf{Unlock})$ and $i \in \mathbb{N}$, let $\mathsf{IterateTimeStep}_i^T$ denote the following function:

$$\mathsf{IterateTimeStep}^T(i, x, a) =$$
$$\underbrace{\mathsf{TimeStep}(\mathsf{TimeStep}(\ldots(\mathsf{TimeStep}(x, a), a)\ldots), a)}_{i}.$$

Define $\mathsf{FullUnlock}^T$ to be the following function:

$$\mathsf{FullUnlock}^T((x, t, b, a)) = \mathsf{Unlock}(\mathsf{IterateTimeStep}^T(t, x, a), b),$$

that is, the function that should be used to unlock a time-lock puzzle outputted by Lock.

The following definitions formalize correctness and security for time-lock puzzle schemes.

DEFINITION 21 (CORRECTNESS). *A time-lock puzzle scheme $T = (\mathsf{Lock}, \mathsf{TimeStep}, \mathsf{Unlock})$ is correct if the following holds (where κ is the security parameter):*

$$\Pr_{(x,t,b,a)\leftarrow\mathsf{Lock}(d,t)} \left[\mathsf{FullUnlock}^T((x, t, b, a)) \neq d \right] \leq \mathsf{negl}(\kappa).$$

DEFINITION 22 (SECURITY). *Let $T = (\mathsf{Lock}, \mathsf{TimeStep}, \mathsf{Unlock})$ be a time-lock puzzle scheme. T is secure if it holds that: for all $d, d' \in \{0,1\}^\ell, t = \mathsf{poly}(\kappa)$, if there exists an adversary $\mathcal{A}$ that solves the time-lock puzzle $\mathsf{Lock}(d, t)$, that is,*

$$\Pr_{P\leftarrow\mathsf{Lock}(d,t)}[\mathcal{A}(P) = d] = \varepsilon \text{ for some non-negligible } \varepsilon,$$

then for each $j \in [t]$, there is an adversary $\mathcal{A}_j$ such that the following probabilities are overwhelming (i.e. $1 - \mathsf{negl}(\kappa)$):

$$\Pr_{P'\leftarrow\mathsf{Lock}(d',j)} \left[\mathcal{A}_j(P') = d' \right], \text{ and}$$

$$\Pr_{\substack{P\leftarrow\mathsf{Lock}(d,t), \\ P'\leftarrow\mathsf{Lock}(d',j)}} \left[\mathsf{time}_{\mathcal{A}}(P) \geq (t/j) \cdot \mathsf{time}_{\mathcal{A}_j}(P') \mid \mathcal{A}(P) = d \right].$$

4.2.2 Protocol based on time-lock puzzles

Because of the use of time-lock puzzles by different parties in the protocol that follows, we require an additional assumption that all players have comparable computing power (within a logarithmic factor).

Relative-Delay Assumption. The difference in speed of computation between any two parties $i, j \in [n]$ is at most a factor of $B = O(\log(\kappa))$.

Protocol 2. Timed-delay MPC with time-lock puzzles

Public parameters. $\kappa \in \mathbb{N}$, the security parameter; $n \in \mathbb{N}$, the number of parties; $f : (\{0,1\}^*)^n \to (\{0,1\}^*)^n$, the function to be computed; $p : (\{0,1\})^* \to ([n] \to [n])$, the ordering function; $B = O(\log(\kappa))$, the maximum factor of difference between any two parties' computing power; $G = \mathsf{poly}(\kappa)$, the number of time-steps between the issuance of one party's output and the next; and $T = \{\mathsf{Lock}, \mathsf{TimeStep}, \mathsf{Unlock}\}$ a time-lock puzzle scheme.

Inputs. Each party i has input x_i.

Protocol steps. Let $(y_1, \ldots, y_n) = f(x_1, \ldots, x_n)$ and $\pi = p(x_1, \ldots, x_n)$. Define $t_1 = 1$ and $t_{i+1} = (B \cdot G + 1) \cdot t_i$ for $i \in [n-1]$. Compute $(P_1, \ldots, P_n)$, where each $P_i = (x_i, t_{\pi(i)}, a_i, b_i)$ is a time-lock puzzle computed as

$$P_i = \mathsf{Lock}(y_i \oplus r_i, t_{\pi(i)}),$$

where each r_i is a random string provided as input randomness by party i.

Outputs. *For each $i \in [n]$, the puzzle P_i is outputted to party i. The players all receive their respective outputs at the same time, then recovers his output y_i by solving his time-lock puzzle, and finally "unmasking" the result by XORing with his random input r_i.*

Check-points. *There are n check-points. For $i \in [n]$, the checkpoint C_i is the event of party $\pi(i)$ learning his eventual output $y_{\pi(i)}$ (i.e. when he finishes solving his time-lock puzzle).*

For the following theorem, we assume that each player i uses the optimal algorithm to solve his puzzle P_i that outputs the correct answer. Without this assumption, any further protocol analysis would not make sense: there can always be a "lazy" player who willfully uses a very slow algorithm to solve his puzzle, who will as a result learn his eventual output much later in the order than he could otherwise have done. The property that we aim to achieve is that every player *could* learn his output at his assigned position in the ordering π, with appropriate delays before and after he learns his output.

THEOREM 23. *Suppose that the Relative-Delay Assumption holds, and each player i uses the optimal algorithm to solve his puzzle P_i that outputs (with overwhelming probability) the correct answer. Then, Protocol 2 securely realizes $\mathcal{F}_{\text{Timed-MPC}}$ when there is an honest majority.*

A few remarks are in order. In Protocol 2, all the parties can stop interacting as soon as all the puzzles are outputted. When the locking algorithm $\text{Lock}(d, t)$ has run-time that is independent of the delay t, the run-time of Protocol 2 is also independent of the delay parameters. (This is achievable using the [19] time-lock construction, for example.)

In our full version, we introduce the more general, novel definition of *time-line* puzzles, which can be useful for locking together many data items with different delays for a single recipient, or for locking data for a group of people. In the latter case, it becomes a concern that computation speed will vary between parties: indeed, the scheme will be unworkable if some parties have orders of magnitude more computing power than others, so some assumption is required on the similarity of computing power among parties. When a time-line puzzle is given to a single recipient, then no additional assumptions are required.

We remark that time-line puzzles could be used (instead of a set of time-lock puzzles) to realize Protocol 2 more efficiently: the time required to generate a time-line puzzle is dependent only on the longest delay t_n, whereas the time required to generate n separate time-lock puzzles depends on the sum of all the delays, $t_1 + \cdots + t_n$. More generally, we believe that time-line puzzles may be of independent interest as a timed-release primitive.

Acknowledgements

We would like to thank Yehuda Lindell for an interesting discussion on the nature of fairness in multiparty computation, and we are grateful to Juan Garay, Björn Tackmann, and Vassilis Zikas for an illuminating discussion about measures of partial fairness in MPC. We thank Silvio Micali and Ron Rivest for helpful comments about the data-sharing model.

References

[1] Pablo Daniel Azar, Shafi Goldwasser, and Sunoo Park. *How to Incentivize Data-Driven Collaboration Among Competing Parties.* http://eprint.iacr.org/2015/178. 2015.

[2] Pablo Daniel Azar and Silvio Micali. "Rational proofs". In: *Proceedings of the forty-fourth annual ACM symposium on Theory of computing.* ACM. 2012, pp. 1017–1028.

[3] Pablo Daniel Azar and Silvio Micali. "Super-efficient rational proofs". In: *Proceedings of the fourteenth ACM conference on Electronic commerce.* ACM. 2013, pp. 29–30.

[4] Siddhartha Banerjee, Ashish Goel, and Anilesh Kollagunta Krishnaswamy. "Re-incentivizing discovery: mechanisms for partial-progress sharing in research". In: *ACM Conference on Economics and Computation, EC '14, Stanford , CA, USA, June 8-12, 2014.* 2014, pp. 149–166.

[5] Yoshua Bengio, Yann LeCun, et al. "Scaling learning algorithms towards AI". In: *Large-scale kernel machines* 34.5 (2007).

[6] Iddo Bentov and Ranjit Kumaresan. "How to Use Bitcoin to Design Fair Protocols". In: *Advances in Cryptology - CRYPTO 2014 - 34th Annual Cryptology Conference, Santa Barbara, CA, USA, August 17-21, 2014, Proceedings, Part II.* 2014, pp. 421–439.

[7] Sarah E. Bergen and Tracey L. Petryshen. "Genome-wide association studies (GWAS) of schizophrenia: does bigger lead to better results?" In: *Current opinion in psychiatry* 25.2 (Mar. 2012), pp. 76–82.

[8] Dan Boneh and Moni Naor. "Timed Commitments". In: *Advances in Cryptology - CRYPTO 2000, 20th Annual International Cryptology Conference, Santa Barbara, California, USA, August 20-24, 2000, Proceedings.* 2000, pp. 236–254.

[9] Yang Cai, Constantinos Daskalakis, and Christos Papadimitriou. "Optimum Statistical Estimation with Strategic Data Sources". In: *ArXiv e-prints* (2014). arXiv: 1408.2539 [stat.ML].

[10] Richard Cleve. "Limits on the Security of Coin Flips when Half the Processors Are Faulty (Extended Abstract)". In: *Proceedings of the 18th Annual ACM Symposium on Theory of Computing, May 28-30, 1986, Berkeley, California, USA.* 1986, pp. 364–369.

[11] Schizophrenia Research Forum. *GWAS Goes Bigger: Large Sample Sizes Uncover New Risk Loci, Additional Overlap in Schizophrenia and Bipolar Disorder.* Sept. 2011.

[12] Oded Goldreich, Silvio Micali, and Avi Wigderson. "How to Play any Mental Game or A Completeness Theorem for Protocols with Honest Majority". In: *Proceedings of the 19th Annual ACM Symposium on Theory of Computing, 1987, New York, New York, USA.* 1987, pp. 218–229.

[13] Siyao Guo et al. "Rational arguments: single round delegation with sublinear verification". In: *Proceedings of the 5th conference on Innovations in theoretical computer science.* ACM. 2014, pp. 523–540.

[14] Robin Hanson. "Logarithmic Market Scoring Rules For Modular Combinatorial Information Aggregation". In: *The Journal of Prediction Markets* 1.1 (2012), pp. 3–15.

[15] Broad Institute. *International team sheds new light on biology underlying schizophrenia.* July 2014. URL: https://www.broadinstitute.org/news/5895.

[16] Jon M. Kleinberg and Sigal Oren. "Mechanisms for (mis)allocating scientific credit". In: *Proceedings of the 43rd ACM Symposium on Theory of Computing, STOC 2011, San Jose, CA, USA, 6-8 June 2011.* 2011, pp. 529–538.

[17] Timothy C. May. *Timed-release crypto.* 1993. URL: http://www.hks.net/cpunks/cpunks-01460.html.

[18] Schizophrenia Working Group of the Psychiatric Genomics Consortium. "Biological insights from 108 schizophrenia-associated genetic loci". In: *Nature* 511 (Mar. 2014), pp. 421–427.

[19] Ronald L. Rivest, Adi Shamir, and David A. Wagner. *Time-lock puzzles and timed-release crypto.* Tech. rep. 1996.

[20] The Wellcome Trust. *Sharing Data from Large-scale Biological Research Projects: A System of Tripartite Responsibility.* Report of a meeting organized by the Wellcome Trust and held on 14–15 January 2003 at Fort Lauderdale, USA. 2003.

From Nash Equilibria to Chain Recurrent Sets: Solution Concepts and Topology

Christos Papadimitriou
University of California, Berkeley
christos@berkeley.edu

Georgios Piliouras
Singapore University of Technology and Design
Simons Institute for the Theory of Computing
University of California, Berkeley
georgios@sutd.edu.sg

ABSTRACT

Nash's universal existence theorem for his notion of equilibria was essentially an ingenious application of fixed point theorems, the most sophisticated result in his era's topology — in fact, recent algorithmic work has established that Nash equilibria are in fact computationally equivalent to fixed points. Here, we shift focus to universal non-equilibrium solution concepts that arise from an important theorem in the topology of dynamical systems that was unavailable to Nash. This approach takes as input both a game and a learning dynamic, defined over mixed strategies. Nash equilibria are guaranteed to be fixed points of such dynamics; however, the system behavior is captured by a more general object that is known in dynamical systems theory as *chain recurrent set*. Informally, once we focus on this solution concept, every game behaves like a potential game with the dynamic converging to these states. We characterize this solution for simple benchmark games under replicator dynamics, arguably the best known evolutionary dynamic in game theory. For potential games it coincides with the notion of equilibrium; however, in simple zero sum games, it can cover the whole state space. We discuss numerous novel computational as well as structural, combinatorial questions that chain recurrence raises.

Categories and Subject Descriptors

F.0 [**Theory of Computation**]: General

Keywords

Algorithmic Game Theory; Replicator Dynamics; Invariant; Entropy

1. INTRODUCTION

Game theory has enjoyed a close relationship with topology of dynamical systems from its very beginnings. Nash's brilliant proof of the universality of equilibria is based on

Permission to make digital or hard copies of all or part of this work for personal or classroom use is granted without fee provided that copies are not made or distributed for profit or commercial advantage and that copies bear this notice and the full citation on the first page. Copyrights for components of this work owned by others than the author(s) must be honored. Abstracting with credit is permitted. To copy otherwise, or republish, to post on servers or to redistribute to lists, requires prior specific permission and/or a fee. Request permissions from Permissions@acm.org.

ITCS'16, January 14–16, 2016, Cambridge, MA, USA.
Copyright is held by the owner/author(s). Publication rights licensed to ACM.
ACM 978-1-4503-4057-1/16/01 ...$15.00.
DOI: http://dx.doi.org/10.1145/2840728.2840757

fixed point theorems, the most sophisticated class of topological theorems of his time. Recent work in algorithmic game theory has coupled these concepts even further arguing that that these ideas are, in fact, in a formal sense computationally equivalent [11]. However, natural dynamics do not always converge to a Nash equilibrium. *To which object do they converge?*

To answer, one must apply the modern pinnacle of dynamical systems theory, the fundamental theorem of dynamical systems, which was introduced in the seminal work of Conley [8] in 1978. The theorem states that, given an arbitrary initial condition, a dynamical system converges to a set of states with a natural recurrence property, an elegant concept that should appeal to a computer scientist, especially a student of cryptography.

Imagine that Alice is trying to simulate the trajectory of a given system on a powerful computer. Every time she computes a single iteration of the dynamical process, there is a rounding error ϵ. Furthermore, imagine that inside the machine there is an infinitely powerful demon, Bob who, before the next computational step is taken, rounds the result in arbitrary fashion of his own choosing (but within distance ϵ of the actual outcome). If, no matter how high the accuracy of Alice's computer is, Bob can always fool her into believing that a specific point is periodic, then this point is a chain recurrent point.

Naturally, periodic points are chain recurrent, since Bob does not have to intervene. Therefore, equilibria are also chain recurrent since they are trivially periodic. On the other hand, there exist chain recurrent point that are not periodic. Imagine for example a system that is defined as the product of two points moving at constant angular speed along circles of equal length, but where the ratio of the speed of the two points is an irrational number, *e.g.*, $\sqrt{2}$. This system will, after some time, get arbitrarily close to its initial position and a slight bump of the state by Bob would convince Alice that the initial condition is periodic.

In a sense, chain recurrent points are the natural generalization of periodic points in a world where measurements work like a PTAS/FPTAS algorithm, with arbitrarily high accuracy. The surprising implication of the fundamental theorem of dynamical system is that this generalization is not just necessary when arguing about computational systems but also sufficient. It captures all possible limit points of the system.

How does this connect back to game theory? We can apply the fundamental theorem of dynamical systems on the system (G, f) that emerges by coupling any game G and a learning dynamic f. (For most of this paper, we take f to be the replicator dynamics, that is, the continuous-time version of Multiplicative Weights Update.) This defines a new solution concept, the set of chain recurrent points of the system, which we denote R(G,f).

Naturally, we wish to understand how this concept compares against the standard game theoretic solution of Nash equilibria. Since Nash equilibria are fixed points for any reasonable learning dynamics the set of chain recurrent points will be a superset of the set of Nash. However, can it be a strict superset and by how much? Also, potential games comprise the one class of games where learning dynamics indeed work well and converge to equilibria. Does this new solution concept reflect this?

We exemplify this solution concept in two simple and well-understood classes of games, in which it is particularly well behaved, namely 2×2 zero-sum games, and potential games.

In 2×2 zero-sum games we show that once a fully mixed Nash equilibrium exists (like in Matching Pennies) then the set of chain recurrent states is the whole state space. This is an extremal example, in the sense that this is a zero-sum game with a unique Nash equilibrium, where the dominant belief is that any natural, self-interested dynamic will "solve" the game. In fact, it is conventional wisdom amongst game theorists that all no-regret dynamics "converge" in a weak sense to Nash equilibria. By that it is meant that the time-averages of the strategies of both agents will converge to the Nash equilibrium. This is true for the replicator dynamic, which indeed is a continuous time analogue of well known regret minimizing dynamics (*i.e.* Multiplicative Weights Update Algorithm). Nevertheless, time averages fail to fully capture the actual system behavior.

The phase space is partitioned into cyclic trajectories that are essentially "co-centric" orbits around the maxmin [12]. Rounding errors can cause the system to jump from one trajectory to a nearby one. No matter how small these jumps are allowed to be one can fully migrate from any point of the phase space to another making the system completely unpredictable in the presence of any arbitrary small and any arbitrary infrequent perturbation. Chain recurrent sets capture perfectly this uncertainty by declaring the system may lie anywhere in its state space. This comes to a direct contrast with the common knowledge belief that zero-sum games are easy. Just because a Nash equilibrium is unique and efficiently computable does not mean that it fully captures the behavior of self-interested agents, especially when we target nonlinear properties of such systems, *i.e.*, the variance of the utilities of the agents. Technically, this analysis requires combining insights from the fundamental theorem of dynamical systems, Poincaré-Bendixson theorem, a powerful theorem for planar dynamical systems along with known connections between replicator dynamics and information theory and entropy (e.g., [12, 22]).

On the contrary, for potential games, it is already well known that replicator (and many other dynamics) converge to equilibria (e.g., [12, 15]). As the name suggests, these games have a potential function that strictly decreases as long as we are not at equilibrium. One could naturally come to hypothesize that in such systems, which are called gradient-like, the chain recurrent set must be equal to the set of equilibria. However, this is not the case.

Here is a counterexample that is due to Conley [8]. Imagine a continuous dynamical system on the $[0,1]^2$ where all

points on the boundary of this square are equilibria and all other trajectories flow straight downwards. That is, the limit behavior given any point (x,y) with $0 < x, y < 1$ is $(x,0)$. This is a gradient-like system since the height y is always strictly decreasing unless we are at an equilibrium. Nevertheless, by allowing hops of size ϵ, for any $\epsilon > 0$, we can return from every point to itself. Starting from any (x,y) we move downwards along the flow, and when we get close enough to the boundary we hop on it on the point $(x,0)$. Afterwards, we use these hops to traverse the boundary till we reach point $(x,1)$ then one last last hop to $(x,1-\epsilon)$ places us on a trajectory that will revisit our starting point. Hence, once again, the whole state space is chain recurrent despite the fact that the system has a potential function. A memorable analogy for these systems is the game of snakes and ladders. The non-equilibrium states corresponds to the snakes where you move downwards alongside it, whereas the equilibrium states given these ϵ perturbations work as ladders that you can traverse upwards. Unlike the standard game of snakes and ladders there is no ending state in this game and you can keep going in circles indefinitely.

In the case of potential games we show that such contrived counterexamples cannot arise. The key components to this proof are techniques developed by Hurley [13], along with a beautiful, simplified and equivalent definition of chain recurrence, connecting chain recurrence of continuous flows and their discrete time maps, as well as tools from analysis (Sard's theorem) to establish that set of all possible potential values amongst all system equilibria is of zero measure. Combining these two, we establish that as we decrease the size of allowable perturbations eventually at the limit these perturbations do not allow for any new recurrent states to emerge and thus the set of equilibria and chain recurrent sets do coincide.

2. RELATED WORK

Studying dynamics in game theoretic settings is an area of research that is effectively as old as game theory itself. However, dating all the way back to the work of Brown and Robinson [6, 24] on dynamics in zero-sum games, the role of dynamics in game theory played a second fiddle to the main tune of Nash equilibria. The role of dynamics in game theory has predominantly been viewed as a way to provide validation and computational tools for equilibria.

At the same time, over the last fifty years and starting with Shapley [27] there has been an ever increasing trickle of counterexamples to the dominant Nash equilibrium paradigm that has been building up to a steady stream within the algorithmic game theory community ([10, 14, 16, 22, 18, 19] and references therein). Several analogous results are well known within evolutionary game theory [12, 25]. Such observations do not fit the current theoretical paradigm. The recent intractability results in terms of computing equilibria [11, 7] have provided an alternate, more formal tone to this growing discontent with the Nash solution concept, however, the key part is still missing. We need a general theory that fully encompasses all these special cases.

The definition of chain recurrent sets as well as a reference to the fundamental theorem of dynamical systems have been actually introduced in what is currently the definitive textbook reference of evolutionary game theory [25], however, the treatment is rather cursory, limited to abridged definitions and references to the dynamical systems literature. No intuition is built and no specific examples are discussed.

One recent paper [3] is quite related to the issues examined here. [3] establishes stability properties for chain recurrence sets in general dynamical systems. Applications to game theory are discussed. It is shown that there exist games where chain recurrent sets for learning dynamics can be more inclusive than Nash. However, no explicit characterization for these sets is established and all interior initial conditions actually converge to Nash. Connections between chain recurrence sets in potential games and equilibria are discussed without formal proofs. Our results provide complete characterizations of chain recurrent sets and reflect the realized behavior given generic initial states. We believe that chain recurrent sets is a central object of interest whose properties need to be carefully analyzed and we set up a series of analytical goals along these lines in the future work section.

3. PRELIMINARIES

3.1 Game Theory

We denote an n-agent game as $(n, \times_i S_i, \times u_i)$. Each agent chooses a strategy s_i from its set of available strategies S_i. Given a strategy profile $s = (s_1, \ldots, s_n)$, the payoff to each agent i is defined via its utility function $u_i : \times_i S_i \to \mathbb{R}$. Every potential game has a potential function $\Phi : \times_i S_i \to \mathbb{R}$, such that at any strategy profile s and for each agent i possible deviation from strategy s_i to s_i': $\Phi(s_i', s_{-i}) - \Phi(s_i, s_{-i}) = u_i(s_i', s_{-i}) - u_i(s_i, s_{-i})$. Naturally the definitions of strategy and utility can be extended in the usual multilinear fashion to allow for randomized strategies. In that case, we usually overload notation in the following manner: if x_i a mixed strategy for each agent i, then we denote by $u_i(x)$ the expected utility of agent i, $\mathbf{E}_{s \sim x}[u_i(s)]$. We denote by x_{is_i} the probability that agent i assigns to strategy $s_i \in S_i$ in (mixed) strategy profile x. To simplify notation, sometimes instead of x_{is_i} we merely write x_{s_i}.

3.2 Replicator Dynamics

The replicator equation [28, 26] is described by:

$$\frac{dp_i(t)}{dt} = \dot{p}_i = p_i[u_i(p) - \hat{u}(p)], \quad \hat{u}(p) = \sum_{i=1}^{n} p_i u_i(p)$$

where p_i is the proportion of type i in the population, $p = (p_1, \ldots, p_m)$ is the vector of the distribution of types in the population, $u_i(p)$ is the fitness of type i, and $\hat{u}(p)$ is the average population fitness. The state vector p can also be interpreted as a randomized strategy. The replicator dynamic enjoys connections to classic models of ecological growth (e.g., Lotka-Volterra equations [12]), as well as discrete time dynamics (e.g., Multiplicative Weights algorithm) [15, 2, 17].

Remarks: In the context of game theory p_i will replaced with $x_{is_i}(t)$, i.e., the probability that agent i plays strategy $s_i \in S_i$ at time t. Also, many times we will drop the explicit reference to time and just use x_{is_i}, or even just x_{s_i}.

3.3 Topology of dynamical systems

Our treatment follows that of [30], the standard text in evolutionary game theory, which itself borrows material from the classic book by Bhatia and Szegö [5]. Our chain recurrent set approach follows from [1].

Definition 1. A flow on a topological space X is a continuous function $\phi : \mathbb{R} \times X \to X$ such that

(i) $\phi(t, \cdot) : X \to X$ is a homeomorphism for each $t \in \mathbb{R}$.

(ii) $\phi(s+t, \mathbf{x}) = \phi(s, (\phi(t, \mathbf{x})))$ for all $s, t \in \mathbb{R}$ and all $x \in X$.

The second property is known as the group property of the flows. The topological space X is called the phase (or state) space of the flow.

Definition 2. Let X be a set. A map (or discrete dynamical system) is a function $f : X \to X$.

Typically, we write $\phi^t(x)$ for $\phi(t, x)$ and denote a flow $\phi : \mathbb{R} \times X \to X$ by $\phi^t : X \to X$, where the group property appears as $\phi^{t+s}(x) = \phi^s(\phi^t(x))$ for all $x \in X$ and $s, t \in \mathbb{R}$. Sometimes, depending on context, we use the notation ϕ^t to also signify the map $\phi(t, \cdot)$ for a fixed real number t. The map ϕ^1 is useful to relate the behavior of a flow to the behavior of a map.

Definition 3. If ϕ^t is a flow on a topological space X, then the function ϕ^1 defines the time-one map of ϕ^t.

Since our state space is compact and the replicator vector field is Lipschitz-continuous, we can present the unique solution of our ordinary differential equation by a flow $\phi : \mathbb{R} \times X \to X$, where X denotes the set of all mixed strategy profiles. Fixing starting point $x \in X$ defines a function of time which captures the trajectory (orbit, solution path) of the system with the given starting point. This corresponds to the graph of $\phi(\cdot, x) : \mathbb{R} \to X$, i.e., the set $\{(t, y) : y = \phi(t, x) \text{ for some } t \in \mathbb{R}\}$.

If the starting point x does not correspond to an equilibrium then we wish to capture the asymptotic behavior of the system (informally the limit of $\phi(t, x)$ when t goes to infinity). Typically, however, such functions do not exhibit a unique limit point so instead we study the set of limits of all possible convergent subsequences. Formally, given a dynamical system $(\mathbb{R}, X, \phi)$ with flow $\phi : \mathbb{R} \times X \to X$ and a starting point $x \in X$, we call point $y \in X$ an ω-limit point of the orbit through x if there exists a sequence $(t_n)_{n \in \mathbb{N}} \in \mathbb{R}$ such that $\lim_{n \to \infty} t_n = \infty$, $\lim_{n \to \infty} \phi(t_n, x) = y$. Alternatively the ω-limit set can be defined as: $\omega_\Phi(x) = \cap_t \overline{\cup_{\tau \geq t} \phi(\tau, x)}$.

We denote the boundary of a set X as $\text{bd}(X)$ and the interior of S as $\text{int}(X)$. In the case of replicator dynamics where the state space X corresponds to a product of agent (mixed) strategies we will denote by $\phi_i(t, x)$ the projection of the state on the simplex of mixed strategies of agent i. In our replicator system we embed our state space with the standard topology and the Euclidean distance metric.

3.4 Poincaré-Bendixson theorem

The Poincaré-Bendixson theorem is useful in proving the existence of periodic orbits and limit cycles[1] in two dimensional systems. The main idea is to find a trapping region, i.e., a region from which trajectories cannot escape. If a trajectory enters and does not leave such a closed and bounded region of the state space that contains no equilibria then this trajectory must approach a periodic orbit as time goes to infinity. Formally, we have:

---

[1] A periodic orbit is called a limit cycle if it is the ω-limit set of some point not on the periodic orbit.

THEOREM 1. *[4, 29] Given a differentiable real dynamical system defined on an open subset of the plane, then every non-empty compact ω-limit set of an orbit, which contains only finitely many fixed points, is either a fixed point, a periodic orbit, or a connected set composed of a finite number of fixed points together with homoclinic and heteroclinic orbits connecting these.*

Homeomorphisms and Conjugacy of Flows

A function f between two topological spaces is called a *homeomorphism* if it has the following properties: f is a bijection, f is continuous, and f has a continuous inverse. A function f between two topological spaces is called a *diffeomorphism* if it has the following properties: f is a bijection, f is continuously differentiable, and f has a continuously differentiable inverse. Two flows $\Phi^t : A \to A$ and $\Psi^t : B \to B$ are conjugate if there exists a homeomorphism $g : A \to B$ such that for each $x \in A$ and $t \in \mathbb{R}$: $g(\Phi^t(x)) = \Psi^t(g(x))$. Furthermore, two flows $\Phi^t : A \to A$ and $\Psi^t : B \to B$ are *diffeomorhpic* if there exists a diffeomorphism $g : A \to B$ such that for each $x \in A$ and $t \in \mathbb{R}$ $g(\Phi^t(x)) = \Psi^t(g(x))$. If two flows are diffeomorphic then their vector fields are related by the derivative of the conjugacy. That is, we get precisely the same result that we would have obtained if we simply transformed the coordinates in their differential equations [20].

3.5 The fundamental theorem of dynamical systems

The standard formulation of the fundamental theorem of dynamical systems is built on the following set of definitions, based primarily on the work of Conley [8].

Definition 4. Let ϕ^t be a flow on a metric space (X, d). Given $\epsilon > 0$, $T > 0$, and $x, y \in X$, an (ϵ, T)-chain from x to y with respect to ϕ^t and d is a pair of finite sequences $x = x_0, x_1, \ldots, x_{n-1}, x_n = y$ in X and $t_0, \ldots, t_{n-1}$ in $[T, \infty)$, denoted together by $(x_0, \ldots, x_n; t_0, \ldots, t_{n-1})$ such that

$$d(\phi_i^t(x_i), x_{i+1}) < \epsilon$$

for $i = 0, 1, 2, \ldots, n - 1$.

Definition 5. Let ϕ^t be a flow on a metric space (X, d). The forward chain limit set of $x \in X$ with respect to ϕ^t and d is the set

$$\Omega^+(x) = \bigcap_{\epsilon, T > 0} \{y \in X \mid \exists \text{ an } (\epsilon, T)\text{-chain from } x \text{ to } y\}.$$

Definition 6. Let ϕ^t be a flow on a metric space (X, d). Two points $x, y \in X$ are chain equivalent with respect to ϕ^t and d if $y \in \Omega^+(x)$ and $x \in \Omega^+(y)$.

Definition 7. Let ϕ^t be a flow on a metric space (X, d). A point $x \in X$ is chain recurrent with respect to ϕ^t and d if x is chain equivalent to itself. The set of all chain recurrent points of ϕ^t, denoted $\mathcal{R}(\phi)$, is the chain recurrent set of ϕ^t.

One key definition is the notion of a complete Lyapunov function. The game theoretic analogue of this idea is the notion of a potential function in potential games. In a potential game, as long as we are not at an equilibrium, the potential is strictly decreasing guiding the dynamics towards

the standard game theoretic solution concept, *i.e.*, equilibria. The notion of a complete Lyapunov function switches the target solution concept from equilibria to chain recurrent points. More formally:

Definition 8. Let ϕ^t be a flow on a metric space X. A complete Lyapunov function for ϕ^t is a continuous function $\gamma : X \to \mathbb{R}$ such that

(i) $\gamma(\phi^t(x))$ is a strictly decreasing function of t for all $x \in X \setminus \mathcal{R}(\phi^t)$,

(ii) for all $x, y \in \mathcal{R}(\phi^t)$ the points x, y are chain equivalent with respect to ϕ^t if and only if $\gamma(x) = \gamma(y)$,

(iii) $\gamma(\mathcal{R}(\phi^t))$ is nowhere dense.

The powerful implication of the fundamental theorem of dynamical systems is that complete Lyapunov functions always exist. In game theoretic terms, every game is a "potential" game, if only we change our solution concept from equilibria to chain recurrent sets.

THEOREM 2. *[8] Every flow on a compact metric space has a complete Lyapunov function.*

Alternative, equivalent formulations of chain equivalence

For the purpose of our investigation, it will be useful to apply the following alternative definitions of chain equivalence, which are due to Hurley [13].

Definition 9. Let (X, d) be a metric space, and let $f : X \to X$. Given $\epsilon > 0$ and $x, y \in X$, an ϵ-chain from x to y is a finite sequence

$$x = x_0, x_1, \ldots, x_{n-1}, x_n = y$$

in X such that $d(f(x_i), x_{i+1}) < \epsilon$ for $i = 0, 1, 2, \ldots, n - 1$.

Definition 10. Let X be a metric space, and let $f : X \to X$. Two points $x, y \in X$ are called chain equivalent if for every $\epsilon > 0$ there exists an ϵ-chain from x to y and there exists an ϵ-chain from y to x.

Next, we provide three alternative formulations of chain equivalence which are equivalent with our original definition for a flow on a compact metric space as shown in [13].

THEOREM 3. *[13] If ϕ^t is a flow on a compact metric space (X, d) and $x, y \in X$, then the following statements are equivalent.*

1. *(i) The points x and y are chain equivalent with respect to ϕ^t.*

2. *(ii) For every $\epsilon > 0$ and $T > 0$ there exists an $(\epsilon, 1)$-chain*

$$(x_0, \ldots, x_n; t_0, \ldots, t_n - 1)$$

from x to y such that

$$t_0 + \cdots + t_{n-1} \geq T$$

and there exists an $(\epsilon, 1)$-chain

$$(y_0, \ldots, y_m; s_0, \ldots, s_m - 1)$$

from y to x such that

$$s_0 + \cdots + s_{m-1} \geq T.$$

3. *(iii) For every $\epsilon > 0$ there exists an $(\epsilon, 1)$-chain from x to y and an $(\epsilon, 1)$-chain from y to x.*

4. *(iv) The points x and y are chain equivalent with respect to ϕ^1.*

4. CHAIN RECURRENT SETS FOR MATCHING PENNIES

Zero-sum games are amongst the most well studied class of games within game theory. Equilibria here are classically considered to completely "solve" the setting. This is due to the fact that the equilibrium prediction is essentially unique, Nash computation is tractable, and many natural classes of learning dynamics are known to "converge weakly" to the set of Nash equilibria.

The notion of weak convergence encodes that the time average of the dynamics converge to the equilibrium set. However, this linguistic overloading of the notion of convergence is unnatural and arguably can lead to a misleading sense of certainty about the complexity that learning dynamics may exhibit in this setting. For example, would it be meaningful to state that the moon "converges weakly" to the earth instead of stating that e.g. the moon follows a trajectory that has earth at its center?

The complexity and unpredictability of the actual behavior of dynamics becomes apparent when we characterize the set of chain recurrent points even for the simplest zero-sum games, Matching Pennies. Despite the uniqueness and symmetry of the Nash equilibrium it is shown to not capture fully the actual dynamics. The set of chain recurrent points is the whole strategy space. This means that in the presence of arbitrary small noise the replicator dynamics can become completely unpredictable. Even in an idealized implementation without noise there exist absolutely no initial conditions that converge to a Nash equilibrium. To argue this we will use the following known lemma, whose proof we provide for completeness in the appendix.

LEMMA 1. *[12, 23] Let ϕ denote the flow of the replicator dynamic when applied to a zero sum game with a fully mixed Nash equilibrium $q = (q_1, q_2)$ then given any starting point $x(0) = (x_1(0), x_2(0))$ then the sum of the KL-divergences between each agent's mixed Nash equilibrium q_i and his evolving strategy $x_i(t)$ is time invariant. Equivalently, $D_{\mathrm{KL}}(q_1\|x_1(t)) + D_{\mathrm{KL}}(q_2\|x_2(t)) = D_{\mathrm{KL}}(q_1\|x_1(0)) + D_{\mathrm{KL}}(q_2\|x_2(0))$ for all t.*

The main theorem of this section is the following:

THEOREM 4. *Let ϕ denote the flow of the replicator dynamic when applied to Matching Pennies then the set of chain recurrent points is the whole state space. This characterization holds for all 2x2 zero-sum games that have a fully mixed Nash equilibrium.*

PROOF. The proof proceeds in two steps. In the first step, which follows along the lines of [22], we establish that every interior point of the state space, i.e., any fully mixed strategy profile, lies on a periodic orbit. The second part of the proof establishes that the geometry of the trajectories implies that for any point in the state space and for any $\epsilon > 0$ we can find an ϵ-orbit connecting this point to itself.

In order to establish periodicity of all orbits starting from a fully mixed initial condition we need to apply the Poincaré-Bendixson theorem. The Poincaré-Bendixson theorem can only be applied for two dimensional systems, whereas our system has four variables ($x_{1Heads}, x_{1Tails}, x_{2Heads}, x_{2Tails}$). Since $x_{1Heads} + x_{1Tails} = 1$ and $x_{2Heads} + x_{2Tails} = 1$ there exists a natural projection to the plane (x_{1Heads}, x_{2Heads}). The two flows are conjugate and periodicity is a topological invariant property [1], so we can identify all periodic points of all four variable system by lifting up all the periodic points of the flow on the (x_{1Heads}, x_{2Heads}) plane.

We know from lemma 2 that in zero-sum games with fully mixed equilibria, and hence in Matching Pennies, the sum of the KL-divergences between the Nash equilibrium strategies and the time evolving strategies of each agent remains constant as we move along the trajectories of the replicator. KL-divergence is a (pseudo)-metric implying the existence of trapping regions in the interior of our state space. Specifically, as long as we start from an interior point other than the unique Nash then the trajectory stays bounded away from the boundary (KL-divergence becomes infinite) and from the unique equilibrium (KL-divergence becomes zero). Naturally, these restrictions also apply to the conjugate flow via the homeomorphic projection. By the Poincaré-Bendixson theorem we have that starting from any point (other than the Nash) the resulting limit set is a periodic orbit. It is straightforward to check that the KL-divergence invariance condition when projected to our subspace translates to an invariance of the quantity $x_{1Head}(1 - x_{1Head})x_{2Head}(1 - x_{2Head})$. This defines a closed continuous curve on our subspace that is symmetric along the axis $x_{1Head} = 1/2$ and $x_{2Head} = 1/2$. In each of the four regions defined by $x_{1Head} = 1/2$, $x_{2Head} = 1/2$ the signs of $\frac{dx_{1Head}}{dt}$, $\frac{dx_{2Head}}{dt}$ are fixed and define a clockwise direction. The periodicity of the interior points now follows from the uniqueness of the solution of the projected replicator flow.

The case of non-interior points is simpler. Naturally each of the four "pure" initial conditions $(H,H)(H,T)(T,H)(T,T)$ are fixed points for the replicator dynamics. Finally, initial conditions where exactly one agent applies a pure strategy lie on an orbit connection two pure states. For example, if the first agent chooses *Heads* with probability one, then as the second agent moves forward in time he will continuously increase his probability of playing strategy *Tails*. Thus, all these points lie on an orbit connecting (H,H) to (H,T). The geometry of these orbits is depicted in Figure 1.

The fact that all states are chain recurrent follows easily. All interior states are chain recurrent since they are periodic. All pure states are chain recurrent since they are equilibria. Let x be any of the remaining states with exactly one randomizing agent. For any $\epsilon > 0$ we can create a $(\epsilon, 1)$-orbit which travels exclusively along the boundary of the state space and as it approaches a fixed point, uses a jump of size at most ϵ to hop onto the next best response ray. Thus, $x \in \Omega^+(x)$ and these states are chain recurrent as well. □

5. CHAIN RECURRENT SETS FOR POTENTIAL GAMES

For gradient systems, it is understood that under sufficient smoothness conditions the set of chain recurrent points coincides with the set of equilibria. Many learning dynamics define gradient-like behavior in potential games (i.e., the potential function always increases), but without being formally a gradient (moving in the direction of maximum increase). We argue that under replicator dynamics the chain

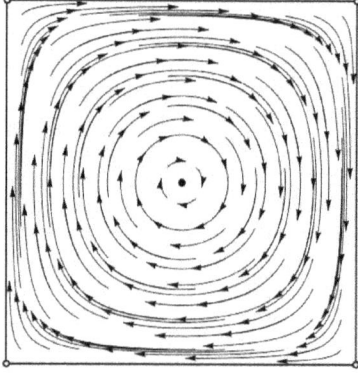

Figure 1: Replicator trajectories in Matching Pennies game. Each point encodes the probability assigned by the agents to their first strategy.

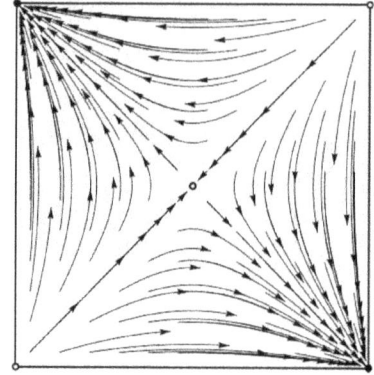

Figure 2: Replicator trajectories in a partnership, coordination game. Each point encodes the probability assigned by the agents to their first strategy.

recurrent sets for any potential games coincides with the set of system equilibria. The set of chain recurrent points of gradient-like systems can be rather complicated and Conley [8] constructs a specific example of a gradient-like system with a zero measurable set of equilibria where the set of chain recurrent points is the whole state space. Nevertheless, we establish that such bad examples do not arise in potential games. For the proof of this characterization we will apply the following theorem due to Hurley that we have already discussed in the preliminaries:

THEOREM 5. *[13] The chain recurrent set of a continuous (semi)flow on an arbitrary metric space is the same as the chain recurrent set of its time-one map.*

THEOREM 6. *Let ϕ denote the flow of the replicator dynamic when applied to a potential game then the set of chain recurrent points coincides with its set of equilibria.*

PROOF. Replicator dynamics defines a gradient-like system, where the (expected) value of the potential function always increases unless we are at a fixed point. Specifically, it is well known that in any potential game the utility of any agent at a state s, $u_i(s)$ can be expressed as a summation of the potential Φ and a dummy term $D_i(s_{-i})$ that depends on the strategies of all agents other than i. Indeed, by the definition of the potential game for any possible deviation of agent i from strategy s_i to s_i': $\Phi(s_i', s_{-i}) - \Phi(s_i, s_{-i}) = u_i(s_i', s_{-i}) - u_i(s_i, s_{-i})$ and hence for each $s_{-i} = \times_{j \neq i} s_j$ and any two possible strategies s_i, s_i' of agent i we have that $u_i(s_i', s_{-i}) - \Phi(s_i', s_{-i}) = u_i(s_i, s_{-i}) - \Phi(s_i, s_{-i})$. Hence these differences are independent of the choice of strategy of agent i and can be expressed as $D_i(s_{-i})$, a function of the choices of all other agents. We can now express $u_i(s) = \Phi(s) + D_i(s_{-i})$ and similarly $u_i(x) = \Phi(x) + D_i(x_{-i})$ for mixed strategy profiles. Furthermore, we have that since $\Phi(x) = \sum_{s_i \in S_i} x_{s_i} \Phi(s_i, x_{-i})$, we have that for each $s_i \in S_i$ $\frac{\partial \Phi(x)}{\partial x_{s_i}} = \Phi(s_i, x_{-i})$. Therefore, we have that:

$$
\begin{aligned}
\dot{\Phi}(x) &= \sum_i \sum_{s_i \in S_i} \frac{\partial \Phi(x)}{\partial x_{s_i}} \dot{x}_{s_i} = \sum_i \sum_{s_i \in S_i} \Phi(s_i, x_{-i}) \dot{x}_{s_i} \\
&= \sum_i \sum_{s_i \in S_i} \Phi(s_i, x_{-i}) x_{s_i} [u_i(s_i, x_{-i}) - u_i(\mathbf{x})] \\
&= \sum_i \sum_{s_i \in S_i} \Phi(s_i, x_{-i}) x_{s_i} [\Phi(s_i, x_{-i}) - \Phi(\mathbf{x})] \\
&= \sum_{i, s_i, s_i' \in S_i} x_{s_i} x_{s_i'} [\Phi(s_i, x_{-i})^2 - \Phi(s_i, x_{-i})\Phi(s_i', x_{-i})] \\
&= \frac{1}{2} \sum_{i, s_i, s_i' \in S_i} x_{s_i} x_{s_i'} [\Phi(s_i, x_{-i}) - \Phi(s_i', x_{-i})]^2 \qquad (1) \\
&= \frac{1}{2} \sum_{i, s_i, s_i' \in S_i} x_{s_i} x_{s_i'} \sum_{i, s_i, s_i' \in S_i} x_{s_i} x_{s_i'} [\Phi(s_i, x_{-i}) - \Phi(s_i', x_{-i})]^2 \\
&\geq \frac{1}{2} \Big[\sum_{i, s_i, s_i' \in S_i} x_{s_i} x_{s_i'} |\Phi(s_i, x_{-i}) - \Phi(s_i', x_{-i})| \Big]^2 \\
&= \frac{1}{2} \Big[\sum_{i, s_i, s_i' \in S_i} x_{s_i} x_{s_i'} |u_i(s_i, x_{-i}) - u_i(s_i', x_{-i})| \Big]^2 \\
&\geq \frac{1}{2} \Big[\sum_{i, s_i, s_i' \in S_i} x_{s_i} |u_i(s_i, x_{-i}) - u_i(x)| \Big]^2 = \frac{1}{2} \|\xi\|_1^2
\end{aligned}
$$

where ξ expresses the replicator vector field. Although the convergence of the replicator dynamics in congestion and hence potential games can be derived by an analogous construction in [15] here we will also use this proof to establish that the set of all potential values attained at equilibrium points, i.e., $\mathcal{V} = \{\Phi(x), x \text{ is an equilibrium}\}$ is of measure zero.

We will argue this by showing that it can be expressed as the finite union of zero measure sets. By the above derivation we have that the potential is strictly decreasing unless we are at a system equilibrium. Furthermore, its establishes that in the places where the potential does not increase, i.e., at equilibrium, we have that for all agents i if $x_{s_i}, x_{s_i'} > 0$, then $\Phi(s_i, x_{-i}) - \Phi(s_i', x_{-i}) = 0$. However, this immediately

232

implies that $\frac{\partial \Phi(x)}{\partial x_{s_i}} - \frac{\partial \Phi(x)}{\partial x_{s'_i}} = 0$. Any equilibrium, either corresponds to a pure state, in which cases the union of their potential values is trivially of zero measure or its corresponds to a mixed state where one or more agents is randomizing. In order to account for the possibility of continuums of equilibria, we will use Sard's theorem that implies that the set of critical values (that is, the image of the set of critical points[2]) of a smooth function from one Euclidean space to another is a null set, i.e., it has Lebesgue measure 0. We define an arbitrary fixed ordering over the strategy set of each agent. Given any mixed system equilibrium x, the expected value of the potential $\Phi(x)$ can be written as a multi-variate polynomial over all strategy variables x_{s_i} played with strictly positive probability. Since the x_{s_i}'s represent probabilities we can replace the lexicographically smaller variable x_{s_i} as one minus the summation of all other variables in the support of the current mixed strategy of agent i. Now, however, all partial derivatives of this polynomial at the equilibrium are equal to zero. Hence, each equilibrium can be expressed as a critical point of a smooth function from some space $\mathbb{R}^k$ to $\mathbb{R}$ and hence its image (i.e. its set of potential values) is a zero measure subset of $\mathbb{R}$. It is clear that the set of polynomials needed to capture all equilibria depends only on the choice of strategies for each agent that are played with positive probability and hence although they are exponential many they are finite. Putting everything together the set of all potential values attained at equilibria is of zero measure.

Naturally, however, the complement of equilibrium values, which we denote $\mathcal{C}$, is dense in the set[3] $[\min_s \Phi(s), \max_s \Phi(s)]$. Indeed, if $\mathcal{C}$ is not dense in $[\min_s \Phi(s), \max_s \Phi(s)]$ then there exists a point $y \in [\min_s \Phi(s), \max_s \Phi(s)]$ such that $y \notin \mathcal{C}$ and at the same time y is not an accumulation point of $\mathcal{C}$. This implies that there exists a neighborhood of y that contains no points of $\mathcal{C}$. We reach contradiction since $[\min_s \Phi(s), \max_s \Phi(s)] \setminus \mathcal{C}$ is of zero measure.

Next, we will apply the fact that the complement of equilibrium values of the potential is dense in the set $[\min_s \Phi(s), \max_s \Phi(s)]$ to establish that the chain recurrent points of the time one map ϕ^1 of the flow coincide with the set of equilibria. As we stated above, Hurley [13] has shown that the chain recurrent points of the flow coincide with those of its time one map and hence the theorem follows.

We have that $\Phi(\phi^1(x)) < \Phi(x)$ for all x, with equality if and only if we are at equilibrium. Suppose that we choose a regular value r of the potential, *i.e.* a value that does not correspond to a fixed point. Let's consider the sets $K_r = \Phi^{-1}((-\infty, r])$, and $U_r = \Phi^{-1}((-\infty, r))$. Note that K_r is closed while U_r is open (in the topology defined by the set of strategy profiles) and contained in K_r. If $\Phi(p) = r$, then $\Phi(\phi^1(p)) < \Phi(p) = r$. This means that $\phi^1(K_r) \subset U_r$. However, since ϕ^1, the time one map of the flow is a homeomorphism, the fact that K_r is closed yields that $\overline{\phi^1(U_r)} \subset \overline{\phi^1(K_r)} = \phi^1(K_r) \subset U_r$.

Any chain recurrent point whose forward orbits meets U_r is furthermore contained in $\overline{\phi^1(U_r)}$ [13, 8]. Let q be a non-equilibrium point, then we have that $\Phi(\phi^1(q)) < \Phi(q)$. How-

ever, due to the fact that the images of the potential values of non-equilibrium points are dense in $(\min_s \Phi(s), \max_s \Phi(s))$ we can choose such a value r such that $\Phi(\phi^1(q)) < r < \Phi(q)$. Then $\phi^1(q) \in U_r$ but $q \notin U_r$ and thus q is not a chain recurrent point of ϕ^1. As such it cannot be a chain recurrent point for the replicator flow as well. The theorem follows immediately since all equilibria are trivially chain recurrent points. $\square$

6. FUTURE WORK

The purpose of this paper is to introduce the fundamental theorem of dynamical systems, and to sketch and motivate its use towards developing a principled, rigorous, and informative discourse on game-theoretic solution concepts. We focused on two simple and evocative examples, namely zero-sum games with fully mixed equilibria and potential games. Naturally, there is much that needs to be done, and below we sample a few research goals that are immediate, important, and each open ended in its own way.

- **The structure of Chain Recurrent Sets (CRSs).** A game may have many CRSs (for example, the coordination game in Figure 2 has five). It is not hard to see that chain equivalence defines an equivalence relation that partitions the set of CRSs to equivalence classes. These classes are called chain components and can be arranged as vertices of a directed acyclic graph, where directed edges signify possible transitions after an infinitesimal jump; for the coordination game in Figure 2 this DAG has two sinks (the pure Nash equilibria), two sources (the other two pure profiles), and a node of degree 4 (the mixed Nash equilibrium). Identifying this DAG is tantamount to analyzing the game, the generalization of finding its Nash equilibria. Understanding the fundamental structure in games of interest is an important challenge.

- **Price of Anarchy through CRSs.** We can define a natural distribution over the sink CRSs of a game, namely, assign to each sink CRS the probability that a trajectory started at a (say, uniformly) random point of the state space will end up, perhaps after infinitesimal jumps, at the CRS. This distribution, together with the CRS's expected utility, yield a new and productive definition of the average price of anarchy in a game, as well as a methodology for calculating it, see for example [21].

- **Inside a CRS.** Equilibria and limit cycles are the simplest forms of a chain recurrent component, in the sense that no "jumps" are necessary for going from one state in the component to another. In Matching Pennies, in contrast, $O(\frac{1}{\epsilon})$ many ϵ-jumps are needed to reach the Nash equilibrium, starting from a pure strategy profile. What is the possible range of this form of complexity of a CRS?

- **Complexity.** There are several intriguing complexity questions posed by this concept. What is the complexity of determining, given a game and two strategy profiles, whether they belong to the same component? What is the complexity of finding a point in a sink chain component? What is the speed of convergence to a CRS?

---

[2]For a differentiable function of several real variables, a critical point is a value in its domain where all partial derivatives are zero.

[3]For simplicity we disregard the trivial potential games where the potential is everywhere constant $\min_s \Phi(s) = \max_s \Phi(s)$. After all in those games are states are equilibria and the theorem is trivially true.

7. ACKNOWLEDGMENTS

This work was supported by NSF grant CCF1408635 and SUTD grant SRG ESD 2015 097.

8. REFERENCES

[1] J. M. Alongi and G. S. Nelson. *Recurrence and topology*, volume 85. American Mathematical Soc., 2007.

[2] S. Arora, E. Hazan, and S. Kale. The multiplicative weights update method: a meta algorithm and applications. Technical report, 2005.

[3] M. Benaïm, J. Hofbauer, and S. Sorin. Perturbations of set-valued dynamical systems, with applications to game theory. *Dynamic Games and Applications*, 2(2):195–205, 2012.

[4] I. Bendixson. Sur les courbes définies par des équations différentielles. *Acta Mathematica*, 24(1):1–88, 1901.

[5] N. P. Bhatia and G. P. Szegö. *Stability theory of dynamical systems*. Berliin: Springer Verlag, 1970.

[6] G. Brown. Iterative solutions of games by fictitious play. *In Activity Analysis of Production and Allocation, T.C. Koopmans (Ed.), New York: Wiley.*, 1951.

[7] X. Chen, X. Deng, and S.-H. Teng. Settling the complexity of computing two-player nash equilibria. *J. ACM*, 56(3):14:1–14:57, May 2009.

[8] C. Conley. Isolated invariant sets and the morse index. cbms regional conference series in mathematics, 38. *American Mathematical Society, Providence, RI*, 16, 1978.

[9] T. M. Cover and J. A. Thomas. *Elements of Information Theory*. Wiley, New York, 1991.

[10] C. Daskalakis, R. Frongillo, C. Papadimitriou, G. Pierrakos, and G. Valiant. On learning algorithms for Nash equilibria. *Algorithmic Game Theory*, pages 114–125, 2010.

[11] C. Daskalakis, P. W. Goldberg, and C. H. Papadimitriou. The complexity of computing a nash equilibrium. pages 71–78. ACM Press, 2006.

[12] J. Hofbauer and K. Sigmund. *Evolutionary Games and Population Dynamics*. Cambridge University Press, Cambridge, 1998.

[13] M. Hurley. Chain recurrence, semiflows, and gradients. *Journal of Dynamics and Differential Equations*, 7(3):437–456, 1995.

[14] R. Kleinberg, K. Ligett, G. Piliouras, and É. Tardos. Beyond the Nash equilibrium barrier. In *Symposium on Innovations in Computer Science (ICS)*, 2011.

[15] R. Kleinberg, G. Piliouras, and É. Tardos. Multiplicative updates outperform generic no-regret learning in congestion games. In *ACM Symposium on Theory of Computing (STOC)*, 2009.

[16] K. Ligett and G. Piliouras. Beating the best Nash without regret. *SIGecom Exchanges 10*, 2011.

[17] V. Losert and E. Akin. Dynamics of games and genes: Discrete versus continuous time. *Journal of Mathematical Biology*, 1983.

[18] R. Mehta, I. Panageas, and G. Piliouras. Natural selection as an inhibitor of genetic diversity: Multiplicative weights updates algorithm and a conjecture of haploid genetics [working paper abstract]. In *Proceedings of the 2015 Conference on Innovations in Theoretical Computer Science*, ITCS '15, pages 73–73, New York, NY, USA, 2015. ACM.

[19] R. Mehta, I. Panageas, G. Piliouras, and S. Yazdanbod. The Complexity of Genetic Diversity: Sex with Two Chromosomes is Advantageous but Unpredictable. *ArXiv e-prints*, Nov. 2014.

[20] J. Meiss. *Differential Dynamical Systems*. SIAM, 2007.

[21] I. Panageas and G. Piliouras. Approximating the geometry of dynamics in potential games: Point-wise convergence, regions of attraction, average case performance analysis and system invariants. *http://arxiv.org/abs/1403.3885*, 2014.

[22] G. Piliouras, C. Nieto-Granda, H. I. Christensen, and J. S. Shamma. Persistent patterns: Multi-agent learning beyond equilibrium and utility. In *Proceedings of the 2014 International Conference on Autonomous Agents and Multi-agent Systems*, AAMAS '14, pages 181–188, Richland, SC, 2014. International Foundation for Autonomous Agents and Multiagent Systems.

[23] G. Piliouras and J. S. Shamma. Optimization despite chaos: Convex relaxations to complex limit sets via Poincaré recurrence. In *SODA*, 2014.

[24] J. Robinson. An iterative method of solving a game. *Annals of Mathematics*, 54:296–301, 1951.

[25] W. H. Sandholm. *Population Games and Evolutionary Dynamics*. MIT Press, 2010.

[26] P. Schuster and K. Sigmund. Replicator dynamics. *Journal of Theoretical Biology*, 100(3):533 – 538, 1983.

[27] L. Shapley. Some topics in two-person games. *Advances in game theory, edited by M. Dresher, R. J. Aumann, L. S. Shapley, A. W. Tucker*, 1964.

[28] P. D. Taylor and L. B. Jonker. Evolutionary stable strategies and game dynamics. *Mathematical Biosciences*, 40(12):145–156, 1978.

[29] G. Teschl. *Ordinary differential equations and dynamical systems*, volume 140. American Mathematical Soc., 2012.

[30] J. Weibull. *Evolutionary Game Theory*. MIT Press; Cambridge, MA: Cambridge University Press., 1995.

APPENDIX

A. INFORMATION THEORY

Entropy is a measure of the uncertainty of a random variable and captures the expected information value from a measurement of the random variable. The entropy H of a discrete random variable X with possible values $\{1, \ldots, n\}$ and probability mass function $p(X)$ is defined as $H(X) = -\sum_{i=1}^{n} p(i) \ln p(i)$.

Given two probability distributions p and q of a discrete random variable their *K-L divergence* (relative entropy) is defined as $D_{\mathrm{KL}}(p\|q) = \sum_i \ln\left(\frac{p(i)}{q(i)}\right) p(i)$. It is the average of the logarithmic difference between the probabilities p and q, where the average is taken using the probabilities p. The K-L divergence is only defined if $q(i) = 0$ implies $p(i) = 0$ for all i[4]. K-L divergence is a "pseudo-metric" in the sense that for it is always non-negative and is equal to zero if and only if the two distributions are equal (almost everywhere). Other useful properties of the K-L divergence is that it is additive for independent distributions and that it is jointly convex in both of its arguments; that is, if (p_1, q_1) and (p_2, q_2) are two pairs of distributions then for any $0 \leq \lambda \leq 1$: $D_{\mathrm{KL}}(\lambda p_1 + (1-\lambda)p_2 \| \lambda q_1 + (1-\lambda)q_2) \leq \lambda D_{\mathrm{KL}}(p_1\|q_1) + (1-\lambda)D_{\mathrm{KL}}(p_2\|q_2)$.

A closely related concept is that of the *cross entropy* between two probability distributions, which measures the average number of bits needed to identify an event from a set of possibilities, if a coding scheme is used based on a given probability distribution q, rather than the "true" distribution p. Formally, the cross entropy for two distributions p and q over the same probability space is defined as follows: $H(p, q) = -\sum_{i=1}^{n} p(i) \ln q(i) = H(p) + D_{\mathrm{KL}}(p\|q)$. For more details and proofs of these basic facts the reader should refer to the classic text by Cover and Thomas [9].

B. MISSING PROOFS OF SECTION 4

LEMMA 2. *[12, 23] Let ϕ denote the flow of the replicator dynamic when applied to a zero sum game with a fully mixed Nash equilibrium $q = (q_1, q_2)$. Given any starting point $x(0) = (x_1(0), x_2(0))$ then the sum of the KL-divergences between each agent's mixed Nash equilibrium q_i and his evolving strategy $x_i(t)$ is time invariant. Equivalently, $D_{\mathrm{KL}}(q_1\|x_1(t)) + D_{\mathrm{KL}}(q_2\|x_2(t)) = D_{\mathrm{KL}}(q_1\|x_1(0)) + D_{\mathrm{KL}}(q_2\|x_2(0))$ for all t.*

PROOF. It suffices to establish that the time derivative of $D_{\mathrm{KL}}(q_1\|x_1(t)) + D_{\mathrm{KL}}(q_2\|x_2(t))$ is everywhere equal to zero. By properties of the KL-divergence, it suffices to show that the time derivative of the quantity $\sum_i H(q_i, \phi_i(t, x_0)) = -\sum_i \sum_{s_i \in S_i} q_{s_i} \cdot \ln(x_{s_i})$ is everywhere zero, where $i \in \{1, 2\}$ and S_i the available strategies of agent i. We denote by $A^{1,2}$ the payoff matrix of agent 1 and $A^{2,1}$ the payoff matrix of agent 2. Since this is a zero-sum game: $A^{1,2} + (A^{2,1})^T = \mathbf{0}$ where $(A^{2,1})^T$ the transpose of $A^{2,1}$.

$$
\begin{aligned}
\sum_i \sum_{s_i \in S_i} q_{s_i} \frac{d\ln(x_{s_i})}{dt} &= \sum_i \sum_{s_i \in S_i} q_{s_i} \frac{\dot{x}_{s_i}}{x_{s_i}} = \\
&= \sum_i \left(\sum_{s_i \in S_i} q_{s_i} u_i(s_i, x_{-i}) - \sum_{s_i \in S_i} x_{s_i} u_i(s_i, x_{-i}) \right) = \\
&= \left(q_1^{\mathrm{T}} A^{1,2} x_2 - x_1^{\mathrm{T}} A^{1,2} x_2 \right) + \left(q_2^{\mathrm{T}} A^{2,1} x_1 - x_2^{\mathrm{T}} A^{2,1} x_1 \right) = \\
&= \left(q_1^{\mathrm{T}} - x_1^{\mathrm{T}} \right) A^{1,2} (x_2 - q_2) + \left(q_2^{\mathrm{T}} - x_2^{\mathrm{T}} \right) A^{2,1} (x_1 - q_1) = \\
&= -\left(q_1^{\mathrm{T}} - x_1^{\mathrm{T}} \right) \left[A^{1,2} + (A^{2,1})^T \right] (q_2 - x_2) = 0
\end{aligned}
$$

$\square$

---

[4]The quantity $0\ln 0$ is interpreted as zero because $\lim_{x \to 0} x \ln(x) = 0$.

Rational Proofs with Multiple Provers[*]

Jing Chen   Samuel McCauley   Shikha Singh

Computer Science Department, Stony Brook University
Stony Brook, NY 11794, USA
{jingchen, smccauley, shiksingh}@cs.stonybrook.edu

ABSTRACT

Interactive proofs model a world where a verifier delegates computation to an untrustworthy prover, verifying the prover's claims before accepting them. These proofs have applications to delegation of computation, probabilistically checkable proofs, crowdsourcing, and more.

In some of these applications, the verifier may pay the prover based on the quality of his work. Rational proofs, introduced by Azar and Micali (2012), are an interactive proof model in which the prover is *rational* rather than untrustworthy—he may lie, but only to increase his payment. This allows the verifier to leverage the greed of the prover to obtain better protocols: while rational proofs are no more powerful than interactive proofs, the protocols are simpler and more efficient. Azar and Micali posed as an open problem whether multiple provers are more powerful than one for rational proofs.

We provide a model that extends rational proofs to allow multiple provers. In this model, a verifier can cross-check the answers received by asking several provers. The verifier can pay the provers according to the quality of their work, incentivizing them to provide correct information.

We analyze rational proofs with multiple provers from a complexity-theoretic point of view. We fully characterize this model by giving tight upper and lower bounds on its power. On the way, we resolve Azar and Micali's open problem in the affirmative, showing that multiple rational provers are strictly more powerful than one (under standard complexity-theoretic assumptions). We further show that the full power of rational proofs with multiple provers can be achieved using only two provers and five rounds of interaction. Finally, we consider more demanding models where the verifier wants the provers' payment to decrease signifi-cantly when they are lying, and fully characterize the power of the model when the payment gap must be noticeable (i.e., at least $1/p$ where p is a polynomial).

Categories and Subject Descriptors

F.1.2 [**Computation by Abstract Devices**]: Modes of Computation—*Interactive computation*; F.1.3 [**Computation by Abstract Devices**]: Complexity Measures and Classes; F.2.2 [**Analysis of Algorithms and Problem Complexity**]: Nonnumerical Algorithms and Problems—*Complexity of proof procedures*

Keywords

Interactive proofs; multi-prover rational interactive proofs; scoring rules; DC uniform circuit families; complexity theory

1. INTRODUCTION

Multi-prover interactive proofs (MIP) [10] and rational interactive proofs (RIP) [5] are two important extensions of interactive proof systems.

In a multi-prover interactive proof, several computationally unbounded, potentially dishonest provers interact with a polynomial time, randomized verifier. The provers can pre-agree on a joint strategy to convince the verifier of the truth of a proposition. However, once the protocol starts, the provers cannot communicate with each other. If the proposition is true, the verifier should be convinced with probability 1; otherwise the verifier should reject with some non-negligible probability. As shown by Babai, Fortnow and Lund, MIP = NEXP [8], which demonstrates the power of multiple provers compared to one-prover interactive proofs (recall that IP = PSPACE [31, 29]).

Rational interactive proofs [5] are a variant of interactive proofs, where the verifier makes a payment to the prover at the end of the protocol. The prover is assumed to be *rational*, that is, he only acts in ways that maximize this payment. Thus, in contrast to interactive proofs, the prover does not care whether the verifier is convinced or not. Rational proofs ensure that the prover's payment is maximized if and only if the verifier learns the correct answer to the proposition. Azar and Micali [5] show that, while rational proofs are no more powerful than interactive proofs (i.e., RIP = PSPACE), the protocols are simpler and more efficient. Previous work on rational proofs [6, 5, 25] considers a *single* rational prover.

Many computation-outsourcing applications have ingredients of both of these models: the verifier pays a *team*

---

[*]We thank several anonymous reviewers for their valuable feedback, and Sanjoy Das, Andrew Drucker, Silvio Micali and Rafael Pass for their comments. The second and third authors are partially supported by NSF Grants CNS 1408695, CCF 1439084, IIS 1247726, IIS 1251137, and CCF 1217708, and Sandia National Laboratories.

Permission to make digital or hard copies of all or part of this work for personal or classroom use is granted without fee provided that copies are not made or distributed for profit or commercial advantage and that copies bear this notice and the full citation on the first page. Copyrights for components of this work owned by others than the author(s) must be honored. Abstracting with credit is permitted. To copy otherwise, or republish, to post on servers or to redistribute to lists, requires prior specific permission and/or a fee. Request permissions from Permissions@acm.org.

ITCS'16, January 14–16, 2016, Cambridge, MA, USA.
Copyright is held by the owner/author(s). Publication rights licensed to ACM.
ACM 978-1-4503-4057-1/16/01 ...$15.00.
DOI: http://dx.doi.org/10.1145/2840728.2840744

of provers based on their responses. For example, in Internet marketplaces such as *Amazon's Mechanical Turk* [1] and *Proof Market* [3], the requesters (verifiers) post labor-intensive tasks on the website along with a monetary compensation they are willing to pay. The providers (provers) accept these offers and perform the job. In these Internet marketplaces and crowdsourcing games [33] correctness is often ensured by verifying one provider's answers against another [32, 2]. Thus, the providers collaborate as a team—their answers need to match, even though they are likely to not know each other and cannot communicate with each other [27].

Inspired by these applications and previous theoretical work, we introduce *multi-prover rational interactive proofs*, which combine elements of rational proofs and classical multi-prover interactive proofs. This model aims to answer the following question: what problems can be solved by a team of rational workers who cannot communicate with each other and get paid based on the joint-correctness of their answers? One of our main contributions is to completely characterize the power of this model.

Previous Work Involving Multiple Rational Provers.

The notion of rational proofs with multiple provers has appeared several times in previous work [5, 6, 25]. However, the authors only use multiple provers to simplify the analysis of single-prover protocols, without formalizing the model. They show that multiple provers in their protocols can be simulated by a single prover by scaling the payments appropriately. Azar and Micali [5] discuss one of the fundamental challenges of using multiple rational provers: in a cooperative setting, one prover may lie to give subsequent provers the opportunity to obtain a larger payment. They pose the following open problem: are multiple provers more powerful than one in rational proofs? In this paper, we show that, in general, a protocol with multiple rational provers cannot be simulated by a single-prover protocol under standard complexity-theoretic assumptions.

The Model of Multi-Prover Rational Proofs.

We briefly summarize our model in order to compare it with the literature and discuss our results. The model is formally defined in Section 2.

In a multi-prover rational interactive proof (MRIP), several computationally-unbounded provers communicate with a polynomial-time randomized verifier who wants to determine the membership of an input string in a language. The provers can pre-agree on how they plan to respond to the verifier's queries. However, they cannot communicate with each other once the protocol begins. At the end of the protocol, the verifier outputs the answer and computes a total payment for the provers based on the input, his own randomness, and the messages exchanged. This total payment may be distributed in any pre-determined way by the verifier or the provers themselves.

A protocol is an MRIP protocol if any strategy of the provers that maximizes their expected payment leads the verifier to the correct answer. The class of languages having such protocols is denoted by MRIP.

Distribution of Payments.

In classical MIP protocols, the provers work collaboratively to convince the verifier of the truth of a proposition

and their goal is to maximize the verifier's acceptance probability. Similarly, the rational provers in MRIP work as a team to maximize the total payment received from the verifier. Any pre-specified distribution of this payment is allowed, as long as it does not depend on the transcript of the protocol (i.e., the messages exchanged, the coins flipped, and the amount of the payment). For instance, the division of the payment can be pre-determined by the provers themselves based on the amount of work each prover must perform, or it can be pre-determined by the verifier based on the reputation of each prover.[1] We ignore the choice of division in our model and protocols, as it does not affect the choices made by the provers in deciding their strategy.

1.1 Results and Discussions

We state our main results and discuss several interesting aspects of our model.

The Power of Multi-Prover Rational Proofs.

We give tight upper and lower bounds on the power of MRIP protocols. As a warm up, we show that MRIP contains NEXP, using an MIP protocol as a black box and paying the provers appropriately. A similar technique shows that MRIP also contains coNEXP. In fact, an important property of MRIP is that it is closed under complement (Lemma 1). Thus, MRIP is strictly more powerful than RIP (assuming PSPACE $\neq$ NEXP), resolving the question raised in [5]. Furthermore, MRIP is also more powerful than MIP (assuming NEXP $\neq$ coNEXP), in contrast to the single-prover case in which classical and rational proofs have the same power.

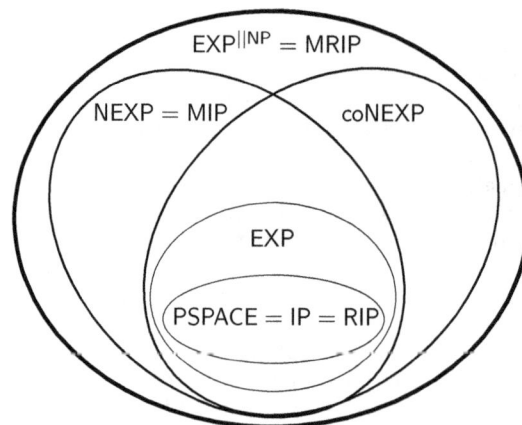

Figure 1: The relative power of rational and classical interactive proof systems. Note that it is widely believed that PSPACE $\neq$ EXP, EXP $\neq$ NEXP, and NEXP $\neq$ coNEXP.

We exactly characterize the class MRIP by showing that a language has a multi-prover rational interactive proof if and only if it is decidable by a deterministic exponential-time oracle Turing machine with non-adaptive access to an NP oracle. That is,

THEOREM 1. MRIP = EXP$^{||NP}$.

---
[1] Note that unbalanced divisions are allowed: for example, it may be that one particular prover always receives half of the total payment, and the other provers split the remainder equally.

We summarize the power of various models of interactive proofs in Figure 1. To prove Theorem 1, we (a) provide a new characterization for $\mathsf{EXP}^{||\mathsf{NP}}$, and (b) decompose the circuit family for $\mathsf{EXP}^{||\mathsf{NP}}$ obtained from this characterization into three stages, construct MRIP protocols for each stage and combine them together appropriately. A similar 3-stage decomposition was used in [6], but their technique results in an exponential blow-up in the number of messages when applied to multi-prover protocols.

It is known that any MIP protocol can be simulated using only two provers and one round of communication between the provers and the verifier [15]. Similarly, we show that only two provers and five rounds are sufficient to capture the full power of MRIP. That is, denoting by $\mathsf{MRIP}(p, r)$ the class of languages that have p-prover rational proofs with r rounds, we have:

THEOREM 2. $\mathsf{MRIP} = \mathsf{MRIP}(2, 5)$.

Note that we count the number of rounds as the total number of interactions (provers' messages and verifier's queries are separate rounds), in contrast to the number of *pairs* of back-and-forth interaction of MIP [15]. We use this convention to simplify our technical discussion.[2] It remains open whether or not the number of rounds in our protocol can be further reduced (see Section 4 for further discussion).

Utility Gaps.

Rational proofs assume that the provers always act to maximize their payment. However, how much do they lose by lying? The notion of *utility gaps*, first introduced in [6], measures the loss in payment (or utility) incurred by a lying prover. Notice that a lying prover may (a) deviate (even slightly) from the truthful protocol but still lead the verifier to the correct answer or (b) deviate and mislead the verifier to an incorrect answer. The authors of [6] demanded their protocols to be robust against provers of type (a): that is, any deviation from the prescribed strategy that the verifier intends the provers to follow results in a significant decrease in the payment. This ideal requirement on utility gaps is quite strong, and even the protocol in [6] fails to satisfy it, as pointed out by Guo, Hubáček, Rosen and Vald [25]. In this paper, we consider multi-prover rational proofs robust against cheating provers of type (b): that is, the provers may respond to some messages of the verifier incorrectly and incur a small payment loss, but if the verifier learns the answer to the membership question of the input string incorrectly, the provers must suffer a significant loss in payment. Note that [25] also considers type (b) utility gap, but for single-prover protocols. Our utility gaps are formally defined in Section 5.

We show that requiring a noticeable utility gap results in protocols for a different, possibly smaller, complexity class. In particular, let $\mathsf{poly(n)}$-gap-MRIP be the class of languages that have MRIP protocols with $1/\alpha(n)$ utility gap for lying provers, where $\alpha(n)$ is a polynomial in n. We completely characterize this class as the class of languages decidable by a polynomial-time oracle Turing machine with non-adaptive access to an NEXP oracle. That is,

THEOREM 3. $\mathsf{poly(n)}$-gap-$\mathsf{MRIP} = \mathsf{P}^{||\mathsf{NEXP}}$.

---

[2]Using the convention of [15], our simulation of any MRIP protocol with two provers would require only three rounds.

Simple and Efficient MRIP protocol for NEXP.

Classical multi-prover interactive proofs for languages in NEXP rely on the MIP protocol for the NEXP-complete language Oracle-3SAT [8]. This MIP protocol is (a) complicated, involving techniques such as multilinearity test of functions and arithmetization, and (b) requires polynomial computation and polynomial rounds of interaction from the verifier. We construct a simple two prover, three round MRIP protocol for Oracle-3SAT using *scoring rules*.[3] Our protocol is very efficient: the verifier performs linear computation along with constant number of basic arithmetic operations to calculate the reward.

Contrasting MRIP with Other Relevant Models.

Existing models, such as *refereed games*, MIP, and single-prover rational proofs all differ from MRIP in distinct and potentially interesting ways.

Refereed games [17] are interactive proof models consisting of two competing provers, who try to convince the verifier of the membership (or non-membership) of a given input string in a language. However, one of them is honest and the other is not. The model of refereed games reflects the strategic nature of the provers, but does not allow collaboration between them.

Classical multi-prover interactive proofs are robust against arbitrary collaborative provers, who may be irrational or even malicious. While MIP protocols provide a stronger guarantee, they are often complicated and computationally-intensive (require polynomial-work from the verifier). In contrast, MRIP restricts provers to be rational, a reasonable assumption in a "mercantile world", as pointed out in [5]. This restriction leads to simple and efficient protocols for the single-prover case [6, 25], making rational proofs a meaningful and interesting model to study.

Finally, MRIP achieves its full power with only five rounds of interaction between the verifier and the provers. In contrast, RIP is less powerful when restricted to constant rounds.[4]

1.2 Additional Related Work

Interactive Proofs.

First introduced by Goldwasser, Micali and Rackoff [23] and in a different form by Babai and Moran [7], interactive proofs (IP) have been extensively studied (see, e.g., [22, 8, 10, 9, 23, 19, 20, 24]) and precisely characterized: that is, $\mathsf{IP} = \mathsf{PSPACE}$ [31, 29]. Ben-Or et al. [10] introduced multi-prover interactive proofs (MIP), which were shown to be exactly equal to NEXP [8]. In fact, two provers and one round is sufficient; in other words, $\mathsf{NEXP} = \mathsf{MIP}(2, 1)$ [15].

Rational Proofs.

Azar and Micali [5] use scoring rules in a novel way to construct simple and efficient single-prover rational protocols. The prover is assumed to be sensitive to exponentially small losses in payment, that is, a negligible utility gap is a sufficient punishment for the prover. In [6], the same authors proposed the idea of utility gaps and constructed super-

---

[3]Scoring rules are powerful tools to elicit information about probabilistic distributions from experts; see Section 2.
[4]As shown in [5], $\mathsf{RIP}\text{-}\mathsf{O}(1) = \mathsf{CH}$, where $\mathsf{RIP}\text{-}\mathsf{O}(1)$ is the class of languages having constant-round rational proofs and CH is the counting hierarchy.

efficient rational proofs, where the verifier performs only logarithmic computation. Guo, Hubáček, Rosen and Vald [25] studied *rational arguments*, which are rational proofs with a single computationally-bounded prover. They constructed rational arguments with single-round interaction and sublinear verification for NC^1. They also mentioned that a rational proof model with multiple provers may have interesting implications in computation delegation schemes, but did not define such a model. Later, they extended their rational argument protocols to P [26], via a novel technique called *rational sumcheck*.

Game-Theoretic Characterization of Complexity Classes.

Game-theoretic characterization of complexity classes has been largely studied in the form of *refereed games* [12, 17, 14, 16, 30, 18, 28].

The classic work of Chandra and Stockmeyer [12] proved that any language in PSPACE is refereeable by a game of perfect information. Feige and Kilian [14] show this is tight for single-round refereed games and that the class of languages with polynomial-round refereed games is exactly EXP.

Feigenbaum, Koller and Shor [18] study a related complexity class $\mathsf{EXP}^{\mathsf{NP}}$ and show that it can be simulated as a zero-sum refereed game between two computationally unbounded provers with *imperfect recall*. Note that imperfect recall is a very strong assumption and makes the computationally unbounded provers essentially act as oracles. In contrast, MRIP consists of collaborative provers having imperfect information (since a prover does not see the messages exchanged between the verifier and other provers) and perfect recall (since a prover remembers the history of messages he exchanged with the verifier). Notice that imperfect information is necessary for multi-prover protocols: if all provers can see all messages exchanged in the protocol, then the model degenerates to a single-prover case. Moreover, perfect recall gives the provers the ability to cheat adaptively across messages. With these differences, MRIP is equivalent to $\mathsf{EXP}^{||\mathsf{NP}}$. To our best knowledge, this is the first game-theoretic characterization of this complexity class.

It is worth pointing out that $\mathsf{EXP}^{\mathsf{NP}}$ is also an important class in the study of circuit lower bounds [34]. It would be interesting to see if the related complexity class $\mathsf{EXP}^{||\mathsf{NP}}$ emerges in similar contexts.

1.3 Outline of the paper

The paper is organized as follows. In Section 2 we define the class of languages that have multi-prover rational interactive proofs, MRIP, and discuss some of its properties. We construct MRIP protocols for NEXP in the same section. We characterize the class MRIP in Section 3. In Section 4 we show how to simulate any MRIP protocol with two provers and five rounds. Finally, in Section 5 we define the notion of *utility gap* and characterize the power of MRIP protocols with a polynomial utility gap.

2. MULTI-PROVER RATIONAL INTERACTIVE PROOFS

In this section we define the model of multi-prover rational interactive proofs and demonstrate several important properties of the class of languages recognized by these proofs.

First, we describe how the verifier and the provers interact, and introduce necessary notations on the way. Let L be a language, x a string whose membership in L is to be decided, and $n = |x|$. An interactive protocol is a pair $(V, \vec{P})$, where V is the *verifier* and $\vec{P} = (P_1, \ldots, P_{t(n)})$ is the vector of *provers*, with $t(n)$ a polynomial.[5] The verifier runs in polynomial time and flips private coins, whereas each P_i is computationally unbounded. The verifier and provers all know x. The verifier can communicate with each prover privately, but no two provers can communicate with each other. In a *round*, either each prover sends a message to the verifier, or the verifier sends a message to each prover, and these two cases alternate. Without loss of generality we assume the first round of messages are sent by the provers, and the first bit sent by P_1, denoted by c, indicates whether $x \in L$ (corresponding to $c = 1$) or not ($c = 0$). Notice that c does not depend on the randomness used by V.

The length of each message and the number of rounds are polynomial in n. Let $p(n)$ be the number of rounds and r the random string used by V. For each $j \in \{1, 2, \ldots, p(n)\}$, let m_{ij} be the message exchanged between V and P_i in round j. In particular, the first bit of m_{11} is c. The transcript that each prover P_i has seen at the beginning of each round j is $(m_{i1}, m_{i2}, \ldots, m_{i(j-1)})$. Let $\vec{m}$ be the vector of all messages exchanged in the protocol (therefore $\vec{m}$ is a random variable depending on r).

At the end of the communication, the verifier computes a payment function R based on x, r, and $\vec{m}$ as the total payment to give to the provers. We restrict $R(x, r, \vec{m}) \in [-1, 1]$ for convenience.[6]

The protocol followed by V, including the payment function R, is public knowledge.

The verifier outputs c as the answer for the membership of x in L: that is, V does not check the provers' answer and follows it blindly. As will become clear from our results, this requirement for the verifier does not change the set of languages that have multi-prover rational interactive proofs. Indeed, we could have allowed V to compute his answer based on x, r, and $\vec{m}$ as well, but the current model eases later discussion on the payment loss of the provers caused by "reporting a wrong answer".

Each prover P_i can choose a *strategy* $s_{ij} : \{0,1\}^* \to \{0,1\}^*$ for each round j, which maps the transcript he has seen at the beginning of round j to the message he sends in that round.[7] Let $\tilde{s}_i = (s_{i1}, \ldots, s_{ip(n)})$ be the vector of strategies P_i uses in rounds $1, \ldots, p(n)$, and $\tilde{s} = (\tilde{s}_1, \ldots, \tilde{s}_{t(n)})$ be the strategy profile of the provers. Given any input x, randomness r, and strategy profile $\tilde{s}$, we denote by $(V, \vec{P})(x, r, \tilde{s})$ the vector of all messages exchanged in the protocol.

The provers are *cooperative* and jointly act to maximize the (total) expected payment received from the verifier. Note that this is equivalent to the provers maximizing their own expected payment when each prover receives a pre-specified division of the payment, that is, for any function γ_i fixed at the beginning of the protocol with $\sum_{i=1}^n \gamma_i = 1$, P_i receives $\gamma_i R$.

---

[5] That is, we allow polynomially many provers.

[6] Note that the payment can be shifted and scaled so that it is in [0, 1]. We use both positive and negative payments in our model to better reflect the intuition behind our protocols: the former are rewards while the latter are punishments.

[7] P_i does not send any message s_{ij} for an even-numbered round j, and these s_{ij}'s can be treated as constant functions.

Thus, before the protocol starts, the provers pre-agree on a strategy profile $\tilde{s}$ that maximizes

$$u_{(V,\vec{P})}(\tilde{s}; x) \triangleq \mathbb{E}_r R(x, r, (V, \vec{P})(x, r, \tilde{s})).$$

When $(V, \vec{P})$ and x are clear from the context, we write $u(\tilde{s})$ for $u_{(V,\vec{P})}(\tilde{s}; x)$. Using the above notions, we define MRIP as follows.

DEFINITION 1 (MRIP). *For any language L, an interactive protocol $(V, \vec{P})$ is a multi-prover rational interactive proof (MRIP) protocol for L if, for any $x \in \{0, 1\}^*$ and any strategy profile $\tilde{s}$ of the provers such that $u(\tilde{s}) = \max_{\tilde{s}'} u(\tilde{s}')$, we have*

1. $u(\tilde{s}) \geq 0$;

2. $c = 1$ if and only if $x \in L$.

We denote the set of languages that have MRIP protocols by MRIP, *and the set of languages that have MRIP protocols with k provers and p rounds by* MRIP(k, p).

LEMMA 1. MRIP *is closed under complement.*

PROOF. Let L be a language in MRIP, $(V, \vec{P})$ an MRIP protocol for L, and R the payment function computed by V. We construct a verifier V' and thus an MRIP protocol $(V', \vec{P})$ for $\overline{L}$, as follows.

- V' runs V to compute the messages he should send in each round, except that, whenever V' gives V as an input the first message m'_{11} sent by P_1, he flips the first bit.
- At the end of the communication, V' computes a payment function R': for any x, r, and $\vec{m}'$, $R'(x, r, \vec{m}') = R(x, r, \vec{m})$, where $\vec{m}$ is $\vec{m}'$ with the first bit flipped.
- V' outputs the first bit sent by P_1.

For each strategy profile $\tilde{s}$ of the provers in the protocol $(V, \vec{P})$, consider the following strategy profile $\tilde{s}'$ in the protocol $(V', \vec{P})$:

- $\tilde{s}'_i = \tilde{s}_i$ for each $i \neq 1$.
- In round 1, $\tilde{s}'_1$ outputs the same message as $\tilde{s}_1$, except that the first bit is flipped.
- For any odd number $k > 1$ and any transcript m'_1 for P_1 at the beginning of round k, $\tilde{s}'_1(m'_1)$ is the same as $\tilde{s}_1(m_1)$, where m_1 is m'_1 with the first bit flipped.

It is easy to see that for any x and r, $(V', \vec{P})(x, r, \tilde{s}')$ is the same as $(V, \vec{P})(x, r, \tilde{s})$ except the first bit. Thus $R'(x, r, (V', \vec{P})(x, r, \tilde{s}')) = R(x, r, (V, \vec{P})(x, r, \tilde{s}))$, which implies

$$u_{(V',\vec{P})}(\tilde{s}'; x) = u_{(V,\vec{P})}(\tilde{s}; x).$$

Also, it is easy to see that the mapping from $\tilde{s}$ to $\tilde{s}'$ is a bijection. Accordingly, arbitrarily fixing a strategy profile $\tilde{s}'$ that maximizes $u_{(V',\vec{P})}(\tilde{s}'; x)$, we have that the corresponding $\tilde{s}$ maximizes $u_{(V,\vec{P})}(\tilde{s}; x)$ as well. Thus

$$u_{(V',\vec{P})}(\tilde{s}'; x) = u_{(V,\vec{P})}(\tilde{s}; x) \geq 0,$$

where the inequality is by Definition 1. Furthermore, $x \in L$ if and only if the first bit sent by $\tilde{s}_1$ is 1, if and only if the first bit sent by $\tilde{s}'_1$ is 0. That is, $x \in \overline{L}$ if and only if the first bit sent by $\tilde{s}'_1$ is 1. $\square$

To demonstrate the power of multi-prover rational proofs, we show that MRIP contains NEXP. With Lemma 1, this implies that MRIP contains coNEXP as well. We show this in two different ways.

First, we construct an MRIP protocol for any language in NEXP using a standard MIP protocol as a subroutine. Given existing MIP protocols, this method is intuitive and its correctness is easy to see. However, the computation and communication complexity of the protocol depends on the MIP protocol.

Second, we construct an MRIP protocol for an NEXP-complete language without relying on MIP protocols, instead by exploiting the rational nature of the provers. This protocol uses *proper scoring rules* to incentivize the provers. In contrast to MIP, this MRIP protocol is very efficient: it only requires the verifier to perform linear amount of computation and communication, along with computing the payment using constant number of arithmetic operations.

2.1 An MRIP Protocol for any Language in NEXP, Based on MIP.

An MIP protocol (see, e.g., [8, 15]) for a language $L \in$ NEXP first reduces L to the NEXP-complete problem Oracle-3SAT (defined below), and then runs an MIP protocol for Oracle-3SAT.

DEFINITION 2 (Oracle-3SAT [8]). *Let w be a binary string of length $r + 3s$. Let B be a 3-CNF of $r + 3s + 3$ variables. A Boolean function $A : \{0, 1\}^s \to \{0, 1\}$ is a 3-satisfying oracle for B if $B(w, A(b_1), A(b_2), A(b_3))$ is satisfied for all w, where $b_1 b_2 b_3$ are the last $3s$ bits of w. The Oracle-3SAT problem is to decide, for a given B, if there is a 3-satisfying oracle for B.*

Our MRIP protocol for NEXP uses a black-box MIP protocol and an appropriate payment scheme.

LEMMA 2. NEXP $\subseteq$ MRIP.

PROOF. The MRIP protocol $(V, \vec{P})$ for L is shown in Figure 2. By construction, the payment to the provers is always non-negative.

Now we show that V outputs 1 if and only if $x \in L$. On the one hand, for any $x \in L$, if the provers send $c = 1$ and execute the MIP protocol with V, then their payment is $R = 1$;[8] while if they send $c = 0$, the payment is $R = 1/2 < 1$. Accordingly, their best strategy profile is to send $c = 1$ and run the MIP protocol correctly. On the other hand, for any $x \notin L$, if the provers send $c = 1$ and run the MIP protocol, then by the definition of MIP, the probability that V accepts is at most $1/3$, and the expected payment is at most $1/3$; while if they send $c = 0$, the payment is $1/2 > 1/3$. Accordingly, their best strategy profile is to send $c = 0$. $\square$

REMARK 1. *Since any language $L \in$ NEXP has a 2-prover 1-round MIP protocol [15], we automatically obtain an MRIP protocol for L with 2 provers and 3 rounds of interaction (using our convention, executing the MIP protocol takes 2 rounds, plus one round for the answer bit c). Note that this is the best possible. However, the computation and communication complexity of the protocol are both polynomial (in addition to the reduction to Oracle-3SAT) and involve complex techniques such as arithmetization and multilinearity test [8].*

---

[8]If the MIP protocol does not have perfect completeness and accepts x with probability at least $2/3$, then the expected payment is at least $2/3$. However, this does not affect the correctness of the MRIP protocol.

For any input string x, the protocol $(V, \vec{P})$ works as follows:

1. P_1 sends a bit c to V. V outputs c at the end of the protocol.
2. If $c = 0$ then the protocol ends and the payment given to the provers is $R = 1/2$;
3. Otherwise, V and $\vec{P}$ run an MIP protocol for proving $x \in L$. If the verifier accepts then $R = 1$, else $R = 0$.

Figure 2: A simple MRIP protocol for NEXP

By Lemmas 1 and 2, we immediately have the following corollary. Also note that we can obtain a 2-prover 3-round MRIP protocol for coNEXP directly by modifying the protocol of Lemma 2.

COROLLARY 1. coNEXP $\subseteq$ MRIP.

2.2 An MRIP Protocol for any Language in NEXP, Using Scoring Rules.

We now construct an MRIP protocol for any language in NEXP without relying on MIP protocols. Instead, we use *proper scoring rules* to compute the payment that should be given to the provers so as to ensure truthful answers.

To begin, we recall the definitions of proper scoring rules in general and the *Brier's scoring rule* in particular, which has been an essential ingredient in the construction of rational proofs [5, 6, 25].

Proper Scoring Rules.

Scoring rules are tools to assess the quality of a probabilistic forecast by assigning a numerical score (that is, a payment to the forecaster) to it based on the predicted distribution and the sample that materializes. More precisely, given any probability space Σ, letting $\Delta(\Sigma)$ be the set of probability distributions over Σ, a *scoring rule* is a function from $\Delta(\Sigma) \times \Sigma$ to $\mathbb{R}$, the set of reals. A scoring rule S is *proper* if, for any distribution D over Σ and distribution $D' \neq D$, we have

$$\sum_{\omega \in \Sigma} D(\omega) S(D, \omega) \geq \sum_{\omega \in \Sigma} D(\omega) S(D', \omega),$$

where $D(\omega)$ is the probability that ω is drawn from D. A scoring rule S is *strictly proper* if the above inequality is strict. Notice that, when the true distribution is D, the forecaster maximizes the expected payment under a strictly proper scoring rule by reporting $D' = D$. For a comprehensive survey on scoring rules, see [21].

Brier's Scoring Rule [11].

This classic scoring rule, denoted by BSR, is defined as follows: for any distribution D and $\omega \in \Sigma$,

$$\mathsf{BSR}(D, \omega) = 2D(\omega) - \sum_{\omega \in \Sigma} D(\omega)^2 - 1.$$

It is well known that BSR is strictly proper.

Notice that BSR requires the computation of $\sum_{\omega \in \Sigma} D(\omega)^2$, which can be hard when $|\Sigma|$ is large. However, similar to [5, 25], in this paper we only consider $\Sigma = \{0, 1\}$. Also notice that, BSR has range $[-2, 0]$ and can be shifted and scaled so that (1) the range is non-negative and bounded, and (2) the resulting scoring rule is still strictly proper. In particular, we shall add 2 to the function when using it.

Next, we construct a simple and efficient MRIP protocol for Oracle-3SAT. Similar to the classical multi-prover case, an MRIP protocol for any language $L \in$ NEXP can be obtained by first reducing L to Oracle-3SAT, and then using our efficient MRIP protocol for Oracle-3SAT. The complexity of the overall protocol for L is thus the same as the reduction.

LEMMA 3. Oracle-3SAT *has an MRIP protocol with 2 provers and 3 rounds where, for any instance B of length n, the randomness used by the verifier, the computation complexity, and the communication complexity of the protocol are all $O(n)$, and the computation of the payment function consists of constant number of arithmetic operations over $O(n)$-bit numbers.*

PROOF. For any instance B with $r + 3s + 3$ variables (thus $n \geq r + 3s + 3$), the provers can, with their unbounded computation power, find an oracle A^* that maximizes the number of satisfying w's for B. Denote this number by a^*. If $B \in$ Oracle-3SAT then $a^* = 2^{r+3s}$, otherwise $a^* < 2^{r+3s}$.

Roughly speaking, in our MRIP protocol $(V, \vec{P})$, the verifier incentivizes the provers to report the correct value of a^*, so that the membership of B can be decided. The protocol is shown in Figure 3.

To see why this protocol works, first notice that, if the provers send $c = 0$ and $a = 0$ in Step 1 and always send 0's in Step 4, then the protocol always ends in Steps 5b or 5c, and the provers' expected payment is 0. Accordingly, the best strategy profile $\tilde{s}^*$ of the provers gives them expected payment at least 0, and Condition 1 of Definition 1 holds. Moreover, $\tilde{s}^*$ must be such that

either $c = 1$ and $a = 2^{r+3s}$, or $c = 0$ and $a < 2^{r+3s}$, (1)

since otherwise the provers' expected payment is -1.

It remains to show that Condition 2 of Definition 1 holds. Notice that P_2 only answers one query of the verifier (in step 4), thus under any strategy $\tilde{s}_2$ and given any c and a, P_2 de facto commits to an oracle $A' : \{0, 1\}^s \to \{0, 1\}$. Assume that P_1, using a strategy $\tilde{s}_1$ and seeing $(b_1, ..., b_6)$, sends V six bits in step 4 that are not consistent with A' —that is, there exists $i \in \{1, \ldots, 6\}$ such that $A(b_i) \neq A'(b_i)$. Let q be the probability that, conditioned on $(b_1, ..., b_6)$, the verifier chooses a k that catches the provers in step 5a. We have $q \geq 1/6$. Let R be the payment to the provers conditioned on $(b_1, ..., b_6)$ and on the event that they are not caught in step 5a. Note that $R \leq \frac{2}{11}$ by the definition of Brier's scoring rule (after shifting and scaling). Thus the expected payment to the provers conditioned on $(b_1, ..., b_6)$ is $-q + (1 - q)R < 0$. However, if P_1 answers the verifier's queries consistently with A', his expected payment conditioned on $(b_1, ..., b_6)$ is non-negative. Accordingly, the best strategy profile $\tilde{s}^*$ must be such that, for any c, a, and the oracle commited by P_2, P_1's answers for any $(b_1, ..., b_6)$ are consistent with A'. Thus under $\tilde{s}^*$ the payment is never computed in step 5a.

Furthermore, given b_1, b_2, b_3 and A', whether B evaluates to 0 in step 5b or not is totally determined. If B evaluates to 0, then it does not matter what a or c is and the provers' received payment is 0. If B does not evaluate to 0 in step 5b, then the expected payment to the provers in step 5c is defined by Brier's scoring rule: the true distribution of b, denoted by D, is such that $D(1) = a'/2^{r+3s}$, with a' being the number of satisfying w's for B under oracle A'; and the realized value is $b = B(z', b_4, b_5, b_6, A(b_4), A(b_5), A(b_6))$. Indeed, since b_4, b_5, b_6 are independent from b_1, b_2, b_3, we have that w' is a uniformly random input to B, and the probability for b to be 1 is exactly $a'/2^{r+3s}$. Since Brier's scoring rule is strictly proper, conditioned on A' the provers maximize their expected utility by reporting

$$a = a', \qquad (2)$$

which implies $(p_1, p_0) = (D(1), D(0))$.

If $B \notin$ Oracle-3SAT, then no matter which oracle A' is committed under $\tilde{s}^*$, we have $a' < 2^{r+3s}$. By Equations 1 and 2, we have $a < 2^{r+3s}$ and $c = 0$, as desired.

If $B \in$ Oracle-3SAT, we show that under $\tilde{s}^*$ the prover P_2 commits to the desired 3-satisfying oracle A^* (so that $a' = 2^{r+3s}$ and $D(1) = 1$). To see why this is true, denote by BSR(D) the expected score for reporting D under Brier's scoring rule, when the true distribution is D. We have

$$
\begin{aligned}
\text{BSR}(D) &= D(1)\left(2D(1) - D(1)^2 - (1 - D(1))^2 - 1\right) \\
&\quad + (1 - D(1))\left(2(1 - D(1)) - D(1)^2\right. \\
&\quad \left. - (1 - D(1))^2 - 1\right) \\
&= 2(D(1)^2 - D(1)).
\end{aligned}
$$

Thus BSR(D) is symmetric at $D(1) = 1/2$, strictly decreasing on $D(1) \in [0, 1/2]$, strictly increasing on $D(1) \in [1/2, 1]$, and maximized when $D(1) = 1$ or $D(1) = 0$. Notice that the shifting and scaling of BSR in step 5c do not change these properties, but make BSR(D) strictly positive when $D(1) = 1$ or $D(1) = 0$. Accordingly, to maximize their expected payment conditioned on the event that step 5c is reached, P_2 should commit to either an oracle A' such that $D(1)$ is as small as possible, or an A' such that $D(1)$ is as large as possible, whichever makes $D(1)$ further from $1/2$.

If there is no oracle A' such that $a' = 0$ given A', then the only way for the provers to maximize their expected payment is to commit to the 3-satisfying oracle A^* (thus $a' = 1$), under which step 5c is reached with probability 1. Again by Equations 1 and 2, we have $c = 1$ and $a = 2^{r+3s}$ as desired.

If there is both a 3-satisfying oracle A^* and an oracle A' such that $a' = 0$, we need to make sure that P_2 does not commit to A': indeed, committing to any other oracle results in an expected payment strictly smaller than that by committing to A^*, since it increases the probability that the protocol ends at step 5b with $R = 0$, and strictly decreases the expected payment conditioned on step 5c being reached. If P_2 commits to A', then B *always* evaluates to 0 in step 5b, and step 5c is actually never reached. Thus, even though by committing to A' the provers maximize their expected payment in step 5c, their actual expected payment is 0. Instead, by committing to A^*, step 5c is reached with probability 1 and the provers get positive payment. Accordingly, the strategy profile $\tilde{s}^*$ must be such that P_2 commits to A^* and P_1 sends $a = 2^{r+3s}$ and $c = 1$, as desired. Notice that if there are multiple 3-satisfying oracles for B, then the provers can pre-agree on any one of them.

In sum, Condition 2 of Definition 1 also holds and $(V, \vec{P})$ is an MRIP protocol for Oracle-3SAT. Moreover, since $n \geq r + 3s + 3$, it is easy to see that the number of coins flipped by V is at most $2n$ (for sampling w, w', and k) and the number of bits exchanged between V and $\vec{P}$ is at most $3n+3$. Finally, given an input string $w = (z, b_1, b_2, b_3)$ for B and the 3-bit answers of the oracle for b_1, b_2, b_3, B can be evaluated in linear time, thus the running time of V is $O(n)$ plus constant number of arithmetic operations to compute the payment in step 5c. Therefore Lemma 3 holds. □

3. CHARACTERIZING MULTI-PROVER RATIONAL INTERACTIVE PROOFS

In this section we prove Theorem 1, that is,

THEOREM 1. MRIP = EXP$^{||\mathsf{NP}}$.

We first show that MRIP is the same as another complexity class, EXP$^{||\mathsf{poly-NEXP}}$, which we define below. We complete the proof of Theorem 1 by showing EXP$^{||\mathsf{NP}}$ = EXP$^{||\mathsf{poly-NEXP}}$.

DEFINITION 3. EXP$^{||\mathsf{poly-NEXP}}$ *is the class of languages decidable by a deterministic exponential-time Turing machine with non-adaptive access to an NEXP oracle, such that the length of each oracle query is polynomial in the length of the input of the Turing machine.*

We use two intermediate lemmas to prove the lower bound. Lemma 4 is from [4] and gives a circuit characterization of EXP.

LEMMA 4 ([4]). *For any language L, $L \in$ EXP if and only if it can be computed by a DC uniform circuit family of size $2^{n^{O(1)}}$.*

LEMMA 5. *Every language L in EXP has an MRIP protocol with two provers and five rounds.*

PROOF. To begin, we recall some definitions and results from the literature that we use in our proof. First of all, a *circuit family* $\{C_n\}_{n=1}^{\infty}$ is a sequence of boolean circuits such that $C_n : \{0,1\}^n \to \{0,1\}$. The gates in the circuits are of type AND, OR, and NOT, with fan-ins 2, 2, and 1 respectively. The input string to a circuit is connected to a special set of "input gates", one for each bit of the input, whose output value is always the value of the corresponding bit. The *size* of a circuit C is the number of gates (including the input gates) in C. For a circuit C of size g, the set of gates in it is denoted by $\{1, 2, ..., g\}$. Without loss of generality we assume that gate g is the output gate of the whole circuit. Moreover, if C has input length n, without loss of generality we assume that gates $1, 2, .., n$ are the input gates. Notice that the number of wires in C is at most $2g$, since each gate has at most 2 fan-ins. The set of wires is denoted by $\{1, 2, ..., 2g\}$.

DEFINITION 4 (DC UNIFORM CIRCUITS [4]). *A circuit family $\{C_n\}_{n=1}^{\infty}$ is a Direct Connect uniform (DC uniform) family if the following questions can be answered in polynomial time:*

1. *$SIZE(n)$: what is the size of C_n?*
2. *$INPUT(n, h, i)$: is wire h an input to gate i in C_n?*
3. *$OUTPUT(n, h, i)$: is wire h the output of gate i in C_n?*

For any instance B, the protocol $(V, \vec{P})$ works as follows:
1. P_1 sends $c \in \{0,1\}$ and $a \in \{0,\ldots,2^{r+3s}\}$ to V. V always outputs c at the end of the protocol.
2. If $c=1$ and $a < 2^{r+3s}$, or if $c=0$ and $a = 2^{r+3s}$, the protocol ends with payment $R = -1$.
3. Otherwise, V randomly chooses two binary strings of length $r + 3s$, $w = (z, b_1, b_2, b_3)$ and $w' = (z', b_4, b_5, b_6)$, as well as a number $k \in \{1,2,3,4,5,6\}$.
   V sends $b_1, b_2, b_3, b_4, b_5, b_6$ to P_1 and b_k to P_2.
4. P_1 sends to V six bits, $A(b_i)$ with $i \in \{1,2,...,6\}$, and P_2 sends one bit, $A'(b_k)$.
5. The protocol ends and V computes the payment R as follows.
   (a) If $A(b_k) \neq A'(b_k)$ then $R = -1$.
   (b) Otherwise, if $B(z, b_1, b_2, b_3, A(b_1), A(b_2), A(b_3)) = 0$ then $R = 0$.
   (c) Else, let $b = B(z', b_4, b_5, b_6, A(b_4), A(b_5), A(b_6))$, $p_1 = a/2^{r+3s}$, and $p_0 = 1 - p_1$.
       V computes R using Brier's scoring rule:
       if $b = 1$ then $R = \frac{2p_1 - (p_1^2 + p_0^2) + 1}{11}$; otherwise $R = \frac{2p_0 - (p_1^2 + p_0^2) + 1}{11}$.

Figure 3: An efficient MRIP protocol for Oracle-3SAT.

4. TYPE(n, i, t): is t the type of gate i in C_n?

That is, the circuits in a DC uniform family may have exponential size, but they have a succinct representation in terms of a polynomial-time Turing machine that can answer all the questions in Definition 4. The class EXP can be characterized by the class of DC uniform circuit families [4]; this is stated formally in Lemma 4.

Now we are ready to prove Lemma 5.

Following Lemma 4, there exists a DC uniform circuit family $\{C_n\}_{n=1}^\infty$ that computes L. Let $g = 2^{n^k}$ be the size of each C_n, where k is a constant that may depend on L. For any input string x of length n and any gate $i \in \{1,2,...,g\}$ in C_n, let $v_i(x) \in \{0,1\}$ be the value of i's output on input x. In particular, $v_i(x) = x_i$ for any $i \in \{1,2,...,n\}$. We call a gate i' in C_n an *input gate* of i if there is a directed wire from i' to i. The MRIP protocol $(V, \vec{P})$ is shown in Figure 4.

Clearly this protocol has two provers and five rounds. To see why it is an MRIP protocol, notice that if P_1 and P_2 always send the correct c and answer V's queries correctly according to C_n, their received payment is always $R = 1$, irrespective of V's coin flips. Thus the expected received payment is 1. Below we show that any other strategy profile gives expected payment strictly less than 1.

First of all, when the gate i chosen by the verifier in step 2 is not an input gate, if any of P_1's answers in step 3 to queries 2a and 2b (namely, about i's type, input gates and input wires) is incorrect, then the verification in step 6a fails, giving the provers a payment $R = 0$. Accordingly, if there exists such a gate then the expected payment to the provers is at most $1 - 1/g < 1$. Similarly, if there exists a non-input gate i such that P_1 answers queries 2a and 2b correctly but the values $v_i(x), v_{i_1}(x), v_{i_2}(x)$ are inconsistent with i's type, then, when i is chosen, step 6b fails, thus the expected payment to the provers is at most $1 - 1/g < 1$. Moreover, if there exists an input gate i such that $v_i(x) \neq x_i$ when i is chosen, or if $v_g(x) \neq c$ when gate g is chosen, then the expected payment to the provers is again at most $1 - 1/g < 1$.

Next, similar to the analysis of Lemma 3, P_2 is only queried once (in step 5). Thus P_2 de facto commits to an oracle $A : \{1, \ldots, g\} \to \{0, 1\}$, which maps any gate to its value under input x. If there exists a gate i such that the values $v_i(x), v_{i_1}(x), v_{i_2}(x)$ in step 3 are not consistent with A, then, conditioned on i being chosen in step 2, with prob-

ability $1/3$ step 6e fails. Since i is chosen with probability $1/g$, the expected payment is at most $1 - \frac{1}{3g} < 1$.

Accordingly, the only strategy profile $\tilde{s}$ that can have expected payment equal to 1 is exactly what we want: that is,
(1) P_1 and P_2 answer queries to the values of gates using the same oracle $A : \{1, \ldots, g\} \to \{0, 1\}$,
(2) $A(i) = x_i$ for any input gate i,
(3) $A(g) = c$, and
(4) for any non-input gate i, $A(i)$ is computed correctly according to i's type and the values of its input gates in C_n.

Thus $A(g)$ is computed according to C_n with input x, and $A(g) = 1$ if and only if $x \in L$. Since $c = A(g)$, we have that $c = 1$ if and only if $x \in L$, implying that $(V, \vec{P})$ is an MRIP protocol for L. Therefore Lemma 5 holds. $\square$

Using these lemmas, Lemma 6 proves the lower bound on MRIP. We describe the main ideas in the proof sketch below. A detailed proof can be found in the full version of this paper [13].

LEMMA 6. $\mathsf{EXP}^{||\mathsf{poly-NEXP}} \subseteq \mathsf{MRIP}$.

PROOF SKETCH: Using the characterization of EXP in terms of DC uniform circuits from Lemma 4, we have an MRIP protocol for EXP with 2 provers and 5 rounds as in Lemma 5 (see Figure 4). We then combine this protocol with the MRIP protocol for Oracle-3SAT in Figure 2 to obtain the desired MRIP protocol for $\mathsf{EXP}^{||\mathsf{poly-NEXP}}$.[9] In particular, we use the protocol for Oracle-3SAT to answer NEXP oracle queries. A similar structure has been used by [6] for single-prover rational proofs. However, the prover in [6] can send the entire proof of a circuit satisfiability problem to the verifier, which is not feasible for us because our circuit may be exponentially large while our verifier is still of polynomial time. We overcome this problem by using a second prover to cross-check whether the first prover is answering questions about the circuit correctly. $\square$

Lemma 7 then shows that the above lower bound is tight, leading to an exact characterization.

---
[9] The MRIP protocol for Oracle-3SAT in Figure 3 can also be used, with appropriate modifications in the computation of the payment. We use the protocol in Figure 2 to simplify the analysis.

244

Given any string x of length n,
1. P_1 sends one bit $c \in \{0,1\}$ to V. V always outputs c at the end of the protocol.
2. V computes $g = SIZE(n)$, picks a gate $i \in \{1, 2, ..., g\}$ uniformly at random, and sends i to P_1. That is, V queries P_1 for:
   (a) the type of gate i,
   (b) the input gates of i and corresponding input wires, and
   (c) the values of gate i and its input gates.
3. P_1 sends to V the concatenation of the following strings: type $t_i \in \{AND, OR, NOT\}$; gates $i_1, i_2 \in \{1, 2, ..., g\}$; wires $h_1, h_2 \in \{1, 2, ..., 2g\}$; and values $v_i(x), v_{i_1}(x), v_{i_2}(x) \in \{0,1\}$.
4. V picks a gate $i' \in \{i, i_1, i_2\}$ uniformly at random and sends i' to P_2.
5. P_2 sends $v_{i'}(x) \in \{0,1\}$ to V.
6. The protocol ends and V computes the payment R by verifying the following statements:
   (a) If $i \notin \{1, 2, ..., n\}$ (that is, i is not an input gate), then $TYPE(n, i, t_i) = 1$, $INPUT(n, h_1, i) = OUTPUT(n, h_1, i_1) = 1$, and, if $t_i \neq NOT$, $INPUT(n, h_2, i) = OUTPUT(n, h_2, i_2) = 1$.
   (b) If $i \notin \{1, 2, ..., n\}$, then $v_i(x)$ is computed correctly based on type t_i from $v_{i_1}(x)$ and (when $t_i \neq NOT$) $v_{i_2}(x)$.
   (c) If $i \in \{1, 2, ..., n\}$ then $v_i(x) = x_i$.
   (d) If $i = g$ (that is, the output gate of the circuit) then $v_i(x) = c$.
   (e) The answers of P_1 and P_2 on the value of gate i' are consistent.
   If any of these verifications fails then $R = 0$; otherwise $R = 1$.

Figure 4: An MRIP protocol for EXP.

LEMMA 7. $\mathsf{MRIP} \subseteq \mathsf{EXP}^{||poly-\mathsf{NEXP}}$.

PROOF. Arbitrarily fix a language $L \in \mathsf{MRIP}$ and let $(V, \vec{P})$ be an MRIP protocol for L. Since V runs in polynomial time, there exists a constant k such that, for any two payments R and R' that can be output by V under some input of length n and some randomness, we have

$$R \neq R' \Rightarrow |R - R'| \geq \frac{1}{2^{n^k}}.$$

For example, n^k can be an upper bound of V's running time. Moreover, since V uses polynomially many random coins, there exists another constant k' such that, when a payment appears with positive probability under some input of length n, it must appear with probability at least $\frac{1}{2^{n^{k'}}}$. Accordingly, for any input x of length n and any two strategy profiles $\tilde{s}$ and $\tilde{s}'$ of the provers, if the expected payments $u(\tilde{s}; x)$ and $u(\tilde{s}'; x)$ are different, then

$$|u(\tilde{s}; x) - u(\tilde{s}'; x)| \geq \frac{1}{2^{n^{k+k'}}}. \quad (3)$$

Consider the following deterministic oracle Turing machine M: Given any input x of length n, it divides the interval $[0,1]$ to $2 \cdot 2^{n^{k+k'}}$ sub-intervals of length $\frac{1}{2 \cdot 2^{n^{k+k'}}}$. For any $i \in \{1, ..., 2 \cdot 2^{n^{k+k'}}\}$, the i-th interval is $[2(i-1) \cdot 2^{n^{k+k'}}, 2i \cdot 2^{n^{k+k'}}]$. M then makes $4 \cdot 2^{n^{k+k'}}$ oracle queries of the form (i, j), where $i \in \{1, ..., 2 \cdot 2^{n^{k+k'}}\}$ and $j \in \{0,1\}$. Notice that the lengths of the queries are upper bounded by $2 + n^{k+k'}$, which is a polynomial as required by the class $\mathsf{EXP}^{||poly-\mathsf{NEXP}}$.

For each query (i, j), if $j = 0$ then the corresponding question is "whether there exists a strategy profile $\tilde{s}$ of the provers such that $u(\tilde{s}; x)$ is in the i-th interval"; and if $j = 1$ then the corresponding question is "whether there exists a strategy profile $\tilde{s}$ such that $u(\tilde{s}; x)$ is in the i-th interval and the first bit sent by P_1 is $c = 1$". Notice that all the queries are indeed non-adaptive. We say that interval i is non-empty if the query $(i, 0)$ is answered 1, and empty otherwise.

Assume for now all the queries are answered correctly. M finds the highest index i^* such that the interval i^* is non-empty. It accepts if $(i^*, 1)$ is answered 1, and rejects otherwise. M clearly runs in exponential time. To see why it decides L (given correct oracle answers), notice that by Definition 1, there exists a strategy profile whose expected payment is non-negative and thus in $[0, 1]$ (since the payment is always in $[-1, 1]$). Thus there exists an interval i such that $(i, 0)$ is answered 1. Also by definition, the best strategy profile $\tilde{s}$ has the highest expected payment, and thus $u(\tilde{s}; x)$ falls into interval i^*.

By Inequality 3, any strategy profile $\tilde{s}'$ with $u(\tilde{s}'; x) < u(\tilde{s}; x)$ has $u(\tilde{s}'; x)$ not in interval i^*, since the difference between $u(\tilde{s}'; x)$ and $u(\tilde{s}; x)$ is larger than the length of the interval. Accordingly, all strategy profiles $\tilde{s}'$ with $u(\tilde{s}'; x)$ in interval i^* satisfies $u(\tilde{s}'; x) = u(\tilde{s}; x)$: they are all the best strategy profiles of the provers. Again by Definition 1, P_1 sends the same first bit c under all these strategy profiles, $c = 1$ if and only if $x \in L$, and there does not exist any other strategy profile whose expected payment falls into interval i^* but the first bit sent by P_1 is different from c. Thus the answer to $(i^*, 1)$ always equals c, and M accepts if and only if $c = 1$, if and only if $x \in L$, as desired.

It remains to show that the oracle queries can be answered by an NEXP oracle. Recall that in the protocol $(V, \vec{P})$ a strategy s_{ij} of each prover P_i for each round j is a function mapping the transcript P_i has seen at the beginning of round j to the message he sends in that round. Since the protocol has polynomially many provers and polynomially many rounds, by definition a strategy profile consists of polynomially many functions from $\{0,1\}^*$ to $\{0,1\}^*$, where for each function both the input length and the output length are polynomial in n (since otherwise the messages cannot be processed by V). Accordingly, it takes exponentially many bits to specify each function: if the input length is $p(n)$ and the output length is $q(n)$, then $2^{p(n)} q(n)$ bits are sufficient to specify the truth table of the function. Therefore a strategy profile can also be specified by exponentially many bits. Below we construct an exponential-time non-deterministic

245

Turing machine M' that decides the questions corresponding to the queries.

Given any input $(i, 0)$, M' non-deterministically chooses a strategy profile $\tilde{s}$, in exponential time. It then goes through all the realizations of V's random string, and for each realization r it runs V with x and r, and generates the provers' messages by looking them up in the corresponding truth table in $\tilde{s}$. M' computes for each r the payment output by V at the end of the protocol, and by combining these payments with corresponding probabilities M' computes the expected payment $u(\tilde{s}; x)$. If $u(\tilde{s}; x)$ is in interval i then M' accepts, otherwise it rejects. Since V's random string is polynomially long, there are exponentially many realizations, and each one of them takes exponential time to run: V runs in polynomial time and it takes M' exponential time to look up the truth tables in $\tilde{s}$ to generate a prover's message. Thus M' runs in non-deterministic exponential time. Also, if interval i is non-empty then there exists a strategy profile $\tilde{s}$ that makes M' accept, and if interval i is empty then M' always rejects.

Similarly, given any input $(i, 1)$, M' non-deterministically chooses a strategy profile $\tilde{s}$ and computes its expected payment $u(\tilde{s}; x)$. If $u(\tilde{s}; x)$ is not in interval i then M' rejects; otherwise, M' accepts if and only if the first bit sent by P_1 is 1. The correctness and the running time of this part follows immediately. $\quad\square$

We have now established that $\mathsf{MRIP} = \mathsf{EXP}^{||\mathsf{poly-NEXP}}$. To finish the proof of Theorem 1, we show that $\mathsf{EXP}^{||\mathsf{poly-NEXP}}$ equals $\mathsf{EXP}^{||\mathsf{NP}}$, by a padding argument. The detailed proof is omitted here and can be found in the full version [13].

LEMMA 8. $\mathsf{EXP}^{||\mathsf{poly-NEXP}} = \mathsf{EXP}^{||\mathsf{NP}}$.

PROOF OF THEOREM 1. Theorem 1 follows immediately from Lemmas 6, 7, and 8. $\quad\square$

4. SIMULATING MRIP USING TWO PROVERS AND FIVE ROUNDS

In this section we prove Theorem 2, that is,

Theorem 2. $\mathsf{MRIP} = \mathsf{MRIP}(2, 5)$.

In particular, in Figure 5, we show how to simulate any MRIP protocol $(V, \vec{P})$ with $t(n)$ provers and $p(n)$ rounds using a verifier V' and two provers P_1' and P_2'. Recall that m_{ij} denotes the message exchanged between V and prover P_i in round j of their protocol. Essentially, V' asks one prover to simulate all other provers in the original protocol, and uses a second prover to cross-check his answers.

PROOF. Let $(V, \vec{P})$ be the MRIP protocol for a language L using $\vec{P} = (P_1, \ldots, P_{t(n)})$ provers and $p(n)$ rounds of communication. Let $\vec{m}$ denote the complete transcript of the protocol and m_{ij} be the message of prover P_i in round j of the protocol. We simulate this protocol using two provers P_1' and P_2' and verifier V' in the protocol $(V', \vec{P'})$ in Figure 5. Let r denote the random coin flips used by V in protocol $(V, \vec{P})$.

To see the correctness of the protocol, notice that,

(a) Even though V' sends the random string r of V to P_1', he uses a different random string $r' \neq r$ to select a message in Step 4. Thus, the expected payment to the provers depends on r', which is not known to them.

(b) P_2' does not know r and essentially commits to a transcript $\vec{m}'$ of $(V, \vec{P})$ in Step 5.

The provers can lie in the following ways, with the corresponding payments:

1. P_1' and P_2' do not commit to the same transcript $\vec{m}$. Without loss of generality assume that, P_1' lies on some message in $\vec{m}$. V catches this lie in Step 6a with probability $\frac{1}{p(n)t(n)}$ and gives a payment $R' = -1$.

2. P_1' and P_2' agree on the transcript $\vec{m}$, but $\vec{m}$ does not correspond to the best strategy profile in protocol $(V, \vec{P})$. In this case, they get a payment $\frac{R}{2p(n)t(n)}$, where R is the payment that the original protocol generates on this suboptimal transcript $\vec{m}$.

First of all, we can rule out Case 2 as a possible strategy of rational provers P_1' and P_2'. This is because V' pays them according to the original protocol $(V, \vec{P})$. Committing to any dishonest transcript earns them a payment strictly less than the best possible. This follows from the correctness of the original MRIP protocol $(V, \vec{P})$.

Now suppose P_1' lies on $y > 0$ messages in $\vec{m}$ —this corresponds to Case 1. The expected payment to P_1' would then be

$$
-1 \left(\frac{y}{p(n)t(n)} \right) + \frac{R}{2p(n)t(n)} \left(\frac{p(n)t(n) - y}{p(n)t(n)} \right)
$$
$$
\leq \frac{1}{p(n)t(n)} \left(\frac{R}{2} - y \right) < 0,
$$

where the last inequality is because $R \leq 1$ and $y \geq 1$. Thus, it is not rational for P_1' to lie on any message in $\vec{m}$ and the result follows. $\quad\square$

REMARK 2. *If we allow 3 provers instead of 2, then the verifier only needs to interact with each prover exactly once. In particular, V' sends r to P_3' instead of P_1'. This property may be desirable for applications that do not allow repeated interactions (e.g., each prover may be available only for a limited amount of time).*

Optimal number of rounds.

We conclude this section with a discussion on the optimal number of rounds required to capture the full power of MRIP. It is well known that MIP can be simulated using two provers and one round [15], which is clearly optimal. It would be interesting to obtain a similar result for MRIP. Note that, because we count the number of rounds differently (provers' messages and verifier's queries are considered to be separate rounds) and we assume the first round of messages are always from the provers, any non-trivial MRIP protocol with at least two provers requires at least three rounds. Indeed, in less than three rounds, the verifier cannot cross-check answers with the second prover (beyond the initial messages received from them), in which case the protocol reduces to a single-prover protocol.

Currently, the protocol in Figure 5 requires two extra rounds because the verifier's queries to each prover are not parallel. The verifier uses the answers from its query to Prover 1 to form its query to Prover 2. Getting rid of this dependency may result in a 2-prover 3-round protocol for MRIP. Interestingly, note that our protocols for NEXP and coNEXP only require 3 rounds (Section 2.1), so we know $\mathsf{NEXP} \cup \mathsf{coNEXP} \subseteq \mathsf{MRIP}(2, 3)$. We leave the following closely related problems open for future study: (1) what is the optimal number of rounds required to capture the full

---

Given any string x of length n,

1. P_1' sends c, which is the first bit of m_{11}, to V'. V' outputs c at the end of the protocol.
2. V' calculates the random bits r used by V in protocol $(V, \vec{P})$. V' sends r to P_1'.
3. P_1' uses r to simulate the entire protocol $(V, \vec{P})$ and sends $\vec{m}$ to V'.
4. V' chooses a round j at random from $\{1, \ldots, p(n)\}$ and a prover index k from $\{1, \ldots, t(n)\}$.
5. V' sends (j, k) and $\vec{m}_k = (m_{k1}, \ldots, m_{k(j-1)})$ (that is, message transcript till $j-1$ rounds of V with P_k) to P_2'.
6. P_2' simulates P_k on the round j and sends m_{kj}' to V.
7. V computes the payment R' as follows,
   (a) If $j = 1$ and $k = 1$, then if the first bit of m_{kj}' is not c, set $R' = -1$.
   (b) If $m_{kj} \neq m_{kj}'$, set $R' = -1$.
   (c) Else, V' computes the payment R given by V in the protocol $(V, \vec{P})$, using $\vec{m}$.
       V' then sets $R' = \frac{R}{2p(n)t(n)}$.

Figure 5: Simulating MRIP with 2 provers and 5 rounds.

power of MRIP, and (2) what is the exact characterization of MRIP$(2,3)$?

5. UTILITY GAPS IN MRIP

In our MRIP protocols until now, the provers are sensitive to arbitrarily small losses in the payment (similar to RIP in [5]). In [6] the authors strengthen their model by requiring the prover deviating from the honest protocol to suffer a non-negligible loss in their received payment (either constant or polynomial). This loss is demanded for *any* deviation from the prescribed behavior (i.e., the optimal strategy) and not just for reporting an incorrect answer to the membership of the input.

Formally, let $\tilde{s}$ be the optimal strategy profile and $\tilde{s}^*$ a suboptimal strategy profile of P. Then the *ideal* utility gap requires that $u(\tilde{s}) - u(\tilde{s}^*) > 1/\alpha(n)$, where $\alpha(n)$ is constant or polynomial in n. Although an ideal utility gap strongly guarantees that the prover uses his optimal strategy, as pointed out by [25], such a utility gap appears to be too strong to hold for many meaningful protocols.

To provide some intuition about the ideal utility gap, consider the MRIP protocol for NEXP given in Figure 2. This protocol does not satisfy the ideal utility gap condition, even though at first glance the gap appears to be significant. Indeed, the provers who *report the incorrect answer* always have a constant utility gap. However, a prover may tell the truth about the membership of x but deviate slightly from the optimal strategy. For example, the prover could lie so that the verifier accepts with probability $1 - \varepsilon$, where ε is exponentially small in $|x|$. In this situation, the verifier may have an exponentially small probability of detecting the deviation, and the expected payment would decrease by an exponentially small amount.

The difficulty in achieving the ideal gap can be seen in previous work as well. For example, the rational proof for MA in [6] fails to satisfy this constraint. Guo, Hubáček, Rosen and Vald in [25] also echo the concern about the ideal utility gap being strong and define a weaker notion of utility gap. However, they impose it on *rational arguments* rather than rational proofs, and they still consider a single prover. They also require that *noticeable deviation* leads to *noticeable loss*: if under a strategy $\tilde{s}'$ of the prover, the probability for the verifier to output the correct answer is noticeably smaller than 1, then the expected payment to the prover under $\tilde{s}'$ is also noticeably smaller than the optimal expected pay-

ment. While we do not impose this requirement, our notion of utility gap as defined below implies it, but not vice-versa.

In particular, our notion allows us to encompass both the protocol in [6] and the NEXP protocol in Figure 2. Intuitively, we require that the provers who report the membership of the input incorrectly suffer noticeable loss in their received payment.

DEFINITION 5 (UTILITY GAP). *Let L be a language in* MRIP, $(V, \vec{P})$ *an MRIP protocol for L, $\tilde{s}$ the strategy profile of $\vec{P}$ that maximizes the expected payment, and c the first bit sent by P_1 according to $\tilde{s}$. For any other strategy profile $\tilde{s}'$, let c' be the first bit sent by P_1 according to $\tilde{s}'$. We say that $(V, \vec{P})$ has an $\alpha(n)$-utility gap if, whenever $c' \neq c$ we have*

$$\mathbb{E}_r R(x, r, (V, \vec{P})(x, r, \tilde{s})) - \mathbb{E}_r R(x, r, (V, \vec{P})(x, r, \tilde{s}')) > 1/\alpha(n).$$

We denote an MRIP protocol with an $\alpha(n)$-utility gap as an $\alpha(n)$-gap-MRIP protocol, and we shorten "polynomial in n" as $poly(n)$. It is easy to see that the protocol for NEXP in Figure 2 has an $O(1)$-utility gap. Following the analysis of Lemma 1 we get the same for coNEXP. That is,

LEMMA 9. NEXP $\subseteq$ $O(1)$-gap-MRIP *and* coNEXP $\subseteq$ $O(1)$-gap-MRIP.

We have shown that with an exponential utility gap, MRIP = EXP$^{||\mathsf{NP}}$. We now characterize MRIP protocols with a polynomial utility gap as exactly the class of languages decided by a polynomial-time oracle Turing machine with non-adaptive access to an NEXP oracle. That is,

Theorem 3. poly(n)-gap-MRIP = P$^{||\mathsf{NEXP}}$.

The proof of Theorem 3 uses similar ideas as that of Lemma 7 and can be found in the full version [13].

REMARK 3. *There is a tradeoff between the utility gap and the computational efficiency in the two MRIP protocols we constructed for NEXP: the protocol in Figure 2 has a constant utility gap, but it relies on the standard MIP protocol; the protocol in Figure 3 is very efficient, but it only has an exponential utility gap. It would be interesting to see if there exists an MRIP protocol for NEXP that has a noticeable utility gap and is (almost) as efficient as the protocol in Figure 3.*

6. REFERENCES

[1] Amazon Mechanical Turk. Online at https://www.mturk.com/mturk.

[2] Effective use of Amazon Mechanical Turk (MTurk). Online at http://neerajkumar.org/writings/mturk/.

[3] Proof Market. Online at https://proofmarket.org.

[4] S. Arora and B. Barak. *Computational complexity: a modern approach.* Cambridge University Press, 2009.

[5] P. D. Azar and S. Micali. Rational proofs. In *Proceedings of the Forty-Fourth Annual Symposium on Theory of Computing (STOC)*, pages 1017–1028, 2012.

[6] P. D. Azar and S. Micali. Super-efficient rational proofs. In *Proceedings of the Fourteenth Annual ACM Conference on Electronic Commerce (EC)*, pages 29–30, 2013.

[7] L. Babai. Trading group theory for randomness. In *Proceedings of the Seventeenth Annual ACM Symposium on Theory of Computing (STOC)*, pages 421–429, 1985.

[8] L. Babai, L. Fortnow, and C. Lund. Non-deterministic exponential time has two-prover interactive protocols. *Computational complexity*, 1(1):3–40, 1991.

[9] L. Babai and S. Moran. Arthur-Merlin games: a randomized proof system, and a hierarchy of complexity classes. *Journal of Computer and System Sciences*, 36(2):254–276, 1988.

[10] M. Ben-Or, S. Goldwasser, J. Kilian, and A. Wigderson. Multi-prover interactive proofs: How to remove intractability assumptions. In *Proceedings of the Twentieth Annual ACM Symposium on Theory of Computing (STOC)*, pages 113–131, 1988.

[11] G. W. Brier. Verification of forecasts expressed in terms of probability. *Monthly weather review*, 78(1):1–3, 1950.

[12] A. K. Chandra and L. J. Stockmeyer. Alternation. In *17th Annual Symposium on Foundations of Computer Science (FOCS)*, pages 98–108, 1976.

[13] J. Chen, S. McCauley, and S. Singh. Rational proofs with multiple provers. *arXiv preprint arXiv:1504.08361*, 2015.

[14] U. Feige and J. Kilian. Making games short. In *Proceedings of the Twenty Ninth Annual ACM Symposium On Theory of Computing (STOC)*, pages 506–516, 1997.

[15] U. Feige and L. Lovász. Two-prover one-round proof systems: their power and their problems. In *Proceedings of the Twenty-Fourth Annual ACM Symposium on Theory of Computing (STOC)*, pages 733–744, 1992.

[16] U. Feige and A. Shamir. Multi-oracle interactive protocols with constant space verifiers. *Journal of Computer and System Sciences*, 44(2):259–271, 1992.

[17] U. Feige, A. Shamir, and M. Tennenholtz. The noisy oracle problem. In *Proceedings of the Tenth Annual Conference on Advances in Cryptology (CRYPTO)*, pages 284–296, 1990.

[18] J. Feigenbaum, D. Koller, and P. Shor. A game-theoretic classification of interactive complexity classes. In *Proceedings of Tenth Annual IEEE Structure in Complexity Theory Conference*, pages 227–237, 1995.

[19] L. Fortnow, J. Rompel, and M. Sipser. On the power of multi-prover interactive protocols. *Theoretical Computer Science*, 134(2):545–557, 1994.

[20] L. Fortnow and M. Sipser. Are there interactive protocols for co-NP languages? *Information Processing Letters (IPL)*, 28(5):249–251, 1988.

[21] T. Gneiting and A. E. Raftery. Strictly proper scoring rules, prediction, and estimation. *Journal of the American Statistical Association*, 102(477):359–378, 2007.

[22] O. Goldreich, S. Micali, and A. Wigderson. Proofs that yield nothing but their validity or all languages in NP have zero-knowledge proof systems. *Journal of the ACM (JACM)*, 38(3):690–728, 1991.

[23] S. Goldwasser, S. Micali, and C. Rackoff. The knowledge complexity of interactive proof systems. *SIAM Journal on Computing*, 18(1):186–208, 1989.

[24] S. Goldwasser and M. Sipser. Private coins versus public coins in interactive proof systems. In *Proceedings of the Eighteenth Annual ACM Symposium on Theory of Computing (STOC)*, pages 59–68, 1986.

[25] S. Guo, P. Hubáček, A. Rosen, and M. Vald. Rational arguments: single round delegation with sublinear verification. In *Proceedings of the Fifth Annual Conference on Innovations in Theoretical Computer Science (ITCS)*, pages 523–540, 2014.

[26] S. Guo, P. Hubáček, A. Rosen, and M. Vald. Rational sumchecks. In *13th Theory of Cryptography Conference (TCC'2016-A), to appear*, 2016.

[27] A. Kittur. Crowdsourcing, collaboration and creativity. *ACM Crossroads*, 17(2):22–26, 2010.

[28] D. Koller and N. Megiddo. The complexity of two-person zero-sum games in extensive form. *Games and economic behavior*, 4(4):528–552, 1992.

[29] C. Lund, L. Fortnow, H. Karloff, and N. Nisan. Algebraic methods for interactive proof systems. *Journal of the ACM (JACM)*, 39(4):859–868, 1992.

[30] J. H. Reif. The complexity of two-player games of incomplete information. *Journal of Computer and System Sciences*, 29(2):274–301, 1984.

[31] A. Shamir. IP = PSPACE. *J. ACM*, 39(4):869–877, 1992.

[32] L. Von Ahn and L. Dabbish. Labeling images with a computer game. In *Proceedings of the SIGCHI conference on Human factors in computing systems*, pages 319–326, 2004.

[33] L. Von Ahn and L. Dabbish. Designing games with a purpose. *Communications of the ACM*, 51(8):58–67, 2008.

[34] R. Williams. Nonuniform ACC circuit lower bounds. *Journal of the ACM (JACM)*, 61(1):2, 2014.

Lower Bounds: From Circuits to QBF Proof Systems

Olaf Beyersdorff
School of Computing
University of Leeds, UK
o.beyersdorff@leeds.ac.uk

Ilario Bonacina
School of Computer Science
and Communication
KTH Royal Institute of
Technology, Sweden
ilario@kth.se

Leroy Chew
School of Computing
University of Leeds, UK
mm12lnc@leeds.ac.uk

ABSTRACT

A general and long-standing belief in the proof complexity community asserts that there is a close connection between progress in lower bounds for Boolean circuits and progress in proof size lower bounds for strong propositional proof systems. Although there are famous examples where a transfer from ideas and techniques from circuit complexity to proof complexity has been effective, a formal connection between the two areas has never been established so far. Here we provide such a formal relation between lower bounds for circuit classes and lower bounds for Frege systems for quantified Boolean formulas (QBF).

Starting from a propositional proof system P we exhibit a general method how to obtain a QBF proof system $P + \forall \mathsf{red}$, which is inspired by the transition from resolution to Q-resolution. For us the most important case is a new and natural hierarchy of QBF Frege systems $\mathcal{C}\text{-Frege} + \forall \mathsf{red}$ that parallels the well-studied propositional hierarchy of $\mathcal{C}\text{-Frege}$ systems, where lines in proofs are restricted to belong to a circuit class $\mathcal{C}$.

Building on earlier work for resolution [Beyersdorff, Chew, and Janota, 2015a] we establish a lower bound technique via strategy extraction that transfers arbitrary lower bounds for the circuit class $\mathcal{C}$ to lower bounds in $\mathcal{C}\text{-Frege} + \forall \mathsf{red}$.

By using the full spectrum of state-of-the-art circuit lower bounds, our new lower bound method leads to very strong lower bounds for QBF Frege systems:

(i) exponential lower bounds and separations for the QBF proof system $\mathsf{AC}^0[p]\text{-Frege} + \forall \mathsf{red}$ for all primes p;

(ii) an exponential separation of $\mathsf{AC}^0[p]\text{-Frege} + \forall \mathsf{red}$ from $\mathsf{TC}^0\text{-Frege} + \forall \mathsf{red}$;

(iii) an exponential separation of the hierarchy of constant-depth systems $\mathsf{AC}^0_d\text{-Frege} + \forall \mathsf{red}$ by formulas of depth independent of d.

In the propositional case, all these results correspond to major open problems.

Permission to make digital or hard copies of all or part of this work for personal or classroom use is granted without fee provided that copies are not made or distributed for profit or commercial advantage and that copies bear this notice and the full citation on the first page. Copyrights for components of this work owned by others than ACM must be honored. Abstracting with credit is permitted. To copy otherwise, or republish, to post on servers or to redistribute to lists, requires prior specific permission and/or a fee. Request permissions from Permissions@acm.org.

ITCS'16, January 14–16, 2016, Cambridge, MA, USA
© 2016 ACM. ISBN 978-1-4503-4057-1/16/01 ...$15.00
DOI: http://dx.doi.org/10.1145/2840728.2840740

Categories and Subject Descriptors

F.2.2 [**Analysis of algorithms and problem complexity**]: Nonnumerical Algorithms and Problems—*Complexity of proof procedures*

Keywords

QBF proof complexity; Frege systems; proof complexity; circuit complexity

1. INTRODUCTION

Proof complexity investigates how difficult it is to prove theorems in different formal systems. The main question asks, given a formula φ and a proof system P, typically comprised of axioms and rules, what is the size of the smallest proof of φ in P. This question bears tight and fruitful relations to a number of further areas, in particular to computational complexity, where lower bounds to the size of proofs offer an approach towards the separation of complexity classes (Cook's Programme), and to first-order logic (bounded arithmetic theories and their separations). More recently, the tremendous success of SAT solving has been a main driver for proof complexity, as the analysis of proof systems underlying SAT solvers provides the main theoretical framework towards understanding the power and limitations of solving, cf. the survey of Buss [2012].

The bulk of research in proof complexity has concentrated on proof systems for classical propositional logic. Regarding the central question above, *propositional proof complexity* has made enormous progress over the past three decades in showing tight lower and upper bounds for many principles in various proof systems. Arguably even more important, a number of general lower bound techniques have been developed that can be employed to show lower bounds to the size of proofs. These include the seminal size-width relationship [Ben-Sasson and Wigderson, 2001], the feasible interpolation technique [Krajíček, 1997], or game-theoretic techniques (cf. the recent overview in [Beyersdorff and Kullmann, 2014]).

Notwithstanding these advances, some of the most natural proof systems have resisted all attempts for lower bounds for decades. Frege systems (also known as Hilbert-type systems) are the typical textbook calculi comprised of axiom schemes and rules, and no non-trivial lower bounds are known for Frege. While the power of Frege does not depend on the choice of axioms or rules [Cook and Reckhow, 1979], their strength can be calibrated by restricting the class of allowed formulas. In particular, a hierarchy of Frege systems can be obtained by considering Boolean circuits of increasing strength as lines in **Frege**. These circuit classes comprise the standard classes $AC^0 \subset AC^0[p] \subset TC^0 \subseteq NC^1 \subseteq P/poly$, giving rise to a similar hierarchy of **Frege** systems.

While the strongest non-uniform lower bounds known in circuit complexity hold for the class $AC^0[p]$ [Razborov, 1987; Smolensky, 1987], AC^0-**Frege** is the strongest of the above **Frege** systems with non-trivial lower bounds [Ajtai, 1994; Krajíček et al., 1995; Pitassi et al., 1993]. Despite enormous efforts, all attempts to transfer Razborov's and Smolensky's $AC^0[p]$ circuit lower to a proof size lower bound in $AC^0[p]$-**Frege** have failed so far. More widely, it seems the common belief in the proof complexity community that substantial progress in circuit complexity would also give rise to major new lower bounds in proof complexity, for **Frege** ($= NC^1$-**Frege**) or even extended **Frege** ($= P/poly$-**Frege**). Though this connection has been often postulated (cf. e.g. [Beame and Pitassi, 2001]), it could never have been made formal so far.

In this paper we establish a technique to transfer circuit lower bounds to proof size lower bounds for proof systems for quantified Boolean formulas (QBF). Our technique lifts arbitrary circuit lower bounds to proof size bounds for QBF **Frege** systems, yielding in particular exponential lower bounds for $AC^0[p]$-**Frege** for QBFs via [Razborov, 1987; Smolensky, 1987].

Before explaining our results in more detail, we discuss recent developments in QBF proof complexity.

QBF proof complexity is a relatively young field studying proof systems for quantified Boolean logic. Similarly as in the propositional case, one of the main motivations for the field comes via its intimate connection to solving. SAT and QBF solvers are powerful algorithms that efficiently solve the classically hard problems of SAT and QBF for large classes of practically relevant formulas, with modern solvers routinely solving industrial instances in millions of variables for various applications. Although QBF solving is at an earlier state, due to its **PSPACE** completeness, QBF even applies to further fields such as formal verification or planning [Benedetti and Mangassarian, 2008; Egly et al., 2014; Rintanen, 2007].

The connection to proof complexity comes from the fact that each successful run of a solver on an unsatisfiable instance can be interpreted as a proof of unsatisfiability; and modern SAT and QBF solvers are known to correspond to the resolution proof system and its variants. In comparison to SAT, the picture is more complex in QBF as there exist two main solving approaches utilising CDCL and expansion-based solving. To model the strength of these QBF solvers, a number of resolution-based QBF proof systems have been developed. Q-resolution (**Q-Res**) by Kleine Büning et al. [1995] forms the core of the CDCL-based systems. To capture further ideas from CDCL solving, **Q-Res** has been augmented to long-distance resolution by Balabanov and Jiang [2012], universal resolution **QU-Res** by Van Gelder [2012], and their combinations [Balabanov et al., 2014]. QBF resolution systems for expansion-based solving were developed in [Beyersdorff et al., 2014; Janota and Marques-Silva, 2015]. Recent progress led to a complete understanding of the relative power of all these resolution-type QBF systems [Balabanov et al., 2014; Beyersdorff et al., 2015a; Janota and Marques-Silva, 2015].

From a proof complexity perspective, resolution is considered as a weak system, witnessed by the wealth of resolution lower bounds (cf. [Segerlind, 2007] for a survey); and the same classification applies to all of the QBF resolution calculi

mentioned above. In addition to these weak QBF systems, there exist a number of very strong sequent calculi [Cook and Morioka, 2005; Egly, 2012; Krajíček and Pudlák, 1990] as well as the general proof checking format QRAT [Heule et al., 2014].

However, compared to propositional proof complexity, a number of other approaches is yet missing in QBF. In particular, algebraic systems such as polynomial calculus [Clegg et al., 1996] or systems based on integer programming as cutting planes [Cook et al., 1987] have received great attention in recent years in propositional proof complexity. These systems are interesting as they are of intermediate strength: stronger than resolution, but weaker than **Frege**. No analogues of these systems have been considered in QBF so far; and even a QBF version of the propositional **Frege** hierarchy mentioned above has not been considered in QBF prior to this paper.

1.1 Our contributions

Below we summarise our main contributions of this paper, sketching the main results and techniques.

A. From propositional to QBF: new QBF proof systems. We exhibit a general method how to transform a propositional proof system to a QBF proof system. Our method is both conceptually simple and elegant. Starting from a propositional proof system P comprised of axioms and rules, we design a system $P + \forall red$ for closed prenex QBFs (Definition 3.1). Throughout the proof, the quantifier prefix is fixed, and lines in the system $P + \forall red$ are conceptually the same as lines in P, i.e. clauses in resolution, circuits from $\mathcal{C}$ in $\mathcal{C}$-**Frege**, or inequalities in cutting planes. Our new system $P + \forall red$ uses all the rules from P, and can apply those on arbitrary lines, irrespective of whether the variables are existentially or universally quantified. To make the system complete, we introduce a $\forall red$ rule that allows to replace universal variables by simple Herbrand functions, which can be represented as lines in P. The link to Herbrand functions provides a clear semantic meaning for the $\forall red$ rule, resulting in a natural and robust system $P + \forall red$.

Our new systems $P + \forall red$ are inspired by the approach taken in the definition of **Q-Res** [Kleine Büning et al., 1995]; and indeed when choosing resolution as the base system P, our system $P + \forall red$ coincides with the previously studied **QU-Res** [Van Gelder, 2012]. While our definitions are quite general and yield for example previously missing QBF versions of polynomial calculus or cutting planes, we concentrate here on exploring the hierarchy $\mathcal{C}$-**Frege** $+ \forall red$ of new QBF **Frege** systems.

B. From circuit to QBF lower bounds: a general technique. As mentioned above, it is a long-standing belief that circuit lower bounds correspond to proof size lower bounds, and clearly some of the strongest lower bounds in proof complexity as those for AC^0-**Frege** are inspired by proof techniques in circuit complexity, cf. the survey of Beame and Pitassi [2001]. Here we give a precise and formal account on how *any* circuit lower bound for $\mathcal{C}$ can be directly lifted to a proof size lower bound in $\mathcal{C}$-**Frege** $+ \forall red$.

Conceptually, our lower bound method uses the idea of *strategy extraction*, an important paradigm in QBF (Theorem 4.3). Semantically, a QBF can be understood as a game between a universal and an existential player, where the universal player wins if and only if the QBF is false. Winning strategies for the universal player can be very complex. However, we show that from each refutation of a false QBF in a system $\mathcal{C}$-Frege + ∀red we can efficiently extract a winning strategy for the universal player in a simple computational model we call $\mathcal{C}$-decision lists. We observe that $\mathcal{C}$-decision lists are easy to transform into $\mathcal{C}$ circuits itself, with only a slight increase in complexity.

To obtain a proof-size lower bound we need a function f that is hard for $\mathcal{C}$. From f we construct a family $\mathcal{Q}$-f_n of false QBFs such that each winning strategy of the universal player on $\mathcal{Q}$-f_n has to compute f. By strategy extraction, refutations of $\mathcal{Q}$-f_n in $\mathcal{C}$-Frege + ∀red yield $\mathcal{C}$-circuits for f; hence all such refutations must be long. In fact, we even show the converse implication to hold, i.e. from small $\mathcal{C}$-circuits for f we construct short proofs of $\mathcal{Q}$-f_n in $\mathcal{C}$-Frege + ∀red.

Our lower bound technique widely generalises ideas recently used by Beyersdorff et al. [2015a] to show lower bounds for Q-Res and QU-Res for formulas originating from the PARITY function.

C. Lower bounds and separations: applying our framework. We apply our proof technique to a number of famous circuit lower bounds, thus obtaining lower bounds and separations for $\mathcal{C}$-Frege + ∀red systems that are yet unparalleled in propositional proof complexity. The following results are contained in Section 5.

C.(a) Lower bounds and separations for the QBF proof system $AC^0[p]$-**Frege + ∀red.** The seminal results of [Razborov, 1987; Smolensky, 1987] showed that PARITY and more generally MOD_q are the classic examples for functions that require exponential-size bounded-depth circuits with MOD_p gates, where p and q are different primes. Using these functions, we define families of QBFs that require exponential-size proofs in $AC^0[p]$-Frege + ∀red by strategy extraction.

To obtain separations of these proof systems, the exact formulation of the QBFs matters. When defining the PARITY or MOD_q formulas directly from (arbitrary) NC^1-circuits computing these functions, we obtain polynomial-size upper bounds in Frege + ∀red. However, when carefully choosing specific and indeed very natural encodings, we can prove upper bounds for the MOD_q formulas even in $AC^0[q]$-Frege + ∀red, thus obtaining exponential separations of all the $AC^0[p]$-Frege + ∀red systems for distinct primes p.

As mentioned before, lower bounds for $AC^0[p]$-Frege (as well as their separations) are major open problems in propositional proof complexity.

C.(b) $AC^0[p]$-**Frege + ∀red and** TC^0-**Frege + ∀red are separated.** MAJORITY is another classic function in circuit complexity, for which exponential lower bounds are known for constant-depth circuits with MOD_p gates for each prime p [Razborov, 1987; Smolensky, 1987]. Using our technique, we transfer these to lower bounds in $AC^0[p]$-Frege + ∀red for all primes p. Carefully choosing the QBF encoding of MAJORITY, we obtain polynomial upper bounds for the MAJORITY formulas in TC^0-Frege + ∀red, thus proving an exponential separation between the two QBF proof systems $AC^0[p]$-Frege + ∀red and TC^0-Frege + ∀red. Again, such a separation is wide open in propositional proof complexity.

C.(c) CNFs separating the AC^0_d-**Frege + ∀red hierarchy.** As a third example for our approach we investigate the fine structure of AC^0-Frege + ∀red, comprising all AC^0_d-Frege + ∀red systems, where all formulas in proofs are required to have at most depth d for a fixed constant d. Resolution is an important example of such a system for depth $d = 1$. In circuit complexity the SIPSER$_d$ functions from [Boppana and Sipser, 1990] provide an exponential separation of depth-$(d-1)$ from depth-d circuits [Håstad, 1986]. With our technique, this separation translates into a separation of AC^0_{d-3}-Frege + ∀red from AC^0_d-Frege + ∀red, where the increased gap of size 3 comes from our transformation of $\mathcal{C}$-decision lists into $\mathcal{C}$-circuits.

The SIPSER$_d$ formulas achieving these separations are prenexed CNFs, i.e. the formulas have depth 2. While in propositional proof complexity the hierarchy of AC^0_d-Frege systems is exponentially separated [Ajtai, 1994; Krajíček et al., 1995; Pitassi et al., 1993], such a separation by formulas of depth *independent of* d is a major open problem.

1.2 Relations to previous work

In addition to the developments in propositional and QBF proof complexity sketched in the beginning, the main precursor of our work is the paper [Beyersdorff, Chew, and Janota, 2015a]. Strategy extraction for Q-Res and QU-Res was shown by Balabanov and Jiang [2012], but the idea to turn this into a lower bound argument for the proof size originates from [Beyersdorff et al., 2015a], where the AC^0 lower bound for PARITY is used to obtain exponential lower bounds for Q-Res and QU-Res. However, the treatment in [Beyersdorff et al., 2015a] is solely confined to the resolution case. Here we widely generalise these concepts and uncover the full potential of that approach. In fact, quite weak circuit lower bounds would suffice for the proof-size lower bounds of [Beyersdorff et al., 2015a], cf. Corollary 5.11 in the present paper; and from [Beyersdorff et al., 2015a] it is not clear how the full spectrum of the state-of-the-art circuit lower bounds could be used to get proof size lower bounds.

Feasible interpolation is another technique relating circuit lower bounds to proof size bounds. Feasible interpolation has been successfully applied to show lower bounds for a number of propositional proof systems, including resolution [Krajíček, 1997] and cutting planes [Pudlák, 1997]. Indeed, Beyersdorff, Chew, Mahajan, and Shukla [2015b] have recently shown that feasible interpolation is also effective for QBF resolution calculi. Interpolation transfers *monotone* circuit lower bounds to proof size lower bounds. Hence, different from strategy extraction, there is no connection between the circuit model and the lines in the proof system. Also, by results of [Bonet et al., 2000, 2004; Krajíček and Pudlák, 1998] feasible interpolation is not applicable to strong systems such as AC^0-Frege and beyond. Another restriction of interpolation is that it only applies to special formulas, and for these — at least in the case of QBF resolution systems — it can be understood as a special case of strategy extraction [Beyersdorff et al., 2015b].

1.3 Innovations

Our work opens up two lines of research that we believe will have a great influence on QBF proof complexity and beyond.

Exploring new QBF proof systems. The first of these is the study of natural and powerful QBF proof systems that correspond to ideas developed in propositional proof complexity for many years. While we concentrate here on the hierarchy $\mathcal{C}$-Frege + ∀red of new QBF Frege systems, our definitions introduce meaningful versions of algebraic and geometric proof systems for QBF. These systems will be very interesting to study from a theoretical perspective and also might provide an important stimulus on QBF solving — analogous to the impact of integer linear programming and polynomial calculus on SAT solving.

Understanding the transfer from circuit to proof complexity. As far as we know, for the first time in the literature, our lower bound technique via strategy extraction gives a formal and rigorous account on the relation between a circuit class $\mathcal{C}$ and proof systems using lines from $\mathcal{C}$. Building on the previous work [Beyersdorff et al., 2015a] we establish this relation for a full hierarchy of QBF systems. This yields very strong results in QBF proof complexity. In the recent survey of Buss [2012], the propositional versions of our results C.(a) and (c) in Section 1.1 are referenced as 'the main open problems at the "frontier" of Cook's program'.

We believe that this transfer has the potential to generate lots of further research, both in QBF and indeed for further logics, possibly even including the most important classical propositional case. As for QBFs, the hard formulas $\mathcal{Q}\text{-}f$ that we generate from a Boolean function f have a special syntactic form, i.e. for all functions we use here they are prefixed by $\exists\forall\exists$. Can we also apply our technique to conceptually different types of QBFs? It is also possible that similar ideas are effective for further logics, possibly modal or intuitionistic logics as they share the same PSPACE complexity, and strong lower bounds are known for Frege systems in these logics as well [Hrubeš, 2009; Jeřábek, 2009].

1.4 Organisation of the paper

Section 2 contains definitions and notations on $\mathcal{C}$-Frege systems and QBF. In Section 3 we define the QBF proof systems $\mathcal{C}\text{-Frege} + \forall\text{red}$ (Definition 3.1) and prove their soundness and completeness (Theorem 3.2). Section 4 contains the proof of the Strategy Extraction Theorem (Theorem 4.3), which is our main technical tool to relate circuit complexity and proof size.

In Section 5 we prove our exponential lower bounds for $\mathcal{C}\text{-Frege} + \forall\text{red}$ for several circuit classes $\mathcal{C}$. All the results in this section ultimately rely on the Strategy Extraction Theorem from Section 4 and on a general way to encode a circuit C in a (false) QBF $\mathcal{Q}\text{-}C$ (Definition 5.1). The structure of Section 5 largely follows the order of the results already sketched in item C of Section 1.1.

Section 6 concludes with some open problems.

2. PRELIMINARIES

We assume familiarity with basic notions from computational complexity, cf. [Arora and Barak, 2009], as well as from logic, cf. [Krajíček, 1995], but define all specific concepts needed in this paper. For a formula φ we denote by $\varphi[x_1/\theta_1, \ldots, x_k/\theta_k]$ the formula φ where variables x_i have been substituted by formulas θ_i.

Circuit classes. We recall the definitions of standard circuit classes used in this paper. The class AC^0 contains all languages recognisable by polynomial-size circuits over the Boolean basis $\neg, \vee, \wedge$ with bounded depth and unbounded fan-in. When fixing the depth to a constant d, we denote the circuit class by AC^0_d. The class $\mathsf{AC}^0[p]$ uses bounded-depth circuits with MOD_p gates determining whether the sum of the inputs is 0 modulo p, and in TC^0 bounded-depth circuits with threshold gates are permitted. Stronger classes

are obtained by using NC^1 circuits of polynomial size and logarithmic depth, and by $\mathsf{P/poly}$ circuits of polynomial size.

Proof systems. According to Cook and Reckhow [1979] a *proof system* for a language $\mathcal{L}$ is a polynomial-time onto function $P : \{0,1\}^* \to \mathcal{L}$. Each string $\varphi \in \mathcal{L}$ is a *theorem* and if $P(\pi) = \varphi$, π is a *proof* of φ in P. Given a polynomial-time function $P : \{0,1\}^* \to \{0,1\}^*$ the fact that $P(\{0,1\}^*) \subseteq \mathcal{L}$ is the *soundness property* for $\mathcal{L}$ and the fact that $P(\{0,1\}^*) \supseteq \mathcal{L}$ is the *completeness property* for $\mathcal{L}$.

Proof systems for the language TAUT of propositional tautologies are called *propositional proof systems* and proof systems for the language TQBF of true QBF formulas are called *QBF proof systems*. Equivalently, propositional proof systems and QBF proof systems can be defined respectively for the languages UNSAT of unsatisfiable propositional formulas and FQBF of false QBF formulas, in this second case we call them *refutational*.

Given two proof systems P and Q for the same language $\mathcal{L}$, P *p-simulates* Q (denoted $Q \leq_p P$) if there exists a polynomial-time function t such that for each $\pi \in \{0,1\}^*$, $P(t(\pi)) = Q(\pi)$. Two systems are called p-equivalent if they p-simulate each other.

A proof system P for $\mathcal{L}$ is called *polynomially bounded* if there exists a polynomial p such that every $x \in \mathcal{L}$ has a P-proof of size $\leq p(|x|)$.

Frege systems. Frege proof systems are the common 'textbook' proof systems for propositional logic based on axioms and rules [Cook and Reckhow, 1979]. The lines in a Frege proof are propositional formulas built from propositional variables x_i and Boolean connectives $\neg, \wedge$, and $\vee$. A Frege system comprises a finite set of axiom schemes and rules, e.g., $\varphi \vee \neg\varphi$ is a possible axiom scheme. A Frege *proof* is a sequence of formulas where each formula is either a substitution instance of an axiom, or can be inferred from previous formulas by a valid inference rule. Frege systems are required to be sound and implicationally complete. The exact choice of the axiom schemes and rules does not matter as any two Frege systems are p-equivalent, even when changing the basis of Boolean connectives [Cook and Reckhow, 1979] and [Krajíček, 1995, Theorem 4.4.13]. Therefore we can assume w.l.o.g. that modus ponens is the only rule of inference.

Usually Frege systems are defined as proof systems where the last formula is the proven formula. To include also weak systems as resolution in this picture we use here the equivalent setting of refutation Frege systems where we start with the negation of the formula that we want to prove and derive the contradiction $\bot$.

Given a circuit class $\mathcal{C}$, a general definition of $\mathcal{C}$-Frege is contained in [Jeřábek, 2005]. Below we explicitly present the definitions of $\mathcal{C}$-Frege for the circuit classes we will need later.

There are several common restrictions that can be imposed on Frege; for example *bounded-depth* Frege systems (or AC^0-Frege) are Frege systems where lines are formulas with negations only on variables and with a bounded number of alternations between $\wedge$'s and $\vee$'s. If the number of alternations is at most d, then the proof system is called AC^0_d-Frege. Bounded-depth Frege is called AC^0-Frege since lines in an AC^0-Frege proof are representable as AC^0-circuits.

Resolution (Res) is a particular kind of AC^0_1-Frege system[1] introduced by Blake [1937] and Robinson [1965]. It is a refutational proof system manipulating unsatisfiable CNFs as sets of clauses. The only inference rule is

$$\frac{C \vee x \qquad D \vee \neg x}{C \vee D} \text{ (Res rule)},$$

where C, D denote clauses and x is a variable. A Res refutation derives the empty clause $\bot$.

Given a prime p, the $\mathsf{AC}^0[p]$-Frege systems are defined to be bounded-depth Frege systems in the language with Boolean connectives $\neg$, $\vee$, $\wedge$ and modular gates $MOD_p(x_1, \ldots, x_n)$. The MOD_p predicate is true when $\sum_i x_i \equiv 0 \pmod{p}$.

The TC^0-Frege systems are defined to be bounded-depth Frege systems in the language with Boolean connectives $\neg$, $\vee$, $\wedge$ and threshold gates $T_k(x_1, \ldots, x_n)$. The T_k predicate is true when at least k of its inputs are true. Two different, but equivalent, formalizations of TC^0-Frege proof systems are given by Buss and Clote [1996] and Bonet et al. [2000].

(Unrestricted) Frege systems correspond to the complexity class NC^1 in the same sense as bounded-depth Frege corresponds to the class AC^0. We will refer sometimes to Frege as NC^1-Frege.

Extended Frege *systems* EF allow the introduction of new extension variables that abbreviate formulas. EF can be understood as a Frege system that directly operates with Boolean circuits rather than formulas, where extension variables can be used to define the circuit gates (see [Jeřábek, 2005] for the precise formulation). Therefore we will refer to EF also as $\mathsf{P/poly}$-Frege. An alternative characterisation of EF is through substitution Frege systems SF that allow arbitrary substitution instances of derived formulas [Cook and Reckhow, 1979; Krajíček and Pudlák, 1989].

The Frege systems defined above form a hierarchy of proof systems

$$\text{Res} \leq_p \mathsf{AC}^0\text{-Frege} \leq_p \mathsf{AC}^0[p]\text{-Frege} \leq_p \mathsf{TC}^0\text{-Frege} \leq_p \text{Frege} \leq_p \text{EF}.$$

Currently lower bounds are only known for Res [Haken, 1985] and AC^0-Frege [Ajtai, 1994; Krajíček et al., 1995; Pitassi et al., 1993], whereas super-polynomial lower bounds for any of the stronger systems constitute major problems in proof complexity.

Quantified Boolean Formulas. A (closed prenix) *Quantified Boolean Formula* (QBF) is a formula in quantified propositional logic where each variable is quantified at the beginning of the formula, using either an existential or universal quantifier. We denote such formulas as $\mathcal{Q} \cdot \varphi$, where φ is a propositional Boolean formula in Conjunctive Normal Form (CNF), called *matrix*, and $\mathcal{Q}$ is its *quantifier prefix*. We typically use x_i for existentially quantified variables and u_i for universally quantified variables.

Given a variable y, either existentially quantified or universally quantified in $\mathcal{Q} \cdot \varphi$, the *quantification level* of y in $\mathcal{Q} \cdot \varphi$, qlv($y$), is the number of alternations of quantifiers y has on its left in the quantifier prefix of $\mathcal{Q} \cdot \varphi$. Given a variable y, we will sometimes refer to the variables with quantification level lower than qlv(y) as variables *left* of y; analogously the variables with quantification lever higher than qlv(y) will be *right* of y.

A QBF $\mathcal{Q}_1 x_1 \cdots \mathcal{Q}_k x_k \cdot \varphi$ can be seen as a game between two players: *universal* ($\forall$) and *existential* ($\exists$). In the i-th step of the game, the player $\mathcal{Q}_i$ assigns a value to the variable x_i. The existential player wins if φ evaluates to 1 under the assignment constructed in the game. The universal player wins if φ evaluates to 0. Given a universal variable u with index i, a *strategy for* u is a function from all variables of index $< i$ to $\{0, 1\}$. A QBF is false if and only if there exists a *winning strategy* for the universal player, that is if the universal player has a strategy for all universal variables that wins any possible game [Arora and Barak, 2009; Goultiaeva et al., 2011].

QBF resolution calculi. *Q-resolution* (Q-Res) by Kleine Büning et al. [1995] is a resolution-like calculus that operates on QBFs in prenex form where the matrix is a CNF. It uses the propositional resolution rule $\frac{C \vee x \qquad D \vee \neg x}{C \vee D}$ with the side conditions that variable x is existential and if $z \in C$, then $\neg z \notin D$. In addition Q-Res has a universal reduction rule

$$\frac{C \vee u}{C},$$

where variable u is universal and all other variables $x \in C$ are left of u in the quantifier prefix.

Universal resolution, QU-Res introduced by Van Gelder [2012], additionally allows to resolve on universal variables, under the same side condition as in Q-Res not to derive tautologous clauses.

For definitions of further resolution-based QBF proof system and their complexity we refer to [Beyersdorff et al., 2015a].

3. DEFINING QBF FREGE SYSTEMS

In this section we provide a general method of transforming a propositional proof system into a QBF proof system. While this method works for a wide range of proof systems operating with lines and rules, we will concentrate here on the hierarchy of $\mathcal{C}$-Frege systems introduced in the previous section. However, our method also works for further propositional proof systems such as polynomial calculus [Clegg et al., 1996] or cutting planes [Cook et al., 1987].

For the following we fix a circuit class $\mathcal{C}$ with some natural properties, e.g., closure under restrictions. In particular, $\mathcal{C}$ can be any of the circuit classes mentioned in Section 2.

DEFINITION 3.1   ($\mathcal{C}$-Frege + $\forall$red). *A refutation of a false QBF $\mathcal{Q} \cdot \varphi$ in the system $\mathcal{C}$-Frege + $\forall$red is sequence of lines $L_1, \ldots, L_\ell$ where each line is a circuit from the class $\mathcal{C}$, $L_1 = \varphi$,[2] $L_\ell = \bot$ and each L_i is inferred from previous lines L_j using the inference rules of $\mathcal{C}$-Frege or using the following rule*

$$\frac{L_j}{L_j[u/B]} \text{ ($\forall$red)},$$

where $L_j[u/B]$ belongs to the class $\mathcal{C}$, u is the innermost variable among the variables of L_j and B is a circuit from the class $\mathcal{C}$ containing only variables left of u.

---

[1]We will consistently treat $\mathcal{C}$-Frege systems as operating with lines from $\mathcal{C}$. As Res operates with clauses we will call it a AC^0_1-Frege system even though it refutes CNFs, which are depth 2.

[2]In the case where $\mathcal{C}$ is AC^0_1 we require that $\varphi = L_1 \wedge \cdots \wedge L_m$ where L_j are lines in AC^0_1-Frege.

The formal justification why $\mathcal{C}$-Frege$+\forall$red is a sound and complete QBF proof system is given in Theorem 3.2 below. However, let us pause a moment to see why adding the $\forall$red rule results in a natural proof system $\mathcal{C}$-Frege$+\forall$red. Recall that we consider $\mathcal{C}$-Frege$+\forall$red as a refutation system; hence we aim to refute false quantified $\mathcal{C}$ formulas. A standard approach to witness the falsity of quantified formulas is through *Herbrand functions*, which replace a universal variable u by a function in the existential variables left of u. These functions can be viewed as 'counterexample functions'. In Definition 3.1, B plays the role of the Herbrand function. Clearly, when restricting formulas to a class $\mathcal{C}$ we should also restrict B to that class, and substituting the Herbrand function into the formula should again preserve $\mathcal{C}$.

Note that we are even allowed to choose different Herbrand functions B for the same variable u in different parts of the proof. In general, this will be unsound (unless variables right of u are renamed). However, it is safe to do if the line L_j does not contain any variables right of u.

It is illustrative to see how our construction compares to previously studied QBF resolution systems. Choosing Res as our propositional proof system, which is an AC_1^0-Frege system, we obtain Res$+\forall$red. In Res$+\forall$red the $\forall$red rule can substitute a universal u by either another variable or by a constant $0/1$. In the former case, we simply obtain a weakening step. In the latter case, if u appears positively in the clause then substituting u by 0 precisely corresponds to an application of the $\forall$red rule in Q-Res, whereas substituting u by 1 results in the useless tautology $\top$.[3] As Res$+\forall$red can resolve on existential and universal variables, our system Res$+\forall$red is exactly the well-known QU-Res (with weakening).

We now proceed to show soundness and completeness of the new QBF systems.

THEOREM 3.2. *For every circuit complexity class $\mathcal{C}$, the system $\mathcal{C}$-Frege$+\forall$red is a refutational QBF proof system.*

PROOF. Res$+\forall$red is complete as it p-simulates Q-Res, which is complete for QBF [Kleine Büning et al., 1995]. To obtain the completness for $\mathcal{C}$-Frege$+\forall$red we first use de Morgan's rules to expand the formula into a CNF. This is possible as, by definition, $\mathcal{C}$-Frege is implicationally complete. Now we can refute the CNF by Res$+\forall$red. $\mathcal{C}$-Frege$+\forall$red p-simulates Res$+\forall$red and hence $\mathcal{C}$-Frege$+\forall$red is complete.

Regarding the soundness of $\mathcal{C}$-Frege$+\forall$red, let $(L_1,\ldots,L_\ell)$ be a refutation of $\mathcal{Q}.\varphi$ in the system $\mathcal{C}$-Frege$+\forall$red and let

$$\varphi_i = \begin{cases} \varphi & \text{if } i = 0, \\ \varphi \wedge L_1 \wedge \cdots \wedge L_i & \text{otherwise.} \end{cases}$$

By induction on i we prove that $\mathcal{Q}.\varphi$ semantically entails $\mathcal{Q}.\varphi_i$, i.e. $\mathcal{Q}.\varphi \models \mathcal{Q}.\varphi_i$. Hence, at step $i = \ell$ we will immediately obtain that $\mathcal{Q}.\varphi$ is false, since $L_\ell = \{\bot\}$ and $\mathcal{Q}.\varphi_\ell \equiv \bot$.

Since $\mathcal{Q}.\varphi = \mathcal{Q}.\varphi_0$ the base case of the induction holds. We show now that $\mathcal{Q}.\varphi \models \mathcal{Q}.\varphi_i$ implies $\mathcal{Q}.\varphi \models \mathcal{Q}.\varphi_{i+1}$. By definition, $\varphi_{i+1} = (\varphi_i \wedge L_{i+1})$ and L_{i+1} was either introduced by a $\mathcal{C}$-Frege rule or by the $\forall$red rule. If L_{i+1} was introduced by a $\mathcal{C}$-Frege rule then $\varphi_i \models L_{i+1}$, so $\varphi_i \models \varphi_{i+1}$ and clearly $\mathcal{Q}.\varphi \models \mathcal{Q}.\varphi_i \models \mathcal{Q}.\varphi_{i+1}$.

---

[3] Note that, contrasting the usual setting of Q-Res [Kleine Büning et al., 1995], our definition of Res$+\forall$red does not need to disallow tautologous resolvents as these will always be reduced to $\top$.

Suppose now that L_{i+1} was introduced by the $\forall$red rule, say $L_{i+1} = L_j[u/B]$ with $j \leq i$, u the innermost variable among the ones in L_j and B relying only on the variables left of u. Moreover suppose that $\mathcal{Q}.\varphi_i = \mathcal{Q}_1\vec{x}\forall u\, \mathcal{Q}_2\vec{y}.\varphi_i$, then we have the following chain of equivalences

$$\mathcal{Q}.\varphi_i = \mathcal{Q}_1\vec{x}\forall u\, \mathcal{Q}_2\vec{y}.\varphi_i \tag{1}$$

$$\equiv \mathcal{Q}_1\vec{x}\forall u\, \mathcal{Q}_2\vec{y}.\varphi_i \wedge L_j \tag{2}$$

$$\equiv \mathcal{Q}_1\vec{x}\Big(\big(\mathcal{Q}_2\vec{y}.\varphi_i[u/0] \wedge L_j[u/0]\big) \wedge \big(\mathcal{Q}_2\vec{y}.\varphi_i[u/1] \wedge L_j[u/1]\big)\Big) \tag{3}$$

$$\equiv \mathcal{Q}_1\vec{x}\Big(L_j[u/0] \wedge L_j[u/1] \wedge \big(\mathcal{Q}_2\vec{y}.\varphi_i[u/0]\big) \wedge \big(\mathcal{Q}_2\vec{y}.\varphi_i[u/1]\big)\Big) \tag{4}$$

$$\equiv \mathcal{Q}_1\vec{x}\Big(L_j[u/0] \wedge L_j[u/1] \wedge \forall u\mathcal{Q}_2\vec{y}.\varphi_i\Big) \tag{5}$$

$$\equiv \mathcal{Q}_1\vec{x}\Big(L_j[u/0] \wedge L_j[u/1] \wedge L_j[u/B] \wedge \forall u\mathcal{Q}_2\vec{y}.\varphi_i\Big) \tag{6}$$

$$\equiv \mathcal{Q}_1\vec{x}\forall u\mathcal{Q}_2\vec{y}.\varphi_i \wedge L_j[u/0] \wedge L_j[u/1] \wedge L_j[u/B]. \tag{7}$$

In (3) and (5) we used the definition of semantic expansion of a universal variable in a QBF; in (4), (6) and (7) we used the fact that $L_j[u/0]$, $L_j[u/1]$ and $L_j[u/B]$ do not contain $\vec{y}$ variables. From (7) follows, by weakening, that

$$\mathcal{Q}.\varphi_i \models \mathcal{Q}_1\vec{x}\forall u\mathcal{Q}_2\vec{y}.\varphi_i \wedge L_j[u/B],$$

hence $\mathcal{Q}.\varphi \models \mathcal{Q}.\varphi_{i+1}$. $\square$

Clearly lower bounds on the complexity of $\mathcal{C}$-Frege$+\forall$red follow from lower bounds on $\mathcal{C}$-Frege. The lower bounds we show later will be of a different kind as they will be 'purely for QBF proof systems' in the sense that they will lower bound the number of occurrences of the $\forall$red rule in refutations.

4. STRATEGY EXTRACTION

We introduce now the simple computational model of $\mathcal{C}$-decision lists.

DEFINITION 4.1 ($\mathcal{C}$-DECISION LIST). *A $\mathcal{C}$-decision list is a programme of the following form*

```
if C₁(x⃗) then u ← B₁(x⃗);
    else if C₂(x⃗) then u ← B₂(x⃗);
        ⋮
            else if Cₗ₋₁(x⃗) then u ← Bₗ₋₁(x⃗);
                else u ← Bₗ(x⃗),
```

where $C_1,\ldots,C_{\ell-1}$ and $B_1,\ldots,B_\ell$ are circuits in the class $\mathcal{C}$. Hence a decision list as above computes a Boolean function $u = g(\vec{x})$.

This definition generalises decision lists from [Rivest, 1987], where the conditions $C_i(\vec{x})$ are expressible as terms. We note that for many cases $\mathcal{C}$-decision lists can be easily transformed into $\mathcal{C}$-circuits.

PROPOSITION 4.2. *Let D be a $\mathcal{C}$-decision list using circuits $C_1,\ldots,C_{\ell-1}$ and $B_1,\ldots,B_\ell$, such that D computes the Boolean function g. Then there exists a circuit $D' \in \mathcal{C}$ computing the same function g, such that the size of D' is linear in the size of D and*

$$\mathrm{depth}(D') \leq \max\left\{ \max_{1\leq i\leq \ell-1}\{\mathrm{depth}(C_i)\}, \max_{1\leq i\leq \ell}\{\mathrm{depth}(B_i)\}\right\}+2.$$

PROOF. We have that

$$u \equiv \bigvee_{j=1}^{\ell} \left(C_j(\vec{x}) \wedge B_j(\vec{x}) \wedge \bigwedge_{k<j} \neg C_k(\vec{x}) \right),$$

where C_ℓ is a circuit computing the constant 1. □

Balabanov and Jiang [2012] proved a strategy extraction result for QU-Res. Here we generalise that result to the full hierarchy of C-Frege + ∀red QBF proof systems. This result is the main tool we use to prove size lower bounds in such systems.

THEOREM 4.3 (STRATEGY EXTRACTION). *Given a false QBF $\mathcal{Q}.\varphi$ and a refutation π of $Q.\varphi$ in C-Frege + ∀red, it is possible to extract in linear time (w.r.t. $|\pi|$) a collection of C-decision lists D computing a winning strategy on the universal variables of φ.*

PROOF. Let $\pi = (L_1, \ldots, L_\ell)$ be a refutation of the false QBF $\mathcal{Q}.\varphi$ and let

$$\pi_i = \begin{cases} \emptyset & \text{if } i = \ell, \\ (L_{i+1}, \ldots, L_\ell) & \text{otherwise.} \end{cases}$$

We show, by downward induction on i, that from π_i it is possible to construct in linear time (w.r.t. $|\pi_i|$) a winning strategy σ^i for the universal player for the QBF formula $\mathcal{Q}.\varphi_i$, where

$$\varphi_i = \begin{cases} \varphi & \text{if } i = 0, \\ \varphi \wedge L_1 \wedge \cdots \wedge L_i & \text{otherwise,} \end{cases}$$

such that for each universal variable u in $\mathcal{Q}.\varphi$, there exists a C-decision list D_u^i computing σ_u^i as a function of the variables in $\mathcal{Q}$ left of u, having size $O(|\pi_i|)$.

The statement of the Strategy Extraction Theorem correspond to the case when $i = 0$. The base case of the induction is for $i = \ell$. In this case σ^ℓ is trivial since φ_ℓ contains the line $L_\ell = \bot$, and we can define all the D_u^ℓ as $u \leftarrow 0$.

We show now how to construct σ_u^{i-1} and D_u^{i-1} from σ_u^i and D_u^i:

• If L_i is derived by some Frege rule, then for each universal variable u we set $\sigma_u^{i-1} = \sigma_u^i$ and $D_u^{i-1} = D_u^i$.

• If L_i is the result of an application of a ∀red rule, that is $\dfrac{L_j}{L_j[u/B]}$, where u is the rightmost variable in L_j, $L_j[u/B]$ is a circuit in $\mathcal{C}$ using only variables on the left of u, and $L_j(u/B) = L_i$. Let $\vec{x}_{u'}$ denote the variables on the left of u' in the quantifier prefix of $\mathcal{Q}.\varphi$. Then we define

$$\sigma_{u'}^{i-1}(\vec{x}_{u'}) = \begin{cases} \sigma_{u'}^i(\vec{x}_{u'}) & \text{if } u' \neq u, \\ B(\vec{x}_u) & \text{if } u' = u \text{ and } L_j[u/B](\vec{x}_u) = 0, \\ \sigma_u^i(\vec{x}_u) & \text{if } u' = u \text{ and } L_j[u/B](\vec{x}_u) = 1. \end{cases}$$

Moreover for each $u' \neq u$ we set $D_{u'}^{i-1} = D_{u'}^i$ and we set D_u^{i-1} as follows:

```
if ¬L_j[u/B](x_u) then u ← B(x_u);
    else D_i^u(x_u).
```

We now check that for each u', $\sigma_{u'}^{i-1}$ respects all the properties of the inductive claim.

▶ $\sigma_{u'}^{i-1}$ and $D_{u'}^{i-1}$ are well defined. By construction $L_j[u/B]$ is a formula in the variables $\vec{x}$ left of u. This immediately

implies that, for each universal variable u', the strategy $\sigma_{u'}^{i-1}$ is well defined and D_u^{i-1} is also well defined. By induction hypothesis D_u^i is a C-decision list, so D_u^{i-1} is also a C-decision list.

▶ σ^{i-1} and $D_{u'}^{i-1}$ *are constructed in linear time w.r.t. $|\pi_{i-1}|$.* This holds by inductive hypothesis and the fact that computing $\neg L_j(u/B)$ is linear in $|\pi_{i-1}|$.

▶ D_u^{i-1} *computes $\sigma_{u'}^{i-1}$.* For $u' \neq u$, by induction hypothesis, $D_{u'}^{i-1}$ computes $\sigma_{u'}^i$. The same happens, by construction, for $u' = u$.

▶ σ^{i-1} *is a winning strategy for $\mathcal{Q}.\varphi_{i-1}$.* Fix an assignment ρ to the existential variables of φ. Let τ_i be the complete assignment to existential and universal variables, constructed in response to ρ under the strategy σ^i. By induction hypothesis τ_i falsifies φ_i. We need to show that τ_{i-1} falsifies φ_{i-1}. To show this we distinguish again two cases.

If L_i is derived by some Frege rule, then $\sigma^{i-1} = \sigma^i$ and $\tau_{i-1} = \tau_i$. Hence by induction hypothesis, τ_i falsifies a conjunct from φ_i. To argue that τ_{i-1} also falsifies a conjunct from φ_{i-1} we only need to look at the case when the falsified conjunct is L_i. As L_i is false under τ_i and L_i is derived by a sound Frege rule, one of the parent formulas of L_i in the application of the Frege rule must be falsified as well. Hence τ_{i-1} falsifies φ_{i-1}.

Let now $L_i = L_j[u/B]$ for some $j < i$. In this case, our strategy σ^{i-1} changes the assignment τ_i only when τ_i made the universal player win by falsifying L_i. As we set u to $B(\tau_i(\vec{x}))$, the modified assignment τ_{i-1} falsifies L_j. Otherwise, if τ_i does not falsify L_i we keep $\tau_{i-1} = \tau_i$ and hence falsify one of the conjuncts of φ_{i-1} by induction hypothesis. □

From the proof of the Strategy Extraction Theorem it is clear that the size of the C-decision list computing the winning strategy extracted from the refutation π has size that is actually linear in the number of applications of the ∀red rule in π. More precisely, the size of the C-decision list computing the winning strategy for variable u corresponds exactly to the number of ∀red rules on u in π.

5. SEPARATIONS AND LOWER BOUNDS VIA CIRCUIT COMPLEXITY

We now introduce a class of QBFs defined from some circuits C_n computing a function f. Choosing different functions f, these formulas will form the basis of our lower bounds.

DEFINITION 5.1 ($\mathcal{Q}$-C_n). *Let n be an integer and C_n be a circuit with inputs $x_1, \ldots, x_n$. Let $t_1, \ldots, t_{m-1}$ be a topological ordering of the internal gates of C_n, and let the output gate of C_n be t_m. We define*

$$\mathcal{Q}\text{-}C_n = \exists x_1 \cdots \exists x_n \forall u \exists t_1 \cdots \exists t_m . (u \leftrightarrow \neg t_m) \wedge \bigwedge_{i=1}^{m} G_i,$$

where $u \leftrightarrow \neg t_m \equiv (u \vee t_m) \wedge (\neg u \vee \neg t_m)$ and G_i expresses as a CNF the function computed in the circuit C_n at gate i, e.g. if node t_i computes the $\wedge$ of t_j and t_k then

$$G_i = t_i \leftrightarrow (t_j \wedge t_k) \equiv (\neg t_i \vee t_j) \wedge (\neg t_i \vee t_k) \wedge (t_i \vee \neg t_j \vee \neg t_k),$$

similarly if gate i computes $\neg$, $\vee$, $\oplus$, MOD_p, T_k or some other Boolean function.

Informally, the QBF $\mathcal{Q}\text{-}C_n$ expresses that there exists an input $\vec{x}$ such that $C_n(\vec{x})$ evaluates to both 0 and 1, an obvious contradiction. Using these formulas together with the Strategy Extraction Theorem, we now establish a deep connection between the circuit class $\mathcal{C}$ and $\mathcal{C}\text{-Frege}+\forall\text{red}$.

THEOREM 5.2. *Let $\mathcal{C}$ be one of the circuit classes AC^0, $\mathsf{AC}^0[p]$, TC^0, NC^1, $\mathsf{P/poly}$ and let $(C_n)_{n\in\mathbb{N}}$ be a non-uniform family of circuits where C_n is a circuit with n inputs. Then the following implications hold:*

(i) *if the QBFs $\mathcal{Q}\text{-}C_n$ have $\mathcal{C}\text{-Frege}+\forall\text{red}$ refutations of size bounded by a function $q(n)$, then for each n, C_n is equivalent to a circuit C'_n where C'_n is of size $O(q(n))$ and uses the gates and depth allowed in $\mathcal{C}$;*

(ii) *if $(C_n)_{n\in\mathbb{N}}$ is a polynomial-size circuit family from $\mathcal{C}$ then the QBFs $\mathcal{Q}\text{-}C_n$ have polynomial-size refutations in $\mathcal{C}\text{-Frege}+\forall\text{red}$.*

PROOF. Regarding (i), by the Strategy Extraction Theorem and Proposition 4.2, if the QBF $\mathcal{Q}\text{-}C_n$ has a refutation in $\mathcal{C}\text{-Frege}+\forall\text{red}$ of size S then a winning strategy for the universal player can be computed by a circuit $C'_n \in \mathcal{C}$ of size $O(S)$. We have that in $\mathcal{Q}\text{-}C_n$ the quantifier prefix looks like $\exists x_1 \cdots \exists x_n \forall u \exists \vec{t}$. Now, by construction, $u \not\equiv C_n(x_1,\ldots,x_n)$, hence a winning strategy for the universal player must consist of playing $u = C_n(x_1,\ldots,x_n)$. This means that the circuit C'_n computing the winning strategy for the universal player is equivalent to the circuit C_n and the size bound follows.

Regarding (ii), let

$$\mathcal{Q}\text{-}C_n = \exists x_1 \cdots \exists x_n \forall u \exists t_1 \cdots \exists t_m . (u \leftrightarrow \neg t_m) \wedge \varphi_n,$$

where φ_n is a formula depending on the circuit C_n. By definition, the t_i are indexed w.r.t. a topological ordering of the nodes of C_n.

We prove, by induction on i, that there exists a circuit $D_i \in \mathcal{C}$ such that $t_i \leftrightarrow D_i$ is derivable in $\mathcal{C}\text{-Frege}$ with size polynomial in $|D_i|$. Suppose that t_i corresponds to a gate $\odot(t_{j_1},\ldots,t_{j_\ell})$ with fan-in ℓ, where $\odot$ could be an $\wedge,\vee,\neg,\oplus,MOD_p,T_k,\ldots$ from the gates allowed in the class $\mathcal{C}$. By the inductive property we know that $t_{j_k} \leftrightarrow D_{j_k}$ is provable in $\mathcal{C}\text{-Frege}$ with proofs of size polynomial in $|D_{j_k}|$. Moreover, $\mathcal{C}\text{-Frege}$ is able to prove

$$\frac{t_{j_1} \leftrightarrow D_{j_1} \quad \cdots \quad t_{j_\ell} \leftrightarrow D_{j_\ell} \quad t_i \leftrightarrow \odot(t_{j_1},\ldots,t_{j_\ell})}{t_i \leftrightarrow \odot(D_{j_1},\ldots,D_{j_\ell})}.$$

Let then $D_i = \odot(D_{j_1},\ldots,D_{j_\ell})$. At the m-th step $\mathcal{C}\text{-Frege}$ proves that $t_m \leftrightarrow D_m$, from which follows that

$$\frac{t_m \leftrightarrow D_m \quad u \leftrightarrow \neg t_m}{u \leftrightarrow \neg D_m}.$$

Since now u is universal and the innermost variable of $u \leftrightarrow \neg D_m$, we can apply the $\forall$red rule and get $0 \leftrightarrow \neg D_m$, $1 \leftrightarrow \neg D_m$, which leads to an immediate contradiction in the QBF proof system $\mathcal{C}\text{-Frege}+\forall\text{red}$. $\square$

In particular, a Boolean function f is computable by polynomial-size $\mathcal{C}$ circuits if and only if $\mathcal{Q}\text{-}C_n$ have polynomial-size $\mathcal{C}\text{-Frege}$ refutations for each choice of Boolean circuits $(C_n)_{n\in\mathbb{N}}$ computing f. Note that the circuits C_n are not necessarily circuits from the class $\mathcal{C}$.

In the remainder of this section we apply Theorem 5.2 to a number of circuit classes and transfer circuit lower bounds to proof size lower bounds.

5.1 Lower bounds for bounded-depth Frege systems

PARITY is one of the best-studied functions in terms of its circuit complexity. With Theorem 5.2 we can immediately transfer circuit lower bounds for PARITY to $\mathsf{AC}^0[p]\text{-Frege}+\forall\text{red}$, regardless of the encoding for PARITY.

COROLLARY 5.3 ($\mathcal{Q}$-PARITY LOWER BOUNDS). *Let C_n be a family of polynomial-size circuits computing PARITY. For each odd prime p the QBFs $\mathcal{Q}\text{-}C_n$ require proofs of exponential size in $\mathsf{AC}^0[p]\text{-Frege}+\forall\text{red}$.*

PROOF. The exponential lower bound for the proof size in $\mathsf{AC}^0[p]\text{-Frege}+\forall\text{red}$ follows from Theorem 5.2 and the fact that for each odd prime p any family of bounded-depth circuits with MOD_p gates computing PARITY must be of exponential size [Razborov, 1987; Smolensky, 1987]. $\square$

We highlight that non-trivial lower bounds for $\mathsf{AC}^0[p]\text{-Frege}$ are one of the major open problems in propositional proof complexity. We complement the lower bound in Corollary 5.3 with an upper bound for arbitrary NC^1 encodings of PARITY in $\mathsf{Frege}+\forall\text{red}$.

COROLLARY 5.4 ($\mathcal{Q}$-PARITY UPPER BOUNDS). *Let C_n be a family of NC^1 circuits computing PARITY. Then the QBFs $\mathcal{Q}\text{-}C_n$ have polynomial-size proofs in $\mathsf{Frege}+\forall\text{red}$.*

PROOF. By a result of Muller and Preparata [1975], PARITY can be computed by circuits in NC^1. Hence if we consider a family C_n of NC^1 circuits computing PARITY then the polynomial upper bound in $\mathsf{Frege}+\forall\text{red}$ follows immediately from Theorem 5.2. $\square$

In fact, this upper bound can be improved to the QBF proof system $\mathsf{AC}^0[2]\text{-Frege}+\forall\text{red}$, albeit not for arbitrary NC^1-encodings of PARITY, as it is not clear how these could be handled in bounded depth. For this purpose, we consider explicit QBFs for PARITY, which can be built from its inductive definition $\text{PARITY}(x_1,\ldots,x_n) = \text{PARITY}(x_1,\ldots,x_{n-1}) \oplus x_n$. This leads to the QBFs

$$\Phi_n = \exists x_1 \cdots \exists x_n \forall u \exists t_2 \cdots \exists t_n . (t_2 \leftrightarrow (x_1 \oplus x_2)) \wedge$$
$$\bigwedge_{i=3}^{n}(t_i \leftrightarrow (t_{i-1} \oplus x_i)) \wedge (u \leftrightarrow \neg t_n),$$

where $a \leftrightarrow (b \oplus c) \equiv (\neg a \vee \neg b \vee \neg c) \wedge (\neg a \vee b \vee c) \wedge (a \vee \neg b \vee c) \wedge (a \vee b \vee \neg c)$. This formulation of $\mathcal{Q}$-PARITY was considered by Beyersdorff et al. [2015a], where the formulas Φ_n are shown to be hard for Q-Res and QU-Res. Here we obtain:

COROLLARY 5.5. *The PARITY-formulas Φ_n require refutations of exponential size in$\mathsf{AC}^0[p]\text{-Frege}+\forall\text{red}$ for each odd prime p, but it have polynomial-size $\mathsf{AC}^0[2]\text{-Frege}+\forall\text{red}$ refutations.*

PROOF. The lower bound follows as in Corollary 5.3. For the upper bound we cannot use Theorem 5.2, but need to give a more direct proof. Without loss of generality we can assume that our $\mathsf{AC}^0[2]\text{-Frege}+\forall\text{red}$ system uses the connectives $\{\wedge,\vee,\neg,\leftrightarrow,\oplus\}$.

Then it is easy to see, by induction on i, that Frege proves $t_i \leftrightarrow \oplus(x_1,x_2,\ldots,x_i)$ with a proof of size linear in i. Hence, similarly to what was done in Theorem 5.2, we get

$$u \leftrightarrow \neg \oplus (x_1,x_2,\ldots,x_n). \tag{8}$$

Then u is the rightmost variable in (9); hence by the $\forall$red rule we have

$$1 \leftrightarrow \neg \oplus (x_1, x_2, \ldots, x_n) \quad \text{and} \quad 0 \leftrightarrow \neg \oplus (x_1, x_2, \ldots, x_n),$$

which gives an immediate contradiction. $\square$

In fact, we can further strengthen Corollary 5.5 and use Smolensky's circuit lower bounds for an even more ambitious separation of *all* $\mathsf{AC}^0[p]$-$\mathsf{Frege} + \forall$red systems. For this we consider the function

$$MOD_p(x_1, \ldots, x_n) = \begin{cases} 1 & \text{if } \sum_{i=1}^n x_i \equiv 0 \pmod{p} \\ 0 & \text{otherwise.} \end{cases}$$

For $r \le p - 1$ let

$$MOD_{p,r}(x_1, \ldots, x_n) = \begin{cases} 1 & \text{if } \sum_{i=1}^n x_i \equiv r \pmod{p} \\ 0 & \text{otherwise.} \end{cases}$$

If we want to use MOD_p for a separation of $\mathsf{AC}^0[p]$-$\mathsf{Frege} + \forall$red and $\mathsf{AC}^0[q]$-$\mathsf{Frege} + \forall$red for different primes p, q, then MOD_p has to be encoded as a QBF in the language common to both proof systems, which means that we cannot use MOD_p or MOD_q gates. As for PARITY, an arbitrary NC^1 encoding as in Corollary 5.3 will also not work (this would just give upper bounds in $\mathsf{Frege} + \forall$red), so we need to devise again explicit QBF encodings for MOD_p. Such QBFs can be built using the fact that MOD_p, that is $MOD_{p,0}$, can be defined for $r \ne 0$ by

$$MOD_{p,r}(x_1, \ldots, x_i) = (MOD_{p,r}(x_1, \ldots, x_{i-1}) \wedge \neg x_i) \vee$$
$$(MOD_{p,r-1}(x_1, \ldots, x_{i-1}) \wedge x_i),$$

and for $r = 0$ by

$$MOD_{p,0}(x_1, \ldots, x_i) = (MOD_{p,0}(x_1, \ldots, x_{i-1}) \wedge \neg x_i) \vee$$
$$(MOD_{p,p-1}(x_1, \ldots, x_{i-1}) \wedge x_i).$$

Using variables s_i^r for $MOD_{p,r}(x_1, \ldots, x_i)$ this leads to the QBFs

$$\Theta_n^p = \exists x_1 \cdots \exists x_n \forall u \exists s_1^0 \exists s_1^1 \exists s_2^0 \exists s_2^1 \exists s_2^2 \cdots \exists s_n^0 \cdots \exists s_n^{p-1} .$$

$$(u \leftrightarrow \neg s_n^0) \wedge (s_1^1 \leftrightarrow x_1) \wedge (s_1^0 \leftrightarrow \neg x_1) \wedge$$

$$\bigwedge_{\substack{1 < i \le n \\ 0 < r \le p-1}} \left(s_i^r \leftrightarrow (s_{i-1}^r \wedge \neg x_i) \vee (s_{i-1}^{r-1} \wedge x_i) \right) \wedge$$

$$\bigwedge_{1 < i \le n} \left(s_i^0 \leftrightarrow (s_{i-1}^0 \wedge \neg x_i) \vee (s_{i-1}^{p-1} \wedge x_i) \right).$$

COROLLARY 5.6. *For each pair p, q of distinct primes the MOD_p-formulas Θ_n^p require proofs of exponential size in $\mathsf{AC}^0[q]$-$\mathsf{Frege} + \forall$red, but have polynomial-size proofs in $\mathsf{AC}^0[p]$-$\mathsf{Frege} + \forall$red.*

PROOF. The exponential lower bound for the QBF proof system $\mathsf{AC}^0[q]$-$\mathsf{Frege} + \forall$red follows from Theorem 5.2 together with the result from [Razborov, 1987; Smolensky, 1987] that for distinct primes p, q any family of bounded-depth circuits with MOD_q gates computing MOD_p must be of exponential size.

Regarding the upper bound, without loss of generality we can assume that our $\mathsf{AC}^0[p]$-Frege system uses the connectives $\{\wedge, \vee, \neg, \leftrightarrow, MOD_p\}$. Then it is easy to see, by induction on

i, that $\mathsf{AC}^0[p]$-Frege proves

$$s_i^r \leftrightarrow MOD_p(x_1, \ldots, x_i, \underbrace{1, 1, \ldots, 1}_{p-r}),$$

with a proof of size linear in i. Hence, similarly to what was done in Theorem 5.2 and Corollary 5.5, we get

$$u \leftrightarrow \neg MOD_p(x_1, \ldots, x_n, \underbrace{1, 1, \ldots, 1}_{p}). \qquad (9)$$

Then u is the rightmost variable in (9); hence by the $\forall$red rule we have

$$1 \leftrightarrow \neg MOD_p(x_1, \ldots, x_n, \underbrace{1, 1, \ldots, 1}_{p}) \quad \text{and}$$

$$0 \leftrightarrow \neg MOD_p(x_1, \ldots, x_n, \underbrace{1, 1, \ldots, 1}_{p}),$$

which gives an immediate contradiction. $\square$

Another notorious function in circuit complexity is MAJORITY. Again we can transform circuit lower bounds to proof size lower bounds for arbitrary encodings of MAJORITY.

COROLLARY 5.7 (LOWER BOUNDS FOR $\mathcal{Q}$-MAJORITY). *Let C_n be a family of polynomial-size circuits computing MAJORITY$(x_1, \ldots, x_n)$. Then for every prime p, the QBFs $\mathcal{Q}$-C_n require proofs of exponential size in $\mathsf{AC}^0[p]$-$\mathsf{Frege} + \forall$red.*

PROOF. The lower bound follows again applying Theorem 5.2 and the fact that MAJORITY requires exponential-size bounded-depth circuits with MOD_p gates [Razborov, 1987; Smolensky, 1987]. $\square$

For general encodings, we can again show $\mathsf{Frege} + \forall$red upper bounds.

COROLLARY 5.8 ($\mathcal{Q}$-MAJORITY UPPER BOUNDS). *Let C_n be a family of NC^1 circuits computing MAJORITY$(x_1, \ldots, x_n)$. Then the QBFs $\mathcal{Q}$-C_n have polynomial-size proofs in the QBF proof system $\mathsf{Frege} + \forall$red.*

PROOF. By a result of Muller and Preparata [1975], the function MAJORITY is computable in NC^1 and hence $\mathcal{Q}$-C_n are well defined. The upper bound then follows from Theorem 5.2. $\square$

As for the MOD_p functions, we can improve on this upper bound by considering explicit QBF encodings of MAJORITY, thereby even obtaining a separation of $\mathsf{AC}^0[p]$-$\mathsf{Frege} + \forall$red systems from TC^0-$\mathsf{Frege} + \forall$red.[4] Explicit QBFs for MAJORITY can be defined using the following property of the k-threshold function

$$T_k(x_1, \ldots, x_i) \equiv T_k(x_1, \ldots, x_{i-1}) \vee (T_{k-1}(x_1, \ldots, x_{i-1}) \wedge x_i). \qquad (10)$$

Using variables t_k^i for $T_k(x_1, \ldots, x_i)$ this gives rise to the QBFs

$$\Psi_n = \exists x_1 \cdots \exists x_n \forall u \exists t_1^1 \cdots \exists t_{n/2}^n . (u \leftrightarrow \neg t_{n/2}^n) \wedge$$
$$\bigwedge_{i \le n} t_0^i \wedge (t_1^1 \leftrightarrow x_1) \wedge \bigwedge_{\substack{k \le n/2 \\ i \le n}} \left(t_k^i \leftrightarrow t_k^{i-1} \vee (t_{k-1}^{i-1} \wedge x_i) \right).$$

---

[4]Clearly, such a separation already follows from Corollary 5.6 together with the simulation of $\mathsf{AC}^0[p]$-$\mathsf{Frege} + \forall$red by TC^0-$\mathsf{Frege} + \forall$red. Here we will prove the stronger result that all these systems are separated by *one* natural principle, namely MAJORITY.

COROLLARY 5.9. *For each prime p the* MAJORITY-*based formulas Ψ_n require proofs of exponential-size in the QBF proof system* $\mathsf{AC}^0[p]$-$\mathsf{Frege}+\forall\mathsf{red}$, *but have polynomial-size proofs in* TC^0-$\mathsf{Frege}+\forall\mathsf{red}$.

PROOF. The exponential lower bound from [Razborov, 1987; Smolensky, 1987] will give us the exponential lower bound w.r.t. the size of Ψ_n in $\mathsf{AC}^0[p]$-$\mathsf{Frege}+\forall\mathsf{red}$, since the size of Ψ_n is $O(n^2)$.

Regarding the polynomial-size proof of the QBF formula Ψ_n in TC^0-$\mathsf{Frege}+\forall\mathsf{red}$ we can proceed similarly as for PARITY in Frege. The crucial feature here is that T_k are, by definition of TC^0, in the language of TC^0-Frege. Hence (10) can be used to prove $t_k^j \leftrightarrow T_k(x_1, \ldots, x_j)$ and we can easily refute Ψ_n in TC^0-$\mathsf{Frege}+\forall\mathsf{red}$. $\square$

We note that a separation of $\mathsf{AC}^0[p]$-Frege from TC^0-Frege constitutes a major open problem in propositional proof complexity as we are currently lacking lower bounds for $\mathsf{AC}^0[p]$-Frege.

5.2 Lower bounds for depth-d Frege systems

We now aim at a fine-grained analysis of AC^0-Frege by studying its subsystems AC^0_d-Frege. Our next result is a version of Theorem 5.2, however, we need to be a bit more careful for circuits of fixed depth d.

THEOREM 5.10. *Let $(C_n)_{n\in\mathbb{N}}$ be a non-uniform family of circuits where C_n is a circuit with n inputs. Then the following implications hold:*

(i) *if the QBFs $\mathcal{Q}$-C_n have AC^0_d-$\mathsf{Frege}+\forall\mathsf{red}$ refutations of size bounded by a function $q(n)$, then for each n, C_n is equivalent to a depth-$(d+2)$ circuit C'_n of size $O(q(n))$;*

(ii) *if $(C_n)_{n\in\mathbb{N}}$ is a family of polynomial-size depth-d circuits, then the QBFs $\mathcal{Q}$-C_n have polynomial-size refutations in AC^0_d-$\mathsf{Frege}+\forall\mathsf{red}$.*

PROOF. The proof of (i) follows the proof of the analogous statement of Theorem 5.2. The Strategy Extraction Theorem in this case tell us that from refutations of $\mathcal{Q}$-C_n in AC^0_d-$\mathsf{Frege}+\forall\mathsf{red}$ of size S we can extract a winning strategy for the universal player that can be computed by AC^0_d-decision lists of size $O(S)$. By Proposition 4.2, this means that the winning strategy can be also computed by AC^0_{d+2} circuits and the size upper bound follows.

The proof of point (ii) follows the proof of the analogous statement of Theorem 5.2. That proof will give us that $\mathcal{Q}$-C_n has polynomial-size refutations in AC^0_{d+2}-$\mathsf{Frege}+\forall\mathsf{red}$. Here we want to prove that $\mathcal{Q}$-C_n has actually polynomial-size proofs in AC^0_d-$\mathsf{Frege}+\forall\mathsf{red}$. Without loss of generality suppose that the last gate t_m of C_n is an $\bigwedge$, that is

$$\mathcal{Q}\text{-}C_n = \exists x_1 \cdots \exists x_n \forall u \exists t_1 \cdots \exists t_m . (u \leftrightarrow \neg t_m) \wedge$$
$$\wedge (t_m \leftrightarrow \bigwedge_{j \leq \ell} t_{i_j}) \wedge \varphi_n,$$

where each t_{i_j} is an $\bigvee$ gate and φ_n is the encoding of the rest of the circuit C_n. We clearly have that

$$\frac{u \leftrightarrow \neg t_m \qquad t_m \leftrightarrow \bigwedge_{j\leq\ell} t_{i_j}}{u \leftrightarrow \bigvee_{j\leq\ell} \neg t_{i_j}}$$

From which we obtain both

$$u \vee \bigwedge_{j\leq\ell} t_{i_j}, \tag{11}$$

$$\neg u \vee \bigvee_{j\leq\ell} \neg t_{i_j}. \tag{12}$$

Now we can proceed, similarly as in Theorem 5.2. By induction (on the depth of C_n) AC^0_d-Frege is able to substitute t_{i_j} with D_{i_j} where D_{i_j} is an AC^0_{d-1}-formula over the $x_1, \ldots, x_n$ variables starting with an $\bigvee$. More precisely by induction we can prove that AC^0_d-Frege proves both

$$t_{i_j} \vee \neg D_{i_j}, \tag{13}$$

$$\neg t_{i_j} \vee D_{i_j}. \tag{14}$$

Hence from (12) and (13) follows that $\neg u \vee \bigvee_{j\leq\ell} \neg D_{i_j}$, which is an AC^0_d-formula only over the variables $u, x_1, \ldots, x_n$. Hence by the $\forall\mathsf{red}$ rule we get

$$\bigvee_{j\leq\ell} \neg D_{i_j}. \tag{15}$$

Similarly from (11) we get first that $\bigwedge_{j\leq\ell}(u \vee t_{i_j})$ and then using (14) we get $\bigwedge_{j\leq\ell}(u \vee D_{i_j})$, which, again, is an AC^0_d-formula over the variables $u, x_1, \ldots, x_n$. By the $\forall\mathsf{red}$ rule we get

$$\bigwedge_{j\leq\ell} D_{i_j}. \tag{16}$$

From (15) and (16) follows immediately a contradiction. $\square$

From Theorem 5.2 we immediately obtain a wealth of lower bounds for $\mathsf{Res}+\forall\mathsf{red}$.

COROLLARY 5.11. *Let $f(x_1, \ldots, x_n)$ be a Boolean function requiring exponential-size depth-3 circuits and let $(C_n)_{n\in\mathbb{N}}$ be polynomial-size circuits (of unbounded depth) computing f. Then the QBFs $\mathcal{Q}$-C_n require exponential-size refutations in AC^0_1-$\mathsf{Frege}+\forall\mathsf{red}$ and hence, in particular, in $\mathsf{Res}+\forall\mathsf{red}$.*

We now prove a separation of constant-depth $\mathsf{Frege}+\forall\mathsf{red}$ systems. For this we employ the Sipser functions separating the hierarchy of constant-depth circuits. We quote the definition of the SIPSER$_d$ function from Boppana and Sipser [1990]:

$$\text{SIPSER}_d = \bigwedge_{i_1 \leq m_1} \bigvee_{i_2 \leq m_2} \bigwedge_{i_3 \leq m_3} \cdots \bigodot_{i_d \leq m_d} x_{i_1 i_2 i_3 \ldots i_d},$$

where $\bigodot = \bigvee$ or $\bigwedge$ depending on the parity of d. The variables $x_1, \ldots, x_n$ appear as $x_{i_1 i_2 i_3 \ldots i_d}$ for $i_j \leq m_j$, where $m_1 = \sqrt{m/\log m}$, $m_2 = m_3 = \cdots = m_{d-1} = m$, $m_d = \sqrt{dm\log m/2}$ and $m = (n\sqrt{2/d})^{1/(d-1)}$.

COROLLARY 5.12. *Fix an integer $d \geq 2$. Let $(C_d^n)_{n\in\mathbb{N}}$ be a family of polynomial-size depth-$(d+3)$ circuits computing the function* SIPSER$_{d+3}(x_1, \ldots, x_n)$. *Then the QBFs $\mathcal{Q}$-C_d^n need exponential-size proofs in AC^0_d-$\mathsf{Frege}+\forall\mathsf{red}$, but have polynomial-size proofs in AC^0_{d+3}-$\mathsf{Frege}+\forall\mathsf{red}$.*

PROOF. The lower bound follows from Theorem 5.10 and from the result that for every d, SIPSER$_{d+3}$ needs exponential-size depth-$(d+2)$ circuits [Håstad, 1986]. Regarding the upper bound, by construction C_d^n has depth $d+3$ and polynomial-size. Hence, by Theorem 5.10, the family $\mathcal{Q}$-C_d^n has polynomial-size proofs in AC^0_{d+3}-$\mathsf{Frege}+\forall\mathsf{red}$. $\square$

Note that the gap of size 1 in the circuit separation of [Håstad, 1986] increases to a gap of size 3 in our proof system separation, due to the transformation in Proposition 4.2. We highlight that in contrast to Corollary 5.12 where our separating formulas are CNFs, a separation of the depth-d Frege hierarchy with formulas of depth independent of d is a major open problem in propositional proof complexity.

5.3 Conditional lower bounds for Frege and extended Frege

We end this section with conditional lower bounds for Frege + ∀red and EF + ∀red. Turning these conditional lower bounds into unconditional ones — at least with our technique — will depend on major breakthroughs in circuit complexity.

THEOREM 5.13. *Let $\mathcal{C}$ be either* P/poly *or non-uniform* NC^1. *If* PSPACE $\not\subset \mathcal{C}$ *then the $\mathcal{C}$-*Frege + ∀red *is not polynomially bounded.*

PROOF. Let f be a Boolean function in PSPACE but not in $\mathcal{C}$. Since QBF is PSPACE-complete there exists a QBF $\mathcal{Q}\vec{w} . \varphi(\vec{w}, x_1, \ldots, x_n)$ with a CNF φ such that

$$f(x_1, \ldots, x_n) \equiv \mathcal{Q}\vec{w} . \varphi(\vec{w}, x_1, \ldots, x_n).$$

We define

$$\mathcal{Q}\text{-}f_n = \exists x_1 \cdots \exists x_n \forall u . (u \leftrightarrow \mathcal{Q}\vec{w} . \varphi(\vec{w}, x_1, \ldots, x_n)),$$

which can be rewritten into formulas Θ_n in prenex form. Notice that the only winning strategy for the universal player on both $\mathcal{Q}\text{-}f_n$ and Θ_n is to compute $u = f(x_1, \ldots, x_n)$. Therefore, the Strategy Extraction Theorem together with $f \notin \mathcal{C}$ immediately implies super-polynomial lower bounds for Θ_n in $\mathcal{C}$-Frege + ∀red. □

We remark that we do have a separation between *uniform* NC^1 and PSPACE, because NC^1 ⊆ L and L ≠ PSPACE by the space hierarchy theorem. Therefore, choosing $f \in$ PSPACE \ NC^1 and considering the prenex formulas Θ_n arising from $\mathcal{Q}\text{-}f_n$ we can infer the weaker result that Frege + ∀red has no uniform short proofs of Θ_n.

6. CONCLUSION AND OPEN PROBLEMS

We already outlined the main directions of this paper's potential for impact in Section 1.3. The most immediate specific open problem arising from this work is to show lower bounds for Frege + ∀red. While such a lower bound via our technique would need a major breakthrough in circuit complexity (cf. Theorem 5.13), we ask the (possibly very challenging) question whether a lower bound can be shown via a different method.

Acknowledgements.
The authors are grateful to Nicola Galesi and Albert Atserias for interesting discussions about this work and circuit complexity in general.
This research was supported by grant no. 48138 from the John Templeton Foundation, EPSRC grant EP/L024233/1, and a Doctoral Training Grant from EPSRC (3rd author).
This work was completed while the 2nd author was affiliated to the Computer Science Department of Sapienza University of Rome (Italy). The 2nd author was funded by the European Research Council under the European Union's Seventh Framework Programme (FP7/2007–2013) / ERC grant agreement no. 279611.

References

Miklós Ajtai. The complexity of the pigeonhole-principle. *Combinatorica*, 14(4):417–433, 1994.

Sanjeev Arora and Boaz Barak. *Computational Complexity - A Modern Approach.* Cambridge University Press, 2009.

Valeriy Balabanov and Jie-Hong R. Jiang. Unified QBF certification and its applications. *Form. Methods Syst. Des.*, 41(1):45–65, August 2012.

Valeriy Balabanov, Magdalena Widl, and Jie-Hong R. Jiang. QBF resolution systems and their proof complexities. In *SAT*, pages 154–169, 2014.

Paul Beame and Toniann Pitassi. Propositional proof complexity: Past, present, and future. In G. Paun, G. Rozenberg, and A. Salomaa, editors, *Current Trends in Theoretical Computer Science: Entering the 21st Century*, pages 42–70. World Scientific Publishing, 2001.

Eli Ben-Sasson and Avi Wigderson. Short proofs are narrow - resolution made simple. *Journal of the ACM*, 48(2): 149–169, 2001.

Marco Benedetti and Hratch Mangassarian. QBF-based formal verification: Experience and perspectives. *JSAT*, 5 (1-4):133–191, 2008.

Olaf Beyersdorff and Oliver Kullmann. Unified characterisations of resolution hardness measures. In *SAT*, pages 170–187, 2014.

Olaf Beyersdorff, Leroy Chew, and Mikoláš Janota. On unification of QBF resolution-based calculi. In *MFCS, II*, pages 81–93, 2014.

Olaf Beyersdorff, Leroy Chew, and Mikolás Janota. Proof complexity of resolution-based QBF calculi. In *32nd International Symposium on Theoretical Aspects of Computer Science (STACS 2015)*, pages 76–89, 2015a.

Olaf Beyersdorff, Leroy Chew, Meena Mahajan, and Anil Shukla. Feasible interpolation for QBF resolution calculi. In *ICALP*. Springer, 2015b.

Archie Blake. *Canonical Expressions in Boolean Algebra.* PhD thesis, 1937. University of Chicago.

Maria Luisa Bonet, Toniann Pitassi, and Ran Raz. On interpolation and automatization for Frege systems. *SIAM Journal on Computing*, 29(6):1939–1967, 2000.

Maria Luisa Bonet, Carlos Domingo, Ricard Gavaldà, Alexis Maciel, and Toniann Pitassi. Non-automatizability of bounded-depth Frege proofs. *Computational Complexity*, 13(1–2):47–68, 2004.

Ravi B. Boppana and Michael Sipser. Handbook of theoretical computer science (vol. A). chapter The Complexity of Finite Functions, pages 757–804. MIT Press, Cambridge, MA, USA, 1990.

Samuel R. Buss. Towards NP-P via proof complexity and search. *Ann. Pure Appl. Logic*, 163(7):906–917, 2012.

Samuel R. Buss and Peter Clote. Cutting planes, connectivity, and threshold logic. *Archive for Mathematical Logic*, 35 (1):33–62, 1996.

Matthew Clegg, Jeff Edmonds, and Russell Impagliazzo. Using the Groebner basis algorithm to find proofs of unsatisfiability. In *Proc. 28th ACM Symposium on Theory of Computing*, pages 174–183, 1996.

Stephen A. Cook and Tsuyoshi Morioka. Quantified propositional calculus and a second-order theory for NC1. *Arch. Math. Log.*, 44(6):711–749, 2005.

Stephen A. Cook and Robert A. Reckhow. The relative efficiency of propositional proof systems. *Journal of Symbolic Logic*, 6:169–184, 1979.

William Cook, Collette R. Coullard, and György Turán. On the complexity of cutting-plane proofs. *Discrete Applied Mathematics*, 18(1):25–38, 1987.

Uwe Egly. On sequent systems and resolution for qbfs. In *Theory and Applications of Satisfiability Testing - SAT 2012*, pages 100–113, 2012.

Uwe Egly, Martin Kronegger, Florian Lonsing, and Andreas Pfandler. Conformant planning as a case study of incremental QBF solving. In *Artificial Intelligence and Symbolic Computation AISC 2014*, pages 120–131, 2014.

Alexandra Goultiaeva, Allen Van Gelder, and Fahiem Bacchus. A uniform approach for generating proofs and strategies for both true and false QBF formulas. In *IJCAI*, pages 546–553, 2011.

Amin Haken. The intractability of resolution. *Theoretical Computer Science*, 39:297–308, 1985.

Johan Håstad. Almost optimal lower bounds for small depth circuits. In *Proc. 18th STOC*, pages 6–20. ACM Press, 1986.

Marijn Heule, Martina Seidl, and Armin Biere. A unified proof system for QBF preprocessing. In *IJCAR*, pages 91–106, 2014.

Pavel Hrubeš. On lengths of proofs in non-classical logics. *Annals of Pure and Applied Logic*, 157(2–3):194–205, 2009.

Mikolás Janota and Joao Marques-Silva. Expansion-based QBF solving versus Q-resolution. *Theor. Comput. Sci.*, 577:25–42, 2015.

Emil Jeřábek. *Weak pigeonhole principle, and randomized computation*. PhD thesis, Faculty of Mathematics and Physics, Charles University, Prague, 2005.

Emil Jeřábek. Substitution Frege and extended Frege proof systems in non-classical logics. *Annals of Pure and Applied Logic*, 159(1–2):1–48, 2009.

Hans Kleine Büning, Marek Karpinski, and Andreas Flögel. Resolution for quantified Boolean formulas. *Inf. Comput.*, 117(1):12–18, 1995.

Jan Krajíček. *Bounded Arithmetic, Propositional Logic and Complexity Theory*. Cambridge University Press, 1995.

Jan Krajíček. Interpolation theorems, lower bounds for proof systems and independence results for bounded arithmetic. *The Journal of Symbolic Logic*, 62(2):457–486, 1997.

Jan Krajíček and Pavel Pudlák. Propositional proof systems, the consistency of first order theories and the complexity of computations. *The Journal of Symbolic Logic*, 54(3):1063–1079, 1989.

Jan Krajíček and Pavel Pudlák. Quantified propositional calculi and fragments of bounded arithmetic. *Zeitschrift für mathematische Logik und Grundlagen der Mathematik*, 36:29–46, 1990.

Jan Krajíček and Pavel Pudlák. Some consequences of cryptographical conjectures for S_2^1 and EF. *Information and Computation*, 140(1):82–94, 1998.

Jan Krajíček, Pavel Pudlák, and Alan Woods. Exponential lower bounds to the size of bounded depth Frege proofs of the pigeonhole principle. *Random Structures and Algorithms*, 7(1):15–39, 1995.

David E. Muller and Franco P. Preparata. Bounds to complexities of networks for sorting and for switching. *J. ACM*, 22(2):195–201, 1975.

Toniann Pitassi, Paul Beame, and Russell Impagliazzo. Exponential lower bounds for the pigeonhole principle. *Computational Complexity*, 3:97–140, 1993.

Pavel Pudlák. Lower bounds for resolution and cutting planes proofs and monotone computations. *The Journal of Symbolic Logic*, 62(3):981–998, 1997.

Alexander A. Razborov. Lower bounds for the size of circuits of bounded depth with basis $\{\&, \oplus\}$. *Math. Notes Acad. Sci. USSR*, 41(4):333–338, 1987.

Jussi Rintanen. Asymptotically optimal encodings of conformant planning in QBF. In *AAAI*, pages 1045–1050. AAAI Press, 2007.

Ronald L. Rivest. Learning decision lists. *Machine Learning*, 2(3):229–246, 1987.

John Alan Robinson. A machine-oriented logic based on the resolution principle. *J. ACM*, 12(1):23–41, 1965.

Nathan Segerlind. The complexity of propositional proofs. *Bulletin of Symbolic Logic*, 13(4):417–481, 2007.

Roman Smolensky. Algebraic methods in the theory of lower bounds for Boolean circuit complexity. In *Proc. of 19th ACM STOC*, pages 77–82, 1987.

Allen Van Gelder. Contributions to the theory of practical quantified Boolean formula solving. In *CP*, pages 647–663, 2012.

Nondeterministic Extensions of the Strong Exponential Time Hypothesis and Consequences for Non-reducibility

Marco L. Carmosino   Jiawei Gao   Russell Impagliazzo
Ivan Mihajlin   Ramamohan Paturi   Stefan Schneider

{mcarmosi, jiawei, russell, imikhail, paturi, stschnei}@cs.ucsd.edu
Department of Computer Science and Engineering
UC, San Diego
La Jolla, CA 92093

ABSTRACT

We introduce the Nondeterministic Strong Exponential Time Hypothesis (NSETH) as a natural extension of the Strong Exponential Time Hypothesis (SETH). We show that both refuting and proving NSETH would have interesting consequences.

In particular we show that disproving NSETH would give new nontrivial circuit lower bounds. On the other hand, NSETH implies non-reducibility results, i.e. the absence of (deterministic) fine-grained reductions from SAT to a number of problems. As a consequence we conclude that unless this hypothesis fails, problems such as 3-SUM, APSP and model checking of a large class of first-order graph properties cannot be shown to be SETH-hard using deterministic or zero-error probabilistic reductions.

Categories and Subject Descriptors

F.1.3 [**Computation By Abstract Devices**]: Complexity Measures and Classes—*Reducibility and Completeness*; F.1.2 [**Computation By Abstract Devices**]: Modes of Computation—*Alternation and Nondeterminism*

Keywords

3-Sum; All-pairs shortest path; Computational Complexity; conditional lower bounds; fine-grained complexity; nondeterminism; SETH

1. INTRODUCTION

Traditionally, complexity theory has been used to distinguish very hard problems, such as NP-complete problems, from relatively easy problems, such as those in P. However, over the past few decades, there has been progress in understanding the exact complexities of problems, both for very hard problems and those within P, under plausible assumptions. For example, under hypotheses such as the

Permission to make digital or hard copies of all or part of this work for personal or classroom use is granted without fee provided that copies are not made or distributed for profit or commercial advantage and that copies bear this notice and the full citation on the first page. Copyrights for components of this work owned by others than ACM must be honored. Abstracting with credit is permitted. To copy otherwise, or republish, to post on servers or to redistribute to lists, requires prior specific permission and/or a fee. Request permissions from Permissions@acm.org.
ITCS'16, January 14–16, 2016, Cambridge, MA, USA.
© 2016 ACM. ISBN 978-1-4503-4057-1/16/01 ...$15.00.
DOI: http://dx.doi.org/10.1145/2840728.2840746

3-SUM conjecture [13] from computational geometry or the Strong Exponential Time Hypothesis for the complexity of SAT [16, 15], it follows that the known algorithms for many basic problems within P, including Fréchet distance [9], edit distance [5], string matching [1], k-dominating set [23], orthogonal vectors [26], stable marriage for low dimensional ordering functions [21], and many others [8], are essentially optimal.

Unfortunately, as our understanding of the relationship between the exact complexities of problems grows, so does the complexity of the web of known reductions and the number of distinct conjectures these results are based on. Ideally, we would like to show that many of these conjectures are in fact equivalent, or that all follow from some basic unifying hypothesis, thereby improving our understanding and simplifying the state of knowledge. For example, it would be nice to show that the 3-SUM conjecture follows from SETH (Strong Exponential Time Hypothesis). It would also be nice to show that SETH implies that HITTINGSET and MAXFLOW require superlinear time. Can we prove that APSP takes n^3 time under SETH?

In this paper, we introduce a new technique which provides evidence that such a simplification (i.e. hardness results under one unifying hypothesis such as SETH) is *unlikely*, at least when restricted to deterministic reductions. Just as one can show that a problem is unlikely to be NP-complete by showing that it belongs to a presumably smaller complexity class (such as NP ∩ coNP), we can get *non-reducibility* results by comparing the complexity of problems in other models of computation.

To obtain our non-reducibility results, we consider the nondeterministic and co-nondeterministic complexities of the problem under question. If a problem has smaller nondeterministic and co-nondeterministic complexities, we show that if there were to be a deterministic *fine-grained* reduction from SAT to such a problem, it follows that SAT can be solved faster in co-nondeterministic time, which may be unlikely. More precisely, we introduce the following variant of SETH for nondeterministic models.

Nondeterministic Strong Exponential Time Hypothesis (NSETH): For every $\epsilon > 0$, there exists a k so that k-TAUT is not in $\mathsf{NTIME}[2^{n(1-\epsilon)}]$, where k-TAUT is the language of all k-DNF which are tautologies.

We feel that NSETH is plausible for many of the same reasons as SETH. Just as many algorithmic techniques have been developed for k-SAT, all of which approach exhaustive search for large k, many proof systems have been considered for k-TAUT, and none have been shown to have significantly less than purely exponential complexity for large k. In fact, the tree-like ([24]) and regular resolution ([6]) proof systems have been proved to require such sizes. Moreover, we observe that results of [17] that obtain circuit lower bounds assuming SETH is false yield the same bounds assuming that NSETH is false. So disproving NSETH would be both a breakthrough in proof complexity and in circuit complexity.

We consider problems together with their *presumed* or *conjectured* complexities. Let the pair (L, T) denote the language L with (presumed) deterministic time complexity T. We use the notion of *fine-grained reducibility* (the special case of subcubic reducibility was defined in [33], the general case was defined in [32]) introduced by Vassilevska Williams [31] to reduce problems with their complexities to one another. We say that (L_1, T_1) is fine-grained reducible (denoted as $\leq_{FGR}$) to (L_2, T_2) if there is a Turing reduction from L_1 to L_2 such that improvement of the sort $T_2^{1-\epsilon}$ for $\epsilon > 0$ in the complexity of L_2 leads to an improvement of $T_1^{1-\delta}$ in the complexity of L_1 for some $\delta > 0$. We say that a language L with time complexity T is SETH-hard if there is a fine-grained reduction from CNFSAT with time 2^n to (L, T).

Using fine-grained reductions, an intricate web of relationships between improving basic algorithms within polynomial time has been established. By considering the nondeterministic and co-nondeterministic complexities of such problems, we show, under NSETH, that deterministic fine-grained reductions between many of these problems *do not exist*. In particular,

- HITTINGSET for sets of total size m and time $T(m) = m^{1+\gamma}$ is not SETH-hard for any $\gamma > 0$, and no problem that is SETH-hard reduces to HITTINGSET for any such time complexity.

- 3-SUM for $T(n) = n^{1.5+\gamma}$ is not SETH-hard for any $\gamma > 0$.

- MAXFLOW, minimum cost MAXFLOW, and maximum cardinality matching on a graph with m edges and $T(m) = m^{1+\gamma}$ are not SETH-hard.

- All-pairs shortest path on a graph with n vertices and $T(n) = n^{\frac{3+\omega}{2}+\gamma}$ is not SETH-hard.

While there are many known SETH-hard problems, few are graph problems, and those few have the same logical structure. In addition to specific problems, our method can be used to explain why the structure of SETH-hard graph problems are all similar. In particular, we consider first-order definable graph properties on sparse graphs (where we view the input size as the number of edges m). We show that, under SETH, the maximum time complexity for such a property expressible with k quantifiers will be close to $O(m^{k-1})$. On the other hand, if NSETH, all SETH-hard properties have the same logical structure: $k-1$ quantifiers of one type, followed by a single quantifier of the other type.

These results are only valid for deterministic or zero-error probabilistic fine-grained reductions. We introduce a non-uniform variant NUNSETH under which they also hold for randomized reductions with bounded error. However, some care should be used to evaluate whether this hypothesis is true, since it has not been the subject to previous study and Williams has recently shown related hypotheses about Merlin-Arthur complexity of k-TAUT are false ([30]).

2. OUTLINE OF THE PAPER

In section 3, we provide definitions of fine-grained reducibilities and establish basic closure properties of these reductions. In section 4, we outline reasons why disproving NSETH is nontrivial. In section 5, we examine the nondeterministic and co-nondeterministic complexities of several problems within polynomial time whose exact complexities have been extensively studied, and show that, under NSETH, none of these problems are SETH-hard. In section 6, we explain why all the known maximally hard SETH-hard first-order graph properties have the same logical structure.

In section 7, we show that NSETH also implies that certain new problems are hard, especially those involving verifying solutions to known SETH-hard problems. Finally, section 8 presents our conclusions and open problems.

3. DEFINITIONS AND BASIC PROPERTIES

Fine-grained reductions are defined with the motivation to control the exact complexity of the reducibility. For this purpose, we consider languages together with their *presumed* or *conjectured* complexities. We use the pair (L, T) to denote a language together with its time complexity T. Intuitively, if (L_1, T_1) fine-grained reduces to (L_2, T_2), then any constant savings in the exponent of the time complexity of L_2 implies some constant savings in the exponent of the time complexity of L_1.

Definition 1 (Fine-Grained Reductions ($\leq_{FGR}$))**.** *Let L_1 and L_2 be languages, and let T_1 and T_2 be time bounds. We say that (L_1, T_1) fine-grained reduces to (L_2, T_2) (denoted $(L_1, T_1) \leq_{FGR} (L_2, T_2)$) if*

(a) $\forall \epsilon > 0 \quad \exists \delta > 0, \exists \mathcal{M}^{L_2}$, a deterministic Turing reduction from L_1 to L_2, such that

$$\mathsf{TIME}[\mathcal{M}] \leq T_1^{1-\delta}$$

(b) Let $\tilde{Q}(\mathcal{M}, x)$ denote the set of queries made by $\mathcal{M}$ to the oracle on an input x of length n. The query lengths obey the following time bound.

$$\sum_{q \in \tilde{Q}(\mathcal{M}, x)} (T_2(|q|))^{1-\epsilon} \leq (T_1(n))^{1-\delta}$$

If a fine-grained reduction exists from (L_1, T_1) to (L_2, T_2), algorithmic savings for L_2 can be transferred to L_1. The definition gives us exactly what is needed to establish savings for L_1 by simulating the machine $\mathcal{M}^{L_2}$ using the faster algorithm for L_2. The role of each parameter in the definition of fine-grained reducibility makes this clear.

T_1: The presumed time to decide L_1, usually given by a trivial algorithm.

T_2: The presumed time to decide L_2.

ϵ: Any savings (assumed or real) on computing L_2.

δ: The savings (as a function of ϵ) that can be obtained over T_1 when deciding L_1 by reducing to L_2.

Definition 2 (Randomized Fine-Grained Reductions ($\leq_{rFGR}^s$)). *Exactly as in the deterministic case, except the Turing reduction from (L_1, T_1) to (L_2, T_2) is a probabilistic machine with some two-sided error bound*

$$\Pr[\mathcal{M}^{L_2}(x) = L_1(x)] \geq s$$

We denote a randomized fine grained reduction from L_1 to L_2 with error bound s by $(L_1, T_1) \leq_{rFGR}^s (L_2, T_2)$. Generally, we will use $s = 2/3$, so we denote $\leq_{rFGR}^{2/3}$ by $\leq_{rFGR}$.

We will have occasion to consider FGRs between function problems. This poses the problem that, in certain situations, just writing down the solution to a problem could exceed the time bound and wipe out fine-grained savings. In the deterministic case, we cope with this by adding another restriction to the definition of a fine-grained reduction:

Definition 3 (Fine-Grained Reductions for Functions ($\leq_{fFGR}$)). *Exactly as in the decision deterministic case, except that the Turing reduction $\mathcal{M}^{f_2}$ is to a function problem f_2 and is expected to produce a functional output. In addition to the existing resource bounds, we bound the size of answers given by the f_2 oracle.*

$$\sum_{q \in \tilde{Q}(\mathcal{M}, x)} (|f_2(q)|) \leq (T_1(n))^{1-\delta}$$

The bound on query answer size ensures that each proof about decision FGRs goes through in the function FGR case, with an additional step corrosponding to the bound on query answers that is identical to checking the bound on query sizes of the definition of a decision FGR.

We will also consider FGRs between nondeterministic computation of function problems. Defining exactly what it means for a nondeterministic machine to compute a function is fairly involved, so we sidestep this issue by using the *graph* of the function as a decision problem. That is, by convention we use the language $gr(f) = \{\langle x, f(x)\rangle | x \in \{0,1\}^*\}$ to assess the nondeterministic complexity of every function f we are interested in. Since here we only only study $(N \cap coN)TIME$ complexity, this convention does not unduly simplify our model. It is equivalent to being able to print the ith bit of $f(x)$ on input x in $(N \cap coN)TIME$, which we would have anyway. Thus, using the graph of a function, all properties of FGRs between the nondeterministic complexity of decision problems hold between function problems as well.

3.1 Deterministic Fine-grained Reductions

The properties of deterministic fine-grained reductions are exactly what one would expect and follow by standard methods. See full version of the paper for proofs.

Lemma 1 (Fine-grained reductions translate savings for DTIME). *Let $(L_1, T_1) \leq_{FGR} (L_2, T_2)$, and $L_2 \in \text{DTIME}[T_2(n)^{1-\epsilon}]$ for $\epsilon > 0$. There exists $\delta > 0$ such that*

$$L_1 \in \text{DTIME}[T_1(n)^{1-\delta}]$$

Lemma 2 (Fine-grained reductions transfer savings for $(N \cap coN)TIME$). *Let $(L_1, T_1) \leq_{FGR} (L_2, T_2)$, and $L_2 \in (N \cap coN)TIME[T_2(n)^{1-\epsilon}]$ for some $\epsilon > 0$. Then there exists a $\delta > 0$ such that*

$$L_1 \in (N \cap coN)TIME[T_1(n)^{1-\delta}]$$

To prove both of these "savings" lemmas, we simply run the reduction TM and simulate oracle calls to L_2 using the efficient algorithm for L_2 to get savings for L_1.

Corollary 1 (Fine-grained reductions translate savings from reductions). *When the true complexity of a problem is meaningfully smaller than the time bound used in a fine-grained reduction, savings are translated.*

1. *Let $(L_1, T_1) \leq_{FGR} (L_2, T_2^{1+\gamma})$, and $L_2 \in \text{DTIME}[T_2]$. Then there exists $\delta > 0$ such that*

$$L_1 \in \text{DTIME}[T_1^{1-\delta}]$$

2. *Let $(L_1, T_1) \leq_{FGR} (L_2, T_2^{1+\gamma})$, and $L_2 \in (N \cap coN)TIME[T_2]$. Then there exists a $\delta > 0$ such that*

$$L_2 \in (N \cap coN)TIME[T_1^{1-\delta}]$$

The above follows from the saving transfer lemmas by a simple substitution.

Lemma 3 (Fine-grained reductions are closed under composition). *Let $(A, T_A) \leq_{FGR} (B, T_B)$ and $(B, T_B) \leq_{FGR} (C, T_C)$. It then follows $(A, T_A) \leq_{FGR} (C, T_C)$.*

Finally, composition is proved by carefully verifying time and query bounds on the obvious "nested" simulation of A using the algorithm for C.

3.2 Randomized FGRs

As we will show, many of the problems such as k-SUM and HITTINGSET which have served as starting points for fine-grained reductions have substantially smaller nondeterministic complexities than their conjectured deterministic complexities. From the above closure properties, it will follow that if NSETH is true, none of these problems is SETH-hard under deterministic (or zero-error probabilistic) fine-grained reductions. This leaves a major loophole: these problems might still be SETH-hard under randomized reductions. In this section, we will outline a reason why even randomized SETH-hardness would be somewhat surprising. We introduce a non-uniform version of NSETH, NUNSETH, and show that this hypothesis would imply the non-existence of even randomized SETH-hardness results.

Definition 4. *Let k-TAUT be the tautology problem restricted to k-DNF's. The Non-uniform Nondeterministic Strong Exponential Time Hypothesis (NUNSETH) is the statement : $\forall \epsilon > 0 \exists k \geq 0$, so that there are no nondeterministic circuit families of size $O(2^{n(1-\epsilon)})$ recognizing the language k-TAUT.*

While we do not have any general conservation of non-uniform nondeterministic time by randomized reductions, we do have a limit for the special case of problems that are SETH-hard under randomized reductions.

Lemma 4. *Assume L is SETH-hard with $T(N)$ via a randomized reduction. If NUNSETH, then there is no $\delta > 0$ so that $L \in (N \cap coN)TIME[T^{1-\delta}(n)]$.*

Proof. Let ϵ be the constant corresponding to δ in the reduction, and let $\mathcal{M}^L$ be the corresponding randomized oracle machine. Let $m < n^k$ be the length in bits of a description of a k-SAT formula on n inputs. By repeating $\mathcal{M}^L$ $O(m)$ times and taking the majority answer, we can make the error probability less than 2^{-m}. Therefore, there is one random tape that has no errors, using the standard argument that BPP $\in$ P/poly. Since $\mathcal{M}$ runs in total time $2^{(1-\epsilon)n}$, this tape will have length at most $m2^{(1-\epsilon)n}$, and so will be an exponential improvement over 2^n. Once we have fixed the tape, we can simulate the oracle queries nondeterministically as in the case of deterministic reductions, with total complexity $O(m)$ times what it is for one run. Thus, we get a nondeterministic circuit with total size $O(m2^{(1-\epsilon)n})$. $\qquad\square$

Note that the above argument, in addition to needing advice, multiplies the complexity by an amount polynomial in the input size. While this is not an issue for SAT, it would render the consequences of randomized reductions for problems within P moot, since we are trying to preserve exact polynomial complexities.

While NUNSETH seems plausible, we should exercise some caution before adopting it as an axiom. First, there are no known consequences if NUNSETH fails to be true. Secondly, we originally were going to add equally plausible (to us) hypotheses concerning the total time for bounded round interactive protocols for k-TAUT. However, Williams recently showed that even the general formula counting problem has a Merlin-Arthur protocol of total complexity $\tilde{O}(2^{n/2})$. Because there is a polynomial overhead in making such a protocol a nondeterministic algorithm with advice, this does not contradict NUNSETH. However, it does remind us that counter-intuitive things can happen when randomness and nondeterminism are combined, so we should be cautious in assuming non-uniformity might not speed up computation in this circumstance.

4. WHAT IF ¬NSETH?

SETH is an interesting hypothesis because both ¬SETH and SETH have interesting consequences that seem difficult to prove unconditionally. In this section, we show that the same proofs that show "¬SETH implies circuit lower bounds" can be applied to ¬NSETH as well. This is evidence that NSETH will be hard to refute.

Algorithms for CKT-SAT or CKT-TAUT imply circuit lower bounds (see [27] and [29]). For some restricted circuit classes $\mathcal{C}$, we can reduce satisfiability or tautology of $\mathcal{C}$-circuits to k-SAT or k-TAUT by decomposing $\mathcal{C}$ circuits into a "big OR" of CNF formulas. Thus, both ¬SETH and ¬NSETH imply faster $\mathcal{C}$-circuit analysis algorithms (tautology or satisfiability) for these classes, which imply lower bounds.

The proofs of [17] optimize the reduction of arbitrary nondeterministic time languages to 3-SAT to obtain new "failure of a hardness hypothesis about k-SAT implies circuit lower bounds" results for a variety of circuit classes. The following (see the full version for details) is implicit in their work:

Theorem 1. *We have the following implications from failure of a k-TAUT hardness hypothesis to circuit lower bounds for restricted classes:*

1. *If the nondeterministic exponential time hypothesis (NETH) is false; i.e., for every $\epsilon > 0$, 3-TAUT is in*

time $2^{\epsilon n}$, *then $\exists f \in \mathsf{E}^{\mathsf{NP}}$ such that f does not have linear-size circuits.*

2. *If the nondeterministic strong exponential time hypothesis (NSETH) is false; i.e., there is a $\delta < 1$ such that for every k, k-TAUT is in time $2^{\delta n}$, then $\exists f \in \mathsf{E}^{\mathsf{NP}}$ such that f does not have linear-size series-parallel circuits.*

3. *If there is $\alpha > 0$ such that n^α-TAUT is in time $2^{n-\omega(n/\log\log n)}$, then $\exists f \in \mathsf{E}^{\mathsf{NP}}$ such that f does not have linear-size log-depth circuits.*

Since (by item 2 above) refuting NSETH would give nontrivial circuit lower bounds, it is unlikely to be easy to refute.

5. THE NONDETERMINISTIC TIME COMPLEXITY OF PROBLEMS IN P

How could we show that one language is not reducible to another language? There is an ever-growing web of problems, hypotheses, and reductions that reflect the fine-grained complexity approach to explaining hardness. Could this structure collapse into a radically simpler graph, with just a few equivalence classes? If we assume NSETH, the answer to this question is *probably not as much as one might hope*.

We can broadly categorize computational problems into two sets. In the first category, the deterministic time complexity is higher than both the nondeterministic and co-nondeterministic time complexity. In the second category, at least one of nondeterminism or co-nondeterminism does not help in solving the problem more efficiently. Corollary 1 shows that savings in $(N \cap coN)TIME$ are preserved under deterministic fine-grained reductions. As a result, we can rule out tight reductions from a problem that is hard using nondeterminism or co-nondeterminism to a problem that is easy in $(N \cap coN)TIME$.

If NSETH holds, then k-TAUT is in the category of problems that do not benefit fron nondeterminism.. benefit from co-nondeterminism. So, any problem that is SETH-hard under deterministic reductions also falls in this category.

In this section we explore problems that do benefit from $(N \cap coN)TIME$, i.e. we give nondeterministic algorithms that are faster than their presumed deterministic time complexities. This rules out deterministic fine-grained reductions from CNFSAT to these problems with their presumed time complexities. As a consequence, it is not possible to show that these problems are SETH-hard using a deterministic reduction.

We begin by formalizing the notion of non-reducibility.

Theorem 2 (NSETH implies no reduction from SAT). *If NSETH and $C \in (N \cap coN)TIME[T_C]$ for some problem C, then $(\mathsf{SAT}, 2^n) \not\leq_{FGR} (C, T_C^{1+\gamma})$ for any $\gamma > 0$.*

Proof. Assume NSETH, $(\mathsf{SAT}, 2^n) \leq_{FGR} (C, T_C^{1+\gamma})$, and $C \in (N \cap coN)TIME[T_C]$. By Corollary 1, preservation of $(N \cap coN)TIME$ savings under fine-grained reductions, there exists $\delta > 0$ such that $\mathsf{SAT} \in (N \cap coN)TIME[2^{n(1-\delta)}]$. This contradicts NSETH, therefore it cannot be the case (under NSETH) that $(\mathsf{SAT}, 2^n) \leq_{FGR} (C, T_C)$. $\qquad\square$

Corollary 2 (NSETH implies no reductions from SETH-hard problems). *If NSETH holds and $C \in (N \cap$*

coN)$TIME[T_C]$, then for any B that is SETH-hard under deterministic reductions with time T_B, and $\gamma > 0$, we have

$$(B, T_B) \not\leq_{FGR} (C, T_C^{1+\gamma})$$

Proof. Assume NSETH, and that (B, T_B) is SETH-hard. Therefore, we know $(\mathsf{SAT}, 2^n) \leq_{FGR} (B, T_B)$. Now assume $(B, T_B) \leq_{FGR} (C, T_C^{1+\gamma})$. Then by Lemma 3, composition of fine-grained reductions, we have that $(\mathsf{SAT}, 2^n) \leq_{FGR} (C, T_C)$. But by Theorem 2 above, this is impossible under NSETH. $\qquad\square$

We now give the main result of this section.

Theorem 3. *Under NSETH, there is no deterministic or zero-error fine-grained reduction from SAT or any SETH-hard problem to the following problems with the following time complexities for any $\gamma > 0$.*

- MAXFLOW, *min-cost* MAXFLOW, *and maximum matching with* $T(m) = m^{1+\gamma}$

- HITTINGSET *with* $T(m) = m^{1+\gamma}$

- 3-SUM *with* $T(n) = n^{1.5+\gamma}$

- *All-pairs shortest path with* $T(n) = n^{\frac{3+\omega}{2}+\gamma}$

Note that for graph problems, n refers to the number of vertices, m refers to the number of edges, and ω is the matrix multiplication exponent.

To prove Theorem 3 we give both nondeterministic and co-nondeterministic algorithms for these problems.

5.1 Maximum Flow

The maximum flow problem has been an extensively studied problem for decades and has a large number of theoretical and practical applications. While approximate maximum flow on undirected graphs has a $\tilde{O}(m)$ algorithm [18], where m is the number of edges, no linear time algorithm is known for the exact version of the problem.

A natural question from the point of conditional hardness is if we can prove a superlinear lower bound by proving that the problem is SETH-hard.

In this section we use the max-flow/min-cut theorem to give a $(N \cap coN)TIME$ algorithm for the decision version of max-flow with time linear in the number of edges. Assuming NSETH, we can then conclude that there is no deterministic fine-grained reduction from any SETH-hard problem to maximum flow with a superlinear time bound.

Definition 5 (Maximum Flow Problem). *Let $G = (V, E)$ be a connected directed graph, $s, t \in V$ be vertices and $k \in \mathbb{R}$.*

The maximum flow problem (MAXFLOW) is to decide if there exists a flow from s to t of value at least k.

The nondeterministic algorithm for maximum flow is straightforward and the co-nondeterministic algorithm follows directly for the max-flow/min-cut theorem.

Lemma 5. MAXFLOW $\in (N \cap coN)TIME[O(m)]$

Proof. For the nondeterministic algorithm, nondeterministically guess the flow on each edge. We can verify in linear time that the value of the flow is at least k, that no edge flow exceeds the edge capacity, and that for all nodes the inflow is equal to the outflow.

For the co-nondeterministic algorithm, nondeterministically guess a cut (S, T) such that $s \in S$ and $t \in T$ with value l where $l < k$. By the max-flow/min-cut theorem there is no flow with value strictly greater than l. The value of a cut can be computed in $O(m)$ time. $\qquad\square$

This completes the part of Theorem 3 concerning maximum flow. In contrast, the single-source maximum flow problem requires quadratic time under SETH [2]. In the single-source maximum flow problem we are given a source s and need to output the maximum flow from s to all other nodes. As a consequence, there is no deterministic fine-grained reduction from single-source maximum flow to maximum flow under NSETH.

5.2 Hitting Set

Given two families of non-empty sets $\mathcal{S}$ and $\mathcal{T}$ defined on universe U, a set $S \in \mathcal{S}$ is a *hitting set* if it has nonempty intersections with all members in $\mathcal{T}$. The HITTINGSET problem accepts input $(\mathcal{S}, \mathcal{T}, U)$ iff

$$\exists S \in \mathcal{S} \; \forall T \in \mathcal{T} \; \exists u \in U \;\; ((u \in S) \wedge (u \in T))$$

Let the size of input be $m = \sum_{S \in \mathcal{S}} |S| + \sum_{T \in \mathcal{T}} |T|$. We assume for any $u \in U$, we can in constant time decide if $u \in S$ or $u \in T$. It is conjectured, that this problem does not admit a subquadratic time algorithm [4]. We show that HITTINGSET and its negation are both solvable in nondeterministic linear time.

Lemma 6. HITTINGSET $\in (N \cap coN)TIME[O(m)]$

HITTINGSET can be solved nondeterministically in linear time, by guessing an S, enumerating all $T \in \mathcal{T}$, and guessing a $u \in T$.

The negation of the HITTINGSET problem ¬HITTINGSET, which is defined as

$$\forall S \in \mathcal{S} \; \exists T \in \mathcal{T} \; \forall u \in U \;\; ((u \notin S) \vee (u \notin T))$$

can be solved by the following algorithm.

```
for each S ∈ S do
    Nondeterministically select T from T;
    for each u ∈ S do
        if u ∈ T then
        │   Reject.
        end
    end
end
Accept.
```

Algorithm 1: Algorithm for ¬HITTINGSET

The algorithm runs in time $O(\sum_{S \in \mathcal{S}} |S|) = O(m)$.

The full version generalizes this algorithm for model checking of arbitrary k-quantifier sentences with at least one existential quantifier and ending with a universal quantifier.

5.3 Min-Cost Maximum Flow

The min-cost maximum flow problem is an important generalization of the maximum flow problem that also generalizes problems such as shortest path and bipartite minimum cost perfect matching.

In the min-cost maximum flow problem on a graph $G = (V, E)$ we consider flow networks where the edges e have aditional costs $\psi(e)$. The cost of a flow is defined as

$$\sum_{e \in E} \psi(e) \text{flow}(e)$$

Definition 6. *Let $G = (V, E)$ be a connected directed graph with capacity constraints and edge costs, let $s, t \in V$ be vertices and $k, c \in \mathbb{R}$.*

The min-cost maximum flow problem *is to decide if there either exists a flow from s to t of value strictly more than k, or if there is a flow from s to t of value exactly k and cost at most c.*

Orlin [22] gives a $O(m^2)$ algorithm for min-cost maxflow. In this section consider the question if it is possible to show SETH-hardness of this problem and show that there is a $O(m)$ nondeterministic and co-nondeterministic algorithm. Therefore, assuming NSETH, this problem is not SETH-hard under deterministic reductions for any superlinear time.

It is easy to see that this problem is in $\mathsf{NTIME}[O(m)]$ where m is the number of edges. Simply either guess a maximum flow with minimum cost and verify that it is indeed a flow with the correct value and cost. We therefore concentrate on the co-nondeterministic time complexity.

Lemma 7. *The min-cost maximum flow problem is in $(N \cap coN)TIME[O(m)]$.*

Proof. Klein [19] showed that a for any flow f, there is a flow of the same value as f but smaller cost if and only if there is a negative cost cycle in the residual graph.

Furthermore, as oserved in the analysis of the Bellmann-Ford algorithm [7, 12], there is a nondeterministic algorithm for the nonexistence of a negative weight cycle in a graph. A potential for a weighted graph $G = (V, E, w)$ is a map $p : V \to \mathbb{R}$ such that for all edges $(u, v) \in E$ we have $p(v) \leq p(u) + w(u, v)$. Bellman and Ford show that there is a negative weight cycle in G if and only if there is no potential for G.

The co-nondeterministic algorithm for min-cost maximum flow has two cases. If there is no flow of value k, then we non-deterministically guess a cut of value less than k. Otherwise, nondeterministically guess a flow of value k with minimum cost. We then certify that the flow is a maximum flow by guessing a cut of value k. Furthermore we guess a potential for the residual graph. The cut certifies that there is no flow of value greater than k, and the potential certifies that there is no maximum flow of smaller cost.

Verifying all nondeterministic guesses can be done in time $O(m)$. $\qquad\square$

Since the maximum flow problem is a generalization of the min-cost maximum flow problem, Lemma 5 also follows as a corollary of 7.

5.4 Maximum Matching

The maximum matching problem in general graphs is one of the most fundamental problems in computer science. The maximum matching problem is in time $O(m\sqrt{n})$ [20], matching the time complexity of the bipartite case [14].

In this section we show that there is a linear time co-nondeterministic algorithm, and that there is therefore no fine-grained reduction from CNFSAT to maximum matching for any superlinear time, assuming NSETH.

Definition 7 (Maximum Matching Problem). *The maximum matching problem is given a graph $G = (V, E)$ and a number k, is to decide if there exists a matching of size at least k.*

We give an $O(m)$ co-nondeterministc algorithm for this problem. The $O(m)$ nondeterministic algorithm is trivial.

Lemma 8. *The maximum matching problem is in $(N \cap coN)TIME[O(m)]$.*

Proof. Edmonds Theorem [11] relates maximum matchings of a graph $G = (V, E)$ with odd set covers. An odd set cover is a map $f : V \to \mathbb{N}$, such that each edge is either adjacent to a vertex v with $f(v) = 1$, or is adjacent to two vertices u, v such that $f(u) = f(v) \geq 2$. Furthermore, for $n_i = |\{v \mid v \in V, f(v) = i\}|$ we have n_i is odd for all $i \geq 2$.

For an odd set cover O, let $val(O) = n_1 + \sum_{i \geq 2} \lfloor \frac{n_i}{2} \rfloor$ be the value of the set cover. Edmonds Theorem says that for any matching M and any odd set cover O, we have $|M| \leq val(O)$. Furthermure, for any maximum matching M there is an odd set cover O such that $|M| = val(O)$. Therefore a matching M is maximum if and only if there is an odd set cover O such that $|M| = val(O)$.

The co-nondeterministic algorithm then guesses a maximum matching M and an odd set cover O such that $|M| = val(O)$.

Verifying that M is a matching and O an odd set cover, as well as computing the value of the set cover can easily be done in time $O(m)$. $\qquad\square$

5.5 3-SUM

The conjecture that the 3-SUM problem admits no $O(n^{2-\epsilon})$ algorithm for any $\epsilon > 0$ has proven immensely useful to show the conditional hardness of a large number of problems (e.g. [13, 10, 3]), most of which are not known to be hard under SETH. A fine-grained reduction from SAT to 3-SUM would therefore have a large impact, proving the 3-SUM conjecture under SETH.

We give a subquadratic algorithm for 3-SUM in $(N \cap coN)TIME$, which rules out a deterministic fine-grained reduction from SAT to 3-SUM under NSETH.

Definition 8. *Given n integers $a_1 \ldots a_n$ in the range $[-n^c, n^c]$ for some constant c, the 3-Sum problem (3-SUM) is the problem of determining if there is a triple $1 \leq i, j, k \leq n$ such that $a_i + a_j + a_k = 0$.*

Lemma 9. $3\text{-SUM} \in (N \cap coN)TIME[\tilde{O}(n^{1.5})]$

Proof. There is a trivial constant time nondeterministic algorithm of guessing the triplet of indices. The more interesting part is to show that there is an efficient nondeterministic algorithm to show that there is no such triplet.

We nondeterministically guess a proof of the form (p, t, S), such that

- p is a prime number, such that $p \leq \mathbf{prime}_{n^{1.5}}$, where $\mathbf{prime}_i$ is i-th prime number.

- t is a nonnegative integer with $t \leq 3cn^{1.5} \log n$ such that $t = |\{(i, j, k) \mid a_i + a_j + a_k = 0 \mod p\}|$ is the number of three-sums modulo p.

- $S = \{(i_1, j_1, k_1), \ldots, (i_t, j_t, k_t)\}$ is a set of t triples of indices, such that for all $r : 0 < r \leq t$ we have $a_{i_r} + a_{j_r} + a_{k_r} = 0 \mod p$ and $a_{i_r} + a_{j_r} + a_{k_r} \neq 0$

We first show that such a proof exists. Let us assume that there is no triple of elements that sum up to zero. Let R be the set of all pairs $((i, j, k), p)$, such that p is a prime $\leq \mathbf{prime}_{n^{1.5}}$ and $a_i + a_j + a_k = 0 \mod p$. Then $|R| \leq n^3 \log(3n^c) < 3cn^3 \log n$, as any integer z can have at most $\log(z)$ prime divisors. Then, by a simple counting argument, there indeed exists a prime $p_0 \leq \mathbf{prime}_{n^{1.5}}$, such that the number of pairs of the form $((i, j, k), p_0)$ in R is at most $\frac{3cn^3 \log n}{n^{1.5}} = 3cn^{1.5} \log n$).

To verify a proof of that form we first need to check that for all $r \leq t$:

$$a_{i_r} + a_{j_r} + a_{k_r} = 0 \mod p$$

$$a_{i_r} + a_{j_r} + a_{k_r} \neq 0$$

Then we compute the number of 3-sums modulo p and compare it with t. In order to do this we expand the following expression using Fast Fourier Transform in time $\tilde{O}(t)$:

$$\left(\sum_i x^{(a_i \mod p)} \right)^3$$

Let b_j be a coefficient before x^j. We need to check that

$$b_0 + b_p + b_{2p} = t$$

If it is true, then the proof is accepted, otherwise it is rejected.

The time complexity of verification is $\tilde{O}(n^{1.5})$ for reading and checking the properties of all the triples and $\tilde{O}(t) = \tilde{O}(n^{1.5})$ for counting the number of triples that sum to 0 modulo p. Therefore the total time complexity is $\tilde{O}(n^{1.5})$. $\square$

5.6 All-pairs shortest paths and related problems

The All-pairs shortest path problem (APSP) is to find the shortest path in a graph between any pair of nodes. Like the 3-SUM conjecture and SETH, the conjecture that APSP does not admit an $O(n^{3-\epsilon})$ time algorithm for any $\epsilon > 0$ has been used successfully to show the conditional hardness of a number of problems, e.g. [33, 25].

We use a similar technique as in the algorithm for 3-SUM to show that the Zero Weight Triangle problem (ZWT), which is hard under APSP, admits an efficient algorithm in $(N \cap coN)TIME$.

Definition 9. *Given a tripartite graph $G(V_1, V_2, V_3, E)$ with $|V_1| = |V_2| = |V_3| = n$ and edge weights in $[-n^a, n^a]$, the Zero Weight Triangle problem is the problem of determining if there is a triangle such that the sum of the edge weights is 0.*

We first show that if the range is small enough, then we can count the number of zero weight triangles efficiently.

Lemma 10. *For a prime p, there is a deterministic algorithm for counting the number of zero weight triangles mod p in time $O(n^\omega p)$*

Proof. For $i \in GF(p)$, let $q(i)$ be the polynomial x^i. Let A be the weight matrix of the input graph G ($\mod p$). We

define matrix B as $B[i, j] = q(A[i, j])$. For a polynomial r and integer i, let $b_{i,r}$ be the coefficient of x^i in r. Every triangle with weight zero mod p has weight either 0, p and $3p$. We have that $b_{j, B^3[i,i]}$ is the number of triangles of weight j that involve vertex i. Therefore

$$\sum_{i=1}^{n} \sum_{j \in \{0, p, 2p\}} b_{j, B^3[i,i]} = 3t \qquad (1)$$

where t is the number of zero weight triangles modulo p.

The time to compute B^3 is $O(n^\omega p)$ if we multiply the polynomials using Fast Fourier Transform. $\square$

In particular, we will be using Lemma 10 to verify that our nondeterministic guess of the number of false positives is correct.

Lemma 11. *The Zero Weight Triangle Problem is in $(N \cap coN)TIME[O(n^{\frac{\omega+3}{2}})]$.*

Proof. As for 3-SUM, the nondeterministic algorithm is trivial and we concentrate on the co-nondeterministic algorithm.

Let $\mu = \frac{3-\omega}{2}$. Further let c be a large constant such that there are at least n^μ primes in the range $R = [n^\mu, cn^\mu \log n]$. We assume that there is no zero weight triangle and consider any fixed triangle. The total weight of the triangle is in the range $[-3n^a, 3n^a]$ and the number of primes $p \in R$ such that the triangle has weight $0 \mod p$ is at most $\log(3n^a)/\log(n^\mu) < \frac{2}{\mu}a$. Since R contains at least n^μ primes, there is a prime $p \in R$ such that the number of triangles with weight $0 \mod p$ is at most $\frac{2}{\mu}an^{\frac{3+\omega}{2}}$.

The nondeterministic algorithm now proceeds as follows: Nondeterministically pick p as above. By Lemma 10 we can deterministically count the number t of triangles with weight $0 \mod p$ in time $O(n^\omega p) = O(n^{\frac{3+\omega}{2}})$. Nondeterministically pick t distinct triangles and check that each of them has weight $w \neq 0$ with $w = 0 \mod p$.

The total time is bounded by $O(n^{\frac{3+\omega}{2}})$ as claimed. $\square$

Corollary 3. *APSP $\in (N \cap coN)TIME[\tilde{O}(n^{\frac{3+\omega}{2}})]$.*

Proof. A deterministic fine-grained reduction from the problem of finding a negative weight triangle to ZWT can be found in [25], such that the negative weight triangle problem is also in $(N \cap coN)TIME[\tilde{O}(n^{\frac{3+\omega}{2}})]$.

Finally, [33] give a deterministic fine-grained reduction from APSP to the negative weight triangle problem with time $\tilde{O}(n^2 T(n^{1/3}))$, where $T(n)$ is the time complexity of the negative weight triangle problem.

Instead of applying this reduction directly, which would still give a subcubic nondeterministic upper bound for APSP, we instead modify their reduction to a nondeterministic reduction that preserves the savings in the exponent. The reduction from [33] loses savings in the exponent when reducing from min-plus product to negative weight triangle. The fine-grained reduction from APSP to min-plus product is folklore and does not change the exponent.

For two matrices A and B the min-plus product C is the matrix such that $C[i, j] = \min_k \{A[i, k] + B[k, j]\}$. Given an instance of min-plus product, nondeterministically guess C as well as a matrix K such that $K[i, j] = \operatorname{argmin}_k \{A[i, k] + B[k, j]\}$. We can easily check that $C[i, j] = A[i, K[i, j]] +$

$B[K[i,j],j]$ for all i and j, which proves that none of the entries in C are too large.

To verify none of the entries in C are too small, we construct a complete $n \times n \times n$ tripartite graph $G = (V_1, V_2, V_3, E)$ such that matrix $-A$ is the weight matrix for the edges between V_1 and V_2, $-B$ corresponds to the weights between V_2 and V_3, and C corresponds to the weights between V_1 and V_3. There are i, j, k such that $C[i,j] < A[i,k] + B[k,j]$ if and only if there is a negative weight triangle in this graph.

This reduction along with the co-nondeterministic algorithm for ZWT gives a nondeterministic algorithm for APSP with the claimed time complexity. $\qquad\square$

Note that [33] in fact give a sizable list of problems that are equivalent to APSP under subcubic deterministic fine-grained reductions (including negative weight triangle, but not zero weight triangle). Our non-reducibility result therefore applies to all of these problems.

6. CHARACTERIZING THE QUANTIFIER STRUCTURE OF SETH-HARD GRAPH PROBLEMS

There are many problems within P that are known to be SETH-hard, but few of them are graph problems. And of the ones that are, they tend to have similar logical forms. For instance, k-Dominating Set [23] is definable by a $\forall^k\exists$ quantified formula; Graph Diameter-2 and Bipartite Graph Dominated Vertex [8] are definable by $\forall\forall\exists$ quantified formulas. Here we study the relations between SETH-hardness and the logical structures of model checking problems. The paper by Ryan Williams [28] explored the first-order graph properties on dense graphs, while in this paper, we look into sparse graphs whose input is a list of edges.

We define "graph property" quite broadly. The input to a graph property is a many-sorted universe that we view as sets of vertices, together with a number of unary relations (node colors), and binary relations, viewed as different categories or colors of edges. The binary relations can in general be directed. We specify the problem to be solved by a first order sentence. Let φ be a first order sentence in prenex normal form, which has k quantifiers.

$$\varphi = Q_1 x_1 \in X_1, Q_2 x_2 \in X_2, \ldots Q_k x_k \in X_k \psi$$

or shortened as

$$\varphi = Q_1 x_1 Q_2 x_2 \ldots Q_k x_k \psi$$

where φ is a quantifier-free formula whose atoms are unary or binary predicates on $x_1, \ldots, x_k$.

An instance of the model checking problem of φ gives k ($k \geq 3$) specifies sets $X_1, \ldots X_k$, where variable x_i is an element of set X_i, and unary or binary relations on these sets. (X_i needn't be disjoint, so allowing them to be viewed as distinct only increases the expressive power. We assume equality is one of the relations, so we can tell when $x_i = x_j$.) The sets $X_1, \ldots, X_k$ can be considered as the sets of nodes in a k-partite graph, and the values of a binary predicate can be considered as edges in the graph, i.e. for predicate P, $P(x_i, x_j) = true$ means there is an edge between nodes x_i and x_j. We refer to the k-partite graph with edges defined by predicate P as G_P, and the union of graphs defined on all predicates as G. The data structures used to code the relations are as follows: For each unary relation, an array of

Booleans indexed by the vertices saying whether the relation holds, and for each binary predicate, the list representation of the corresponding directed graph. We want to see if φ is true for the input model.

Examples of this problem include k-Clique, which is defined by

$$\varphi = \exists x_1 \ldots \exists x_k \bigwedge_{i,j \in \{1,\ldots,k\}, i \neq j} E(x_i, x_j)$$

and k-Dominating Set, defined by

$$\varphi = \exists x_1 \ldots \exists x_k \forall x_{k+1} \left(E(x_1, x_{k+1}) \vee \cdots \vee E(x_k, x_{k+1}) \right)$$

and Graph Radius-2, defined by

$$\varphi = \exists x_1 \forall x_2 \exists x_3 \left(E(x_1, x_3) \wedge E(x_3, x_2) \right)$$

We let $n = \max_i |X_i|$ be the maximum size of the node parts, and m be the number of edges in the union of the graphs. The size is $n + m$, but for convenience, we will assume $m > n$ and use m as the size.

The maximum deterministic complexity of a k-quantifier formula for $k \geq 2$ is $O(m^{k-1})$. For $k = 2$, this is just linear in the input size, so matching lower bounds follow. So the interesting case is $k \geq 3$. If SETH is true, some formulas require approximately this time. But if NSETH holds, all such formulas that are SETH hard are of the same logical form. This is made precise as follows:

Theorem 4. *Let $k \geq 3$. If NSETH is true, then there is a k-quantifier formula whose model checking problem is $O(m^{k-1})$ SETH-hard, and all such formulas have the form $\forall^{k-1}\exists$ or $\exists^{k-1}\forall$.*

Theorem 4 comes directly from the following lemmas:

Lemma 12. *If SETH or NSETH is true, then there are $\forall^{k-1}\exists$ problems that are SETH-hard for time $O(m^{k-1})$.*

Thus by negating φ, the $\exists^{k-1}\forall$ problems are also hard under SETH.

On the other hand if a problem is of any form other than $\forall^{k-1}\exists$, we will show it has smaller nondeterministic complexity. Such a problem has either exactly one existential quantifier not in the innermost position, no existential quantifiers, or at least two existential quantifiers.

Lemma 13. *If φ has exactly one existential quantifier, but it is not on the innermost position, then it can be solved in $O(m^{k-2})$ nondeterminisitic time.*

Lemma 14. *If φ has more than one existential quantifiers, then it can be solved in time $O(m^{k-2})$ nondeterministically.*

These problems can be solved by guessing the existentially quantified variables, and exhaustive search on universally quantified variables. Because there are at most $k - 2$ universal quantifiers, the algorithm runs in time $O(m^{k-2})$.

Lemma 15. *If all quantifiers are universal, then it can be solved in deterministic time $O(m^{k-1.5})$.*

Thus, only $\forall^{k-1}\exists$ formulas require $O(m^{k-1})$ nondeterministic time, and by looking at the complements, only $\exists^{k-1}\forall$ formulas require $O(m^{k-1})$ co-nondeterministic time. Thus, assuming NSETH, only these two types of first-order properties might be SETH-hard for the maximum difficulty of a k-quantifier formula.

Proofs of lemmas 12, 13 and 15 can be found in the full version of the paper.

7. CONSEQUENCES FOR VERIFICATION OF SOLUTIONS

Besides implying that some problems are not SETH-hard, NSETH also implies some new lower bounds on problems in P. Namely, if NSETH is true, then problems such as Fréchet distance, edit distance, and longest common substring also require quadratic co-nondeterministic time (i.e., to show that the optimal solution has cost that exceeds a given value). This immediately implies that, even given a solution, testing optimality requires quadratic time. We can formalize this as follows:

Theorem 5. *Let* $\mathrm{Opt}(x)$ *be the optimization problem, given* x, *find* $\max_{y,|y|=l(|x|)} F(x,y)$, *for some* F *that is computable in time* $T_F(n+l(n)) \geq n+l(n)$. *The verification problem* Ver *is: given* x *and* y, *is* y *an optimal solution for* Opt, *i.e., is there no* y' *with* $F(x,y') > F(x,y)$. *Assume that* Opt *is* SETH-*hard for some* $T(n)$ *which is greater than* $T_F^{1+\gamma}(n+l(n))$ *for some* $\gamma > 0$. *Then if* NSETH, Ver *cannot be solved in any time* T' *so that* $T_{\mathrm{Ver}}(n+l(n)) < T'^{1-\epsilon}(n)$ *for any* $\epsilon > 0$.

Proof. Assume not, that Ver can be solved in some time T' with $T_{\mathrm{Ver}}(n+l(n)) < T'^{1-\epsilon}(n)$. Then we can compute the function Opt in $\mathsf{NTIME}((T_{\mathrm{Ver}}(n+l(n)) + T_F(n+l(n))))$ as follows:

Non-deterministically guess an optimal solution y and run the algorithm for Ver on the pair (x,y). If it is optimal (i.e., in Ver), return $F(x,y)$. The total time is $l(n)$ to guess y, plus $T_F(n+l(n))$ to compute F, plus $T_{\mathrm{Ver}}(n+l(n))$.

From the assumption that Opt is SETH-hard for time $T(n)$, and since the time complexity of the above procedure is $O(T(n)^{1-\epsilon})$ for some $\epsilon > 0$, it follows that TAUT is in time $2^{n(1-\delta)}$ for some $\delta > 0$. This contradicts NSETH. $\square$

So NSETH gives us a way to argue that not only finding but verifying optimal solutions is computationally intensive.

8. CONCLUSIONS AND OPEN PROBLEMS

A theme running through computational complexity is that looking at general relationships between models of computing and complexity classes can frequently shed light on the difficulty of specific problems. In this paper, we introduce this general technique to the study of fine-grained complexity by comparing nondeterministic complexities of problems. This raises the more general question of what other notions and models of complexity might be useful in distinguishing the fine-grained complexity of problems. For example, we show that neither 3-SUM or all-pairs shortest path can be SETH-hard if NSETH holds. This still leaves open the possibility that the two conjectures are equivalent to each other (if not to SETH). One might be able to prove such an equivalence, or give evidence against it by showing a different notion of complexity that distinguishes the two and is preserved by FGR.

9. ACKNOWLEDGMENTS

We would like to thank Amir Abboud, Karl Bringmann, Bart Jansen, Sebastian Krinninger, Virginia Vassilevska Williams, Ryan Williams and the anonymous reviewers for many helpful comments on an earlier draft.

This research is supported by NSF grant CCF-1213151 from the Division of Computing and Communication Foundations. Any opinions, findings and conclusions or recommendations expressed in this material are those of the authors and do not necessarily reflect the views of the National Science Foundation. This work was done in part while the author was visiting the Simons Institute for the Theory of Computing, supported by the Simons Foundation and by the DIMACS/Simons Collaboration in Cryptography through NSF grant #CNS-1523467.

10. REFERENCES

[1] A. Abboud, A. Backurs, and V. V. Williams. Quadratic-time hardness of LCS and other sequence similarity measures. *CoRR*, abs/1501.07053, 2015.

[2] A. Abboud, V. Vassilevska Williams, and H. Yu. Matching triangles and basing hardness on an extremely popular conjecture. In *Proceedings of the Forty-Seventh Annual ACM on Symposium on Theory of Computing*, STOC '15, pages 41–50, New York, NY, USA, 2015. ACM.

[3] A. Abboud and V. V. Williams. Popular conjectures imply strong lower bounds for dynamic problems. In *55th IEEE Annual Symposium on Foundations of Computer Science, FOCS 2014, Philadelphia, PA, USA, October 18-21, 2014*, pages 434–443, 2014.

[4] V. V. W. Amir Abboud and J. Wang. Approximation and fixed parameter subquadratic algorithms for radius and diameter. *arXiv preprint arXiv:1506.01799 (2015)*, pages 434–443, 2015.

[5] A. Backurs and P. Indyk. Edit distance cannot be computed in strongly subquadratic time (unless SETH is false). In *Proceedings of the Forty-Seventh Annual ACM on Symposium on Theory of Computing, STOC 2015, Portland, OR, USA, June 14-17, 2015*, pages 51–58, 2015.

[6] C. Beck and R. Impagliazzo. Strong ETH holds for regular resolution. In *Symposium on Theory of Computing Conference, STOC'13, Palo Alto, CA, USA, June 1-4, 2013*, pages 487–494, 2013.

[7] R. Bellman. On a routing problem. Technical report, DTIC Document, 1956.

[8] M. Borassi, P. Crescenzi, and M. Habib. Into the square - on the complexity of quadratic-time solvable problems. *CoRR*, abs/1407.4972, 2014.

[9] K. Bringmann. Why walking the dog takes time: Frechet distance has no strongly subquadratic algorithms unless SETH fails. *CoRR*, abs/1404.1448, 2014.

[10] M. De Berg, M. M. de Groot, and M. H. Overmars. Perfect binary space partitions. *Computational Geometry*, 7(1):81–91, 1997.

[11] J. Edmonds. Maximum matching and a polyhedron with 0, l-vertices. *J. Res. Nat. Bur. Standards B*, 69(1965):125–130, 1965.

[12] L. R. Ford Jr. Network flow theory. Technical report, DTIC Document, 1956.

[13] A. Gajentaan and M. H. Overmars. On a class of o (n 2) problems in computational geometry. *Computational geometry*, 5(3):165–185, 1995.

[14] J. E. Hopcroft and R. M. Karp. An n^5/2 algorithm for maximum matchings in bipartite graphs. *SIAM Journal on computing*, 2(4):225–231, 1973.

[15] R. Impagliazzo and R. Paturi. On the complexity of k-sat. *Journal of Computer and System Sciences*, 62(2):367 – 375, 2001.

[16] R. Impagliazzo, R. Paturi, and F. Zane. Which problems have strongly exponential complexity? *Journal of Computer and System Sciences*, 63(4):512 – 530, 2001.

[17] H. Jahanjou, E. Miles, and E. Viola. Local reductions. *Electronic Colloquium on Computational Complexity (ECCC)*, 20:99, 2013.

[18] J. A. Kelner, Y. T. Lee, L. Orecchia, and A. Sidford. An almost-linear-time algorithm for approximate max flow in undirected graphs, and its multicommodity generalizations. In *Proceedings of the Twenty-Fifth Annual ACM-SIAM Symposium on Discrete Algorithms*, SODA '14, pages 217–226. SIAM, 2014.

[19] M. Klein. A primal method for minimal cost flows with applications to the assignment and transportation problems. *Management Science*, 14(3):205–220, 1967.

[20] S. Micali and V. V. Vazirani. An o (v| v| c| e|) algoithm for finding maximum matching in general graphs. In *Foundations of Computer Science, 1980., 21st Annual Symposium on*, pages 17–27. IEEE, 1980.

[21] D. Moeller, R. Paturi, and S. Schneider. Subquadratic algorithms for succinct stable matching. 2015.

[22] J. B. Orlin. A faster strongly polynomial minimum cost flow algorithm. *Operations research*, 41(2):338–350, 1993.

[23] M. Patrascu and R. Williams. On the possibility of faster SAT algorithms. In *Proceedings of the Twenty-First Annual ACM-SIAM Symposium on Discrete Algorithms, SODA 2010, Austin, Texas, USA, January 17-19, 2010*, pages 1065–1075, 2010.

[24] P. Pudlak and R. Impagliazzo. A lower bound for dll algorithms for k-sat. In *Proceedings of the Eleventh Annual ACM-SIAM Symposium on Discrete Algorithms, SODA 2000, San Francisco, CA, USA, January 9-11, 2000*, pages 128–136, 2000.

[25] V. Vassilevska and R. Williams. Finding, minimizing, and counting weighted subgraphs. In *Proceedings of the forty-first annual ACM symposium on Theory of computing*, pages 455–464. ACM, 2009.

[26] R. Williams. A new algorithm for optimal constraint satisfaction and its implications. *Electronic Colloquium on Computational Complexity (ECCC)*, (032), 2004.

[27] R. Williams. Improving exhaustive search implies superpolynomial lower bounds. *SIAM J. Comput.*, 42(3):1218–1244, 2013.

[28] R. Williams. Faster decision of first-order graph properties. In *Joint Meeting of the Twenty-Third EACSL Annual Conference on Computer Science Logic (CSL) and the Twenty-Ninth Annual ACM/IEEE Symposium on Logic in Computer Science (LICS), CSL-LICS '14, Vienna, Austria, July 14 - 18, 2014*, pages 80:1–80:6, 2014.

[29] R. Williams. Nonuniform ACC circuit lower bounds. *J. ACM*, 61(1):2:1–2:32, 2014.

[30] R. Williams. Personal communication. 2015.

[31] V. V. Williams. Stoc tutorial: Hardness and equivalences in p. http://theory.stanford.edu/~virgi/stoctutorial.html.

[32] V. V. Williams. Hardness of easy problems: Basing hardness on popular conjectures such as the strong exponential time hypothesis (invited talk). In *LIPIcs-Leibniz International Proceedings in Informatics.*, volume 43, 2015.

[33] V. V. Williams and R. Williams. Subcubic equivalences between path, matrix and triangle problems. In *Foundations of Computer Science (FOCS), 2010 51st Annual IEEE Symposium on*, pages 645–654. IEEE, 2010.

The Space "Just Above" BQP

Scott Aaronson
Massachusetts Institute of
Technology
Cambridge, MA, USA
aaronson@csail.mit.edu

Adam Bouland
Massachusetts Institute of
Technology
Cambridge, MA, USA
adam@csail.mit.edu

Joseph Fitzsimons
Singapore University of
Technology and Design
Centre for Quantum
Technologies, National
University of Singapore
Singapore
joe.fitzsimons@nus.edu.sg

Mitchell Lee
Massachusetts Institute of
Technology
Cambridge, MA, USA
mitchlee@mit.edu

ABSTRACT

We explore the space "just above" BQP by defining a complexity class naCQP (non-adaptive Collapse-free Quantum Polynomial time) which is larger than BQP but does not contain NP relative to an oracle. The class is defined by imagining that quantum computers can perform (non-adaptive) measurements that do not collapse the wavefunction. This non-physical model of computation can efficiently solve problems such as Graph Isomorphism and Approximate Shortest Vector which are believed to be intractable for quantum computers. Furthermore, it can search an unstructured N-element list in $\tilde{O}(N^{1/3})$ time, but no faster than $\Omega(N^{1/4})$, and hence cannot solve NP-hard problems in a black box manner. In short, this model of computation is more powerful than standard quantum computation, but only slightly so. This is surprising as most modifications of BQP increase the power of quantum computation to NP or beyond.

1. INTRODUCTION

Quantum computers are believed to be strictly more powerful than classical computers, but not so much more powerful that they can solve NP-hard problems efficiently. In particular, it is known that BQP, the class of languages recognizable in polynomial time by a quantum algorithm [11], does not contain NP "relative to an oracle." This means that there is some "black box" problem $\mathcal{O}$ for which $\mathsf{BQP}^{\mathcal{O}} \not\supseteq \mathsf{NP}^{\mathcal{O}}$. (For more information about the terminology, see [8].) On the other hand, many seemingly innocuous modifications of quantum mechanics—for example, allowing nonlinear transformations, non-unitary transformations, postselec-

Permission to make digital or hard copies of all or part of this work for personal or classroom use is granted without fee provided that copies are not made or distributed for profit or commercial advantage and that copies bear this notice and the full citation on the first page. Copyrights for components of this work owned by others than the author(s) must be honored. Abstracting with credit is permitted. To copy otherwise, or republish, to post on servers or to redistribute to lists, requires prior specific permission and/or a fee. Request permissions from Permissions@acm.org.

ITCS'16, January 14–16, 2016, Cambridge, MA, USA.
Copyright is held by the owner/author(s). Publication rights licensed to ACM.
ACM 978-1-4503-4057-1/16/01 ...$15.00.
DOI: http://dx.doi.org/10.1145/2840728.2840739 .

tion, or measurement statistics based on the pth power of the amplitudes for $p \neq 2$—increase the power of quantum computation drastically enough that they can solve NP-hard problems (and even #P-hard problems) efficiently [6][3]. As a result, it is difficult to find natural complexity classes which are bigger than BQP but which don't contain NP. Quantum mechanics appears to be an "island in theoryspace" in terms of its complexity-theoretic properties [3].

In this work, we explore a natural modification of quantum mechanics to obtain a complexity class which is only "slightly more powerful" than BQP. In quantum mechanics, when a system is measured, the state of the system "collapses" to its observed value; one cannot observe a quantum system without perturbing it. Here we consider the power of quantum computers which can also make "non-collapsing measurements," which are identical to usual quantum measurements except that they do not perturb the state. We call the class of problems decidable in polynomial time in this model CQP, which stands for "Collapse-free Quantum Polynomial time." We additionally consider a weaker version of this model, naCQP (non-adaptive CQP) in which the quantum operations performed must be independent of the non-collapsing measurement outcomes.

We show that quantum computers equipped with this power (even in the non-adaptive case) can solve the Graph Isomorphism problem in polynomial time, and in fact can solve any problem in SZK in a black-box manner. Since standard quantum computers cannot solve SZK-hard problems in a black-box manner [1], this implies that there is an oracle $\mathcal{O}$ for which $\mathsf{BQP}^{\mathcal{O}} \neq \mathsf{naCQP}^{\mathcal{O}}$. This is evidence that quantum computation with non-collapsing measurements is more powerful than standard quantum computation. Furthermore, we upper bound the power of both CQP and naCQP by showing that $\mathsf{naCQP} \subseteq \mathsf{CQP} \subseteq \mathsf{BPP}^{\mathsf{PP}}$, so both naCQP and CQP are in the counting hierarchy. In comparison the best known classical upper bound for BQP is AWPP which is contained in PP [14][7].

We also demonstrate that if (even non-adaptive) non-collapsing measurements are possible, then there is a quantum algorithm that searches an unstructured list of N elements in $\tilde{O}(N^{1/3})$ time. Furthermore any such algorithm takes at least $\Omega(N^{1/4})$ time in the non-adaptive case. While the upper bound is simple, the proof of the lower bound uses a hybrid argument [10] and properties of Markov chains. We conclude that naCQP does not contain NP relative to an oracle. To our knowledge this represents the only known complexity class larger than BQP which provably does not admit polynomial time black-box algorithms for NP-hard problems. This is what we mean when we say naCQP is only "slightly more powerful" than BQP. Proving the analogous lower bound for CQP remains open, so it is possible that CQP could be more powerful than naCQP.

Note that introducing non-collapsing measurements into quantum mechanics allows for many strange phenomena. In particular, it allows for faster-than-light communication, it allows for quantum cloning[1], and it renders quantum query complexity and quantum communication complexity meaningless. We describe these strange consequences of non-collapsing measurements in detail in Appendix A. For this reason, we are not suggesting that "non-collapsing measurements" should be considered seriously as an amendment to quantum theory. Rather we are simply showing that non-collapsing measurements have interesting complexity-theoretic properties - namely, that they can be used to define an complexity class which is "just above" BQP.

2. RELATION TO PRIOR WORK

Our work is inspired by previous work on quantum computing with hidden variables by Aaronson [2]. Aaronson defines a class DQP ("Dynamical Quantum Polynomial Time") by imagining a hidden variable theory is true, and that an experimenter can view the evolution of the hidden variables in real time. Additionally, he requires that the quantum operations are non-adaptive to the hidden variable values (similar to our class naCQP). He shows that with this power one can search in $\tilde{O}(N^{1/3})$ time and solve any problem in SZK in polynomial time. He additionally claims one cannot search in faster than $\Omega(N^{1/3})$ time in this model. Unfortunately, there is an error which invalidates his proof of the lower bound for search. For the interested reader, we describe this error in and correct it for a modified version of the computational model in the full version of this paper [5]. Proving the lower bound for search under Aaronson's original computational model is challenging because we have few examples of working hidden variable theories, and therefore have little understanding of how hidden variable values could correlate over time. Note, however, that an $\Omega(N^{1/3})$ lower bound for search might hold even for Aaronson's original model.

The classes CQP and naCQP, which we define by imagining one can perform (non-adaptive) non-collapsing measurements, seem incomparable to DQP - we do not know if either CQP $\subseteq$ DQP, nor if DQP $\subseteq$ CQP. However, we suspect that naCQP is a weaker class than DQP for several reasons. First, we can prove a polynomial lower bound for search in naCQP, which we don't know how to do in DQP. Second, we can prove an upper bound that naCQP $\subseteq$ BPP^{PP} $\subseteq$ PSPACE.

---

[1]Note, however, that this only arises when the quantum operations can depend on the non-collapsing measurement results. Our definition of naCQP does not allow cloning due to the non-adaptivity restriction. In contrast the class CQP does admit cloning, so might be a more powerful computational model. We discuss this issue in detail in Appendix A, and describe a related open problem in Section 8.

In contrast the best known upper bound for DQP is EXP. Table 1 summarizes the relationship between BQP, naCQP, CQP and DQP.

3. DEFINITION OF CQP AND NACQP

We assume the reader is familiar with the standard definition of BQP and the basics of quantum computing; for an introduction to this topic see [16]. We now give a formal definition of our model of quantum computing with non-collapsing measurements.

Let $\mathcal{Q}$ be an oracle that takes as input a quantum circuit $C = (U_1, M_1, U_2, M_2, \cdots, U_T, M_T)$ and an integer $\ell \geq 0$. Here each U_i is a unitary operator on ℓ qubits composed of gates from some finite universal gate set $\mathcal{U}$, and each M_i is a standard (collapsing) measurement of zero or more qubits in the computational basis. Define a (random) sequence $\{|\psi_t\rangle\}_{t=0}^{T}$ of quantum states by $|\psi_0\rangle = |0\rangle^{\otimes \ell}$ and for $t > 0$, $|\psi_t\rangle$ is the resulting (random) pure state obtained when measurement M_t is applied to $U_t |\psi_{t-1}\rangle$. Note that we imagine the state of the system $|\psi_t\rangle$ is a (random) pure state for $0 \leq t \leq T$. The oracle $\mathcal{Q}$ samples the sequence $\{|\psi_t\rangle\}_{t=0}^{T}$ (note that the random variables $|\psi_t\rangle$ are not independent), measures $|\psi_t\rangle$ in the computational basis for every t independently, and outputs the $T+1$ measurement results, which we label $v_0, v_1, \ldots v_T$, respectively. The output of $\mathcal{Q}$ is an element of $(\{0,1\}^\ell)^{T+1}$. Note that once the $|\psi_t\rangle$ are fixed, the $T + 1$ measurement results are independent, however since the $|\psi_t\rangle$ are correlated, the measurement outcomes may be correlated.

naCQP (non-adaptive Collapse-free Quantum Polynomial-time) is then defined as the class of all languages that can be recognized in polynomial time by a deterministic Turing machine with one query to $\mathcal{Q}$, with error probability at most $\frac{1}{3}$. Note that because the base machine is polynomially bounded, the circuit C with which it queries $\mathcal{Q}$ must be polynomially sized. Furthermore, since the base machine can use the oracle to output coin flips, it makes no difference if we define the base machine to be deterministic or randomized. This class contains BQP, because one can always query the oracle $\mathcal{Q}$ with a BQP circuit, and then ignore all output except the final measurement outcome. The constant $\frac{1}{3}$ is arbitrary: we can decrease the error probability arbitrarily close to 0 by repetition, which can be accomplished by packing multiple copies of a quantum circuit into a single call to $\mathcal{Q}$. Furthermore, it turns out that the definition of naCQP is not affected by the choice of universal gate set $\mathcal{U}$; this is a consequence of the Solovay-Kitaev Theorem. The proof is omitted here due to lack of space, but can be found in the full version of this paper [5].

We can think of the $T+1$ measurement samples from $\mathcal{Q}$ as the results of *non-collapsing* measurements on the state vector, which give information about the state without changing it. For instance, let $|\psi_1\rangle = U_1 |0\rangle^{\otimes \ell}$, let M_1, M_2 and M_3 be empty measurements, and let U_2, U_3 be the identity. Then the oracle $\mathcal{Q}$ will output the result of three independent non-collapsing measurements of $|\psi_1\rangle$ in the computational basis. The key point is that the oracle's samples do not disturb the state of the system; only the unitary operators U_i and collapsing measurements M_i do. The oracle $\mathcal{Q}$ gives us information about the intermediate stages of the quantum computation without collapsing the state; this is what gives naCQP additional power over BQP.

Table 1: Comparison between BQP, naCQP, CQP and DQP

Property	BQP	naCQP	CQP	DQP
Contains SZK	Unknown	Yes	Yes	Yes
Contains SZK relative to all oracles	No	Yes	Yes	Yes
Upper Bound for Search	$O(N^{1/2})$	$\tilde{O}(N^{1/3})$	$\tilde{O}(N^{1/3})$	$\tilde{O}(N^{1/3})$
Lower Bound for Search	$\Omega(N^{1/2})$	$\Omega(N^{1/4})$	$\Omega(1)$	$\Omega(1)$
Upper Bound	AWPP	BPP^{PP}	BPP^{PP}	EXP

Note that by requiring the quantum circuit C to be specified up front, we have enforced the condition that the circuit is non-adaptive to the non-collapsing measurement outcomes (hence the name naCQP). To define CQP, we consider the case where the base machine can query the oracle $\mathcal{Q}$ adaptively. That is, the base machine can first specify $U_1, M_1, \ldots U_t, M_t$ and receive samples $v_1 \ldots v_t$, then based on those samples select $U_{t+1}, M_{t+1} \ldots U_{t'}, M_{t'}$ and receive samples $v_{t+1} \ldots v_{t'}$, etc. CQP is then defined analogously to be the class of languages which can be decided in polynomial time with adaptive queries to $\mathcal{Q}$, with error probability at most 1/3. This class captures the power of generic computations with non-collapsing measurements.

Note that we explicitly allow for intermediate (collapsing) measurements in our model. In the definition of BQP, the principle of deferred measurement tells us that this is not necessary; the power of standard quantum computers is unchanged by the inclusion of intermediate collapsing measurements. However, in our model this makes a crucial difference. Indeed, suppose that we did not allow for intermediate collapsing measurements; then this model would be simulable in BQP with a polynomial amount of overhead. If there are no intermediate measurements M_i, then $|\psi_t\rangle = U_t U_{t-1} \ldots U_1 |0\rangle^{\otimes \ell}$ are no longer random variables but are deterministic pure states, each preparable with a polynomially sized quantum circuit. So a BQP machine could simply prepare $|\psi_1\rangle$ and measure it, then prepare $|\psi_2\rangle$ from scratch and measure it, etc. to obtain the samples $v_0, \ldots, v_T$. This would incur at most quadratic overhead.

When we add intermediate measurements into our model, this simulation strategy no longer works. Indeed, suppose that we performed measurement M_1 to obtain a random state $|\psi_1\rangle$. If we wanted to reproduce this state with a BQP machine, we could try applying M_1 to $U_1 |0\rangle^{\otimes \ell}$. However, it might be that the probability of obtaining the same outcome for M_1 is exponentially small, and hence the BQP machine could not prepare another copy of $|\psi_1\rangle$ in polynomial time.

In short, the power of this model comes from the fact that we can perform intermediate measurements which collapse the wave function, and afterwards we can examine the resulting pure state $|\psi_t\rangle$ (which might not be efficiently preparable with a BQP machine) using multiple non-collapsing measurements. In the next section we will show how to leverage these properties to solve any problem in SZK in polynomial time.

4. SZK IS CONTAINED IN NACQP

We will now describe how to use the peculiarities of non-collapsing measurements to solve any problem in SZK in polynomial time. The proof uses essentially the ideas of Aaronson [2], with minor simplifications.

SZK was originally defined as the class of languages admitting statistical zero-knowledge proofs. The precise definition of a statistical zero-knowledge proof can be found in [18], but it is not important here. SZK includes important problems such as Graph Isomorphism and Approximate Shortest Vector. It has been a long-standing open problem whether or not these problems can be solved in quantum polynomial time. Ettinger, Høyer and Knill showed that Graph Isomorphism (and indeed any hidden subgroup problem) can be solved in a black box manner with a polynomial number of queries to the black box, but with exponential post-processing time [13]. On the other hand, Aaronson [1] showed that BQP does not admit a black-box algorithm for the collision problem, and hence there is an oracle relative to which SZK is not in BQP.

In contrast, we show that quantum computers with non-collapsing measurements can solve any problem in SZK efficiently, i.e. SZK $\subseteq$ naCQP. It is enough to prove that Statistical Difference, a problem shown in [18] to be SZK-complete, is in naCQP. The statistical difference problem is to determine, for two functions $P_0, P_1 : \{0,1\}^n \rightarrow \{0,1\}^m$ specified by classical circuits, whether the distributions of $P_0(X), P_1(X)$ for uniformly random X are close or far. Here, two distributions are "close" if their total variation distance is less than $\frac{1}{3}$ and they are "far" if their total variation distance is more than $\frac{2}{3}$.

We now show how to solve this efficiently if we have access to non-collapsing measurements.

THEOREM 4.1. *The Statistical Difference problem can be solved in polynomial time in* naCQP*, and therefore* SZK $\subseteq$ naCQP.

PROOF. By the Polarization Lemma of Sahai and Vadhan [18, Lemma 3.3], we can assume that the distributions $P_0(X)$ and $P_1(X)$ have total variation distance less than 2^{-n^c} or more than $1 - 2^{-n^c}$, for any constant c. For now, assume that the distributions have total variation distance equal to either 1 or 0.

Our algorithm for the statistical difference problem is as follows. Prepare the state

$$\frac{1}{2^{(n+1)/2}} \sum_{b \in \{0,1\}, x \in \{0,1\}^n} |b\rangle |x\rangle |P_b(x)\rangle.$$

Now, measure the third register with a collapsing measurement to obtain a state $|\phi\rangle$ on the first two registers. If the distributions P_0, P_1 have total variation distance 1, then $|\phi\rangle$ will be of the form $|b\rangle |\psi\rangle$ for some b and $|\psi\rangle$. On the other hand, if they have total variation distance 0, then $|\phi\rangle$ will be an equal superposition $\frac{1}{\sqrt{2}}(|0\rangle |\psi_0\rangle + |1\rangle |\psi_1\rangle)$ where $|\psi_0\rangle$ and $|\psi_1\rangle$ have unit norm. We can distinguish the two cases by now repeatedly performing non-collapsing measurements and examining the value of the first register. If P_0, P_1 have total variation distance 1, then all of these measurements will give the same value b; if P_0 and P_1 have total variation distance 0, then each of these measurements will independently give 0 with probability $\frac{1}{2}$ and 1 with probability $\frac{1}{2}$. We can distinguish the two cases with probability 3/4 by performing three non-collapsing measurements and looking at whether or not they yielded identical values of the first register.

Furthermore, the fact that the total variation distances are merely exponentially close to 0 or 1, rather than actually being equal to 0 or 1, makes little difference. One can show that the probability of seeing the same measurement outcome three times is at most $\frac{1}{4} + O(2^{-n^c})$ if P_0 and P_1 are exponentially close and at least $1 - O(2^{-n^c})$ if P_0 and P_1 are exponentially far apart. We provide a detailed proof of this fact in Appendix B. Therefore our algorithm will have error probability at most 1/3.

□

Hence SZK is in naCQP, and furthermore we can solve SZK problems in naCQP in a black box manner, i.e. relative to any oracle. Since [1] has the result that SZK $\not\subset$ BQP relative to an oracle, we have the immediate corollary[2]:

COROLLARY 4.1. *There exists an oracle $\mathcal{O}$ such that* naCQP$^{\mathcal{O}} \neq$ BQP$^{\mathcal{O}}$.

5. SEARCH IN O($N^{1/3}$) TIME

Suppose that we are given query access to a function $f : \{0,1\}^n \to \{0,1\}$ such that the preimage $f^{-1}(1)$ contains exactly one element, x. In the classical randomized computational model, we can find x in $O(N)$ time, where $N = 2^n$, but no faster. In the quantum computational model, on the other hand, we can find x in $O(N^{1/2})$ time using Grover's search algorithm [15], but no faster [10].

Here we show that quantum computers equipped with (non-adaptive) non-collapsing measurements can search in $\tilde{O}(N^{1/3})$ time, where the tilde hides factors in $\log N$. The basic idea is to run $N^{1/3}$ Grover iterations, and then make $N^{1/3}$ non-collapsing measurements of the resulting state. Then with high probability the the marked item will be seen. This is a simplification of the proof given in [2, Theorem 10] for DQP. We now formalize this idea below:

THEOREM 5.1. *Suppose, in the definition of* naCQP, *that the unitary operators $U_1, \cdots, U_T$ are now allowed to query f. That is, we are given access to the n-qubit gate U_f defined by $U_f |y\rangle = (-1)^{f(y)} |y\rangle$ for all $y \in \{0,1\}^n$, as well as controlled-U_f. Then there is a* naCQP *algorithm to find the value of x that uses $O(N^{1/3})$ queries and $\tilde{O}(N^{1/3})$ time.*

PROOF. Prepare the uniform superposition of all basis states, apply $i = N^{1/3}$ Grover iterations [15], then query the oracle to record whether or not each basis state is marked in an ancilla. We obtain the state

$$\sin((2i+1)\theta) |x\rangle |1\rangle + \cos((2i+1)\theta) \sum_{y \in \{0,1\}^n, y \neq x} 2^{-\frac{N-1}{2}} |y\rangle |0\rangle$$

where $\sin(\theta) = 2^{-n/2}$ and $i = 2^{n/3}$. For small x we have $\sin(x) \approx x$, so for large n we have $\theta = \Theta(2^{-n/2})$, so $\sin((2i+1)\theta) = \Theta(2^{-n/6})$.

Now make $O(N^{1/3} \log N)$ non-collapsing measurements. We claim that with high probability, the marked item x will appear at least once. Indeed, the marked item x appears with probability at least $\Omega\left(N^{-1/3}\right)$ in each non-collapsing measurement outcome, so it occurs at least once with probability more than $1 - (\log N + 1)e^{-\log N} = 1 - o(1)$. □

Note that if we are willing to use an enormous amount of *time*, we can search in the naCQP model using only one *query*: just query the oracle in superposition and then perform $O(N)$ non-collapsing measurements. Indeed as we note in the introduction, any function f has query complexity 1 in this model, although this approach requires exponentially many non-collapsing measurements. Therefore in this model of computation, the relevant measure of complexity of an algorithm is the number of queries Q plus the number of non-collapsing measurements T used by the algorithm. Our above algorithm uses $Q + T = \tilde{O}(N^{1/3})$ of each, with $O(N^{1/3})$ post-processing time, so we say it "runs in time $\tilde{O}(N^{1/3})$".

6. LOWER BOUNDS FOR SEARCH

We now show that our search algorithm in section 5 cannot be improved by much; in particular there is no way to solve search in faster than $N^{1/4}$ time, even with non-adaptive non-collapsing measurements. Proving the analogous lower bound for adaptive non-collapsing measurements (i.e. for the class CQP) remains open.

THEOREM 6.1. *Suppose, in the definition of* naCQP, *that the unitary operators $U_1, \cdots, U_T$ are now allowed to query f. Let Q be the number of queries to f made by a* naCQP *algorithm, and T be the number of non-collapsing measurements. Then any* naCQP *algorithm to find the value of x obeys $Q + T = \Omega(N^{1/4})$, and hence search requires $\Omega(N^{1/4})$ time.*

In other words, there is no "black box" polynomial-time algorithm for NP-hard problems, even when given access to non-collapsing measurements. This is evidence that the class naCQP does not contain NP. The following corollary follows immediately from the well-known "diagonalization method" of Baker, Gill, and Solovay [9]:

COROLLARY 6.1. *There exists an oracle $\mathcal{O}$ such that* NP$^{\mathcal{O}} \not\subset$ naCQP$^{\mathcal{O}}$.

We now outline the proof of Theorem 6.1. The following lemma is essential: it bounds the total variation distance between two Markov distributions.

LEMMA 6.1. *Suppose that $T \geq 1$, and that $v = (v_0, \cdots, v_T)$ is a random variable governed by a Markov distribution. That is, for all $1 \leq i \leq T$, v_i is independent of $v_0, \cdots, v_{i-2}$ conditioned on a particular value of v_{i-1}. Let $w = (w_0, \cdots, w_T)$ be another random variable governed by a Markov distribution. If $d_{TV}(\cdot, \cdot)$ denotes the total variation distance between random variables, then*

$$d_{TV}(v, w) \leq 2 \sum_{i=1}^{T} d_{TV}((v_{i-1}, v_i), (w_{i-1}, w_i)).$$

---

² Note that when we say naCQP$^{\mathcal{O}}$, we mean that circuits given in the input to $\mathcal{Q}$ in the definition of naCQP can contain quantum calls to the oracle.

PROOF. We proceed by induction on T. The base case $T = 1$ is trivial. For $T > 1$, since w_T depends only on w_{T-1} (by the Markov property), it is equal to $A(w_{T-1})$ for some randomized process A; let $w'_T := A(v_{T-1})$ be a variable that depends on v_{T-1} in exactly the same way that w_T depends on w_{T-1}. Then, define the random variable $v' = (v_0, \cdots, v_{T-1}, w'_T)$. By the triangle inequality,

$$d_{TV}(v, w) \leq d_{TV}(v, v') + d_{TV}(v', w). \tag{1}$$

Applying the same randomized process to two random variables cannot increase their total variation distance [18]. We can generate random variables identically distributed to v and v' by applying a suitable randomized process to (v_{T-1}, v_T) and (v_{T-1}, w'_T). We can also generate random variables identically distributed to v' and w by applying a suitable randomized process to $(v_0, \cdots, v_{T-1})$ and $(w_0, \cdots, w_{T-1})$. Therefore, the right hand side of (1) is bounded above by

$$d_{TV}((v_{T-1}, v_T), (v_{T-1}, w'_T))$$
$$+ d_{TV}((v_0, \cdots, v_{T-1}), (w_0, \cdots, w_{T-1})).$$

By the triangle inequality, $d_{TV}((v_{T-1}, v_T), (v_{T-1}, w'_T))$ is upper bounded by

$$d_{TV}((v_{T-1}, v_T), (w_{T-1}, w_T))$$
$$+ d_{TV}((w_{T-1}, w_T), (v_{T-1}, w'_T))$$
$$= d_{TV}((v_{T-1}, v_T), (w_{T-1}, w_T))$$
$$+ d_{TV}(v_{T-1}, w_{T-1})$$
$$\leq 2d_{TV}((v_{T-1}, v_T), (w_{T-1}, w_T)).$$

Putting all of this together, we get that $d_{TV}(v, w)$ is upper bounded by

$$2d_{TV}((v_{T-1}, v_T), (w_{T-1}, w_T))$$
$$+ d_{TV}((v_0, \cdots, v_{T-1}), (w_0, \cdots, w_{T-1})).$$

The result follows from induction. $\square$

LEMMA 6.2. *The trace distance between two pure states $|\psi\rangle$ and $|\phi\rangle$ is less than or equal to the 2-norm $\| |\psi\rangle - |\phi\rangle \|_2$.*

PROOF. The trace distance between $|\psi\rangle$ and $|\phi\rangle$ is equal to $\sqrt{1 - |\langle\psi|\phi\rangle|^2}$ [16], and the 2-norm $\| |\psi\rangle - |\phi\rangle \|_2$ is $\sqrt{2 - 2\text{Re}(\langle\psi|\phi\rangle)}$. The inequality follows from $|\langle\psi|\phi\rangle| \leq 1$. $\square$

From the hybrid argument of [10], we have the following:

LEMMA 6.3. *For all t, if there are no measurements made before time t, we have*
$\sum_{x=0}^{N-1} \| |\psi_t\rangle - |\psi_t(x)\rangle \|_2^2 \leq 4Q^2.$

With these facts, we can now prove Theorem 6.1. We provide an outline of the proof here, and the full proof can be found in Appendix C. The basic idea is to realize that the non-collapsing measurement outcomes form a Markov chain, because the distribution of any non-collapsing measurement is independent once the results of the previous intermediate collapsing measurements are fixed. So, letting v and $v(x)$ be the distributions on non-collapsing measurement outcomes when the marked item is absent or present at x, by applying Lemma 6.1, we have that

$$\frac{1}{3} \leq d_{TV}(v, v(x)) \leq 2 \sum_{i=1}^{T} d_{TV}((v_{i-1}, v_i), (v_{i-1}(x), v_i(x))).$$

Here the lower bound on d_{TV} comes from the fact that our algorithm can distinguish whether or not a marked item is present with probability $2/3$, and hence these distributions must be $1/3$-far apart for all x.

Lemma 6.3 tells us that there is some x for which the marginal distributions v_i and $v_i(x)$ are close. However, this isn't sufficient to upper bound the quantity on the right of this inequality, because the correlations between the distributions at steps $i - 1$ and i (which are induced by the intermediate collapsing measurements) might make the distributions easier to distinguish[3]. Hence in order to prove this lower bound, we have to substantially strengthen the hybrid argument [10] to show that the correlations induced by the collapsing measurement outcomes do not allow $d_{TV}((v_{i-1}, v_i), (v_{i-1}(x), v_i(x)))$ to be large. By carefully keeping track of these induced correlations, we show in Appendix C that there is some x for which

$$d_{TV}(v, v(x)) \leq 2 \sum_{i=1}^{T} d_{TV}((v_{i-1}, v_i), (v_{i-1}(x), v_i(x))) \leq \frac{20TQ}{\sqrt{N}}.$$

where Q is the number of queries made by the algorithm and T is the number of non-collapsing measurements. Combining this with the fact that $d_{TV}(v, v(x)) \geq \frac{1}{3}$ for all x, this implies

$$\frac{20TQ}{\sqrt{N}} \geq \frac{1}{3},$$

and hence the running time of the algorithm is at least $T + Q = \Omega(N^{1/4})$.

7. AN UPPER BOUND ON CQP

We now show that CQP is contained in the class BPP^{PP}. Since $\text{naCQP} \subseteq \text{CQP}$, this places both classes in the second level of the counting hierarchy. By comparison, the best known upper bound for BQP is AWPP which is contained in PP [14][7].

THEOREM 7.1. $\text{CQP} \subseteq \text{BPP}^{\text{PP}}$.

PROOF. First note that $\text{BPP}^{\text{PP}} = \text{BPP}^{\#P}$, because one can always use a PP oracle to count with only polynomial overhead. Therefore it suffices to show $\text{CQP} \subseteq \text{BPP}^{\#P}$. We now show how to simulate the sampling oracle $\mathcal{Q}$ in $\text{BPP}^{\#P}$. Our algorithm will work for adaptive queries as well. Since $\text{CQP} = \text{BPP}^{\mathcal{Q},1}$, this implies the claim.

Suppose we wish to simulate a sample from the oracle $\mathcal{Q}$ with input circuit $C = (U_1, M_1, \ldots U_T, M_T)$ on n qubits. Since the choice of gate set does not matter (for a proof of this, please refer to the full version of this paper [5]), without loss of generality we can assume our circuit is composed of only Toffoli and Hadamard gates, which are universal by a result of Shi [19].

We first simulate the result of the measurement M_1. Suppose without loss of generality that M_1 measures the first k qubits and gets outcome $x_1 \ldots x_k \in \{0,1\}^k$. Following the techniques of Adleman, DeMarrais, and Huang [7], we can write the probability that x_1 is 0 or 1 as an exponential sum

---

[3] To see how this could happen in general, consider the following two Markov distributions on two bits: D_1 outputs 00 or 11 with equal probability, and D_2 outputs 01 or 10 with equal probability. These have identical marginals on each bit, but are perfectly distinguishable due to the correlations between their bits.

of poly-time-computable terms (since U_1 is specified by a poly-sized circuit). Since we chose Hadamard and Toffoli as our gate set, all terms in the sum are of the form $\frac{\pm 1}{2^k}$, where k is the number of Hadamard gates in U_1. Hence using the #P oracle, we can compute $\Pr[x_1 = 1]$ exactly in binary, and then flip a coin with bias p using the base BPP machine to obtain outcome $x_1 \in 0, 1$ with this probability.

We've now sampled the value of x_1. To sample the value of x_2, note that we can also express $\Pr[x_2 = 1|x_1 = 0]$ as a sum of exponentially many terms, each of which is poly-time computable and takes values in $\frac{\pm 1}{2^k}$. Therefore using the #P oracle, we can exactly compute the *conditional* probability that $x_2 = 1$ given our sampled value of x_1; in other words the #P oracle can compute the probabilities of measurement outcomes under post-selection. In this way we can sample x_2, then x_3, etc. obtain a sample $x_1 \dots x_k \in \{0,1\}^k$ as desired.

Now suppose we wish to sample the variable $v_1 \in \{0,1\}^n$ which is the result of a non-collapsing measurement on the state remaining after measurement M_1 yields value $x_1 \dots x_k$. As noted above, using the #P oracle, we can compute the marginal probability that any qubit is 1, postselected on a particular measurement outcome. Hence using the #P oracle, we can draw the sample v_1 using n queries to the oracle. We can continue this process to simulate M_2, then sample v_2, etc. Therefore we can draw a sample from $\mathcal{Q}$ using $O(nT)$ queries to the #P oracle. Note that this simulation works when the U_i and the M_i are chosen adaptively, since for each t the base BPP machine receives the non-collapsing measurement samples $v_0 \dots v_t$ before proposing the next unitary U_{t+1} and measurement M_{t+1}. Hence this shows $\mathsf{CQP} \subseteq \mathsf{BPP}^{\mathsf{PP}}$.

$\square$

An open question is whether or not we can improve this upper bound to show $\mathsf{naCQP} \subseteq \mathsf{PP}$. This seems difficult because $\mathsf{SZK} \subseteq \mathsf{naCQP}$, and it is open whether or not $\mathsf{SZK} \subseteq \mathsf{PP}$. In fact, Aaronson [4] showed that there is an oracle separation between SZK and a weaker class $\mathsf{A_0PP}$, and left open the problem of finding an oracle relative to which SZK is not contained in PP. If such an oracle exists, it would imply one could not show $\mathsf{naCQP} \subseteq \mathsf{PP}$ with a relativizing proof.

One natural approach to showing $\mathsf{naCQP} \subseteq \mathsf{PP}$ is to use the fact that $\mathsf{PP} = \mathsf{PostBQP}$ [3], and design a post-selected quantum circuit to simulate the oracle $\mathcal{Q}$. However, the most naive way of trying to do this fails. Suppose that one tried the following: to simulate the oracle's output under $C = (U_1, M_1, \dots U_T, M_T)$ on n qubits, create a post-selected circuit C' on nT qubits which runs $U_1 M_1$ on the first n qubits, $U_1 M_1 U_2 M_2$ on the second n qubits, etc, and post-selects on them receiving the same outcomes for the intermediate measurements. While this superficially looks like what the oracle $\mathcal{Q}$ performs, this approach does not sample from the correct distribution on outputs. Suppose the probability that the outcome of M_1 is 1 is p. Then the probability one sees $M_1 = 1$ in the final output of C' will be $\frac{p^T}{p^T + (1-p)^T}$, while the quantum oracle $\mathcal{Q}$ will sample $M_1 = 1$ with probability p. For this reason it seems difficult to generate a sample from $\mathcal{Q}$ with a post-selected circuit, and hence difficult to place naCQP in PP.

8. OPEN QUESTIONS

We leave many questions about the complexity classes DQP, CQP and naCQP unanswered.

1. We demonstrated a $\tilde{O}(N^{1/3})$-time algorithm for the search problem in the naCQP model, as well as the result that any search algorithm takes $\Omega(N^{1/4})$ time. Is it possible to close the gap between these two bounds? If we disallow intermediate collapsing measurements, then we can prove an $N^{1/3}$ lower bound for search (a proof is included in Appendix D). However proving an $N^{1/3}$ lower bound when there are intermediate measurements remains open.

2. Can we demonstrate a lower bound, superpolynomial in $\log N$, for the running time of a search algorithm in the DQP model? The proof given in [2] of an $\Omega(N^{1/3})$ lower bound is flawed (as discussed in the full version of this paper [5]).

3. Is there a hierarchy of computational models for which the kth allows searching in $\tilde{O}(N^{1/k})$ time?

4. Can we improve the upper bound $\mathsf{naCQP} \subseteq \mathsf{BPP}^{\mathsf{PP}}$ to $\mathsf{naCQP} \subseteq \mathsf{P}^{\mathsf{PP}}$ or $\mathsf{naCQP} \subseteq \mathsf{PP}$? One possible way to approach this problem is to use the alternative formulation of PP as $\mathsf{PostBQP}$ [3], however a straightforward application of this result does not seem to work.

5. How powerful is the class CQP? In particular, can one prove a polynomial lower bound for search in CQP?

6. More generally, what is the power of quantum computers which have the ability to clone quantum states? Such devices could clearly simulate computations in naCQP and CQP - to simulate a non-collapsing measurement, simply clone the state and measure in the computational basis - but may be more powerful than either class. For a further discussion see Appendix A.

9. ACKNOWLEDGEMENTS

S.A. was supported in part by an Alan T. Waterman Award. A.B. was supported in part by the National Science Foundation Graduate Research Fellowship under Grant No. 1122374 and by the Center for Science of Information (CSoI), an NSF Science and Technology Center, under grant agreement CCF-0939370. J.F. was supported in part by the Singapore National Research Foundation under NRF Award No. NRF-NRFF2013-01. M.L. was supported by the MIT SPUR program.

10. REFERENCES

[1] Scott Aaronson. Quantum lower bound for the collision problem. In *Proceedings of the thiry-fourth annual ACM symposium on Theory of computing*, STOC '02, pages 635–642, New York, NY, USA, 2002. ACM.

[2] Scott Aaronson. Quantum computing and hidden variables. *Phys. Rev. A*, 71:032325, Mar 2005.

[3] Scott Aaronson. Quantum computing, postselection, and probabilistic polynomial-time. In *Proceedings of the Royal Society A*, page 0412187, 2005.

[4] Scott Aaronson. Impossibility of Succinct Quantum Proofs for Collision-Freeness. *Quantum Information and Computation*, 12:21-28, 2012.

[5] Scott Aaronson, Adam Bouland, Joseph Fitzsimons, and Mitchell Lee. The space "just above" BQP. Technical report, arXiv:1412.6507, 2014.

[6] Daniel S. Abrams and Seth Lloyd. Nonlinear quantum mechanics implies polynomial-time solution for NP-complete and #P problems. Phys. Rev. Lett., 81, 3992–3995, 1998.

[7] Leonard M. Adleman, Jonathan Demarrais, Ming-deh, and A. Huang. Quantum computability. *SIAM Journal of Computation*, pages 1524–1540, 1997.

[8] Sanjeev Arora and Boaz Barak. *Computational Complexity: A Modern Approach*. Cambridge University Press, New York, NY, USA, 1st edition, 2009.

[9] T. Baker, J. Gill, and R. Solovay. Relativizations of the $\mathcal{P} =? \mathcal{NP}$ question. *SIAM Journal on Computing*, 4(4):431–442, 1975.

[10] Charles H. Bennett, Ethan Bernstein, Gilles Brassard, and Umesh Vazirani. Strengths and weaknesses of quantum computing. *SIAM J. Comput.*, 26(5):1510–1523, October 1997.

[11] Ethan Bernstein and Umesh Vazirani. Quantum complexity theory. In *in Proc. 25th Annual ACM Symposium on Theory of Computing, ACM*, pages 11–20, 1993.

[12] Christopher M. Dawson and Michael A. Nielsen. The Solovay-Kitaev algorithm. *Quantum Info. Comput.*, 6(1):81–95, January 2006.

[13] Mark Ettinger, Peter Høyer, and Emanuel Knill. The quantum query complexity of the hidden subgroup problem is polynomial. Information Processing Letters, 91(1):43-48, July 2004.

[14] Lance Fortnow and John Rogers. Complexity limitations on quantum computation. In *Proc. IEEE CCC'98*, p. 202-209, 1998.

[15] Lov K. Grover. A fast quantum mechanical algorithm for database search. In *Proceedings of the twenty-eighth annual ACM symposium on Theory of computing*, STOC '96, pages 212–219, New York, NY, USA, 1996. ACM.

[16] Michael A. Nielsen and Isaac L. Chuang. *Quantum Computation and Quantum Information (Cambridge Series on Information and the Natural Sciences)*. Cambridge University Press, 1 edition, January 2004.

[17] A Peres. Two simple proofs of the Kochen-Specker theorem. *Journal of Physics A: Mathematical and General*, 24(4):L175, 1991.

[18] A. Sahai and S.P. Vadhan. A complete promise problem for statistical zero-knowledge. In *Foundations of Computer Science, 1997. Proceedings., 38th Annual Symposium on*, pages 448–457, 1997.

[19] Y. Shi. Both Toffoli and controlled-NOT need little help to do universal quantum computing. *Quantum Information & Computation*, 3:1 pp. 84-92 (2003).

APPENDIX

Appendix

A. STRANGE PROPERTIES OF NONCOLLAPSING MEASUREMENTS

Here we show why allowing non-collapsing measurements in quantum mechanics allows for faster than light communication, renders quantum query complexity and quantum communication complexity meaningless, and allows for quantum cloning. We also discuss the relationship between naCQP and quantum computers which have the ability to clone.

To see that non-collapsing measurements allow for faster-than-light communication: suppose two players Alice and Bob share n EPR pairs. Then Alice can send a bit of information to Bob with probability $1-2^{-n}$. To see this, suppose Alice makes collapsing measurements in the 0/1 basis on her share of the EPR pairs to send a 0, and measures in the +/- basis to send a 1. Now Bob makes two non-collapsing measurements in the 0/1 basis on his half of the EPR pairs. If Alice had sent a 0, then Bob will see the same outcome each time. If Alice had sent a 1, then Bob will see a random string each time, so with probability $1 - 2^{-n}$ Bob will see two different outcomes. Thus Bob can tell which basis Alice measured in with high probability, and Alice and Bob can communicate faster than light.

We now explain why with non-collapsing measurements, the quantum query complexity and quantum communication complexity of any function is 1. Suppose one wishes to evaluate $f(x)$ where $x = x_1 \ldots x_N$. Then one can prepare the superposition $\sum_i |i\rangle |x_i\rangle$ with one query to the oracle, and make $O(N \log N)$ non-collapsing measurements of this state to observe the value of each x_i and compute the function. Similarly, in the context of communication complexity, one player can simply encode their input $x \in \{0,1\}^n$ into the state $\cos \theta_x |0\rangle + \sin \theta_x |1\rangle$ where $\theta_x = \frac{x}{2^n} \frac{\pi}{2}$. By performing roughly 2^n non-collapsing measurements, the other player can learn θ_x and hence x, with only one quantum bit of communication. Note that although these example algorithms use only one query or one qubit of communication, respectively, they use a large number of non-collapsing measurements. For this reason, when we prove lower bounds for naCQP, we lower bound the number of queries *plus* the number of non-collapsing measurements required, rather than the number of queries alone.

To see that non-collapsing measurements allow for cloning: given a quantum state ψ on n qubits, one could perform $2^{O(n)}$ non-collapsing measurements to characterize the state using tomography, and then (approximately) reproduce the state. This "approximate cloning" operation take exponential time for generic states, and is non-unitary.

Note, that the class of computations considered in naCQP cannot clone, even for states of $O(\log(n))$ qubits, since the naCQP machine cannot perform further quantum computations after receiveing the non-collapsing measurement results (i.e. because of the non-adaptivity restriction). In contrast, if the circuit could depend on the non-collapsing measurement results (as in CQP), then one could clone states of $O(\log(n))$ qubits to polynomial accuracy, which is a non-unitary operation. Hence following the result of Abrams and Lloyd [6], the power of CQP class might include NP or even #P, though we do not know if this is the case. A broader related open problem is: what is the power of quantum computers which are given the ability to clone? Such devices could clearly simulate naCQP and CQP computations - to simulate a non-collapsing measurement, simply clone and measure in the computational basis. However, it's unclear how powerful such quantum devices would be.

B. A DETAILED PROOF THAT SZK IS IN NACQP

Here we provide a detailed analysis of the probability of error in our naCQP algorithm for solving the Statistical Difference problem, which is SZK-complete.

Let's briefly recap the algorithm. Suppose we're given an instance of Statistical Difference, and apply the Polarization Lemma of Sahai and Vadhan [18] to obtain two circuits P_0 and P_1 which encode probability distributions D_0 and D_1 which satisfy either $d_{TV}(D_0, D_1) \leq \epsilon$ or $d_{TV}(D_0, D_1) \geq 1 - \epsilon$, where $\epsilon = 2^{-O(n^c)}$ for some constant c. We now prepare the state

$$\frac{1}{2^{(n+1)/2}} \sum_{b \in \{0,1\}, x \in \{0,1\}^n} |b\rangle \, |x\rangle \, |P_b(x)\rangle$$

Now, measure the third register with a collapsing measurement to obtain some outcome y, and then perform three non-collapsing measurements on the b register to obtain outcomes b_1, b_2, b_3. If $b_1 = b_2 = b_3$ then output the distributions were $(1-\epsilon)$-far in total variation distance, otherwise output they were ϵ-close in total variation distance.

We will now compute the probability this algorithm makes an error when the input distributions are ϵ-close in total variation distance.

Let $D_b(x)$ denote the probability that distribution D_b outputs string x. The probability of seeing outcome y in the $P_b(x)$ register under our collapsing measurement is

$$\frac{1}{2}(D_0(y) + D_1(y)).$$

Conditioned on seeing outcome y, one can easily compute that the probability of obtaining outcome $b_1 = b_2 = b_3$ (which causes the algorithm to err) is $\frac{D_0(y)^3 + D_1(y)^3}{(D_0(y) + D_1(y))^3}$.

Hence the total probability of error is this case is given by

$$\Pr[\text{error}] - \sum_y \frac{D_0(y) + D_1(y)}{2} \frac{D_0(y)^3 + D_1(y)^3}{(D_0(y) + D_1(y))^3}$$

Let $\delta(y) = D_1(y) - D_0(y)$. So $\sum_y \delta(y) = 0$ and $\sum_y |\delta(y)| \leq 2\epsilon$ by our promise on the total variation distance between D_0 and D_1. Hence we have by direct calcuation that

$$\Pr[\text{error}] = \frac{1}{2} \sum_y \frac{D_0(y)^3 + D_1(y)^3}{(D_0(y) + D_1(y))^2}$$

$$= \frac{1}{2} \sum_y \frac{D_0(y)^3 + (D_0(y) + \delta(y))^3}{(2D_0(y) + \delta(y))^2}$$

$$= \frac{1}{2} \sum_y \frac{2D_0(y)^3 + 3D_0(y)^2\delta(y) + 3D_0(y)\delta(y)^2 + \delta(y)^3}{4D_0(y)^2 + 4D_0(y)\delta(y) + \delta(y)^2}$$

$$= \frac{1}{2} \sum_y \frac{D_0(y)}{2} + \frac{D_0(y)^2\delta(y) + \frac{5}{2}D_0(y)\delta(y)^2 + \delta(y)^3}{4D_0(y)^2 + 4D_0(y)\delta(y) + \delta(y)^2}$$

$$= \frac{1}{4} + \frac{1}{2} \sum_y \delta(y) \frac{D_0(y)^2 + \frac{5}{2}D_0(y)\delta(y) + \delta(y)^2}{4D_0(y)^2 + 4D_0(y)\delta(y) + \delta(y)^2}$$

$$\leq \frac{1}{4} + \frac{1}{2} \sum_y |\delta(y)| \frac{D_0(y)^2 + \frac{5}{2}D_0(y)|\delta(y)| + |\delta(y)^2|}{4D_0(y)^2 + 4D_0(y)\delta(y) + \delta(y)^2}$$

$$\leq \frac{1}{4} + \frac{1}{2} \sum_y |\delta(y)| \frac{4D_0(y)^2 + 4D_0(y)|\delta(y)| + |\delta(y)^2|}{4D_0(y)^2 + 4D_0(y)\delta(y) + \delta(y)^2}$$

$$= \frac{1}{4} + \frac{1}{2} \sum_y |\delta(y)| \leq \frac{1}{4} + \epsilon$$

Where the last two lines follow from the fact that all terms in the sum are non-negative, and the fact that $\sum_y |\delta(y)| \leq 2\epsilon$. Hence the probability of error in the case is upper bounded by $\frac{1}{4} + \epsilon = \frac{1}{4} + O(2^{-n^c})$, so the algorithm has probability of error $< \frac{1}{3}$ for sufficiently large n as desired.

We now bound the probability of error in the case that the distributions are far apart. In this case, the probability of getting an outcome where b_1, b_2, b_3 are not all at the same, conditioned on measuring y, is given by

$$\frac{3D_0(y)^2 D_1(y) + 3D_0(y)D_1(y)^2}{(D_0(y) + D_1(y))^3}.$$

Hence by direct calculation we have that the probability of error is

$$\sum_y \frac{D_0(y) + D_1(y)}{2} \frac{3D_0(y)^2 D_1(y) + 3D_0(y)D_1(y)^2}{(D_0(y) + D_1(y))^3}$$

$$= \frac{3}{2} \sum_y \frac{D_0(y)^2 D_1(y)}{(D_0(y) + D_1(y))^2} + \frac{D_0(y)D_1(y)^2}{(D_0(y) + D_1(y))^2}$$

Let us upper bound the first of these terms; the upper bound on the second term follows analogously by switching D_0 and D_1.

Since D_0 and D_1 are $1 - \epsilon$-far in total variation distance, there must exist some set S of y's, and its complement $\bar{S}$, such that $\sum_{y \in S} D_0(y) \geq 1 - \epsilon$ and $\sum_{y \in S} D_1(y) \leq \epsilon$, which implies that $\sum_{y \in \bar{S}} D_0(y) \leq \epsilon$ and $\sum_{y \in \bar{S}} D_1(y) \geq 1 - \epsilon$. Hence we have that

$$\sum_y \frac{D_0(y)^2 D_1(y)}{(D_0(y) + D_1(y))^2} = \sum_{y \in S} \frac{D_0(y)^2 D_1(y)}{(D_0(y) + D_1(y))^2}$$

$$+ \sum_{y \in \bar{S}} \frac{D_0(y)^2 D_1(y)}{(D_0(y) + D_1(y))^2}$$

$$\leq \sum_{y \in S} \frac{D_0(y)^2 D_1(y)}{(D_0(y))^2}$$

$$+ \sum_{y \in \bar{S}} \frac{D_0(y)^2 D_1(y)}{(D_1(y))^2}$$

$$\leq \sum_{y \in S} D_1(y) + \sum_{y \in \bar{S}} D_0(y)$$

$$\leq 2\epsilon$$

By applying an analogous bound to the second term, we have that $\Pr[\text{error}] = O(\epsilon) = O(2^{-n^c})$ as desired, so the probability of error in this case is vanishingly small.

Hence the net probability that the algorithm errs is $\frac{1}{4} + \epsilon$ in the case the distributions are ϵ-close and $O(\epsilon)$ in the case the distributions are $(1 - \epsilon)$-far.

C. AN $N^{1/4}$ LOWER BOUND FOR SEARCH IN NACQP

Here we show that any `naCQP` algorithm for search requires at least $N^{1/4}$ time.

PROOF PROOF OF THEOREM 6.1. Since it is always possible to copy measured qubits, we can assume that qubits which are measured in an intermediate step of the algorithm are never directly modified again. Now, assume that the algorithm uses ℓ qubits and applies unitary operators $U_1, \cdots, U_T$, each of which is either a (controlled) query to the search function f or a gate from the finite universal gate set $\mathcal{U}$. The measurements $M_1 \ldots M_T$ (which may or may not be empty) are applied between the operators $U_1 \ldots U_T$.

Let $v(x) = (v_0(x), v_1(x), \cdots, v_T(x))$ be the non-collapsing measurement results when the marked item is x, so that $v_i(x)$ is sampled immediately before the application of U_{i+1}. Let $v = (v_0, \cdots, v_T)$ be the non-collapsing measurement results when there is no marked item. In general, both $v(x)$ and v are random variables. Since the postprocessing step can distinguish the distributions of v and $v(x)$ with success probability $2/3$, $d_{TV}(v, v(x)) \geq \frac{1}{3}$ for all x. On the other hand, each v and $v(x)$ is a Markov process. Therefore, by Lemma 6.1,

$$d_{TV}(v, v(x)) \leq 2 \sum_{i=1}^{T} d_{TV}((v_{i-1}, v_i), (v_{i-1}(x), v_i(x))).$$

Now, we bound the term

$$d_{x,i} := d_{TV}((v_{i-1}, v_i), (v_{i-1}(x), v_i(x))).$$

Since it is possible to defer measurements in a quantum circuit to a later stage [16], we can assume that all intermediate measurements that occurred before the application of U_i occurred immediately before the sampling of v_i. Suppose that these measurements were applied to the first k qubits of the state. Let $|\phi\rangle$ and $|\phi(x)\rangle$ be the state vectors immediately before these measurements. Then, we decompose $|\phi\rangle = \sum_{s \in \{0,1\}^k} \alpha_s |s\rangle |\phi_s\rangle$ and $|\phi(x)\rangle = \sum_{s \in \{0,1\}^k} \beta_s |s\rangle |\phi_s(x)\rangle$. Possible values for (v_{i-1}, v_i) and $(v_{i-1}(x), v_i(x))$ can be written in the form (st_1, st_2), where s is a k-bit string and t_1, t_2 are $(\ell - k)$-bit strings.

Assume for now that U_i does not contain a query to f. Then, since it does not affect the first k qubits, it can be decomposed into the sum $\sum_{s \in \{0,1\}^k} |s\rangle V_s \langle s|$ for some unitary operators V_s. The transformation U_i can be thought of as applying the unitary V_s to the last $\ell - k$ qubits if the (measured) first k qubits are equal to s. Then, the probability that $(v_{i-1}, v_i) = (st_1, st_2)$ is equal to

$$|\alpha_s|^2 |\langle t_1 | \phi_s \rangle|^2 |\langle t_2 | V_s | \phi_s \rangle|^2,$$

and the probability that $(v_{i-1}(x), v_i(x)) = (st_1, st_2)$ is equal to $|\beta_s|^2 |\langle t_1 | \phi_s(x) \rangle|^2 |\langle t_2 | V_s | \phi_s(x) \rangle|^2$. Therefore, the total variation distance $d_{x,i}$ is by the triangle inequality

$$d_{x,i} = \frac{1}{2} \sum_{s,t_1,t_2} \Big| |\alpha_s|^2 |\langle t_1 | \phi_s \rangle|^2 |\langle t_2 | V_s | \phi_s \rangle|^2$$
$$- |\beta_s|^2 |\langle t_1 | \phi_s(x) \rangle|^2 |\langle t_2 | V_s | \phi_s(x) \rangle|^2 \Big|$$
$$\leq \frac{1}{2} \sum_{s,t_1,t_2} \Big(\big| |\alpha_s|^2 |\langle t_1 | \phi_s(x) \rangle|^2 |\langle t_2 | V_s | \phi_s(x) \rangle|^2$$
$$- |\beta_s|^2 |\langle t_1 | \phi_s(x) \rangle|^2 |\langle t_2 | V_s | \phi_s(x) \rangle|^2 \big|$$

$$+ \frac{1}{2} \sum_{s,t_1,t_2} \Big(|\alpha_s|^2 \big| |\langle t_1 | \phi_s \rangle|^2 |\langle t_2 | V_s | \phi_s \rangle|^2$$
$$- |\langle t_1 | \phi_s(x) \rangle|^2 |\langle t_2 | V_s | \phi_s \rangle|^2 \big| \Big)$$
$$+ \frac{1}{2} \sum_{s,t_1,t_2} \Big(|\alpha_s|^2 \big| |\langle t_1 | \phi_s(x) \rangle|^2 |\langle t_2 | V_s | \phi_s \rangle|^2$$
$$- |\langle t_1 | \phi_s(x) \rangle|^2 |\langle t_2 | V_s | \phi_s(x) \rangle|^2 \big| \Big)$$
$$=: \frac{1}{2}(S_1 + S_2 + S_3)$$

where S_1, S_2, S_3 are the three sums written above, which range over $s \in \{0,1\}^k$ and $t_1, t_2 \in \{0,1\}^{\ell - k}$. Now, we have:

$$S_1 := \sum_{s,t_1,t_2} \Big(\big| |\alpha_s|^2 |\langle t_1 | \phi_s(x) \rangle|^2 |\langle t_2 | V_s | \phi_s(x) \rangle|^2$$
$$- |\beta_s|^2 |\langle t_1 | \phi_s(x) \rangle|^2 |\langle t_2 | V_s | \phi_s(x) \rangle|^2 \big| \Big)$$
$$= \sum_s \big| |\alpha_s|^2 - |\beta_s|^2 \big| \left(\sum_{t_1,t_2} |\langle t_1 | \phi_s(x) \rangle|^2 |\langle t_2 | V_s | \phi_s(x) \rangle|^2 \right)$$
$$= \sum_s \big| |\alpha_s|^2 - |\beta_s|^2 \big|$$
$$\leq \| |\phi\rangle \langle\phi| - |\phi(x)\rangle \langle\phi(x)| \|_{tr}$$
$$\leq 2 \| |\phi(x)\rangle - |\phi\rangle \|_2.$$

Additionally,

$$S_2 := \sum_{s,t_1,t_2} \Big(|\alpha_s|^2 \big| |\langle t_1 | \phi_s \rangle|^2 |\langle t_2 | V_s | \phi_s \rangle|^2$$
$$- |\langle t_1 | \phi_s(x) \rangle|^2 |\langle t_2 | V_s | \phi_s \rangle|^2 \big| \Big)$$
$$= \sum_{s,t_1} \big(|\alpha_s|^2 \big| |\langle t_1 | \phi_s \rangle|^2 - |\langle t_1 | \phi_s(x) \rangle|^2 \big| \big)$$
$$\leq \sum_{s,t_1} \big(\big| |\alpha_s|^2 |\langle t_1 | \phi_s \rangle|^2 - |\beta_s|^2 |\langle t_1 | \phi_s(x) \rangle|^2 \big| \big)$$
$$+ \sum_{s,t_1} \big(\big| |\alpha_s|^2 |\langle t_1 | \phi_s(x) \rangle|^2 - |\beta_s|^2 |\langle t_1 | \phi_s(x) \rangle|^2 \big| \big)$$
$$= \sum_{s,t_1} \big(\big| |\alpha_s|^2 |\langle t_1 | \phi_s \rangle|^2 - |\beta_s|^2 |\langle t_1 | \phi_s(x) \rangle|^2 \big| \big)$$
$$+ \sum_s \big(\big| |\alpha_s|^2 - |\beta_s|^2 \big| \big)$$
$$\leq 2 \| |\phi\rangle \langle\phi| - |\phi(x)\rangle \langle\phi(x)| \|_{tr}$$
$$\leq 4 \| |\phi(x)\rangle - |\phi\rangle \|_2.$$

Finally,

$$S_3 = \sum_{s,t_1,t_2} \Big(|\alpha_s|^2 \big| |\langle t_1 | \phi_s(x) \rangle|^2 |\langle t_2 | V_s | \phi_s \rangle|^2$$
$$- |\langle t_1 | \phi_s(x) \rangle|^2 |\langle t_2 | V_s | \phi_s(x) \rangle|^2 \big| \Big)$$
$$= \sum_{s,t_2} \big(|\alpha_s|^2 \big| |\langle t_2 | V_s | \phi_s \rangle|^2 - |\langle t_2 | V_s | \phi_s(x) \rangle|^2 \big| \big)$$
$$\leq \sum_{s,t_2} \big(\big| |\alpha_s|^2 |\langle t_2 | V_s | \phi_s \rangle|^2 - |\beta_s|^2 |\langle t_2 | V_s | \phi_s(x) \rangle|^2 \big| \big)$$
$$+ \sum_{s,t_2} \big(\big| |\alpha_s|^2 |\langle t_2 | V_s | \phi_s(x) \rangle|^2 - |\beta_s|^2 |\langle t_2 | V_s | \phi_s(x) \rangle|^2 \big| \big)$$

$$= \sum_{s,t_2} \left(||\alpha_s|^2 |\langle t_2| V_s |\phi_s\rangle|^2 - |\beta_s|^2 |\langle t_2| V_s |\phi_s(x)\rangle|^2| \right)$$

$$+ \sum_s \left(||\alpha_s|^2 - |\beta_s|^2| \right)$$

$$\leq 2 \, ||\, |\phi\rangle \langle\phi| - |\phi(x)\rangle \langle\phi(x)|\,||_{tr}$$

$$= 4 \, ||\, |\phi(x)\rangle - |\phi\rangle \, ||_2$$

Therefore,

$$d_{x,i} \leq \frac{1}{2}(S_1 + S_2 + S_3) \leq 5 \, ||\, |\phi(x)\rangle - |\phi\rangle \, ||_2 \,.$$

On the other hand, if U_i is a query to f, then it only applies a local phase of -1 to some of the probability amplitudes of $|\phi\rangle$ and $|\phi_x\rangle$. Therefore, the same argument still shows that $d_{x,i} \leq 5 \, ||\, |\phi(x)\rangle - |\phi\rangle \, ||_2$.

By the Cauchy-Schwarz inequality and Lemma 6.3,

$$\frac{1}{N} \sum_{x=0}^{N-1} d_{x,i} \leq 5 \cdot \frac{1}{N} \sum_{x=0}^{N-1} ||\, |\phi(x)\rangle - |\phi\rangle \, ||_2$$

$$\leq 5 \sqrt{\frac{1}{N} \sum_{x=0}^{N-1} ||\, |\phi(x)\rangle - |\phi\rangle \, ||_2^2}$$

$$\leq \frac{10Q}{\sqrt{N}}$$

for all i. Therefore, there is some x for which

$$d_{TV}(v, v(x)) \leq 2 \sum_{i=1}^{T} d_{x,i} \leq \frac{20TQ}{\sqrt{N}}.$$

On the other hand, $d_{TV}(v, v(x)) \geq \frac{1}{3}$ for all x, so

$$\frac{20TQ}{\sqrt{N}} \geq \frac{1}{3},$$

and the running time of the algorithm is at least $T + Q = \Omega(N^{1/4})$. $\quad\square$

D. AN $N^{1/3}$ LOWER BOUND FOR SEARCH IN NACQP IF THERE ARE NO COLLAPSING MEASUREMENTS

Assume that intermediate measurements are not allowed in our search algorithm. As we discuss in Section 3, this gives a model with only the power of BQP, because then the states $|\psi_t\rangle = U_t U_{t-1} \ldots U_1 |0\rangle^{\otimes n}$ can be generated with poly-sized circuits, and hence a BQP machine could prepare and and measure them to sample from $\mathcal{Q}$. Trivially one can prove a lower bound of $N^{1/4}$ for search in this model, either by noting that this class can achieve at most quadratic speedups over BQP by the previous comment, or by using the argument put forth in Theorem 6.1. Here we tighten this result to give an $N^{1/3}$ lower bound for search in this class.

Suppose that an algorithm A searches with Q queries and T timesteps, where $Q + T = o(N^{1/3})$. Let ψ_t be the quantum state after t steps with no marked item, and let ψ_t^x be defined likewise when the marked item is at location x.

By the hybrid argument we have that $\forall t$

$$\sum_x ||\psi_t - \psi_t^x||_2^2 \leq 4Q^2$$

where $||a||_2^2$ is the 2-norm squared of a. This implies

$$\sum_t \sum_x ||\psi_t - \psi_t^x||_2^2 \leq 4TQ^2$$

Hence there must exist x such that

$$\sum_t ||\psi_t - \psi_t^x||_2^2 \leq \frac{4TQ^2}{N} \qquad (2)$$

Since we assumed $Q + T = o(N^{1/3})$, we have that $\frac{4TQ^2}{N} = o(1)$. Therefore for sufficiently large N and for all t we have

$$||\psi_t - \psi_t^x||_2^2 \leq 0.01$$

(The choice of constant here is arbitrary, we simply need it to be less than around 0.5.) Now consider the states $\Psi := \bigotimes_t |\psi_t\rangle$ and $\Psi^x := \bigotimes_t |\psi_t^x\rangle$. Let V the distribution on samples with no marked item, and let V^x be defined likewise. Then clearly we have that

$$|V - V^x|_1 \leq ||\Psi - \Psi^x||$$

where $||a||$ denotes the trace norm of a. This is because the output distributions of V and V^x can be obtained by (independent) measurements on the states Ψ and Ψ_x in the computational basis. Note that $|V - V^x|_1$ must be $\Omega(1)$ in order to distinguish the presence of a marked item at x in postprocessing. Therefore we have

$$\Omega(1) \leq |V - V_x|_1 \leq ||\Psi - \Psi^x|| \qquad (3)$$

$$= \sqrt{1 - |\langle \Psi | \Psi^x \rangle|^2} \qquad (4)$$

$$= \sqrt{1 - |\Pi_t \langle \psi_t | \psi_t^x \rangle|^2} \qquad (5)$$

$$\leq \sqrt{1 - \Pi_t e^{-||\psi_t - \psi_t^x||_2^2}} \qquad (6)$$

$$= \sqrt{1 - e^{-\Sigma_t ||\psi_t - \psi_t^x||_2^2}} \qquad (7)$$

$$\leq \sqrt{1 - e^{-\frac{4TQ^2}{N}}} \qquad (8)$$

$$= o(1) \qquad (9)$$

Where in line 4 we use the formula for trace distance of pure states, in line 8 we used equation 2, in line 9 we used the fact that $T + Q = o(N^{1/3})$, and in line 6 we use the inequality

$$|\langle \psi_t | \psi_t^x \rangle| \geq \mathrm{Re}\left(\langle \psi_t | \psi_t^x \rangle \right) \qquad (10)$$

$$= 1 - \frac{||\psi_t - \psi_t^x||_2^2}{2} \qquad (11)$$

$$\geq e^{-||\psi_t - \psi_t^x||_2^2} \qquad (12)$$

where we have use the fact that $1 - x \geq e^{-2x}$ for $0 \leq x \leq 0.01$. Therefore we have shown $\Omega(1) = o(1)$, a contradiction. Hence such an algorithm A cannot exist, so searching takes $Q + T = \Omega(N^{1/3})$ time when there are non-collapsing measurements, but no collapsing measurements, in the model.

Coordination Complexity:
Small Information Coordinating Large Populations

[Extended Abstract] *

Rachel Cummings [†]
Caltech

Katrina Ligett [‡]
Caltech

Jaikumar Radhakrishnan
Tata Institute of Fundamental
Research

Aaron Roth [§]
University of Pennsylvania

Zhiwei Steven Wu [¶]
University of Pennsylvania

ABSTRACT

We study a quantity that we call *coordination complexity*. In a distributed optimization problem, the information defining a problem instance is distributed among n parties, who need to each choose an action, which jointly will form a solution to the optimization problem. The coordination complexity represents the minimal amount of information that a centralized coordinator, who has full knowledge of the problem instance, needs to broadcast in order to coordinate the n parties to play a nearly optimal solution.

We show that upper bounds on the coordination complexity of a problem imply the existence of good jointly differentially private algorithms for solving that problem, which in turn are known to upper bound the price of anarchy in certain games with dynamically changing populations.

We show several results. We fully characterize the coordination complexity for the problem of computing a many-to-one matching in a bipartite graph by giving almost matching lower and upper bounds. Our upper bound in fact extends much more generally, to the problem of solving a linearly separable convex program. We also give a different upper

*A full version of this paper is available on arXiv at http://arxiv.org/abs/1508.03735

†Supported by Simons Award for Graduate Students in Theoretical Computer Science and NSF CNS-1254169.

‡Supported in part by NSF grant CNS-1254169, NSF grant CNS-1518941 US-Israel Binational Science Foundation grant 2012348, the Charles Lee Powell Foundation, a Google Faculty Research Award, an Okawa Foundation Research Grant, a Microsoft Faculty Fellowship.

§Supported in part by NSF Grant CCF-1101389, an NSF CAREER award, and an Alfred P. Sloan Foundation Fellowship.

¶Supported in part by NSF Grant CCF-1101389.

Permission to make digital or hard copies of all or part of this work for personal or classroom use is granted without fee provided that copies are not made or distributed for profit or commercial advantage and that copies bear this notice and the full citation on the first page. Copyrights for components of this work owned by others than ACM must be honored. Abstracting with credit is permitted. To copy otherwise, or republish, to post on servers or to redistribute to lists, requires prior specific permission and/or a fee. Request permissions from Permissions@acm.org.

ITCS'16, January 14-16, 2016, Cambridge, MA, USA

© 2016 ACM. ISBN 978-1-4503-4057-1/16/01... $15.00

DOI: http://dx.doi.org/10.1145/2840728.2840767

bound technique, which we use to bound the coordination complexity of coordinating a Nash equilibrium in a routing game, and of computing a stable matching.

CCS Concepts

•**Theory of computation** → **Communication complexity; Approximation algorithms analysis; Algorithmic game theory;**

Keywords

coordination complexity, privacy

1. INTRODUCTION

In this paper, we study a quantity which we call *coordination complexity*. This quantity measures the amount of information that a centralized coordinator needs to broadcast in order to coordinate n parties, each with only local information about a problem instance, to jointly implement a globally optimal solution. Unlike in *communication complexity*, there is no need for the communication protocols in our setting to derive the optimal solution starting with nothing but local information, nor even *verify* that a proposed solution is optimal (as is the goal in non-deterministic communication complexity). Instead, in our setting, there is a central coordinator who already has complete knowledge of the problem instance — and hence also of the optimal solution. His goal is simply to publish a concise message to guide the n parties making up the problem instance to coordinate on the desired solution – ideally using fewer bits than would be (trivially) needed to simply publish the optimal solution itself.[1]

Aside from its intrinsic interest, our motivation for studying this quantity is two-fold. First, as we show, problems with low coordination complexity also have good protocols for implementing nearly optimal solutions under the constraint of *joint differential privacy* [DMNS06, KPRU14] – i.e. protocols that allow the joint implementation of a nearly

---

[1]Within our framework of coordination complexity, we assume that the players are not strategic — they will faithfully follow the coordination protocol upon observing the message broadcast by the coordinator. We do study the interface between the coordination complexity and the strategic variants of some problems in Section 5.

optimal solution in a manner such that no coalition of parties can learn much about the portion of the instance known by any party not in the coalition. The existence of jointly differentially private protocols in turn have recently been shown to imply a low "price of anarchy" for no-regret players in the strategic variant of the optimization problem when the game in question is smooth – even when the population is dynamically changing [LST15]. Hence, as a result of the connection we develop in this paper, in order to show dynamic price of anarchy bounds of the sort given in [LST15], it is sufficient to show that the game in question has low coordination complexity, without needing to directly develop and analyze differentially private algorithms. Using this connection we also derive new results for what can be implemented under the constraint of pure joint differential privacy – results that were previously only known subject to approximate joint differential privacy.

Second, coordination complexity is a stylized measure of the power of concise broadcasts (e.g. prices in the setting of allocation problems, or congestion information in the setting of routing problems) to coordinate populations in the absence of any interaction.[2] Here we note that prices seem to coordinate markets, despite the fact that individuals do not actually participate in any kind of interactive "Walrasian mechanism" of the sort that would be needed to compute the allocation itself, in addition to the prices (see e.g. [KC82, DNO14]). Indeed, prices alone are generally not sufficient to coordinate high welfare allocations because prices on their own can induce a large number of indifferences that might need to be resolved in a coordinated way – and hence Walrasian equilibria are defined not just as vectors of equilibrium prices, but as vectors of prices paired with optimal allocations. Publishing a Walrasian equilibrium would be a trivial solution in our setting, because it involves communicating the entire solution that we wish to coordinate – the optimal allocation. Nevertheless, we show that the coordination complexity of the allocation problem is – up to log factors – equal to the number of types of goods in a commodity market. This is the same as what would be needed to communicate prices (indeed, our solution can be viewed as communicating prices in a slightly different, "regularized" market), and can be substantially smaller than what would be needed to communicate the optimal allocation itself.

1.1 Our Results and Techniques

In our model (which we formally define in Section 2), a *problem instance* D is defined by an n-tuple from some abstract domain $\mathcal{X}$: $D \in \mathcal{X}^n$. We write $D = (D^{(1)}, \ldots, D^{(n)})$ to denote the fact that the information defining the problem instance is partitioned among n agents, and each agent i knows only his own part $D^{(i)}$. The solution space is also a product space: $\mathcal{A}^n$, and each agent i can choose a single *action* $a_i \in \mathcal{A}$ – the choices of all of the agents jointly form a solution $a = (a_1, \ldots, a_n)$. The *coordinator* knows the entire problem instance D, and publishes a signal $\sigma(D) \in \{0, 1\}^\ell$. Each agent then chooses an action $a_i := \pi(D^{(i)}, \sigma(D))$ based only on the coordinator's signal and her own part of the problem instance. The jointly induced solution $a = (a_1, \ldots, a_n)$

is the output of the interaction. The pair of functions σ, π jointly form a protocol, and ℓ, the length of the coordinator's signal is the coordination complexity of the protocol. The coordination complexity of a problem is the minimal coordination complexity of any protocol solving the problem.

A canonical example to keep in mind is many-to-one matchings: Here, a problem instance is defined by a bipartite graph between n agents and k types of goods. Each good j has a supply s_j, and the goal is to find a maximum cardinality matching such that no agent is matched to more than one good, and no good j is matched to more than s_j agents. Here, the portion of the instance known to agent i is the set of goods adjacent to agent i– but nothing about the goods adjacent to other agents. Note that describing a matching requires $\Omega(n \log k)$ bits, which is the trivial upper bound on the coordination complexity for this problem. For this problem, we show nearly matching upper and lower bounds: no protocol with coordination complexity $o(k)$ can guarantee a constant approximation to the optimal solution, whereas there is a protocol with coordination complexity $O(k \log n)$ that can obtain a $(1 + o(1))$-approximation to the optimal solution. Our upper bound in fact extends much more generally, to any problem that can be written down as a convex program whose objective and constraints are linearly separable between agents' data.

The idea of the upper bound is to broadcast a portion of the optimal dual solution to the convex program – one dual variable for every constraint that is defined by the data of multiple agents (there is no need to publish the dual variables corresponding to constraints that depend only on the data of a single agent). For the many-to-one matching problem, these dual variables correspond to "prices" – one for each of the k types of goods. This idea on its own does not work, however, because a dual optimal solution to a convex program is not generally sufficient to specify the primal optimal solution. When specialized to the case of matchings, this is because optimal "market clearing prices" can induce a large number of indifferences among goods for each of the n agents, and these indifferences might need to be broken in a coordinated way to induce an optimal matching. To solve this problem, we instead release the dual variables corresponding to a slightly different convex program, in which a *strongly convex regularizer* has been added to the objective. The effect of the strongly convex regularizer is that the optimal dual solution now uniquely specifies the optimal primal solution – although now the optimal primal solution to a modified problem. The rest of our approach deals with trading off the weight of the regularizer with the number of bits needed to approximately specify each of the dual variables, and the error of the regularized optimal solution relative to the optimal solution to the original problem.

We also give several other positive results, based on a different technique: broadcasting the truncated transcript of a process known to converge to a solution of interest. Using this technique, we give low coordination complexity protocols for the problem of coordinating on an equilibrium in a routing game, and for the problem of coordinating on a *stable* many-to-one matching.

Finally, we show that problems that have both low sensitivity objectives (as all of the problems we study do) and low coordination complexity also have good *jointly differentially private* protocols. Using the results of [LST15], this also shows a bound on the price of anarchy of the strategic

---

[2]Of course, the connection here is in a stylized model – in a market, there is not in fact any party with complete information of the problem instance – but the market is nevertheless encoding good "distributional information" about the population of buyers likely to arrive.

variant of these problems, whenever they are *smooth games*, which holds even under a dynamically changing population.

1.2 Related Work

Our model of coordination complexity is related to, but distinct from, the well-studied notion of communication complexity – see [KN97] for a textbook introduction. While both complexity notions measure the number of bits that must be transmitted among decentralized parties to reach a particular outcome, they differ in the initial endowment of information, as well as in the requirements of each player to know the final outcome. In communication complexity, the information describing the problem instance is fully distributed, and communication is necessary for all parties to know the outcome. Coordination complexity in contrast assumes the existence of a coordinator who knows the entire problem instance, and must broadcast information to the players which will allow them to each compute their part of the output – there is no need for any of the parties to know the entire output. More similar to our setting is *non-deterministic communication complexity*, in which we may imagine that there is an oracle who knows the inputs of all players and broadcasts a message (perhaps partially) describing a solution together with a certificate that allows the parties to verify the optimality of the solution. In contrast, in our model of coordination complexity, the coordinator does not need to provide any certificate allowing parties to verify that the coordinated solution is optimal (indeed, each party need not have any information about the portion of the solution proposed to other parties).

The informational requirements of coordinating matchings has a long history of study in economics, and has recently gained attention in theoretical computer science. Hayek's classic paper [Hay45] conjectured that Walrasian price mechanisms, which coordinate matchings via a tâtonnement process that updates market-clearing prices based on demand, are "informationally efficient," in that they verify optimal allocations with the least amount of information. This was later formalized by [Hur60] and [MR74] in specific settings of interest, using an informational metric that measured smooth real-valued communication. Nisan and Segal study the communication complexity of matchings using the tools of communication complexity as developed in computer science, and show that any communication protocol that determines an optimal allocation must also determine supporting prices [NS06]. Recently, [DNO14] and [ANRW15] studied the problem of computing an optimal matching through the lens of interactive communication complexity, showing that interactive protocols can have significantly lower communication complexity than non-interactive ones. Note that the communication complexity bounds given in these papers are always larger than the description length of the matching itself – in contrast, here when we study coordination complexity, nontrivial bounds must not just be smaller than the input, but must also be smaller than the size of the optimal matching.

Finally, there are two papers that study a very similar setting to ours, although they obtain rather different results.[3] Calsamiglia [Cal84] studies a real-valued communication model in which a central coordinator with full knowledge of the instance needs to broadcast a concise signal to

coordinate an allocation in an exchange market—see [Seg06] for context on how this result fits into the economic literature on communication complexity. Deng, Papadimitriou, and Safra also study a similar model in Section 4 of [DPS02], which they call "Market Communication". Despite the similarity in models, the results of both [Cal84] and [DPS02] stand in sharp contrast to ours—they both give *lower bounds*, showing that the amount of communication necessary needs to grow linearly with the number of buyers n, while we give upper bounds showing that it is necessary to grow only with the number of different types of goods k. Calsamiglia does not allow approximation in his model, which is necessary for our results. Deng, Papadimitriou, and Safra allow for approximation, but study an instance of a problem that cannot be expressed as a linearly separable convex program, which shows that structure of the sort that we use is necessary.

A line of work [KPRU14, RR14, CKRW14, HHR+14, HHRW14, RRUW15] has studied protocols for implementing outcomes in various settings under the constraint of joint differential privacy [DMNS06, KPRU14], which allows n parties to jointly implement some solution while ensuring that no coalition of parties can learn much about the input of any party outside the coalition. Most (but not all) of these algorithms are actually private coordination protocols of the sort we study here, in which the algorithm can be viewed as a coordinator who is constrained to broadcast a private signal. These jointly private algorithms are not constrained to transmit a short signal – and indeed, the private signals can sometimes be verbose. But as we show, problems with low coordination complexity also have good jointly differentially private algorithms, which was one of our original motivations for studying this quantity.

Lykouris, Syrgkanis, and Tardos [LST15] show that the existence of a jointly differentially private algorithm for solving an optimization problem implies that the strategic variant of the problem has a low "price of anarchy" for learning agents, even in dynamic settings, in which player types change over time, as long as the game is smooth. Because we show in Section 5 that any problem with a low sensitivity objective and low coordination complexity has a good jointly differentially private algorithm, using the results of [LST15], to prove a bound on the price of anarchy in a smooth dynamic game, we show it suffices to bound the coordination complexity of the game.

2. PRELIMINARIES

A *coordination problem* is defined by a set of n agents, a data domain $\mathcal{X}$, an action range $\mathcal{A}$, and a social objective function $S\colon \mathcal{X}^n \times \mathcal{A}^n \to \mathbb{R}$. An *instance* of a coordination problem consists of a set of n elements from the data domain: $D = (D^{(1)}, \ldots, D^{(n)}) \in \mathcal{X}^n$. Each agent i has knowledge only of $D^{(i)}$, his own portion of the problem instance, and the goal is for a centralized *coordinator* to broadcast a concise message to the agents to allow them to arrive at a solution $a = (a_1, \ldots, a_n) \in \mathcal{A}^n$ that approximately maximizes the objective function $S(D, a)$.

A *coordination protocol* consists of two functions, an *encoding function* $\sigma\colon \mathcal{X}^n \to \{0,1\}^*$ and a *decoding function* $\pi\colon \mathcal{X} \times \{0,1\}^* \to \mathcal{A}$. A coordination protocol (σ, π) proceeds in two stages:

- First the coordinator broadcasts the message $\sigma(D)$ to all agents using the encoding function.

---

[3]We thank Ilya Segal for pointing out [Cal84] to us, and thank Sepehr Assadi for pointing out Section 4 of [DPS02].

- Then each agent selects an action a_i on the basis of her own portion of the problem instance and the broadcast message, using the decoding function: $a_i := \pi(D^{(i)}, \sigma(D))$.

Both functions σ and π may be randomized. The approximation ratio of a protocol is the ratio of the optimal objective value to the expected objective value of the solution induced by the protocol, in the worst case over problem instances.

DEFINITION 1 (APPROXIMATION RATIO). *A coordination protocol (σ, π) obtains a ρ approximation to a problem if:*

$$\max_{D \in \mathcal{X}^n} \frac{\mathrm{OPT}(D)}{\mathbb{E}_{a_1,\ldots,a_n}[S(D, a)]} \leq \rho$$

where each $a_i = \pi(D^{(i)}, \sigma(D))$, and the expectation is taken over the randomness of σ and π.

The coordination complexity of a protocol is the maximum number of bits the encoding function broadcasts, in the worst case over problem instances.

DEFINITION 2 (COORDINATION COMPLEXITY). *A coordination protocol (σ, π) has coordination complexity ℓ if:*

$$\max_{D \in \mathcal{X}^n} |\sigma(D)| = \ell.$$

The coordination complexity of obtaining a ρ approximation to a problem is the minimum value of the coordination complexity of all protocols (σ, π) that obtain a ρ approximation to the problem.

We conclude by making several observations about coordination protocols. First, as we have defined them, they are *non-interactive* – the coordinator first broadcasts a signal, and then the agents respond. This is without loss of generality, since the coordinator has full knowledge of the problem instance. Any interactive protocol could be reduced at no additional communication cost to a non-interactive protocol, simply by having the coordinator publish the transcript that would have arisen from the interactive protocol. This is in contrast to the setting of communication complexity, in which interactive protocols can be more powerful than non-interactive protocols (and makes it easier to prove lower bounds for coordination complexity).

Second, the coordination complexity of a problem is trivially upper bounded both by the description length of the problem instance (as is communication complexity), *and* by the description length of the problem's optimal solution (unlike in non-deterministic communication complexity, there is no need to pair the optimal solution with a certificate allowing individual agents to verify it). Hence, non-trivial bounds will be asymptotically smaller than both of these quantities.

Bipartite Matching.

The primary coordination problem we study in this paper is the *bipartite matching problem*. In this problem, there is a bipartite graph $G = (V, W, E)$, in which every node in V is associated with a player and every node in W represents a good. Each player i's private data is the set of edges incident to her node – i.e. $D^{(i)} = \{j : (i, j) \in E\}$. We study two variants of this problem. In the *one-to-one* matching problem, W represents a set of distinct goods, and the goal is to coordinate a maximum cardinality matching $E' \subseteq E$ such that for every $i \in V$, $|\{j \in W : (i, j) \in E'\}| \leq 1$

and for every $j \in W$, $|\{i \in V : (i, j) \in E'\}| \leq 1$. In the *many-to-one* matching problem, W represents a set of k commodities j, each with a supply b_j. The goal is to coordinate a maximum cardinality many-to-one matching $E' \subseteq E$ such that for every $i \in V$, $|\{j \in W : (i, j) \in E'\}| \leq 1$ and for every $j \in W$, $|\{i \in V : (i, j) \in E'\}| \leq b_j$. The social objective in this setting is the welfare or the cardinality of the matching, and we will use $\mathrm{OPT}(G)$ to denote the optimal welfare objective.

Note that the resulting solution might not be feasible since the players' demands are not always satisfied. We need to make sure that we are not over-counting when measuring the welfare. In one-to-one matchings, if more than one players select a good, only the first player is matched to it. In many-to-one matchings, if more than b_j players select a good of type j, only the first b_j players are matched the good j.

Notation.

We use $\|\cdot\|$ to denote the ℓ_2 norm, and more generally use $\|\cdot\|_p$ to denote the ℓ_p norm.

3. LOWER BOUNDS FOR MATCHINGS

In this section, we present lower bounds on the coordination complexity of bipartite matching problems. As a building block, we prove a lower bound for the one-to-one matching problem on a bipartite graph with n vertices on each side, showing an $\Omega(n)$ lower bound – i.e. that no substantial improvement on the trivial solution is possible. We then extend this lower bound to the problem of many-to-one matchings, in which there are n agents who must be matched to k goods (each good can be matched to many agents, up to its supply). Here, we show an $\Omega(k)$ lower bound. In the next section, we give a nearly matching upper bound, which substantially improves over the trivial solution.

3.1 A Variant of the Index Function Problem

Before we present our lower bound, we introduce a variant of the *random index function* problem [KNR99], which will be useful for our proof.

MULTIPLE-INDEX.

There are two players Alice and Bob. Alice receives as input a sequence of t pairs, $I = \langle (S_i, u_i) : i = 1, 2, \ldots, t \rangle$, where the S_i are disjoint sets each with k elements, and u_i is uniformly distributed in S_i. Based on her input Alice sends Bob a message $M(I)$. Bob then receives (S_j, j), where j is chosen from $[t]$. Bob must determine u_j; let his output be $B(S_j, j, M(I)) \in S_j$. We say that the protocol succeeds if $B(S_j, j, M(I)) = u_j$. Let $\ell(t, k, p)$ be the minimum number of bits (for the worst input) that Alice must send in order for Bob to succeed with probability at least p.

Note that if Bob guesses randomly, then the protocol already succeeds with probability $p = 1/k$. The following result shows that any significant improvement over this trivial probability of success will require Alice to send Bob a long message. See the full version for a full proof.

LEMMA 1. *For $p \geq 1/k$, we have $\ell(t, k, p) \geq (8 \log e) t (p - 1/k)^2$.*

3.2 Lower Bound for One-to-One Matchings

We will first focus on the lower bound on one-to-one matching and show the following.

THEOREM 1. *Suppose the coordination protocol* Π *for one-to-one matching guarantees an approximation ratio of* ρ *in expectation. Then, the coordinator of* Π *must broadcast* $\Omega(n/\rho^4)$ *bits on problem instances of size* n *(in the worst case).*

Fix the protocol Π. We will extract a two-party communication protocol for the **MULTIPLE-INDEX** problem from Π, and use the above lemma. As a first step for our lower bound proof, we will consider the following random graph construction process RanG.

Random Graph Construction RanG(ρ, n):.

Let $\kappa = \frac{n}{8\rho}$ and $A = \frac{n}{16\rho^2}$. Consider the following random bipartite graph G with vertex set (V, W) such that $|V| = |W| = n$.

- Randomly generate an ordering $w_1, w_2, \ldots, w_n$ of W (all $n!$ orderings being equally likely), and partition W as $W_1 \cup W_2$ such that $W_1 = \{w_1, w_2, \ldots, w_\kappa\}$, and $W_2 = \{w_{\kappa+1}, w_{\kappa+2}, \ldots, w_n\}$.

- Similarly, randomly generate an ordering $v_1, v_2, \ldots, v_n$ of V, and parition V into n/A bocks, $B_1, B_2, \ldots, B_{n/A}$ (each with A vertices), where

$$B_j := \{v_i : (j-1)A + 1 \leq i \leq j A\}.$$

- Connect B_j and W as follows. First, we describe the connections between V and W_1. The neighbourhoods of the vertices in each B_j will be disjoint: we partition W_1 into equal-sized disjoint sets $(T_v : v \in B_j)$, and let the neighbours of $v \in B_j$ be exactly the 2ρ vertices in T_v.

- In addition, assign each vertex in v one neighbor in W_2, by connecting V with W_2 in round-robin fashion — connect vertex v_i to vertex w_j, where $j = (\kappa + i \mod (n - \kappa))$.

Before we prove Theorem 1, let us first observe that a graph generated by RanG always has a matching with high welfare.

LEMMA 2. *Each graph* G *generated by the above process* RanG$(\cdot, n)$ *has optimal welfare* $\text{OPT}(G) \geq \frac{7n}{8}$.

PROOF PROOF OF THEOREM 1. Let Π be a coordination protocol with coordination complexity ℓ and approximation ratio ρ. This means that on a graph instance generated by RanG, the parties can coordinate on a matching with expected weight at least $\frac{7n}{8\rho}$. Since $|W_1| = \frac{n}{8\rho}$, we know in expectation at least $\frac{7n}{8\rho} - \frac{n}{8\rho} = \frac{3n}{4\rho}$ of the vertices in W_2 are matched. Let α_v be the probability that in Π, agent v picks her neighbor in W_2. Then, by linearity of expectation, $\sum_{v \in V} \alpha_v \geq \frac{3n}{4}$, that is, $\mathbb{E}_{v \in V}[\alpha_v] \geq \frac{3}{4}$. Hence, there must be some block B_j such that $\mathbb{E}_{v \in B_j}[\alpha_v] \geq \frac{3}{4}$. We will now restrict attention to the block B_j and consider the following instance of **MULTIPLE-INDEX**: for each $v \in B_j$, set $S_v = N(v)$—the neighborhood of vertex v, and let u_v be the vertex unique vertex in $S_v \cap W_2$. Since the message broadcast by the coordination protocol allows the players to identify the special element with average success probability

of $\frac{3}{4\rho}$, by Lemma 1 the length of message

$$\ell \geq (8 \log e)|B_j| \left(\frac{3}{4\rho} - \frac{1}{2\rho + 1}\right)^2$$

$$\geq (8 \log e) \left(\frac{n}{16\rho^2}\right) \left(\frac{3}{4\rho} - \frac{1}{2\rho + 1}\right)^2 \geq \Omega\left(\frac{n}{\rho^4}\right),$$

which completes the proof. $\square$

3.3 Lower Bound for Many-to-One Matchings

Finally, we give the following lower bound on coordination complexity for many-to-one matchings. The lower bound relies on the result from Section 3.2—we show that any coordination protocol for many-to-one matchings can also be reduced to a protocol for one-to-one matchings, and so the lower bound in Section 3.2 can be extended to give a lower bound for the many-to-one setting.

For our lower bound instance, we consider bipartite graphs $G = (V, E)$ such that the vertices in V represent n different players and W represent a set of k goods j, each with a supply b.

THEOREM 2. *Suppose that there exists a coordination protocol for many-to-one matchings that guarantees an approximation ratio of* ρ *in expectation. Then such a protocol has coordination complexity of* $\Omega(k/\rho^4)$.

We will start by considering a one-to-one matching instance generated by RanG with k vertices on each side of the graph $G' = (V', W', E')$. By Lemma 2, the optimal matching of G' has size $\text{OPT}' \geq \frac{7k}{8}$.

Now we will turn this into an instance of a many-to-one matching problem: make b copies of each vertex in V' to obtain vertex set V, and set $W := W'$ such that the supply of each good j is b; then for an edge (v', w') in the original graph, connect all copies of v' to w' in the new graph. This gives a bipartite graph $G = (V, W, E)$. The following claim is straightforward.

CLAIM 1. *The new graph* G *has a matching of size at least* $(b\,\text{OPT}')$.

Now suppose that we could coordinate the players in V to obtain a matching M^* of size $\frac{b\,\text{OPT}'}{\rho}$ in G. Then with a simple sampling procedure, we can extract a high cardinality matching for the original graph: for each vertex in $v' \in V'$, sample one of the b copies of v' in G uniformly at random along with its incident matched edge. If two vertices in V' are connected to the same type of good in W', break ties arbitrarily and keep only one of the edges.

LEMMA 3. *The sampled matching in* G' *has expected size at least* $\frac{\text{OPT}'}{3\rho}$.

We will defer the proof to the full version. We now have all the pieces to prove Theorem 2.

PROOF PROOF OF THEOREM 2. Suppose that there exists a coordination protocol (σ, π) for many-to-one matchings with a guaranteed approximation ratio of ρ. By the result of Lemma 3, we know that this coordination protocol for one-to-one matchings has an approximation ratio most $O(\rho)$. By the lower bound in Theorem 1, we know that the length of $\sigma(G)$ is at least $\Omega(k/\rho^4)$. $\square$

4. COORDINATION PROTOCOL FOR LINEARLY SEPARABLE CONVEX PROGRAMS

In this section, we give a coordination protocol for problems which can be expressed as linearly separable convex programs, with coordination complexity scaling only with the number of constraints that bind between agents (so called *coupling constraints*, defined below). In the next section, we show how to specialize this protocol to the special case of many-to-one matchings, which gives coordination complexity nearly matching our lower bound.

DEFINITION 3. *A linearly separable convex optimization problem consists of n players and for each player i,*

- *a compact and bounded convex feasible set $\mathcal{F}^{(i)} \subseteq \{x^{(i)} \in \mathbb{R}^l \mid \|x^{(i)}\| \leq 1\}$,*
- *a concave objective and 1-Lipschitz function $v^{(i)} \colon \mathcal{F}^{(i)} \to \mathbb{R}$ such that $v^{(i)}(\mathbf{0}) = 0$,*
- *and k convex constraint function $c_j^{(i)} \colon \mathcal{F}^{(i)} \to [0,1]$ (indexed by $j = 1, \ldots, k$).*

The convex optimization problem is:

$$\max_x \sum_{i=1}^n v^{(i)}(x^{(i)})$$

$$\text{subject to } \sum_{i=1}^n c_j^{(i)}(x^{(i)}) \leq b_j \quad \text{for } j = 1, \ldots, k$$

$$x^{(i)} \in \mathcal{F}^{(i)} \quad \text{for } i = 1, \ldots, n$$

where each player i controls the block of decision variable $x^{(i)}$.

Viewed as a coordination problem, the data held by each agent i is $D^{(i)} = \{\mathcal{F}^{(i)}, v^{(i)}, c_1^{(i)}, \ldots, c_k^{(i)}\}$, his action range is $\mathcal{A}_i = \mathcal{F}^{(i)}$, and the social objective function is S the objective of the convex program. We will call the first set of constraints the *coupling constraints*, and the second set of constraints the *personal constraints*.

We will denote the product of the personal constraints by $\mathcal{F} = \mathcal{F}^{(1)} \times \ldots \times \mathcal{F}^{(n)}$, the objective function by $v(x)$, and the optimal value by OPT. In this notation we can write the problem as

$$\max_{x \in \mathcal{F} \text{ and } \sum_{i=1}^n c_j^{(i)}(x^{(i)}) \leq b_j \text{ for all } j} v(x).$$

Note that here the problem is constrained both by the personal constraints $\mathcal{F}$ and by the coupling constraints. We will assume the problem above is feasible and our goal is coordinate the players to play an aggregate solution $x = (x^{(i)})_{i \in [n]}$ that is approximately feasible and optimal. Our solution consists of two steps:

1. We will first introduce a regularization term $\eta \|x\|^2$ to our objective function, and coordinate the players to maximize the regularized objective. The purpose of adding this regularization term is to make the objective function *strongly concave*, which will cause it to have the property that an optimal dual solution will uniquely specify the optimal primal solution.

2. Then we will show that the resulting optimal solution to the regularized problem is close to being optimal for the original (unregularized) problem. The weight of the regularization has to be traded off against the bit precision to which we need to communicate the optimal dual variables.

4.1 Coordination through Regularization

In the first step, we add a small regularization term to our original objective function. Consider the following convex optimization problem:

$$\max_{x \in \mathcal{F} \text{ and } \sum_{i=1}^n c_j^{(i)}(x^{(i)}) \leq b_j \text{ for all } j} v'(x) = \sum_{i=1}^n v^{(i)}(x^{(i)}) - \frac{\eta}{2}\|x\|^2$$

CLAIM 2. *The objective function v' is η-strongly concave.*

To solve the convex program, we will work with the partial *Lagrangian* $\mathcal{L}(x, \lambda)$, which results from bringing only the coupling constraints into the objective via Lagrangian dual variables, but leaving the personal constraints to continue to constrain the primal feasible region:

$$\sum_{i=1}^n \left(v^{(i)}\left(x^{(i)}\right) - \frac{\eta}{2}\|x^{(i)}\|^2 - \sum_{j=1}^k \lambda_j \left(\sum_{i=1}^n c_j^{(i)}\left(x^{(i)}\right) - b_j \right) \right)$$

Let OPT$'$ denote the optimum of the convex program, and by *strong duality* we have

$$\max_{x \in \mathcal{F}} \min_{\lambda \in \mathbb{R}_+^k} \mathcal{L}(x, \lambda) = \min_{\lambda \in \mathbb{R}_+^k} \max_{x \in \mathcal{F}} \mathcal{L}(x, \lambda) = \text{OPT}'$$

Fixing the optimal dual variables, λ, the optimal primal solution y satisfies

$$y = \operatorname*{argmax}_{x \in \mathcal{F}} \mathcal{L}(x, \lambda)$$

Note that the result of moving the coupling constraints into the Lagrangian is that we can now write the primal optimization problem over a feasible region defined only by the personal constraints. Because of this fact, and because the Lagrangian objective is linearly separable across players, given λ, each player's portion of the solution $y^{(i)}$ is

$$\operatorname*{argmax}_{x \in \mathcal{F}_i} \left[v^{(i)}\left(x^{(i)}\right) - \frac{\eta}{2}\|x^{(i)}\|^2 - \sum_{j=1}^k \lambda_j c_j^{(i)}\left(x^{(i)}\right) \right]. \quad (1)$$

Thus, if the argmax were unique, this means that the optimal dual variables λ would be sufficient to coordinate each of the parties to find their portion of the optimal solution, without the need for further communication (the problem, in general, is that the argmax need not be unique, and ties may need to be broken in a coordinated fashion). However, because we have added a strongly concave regularizer, the argmax is unique in our setting:

CLAIM 3. *The solution to*

$$\operatorname*{argmax}_{x \in \mathcal{F}_i} v^{(i)}\left(x^{(i)}\right) - \frac{\eta}{2}\|x^{(i)}\|^2 - \sum_{j=1}^k \lambda_j \left(\sum_{i=1}^n c_j^{(i)}\left(x^{(i)}\right) \right)$$

is unique.

This gives rise to our simple coordination mechanism ReC. The mechanism first computes the optimal dual variables in our regularized partial Lagrangian problem, rounds them to finite precision, and then publishes these variables. Then each individual player finds her part of the near optimal solution by performing the optimization in Equation (1). The details are in Algorithm 4.1.

Algorithm 1 Coordination Protocol for Linearly Separable Convex Programs $\mathsf{ReC}(\eta, \varepsilon)$

Input: a linearly separable convex program instance I, regularization parameter η and target accuracy ε

Initialize: $\alpha = \frac{\eta \varepsilon^2}{4\sqrt{nk}}$

Modify the objective of I into

$$\max_{x \in \mathcal{F}} v(x) - \frac{\eta \|x\|^2}{2}$$

Compute the optimal dual solution $\lambda^\bullet$ for the modified convex program

Round each coordinate of $\lambda^\bullet$ into a multiple of $\alpha/\sqrt{k}$ and obtain $\widehat{\lambda}$

Broadcast the rounded dual solution $\widehat{\lambda}$. To decode, each player i computes $\widehat{x}^{(i)}(\lambda)$:

$$\operatorname*{argmax}_{x \in \mathcal{F}_i} \left[v^{(i)}\left(x^{(i)}\right) - \frac{\eta}{2}\|x^{(i)}\|^2 - \sum_{j=1}^{k} \widehat{\lambda}_j c_j^{(i)}\left(x^{(i)}\right) \right]$$

Next we show that the resulting solution is close to the optimal solution of the regularized convex program (i.e. that we do not lose much by truncating the dual variables to have finite bit precision). Let $(x^\bullet, \lambda^\bullet)$ be an optimal primal-dual pair for the regularized convex program. Note that since the objective of the program is strongly concave, $x^\bullet$ is unique. First, we will show that if the broadcast dual vector $\widehat{\lambda}$ is close to an optimal dual solution $\lambda^\bullet$, the resulting solution $\widehat{x}$ will also be close to the optimal primal solution $x^\bullet$.

LEMMA 4. *Suppose we have a dual vector $\widehat{\lambda}$ such that $\|\lambda^\bullet - \widehat{\lambda}\| \leq \alpha$. Let $\widehat{x} = \operatorname{argmax}_{x \in \mathcal{F}} \mathcal{L}(x, \widehat{\lambda})$, then*

$$\|\widehat{x} - x^\bullet\| \leq \frac{2\sqrt{\alpha}(nk)^{1/4}}{\sqrt{\eta}}$$

The proof relies on some basic properties of the Lagrangian and strong concavity and is deferred to the full version.

LEMMA 5. *The coordination mechanism ReC instantiated with regularization parameter η and target accuracy parameter ε will coordinate the players to play a solution $\widehat{x}$ that satisfies $\|\widehat{x} - x^\bullet\| \leq \varepsilon$, and has a coordination complexity of $O(k \log(nk/\eta\varepsilon))$.*

PROOF. Note that $\alpha = \frac{\eta \varepsilon^2}{4\sqrt{nk}}$, and the mechanism rounds each coordinate of the optimal dual solution $\lambda^\bullet$ to a multiple of $\alpha/\sqrt{k}$, so the approximate dual vector $\widehat{\lambda}$ can be specified with $O(k \log(\sqrt{k}/\alpha))$ bits.

Since for each coordinate j, $|\lambda_j^\bullet - \widehat{\lambda}_j| \leq \alpha/\sqrt{k}$, we also have that that $\|\lambda^\bullet - \widehat{\lambda}\| \leq \alpha$. By Lemma 4, we know that $\|\widehat{x} - x^\bullet\| \leq \varepsilon$. $\square$

4.2 Approximate Feasibility and Optimality

Now we carry out the second step to show that if we choose the regularization parameter η carefully, the solution resulting from the coordination mechanism above is both approximately feasible and optimal. Let x^* denote the optimal

solution of the original convex program, $x^\bullet$ denote the optimal solution of the regularized convex program, and $\widehat{x}(\eta)$ denote the solution resulting from the coordination mechanism when we use parameter η.

As an intermediate step, we will first bound the objective difference between $x^\bullet$ and x^*.

LEMMA 6. *For any choice of η, $v(x^*) - v(x^\bullet) \leq \frac{\eta n}{2}$.*

Next we bound the objective difference between $\widehat{x}$ and $x^\bullet$ using Lipschitzness.

LEMMA 7. *Suppose that $\|\widehat{x} - x^\bullet\| \leq \varepsilon$, then*

$$v(x^\bullet) - v(\widehat{x}) \leq n\varepsilon.$$

THEOREM 3. *The coordination mechanism $\mathsf{ReC}(\eta, \varepsilon)$ coordinates the players to play a joint solution $\widehat{x}$ that satisfies*

$$v(\widehat{x}) \geq \mathrm{OPT} - n(\varepsilon + \eta) \qquad and \qquad \min_{x \in \mathcal{F}} \|x - \widehat{x}\| \leq \varepsilon$$

and has coordination complexity of $O(k \log(nk/\eta\varepsilon))$.

PROOF. Follows easily from the previous lemmas. $\square$

4.3 Application to Many-to-One Matchings

Next we show a simple instantiation of our coordination mechanism for linearly separable convex programs to give a coordination complexity upper bound for many-to-one matchings. First, let's consider the following linear program formulation of the matching problem.

$$\max_{x} \sum_{i=1}^{n} \sum_{j=1}^{k} v_{i,j}\, x_{i,j} \tag{2}$$

$$\text{subject to } \sum_{i=1}^{n} x_{i,j} \leq b_j \quad \text{for } j = 1, \dots, k \tag{3}$$

$$\sum_{j=1}^{k} x_{i,j} \leq 1 \quad \text{for } j = 1, \dots, k \tag{4}$$

$$x_{i,j} \geq 0 \quad \text{for } i = 1, \dots, n \text{ and } j = 1, \dots, k \tag{5}$$

Observe that the matching linear program is an example of a linearly separable convex program as defined in Definition 3. Each player i has valuation $v_{i,j} \in \{0, 1\}$ for each type of good j and controls the decision variables $\{x_{i,j}\}_{j=1}^{k}$. Each supply constraint in Equation (3) corresponds to a coupling constraint, and constraints in both Equation (4) and Equation (5) are personal constraints.

A nice property about the matching linear program is that any extreme point is integral. However, this structure no longer holds if we add a regularization term to the welfare objective, so the resulting solution $\widehat{x}$ resulting from the coordination mechanism will be fractional. To obtain an integral solution, we can simply use independent rounding, which does not require any further coordination. In order to obtain an integral solution, each player i will take their portion of the fractional solution $(\widehat{x}_{i,j})_{j=1}^{k}$ and will independently sample a good by selecting each good j with probability $\widehat{x}_{i,j}$. We will continue to use similar notation: let $v(\cdot)$ denote the welfare objective in the linear program, let x^* be the optimal solution for the matching linear program with welfare OPT, $\widehat{x}$ be the optimal solution for the regularized program with welfare $\widehat{V}$, x' be the rounded solution of $\widehat{x}$, and let $\mathcal{F}$ denote the feasible region defined by all the constraints of Equation (3) in the linear program. The following lemma bounds the loss of welfare due to rounding.

LEMMA 8. *Let $\beta \in (0,1)$. Then with probability at least $1 - \beta$, the rounded solution x' satisfies*

$$v(x') \geq \left(1 - \frac{\log(2/\beta)}{\sqrt{\widehat{V}}}\right) \widehat{V}$$

Now we look at approximate feasibility of x'.

LEMMA 9. *Suppose that $\min_{x \in \mathcal{F}} \|x - \widehat{x}\| \leq \varepsilon$. Then with probability $1 - \beta$, x' satisfies*

$$\sum_{j=1}^{k} \left(\sum_{i=1}^{n} x'_{i,j} - b_j\right)_+ \leq \sqrt{3k \log(k/\beta)\widehat{V}} + \sqrt{nk}\varepsilon$$

Observe that since this is a packing linear program, if desired, it is easy to obtain exact feasibility by simply scaling down the supply constraints: this transfers the approximation factor in the feasibility bound to the become an approximation factor in the objective.

Lastly, we are ready to establish the welfare guarantee for the rounded solution. Since the solution we obtain might slightly violate the feasibility constraints, we want to make sure we are not over-counting. If more than b_j parties select a particular good of type j, we only count the first b_j parties to select it when measuring our welfare guarantee.

THEOREM 4. *There exists a coordination protocol with coordination complexity $O(k \log(nk))$ such that the parties coordinate on a matching x' with total weight:*

$$\sum_{j=1}^{k} \min\left\{\sum_{i=1}^{n} v_{i,j} x'_{i,j}, b_j\right\} \geq \left(1 - O\left(\frac{\sqrt{k}\log(k/\beta)}{\sqrt{\mathrm{OPT}}}\right)\right) \mathrm{OPT}$$

as long as $\mathrm{OPT} \geq 1$.

Observe that in the setting of many-to-one matchings, when the supply of each good is $s_j \gg 1$, we expect that $\mathrm{OPT} \gg k$, and hence in this setting, the above theorem guarantees a solution with weight $(1 - o(1))\mathrm{OPT}$.

5. INTERFACE WITH PRIVACY AND EFFICIENCY IN GAMES

In this section, we explain a simple implication of our results: Problems that have low sensitivity objectives (i.e. problems such that one party's data and action do not substantially affect the objective value) and low coordination complexity also have good algorithms for solving them subject to *joint differential privacy*. When the strategic variant of the optimization problem is a smooth game, they also have good welfare properties for no-regret players, even when agent types are dynamically changing.

5.1 Privacy Background

A *database* $D \in \mathcal{X}^n$ is an n-tuple of private records, each from one of n agents. Two databases D, D' are *i-neighbors* if they differ only in their i-th index: that is, if $D_j = D'_j$ for all $j \neq i$. If two databases D and D' are i-neighbors for some i, we say that they are *neighboring databases*. We write $D \sim D'$ to denote that D and D' are neighboring. We will be interested in randomized algorithms that take a database as input, and output an element from some abstract range $\mathcal{R}$.

DEFINITION 4 ([DMNS06]). *A mechanism $\mathcal{M}: \mathcal{X}^n \to \mathcal{R}$ is (ε, δ)-differentially private if for every pair of neighboring databases $D, D' \in \mathcal{X}^n$ and for every subset of outputs $\mathcal{S} \subseteq \mathcal{R}$,*

$$\Pr[\mathcal{M}(D) \in \mathcal{S}] \leq \exp(\varepsilon) \Pr[\mathcal{M}(D') \in \mathcal{S}] + \delta.$$

For the class of problems we consider, elements in both the domain and the range of the mechanism are partitioned into n components, one for each player. In this setting, *joint differential privacy* [KPRU14] is a more natural constraint: For all i, the *joint* distribution on outputs given to players $j \neq i$ is differentially private in the input of player i. Given a vector $x = (x_1, \ldots, x_n)$, we write $x_{-i} = (x_1, \ldots, x_{i-1}, x_{i+1}, \ldots, x_n)$ to denote the vector of length $(n-1)$ which contains all coordinates of x except the i-th coordinate.

DEFINITION 5 ([KPRU14]). *A mechanism $\mathcal{M}: \mathcal{X}^n \to \mathcal{R}^n$ is (ε, δ)-jointly differentially private if for every i, for every pair of i-neighbors $D, D' \in \mathcal{X}^n$, and for every subset of outputs $\mathcal{S} \subseteq \mathcal{R}^{n-1}$,*

$$\Pr[\mathcal{M}(D)_{-i} \in \mathcal{S}] \leq \exp(\varepsilon) \Pr[\mathcal{M}(D')_{-i} \in \mathcal{S}] + \delta.$$

If $\delta = 0$, we say that $\mathcal{M}$ is ε-differentially private. The case of $\delta > 0$ is sometimes referred to as approximate differential privacy.

Note that this is still a very strong privacy guarantee; the mechanism preserves the privacy of any player i against arbitrary coalitions of other players. It only weakens the constraint of differential privacy by allowing player i's output to depend arbitrarily on her *own* input.

An important class of jointly differentially private algorithms – particularly amenable to our purposes – are those that work in the so-called *billboard model*. Algorithms in the billboard model compute a differentially private signal as a function of the input database; then each player i's portion of the output is computed as a function only of this private signal and the private data of player i. The following lemma shows that algorithms operating in the billboard model satisfy joint differential privacy.

LEMMA 10 ([HHR+14]). *Suppose $\mathcal{M}: \mathcal{X}^n \to \mathcal{R}$ is (ε, δ)-differentially private. Consider any set of functions $f_i : \mathcal{X} \times \mathcal{R} \to \mathcal{R}'$. Then the mechanism $\mathcal{M}'$ that outputs to each player i: $f_i(D_i, \mathcal{M}(D))$ is (ε, δ)-jointly differentially private.*

Note the similarity between algorithms operating in the billboard model and coordination complexity protocols: a signal is computed by a central party, and then the action of each agent is a function only of this signal and of their own portion of the problem instance. Thus, the following lemma is immediate:

LEMMA 11. *A coordination protocol (σ, π) satisfies (ε, δ)-joint differential privacy if the coordinator's encoding function σ satisfies (ε, δ)-differential privacy.*

5.2 A Generic Private Coordination Protocol

Next, we give a general way to convert any coordination protocol to a jointly differentially private algorithm – and the lower the coordination complexity of the protocol, the better the utility guarantee of the private algorithm. The tool we use is the *exponential mechanism* of [MT07], one of the most basic tools in differential privacy. To formally define this mechanism, we consider some arbitrary range $\mathcal{R}$ and some quality score function $q: \mathcal{X}^n \times \mathcal{R} \to \mathbb{R}$, which maps database-output pairs to quality scores.

DEFINITION 6 (THE EXPONENTIAL MECHANISM [MT07]). *The exponential mechanism $\mathcal{M}_E(D, q, \mathcal{R}, \varepsilon)$ selects and outputs an element $r \in \mathcal{R}$ with probability proportional to*

$$\exp\left(\frac{\varepsilon q(D, r)}{2\Delta(q)}\right),$$

where

$$\Delta(q) \equiv \max_{D, D' \in \mathcal{X}^n, D \sim D'} |q(D) - q(D')|.$$

McSherry and Talwar showed that the exponential mechanism is private and with high probability selects an outcome with high quality.

THEOREM 5 ([MT07]). *The exponential mechanism satisfies $(\varepsilon, 0)$-differential privacy, and for any $D \in \mathcal{X}^n$ it outputs an outcome $r \in \mathcal{R}$ that satisfies*

$$q(D, r) \geq \max_{r'} q(D, r') - \frac{2\Delta(q)(\log(|\mathcal{R}|/\beta))}{\varepsilon}$$

with probability at least $1 - \beta$.

Using the exponential mechanism, we can take any coordination protocol (σ, π), and construct a jointly differentially private coordination protocol (σ', π) with the same coordination complexity, and almost the same approximation factor. The idea is to construct a differentially private encoding function σ' that selects from the message space of σ using the exponential mechanism. Without loss of generality, we assume that the social objective function S has low-sensitivity:

$$\max_{i \in [n], a \in \mathcal{A}^n, D \sim D', a'_i \in \mathcal{A}_i} |S(D, a) - S(D', (a'_i, a_{-i}))| \leq 1.^4$$

Now we present the private protocol as follows:

Algorithm 2 Jointly private algorithm $\mathsf{PriCoor}((\sigma, \pi), q, \varepsilon, D)$

Input: A coordination protocol (σ, π), objective function f, and input instance D
    Let $\mathcal{R} = \{\sigma(D') \mid D' \in \mathcal{X}^n\}$ be the space of all possible messages in the range of σ
    Let quality function q be defined as $q(D, r) = \mathbb{E}_\pi[S(D, (\pi(r, D^{(i)}))_{i \in [n]})] \ \forall D \in \mathcal{X}^n, r \in \mathcal{R}$
    Let $\sigma'(D) = \mathcal{M}_E(D, q, \mathcal{R})$ be the message selected by the exponential mechanism
Output $a = (\pi(\sigma'(D), D^{(i)}))_{i=1}^n$

LEMMA 12. *Suppose that (σ, π) has coordination complexity ℓ and approximation ratio ρ for the objective f. Then the algorithm $\mathsf{PriCoor}((\sigma, \pi), f, \varepsilon, D)$ satisfies $(\varepsilon, 0)$-joint differential privacy, and with probability at least $1 - \beta$, the resulting action profile a satisfies*

$$\mathbb{E}[S(D, a)] \geq \frac{\mathrm{OPT}(D)}{\rho} - \frac{2(\ell + \log(1/\beta))}{\varepsilon},$$

---
[4]We can always obtain this condition by scaling. It is already satisfied in the matching problem.

where the expectation is taken over the internal randomness of the encoding function σ' and decoding function π.

5.3 Efficiency in Games with Dynamic Population

Now we briefly discuss a connection between coordination complexity and the efficiency in games with dynamic population, which leverages the connection to joint differential privacy discovered by [LST15]. We briefly introduce the model in [LST15], but the discussion will necessarily be lacking in detail – see [LST15] for a formal treatment.

Let G be an n-player normal form *stage game*. We consider this game played repeatedly with a changing population of players over T rounds. Each player i has an action set $\mathcal{A}_i$, type $D^{(i)}$, and a utility function $u(D^{(i)}, a) = u_i(a)$. For concreteness, we can think about allocation games defined by auction rules M, which take as input an action profile and output an allocation $X_i(a)$ and a payment $P_i(a)$ for each player. Players have quasi-linear utility $u_i(a) = v(D^{(i)}, X_i(a)) - P_i(a) = v_i(X_i(a)) - P_i(a)$, where $v_i: \mathcal{A}^n \to [0, 1]$ denotes the valuation of player i over the allocation. In these games, a natural objective function is social welfare: $S(D, a) = \sum_{i=1}^n v_i(X_i(a))$. We write $\mathrm{OPT}(D) = \max_{a \in \mathcal{A}^n} S(D, a)$ to denote the optimal welfare with respect to an instance D.

In the model of [LST15], after each round, every player independently exits with some probability p. Whenever a player leaves the game, she is replaced a new player, whose type is chosen adversarially. We will write D^t to denote the game instance, and a^t to denote the action profile played at round t. Lastly, we also assume that each player in the game is a *no-regret learner* and plays some *adaptive learning algorithm*.[5]

The main result of [LST15] is that the existence of jointly differentially private algorithms that find action profiles approximately optimizing the welfare in a game implies that when the dynamically changing game is played by no-regret players, their average welfare is high.

THEOREM 6 (COROLLARY 5.2 OF [LST15]). *Consider a mechanism with dynamic population (M, T, p), such that the stage mechanism M is allocation based (λ, μ)-smooth and $T \geq 1/p$. Assume that there exists an (ε, δ)-joint differentially private allocation algorithm $X^\bullet: \mathcal{X}^n \to \mathcal{A}^n$ such that for any input instance $D \in \mathcal{X}^n$ it computes a feasible outcome that is ρ-approximately optimal*

$$\mathbb{E}[S(D, X^\bullet(D))] \geq \mathrm{OPT}(D)/\rho.$$

If all players use adaptive learning in the repeated mechanism, then the overall welfare satisfies

$$\sum_t \mathbb{E}[S(D^t, a^t)] \geq \frac{\lambda}{\rho \max\{1, \mu\}} \sum_t \mathbb{E}[\mathrm{OPT}(D^t)] -$$
$$\frac{nT}{\max\{1, \mu\}} \sqrt{2p(1 + n(\varepsilon + \delta)) \ln(NT)},$$

where $N = \max_i |\mathcal{A}_i|$.

We show the following result connecting low coordination complexity with the welfare guarantee in games with dynamic population. (See the full version for details).

---
[5]For more details of adaptive learning algorithms and adaptive regret, see [HS07].

LEMMA 13. *Consider a mechanism with dynamic population (M, T, p) such that the stage mechanism M is allocation based (λ, μ)-smooth and $T \geq 1/p$. Assume there is a coordination protocol (σ, π) with coordination complexity ℓ and approximation ratio ρ for the corresponding welfare maximization problem.*

Then if all players use adaptive learning in the repeated mechanism, the average welfare satisfies

$$\sum_t \mathbb{E}\left[S(D^t, a^t)\right] \geq \frac{\lambda}{\rho \max\{1, \mu\}} \sum_t \mathbb{E}[\mathrm{OPT}(D^t)]$$

$$- \frac{T}{\max\{1, \mu\}} \cdot \inf_{\varepsilon > 0} \left\{ n\sqrt{4pn\varepsilon \ln(NT)} + \frac{\lambda}{\rho} \frac{2(\ell + \log(n))}{\varepsilon} \right\}.$$

6. FURTHER RESULTS

In the full version, we also present coordination protocols for coordinating a Nash equilibrium in atomic routing games and many-to-one stable matchings.

References

[ANRW15] Noga Alon, Noam Nisan, Ran Raz, and Omri Weinstein. Welfare maximization with limited interaction. *CoRR*, abs/1504.01780, 2015.

[Cal84] Xavier Calsamiglia. *Informational requirements of parametric resource allocation processes*. Asociación Sudeuropea de Economía Teórica, 1984.

[CKRW14] Rachel Cummings, Michael Kearns, Aaron Roth, and Zhiwei Steven Wu. Privacy and truthful equilibrium selection for aggregative games. *CoRR*, abs/1407.7740, 2014.

[DMNS06] Cynthia Dwork, Frank McSherry, Kobbi Nissim, and Adam Smith. Calibrating noise to sensitivity in private data analysis. In *Proceedings of the 3rd Theory of Cryptography Conference, TCC '06*, pages 265–284, 2006.

[DNO14] Shahar Dobzinski, Noam Nisan, and Sigal Oren. Economic efficiency requires interaction. In *Proceedings of the 46th ACM Symposium on Theory of Computing, STOC '14*, pages 233–242, 2014.

[DPS02] Xiaotie Deng, Christos Papadimitriou, and Shmuel Safra. On the complexity of equilibria. In *Proceedings of the thiry-fourth annual ACM symposium on Theory of computing*, pages 67–71. ACM, 2002.

[Hay45] Friedrich A. Hayek. The use of knowledge in society. *American Economic Review*, 35(4):519–530, 1945.

[HHR+14] Justin Hsu, Zhiyi Huang, Aaron Roth, Tim Roughgarden, and Zhiwei Steven Wu. Private matchings and allocations. In *Proceedings of the 46th ACM Symposium on Theory of Computing, STOC '14*, pages 21–30, 2014.

[HHRW14] Justin Hsu, Zhiyi Huang, Aaron Roth, and Zhiwei Steven Wu. Jointly private convex programming. *CoRR*, abs/1411.0998, 2014.

[HS07] Elad Hazan and C. Seshadhri. Adaptive algorithms for online decision problems. *Electronic Colloquium on Computational Complexity (ECCC)*, 14(088), 2007.

[Hur60] Leonid Hurwicz. *Optimality and Informational Efficiency in Resource Allocation Processes*. Mathematical Methods in the Social Sciences. Stanford University Press, 1960.

[KC82] Alexander S Kelso and Vincent P Crawford. Job matching, coalition formation, and gross substitutes. *Econometrica*, pages 1483–1504, 1982.

[KN97] Eyal Kushilevitz and Noam Nisan. Communication complexity. *Advances in Computers*, 44:331–360, 1997.

[KNR99] Ilan Kremer, Noam Nisan, and Dana Ron. On randomized one-round communication complexity. *Computational Complexity*, 8(1):21–49, 1999.

[KPRU14] Michael Kearns, Mallesh M. Pai, Aaron Roth, and Jonathan Ullman. Mechanism design in large games: incentives and privacy. In *Proceedings of the 5th Innovations in Theoretical Computer Science, ITCS '14*, pages 403–410, 2014.

[LST15] Thodoris Lykouris, Vasilis Syrgkanis, and Éva Tardos. Learning and efficiency in games with dynamic population. *CoRR*, abs/1505.00391, 2015.

[MR74] Kenneth Mount and Stanley Reiter. The information size of message spaces. *Journal of Economic Theory*, 8(2):161–192, June 1974.

[MT07] Frank McSherry and Kunal Talwar. Mechanism design via differential privacy. In *Proceedings of the 48th Annual IEEE Symposium on Foundations of Computer Science, FOCS '07*, pages 94–103, 2007.

[NS06] Noam Nisan and Ilya Segal. The communication requirements of efficient allocations and supporting prices. *Journal of Economic Theory*, 129(1):192–224, 2006.

[RR14] Ryan M. Rogers and Aaron Roth. Asymptotically truthful equilibrium selection in large congestion games. In *Proceedings of the 16th ACM Conference on Economics and Computation, EC '14*, pages 771–782, 2014.

[RRUW15] Ryan M. Rogers, Aaron Roth, Jonathan Ullman, and Zhiwei Steven Wu. Inducing approximately optimal flow using truthful mediators. In *Proceedings of the Sixteenth ACM Conference on Economics and Computation, EC '15, Portland, OR, USA, June 15-19, 2015*, pages 471–488, 2015.

[Seg06] Ilya Segal. Communication in economic mechanisms. *ECONOMETRIC SOCIETY MONOGRAPHS*, 41:222, 2006.

On a Natural Dynamics for Linear Programming

Damian Straszak
École Polytechnique Fédérale de Lausanne
damian.straszak@epfl.ch

Nisheeth K. Vishnoi
École Polytechnique Fédérale de Lausanne
nisheeth.vishnoi@epfl.ch

Abstract

There is growing evidence that several fundamental processes in nature are inherently computational and are best viewed from the standpoint of computation. Consider the case of *Physarum polycephalum* (slime mold), a single celled organism which has been the source of much excitement among biologists and computer scientists due to its ability to solve complex optimization problems. This started with an experiment (Nakagaki et al. in Nature 2000) that showed the slime mold could solve the shortest path problem on a maze. Subsequently, the time evolution of Physarum was captured by mathematical biologists using the language of dynamical systems giving rise to a broad class of dynamics for basic computational problems such as shortest paths, transshipment problems, and linear programs (Tero et al. in 2007, Ito et al. in 2011, Johannson and Zou in 2012).

The Physarum dynamics are highly nonlinear and decentralized and, thus, there is no a priori reason for them to converge anywhere, let alone to solutions of problems, such as those listed above, where a global optima is sought. However, experiments and simulations suggest that the solution not only converges, it converges quickly. Two sets of questions arise naturally from a computational viewpoint: (1) While the dynamical system gives a mechanistic insight into the workings of a Physarum, it fails to explain what is going on globally. Can we explain Physarum dynamics from an optimization perspective? (2) Can we rigorously explain what experiments, simulations and partial results about the Physarum dynamics suggest, namely the (a) existence of a solution, (b) convergence to an optimal solution and (c) time to convergence of the (continuous *and* discretized) dynamics?

We study these questions for the Physarum dynamics for linear programming proposed by (Johannson and Zou in 2012) which generalizes earlier models for shortest path and the transshipment problem. For question (1) there are no known answers even in the simplest setting of shortest path: on the one hand the Physarum dynamics resemble the gradient descent method; however, one can show that it is not. On the other hand, the dynamics are reminiscent of interior point methods; however, what makes the Physarum dynamics remarkable is that one can start from *outside* the feasible region of the linear program and yet converge to the optimal point. For question (2), the situation is slightly better. For various special cases such as shortest path (Bonifaci et al. in 2012, Becchetti et al. in 2013) and the transshipment problem (Ito et al. in 2011, a prior work of the current authors in SODA 2016) (a)-(c) have been answered. However, these results heavily rely on the special structure of the problem. For LPs, the prior results prove convergence *assuming* that (i) the solution exists (ii) the feasible region of the LP is bounded and (iii) the optimizer is unique. As we argue later, justifying or removing these ends up being quite hard. Current results do not bound the convergence time.

We provide answers to all of these questions: We show that Physarum dynamics can be seen as a steepest-descent type algorithm, however, not in Euclidean space, rather in a space endowed with a *Riemannian metric* obtained from an *entropy-like function*. As a consequence, we show that Physarum dynamics for linear programming are obtained by balancing two forces in this Riemannian manifold: the need to reduce cost and the need to be feasible. Moreover, we show that the continuous trajectories of Physarum are in fact paths of optimizers to a parametrized family of convex programs, in which the objective is a linear cost function regularized by an entropy barrier. Subsequently, we establish the global existence of solutions of Physarum dynamics and show that they have limits, being optimal solutions of the underlying LP. Finally, we present a time-bound on a discretization of the dynamics to yield an algorithm that is provably efficient for a class of linear programs, which include unimodular constraint matrices. Our proofs synthesize concepts and tools from several distinct areas such as Riemannian manifolds, convex optimization and dynamical systems and should be of independent interest. The paper can be found here: http://arxiv.org/abs/1511.07020.

Permission to make digital or hard copies of all or part of this work for personal or classroom use is granted without fee provided that copies are not made or distributed for profit or commercial advantage and that copies bear this notice and the full citation on the first page. Copyrights for components of this work owned by others than the author(s) must be honored. Abstracting with credit is permitted. To copy otherwise, or republish, to post on servers or to redistribute to lists, requires prior specific permission and/or a fee. Request permissions from permissions@acm.org.

ITCS'16, January 14 - 16, 2016, Cambridge, MA, USA

© 2016 Copyright held by the owner/author(s). Publication rights licensed to ACM.
ISBN 978-1-4503-4057-1/16/01...$15.00

DOI: http://dx.doi.org/10.1145/2840728.2840762

On the Space Complexity of Linear Programming with Preprocessing

Yael Tauman Kalai[*]
Microsoft Research
yael@microsoft.com

Ran Raz[†]
Weizmann Institute of
Science, Israel, and the
Institute for Advanced Study,
Princeton, NJ
ran.raz.mail@gmail.com

Oded Regev[‡]
Courant Institute of
Mathematical Sciences, New
York University

ABSTRACT

It is well known that Linear Programming is P-complete, with a log-space reduction. In this work we ask whether Linear Programming remains P-complete, even if the polyhedron (i.e., the set of linear inequality constraints) is a fixed polyhedron, for each input size, and only the objective function is given as input. More formally, we consider the following problem: maximize $c \cdot x$, subject to $Ax \leq b; x \in \mathbb{R}^d$, where A, b are fixed in advance and only c is given as an input.

We start by showing that the problem remains P-complete with a log-space reduction, thus showing that $n^{o(1)}$-space algorithms are unlikely. This result is proved by a direct classical reduction.

We then turn to study *approximation* algorithms and ask what is the best approximation factor that could be obtained by a small space algorithm. Since approximation factors are mostly meaningful when the objective function is non-negative, we restrict ourselves to the case where $x \geq 0$ and $c \geq 0$. We show that (even in this possibly easier case)

approximating the value of max $c \cdot x$ (within any polynomial factor) is P-complete with a polylog space reduction, thus showing that $2^{(\log n)^{o(1)}}$-space approximation algorithms are unlikely.

The last result is proved using a recent work of Kalai, Raz, and Rothblum, showing that every language in P has a no-signaling multi-prover interactive proof with poly-logarithmic communication complexity. To the best of our knowledge, our result gives the first space hardness of approximation result proved by a PCP-based argument.

Categories and Subject Descriptors

G.1.6 [**Optimization**]: Linear programming; F.1.3 [**Complexity Measures and Classes**]: Reducibility and completeness

Keywords

Linear programming, P-completeness, space complexity, pre-processing

1. INTRODUCTION

Linear programs often arise in practice, and algorithms for Linear Programming are widely deployed. There has been a major effort to construct fast algorithms for Linear Programming, resulting with very efficient (polynomial time) algorithms (e.g., [7, 18, 15, 9, 6, 16]).

Recall that a linear program is a constrained optimization problem of the form:

$$\text{maximize } c \cdot x$$

$$\text{subject to } Ax \leq b; x \in \mathbb{R}^d$$

where $c \in \mathbb{R}^d$ and $b \in \mathbb{R}^n$, and A is an $n \times d$ matrix. The vector c is the objective function, and the set $H = \{x : A \cdot x \leq b\}$ is the set of feasible points. If it is non-empty, H is a convex polyhedron.

1.1 The Space Complexity of Linear Programming

A fundamental question is: what is the *space complexity* of Linear Programming?

The space complexity of Linear Programming was first studied in the late 70's. Dobkin, Lipton, and Reiss [8], followed by Serna [23], proved that approximating Linear Programming is P-complete with a log-space reduction, thus

[*]This work was done (in part) while the author was visiting the Simons Institute for the Theory of Computing, supported by the Simons Foundation and by the DIMACS/Simons Collaboration in Cryptography through NSF grant #CNS-1523467.

[†]Research supported by the Israel Science Foundation grant No. 1402/14, by the I-CORE Program of the Planning and Budgeting Committee and the Israel Science Foundation, by the Simons Collaboration on Algorithms and Geometry, by the Fund for Math at IAS, and by the National Science Foundation grant No. CCF-1412958.

[‡]Supported by the Simons Collaboration on Algorithms and Geometry and by the National Science Foundation (NSF) under Grant No. CCF-1320188. Any opinions, findings, and conclusions or recommendations expressed in this material are those of the authors and do not necessarily reflect the views of the NSF.

Permission to make digital or hard copies of all or part of this work for personal or classroom use is granted without fee provided that copies are not made or distributed for profit or commercial advantage and that copies bear this notice and the full citation on the first page. Copyrights for components of this work owned by others than ACM must be honored. Abstracting with credit is permitted. To copy otherwise, or republish, to post on servers or to redistribute to lists, requires prior specific permission and/or a fee. Request permissions from Permissions@acm.org.

ITCS'16, January 14–16, 2016, Cambridge, MA, USA.
© 2016 ACM. ISBN 978-1-4503-4057-1/16/01 ...$15.00.
DOI: http://dx.doi.org/10.1145/2840728.2840750.

showing that $n^{o(1)}$-space algorithms for (approximating) Linear Programming are unlikely. (See also Feige and Kilian's paper [10] for an alternative proof.)

For the special case of positive Linear Programming (where all variables in x, as well as all the coefficients in c, A, b are non-negative), Luby and Nisan [20] gave a polynomial time and polylog-space approximation algorithm.

1.2 Our Results

The above results, by Dobkin, Lipton and Reiss [8] and Serna [23], show that any language $L \in P$ has a log-space reduction that converts any instance $x^* \in \{0, 1\}^n$ into a linear program of size poly(n), such that if $x^* \in L$ then the the maximum value of the objective function on the polyhedron is 1, and if $x^* \notin L$ then the maximum value of the objective function on the polyhedron is 0. The polyhedron of the resulting linear program is not fixed and depends on x^*. In this work we ask whether a similar result can be obtained when the polyhedron is some fixed polyhedron that depends only on the input size and the running time, and doesn't depend on the instance x^* or the language L. A positive answer implies that small-space algorithms for Linear Programming are unlikely, even if one allows a *preprocessing* phase that takes the polyhedron as input and runs in unbounded time and space. Similarly, a positive answer implies that parallel algorithms for this problem running in polylog(n) time on a polynomial number of processors are unlikely.

Our first result shows that Linear Programming remains P-complete (with a log-space reduction) even when the polyhedron is fixed: We show that any language $L \in P$ has a log-space reduction that converts any instance $x^* \in \{0, 1\}^n$ into a linear program of size poly(n), such that if $x^* \in L$ then the the maximum value of the objective function on the polyhedron is at least 1, and if $x^* \notin L$ then the maximum value of the objective function on the polyhedron is at most 0. The polyhedron of the resulting linear program is a *fixed* polyhedron that depends on n but is otherwise independent of x^*,[1] and only the objective function depends on x^*. This shows that (for some polyhedrons) $n^{o(1)}$-space algorithms for Linear Programming are unlikely, even if the polyhedron is fixed and is not part of the input. This result is proved by a direct classical reduction, building on the techniques of [8] and [23].

We then turn to study approximation algorithms and ask what is the best factor of approximation that can be obtained by a small-space algorithm. We note that in the most general case of Linear Programming, any gap (in the value of the program), say a gap between 1 and $1 - \varepsilon$, can be easily amplified to a gap between 1 and 0, by applying the linear transformation $f(z) = (z - (1 - \varepsilon))/\varepsilon$ on the objective function. Therefore, in order for the approximation question to be meaningful, we restrict ourselves to the *semi-positive* case, where $x \geq 0$ and $c \geq 0$. We believe that in the semi-positive case, gaps cannot be easily amplified, and hence are much harder to establish, and that the semi-positive case is a particularly interesting one from the point of view of hardness of approximation.

Our second result shows that in the semi-positive case (where $x, c \geq 0$), and even when the polyhedron is fixed, approximating Linear Programming is P-complete under a quasi-poly time and polylog space reduction: We show that

---

[1] The polyhedron also does not depend on the language L, only on its runtime.

any language $L \in P$ has a quasi-poly time and polylog space reduction that converts any instance $x^* \in \{0, 1\}^n$ into a linear program of quasi-polynomial size, such that if $x^* \in L$ then the the maximum value of the objective function on the polyhedron is 1, and if $x^* \notin L$ then the maximum value of the objective function on the polyhedron is less than $2^{-\text{polylog}(n)}$. The polyhedron of the resulting linear program is a *fixed* polyhedron that depends on n (and the running time) but is otherwise independent of x^* (and L), and only the objective function depends on x^*. This shows that (for some polyhedrons) $2^{(\log n)^{o(1)}}$-space approximation algorithms for semi-positive Linear Programming (within a quasi-polynomial factor) are unlikely, even if the polyhedron is fixed and is not part of the input.

The proof of this second result uses the recent work of [14], that shows that any language in P has a multi-prover interactive proof with polylog communication complexity, which is secure against *no-signaling* cheating provers.

We note that our first result can be modified to yield semi-positive instances, however the resulting hardness of approximation factors are miniscule. We also note that if in addition to $x, c \geq 0$ we have that all coefficients in A, b are also larger or equal to 0 (i.e., the positive case), the above-mentioned result of Luby and Nisan [20] gives a fast polylog-space approximation algorithm. In contrast, by our second result, if only $x, c \geq 0$, a small space approximation algorithm is unlikely.

1.3 Organization of the Paper

We prove the first result in Section 2 and the second in Section 3.

2. A CLASSICAL APPROACH

THEOREM 1. *There exists a fixed family of polyhedrons $H = \{H_t\}_{t \in \mathbb{N}}$ such that the following holds: For every language L computable by a Turing Machine with polynomial runtime $t = t(n)$, there exists a log-space reduction, that converts any instance $x^* \in \{0, 1\}^n$ into a linear program with the polyhedron $H_{t(n)}$ (and an objective function that depends on x^*), such that if $x^* \in L$ then the maximum value of the objective function on the polyhedron is at least 1, and if $x^* \notin L$ then the maximum value of the objective function on the polyhedron is at most 0.*

High-level idea.

Our starting point is the results by Dobkin, Lipton and Reiss [8] and Serna [23], that show that any language L, computable by a Turing Machine with polynomial runtime $t = t(n)$, has a log-space reduction that converts any instance $x^* \in \{0, 1\}^n$ into a linear program of size poly($t(n)$), such that if $x^* \in L$ then the the maximum value of the objective function on the polyhedron is 1, and if $x^* \notin L$ then the maximum value of the objective function on the polyhedron is 0. The polyhedron of the resulting linear program is not fixed and *does depend* on x^*.

We show how to convert this linear program into a linear program with almost the same value, and with an a priori *fixed* polyhedron that is *independent* of x^* and L, and depends only on the runtime t (and the length of x^*).

The main idea is to show that there exists a universal set of inequalities such that by "switching off" some of them one

---

can obtain *any* polyhedron. Then we show how one can use the objective function to effectively "switch off" inequalities.

2.1 Linear Programming is P-Complete

Before we prove Theorem 1, we need to recall the reduction of [8].

THEOREM 2 ([8]). *Any language L computable by a Turing Machine with polynomial runtime $t = t(n)$, has a log-space reduction that converts any instance $x^* \in \{0,1\}^n$ into a linear program* LP:

$$\text{maximize } c \cdot x$$
$$\text{subject to } Ax \geq b,$$

such that the following holds:

1. *All the coefficients in c, b and A are in $\{0, 1, -1\}$.*

2. *If $x^* \in L$ then the value of* LP *is 1, and if $x^* \notin L$ then the value of* LP *is 0.*

3. *The number of variables in* LP *is $d = t^2(n)$, and the number of linear constraints is at most $5d$.*

PROOF. Fix any language L computable by a Turing machine with polynomial runtime $t = t(n)$. The log-space reduction that converts any $x^* \in \{0,1\}^n$ into a linear program LP, is defined as follows.

Let C be a Boolean circuit of size $t^2(n)$ that takes as input $x^* \in \{0,1\}^n$ and outputs 1 if and only if $x^* \in L$. (Such a circuit can be built from the Turing machine computing L; see, e.g., [1, Theorem 6.6].) Assume (without loss of generality) that the circuit C has only NOT and AND gates. Denote the number of wires in C by $d = t^2(n)$. The linear program LP consists of d variables, $x_1, \ldots, x_d$, one variable for each wire of C. Denote the n input wires by $x_1, \ldots, x_n$, and denote the output wire by x_d. The objective function of LP is

$$\max x_d.$$

The linear constraints of LP are the following: For every $i \in [d]$, we have the constraint $0 \leq x_i \leq 1$, that can be written as

$$x_i \geq 0$$
$$-x_i \geq -1.$$

For every $i \in [n]$ (corresponding to an input wire), we have the constraint $x_i = x_i^*$, that can be written as

$$x_i \geq x_i^* \tag{1}$$
$$-x_i \geq -x_i^*. \tag{2}$$

For every NOT gate in C, with output wire i and input wire j, we have the constraint $x_i = 1 - x_j$, that can be written as

$$x_i + x_j \geq 1 \tag{3}$$
$$-x_i - x_j \geq -1. \tag{4}$$

For every AND gate with output wire i and input wires j and k, we have the constraints $x_i \leq x_j$, $x_i \leq x_k$, and $x_i \geq x_j + x_k - 1$. These constraints can be written as

$$x_j - x_i \geq 0 \tag{5}$$
$$x_k - x_i \geq 0 \tag{6}$$
$$x_i - x_j - x_k \geq -1. \tag{7}$$

Note that all the coefficients (both in the objective function and in the linear constraints) are in $\{0, 1, -1\}$, as desired. Note that the polyhedron consists of a single element, corresponding to the value of the wires of C on input x^*. Thus, if $x^* \in L$, then $x_d = 1$, and hence the value of LP is 1, and if $x^* \notin L$ then $x_d = 0$, and hence the value of LP is 0, as desired. Note that the number of variables in LP is $d = t^2(n)$ and the number of linear constraints is $\leq 5d$, as desired. $\square$

2.2 Proof of Theorem 1

PROOF. Our starting point is the proof of Theorem 2 (see Section 2.1) that for a language L, computable by a Turing Machine with a polynomial runtime $t = t(n)$, gives a log-space reduction that converts any instance $x^* \in \{0,1\}^n$ into a linear program LP:

$$\max c \cdot x$$
$$\text{s.t. } Ax \geq b.$$

We define a universal family of polyhedrons $\{H_d\}$, and show a log-space reduction that converts the linear program LP into a linear program LP$'$, with the polyhedron H_d. The polyhedron H_d depends on d, but is otherwise independent of x^* and L.

Let

$$T = 2^{4d}. \tag{8}$$

Let $m = 5d$. We will assume for simplicity and without loss of generality that $d \geq 10$. The linear program LP$'$ consists of $4dm + 3m + d$ variables: For every $i \in [d]$, it has the variables x_i corresponding to x_i in the original LP. For every $i \in [d]$ and every $j \in [m]$, it has the variable $y_{j,i}$, where each $y_{j,i}$ supposedly corresponds to the value of $A_{j,i} \cdot x_i$. In addition, for every $i \in [d]$ and every $j \in [m]$, it contains auxiliary variables

$$z_{j,i,0}, z_{j,i,1}, z_{j,i,-1},$$

and for every $j \in [m]$ it contains auxiliary variables

$$w_{j,0}, w_{j,1}, w_{j,-1}.$$

These auxiliary variables are used to "turn off" some of the constraints.

We next define the polyhedron H_d to consist of the following inequalities:[2]

1. For every $i \in [d]$ and $j \in [m]$,

$$y_{j,i} - z_{j,i,0} \leq 0$$
$$y_{j,i} - z_{j,i,1} \leq x_i$$
$$y_{j,i} - z_{j,i,-1} \leq -x_i$$
$$z_{j,i,0} \geq 0$$
$$z_{j,i,1} \geq 0$$
$$z_{j,i,-1} \geq 0$$

---

[2] We remark that the A part of the linear program LP produced by Theorem 2 is already independent of the input x^*. Using this fact, we could slightly simplify our proof by avoiding Item 1 below. We choose not to use this fact in order to keep the reduction more general, and also in order for the resulting polyhedron to be more natural.

High-level idea.
Intuitively, these six inequalities encode the single inequality $y_{j,i} \leq A_{j,i} \cdot x_i$, in a way that does not depend on $A_{j,i}$. More specifically, we use the objective function to effectively "turn off" the inequalities $y_{j,i} - z_{j,i,\ell} \leq \ell \cdot x_i$, for $\ell \neq A_{j,i}$. This is done by keeping the variables $\{z_{j,i,\ell}\}_{\ell \neq A_{j,i}}$ free, by not including them in the objective function, so that by choosing $z_{j,i,\ell}$ large enough these inequalities can be trivially satisfied without affecting the objective function. On the other hand, we add the term $-T \cdot z_{j,i,A_{j,i}}$ to the objective function, so that even taking $z_{j,i,A_{j,i}}$ exponentially small, would add an exponential large penalty to the objective value. Thus, effectively the remaining inequality $y_{j,i} - z_{j,i,A_{j,i}} \leq A_{j,i} \cdot x_i$ is almost equivalent to the inequality $y_{j,i} \leq A_{j,i} \cdot x_i$.

2. For every $j \in [m]$,

$$y_{j,1} + \cdots + y_{j,d} + w_{j,0} \geq 0$$
$$y_{j,1} + \cdots + y_{j,d} + w_{j,1} \geq 1$$
$$y_{j,1} + \cdots + y_{j,d} + w_{j,-1} \geq -1$$
$$w_{j,0} \geq 0$$
$$w_{j,1} \geq 0$$
$$w_{j,-1} \geq 0$$

High-level idea.
Intuitively, these six inequalities encode the single inequality

$$y_{j,1} + \cdots + y_{j,d} \geq b_j,$$

in a way that does not depend on b_j. More specifically, as before, this is done by "turning off" the inequalities $y_{j,1} + \cdots + y_{j,d} + w_{j,\ell} \geq \ell$ for $\ell \neq b_j$, and using the objective function to effectively restrict w_{j,b_j} to be exponentially small, and as a result the equation $y_{j,1} + \cdots + y_{j,d} + w_{j,b_j} \geq b_j$ is almost equivalent to the equation $y_{j,1} + \cdots + y_{j,d} \geq b_j$.

3. For every $i \in [d]$,

$$0 \leq x_i \leq 1$$

Note that the polyhedron H_d is indeed independent of LP, given d.

We next define the linear objective function of LP′. Intuitively, the objective function is the same as that of LP, with additional terms that are used to "turn on" all the inequalities in H_d that correspond to $Ax \geq b$.

We define the linear objective function of LP′ to be

$$\max \sum_{i=1}^{d} c_i \cdot x_i - T \cdot \sum_{i \in [d], j \in [m]} z_{j,i,A_{j,i}} - T \cdot \sum_{j \in [m]} w_{j,b_j}. \quad (9)$$

High-level idea.
Intuitively, all the linear constraints that include a variable in $\{z_{j,i,\ell}\}_{\ell \neq A_{j,i}} \cup \{w_{j,\ell}\}_{\ell \neq b_j}$ are "turned off" since we are free to choose these variables to be as large as we want, *without affecting the objective function*. Moreover, as we argue formally below, since we chose T to be large enough (recall that we set $T = 2^{4d}$, see Equation (8)), the maximal value

of LP′ is obtained when $z_{j,i,A_{j,i}}$ and w_{j,b_j} are exponentially small, and thus the value of LP′ is exponentially close to the value of LP.

Formally, we argue that the values of the linear programs LP and LP′ are exponentially close, as follows. We define another linear program LP″. We prove that LP″ has the same value as LP′, and we prove that the values of LP″ and LP are exponentially close.

The linear program LP″ is defined as follows: The objective function of LP″ is identical to that of LP′ (Equation (9)), and the linear constraints consist of a subset of the linear constraints of H_d. Specifically, LP″ only contains the linear constraints in LP′ that are "turned on". In other words, LP″ only contains the constraints in LP′ that do not contain variables from the set

$$\{z_{j,i,\ell}\}_{\ell \neq A_{j,i}} \cup \{w_{j,\ell}\}_{\ell \neq b_j}.$$

In other words, the linear program LP″ contains the following constraints:

1. For every $i \in [d]$ every $j \in [m]$,

$$y_{j,i} - z_{j,i,A_{j,i}} \leq A_{j,i} \cdot x_i$$
$$z_{j,i,A_{j,i}} \geq 0$$

2. For every $j \in [m]$,

$$y_{j,1} + \cdots + y_{j,d} + w_{j,b_j} \geq b_j$$
$$w_{j,b_j} \geq 0.$$

3. For every $i \in [d]$,

$$0 \leq x_i \leq 1$$

We next prove that LP′ and LP″ have the same value. Clearly the value of LP″ is at least as large as the value of LP′, since it has the same objective function and contains only a subset of the constraints. On the other hand, the value of LP″ is not larger than the value of LP′, since any solution for LP″ can be extended to a solution in H_d. This is the case since by the definition of LP″, any linear constraint in H_d that does not appear in LP″ contains a variable from

$$\{z_{j,i,\ell}\}_{\ell \neq A_{j,i}} \cup \{w_{j,\ell}\}_{\ell \neq b_j}.$$

Note that these variables do not appear in the objective function, and thus can be set to be arbitrarily large, so as to satisfy the inequalities in LP′ that are not in LP″, without affecting the linear objective function.

It remains to argue that the value of LP″ is exponentially close to the value of LP. To this end, we first note that the value of LP″ is at least as large as the value of LP, since by setting all the auxiliary variables $z_{j,i,A_{j,i}}$ and w_{j,b_j} in LP″ to be 0, we obtain a linear program that is equivalent to LP.

We next argue that if the value of LP″ is v then the value of LP is at least $v - 2^{-d}$. To this end, let (x, y, z, w) be a point in the polyhedron of LP″ which yields the maximal value v. We note that it must be the case that all the coordinates of z and all the coordinates of w are of size at most 2^{-3d}. This is the case since otherwise, the linear objective function of LP″ on the point (x, y, z, w) obtains the value

$$\sum_{i=1}^{d} c_i \cdot x_i - T \cdot \sum_{i \in [d], j \in [m]} z_{j,i,A_{j,i}} - T \cdot \sum_{j \in [m]} w_{j,b_j} \leq d - T \cdot 2^{-3d} < 0,$$

296

which we know is not the maximal value on the polyhedron, since the value of LP'' is at least as large as the value of LP, which is at least 0.

The fact that the coordinates of z and w are exponentially small implies that the point (x, y, z, w) satisfies the constraint

$$Ax \geq b - \varepsilon, \tag{10}$$

for

$$\varepsilon := \sum z_{j,i,A_{j,i}} + \sum w_{j,b_j} \leq 2^{-2d}.$$

We next argue that this implies that there exists x' in the polyhedron of LP (i.e., $Ax' \geq b$), such that for every $i \in [d]$,

$$|x_i - x'_i| \leq 2^{-d}.$$

Recall that $x_1, \ldots, x_d$ correspond to the wires of a circuit C that takes as input $x^* \in \{0,1\}^n$ and outputs 1 if and only if $x^* \in L$ (see the proof of Theorem 2 in Section 2.1). Recall that the n input wires are $x_1, \ldots, x_n$, and the output wire is x_d. Assume without loss of generality that $x_1, \ldots, x_d$ are ordered in an order that agrees with the circuit, that is, for every gate in the circuit, the variable that corresponds to the output of the gate appears after all variables that correspond to the inputs for the gate. Denote by $x'_1, \ldots, x'_d$ the true values of the wires of C on the input $x^* \in \{0,1\}^n$, and note that for every $i \in [n]$ we have $x'_i = x^*_i$, and that the point $x' = (x'_1, \ldots, x'_d)$ is in the polyhedron of LP (it is actually the unique point in the polyhedron of LP).

We next argue that for every $i \in [d]$,

$$|x_i - x'_i| \leq 2^i \cdot \varepsilon.$$

This is proved by induction on i, using Equation (10) and by the definition of LP (see the Proof of Theorem 2 in Section 2.1) as follows:

1. If i corresponds to an input of the circuit C, then by Equation (10), Equation (1) and Equation (2), we have

   $$|x_i - x'_i| \leq \varepsilon \,.$$

2. If i corresponds to the output of a NOT gate with input wire j, then by Equation (10), Equation (3) and Equation (4), and by the inductive hypothesis and the triangle inequality, and since $x'_i = (1 - x'_j)$ we have

   $$|x_i - x'_i| \leq |x_i - (1 - x_j)| + |(1 - x_j) - (1 - x'_j)| + |(1 - x'_j) - x'_i|$$

   $$\leq \varepsilon + 2^j \cdot \varepsilon + 0 \leq 2^i \cdot \varepsilon$$

3. If i corresponds to the output of an AND gate with input wires j, k (for simplicity and without loss of generality, we assume $j \neq k$), then by Equation (10), Equation (5), Equation (6), Equation (7) and by the inductive hypothesis and since $0 \leq x_i, x_j, x_k \leq 1$ and $j, k < i$, we have

   (a) If $x'_i = 0$ then either $x'_j = 0$ or $x'_k = 0$. Without loss of generality assume $x'_j = 0$. Thus,

   $$x_i - x'_i = x_i \leq x_j + \varepsilon \leq x'_j + 2^j \cdot \varepsilon + \varepsilon \leq 0 + 2^i \cdot \varepsilon$$

   and

   $$x_i - x'_i = x_i \geq 0$$

   (b) If $x'_i = 1$ then $x'_j = x'_k = 1$. Thus,

   $$x_i - x'_i = x_i - 1 \leq 0$$

   and

   $$x_i - x'_i \geq (x_j + x_k - 1 - \varepsilon) - 1$$
   $$= (x_j - x'_j) + (x_k - x'_k) - \varepsilon$$
   $$\geq -2^j \cdot \varepsilon - 2^k \cdot \varepsilon - \varepsilon \geq -2^i \cdot \varepsilon$$

In particular, we proved that $|x_d - x'_d| \leq 2^d \cdot \varepsilon \leq 2^{-d}$. Since the value of LP'' is at most x_d and the value of LP is x'_d, we proved that if the value of LP'' is v then the value of LP is at least $v - 2^{-d}$.

Thus LP'', and hence also LP' satisfies that if $x^* \in L$ then the maximum value of the objective function on the polyhedron is at least $1 - 2^{-d}$, and if $x^* \notin L$ then the maximum value of the objective function on the polyhedron is at most 2^{-d}. The gap between $1 - 2^{-d}$ and 2^{-d} can be easily amplified to a gap between 1 and 0, by applying a linear function on the objective function, as described in the introduction. $\square$

3. A PCP-BASED APPROACH

In this section, we consider the problem of *approximating* Linear Programming with a fixed polyhedron. For us to be able to meaningfully talk about approximation, we restrict to the case of semi-positive linear programs, i.e, when $c, x \geq 0$. While the hardness result of Section 2 can be adapted to this case, the resulting approximation factors are miniscule. In this section we show hardness for approximation factors $2^{\text{polylog}(n)}$ through a polylog space and quasi-poly time reduction, thus showing that $2^{(\log n)^{o(1)}}$-space approximation algorithms are unlikely.

THEOREM 3. *There exists a fixed family of polyhedrons $H = \{H_t\}_{t \in \mathbb{N}}$ such that the following holds: For every language $L \in \mathsf{P}$ computable by a Turing Machine with polynomial runtime $t = t(n)$, there exists a polylog space and quasi-poly time reduction, that converts any instance $x^* \in \{0,1\}^n$ into a linear program with the polyhedron $H_{t(n)}$, and an objective function $\max c \cdot x$, such that $x, c \geq 0$, and such that if $x \in L$ then the maximum value of the objective function on the polyhedron is 1, and if $x \notin L$ then the maximum value of the objective function on the polyhedron is smaller than $2^{-\text{polylog}(n)}$.*

The proof of Theorem 3 uses a recent result of Kalai, Raz and Rothblum (stated in Theorem 5 below), showing that every language in P has a no-signaling multi-prover interactive proof with poly-logarithmic communication complexity.

In Section 3.1 below, we provide the necessary background for proving Theorem 3, and then in Section 3.2 we prove Theorem 3.

3.1 Preliminaries

3.1.1 Notation

For a vector $a = (a_1, \ldots, a_k)$ and a subset $S \subseteq [k]$, we denote by a_S the sequence of elements of a that are indexed by indices in S, that is, $a_S = (a_i)_{i \in S}$. In general, we denote by a_S a sequence of elements indexed by S, and we denote by a_i the ith coordinate of a vector a.

For a distribution $\mathcal{A}$, we denote by $a \in_R \mathcal{A}$ a random variable distributed according to $\mathcal{A}$ (independently of all other random variables).

3.1.2 Multi-Prover Interactive Proofs

Multi-prover interactive proofs (MIPs) were introduced by [5]. In such a proof system a set of provers wish to convince a verifier of the validity of a statement. Specifically, let L be a language and let x be an input of length n. In a one-round k-prover interactive proof, k computationally unbounded provers, $P_1, \ldots, P_k$, try to convince a (probabilistic) $\mathsf{poly}(n)$-time verifier, V, that $x \in L$. The input x is known to all parties.

The proof consists of only one round. Given x and her random string, the verifier generates k queries, $q_1, \ldots, q_k$, one for each prover, and sends them to the k provers. Each prover responds with an answer that depends only on her own individual query. That is, the provers respond with answers $a_1, \ldots, a_k$, where for every i we have $a_i = P_i(q_i)$. Finally, the verifier decides whether to accept or reject based on the answers that she receives (as well as the input x and her random string).

We say that $(V, P_1, \ldots, P_k)$ is a one-round multi-prover interactive proof system (MIP) for L if the following two properties are satisfied:

1. **Completeness:** For every $x \in L$, the verifier V accepts with probability 1, after interacting with $P_1, \ldots, P_k$.

2. **Soundness:** For every $x \notin L$, and any (computationally unbounded, possibly cheating) provers $P_1^*, \ldots, P_k^*$, the verifier V rejects with probability $\geq 1 - \varepsilon$, after interacting with $P_1^*, \ldots, P_k^*$, where ε is a parameter referred to as the *error* or *soundness* of the proof system.

Other important parameters of an MIP include the number of provers, the length of queries, the length of answers, and the error. One celebrated result in this line of work is that of Babai, Fortnow, and Lund [3] who showed that any language in NEXP has an MIP with negligible soundness.

3.1.3 No-Signaling MIPs

We consider a variant of the MIP model, where the cheating provers are more powerful. In the MIP model, each prover answers her own query locally, without knowing the queries that were sent to the other provers. The no-signaling model allows each answer to depend on all the queries, as long as for any subset $S \subset [k]$, and any queries q_S for the provers in S, the distribution of the answers a_S, conditioned on the queries q_S, is independent of all the other queries.

Intuitively, this means that the answers a_S do not give the provers in S information about the queries of the provers outside S, except for information that they already have by seeing the queries q_S.

Formally, denote by D the alphabet of the queries and denote by Σ the alphabet of the answers. For every $q = (q_1, \ldots, q_k) \in D^k$, let $\mathcal{A}_q$ be a distribution over Σ^k. We think of $\mathcal{A}_q$ as the distribution of the answers for queries q.

We say that the family of distributions $\{\mathcal{A}_q\}_{q \in D^k}$ is *no-signaling* if for every subset $S \subset [k]$ and every two sequences of queries $q, q' \in D^k$, such that $q_S = q'_S$, the following two random variables are identically distributed:

- a_S, where $a \in_R \mathcal{A}_q$, and

- a'_S, where $a' \in_R \mathcal{A}_{q'}$.

An MIP $(V, P_1, \ldots, P_k)$ for a language L is said to have soundness ε against no-signaling strategies (or provers) if the following (more general) soundness property is satisfied:

2. **Soundness:** For every $x \notin L$, and any no-signaling family of distributions $\{\mathcal{A}_q\}_{q \in D^k}$, the verifier V rejects with probability $\geq 1 - \varepsilon$, where on queries $q = (q_1, \ldots, q_k)$ the answers are given by $(a_1, \ldots, a_k) \in_R \mathcal{A}_q$, and ε is the error parameter.

The study of multi-prover interactive proofs (MIPs) that are secure against no-signaling provers was motivated by the study of MIPs with provers that share entangled quantum states. No-signaling provers are more powerful than entangled provers, since no-signaling provers are allowed to use arbitrary strategies, as long as their strategies cannot be used for communication between any two disjoint sets of provers. By the physical principle that information cannot travel faster than light, a consequence of Einstein's special relativity theory, it follows that all the strategies that can be realized by provers that share entangled quantum states are no-signaling strategies.

No-signaling strategies were first studied in physics in the context of Bell inequalities by Khalfin and Tsirelson [19] and Rastall [22], and they gained much attention after they were reintroduced by Popescu and Rohrlich [21]. MIPs that are secure against no-signaling provers were extensively studied in the literature (see for example [24, 4, 2, 17, 13, 11, 12]). It was known that they are contained in EXP, and recently [14] showed that they also contain EXP, thus giving a full characterization of their exact power.

INFORMAL THEOREM 4 ([14]). *For any language L computable in time $t = t(n)$, there exists an MIP with soundness error $2^{-\mathsf{polylog}(t)}$ against no-signaling cheating provers. The number of provers and the communication complexity is $\mathsf{polylog}(t)$. The verifier runs in time $n \cdot \mathsf{polylog}(t)$ (and the provers run in time $\mathsf{poly}(t)$). Moreover, the verifier only runs in time $\mathsf{polylog}(t)$ if he is given oracle access to a (specific) encoding of x,[3] where each entry of the encoding can be computed deterministically from x in time $\tilde{O}(n)$ and space $O(\log n)$.*

In this work, we use this theorem for languages in P. Note that this theorem implies that for languages in P the verifier runs in $\tilde{O}(n)$ time and in $\mathsf{polylog}(n)$ space. Thus, we restate the theorem as follows.

THEOREM 5 ([14]). *If $L \in$ P, then there exists an MIP for L with $\mathsf{polylog}(n)$ provers, and with soundness error $2^{-\mathsf{polylog}(n)}$ against no-signaling strategies. The verifier runs in time $\tilde{O}(n)$, space $\mathsf{polylog}(n)$, and tosses at most $\mathsf{polylog}(n)$ coins (and the provers run in polynomial time). Each query and answer is of length $\mathsf{polylog}(n)$.*

We use Theorem 5 to show a reduction from any language $L \in$ P to a linear program. Our reduction runs in quasi-poly time and polylog space. In particular, our reduction takes an instance of size n and converts it into a linear program of size quasi-polynomial in n, where the polyhedron is on

---

[3]This encoding is the low-degree extension encoding. We refer the reader to [14] for details.

quasi-polynomial number of variables (i.e., quasi-polynomial dimensions). This polyhedron is fixed, independent of the instance x (and depends only on its size $n = |x|$).[4]

3.2 Proof of Theorem 3

PROOF. Let L be any language in P. By Theorem 5, the language L has an MIP, $(V, P_1, \ldots, P_k)$, where $k = \mathsf{polylog}(n)$, with communication complexity $\mathsf{polylog}(n)$ and soundness $2^{-\mathsf{polylog}(n)}$ against no-signaling provers (where n is the instance size).

We define a reduction $\mathcal{R}$ that takes as input an instance $x \in \{0, 1\}^n$ and converts it into a linear program, as follows: Consider all possible no-signaling families of distributions of cheating provers in the MIP. For each such possible no-signaling family of distributions $\{\mathcal{A}_q\}_{q \in D^k}$, denote by

$$p_{q,a} = \Pr_{A \in_R \mathcal{A}_q}[A = a].$$

Note that $\{\mathcal{A}_q\}_{q \in D^k}$ is a no-signaling family of distributions if and only if the following conditions are satisfied (the first two conditions hold if and only if each $\mathcal{A}_q$ is a distribution, and the last condition holds if and only if these distributions are no-signaling):

1. For every $q = (q_1, \ldots, q_k) \in D^k$ and for every $a \in \Sigma^k$,

$$p_{q,a} \geq 0.$$

2. For every $q = (q_1, \ldots, q_k) \in D^k$,

$$\sum_{a \in \Sigma^k} p_{q,a} = 1.$$

3. For every $S \subseteq [k]$, for every $q = (q_1, \ldots, q_k) \in D^k$ and $q' = (q'_1, \ldots, q'_k) \in D^k$ for which $q_S = q'_S$, and for every $a_S \in \Sigma^S$, it holds that

$$\sum_{a' : a'_S = a_S} p_{q,a'} = \sum_{a' : a'_S = a_S} p_{q',a'}.$$

Denote by p_q the probability that V sends the provers queries $q = (q_1, \ldots, q_k) \in \mathcal{D}^k$. The fact that $(V, P_1, \ldots, P_k)$ is an MIP that is secure against no-signaling strategies (with soundness $2^{-\mathsf{polylog}(n)}$ and perfect completeness), implies that if $x \notin L$ then[5]

$$\sum_q p_q \sum_{a : V(x,q,a)=1} p_{q,a} \leq 2^{-\mathsf{polylog}(n)},$$

and if $x \in L$ then there exists a (classical) strategy for which

$$\sum_q p_q \sum_{a : V(x,q,a)=1} p_{q,a} = 1.$$

Thus, the reduction $\mathcal{R}$ converts $x \in \{0, 1\}^n$ into the linear program with the polyhedron defined by:

$$p_{q,a} \geq 0, \ \forall q \in D^k \text{ and } \forall a \in \Sigma^k.$$

$$\sum_{a \in \Sigma^k} p_{q,a} = 1, \ \forall q \in D^k.$$

$$\sum_{a' : a'_S = a_S} p_{q,a'} = \sum_{a' : a'_S = a_S} p_{q',a'},$$

$$\forall S \subseteq [k], \ \forall q, q' \in D^k \text{ s.t. } q_S = q'_S, \ \forall a_S \in \Sigma^S.$$

Note that this polyhedron is fixed and does not depend on the instance x. The objective function is

$$\max_{\{p_{q,a}\}} \sum_q p_q \sum_{a : V(x,q,a)=1} p_{q,a}, \quad (11)$$

where for every q, p_q is a fixed value defined by the verifier in the underlying MIP, and $\{p_{q,a}\}$ are the variables. Note that if $x \in L$ then the maximum of this objective function on the polyhedron is 1, whereas if $x \notin L$ then the maximum of this objective function on the polyhedron is at most $2^{-\mathsf{polylog}(n)}$. Thus, determining whether x is in the language or not reduces to approximating the objective function.

It remains to prove that the space complexity of $\mathcal{R}$ is $\mathsf{polylog}(n)$ (and hence the runtime is at most $\mathsf{quasi\text{-}poly}(n)$). Since the polyhedron is fixed, it suffices for the reduction $\mathcal{R}$ to generate the objective function, as defined in Equation (11).[6] Namely, $\mathcal{R}$ needs to compute p_q for every q, and $V(x, q, a)$ for every q and a. $\mathcal{R}$ computes p_q by enumerating over all possible random coin tosses of the MIP verifier (recall that the MIP verifier tosses at most $\mathsf{polylog}(n)$ coins). This, together with the fact that the space complexity of V is $\mathsf{polylog}(n)$, implies that the space complexity of $\mathcal{R}$ is $\mathsf{polylog}(n)$, as desired. $\square$

Acknowledgments.
We thank Boaz Barak for illuminating discussions.

4. REFERENCES

[1] S. Arora and B. Barak. *Computational complexity: A modern approach.* Cambridge University Press, Cambridge, 2009.

[2] D. Avis, H. Imai, and T. Ito. On the relationship between convex bodies related to correlation experiments with dichotomic observables. *Journal of Physics A: Mathematical and General, 39(36),* 39(36):11283, 2006.

[3] L. Babai, L. Fortnow, and C. Lund. Non-deterministic exponential time has two-prover interactive protocols. In *31st Annual Symposium on Foundations of Computer Science, St. Louis, Missouri, USA, October 22-24, 1990, Volume I*, pages 16–25. IEEE Computer Society, 1990.

[4] J. Barrett, N. Linden, S. Massar, S. Pironio, S. Popescu, and D. Roberts. Nonlocal correlations as an information-theoretic resource. *Physical Review A, 71(022101),* 71(2):022101, 2005.

[5] M. Ben-Or, S. Goldwasser, J. Kilian, and A. Wigderson. Multi-prover interactive proofs: How to

---

[4]The polyhedron is also independent of the language L, and depends only on its time complexity.

[5]Here we assume for simplicity that the verifier's decision is a function only of the input x, the queries q, and the answers a, and not of the verifier's randomness. This is indeed the case for the verifier given by Theorem 5 (and in fact can always be assumed without loss of generality).

[6]We remark that the inequalities describing the polyhedron can easily be computed in $\mathsf{polylog}(n)$ space.

remove intractability assumptions. In *Proceedings of the 20th Annual ACM Symposium on Theory of Computing, May 2-4, 1988, Chicago, Illinois, USA*, pages 113–131, 1988.

[6] D. Bertsimas and S. Vempala. Solving convex programs by random walks. *J. ACM*, 51(4):540–556, 2004.

[7] G. B. Dantzig. Maximization of linear function of variables subject to linear inequalities. pages 339–347, 1951.

[8] D. P. Dobkin, R. J. Lipton, and S. P. Reiss. Linear programming is log-space hard for P. *Inf. Process. Lett.*, 8(2):96–97, 1979.

[9] J. Dunagan and S. Vempala. A simple polynomial-time rescaling algorithm for solving linear programs. In *Proceedings of the 36th Annual ACM Symposium on Theory of Computing, Chicago, IL, USA, June 13-16, 2004*, pages 315–320, 2004.

[10] U. Feige and J. Kilian. Making games short (extended abstract). In F. T. Leighton and P. W. Shor, editors, *Proceedings of the Twenty-Ninth Annual ACM Symposium on the Theory of Computing, El Paso, Texas, USA, May 4-6, 1997*, pages 506–516. ACM, 1997.

[11] T. Holenstein. Parallel repetition: Simplification and the no-signaling case. *Theory of Computing*, 5(1):141–172, 2009.

[12] T. Ito. Polynomial-space approximation of no-signaling provers. In *ICALP (1)*, pages 140–151, 2010.

[13] T. Ito, H. Kobayashi, and K. Matsumoto. Oracularization and two-prover one-round interactive proofs against nonlocal strategies. In *IEEE Conference on Computational Complexity*, pages 217–228, 2009.

[14] Y. T. Kalai, R. Raz, and R. D. Rothblum. How to delegate computations: the power of no-signaling proofs. In *Symposium on Theory of Computing, STOC 2014, New York, NY, USA, May 31 - June 03, 2014*, pages 485–494, 2014.

[15] N. Karmarkar. A new polynomial-time algorithm for linear programming. *Combinatorica*, 4(4):373–396, 1984.

[16] J. A. Kelner and D. A. Spielman. A randomized polynomial-time simplex algorithm for linear programming. In *Proceedings of the 38th Annual ACM Symposium on Theory of Computing, Seattle, WA, USA, May 21-23, 2006*, pages 51–60, 2006.

[17] J. Kempe, H. Kobayashi, K. Matsumoto, B. Toner, and T. Vidick. Entangled games are hard to approximate. In *FOCS*, pages 447–456, 2008.

[18] L. G. Khachiyan. A polynomial algorithm in linear programming. *In Doklady Akademia Nauk SSSR*, pages 1093–1096, 1979.

[19] L. A. Khalfin and B. S. Tsirelson. Quantum and quasi-classical analogs of Bell inequalities. In *In Symposium on the Foundations of Modern Physics*, pages 441–460, 1985.

[20] M. Luby and N. Nisan. A parallel approximation algorithm for positive linear programming. In S. R. Kosaraju, D. S. Johnson, and A. Aggarwal, editors, *Proceedings of the Twenty-Fifth Annual ACM Symposium on Theory of Computing, May 16-18, 1993, San Diego, CA, USA*, pages 448–457. ACM, 1993.

[21] S. Popescu and D. Rohrlich. Quantum nonlocality as an axiom. *Foundations of Physics*, 24(3):379–385, 1994.

[22] P. Rastall. Locality, Bell's theorem, and quantum mechanics. *Foundations of Physics*, 15(9):963–972, 1985.

[23] M. J. Serna. Approximating linear programming is log-space complete for P. *Inf. Process. Lett.*, 37(4):233–236, 1991.

[24] B. Toner. Monogamy of non-local quantum correlations. *Proceedings of the Royal Society A: Mathematical, Physical and Engineering Science*, 465(2101):59–69, 2009.

Spectral Embedding of k-Cliques, Graph Partitioning and k-Means

Pranjal Awasthi
Rutgers University
pa336@cs.rutgers.edu

Moses Charikar
Stanford University
moses@cs.stanford.edu

Ravishankar Krishnaswamy
Microsoft Research
ravishan@cs.cmu.edu

Ali Kemal Sinop
Simons Institute for the Theory of Computing
asinop@cs.cmu.edu

ABSTRACT

We introduce and study a new notion of graph partitioning, intimately connected to spectral clustering and k-means clustering. Formally, given a graph G on n vertices, we ask to find a graph H that is the union of k cliques on n vertices, such that $L_G \succeq \lambda L_H$ where λ is maximized. Here L_G and L_H are the (normalized) Laplacians of the graphs G and H respectively. Informally, our graph partitioning objective asks for the *optimal spectral simplification* of a given graph as a disjoint union of k cliques.

We justify this objective function in several ways. First and foremost, we show that a commonly used spectral clustering algorithm *implicitly optimizes* this objective function, up to a factor of $O(k)$. Using this connection, we immediately get an $O(k)$-approximation algorithm to our new objective function by simply using the spectral clustering algorithm on G. Next, we demonstrate another application of our objective function: we use it as a means to proving that simple spectral clustering algorithms can solve some well-studied graph partitioning problems (such as partitioning into expanders). Additionally, we also show that (a relaxation of) this optimization problem naturally arises as the dual problem to the question of finding the worst-case integrality gap instance for the classical k-means SDP. Finally, owing to these close connection between some classical clustering techniques (such as k-means and spectral clustering), we argue that a more complete understanding of this optimization problem could lead to new algorithmic insights and techniques for the area of graph partitioning.

Permission to make digital or hard copies of all or part of this work for personal or classroom use is granted without fee provided that copies are not made or distributed for profit or commercial advantage and that copies bear this notice and the full citation on the first page. Copyrights for components of this work owned by others than ACM must be honored. Abstracting with credit is permitted. To copy otherwise, or republish, to post on servers or to redistribute to lists, requires prior specific permission and/or a fee. Request permissions from Permissions@acm.org.

ITCS'16, January 14–16, 2016, Cambridge, MA, USA.
© 2016 ACM. ISBN 978-1-4503-4057-1/16/01 ...$15.00.
DOI: http://dx.doi.org/10.1145/2840728.2840751

1. INTRODUCTION

Graph partitioning is a fundamental problem in computer science with various applications in computer vision, machine learning and bioinformatics, among others. Such problems have been studied extensively in theoretical computer science (e.g. sparsest cut, multicut, multiway cut, etc) [28, 16, 18, 13]. Designing a good objective function for graph partitioning is a balancing act between several, often conflicting, desiderata. For instance, the objective function formulation should be succinct and mathematically tractable. In traditional graph partitioning objectives, this is captured by formulating the function as a combinatorial measure of the number of edges cut. From a practitioner's point of view, the hope is that the study of the objective function will naturally lead to good algorithms which succeed on practical instances of the problem, if not on all. In this paper, we introduce and study a new spectral notion of graph partitioning, intimately connected to spectral clustering and k-means clustering. We make the claim, and formally justify, that our objective function has many of the desirable properties mentioned above.

Formally, we study the following problem (see Section 2 and 3 for definitions of these concepts): Given a graph G with normalized Laplacian L_G, the goal is to find a partition of the vertices $\Gamma = \{C_1, \ldots, C_k\}$ into k normalized cliques with associated Laplacian matrix K_Γ whose (i,j)th entry is $1 - \frac{1}{|C_\ell|}$ if $i = j \in C_\ell$, $\frac{-1}{|C_\ell|}$ if both $i, j \in C_\ell$, and 0 otherwise. The objective is to find a partition Γ such that $L_G \succeq \lambda K_\Gamma$ and λ is maximized. Informally, our graph partitioning objective asks for the optimal spectral simplification of the graph as a disjoint union of cliques. It can be seen as a spectral variant of the problem of graph partitioning into expanders (where expansion is just measured w.r.t the induced graph in each piece of the decomposition); in contrast, our objective function also captures the edges going across pieces, and can be loosely viewed as partitioning a graph into weakly embedded expanders. Moreover, our notion of embedding cliques is a one-sided version of the notion of spectral similarity of graph Laplacians used in the recent influential sequence of work on spectral sparsification [38, 36, 9]. It is also akin to the notion of spectrally thin trees that have been studied before [19], except that we look for a decomposition into cliques that is spectrally thin, instead of trees. Finally, we would like to mention that a very similar notion has been used in [8] where the authors address the question of whether a metric space which does not coarsely embed into a Hilbert space necessarily contains a weakly embedded expander.

1.1 Why Study Another Objective Function?

A) Precise Equivalence Between Partitioning and Clustering. Our first main result is an equivalence between *optimizing our objective and optimizing the clustering cost[1] of the "resistive embedding" of the given graph.* That is, we show that a partitioning of the vertices into k pieces is good for our objective function if and only if the same partitioning is a good clustering of the resistive embedding vectors (which are the column vectors of $L^{\dagger/2}$). Our result also suggests that a natural variant of spectral clustering is a good algorithm for our objective function. Typically, the graph Laplacian is projected to the top k eigenvectors, and then the resulting row vectors are clustered. In our case, we project the resistive embedding vectors into a k dimensional space, and run a standard clustering algorithm on these vectors. Using the equivalence, we show that the resulting graph partitioning is a good solution — an $O(k)$ approximation — for our new objective function, thereby giving us provable guarantees, and more intuition, on the types of clusterings our algorithm finds.

We next show that we can improve the provable guarantees, if we are allowed to output a distribution over partitionings. In Section 4, we show how we can use the matrix multiplicative weights algorithm of Arora and Kale [4] to obtain a *distribution of partitions* that, in expectation, can embed into G with a constant factor approximation in terms of our objective function. Interestingly, we obtain this result by exhibiting a connection between our problem and that of finding the worst-case integrality gap instance for a natural SDP relaxation for the classical k-means problem.

B) New Smoothing Step. While effective resistances (i.e. the values) themselves have been used [36] in spectral sparsification, and the resistive distance embedding has been used in graph partitioning heuristics [24, 25, 34], we believe that this is the first provable justification of their use in graph partitioning algorithms. Moreover, by understanding how our algorithm works on our objective function, we also suggest an additional iterative step in the process, called *smoothing*: iteratively *average* each vector with the vectors corresponding to the neighboring vertices in the original graph, and cluster the smoothed vectors. We are able to get provably better guarantees in certain situations, and also empirically get better guarantees in some large datasets. Going forward, we believe that an analysis of multiple steps of smoothing will lead to improved guarantees for our objective function in theory and in practice.

C) Applications. Then, in Section 5, in order to illustrate the power of our new notion of graph decomposition, we show that approximation algorithms for our new objective can be used as a black box to find a partition of a graph into k pieces with sufficiently large gaps between internal and external conductance. Partitions with such properties were studied by [22] (see also [17]); they also arise in the work of Ng, Jordan and Weiss [33]. Given the promise that

such a partition exists, any good algorithm for our objective directly produces a partition that is guaranteed to have small symmetric difference with this unknown partition. In particular, we show that our variant of spectral clustering (using effective resistance vectors) works! Finally in Section 6, we further strengthen the connection to spectral clustering by showing that the most popular variant of this approach also gives guarantees for our new objective function. Combining the above connections and applications, we thus believe our new graph partitioning objective function and associated algorithm makes a meaningful contribution to the existing body of work trying to motivate and justify spectral clustering algorithms, which we detail in Section 1.3.

1.2 Related Work

Graph partitioning objectives have received a lot of attention in theoretical computer science. Most notable among them is the sparsest cut objective [28, 7, 6] which attempts to find a 2-partition with minimum conductance. Conductance is also closely related to the second smallest eigenvalue of the graph Laplacian [12, 1, 3]. Generalizations of this to k-partitions aim at finding k clusters with small conductance [27, 30] as well as high conductance within each cluster [22, 17]. These works exploit gaps in the higher eigenvalues of the graph Laplacian to design algorithms which achieve a good clustering. The most relevant to our work is the result of [17] which uses the spectrum of the graph Laplacian to design a good clustering if one exists (See Section 6 for a result of similar flavor using our new objective). However as opposed to our algorithm, the algorithm proposed in [17] does not fit naturally into the framework of spectral clustering as used in practice. See the next section for details. A sequence of work has also shown that spectral partitioning works well in geometric settings [37, 23, 10].

1.3 Spectral clustering and k-means

Spectral clustering approaches in practice consist of two main steps: a) transforming the original set of points to be clustered using the spectrum of the data matrix (or an associated matrix), and b) optimizing the k-means objective in the new space to obtain a k-partition. The choice of using the k-means objective in the new space is not arbitrary and several prior works have hinted at a deeper connection. The simplest scenario consists of the original set of points in $\Re^d$ such that there is a true unknown k-partition with the mean vectors of each partition being far away from each other. In this case, Kumar and Kannan [26] show that performing a linear embedding of the points onto the span of the top k singular vectors of the data matrix and optimizing for k-means in the new space leads to good approximations to the true mean vectors. This approach also has applications in the planted partition model of Mcsherry [31].

In many real world applications however, one does not have a true clustering with well separated mean vectors. In such scenarios spectral clustering approaches prove to be immensely successful again. The idea is to now look at non-linear embeddings. This approach pioneered by the work of Weiss, Meila and Shi and Ng, Jordan and Weiss [40, 32, 33] looks at the spectrum of the Laplacian L of the affinity graph. The affinity graph A is an $n \times n$ matrix where the entry $A(i, j) \propto \exp(-\|x_i - x_j\|^2)$. The k dimensional embedding of a point is obtained by using the corresponding coordinates in the top k eigenvectors of L. Ng, Jordan and Weiss

---

[1] Formally, the equivalence holds if the metric used to evaluate a clustering is the spectral radius objective, i.e., $\min_C \|A - C\|_2^2$ where the rows of A are the data points, and the rows of C are the cluster centers each data point is assigned to; in contrast, $\|A - C\|_F^2$ is the k-means cost.

[33] justify this approach by showing that if the true clustering is well separated in the sense that it has densely connected clusters with sparse connections across them then in the new space the optimal k means clustering will have a small cost. In many instances, it has been observed that replacing the Laplacian based embedding with the resistive embedding (using the eigen vectors of $L^{\frac{1}{2}}$) works better as it induces a stronger block structure in the induced distance metric [34]. As an application of our result we strengthen this connection by showing in Section 5 how to recover a good point wise approximation to a well separated clustering using our algorithm which is based on resistive embeddings followed by solving k-means. Spectral approaches have also been used with great success in partitioning problems where one is naturally interested in optimizing a cut based objective function [32, 35, 42]. It has also been observed that such approaches have connections, and in some cases are equivalent to optimizing a kernel k-means objective in the original space [14, 15]. Finally, our approach of modifying the metric for the clustering problem (via our smoothing step) can be loosely connected with that of learning the metric for clustering [41].

2. PRELIMINARIES

2.1 Linear Algebra

Let $\mathbb{R}^{m \times n}$ be the set of all $m \times n$ real matrices; $\mathbb{S}^m$ be the set of $m \times m$ symmetric matrices; $\mathbb{S}_+^m \subset \mathbb{S}^m$ be the set of $m \times m$ positive semidefinite (PSD) matrices. Alternatively, we will use $A \succeq 0$ to denote $A \in \mathbb{S}_+^m$. The $m \times m$ identity matrix is denoted by I_m. For any subset $C \subseteq [n]$, $\mathbf{e}_C \in \mathbb{R}^n$ is the indicator vector for C so that $(\mathbf{e}_C)_i = 1$ iff $i \in C$; 0 else. Define $J_C \stackrel{\text{def}}{=} \mathbf{e}_C \mathbf{e}_C^T$ as the matrix whose entries are 0 except the principal minor on C, which is all-1's.

For any $A \in \mathbb{R}^{m \times n}$, we will use $A^\Pi, A^\perp \in \mathbb{S}_+^m$ to refer to the projection matrix onto the column span of A and its orthogonal complement, respectively. Note that $A^\Pi + A^\perp = I_m$. Finally, we will use $\sigma_{\max}(A)$ and $\sigma_{\min}(A)$ to denote the maximum and minimum singular values of A.

Given $A \in \mathbb{S}^m$, we define $A^\dagger$ to be the pseudo-inverse of A; and $\lambda_{\min}(A), \lambda_{\max}(A)$ as the the minimum and maximum eigenvalues of A, respectively: $\lambda_{\min}(A) \stackrel{\text{def}}{=} \min_{q \neq 0} \frac{q^T A q}{\|q\|^2}$; $\lambda_{\max}(A) \stackrel{\text{def}}{=} \max_{q \neq 0} \frac{q^T A q}{\|q\|^2}$. Likewise, given $A, B \in \mathbb{S}_+^m$, let $\lambda_{\min}(A, B)$ be the minimum generalized eigenvalue of A and B, $\lambda_{\min}(A, B) \stackrel{\text{def}}{=} \min_{q:Bq \neq 0} \frac{q^T A q}{q^T B q}$. An equivalent definition is $\lambda_{\min}(A, B) \stackrel{\text{def}}{=} \max\{\lambda | A \succeq \lambda B\}$.

2.2 Graphs

Given a graph G with adjacency matrix A, let D be the diagonal matrix with $D_{ii} = d_i$ where d_i is the weighted degree of node i. We define the Laplacian matrix of G as $L_G = D - A$. We define the normalized adjacency matrix to be $D^{-1/2} A D^{-1/2}$, and the normalized Laplacian to be $I - D^{-1/2} A D^{-1/2}$. Also, let $K \in \mathbb{S}_+^n$ be the Laplacian matrix of a normalized clique, $K \stackrel{\text{def}}{=} I - \frac{1}{n} J$.

2.3 Partitions

Define $\Gamma_k(n)$ to be the set of all proper k-partitions of $[n]$:

$$\Gamma_k(n) \stackrel{\text{def}}{=} \Big\{ \Gamma = \{S_1, \dots, S_k\} \mid S_i \neq \emptyset, \; S_1 \uplus \dots \uplus S_k = [n] \Big\}.$$

We can construct an associated graph for Γ by placing a normalized clique on each $S \in \Gamma$. We will use K_Γ to denote the Laplacian matrix of corresponding graph. Finally, given a subset S, we use $\mathbf{e}_S$ to denote the indicator vector for S so that $[\mathbf{e}_S]_i = 1$ iff $i \in S$; we also use $\mathbf{e}$ for the all-1's vector.

3. SPECTRAL EMBEDDING OF CLIQUES

We now formally define the spectral embedding we study in this work. Given as input a connected graph G with the corresponding normalized Laplacian matrix L_G, the goal is to find a partition Γ into k normalized cliques while optimizing the following objective:

$$\max \lambda \text{ st } L_G \succeq \lambda K_\Gamma.$$

Before we get into the technical details of our algorithm, we present some simple observations about the objective function. To begin with, note that $\lambda \geq 0$ because $L \succeq 0$. Next observe that when $k = 1$, the optimal value OPT of our problem will be the second smallest eigenvalue of the Laplacian, which is the algebraic expansion of the graph (in words, it captures how well we can embed a complete graph into G). Thus our objective can be seen as a generalization of algebraic expansion to k-way partitionings. It is also a smooth transition between completely combinatorial ways of measuring a good k-way partitioning (such as normalized cuts), which are often hard to compute, and purely algebraic ways (such as measuring the kth smallest eigenvalue), which are more difficult to understand and relate to k-way partitionings. Indeed, if the graph G is a disjoint union of k pieces, then OPT is the smallest algebraic expansion of the different pieces. Moreover, as mentioned above, OPT is also related to λ_{k+1} of the graph — by relaxing K_Γ to be any $n - k$ dimensional projection, we get that OPT $\leq \lambda_{k+1}$. It is also easy to show that OPT $\geq \lambda_2$. To see this, fix any partitioning Γ and only consider vectors x such that $\sum_i x_i = 0$ for each cluster in Γ. Then

$$\frac{x^T L_G x}{x^T K_\Gamma x} = \frac{x^T L_G x}{x^T x} = \lambda_2$$

Finally, OPT only increases with larger k, because $K_\Gamma \succeq K_{\Gamma'}$ whenever Γ' is a refinement of Γ.

In order to understand this objective better consider the following simple scenario first. Given a Laplacian matrix L and k-partition, for some λ, how can we even verify $L \succeq \lambda K_\Gamma$? From an algorithmic perspective, this is easy: Compute the minimum generalized eigenvalue of L and K_Γ and compare it against λ. From an analysis perspective on the other hand, this yields little to no insight for us on how to certify that the graph admits a good spectral k-clique-embedding. There is no analogue of Cheeger's inequality for the generalized case, and indeed there is strong evidence to believe none exists [39]. As a result, we first present a characterization of k-clique embeddability and, using this, derive a sufficient condition for the existence of one. This condition then leads to a natural algorithm for finding such clustering. We would like to mention that the above formulation has also been studied in the context of expansion relative to a sequence of subgroups [8]. This notion of relative expansion has also been used to show that certain finite semi-direct products form an expander [2].

Good and bad cases: As mentioned above, if the grah is a disjoint union of k pieces, then the optimal value of λ will be the smallest algebraic expansion of any piece. It is also an

303

easy calculation to show that the partitioning corresponding to the optimal λ will correspond to each piece being a clique. In general, our objective function will represent well cases when there is a ground truth partitioning with internal connectivity more than the external connectivity of each piece. We formalize this in Section 5. On the other hand, if there is no "clear" k-partitioning of the graph, our objective may fail to capture the instance. Consider, for example the case of grid graphs with $k = 2$. From the above discussion, we know that the optimal value of our objective will lie between λ_2 and λ_3. However, for grid graphs these two values are the same and hence according to our objective, any 2-partitioning will be equally good!

3.1 Necessary and Sufficient Conditions

Our starting point is relating the minimum generalized eigenvalue to a standard maximum eigenvalue problem. While there are other bounds for this [11], we prove one most amenable to us.

LEMMA 3.1. *Given a connected graph G and a k-partition Γ of V, we have $\max\{\lambda \mid L_G \succeq \lambda K_\Gamma\} = \frac{1}{\lambda_{\max}(K_\Gamma L_G^\dagger K_\Gamma)}$. Furthermore the maximum eigenvector p of $K_\Gamma L_G^\dagger K_\Gamma$ satisfies $K_\Gamma p = p$.*

For simplicity in notation, we define $L \stackrel{\text{def}}{=} L_G$, $M \stackrel{\text{def}}{=} K_\Gamma$ and $K \stackrel{\text{def}}{=} L \cdot L^\dagger$. Additionally, let $\lambda_{\min}(L, M) = \lambda_{\min}$ and $\lambda_{\max}(ML^\dagger M) = \lambda_{\max}$. Since any cluster $C \in \Gamma$ is connected in G, $\lambda_{\min} > 0$.

The first identity (i) follows immediately from the definition of $\lambda_{\min}$: $\lambda_{\min}(L, M) = \min_{q:Mq \neq 0} \frac{q^T L q}{q^T M q}$, So for all q, $q^T L q \geq \lambda_{\min} q^T M q$ implying $L \succeq \lambda_{\min} M$. We prove (ii) in two parts.

PROOF OF $\lambda_{\max} \geq 1/\lambda_{\min}$. Given any g such that $Lg = \lambda_{\min} M g$, we can assume $Kg = g$, since Kg also satisfies this identity. Therefore:

$$g = Kg = L^\dagger L g = \lambda_{\min} L^\dagger M g.$$

Multiplying with $\frac{1}{\lambda_{\min}} M$ on both sides,

$$\frac{1}{\lambda_{\min}} Mg = ML^\dagger Mg.$$

For $p \stackrel{\text{def}}{=} Mg$, together with the fact that $M^2 = M$, this becomes

$$\frac{1}{\lambda_{\min}} p = ML^\dagger M p.$$

Therefore $\lambda_{\max}(ML^\dagger M) \geq \frac{1}{\lambda_{\min}}$. $\square$

PROOF OF $\lambda_{\max} \leq 1/\lambda_{\min}$. We always have $\lambda_{\min} \geq 0$ so we only need to consider the case of $\lambda_{\max} > 0$. Given corresponding eigenvector p with $M(L^\dagger M p) = \lambda_{\max} p$, it is easy to see that $Mp = p$. Therefore

$$ML^\dagger p = \lambda_{\max} p.$$

Eigenvalues of a matrix and its transpose are the same, thus

$$(ML^\dagger)^T = L^\dagger M$$

has maximum eigenvalue $\lambda_{\max}$ with eigenvector g, so that $L^\dagger M g = \lambda_{\max} g$. Multiplying both sides by L and observing that $LL^\dagger = K$ with $KM = M$,

$$\lambda_{\max} \cdot Lg = LL^\dagger Mg = KMg = Mg.$$

Hence

$$\lambda_{\min}(L, M) \leq \frac{g^T L g}{g^T M g} = \frac{1}{\lambda_{\max}}.$$

$\square$

Equipped with Theorem 3.1, our goal is now much simpler: Instead of lower bounding the minimum generalized eigenvalue of a pair of matrices, we want to upper bound the maximum eigenvalue of a single matrix. Indeed, the largest eigenvalue of $K_\Gamma L_G^\dagger K_\Gamma$ is equal to the $\|L_G^{\dagger/2} K_\Gamma\|_2^2$, the largest singular value of the matrix. However, $L_G^{\dagger/2} K_\Gamma$ is the matrix $L_G^{\dagger/2} - C_\Gamma$, where we think of the columns of $L_G^{\dagger/2}$ as being the data points in Euclidean space, and C_Γ is the center matrix of the corresponding centroid each point/column is assigned to, depending on the cluster it belongs to in Γ. Therefore, finding a good Γ for our partitioning objective is equivalent to clustering the columns of $L_G^{\dagger/2}$, in the spectral norm sense (note that we want to bound the $\|L_G^{\dagger/2} - C_\Gamma\|_2^2$; in relation, $\|L_G^{\dagger/2} - C_\Gamma\|_F^2$ is the k-means cost of clustering the same points). This is precisely the setting considered in Kumar-Kannan [26, 20], where they give an $O(k)$ approximation for this problem using SVD and k-means clustering. However, we give an alternate proof of this result which is more amenable, and in fact, leads naturally to our smoothing step.

THEOREM 3.2. *Given a connected graph G with normalized adjacency (normalized Laplacian) matrix A (L resp.), suppose Γ is a k-partition. Then, for all $\tau \in \mathbb{Z}_+$, we have:*

$$\lambda_{\min}(L, K_\Gamma) \geq \left\{ \max(\lambda^{-1}, 2\tau) + \text{Tr}\left[K_\Gamma A^\tau (L^\dagger)_k A^\tau \right] \right\}^{-1}.$$

Here λ is the kth smallest eigenvalue of L, and $(L^\dagger)_k$ is the matrix $L^\dagger$ projected onto its top k-eigenvectors. [2] *In particular, for the choice of $\tau \leftarrow 0$:*

$$\lambda_{\min}(L, K_\Gamma) \geq \left\{ \frac{1}{\lambda_k} + \text{Tr}\left[K_\Gamma (L^\dagger)_k \right] \right\}^{-1}.$$

PROOF. Let λ_i and q_i be the ith smallest eigenvalue and corresponding eigenvector of L. Suppose G has c-connected components. Then $0 = \lambda_1 = \ldots = \lambda_c < \lambda_{c+1} \leq \ldots \leq \lambda_n \leq 2$. Moreover if we define $K \stackrel{\text{def}}{=} L \cdot L^\dagger$ (the projection matrix onto the complement of connected components of G), then $K = \sum_{j>c} q_j q_j^T$. By our assumption, $K_\Gamma K = K K_\Gamma = K_\Gamma$. For any $x \in [0, 2]$, $\frac{1}{x} = \frac{1}{1-(1-x)} \leq 2\tau + \frac{(1-x)^{2\tau}}{x}$. Using this, we can now upper bound $L^\dagger$:

$$L^\dagger = \sum_{j>c} \frac{1}{\lambda_j} q_j q_j^T \preceq \sum_{c<j<k} \left(2\tau + \frac{(1-\lambda_i)^{2\tau}}{\lambda_i} \right) q_j q_j^T$$

$$+ \frac{1}{\lambda_r} \sum_{j \geq r} q_j q_j^T$$

$$\preceq \max(2\tau, \lambda_r^{-1}) K + A^\tau (L)_k A^\tau.$$

$$K_\Gamma L^\dagger K_\Gamma \preceq \max(2\tau, \lambda_r^{-1}) K_\Gamma + K_\Gamma A^\tau (L)_k A^\tau K_\Gamma.$$

---

[2] In words, for y_i's being the columns of $[L^\dagger]_k^{1/2} A^\tau$, a simple calculation shows that the trace term is equal to the k-means cost of clustering these vectors using Γ.

Since $\lambda_{\max}(X+Y) \leq \lambda_{\max}(X) + \lambda_{\max}(Y)$,

$$\lambda_{\max}(K_\Gamma L^\dagger K_\Gamma) \leq \max(2\tau, \lambda_r^{-1}) \underbrace{\lambda_{\max}(K_\Gamma)}_{=1}$$
$$+ \lambda_{\max}(K_\Gamma \underbrace{A^\tau (L)_k A^\tau}_{\succeq 0} K_\Gamma)$$
$$\leq \max(2\tau, \lambda_r^{-1}) + \mathrm{Tr}(K_\Gamma A^\tau (L)_k A^\tau K_\Gamma).$$

The proof is complete by using the identity from Theorem 3.1. $\square$

3.2 Main Algorithm

The lower bound presented in Theorem 3.2 corresponds to a natural algorithm for finding Γ. We state the algorithm only for connected graphs. The disconnected case can easily be handled by recursing on each component separately. Even though this algorithm has polynomial running time, it can be implemented much more efficiently, and we leave the details to the final version.

Input..
Number of clusters k, normalized adjacency and Laplacian matrices $A, L = I - A$ respectively, and maximum smoothing count $\tau_{\max}$.

Output..
λ and k-partition Γ such that $L \succeq \lambda K_\Gamma$.

1. *(Resistive Embedding)* For every $i \in V$, let $Y_i^{(0)} \leftarrow (L^{\dagger/2})_k \mathbf{e}_i$ be the resistive embedding of node i projected onto top k-eigenvalues.

2. *(Best k-Partition So Far)* Let Γ_{best} be an arbitrary k-partition. $\lambda_{\mathrm{best}} \leftarrow 0$.

3. For $\tau \leftarrow 0$ to $\tau_{\max}$ do:

   (a) Find a k-means solution Γ for
   $$Y^{(t)} = \left[Y_i^{(t)} \mid i \in V \right]$$
   $$\lambda_{cur} \leftarrow \left[\max(2\tau, \lambda_k^{-1}) + \|Y^{(t)} K_\Gamma\|_F^2 \right]^{-1}.$$

   (b) If $\lambda_{cur} > \lambda_{\mathrm{best}}$, then $\Gamma_{\mathrm{best}} \leftarrow \Gamma$, $\lambda_{\mathrm{best}} \leftarrow \lambda_{cur}$.

   (c) *(Smoothing)* $\forall i \in V$, $Y_i^{(t+1)} \leftarrow \sum_j A_{ij} Y_j^{(t)}$.

In the algorithm above, steps (b) and (c) are optional (our current proof does not use any power derived from these steps); however, we believe that they could help in getting an improved quality of solution w.r.t our objective function. In words, the algorithm (without the smoothing step) simply projects the resistive embedding vectors onto the top k eigenvectors, and runs a k-means algorithm on the projected points.

THEOREM 3.3. *(Correctness) The output of this algorithm, Γ_{best} and λ_{best}, satisfies $L \succeq \lambda_{\mathrm{best}} K_{\Gamma_{\mathrm{best}}}$. Furthermore, we have that $\lambda_{\mathrm{best}} \geq \frac{\lambda_{\mathrm{OPT}}}{O(k)}$, where λ_{OPT} is the optimum.*

PROOF. Correctness follows immediately from Theorem 3.2. For the approximation guarantee, let Γ_{opt} be an optimal solution with $L \succeq \lambda_{\mathrm{OPT}} K_{\Gamma_{\mathrm{opt}}}$. Consider the projection matrix onto top k-eigenvectors of $L^\dagger$, Q_k: $Q_k = \sum_{j<k} q_j q_j^T$. Note that Q_k commutes with L. Thus, if we multiply the first expression on both sides with $Q_k L^{\dagger/2} Q_k = (Y^{(0)})^T (Y^{(0)})$:

$$Q_k \succeq \lambda_{\mathrm{OPT}} \cdot (Q_k L^{\dagger/2} Q_k) K_{\Gamma_{\mathrm{opt}}} (Q_k L^{\dagger/2} Q_k).$$

Taking the trace, $k \geq \lambda_{\mathrm{OPT}} \|Y^{(0)} K_{\Gamma_{\mathrm{opt}}}\|_F^2$. Therefore at time $\tau = 0$, there exists a k-means solution of cost $\leq \frac{k}{\lambda_{\mathrm{OPT}}}$. Hence the algorithm will find some Γ_{best} with

$$\|Y^{(0)} K_{\Gamma_{\mathrm{best}}}\|_F^2 \leq \frac{O(k)}{\lambda_{\mathrm{OPT}}}.$$

Consequently $\lambda_{best} \leq \frac{1}{\lambda_k} + \frac{O(k)}{\lambda_{\mathrm{OPT}}} \leq \frac{O(k)}{\lambda_{\mathrm{OPT}}}$ where we used the fact that $\lambda_{\mathrm{OPT}} \leq \lambda_k$. $\square$

Remark: Connection with Spectral Clustering. In machine learning, data mining and similar fields, a very common approach for clustering is to apply k-means on either the resistive embedding, or the embedding obtained by the smallest k-eigenvectors. In these cases, our algorithm above, or more the discussion following Theorem 3.1, could be seen to offer an explanation for *what kind of k-partitions* such methods implicitly seek. For example, if an algorithm of the above types finds a k-partition with small cost in the resistive embedding, then it means the underlying clusters are better connected to each other than across clusters, i.e., they have high value in our objective function. We give a more rigorous connection in Section 6. Given this connection, an intriguing practical problem is whether the applying the smoothing step helps clustering in such domains.

3.3 Smoothing for Multiple Steps

We end this section with a small remark regarding the use of single versus multiple steps of smoothing. While we don't require smoothing for our current guarantee of a factor of $O(k)$, we leave open the question of whether smoothing can provably yield better bounds in practical settings. To support our belief, we empirically demonstrate that the performance of traditional spectral clustering itself improves with a small number of steps of smoothing on large-scale real-world datasets [43].

Dataset	n	k	SC	SC+smoothing
Musk	6598	2	74.63%	83.2%(1)
Gamma	19020	2	69.36%	75.09%(2)
USCI	285779	2	93.9%	93.76%(1)
Segmentation	19020	7	33.23%	37.4%(5)
Poker	1000000	3	47.7%	49.8%(3)

Table 1: The clustering accuracy of the spectral clustering method used in [43] as compared to the same method applied with smoothing. The quantity in bracket denotes the number of rounds of smoothing which provides the best result. The datasets are from the UCI repository [29]. SC stands for Spectral Clustering.

4. SPECTRALLY EMBEDDING A DISTRIBUTION OF PARTITIONINGS

In this section, we show that we can get much better approximation guarantees if we allow ourselves to find a distribution over k-partitions.

THEOREM 4.1. *Given a feasible fractional solution X to the k-partitioning problem, we can efficiently find a distribution $\mathcal{X}$ over k-partitions such that $L_X \succeq \alpha E_{\Gamma \sim \mathcal{X}}[K_\Gamma]$ where $\alpha > \frac{1}{216}$ is a constant.* [3]

A nice additional property this says is that if X is a fractional solution for the *Euclidean k-means problem*, then we can round X **obliviously** into an integral clustering *even without looking at the point-set, or their distances*, and still achieve the best possible approximation factor.

We prove this by writing down the SDP for the best convex combination of k-partitions into X, and analyzing its dual. Consider the following SDP, which, given a feasible fractional k-means solution, tries to find the best convex combination of K_Γ's which embed into X, and its dual. Here, let $\mathbf{\Gamma}$ denote the set of all possible k-partitions of G.

$$(\text{Primal}) \qquad \max \sum_\Gamma w_\Gamma \text{ st } \sum_\Gamma w_\Gamma K_\Gamma \preceq L_X.$$

$$(\text{Dual}) \qquad \min L_X \cdot Y \text{ st } K_\Gamma \cdot Y \geq 1, \; \forall \Gamma \in \mathbf{\Gamma}, \; Y \succeq 0,$$

Clearly, notice that if we show that the primal solution has objective value at least α, then we're done (by scaling by $1/\sum_\Gamma w_\Gamma$, we'll get a convex combination which embeds into $(1/\alpha)L_X$). In what follows, we'll first show that, indeed, this is true, and subsequently show how to approximately solve this SDP using the Multiplicative Weights framework of Arora and Kale [5].

To show that the objective value is at least α, consider the dual. We show that the dual optimal has value at least α. Indeed, what is the dual trying to solve? Upon careful inspection, it is trying to find, given X, the *worst-case* set of points in Euclidean space, for which the k-means LP has the largest integrality gap. Indeed, suppose the set of points $\{y_1, y_2, \ldots, y_n\}$ are such that their gram matrix is Y, then $K_\Gamma \cdot Y = \text{Tr}(K_\Gamma Y)$ is precisely the k-means cost of the data set according to clustering Γ. So the dual asks for all the true clusterings to have cost at least 1 while minimizing the fractional cost of the k-means LP. But this is precisely the integrality gap instance! From existing rounding algorithms (most relevant to our work is that of Jain and Vazirani [21]), we know that the integrality gap is bounded by a small constant $c_{JV} \leq 216$, and hence the dual objective is at least a constant $1/c_{JV} \geq \alpha$. We hence know that the dual SDP has optimal value at least $\alpha = \frac{1}{216}$. Hence, the primal objective has value at least α, which completes the existential result. It remains to show that we can efficiently construct the distribution $\mathcal{X}$. Indeed, we show that we can achieve this using the Matrix Multiplicative Weights framework of Arora and Kale [5]. Perhaps not surprisingly, the "oracle" needed in their algorithm amounts to running the Jain-Vazirani approximation algorithm for k-means. We provide complete details in Appendix A.

5. AN APPLICATION: PARTITIONING OF WELL SEPARATED GRAPHS

In this section, we demonstrate the power of our objective by presenting an application in a traditional k-way clustering problem. In order to simplify the exposition, we assume

G is regular, with normalized adjacency and Laplacian matrices given by A and $L = I - A$, respectively. Indeed, suppose a graph G has a good *k-partition into expanders*, such that each cluster has low external sparsity and every cluster is internally an expander. Then we show that, as long as the internal expansion is sufficiently more than the external sparsity[4], we can recover a clustering which is ϵ-close in symmetric difference, by simply running our spectral clustering algorithm from Section 3. Before we delve into the details, let us introduce some notation.

DEFINITION 5.1. *Given a graph G and a k-partition Γ, we say that Γ is a (k, ϕ, λ) partition for G provided the following: (i) Every $S \in \Gamma$ has small sparsity in G, i.e., $\phi_G(S) \leq \phi$. (ii) Every $S \in \Gamma$ induces an algebraic expander, i.e., $\lambda_2(L[S]) \geq \lambda$.*

A similar notion appeared in the work of Gharan and Trevisan [17]. Unfortunately a direct comparison of both algorithms is not possible, as the goals are different: They first proved the existence of such a (k, λ, ϕ) clustering when there is a (sufficiently large) gap between λ_k and λ_{k+1}, and their constructive algorithm to efficiently find such a clustering requires an even larger gap between λ_k and λ_{k+1}. However, our algorithm works simply by assuming the existence of such a (k, λ, ϕ) partition and finding one which is close to this ground truth.

THEOREM 5.2. *There exists a constant $1 > \alpha > 0$ such that the following holds. Given graph G with (k, ϕ, λ)-partition $\Gamma_{\text{opt}} = \{T_1, \ldots, T_k\}$ and $\varepsilon \overset{\text{def}}{=} \frac{k\phi}{\lambda} \leq \alpha$, our algorithm will output a k-partition Γ of the form $\Gamma = \{S_1, \ldots, S_k\}$ such that: $\forall i \in [k] : |S_i \Delta T_i| \leq O(\varepsilon) \min(|S_i|, |T_i|)$.*

We devote the remainder of this section to the proof of Theorem 5.2. We use $\Gamma_{\text{opt}} = \{T_1, \ldots, T_k\}$ to denote a (k, ϕ, λ)-partition of G with $\frac{k\phi}{\lambda} = \varepsilon$ for some $\varepsilon \leq O(1)$. We will use $\Gamma = \{S_1, \ldots, S_k\}$ to refer to the partition found by our algorithm. Unless noted otherwise, we use S (solution we found) to refer to the clusters in Γ and T (ground truth) to refer to the clusters in Γ_{opt}.

For further convenience, we define $A_{\Gamma_{\text{opt}}}$ and A_Γ as the normalized adjacency matrices for the union of cliques on Γ_{opt} and Γ, respectively:

$$A_{\Gamma_{\text{opt}}} \overset{\text{def}}{=} \sum_T \frac{1}{|T|} J_T \text{ and } A_\Gamma \overset{\text{def}}{=} \sum_S \frac{1}{|S|} J_S.$$

Note that $K_{\Gamma_{\text{opt}}} = I - A_{\Gamma_{\text{opt}}}$ and $K_\Gamma = I - A_\Gamma$.

We begin with some useful preliminary definitions pertaining to how we measure the proximity of a partitioning to the ground truth (which is stronger than the commonly used notion of total number of mis-clustered points which can heavily be biased towards larger clusters and ignoring small clusters altogether), and a theorem connecting nearby partitionings and the corresponding closeness of their indicator matrices.

DEFINITION 5.3. *Given two k-partitions $\Gamma_1, \Gamma_2 \in \Gamma_k(n)$; we say Γ_1 and Γ_2 are ε-close if there is a perfect matching $M \subseteq \Gamma_1 \times \Gamma_2$ such that any matched pair $(S, T) \in M$ has $|S \Delta T| \leq \varepsilon \min(|S|, |T|)$.*

---

[3]For the curious reader, $1/\alpha$ is the approximation ratio (more specifically, integrality gap) of the best known rounding algorithm for the Euclidean k-means problem using the natural LP. If running time is not a concern, then $1/\alpha$ is the true integrality gap of the natural k-means LP.

[4]To the best of our knowledge, all known constructive algorithms need some such assumption which may appear in different manifestations, like an eigenvalue gap, for instance.

THEOREM 5.4. *Given two k-partitions Γ_1, $\Gamma_2 \in \Gamma_k(n)$, consider the matrices $\mathbf{\Gamma_1}, \mathbf{\Gamma_2} \in \mathbb{R}^{n \times k}$ where $\mathbf{\Gamma_1}$ is the orthonormal basis corresponding to Γ_1 ($\mathbf{\Gamma_2}$ is defined similarly):*

$$\mathbf{\Gamma_1} = \left[\frac{1}{\sqrt{|S|}} \mathbf{e}_S \,\middle|\, S \in \Gamma_1 \right],$$

Suppose there exists $\varepsilon < 1/2$ with $\sigma_{\min}(\mathbf{\Gamma_1}^T \mathbf{\Gamma_2}) \geq \sqrt{1 - \varepsilon}$. Then Γ_1 and Γ_2 are 2ε-close.

We give the proof in Appendix B.

Next, in Theorem 5.5, we will show that L spectrally dominates the union of cliques on Γ_{opt} and Γ, the solution we find after running spectral clustering.

PROPOSITION 5.5. *If each $T \in \Gamma_{\mathrm{opt}}$ induces a λ-algebraic expander, then $L \succeq \lambda K_{\Gamma_{\mathrm{opt}}}$ and $L \succeq \frac{\beta \lambda}{k} K_\Gamma$ for some universal constant $\beta > 0$.*

PROOF. For any pair of subsets A, B, define $L[A, B]$ as the Laplacian matrix induced between A and B including only the edges between A and B. Observe $L[A, B] \succeq 0$. By abusing notation, we can express L as $L = \sum_{i \leq j} L[T_i, T_j] \succeq \sum_i L[T_i]$. Since $L[T]$ is an algebraic expander for every $T \in \Gamma_{\mathrm{opt}}$, $L[T] \succeq \lambda K_T$. Therefore $L \succeq \lambda \sum_T K_T = \lambda K_{\Gamma_{\mathrm{opt}}}$. Second part follows from Theorem 3.3. $\square$

Next, we will prove that $A_\Gamma \approx A_{\Gamma_{\mathrm{opt}}}$ so as to relate Γ and Γ_{opt}. To this end, we upper bound the spectral radius of the Laplacian obtained by contracting each cluster in Γ_{opt}.

LEMMA 5.6. *Let*

$$\phi \overset{\text{def}}{=} \max_{T \in \Gamma_{\mathrm{opt}}} \phi_G(T)$$

. Then $\phi \leq \lambda_{\max}(A_{\Gamma_{\mathrm{opt}}} L A_{\Gamma_{\mathrm{opt}}}) \leq 2\phi$.

PROOF. Define $D \in \mathbb{S}_+^k$ as the diagonal matrix with entries $(|T| \mid T \in \Gamma_{\mathrm{opt}})$ and $P \in \{0,1\}^{n \times k}$ as the matrix whose columns are indicator vectors for each $T \in \Gamma_{\mathrm{opt}}$. Note that $U \overset{\text{def}}{=} PD^{-1/2} \in \mathbb{R}^{n \times k}$ is an orthonormal basis, $U^T U = I_k$. Moreover $UU^T = \Pi$. The entry of matrix $\widehat{L} \overset{\text{def}}{=} P^T L P$ at (S, T) for $S, T \in \Gamma_{\mathrm{opt}}$ is

$$\widehat{L}_{S,T} = \begin{cases} \text{Weight } C(S, \overline{S}) \text{ of edges crossing } S & \text{if } S = T, \\ -\text{Weight of edges between } S \text{ and } T & \text{else.} \end{cases}$$

It is easy to see that $\widehat{L}$ is a Laplacian matrix and $\widehat{L} \preceq 2 \operatorname{diag}(C(T, \overline{T}))_{T \in \Gamma_{\mathrm{opt}}}$. If we multiply with $D^{-1/2}$ on both sides, on RHS we obtain a diagonal matrix with entries $\frac{2C(T, \overline{T})}{|T|} \leq 2\phi_G(T) \leq 2\phi$:

$$U^T L U = D^{-1/2} \widehat{L} D^{-1/2} \preceq 2\phi I_k.$$

Again, multiplying with U, U^T on the left and right, respectively:

$$2\phi \Pi = 2\phi U U^T \succeq U U^T L U U^T = A_{\Gamma_{\mathrm{opt}}} L A_{\Gamma_{\mathrm{opt}}}.$$

For the lower bound, consider $q \leftarrow K \mathbf{e}_T$ where

$$T = \underset{T \in \Gamma_{\mathrm{opt}}}{\operatorname{argmax}} \phi_G(T)$$

$$\Pi q = q \implies q^T A_{\Gamma_{\mathrm{opt}}} L A_{\Gamma_{\mathrm{opt}}} q = q^T L q$$

$$= \phi_G(T) \frac{|T| \cdot |\overline{T}|}{n} = \phi_G(T) \|q\|^2.$$

$\square$

We are ready to relate $A_{\Gamma_{\mathrm{opt}}}$ and A_Γ to each other via Theorem 5.6. Recall $L \succeq \frac{\lambda}{O(k)} K_\Gamma$. Multiply with $A_{\Gamma_{\mathrm{opt}}}$:

$$\frac{\lambda}{O(k)} A_{\Gamma_{\mathrm{opt}}} K_\Gamma A_{\Gamma_{\mathrm{opt}}} \preceq A_{\Gamma_{\mathrm{opt}}} L A_{\Gamma_{\mathrm{opt}}} \preceq 2\phi A_{\Gamma_{\mathrm{opt}}}$$

where we used Theorem 5.6 in the last step. In particular, for $\mathbf{\Gamma}$ and $\mathbf{\Gamma_{\mathsf{OPT}}}$ being the orthonormal matrices corresponding to Γ and Γ_{OPT} as described in **??**, then we see that $I_k - \mathbf{\Gamma}^T \mathbf{\Gamma} = K_\Gamma$, $\Gamma_{\mathsf{OPT}}^T \Gamma_{\mathsf{OPT}} = A_{\Gamma_{\mathrm{opt}}}$:

$$A_{\Gamma_{\mathrm{opt}}} K_\Gamma A_{\Gamma_{\mathrm{opt}}} \preceq O(\varepsilon) A_{\Gamma_{\mathrm{opt}}} \implies$$

$$(1 - O(\varepsilon)) I_k \preceq \mathbf{\Gamma_{\mathsf{OPT}}}^T \mathbf{\Gamma} \mathbf{\Gamma}^T \mathbf{\Gamma_{\mathsf{OPT}}}.$$

Theorem 5.4 immediately implies that Γ and Γ_{opt} are $O(\varepsilon)$ close.

6. CONNECTION WITH SPECTRAL CLUSTERING

Finally, we present yet another connection with a traditional spectral clustering approach often deployed in practice. In this approach, given a graph, the algorithm for graph partitioning is to essentially compute the top k eigenvectors of the graph Laplacian, project every vertex to the top k eigenvectors, and simply run a k-means clustering algorithm on these vectors. We now show that, implicitly, there is a connection to our objective function. Indeed, we show that if the spectral clustering has low cost for some k, then the same clustering is a good solution for our PSD-embedding of k-cliques problem as well!

Given graph G, let (λ_i, q_i) be the pair of ith smallest eigenvalue and corresponding eigenvector. Consider

$$Q_i \overset{\text{def}}{=} \sum_{2 \leq j \leq i} q_i q_i^T.$$

Observe that $Q_n = K$. Recall the basic spectral clustering heuristic for k-clusters: Output the partition found by running k-means on Q_k. In the next theorem, we will show that if this heuristic finds a small cost solution, then the solution is spectrally embeddable into G.

THEOREM 6.1. *Suppose there exists a k-partition Γ such that: $\operatorname{Tr}(K_\Gamma \cdot Q_k) \leq \kappa \frac{\lambda_2}{\lambda_k - \lambda_2}$. Then $L \succeq \frac{\lambda_k}{\kappa + 1} K_\Gamma$. Moreover this is within factor $\kappa + 1$ of the best possible.*

The proof is in Appendix C.

7. CONCLUSIONS

In this paper we propose a new notion of graph partitioning which involves spectrally embedding a disjoint union of k (normalized) cliques into the original graph. We motivate and justify the study of our notion of spectral embedding by exhibiting several interesting connections to k-means, spectral clustering and the use of resistive embeddings which is a common heuristic in practical applications. Along the way, we give a formal connection bringing forth the implicit objective function being optimized by the clustering heuristic involving the resistive embedding for graph partitioning. As an application of our framework we also show how to recover good partitions on graphs where one exists.

When studying graph partitioning problems, the modeling aspect of choosing a good objective function is often overlooked in favor of the study of more traditional objectives. Our work illustrates that a well chosen objective function can lead to insights into the operation of heuristic algorithms as well as bring up intriguing algorithmic questions. One such question concerns the use of a novel smoothing step that we use in our algorithm. We empirically demonstrate that smoothing helps in practice in conjunction with current spectral clustering heuristics. It would be interesting to make a rigorous claim about the benefits of smoothing.

8. ACKNOWLEDGMENTS

Moses Charikar is supported by National Science Foundation grants CCF-1565581, CCF-1302518 and a Simons Investigator Award.

9. REFERENCES

[1] N. Alon. Eigenvalues and expanders. *Combinatorica*, 6(2):83–96, 1986.

[2] N. Alon, A. Lubotzky, and A. Wigderson. Semi-direct product in groups and zig-zag product in graphs: connections and applications. In *Foundations of Computer Science, 2001. Proceedings. 42nd IEEE Symposium on*, pages 630–637. IEEE, 2001.

[3] N. Alon and V. D. Milman. λ_1, isoperimetric inequalities for graphs, and superconcentrators. *Journal of Combinatorial Theory, Series B*, 38(1):73–88, 1985.

[4] S. Arora and S. Kale. A combinatorial, primal-dual approach to semidefinite programs. In *Proceedings of the thirty-ninth annual ACM symposium on Theory of computing*, pages 227–236. ACM, 2007.

[5] S. Arora and S. Kale. A combinatorial, primal-dual approach to semidefinite programs. In *Proceedings of the thirty-ninth annual ACM symposium on Theory of computing*, pages 227–236. ACM, 2007.

[6] S. Arora, J. Lee, and A. Naor. Euclidean distortion and the sparsest cut. *Journal of the American Mathematical Society*, 21(1):1–21, 2008.

[7] S. Arora, S. Rao, and U. Vazirani. Expander flows, geometric embeddings and graph partitioning. *Journal of the ACM (JACM)*, 56(2):5, 2009.

[8] G. Arzhantseva and R. Tessera. Relatively expanding box spaces with no expansion. *arXiv preprint arXiv:1402.1481*, 2014.

[9] J. Batson, D. A. Spielman, and N. Srivastava. Twice-ramanujan sparsifiers. *SIAM Journal on Computing*, 41(6):1704–1721, 2012.

[10] P. Biswal, J. R. Lee, and S. Rao. Eigenvalue bounds, spectral partitioning, and metrical deformations via flows. *Journal of the ACM (JACM)*, 57(3):13, 2010.

[11] E. G. Boman and B. Hendrickson. Support theory for preconditioning. *SIAM Journal on Matrix Analysis and Applications*, 25(3):694–717, 2003.

[12] J. Cheeger. A lower bound for the smallest eigenvalue of the laplacian. *Problems in analysis*, 625:195–199, 1970.

[13] E. Dahlhaus, D. S. Johnson, C. H. Papadimitriou, P. D. Seymour, and M. Yannakakis. The complexity of multiterminal cuts. *SIAM Journal on Computing*, 23(4):864–894, 1994.

[14] I. Dhillon, Y. Guan, and B. Kulis. *A unified view of kernel k-means, spectral clustering and graph cuts.* Citeseer, 2004.

[15] I. S. Dhillon, Y. Guan, and B. Kulis. Kernel k-means: spectral clustering and normalized cuts. In *Proceedings of the tenth ACM SIGKDD international conference on Knowledge discovery and data mining*, pages 551–556. ACM, 2004.

[16] N. Garg, V. V. Vazirani, and M. Yannakakis. Approximate max-flow min-(multi) cut theorems and their applications. *SIAM Journal on Computing*, 25(2):235–251, 1996.

[17] S. O. Gharan and L. Trevisan. Partitioning into expanders. In *SODA*, pages 1256–1266. SIAM, 2014.

[18] O. Goldschmidt and D. S. Hochbaum. Polynomial algorithm for the k-cut problem. In *2013 IEEE 54th Annual Symposium on Foundations of Computer Science*, pages 444–451. IEEE, 1988.

[19] N. J. Harvey and N. Olver. Pipage rounding, pessimistic estimators and matrix concentration. In *SODA*, pages 926–945. SIAM, 2014.

[20] J. Hopcroft and R. Kannan. *Foundations of Data Science.* 2014.

[21] K. Jain and V. V. Vazirani. Approximation algorithms for metric facility location and k-median problems using the primal-dual schema and lagrangian relaxation. *Journal of the ACM (JACM)*, 48(2):274–296, 2001.

[22] R. Kannan, S. Vempala, and A. Vetta. On clusterings: Good, bad and spectral. *Journal of the ACM (JACM)*, 51(3):497–515, 2004.

[23] J. A. Kelner. Spectral partitioning, eigenvalue bounds, and circle packings for graphs of bounded genus. *SIAM Journal on Computing*, 35(4):882–902, 2006.

[24] N. L. D. Khoa and S. Chawla. Large scale spectral clustering using resistance distance and spielman-teng solvers. In *Discovery Science*, pages 7–21. Springer, 2012.

[25] N. L. D. Khoa and S. Chawla. A scalable approach to spectral clustering with sdd solvers. *Journal of Intelligent Information Systems*, pages 1–20, 2013.

[26] A. Kumar and R. Kannan. Clustering with spectral norm and the k-means algorithm. In *Foundations of Computer Science (FOCS), 2010 51st Annual IEEE Symposium on*, pages 299–308. IEEE, 2010.

[27] J. R. Lee, S. Oveis Gharan, and L. Trevisan. Multi-way spectral partitioning and higher-order cheeger inequalities. In *Proceedings of the forty-fourth annual ACM symposium on Theory of computing*, pages 1117–1130. ACM, 2012.

[28] T. Leighton and S. Rao. Multicommodity max-flow min-cut theorems and their use in designing approximation algorithms. *Journal of the ACM (JACM)*, 46(6):787–832, 1999.

[29] M. Lichman. UCI machine learning repository, 2013.

[30] A. Louis, P. Raghavendra, P. Tetali, and S. Vempala. Many sparse cuts via higher eigenvalues. In *Proceedings of the forty-fourth annual ACM*

symposium on Theory of computing, pages 1131–1140. ACM, 2012.

[31] F. McSherry. Spectral partitioning of random graphs. In *Foundations of Computer Science, 2001. Proceedings. 42nd IEEE Symposium on*, pages 529–537. IEEE, 2001.

[32] M. Meila and J. Shi. A random walks view of spectral segmentation. 2001.

[33] A. Y. Ng, M. I. Jordan, Y. Weiss, et al. On spectral clustering: Analysis and an algorithm. *Advances in neural information processing systems*, 2:849–856, 2002.

[34] H. Qiu and E. R. Hancock. Clustering and embedding using commute times. *Pattern Analysis and Machine Intelligence, IEEE Transactions on*, 29(11):1873–1890, 2007.

[35] J. Shi and J. Malik. Normalized cuts and image segmentation. *Pattern Analysis and Machine Intelligence, IEEE Transactions on*, 22(8):888–905, 2000.

[36] D. A. Spielman and N. Srivastava. Graph sparsification by effective resistances. *SIAM Journal on Computing*, 40(6):1913–1926, 2011.

[37] D. A. Spielman and S.-H. Teng. Spectral partitioning works: Planar graphs and finite element meshes. *Linear Algebra and its Applications*, 421(2):284–305, 2007.

[38] D. A. Spielman and S.-H. Teng. Spectral sparsification of graphs. *SIAM Journal on Computing*, 40(4):981–1025, 2011.

[39] L. Trevisan. Is cheeger-type approximation possible for nonuniform sparsest cut? *arXiv preprint arXiv:1303.2730*, 2013.

[40] Y. Weiss. Segmentation using eigenvectors: a unifying view. In *Computer vision, 1999. The proceedings of the seventh IEEE international conference on*, volume 2, pages 975–982. IEEE, 1999.

[41] E. Xing, A. Ng, M. Jordan, and S. Russell. Distance metric learning, with application to clustering with side-information. In *Advances in Neural Information Processing Systems*, volume 15, 2003.

[42] E. Xing, E. P. Xing, M. Jordan, and M. I. Jordan. On semidefinite relaxations for normalized k-cut and connections to spectral clustering. 2003.

[43] D. Yan, L. Huang, and M. I. Jordan. Fast approximate spectral clustering. In *Proceedings of the 15th ACM SIGKDD international conference on Knowledge discovery and data mining*, pages 907–916. ACM, 2009.

APPENDIX

A. PROOF OF Theorem 4.1

In order to constructively solve the SDP in Section 4 (note that the SDP has exponentially many variables), we appeal to the Matrix Multiplicative Weights framework due to Arora and Kale [5]. Let c_{JV} denote the integrality gap of the Jain-Vazirani algorithm for k-means clustering. We will solve the primal using Arora-Kale approach to get a feasible solution of value $(1-\delta)(1/c_{JV})$ for any constant δ. Formally, we appeal black-box to the following result of Arora and Kale [5]:

THEOREM A.1. *Consider the following SDP optimization problem with target solution value* val *(that is feasible):*

$$\max \mathbf{b} \bullet \mathbf{y}$$
$$\sum_j \mathbf{A}_j y_j \preceq \mathbf{C}$$
$$\mathbf{y} \geq \mathbf{0}$$

Also suppose there is an efficient "oracle" algorithm for solving the following linear system given any positive semi-definite $\mathbf{Z}$: $\{\mathbf{y} : \mathbf{y} \geq \mathbf{0}; \mathbf{b} \bullet \mathbf{y} \geq$ val; $\sum_{j=1}^{m} (\mathbf{A}_j \bullet \mathbf{Z}) y_j - \mathbf{C} \bullet \mathbf{Z} \leq 0\}$. *Then, for any* δ, *there is an efficient algorithm which runs in time polynomial in* $n, 1/$val$, 1/\delta$ *and* ρ *which finds a feasible* $\mathbf{y}$ *with objective value at least* $(1 - \delta)$val. *Here* ρ *is the width, i.e.,* $\max_j \|A_j y_j - C\|$ *of the system.*

In our case, the $\mathbf{A}_j$'s correspond to the K_Γ's, the vector $\mathbf{y}$ corresponds to the vector $\mathbf{w}$, the vector $\mathbf{b}$ is the all ones vector, the matrix $\mathbf{C}$ corresponds to $L(X)$, and finally we set val to be $1/c_{JV}$. Indeed, due to the nice structure of both the matrix $L(X)$ and the set of matrices K_Γ, it is easy to see that the width ρ is at most 2, which bounds the overall runtime. Moreover, the oracle algorithm is also simple: plugging in our values of $\mathbf{A}, \mathbf{b}, \mathbf{C}$, we get that it amounts to solving the following system: $\{\mathbf{y} : \mathbf{y} \geq \mathbf{0}; \sum_\Gamma y_\Gamma \geq 1/c_{JV}; \sum_\Gamma (K_\Gamma \bullet \mathbf{Z}) y_\Gamma - L(X) \bullet \mathbf{Z} \leq 0\}$. Indeed, as mentioned earlier, if we view the psd matrix $\mathbf{Z}$ as the gram matrix of a set of n points P in Euclidean space, then $L(X) \bullet \mathbf{Z}$ is precisely the fractional k-means cost of solution X on dataset P. And using the Jain-Vazirani algorithm, we can find a integer clustering Γ' such that its cost $K_{\Gamma'} \bullet \mathbf{Z} \leq c_{JV} L(X) \bullet \mathbf{Z}$, and so we can set $y_{\Gamma'} = 1/c_{JV}$ and satisfy the system of equations we are checking! This completes the proof of our multiplicative-weights based algorithm. For an informal explanation of how the Arora-Kale algorithm works, please read on.

Explanation of Matrix Multiplicative Weights We will now sketch the informal description of how the Matrix Multiplicative Weights algorithm of Arora and Kale [5] works. Readers familiar with the framework can entirely skip this section, as it only provides a rough overview of the steps of the algorithm. The basis of the algorithm is the following identity: $A \succeq B$ if and only if $A \bullet C \geq B \bullet C$ for all PSD-matrices C. So, the Arora-Kale algorithm intuitively views each psd matrix C as an expert, and maintains a distribution $\mathcal{D}_t$ over experts at each time step t (all of this is succinctly implemented in the final algorithm). Initially, $\mathcal{D}_t$ has all its mass on I, and it updates this over time with the goal of in fact trying to show *infeasibility* of the primal SDP! Indeed, suppose it finds a distribution $\mathcal{D}_t$[5] (with expectation $M_t = E_{M \sim \mathcal{D}_t}[M]$) such that the system $\{\mathbf{w} : \sum_\Gamma w_\Gamma \geq 1/c_{JV}, \sum_\Gamma w_\Gamma K_\Gamma \bullet M_t \leq L(X) \bullet M_t\}$ is infeasible, then we would have found our proof of infeasibility. On the other hand, suppose the above system is indeed feasible, and suppose we find a vector $\mathbf{w}_t$ which satisfies these constraints, then the Arora-Kale algorithm updates $\mathcal{D}_t$ to $\mathcal{D}_{t+1}$ by looking at the *reward matrix* $\sum_\Gamma w_{t,\Gamma} K_\Gamma - L(X)$. Indeed, if an expert C is such that $(\sum_\Gamma w_{t,\Gamma} K_\Gamma - L(X)) \bullet C$ is very positive, then we increase its weight a lot, and if its very negative, we decrease its weight.[6]

---

[5]Of course, the algorithm does all of this implicitly.

[6]Recall that we are still trying to establish a proof of infeasibility, and when we will have failed, we'd have found a good feasible solution!

Then, after T rounds, if we haven't found a proof of infeasibility, then the experts algorithm guarantees that our overall expected reward is almost at least the reward of the best expert in hindsight. Our overall reward is simply,

$$0 \geq \frac{1}{T} \sum_{t=1}^{T} \Big(\sum_{\Gamma} w_{t,\Gamma} K_{\Gamma} - L(X) \Big) \bullet M_t$$

Here, this sum is at most 0 because we have assumed that always found a feasible $\mathbf{w}_t$ for all steps of our algorithm. And the reward of any expert C is

$$\frac{1}{T} \sum_{t=1}^{T} \Big(\sum_{\Gamma} w_{t,\Gamma} K_{\Gamma} - L(X) \Big) \bullet C$$

The experts algorithm guarantees that, for all experts C, our reward is at least its reward, and in particular,

$$0 \geq \frac{1}{T} \sum_{t=1}^{T} \Big(\sum_{\Gamma} w_{t,\Gamma} K_{\Gamma} - L(X) \Big) \bullet C - \delta$$

for some small constant δ. But this says that the solution $\hat{\mathbf{w}} = \frac{1}{T} \sum_{t=1}^{T} \mathbf{w}_t$ is almost a feasible dual solution. It's dual objective value is at least $1/c_{JV}$ (as the individual $\mathbf{w}_t$'s satisfied this), and moreover, for all psd C, it satisfies

$$\sum_{\Gamma} \hat{w}_{\Gamma} K_{\Gamma} \bullet C \leq L(X) \bullet C + \delta$$

Intuitively, this almost means that $\sum_{\Gamma} \hat{w}_{\Gamma} K_{\Gamma} \preceq L(X) + \delta I$. They also show that T only depends polynomially on n and $1/\delta$. And we can make it strictly feasible by scaling the $\hat{\mathbf{w}}$ by a bit while only losing out on a little in the objective function. Throughout this above analysis, we have assumed that we will always find a feasible $\mathbf{w}_t$ for all of the T steps. Why is that? Indeed, here is where we use the rounding algorithm due to Jain and Vazirani [21]. Let us revisit what the linear system corresponds to. Given a distribution $\mathcal{D}_t$ with expectation $M_t = E_{M \sim \mathcal{D}_t}[M]$ (which is positive semi-definite), it is $\{\mathbf{w} : \sum_{\Gamma} w_{\Gamma} \geq 1/c_{JV}, \sum_{\Gamma} w_{\Gamma} K_{\Gamma} \bullet M_t \leq L(X) \bullet M_t\}$. But if we view M_t as the gram matrix of a set of n points P_t in Euclidean space, then $L(X) \bullet M_t$ is precisely the fractional k-means cost of solution X on dataset P_t. And using the Jain-Vazirani algorithm, we can find a integer clustering Γ_t such that its cost $K_{\Gamma_t} \bullet M_t \leq c_{JV} L(X) \bullet M_t$, and so we can set $w_{\Gamma_t} = 1/c_{JV}$ and satisfy the system of equations we are checking! Essentially, this completes the high level overview of the Arora-Kale algorithm.

B. PROOF OF THEOREM 5.4

We define $\pi_1 : \Gamma_1 \to \Gamma_2$ and $\pi_2 : \Gamma_2 \to \Gamma_1$ as the following:

$$\forall S \in \Gamma_1 : \pi_1(S) \stackrel{\text{def}}{=} \operatorname*{argmax}_{T \in \Gamma_2} \frac{|S \cap T|}{|T|} \quad \text{and}$$

$$\forall T \in \Gamma_2 : \pi_2(T) \stackrel{\text{def}}{=} \operatorname*{argmax}_{S \in \Gamma_1} \frac{|S \cap T|}{|S|}.$$

Consider $M = \{(S, \pi_1(S)) \mid S \in \Gamma_1\}$: By B.2 and B.3, M is indeed a perfect matching between Γ_1 and Γ_2. Now consider any matched pair $(S, T) \in M$. Without loss of generality, say $|S| \geq |T|$. By B.1, $|S \cap T| \geq (1 - \varepsilon)|S|$. Since $|S \triangle T| = |S| + |T| - 2|S \cap T|$:

$$|S \triangle T| \leq |S| + |T| - 2(1 - \varepsilon)|S| = 2\varepsilon|S| + (|T| - |S|) \leq 2\varepsilon|S|.$$

We finish our proof with proving Theorems B.1, B.2, and B.3 below.

CLAIM B.1. *If* $\pi_1(S) = T$, *then* $|S \cap T| \geq (1 - \varepsilon)|T|$. *Similarly, if* $\pi_2(T) = S$, *then* $|S \cap T| \geq (1 - \varepsilon)|S|$.

PROOF. Consider the matrix $P = \mathbf{\Gamma_1}^T \mathbf{\Gamma_2} \mathbf{\Gamma_2}^T \mathbf{\Gamma_1} \in \mathbb{S}_+^k$ so that $\lambda_{\min}(P) = \sigma_{\min}^2(\mathbf{\Gamma_1}^T \mathbf{\Gamma_2})$. It is easy to notice that $\lambda_{\min}(P) = \sigma_{\min}^2(\mathbf{\Gamma_1}^T \mathbf{\Gamma_2}) \geq 1 - \varepsilon$. In particular, all diagonals of P are at least $1 - \varepsilon$. Consider any diagonal corresponding to $S \in \Gamma_1$:

$$1 - \varepsilon \leq \frac{\mathbf{e}_S^T \mathbf{\Gamma_2} \mathbf{\Gamma_2}^T \mathbf{e}_S}{|S|} = \sum_{T \in \Gamma_2} \frac{|S \cap T|^2}{|S||T|}$$

$$\leq \Big(\max_{T' \in \Gamma_2} \frac{|S \cap T'|}{|T'|} \Big) \sum_{T \in \Gamma_2} \frac{|S \cap T|}{|S|} = \max_{T' \in \Gamma_2} \frac{|S \cap T'|}{|T'|},$$

which, by construction, is equal to $\frac{|S \cap \pi_1(S)|}{|\pi_1(S)|}$. This proves the first part of the claim. The second part follows immediately by applying the same argument on Γ_2 and Γ_1. $\square$

CLAIM B.2. *Both* π_1 *and* π_2 *are bijections.*

PROOF. Suppose $\pi_1(S) = \pi_1(S') = T$ for some $S \neq S'$. Since S, S' are disjoint and $\varepsilon < \frac{1}{2}$:

$$|T| \geq |S \cap T| + |S' \cap T| \geq 2(1 - \varepsilon)|T| > |T|,$$

a contradiction. A similar argument shows that π_2 is a bijection as well. $\square$

This completes the proof of the theorem.

CLAIM B.3. $\pi_1 = \pi_2^{-1}$.

PROOF. Suppose not. Since both Γ_1 and Γ_2 are bijections by B.2, there exists a cycle of the form

$$(S_0, T_0, \ldots, S_{m-1}, T_{m-1}, S_m = S_0)$$

where $\pi_1(S_i) = T_i$ and $\pi_2(T_i) = S_{i+1}$ for some $m \geq 2$. By construction, $|S_i \cap T_i| \geq (1 - \varepsilon)|T_i|$ which means $\varepsilon|T_i| \geq |T_i \setminus S_i|$. Since S_i and S_{i+1} are disjoint, $|T_i \setminus S_i| \geq |T_i \cap S_{i+1}|$. Again, by construction, $|T_i \cap S_{i+1}| \geq (1 - \varepsilon)|S_{i+1}|$. Therefore:

$$\varepsilon|T_i| \geq (1 - \varepsilon)|S_{i+1}| \implies |T_i| \geq \frac{1 - \varepsilon}{\varepsilon}|S_{i+1}| > |S_{i+1}|$$

The last inequality holds because $\varepsilon < 1/2$. By a similar argument, we can also show that $|S_i| > |T_i|$. Consequently, $|S_0| > |S_1| > \ldots > |S_m| = |S_0|$ which is a contradiction. So all cycles have length 2, which implies $\pi_1 = \pi_2^{-1}$. $\square$

C. PROOF OF THEOREM 6.1

For some r (we will fix r to k later) Γ satisfies:

$$\text{Tr}(K_{\Gamma} \cdot Q_r) \leq \kappa \frac{\lambda_2}{\lambda_r - \lambda_2}.$$

It is easy to see that $L^{\dagger} \preceq \frac{1}{\lambda_r} \Big(\frac{\lambda_r - \lambda_2}{\lambda_2} Q_r + K \Big)$. We want to upper bound $\lambda_{\max}(K_{\Gamma} L^{\dagger} K_{\Gamma})$ which is at most

$$\frac{1}{\lambda_r} \Big[\frac{\lambda_r - \lambda_2}{\lambda_2} \text{Tr}(K_{\Gamma} Q_r) + 1 \Big] \leq \frac{1}{\lambda_r}(\kappa + 1).$$

By Theorem 3.1, $L \succeq \frac{\lambda_r}{\kappa + 1} K_{\Gamma}$. Substituting $r = k$ yields the first claim. Second one follows from $\lambda_{\min}(L, K_{\Gamma'}) \leq \lambda_k$ for any k-partitioning Γ'.

On Sketching Quadratic Forms*

Alexandr Andoni†
Columbia University
New York, NY, USA
andoni@cs.columbia.edu

Jiecao Chen‡
Indiana University
Bloomington, IN, USA
jiecchen@indiana.edu

Robert Krauthgamer§
Weizmann Institute of Science
Rehovot, Israel
robert.krauthgamer@weizmann.ac.il

Bo Qin¶
Hong Kong University of
Science and Technology
Clear Water Bay, Hong Kong
bqin@cse.ust.hk

David P. Woodruff∥
IBM Almaden Research
San Jose, CA, USA
dpwoodru@us.ibm.com

Qin Zhang‡
Indiana University
Bloomington, IN, USA
qzhangcs@indiana.edu

ABSTRACT

We undertake a systematic study of sketching a quadratic form: given an $n \times n$ matrix A, create a succinct sketch $\mathrm{sk}(A)$ which can produce (without further access to A) a multiplicative $(1+\varepsilon)$-approximation to $x^T A x$ for any desired query $x \in \mathbb{R}^n$. While a general matrix does not admit non-trivial sketches, positive semi-definite (PSD) matrices admit sketches of size $\Theta(\varepsilon^{-2}n)$, via the Johnson-Lindenstrauss lemma, achieving the "for each" guarantee, namely, for each query x, with a constant probability the sketch succeeds. (For the stronger "for all" guarantee, where the sketch succeeds for all x's simultaneously, again there are no non-trivial sketches.)

We design significantly better sketches for the important subclass of graph Laplacian matrices, which we also extend to symmetric diagonally dominant matrices. A sequence of work culminating in that of Batson, Spielman, and Srivastava (SIAM Review, 2014), shows that by choosing and reweighting $O(\varepsilon^{-2}n)$ edges in a graph, one achieves the "for all" guarantee. Our main results advance this front.

---

*A full version of this paper is available at arXiv:1511.06099.

†Work done in part while the author was at Microsoft Research Silicon Valley.

‡Work supported in part by NSF CCF-1525024, and IU's Office of the Vice Provost for Research through the Faculty Research Support Program.

§Work supported in part by a US-Israel BSF grant #2010418, an Israel Science Foundation grant #897/13, and by the Citi Foundation. Part of the work was done at Microsoft Research Silicon Valley.

¶Work of this author partially supported by Hong Kong RGC GRF grant 16208415.

∥Supported in part by the XDATA program of the Defense Advanced Research Projects Agency (DARPA), administered through Air Force Research Laboratory contract FA8750-12-C-0323.

Permission to make digital or hard copies of all or part of this work for personal or classroom use is granted without fee provided that copies are not made or distributed for profit or commercial advantage and that copies bear this notice and the full citation on the first page. Copyrights for components of this work owned by others than the author(s) must be honored. Abstracting with credit is permitted. To copy otherwise, or republish, to post on servers or to redistribute to lists, requires prior specific permission and/or a fee. Request permissions from permissions@acm.org.

ITCS'16, January 14 - 16, 2016, Cambridge, MA, USA

ⓒ 2016 Copyright held by the owner/author(s). Publication rights licensed to ACM.
ISBN 978-1-4503-4057-1/16/01...$15.00

DOI: http://dx.doi.org/10.1145/2840728.2840753

1. For the "for all" guarantee, we prove that Batson et al.'s bound is optimal even when we restrict to "cut queries" $x \in \{0,1\}^n$. Specifically, an arbitrary sketch that can $(1+\varepsilon)$-estimate the weight of *all* cuts $(S, \bar{S})$ in an n-vertex graph must be of size $\Omega(\varepsilon^{-2}n)$ bits. Furthermore, if the sketch is a cut-sparsifier (i.e., itself a weighted graph and the estimate is the weight of the corresponding cut in this graph), then the sketch must have $\Omega(\varepsilon^{-2}n)$ edges.

   In contrast, previous lower bounds showed the bound only for *spectral-sparsifiers*.

2. For the "for each" guarantee, we design a sketch of size $\tilde{O}(\varepsilon^{-1}n)$ bits for "cut queries" $x \in \{0,1\}^n$. We apply this sketch to design an algorithm for the distributed minimum cut problem. We prove a nearly-matching lower bound of $\Omega(\varepsilon^{-1}n)$ bits. For general queries $x \in \mathbb{R}^n$, we construct sketches of size $\tilde{O}(\varepsilon^{-1.6}n)$ bits.

Our results provide the first separation between the sketch size needed for the "for all" and "for each" guarantees for Laplacian matrices.

Categories and Subject Descriptors

F.2.0 [**Theory of Computation**]: ANALYSIS OF ALGORITHMS AND PROBLEM COMPLEXITY—*General*

Keywords

Quadratic Forms, Sketching, Graph Sparsification, Lower Bound

1. INTRODUCTION

Sketching emerges as a fundamental building block used in numerous algorithmic contexts to reduce memory, run-time, or communication requirements. Here we focus on sketching *quadratic forms*, defined as follows: Given a matrix $A \in \mathbb{R}^{n \times n}$, compute a sketch of it, $\mathrm{sk}(A)$, which suffices to estimate the quadratic form $x^T A x$ for every query vector $x \in \mathbb{R}^n$. Typically, we aim at $(1+\varepsilon)$-approximation, i.e., the estimate is in the range $(1 \pm \varepsilon)x^T A x$, and sketches that are randomized. The randomization guarantee comes in two flavors. The first one requires that the sketch $\mathrm{sk}(A)$ succeeds (produces a $(1+\varepsilon)$-approximation) on all queries x simultaneously. The second one requires that for every fixed query

x, the sketch succeeds with high probability. The former is termed the "for all" guarantee and the latter the "for each" guarantee, following the prevalent terminology in compressive sensing. The main goal is then to design a sketch $\mathrm{sk}(A)$ of small size.

Sketching quadratic forms is a basic task with many applications. In fact, the definition from above abstracts several specific concepts studied before. One important example is the sparsification of a graph G, where we take the matrix A to be the Laplacian of G and restrict the sketch to be of a specific form, namely, a Laplacian of a sparse subgraph G'. Then a cut-sparsifier corresponds to the setting of query vectors $x \in \{0,1\}^n$, in which case $x^T A x$ describes the weight of the corresponding cut in G. Also, a spectral-sparsifier corresponds to query vectors $x \in \mathbb{R}^n$ in which case $x^T A x$ is a Laplacian Rayleigh quotient. Cut queries to a graph have been studied in the context of privacy in databases [GRU12, JT12, BBDS13, Upa13, Upa14] where, for example, vertices represent users and edges represent email correspondence between users, and email correspondences between groups of users are of prime interest. These papers study also directional covariance queries on a matrix, which correspond to evaluating the quadratic form of a positive semidefinite (PSD) matrix, as well as evaluating the quadratic form of a low-rank matrix, which could correspond to, e.g., a user-movie rating matrix. Finally, sketching quadratic forms has appeared and has been studied in other contexts [AHK05, AGM12a, AGM12b, KLM+14, McG14].

Quadratic form computations also arise in numerical linear algebra. Consider the least squares regression problem of minimizing $\|By - c\|_2^2$ for an input matrix B and vector c. Writing the input as an adjoined matrix $M = [B, c]$ and denoting $x = (y, -1)$, the objective is just $\|By - c\|_2^2 = \|Mx\|_2^2 = x^T M^T M x$, and thus regression queries can be modeled by a quadratic form over the PSD matrix $A = M^T M$. Indeed, for a concrete example where a small-space sketch $\mathrm{sk}(A)$ leads to memory savings (in the data-stream model) in regression problems, see [CW09].

To simplify the exposition, let us assume that the matrix A is of size $n \times n$ and its entries are integers bounded by a polynomial in n, and fix the success probability to be 90%. When we consider a graph G, we let n denote its number of vertices, with edge-weights that are positive integers bounded by a polynomial in n. We use $\tilde{O}(f)$ to denote $f \cdot (\log f)^{O(1)}$, which suppresses the distinction between counting bits and machine words.

The general quadratic forms, i.e., when the square matrix A is arbitrary, require a sketch of size $\tilde{\Omega}(n^2)$ bits, even in the "for each" model (see Appendix A).

Hence we restrict our attention to the class of PSD matrices A, and its subclasses like graph Laplacians, which occur in many applications. We provide tight or near-tight bounds for these classes, as detailed in Table 1. Overall, our results show that the specific class of matrices as well as the model ("for each" vs. "for all" guarantee) can have a dramatic effect on the sketch size, namely, quadratic vs. linear dependence on n or on ε.

1.1 Our Contributions

We start by characterizing the sketching complexity for general PSD matrices A, in both the "for all" and "for each" models. First, we show that, for the "for all" model, sketching an arbitrary PSD matrix A requires $\Omega(n^2)$ bits (Theo-

rem 2.1); i.e., storing the entire matrix is essentially optimal. In contrast, for the "for each" model, we show that the Johnson-Lindenstrauss lemma immediately yields a sketch of size $O(n\varepsilon^{-2} \log n)$ bits and this is tight up to the logarithmic factor (see Section 2.1). We conclude that the bounds for the two models are quite different: quadratic vs. linear in n.

Surprisingly, one can obtain significantly smaller sketches when A is the Laplacian of a graph G, a subclass of PSD matrices that occurs in many applications. Specifically, we refer to a celebrated result of Batson, Spielman, and Srivastava [BSS14], which is the culmination of a rich line of research on graph sparsification [BK96, ST04, ST11, SS11, FHHP11, KP12]. They show that every graph Laplacian A admits a sketch in the "for all" model whose size is $O(n\varepsilon^{-2} \log n)$ bits. This stands in contrast to the $\tilde{\Omega}(n^2)$ lower bound for general PSD matrices. Their sketch has a particular structure: it is itself a graph, consisting of a reweighted subset of edges in G and works in the "for all" model. Batson et al. [BSS14] also prove a lower bound for the case of *spectral sparsification* (for cut sparsifiers, the bound remained open).

The natural question is whether there are qualitatively better sketches we can construct by relaxing the guarantees or considering more specific cases. Indeed, we investigate this research direction by pursuing the following concrete questions:

Q1. Can we improve the "for all" upper bound $O(n\varepsilon^{-2})$ by using an arbitrary data structure?

Q2. Can we improve the bound by restricting attention to *cut* queries? Specifically, can the optimal size of *cut-sparsifiers* be smaller than that of spectral-sparsifier?

Q3. Can we improve the "for each" bound beyond the $\tilde{O}(n\varepsilon^{-2})$ bound that follows from general PSD matrices result (and also from the "for all" model via [BSS14])?

We make progress on all of the above questions, often providing (near) tight results.

In all of these questions, the main quantitative focus is the dependence on the accuracy parameter ε. We note that improving the dependence on ε is important for a variety of reasons. From a theoretical angle, a quadratic dependence is common for estimates with two-sided error, and hence sub-quadratic dependence elucidates new interesting phenomena. From a practical angle, we can set ε to be the smallest value for which the sketch still fits in memory (i.e., we can get *better* estimates with the same memory). In general, quadratic dependence might be prohibitive for large-scale matrices: if, say, ε is 1% then $1/\varepsilon^2 = 10000$.

We answer Q1 negatively by showing that every sketch that satisfies the "for all" guarantee requires $\Omega(n\varepsilon^{-2})$ bits of space, even if the sketch is an arbitrary data structures (see Section 2.2). This matches the upper bound of [BSS14] (up to a logarithmic factor, which stems from the difference between counting words and bits).

Our answer to Q1 essentially answers Q2 as well: our lower bound actually holds even if we only consider cut queries $x \in \{0,1\}^n$. Indeed, an immediate consequence of the $\Omega(n\varepsilon^{-2})$ bits lower bound is that a cut-sparsifier G' must have $\Omega(n\varepsilon^{-2}/\log n)$ edges. We strengthen this further and obtain a tight lower bound of $\Omega(n\varepsilon^{-2})$ edges (even in the case when the cut-sparsifier G' is a not necessarily a subgraph of G). Such an edge lower bound was not known before. The previous lower bound for a cut-sparsifier G', due to Alon [Alo97], uses two additional requirements — that the sparsifier G' has *regular degrees* and *uniform edge weights* — to reach the same conclusion that G' has $\Omega(n/\varepsilon^2)$ edges. Put differently, Alon's lower bound is *quantitatively* optimal — it concludes the tight lower bound of $\Omega(n/\varepsilon^2)$ edges — but it is unsatisfactory *qualitatively*, as it does not cover a cut-sparsifier G' that has edge weights or has non-regular degrees, which may potentially lead to a smaller sparsifier. Similarly, the results of [Nil91, BSS14] apply to spectral-sparsification, which is a harder problem than cut-sparsification. Our result subsumes all of these bounds, and for cut sparsifiers it is in fact the first lower bound under no assumption. Our lower bound holds even for input graphs G that are unweighted.

On the upside, we answer Q3 positively by showing how to achieve the "for each" guarantee using $n\varepsilon^{-1}$ polylog(n) bits of space (see Section 2.3.1). This bound can be substantially smaller than in the "for all" model when ε is small: e.g., when $\varepsilon = 1/\sqrt{n}$ we obtain size $n^{3/2}$ polylog(n) instead of the $O(n^2)$ needed in the "for all" model. We also show that $\Omega(n\varepsilon^{-1})$ bits of space is necessary for the "for each" guarantee (Theorem 2.8).

We then give an application for the "for each" sketch to showcase that it is useful algorithmically despite having a guarantee that is is weaker than that of a "for all" cut-sparsifier. In particular, we show how to $(1+\varepsilon)$-approximate the global minimum cut of a graph whose edges are distributed across multiple servers (see Section 1.3).

Finally, we consider a "for each" sketch of a Laplacian matrix under arbitrary query vectors $x \in \mathbb{R}^n$, which we refer to as *spectral queries* on the graph G. Such spectral queries give more flexibility than cut queries. For example, if the graph corresponds to a physical system, e.g., the edges correspond to electrical resistors, then spectral queries can evaluate the total heat dissipation of the system for a given set of potentials on the vertices. Also, a spectral query x that is a permutation of $\{1, 2, \ldots, n\}$ gives the average squared distortion of a line embedding of G. We design in Section 2.3.2 a sketch for spectral queries that uses $n\varepsilon^{-1.6}$ polylog(n) bits of space. These upper bounds also apply to the symmetric diagonally-dominant (SDD) matrices.

Our results and previous bounds are summarized in Table 1.

1.2 Highlights of Our Techniques

In this section we give technical overviews for our three main results: (1) the lower bound for cut queries on Laplacian matrices (answering Q1 and Q2); (2) the upper bound for cut queries on Laplacian matrices; and (3) the upper bound for spectral queries on Laplacian matrices (answering Q3). We always use G to denote the corresponding graph of the considered Laplacian matrix.

1.2.1 Lower Bound for Sketching Laplacian Matrices with Cut Queries, "For All" Model

We first prove our $\Omega(n\varepsilon^{-2})$-bit lower bound using communication complexity for arbitrary data structures. We then show how to obtain an $\Omega(n\varepsilon^{-2})$ edge lower bound for cut sparsifiers by encoding a sparsifier in a careful way so that if it had $o(n/\varepsilon^2)$ edges, it would violate an $\Omega(n\varepsilon^{-2})$ bit lower bound in the communication problem.

For the $\Omega(n\varepsilon^{-2})$ bit lower bound, the natural thing to

do would be to give Alice a graph G, and Bob a cut S. Alice produces a sketch of G and sends it to Bob, who must approximate the capacity of S. The communication cost of this problem lower bounds the sketch size. However, as we just saw, Alice has an upper bound with only $\tilde{O}(n\varepsilon^{-1})$ bits of communication. We thus need for Bob to solve a much harder problem which uses the fact that Alice's sketch preserves all cuts.

We let G be a disjoint union of $\varepsilon^2 n/2$ graphs G_i, where each G_i is a bipartite graph with $\frac{1}{\varepsilon^2}$ vertices in each part. Each vertex in the left part is independently connected to a random subset of half the vertices in the right part. Bob's problem is now, given a vertex v in the left part of one of the G_i, as well as a subset T of half of the vertices in the right part of that G_i, decide if $|N(v) \cap T| > \frac{1}{4\varepsilon^2} + \frac{c}{\varepsilon}$ ($N(v)$ is the set of neighboring vertices of v), or if $|N(v) \cap T| < \frac{1}{4\varepsilon^2} - \frac{c}{\varepsilon}$, for a small constant $c > 0$. Most vertices v will satisfy one of these conditions, by anti-concentration of the binomial distribution. Note that this problem is not a cut query problem, and so *a priori* it is not clear how Bob can use Alice's sketch to solve it.

To solve the problem, Bob will do an exhaustive enumeration on cut queries, and here is where we use that Alice's sketch preserves all cuts. Namely, for each subset S of half of the vertices in the left part of G_i, Bob queries the cut $S \cup T$. As Bob ranges over all (exponentially many) such cuts, what will happen is that for most vertices u in the left part for which $|N(u) \cap T| > \frac{1}{4\varepsilon^2} + \frac{c}{\varepsilon}$, the capacity of $S \cup T$ is a "little bit" larger if u is excluded from S. This little bit is not enough to be detected, since $|N(u) \cap T| = \Theta\left(\frac{1}{\varepsilon^2}\right)$ while the capacity of $S \cup T$ is $\Theta\left(\frac{1}{\varepsilon^4}\right)$. However, as Bob range over all such S, he will eventually get lucky in that S contains all vertices u for which $|N(u) \cap T| > \frac{1}{4\varepsilon^2} + \frac{c}{\varepsilon}$, and now since there are about $\frac{1}{2\varepsilon^2}$ such vertices, the little $\frac{c}{\varepsilon}$ bit gets "amplified" by a factor of $\frac{1}{2\varepsilon^2}$, which is just enough to be detected by a $(1+\varepsilon)$-approximation to the capacity of $S \cup T$. If Bob finds the S which maximizes the (approximate) cut value $S \cup T$, he can check if his v is in S, and this gives him a correct answer with large constant probability.

We believe our main contribution is in designing a communication problem which requires Alice's sketch to preserve all cuts instead of only a single cut. There are also several details in the communication lower bound for the problem itself, including a direct-sum theorem for a constrained version of the Gap-Hamming-Distance problem, which could be independently useful.

For the $\Omega(n\varepsilon^{-2})$ edge lower bound for cut sparsifiers, the straightforward encoding would encode each edge using $O(\log n)$ bits, and cause us to lose a $\log n$ factor in the lower bound. Instead, we show how to randomly round each edge weight in the sparsifier to an adjacent *integer*, and observe that the integer weights sum up to a small value in our communication problem. This ultimately allows to transmit, in a communication-efficient manner, all the edge weights together with the edge identities.

1.2.2 Upper Bound for Sketching Laplacian Matrices with Cut Queries, "For Each" Model

To discuss the main ideas behind our $\tilde{O}(n\varepsilon^{-1})$-bit sketch construction for Laplacian matrices with queries $x \in \{0, 1\}^n$, let us first give some intuition on why the previous algorithms cannot yield a $\tilde{O}(n\varepsilon^{-1})$ bound, and show how our algorithm circumvents these roadblocks on a couple of illus-

Matrix family	"for all" model		"for each" model	
	upper bound	lower bound	upper bound	lower bound
General	$\tilde{O}(n^2)$	$\Omega(n^2)$	$\tilde{O}(n^2)$	$\Omega(n^2)$ App. A
PSD	$\tilde{O}(n^2)$	$\Omega(n^2)$ Sec. 2.1	$\tilde{O}(n\epsilon^{-2})$ Sec. 2.1	$\Omega(n\varepsilon^{-2})$ Sec. 2.1
Laplacian, SDD	$\tilde{O}(n\varepsilon^{-2})$ [BSS14]	$\Omega(n\varepsilon^{-2})$ [BSS14]	$\tilde{O}(n\varepsilon^{-1.6})$ Sec. 2.3.2	$\Omega(n\varepsilon^{-1})$ Sec. 2.3.1
edge-count:	$O(n\varepsilon^{-2})$ [BSS14]	$\Omega(n\varepsilon^{-2})$ [BSS14]		
Laplacian+cut queries	$\tilde{O}(n\varepsilon^{-2})$ [BSS14]	$\Omega(n\varepsilon^{-2})$ Sec. 2.2	$\tilde{O}(n\varepsilon^{-1})$ Sec. 2.3.1	$\Omega(n\varepsilon^{-1})$ Sec. 2.3.1
edge-count:	$O(n\varepsilon^{-2})$ [BSS14]	$\Omega(n\varepsilon^{-2})$ Sec. 2.2		

Table 1: Bounds for sketching quadratic forms, expressed in bits, except when counting edges.

trative examples. For concreteness, it is convenient to think of $\varepsilon = 1/\sqrt{n}$.

All existing cut (and spectral) sparsifiers algorithms construct the sparsifier by taking a subgraph of the original graph G, with the "right" re-weightening of the edges [BK96, SS11, BSS14, FHHP11, KP12]. In fact, except for [BSS14], they all proceed by sampling edges independently, each with its own probability (that depends on the graph).

Consider for illustration the complete graph. In this case, these sampling schemes employ a uniform probability $p \approx \frac{1/\varepsilon^2}{n}$ of sampling every edge. It is not hard to see that one cannot sample edges with probability less than p, as otherwise anti-concentration results suggest that even the degree of a vertex (i.e., the cut of a "singleton") is not preserved within $1 + \varepsilon$ approximation. Perhaps a more interesting example is a random graph $\mathcal{G}_{n,1/2}$; if edges are sampled independently with (roughly) uniform probability, then again it cannot be less than p, because of singleton cuts. However, if we aim for a sketch for the complete graph or $\mathcal{G}_{n,1/2}$, we can just store the degree of each vertex using only $O(n)$ space, and this will allow us to report the value of every singleton cut (which is the most interesting case, as the standard deviation for these cut values have multiplicative order roughly $1 \pm \varepsilon$). These observations suggest that *sketching* a graph may go beyond considering a subgraph (or a different graph) to represent the original graph G.

Our general algorithm proceeds in several steps. The core of our algorithm is a procedure for handling cuts of value $\approx 1/\varepsilon^2$ in a graph with unweighted edges, which proceeds as follows. First, repeatedly partition the graph along every *sparse* cut, namely, any cut whose sparsity is below $1/\varepsilon$. This results with a partition of the vertices into some number of parts. We store the cross-edges (edge connecting different parts) explicitly. We show the number of such edges is only $\tilde{O}(n\varepsilon^{-1})$, and hence they fit into the space allocated for the sketch. Obviously, the contribution of these edges to any desired cut $w(S, \bar{S})$ is easy to compute from this sketch.

The sketching algorithm still needs to estimate the contribution (to a cut $w(S, \bar{S})$ for a yet unknown $S \subset V$) from edges that are inside any single part P of the partition. To accomplish this, we sample $\approx 1/\varepsilon$ edges out of each vertex, and also store the exact degrees of all vertices. Then, to estimate the contribution of edges inside a part P to $w(S, \bar{S})$, we take the sum of (exact) degrees of all vertices in $S \cap P$, *minus* an estimate for (twice) the number of edges inside $S \cap P$ (estimated from the edge sample). This "difference-based" estimate has a smaller variance than a direct estimate for the number edges in $(S \cap P, \bar{S} \cap P)$ (which would be the "standard estimate", in some sense employed by previous work). The smaller variance is achieved thanks to the facts

that (1) the assumed cut is of size (at most) $1/\varepsilon^2$; and (2) there are no sparse cuts in P.

Overall, we achieve a sketch size of $\tilde{O}(n\varepsilon^{-1})$. We can construct the sketch in polynomial time by employing an $O(\sqrt{\log n})$-approximation algorithm for sparse cut [ARV09, She09] or faster algorithms with $(\log^{O(1)} n)$-approximation [Mad10].

1.2.3 Upper Bound for Sketching Laplacian Matrices with Spectral Queries, "For Each" Model

Now we consider spectral queries $x \in \mathbb{R}^n$, starting first with a space bound of $n\varepsilon^{-1.66}\text{polylog}(n)$ bits, and then discuss how to improve it further to $n\varepsilon^{-1.6}\text{polylog}(n)$.

We start by making several simplifying assumptions. The first is that the total number of edges is $O(n\varepsilon^{-2})$. Indeed, we can first compute a spectral sparsifier [BSS14]. It is useful to note that if all edges weights were between 1 and $\text{poly}(n)$, then after spectral sparsification the edge weights are between 1 and $\text{poly}(n)$, for a possibly larger polynomial. Next, we can assume all edge weights are within a factor of 2. Indeed, by linearity of the Laplacian, if all edge weights are in $[1, \text{poly}(n)]$, then we can group the weights into powers of 2 and sketch each subset of edges separately, incurring an $O(\log n)$ factor blowup in space. Third, and most importantly, we assume that Cheeger's constant h_G of each resulting graph $G = (V, E)$ satisfies $h_G > \varepsilon^{1/3}$, where recall that $h_G = \inf_{S \subset V} \Phi_G(S)$ where

$$\Phi_G(S) = \frac{w(S, \bar{S})}{\min\{\text{vol}(S), \text{vol}(\bar{S})\}} \quad \text{and} \quad \text{vol}(S) = \sum_{u \in S} w(\{u\}, V \setminus \{u\}).$$

We can assume $h_G > \varepsilon^{1/3}$ because if it were not, then by definition of h_G there is a sparse cut, that is, $\Phi_G(S) \le \varepsilon^{1/3}$. We can find a sparse cut (a polylogarithmic approximation suffices), store all sparse cut edges in our data structure, and remove them from the graph G. We can then recurse on the two sides of the cut. By a charging argument we can bound the total number of edges stored across all sparse cuts.

As for the actual data structure achieving our $n\varepsilon^{-1.66}\text{polylog}(n)$ upper bound, we first store the weighted degree $\delta_u(G) = \sum_{v:(u,v)\in E} w(u, v)$ of each node (as that for the cut queries). A difference is that we now partition vertices into "heavy" and "light" classes V_L and V_H, where V_H contains those vertices whose weighted degree exceeds a threshold, and light consists of the remaining vertices. We include all edges incident to light vertices in the data structure. The remaining edges have both endpoints heavy and for each heavy vertex, we randomly sample about $\varepsilon^{-5/3}$ of its neighboring heavy edges; edge u, v is sampled with probability $\frac{w(u,v)}{\delta_u(G_H)}$ where $\delta_u(G_H)$ is the sum of weighted edges from the heavy vertex u to neighboring heavy vertices v.

For the estimation procedure, we write $x^T L x = \sum_{(u,v)\in E}(x_u - x_v)^2 w(u,v)$ as

$$x^T L x = \sum_{u \in V} \delta_u(G) x_u^2 - \sum_{u \in V_L, v \in V} x_u x_v w(u,v)$$
$$- \sum_{u \in V_H, v \in V_L} x_u x_v w(u,v) - \sum_{u \in V_H}\sum_{v \in V_H} x_u x_v w(u,v)$$

and observe that our data structure has the first three summations on the right exactly; error can only come from estimating $\sum_{u \in V_H}\sum_{v \in V_H} x_u x_v w(u,v)$, for which we use our sampled heavy edges. Since this summation has only heavy edges, we can control its variance and upper bound it by $\varepsilon^{10/3}\|D^{1/2}x\|_2^4$, where D is a diagonal matrix with the degrees of G on the diagonal. We can then upper bound this norm by relating it to the first non-zero eigenvalue $\lambda_1(\tilde{L})$ of the normalized Laplacian $\tilde{L}$, which cannot be too small, since by Cheeger's inequality, $\lambda_1(\tilde{L}) \geq h_G^2/2$, and we have ensured that h_G is large.

To improve the upper bound to $n\varepsilon^{-1.6}\mathrm{polylog}(n)$ bits, we partition the edges of G into more refined groups, based on the degrees of their endpoints. More precisely, we classify edges e by the minimum degree of their two endpoints, call this number $m(e)$, and two edges e, e' are in the same class if the nearest power of 2 of $m(e)$ and of $m(e')$ is the same. We note that the total number of vertices with degree in $\omega(\varepsilon^{-2})$ is $o(n)$, since we are starting with a graph with only $O(n\varepsilon^{-2})$ edges; therefore, all edges e with $m(e) = \omega(\varepsilon^{-2})$ can be handled by applying our entire procedure recursively on say, at most $n/2$ nodes. Thus, it suffices to consider $m(e) \leq \varepsilon^{-2}$.

The intuition now is that as $m(e)$ increases, the variance of our estimator decreases since the two endpoints have even larger degree now and so they are even "heavier" than before. Hence, we need fewer edge samples when processing a subgraph restricted to edges with large $m(e)$. On the other hand, a graph on edges e for which every value of $m(e)$ is small simply cannot have too many edges; indeed, every edge is incident to a low degree vertex. Therefore, when we partition the graph to ensure that Cheeger's constant h_G is small, since there are fewer total edges (before we just assumed this number was upper bounded by $n\varepsilon^{-2}$), now we pay less to store all edges across sparse cuts. Thus, we can balance these two extremes, and doing so we arrive at our overall $n\varepsilon^{-1.6}\mathrm{polylog}(n)$ bit space bound.

Several technical challenges arise when performing this more refined partitioning. One is that when doing the sparse cut partitioning to ensure the Cheeger's constant is small, we destroy the minimum degree of endpoints of edges in the graph. Fortunately we can show that for our setting of parameters, the total number of edges removed along sparse cuts is small, and so only a small number of vertices have their degree drop by more than a factor of 2. For these vertices, we can afford to store all edges incident to them directly, so they do not contribute to the variance. Another issue that arises is that to have small variance, we would like to "assign" each edge $\{u,v\}$ to one of the two endpoints u or v. If we were to assign it to both, we would have higher variance. This involves creating a companion or "buddy graph" which is a directed graph associated with the original graph. This directed graph assists us with the edge partitioning, and tells us which edges to potentially sample from which vertices.

1.3 Application to Distributed Minimum Cut

We now illustrate how a "for each" sketch can be useful algorithmically despite its relaxed guarantees compared to a cut sparsifier. In particular, we show how to $(1 + \varepsilon)$-approximate the global minimum cut of a graph whose edges are distributed across multiple servers. Distributed large-scale graph computation has received recent attention, where protocols for distributed minimum spanning tree, breadth-first search, shortest paths, and testing connectivity have been studied, among other problems, see, e.g., [KNPR15, WZ13]. In our case, each server locally computes the "for each" data structure of Sec. 2.3.1 on its subgraph (for accuracy ε), and sends it to a central server. Each server also computes a classical cut sparsifier, with fixed accuracy $\varepsilon' = 0.2$, and sends it to the central server. Using the fact that cut-sparsifiers can be merged, the central server obtains a $(1 \pm \varepsilon')$-approximation to all cuts in the union of the graphs. By a result of Henzinger and Williamson [HW96] (see also Karger [Kar00]), there are only $O(n^2)$ cuts strictly within factor 1.5 of the minimum cut, and they can be found efficiently from the sparsifier (see [Kar00] for an $\tilde{O}(n^2)$ time way of implicitly representing all such cuts). The central server then evaluates each "for each" data structure on each of these cuts, and sums up the estimates to evaluate each such cut up to factor $1 + \varepsilon$, and eventually reports the minimum found. Note that the "for each" data structures can be assumed, by independent repetitions, to be correct with probability $1 - 1/n^4$ for any fixed cut (and at any server), and therefore correct with high probability on all $O(n^2)$ candidate cuts.

2. MAIN THEOREMS

Due to space constraints, this extended abstract lists only the main results of our paper. We refer the reader to the full version of the paper for other results and the proof details.

2.1 Positive-Semidefinite Matrices

For PSD matrices, we show the following two lower bounds, for the "for all" and "for each" models, respectively, which resolve the sketching complexities for PSD matrices up to a logarithmic factor. Indeed, the first lower bound matches the trivial upper bound of storing the whole matrix, and the second one matches a straightforward application of the Johnson-Lindenstrauss dimension reduction lemma.

THEOREM 2.1. *For a general PSD matrix A and relative approximation $\varepsilon > 0$ that is a sufficiently small constant, every sketch $sk(A)$ that satisfies the "for all" guarantee (with constant probability of success), must use $\Omega(n^2)$ bits of space. This is true even if all of entries of A are promised to be in the range $\{-1, -1 + 1/n^C, -1 + 2/n^C, \ldots, 1 - 1/n^C, 1\}$ for a sufficiently large constant $C > 0$,*

THEOREM 2.2. *For a general PSD matrix A and relative approximation $\varepsilon \in (1/\sqrt{n}, 1)$, every sketch $sk(A)$ that satisfies the "for each" guarantee (with constant probability) must use $\Omega(n/\varepsilon^2)$ bits of space.*

2.2 Symmetric Diagonally Dominant Matrices, "For All" Model

Our first main result is an $\Omega(n/\varepsilon^2)$ space lower space for sketching SDD matrices under the "for all" guarantee. In fact, we prove the lower bound $\Omega(n/\varepsilon^2)$ for the special case where A is a Laplacian matrix and for cut queries $x \in \{0,1\}^n$.

We additionally show in Appendix B that the quadratic form of an SDD matrix can be reduced to that of a Laplacian matrix, with only a modest increase in the matrix size, from order n to order $2n$. Thus, the upper bound of sketching SDD matrices in both "for each" and "for all" cases will be the same as that for Laplacians. Since in the "for all" case, we can build the cut (or spectral) sparsifier for a graph using $\tilde{O}(n/\varepsilon^2)$ bits (using e.g. [BSS14]), we can also construct a "for all" sketch for an SDD matrix using $\tilde{O}(n/\varepsilon^2)$ bits of space. This means that our $\Omega(n/\varepsilon^2)$ lower bound is tight up to a logarithmic factor.

THEOREM 2.3. *Fix an integer n and $\varepsilon \in (1/\sqrt{n}, 1)$, and let $\mathbf{sk} = \mathbf{sk}_{n,\varepsilon}$ and $\mathbf{est} = \mathbf{est}_{n,\varepsilon}$ be possibly randomized sketching and estimation algorithms for unweighted graphs on vertex set $[n]$. Suppose that for every such graph $G = ([n], E)$, with probability at least $3/4$ we have[1]*

$$\forall S \subset [n], \quad \mathbf{est}\,(S, \mathbf{sk}(G)) \in (1 \pm \varepsilon) \cdot w(S, \bar{S}).$$

Then the worst-case size of $\mathbf{sk}(G)$ is $\Omega(n/\varepsilon^2)$ bits.

If the sketch must take the form of a graph H (i.e., be a cut sparsifier), then a straightforward application of Theorem 2.3 implies that H must have $\Omega(n/(\varepsilon^2 \log n))$ edges. The following theorem improves this lower bound by a logarithmic factor, and obtains a bound that is tight up to constant factors.

THEOREM 2.4. *For every integer n and $\varepsilon \in (1/\sqrt{n}, 1)$, there is an n-vertex graph G for which every $(1 + \varepsilon)$-cut sparsifier H has $\Omega(n/\varepsilon^2)$ edges, even if H is not required to be a subgraph of G.*

Proof outline for Theorem 2.3.

The proof uses the following communication lower bound for a version of the Gap-Hamming-Distance problem. Fix $c = 10^{-3}$.

THEOREM 2.5. *Consider a distributional communication problem, where Alice has as input $n/2$ strings $s_1, \ldots, s_{n/2} \in \{0,1\}^{1/\varepsilon^2}$ of Hamming weight $\frac{1}{2\varepsilon^2}$, and Bob has an index $i \in [n/2]$ together with one string $t \in \{0,1\}^{1/\varepsilon^2}$ of Hamming weight $\frac{1}{2\varepsilon^2}$, drawn as follows:[2]*

- *i is chosen uniformly at random;*
- *s_i and t are chosen uniformly at random but conditioned on their Hamming distance $\Delta(s_i, t)$ being, with equal probability, either $\geq \frac{1}{2\varepsilon^2} + \frac{c}{\varepsilon}$ or $\leq \frac{1}{2\varepsilon^2} - \frac{c}{\varepsilon}$;*
- *the remaining strings $s_{i'}$ for $i' \neq i$ are chosen uniformly at random.*

Consider a (possibly randomized) one-way protocol, in which Alice sends to Bob an m-bit message, and then Bob determines, with success probability at least $2/3$, whether $\Delta(s_i, t)$ is $\geq \frac{1}{2\varepsilon^2} + \frac{c}{\varepsilon}$ or $\leq \frac{1}{2\varepsilon^2} - \frac{c}{\varepsilon}$. Then Alice's message size is $m \geq \Omega(n/\varepsilon^2)$ bits.

---

[1] The probability is over the randomness of the two algorithms; more precisely, the two algorithms have access to a common source of random bits.

[2] Alice's input and Bob's input are *not* independent, but the marginal distribution of each one is uniform over its domain, namely, $\{0,1\}^{(n/2) \times (1/\varepsilon^2)}$ and $[n] \times \{0,1\}^{1/\varepsilon^2}$, respectively.

We then prove Theorem 2.3 by a reduction to the above communication problem, interpreting the one-way protocol as a sketching algorithm, as follows. Given the instance $(s_1, \ldots, s_{n/2}, i, t)$, define an n-vertex graph G that is a disjoint union of the graphs $\{G_j : j \in [\varepsilon^2 n/2]\}$, where each G_j is a bipartite graph, whose two sides, denoted $L(G_j)$ and $R(G_j)$, are of size $|L(G_j)| = |R(G_j)| = 1/\varepsilon^2$. The edges of G are determined by $s_1, \ldots, s_{n/2}$, where each string s_u is interpreted as a vector of indicators for the adjacency between vertex $u \in \cup_{j \in [\varepsilon^2 n/2]} L(G_j)$ and the respective $R(G_j)$.

Observe that Alice can compute G without any communication, as this graph is completely determined by her input. She then builds a sketch of this graph, that with probability $\geq 99/100$, succeeds in simultaneously approximating all cut queries within factor $1 \pm \gamma\varepsilon$, where $\gamma > 0$ is a small constant to be determined later. This sketch is obtained from the theorem's assumption about m-bit sketches by standard amplification of the success probability from $3/4$ to 0.99 (namely, repeating $r = O(1)$ times independently and answering any query with the median value of the r answers). Alice then sends this $O(m)$-bit sketch to Bob.

Bob then uses his input i to compute $j = j(i) \in [\varepsilon^2 n/2]$ such that the graph G_j contains vertex i (i.e., the vertex whose neighbors are determined by s_i). Bob also interprets his input string t as a vector of indicators determining a subset $T \subseteq R(G_j)$. Let $N(v)$ be the neighbor set of the vertex v. We have the following lemma.

LEMMA 2.6. *Using the $O(m)$-bit sketch he received from Alice, Bob can compute a "list" $B \subset L(G_j)$ of size $|B| = \frac{1}{2}|L(G_j)| = \frac{1}{2\varepsilon^2}$, and with probability at least 0.96, this list contains at least $\frac{4}{5}$-fraction of the vertices in the set*

$$L_{\text{high}} := \{v \in L(G_j) : |N(v) \cap T| \geq \frac{1}{4\varepsilon^2} + \frac{c}{\varepsilon}\}. \quad (1)$$

Moreover, Bob uses no information about his input i other than $j = j(i)$.

Finally, Bob can decide whether $\Delta(s_i, t)$ is $\geq \frac{1}{2\varepsilon^2} + \frac{c}{\varepsilon}$ or $\leq \frac{1}{2\varepsilon^2} - \frac{c}{\varepsilon}$ using L_{high}, thereby solving the (variation of the) Gap-Hamming problem, which implies that $m \geq \Omega(n/\varepsilon^2)$, and proves Theorem 2.3.

2.3 Symmetric Diagonally Dominant Matrices, "For Each" Model

Our second and third main results design sketches of SDD matrices in the "for each" model, namely, sketch-size $\tilde{O}(n/\varepsilon)$ for cut queries $x \in \{0,1\}^n$ and sketch-size $\tilde{O}(n/\varepsilon^{1/6})$ for spectral queries $x \in \mathbb{R}^n$. Again, due to the reduction shown in Appendix B, sketching of SDD matrices and of Laplacian matrices are equivalent, hence we only need to prove these bounds for Laplacian matrices.

2.3.1 Laplacian Matrices with Cut Queries

Given a Laplacian matrix L, let $G = G(L) = (V, E, w)$ be the corresponding graph, and let $n = |V|$. For cut queries, we obtain the following upper bound.

THEOREM 2.7. *Fix an integer n and $\varepsilon \in (1/n, 1/30)$. Then every n-vertex graph $G = (V, E, w)$ with edge weights in the range $[1, W]$ admits a cut sketch of size $\tilde{O}(n\varepsilon^{-1} \cdot \log \log W)$ bits with the "for each" guarantee. Specifically, for every query $S \subset V$ (equivalently, $x \in \{0,1\}^n$), the sketch can produce with high probability a $1 + O(\varepsilon)$ approximation to $w(S, \bar{S})$.*

We can also show a matching lower bound (up to logarithmic factors).

THEOREM 2.8. *Fix an integer n and $\varepsilon \in [2/n, 1/2]$. Suppose $sk(\cdot)$ is a sketching algorithm that outputs at most $s = s(n, \varepsilon)$ bits, and* **est** *is an estimation algorithm, such that together for every n-vertex graph G,*

$$\forall S \subset V, \qquad \mathbf{Pr}\Big[\mathbf{est}(S, sk(G)) \in (1 \pm \varepsilon) \cdot w(S, \bar{S})\Big] \geq 9/10.$$

Then $s \geq \Omega(n/\varepsilon)$.

We next outline the proof of Theorem 2.7. The starting point of our algorithm design is to consider the a special graph (S1-graph) under a special set of queries (the weighted cut value $w(S, \bar{S}) \leq 5$). We then show how to massage a general graph with polynomial weights to a set of S1-graph's (using the importance sampling and a hierarchical partition on the edge weights, and by repeatedly finding sparse cuts), and how to handle general cut queries. Finally we remove the polynomial weight constraints using a finer grade of "pruning and partition" step making use of a minimum-weight spanning tree of the graph. Due to the space constraints, we only present here the definition of the S1-graph and the algorithm for sketching S1-graph for cut queries $w(S, \bar{S}) \leq 5$.

DEFINITION 2.9 (S1-GRAPH). *We say an undirected weighted graph $G = (V, E, w)$ is an S1-graph if it satisfies the following.*

1. *All edge weights are within a factor of 2, i.e. $\forall e \in E$, $w(e) \in [\gamma, 2\gamma]$ for some $\gamma > 0$.*

2. *The expansion constant of G is $\Gamma_G \geq \frac{1}{\varepsilon}$, where $\Gamma_G := \min_{|S| \leq n/2} \frac{|E(S, \bar{S})|}{|S|}$, where $E(S, \bar{S}) = \{(u, v) \in E \mid u \in S, v \in \bar{S}\}$.*

The sketching algorithm for S1-graph and the special cut queries $w(S, \bar{S}) \leq 5$ is fairly simple: we first add all weighted degrees of vertices to the sketch, and then for each vertex we sample uniformly with replacement a set of $1/\varepsilon$ adjacent edges and store them in the sketch. As mentioned in the techniques overview (Section 1.2), using a "difference-based" estimator together with the fact that there is no sparse cut and the assumption that $w(S, \bar{S}) \leq 5$ (and consequently the cut is of size at most $O(1/\varepsilon^2)$ because the weight of each edge of an S1-graph is at least ε^2), we can tightly bound the variance of the estimator of a cut $w(S, \bar{S})$ in an S1-graph, which allows a small set of edge samples and thus the small space usage.

2.3.2 Laplacian Matrices with Spectral Queries

THEOREM 2.10. *Given a Laplacian matrix L with polynomially-bounded entries, and $\varepsilon \in (0, 1)$, there exists a spectral sketch of size $\tilde{O}(n/\varepsilon^{8/5})$ bits such that for every query $x \in \mathbb{R}^n$, the sketch can produce with high probability a $(1 + \varepsilon)$ to $x^T L x$.*

We next outline the proof of Theorem 2.10. Let G be the corresponding graph of the Laplacian matrix L. To prove Theorem 2.10 we again start from a simple type of graphs we call S2-graph, whose definition is given below. Note that an S2-graph again has almost uniform edge weights, and a small Cheeger's constant which is similar in spirit to the expansion

constant, but has more to do with the spectral properties of the graph. We then finish the proof via a long sequence of generalizations and optimizations, as partly discussed in the technique overview (Section 1.2).

DEFINITION 2.11 (S2-GRAPH). *We say an undirected weighted graph $G = (V, E, w)$ is an S2-graph if it satisfies the following.*

1. *All edge weights are within a factor of 2, i.e. $\forall e \in E$, $w(e) \in [\gamma, 2\gamma]$ for some $\gamma > 0$.*

2. *Cheeger's constant $h_G > c_\alpha \varepsilon^{\frac{1}{3}}$ for a large constant $c_\alpha > 0$.*

The sketching algorithm for S2-graph is slightly more complicated than that for S1-graph in the cut query case: We first add all weighted degrees of vertices to the sketch. Next, we partition the vertices to two sets $\mathcal{S}$ and $\mathcal{L}$, where $\mathcal{S}$ contains all vertices of weighted degrees less than $\gamma c_\alpha \varepsilon^{-5/3}$, and $\mathcal{L}$ contains the rest of the vertices. We then store all adjacent edges of vertices in $\mathcal{S}$ in the sketch, and then delete these vertices and edges from G, obtaining a graph $G' = (V', E', w')$. For each vertex in G', we sample with replacement $c_\alpha \varepsilon^{-5/3}$ of its adjacent edges with probability proportional to the edge weights, and store them in the sketch.

This algorithm, however, only gives a sketch of size $\tilde{O}(n/\varepsilon^{5/3})$ bits (even for this special type of graphs). To improve it to $\tilde{O}(n/\varepsilon^{1.6})$ we need a finer process of edge partition.

3. REFERENCES

[AGM12a] K. J. Ahn, S. Guha, and A. McGregor. Analyzing graph structure via linear measurements. In *23rd Annual ACM-SIAM Symposium on Discrete Algorithms*, pages 459–467, 2012.

[AGM12b] K. J. Ahn, S. Guha, and A. McGregor. Graph sketches: sparsification, spanners, and subgraphs. In *31st ACM SIGMOD-SIGACT-SIGART Symposium on Principles of Database Systems*, pages 5–14, 2012.

[AHK05] S. Arora, E. Hazan, and S. Kale. Fast algorithms for approximate semidefinite programming using the multiplicative weights update method. In *46th Annual IEEE Symposium on Foundations of Computer Science*, FOCS '05, pages 339–348. IEEE Computer Society, 2005. doi:10.1109/SFCS.2005.35.

[Alo97] N. Alon. On the edge-expansion of graphs. *Comb. Probab. Comput.*, 6(2):145–152, June 1997. doi:10.1017/S096354839700299X.

[ARV09] S. Arora, S. Rao, and U. Vazirani. Expander flows, geometric embeddings and graph partitioning. *J. ACM*, 56(2):1–37, 2009. doi:10.1145/1502793.1502794.

[BBDS13] J. Blocki, A. Blum, A. Datta, and O. Sheffet. Differentially private data analysis of social networks via restricted sensitivity. In *Innovations in Theoretical Computer Science, ITCS 2013*, pages 87–96, 2013.

[BK96] A. A. Benczúr and D. R. Karger. Approximating s-t minimum cuts in $\tilde{O}(n^2)$ time. In *28th Annual ACM Symposium on Theory of Computing*, pages 47–55. ACM, 1996. doi:10.1145/237814.237827.

[BSS14] J. D. Batson, D. A. Spielman, and N. Srivastava. Twice-ramanujan sparsifiers. *SIAM Review*, 56(2):315–334, 2014. doi:10.1137/130949117.

[CW09] K. L. Clarkson and D. P. Woodruff. Numerical linear algebra in the streaming model. In *Proceedings of the 41st Annual ACM Symposium on Theory of Computing, STOC 2009*, pages 205–214, 2009.

[FHHP11] W. S. Fung, R. Hariharan, N. J. Harvey, and D. Panigrahi. A general framework for graph sparsification. In *Proceedings of the Symposium on Theory of Computing (STOC)*, pages 71–80. ACM, 2011. doi:10.1145/1993636.1993647.

[GRU12] A. Gupta, A. Roth, and J. Ullman. Iterative constructions and private data release. In *9th International Conference on Theory of Cryptography*, TCC'12, pages 339–356. Springer-Verlag, 2012. doi:10.1007/978-3-642-28914-9_19.

[HW96] M. R. Henzinger and D. P. Williamson. On the number of small cuts in a graph. *Inf. Process. Lett.*, 59(1):41–44, 1996.

[JT12] P. Jain and A. Thakurta. Mirror descent based database privacy. In *15th International Workshop, APPROX 2012, and 16th International Workshop, RANDOM 2012*, pages 579–590, 2012.

[Kar00] D. R. Karger. Minimum cuts in near-linear time. *J. ACM*, 47(1):46–76, 2000. doi:10.1145/331605.331608.

[KLM+14] M. Kapralov, Y. T. Lee, C. Musco, C. Musco, and A. Sidford. Single pass spectral sparsification in dynamic streams. In *55th Annual Symposium on Foundations of Computer Science*, FOCS '14, pages 561–570. IEEE Computer Society, 2014. arXiv:1407.1289, doi:10.1109/FOCS.2014.66.

[KNPR15] H. Klauck, D. Nanongkai, G. Pandurangan, and P. Robinson. Distributed computation of large-scale graph problems. In *26th Annual ACM-SIAM Symposium on Discrete Algorithms*, SODA '15, pages 391–410. SIAM, 2015. arXiv:1311.6209, doi:10.1137/1.9781611973730.28.

[KP12] M. Kapralov and R. Panigrahy. Spectral sparsification via random spanners. In *3rd Innovations in Theoretical Computer Science Conference*, pages 393–398. ACM, 2012. doi:10.1145/2090236.2090267.

[Mad10] A. Madry. Fast approximation algorithms for cut-based problems in undirected graphs. In *Proceedings of the Symposium on Foundations of Computer Science (FOCS)*, pages 245–254. IEEE, 2010.

[McG14] A. McGregor. Graph stream algorithms: a survey. *SIGMOD Record*, 43(1):9–20, 2014.

[Nil91] A. Nilli. On the second eigenvalue of a graph. *Discrete Math*, 91:207–210, 1991. doi:10.1016/0012-365X(91)90112-F.

[She09] J. Sherman. Breaking the multicommodity flow barrier for $O(\sqrt{\log n})$-approximations to sparsest cut. In *Proceedings of the Symposium on Foundations of Computer Science (FOCS)*, pages 363–372, 2009.

[SS11] D. A. Spielman and N. Srivastava. Graph sparsification by effective resistances. *SIAM J. Comput.*, 40(6):1913–1926, December 2011. doi:10.1137/080734029.

[ST04] D. A. Spielman and S.-H. Teng. Nearly-linear time algorithms for graph partitioning, graph sparsification, and solving linear systems. In *Proceedings of the Symposium on Theory of Computing (STOC)*, pages 81–90. ACM, 2004. doi:10.1145/1007352.1007372.

[ST11] D. A. Spielman and S.-H. Teng. Spectral sparsification of graphs. *SIAM J. Comput.*, 40(4):981–1025, 2011. doi:10.1137/08074489X.

[Upa13] J. Upadhyay. Random projections, graph sparsification, and differential privacy. In *19th International Conference on Advances in Cryptology*, ASIACRYPT 2013, pages 276–295. Springer-Verlag, 2013. doi:10.1007/978-3-642-42033-7_15.

[Upa14] J. Upadhyay. Circulant matrices and differential privacy. *CoRR*, abs/1410.2470, 2014. arXiv:1410.2470.

[WZ13] D. P. Woodruff and Q. Zhang. When distributed computation is communication expensive. In *Distributed Computing - 27th International Symposium, DISC 2013*, pages 16–30, 2013. doi:10.1007/978-3-642-41527-2_2.

APPENDIX

A. GENERAL MATRICES, "FOR EACH" MODEL

THEOREM A.1. *Any sketch $sk(A)$ of a general $n \times n$ matrix A that satisfies the "for each" guarantee with probability 0.9, even when all entries of A are promised to be in the set $\{0,1\}$, must use $\Omega(n^2)$ bits of space.*

PROOF. Let A be a symmetric matrix with zero on the diagonal, and a random bit in every other entry. Set the query vector $x = (e_i + e_j)$. Then using $\frac{1}{2}x^T A x$ we can recover the entry $A_{i,j}$, with probability 0.9. Think the sketching problem as a communication problem where Alice holds the matrix A; she sends a message (the sketch) M to Bob such that Bob can recover each entries of A with probability 0.9 (except for the diagonal entries, which are fixed to be 0, Bob can recover exactly). Then,

$$H(A \mid M) = \sum_{i,j \in [n]} H(A_{i,j} \mid M) \quad (A_{i,j} \text{ are independent})$$
$$\leq (H_2(0.9) + 0.1) \cdot n^2 \quad (\text{Fano's inequality})$$
$$< 0.6n^2.$$

Thus $H(M) \geq H(A) - H(A \mid M) = \Omega(n^2)$. ☐

B. REDUCTION FROM SDD MATRICES TO LAPLACIAN MATRICES

In this section we show that the quadratic form of an SDD matrix, $x^T A x$, can be reduced to the quadratic form of a Laplacian, therefore our upper bounds for Laplacian matrices in Section 2.3.1 and Section 2.3.2 can be extended to SDD matrices.

An SDD matrix A has the property that $A_{i,i} \geq \sum_{j \neq i} |A_{i,j}|$ for all i. In the case when $A_{i,i} = \sum_{i \neq j} |A_{i,j}|$ for all i, we can write A as $A_p + A_n + D$ where D is the diagonal of A, A_n is the matrix consisting of only the negative off-diagonal entries of A, and A_p is the matrix consisting of only the positive off-diagonal entries of A. It is straightforward to verify that

$$\begin{pmatrix} x^T & -x^T \end{pmatrix} \begin{pmatrix} D + A_n & -A_p \\ -A_p & D + A_n \end{pmatrix} \begin{pmatrix} x \\ -x \end{pmatrix} = 2 x^T A x.$$

The matrix $\begin{pmatrix} D + A_n & -A_p \\ -A_p & D + A_n \end{pmatrix}$ is clearly a Laplacian matrix.

For the general case when $A_{i,i} \geq \sum_{i \neq j} |A_{i,j}|$. We can remove some "weights" from the diagonal entries of A, so that A can be written as $A = D + B$ where D is a diagonal matrix and B satisfies the requirement $B_{i,i} = \sum_{i \neq j} |B_{i,j}|$ for all i. We then have $x^T A x = x^T D x + x^T B x$. The matrix D can be stored explicitly, and $x^T B x$ can be reduced to the quadratic form of a Laplacian matrix as discussed above.

THEOREM B.1. *Given an $n \times n$ SDD matrix A, let $w_{\max} = \max_{i,j} |A_{i,j}|$ and $w_{\min} = \min_{i,j \text{ with } A_{i,j} \neq 0} |A_{i,j}|$, and assume $w_{\max}/w_{\min} = poly(n)$ We can then construct a sketch of A that gives a $(1 + \varepsilon, 0.99)$-approximation to $x^T A x$ for any fixed $x \in \mathbb{R}^n$. The size of this sketch is $\tilde{O}(n/\varepsilon^{8/5})$ bits.*

Energy-Efficient Algorithms

Erik D. Demaine *
MIT CSAIL
32 Vassar Street
Cambridge, MA 02139
edemaine@mit.edu

Jayson Lynch*
MIT CSAIL
32 Vassar Street
Cambridge, MA 02139
jaysonl@mit.edu

Geronimo J. Mirano*
MIT CSAIL
32 Vassar Street
Cambridge, MA 02139
geronm@mit.edu

Nirvan Tyagi*
MIT CSAIL
32 Vassar Street
Cambridge, MA 02139
ntyagi@mit.edu

ABSTRACT

We initiate the systematic study of the *energy complexity* of algorithms (in addition to time and space complexity) based on Landauer's Principle in physics, which gives a lower bound on the amount of energy a system must dissipate if it destroys information. We propose energy-aware variations of three standard models of computation: circuit RAM, word RAM, and transdichotomous RAM. On top of these models, we build familiar high-level primitives such as control logic, memory allocation, and garbage collection with zero energy complexity and only constant-factor overheads in space and time complexity, enabling simple expression of energy-efficient algorithms. We analyze several classic algorithms in our models and develop low-energy variations: comparison sort, insertion sort, counting sort, breadth-first search, Bellman-Ford, Floyd-Warshall, matrix all-pairs shortest paths, AVL trees, binary heaps, and dynamic arrays. We explore the time/space/energy trade-off and develop several general techniques for analyzing algorithms and reducing their energy complexity. These results lay a theoretical foundation for a new field of semi-reversible computing and provide a new framework for the investigation of algorithms.

CCS Concepts

●**Theory of computation → Models of computation; Design and analysis of algorithms;**

Keywords: Reversible Computing; Landauer's Principle; Algorithms; Models of Computation

1. INTRODUCTION

Landauer limit. CPU power efficiency (number of computations per kilowatt hour of energy) has doubled every 1.57 years from 1946 to 2009 [14]. Within the next 15–60 years, however, this trend will hit a fundamental limit in physics, known as Landauer's

Principle [19]. This principle states that discarding one bit of information (increasing the entropy of the environment by one bit) requires $kT \ln 2$ energy, where k is Boltzmann's constant and T is ambient temperature, which is about $2.8 \cdot 10^{-21}$ joules or $7.8 \cdot 10^{-28}$ kilowatt hours at room temperature (20°C). (Even at liquid nitrogen temperatures, this requirement goes down by less than a factor of 5.) Physics has proved this principle under a variety of different assumptions [19, 30, 17, 26, 18], and a recent *Nature* paper verified it experimentally [6]. Most CPUs discard many bits of information per clock cycle, as much as one per gate; for example, an AND gate with output 0 or an OR gate with output 1 "forgets" the exact values of its inputs. To see how this relates to Landauer's principle, consider the state-of-the-art 15-core Intel Xeon E7-4890 v2 2.8GHz CPU. In a 4-processor configuration, it achieves $1.2 \cdot 10^{12}$ computations per second at 620 watts, [1] for a ratio of $7.4 \cdot 10^{15}$ computations per kilowatt hour. At the pessimistic extreme, if every one of the $4.3 \cdot 10^9$ transistors discards a bit, then the product $3.2 \cdot 10^{25}$ is only three orders of magnitude greater than Landauer limit. If CPUs continue to double in energy efficiency every 1.57 years, this gap will close in less than 18 years. At the more optimistic extreme, if a 64-bit computation discards only 64 bits (to overwrite one register), the gap will close within 59 years. The truth is probably somewhere in between these extremes.

Reversible computing. The only way to circumvent the Landauer limit is to do logically *reversible* computations, whose inputs can be reconstructed from their outputs, using physically *adiabatic* circuits. According to current knowledge, such computations have no classical fundamental limitations on energy consumption. General-purpose CPUs with adiabatic circuits were constructed by Frank and Knight at MIT [10]. The design of reversible computers is still being actively studied, with papers on designs for adders [29], multipliers [28], ALUs [27], clocks [31], and processors [32] being published within the last five years. AMD's CPUs since Oct. 2012 (Piledriver) use "resonant clock mesh technology" (essentially, an adiabatic clock circuit) to reduce overall energy consumption by 24% [8]. Thus the ideas from reversible computing are already creating energy savings today.

But what can be done by reversible computation? Reversible computation is an old idea, with reversible Turing machines being proved universal by Lecerf in 1963 [21] and ten years later by Bennett [3]. Early complexity results showed that any computation can be made reversible, but with a quadratic space overhead [4] or an exponential time overhead [20, 37], in particular models of computation. More recent results give a trade-off with subquadratic space and subexponential time [7]. These general transforms are

---

* Supported in part by the MIT Energy Initiative and by MADALGO — Center for Massive Data Algorithmics — a Center of the Danish National Research Foundation.

Permission to make digital or hard copies of all or part of this work for personal or classroom use is granted without fee provided that copies are not made or distributed for profit or commercial advantage and that copies bear this notice and the full citation on the first page. Copyrights for components of this work owned by others than the author(s) must be honored. Abstracting with credit is permitted. To copy otherwise, or republish, to post on servers or to redistribute to lists, requires prior specific permission and/or a fee. Request permissions from Permissions@acm.org.

ITCS'16, January 14–16, 2016, Cambridge, MA, USA.
Copyright is held by the owner/author(s). Publication rights licensed to ACM.
ACM ACM 978-1-4503-4057-1/16/01...$15.00.
DOI: http://dx.doi.org/10.1145/2840728.2840756

---

[1] We follow Koomey et al.'s [14] definitions, using Cisco's measured SPECint_rate_base2006 of 2,320 to estimate millions of computations per second (MCPS).

too expensive; in particular, in a bounded-space system, consuming extra space to make computations reversible is just delaying the inevitable destruction of bits.

The relationship between thermodynamics and information theory is described by Zurek [40]. In a series of papers, Li, Tromp, and Vitanyi discuss irreversible operations as a useful metric for energy dissipation in computers and study the trade-off between time, space, and irreversible operations. An energy cost based on Kolmogorov complexity [24], a precise but uncomputable measure of the information content of a string, is introduced in [22] and further explored in [5, 36, 23]. These papers study algorithms for Bennett's pebble game as well as simulating Turing machines; however, they still focus on universal results, eshrew RAM models, and analyze problems more from a complexity than an algorithms perspective.

Irreversibility is just one source of energy consumption in current chips, and several other models of computation attempt to capture them individually: switching energy of VLSI circuits [12], dynamic and leakage power loss in CMOS circuits [15, 16], and I/O or memory access [11]. Albers [1] surveys many algorithmic techniques for reducing energy consumption of current computers, including techniques like sleep states and power-down mechanisms, dynamic speed scaling, temperature management, and energy-minimizing scheduling. Ultimately, however, we believe that irreversibility will become a critical energy cost shaping the future of computing, and a topic now ripe for algorithmic analysis.

Our results. This paper is the first to perform a thorough algorithmic study of partially reversible computing, and to analyze realistic time/space/energy trade-offs. We define the (Landauer/irreversibility) energy cost, and use it to explore reversible computing in a novel manner. Although there are many other sources of energy inefficiency in a computer we believe the Landauer energy cost is a fundamental and useful measure. A key perspective shift from most of the reversible computing literature (except [23]) is that we allow algorithms to destroy bits, and measure the number of destroyed bits as the energy cost. This approach enables the unification of classic time/space measures with a new energy measure. In particular, it enables us to require algorithms to properly clean up all additional space by the end of their execution, and data structures to be properly charged for their total space allocation.

We introduce three basic models for analyzing the energy cost of word-level operations, similar to the standard word models used in most algorithms today: the word RAM, the more general transdichotomous RAM, and the realistically grounded circuit RAM. Our models allow arbitrary computation to be performed, but define a spectrum of "irreversibility", from reversible (free) computation to completely destructive (expensive) computation. On top of these basic models (akin to assembly language), we build a high-level pseudocode for easy algorithm specification, by showing how to implement many of the familiar high-level programming structures, as well as some new structures, with zero energy overhead and only constant-factor overheads in time and space:

1. **Control logic:** If/then/else, for/while loops, jumps, function calls, stack-allocated variables.
2. **Memory allocation:** Dynamic allocation and deallocation of fixed-size or variable-size blocks, in particular implementing pointer-machine algorithms.
3. **Garbage collection:** Reference-counting and mark-and-sweep algorithms for finding no-longer-used memory blocks for automatic deallocation.
4. **Logging and unrolling:** Specific to energy-efficient computation, we describe a new programming-language feature that makes it easy to turn energy into space overhead, and later remove that space overhead by playing it backwards.

Primitive	Time (ops)	Space in Log (bits)	Energy (bits)	Thm.
Control Logic				
Paired Jump	$\Theta(1)$	1	0	3.1
Variable Jump	$\Theta(1)$	$1 + w$	0	3.1
Protected If	$\Theta(1)$	0	0	3.2
General If	$\Theta(1)$	1	0	3.2
Simple For loop	$\Theta(l)$	0	0	3.3
Protected For loop	$\Theta(l)$	0	0	3.4
General For loop	$\Theta(l)$	$\lg l$	0	3.5
Function call	$\Theta(1)$	0	0	3.6
Memory Management				
Free lists	$\Theta(N)$	$\Theta(wN)$	0	3.7
Reference Counting	$\Theta(N)$	$\Theta(wN)$	0	3.8
Mark & Sweep	$\Theta(N)$	$\Theta(wN)$	0	3.9

Table 1: Summary of our reversible primitives analyses and results including control logic, memory management, and garbage collection. In this table, w is the word size, l is the number of loop iteration, and N represents number of memory objects.

These models open up an entire research field, which we call *energy-efficient algorithms*, to find the minimum energy required to solve a desired computational problem within given time and space bounds. We launch this field with several initial results about classic algorithmic problems, first analyzing the energy cost of existing algorithms, and then modifying or designing new algorithms to reduce the energy cost without significantly increasing the time and space costs. Table 2 summarizes these results.

Although there are many practical papers about minimizing energy in computation (favoring instructions that use somewhat less energy than others), the algorithms community has not made it a standard measure to complement time and space because, without the idea of reversibility, energy is simply within a constant-factor of time. By contrast, in our model, the energy cost can be anywhere between 0 (for reversible computation) and $t \cdot w$ where t is the running time (number of word operations) and w is the number of bits in a word.

Consequences. Reducing the energy consumption of many computations by several orders of magnitude (n) will have tremendous impact on practice. Computer servers alone constitute 23–31 gigawatts of power consumption, which translates to $14–18 billion annually and 1.1–1.5% of worldwide electricity use [13]; there are roughly 50 times as many PCs with an annual growth rate of 12% [38]; and there are about as many smartphones as PCs [9]. Improved energy efficiency would save both environmental impact and money. Reducing energy consumption would also improve the longevity of batteries in portable devices (laptops, phones, watches, etc.), or enable the use of smaller and lighter batteries for similar performance. Perhaps most interestingly, lower energy consumption would lead to faster CPUs, as cooling is the main bottleneck in increasing clock speeds; reducing the energy consumption by a factor of α, we expect to be able to run the CPU roughly α times faster. For example, the world record for CPU clock speed of 8.429 GHz was set by AMD with liquid nitrogen cooling [33].

Our approach is ambitious in that it requires rethinking both software (algorithms) and hardware. Our belief is that building a rich algorithmic theory for (partially) reversible computation, and showing the orders of magnitude in possible energy reduction for important problems, will prove to hardware makers that reversibility is a lucrative feature worth exploring intensely, even before it becomes inevitable by hitting the Landauer Limit.

Algorithm	Time	Space (words)	Energy (bits)	Thm.
Sorting Algorithms				
Comparison Sort	$\Theta(n \lg n)$	$\Theta(n)$	$\Theta(n \lg n)$	6.2
Reversible Comparison Sort	$\Theta(n \lg n)$	$\Theta(n)$	0	6.3, 6.4
Reversible Insertion Sort	$\Theta(n^2)$	$\Theta(n)$	0	6.5
Counting Sort	$\Theta(n + k)$	$\Theta(n + k)$	$\Theta(n + k)$	6.6
Reversible Counting Sort	$\Theta(n + k)$	$\Theta(n + k)$	0	6.8
Graph Algorithms				
Breadth-first Search	$\Theta(V + E)$	$\Theta(V + E)$	$\Theta(wV + E)$	6.9
Reversible BFS[10]	$\Theta(V + E)$	$\Theta(V + E)$	0	6.10
Bellman-Ford	$\Theta(VE)$	$\Theta(V)$	$\Theta(VEw)$	6.12
Reversible Bellman-Ford	$\Theta(VE)$	$\Theta(VE)$	0	6.13
Floyd-Warshall	$\Theta(V^3)$	$\Theta(V^2)$	$\Theta(V^3 w)$	6.14
Reversible Floyd-Warshall [10]	$\Theta(V^3)$	$\Theta(V^3)$	0	6.15
Matrix APSP	$\Theta(V^3 \lg V)$	$\Theta(V^2)$	$\Theta(wV^3 \lg V)$	6.17
Reversible Matrix APSP [10]	$\Theta(V^3 \lg V)$	$\Theta(V^2 \lg V)$	0	6.16
Semi-reversible Matrix APSP	$\Theta(V^3 \lg V)$	$\Theta(V^2)$	$wV^2 \lg V$	6.16
Data Structures				
Standard AVL Trees (build)	$O(n \lg n)$	$O(n)$	$O(w \cdot n \lg n)$	
(search)	$O(\lg n)$	$O(1)$	$O(\lg n)$	5.4
(insert)	$O(\lg n)$	$O(1)$	$O(w \lg n)$	5.5
(k deletes)	$O(k \lg n)$	$O(1)$	$O(w \lg n)$	5.6
Reversible AVL Trees (build)	$O(n \lg n)$	$O(n)$	0	
(search)	$O(\lg n)$	$O(1)$	0	5.7
(insert)	$O(\lg n)$	$O(1)$	0	5.8
(k deletes)	$O(k \lg n)$	$O(k)$	0	5.9
Standard Binary Heap (insert)	$O(\lg n)$	$O(1)$	$O(\lg n)$	5.10
(delete max)	$O(\lg n)$	$O(\lg n)$	$O(w \lg n)$	5.11
Reversible Binary Heap (insert)	$O(\lg n)$	$O(1)$	0	5.10
(delete max)	$O(\lg n)$	$O(\lg n)$	0	5.12
Dynamic Array (build)	$O(n)$	$O(n)$	0	
(query)	$O(1)$	$O(1)$	0	5.3
(add)	$O(1)$	$O(1)$	0	5.3
(delete)	$O(1)$	$O(1)$	0	5.3

Table 2: Summary of our algorithmic analyses and results. In this table, n is the problem size or number of elements in the data-structure, w is the word size, lg is $\log_2$, and in graph algorithms, V is the number of vertices, and E is the number of edges.

Guide. This paper has several sections and does not necessarily need to be read in order or in full, depending on the reader's interest. We recommend reading Sections 2.2 and 2.4 before continuing onto later parts of the paper, to set up the model which is used extensively in the rest of the paper. The remainder of Section 2 further explores our energy models and useful variations. The remaining sections of the paper can be read in any preferred order. Parts of Sections 3–6 use results from previous sections, but these should remain understandable without having seen the prior proofs. Section 3 constructs and analyzes basic control logic and memory management, to enable high-level pseudocode for algorithm specification. Section 4 provides some general techniques we have developed for constructing (semi-)reversible algorithms. Sections 5 and 6 analyze several classic algorithms and data structures, and construct new algorithms and data structures that are more energy efficient. Section 7 poses open problems.

2. ENERGY MODELS

In the following sections we present three different models of computation which define an energy complexity that attempts to capture the energy loss from Landauer's Principle. We begin with a circuit model due to its intuitiveness and similarity to early work done on reversible logic and computation. We then build up RAM mod-

els which bear far more similarity to those used for the analysis of algorithms.

2.1 Energy Circuit Model

At the lowest level we will consider logical gates. Every gate is a Boolean function $g : x \to y$. The energy cost of a gate is defined as the log of the size ratio of the input space, X, to the output space, $Y = g(X)$. Thus, energy $E = \lg\left(\frac{X}{Y}\right)$, whose units are bits. The energy cost cannot be negative because a given input cannot map to more than one output. Here we forbid randomized computation. Alternatively, one could allow the creation of b random bits at an energy cost of b. Also, the energy cost is zero exactly when the function is bijective in which case we call the gate *reversible*.

2.2 Energy Word RAM Model

The Energy Word RAM model allows any contiguous segment of memory of size w to be accessed in constant time and defines a fixed set of operations that can take in $O(1)$ word sized inputs in constant time. We also assume memory allocation is handled in a reversible manner. This will become a more reasonable assumption later, when we show linked-lists and stacks can be implemented reversibly. The program and operations have the following restrictions. First, we restrict ourselves to the operations typically found

323

in high-level languages as well as their reversible analogues. Second, the operation's energy costs should be calculated based off of what can be constructed in the circuit model. Third, all reversible operations must come paired with their inverse operation. Finally, all Energy Word RAM programs must return the machine to its original state, with the exception of a copy of the output living somewhere in memory. This can be done simply but expensively by irreversibly zeroing out every bit and paying the associated energy cost.

The reversible operations we allow include in-place addition and subtraction (e.g., $a \mathrel{+}= b$), increment and decrement (e.g., $a \mathrel{+}= 1$), swapping two variables, testing for equality or less-than relation, copying a variable into an initially empty variable

$$(\text{COPY}(a, \underline{b}) \equiv b \mathrel{+}= a)$$

and destroying a known copy of a variable

$$(\text{DESTROYCOPY}(a, b) \equiv b \mathrel{-}= a)$$

We have introduced here a useful notation, that of underlining variables whose values are empty, which shall serve us in writing pseudocode as well. The irreversible operations we allow include overwriting one variable with another, and computing the bitwise AND or OR of two variables.

In this model, we intend that our lowest level pseudocode correspond to an assembly-like language. For simplicity we will continue to work with variables and locations in memory as though they are all stored in RAM, rather than deal with registers, paging, and other complications that may arise depending on the computer architecture. At this level we also explicitly number every line of our program and grant the code access to the program counter, PC, which is the location in memory of the current instruction. At every instruction the PC is incremented, but it can also be manipulated manually, allowing jumps among other operations. It is very easy to make code irreversible by manipulating the PC, as this is implicitly adding control logic to the program. The instruction set we will be using in this paper is the same as the one with which we defined our Word RAM model. For an instruction set for a reversible computer that has been built see Appendix B of Frank's Thesis [10] or [32].

2.3 Energy Transdichotomous RAM Model

The Energy Transdichotomous RAM model is computationally the most powerful and flexible. As with the Word RAM model, we allow access to memory segments of size w in constant time and assume memory allocation is done reversibly. Generally we will assume that $w = \Omega(\lg n)$, making the word size capable of indexing the entire input of the problem. We also allow any operations on $O(1)$ words to be performed in constant time; however, every algorithm can only use a constant number of different operations. The energy cost of an operation is simply the log of the ratio of the input space to the output space, as in the circuit model. Note that this is a lower bound on the energy cost of the operation in the circuit model, and thus a lower bound in the Energy Word RAM model. Finally, we still need to leave the computer in its initial state, except for a copy of the output.

This model is convenient to work in because it is relatively easy to calculate the energy cost of many operations and the flexibility of choosing operations allows us to exploit information in the system without having to work out the details of how it would be implemented. For example, when dividing an integer by four would generally incur two bits of energy loss or two bits of garbage; however, if we happen to know that the number is even, there is really

only a single bit of information being lost. Instead of having to worry about how to perform shifts and additions to save this bit, the Transdichotomous RAM model allows us to have a 'divide by four when evenly divisible by 2' operation with the restriction that it only takes even inputs.

We now develop some conventions for writing programs in the Transdichotomous RAM Model. All lines are of the form $TUPLE = TUPLE$. Both tuples must contain the same number of elements, and the number of elements must be $O(1)$. The left tuple is a list of all of the values in memory which are used in the computation being performed on this line, including those simply being overwritten. The right tuple contains expressions representing the values that will be in the corresponding variables on the left. These expressions must contain no more than $O(1)$ constant time operations. One interesting convention about this language is every variable implicitly serves two purposes depending on its location. On the left, all variables refer to the memory location where they are stored, and on the right they refer to the values being represented at those memory locations.

As we did above, here we shall annotate variables whose value is known to be zero (often new, unassigned variables) with an underline. This information is often critical to the energy cost of an expression. For example, $(a, b, c) = (a, b, a + b)$ would cost w units of energy because we are erasing every bit in c before replacing it with the value $a + b$. However, $(a, b, \underline{c}) = (a, b, a + b)$ has no energy cost because the input has the value of c assumed to be zero, thus reducing the input space by a factor of 2^w and making the number of inputs and outputs the same.

The following are some examples of common operations written in the format. All operations are assumed to be integer operations with reasonable overflow and rounding conventions. The following examples cost zero energy:

- COPY: $(a, \underline{b}) = (a, a)$
- DESTROYCOPY: $(a, b) = (a, b - a)$
- ADD: $(a, b) = (a + b, b)$
- LESSTHAN: $(a, b, \underline{c}) = (a, b, a < b)$

2.4 High-level Pseudocode

Although the previous section provides a nice, clean way to analyze the energy, space, and time complexity of an algorithm; we may want a more concise and C-like language. Past research on reversible programming languages has focused on fully reversible programming languages and architectures. The first high-level reversible programming languages developed were Janus [25][39] and R [10]. The first reversible architecture, Pendulum, was developed by Vieri [35][34]. Along with Pendulum, Vieri introduced a reversible low-level instruction set, PISA, which is used as a basic reversible instruction set for many future works. Most recently, this architecture has been further improved with the development of Bob [32] using a slightly modified version of PISA known as BobISA, providing more efficient branch handling and address calculation. Axelsen [2] presented the first compilation techniques to translate high-level Janus to low-level PISA, two independently developed reversible languages, and showed that his techniques can be extended for use in any high-level reversible language.

We modeled our pseudocode off of these previous high and low level reversible languages while also adding a few new commands to allow for partial reversibility. We now allow lines of the form $VARIABLE = EXPRESSION$ as well as for loops, while loops, if/else statements, and subroutine calls. We also introduce log blocks

$$x = x + y + z \qquad \textbf{high}$$

$$(x, y, z) = (x + y + z, x, z) \qquad \textbf{intermediate}$$

$$\begin{aligned}
&101 \;\; \overline{tempx = x} \qquad\qquad \textbf{low}\\
&102 \;\; x \mathrel{+}= y\\
&103 \;\; y \mathrel{-}= x\\
&104 \;\; x \mathrel{+}= z\\
&105 \;\; y \mathrel{+}= tempx\\
&106 \;\; y \mathrel{+}= tempx\\
&107 \;\; tempx \mathrel{-}= y
\end{aligned}$$

Figure 1: Simple example of code in high, intermediate, and low-level pseudocode.

	log:	$\underline{a} = x > y$
$\underline{a} = x > y$	$\quad\underline{a} = x > y$	$counter \mathrel{+}= a$
$counter \mathrel{+}= a$	$\quad counter \mathrel{+}= a$	$a \mathrel{-}= x > y$
	unroll	**dealloc**(a)
(a) garbage data not unrolled	(b) logged high-level	(c) logged low-level / automatic unroll

Figure 2: Three examples detailing the mechanics of logged code.

and unroll statements in Section 2.4.1. On lines where we are assigning a variable, we assume that every input in the expression will remain unchanged in its memory location after the computer performs the operation and that the variable on the left-hand side will have its value replaced by the value of the expression. If this is a reversible operation, the variable will merely be changed as appropriate; if it is an irreversible operation, then the variable will be changed and an additional energy cost will be incurred based on the model being used.

Figure 1 gives some simple examples of equivalent code in the three different levels of pseudocode conventions we've developed (high, intermediate, low). The high level is our C-like language. The intermediate language converts high level control logic to jumps and labels. The low level breaks it down further to an assembly-like language. Future sections will use one or more conventions as needed for clarity.

2.4.1 Logging and Unrolling

Dealing with garbage data tends to become tedious when writing reversible computer code. For example, suppose that we were comparing two variables, a and b, and that we wanted to use the result of this comparison to increase some counter; see Figure 2a.

In a normal computer, by the function's end, a would be garbage-collected automatically; however, in our reversible computer a naive garbage collection algorithm would destroy the information stored in a, clearing whatever value it held and costing a word of energy. Thus, the reversible algorithm programmer must handle the task of deallocating a manually.

We call the process of using a series of commands to directly reverse some portion of the code *unrolling*. Manually writing all such commands can be tedious and is prone to error. To expedite the process, we introduce the high-level keywords **log** and **unroll**:

In Figure 2b, the line $\underline{a} = x > y$ is included inside the **log** indentation block, and so is to be reversed at the call to **unroll**. For much longer programs, this extra syntax can save the programmer a great deal of effort that would otherwise be spent writing reverse code. Note that the **log** and **unroll** commands only exist in the highest-level language, and are translated into their manual equivalent at compile-time. The above program, therefore, would compile to the low-level program seen in Figure 2c.

The rules for unrolling are straightforward. Reversible commands can be unrolled simply by including their inverse commands in reverse calling order. Unrolling reversible control logic is discussed in Section 3.1.

To allow our model to unroll semi-reversible programs, which may include irreversible commands, we introduce the *log stack*, a data structure onto which the program can push extra bits of information to be used later to invert the otherwise-irreversible operations. We keep track of our position in the log stack with the log pointer, lp. In the Transdichotomous model, every operation must have its inverse and the process for logging that operation explicitly specified. Furthermore, we assume that this garbage is encoded as efficiently as possible and thus only requires as many bits of space as are needed to distinguish the input space from the output space. Once again, when we log lines with operations that were previously irreversible, we are implicitly defining new operations and should take appropriate precautions. In our Word RAM model, these operations, their inverses, and operations capable of interfacing with lp and memory must be specified.

2.4.2 Promise Notation

We introduce another notational convention that will assist in writing low-energy pseudocode for the Transdichotomous RAM model. At the end of a standard line of code, one may add a comma, the keyword "assert", and then a claimed Boolean expression restricting the values of the involved variables. Some useful examples include:

$$IsTrue = 0, \textbf{ assert } 0 \leq IsTrue \leq 1$$
$$x = x/y, \textbf{ assert } 6 \mid x$$

Here $IsTrue$ may have been the result of a comparison and is known to be either 0 or 1. Thus the energy cost of destroying it is only 1 bit instead of w bits. In the second example, we might know that the problem being computed has some symmetries that a compiler might not see which restrict the values x can take on. Asserts allow us to implicitly define functions which have a restricted input space and thus reduce energy costs. Given the convenience of defining functions in this manner, we must be very careful that we are still using only $O(1)$ different operations in our algorithm.

3. REVERSIBLE PRIMITIVES

In this section, we develop many high-level primitives commonly used throughout algorithms, but which need special care to be done in an energy-efficient manner. Before proceeding, we should discuss in slightly more detail the architecture of our theoretical semi-reversible computer. Our computer only has a single mode of operation, always incrementing the program counter with every instruction. Reversing operations comes from writing the inverse operation in a later section of code, rather than having a separate reversal mode which travels backward along the program counter, inverting those operations. This gives us more flexibility in how to handle irreversible sections of code, and the manner in which we reverse operations which are not dependent upon each other. However, it comes at the cost that we cannot recover the value of the program counter. Thus this design will have to incur an energy cost of w every time the computer is reset. Because we can run many programs between restarts, we do not consider this to be of major consequence.

3.1 Control Logic

Following Frank [10], we can make branching logic reversible with constant space overhead using paired branching with the destination of a branch being a branch that points back. Thus, we have symmetry, and when running backward, we can just follow the branch we arrived on. However, because we are not working in a fully reversible model, there are some caveats we must pay attention to: all reversible control logic in this section depends on all of the code within the control sequence being reversible. If this is not the case, we can make no guarantees about the correctness when irreversible operations are being performed within some control logic, especially if they are manipulating the variables the control logic depends on.

In Section 2.2 we noted that we can do comparisons reversibly with a single bit of extra space. In this section, we look at jumps, branches, conditionals, for loops, and function calls.

Here we consider the most basic building blocks of control logic, alterations to the program counter in the form of jumps and branches (conditional jumps). Jumps can be performed by a reversible addition to the program counter, we use notation **goto**, **gotoifeq**, and **gotoifneq**. However, if the program counter is allowed to change, we can no longer assume every line was reached by an increment to the program counter, thus creating an irreversible situation. To deal with this, all program counter jumps must be paired with a **comefrom**, **comefromifeq**, or **comefromifneq** statement. In our pseudocode, we allow for **goto** to direct an absoloute or relative jump and note that a compiler can transform absolute to relative, as is used in most reversible architectures.

THEOREM 3.1. *Jumps can be implemented reversibly with constant factor increases in time and space and up to an additive extra word of space per jump.*

PROOF. All jumps must be paired with **comefrom** statements. In the case of a regular **comefrom** statement, the program knows that it reached this location via a jump and thus will jump back in the reverse. However, it is rare that an unconditional jump such as this exist. In the more general case, the program must decide whether the comefrom was reached via a jump or from the line above by an increment in the program counter. To address this, we log two things upon jumping: (1) the length of the jump and (2) a bit indicating that a jump occurred. We then use a **comefromif** to check this bit upon reversing. At the corresponding reverse **comefromif** we'll pop the value off the log stack and use it to either change the program counter or not depending on whether the code jumped to that location.

We can make an additional optimization if a **comefrom** statement only has one corresponding **goto**. Because we know the jump location corresponding with the **comefrom**, this can be implemented reversibly by noting the jump length directly in the source code and not logging. In this case we only have a single bit of storage for logging whether the jump was taken. □

3.1.1 Conditional Statements

We distinguish between two different types of conditionals, a *protected* **if** statement and a general **if** statement. A protected **if** state-

ment is one in which the conditional is not modified within the **if** statement.

THEOREM 3.2. *Protected If statements can be implemented reversibly with constant-factor increases in time and space, and general If statements with an extra bit of overhead in space.*

We now examine a special case of **for** loops. A *simple for loop* is one in which a variable i iterates over the values 1 through k, each time executing some piece of code which does not alter i or k.

THEOREM 3.3. *Simple for loops can be implemented reversibly with constant-factor increases in time and space.*

We consider an extension of the simple for loop. A for loop has *internal conditions* if all variables used in the condition of the for loop only exist within the scope of the for loop. That value is *protected* if it is never changed irreversibly. We define a *protected* for loop as a for loop with protected, internal conditions.

THEOREM 3.4. *A protected for loop can be performed reversibly with constant factor overhead in time and space.*

THEOREM 3.5. *A general for loop can be performed reversibly with constant factor overhead in time and an extra word of space representing the number of loop executions.*

THEOREM 3.6. *Function calls can be implemented reversibly with constant-factor increases in time and space.*

THEOREM 3.7. *Memory allocation using free lists can be done reversibly with constant-factor overheads in time and space.*

Garbage collection often uses a technique known as reference counting. Reference counting keeps track of the number of references to an object or resource and deallocates the space when it is no longer referenced. In our analysis, we do not charge the cost of freeing or destroying the objects to the algorithm. Since this destruction would need to happen regardless of what sort of garbage collection, if any, was performed we believe the energy costs involved are not a fair representation of the work done by the garbage collector itself.

THEOREM 3.8. *Reference Counting can be done reversibly with constant-factor overhead in space and time.*

THEOREM 3.9. *Mark and Sweep can be done reversibly with constant-factor overhead in space and time.*

4. ENERGY REDUCTION TECHNIQUES

This section overviews some general techniques that have been helpful in constructing reversible algorithms and proves some general theorems about algorithms sharing certain properties.

4.1 Complete Logging

One very simple, yet surprisingly useful technique is to simply log every step of an algorithm. This incurs a space cost of $O(t(n))$ words where $t(n)$ is the runtime of the algorithm. Although this seems wasteful, the prevalence of linear time algorithms or linear time sub-routines in algorithms makes this important to remember.

4.2 Reversible Subroutine

Earlier we saw that function calls can be implemented reversibly. We now give a stronger result for being able to use some reversible subroutines efficiently.

THEOREM 4.1. *If we have a fully reversible subroutine whose only effect on the program is through its return value, one need only store the inputs and outputs to this subroutine to later unroll it with only a constant-factor overhead in time.*

PROOF. To do this, we use a slightly more complicated, two-step unrolling process. First, after the subroutine has initially run, we copy out the output and immediately unroll the subroutine. This copy of the output looks no different to the rest of the program from what would normally be computed, and we've already stipulated that the subroutine cannot alter the program through any other means. When it comes time to unroll the subroutine, we may have lost important logged information needed to take us from the output back to the input. At this point, we run the subroutine forward, recovering all of that needed information. Next we delete the copy of the output and unroll the subroutine normally. □

4.3 Data Structure Rebuilding

When attempting to implement data structures which support insert and delete operations reversibly, we run into a new challenge. Often the insertion or deletion operation will create some amount of garbage data which is necessary to reverse it in the future. We also need the result of the operation to remain in place, so we cannot immediately reverse the operation. Thus over the life of the data structure, its size will depend on the total number of insert and delete operations, rather than just the number of elements in the data structure. To circumvent this we can use a technique we call *periodic unwinding*. Note, this technique depends exceedingly on what is considered the data-structure and what is an algorithm that uses the data-structure. This is discussed more below and in Section 5.

THEOREM 4.2. *If a data structure which allows reversible insertions, deletions, and traversals can be constructed reversibly from k insertions in $O(k)$ time and space, and its operations can be performed reversibly with constant-factor overhead in time and space, then it can be maintained reversibly in amortized time with constant-factor overheads in space and time via periodic unwinding.*

PROOF. If there are only $O(n)$ deletions, then we can simply log and unroll all of the operations. If not, we need to keep track of the number of insertions and deletions that have occurred because the last rebuilding. We will keep track of these counts and increment them as part of the insertion or deletion routine. We also track the number of elements in the data structure. Whenever a delete is called, we then check to see whether the number of deletions is more than twice the number of nodes in the data structure. If this is true, we will proceeded to rebuild the data structure. We perform a reversible traversal of the tree, with the addition that we make an extra copy of the inserted data at every node. Now that we have this copy, we can proceed to unroll the data structure, clearing the log. Once this is done we construct a new data structure with the same values as before the reversing, but with none of the accumulated garbage. Construction of the new data structure takes $O(n)$ time. To trigger a rebuilding, we must have called delete a larger number of times than the size of the data structure we are building. We charge the amortized constant cost per element being added to

the new data structure to the number of deletes performed, giving us constant amortized time. Our counters and copies of the data all require $O(n)$ space, meaning we never use more than a constant-factor overhead in space. □

With this method, after rebuilding and clearing the log, the data structure can no longer provide any information about past items which were deleted from the data structure. This is covered by the assumption that the algorithm interacting with the data structure makes copies of all of its inputs and if it needs them to reverse itself, it is responsible for maintaining that information. Thus, depending on how the data structure is being used, this technique can be superfluous or very powerful.

5. DATA STRUCTURES

Data structures are meant to be used in the context of an algorithm. In the standard model for algorithms, we can draw a nice abstraction between these two and analyze their properties separately. We also wish to do so in the energy complexity model; however, we need to be more careful about the responsibilities of the data structure and the algorithm for maintaining information and reversibility. First, we assume the data structure is only accessed through the prescribed operations; we don't want the algorithm irreversibly altering stored elements or manually altering the data structure in an unknown way. Second, if it is a reversible data structure, every operation must have a reverse operation. Third, when inserting, the algorithm gives a copy of the data to the data structure and is responsible for maintaining its own reversibility after an insert has been reversed. Fourth, the algorithm will handle zeroing of the bits of elements removed from the data structure. For this purpose, the common delete operation will be replaced with $Extract(x)$ which removes an element from a data structure and returns it; however, we will generally still call this operation delete. Fifth, for a reversible algorithm, it is responsible for making the correct calls to reverse functions to reset the data structure.

This is certainly not the only way to treat this interface. We could just as well require the data structure to remember all of the calls performed on it so it could reverse itself upon command. Similarly, we could imagine that a deleted item cannot be handed back to the algorithm, but must in some way be removed by the data structure, most likely when unrolling. We've chosen our conventions because it more closely matches our idea of how subroutines should work and because it is clearer to us how to analyze such cases.

5.1 Stacks and Linked Lists

THEOREM 5.1. *Doubly-linked lists can be implemented reversibly with constant-factor overheads in time and space.*

COROLLARY 5.2. *Stacks, queues, and dequeues can be implemented reversibly with constant-factor overheads in time and space.*

5.2 Dynamic Arrays

THEOREM 5.3. *Dynamic arrays can be implemented reversibly with constant time and space overhead with an extra bit of space for* ADD/DELETE *operations. Size of the structure grows with the number of* ADD/DELETE *operations.*

PROOF. We now consider how to handle these operations reversibly. Because both ADD/DELETE operations work at the end of the array, we check the *length* attribute to find where to perform the reverse operation. For REVERSE-ADD, we remove the element and decrement *length*. And for REVERSE-DELETE, we must log the deleted element to add it back and increment *length*. We must also consider how to handle table doubling. On an ADD/DELETE operation, table doubling (or halving) occurs based on the result of a single comparison of *length* and *size*. We can log a single bit representing the result of this comparison for each ADD/DELETE operation that will indicate whether a table doubling (or halving) needs to be reversed.

This bit is necessary in order to undo table doubling because we can not determine whether a table doubling operation occurred just by looking at the resulting *length* and *size* attributes. For example, consider a table with length n and size $2n$ where the last operation was an ADD. This state could have been reached in two ways. (1) length $n-1$, size n incurring a table double ; (2) length $n-1$, size $2n$.

We maintain the dynamic array to preserve the order and length of its elements in the reverse direction, thus a REVERSE-QUERY operation can be run in the same way as a QUERY operation by simply making the same query again. Periodic rebuilding of this data structure follows from Theorem 4.2 because all operations are reversible with constant factor overhead and rebuild can be done in linear time. □

5.3 AVL Trees

Using and maintaining standard AVL trees incurs an energy cost proportional to the time of the associated operations.

THEOREM 5.4. SEARCH(x) *can be performed on standard AVL trees in* $\Theta(\lg n)$ *time,* $O(1)$ *auxiliary space and* $O(\lg n)$ *energy.*

THEOREM 5.5. INSERT(x) *can be performed on standard AVL trees in* $\Theta(\lg n)$ *time,* $O(1)$ *auxiliary space and* $O(w \lg n)$ *energy.*

THEOREM 5.6. DELETE(x) *can be performed on standard AVL trees in* $\Theta(\lg n)$ *time,* $O(1)$ *auxiliary space and* $O(w \lg n)$ *energy.*

We will show that, provided only SEARCH and INSERT operations are invoked, reversible AVL trees can be maintained with only constant-factor auxiliary space consumption. If DELETE is to be invoked, then the structure will accumulate an extra $\Theta(k)$ words of space for k DELETE operations invoked over the lifetime of the tree. Such space consumption can still be made reasonable within the context of a larger algorithm, provided that runs of INSERT and DELETE form a small part of the algorithm, and are unwound periodically to refresh log space.

Since these algorithms employ only conditional branches which do not modify their conditions (for example, in SEARCH when comparing a value against a node of the tree to choose a branch, we leave the value of the comparison intact post-search), they are completely reversible with no logging penalty.

THEOREM 5.7. SEARCH(x) *can be performed on reversible AVL trees in* $\Theta(\lg n)$ *time,* $O(1)$ *auxiliary space and 0 energy.*

PROOF. Provided that our reversible AVL tree is constructed using two-way nodes, performing SEARCH(x) reversibly is straightforward. Upon reaching a node v in the tree, we compare its value with x and use the resulting bit to determine whether to jump left or right. After jumping, as we have maintained in memory a pointer back to v, we can compare x to v again to destroy this bit and free the space gain. Once the final node is reached and our answer is found or determined to be absent, we can log our result somewhere and reverse our computation to destroy any remaining garbage bits. This procedure uses constant auxiliary space, and produces our answer reversibly in $O(\lg n)$ time. □

INSERT is the next operation we address. It includes the task of reversibly rebalancing the tree, a slightly more complicated task than that of SEARCH.

From a given tree, there may be multiple legal trees that underwent a different rotation to produce it. Thus, if we didn't store any auxiliary information about the AVL rotations as we performed them, it would not be possible to immediately reverse a tree's configuration. A key insight into the space consumption of this process is to note that, for a tree containing n unique elements, each of those elements must occupy at least $\Omega(\lg n)$ bits of space each on average (in the word model in particular, each element takes a constant $w = \Theta(\lg n)$ bits of space). Thus, we must store a $\Theta(\lg n)$-sized entry to a rotation log for each inserted element. The space cost of this logging is absorbed into the space cost of the element's value in the tree itself. This is the premise of the following theorem:

THEOREM 5.8. INSERT(x) *for x not yet present in the reversible AVL tree can be performed in* $\Theta(\lg n)$ *time, preserving the* $\Theta(n)$ *space cost of the tree and using 0 energy.*

PROOF. Insertion consists of traversing the reversible AVL tree, adding the new element to the tree, and making any rotations that are necessary to balance the tree.

Traversing the tree can be done reversibly as in SEARCH(x), and we refer to its proof for reversibility. Once we know where x is to be added into the tree, we create a new node for it and proceed to rebalance the tree.

During the balancing step, rotations begin at the lowest level and proceed upward. To perform our operations reversibly, we will keep a log of every rotation performed at each of the $\lg n$ levels of the tree. For each level, we will store 01 for a right-rotation, 10 for a left-rotation, and 00 for no rotation. By keeping this log, we have enough information to go in the reverse direction, proceeding from the top of the tree to its bottom and checking x's value against those of the encountered nodes to progress. In this way, we keep our INSERT(x) action reversible.

Each log entry need only store a number of bits proportional in size to the maximum height of the tree. Because there are n unique entries in the tree at any given time, each call to INSERT incurs only $O(\lg n)$ bits of space cost. Thus our log, which stores $\Theta(\lg n)$ additional bits per element, results in only a constant-factor increase in the space consumption of the tree. This holds even if deletions from the tree have also been performed, as inserting into a tree will always grow the tree's space consumption asymptotically by $\Omega(\lg n)$ bits per insertion, while the log size will grow by $O(\lg n)$ bits per insertion. The space consumption of the tree is thus preserved to within constant factors. □

THEOREM 5.9. DELETE(x) *can be incorporated into reversible AVL trees, taking* $O(\lg n)$ *time and incurring an additional* $\Theta(k \lg n) = O(kw)$ *bits or* $O(k)$ *words of space for k delete operations.*

5.4 Binary Heaps

THEOREM 5.10. *Binary Heaps can have items inserted irreversibly with* $\Theta(\lg n)$ *time,* $\Theta(1)$ *space, and* $\Theta(\lg n)$ *energy; or reversibly with* $\Theta(\lg n)$ *time,* $\Theta(1)$ *space, and 0 energy.*

THEOREM 5.11. *Binary Heaps can have the root node deleted irreversibly with* $\Theta(\lg n)$ *time,* $\Theta(\lg n)$ *space, and* $\Theta(w \lg n)$ *energy.*

THEOREM 5.12. *Binary Heaps can have the root node deleted reversibly with* $\Theta(\lg n)$ *time,* $\Theta(\lg n)$ *space, and 0 energy.*

As with AVL trees, binary heaps subject to k insertions and deletions will accumulate an extra $O(k)$ space to be maintained. In some cases this can be resolved by periodic unwinding.

6. ALGORITHMS

This section includes the analysis for the time, space, and energy complexity of several standard algorithms in our model. We also give a number of improved algorithms. Some of our results for algorithms with zero energy complexity are similar to results claimed or proved in [10] about reversible algorithms. However, we prove these results within our own model, which differers slightly from [10].

6.1 Sorting

Sorting is among most fundamental and well understood algorithmic problems. In this section we give reversible algorithms for comparison and counting sorts which match the time and space complexities of know irreversible algorithms. It is especially interesting to see this is achievable despite the known entropy change during comparison sorts which give us a lower bound on their time complexity.

6.1.1 Comparison Sort

THEOREM 6.1. *A comparison sort destroying its input must consume* $\Omega(\lg n!)$ *energy.*

We can achieve this energy bound with Merge Sort. Merge Sort takes in an array of numbers, recursively calls itself on half of the array until it reaches the sorted array of size 1. It then merges the returned arrays by iteratively comparing the smallest values in each array and moving it to the beginning of a new sorted array.

THEOREM 6.2. *Comparison sort destroying its input can be done in* $\Theta(n \lg n)$ *time,* $\Theta(n)$ *space, and* $\Theta(n \lg n)$ *energy.*

If we do not destroy the input and are careful with our algorithm, we can do better:

THEOREM 6.3. *Comparison sort, not destroying its input, if performed on an array of* n *w-bit elements with* $\lg n = O(w)$*, can be done reversibly in* $\Theta(n \lg n)$ *time,* $\Theta(n)$ *auxiliary space, and* 0 *energy.*

PROOF. This algorithm is a modification of Merge Sort. In summary, we will we augment each element of the array with its index in the array, and so-equipped shall reversibly merge sort the elements in $\Theta(n \lg n)$ time. After we remove these indices from the sorted array, the output of the algorithm will be the original array L and a sorted copy of the array L_{sorted}.

During a traditional Merge Sort, there are three main steps: dividing the array in two, recursing on each half of the array, and merging the two resultant arrays into a complete, sorted array.

The first step, dividing an array in two, is reversed trivially: Given the two resultant lists of such an operation $L[r:s]$ and $L[s+1:t]$, the original subarray $L[r:t]$ is their concatenation.

The second step, recursing, will be reversible if our entire algorithm is reversible. We know the base case of sorting a size-1 array is reversible, and thus if steps 1 and 3 of our algorithm are also reversible, then this recursive step will be as well.

The third step, in contrast to the first two, presents us with some difficulties. Given a resultant, fully-merged subarray $L_{sorted}[r:t]$,

it is not at all obvious how to go backwards, i.e. how to reproduce the input subarrays $L_{sorted}[r:s]$ and $L_{sorted}[s+1:t]$. Information will be lost in this merge step, and to allow our algorithm to be done reversibly, we must find some way to preserve it.

Our augmentation makes this step possible. Before sorting, we transform L into a new array L' of twice the size, which consists of the elements of L each augmented with their index in L. Thus, the elements of our array are 2-tuples (v, i) of each element's value and original location in L. The above transformation is sufficient to make the merge step reversible. To see why, consider any step in the algorithm in which we are trying to merge two sorted subarrays $L[r:s]$ and $L[s+1:t]$. Denote the merge subroutine that we are trying to compute as $M_{s+\frac{1}{2}}(L[r:s], L[s+1:t])$; that is, we are merging around a pivot $s + \frac{1}{2}$, determined by which step of the algorithm we are presently carrying out. All elements (v, i) with $i < s + \frac{1}{2}$ must have come from $L[r:s]$, and elements with $i > s + \frac{1}{2}$ from $L[s+1:t]$. Given a resultant array $L_{sorted}[r:t] = M_{s+\frac{1}{2}}(L_{sorted}[r:s], L_{sorted}[s+1:t])$, we can reverse the merge operation step-by-step simply by checking each element's index against the pivot $s + \frac{1}{2}$ to determine where it came from. This enables us to construct two-way branches that perform the merge in a way that is instantaneously reversible. Because the pivot is fixed for each step in the algorithm, no information is lost in computing and decomputing it, and thus this step of the algorithm may be implemented reversibly with only constant additional auxiliary space.

The output of the above algorithm is a list L'_{sorted} of (v, i) tuples sorted in the v keys (whereas our original list L' was "sorted" in the i keys).

Now we need only remove the auxiliary indices from the elements (v, i) to produce our unaugmented sorted list L_{sorted}. This step must be handled with care to ensure that every step is reversible. We begin by reproducing the original array L via a single pass over L'_{sorted}, a simple operation that has not yet destroyed any data. Next, we copy out L_{sorted}, the final, sorted array that we care about. What remains is to dismantle L'_{sorted}, and here we shall employ a special trick: We will perform a single pass over the *original* array L, and for every value v encountered we will perform a logged binary search for this element in the *unaugmented* sorted list L_{sorted}. When the element is found, we will know the value v, index i, and the location of the element (v, i) in the augmented sorted array L'_{sorted}. This is sufficient to destroy this element, setting its entry to zero before unrolling the log of our binary search. The complete dismantling operation uses only $\Theta(\lg n)$ additional logging space total, and only takes time $\Theta(n \lg n)$, so our runtime and space consumption are preserved.

This algorithm is instantaneously reversible at every step, and could be implemented using only simple for loops and two-way conditional branches. Thus, the algorithm is completely reversible under our model. Given an array of size $n = O(2^w)$ which occupies nw space in memory, we can reversibly comparison-sort the array using $\Theta(nw)$ bits of auxiliary space in $\Theta(n \lg n)$ time, matching the best irreversible algorithm to within constant-factors of space and time. □

THEOREM 6.4. *Comparison sort, not destroying its input, can be done reversibly on an array of* n *d-bit elements which require* nd *space in* $\Theta(n \lg n)$ *time,* $\Theta(nd)$ *auxiliary space, and* 0 *energy.*

PROOF. As we saw in the preceding theorem, reversible comparison sort is straightforward to perform if we first augment each element in the array with a number corresponding to its index in the original list. When the size of the values d is $\Omega(\lg n)$, then we attain the optimum space bound as the $\lg n$-sized indices get absorbed into the space cost of the d-bit elements. However, we are faced with a conundrum when d is $o(\lg n)$.

To handle this case, we shall employ counting sort in order to reduce the problem of sorting L to the problem of sorting the *unique keys* of L. We utilize a reversible AVL tree (described in Section 5.3) to achieve this.

This algorithm works by reducing the array L only to its unique elements, to sort those elements, and finally to perform a Counting Sort of the original array, consulting our sorted elements to determine the final order. Let k be the number of distinct elements of L. We employ a reversible AVL tree, with actions carefully specified so as to keep them reversible. First, we read the distinct elements of L into the tree, bringing it to a size $O(kd)$, and keeping an $O(n)$-bit uniqueness log and an $O(nd)$-bit rotation log (see reversible AVL trees discussion) as we go. This step takes $O(n \lg n)$ time. Next, we apply Counting Sort on the original array (see Section 6.1.2), consulting the static tree in $O(\lg n)$ time for each element and achieving the $O(n \lg n)$ runtime in this step as well. The output array may be copied and the entire algorithm reversed (Note: not an unrolling of a log, but rather an execution of a reversed version of the algorithm) to leave us with our desired arrays L and L_{sorted}.

This algorithm works by reducing the array L only to its unique elements, to sort those elements, and finally to perform a Counting Sort of the original array, consulting our sorted elements to determine the final order. Let k be the number of distinct elements of L. We employ a reversible AVL tree, with actions carefully specified so as to keep them reversible. First, we read the distinct elements of L into the tree, bringing it to a size $O(kd)$, and keeping an $O(n)$-bit uniqueness log and an $O(nd)$-bit rotation log (see reversible AVL trees discussion) as we go. This step takes $O(n \lg n)$ time. Next, we apply Counting Sort on the original array (see Section 6.1.2), consulting the static tree in $O(\lg n)$ time for each element and achieving the $O(n \lg n)$ runtime in this step as well. The output array may be copied and the entire algorithm reversed (Note: not an unrolling of a log, but rather an execution of a reversed version of the algorithm) to leave us with our desired arrays L and L_{sorted}.

In terms of the intricate details glossed over above, the most involved are in the first step: reversibly constructing a reversible AVL tree out of the unique elements of L. We proceed as follows: making a single pass over our array L, we add every element into the tree. If an element is the first of its exact value to be encountered, we store a corresponding uniqueness bit as true and add the element to the tree. If an element's value already exists in our tree, we store its uniqueness bit as false and move on (never adding duplicates to the tree). These n uniqueness bits allow us to reverse the algorithm, as we know for which elements we modified the tree and on which ones we did not. By theorem 5.8, these insertions take $\Theta(nd)$ space and $O(n \lg n)$ time.

Once the AVL tree is constructed, the rest of the algorithm is a straightforward Counting Sort with a slower $\Theta(\lg k)$ lookup time, yielding the $O(n \lg k)$ time which is optimal for Comparison-based Sort. In addition to the fully-reversible AVL tree data structures, our algorithm employs only simple for-loop passes over the input and reversible two-way branching in the AVL tree, ensuring its reversibility. The entire algorithm takes $\Theta(nd)$ space and $O(n \lg n)$ time, matching the best irreversible comparison sorts up to constant-factors of space and time. □

THEOREM 6.5. *Reversible Duplicated Insertion Sort runs in* $\Theta(n^2)$ *time,* $\Theta(n)$ *space, and* 0 *energy.*

6.1.2 Counting Sort

Counting sort involves counting the number of elements at or below a specific value, and then running through them and adding them to an array based on how many elements are below them. This achieves $\Theta(n + k)$ time and space where k is the size of the maximum integer to be sorted.

THEOREM 6.6. *Counting Sort can be done in* $\Theta(n + k)$ *time,* $\Theta(n + k)$ *space, and* $\Theta(wn + \lg k)$ *energy.*

THEOREM 6.7. *If all entries are unique, then Counting Sort has an energy complexity of* $\Theta(\lg n + \lg k)$ *energy.*

THEOREM 6.8. *Reversible Counting Sort can be done in* $\Theta(n + k)$ *time,* $\Theta(n + k)$ *space, and* 0 *energy.*

6.2 Graph Algorithms

Frank [10] argues that Breadth-first Search and Depth-first search can be done reversibly. We reproduce this result in our model and give a different analysis.

THEOREM 6.9. *Breadth-first Search runs in* $\Theta(V + E)$ *time,* $\Theta(V)$ *space, and* $\Theta(wV + E)$ *energy.*

THEOREM 6.10. *Reversible Breadth-first Search can runs in* $\Theta(V)$ *time,* $\Theta(V + E)$ *space, and* 0 *energy.*

COROLLARY 6.11. *Reversible Depth First Search can runs in* $\Theta(V + E)$ *time,* $\Theta(V)$ *space, and* 0 *energy.*

6.3 Bellman-Ford

THEOREM 6.12. *Bellman-Ford runs in* $\Theta(VE)$ *time,* $\Theta(V + E)$ *space, and* $\Theta(VEw)$ *energy.*

THEOREM 6.13. *Reversible Bellman-Ford runs in* $\Theta(VE)$ *time,* $\Theta(VE)$ *space, and* 0 *energy.*

6.4 Floyd-Warshall

Frank [10] argues that the Floyd-Warshall algorithm can be adapted to run reversibly with $\Theta(V^3)$ space. This is a substantial increase in space to make the program reversible and thus save energy.

THEOREM 6.14. *Floyd-Warshall runs in* $\Theta(V^3)$ *time,* $\Theta(V^2)$ *space, and* $\Theta(V^3 w)$ *energy.*

THEOREM 6.15. *Reversible Floyd-Warshall runs in* $\Theta(V^3)$ *time,* $O(V^3)$ *space, and* 0 *energy.*

6.5 All Pairs Shortest Path via (min, +) Matrix Multiplication

Another algorithm for solving APSP involves using the adjacency matrix representation of a graph A and noticing that the relaxations over the edges can be expressed by calculating a new matrix, C, whose entries are given by $c_{ij} = \min_k(a_{ik} + a_{kj})$. Further, this operation is associative, so we can speed up the calculation by using repeated squaring. Thus we have $O(\lg V)$ iterations over (V^2) elements which take $O(V)$ time to compute. Frank [10] claims without proof that this leads to a reversible algorithm that runs in $\Theta(V^3 \lg V)$ time and $\Theta(V^2 \lg V)$ space. We give a proof of this result.

THEOREM 6.16. *Reversible APSP using repeated squaring with (min,+) matrix multiplication runs in $O(V^3 \lg V)$ time, $O(V^2 \lg V)$ space, and 0 energy.*

THEOREM 6.17. *APSP using repeated squaring with (min,+) matrix multiplication runs in $O(V^3 \lg V)$ time, $O(V^2)$ space, and $O(wV^3 \lg V)$ energy.*

We now present a new variation on APSP which demonstrates a non-trivial trade-off between energy and space. By exploiting reversible subroutines, we're able to reach the APSP with repeated squaring bounds on time and space, but beat it in energy cost. The reversible, semi-reversible, and standard APSP using repeated squaring demonstrate there are semi-reversible algorithms that actually achieve bounds not reached by the fully reversible or fully irreversible counterparts.

THEOREM 6.18. *Semi-reversible APSP using repeated squaring with (min,+) matrix multiplication runs in $O(V^3 \lg V)$ time, $O(V^2)$ space, and $O(wV^2 \lg V)$ energy.*

PROOF. To begin, we will examine how each individual entry in the matrix is updated. Say we have a graph represented by adjacency matrix $W = (w_{i,j})$, and a matrix $L^{(m)} = (l_{i,j}^{(m)})$ representing the shortest paths between two vertices with path length at most m. Each entry is updated as

$$l_{i,j}^{(m+1)} = \min_{1 \le k \le |V|} \left(l_{i,j}^{(m)} + w_{k,j} \right)$$

This subroutine runs in $O(V)$ time and $O(wV)$ energy and can thus be trivially made reversible by logging everything, using $O(V)$ time and space. We replace our normal update function with the new reversible one, and by Theorem 3.6 we have a new, more energy efficient algorithm. The subroutine does not use asymptotically more time than before, the temporary use of $O(V)$ space is much smaller than that needed to store the matrices and is freed upon completion of the subroutine, and the energy cost drops by a factor of V which reduces the algorithms total energy cost by a factor of V. □

7. FUTURE DIRECTIONS

This paper built up a framework for designing and analyzing the energy cost of algorithms caused by irreversibility, and started the quest for positive results for basic algorithms and data structures. In many cases, we obtained fully reversible versions of algorithms, but other problems seem more resistant. For example, is there a reversible all-pairs shortest path algorithm with only constant factor overheads in time and space? We managed to give a reduced-energy semi-reversible algorithm for the problem, but a fully reversible algorithm still seems elusive. Shortest-path algorithms more generally seem like a category that are difficult to make reversible, as they use very little space and make frequent use of rewriting old values. We anticipate other graph problems such as max-flow/min-cut may also be challenging and interesting for similar reasons.

There are more fundamental algorithms that should be given high priority given their use in many other results: hashing, predecessor data structures (e.g., van Emde Boas trees), max-flow/min-cut, Fast Fourier Transforms, and dynamic programming. Geometric algorithms offer more nontrivial challenges to attain reversibility, such as line intersection, orthogonal range finding, convex hull, and Delaunay triangulations. We also see the field of machine learning being an interesting target for analysis in the semi-reversible

model: these algorithms often have significantly higher time complexities than space complexities, fundamental updates (such as Bayes' rule) which appear reversible, and many conditional updates or data overwrites.

One important question for any practical application is how to deal with long-running programs. Although we are perfectly happy to log some auxiliary information during the execution of a specific program, it may be more problematic to maintain reversibility for the entire operating system of a computer or a long-lived database. This is an area we believe ideas like semi-reversibility and periodic rebuilding will become particularly important.

There are some areas where we see slight extensions of the model opening up interesting questions. First, incorporating randomness seems a practical necessity and carries interesting thermodynamic implications depending on how it is modeled. Assuming there is an energy cost associated with the production of randomness (say, equal to the number of random bits), this may give further reason to investigate exactly how much randomness is needed for an algorithm's correctness. Streaming algorithms and other models where the working space is much smaller than the problem input seem like a rich source of problems. Because we now use sublinear space, our trivial transform is no longer applicable. Further, the larger the gap in space and time, the less ability we have to accrue garbage. Finally, succinct data structures, which try to minimize the bits of space used up to sublinear factors, seem like another challenge: many of our transforms double or triple the space being used by an algorithm, while in the succinct setting, this overhead must be considered.

Finally, a major open direction is to obtain lower bounds. The additional constraints on semi-reversible algorithm design might allow showing algorithms cannot be obtained without some minimum time-space-energy trade-off.

Acknowledgments

We thank Martin Demaine and Kevin Kelley for helpful early discussions about this project, in particular early formulations of the models of computation. We also thank Maria L. Messick and Licheng Rao for useful discussion and help clarifying our pseudocode and model.

References

[1] S. Albers. Energy-efficient algorithms. *Commun. ACM*, 53(5):86–96, May 2010.

[2] H. B. Axelsen. Clean translation of an imperative reversible programming language. In *Compiler Construction*, pages 144–163. Springer, 2011.

[3] C. H. Bennett. Logical reversibility of computation. *IBM Journal of Research and Development*, 17(6):525–532, 1973.

[4] C. H. Bennett. Time/space trade-offs for reversible computation. *SIAM Journal on Computing*, 18(4):766–776, Aug. 1989.

[5] C. H. Bennett, P. Gács, M. Li, P. M. Vitányi, and W. H. Zurek. Information distance. *IEEE Transactions on Information Theory*, 44(4):1407–1423, 1998.

[6] A. Berut, A. Arakelyan, A. Petrosyan, S. Ciliberto, R. Dillenschneider, and E. Lutz. Experimental verification of Landauer's principle linking information and thermodynamics. *Nature*, 483(7388):187–189, 2012.

[7] H. Buhrman, J. Tromp, and P. Vitãₐnyi. Time and space bounds for reversible simulation. In F. Orejas, P. G. Spirakis,

and J. van Leeuwen, editors, *Proceedings of the 28th International Colloquium on Automata, Languages and Programming*, volume 2076 of *Lecture Notes in Computer Science*, pages 1017–1027. Springer Berlin Heidelberg, 2001.

[8] Cyclos Semiconductor. Cyclos Semiconductor announces first commercial implementation of resonant clock mesh technology. http://www.cyclos-semi.com/news/first_commercial_implementation.html, Feb. 2012.

[9] eMarketer. Smartphone users worldwide will total 1.75 billion in 2014. http://www.emarketer.com/Article/Smartphone-Users-Worldwide-Will-Total-175-Billion-2014/1010536, Jan. 2014.

[10] M. P. Frank. *Reversibility for efficient computing*. PhD thesis, Massachusetts Institute of Technology, 1999.

[11] R. Jain, D. Molnar, and Z. Ramzan. Towards a model of energy complexity for algorithms. In *Proceedings of the 2005 IEEE Wireless Communications and Networking Conference*, volume 3, pages 1884–1890, 2005.

[12] G. Kissin. Upper and lower bounds on switching energy in vlsi. *J. ACM*, 38(1):222–254, Jan. 1991.

[13] J. G. Koomey. *Growth in data center electricity use 2005 to 2010*. Analytics Press, Aug. 2011.

[14] J. G. Koomey, S. Berard, M. Sanchez, and H. Wong. Implications of historical trends in the electrical efficiency of computing. *IEEE Annals of the History of Computing*, 33(3):46–54, March 2011.

[15] V. A. Korthikanti and G. Agha. Towards optimizing energy costs of algorithms for shared memory architectures. In *Proceedings of the 22nd Annual ACM Symposium on Parallelism in Algorithms and Architectures*, pages 157–165, New York, NY, USA, 2010. ACM.

[16] V. A. Korthikanti, G. Agha, and M. R. Greenstreet. On the energy complexity of parallel algorithms. In G. R. Gao and Y.-C. Tseng, editors, *Proceedings of the 2011 International Conference on Parallel Processing*, pages 562–570, 2011.

[17] J. Ladyman, S. Presnell, A. J. Short, and B. Groisman. The connection between logical and thermodynamic irreversibility. *Studies In History and Philosophy of Science Part B: Studies In History and Philosophy of Modern Physics*, 38(1):58–79, 2007.

[18] B. Lambson, D. Carlton, and J. Bokor. Exploring the thermodynamic limits of computation in integrated systems: magnetic memory, nanomagnetic logic, and the Landauer limit. *Phys Rev Lett*, 107(1):010604, 2011.

[19] R. Landauer. Irreversibility and heat generation in the computing process. *IBM Journal of Research and Development*, 5(3):261–269, 1961.

[20] K.-J. Lange, P. Mckenzie, and A. Tapp. Reversible space equals deterministic space. In *Proceedings of the 12th Annual IEEE Conference on Computational Complexity*, pages 45–50, 1997.

[21] Y. Lecerf. Logique mathematique. machines de Turing réversibles. récursive insolubilité en $n \in N$ de l'équation $u = \theta^n u$, où θ est un "isomorphisme de codes". note. *Comptes rendus hebdomadaires des séances de l'Academie des sciences*, 257(18):2597–2600, October 1963.

[22] M. Li and P. Vitányi. Theory of thermodynamics of computation. In *Proceedings of the IEEE Physics of Computation Workshop*, pages 42–46, 1992.

[23] M. Li and P. Vitányi. Reversibility and adiabatic computation: trading time and space for energy. *Proceedings of the Royal Society of London A: Mathematical, Physical and Engineering Sciences*, 452(1947):769–789, 1996.

[24] M. Li and P. Vitányi. *An introduction to Kolmogorov Complexity and its Applications*. Springer, 3rd edition, 2008.

[25] C. Lutz and H. Derby. Janus: a time-reversible language. *Caltech class project*, 1982.

[26] O. J. E. Maroney. Generalizing Landauer's principle. *Phys. Rev. E*, 79:031105, Mar 2009.

[27] M. Morrison and N. Ranganathan. Design of a reversible alu based on novel programmable reversible logic gate structures. In *Proceedings of the 2011 IEEE Computer Society Annual Symposium on VLSI*, pages 126–131, 2011.

[28] M. Nachtigal, H. Thapliyal, and N. Ranganathan. Design of a reversible single precision floating point multiplier based on operand decomposition. In *Proceedings of the 10th IEEE Conference on Nanotechnology*, pages 233–237, Aug 2010.

[29] M. Nachtigal, H. Thapliyal, and N. Ranganathan. Design of a reversible floating-point adder architecture. In *Proceedings of the 11th IEEE Conference on Nanotechnology*, pages 451–456, Aug 2011.

[30] B. Piechocinska. Information erasure. *Phys. Rev. A*, 61:062314, May 2000.

[31] V. S. Sathe, A. Arekapudi, A. T. Ishii, C. Ouyang, M. C. Papaefthymiou, and S. Naffziger. Resonant-clock design for a power-efficient, high-volume x86-64 microprocessor. *IEEE Journal of Solid-State Circuits*, 48(1):140–149, 2013.

[32] M. K. Thomsen, H. B. Axelsen, and R. Glück. A reversible processor architecture and its reversible logic design. In *Proceedings of the 3rd International Conference on Reversible Computation*, pages 30–42, Gent, Belgium, 2012.

[33] C. Velazco. AMD's new FX processor reaches world record clock speed. http://techcrunch.com/2011/09/13/amds-new-fx-processor-reaches-world-record-clock-speed/, Sept. 2011.

[34] C. Vieri, M. J. Ammer, M. Frank, N. Margolus, and T. Knight. A fully reversible asymptotically zero energy microprocessor. In *Proceedings of the Power Driven Microarchitecture Workshop*, pages 138–142, 1998.

[35] C. J. Vieri. *Reversible computer engineering and architecture*. PhD thesis, Massachusetts Institute of Technology, 1999.

[36] P. Vitányi. Time, space, and energy in reversible computing. In *Proceedings of the 2Nd Conference on Computing Frontiers*, CF '05, pages 435–444, New York, NY, USA, 2005. ACM.

[37] R. Williams. Space-efficient reversible simulations. Technical report, DIMACS REU report, 2000. http://web.stanford.edu/~rrwill/spacesim9_22.pdf.

[38] S. Yates, E. Daley, B. Gray, J. P. Gownder, and R. Batiancila. *Worldwide PC Adoption Forecast, 2007 To 2015*. Forrester, June 2007. http://www.foresightfordevelopment.org/sobipro/download-file/46-724/54.

[39] T. Yokoyama. Reversible computation and reversible programming languages. *Electronic Notes in Theoretical Computer Science*, 253(6):71–81, 2010.

[40] W. H. Zurek. Thermodynamic cost of computation, algorithmic complexity and the information metric. *Nature*, 341:119–124, Sept. 1989.

How to Bootstrap Anonymous Communication

Sune K. Jakobsen
School of Mathematical Sciences and School of
Electronic Engineering and Computer Science
Queen Mary University of London
S.K.Jakobsen@qmul.ac.uk

Claudio Orlandi
Department of Computer Science
Aarhus University
orlandi@cs.au.dk

ABSTRACT

We ask whether it is possible to anonymously communicate a large amount of data using only public (non-anonymous) communication together with a small anonymous channel. We think this is a central question in the theory of anonymous communication and to the best of our knowledge this is the first formal study in this direction.

Towards this goal, we introduce the novel concept of *anonymous steganography*: think of a leaker Lea who wants to leak a large document to Joe the journalist. Using anonymous steganography Lea can embed this document in innocent looking communication on some popular website (such as cat videos on *YouTube* or funny memes on *9GAG*). Then Lea provides Joe with a short decoding key dk which, *when applied to the entire website*, recovers the document while hiding the identity of Lea among the large number of users of the website. Our contributions include:

- Introducing and formally defining *anonymous steganography*,

- A construction showing that anonymous steganography is possible (which uses recent results in circuits obfuscation),

- A lower bound on the number of bits which are needed to bootstrap anonymous communication.

1. INTRODUCTION

The problem. Lea the leaker wants to leak a big document to Joe the journalist in an anonymous way.[1] Lea has a way of anonymously communicating a small number of bits to Joe, but the size of the document she wants to leak is orders of magnitudes greater than the capacity of the anonymous channel between them. In this paper we ask whether it is possible to "bootstrap" anonymous communication, in the sense that we want to construct a "large" anonymous

[1]This naming convention is courtesy of Nadia Heninger.

Permission to make digital or hard copies of all or part of this work for personal or classroom use is granted without fee provided that copies are not made or distributed for profit or commercial advantage and that copies bear this notice and the full citation on the first page. Copyrights for components of this work owned by others than the author(s) must be honored. Abstracting with credit is permitted. To copy otherwise, or republish, to post on servers or to redistribute to lists, requires prior specific permission and/or a fee. Request permissions from Permissions@acm.org.

ITCS'16, January 14–16, 2016, Cambridge, MA, USA.
Copyright is held by the owner/author(s). Publication rights licensed to ACM.
ACM 978-1-4503-4057-1/16/01 ...$15.00.
DOI: http://dx.doi.org/10.1145/2840728.2840743

channel using only public (non-anonymous) communication channels together with a "small" anonymous channel. We find the question to be central to the theory of anonymous communication and to the best of our knowledge this is the first formal study in this direction.

Steganography. The goal of (traditional) steganography is to hide that a certain communication is taking place, by embedding sensitive content in innocent looking traffic (such as pictures, videos, or other redundant documents). There is no doubt that steganography is a useful tool for Lea the leaker: using steganography she could send sensitive documents to Joe the journalist in such a way that even someone monitoring all internet traffic would not be able to notice that this communication is taking place. However, steganography alone cannot help Lea if she wants to make sure that *even Joe* does not learn her identity.

Anonymous Steganography. To solve this problem, we introduce a novel cryptographic primitive, which we call *anonymous steganography*. Very informally, anonymous steganography works in the following way: Lea wants to communicate a sensitive (large) message x to Joe. To do so, she embeds x in some (large) innocent looking document c which she uploads to a popular website (not necessarily in an anonymous way). Then Lea produces some (short) decoding key dk (which is a function of c and all other documents on the website – or at least a set large enough so that her identity is hidden in a large group of users, such as "all videos uploaded last week") which she then communicates to Joe using an anonymous channel. Now Joe is able to recover the original message x from the website using the decoding key dk, but at the same time Joe has no way of telling which document contains the message (and therefore which of the website users is the leaker). Intuitively, it is crucial for Lea's anonymity that Joe can only decode *the entire website*: if Joe had a way of decoding single documents (or portions) he would easily be able to pinpoint which document actually contains the leaked message.

In Section 2 we formally introduce anonymous steganography and in Section 3 we show how to construct such a scheme. Unfortunately our positive result crucially relies on heavy tools such as homomorphic encryption and indistinguishability obfuscation for circuits ($i\mathcal{O}$ for short), making it very far from being useful in practice. We leave it as a major open question to construct such schemes using simpler and more efficient cryptographic tools (perhaps even at the price of relaxing the definition of anonymity). Other open problems include studying whether the computational complexity for the leaker must depend on the size of the anonymity set if the leaker is given a hash of all the documents, and whether it is possible to construct more efficient protocols if multiple leakers are leaking to Joe at once.

Lower Bounds. In the scheme described above, Lea sends Joe a decoding key dk using a (pre-existing) anonymous channel. It is a natural question to ask whether this is necessary, or if we can construct a scheme where all communication between Lea and Joe takes place over regular channels. Unfortunately the latter is too good to be true, and in Section 5 we prove that it is impossible to construct an anonymous steganography scheme unless Lea sends a key (of super-logarithmic size) to Joe. The idea behind the proof is: if the scheme is correct at some point the probability that Joe outputs x has to increase from polynomially small to 1. Joe can estimate how each message (sent by any of the users over the non-anonymous channel) affects this probability and concludes that the message which changes this probability the most must come from Lea. Hence, the messages that causes this increase has to be sent over an anonymous channel.

Related Work. Steganography and information-hiding are an important line of research in the signal-processing community. For a background on steganographic techniques see one of the textbooks on the subject e.g., [Fri09]. For a more complexity-theoretic treatment of steganography (both in the private- and in the public-key setting) see e.g. [HLA02, HAL09, AH04, BC05, FNP14] and references therein. There exist practical tools which allow whistleblowers to anonymously communicate with journalists, such as SecureDrop, which in turns relies on Tor [DMS04]. Tor is by far the most popular anonymous internet communication system, and relies on a volunteer network of relays. Several countries have tried, with different degrees of success, to block or limit Tor traffic [WL12]. While anonymous steganography is in no way practical at this stage, we find the question of whether similar ideas could be used to amplify the bandwidth offered by systems like Tor combining anonymous and non-anonymous channels extremely intriguing. *Message In A Bottle* [IKV13] is a protocol where Lea can encrypt her message under Joe's public key, embed it in an image using steganography and post the image on any blog. Joe will now monitor all blogs to see if someone left a (concealed) message for him. Interestingly [IKV13] shows that this approach is feasible in practice and because Lea can use any blog, it will be costly for e.g. a government to prevent Lea from sending the message to Joe. However, in this protocol Joe learns Lea's identity, which is what we are trying to prevent in our work. In *cryptogenography* [BJSW14, Jak14] a group of users cooperate to allow a leaker to publish a message with some reasonable degree of anonymity: here we want that anyone should be able to recover the message from the protocol transcript, but no one (even a computationally unbounded observers) should be able to determine with certainty the identity of the leaker. In other words in cryptogenography we are happy as long as the observer cannot produce evidence which proves with certainty the identity of the leaker (which could be used e.g., in a court case). In [BJSW14] the leaker can publish one bit correctly but no observer can guess the identity of the leaker with probability more than 44%. In [Jak14] instead a different setting is considered, where multiple leakers agree to publish some information while hiding their identity by blending into an arbitrarily large group. The leakers do not need perfect anonymity, but just want to ensure that for each leaker, an observer will never assign a probability greater that c to the event that that person is a leaker. It is shown that for any $\epsilon > 0$ and sufficiently large n, n leakers can publish $\left(-\frac{\log(1-c)}{c} - \log(e) - \epsilon\right) n$ bits, where e is the base of the natural logarithm. Our work is inspired by the model in [Jak14]. The main difference is that we assume the adversary has bounded computational power, so we only need one leaker and we get all but negligible anonymity. In [IKOS06] the authors investigated how an anonymous channel could be used to implement other cryptographic primitives, but not if it could be used to bootstrap a larger anonymous channel. From a technical point of view, our positive result is inspired by the clever techniques of Hubáček and Wichs [HW15] to compress communication using $i\mathcal{O}$ for circuits.

2. DEFINITIONS

Notation. We write $[x, y]$ with $x < y \in \mathbb{N}$ as a shorthand for $\{x, \ldots, y\}$ and $[x]$ as a shorthand for $[1, x]$. If v is a vector $(v_1, \ldots, v_n)$ then v_{-i} is a vector such that $(v_1, \ldots, v_{i-1}, \perp, v_{i+1}, \ldots v_n)$ and $(v_{-i}, v_i) = v$. (This notation trivially extends to multiple indices). A function is *negligible* if it goes to 0 faster than the inverse of any polynomial. We write $\mathsf{poly}(\cdot)$ and $\mathsf{negl}(\cdot)$ for a generic polynomial and negligible function respectively (When we write about asymptotic behaviour, e.g. "super-logarithmic size", "polynomial size" or "exponentially small" without explicitly mentioning which parameter we are comparing with, the implicit parameter is always the security parameter λ.). $x \leftarrow S$ denotes sampling a uniform element x from a set S. If A is an algorithm $x \leftarrow A$ is the output of A on a uniformly random tape. We highlight constants $\alpha, \beta, \ldots$, hardwired in a circuit C using the notation $C[\alpha, \beta, \ldots]$.

Anonymous Steganography. For the sake of presentation, we make the simplifying assumption that honest users sample their documents independently from the uniform distribution. It is then possible to combine our scheme with a regular steganographic scheme to obtain anonymous steganography for arbitrary sources, as discussed in Section 4.

We define an *anonymous steganography* scheme as a tuple of algorithms $\pi = (\mathsf{Gen}, \mathsf{Enc}, \mathsf{KeyEx}, \mathsf{Dec})$. All algorithms, even when not specified, take as input the security parameter λ, and the length parameters s, ℓ, ℓ', d (s is *short*, ℓ is *long*). The syntax of the algorithm is as follows:

- $ek \leftarrow \mathsf{Gen}(1^\lambda)$ is a randomized algorithm which generates an encoding key ek.

- $c \leftarrow \mathsf{Enc}_{ek}(x)$ is a randomized algorithm which encodes a secret message $x \in \{0,1\}^{\ell'}$ into a (random looking) document $c \in \{0,1\}^\ell$.

- $dk \leftarrow \mathsf{KeyEx}_{ek}(t, i)$ takes as input a public vector of documents $t \in (\{0,1\}^\ell)^d$, an index $i \in [d]$ such that $t_i = c$ and extracts a (short) decoding key $dk \in \{0,1\}^s$.

- $x' = \mathsf{Dec}_{dk}(t)$ recovers a message x' using the decoding key dk and the public vector of documents t in a deterministic way.

Remark. We chose to keep Gen separated from Enc since a single key could be used to encode multiple messages –

in a natural extension of the scheme Lea hides her secret(s) in a subset of documents $I \subset [d]$. Finally, KeyEx is a separated algorithm since it takes as input documents which are generated from honest users *after* c is published.

How to Use The Scheme. To use anonymous steganography, Lea generates the encoding key ek using Gen, waits until some honest users publish content online and then encodes her secret x using Enc_{ek} to get the c. Lea then uploads c to this website, and waits until more honest content is published. Then she chooses the set of documents she is hiding among, for example, all files uploaded to this website during that day/week. Lea then downloads all these documents t and finds the index i of her own document in this set. Finally she computes $dk \leftarrow \mathsf{KeyEx}_{ek}(t, i)$, and uses the small anonymous channel to send dk to Joe together with a pointer to t.

Properties. We require the following properties: *correctness* (meaning that $x' = x$ with overwhelming probability), *compactness* (meaning that $s < \ell'$) and *anonymity* (meaning that the receiver does not learn any information about i). Another natural requirement is *confidentiality* (meaning that one should not be able to learn the message without the decoding key dk), but it is easy to see that this follows from *anonymity*. Formal definitions follow:

Definition 1 (Correctness). *We say an anonymous steganography scheme is q-correct if for all $\lambda \in \mathbb{N}, x \in \{0, 1\}^{\ell'}$, $i \in [d], t_{-i} \in (\{0, 1\}^{\ell})^{d-1}$ over $\{0, 1\}^{\ell}$ the following holds:*

$$\Pr\left[\mathsf{Dec}_{dk}\left((t_{-i}, c)\right) = x\right] \geq q,$$

where $ek \leftarrow \mathsf{Gen}(1^{\lambda})$, $c \leftarrow \mathsf{Enc}_{ek}(x)$, $dk \leftarrow \mathsf{KeyEx}_{ek}((t_{-i}, c), i)$ and the probabilities are taken over all the random coin flips. We simply say that a scheme is correct *when $q \geq 1 - \mathsf{negl}(\lambda)$.*

Definition 2 (Anonymity). *We define a game between an adversary $\mathcal{A}$ and a challenger $\mathcal{C}$:*

1. *The challenger $\mathcal{C}$ generates a key $ek \leftarrow \mathsf{Gen}(1^{\lambda})$;*

2. *The adversary $\mathcal{A}$ outputs a message $x \in \{0, 1\}^{\ell'}$, two indices $i_0 \neq i_1 \in [d]$, and a vector $t_{-(i_0, i_1)}$;*

3. *The challenger $\mathcal{C}$:*

   (a) *samples a bit $b \leftarrow \{0, 1\}$;*

   (b) *computes $t_{i_b} \leftarrow \mathsf{Enc}_{ek}(x)$ and samples $t_{i_{1-b}} \leftarrow \{0, 1\}^{\ell}$;*

   (c) *computes $dk \leftarrow \mathsf{KeyEx}_{ek}\left((t_{-(i_0, i_1)}, (t_{i_0}, t_{i_1})), i_b\right)$*

   (d) *outputs dk, t;*

4. *$\mathcal{A}$ outputs a guess bit g;*

We say π satisfies anonymity *if for all PPT $\mathcal{A}$*

$$\left| \Pr[g = b] - \frac{1}{2} \right| = \mathsf{negl}(\lambda).$$

Building Blocks. We will need the following ingredients in our construction: 1) an *indistinguishability obfuscator* ($i\mathcal{O}$) $\bar{C} \leftarrow \mathcal{O}(C)$ which takes any polynomial size circuit C and outputs an obfuscated version $\bar{C}$ [GGH+13]; 2) A *compact* homomorphic encryption scheme (HE.G, HE.E, HE.D, HE.Eval); 3) A pseudorandom function f; 4) A vector commitment scheme (VC.G, VC.C, VC.D, VC.V) which allows to commit to a long string x using VC.C, and where it is possible to decommit to individual bits of x using VC.D. Crucially, the proof of correct decommitting π^j for any bit j has size at most polylogarithmic in $|x|$. In addition, we need that the vector commitment scheme is *somewhere statistically binding* according to the definition of Hubáček and Wichs [HW15]: in a nutshell, this means that when generating a commitment key ck it is possible to specify a special position i such that a) any commitment generated using the key ck is statistically binding for the i-th bit of x (this property is crucial to be able to verify these commitments inside circuits obfuscated using $i\mathcal{O}$) and that b) ck computationally hides the index i. Such a vector commitment scheme can be constructed from fully-homomorphic encryption [HW15]. Formal definitions of these tools can be found in the full version of this paper [?].

3. A PROTOCOL FOR ANONYMOUS STEGANOGRAPHY

We start with a high-level description of our protocol (in steps) before presenting the actual construction and proving that it satisfies our notion of anonymity.

First attempt. Let the encoding key ek be a key for a PRF f, and let the encoding procedure simply be a random looking "symmetric encryption" of x using this PRF. Clearly now the resulting document c is indistinguishable from other elements sampled from the uniform distribution over $\{0, 1\}^{\ell}$.

In this first attempt we let the decoding key dk be the obfuscation of a circuit $C[i, ek, \gamma](t)$: The circuit contains two hard-wired secrets, the index of Lea's document $i \in [d]$ and the key for the PRF ek. It also contains the hash of the entire set of documents $\gamma = H(t)$. On input a database t the circuit checks if $\gamma = H(t)$ and if this is the case outputs x by decrypting t_i with ek.

Clearly this first attempt fails miserably since the size of the circuit is now proportional to the size of the entire database $t = d\ell$, which is even larger than the size of the secret message $|x| = \ell' \leq \ell$.

Second attempt.[2] To remove the dependency on the number of documents d, we include in the decoding key an encryption $\alpha = \mathsf{HE.E}_{pk}(i)$ of the index i (using the homomorphic encryption scheme), and an obfuscation of a (new) circuit $C[ek, sk, \gamma](\beta)$, which contains hardwired secrets ek and sk (the secret key for the homomorphic encryption scheme), as well as a hash $\gamma = H(\mathsf{HE.Eval}(\mathsf{mux}[t], \alpha))$, where the circuit $\mathsf{mux}[t](i)$ outputs t_i. The circuit C now checks that $\gamma = H(\beta)$ and if this is the case computes $t_i \leftarrow \mathsf{HE.D}_{sk}(\beta)$ using the secret key of the HE scheme, then decrypts t_i using the PRF key ek and outputs the secret message x. When Joe receives the decoding key dk, Joe constructs the circuit $\mathsf{mux}[t]$ (using the public t) and (re)-computes $\beta = \mathsf{HE.Eval}(\mathsf{mux}[t], \alpha)$. To learn the secret, he runs the obfuscated circuit on β.

In other words, we are now exploiting the compactness of the homomorphic encryption scheme to let Joe compute an encryption of the document $c = t_i$ from the public database t and the encryption of i. Since Lea the leaker can predict

---
[2] A different approach at this stage could be to use $i\mathcal{O}$ for Turing machines [KLW15]. Unfortunately, [KLW15] uses *complexity-leveraging* and therefore must assume *subexponentially hard* $i\mathcal{O}$ for circuits, while the solution described next will be secure using only standard hardness.

this ciphertext[3], she can construct a circuit which only decrypts when this particular ciphertext is provided as input. However, the size of β (and therefore C) is proportional to $\mathsf{poly}(\lambda) + \ell$, thus we are still far from our goal.[4]

Third attempt. To remove the dependency from the length of the document ℓ, we construct a circuit which takes as input an encryption of a single bit j of t_i instead of the whole ciphertext. However, we also need to make sure that the circuit only decrypts these particular ciphertexts, and does not help Joe in decrypting anything else. Moreover, the circuit must perform this check in an efficient way (meaning, independent of the size of ℓ), so we cannot simply "precompute" these ℓ ciphertexts and hardwire them into C.

This is where we use the vector commitment scheme: we let the decoding key include a (short) commitment key ck. We include in the obfuscated circuit a (short) commitment $\gamma = \mathsf{VC.C}_{ck}(\beta)$ (where $\beta = (\beta^1, \ldots, \beta^\ell)$ is a vector of encryptions of bits) and we make sure that the circuit only helps Joe in decrypting these ℓ ciphertexts (and nothing else). In other words, we obfuscate the circuit $C[ek, sk, ck, \gamma](\beta', \pi', j)$ which first checks if $\mathsf{VC.V}_{ck}(\gamma, j, \beta', \pi') = 1$ and if this is the case it outputs the j-th bit of x from the j-th bit of the ciphertext $t_i^j \leftarrow \mathsf{HE.D}_{sk}(\beta')$.[5] We have now almost achieved our goal, since the size of the decoding key is $\mathsf{poly}(\lambda \log(d\ell))$.

Final attempt. We now have to argue that our scheme is secure. Intuitively, while it is true that the index i is only sent in encrypted form, we have a problem since the obfuscated circuit contains the secret key for the homomorphic encryption scheme, and we therefore need a final fix to be able to argue that the adversary does not learn any information about i.

The final modification to our construction is to encrypt the index i twice under two independent public keys. From these encryptions Joe computes two independent encryptions of the bit t_i^j which he inputs to the obfuscated circuits together with proofs of decommitment. The circuit now outputs $\perp$ if any of the two decommitment proofs are incorrect, otherwise the circuit computes and outputs x^j from one of the two encryptions (and ignores the second ciphertext).

Anonymity. Very informally, we can now prove that Joe cannot distinguish between the decoding keys computed using indices i_0 and i_1 in the following way: we start with the case where the decoding key contains two encryptions of i_0 (this corresponds to the game in the definition with $b = 0$). Then we define a hybrid game where we change one of the two ciphertext from being an encryption of i_0 with an encryption of i_1. In particular, since we change the ciphertext which is ignored by the obfuscated circuit, this does not change the output of the circuit at all (and we can argue indistinguishability since the obfuscated circuit does not contain the secret key for this ciphertext). We also replace the random document c_{i_1} with an encryption of x with a new key for the PRF. Finally we change the obfuscated circuit and let it recover the message x from the second ci-

phertext. Thanks to the SSB property of the commitment scheme it is possible to prove, in a series of hybrids, that the adversary cannot notice this change. To conclude the proof we repeat the hybrids (in inverse order) to reach a game which is identical to the definition of anonymity when $b = 1$.

Before moving on to the actual construction, we describe an attack that is implicitly ruled out by our construction: Consider an adversary that picks a random t^* and computes

$$\beta^* = \mathsf{HE.Eval}(\mathsf{mux}[(t_{-i_0}, t^*)], \alpha)$$

and feeds it to the obfuscated program. It might seem that the adversary can find b by checking if the decoding program returns x on input β^* or not. However, this does not work since it is hard to find two databases $t \neq t^*$ such that $\beta = \beta^*$ where $\beta = \mathsf{HE.Eval}(\mathsf{mux}[t], \alpha)$ and $\beta^* = \mathsf{HE.Eval}(\mathsf{mux}[t^*], \alpha)$: suppose wlog $t[1] \neq t^*[1]$. If $\mathsf{HE.D}(\alpha) = 1$ then $\mathsf{HE.D}(\beta) \neq \mathsf{HE.D}(\beta^*)$ which implies (since the HE is correct and decryption is deterministic) that $\beta \neq \beta^*$. But then one can use this as a test to distinguish encryptions of 1 from encryptions of other indices, contradicting the IND-CPA security of the HE scheme.

The Actual Construction. A complete specification of our anonymous steganography scheme follows. Note that in our construction $\ell' = \ell$.

Key Generation: On input the security parameter λ the algorithm Gen samples a random key $ek \in \{0,1\}^\lambda$ for the PRF and outputs ek.

Encoding: On input a message $x \in \{0,1\}^\ell$ and an encoding key ek the algorithm Enc outputs an encoded message $c \in \{0,1\}^\ell$ where for each bit $j \in [\ell]$, $c^j = x^j \oplus f_{ek}(j)$.

Key Extraction: On input the encoding key ek, the database of documents t, and index i such that $t_i = c$ the algorithm KeyEx outputs a decoding key dk generated as follows:

1. For all $u \in \{0,1\}$ run

$$(pk_u, sk_u) \leftarrow \mathsf{HE.G}(1^\lambda)$$

and

$$\alpha_u \leftarrow \mathsf{HE.E}_{pk_u}(i) .$$

2. For all $j \in [\ell], u \in \{0,1\}$ run[6]

$$\beta_u^j = \mathsf{HE.Eval}_{pk_u}(\mathsf{mux}[t, j], \alpha_u)$$

where the circuit $\mathsf{mux}[t, j](i)$ outputs the j-th bit of the i-th document t_i^j;

3. For all $u \in \{0,1\}$ run

$$ck_u \leftarrow \mathsf{VC.G}(1^\lambda, \ell, 1)$$

and

$$\gamma_u \leftarrow \mathsf{VC.C}_{ck_u}(\beta_u^1, \ldots, \beta_u^\ell) .$$

4. Pick a random bit $\sigma \in \{0,1\}$.

5. Define the following circuit:

$$C[ek, \sigma, sk_\sigma, ck_0, ck_1, \gamma_0, \gamma_1](\beta_0', \beta_1', \pi_0', \pi_1', j):$$

---

[3]The evaluation algorithm $\mathsf{HE.Eval}$ can always be made deterministic since we do not need circuit privacy.

[4]Note that the decoding key also contains an encryption of i which depends logarithmically on d, but we are going to ignore all logarithmic factors.

[5]This means that we need to use a symmetric encryption scheme where it is possible to recover a single bit of the plaintext from a single bit of the ciphertext. This can easily be done by encrypting x bit by bit using the PRF.

[6]Note that we consider $\mathsf{HE.Eval}$ to be a deterministic algorithm. This can always be achieved by fixing the random tape of $\mathsf{HE.Eval}$ to some constant value.

(a) if$(\forall u \in \{0,1\} : \mathsf{VC.V}_{ck_u}(\gamma_u, j, \beta'_u, \pi'_u))$

   output $\mathsf{HE.D}_{sk_\sigma}(\beta'_\sigma) \oplus f_{ek}(j)$;

(b) else output $\bot$;

6. Compute an obfuscation $\bar{C} \leftarrow \mathcal{O}(C_\sigma)$ where C_σ is a shorthand for the circuit defined before, padded to length equal to $\max_{\tau,\rho}(C, C'_{\tau,\rho})$ (where the circuits $C'_{\tau,\rho}$ are defined in the proof of security).

7. Output $dk = (pk_0, pk_1, \alpha_0, \alpha_1, ck_0, ck_1, \bar{C})$

Decoding: On input a decoding key dk and a database of document t the algorithm Dec outputs a message x' in the following way:

1. Parse $dk = (pk_0, pk_1, \alpha_0, \alpha_1, ck_0, ck_1, \bar{C})$;

2. For all $j \in [\ell], u \in \{0,1\}$ run

   $$\beta^j_u = \mathsf{HE.Eval}_{pk_u}(\mathsf{mux}[t,j], \alpha_u) \; ;$$

3. For all $u \in \{0,1\}$ run

   $$\gamma_u \leftarrow \mathsf{VC.C}_{ck_u}(\beta^1_u, \ldots, \beta^\ell_u) \; .$$

4. For all $j \in [\ell], u \in \{0,1\}$ compute

   $$\pi^j_u \leftarrow \mathsf{VC.D}_{ck_u}((\beta^1_u, \ldots, \beta^\ell_u), j) \; ;$$

5. For all $j \in [\ell]$ output $(x')^j \leftarrow \bar{C}(\beta^j_0, \beta^j_1, \pi^j_0, \pi^j_1, j)$;

Theorem 1. *If a) f is PRF b) $(\mathsf{VC.G}, \mathsf{VC.C}, \mathsf{VC.D}, \mathsf{VC.V})$ is a somewhere-statistically binding vector commitment scheme c) $(\mathsf{HE.G}, \mathsf{HE.E}, \mathsf{HE.D}, \mathsf{HE.Eval})$ is a compact homomorphic encryption scheme and d) $\mathcal{O}$ is an indistinguishability obfuscator for all polynomial size circuits then the anonymous steganography scheme $(\mathsf{Gen}, \mathsf{Enc}, \mathsf{KeyEx}, \mathsf{Dec})$ which satisfies Definitions 1, 2 and has*

$$|dk| = \mathsf{poly}(\lambda \log(d\ell)) \; .$$

Proof. **Correctness (Definition 1).** Correctness follows from inspection of the protocol. In particular, for each bit $j \in [\ell]$ it holds that

$$\bar{C}(\beta^j_0, \beta^j_1, \pi^j_0, \pi^j_1, j) =$$

$$C[ek, \sigma, sk_\sigma, ck_0, ck_1, \gamma_0, \gamma_1](\beta^j_0, \beta^j_1, \pi^j_0, \pi^j_1, j)$$

since the obfuscator is correct. It is also true (since the HE scheme is correct) that $\forall u \in \{0,1\}$ the ciphertext β^j_u is such that

$$\mathsf{HE.D}_{sk_u}(\beta^j_u) = \mathsf{mux}[t,j](\mathsf{HE.D}_{sk_u}(\alpha_u)) = \mathsf{mux}[t,j](i) = t^j_i.$$

Now, since $t^j_i = x^j \oplus f_{ek}(j)$ it follows that the output z of $\bar{C}$ is either $\bot$ or x^j. Finally, the circuit only outputs $\bot$ if $\exists u \in \{0,1\}$ s.t. $\mathsf{VC.V}_{ck_u}(\gamma_u, j, \beta^j_u, \pi^j_u) = 0$. But since

$$ck_u \leftarrow \mathsf{VC.G}(1^\lambda, \ell, 1),$$

$$\gamma_u \leftarrow \mathsf{VC.C}_{ck_u}(\beta^1_u, \ldots, \beta^\ell_u), \pi^j_u \leftarrow \mathsf{VC.D}_{ck_u}((\beta^1_u, \ldots, \beta^\ell_u), j)$$

then the probability that $\bar{C}$ (and therefore Dec) outputs $\bot$ is 0 since the vector commitment is correct.

Anonymity (Definition 2). We prove anonymity using a series of hybrid games. We start with a game which is equivalent to the definition when $b = 0$ and we end with a game which is equivalent to the definition when $b = 1$. We prove at each step that the next hybrid is indistinguishable from the previous. Therefore, at the end we conclude that the adversary cannot distinguish whether $b = 0$ or $b = 1$.

Hybrid 0. This is the same as the definition when $b = 0$. In particular, here it holds that

$$(\alpha_0, \alpha_1) \leftarrow (\mathsf{HE.E}_{pk_0}(i_0), \mathsf{HE.E}_{pk_1}(i_0)).$$

Hybrid 1. In the first hybrid we replace $\alpha_{1-\sigma}$ with

$$\alpha_{1-\sigma} \leftarrow \mathsf{HE.E}_{pk_{1-\sigma}}(i_1)$$

Note that the circuit $C[ek, \sigma, sk_\sigma, ck_0, ck_1, \gamma_0, \gamma_1](\cdot)$ does *not* contain the secret key $sk_{1-\sigma}$, therefore any adversary that can distinguish between Hybrid 0 and 1 can be turned into an adversary which breaks the IND-CPA security of the HE scheme.

Hybrid 2. In the previous hybrids t_{i_1} is a random string from $\{0,1\}^\ell$. In this hybrid we replace t_{i_1} with an encryption of x using a new PRF key ek'. That is, for each bit $j \in [\ell]$ we set $t^j_{i_1} = x^j \oplus f_{ek'}(j)$. Clearly, any adversary that can distinguish between Hybrid 1 and Hybrid 2 can be used to break the PRF.

Hybrid 3.(τ, ρ). We now define a series of 2ℓ hybrids indexed by $\tau \in [\ell], \rho \in \{0,1\}$. In Hybrid 3.$(\tau, \rho)$ we replace the obfuscated circuit with the circuit:

$C'[\tau, \rho, ek, ek', \sigma, sk_0, sk_1, ck_0, ck_1, \gamma_0, \gamma_1](\beta'_0, \beta'_1, \pi'_0, \pi'_1, j)$:

1. if$(\exists u \in \{0,1\} : \mathsf{VC.V}_{ck_u}(\gamma_u, j, \beta'_u, \pi'_u) = 0)$ output $\bot$

2. else if$(j \geq \tau + \rho)$ output $\mathsf{HE.D}_{sk_\sigma}(\beta'_\sigma) \oplus f_{ek}(j)$;

3. else output $\mathsf{HE.D}_{sk_{1-\sigma}}(\beta'_{1-\sigma}) \oplus f_{ek'}(j)$;

We use $C'_{\tau,\rho}$ as a shorthand for a circuit defined as above, and which, if necessary, is padded to make C_σ and all the $C'_{\tau,\rho}$'s equally long.

In addition, we also replace the way the keys for the vector commitment schemes are generated. Remember that in the previous hybrids

$$\forall u \in \{0,1\} \quad ck_u \leftarrow \mathsf{VC.G}(1^\lambda, \ell, 1),$$

which are now replaced with

$$\forall u \in \{0,1\} \quad ck_u \leftarrow \mathsf{VC.G}(1^\lambda, \ell, \tau).$$

We now argue that Hybrid 3.$(1, 0)$ is computationally indistinguishable from Hybrid 2 thanks to the $i\mathcal{O}$ property of the obfuscator. This holds since: 1) the keys ck_0, ck_1 are identically distributed and 2) the circuit $C'_{1,0}$ computes the same function as the circuit C obfuscated in Hybrid 2: since j is indexed starting from 1 we always have $j \geq 1 + 0$ and the branch (3) is never taken.

Next, we argue that Hybrid 3.$(\tau, 0)$ is indistinguishable from Hybrid 3.$(\tau, 1)$. First we note that the commitment keys ck_0, ck_1 are identically distributed in these two hybrids i.e., in both hybrids

$$\forall u \in \{0,1\} \quad ck_u \leftarrow \mathsf{VC.G}(1^\lambda, \ell, \tau).$$

The only difference between the two hybrids is what circuits are being obfuscated: in Hybrid 3.$(\tau, 0)$ we obfuscate $C'_{\tau,0}$ and in Hybrid 3.$(\tau, 1)$ we obfuscate $C'_{\tau,1}$. We now argue that these two circuits give the same output on every input, and therefore an adversary that can distinguish between Hybrid 3.$(\tau, 0)$ and Hybrid 3.$(\tau, 1)$ can be used to break the indistinguishability obfuscator.

It follows from inspection that the two circuits behave differently only on inputs of the form $(\beta_0', \beta_1', \pi_0', \pi_1', \tau)$. On input of this form:

- $C_{\tau,0}'$ (since $j = \tau \geq \tau$) chooses branch (2) and outputs

$$x_0^j \leftarrow \mathsf{HE.D}_{sk_\sigma}(\beta_\sigma') \oplus f_{ek}(j),$$

- $C_{\tau,1}'$ (since $j = \tau \not\geq \tau + 1$) chooses branch (3) and outputs

$$x_1^j \leftarrow \mathsf{HE.D}_{sk_{1-\sigma}}(\beta_{1-\sigma}') \oplus f_{ek'}(j).$$

Now, the *somewhere-statistically binding* property of the vector commitment scheme allows us to conclude that there exists only one single pair (β_0', β_1') for which $C_{\tau,0}'$ and $C_{\tau,1}'$ do not output $\perp$ (remember that in both hybrids the commitment keys ck_0, ck_1 are statistically binding on index τ), namely the pair

$$\forall u \in \{0,1\} \quad \beta_u^j = \mathsf{HE.Eval}_{pk_u}(\mathsf{mux}[t, \tau], \alpha_u)$$

which decrypts to the pair $(t_{i_0}^j, t_{i_1}^j)$ (since we changed $\alpha_{1-\sigma}$ in Hybrid 1), which in turns were defined as (since we changed $t_{i_1}^j$ in Hybrid 2)

$$(t_{i_0}^j, t_{i_1}^j) = (x^j \oplus f_{ek}(j), x^j \oplus f_{ek'}(j))$$

which implies that $x_0^j = x_1^j$ and therefore the two circuits have the exact same input/output behavior.

Finally, we argue that Hybrid 3.$(\tau, 1)$ is indistinguishable from Hybrid 3.$(\tau + 1, 0)$ for all $\tau \in [\ell]$ since by definition the circuits $C_{\tau,1}'$ and $C_{\tau+1,0}'$ are identical and the only difference between these hybrids is in the way the commitment keys ck_0, ck_1 are generated. In particular, the only difference is the index on which the keys are statistically binding. Therefore, any adversary who can distinguish between 3.$(\tau, 1)$ and Hybrid 3.$(\tau + 1, 0)$ can be used to break the *index hiding property* of the vector commitment scheme.

This concludes the technical core of our proof, what is left now is to make few simple changes to go from Hybrid 3.$(\ell, 0)$ to the game from Definition 2 when $b = 1$.

Hybrid 4. In this hybrid we replace the obfuscated circuit with

$$C[ek', \sigma', sk_{\sigma'}, ck_0, ck_1, \gamma_0, \gamma_1](\cdot)$$

where $\sigma' = 1 - \sigma$. It is easy to see that the input/output behavior of this circuit is exactly the same as $C_{\ell,1}'$: since $\forall j \in [\ell] : j \not\geq \ell + 1$ the circuit $C_{\ell,1}'$ always executes branch 3) and therefore an adversary that can distinguish between Hybrid 4 and Hybrid 3.$(\ell, 0)$ can be used to break the indistinguishability obfuscator.

Hybrids 5, 6, 7. In Hybrid 5 we change the distribution of both commitment keys ck_0, ck_1 to $\mathsf{VC.G}(1^\lambda, \ell, 1)$ whereas in Hybrid 4 they were both sampled as $\mathsf{VC.G}(1^\lambda, \ell, \ell)$. Indistinguishability follows from the index hiding property. In Hybrids 6 we replace t_{i_0} with a uniformly random string in $\{0,1\}^\ell$ whereas in the previous hybrid it was an encryption of x using the PRF f with key ek. Since the obfuscated circuit no longer contains ek we can use an adversary which distinguishes between Hybrids 5 and 6 to break the PRF. In Hybrid 7 we replace $\alpha_{1-\sigma'}$ (which in the previous hybrid

is an encryption of i_0) with an encryption of i_1. Since the obfuscated circuit no longer contains $sk_{1-\sigma'} = sk_\sigma$ we can use an adversary which distinguishes between Hybrids 6 and 7 to break the IND-CPA property of the encryption scheme. Now Hybrid 7 is exactly as the definition of anonymity with $b = 1$ with a random bit $\sigma' = 1 - \sigma$ (which is distributed uniformly at random) and a random encoding key ek'. This concludes therefore the proof. □

Our theorem, together with the results of [HW15] implies the following.

Corollary 1. *Assuming the existence of homomorphic encryption and indistinguishability obfuscators for all polynomially sized circuits, there exists an anonymous steganography scheme.*

4. DEALING WITH GENERAL DISTRIBUTIONS

In our study we have made the simplifying assumption that the honestly generated documents are sampled independently from the uniform distribution, and we have shown under this constraint that it is possible to construct an anonymous steganography scheme. However, real media (such as video, pictures, etc.) is clearly not generated according to this distribution. We briefly review here "regular" steganography as defined by [HAL09] and discuss how it can be combined with our scheme in order to obtain anonymous steganography for realistic distributions.

Distribution of honest users. In [HAL09] the "innocent looking" traffic is modelled using a distribution $\mathcal{D}$ which samples a sequence of documents in $\{0,1\}^\ell$. Crucially, samples are not independent and we denote with $\mathcal{D}_h$, the marginal distribution of a single document conditioned on a history $h = (t_1, \ldots, t_j)$.

Steganography for $\mathcal{D}$. In [HAL09] a steganographic scheme is defined as a tuple of algorithms $(\mathsf{StG}, \mathsf{StE}, \mathsf{StD})$ such that:

- The generation algorithm $k \leftarrow \mathsf{StG}(1^\lambda, \mathcal{D})$ on input the security parameter λ and the distribution $\mathcal{D}$ samples a key k;

- The encoding algorithm $c \leftarrow \mathsf{StE}(k, h, x)$ embeds a message x in an innocent looking document c given a history of documents $h = (t_1, \ldots, t_j)$.

- The decoding algorithm $x' \leftarrow \mathsf{StD}(k, c)$ recovers a message x' using the key k and the document c;

As usual we require *correctness* (i.e., $x' = x$ except with negligible probability) and *security* with the following game:

Definition 3 (Chosen Hiddentext Attack). *We define a game between an adversary $\mathcal{A}$ and a challenger $\mathcal{C}$:*

1. *The challenger $\mathcal{C}$ generates a key $k \leftarrow \mathsf{StG}(1^\lambda, \mathcal{D})$ and samples a bit $b \leftarrow \{0,1\}$;*

2. *The adversary $\mathcal{A}$ asks polynomially many queries of the form (h, x) with $h = (t_1, \ldots, t_j)$;*

3. *The challenger $\mathcal{C}$ returns:*

   (a) $c \leftarrow \mathcal{D}_h$ if $b = 0$;

   (b) $c \leftarrow \mathsf{StE}(k, h, x)$ if $b = 1$;

4. $\mathcal{A}$ outputs a guess bit g;

We say π satisfies chosen hiddentext attack if for all PPT $\mathcal{A}$ $\left| \Pr[g = b] - \frac{1}{2} \right| = \mathsf{negl}(\lambda)$.

In [HAL09] several constructions provably secure steganography schemes are provided. In particular we are going to use the scheme MultiBit which allows to embed ℓ' bit long messages x into $\ell = \lambda \cdot \ell'$ long documents c, and has the property that each bit of x can be recovered looking only at λ bits of c.

Anonymous Steganography for $\mathcal{D}$. We slightly tweak the definition of anonymous steganography given in Section 2 to handle the distribution $\mathcal{D}$ and the history h. In particular, the interface of Gen and Enc are modified as follows (while KeyEx, Dec are left unchanged):

- $ek \leftarrow \mathsf{Gen}(1^\lambda, \mathcal{D})$ is a randomized algorithm which generates an encoding key ek on input a distribution $\mathcal{D}$.

- $c \leftarrow \mathsf{Enc}_{ek}(h, x)$ is a randomized algorithm which encodes a secret message $x \in \{0,1\}^{\ell'}$ into a (random looking) document $c \in \{0,1\}^\ell$, given a history $h = (t_1, \ldots, t_j)$.

The new definition of correctness is straightforward. Anonymity is now defined as

Definition 4 (Anonymity). *We define a game between an adversary $\mathcal{A}$ and a challenger $\mathcal{C}$:*

1. *The challenger $\mathcal{C}$ generates a key $ek \leftarrow \mathsf{Gen}(1^\lambda, \mathcal{D})$;*

2. *The adversary $\mathcal{A}$ outputs a message $x \in \{0,1\}^{\ell'}$, and index i_0, and a set of documents $(t_1, \ldots, t_{i_0 - 1})$;*

3. *The challenger $\mathcal{C}$ defines $h_0 = (t_1, \ldots, t_{i_0 - 1})$ and:*

    (a) if $b = 0$ computes and outputs $t_{i_0} \leftarrow \mathsf{Enc}_{ek}(h_0, x)$;

    (b) if $b = 1$ computes and outputs $t_{i_0} \leftarrow \mathcal{D}_{h_0}$;

4. *The adversary $\mathcal{A}$ outputs an index i_1 and a set of documents $(t_{i_0 + 1}, \ldots, t_{i_1 - 1})$;*

5. *The challenger $\mathcal{C}$ defines $h_1 = (t_1, \ldots, t_{i_1 - 1})$ and:*

    (a) if $b = 1$ computes and outputs $t_{i_1} \leftarrow \mathsf{Enc}_{ek}(h_1, x)$;

    (b) if $b = 0$ computes and outputs $t_{i_0} \leftarrow \mathcal{D}_{h_1}$;

6. *The adversary $\mathcal{A}$ outputs a set of documents $(t_{i_1}, \ldots, t_d)$;*

7. *The challenger $\mathcal{C}$ computes and outputs*

    $$dk \leftarrow \mathsf{KeyEx}_{ek}((t_1, \ldots, t_d), i_b) \ ;$$

8. *$\mathcal{A}$ outputs a guess bit g;*

We say π satisfies anonymity if for all PPT $\mathcal{A}$ $\left| \Pr[g = b] - \frac{1}{2} \right| = \mathsf{negl}(\lambda)$.

To achieve this definition we only need a few simple changes to the construction from Section 3, highlighted here:

Key Generation: sample $ek \leftarrow \mathsf{StG}(1^\lambda, \mathcal{D})$ (instead of sampling a PRF key);

Encoding: compute $c \leftarrow \mathsf{StE}(k, h, x)$ (instead of using the PRF);

Key Extraction: In Step 5.(a) (the construction of the circuit), let the circuit decode using $\mathsf{StD}(k, \mathsf{HE.D}_{sk_\sigma}(\beta'_\sigma))$ (instead of using the PRF);

Decoding: Unchanged.

Correctness of the modified scheme follows from correctness of the original construction and of $(\mathsf{StG}, \mathsf{StE}, \mathsf{StD})$. The proof that the modified construction satisfies Definition 4 trivially follows from the original proof, where in Hybrid 2 and 6 we rely on the *chosen hiddentext attack* instead of using the PRF f.

5. LOWER BOUND

In this section we show that no (correct) anonymous steganography scheme can have a decoding key of size $O(\log(\lambda))$. Since the decoding key must be sent over an anonymous channel, this gives a lower bound on the number of bits which are necessary to bootstrap anonymous communication.

To show this, we find a strategy for Joe that gives him a higher probability of guessing the leaker than if he guessed uniformly at random.

Our lower bound applies to a more general class of anonymous steganography schemes than defined earlier, in particular it also applies to *reactive* schemes where the leaker can post multiple documents to the website, as a function of the documents posted by other users. We define a *reactive anonymous steganography* scheme as a tuple of algorithms $\pi = (\mathsf{Enc}, \mathsf{KeyEx}, \mathsf{Dec})$ where:

- $(t_k, state_j) \leftarrow \mathsf{Enc}_{ek}(x, t^{k-1}, state_{j-1})$ is an algorithm which takes as input a message $x \in \{0,1\}^{\ell'}$, a sequence of documents t^{k-1} (which represents the set of documents previously sent) and a state of the leaker, and outputs a new document $t_k \in \{0,1\}^\ell$, together with a new state.

- $dk \leftarrow \mathsf{KeyEx}_{ek}(t^d, state)$ is an algorithm which takes as input a transcript of all documents sent and the current state of the leaker and outputs a decryption key $dk \in \{0,1\}^s$.

- $x' = \mathsf{Dec}_{dk}(t^d)$ is an algorithm that given transcript t^d returns a guess x of what the secret is in a deterministic way.

To use a reactive anonymous steganography scheme, the leaker's index i is chosen uniformly at random from $\{1, \ldots, n\}$ where n is the number of players. For each k from 1 to d we generate a document t_k. If $k \not\equiv i \mod n$ we let $t_k \leftarrow \{0,1\}^\ell$. This corresponds to the non-leakers sending a message. When $k \equiv i \mod n$ we define $(t_k, state_j) \leftarrow \mathsf{Enc}_{ek}(x, t^{k-1}, state_{j-1})$, where $t^{k-1} = (t_1, \ldots, t_{k-1})$. Then we define $dk \leftarrow \mathsf{KeyEx}_{ek}(t^d, state)$ and $x' = \mathsf{Dec}_{dk}(t^d)$. Here dk is the message that Lea would send over the small anonymous channel.[7]

The definition of q-correctness for reactive schemes is the same as for standard schemes, but our definition of anonymity is weaker because we do not allow the adversary to choose

---

[7] Note that a "standard" anonymous steganography scheme can easily be turned into an reactive anonymous steganography scheme by combining Gen and Enc into one algorithm and storing ek in the *state*.

the documents for the honest users. This implies that our lower bound is stronger.

Definition 5 (Correctness). *A reactive anonymous steganography scheme is q-correct if for all λ and $x \in \{0,1\}^{\ell'(\lambda)}$ we have*

$$\Pr\left[\mathsf{Dec}_{dk}\left(t^d\right) = x\right] \geq q.$$

where t and dk is chosen as above and the probability is taken over all the random coin flips.

Definition 6 (Weak Anonymity). *Consider the following game between an adversary A and a challenger C*

1. *The adversary A outputs a message $x \in \{0,1\}^{\ell'}$;*

2. *The challenger C samples random $i \in [n]$, and generates t^d, dk as described above*

3. *The challenger C outputs t^d, dk*

4. *A outputs a guess g;*

We say an adversary has advantage $\epsilon(\lambda)$ if $\left|\Pr[g = i] - \frac{1}{n}\right| \geq \epsilon(\lambda)$. We say a reactive anonymous steganography scheme provides anonymity if, for any adversary, the advantage is negligible.

In the model we assume that the non-leakers' documents are chosen uniformly at random. This is realistic in the case where we use steganography, so that each t_k is the result of extracting information from a larger file. We could also define a more general model where the distribution of each non-leaker's documents t_k depends on the previous transcript. The proof of our impossibility results works as long as the adversary can sample from $T_k|_{T^{k-1}=t^{k-1}, i \not\equiv k \mod n}$ in polynomial time. Using this general model, we can also model the more realistic situation where the players do not take turns in sending documents, but at each step only send a document with some small probability. To do this, we just consider "no document" to be a possible value of t_k.

We could also generalise the model to let the leaker use the anonymous channel at any time, not just after all the documents have been sent. However, in such a model, the anonymous channel transmits more information than just the number of bits send over the channel: the times at which the bits are sent can be used to transmit information [IW10]. For the number of bits sent to be a fair measure of how much information is transferred over the channel, we should only allow the leaker to use the channel when Joe knows she would use the anonymous channel[8], and the leaker should only be allowed to send messages from a prefix-free code (which might depend on the transcript, but should be computable in polynomial time for Joe). Our impossibility result also holds for this more general model, however, to keep the notation simple, we will assume that the anonymous channel is only used at the end.

Finally, we could generalise the model by allowing access to public randomness. However, this does not help the players: as none of the players are controlled by the adversary, the players can generate trusted randomness themselves.

We let $T' = (T'_1, \ldots, T'_d)$ denote the random variable where each T'_i is uniformly distributed on $\{0,1\}^\ell$. In particular $T'|_{T'^k=t^k}$ is the distribution the transcript would follow if the first k documents are given by t^k and all the players were non-leakers. We let dk' be uniformly distributed on $\{0,1\}^s$. Joe can sample from both $T'|_{T'^k=t^k}$ and dk' and he can compute Dec. His strategy to guess the leaker, given a transcript t, will be to estimate $\Pr(\mathsf{Dec}_{dk'}(T') = x|T'^k = t^k)$ for each $k \leq d$. That is, given that the transcript of the first k documents is t^k and all later documents are chosen as if the sender was not a leaker and the anonymous channel just sends random bits, what is the probability that the result is x? He can estimate this by sampling: given t^k he randomly generates t^d and dk, and then he computes Dec of this extended transcript.

If we assume that the protocol π is symmetric[9] in the messages x, then before any documents are sent, we have $\Pr(\mathsf{Dec}_{dk'}(T') = x|T'^0 = t^0) = 2^{-\ell'}$. Assuming that after all the documents are sent, there exists a key $dk' \in \{0,1\}^s$ such that $\mathsf{Dec}_{dk'}(t^d) = x$, then for a random dk' we must have $\Pr(\mathsf{Dec}_{dk'}(T') = x|T'^d = t^d) \geq 2^{-s}$. As $s < \ell'$ the documents in t^d must have increased the probability of decoding to x. The non-leakers' documents affect this probability, but *in expectation* they do not, so in most cases most of this increase will have to come from the leaker, that is, these probabilities would tend to be higher just after the leaker's documents than just before. Of course, a leaking player might send some documents that lowers $\Pr(\mathsf{Dec}_{dk'}(T') = x|T'^k = t^k)$ to confuse Joe, so we need a way to add up all the changes a players does to $\Pr(\mathsf{Dec}_{dk'}(T') = x|T'^k = t^k)$. The simplest idea would be to compute the additive difference

$$\Pr(\mathsf{Dec}_{dk'}(T') = x|T'^k = t^k)$$
$$- \Pr(\mathsf{Dec}_{dk'}(T') = x|T'^{k-1} = t^{k-1})$$

and add these for each player. However, the following example shows that this strategy does not work in general.

Example 1. *Consider this protocol for two players, where one of them wants to leak one bit. We have $s = 0$, that is dk is the empty sting and will be omitted from the notation. First we define the function Dec. This function looks at the two first documents. If none of these are 0^ℓ, it returns the first bit of the third document. Otherwise it defines the leader to be the first player who send 0^ℓ. Next Dec looks at the first time the leader sent a document different from 0^ℓ. If this number represents a binary number less than $\frac{9}{10} \cdot 2^\ell$, then Dec returns the last bit of the document before, otherwise it outputs the opposite value of that bit. If the leader only sends the document 0^ℓ the output of Dec is just the last bit sent by the other player.*

The leaker's strategy is to become the leader. There is extremely small probability that the non-leaker sends 0^ℓ in his first document, so we will ignore this case. Otherwise the leaker sends 0^ℓ in her first document and becomes the leader. When sending her next document, she looks at the last document from the non-leaker. If it ended in 0, Joe will think there is 90% chance that 0 it is output and 10% chance that the output will be 1, and if it ended in 1 it is the other way around. If the last bit in the non-leakers document is

---

[8]That is, there should be a polynomial time algorithm that given previous transcript t^k and previous messages over the anonymous channel decides if the leaker sends a message over the anonymous channel.

[9]By this we mean that for random transcript T' and random dk' the result $\mathsf{Dec}_{dk'}(T')$ is uniformly distributed. In the formal proof we will show why we can make this assumption.

340

the bit the leakers wants to leak, she just sends the document $0^{\ell-1}1$. To Joe, this will look like the non-leaker raised the probability of this outcome from 50% to 90% and then the leaker raised it to 100%. Thus, Joe will guess that the non-leaker was the leaker.

If the last bit of the previous document was the opposite of what the leaker wanted to reveal, she will "reset" by sending 0^ℓ. This brings Joe's estimate that the result will be 1 back to 50%. The leaker will continue "resetting" until the non-leaker have sent a document ending in the correct bit more times than he has sent a document ending in the wrong bit. For sufficiently high d, this will happen with high probability, and then the leaker sends $0^\ell 1$. This ensures that $\mathsf{Dec}(T)$ gives the correct value and that Joe will guess that the non-leaker was the leaker.

If the leaker wants to send many bits, the players can just repeat this protocol.

Obviously, the above protocol for revealing information is not a good protocol: it should be clear to Joe that the leader is not sending random documents.

As the additive difference does not work, Joe will instead look at the multiplicative factor

$$\frac{\Pr(\mathsf{Dec}_{dk'}(T') = x | T'^k = t^k)}{\Pr(\mathsf{Dec}_{dk'}(T') = x | T'^{k-1} = t^{k-1})}.$$

Definition 7. *For a transcript t the multiplicative factor $mf_{j,[k_0,k_1]}$ of player j over the time interval $[k_0,k_1]$ is given by*

$$mf_{j,[k_0,k_1]}(t)$$
$$= \prod_{k \in [k_0,k_1] \cap (j+n\mathbb{N})} \frac{\Pr(\mathsf{Dec}_{dk'}(T') = x | T'^k = t^k))}{\Pr(\mathsf{Dec}_{dk'}(T') = x | T'^{k-1} = t^{k-1})}.$$

We also define

$$mf_{-j,[k_0,k_1]}(t)$$
$$= \prod_{k \in [k_0,k_1] \setminus (j+n\mathbb{N})} \frac{\Pr(\mathsf{Dec}_{dk'}(T') = x | T'^k = t^k)}{\Pr(\mathsf{Dec}_{dk'}(T') = x | T'^{k-1} = t^{k-1})}.$$

If we use the multiplicative factor on the non-leaker in the protocol in Example 1 we see that for each document sent by the non-leaker there is probability 0.5 that his multiplicative factor increases by a factor 1.8 and probability 0.5 that it is multiplied by a factor 0.2. Thus, if the non-leaker first sends a document which decrease $\Pr(\mathsf{Dec}_{dk'}(T') = x | T'^k = t^k)$ from 0.5 to 0.1 and later a document that increases it from 0.5 to 0.9, the two document no longer chancel each other out: they result in multiplying the multiplicative factor by 0.36.

For fixed k_0 and non-leaking player j the sequence

$$mf_{j,[k_0,k_0]}(T), mf_{j,[k_0,k_0+1]}(T), \ldots$$

is a martingale. Furthermore, if we consider the first $k_1 - 2$ documents to be fixed and player 1 sends a document at time $k_1 - 1$ and player 2 at time k_1, then player 1's document can affect the distribution of

$$mf_{2,[k_0,k_1]}(T')|_{T'^{k_1-1}=t^{k_1-1}}$$

but no matter what document t_{k_1-1} player 1 sends,

$$mf_{2,[k_0,k_1]}(T')|_{T'^{k_1-1}=t^{k_1-1}}$$

will have expectation

$$mf_{2,[k_0,k_1-1]}(t^{k_1-1}).$$

Similar statements holds for the sum of additive differences, but the advantage of the multiplicative factor is that it is non-negative. For example, as the multiplicative factor starts at 1 there is probability at most 0.1 that it will ever be at least 10. Thus, while the leaker's multiplicative factor has to be large in most cases, all the non-leakers will with high probability have small multiplicative factors. The same does not hold for the sum of additive differences, because as Example 1 shows, you can have a probability arbitrarily close to 1 that a non-leaker's sum of additive differences increases to 0.4 (or any other positive number) as long as there is a small probability that it decreases to negative values of large absolute value.

Proposition 2. *For j and k_0, k_1 we have:*

$$\mathbb{E}_{T' | T^{k_1-1} = t^{k_1-1}} mf_{j,[k_0,k_1]}(T) = mf_{j,[k_0,k_1-1]}(t^{k_1-1})$$

Proof. For $k_1 \not\equiv j \mod n$ we have

$$mf_{j,[k_0,k_1]}(t) = mf_{j,[k_0,k_1-1]}(t^{k_1-1})$$

for any t so the statement is trivially true. For $k_1 \equiv j \mod n$ it follows from Bayes' Theorem. □

Proposition 3. *For fixed $m_0 > 2$ and x and random T there is probability at most $\frac{4d}{m_0}$ that there exists $j \neq i$ and k_0 such that $mf_{j,[k_0,d]}(T)$ or $mf_{-i,[k_0,d]}(T)$ is at least $\frac{m_0}{2}$.*

Proof. For a fixed value of k_0, and a non-leaker j we have $\mathbb{E}\left(mf_{j,[k_0,d]}(T)\right) = 1$. As

$$mf_{j,[k_0,d]}(t) \geq 0$$

this implies that

$$\Pr\left(mf_{j,[k_0,d]}(T) \geq \frac{m_0}{2} \,\Big|\, T\right) \leq \frac{2}{m_0}.$$

Similarly for $mf_{-i,[k_0,d]}$. If player j does not send the k_0'th document we have

$$mf_{j,[k_0,d]}(t) = mf_{j,[k_0-1,d]}(t),$$

so for fixed t there are only d different values (not counting 1) of $mf_{j,[k_0,d]}(t)$ with $j \neq i$ and $k_0 \leq d$. By the union bound, the probability that one of the $mf_{j,[k_0,d]}(t)$'s or one of the $mf_{-i,[k_0,d]}(t)$'s are above $\frac{m_0}{2}$ is at most $\frac{4d}{m_0}$. □

For fixed value of k Joe can estimate $\Pr(\mathsf{Dec}_{dk'}(T') = x | T'^k = t^k)$ with a small *additive* error, by sampling $T'^d|_{T'^k=t^k}$ and dk'. However, when the probability is small, there might still be a large *multiplicative* error. Joe can only do polynomially many samples, so when $\Pr(\mathsf{Dec}_{dk'}(T') = x | T'^k = t^k)$ is less than polynomially small Joe will most likely estimate it to be 0.[10] Instead, the idea is to estimate the multiplicative factor starting from some time k_0 such that $\Pr(\mathsf{Dec}_{dk'}(T') = x | T'^k = t^k)$ is not too small for any $k \geq k_0$. The following proposition is useful when choosing k_0 and choosing how many samples we make.

---

[10]This is the reason that anonymous steganography with small anonymous channel works at all: we keep $\Pr(\mathsf{Dec}_{dk'}(T') = x | T'^k = t^k)$ exponentially small until Lea uses the anonymous channel. When Lea then uses the anonymous channel to send dk, the probability of x being the output increases from exponentially small to 1.

Definition 8. *In the following we say that Joe's estimate of* $\Pr(\mathsf{Dec}_{dk'}(T') = x | T'^k = t^k)$ *is bad if* $\Pr(\mathsf{Dec}_{dk'}(T') = x | T'^k = t^k) \geq \frac{\epsilon^2}{2^{s+7}d^2}$ *but his estimate is not in the interval*

$$\left[\left(1 - \frac{1}{2d}\right) \Pr(\mathsf{Dec}_{dk'}(T') = x | T'^k = t^k) \right.$$
$$\left. , \left(1 + \frac{1}{2d}\right) \Pr(\mathsf{Dec}_{dk'}(T') = x | T'^k = t^k) \right].$$

Proposition 4. *Assume that Joe makes* $\frac{3 \cdot 2^{s+9} d^4}{\epsilon^2} \log\left(\frac{4d}{\epsilon}\right)$ *samples of* $\mathsf{Dec}_{dk'}(T')|_{T'^k = t^k}$ *to estimate* $\Pr(\mathsf{Dec}_{dk'}(T') = x | T'^k = t^k).$

No matter the true value of $\Pr(\mathsf{Dec}_{dk'}(T') = x | T'^k = t^k) \geq \frac{\epsilon^2}{2^{s+7}d^2}$, *there is probability at most* $\frac{\epsilon}{2d}$ *that his estimate is bad.*

Proof. Follows from the multiplicative Chernoff bound. $\square$

Now we are ready to prove the impossibility result.

Theorem 5. *Let ϵ be a function in λ such that $\frac{1}{\epsilon}$ is bounded by a polynomial, and let π be a $q(\lambda)$-correct reactive anonymous steganography scheme with $s(\lambda) = O(\log(\lambda))$, $\ell' \geq s + 7 + 2\log_2(d) - 2\log_2(\epsilon)$. Now there is a probabilistic polynomial time Turing machine A that takes input t and x and outputs the leaker identity with probability*

$$q(\lambda) + \frac{1 - q(\lambda)}{n(\lambda)} - \epsilon(\lambda)$$

Notice that we cannot do better than $q + \frac{1-q}{n}$. The players could use a protocol where with probability q the leaker reveals herself and the information and otherwise no-one reveals any information. This protocol succeeds with probability q, and when is does, Joe will guess the leaker. With probability $1-q$ it does not succeed, and Joe has probability $\frac{1}{n}$ of guessing the leaker. In total Joe will guess the leaker with probability $q + \frac{1-q}{n}$.

Proof. Let π be a reactive anonymous steganography scheme. We assume that for random T' and dk' the random variable $\mathsf{Dec}_{dk'}(T')$ is uniformly distributed[11] on $\{0,1\}^{\ell'}$ and we will just let Joe send $0^{\ell'}$ in the anonymity game.

Let $m_0 = \frac{8d}{\epsilon}$. Consider a random transcript t. If for some k_0 and some non-leaker j we have $mf_{j,[k_0,d]} \geq \frac{m_0}{2}$ or $mf_{-i,[k_0,d]} \geq \frac{m_0}{2}$ we set $E = 1$.

First Joe will estimate $\Pr(\mathsf{Dec}_{dk'}(T') = 0^{\ell'} | T'^k = t^k)$ for all k using

$$\frac{3 \cdot 2^{s+9} d^4}{\epsilon^2} \log\left(\frac{4d}{\epsilon}\right)$$

samples for each k. Set $E = 1$ if at least one of these estimates is bad. In all cases where E has not been defined yet we set $E = 0$. By the above propositions and the union bound, $\Pr(E = 1) \leq \epsilon(\lambda)$.

---

[11]If this is not the case, we can define a reactive anonymous scheme $\widetilde{\pi}$ where this is the case: just let X' be uniformly distributed on $\{0,1\}^{\ell'}$, let $\widetilde{\mathsf{Enc}}(x, t^k, state) = \mathsf{Enc}(x \oplus X', t^k, state)$ and $\widetilde{\mathsf{Dec}}_{dk}(t) = X' \oplus \mathsf{Dec}_{dk}(t)$, where $\oplus$ is bit-wise addition modulo 2. To use $\widetilde{\pi}$ we would need ℓ' bits of public randomness to give us X'. To get this, we can just increase ℓ by ℓ' and let X' be the last ℓ' bits of the first document.

Now let k_0 be the smallest number such that for all $k \geq k_0$ Joe's estimate of $\Pr(\mathsf{Dec}_{dk'}(T') = 0^{\ell'} | T'^k = t^k)$ is at least $\frac{\epsilon^2}{2^{s+7}d^2}$. The idea would be to estimate the multiplication factors $mf_{j,[k_0+1,d]}$. However, the problem is that $\Pr(\mathsf{Dec}_{dk'}(T') = 0^{\ell'} | T'^{k_0} = t^{k_0})$ could be large (even 1) even though $\Pr(\mathsf{Dec}_{dk'}(T') = 0^{\ell'} | T'^{k_0-1} = t^{k_0-1})$ is small, so the players might not reveal any information after the $k_0 - 1$'th document. Thus, Joe needs to include the $k_0 - 1$'th document in his estimate of the multiplication factors, but his estimate of $\Pr(\mathsf{Dec}_{dk'}(T') = 0^{\ell'} | T'^{k_0-1} = t^{k_0-1})$ might be off by a large constant factor. To solve this problem, we define

$$mf_j = \begin{cases} mf_{j,[k_0+1,d]}, \\ \qquad\qquad \text{if } j \not\equiv_n k_0 - 1 \mod n \\ mf_{j,[k_0+1,d]} \frac{\Pr(\mathsf{Dec}_{dk'}(T') = 0^{\ell'} | T'^{k_0} = t^{k_0})}{(1 - \frac{1}{2d})^{-1} \frac{\epsilon^2}{2^{s+7}d^2}}, \\ \qquad\qquad \text{if } j \equiv_n k_0 - 1 \mod n \end{cases}$$

that is, we pretend that $\Pr(\mathsf{Dec}_{dk'}(T') = 0^{\ell'} | T'^{k_0} = t^{k_0}) = (1 - \frac{1}{2d})^{-1} \frac{\epsilon^2}{2^{s+7}d^2}$ and then use $mf_{j,[k_0,d]}$. We define mf_{-i} the similar way. Joe's estimate of $\Pr(\mathsf{Dec}(T) = X | T^{k_0-1} = t^{k_0-1})$ less that $\frac{\epsilon^2}{2^{s+7}d^2}$, otherwise k_0 would have been lower (here we are using the assumption $h \geq s + 7 + 2\log_2(d) - 2\log_2(\epsilon)$. Without this, k_0 could be 1). Thus, if this estimate it not bad we must have

$$\Pr(\mathsf{Dec}_{dk'}(T') = 0^{\ell'} | T'^{k_0-1} = t^{k_0-1}) \leq \left(1 - \frac{1}{2d}\right)^{-1} \frac{\epsilon^2}{2^{s+7}d^2}$$

So if $E = 0$ then $mf_j \leq mf_{j,[k_0,d]} \leq \frac{m_0}{2}$. Similar for mf_{-i}.

If $E = 0$ then $mf_j \leq \frac{m_0}{2}$ for all $j \neq i$ and $mf_{-i} \leq \frac{m_0}{2}$. Furthermore, as all of Joe's estimate are good, his estimate of mf_j is off by at most a factor $\left(1 - \frac{1}{2d}\right)^{-d} < 2$. Now we define Joe's guess: if exactly one of his estimated mf_j's are above m_0 he guesses that this player j is the leaker. Otherwise he chooses his guess uniformly at random from all the players. There are two ways $\Pr(\mathsf{Dec}_{dk'}(T') = 0^{\ell'} | T'^k = t^k)$ can increase as k increases[12]: by the leaker sending documents or by a non-leaker sending documents. In the cases where $E = 0$ and Joe's estimate of mf_i is less than m_0 we know that the contribution from the leaker's documents is a factor less than $2m_0$. As $E = 0$ we also know that the total contribution from all the non-leakers is at most a factor $\frac{m_0}{2}$. So when only dk' has not been revealed to Joe we have

$$\Pr(\mathsf{Dec}_{dk'}(T) = X | T = t^d) < \frac{\epsilon^2}{2^{s+7}d^2} 2m_0 \frac{m_0}{2}$$
$$\leq \frac{\epsilon^2}{2^{s+6}d^2} m_0^2$$
$$= 2^{-s}$$

---

[12]If we allow the leaker to send anonymous bits before the end of the open communication, this is a third way $\Pr(\mathsf{Dec}_{dk'}(T') = 0^{\ell'} | T'^k = t^k)$ can increase. However, if the times where the anonymous channel is used are predictable by Joe, he can still sample as if the anonymous bits where random. This way, each anonymous bits makes $\Pr(\mathsf{Dec}_{dk'}(T') = 0^{\ell'} | T'^k = t^k)$ increase by at most a factor 2. If the leaker can only send s anonymous bit in total this only moves a factor 2^s increase in $\Pr(\mathsf{Dec}_{dk'}(T') = 0^{\ell'} | T'^k = t^k)$ from a later point in the proof to here.

As the only randomness left to be revealed[13] is dk' which is uniformly distributed on a set of size 2^{-s}, we know that

$$\Pr(\mathsf{Dec}_{dk'}(T) = 0^{\ell'} | T = t^d)$$

is a multiple of 2^{-s}. This implies

$$\Pr(\mathsf{Dec}_{dk'}(T) = 0^{\ell'} | T = t^d) = 0$$

In other words, if $\mathsf{Dec}_{dk}(T) = 0^{\ell'}$ and $E = 0$ then A must output i. Furthermore, in all other cases where $E = 0$ Joe will either guess the leaker correctly (because Joe's estimate of mf_i is sufficiently high) or guess uniformly among all the players. The probability that Joe is correct is now

$$\Pr(g = i) \geq \Pr(\mathsf{Dec}_{dk}(T) = 0^{\ell'}, E = 0)$$
$$+ \frac{\Pr(\mathsf{Dec}_{dk}(T) \neq 0^{\ell'}, E = 0)}{n}$$
$$= \Pr(\mathsf{Dec}_{dk}(T) = 0^{\ell'}) - \Pr(\mathsf{Dec}_{dk}(T) = 0^{\ell'}, E = 1)$$
$$+ \frac{\Pr(\mathsf{Dec}_{dk}(T) \neq 0^{\ell'})}{n}$$
$$- \frac{\Pr(\mathsf{Dec}_{dk}(T) \neq 0^{\ell'}, E = 1)}{n}$$
$$\geq q + \frac{1-q}{n} - \Pr(E = 1) \geq q + \frac{1-q}{n} - \epsilon. \qquad \square$$

Finally we can conclude that:

Corollary 2. *If π is a reactive anonymous steganography scheme with $s = O(\log(\lambda))$, d polynomial in λ and $\frac{\ell'}{\log(\lambda)} \to \infty$ that ensures weak anonymity, then the probability of correctness q tends to 0 as $\lambda \to \infty$.*

Proof. Let π be as in the assumption and define

$$\epsilon = \max\left(\lambda^{-1}, 2^{-\frac{s+7+2\log_2(d)-\ell'}{2}}\right)$$

By assumption, $s = O(\log(\lambda))$, $\log(d) = O(\log(\lambda))$, and $\frac{\ell'}{\log(\lambda)} \to \infty$, so $\epsilon \to 0$. The parameters satisfy the assumptions in Theorem 5 so there is an adversary that can guess the leaker with probability

$$q + \frac{1-q}{n} - \epsilon = \frac{1}{n} + \frac{n-1}{n}q - \epsilon \geq \frac{1}{n} + \frac{q(n-1) - n\epsilon}{n}.$$

As π ensures anonymity, $\frac{q(n-1) - n\epsilon}{n}$ must be negligible and as $\epsilon \to 0$ we must have $q \to 0$. $\qquad \square$

Acknowledgements. This research was supported by the Danish National Research Foundation and The National Science Foundation of China (grant 61361136003) for the Sino-Danish Center for the Theory of Interactive Computation and from the Center for Research in Foundations of Electronic Markets (CFEM) and COST Action IC1306.

---

[13]Here we are using that Dec is deterministic. However, allowing it to be non-deterministic does not help: we could just increase ℓ and let Dec use the extra bits in each document as randomness instead of using a random tape.

6. REFERENCES

[AH04]   Luis von Ahn and Nicholas J. Hopper. Public-key steganography. In *Advances in Cryptology - EUROCRYPT 2004, International Conference on the Theory and Applications of Cryptographic Techniques, Interlaken, Switzerland, May 2-6, 2004, Proceedings*, pages 323–341, 2004.

[BC05]   Michael Backes and Christian Cachin. Public-key steganography with active attacks. In *Theory of Cryptography, Second Theory of Cryptography Conference, TCC 2005, Cambridge, MA, USA, February 10-12, 2005, Proceedings*, pages 210–226, 2005.

[BJSW14]   Joshua Brody, Sune Jakobsen, Dominik Scheder, and Peter Winkler. Cryptogenography. In *ITCS*, 2014.

[DMS04]   Roger Dingledine, Nick Mathewson, and Paul Syverson. Tor: The second-generation onion router. In *Proceedings of the 13th USENIX Security Symposium*, August 2004.

[FNP14]   Nelly Fazio, Antonio Nicolosi, and Irippuge Milinda Perera. Broadcast steganography. In *Topics in Cryptology - CT-RSA 2014 - The Cryptographer's Track at the RSA Conference 2014, San Francisco, CA, USA, February 25-28, 2014. Proceedings*, pages 64–84, 2014.

[Fri09]   Jessica Fridrich. *Steganography in Digital Media: Principles, Algorithms, and Applications*. Cambridge University Press, New York, NY, USA, 1st edition, 2009.

[GGH+13]   Sanjam Garg, Craig Gentry, Shai Halevi, Mariana Raykova, Amit Sahai, and Brent Waters. Candidate indistinguishability obfuscation and functional encryption for all circuits. In *54th Annual IEEE Symposium on Foundations of Computer Science, FOCS 2013, 26-29 October, 2013, Berkeley, CA, USA*, pages 40–49, 2013.

[HAL09]   Nicholas J. Hopper, Luis von Ahn, and John Langford. Provably secure steganography. *IEEE Trans. Computers*, 58(5):662–676, 2009.

[HLA02]   Nicholas J. Hopper, John Langford, and Luis von Ahn. Provably secure steganography. In *Advances in Cryptology - CRYPTO 2002, 22nd Annual International Cryptology Conference, Santa Barbara, California, USA, August 18-22, 2002, Proceedings*, pages 77–92, 2002.

[HW15]   Pavel Hubáček and Daniel Wichs. On the communication complexity of secure function evaluation with long output. In *ITCS*, 2015.

[IKOS06]   Yuval Ishai, Eyal Kushilevitz, Rafail Ostrovsky, and Amit Sahai. Cryptography from Anonymity. *Proceedings of the 47th Annual IEEE Symposium on Foundations of Computer Science (FOCS'06)-Volume 00*, pages 239–248, October 2006.

[IKV13]   Luca Invernizzi, Christopher Kruegel, and Giovanni Vigna. Message in a bottle: Sailing past censorship. In *Proceedings of the Annual*

Computer Security Applications Conference (ACSAC). ACM, 2013.

[IW10] Russell Impagliazzo and Ryan Williams. Communication complexity with synchronized clocks. In *Computational Complexity (CCC), 2010 IEEE 25th Annual Conference on*, pages 259–269. IEEE, 2010.

[Jak14] Sune K. Jakobsen. Information theoretical cryptogenography. In *ICALP (1)*, pages 676–688, 2014.

[KLW15] Venkata Koppula, Allison Bishop Lewko, and Brent Waters. Indistinguishability obfuscation for turing machines with unbounded memory. In *Proceedings of the Forty-Seventh Annual ACM on Symposium on Theory of Computing, STOC 2015, Portland, OR, USA, June 14-17, 2015*, pages 419–428, 2015.

[WL12] Philipp Winter and Stefan Lindskog. How the Great Firewall of China is blocking Tor. In *Proceedings of the USENIX Workshop on Free and Open Communications on the Internet (FOCI 2012)*, August 2012.

Time-Lock Puzzles from Randomized Encodings

Nir Bitansky[*]
MIT

Shafi Goldwasser[†]
MIT and Weizmann Institute

Abhishek Jain[‡]
Johns Hopkins University

Omer Paneth[§]
Boston University

Vinod Vaikuntanathan[¶]
MIT

Brent Waters[‖]
UT Austin

ABSTRACT

Time-lock puzzles are a mechanism for sending messages "to the future". A sender can quickly generate a puzzle with a solution s that remains hidden until a moderately large amount of time t has elapsed. The solution s should be hidden from any adversary that runs in time significantly less than t, including resourceful parallel adversaries with polynomially many processors.

While the notion of time-lock puzzles has been around for 22 years, there has only been a *single* candidate proposed. Fifteen years ago, Rivest, Shamir and Wagner suggested a beautiful candidate time-lock puzzle based on the assumption that exponentiation modulo an RSA integer is an "inherently sequential" computation.

We show that various flavors of *randomized encodings* give rise to time-lock puzzles of varying strengths, whose security can be shown assuming *the mere existence* of non-parallelizing languages, which are languages that require circuits of depth at least t to decide, in the worst-case. The existence of such languages is necessary for the existence of time-lock puzzles. We instantiate the construction with different randomized encodings from the literature, where increasingly better efficiency is obtained based on increasingly stronger cryptographic assumptions, ranging from one-way functions to indistinguishability obfuscation. We also ob-

serve that time-lock puzzles imply one-way functions, and thus the reliance on some cryptographic assumption is necessary.

Finally, generalizing the above, we construct other types of puzzles such as *proofs of work* from randomized encodings and a suitable worst-case hardness assumption (that is necessary for such puzzles to exist).

1. INTRODUCTION

A central theme in cryptography is the design of schemes that are secure against adversaries whose running time is bounded by *some* polynomial. Nevertheless, in some scenarios a more precise quantification of the adversary's computational resources may be called for. A useful notion in such scenarios is that of *cryptographic puzzles* that require some precise amount of time or space to solve. Such puzzles are utilized in a wide range of applications including digital-currency, combating junk mail, and timed-release encryption [9, 28, 21, 27].

As a leading example, consider the notion of *time-lock puzzles* introduced by Rivest, Shamir, and Wagner [28], following May's work on timed-release cryptography [26]. Informally, this is a mechanism for sending messages to the future. The sender generates a puzzle with a solution s that remains hidden until time t has elapsed allowing the puzzle to be solved. Concretely, s should be hidden from adversaries that run in time significantly less than t, including parallel adversaries with polynomially many processors, or more broadly, polynomial size circuits of depth much less than t.

While the notion of time-lock puzzles has been around for 22 years, there has essentially only been a *single* candidate proposed. Fifteen years ago Rivest, Shamir, and Wagner [28] suggested candidate time-lock puzzles based on the assumption that exponentiation modulo an RSA integer is an "inherently sequential" computation. Since then, besides variants of the same construction [6, 10], there have been no other candidates meeting the standard notion of time-lock puzzles.[1][2] This is in contrast to other cryptographic primitives such as one-way functions for which several candidates

[*]Supported by NSF Grants CNS-1350619 and CNS-1414119.

[†]Supported by NSF Eager CNS-1347364, NSF Frontier CNS-1413920, and the Simons Foundation.

[‡]Supported in part by DARPA/ARL Safeware grant W911NF-15-C-0213.

[§]Supported by the Simons award for graduate students in theoretical computer science and an NSF Algorithmic foundations grant 1218461.

[¶]Supported by NSF Grants CNS-1350619 and CNS-1414119, DARPA Safeware grant, Alfred P. Sloan Research Fellowship, Microsoft Faculty Fellowship, the NEC Corporation, and a Steven and Renee Finn Career Development Chair from MIT.

[‖]Supported by NSF CNS-1228599 and CNS-1414082, DARPA SafeWare, Google Faculty Research award, the Alfred P. Sloan Fellowship, Microsoft Faculty Fellowship, and Packard Foundation Fellowship.

Permission to make digital or hard copies of all or part of this work for personal or classroom use is granted without fee provided that copies are not made or distributed for profit or commercial advantage and that copies bear this notice and the full citation on the first page. Copyrights for components of this work owned by others than ACM must be honored. Abstracting with credit is permitted. To copy otherwise, or republish, to post on servers or to redistribute to lists, requires prior specific permission and/or a fee. Request permissions from permissions@acm.org.

ITCS'16, January 14-16, 2016, Cambridge, MA, USA

© 2016 ACM. ISBN 978-1-4503-4057-1/16/01. . . $15.00

DOI: http://dx.doi.org/10.1145/2840728.2840745

[1]In nonstandard models, other constructions are known. For example, Mahmoody, Moran and Vadhan [25] constructed *weak* time-lock puzzles in the *random oracle model* where the puzzle generator must spend roughly the same amount of computation to make the puzzle as the solver must use to solve it. What makes this non-trivial is that the generator should be able to spread its computation in parallel over several machines, yet a solver must work sequentially.

[2]We note that, when dropping the requirement regarding paral-

have been discovered and studied over the years. Moreover, the hardness of several such candidates can be based on the worst-case hardness of lattice problems that are currently resilient against quantum algorithms (unlike the existing candidate for time-lock puzzles, which necessitates, at the very least, the hardness of factoring).

We identify two main challenges in designing time-lock puzzles based on natural cryptographic assumptions.

- *Complexity-theoretic bounds on parallelism.* While *typical* cryptographic assumptions address adversaries of *any* polynomial size,[3] very crudely, the time-lock puzzle notion requires differentiating between polynomial size adversaries that are of different polynomial depth (i.e., different parallel running time). For example, the existence of time-lock puzzles implies that P $\not\subseteq$ NC, whereas cryptographic primitives such as one-way functions, fully-homomorphic encryption, or even indistinguishability obfuscation may exist even if P = NC.

- *Inherent sequentiality vs. fast generation.* While there are several candidates for problems that are "inherently sequential to solve" (even on the average-case), the notion of time-lock puzzles further requires that instances for such problems can be generated fast *together with their solution.* Finding candidate constructions satisfying both of these requirements has proved to be rather elusive.

We thus set out to study what is the *weakest complexity-theoretic condition that, combined with well studied cryptographic assumptions,* suffice for the construction of time-lock puzzles.

1.1 This work

Time-Lock Puzzles from Randomized Encodings and Non-Parallelizing Languages. We put forth the notion of *t-non-parallelizing languages:* decidable in time t, but hard for circuits of depth significantly smaller than t. We focus our attention on languages that are non-parallelizing *in the worst case,* meaning that every shallow decider fails on some instance. The assumption that worst-case non-parallelizing languages exist can be seen as a natural generalization of the assumption that P $\not\subseteq$ NC, and has universal candidates. Indeed, any language $\mathcal{L} \in \text{Dtime}(t(\cdot))$ that is P-complete [15] under linear reductions (e.g. *the bounded halting problem*) would be non-parallelizing, assuming that t-non-parallelizing languages exist.

It is easy to see that worst-case non-parallelizing languages are necessary for time-lock puzzles. Indeed, time-lock puzzles can be seen as samplable and *hard on average* non-parallelizing languages: they yield a pair of samplable distributions over yes-instances and no-instances that cannot be distinguished by circuits that are too shallow. In this work, we ask whether worst-case non-parallelizing languages are also sufficient, which is somewhat analogous to the fundamental problem of basing one-way functions on

NP-hardness. While the latter question concerns the nature of general polynomial-time computation, the former concerns computations with some precise depth complexity.

Our main result shows how to construct time-lock puzzles starting from any efficient *randomized encoding* scheme, assuming the existence of a *worst-case* non-parallelizing language.

Randomized encodings [18, 2], pioneered in the works of Applebaum, Ishai and Kushilevitz, allow one to express a complex computation given by a function f and input x, by a *simpler-to-compute* representation $\widehat{f}(x)$ whose distribution encodes the output $f(x)$, but computationally hides any other information. Looking ahead, the efficiency of generating (or "locking") the new time-lock puzzles will be tightly related to the complexity parameters of the randomized encoding used.

Our construction possesses a salient universality feature: its security can be based on the existence of *any* family of non-parallelizing languages. This is unlike the candidate of Rivest, Shamir and Wagner [28] who rely on the (average-case) non-parallelizability of a particular computation with respect to a particular distribution.

Instantiations of New Time Lock Puzzles. We instantiate the construction with different randomized encodings from the literature, where increasingly better efficiency is obtained based on increasingly stronger cryptographic assumptions, ranging from one-way functions to indistinguishability obfuscation (IO). We also observe that time-lock puzzles imply one-way functions, and thus the reliance on some cryptographic assumption is necessary.

At one end of the spectrum, the standard (and strongest) notion of time-lock puzzles requires that the time to generate a puzzle is essentially independent of the time t required to solve the puzzle. To obtain such puzzles, we rely on *succinct randomized encodings* where the complexity of encoding is essentially independent of the complexity of the encoded computation. Such succinct randomized encodings have been constructed recently based on indistinguishability obfuscation [4, 7, 22].[4]

At the other end of the spectrum, we consider *weak time-lock puzzles* where only the parallel-time of generating a puzzle is independent of the time t required to solve the puzzle, whereas the overall (sequential) time may be proportional to t. Such puzzles were constructed by Mahmoody, Moran, and Vadhan in the random oracle model [25]. We construct weak time-lock puzzles based on the traditional notion of (non-succinct) randomized encodings (in another language, Yao's garbled circuits [30]), which can be based on one-way functions. In such randomized encodings, encoding is indeed highly parallelizable as required.

We also consider an intermediate notion of *time-lock puzzles with pre-processing.* Here the puzzle generator performs a one-time expensive preprocessing phase and can subsequently generate an unbounded number of puzzles with low additional cost. Concretely, preprocessing takes total time t but can be parallelized as in weak time-lock puzzles, and

---

lelism, additional solutions exist [6], including recent ones which harness the public bit-coin network for the solution of puzzles [24, 20].

[3]We restrict our discussion to non-uniform adversaries.

---

[4]We note that a strong form of succinct randomized encoding that is *output compressing* implies succinct functional encryption [1], which in turn implies indistinguishability obfuscation [1, 5, 23]. Such output compression is not required for our results, and as far as we know succinct randomized encodings may exist based on much weaker assumptions.

then generating each puzzle is done in time independent of t as in standard time-lock puzzles. Such puzzles can be obtained from *reusable randomized encodings* (also known as *reusable garbled circuits*), where a function f is encoded in an expensive preprocessing phase, and subsequently any input x for the function can be encoded in time that is independent of the complexity of f. Reusable randomized encodings are, in turn, known based on the sub-exponential LWE assumption [14].

A caveat of the two latter constructions is that the size of the puzzle (a garbled circuit) is proportional to the time t required to solve the puzzle, thus making it meaningful only in a model where communication is cheaper than computation.[5]

Other puzzles. Finally, generalizing the above, we construct other types of puzzles such as *proofs of work* [9] where the measure of parallel-time is replaced by another complexity measure. Proofs of work are puzzles that require some precise amount of computational effort to solve and are non-amortizable. Concretely, we require that, for any t chosen by the generator, a single puzzle can be solved in time t, but any polynomial number of puzzles k cannot be solved by a circuit of size significantly smaller than $t \cdot k$.

Analogous to the time-lock puzzles construction, we prove the security of the proof-of-work thus constructed, based on randomized encodings and on a suitable worst-case hardness assumption that is necessary for such puzzles to exist. That is, the existence of *non-amortizing languages* (instead of non-parallelizing languages). A language $\mathcal{L}$ decidable in time t is worst-case non-amortizing if for every k, no circuit of size significantly smaller than $t \cdot k$ can decide the direct product language $\mathcal{L}^k$. The proof of security follows the same lines as above.

We note that even more generally, one can apply the above approach with different complexity measures, relying on an appropriate worst-case assumption.

1.2 The Main Idea: Construction and Proof

Let f be a function, x an input, and $\widehat{f}(x)$ its randomized encoding. By the definition of randomized encodings, the encodings of two computations with the same output are indistinguishable, even if the computations behave differently before producing this output. For instance, one computation might solve some hard problem, whereas the other one stalls and then outputs a hard-coded solution to a hard problem. Our construction follows this intuition: a time-lock puzzle with solution s solvable in time t, consists of a randomized encoding of a "dummy computation" that outputs s after t dummy steps.

In the security proof, we will show that any adversary $\mathcal{A}$ of depth significantly smaller than t that distinguishes puzzles with different solutions s_0 and s_1, can be turned into a circuit $\mathcal{D}$ deciding *any given non-parallelizing language $\mathcal{L}$* using a circuit of roughly the same depth as $\mathcal{A}$. The decider $\mathcal{D}$, given an input x, first computes a randomized encoding of the program $M^{\mathcal{L}}_{s_0,s_1}$ that decides (in time t) whether $x \in \mathcal{L}$, and outputs s_0 or s_1 accordingly. By the guarantee of the randomized encoding, the encoding $\widehat{M^{\mathcal{L}}_{s_0,s_1}}$ is either indistinguishable from a time-lock puzzle with solution s_0

or from one with solution s_1 according to whether $x \in \mathcal{L}$. Since $\mathcal{A}$ can distinguish between the two, $\mathcal{D}$ can invoke $\mathcal{A}$ to successfully decide the language. The depth of the decider $\mathcal{D}$ is the same as the depth of $\mathcal{A}$ plus the depth required to compute the randomized encoding. To reach a contradiction we therefore rely on encodings that can be computed in depth that is significantly smaller than t.

We stress that the construction itself is independent of any particular non-parallelizing language. Rather, we use the existence of a non-parallelizing language only in the proof of security.

1.3 Alternative Approaches

A Refined Approach via Message-hiding Encodings. We observe that a different construction of time-lock puzzles can be obtained from a relaxation of randomized encodings called *message-hiding encodings* [19, 22], at the price of assuming stronger non-parallelizing languages.

In message-hiding encodings, a secret message m is encoded with respect to some public predicate P and input x. Decoding m is possible only if $P(x) = 1$, and otherwise the encoding computationally hides m. As in succinct randomized encodings, the complexity of encoding the message is essentially independent of the complexity of P.

The strengthening of non-parallelizing languages requires that, not only do shallow circuits fail to decide the language $\mathcal{L}$ in the worst-case, but they also fail on some samplable instance distribution $\mathcal{X}$ with probability approximately half. While this is already an average-case guarantee, it is still seemingly weaker than the average-case hardness that is equivalent to time-lock puzzles outlined before; there, both yes-instances and no-instances are required to be efficiently samplable.

In the new construction, the solution s is encoded as the message twice, once with respect to $(P_{\mathcal{L}}, x)$ and then with respect to $(1 - P_{\mathcal{L}}, x)$, where the predicate $P_{\mathcal{L}}$ tests membership in $\mathcal{L}$ and x is sampled from $\mathcal{X}$. We note that, unlike in our previous construction from randomized encodings, the construction from message-hiding encodings explicitly depends on the specific non-parallelizing language together with the corresponding hard distribution $\mathcal{X}$.

Currently, message-hiding encodings are only known based on the same assumption required for succinct randomized encodings, namely, indistinguishability obfuscation. However, the above construction may be appealing if message-hiding encodings can be shown from qualitatively weaker assumptions. We observe that this "gap" can always be bridged based on fully-homomorphic encryption (FHE). Concretely, FHE lets us transform any message-hiding encoding into a succinct randomized encoding, relying on ideas similar to those used by Goldwasser, Kalai, Popa, Vaikuntanathan and Zeldovich [14] to transform attribute-based encryption to functional-encryption. See further details in the full version of this work.

The above suggests a refined view of our original approach separated into two steps. The first step translates worst-case hardness to average-case hardness (and also removes the need to explicitly know the language and hard distribution). The second step translates average-case hardness with oblivious instance sampling to average-case hardness where instances can be sampled with a solution. Whereas randomized encodings achieve both effects together, they can be separated: the second step can be achieved based

---

[5] In the random oracle model, [25] show how to trade between communication and the parallel puzzle generation time d, achieving a solution with communication t/d.

on message-hiding encodings, and the first, by adding fully-homomorphic encryption. Indeed, fully-homomorphic encryption was previously used to yield similar worst-case to average-case connections for functions in deterministic time classes (e.g., in [11, 8]).

A Heuristic Approach Using Obfuscation. We briefly note that there is a natural heuristic approach to designing time lock puzzles using obfuscation. The puzzle generator on input time t and solution s will first create a MAC key k and a signature σ_1 on the message $m = 1$. Next, it creates an obfuscation of the following program. The program will take as input a message, signature pair (m, σ) for $m \in [1, t]$. For $m < t$ it first verifies (using k) that σ is a signature on m, if this check passes the program outputs a signature σ' on message $m + 1$. Finally, if $m = t$ and the signature verifies, the program will output the solution s. The published puzzle is σ_1 together with the obfuscated program. To solve the puzzle, one simply starts by inputting the initial signature into the obfuscated program and receiving a new signature. This process is repeated t times until the solution s is received.

Heuristically, it might appear that this is a potential candidate for a time lock puzzle. Unfortunately, we do not currently see any way to analyze its security.

1.4 On the Necessity of One-way Functions

We observe that (standard) time-lock puzzles imply the existence of one-way functions. To convey the idea behind the implication, assume for starters that we are given time-lock puzzles where it is possible to generate, in fixed polynomial time, puzzles that are solvable only in some super-polynomial time, e.g. $t = \lambda^{\log \lambda}$. Then, we claim that the function that maps the random coins r of the generator to a puzzle with solution $s = 0$ solvable in time t is a one-way function. First, since the puzzle can be computed fast, so can the function. Second, any polynomial inverter for the function can also distinguish in polynomial time $\lambda^{O(1)} \ll t = \lambda^{\log \lambda}$ a puzzle with solution $s = 0$ from one with solution $s = 1$.

In standard time-lock puzzles, however, while correctness is guaranteed for any value of t, security is only guaranteed for t that is polynomial in the security parameter. At high-level, we can bridge this gap by choosing the time t at random from an appropriate set resulting in a weak one-way function, and then use standard amplification [12]. See further details in Appendix A.

2. PRELIMINARIES

The cryptographic definitions in the paper follow the convention of modeling security against non-uniform adversaries. An efficient adversary $\mathcal{A}$ is modeled as a sequence of circuits $\mathcal{A} = \{\mathcal{A}_\lambda\}_{\lambda \in \mathbb{N}}$, such that, for security parameter λ, the circuit $\mathcal{A}_\lambda$ is of polynomial size $\lambda^{O(1)}$ with $\lambda^{O(1)}$ input and output bits. Accordingly, the hardness assumptions made throughout the paper address non-uniform circuits. The results can be cast into the uniform setting, with some adjustments. As usual, all honest algorithms are modeled as uniform machines.

Parallelism. Throughout, we shall also be interested in the *parallel complexity* of certain tasks. To unify terminology, we shall also model parallel algorithms as (uniform or non-uniform) circuits. Here the parallel time of a given algorithm is determined by the depth $\mathsf{dep}(C)$ of the corresponding circuit C and the total running time (which in particular bounds the number of processors) is determined by the total size of the circuit $|C|$.

3. TIME-LOCK PUZZLES

In this section, we define time-lock puzzles and construct them based on succinct randomized encodings. The security of the construction also assumes the existence of a hard language that is non-parallelizing in the worst case.

3.1 Definitions

We start by defining the notion of puzzles. Then we define the security requirement for time-lock puzzles.

Puzzles. A puzzle is associated with a pair of parameters: a security parameter λ determining the cryptographic security of the puzzle, as well as a *difficulty parameter* t that determines how difficult it is to solve the puzzle.

DEFINITION 3.1 (PUZZLES). *A puzzle is a pair of algorithms* $(\mathsf{Puz.Gen}, \mathsf{Puz.Sol})$ *satisfying the following requirements.*

- *Syntax:*
  - $Z \leftarrow \mathsf{Puz.Gen}(t, s)$ *is a probabilistic algorithm that takes as input a difficulty parameter t and a solution $s \in \{0, 1\}^\lambda$, where λ is a security parameter, and outputs a puzzle Z.*
  - $s \leftarrow \mathsf{Puz.Sol}(Z)$ *is a deterministic algorithm that takes as input a puzzle Z and outputs the solution s.*

- *Completeness: For every security parameter λ, difficulty parameter t, solution $s \in \{0, 1\}^\lambda$ and puzzle Z in the support of $\mathsf{Puz.Gen}(t, s)$, $\mathsf{Puz.Sol}(Z)$ outputs s.*

- *Efficiency:*
  - $\mathsf{Puz.Gen}(t, s)$ *can be computed in time $\mathrm{poly}(\log t, \lambda)$.*
  - $\mathsf{Puz.Sol}(Z)$ *can be computed in time $t \cdot \mathrm{poly}(\lambda)$.*

Time-Lock Puzzles In a time-lock puzzle, we require that the parallel time required to solve a puzzle is proportional to the time it takes to solve the puzzle honestly, up to some fixed polynomial loss.

DEFINITION 3.2 (TIME-LOCK PUZZLES). *A puzzle* $(\mathsf{Puz.Gen}, \mathsf{Puz.Sol})$ *is a time-lock puzzle with gap $\varepsilon < 1$ if there exists a polynomial $\underline{t}(\cdot)$, such that for every polynomial $t(\cdot) \geq \underline{t}(\cdot)$ and every polysize adversary $\mathcal{A} = \{\mathcal{A}_\lambda\}_{\lambda \in \mathbb{N}}$ of depth $\mathsf{dep}(\mathcal{A}_\lambda) \leq t^\varepsilon(\lambda)$, there exists a negligible function μ, such that for every $\lambda \in \mathbb{N}$, and every pair of solutions $s_0, s_1 \in \{0, 1\}^\lambda$:*

$$\Pr\left[b \leftarrow \mathcal{A}_\lambda(Z) : \begin{array}{l} b \leftarrow \{0, 1\}, \\ Z \leftarrow \mathsf{Puz.Gen}(t(\lambda), s_b) \end{array}\right] \leq \frac{1}{2} + \mu(\lambda) .$$

3.2 Succinct Randomized Encodings

The main tool used in the construction is a *succinct randomized encoding* scheme. A randomized encoding [18] allows to express a complex computation given by a function f and input x, by a *simpler-to-compute* representation $\widehat{f}(x)$

that encodes the output $f(x)$, but computationally hides any other information. In a succinct randomized encoding, the function f is given by a Turing machine M and the (sequential) time required to compute $\widehat{M}(x)$ is independent of the running time of M.

DEFINITION 3.3 (SUCCINCT RANDOMIZED ENCODING).
A succinct randomized encoding scheme RE *consists of two algorithms* (RE.Enc, RE.Dec) *satisfying the following requirements.*

- *Syntax:*

  - $\widehat{M}(x) \leftarrow \mathsf{RE.Enc}(M, x, t, 1^\lambda)$ *is a probabilistic algorithm that takes as input a machine M, input x, time bound t, and a security parameter 1^λ. The algorithm outputs a randomized encoding $\widehat{M}(x)$.*

  - $y \leftarrow \mathsf{RE.Dec}(\widehat{M}(x))$ *is a deterministic algorithm that takes as input a randomized encoding $\widehat{M}(x)$ and computes an output $y \in \{0,1\}^\lambda$.*

- *Functionality: for every input x and machine M such that, on input x, M halts in t steps and produces a λ-bit output, it holds that $y = M(x)$ with overwhelming probability over the coins of* RE.Enc.

- *Security: there exists a PPT simulator* Sim *satisfying: for any poly-size distinguisher $\mathcal{D} = \{\mathcal{D}_\lambda\}_{\lambda \in \mathbb{N}}$ and polynomials $m = m(\cdot), n = n(\cdot), t = t(\cdot)$, there exists a negligible $\mu(\cdot)$, such that for any $\lambda \in \mathbb{N}$, machine $M \in \{0,1\}^m$, input $x \in \{0,1\}^n$:*

$$\left| \Pr[\mathcal{D}_\lambda(\widehat{M}(x)) = 1 : \widehat{M}(x) \leftarrow \mathsf{RE.Enc}(M, x, t, 1^\lambda)] - \Pr[\mathcal{D}_\lambda(\widehat{S}_y) = 1 : \widehat{S}_y \leftarrow \mathsf{Sim}(y, 1^m, 1^n, t, 1^\lambda)] \right| \leq \mu(\lambda)$$

  where y is the output of $M(x)$ after t steps.

- *Efficiency: For any machine M that on input x produces a λ-bit output in t steps:*

  - $\mathsf{RE.Enc}(M, x, t, 1^\lambda)$ *can be computed in* sequential time $\mathrm{polylog}(t) \cdot \mathrm{poly}(|M|, |x|, \lambda)$.

  - $\mathsf{RE.Dec}(\widehat{M}(x))$ *can be computed in* sequential time $t \cdot \mathrm{poly}(|M|, |x|, \lambda)$.

Succinct randomized encodings were constructed in [4, 7, 22] based on *indistinguishability obfuscation*. The works of [4, 7] gave constructions that met the above efficiency property with the exception that the encoding took time (and have size) proportional to the maximum memory used by the computation. This restriction was removed in [22].

THEOREM 3.4 ([22]). *Assuming one-way functions and indistinguishability obfuscation for all circuits, there exists a succinct randomized encoding scheme.*

3.3 Construction

We describe the construction of time-lock puzzles from succinct randomized encodings.

CONSTRUCTION 3.5 (TIME-LOCK PUZZLES). *Let* RE *be a succinct randomized encoding scheme. For $s \in \{0,1\}^\lambda$ and $t \leq 2^\lambda$, let M_s^t be a machine that, on any input $x \in \{0,1\}^\lambda$,*

outputs the string s after t steps (here we assume that $t \geq \lambda + \omega(1)$). Further assume that M_s^t is described by 3λ bits (which is possible for large enough λ).

The time-lock puzzle is constructed as follows:

- Puz.Gen(t, s) *samples* $\widehat{M_s^t}(0^\lambda) \leftarrow \mathsf{RE.Enc}(M_s^t, 0^\lambda, t, 1^\lambda)$ *and outputs $Z = \widehat{M_s^t}(0^\lambda)$.*

- Puz.Sol(Z) *outputs* RE.Dec(Z).

3.4 Proof of Security

The security of Construction 3.5 relies on the existence of a language with a specific kind of *worst-case hardness* that we refer to as a "non-parallelizing" language. A poly-time decidable language $\mathcal{L}$ is *non-parallelizing* if parallel algorithms cannot do significantly better (than sequential algorithms) in deciding it. That is, the circuit depth of any family of circuits deciding the language $\mathcal{L}$ is as large as the (sequential) time required to decide $\mathcal{L}$ up to some fixed polynomial loss.

DEFINITION 3.6 (NON-PARALLELIZING LANGUAGE).
A language $\mathcal{L} \in Dtime(t(\cdot))$ is non-parallelizing with gap $\varepsilon < 1$ if for every family of non-uniform polysize circuits $\mathcal{B} = \{\mathcal{B}_\lambda\}_{\lambda \in \mathbb{N}}$ where $\mathsf{dep}(\mathcal{B}_\lambda) \leq t^\varepsilon(\lambda)$ and every large enough λ, $\mathcal{B}_\lambda$ fails to decide $\mathcal{L}_\lambda = \mathcal{L} \cap \{0,1\}^\lambda$.

The security of Construction 3.5 is stated in the following theorem.

THEOREM 3.7. *Let $\varepsilon < 1$. Assume that, for every polynomial bounded function $t(\cdot)$, there exists a non-parallelizing language $\mathcal{L} \in Dtime(t(\cdot))$ with gap ε. Then, for any $\underline{\varepsilon} < \varepsilon$, Construction 3.5 is a time-lock puzzle with gap $\underline{\varepsilon}$.*

3.4.1 Proof of Theorem 3.7

The completeness and efficiency properties of the puzzle follow directly from the completeness and efficiency properties of the succinct randomized encoding scheme. We proceed to argue that the puzzle is a secure time-lock puzzle. Let $q_{\mathsf{RE}}(\lambda)$ be the fixed polynomial given by the efficiency property of the succinct randomized encoding scheme, bounding the time required to compute a randomized encoding with machine size 3λ, input size λ, and any time bound $t \leq 2^\lambda$. Let $\underline{t}(\lambda) := (q_{\mathsf{RE}}(\lambda))^{1/\varepsilon}$.

Assume towards contradiction that there exists a polysize adversary $\mathcal{A} = \{\mathcal{A}_\lambda\}_{\lambda \in \mathbb{N}}$, and a polynomially bounded function $t(\cdot) \geq \underline{t}(\cdot)$ such that $\mathsf{dep}(\mathcal{A}_\lambda) < t^{\underline{\varepsilon}}(\lambda)$ and for some polynomial $p(\cdot)$ and infinitely many $\lambda \in \mathbb{N}$ there exists a pair of solutions $s_0, s_1 \in \{0,1\}^\lambda$ such that:

$$\Pr\left[b \leftarrow \mathcal{A}_\lambda(Z) : \begin{array}{l} b \leftarrow \{0,1\}, \\ Z \leftarrow \mathsf{Puz.Gen}(t(\lambda), s_b) \end{array} \right] \geq \frac{1}{2} + \frac{1}{p(\lambda)} \quad . \quad (1)$$

Let $\mathcal{L} \in \mathrm{Dtime}(t(\cdot))$ be a non-parallelizing language with gap ε, which exists by assumption. We construct a polysize circuit family $\mathcal{B} = \{\mathcal{B}_\lambda\}_{\lambda \in \mathbb{N}}$ of depth $\mathsf{dep}(\mathcal{B}_\lambda) \leq t^\varepsilon(\lambda)$ that decides $\mathcal{L}_\lambda = \mathcal{L} \cap \{0,1\}^\lambda$ for any λ as above, contradicting the fact that $\mathcal{L}$ is non-parallelizing.

We start by constructing a *probabilistic* polysize adversary $\mathcal{B}'$ such that that $\mathsf{dep}(\mathcal{B}'_\lambda) = o(t^\varepsilon(\lambda))$ and $\mathcal{B}'_\lambda$ decides $\mathcal{L}_\lambda$ *with some noticeable advantage*. Then, we conclude the proof using a standard parallel repetition argument.

Fix any λ as above with corresponding $s_0, s_1 \in \{0,1\}^\lambda$. Let $M_{s_0, s_1}^{\mathcal{L}, t}$ be a machine that, on input $x \in \{0,1\}^\lambda$, outputs

s_1 if $x \in \mathcal{L}$ and and s_0 if $x \notin \mathcal{L}$, after exactly $t(\lambda)$ steps. Such a machine indeed exists since $\mathcal{L} \in \mathrm{Dtime}(t(\cdot))$. Further assume that $M_{s_0,s_1}^{\mathcal{L},t}$ is described by 3λ bits (which is possible for large enough λ), and thus has the same description length as $M_{s_b}^t$.

Given input $x \in \{0,1\}^\lambda$, to decide if $x \in \mathcal{L}$, the randomized $\mathcal{B}'_\lambda$ acts as follows:

- Sample $Z := \widehat{M_{s_0,s_1}^{\mathcal{L},t}}(x) \leftarrow \mathsf{RE.Enc}(M_{s_0,s_1}^{\mathcal{L},t}, x, t(\lambda), 1^\lambda)$.

- Obtain $b \leftarrow \mathcal{A}_\lambda(Z)$ and output b.

First, note that $\mathcal{B}'$ is of polynomial size and its depth is given by:

$$\mathsf{dep}(\mathcal{B}'_\lambda) = q_{\mathsf{RE}}(\lambda) + \mathsf{dep}(\mathcal{A}_\lambda) = \underline{t}^\varepsilon(\lambda) + t^\varepsilon(\lambda)$$
$$\leq 2t^\varepsilon(\lambda) = o(t^\varepsilon(\lambda)) \ .$$

We next show that $\mathcal{B}'$ distinguishes instances $x \in \mathcal{L}$ from instances $x \notin \mathcal{L}$ with noticeable advantage. For any $x \in \{0,1\}^\lambda$, let $b \in \{0,1\}$ indicate whether $x \in \mathcal{L}_\lambda$. We have that $s_b = M_{s_0,s_1}^{\mathcal{L},t}(x) = M_{s_b}^t(0^\lambda)$. Therefore, by the security of the randomized encoding scheme there exists a PPT simulator Sim and a negligible function $\mu(\cdot)$ such that for any $x \in \{0,1\}^\lambda$:

$$\Pr[\mathcal{B}'_\lambda(x) = 1] =$$
$$\Pr\left[\mathcal{A}'_\lambda(\widehat{M_{s_0,s_1}^{\mathcal{L},t}}(x)) = 1 : \widehat{M_{s_0,s_1}^{\mathcal{L},t}}(x) \leftarrow \mathsf{RE.Enc}(M_{s_0,s_1}^{\mathcal{L},t}, x, t(\lambda), 1^\lambda)\right]$$
$$= \Pr\left[\mathcal{A}'_\lambda(\widehat{S}_{s_b}) = 1 : \widehat{S}_{s_b} \leftarrow \mathsf{Sim}\left(s_b, 1^{3\lambda}, 1^\lambda, t(\lambda), 1^\lambda\right)\right] \pm \mu(\lambda) \ ,$$

and:

$$\Pr[\mathcal{A}_\lambda(Z) = 1 : Z \leftarrow \mathsf{Puz.Gen}(t(\lambda), s_b)] =$$
$$\Pr\left[\mathcal{A}'_\lambda(\widehat{M_{s_b}^t}(0^\lambda)) = 1 : \widehat{M_{s_b}^t}(0^\lambda) \leftarrow \mathsf{RE.Enc}(M_{s_b}^t, 0^\lambda, t(\lambda), 1^\lambda)\right] =$$
$$\Pr\left[\mathcal{A}'_\lambda(\widehat{S}_{s_b}) = 1 : \widehat{S}_{s_b} \leftarrow \mathsf{Sim}\left(s_b, 1^{3\lambda}, 1^\lambda, t(\lambda), 1^\lambda\right)\right] \pm \mu(\lambda) \ .$$

It follows by our assumption towards contradiction (Equation 1) that for large enough λ and any $x \in \mathcal{L}_\lambda$, $\bar{x} \notin \mathcal{L}_\lambda$:

$$\left|\Pr[\mathcal{B}'_\lambda(x) = 1] - \Pr[\mathcal{B}'_\lambda(\bar{x}) = 1]\right| \geq \frac{2}{p(\lambda)} - 2\mu(\lambda) \geq \frac{1}{p(\lambda)} \ .$$

To obtain the required $\mathcal{B}$ that deterministically works for any $x \in \{0,1\}^\lambda$, we rely on the standard parallel repetition argument showing that $\mathrm{BPP}/poly \subseteq \mathrm{P}/poly$ [13]. Note that following this argument, $|\mathcal{B}| = \mathrm{poly}(\mathcal{B}') = \mathrm{poly}(\lambda)$ and $\mathsf{dep}(\mathcal{B}) = \mathsf{dep}(\mathcal{B}) + \mathrm{polylog}(\lambda) = o(t^\varepsilon(\lambda))$ contradicting the fact that $\mathcal{L}$ is non-parallelizing.

3.5 Weak Time-Lock Puzzles from One-Way Functions

In this section, we provide a construction of *weak* time-lock puzzles based on one-way functions. Weak puzzles are defined similarly to standard puzzles (Definition 3.1) except that we only require that the puzzle can be generated in fast *parallel* time even though the sequential time to generate a puzzle may be as much or even more than the time to solve it. The security requirement for weak time-lock puzzles is unchanged (see Definition 3.2).

DEFINITION 3.8 (WEAK PUZZLES). *A weak puzzle is defined by a pair of algorithms* (Puz.Gen, Puz.Sol) *satisfying the syntax and completeness requirements as per Definition 3.1, and the following weak efficiency requirement.*

Weak Efficiency:

- Puz.Gen(t, s) *can be computed by a uniform circuit of size* $\mathrm{poly}(t, \lambda)$ *and depth* $\mathrm{poly}(\log t, \lambda)$.

- Puz.Sol(Z) *can be computed in time* $t \cdot \mathrm{poly}(\lambda)$.

Our construction of weak time-lock puzzles is essentially the same as Construction 3.5 of that of standard time-lock puzzles except that instead of using a succinct randomized encoding, we use a standard *non-succinct* randomized encoding that can be obtained from any one-way function.

DEFINITION 3.9 (RANDOMIZED ENCODING). *A randomized encoding scheme* RE *consists of two algorithms* (RE.Enc, RE.Dec) *satisfying the syntax, functionality and security requirements as per Definition 3.3, and the following efficiency requirement.*

Efficiency: For any machine M that on input x produces a λ-bit output in t steps:

- $\widehat{M}(x) \leftarrow \mathsf{RE.Enc}(M, x, t, 1^\lambda)$ *can be computed by a uniform circuit of depth* $\mathrm{polylog}(t) \cdot \mathrm{poly}(|M|, |x|, \lambda)$ *and total size* $t \cdot \mathrm{poly}(|M|, \lambda)$.

- $\mathsf{RE.Dec}(\widehat{M}(x))$ *can be computed in (sequential) time* $t \cdot \mathrm{poly}(|M|, |x|, \lambda)$.

The celebrated garbled circuits construction of Yao [30] gives us a randomized encoding scheme for all of $P/poly$, assuming the existence of one-way functions.

THEOREM 3.10 ([30]). *Assuming the existence of one-way functions, there exists a randomized encoding scheme for P/poly.*

We are now ready to state the main theorem of this section:

THEOREM 3.11. *Let $\varepsilon < 1$. Assume that, for every polynomial bounded function $t(\cdot)$, there exists a non-parallelizing language $\mathcal{L} \in Dtime(t(\cdot))$ with gap ε. Then, for any $\underline{\varepsilon} < \varepsilon$, Construction 3.5 instantiated with a standard randomized encoding is a weak time-lock puzzle with gap $\underline{\varepsilon}$.*

The proof of Theorem 3.11 follows closely the proof of Theorem 3.7 in Section 3.4 with the following modifications. The weak efficiency of the puzzle follows from the efficiency of randomized encodings since $\mathsf{RE.Enc}(M_{t,s}, 0^\lambda, t, 1^\lambda)$ runs in *parallel* time $\mathrm{polylog}(t) \cdot \mathrm{poly}(|M_{t,s}|, \lambda) = \mathrm{polylog}(t) \cdot \mathrm{poly}(\lambda)$. In security proof we now think of $q_{\mathsf{RE}}(\lambda)$ as bounding the depth of the circuit RE.Enc instead of its sequential running time.

4. TIME-LOCK PUZZLES WITH PREPROCESSING

In this section, we consider time-lock puzzles with *preprocessing*. Generating such puzzles requires a one-time preprocessing phase that is as expensive as solving the puzzle; however, subsequent to the pre-processing phase, one can generate any polynomial number of puzzles inexpensively.

We provide a construction of time-lock puzzles with preprocessing based on *reusable* randomized encodings. While known constructions of succinct randomized encodings (used in Section 3) are based on indistinguishability obfuscation, reusable randomized encodings can be constructed based on sub-exponential LWE [14]. Unlike succinct randomized encodings, the time to compute a reusable randomized encoding $\widehat{M}$ of a Turing machine M does depend on the running time of M. However, generating encodings of inputs x is cheap. The encoded machine $\widehat{M}$ can then be evaluated on many encoded inputs and therefore the cost of encoding M is amortized over many evaluations.

4.1 Definitions

We start with the definition of puzzles with pre-processing and then define security of such time-lock puzzles.

Puzzles with pre-processing. We first define puzzles with pre-processing whose efficiency lies in between that of standard (succinct) puzzles and weak puzzles. Concretely, in puzzles with pre-processing, most of the puzzle is generated ahead of time in a preprocessing phase, independently of any specific desired solution s. Subsequently, a puzzle with any solution s can be generated as efficiently as in standard (succinct) puzzles.

DEFINITION 4.1 (PUZZLES WITH PRE-PROCESSING).
A puzzle with pre-processing is defined by a triple of algorithms (Puz.Prep, Puz.Gen, Puz.Sol) *satisfying the following requirements.*

- *Syntax:*

  - $(P, K) \leftarrow$ Puz.Prep$(1^t, 1^\lambda)$ *is a probabilistic algorithm that takes as input a difficulty parameter t and a security parameter λ, and outputs a state P and a short $K \in \{0,1\}^\lambda$.*

  - $Z \leftarrow$ Puz.Gen(s, K) *is a probabilistic algorithm that takes as input a solution $s \in \{0,1\}^\lambda$ and secret key K and outputs a puzzle Z.*

  - $s \leftarrow$ Puz.Sol(P, Z) *is a deterministic algorithm that takes as input a state P and puzzle Z and outputs a solution s.*

- *Completeness: For every security parameter λ, difficulty parameter t, solution $s \in \{0,1\}^\lambda$, state P, key K in the support of* Puz.Prep$(1^t, 1^\lambda)$, *and puzzle Z in the support of* Puz.Gen(s, K), Puz.Sol(P, Z) *outputs s.*

- *Efficiency:*

  - $(P, K) \leftarrow$ Puz.Prep$(1^t, 1^\lambda)$ *can be computed by a uniform circuit of depth* poly$(\log t, \lambda)$ *and total size $t \cdot$ poly(λ).*

  - $Z \leftarrow$ Puz.Gen(s, K) *can be computed in* sequential time poly$(\log t, \lambda)$.

  - Puz.Sol(Z) *can be computed in time $t \cdot$ poly(λ).*

Time-Lock Puzzles with Pre-processing. We now define time-lock puzzles with pre-processing where the adversary is given *multiple* challenge puzzles. We require that the parallel time required to solve any of the puzzles is proportional to the time it takes to solve a puzzle honestly, up to some fixed polynomial loss. To the best of our knowledge, such a notion of time-lock puzzles was not considered previously.

DEFINITION 4.2 (PUZZLES WITH PREPROCESSING).
A puzzle with pre-processing (Puz.Prep, Puz.Gen, Puz.Sol) *is a time-lock puzzle with gap $\varepsilon < 1$ if there exists a polynomial $\underline{t}(\cdot)$, such that for every polynomial $t(\cdot) \geq \underline{t}(\cdot)$ and every polysize adversary $\mathcal{A} = \{\mathcal{A}_\lambda\}_{\lambda \in \mathbb{N}}$ of depth $\mathsf{dep}(\mathcal{A}_\lambda) \leq t^\varepsilon(\lambda)$, there exists a negligible function μ, such that for every $\lambda \in \mathbb{N}$, and pairs of solutions $(s_{1,0}, s_{1,1}), \ldots, (s_{k,0}, s_{k,1}) \in \{0,1\}^{\lambda+\lambda}$ for $k = $ poly(λ):*

$$\Pr\left[b \leftarrow \mathcal{A}_\lambda\left(P, \{Z_i\}_{i=1}^k\right) : \begin{array}{l} b \leftarrow \{0,1\} , \\ (P, K) \leftarrow \mathsf{Puz.Prep}(1^t, 1^\lambda), \\ Z_i \leftarrow \mathsf{Puz.Gen}(s_{i,b}, K) \end{array} \right] \leq \frac{1}{2} + \mu(\lambda) .$$

REMARK 4.3 (*Security with pre-processing*). *Defn. 4.2 should be compared with a weaker definition where the adversary is given only* one *challenge puzzle. Indeed, there might exist a construction that satisfies this weaker definition but is insecure w.r.t. Definition 4.2.*

REMARK 4.4 (*On the efficiency of pre-processing phase*). *In Definition 4.1, we require that the pre-processing algorithm must be computable by a uniform circuit of* poly$(\log t, \lambda)$ *depth. One could consider an alternative, natural definition where this efficiency requirement is removed. We note that this definition is technically incomparable to weak time-lock puzzles (see Definition 3.8).*

4.2 Reusable Randomized Encodings

Here we define reusable randomized encodings whose efficiency lies in between that of standard randomized encodings and succinct ones. Concretely, in reusable randomized encodings, most of the expensive encoding phase is done ahead of time in a preprocessing phase, independently of any specific (M, x). Subsequently, any (M, x) can be encoded as efficiently as in succinct randomized encodings.

DEFINITION 4.5 (REUSABLE RANDOMIZED ENCODING).
A reusable randomized encoding scheme RE *consists of a triple of algorithms* (RE.Prep, RE.Enc, RE.Dec) *satisfying the following requirements.*

- *Syntax:*

  - $(\widehat{U}, K) \leftarrow$ RE.Prep$(m, n, t, 1^\lambda)$ *is a probabilistic algorithm that takes as input bounds m, n, t on machine size, input size, and time, as well as a security parameter 1^λ. The algorithm outputs an encoded state $\widehat{U}$ and a short secret key $K \in \{0,1\}^\lambda$.*

  - $\widehat{M}(x) \leftarrow$ RE.Enc(M, x, K) *is a probabilistic algorithm that takes as input a machine M, input x, and secret key $K \in \{0,1\}^\lambda$. The algorithm outputs a randomized encoding $\widehat{M}(x)$.*

  - $y \leftarrow$ RE.Dec$(\widehat{U}, \widehat{M}(x))$ *is a deterministic algorithm that takes as input an encoded state $\widehat{U}$ and a randomized encoding $\widehat{M}(x)$, and computes an output $y \in \{0,1\}^\lambda$.*

- *Functionality: for every m, n, t, security parameter λ, n-bit input x, and m-bit machine M such that $M(x)$ halts in t steps, it holds that $y = M(x)$ with overwhelming probability over the coins of* RE.Prep, RE.Enc.

- *Security: there exists a PPT simulator* Sim *satisfying: for any poly-size distinguisher* $\mathcal{D} = \{\mathcal{D}_\lambda\}_{\lambda \in \mathbb{N}}$ *and polynomials* $m(\cdot), n(\cdot), t(\cdot)$, *there exists a negligible* $\mu(\cdot)$, *such that for any* $\lambda \in \mathbb{N}$, *machines and inputs* (M_1, x_1), $\ldots, (M_k, x_k) \in \{0,1\}^{n(\lambda) + m(\lambda)}$:

$$\left| \Pr\left[\mathcal{D}_\lambda(\widehat{U}, \widehat{M_1}(x_1), \ldots, \widehat{M_k}(x_k)) = 1 : \begin{array}{l} (\widehat{U}, K) \leftarrow \mathsf{RE.Prep}(m(\lambda), n(\lambda), t(\lambda), 1^\lambda) \\ \widehat{M_i}(x_i) \leftarrow \mathsf{RE.Enc}(M_i, x_i, K) \end{array} \right] - \right.$$
$$\left. \Pr\left[\mathcal{D}_\lambda(\widehat{U}, \widehat{S}_{y_1}, \ldots, \widehat{S}_{y_k}) = 1 : \widehat{U}, \left\{\widehat{S}_{y_i}\right\} \leftarrow \mathsf{Sim}\left(\{y_i\}, m(\lambda), n(\lambda), t(\lambda), 1^\lambda\right) \right] \right| \leq \mu(\lambda) ,$$

where y_i *is the output of* $M_i(x_i)$ *after* $t(\lambda)$ *steps.*

- *Efficiency: For any* m, n, t *and machine* $M \in \{0,1\}^m$ *that on input* $x \in \{0,1\}^n$ *produces a* λ-bit *output in* t *steps:*

  - $(\widehat{U}, K) \leftarrow \mathsf{RE.Prep}(m, n, t, 1^\lambda)$ *can be computed by a uniform circuit of depth* $\mathrm{polylog}(t) \cdot \mathrm{poly}(m, n, \lambda)$ *and total size* $t \cdot \mathrm{poly}(m, \lambda)$.

  - $\widehat{M}(x) \leftarrow \mathsf{RE.Enc}(M, x, K)$ *can be computed in sequential time* $\mathrm{polylog}(t) \cdot \mathrm{poly}(m, n, \lambda)$ *(rather than just parallel time).*

  - $\mathsf{RE.Dec}(\widehat{U}, \widehat{M}(x))$ *can be computed in (sequential) time* $t \cdot \mathrm{poly}(m, n, \lambda)$.

THEOREM 4.6 ([14]). *Assuming sub-exponential hardness of the LWE problem, there exists a reusable randomized encoding scheme.*

4.3 Construction

We now describe our construction of time-lock puzzles with pre-processing from reusable randomized encodings.

CONSTRUCTION 4.7 (PUZZLES WITH PRE-PROCESSING). *Let* RE *be a reusable randomized encoding scheme. For* $s \in \{0,1\}^\lambda$ *and* $t \leq 2^\lambda$, *let* M_s^t *be a machine that, on any input* $x \in \{0,1\}^\lambda$, *outputs the string* s *after* t *steps (here we assume that* $t \geq \lambda + \omega(1)$). *Further assume that* M_s^t *is described by* 3λ *bits (which is possible for large enough* λ).

The time-lock puzzle with pre-processing is constructed as follows:

- $\mathsf{Puz.Prep}(1^t, 1^\lambda)$ *samples*

$$(\widehat{U}, K') \leftarrow \mathsf{RE.Prep}(3\lambda, \lambda, t, 1^\lambda)$$

  and outputs $(P = \widehat{U}, K = K')$.

- $\mathsf{Puz.Gen}(s, K)$ *samples*

$$\widehat{M_s^t}(0^\lambda) \leftarrow \mathsf{RE.Enc}(M_{t,s}, 0^\lambda, t, 1^\lambda)$$

  and outputs $Z = \widehat{M_s^t}(0^\lambda)$.

- $\mathsf{Puz.Sol}(Z)$ *outputs* $\mathsf{RE.Dec}(P, Z)$.

THEOREM 4.8. *Let* $\varepsilon < 1$. *Assume that, for every polynomial bounded function* $t(\cdot)$, *there exists a non-parallelizing language* $\mathcal{L} \in Dtime(t(\cdot))$ *with gap* ε. *Then, for any* $\underline{\varepsilon} < \varepsilon$, *Construction 4.7 is a time-lock puzzle with pre-processing with gap* $\underline{\varepsilon}$.

4.4 Proof of Security

The completeness and efficiency properties of the puzzle follow directly from the completeness and efficiency properties of the reusable randomized encoding scheme. We proceed to argue that the puzzle is a secure time-lock puzzle with pre-processing. Let $q_{\mathsf{RE}}(\lambda)$ be the fixed polynomial given by the efficiency property of the reusable randomized encoding scheme, bounding the time required to compute a randomized encoding with machine size 3λ, input size λ, and any time bound $t \leq 2^\lambda$. Let $\underline{t}(\lambda) := (q_{\mathsf{RE}}(\lambda))^{1/\varepsilon}$.

Assume towards contradiction that there exists a polysize adversary $\mathcal{A} = \{\mathcal{A}_\lambda\}_{\lambda \in \mathbb{N}}$, and a polynomially bounded function $t(\cdot) \geq \underline{t}(\cdot)$ such that $\mathsf{dep}(\mathcal{A}_\lambda) < t^{\underline{\varepsilon}}(\lambda)$ and for some polynomial $p(\cdot)$ and infinitely many $\lambda \in \mathbb{N}$ there exist pairs of solutions $(s_{1,0}, s_{1,1}), \ldots, (s_{k,0}, s_{k,1}) \in \{0,1\}^{\lambda+\lambda}$ such that:

$$\Pr\left[b \leftarrow \mathcal{A}_\lambda(Z) : \begin{array}{l} b \leftarrow \{0,1\} , \\ (P, K) \leftarrow \mathsf{Puz.Prep}(1^t, 1^\lambda), \\ Z \leftarrow \mathsf{Puz.Gen}(s_{i,b}, K) \end{array} \right] \geq \frac{1}{2} + \frac{1}{p(\lambda)} . \tag{2}$$

Let $\mathcal{L} \in Dtime(t(\cdot))$ be a non-parallelizing language with gap ε, which exists by assumption. We construct a polysize circuit family $\mathcal{B} = \{\mathcal{B}_\lambda\}_{\lambda \in \mathbb{N}}$ of depth $\mathsf{dep}(\mathcal{B}_\lambda) \leq t^\varepsilon(\lambda)$ that decides $\mathcal{L}_\lambda = \mathcal{L} \cap \{0,1\}^\lambda$ for any λ as above, contradicting the fact that $\mathcal{L}$ is non-parallelizing.

We start be constructing a *probabilistic* polysize adversary $\mathcal{B}'$ such that that $\mathsf{dep}(\mathcal{B}'_\lambda) = o(t^\varepsilon(\lambda))$ and $\mathcal{B}'_\lambda$ decides $\mathcal{L}_\lambda$ with some noticeable advantage. Fix any λ with corresponding $(s_{1,0}, s_{1,1}), \ldots, (s_{k,0}, s_{k,1}) \in \{0,1\}^{\lambda+\lambda}$ as above. For every $i \in [k]$, let $M^{\mathcal{L},t}_{s_{i,0}, s_{i,1}}$ be a machine that, on input $x \in \{0,1\}^\lambda$, outputs $s_{i,1}$ if $x \in \mathcal{L}$ and and $s_{i,0}$ if $x \notin \mathcal{L}$, after exactly $t(\lambda)$ steps. Such machines indeed exist since $\mathcal{L} \in Dtime(t(\cdot))$. Further assume that $M^{\mathcal{L},t}_{s_{i,0}, s_{i,1}}$ is described by 3λ bits (which is possible for large enough λ), and thus has the same description length as $M^t_{s_{i,b}}$.

Given input $x \in \{0,1\}^\lambda$, to decide if $x \in \mathcal{L}$, the randomized $\mathcal{B}'_\lambda$ acts as follows:

- Sample $(\widehat{U}, K) \leftarrow \mathsf{RE.Prep}(1^{3\lambda}, 1^\lambda, t, 1^\lambda)$.

- Sample $Z_i := \widehat{M}^{\mathcal{L},t}_{s_{i,0}, s_{i,1}}(x) \leftarrow \mathsf{RE.Enc}(M^{\mathcal{L},t}_{s_{i,0}, s_{i,1}}, x, K)$ for every $i \in [k]$.

- Obtain $b \leftarrow \mathcal{A}_\lambda\left(\widehat{U}, \{Z_i\}_{i=1}^k\right)$ and output b.

First, note that $\mathcal{B}'$ is of polynomial size and its depth is given by:

$$\mathsf{dep}(\mathcal{B}'_\lambda) = q_{\mathsf{RE}}(\lambda) + \mathsf{dep}(\mathcal{A}_\lambda) = \underline{t}^\varepsilon(\lambda) + t^{\underline{\varepsilon}}(\lambda) \leq 2t^{\underline{\varepsilon}}(\lambda) = o(t^\varepsilon(\lambda)) .$$

We next show that $\mathcal{B}'$ distinguishes instances $x \in \mathcal{L}$ from instances $x \notin \mathcal{L}$ with noticeable advantage. For any $x \in \{0,1\}^\lambda$, let $b \in \{0,1\}$ indicate whether $x \in \mathcal{L}_\lambda$ we have that $s_{i,b} = M^{\mathcal{L},t}_{s_{i,0}, s_{i,1}}(x) = M^t_{s_{i,b}}(0^\lambda)$. Therefore, by the security of the reusable randomized encoding scheme there exists a PPT simulator Sim and a negligible function $\mu(\cdot)$ such that for any $x \in \{0,1\}^{\lambda}$:

$$\Pr[\mathcal{B}'_{\lambda}(x) = 1] =$$

$$\Pr\left[\mathcal{A}_{\lambda}\left(\widehat{U}, \left\{\widehat{M}^{\mathcal{L},t}_{s_{i,0},s_{i,1}}(x)\right\}_{i=1}^{k}\right) = 1 : \right.$$

$$(\widehat{U}, K) \leftarrow \mathsf{RE.Prep}\left(1^{3\lambda}, 1^{\lambda}, t, 1^{\lambda}\right), \\ \left. \widehat{M}^{\mathcal{L},t}_{s_{i,0},s_{i,1}}(x) \leftarrow \mathsf{RE.Enc}\left(M^{\mathcal{L},t}_{s_{i,0},s_{i,1}}, x, K\right) \right] =$$

$$\Pr\left[\mathcal{A}_{\lambda}\left(\widehat{U}, \left\{\widehat{S}_{s_{i,b}}\right\}_{i=1}^{k}\right) = 1 : \right.$$

$$\left. \widehat{U}, \left\{\widehat{S}_{s_{i,b}}\right\}_{i=1}^{k} \leftarrow \mathsf{Sim}\left(\left\{s_{i,b}\right\}_{i=1}^{k}, 1^{3\lambda}, 1^{\lambda}, t(\lambda), 1^{\lambda}\right) \right] \pm \mu(\lambda) .$$

and

$$\Pr\left[\mathcal{A}_{\lambda}\left(P, \{Z_i\}_{i=1}^{k}\right) = 1 : \begin{array}{l} (P, K) \leftarrow \mathsf{Puz.Prep}(1^t, 1^{\lambda}), \\ Z_i \leftarrow \mathsf{Puz.Gen}(s_{i,b}, K) \end{array} \right] =$$

$$\Pr\left[\mathcal{A}_{\lambda}\left(\widehat{U}, \left\{\widehat{M}^{t}_{s_{i,b}}(0^{\lambda})\right\}_{i=1}^{k}\right) = 1 : \right.$$

$$(\widehat{U}, K) \leftarrow \mathsf{RE.Prep}\left(1^{3\lambda}, 1^{\lambda}, t, 1^{\lambda}\right), \\ \left. \widehat{M}^{t}_{s_{i,b}}(0^{\lambda}) \leftarrow \mathsf{RE.Enc}(M^{t}_{s_{i,b}}, x, K) \right] =$$

$$\Pr\left[\mathcal{A}_{\lambda}\left(\widehat{U}, \left\{\widehat{S}_{s_{i,b}}\right\}_{i=1}^{k}\right) = 1 : \right.$$

$$\left. \widehat{U}, \left\{\widehat{S}_{s_{i,b}}\right\}_{i=1}^{k} \leftarrow \mathsf{Sim}\left(\left\{s_{i,b}\right\}_{i=1}^{k}, 1^{3\lambda}, 1^{\lambda}, t(\lambda), 1^{\lambda}\right) \right] \pm \mu(\lambda) .$$

It follows by our assumption towards contradiction (Equation 2) that for large enough λ and any $x \in \mathcal{L}_{\lambda}$, $\bar{x} \notin \mathcal{L}_{\lambda}$:

$$\left|\Pr[\mathcal{B}'_{\lambda}(x) = 1] - \Pr[\mathcal{B}'_{\lambda}(\bar{x}) = 1]\right| \geq \frac{2}{p(\lambda)} - 2\mu(\lambda) \geq \frac{1}{p(\lambda)} .$$

To obtain the required $\mathcal{B}$ that deterministically works for any $x \in \{0,1\}^{\lambda}$, we rely on the standard parallel repetition argument showing that $\mathrm{BPP}/poly \subseteq \mathrm{P}/poly$ [13]. Note that following this argument, $|\mathcal{B}| = \mathrm{poly}(\mathcal{B}') = \mathrm{poly}(\lambda)$ and $\mathsf{dep}(\mathcal{B}) = \mathsf{dep}(\mathcal{B}) + \mathrm{polylog}(\lambda) = o(t^{\varepsilon}(\lambda))$ contradicting the fact that $\mathcal{L}$ is non-parallelizing.

5. PROOFS OF WORK

In this section, we define proofs of work and construct them based on succinct randomized encodings. The security of the construction also assumes the existence of a hard language that is non-amortizing in the worst case.

Definition. In proofs of work, we require that the minimal time required to solve k random puzzles is proportional to k times the time it takes to solve the puzzle honestly, up to some fixed polynomial loss. We give the formal definition below.

DEFINITION 5.1 (PROOFS OF WORK). *A puzzle* $(\mathsf{Puz.Gen}, \mathsf{Puz.Sol})$ *is a proof of work with gap* $\varepsilon < 1$ *if there exists a polynomial* $\underline{t}(\cdot)$, *such that for every polynomials* $t(\cdot) \geq \underline{t}(\cdot)$ *and* $k(\cdot)$, *and every polysize adversary* $\mathcal{A} = \{\mathcal{A}_{\lambda}\}_{\lambda \in \mathbb{N}}$ *such that* $|\mathcal{A}_{\lambda}| \leq k(\lambda) \cdot t^{\varepsilon}(\lambda)$, *there exists a negligible function* μ *such that for every* $\lambda \in \mathbb{N}$:

$$\Pr\left[(s_1, \ldots, s_{k(\lambda)}) \leftarrow \mathcal{A}_{\lambda}(Z_1, \ldots, Z_{k(\lambda)}) : \right.$$
$$\left. \begin{array}{l} s_i \leftarrow \{0,1\}^{\lambda}, \\ Z_i \leftarrow \mathsf{Puz.Gen}(t(\lambda), s_i) \end{array} \right] \leq \mu(\lambda) .$$

Construction. Our construction of proofs of work is the same as the construction of time-lock puzzles given in Section 3.3.

5.1 Security

In order to prove security of our construction, we will rely on a specific kind of language with *worst-case hardness* that we refer to as "non-amortizing" language. We first present its definition. The definition addresses non-uniform families of circuits, and can be naturally augmented to the uniform case.

Non-amortizing language. A poly-time decidable language $\mathcal{L}$ is *non-amortizing* if solving multiple instances together is not significantly easier than solving each of them separately. That is, the circuit size of any family of circuits deciding the k-fold direct product $\mathcal{L}^k$ is as large as k times the time required to decide $\mathcal{L}$ up to some fixed polynomial loss.

DEFINITION 5.2 (NON-AMORTIZING LANGUAGE). *A language* $\mathcal{L} \in Dtime(t(\cdot))$ *is non-amortizing with gap* $\varepsilon < 1$ *if for every polynomial* $k(\cdot)$ *and family of non-uniform polysize circuits* $\mathcal{B} = \{\mathcal{B}_{\lambda}\}_{\lambda \in \mathbb{N}}$ *such that* $\mathcal{B}_{\lambda}$ *operates on inputs in* $\{0,1\}^{\lambda \times k(\lambda)}$ *and* $|\mathcal{B}_{\lambda}| \leq k(\lambda) \cdot (t(\lambda))^{\varepsilon}$, *and every large enough* λ, $\mathcal{B}_{\lambda}$ *fails to decide* $\mathcal{L}^k_{\lambda} = \mathcal{L}^{k(\lambda)} \cap \{0,1\}^{\lambda \times k(\lambda)}$.

The security of our construction is stated in the following theorem.

THEOREM 5.3. *Let* $\varepsilon < 1$. *Assume that, for every polynomial bounded function* $t(\cdot)$, *there exists a non-amortizing language* $\mathcal{L} \in Dtime(t(\cdot))$ *with gap* ε. *Then, for any* $\underline{\varepsilon} < \varepsilon$, *Construction 3.5 is a proof of work with gap* $\underline{\varepsilon}$.

5.2 Proof of Theorem 5.3

The completeness and efficiency properties of the puzzle follows directly from the completeness and efficiency properties of the succinct randomized encoding scheme. We proceed to argue that that the puzzle is a secure proof of work. Let $q_{\mathsf{RE}}(\lambda)$ be the fixed polynomial given by the efficiency property of the succinct randomized encoding scheme, bounding the time required to compute a randomized encoding with machine size 3λ, input size λ, and any time bound $t \leq 2^{\lambda}$. Let $\underline{t}(\lambda) := (q_{\mathsf{RE}}(\lambda))^{1/\underline{\varepsilon}}$.

Assume towards contradiction that there exists an adversary $\mathcal{A} = \{\mathcal{A}_{\lambda}\}_{\lambda \in \mathbb{N}}$, and polynomially bounded functions $t(\cdot) \geq \underline{t}(\cdot)$ and $k(\cdot)$ such that for some polynomial $p(\cdot)$ and infinitely many $\lambda \in \mathbb{N}$, $|\mathcal{A}_{\lambda}| < k(\lambda) \cdot (t(\lambda))^{\underline{\varepsilon}}$, and:

$$\Pr\left[(s_1, \ldots, s_{k(\lambda)}) \leftarrow \mathcal{A}_{\lambda}(Z_1, \ldots, Z_{k(\lambda)}) : \right.$$
$$\left. \begin{array}{l} s_i \leftarrow \{0,1\}^{\lambda}, \\ Z_i \leftarrow \mathsf{Puz.Gen}(t(\lambda), s_i) \end{array} \right] \geq \frac{1}{p(\lambda)} .$$

Let $\mathcal{L} \in \mathrm{Dtime}(t(\cdot))$ be a non-amortizing language with gap ε, which exists by assumption. We construct a polysize circuit family $\mathcal{B} = \{\mathcal{B}_{\lambda}\}_{\lambda \in \mathbb{N}}$ operating on inputs in $\{0,1\}^{\lambda \times k(\lambda)}$ and of size $|\mathcal{B}_{\lambda}| \leq k(\lambda) \cdot (t(\lambda))^{\varepsilon}$ such that, for any λ as above, $\mathcal{B}$ decides $\mathcal{L}^k_{\lambda} = \mathcal{L}^{k(\lambda)} \cap \{0,1\}^{\lambda \times k(\lambda)}$, contradicting the fact that $\mathcal{L}$ is non-amortizing.

We start be constructing a *probabilistic* adversary $\mathcal{B}'$ such that that $|\mathcal{B}'_{\lambda}| = o(k(\lambda) \cdot (t(\lambda))^{\varepsilon})$ and $\mathcal{B}'_{\lambda}$ decides $\mathcal{L}_{\lambda}$ *with some noticeable advantage*. Then, we conclude the proof using a standard parallel repetition argument.

Fix any λ as above and choose random $s_1, \ldots, s_k \in \{0,1\}^{\lambda}$. Let $M^{\mathcal{L},t}_{s_1}, \ldots, M^{\mathcal{L},t}_{s_k}$ be k machines where the ith machine $M^{\mathcal{L},t}_{s_i}$, on input $x_i \in \{0,1\}^{\lambda}$, outputs s_i if $x_i \in \mathcal{L}$ and a randomly chosen $r'_i \in \{0,1\}^{\lambda}$ if $x_i \notin \mathcal{L}$, after exactly $t(\lambda)$ steps.

Note that such machines indeed exist since $\mathcal{L} \in \text{Dtime}(t(\cdot))$. Further assume that $M_{s_i}^{\mathcal{L},t}$ is described by the same number of bits as $M_{s_b}^t$, e.g. 3λ bits (which is possible for large enough λ).

Given input $(x_1, \ldots, x_k) \in \{0,1\}^{\lambda \times k(\lambda)}$, to decide if $(x_1, \ldots, x_k) \in \mathcal{L}_\lambda^k$, the randomized $\mathcal{B}_\lambda'$ acts as follows:

- Sample $Z_i := \widehat{M_{s_i}^{\mathcal{L},t}}(x) \leftarrow \mathsf{RE.Enc}(M_{s_i}^{\mathcal{L},t}, x_i, t(\lambda), 1^\lambda)$.

- Obtain $(s_1', \ldots, s_k') \leftarrow \mathcal{A}_\lambda(Z_1, \ldots, Z_k)$. If $s_i' = s_i$ for every $i \in [k]$, output 1; else output 0.

First, note that the size of $\mathcal{B}'$ is given by:

$$|\mathcal{B}_\lambda'| = k(\lambda) \cdot q_{\mathsf{RE}}(\lambda) + |\mathcal{A}_\lambda| = k(\lambda) \cdot (t(\lambda))^\varepsilon + k(\lambda) \cdot (t(\lambda))^\varepsilon \leq$$
$$2k(\lambda) \cdot (t(\lambda))^\varepsilon = o\left(k(\lambda) \cdot (t(\lambda))^\varepsilon\right) \ .$$

We next show that $\mathcal{B}'$ distinguishes instances $(x_1, \ldots, x_k) \in \mathcal{L}^k$ from instances $(x_1, \ldots, x_k) \notin \mathcal{L}^k$ with noticeable advantage. By the security of the randomized encoding scheme there exists a PPT simulator Sim and a negligible function $\mu(\cdot)$ such that:

$$\Pr[\mathcal{B}_\lambda'(x_1, \ldots, x_k) = 1] =$$
$$\Pr\left[\mathcal{A}_\lambda\left(\left\{\widehat{M_{s_i}^{\mathcal{L},t}}(x_i)\right\}_{i=1}^k\right) = (s_1, \ldots, s_k) :\right.$$
$$\left.\widehat{M_{s_i}^{\mathcal{L},t}}(x_i) \leftarrow \mathsf{RE.Enc}(M_{s_i}^{\mathcal{L},t}, x_i, t(\lambda), 1^\lambda)\right] =$$
$$\Pr\left[\mathcal{A}_\lambda\left(\left\{\widehat{S}_{a_i}\right\}_{i=1}^k\right) = (s_1, \ldots, s_k) :\right.$$
$$\left.\begin{array}{c} a_i = M_{s_i}^{\mathcal{L},t}(x_i) \\ \widehat{S}_{a_i} \leftarrow \mathsf{Sim}\left(a_i, 1^{3\lambda}, 1^\lambda, t(\lambda), 1^\lambda\right) \end{array}\right] \pm k \cdot \mu(\lambda),$$

and:

$$\Pr\left[\mathcal{A}_\lambda\left(\{Z_i\}_{i=1}^k\right) = (s_1, \ldots, s_k) :\right.$$
$$\left. Z_i \leftarrow \mathsf{Puz.Gen}(t(\lambda), a_i)\right] =$$
$$\Pr\left[\mathcal{A}_\lambda\left(\left\{\widehat{M_{a_i}^t}\left(0^\lambda\right)\right\}_{i=1}^k\right) = (s_1, \ldots, s_k) :\right.$$
$$\left.\widehat{M_{a_i}^t}(0^\lambda) \leftarrow \mathsf{RE.Enc}(M_{a_i}^t, 0^\lambda, t(\lambda), 1^\lambda)\right] =$$
$$\Pr\left[\mathcal{A}_\lambda\left(\left\{\widehat{S}_{a_i}\right\}_{i=1}^k\right) = (s_1, \ldots, s_k) :\right.$$
$$\left.\widehat{S}_{a_i} \leftarrow \mathsf{Sim}\left(a_i, 1^{3\lambda}, 1^\lambda, t(\lambda), 1^\lambda\right)\right] \pm k \cdot \mu(\lambda).$$

It follows by our assumption towards contradiction that for large enough λ and any $(x_1, \ldots, x_k) \in \mathcal{L}_\lambda^k$, $(\bar{x}_1, \ldots, \bar{x}_k) \notin \mathcal{L}_\lambda^k$:

$$\left|\Pr[\mathcal{B}_\lambda'(x_1, \ldots, x_k) = 1] - \Pr[\mathcal{B}_\lambda'(\bar{x}_1, \ldots, \bar{x}_k) = 1]\right|$$
$$\geq \frac{2}{p(\lambda)} - 2k \cdot \mu(\lambda) \geq \frac{1}{p(\lambda)} \ .$$

To obtain the required $\mathcal{B}$ that deterministically works for any $(x_1, \ldots, x_k) \in \{0,1\}^{\lambda \times k(\lambda)}$, we rely on the standard parallel repetition argument showing that $\mathsf{BPP}/poly \subseteq \mathsf{P}/poly$ [13].

Acknowledgments. We thank Ryan Williams for his patient and thorough answers to our questions. We thank Benny Applebaum for valuable comments. We also thank Juan Garay for referring us to [10].

6. REFERENCES

[1] P. Ananth and A. Jain. Indistinguishability obfuscation from compact functional encryption. In *Crypto*, 2015.

[2] B. Applebaum, Y. Ishai, and E. Kushilevitz. Computationally private randomizing polynomials and their applications. *Computational Complexity*, 15(2):115–162, 2006.

[3] B. Barak. A probabilistic-time hierarchy theorem for "slightly non-uniform" algorithms. In *Randomization and Approximation Techniques, 6th International Workshop, RANDOM 2002, Cambridge, MA, USA, September 13-15, 2002, Proceedings*, pages 194–208, 2002.

[4] N. Bitansky, S. Garg, H. Lin, R. Pass, and S. Telang. Succinct randomized encodings and their applications. In *Symposium on Theory of Computing, STOC 2015*, 2015.

[5] N. Bitansky and V. Vaikuntanathan. Indistinguishability obfuscation from functional encryption. In *FOCS*, 2015.

[6] D. Boneh and M. Naor. Timed commitments. In *Advances in Cryptology - CRYPTO 2000, 20th Annual International Cryptology Conference, Santa Barbara, California, USA, August 20-24, 2000, Proceedings*, pages 236–254, 2000.

[7] R. Canetti, J. Holmgren, A. Jain, and V. Vaikuntanathan. Indistinguishability obfuscation of iterated circuits and ram programs. In *Symposium on Theory of Computing, STOC 2015*, 2015.

[8] K. Chung, Y. T. Kalai, and S. P. Vadhan. Improved delegation of computation using fully homomorphic encryption. In *Advances in Cryptology - CRYPTO 2010, 30th Annual Cryptology Conference, Santa Barbara, CA, USA, August 15-19, 2010. Proceedings*, pages 483–501, 2010.

[9] C. Dwork and M. Naor. Pricing via processing or combatting junk mail. In *Advances in Cryptology - CRYPTO '92, 12th Annual International Cryptology Conference, Santa Barbara, California, USA, August 16-20, 1992, Proceedings*, pages 139–147, 1992.

[10] J. A. Garay, P. D. MacKenzie, M. Prabhakaran, and K. Yang. Resource fairness and composability of cryptographic protocols. *J. Cryptology*, 24(4):615–658, 2011.

[11] R. Gennaro, C. Gentry, and B. Parno. Non-interactive verifiable computing: Outsourcing computation to untrusted workers. In T. Rabin, editor, *Advances in Cryptology - CRYPTO 2010, 30th Annual Cryptology Conference, Santa Barbara, CA, USA, August 15-19, 2010. Proceedings*, volume 6223 of *Lecture Notes in Computer Science*, pages 465–482. Springer, 2010.

[12] O. Goldreich. *The Foundations of Cryptography - Volume 1, Basic Techniques*. Cambridge University Press, 2001.

[13] O. Goldreich. *The Foundations of Cryptography - Volume 1, Basic Techniques*. Cambridge University Press, 2001.

[14] S. Goldwasser, Y. T. Kalai, R. A. Popa, V. Vaikuntanathan, and N. Zeldovich. Reusable garbled circuits and succinct functional encryption. In *Symposium on Theory of Computing Conference, STOC'13, Palo Alto, CA, USA, June 1-4, 2013*, pages 555–564, 2013.

[15] R. Greenlaw, H. J. Hoover, and W. L. Ruzzo. *Limits to Parallel Computation: P-completeness Theory*. Oxford University Press, Inc., New York, NY, USA, 1995.

[16] J. Hartmanis and R. Stearns. On the computational complexity of algorithms. *Transactions of the American Mathematical Society*, 117:285–âĂŞ306, 1965.

[17] R. Impagliazzo and A. Wigderson. Randomness vs time: Derandomization under a uniform assumption. *J. Comput. Syst. Sci.*, 63(4):672–688, 2001.

[18] Y. Ishai and E. Kushilevitz. Randomizing polynomials: A new representation with applications to round-efficient secure computation. In *41st Annual Symposium on Foundations of Computer Science, FOCS 2000, 12-14 November 2000, Redondo Beach, California, USA*, pages 294–304, 2000.

[19] Y. Ishai and H. Wee. Partial garbling schemes and their

applications. In *Automata, Languages, and Programming - 41st International Colloquium, ICALP 2014, Copenhagen, Denmark, July 8-11, 2014, Proceedings, Part I*, pages 650–662, 2014.

[20] T. Jager. How to build time-lock encryption. *IACR Cryptology ePrint Archive*, 2015:478, 2015.

[21] M. Jakobsson and A. Juels. Proofs of work and bread pudding protocols. In *Secure Information Networks: Communications and Multimedia Security, IFIP TC6/TC11 Joint Working Conference on Communications and Multimedia Security (CMS '99), September 20-21, 1999, Leuven, Belgium*, pages 258–272, 1999.

[22] V. Koppula, A. B. Lewko, and B. Waters. Indistinguishability obfuscation for turing machines with unbounded memory. In *Symposium on Theory of Computing, STOC 2015*, 2015.

[23] H. Lin, R. Pass, K. Seth, and S. Telang. Output-compressing randomized encodings and applications. *IACR Cryptology ePrint Archive*, 2015:720, 2015.

[24] J. Liu, F. Garcia, and M. Ryan. Time-release protocol from bitcoin and witness encryption for SAT. *IACR Cryptology ePrint Archive*, 2015:482, 2015.

[25] M. Mahmoody, T. Moran, and S. P. Vadhan. Time-lock puzzles in the random oracle model. In *Advances in Cryptology - CRYPTO 2011 - 31st Annual Cryptology Conference, Santa Barbara, CA, USA, August 14-18, 2011. Proceedings*, pages 39–50, 2011.

[26] T. C. May. Timed-release crypto, 1993. http://www.hks.net/cpunks/cpunks-0/1460.html.

[27] S. Nakamoto. Bitcoin: A peer-to-peer electronic cash system, 2000. http://bitcoin.org/bitcoin.pdf.

[28] R. L. Rivest, A. Shamir, and D. A. Wagner. Time-lock puzzles and timed-release crypto. Technical Report MIT/LCS/TR-684, MIT, February 2000.

[29] A. C. Yao. Theory and applications of trapdoor functions (extended abstract). In *23rd Annual Symposium on Foundations of Computer Science, Chicago, Illinois, USA, 3-5 November 1982*, pages 80–91, 1982.

[30] A. C. Yao. How to generate and exchange secrets (extended abstract). In *27th Annual Symposium on Foundations of Computer Science, Toronto, Canada, 27-29 October 1986*, pages 162–167. IEEE Computer Society, 1986.

APPENDIX

A. NECESSITY OF ONE-WAY FUNCTIONS

In this section, we show that time-lock puzzles imply one-way functions. As a corollary, we can deduce that succinct randomized encodings and non-parallelizing languages imply one-way functions. Extended these ideas, we show that succinct randomized encodings alone imply one-way functions against uniform adversaries (without the additional assumption regarding non-parallelizing languages).

A weak one-way function from time-lock puzzles. As a first step, we construct weak one-way functions from time-lock puzzles. Then, one can obtain strong one-way functions using standard amplification [29].

Let $(\mathsf{Puz.Gen}, \mathsf{Puz.Sol})$ be a time-lock puzzle with gap $\varepsilon < 1$ and assume that for security parameter $\lambda \in \mathbb{N}$, and any $s \in \{0,1\}^\lambda$, $t \leq 2^\lambda$, $\mathsf{Puz.Gen}(t, s; r)$ uses random coins r of length $\ell(\lambda) = \lambda^{O(1)}$. We define a function f that takes as input random coins r and a random parameter τ sampled from some small set, and outputs a puzzle with some fixed solution $s_0 \in \{0,1\}^\lambda$ that opens in time $t = 2^\tau$. Formally, $f : \{0,1\}^{\ell(\lambda)} \times [\log^2 \lambda] \to \{0,1\}^*$ is defined by:

$$f(r, \tau) = \mathsf{Puz.Gen}(2^\tau, s_0; r) \ .$$

CLAIM A.1. *f is $\Omega\left(\frac{1}{\log^2 \lambda}\right)$-one-way.*

PROOF. Fix any poly-size $\mathcal{A} = \{\mathcal{A}_\lambda\}$ and let $d(\lambda)$ be a polynomial bound on $\mathcal{A}$'s depth. We essentially show that when $2^{\varepsilon \tau} > d(\lambda)$, $\mathcal{A}$ fails to distinguish the output of the one-way function $f(r, \tau)$ from a random puzzle with some other fixed solution $s_1 \neq s_0$, which has no preimage under f (by the completeness of the puzzle). Since $2^{\varepsilon \tau} > d(\lambda)$ with probability at least $\frac{1}{\log^2 \lambda}$, the result will follow.

Formally, recall that by the definition of time-lock puzzles there exists a polynomial $\underline{t}(\cdot)$, such that for every polynomial $t(\lambda) \geq \underline{t}(\lambda)$ such that $d(\lambda) \leq t^\varepsilon(\lambda)$:

$$\Big| \Pr\left[\mathcal{A}_\lambda(Z) \in f^{-1}(Z) : Z \leftarrow \mathsf{Puz.Gen}(t(\lambda), s_0)\right] -$$
$$\Pr\left[\mathcal{A}_\lambda(Z) \in f^{-1}(Z) : Z \leftarrow \mathsf{Puz.Gen}(t(\lambda), s_1)\right] \Big| \leq \mu(\lambda) \ ,$$

for some negligible μ and any $s_0, s_1 \in \{0,1\}^\lambda$.

We consider any polynomial $t^*(\lambda) = 2^{\tau^*(\lambda)}$ that satisfies both conditions in the above definition. Then

$$\Pr\left[\mathcal{A}_\lambda(f(r, \tau)) \notin f^{-1}(f(r, \tau)) : (r, \tau) \leftarrow \{0,1\}^{\ell(\lambda)} \times [\log^2(\lambda)]\right] =$$

$$\Pr\left[\mathcal{A}_\lambda(Z) \notin f^{-1}(Z) : \begin{array}{l} (r, \tau) \leftarrow \{0,1\}^{\ell(\lambda)} \times [\log^2(\lambda)] \\ Z = \mathsf{Puz.Gen}(2^\tau, s_0; r) \end{array}\right] \geq$$

$$\frac{1}{\log^2 \lambda} \Pr\left[\mathcal{A}_\lambda(Z) \notin f^{-1}(Z) : \begin{array}{l} r \leftarrow \{0,1\}^{\ell(\lambda)} \\ Z = \mathsf{Puz.Gen}(t^*(\lambda), s_0; r) \end{array}\right] \geq$$

$$\frac{1}{\log^2 \lambda} \left(\Pr\left[\mathcal{A}_\lambda(Z) \notin f^{-1}(Z) : \begin{array}{l} r \leftarrow \{0,1\}^{\ell(\lambda)} \\ Z = \mathsf{Puz.Gen}(t^*(\lambda), s_1; r) \end{array}\right] - \mu(\lambda)\right)$$

$$\geq \frac{1}{\log^2 \lambda} - \lambda^{-\omega(1)} \ .$$

$\square$

A.1 Reducing Complexity Assumptions: One-Way Functions from Relaxed Time-Lock Puzzles

Note that, in the above proof, we did not really invoke the full power of time-lock puzzles. Concretely, time-lock puzzles that are secure against adversaries of a certain bounded *size* rather than bounded *depth* would have sufficed. For such time-lock puzzles non-parallelizing languages are not needed. Instead we can use languages that are decidable in uniform polynomial-time t, but cannot be decided by circuits of significantly smaller size $s < t^\varepsilon$ (in the spirit of the assumptions made in the context of derandomizing BPP [17]).

We observe that if we settle for one-way functions against *uniform* adversaries, we can rely only on succinct randomized encodings and remove additional complexity assumptions altogether. The intuition behind this observation is that for the class of uniform polynomial time languages we have an unconditional *time hierarchy theorem* [16]. This intuition cannot be fulfilled as is since our reduction from breaking time-lock puzzles to violating the hierarchy theorem is a randomized, and a time hierarchy theorem is not known for BPP. However, the intuition can be salvaged using a hierarchy theorem for *slightly non-uniform BPP* [3]. We elaborate below.

We first define the required relaxation of time-lock puzzles.

DEFINITION A.2 (RELAXED TIME-LOCK PUZZLES). *A puzzle $(\mathsf{Puz.Gen}, \mathsf{Puz.Sol})$ is a relaxed time-lock puzzle with gap $\varepsilon < 1$ if there exists a polynomial $\underline{t}(\cdot)$, such that for every polynomial $t(\cdot) \geq \underline{t}(\cdot)$ and every probabilistic poly-time (uniform) adversary $\mathcal{A}$ with running time $\mathsf{time}_\mathcal{A}(\lambda) \leq t^\varepsilon(\lambda)$, there exists a negligible function μ, such that for every $\lambda \in \mathbb{N}$,* and every pair of (uniformly computable) solutions $s_0, s_1 \in \{0,1\}^\lambda$:

$$\Pr\left[b \leftarrow \mathcal{A}(Z): \begin{array}{l} b \leftarrow \{0,1\}, \\ Z \leftarrow \mathsf{Puz.Gen}(t(\lambda), s_b) \end{array}\right] \leq \frac{1}{2} + \mu(\lambda) \ ,$$

where the probability is also over the coin tosses of $\mathcal{A}$.

CLAIM A.3. If $(\mathsf{Puz.Gen}, \mathsf{Puz.Sol})$ is a relaxed time-lock puzzle, then f defined above is $\Omega\left(\frac{1}{\log^2 \lambda}\right)$-one-way against uniform inverters.

The proof of the claim is essentially identical to the proof of Claim A.1, except that instead of considering poly-size circuit inverters and their depth, we consider uniform inverters and their running time.

A.1.1 Constructing Relaxed Time-Lock Puzzles

The construction of relaxed time-lock puzzles is, in fact, identical to Construction 3.5 of (standard) time-lock puzzles. The existence of non-parallelizing languages is replaced by the following unconditional theorem by Barak.

THEOREM A.4 ([3]). For any constant $\varepsilon < 1$ and any (uniformly computable) polynomially-bounded function $t(\cdot)$, there exists a language $\mathcal{L} \in Ptime(t(\cdot))/\log\log(\cdot)$ such that every probabilistic polynomial time $\mathcal{B}$ with running time $\mathsf{time}_\mathcal{B}(\lambda) \leq t^\varepsilon(\lambda)$, and non-uniform advice of size $\log\log(\lambda)$, and every large enough λ, $\mathcal{B}$ fails to decide $\mathcal{L}_\lambda = \mathcal{L} \cap \{0,1\}^\lambda$.

Above $Ptime(t(\cdot))/\log\log(\cdot)$ is the set of languages decidable by a BPP machine with non-uniform advice of size $\log\log(\lambda)$ in the input size λ. We shall assume w.l.o.g that the error of all BPP machines is bounded by $2^{-\lambda}$.

THEOREM A.5. For any $\underline{\varepsilon} < 1$, Construction 3.5 is a relaxed time-lock puzzle with gap $\underline{\varepsilon}$.

The proof of the theorem is an adaptation of the proof of Theorem 3.7. At high-level, the only difference is that now when proving security, rather than constructing a circuit decider for a non-parallelizing language we construct a decider that only has slight non-uniform advice for a language given by Theorem A.4. For the sake of completeness, we give the details below.

A.1.2 Proof of Theorem A.5

The completeness and efficiency properties of the puzzle follow directly from the completeness and efficiency properties of the succinct randomized encoding scheme. We proceed to argue that the puzzle is a secure relaxed time-lock puzzle. Let $q_{\mathsf{RE}}(\lambda)$ be the fixed polynomial given by the efficiency property of the succinct randomized encoding scheme, bounding the time required to compute a randomized encoding with machine size 3λ, input size λ, and any time bound $t \leq 2^\lambda$. Let $\underline{t}(\lambda) := (q_{\mathsf{RE}}(\lambda))^{1/\varepsilon}$.

Assume towards contradiction that there exists a uniform adversary $\mathcal{A}$, and a polynomially bounded function $t(\cdot) \geq \underline{t}(\cdot)$ such that $\mathsf{time}_\mathcal{A}(\lambda) < t^\varepsilon(\lambda)$ and for some polynomial $p(\cdot)$ and infinitely many $\lambda \in \mathbb{N}$ there exists a pair of solutions $s_0, s_1 \in \{0,1\}^\lambda$ (computable in uniform polytime) such that:

$$\Pr\left[b \leftarrow \mathcal{A}(Z): \begin{array}{l} b \leftarrow \{0,1\}, \\ Z \leftarrow \mathsf{Puz.Gen}(t(\lambda), s_b) \end{array}\right] \geq \frac{1}{2} + \frac{1}{p(\lambda)} \ . \quad (3)$$

Fix any $\underline{\varepsilon} < \varepsilon < 1$, and let $\mathcal{L} \in Ptime(t(\cdot))/\log\log(\cdot)$ be the language with gap ε given by Theorem A.4. We construct a probabilistic machine $\mathcal{B}$ with running time $\mathsf{time}_\mathcal{B}(\lambda) \leq t^\varepsilon(\lambda)$ with advice of size $\log\log(\lambda)$ that decides $\mathcal{L}_\lambda = \mathcal{L} \cap \{0,1\}^\lambda$ for any λ as above, contradicting Theorem A.4.

Fix any λ as above with corresponding $s_0, s_1 \in \{0,1\}^\lambda$. Let $M_{s_0,s_1}^{\mathcal{L},t}$ be a probabilistic machine that, on input $x \in \{0,1\}^\lambda$, outputs s_1 if $x \in \mathcal{L}$ and and s_0 if $x \notin \mathcal{L}$, after exactly $t(\lambda)$ steps. Such a machine, with error $2^{-\lambda}$, can be uniformly constructed given $\log\log(\lambda)$ bits of non-uniform advice since $\mathcal{L} \in Ptime(t(\cdot))/\log\log(\cdot)$ (and s_0, s_1 can be generated in uniform polytime). Further, denote by $M_{s_0,s_1}^{\mathcal{L},t,r}$ this machine with fixed random coins r, and assume that each such machine is described by 3λ bits (which is possible for large enough λ), and thus has the same description length as $M_{s_b}^t$.

Given input $x \in \{0,1\}^\lambda$, to decide if $x \in \mathcal{L}$, the $\mathcal{B}_\lambda$ acts as follows:

- Sample $Z := \widehat{M}_{s_0,s_1}^{\mathcal{L},t,r}(x) \leftarrow \mathsf{RE.Enc}(M_{s_0,s_1}^{\mathcal{L},t,r}, x, t(\lambda), 1^\lambda)$, where r are uniformly random coins.

- Obtain $b \leftarrow \mathcal{A}_\lambda(Z)$ and output b.

First, note that $\mathcal{B}$ can be implemented with $\log\log(\lambda)$ bits of non-uniform advice and runs in polynomial time:

$$\mathsf{time}(\mathcal{B}_\lambda) = q_{\mathsf{RE}}(\lambda) + \mathsf{time}_\mathcal{A}(\lambda) = \underline{t}^\varepsilon(\lambda) + t^\varepsilon(\lambda) \leq 2t^\varepsilon(\lambda) = o(t^\varepsilon(\lambda)) \ .$$

We next show that $\mathcal{B}$ distinguishes instances $x \in \mathcal{L}$ from instances $x \notin \mathcal{L}$ with noticeable advantage. For any $x \in \{0,1\}^\lambda$, let $b \in \{0,1\}$ indicate whether $x \in \mathcal{L}_\lambda$ we have that $s_b = M_{s_0,s_1}^{\mathcal{L},t}(x) = M_{s_b}^t(0^\lambda)$. Therefore, by the security of the randomized encoding scheme there exists a PPT simulator Sim and a negligible function $\mu(\cdot)$ such that for any $x \in \{0,1\}^\lambda$:

$$\Pr[\mathcal{B}_\lambda(x) = 1] =$$
$$\Pr\left[\mathcal{A}_\lambda(\widehat{M}_{s_0,s_1}^{\mathcal{L},t,r}(x)) = 1: \begin{array}{l} r \leftarrow \{0,1\}^{\mathrm{poly}(\lambda)} \\ \widehat{M}_{s_0,s_1}^{\mathcal{L},t}(x) \leftarrow \mathsf{RE.Enc}(M_{s_0,s_1}^{\mathcal{L},t}, x, t(\lambda), 1^\lambda) \end{array}\right] =$$
$$\Pr\left[\mathcal{A}_\lambda(\widehat{S}_{s_b}) = 1: \widehat{S}_{s_b} \leftarrow \mathsf{Sim}\left(s_b, 1^{3\lambda}, 1^\lambda, t(\lambda), 1^\lambda\right)\right] \pm (\mu(\lambda) + 2^{-\lambda}) \ ,$$

and:

$$\Pr[\mathcal{A}_\lambda(Z) = 1: Z \leftarrow \mathsf{Puz.Gen}(t(\lambda), s_b)] =$$
$$\Pr\left[\mathcal{A}_\lambda(\widehat{M}_{s_b}^t(0^\lambda)) = 1: \widehat{M}_{s_b}^t(0^\lambda) \leftarrow \mathsf{RE.Enc}(M_{s_b}^t, 0^\lambda, t(\lambda), 1^\lambda)\right] =$$
$$\Pr\left[\mathcal{A}_\lambda(\widehat{S}_{s_b}) = 1: \widehat{S}_{s_b} \leftarrow \mathsf{Sim}\left(s_b, 1^{3\lambda}, 1^\lambda, t(\lambda), 1^\lambda\right)\right] \pm \mu(\lambda) \ .$$

It follows by our assumption towards contradiction (Equation 3) that for large enough λ and any $x \in \mathcal{L}_\lambda, \bar{x} \notin \mathcal{L}_\lambda$:

$$|\Pr[\mathcal{B}_\lambda(x) = 1] - \Pr[\mathcal{B}_\lambda(\bar{x}) = 1]| \geq \frac{2}{p(\lambda)} - 2\mu(\lambda) \geq \frac{1}{p(\lambda)} \ .$$

This completes the proof.

Is There an Oblivious RAM Lower Bound?

Elette Boyle[*]
IDC Herzliya
eboyle@alum.mit.edu

Moni Naor[†]
Weizmann Institute of Science
moni.naor@weizmann.ac.il

ABSTRACT

An Oblivious RAM (ORAM), introduced by Goldreich and Ostrovsky (JACM 1996), is a (probabilistic) RAM that hides its access pattern, i.e. for every input the observed locations accessed are similarly distributed. Great progress has been made in recent years in minimizing the overhead of ORAM constructions, with the goal of obtaining *the smallest* overhead possible.

We revisit the lower bound on the overhead required to obliviously simulate programs, due to Goldreich and Ostrovsky. While the lower bound is fairly general, including the offline case, when the simulator is given the reads and writes ahead of time, it does assume that the simulator behaves in a "balls and bins" fashion. That is, the simulator must act by shuffling data items around, and is not allowed to have sophisticated encoding of the data.

We prove that for the *offline* case, showing a lower bound without the above restriction is related to the size of the circuits for sorting. Our proof is constructive, and uses a bit-slicing approach which manipulates the bit representations of data in the simulation. This implies that without obtaining yet unknown superlinear lower bounds on the size

of such circuits, we cannot hope to get lower bounds on offline (unrestricted) ORAMs.

1. INTRODUCTION

An *Oblivious RAM* (ORAM), introduced by Goldreich and Ostrovsky [19, 20] is a (probabilistic) RAM machine whose memory accesses do not reveal anything about the input—including both program and data—on which it is executed. More specifically, for any two inputs (Π_1, x_1) and (Π_2, x_2) with an equal number of memory accesses, the resulting distributions of accessed memory locations is the same, or similar.

Since their inception, oblivious RAM machines (more specifically, simulations of RAM on oblivious RAMs) have become an invaluable tool in designing cryptographic systems, where observable memory access patterns crucially must not leak sensitive information. This arises in the context of software protection (already in the original work by [20]), secure computation protocols utilizing the random access nature of computation [33, 14, 24, 29, 17, 41, 8], building secure hardware with untrusted memory [16], outsourcing data [37], protection against cache attacks [31], further server-delegation scenarios (e.g., [9, 18]), and much more.

One can trivially simulate a RAM program by an oblivious one by simply replacing each data access with a scan of the entire memory. To be useful, an ORAM simulation should only introduce a small overhead. The primary metric analyzed is the overhead in *bandwidth*: that is, how many data items must be accessed in the oblivious simulation as compared to the original. A great deal of research has gone toward simplifying and optimizing the efficiency of ORAM constructions (e.g., [20, 1, 14, 22, 23, 28, 12, 11, 17, 38, 11, 41, 36, 40]), with a clear goal of obtaining *the smallest* overhead possible.

This spurs the immediate question: *what is the best ORAM overhead possible?* The original Goldreich-Ostrovsky constructions [20] incurred multiplicative overhead $\mathsf{polylog}(n)$ for data size n. After years of progress, the most asymptotically optimized constructions to date achieve overhead $\Omega(\log n)$ for particular choices of block sizes [40]. How much further, if at all, can this be pushed?

The lower bound of Goldreich-Ostrovsky [20].

Presumably, the answer to this question is widely known. As an additional contribution within the original work that introduced and attained ORAMs, Goldreich and Ostrovsky [20] also showed a $\Omega(\log n)$ lower bound for ORAM overhead, for data size n. This has been described as:

[*]The research of the first author has received funding from the European Union's Tenth Framework Programme (FP10/2010-2016) under grant agreement no. 259426 ERC-CaC, and ISF grant 1709/14. Supported by the ERC under the EU's Seventh Framework Programme (FP/2007-2013) ERC Grant Agreement no. 307952.

[†]Weizmann Institute of Science. Incumbent of the Judith Kleeman Professorial Chair. Research supported in part by grants from the Israel Science Foundation, BSF and Israeli Ministry of Science and Technology and from the I-CORE Program of the Planning and Budgeting Committee and the Israel Science Foundation (grant No. 4/11).
This work was done in part while the authors were visiting the Simons Institute for the Theory of Computing, supported by the Simons Foundation and by the DIMACS/Simons Collaboration in Cryptography through NSF grant #CNS-1523467.

Permission to make digital or hard copies of all or part of this work for personal or classroom use is granted without fee provided that copies are not made or distributed for profit or commercial advantage and that copies bear this notice and the full citation on the first page. Copyrights for components of this work owned by others than the author(s) must be honored. Abstracting with credit is permitted. To copy otherwise, or republish, to post on servers or to redistribute to lists, requires prior specific permission and/or a fee. Request permissions from Permissions@acm.org.
ITCS'16, January 14–16, 2016, Cambridge, MA, USA.
Copyright is held by the owner/author(s). Publication rights licensed to ACM.
ACM 978-1-4503-4057-1/16/01 ...$15.00.
DOI: http://dx.doi.org/10.1145/2840728.2840761 .

- *"In their seminal work [20], Goldreich and Ostrovsky showed that an ORAM of n blocks must incur a $O(\log n)$ lower bound in bandwidth blowup, under $O(1)$ blocks of client storage."* [15]

- *"[M]emory bandwidth is always a bottleneck of ORAM. All ORAMs are subject to a $O(\log n)$ lower bound on memory bandwidth overhead [19, 20], where n is the number of blocks in ORAM."* [35]

- *"Even if new methods for oblivious RAM are discovered, there is an inherent limit to how much these schemes can be improved. It was shown in the original work of Goldreich and Ostrovsky [20] that there is a lower bound for oblivious RAM in this model.*
  Theorem ([20], Theorem 6): To obliviously perform n queries using only $O(1)$ client memory, there is a lower bound of $O(\log n)$ amortized overhead per access." [29]

- *"...due to the lower bound by Goldreich and Ostrovsky, any ORAM scheme must have bandwidth cost $\Omega(\beta \log n)$ to read or write a block of β bits.* [4]

As noted in [20, 41], the [20] lower bound is very powerful, applying also for the offline case (where all the accesses are given in advance), for arbitrary block sizes, for several relevant overhead metrics, and even when tolerating up to $O(1)$ statistical failure probability. E.g.,

- *"This is almost optimal since the well-known logarithmic ORAM lower bound [20] is immediately applicable to the circuit size metric as well."* [40].

Altogether, the solidity of the $\Omega(\log n)$ barrier would seem to be inescapable. Or is it?

Reexamining the Goldreich-Ostrovsky [20] bound.

As is well recognized, the Goldreich-Ostrovsky work [20] provided a seminal foundation for understanding ORAM and its restrictions. Upon closer observation, however, one begins to see that the lower bound of [20] is not the end of the story. Despite being broadly interpreted as a hard lower bound, applying to all scenarios, the [20] bound actually bears significant limitations.

1. "Balls and bins" storage. Perhaps most important, the [20] lower bound is within the restricted model of *"balls and bins"* data manipulation. Namely, the n data items are modeled as "balls," CPU registers and server-side data storage locations are modeled as "bins," and the set of allowed data operations consists *only* of moving balls between bins.

This is a meaningful model and captures the natural class of approaches that was the focus of [20] and many others. However, it immediately precludes any ORAM construction approach making use of data encoding, leveraging alternative representations of information, or any other form of non-black-box data manipulation. Such techniques have been shown to surpass performance of analogous "black-box" approaches in several related tasks within computer science, such as improving overhead in distributed file sharing, and optimizing network throughput via network coding (e.g., [32, 30]). It is not clear whether the $\Omega(\log n)$ bound extends at all once these strong restrictions are lifted, and in light of our work this is not going to be simple to show.

2. Statistical security. The bound applies to ORAMs with *statistical* security: i.e., where the distribution of access patterns for two different inputs are statistically close.

This statistical relation is crucial for the proof approach to proceed.

However, in many cases statistical guarantees may be stronger than necessary. Interestingly enough, the constructions presented within the same original ORAM paper [20]—and in fact, all ORAM constructions for the following 15 years, until the works of Ajtai [1] and Damgard *et al.* [14] in 2010— were *not* statistically secure. Rather, due to use of pseudorandom functions and related tools, they guaranteed only that the distributions of memory accesses were *computationally* indistinguishable. Whether such constructions could bypass the $\Omega(\log n)$ bound is unknown.

1.1 Our results

In this work, we further explore the [20] lower bound, its extensions, and its limitations. As our main technical contribution, we provide evidence that the [20] lower bound does *not* extend directly beyond the "balls and bins" storage model (in the offline case)[1], or at least that such an assertion will require developing dramatically new techniques.

Think of a RAM machine that has an external memory of size n words, each of length w bits (where $\log n \leq w \ll n$). Loosely speaking, an *offline* oblivious simulation RAM' of a RAM machine guarantees obliviousness of memory accesses only for inputs $y_i = (\Pi_i, x_i)$ (consisting of program and data) for which the program Π_i specifies its desired memory access instructions up front, within its description. We demonstrate that general logarithmic lower bounds $\Omega(\log n)$ on the overhead of offline ORAM compilers—as is implied by the [20] lower bound within the "balls and bins" setting— would directly imply *new circuit lower bounds*. Our proof is constructive: We show that the existence of n-word sorting circuits of size $o(\log n)$ times linear (i.e., $o(nw \log n)$ gates, for word size w) yields secure offline ORAM with sublogarithmic overhead. While simple $\Omega(n \log n)$ lower bounds are known on the complexity of *comparator-gate* sorting circuits (sorting networks), in which data items can only be swapped as whole entities, no such lower bounds exist for the case of Boolean circuits which may further utilize the bit representation of the data being sorted.[2] In fact, in the RAM model one can obtain *near-linear* $O(n \log \log n)$ complexity sorting algorithms [3, 25]; it is not known whether these algorithms can lead to small sorting circuits.

THEOREM 1.1 (INFORMAL). *Suppose there exists a Boolean circuit family for sorting n words of size w-bits with size $o(nw \log n)$. Then there exists an offline ORAM compiler for $O(1)$ CPU registers, with bandwidth overhead $o(\log n)$. The oblivious simulation uses only* public *randomness to hide its access patterns.*

We remark that sorting networks appear frequently as tools within existing ORAM constructions, dating back to the original works [19, 20]. Our result can be interpreted as observing that, for the offline case, sorting is essentially *all* you need; and, further, that one need not restrict themselves to circuits with this special comparator-gate structure.

Our offline ORAM construction makes heavy "non-black-box" use of data storage and manipulation, violating the

---

[1]Recall that offline ORAM corresponds to answering a sequence of requests all specified at once.

[2]An $O(n \log n)$ sorting network (such as the famed AKS [2] or the most recent work of Goodrich [21]), translates to a Boolean circuit of size $O(nw \log n)$ gates.

balls and bins restriction of the [20] bound. For example, our ORAM-compiled CPU will "re-pack" words to be stored on the server side such that a single word will contain bits of information from several data items. We do not assume much on the computational power of the (compiled) CPU, except that it be able to perform bitwise logical operations and be able to extract parts of a word.

Aside from offline ORAM, our construction also obliviously simulates a different restricted class of RAM programs: those that do not necessarily contain their access instructions in explicit form (in contrast to the offline setting), but which can be *heavily parallelized*. Namely, we can provide oblivious simulation of *Parallel* RAM (PRAM) of the CRCW-Priority variety (see [26, 39] for a survey) that has n processors and memory of size n. The overhead in simulating such PRAM programs is as above, yielding an improved complexity for this special highly-parallel case.[3] Intuitively, the offline and the PRAM cases fall within the same general framework with respect to our techniques, where in the offline case the explicit specification of access instructions allows us to parallelize the oblivious simulation over time. We elaborate on this topic in Section 3.3.

In the full version of this work, we include a complete restatement and proof of the Goldreich-Ostrovksy [20] lower bound, together with a collection of specific extensions. For example, the bound's strict balls and bins data storage model can be mildly relaxed, allowing the CPU to copy and delete balls, and to also write non-data information in "bins" (but cannot output such information). Note that several recent positive results in ORAM make use of the latter technique, storing "helper" information in memory unrelated to the data values themselves, used to locate where within memory the data is stored.

Additionally, in Section 1.2, we highlight several key research questions that remain open. In this context, we propose additional notions of ORAM security (both stronger and weaker) within which we can hope to either prove full lower bounds, or to extend our circuit-based upper bounds.

Technical Overview.
Our offline ORAM compiler construction proceeds in two primary steps.

Step 1: Sorting Circuit → Oblivious-Access Sort.
We first demonstrate how to use the structure of the given sorting circuit to obtain an efficient *Oblivious-Access Sorting* algorithm: that is, a (randomized) RAM program for sorting the values within an n-word database, where the distribution of access patterns is statistically close over any two choices of the input database (analogous to the definition of obliviousness in ORAM).

The challenge is in making this transformation tight. We can of course immediately obtain an oblivious algorithm, by directly emulating the circuit structure with the RAM (i.e., for each Boolean gate, read into memory the 2 words in which the desired bits reside, evaluate the gate on the bits, and write the result back to memory). However, unless the Boolean circuit has a very specific "word-preserving" structure, for which all bits within a single word are operated on at the same time, this approach will generically incur over-

head equal to the word size w—since we are stuck reading an entire word just to operate on a single bit. In our solution, we show how to avoid this w multiplicative overhead, suffering only an additive term comparable to $\log w$.

Two important ideas we employ in our solution are: (i) a bit-slicing/SIMD approach where we utilize the inherent w parallelism of a CPU with words of size w in order to simulate w circuits in parallel. This approach was used by Biham in 1997 [6] in order to speed up software implementations of DES. To do so, we make use of efficient (recursive) algorithms for *transposing* data.[4] The main issue with using this idea is to get w independent problems. (ii) When we randomly split the data into w parts, and sort each one separately, then for each element we have a pretty good idea where its location in the full sorted list should be, up to $\sqrt{n}$ accuracy. We can then refine this almost-sorted via a new set of w parallel sorts, this time independently within local regions.

Step 2: Oblivious-Access Sort → Offline ORAM.
Next, we use this oblivious-access sort algorithm as a black box in order to construct the final offline ORAM compiler. The main idea within this step is to treat the program Π and the data x *together*, and to make use of the Oblivious-Access Sort procedure to enable routing of values to particular desired sub-orderings.

Consider, for example, a slightly simplified case where the programs simply indicate a length-n sequence of Read operations at fixed addresses in $[n]$. This can be obliviously simulated via the following sub-steps. First, the entire size-$2n$ memory contents—including both the query sequence and the data—are labeled and sorted so as to move memory into blocks each associated with a single index of data: starting with the data value itself x_i, and followed by the chronological sequence of Read requests to this address i. This is depicted in the first figure below (where "Ri" denotes Read request at address i). Once we have this structure, each Read request can be satisfied by a single pass through the database, "filling in" the correct value by (always) looking at the preceding word. This is depicted in the second figure below.

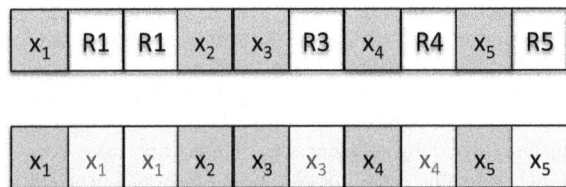

x_1	R1	R1	x_2	x_3	R3	x_4	R4	x_5	R5

x_1	x_1	x_1	x_2	x_3	x_3	x_4	x_4	x_5	x_5

Then, the memory contents are returned to their original ordering by a reverse label and sort, yielding the n data items followed by the n requested items in desired order.

We remark that in this work we consider a somewhat restricted offline setting, where access Read/Write instructions are pre-specified, as opposed to simply access addresses. However, this case is already strong enough to be covered by the [20] lower bound, assuming balls and bins.

1.2 Open Questions

The observations and results above draw forth several interesting open questions in oblivious RAM research. We

---

[3]Note, however, that the resulting system is still a sequential RAM, and not an Oblivious Parallel RAM as in [7].

[4]This transpose step is the source of the $\log w$ additive complexity overhead term.

view these research directions as a further contribution of the present work.

Online lower bound? A good starting point toward proving general ORAM lower bounds (without balls and bins restrictions) is within an even stronger *online* model, where the simulation must successfully answer each data access request before learning the next. This more stringent variant is, in fact, the notion satisfied by essentially all known positive results in ORAM. We propose a definition of online ORAM in Section 2.2 (Definition 2.10).

Relaxing Balls and Bins? One can orthogonally relax the balls and bins model restriction. For example, does the [20] lower bound extend to a setting of *Balls and Bins with Linear Encoding*, where the CPU may generate balls of a different "color" (say, black) as linear combinations of original white balls (treated as formal monomials), may only output white balls at the conclusion of simulation, and can convert a black ball back to white only if its formal polynomial reduces to a single monomial. Note that this model captures approaches in the style of network coding, but does not allow for the type of bit-slicing manipulation we employ in our offline ORAM solution.

Strong offline ORAM from circuits? Is it possible to extend our circuit-based ORAM construction to a more expressive class of programs? For example, suppose the programs explicitly specify the addresses of memory accesses, but only know *at runtime* (e.g., as a result of partial computation) what actual read/write instruction will be performed at this location. We refer to this as a "strong offline" case.

Converse Relation? We show that small sorting circuits imply efficient offline ORAMs; does the converse also hold? Namely, given an offline (or even online) n-word ORAM with $O(1)$ registers and bandwidth and/or computation overhead $o(\log n)$, does this imply the existence of sorting circuits of size $o(nw \log n)$? The challenge here is that, although the access patterns of the ORAM are (essentially) input-independent, they may rely on randomness generated at runtime in order to attain low overhead.

Computationally Secure ORAM? As mentioned, the [20] lower bound crucially relies on the *statistical* closeness of access pattern distributions for any two inputs. As soon as this is relaxed to *computational* indistinguishability, where distributions of access patterns generated from two inputs cannot be distinguished by efficient algorithms (but may even be disjoint), we could even hope to attain constant overhead in bandwidth and computation.[5]

1.3 Related Work

Pippenger and Fischer [34] were the first to consider the issue of oblivious access patterns, in their case, for Turing Machines (TM). Our work can be seen as a converse of the Pippenger-Fischer approach who showed how to efficiently translate a TM into a circuit via *Oblivious* TMs, whereas we obtain Oblivious RAM via circuits. Note that they obtain an $\Omega(\log n)$ lower bound for online oblivious simulation of

Turing Machines, but it is not clear that their bound is relevant to the question of online oblivious simulation of RAM.

Beame and Machmouchi [5] showed a super-logarithmic lower bound for *oblivious branching programs*. However, as they noted, this bound is not applicable to the standard model of Oblivious RAM: The standard ORAM model requires the probability distribution of the observed access patterns to be statistically close regardless of the input; in contrast, Beame's model requires that this holds *for every random string* chosen. Hence, to date, Goldreich and Ostrovsky's original lower bound is the only applicable bound known.

Damgård, Medlegard, and Nielsen [14] proved a lower bound on the amount of secret randomness required for a probabilistic RAM to obliviously simulate an arbitrary RAM in an online setting. Namely, if fewer than $n/8$ items are accessed per original access, then the simulation must use at least $\theta(1)$ *secret* random bits on average per simulated read operation. Their lower bound applies to *online* ORAMs. Our work (on *offline* ORAMs) demonstrates that this is essential, since instantiating our construction with known sorting circuit constructions yields an unconditional offline ORAM that does not make use of any secret randomness.

It was observed by Apon *et al.* [4] that the Goldriech-Ostrovsky [20] bandwidth lower bound does not hold if one allows *server-side computation* on data before sending. Recent constructions (e.g., [4, 15]) provide ORAM-like access pattern security with *constant* bandwidth per data query, by leveraging polylogarithmic server computation (and computational assumptions). In fact, we argue that the reason these works overcome the lower bound is that they 'violated' the balls and bins restriction (and provide computational security).

An alternative weaker "Oblivious *Network* RAM" model was proposed by Dachman-Soled *et al.* [13] which does not fall within the [20] lower bound, where the adversary sees only the most significant bits of accessed addresses (and the lower-order bits are hidden from adversarial view).

We emphasize that our offline ORAM construction is in the oblivious RAM computation model of [20], where server-side computation is not allowed, and the adversary sees the full addresses of accessed memory.

2. RAM AND OBLIVIOUS RAM

We follow the terminology in [20].

2.1 Random Access Machines

A Random Access Machine (RAM) is modeled as a pair of interactive Turing machines (ITM), corresponding to CPU and Memory, which "interact" with each other via a set of specified actions. In what follows, n, w, and $r \in \mathbb{N}$ will be used to denote the memory size, word size, and number of registers (i.e., CPU memory size) of the system.

DEFINITION 2.1 (MEMORY). *For every* $n, w, r \in \mathbb{N}$, *let* $\mathsf{MEM}_{n,w,r}$ *be an ITM with communication tape and input / output / work tapes of size* $O(rw)$ *and* $O(nw)$, *respectively. It partitions its work tape into* n *words, each of size* $O(w)$. *After copying its input to its work tape, machine* $\mathsf{MEM}_{n,w,r}$ *is message-driven. Upon receiving a message* (inst, addr, val), *where* inst $\in \{\mathsf{store}, \mathsf{fetch}, \mathsf{halt}\}$ *(an instruction),* addr $\in [n]$ *(an address), and* val $\in \{0,1\}^{O(w)}$ *(a value), machine* $\mathsf{MEM}_{n,w,r}$ *acts as follows:*

---

[5] Constructions attaining $O(1)$ bandwidth overhead in the computational setting have recently been demonstrated, however fall outside of the standard ORAM model since they assume the RAM memory can perform local computations on data before sending to the CPU: See Related Work.

- If inst = store, *then machine* MEM$_{n,w,r}$ *copies the value* val *from the current message into word number* addr *of its work tape.*

- If inst = fetch, *then machine* MEM$_{n,w,r}$ *sends a message consisting of the current contents of word number* addr *(of its work tape).*

- If inst = halt, *then machine* MEM$_{n,w,r}$ *copies a prefix of its work tape (until a special symbol) to its output tape, and halts.*

DEFINITION 2.2 (CPU). *For every* $n, w, r \in \mathbb{N}$, *let* CPU$_{n,w,r}$ *be an ITM with communication and work tapes of size* $O(rw)$, *operating as hereby specified. After copying its input to its work tape, machine* CPU$_{n,w,r}$ *conducts a computation on its work tape, and sends a message determined by this computation. In subsequent rounds,* CPU$_{n,w,r}$ *is message driven. Upon receiving a new message, machine* CPU$_{n,w,r}$ *copies the message to its work tape, and based on its computation on the work tape, sends a message. In case the* CPU$_{n,w,r}$ *sends a* halt *message, the* CPU$_{n,w,r}$ *halts immediately (with no output).*

DEFINITION 2.3 (RAM). *For every* $n, w, r \in \mathbb{N}$, *let* RAM$_{n,w,r}$ *be a pair of* (CPU$_{n,w,r}$, MEM$_{n,w,r}$), *where* CPU$_{n,w,r}$*'s read-only message tape coincides with* MEM$_{n,w,r}$*'s write-only message tape, and vice versa. The* input *to* RAM$_{n,w,r}$ *is a pair* (s, y), *where* s *is an initialization input for* CPU$_{n,w,r}$,[6] *and* y *is the input to* MEM$_{n,w,r}$. *The output of* RAM$_{n,w,r}$ *on input* (s, y), *denoted* RAM$_{n,w,r}(s,y)$, *is defined as the output of* MEM$_{n,w,r}(y)$ *when interacting with* CPU$_{n,w,r}(s)$.

A probabilistic-RAM$_{n,w,r}$ *is a* RAM$_{n,w,r}$ *in which* CPU$_{n,w,r}$ *additionally has the ability to generate randomness on the fly as part of its local computation.*

To view RAM$_{n,w,r}$ as a universal machine, we separate the input y to MEM$_{n,w,r}$ as $y = (\Pi, x)$ containing both the "program" and "data."

REMARK 2.4. *For purposes of lower bounds, it is generally considered that the running time of* RAM$_{n,w,r}$ *is always greater than the length of the input (i.e.,* $|y|$*). Under this assumption, we may ignore the "loading time" and count only the number of machine cycles in the execution of* Π *on* x *(ie., the number of rounds of message exchange between* CPU$_{n,w,r}$ *and* MEM$_{n,w,r}$*).*

2.2 Oblivious RAM

To define oblivious simulation of RAMs, we first define oblivious RAM machines. Loosely speaking, the "memory access pattern" in an oblivious RAM, on each input, depends only on its running time (on this input). Note that we do not regard hiding the *contents* of memory, which can be achieved independently (e.g., using encryption).

DEFINITION 2.5 (ACCESS PATTERN). *The* access pattern *of a (probabilistic-)*RAM$_{n,w,r}$ *on input* y, *denoted by*

$$\mathscr{A}ccess(\text{RAM}_{n,w,r}, y),$$

is a distribution (over the random coins of CPU$_{n,w,r}$*) of sequences* $(\text{addr}_1, \ldots, \text{addr}_i, \ldots)$, *such that for every* i, *the* i*th message sent by* CPU$_{n,w,r}$, *when interacting with* MEM$_{n,w,r}(y)$ *with corresponding random coins, is of the form* $(\cdot, \text{addr}_i, \cdot)$.

---

[6]Without loss of generality, s may be a fixed "start symbol."

We define an oblivious RAM to be a probabilistic RAM for which the probability distribution of memory access patterns during an execution depends only on the running time (i.e., is independent of the particular input $y = (\Pi, x)$).

DEFINITION 2.6 (OBLIVIOUS RAM). *For every* $n, w, r \in \mathbb{N}$, *we define an* oblivious RAM$_{n,w,r}$ *as a probabilistic* RAM$_{n,w,r}$ *satisfying the following condition. For every two strings* y_1, y_2, *if* $|\mathscr{A}ccess(\text{RAM}_{n,w,r}, y_1)|$ *and* $|\mathscr{A}ccess(\text{RAM}_{n,w,r}, y_2)|$ *are identically distributed, then* $\mathscr{A}ccess(\text{RAM}_{n,w,r}, y_1)$ *and* $\mathscr{A}ccess(\text{RAM}_{n,w,r}, y_2)$ *are identically distributed.*

We consider three primary notions (of varying strength) for oblivious simulation of an arbitrary RAM program on an oblivious RAM. The first, *"standard"* notion (as in [20]) holds for all RAM programs, and requires only that both machines compute the same function. In contrast, the [20] lower bound holds also within a weaker *"offline"* setting—considering only those programs whose memory access addresses are specified explicitly within their descriptions. We additionally propose a definition of a stronger *"online"* notion of oblivious simulation (that is obtained by most ORAM constructions)—where the compiler must satisfy each access query on the fly.

DEFINITION 2.7 (OBLIVIOUS RAM SIMULATION). *We say that a probabilistic-*RAM$'_{n',w',r'}$ *obliviously simulates* RAM$_{n,w,r}$ *if the following conditions hold:*

- **Correctness.** *There exists a negligible function* ν *for which the probabilistic-*RAM$'_{n',w',r'}$ *simulates* RAM$_{n,w,r}$ *with probability* $1 - \nu(n)$. *That is, for every input* y, *with probability* $1 - \nu(n)$ *over the choice of random coins of* CPU$'_{n',w',r'}$, *the output of* RAM$'_{n',w',r'}$ *on input* y *equals the output* RAM$_{n,w,r}(y)$ *of* RAM$_{n,w,r}$ *on the input* y.

- **Obliviousness.** *The probabilistic-*RAM$'_{n',w',r'}$ *is oblivious (as per Definition 2.6).*

- **Non-triviality.** *The random variable representing the running-time of probabilistic-*RAM$'_{n',w',r'}$ *(on input* y*) is fully specified by the running-time of* RAM$_{n,w,r}$ *(on input* y*).*

DEFINITION 2.8 (*Offline* OBLIVIOUS RAM SIMULATION). *We say that a probabilistic-*RAM$'_{n',w',r'}$ *is an* offline *oblivious simulation of* RAM$_{n,w,r}$ *if the Correctness, Obliviousness, and Non-triviality properties of Definition 2.7 hold for the restricted class of* $y = (\Pi, x)$ *corresponding to* Fixed-Access *programs: A Fixed-Access program* Π *contains within its description the explicit sequence of communication triples of the form* (fetch, addr, $\bot$) *or* (store, addr, val) *for pre-specified* val.

Note that, for the above definition to be non-trivial, each fetch operation will implicitly be followed by an output of the fetched value.

Intuitively, an *online* ORAM simulation requires that each access instruction (and output) is successfully completed before learning the next. This prevents the simulation from "pre-processing" any of its access patterns in order to aid future lookups. We formalize this by splitting the program into sequential sub-programs $\Pi = \Pi_1, \Pi_2, \ldots, \Pi_t$ (determined at runtime based on execution), each with a single memory access (and, we will assume, a single output), and introducing an oracle $\mathcal{O}^{\mathsf{NextStep}}$. Instead of the entire input program Π being loaded into memory at initialization, Π is instead given only oracle access to $\mathcal{O}^{\mathsf{NextStep}}$. At any time during execution, the CPU may send a message next to $\mathcal{O}^{\mathsf{NextStep}}$, who responds by loading the next piece Π_{i+1} of the program into memory (i.e., the work tape of $\mathsf{MEM}_{n,w,r}$). However, the CPU must specify its output to the previous Π_i before requesting Π_{i+1}: namely, the ith output cannot be modified after the ith next request is made.

DEFINITION 2.9 (ONLINE RAM MODEL). *For every* $n, w, r \in \mathbb{N}$, *let a (probabilistic) online RAM* $\mathsf{onlineRAM}_{n,w,r}$ *be a triple of ITMs* $(\mathsf{CPU}_{n,w,r}, \mathsf{MEM}_{n,w,r}, \mathcal{O}^{\mathsf{NextStep}})$. *The input to* $\mathsf{onlineRAM}_{n,w,r}$ *is a triple* (s, x, Π), *where* s *is an initialization start input for* $\mathsf{CPU}_{n,w,r}$, x *is the (data) input to* $\mathsf{MEM}_{n,w,r}$, *and* Π *is the (program) input to* $\mathcal{O}^{\mathsf{NextStep}}$. $\mathsf{CPU}_{n,w,r}$ *begins by performing a computation on its work tape, and then may send a message to either* $\mathsf{MEM}_{n,w,r}$ *or* $\mathcal{O}^{\mathsf{NextStep}}$ *based on this computation. In subsequent rounds,* $\mathsf{CPU}_{n,w,r}$ *is message driven, as before.*

Messages sent from $\mathsf{CPU}_{n,w,r}$ *to* $\mathsf{MEM}_{n,w,r}$ *take the same form as in the standard RAM model, and are responded to identically. Messages sent from* $\mathsf{CPU}_{n,w,r}$ *to* $\mathcal{O}^{\mathsf{NextStep}}$ *take the form* $(\mathsf{inst}, \mathsf{state}, \mathsf{out})$, *corresponding to an instruction* $\mathsf{inst} \in \{\mathsf{next}, \mathsf{halt}\}$, *the current contents* $\mathsf{state} \in \{0,1\}^{rw}$ *of the work tape of* $\mathsf{CPU}_{n,w,r}$, *and an intermediate output value* $\mathsf{out} \in \{0,1\}^w$. $\mathcal{O}^{\mathsf{NextStep}}$ *maintains a local counter* i *(initialized at the beginning of execution to* $i = 0$*), and upon receiving such message from* $\mathsf{CPU}_{n,w,r}$, *does the following.*

- *If* $\mathsf{inst} = \mathsf{next}$, *then* $\mathcal{O}^{\mathsf{NextStep}}$ *determines the* $(i+1)$*th instruction* Π_{i+1} *of* Π *given the received value* state, *and sends a description* Π_{i+1} *to* $\mathsf{MEM}_{n,w,r}$, *who copies it into a designated location in its work tape. In addition,* $\mathcal{O}^{\mathsf{NextStep}}$ *writes* out *to the* i*th position of its output tape.*

- *If* $\mathsf{inst} = \mathsf{halt}$, *then* $\mathcal{O}^{\mathsf{NextStep}}$ *outputs the full contents of its output tape.*

The output *of* $\mathsf{onlineRAM}_{n,w,r}$ *on input* (s, d, Π), *denoted* $\mathsf{onlineRAM}_{n,w,r}(s, x, \Pi)$, *is defined as the output of* $\mathcal{O}^{\mathsf{NextStep}}(\Pi)$ *when interacting with* $\mathsf{CPU}_{n,w,r}(s)$ *and* $\mathsf{MEM}_{n,w,r}(x)$.

An online oblivious RAM *is on online RAM satisfying the obliviousness requirement of Definition 2.6, where* $\mathcal{A}ccess(\mathsf{RAM}_{n,w,r}, y)$ *is as in Definition 2.5 (i.e., the sequence of accessed memory addresses, without information on calls to* $\mathcal{O}^{\mathsf{NextStep}}$*).*

Note that the CPU commits itself to the ith step output *before* it gains access to the next instruction Π_{i+1} (through MEM).

DEFINITION 2.10 (*Online* OBLIVIOUS RAM SIMULATION). *We say that a probabilistic-*$\mathsf{RAM}'_{n',w',r'}$ *is an* online oblivious simulation *of* $\mathsf{RAM}_{n,w,r}$ *if the Correctness, Obliviousness and Non-triviality properties of Definition 2.7 hold in the* Online RAM Model, *as per Definition 2.9.*

In any case (standard, offline, etc.), simulation of a RAM by an oblivious RAM incurs certain overhead costs. In this work, we focus on the overhead in *computation* and *bandwidth*.

DEFINITION 2.11 (OVERHEAD OF OBLIVIOUS SIMULATION). *Suppose that a probabilistic-*$\mathsf{RAM}'_{n',w',r'}$ *obliviously simulates the computations of* $\mathsf{RAM}_{n,w,r}$.

- *We say that the* bandwidth overhead *of the simulation is at most* g *for some function* $g : \mathbb{N} \to \mathbb{N}$ *if, for every* y, *at most* $g(B) \cdot B$ *bits are written by* $\mathsf{MEM}'_{n',w',r'}$ *to its communication tape throughout the course of the simulation, where* B *denotes the number of bits written by* $\mathsf{MEM}_{n,w,r}$ *to its communication tape in the original execution.*

- *We say that the* computation overhead *of the simulation is at most* g *for some function* $g : \mathbb{N} \to \mathbb{N}$ *if, for every* y, *at most* $g(t) \cdot t$ *computation steps are taken during the execution of* $\mathsf{RAM}'_{n',w',r'}(y)$, *where* t *denotes the number of computation steps taken in the original execution* $\mathsf{RAM}_{n,w,r}(y)$.

3. OFFLINE ORAM LOWER BOUNDS IMPLY CIRCUIT LOWER BOUNDS

Our main theorem demonstrates that in the *offline* case, lifting the "balls and bins" restriction from the Goldreich-Ostrovsky lower bound will require proving yet unknown circuit lower bounds on the size of Boolean sorting circuits. This conclusion is obtained constructively: Given a small sorting circuit, we show how to build a secure offline ORAM with sub-logarithmic overhead.

THEOREM 3.1. *Suppose there exists a Boolean circuit ensemble* $C = \{C(n, w)\}_{n,w}$ *of size* $s(n, w)$, *such that each* $C(n, w)$ *takes as input* n *words each of size* w *bits, and outputs the words in sorted order. Then for word size* $w \in \Omega(\log n) \cap n^{o(1)}$ *and constant CPU registers* $r \in O(1)$, *there exists a secure offline ORAM (as per Definition 2.8) with total bandwidth and computation* $O(n \log w + s(2n/w, w))$.

In particular, given the existence of any sorting circuit ensemble with size $o(nw \log n)$, we obtain an offline ORAM construction that bypasses the [20] lower bound:

COROLLARY 3.2. *If there exist Boolean sorting circuits* $C = \{C(n, w)\}_{n,w}$ *of size* $s(n, w) \in o(nw \log n)$ *(for* $w \in \Omega(\log n) \cap n^{o(1)}$*), then there exists secure offline ORAM with* $O(1)$ *CPU registers and bandwidth and computation overhead* $o(\log n)$.

The total storage requirement of our offline ORAM construction is $O(n + s(2n/w, w))$. For circuits of size $s(m, w) \in o(mw \log m)$, this corresponds to $o(\log n)$ storage overhead. We do not assume much on the computational power of the (compiled) CPU, except that it be able to perform bitwise logical operations and be able to extract parts of a word.

The proof of Theorem 3.1 proceeds via two steps. First, in Section 3.2, we begin by constructing and analyzing an efficient *Oblivious-Access Sort* algorithm: i.e., a (randomized) RAM program for sorting an n-word database, where the distribution of access patterns is statistically close over any two choices of the input database. We remark that this notion of oblivious-access aligns directly with that of ORAM. (In contrast, the term "Oblivious Sort" refers in the literature to sorting algorithms whose access patterns are *fixed*).

DEFINITION 3.3 (OBLIVIOUS-ACCESS SORT). *An* Oblivious-Access Sort *algorithm for input size* n *(and word size* w*) and computation* $\mathsf{comp}(n, w)$ *is a (possibly randomized) RAM program* Π *in which the following properties hold:*

- *Efficiency: The program Π terminates in $\mathsf{comp}(n,w)$ computation steps.*

- *Correctness: With overwhelming probability in n, at the conclusion of Π, the database contains the n inputs, in sorted order.*

- *Oblivious Access: There exists a negligible function ν such that for any two inputs x, x' of size n, then $\mathscr{A}ccess(\mathsf{RAM}_{n,w,r}, (\Pi, x))$ is $\nu(n)$-close statistically to $\mathscr{A}ccess(\mathsf{RAM}_{n,w,r}, (\Pi, x'))$ (see Definition 2.5).*

Then, in Section 3.3, this oblivious-access sort algorithm will be used as a black box in order to construct the final offline ORAM compiler.

We first begin in Section 3.1 by introducing some useful notation.

3.1 Notation

Throughout this work, n, w, and $r \in \mathbb{N}$ will be used to denote the (external) memory size, word size, and number of registers (i.e., CPU memory size) of the system. We consider the range in which $w \in \Omega(\log n) \cap n^{o(1)}$ and $r \in O(1)$.

We denote the work tapes of $\mathsf{CPU}_{n,w,r}$ and $\mathsf{MEM}_{n,w,r}$ as arrays $\mathsf{Reg}, \mathsf{Mem}$.

In general, capital letters are used to denote arrays (e.g., $\mathsf{Reg}, \mathsf{Mem}$), lowercase letters to denote words (sometimes interpreted as bit strings). Indexing: for an array (e.g., memory Mem), $\mathsf{Mem}[i]$ denotes word i in the array; $\mathsf{Mem}[i][j]$ denotes the jth bit of $\mathsf{Mem}[i]$ in the array. For a single word, $x[j]$ denotes the jth bit of x. When describing addresses of the head of an array (in particular, to be passed as an argument to a function call), we will denote by $D' :=$ "$D[\times n]$" the array D' for which each $D'[i+1] = D[n \cdot i + 1]$

For $n \in \mathbb{N}$, we denote by S_n the symmetric group on n items.

We consider general binary circuits of fan-in 2. Denote by $G = \{f : \{0,1\}^2 \to \{0,1\}\}$ the set of all possible boolean gate functions on two inputs, indexed by an integer in $\{1, \ldots, 16\}$.

NOTATION 3.4 (BOOLEAN CIRCUIT MODEL). *A (fan-in 2) boolean circuit C with n-bit inputs, m-bit outputs, and size $|C| = s$ is a collection of s gates g_i of the following form:*

- *Input gates: $\{g_i\}_{1 \le i \le n}$ each directly associated with bit i of the input bit string.*

- *Computation gates: $\{g_i\}_{n < i \le s-m}$ each specified by a triple (f, i_L, i_R), where $f \in G$ (see above), and $1 \le i_L, i_R < i$.*

- *Output gates: $\{g_i\}_{s-m < i \le s}$ each specified by a single index $i_{\mathsf{out}} < i$.*

3.2 From Sort Circuits to Oblivious-Access Sort

For simplicity of exposition, we treat the case of oblivious-access sorting of *distinct* data items. This will suffice for our Offline ORAM application. However, a few modifications to the algorithm will enable sorting of non-distinct items.

PROPOSITION 3.5 (OBLIVIOUS-ACCESS SORT). *If there exist Boolean sorting circuits $C = \{C(n,w)\}_{n,w}$ of size $s(n,w)$, then there exists an Oblivious-Access Sort algorithm for n distinct elements using $O(1)$ CPU resisters, with total bandwidth and computation complexity each $O(n \log w + s(2n/w, w))$, and probability of error $e^{-n^{\Omega(1)}}$.*

In order to avoid the factor of w overhead in directly emulating the circuit by RAM, in our sorting algorithm the CPU will manipulate the bit structure of words stored in memory, so that we can "make progress" on *all* bits within words pulled into memory. The governing observation is that the above circuit-emulation approach is not too costly when executing independently *on w groups of only n/w words in parallel*, taking a bit-slicing/SIMD approach.

At a high level, our Oblivious-Access Sort RAM program OASort takes the following form. Phases 1 and 2 are depicted visually in Figure 1; Phases 3 and 4 are depicted in Figure 2.

1. First, we perform a random public shuffle of database items. Since the permutation may be public (without attempting to hide the effective permutation), this step may be executed straightforwardly, e.g. via Knuth (Fisher-Yates) shuffle [27]. The purpose of this initial shuffle is to reduce the problem of worst-case sorting to that of sorting a list in random order. Note, however, that no *secret* randomness is required.

2. Second, we sort w separate groups of only n/w words each, *in parallel*. This requires the algorithm to first "repack" words to contain consistent bits from each of the w parallel executions (corresponding to transpose of bits in memory), then to emulate the circuit on "packed" words SIMD-style, and finally to transpose the words back to original form.

   At the conclusion of this step, we have w interleaved sets of n/w sorted words. Our remaining task is to merge these sorted lists into a single sorted list of n words.

3. Because of the random shuffle in Step 1, we are guaranteed with overwhelming probability that no element's current position is too far from its position in the final sorted list. We may thus split the list into new blocks of size $n/w \in \omega(\sqrt{n})$ and sort each block independently, in parallel. To handle elements near the boundary of these blocks, we extend the "window" of each block by an extra $n/(2w)$ on either side, introducing overlaps between blocks.

   At the conclusion of this step, we have a database of size $2n$ (because of overlaps), where each ith consecutive block of $2n/w$ words is individually sorted, and is guaranteed to contain as a subsequence the ith set of n/w words in the *final* sorted list. The goal is now to remove duplicated words, leaving behind this complete sorted subsequence.

4. Removing duplicates takes place via three sub-steps. First, the duplicate items are *identified* (and replaced by $-\infty$ symbols) by a one-pass over the data. In order to remove them *obliviously* (since their location is input-dependent), we re-sort each of the $2n/w$-sized blocks, allowing the $-\infty$ garbage items to sift to the first n/w positions of each $2n/w$-block. Then, we may deterministically remove garbage items and compress back to a sorted list of size n.

REMARK 3.6 (SUB-ALGORITHMS). *We defer the reader to the full version of this work for a full description and analysis of useful sub-algorithms $\mathsf{RandPerm}, \mathsf{Transpose}, \mathsf{EmulateCircuit}$, and $\mathsf{RemRedundant}$. $\mathsf{RandPerm}(D, n)$ shuffles the n words in D to random order, in time $O(n)$. $\mathsf{Transpose}(D, n, w)$ implements a bitwise transpose within each block of w words* within the n-word database D; for $O(1)$ local CPU registers, this can be performed in time $O(n \log w)$. EmulateCircuit(D, C, s, n, m) performs a SIMD execution (i.e., component-wise for each bit in the RAM words) of the circuit C, with n words of input, m words of output, and s boolean gates, on the data held in D, in time $O(s)$. RemRedundant(E, n) steps through an n-item database sorted in blocks with overlap, and identifies and zeroes out redundant items, in linear $O(n)$ time.

Oblivious-Access Sort.

A description of OASort is given in Figure 3.

PROOF OF PROPOSITION 3.5. The complexity (both computation and bandwidth) of each step in OASort is indicated in grey below each arrow within Figures 1 and 2, yielding a total complexity of $O(n \log w + s(2n/w, w))$. These individual values are derived from the complexities of the underlying sub-algorithms RandPerm, Transpose, etc.

The correctness and obliviousness of the OASort procedure (Figure 3) hold via the following sequence of intermediate claims.

The first claim shows that, in a slightly tweaked version of the OASort Steps 3.2-3.2, the items of the n/w individually sorted lists will *not* appear too far from their final positions in the complete n-sorted list, with overwhelming probability over the randomness of the initial shuffle. In the experiment below, the values stored in D represent the *indices* of the distinct values to be sorted, with respect to their correct sorted order (i.e., smallest is 1, largest is n). (The difference between this experiment and the OASort Steps 3.2-3.2 is that here we begin with elements already in sorted order $D[i] = i$, and then apply a random permutation, whereas in OASort the values begin in arbitrary unsorted order). The experiment fails in abort if after randomly permuting and then sorting the interleaved groups (each of size $\ell := n/w$), any position of D holds a value that is "far" from its target value (specifically, if it falls outside the 2ℓ-size region assigned to the ℓ-size region in which it belongs).

CLAIM 3.7. *Fix $\ell := n/w \in \omega(\sqrt{n})$. (Recall $w \in n^{o(1)}$). With overwhelming probability in n (over $\sigma \leftarrow S_n$), the following experiment does* not *end in* abort:

1. *Sample random $\sigma \leftarrow S_n$; $\forall i \in [n]$, set $D[\sigma(i)] \leftarrow i$.*

2. *Individually sort each of the w interleaved groups of (n/w) words of D: i.e., $\forall i \in [w]$, $D[i] \leq D[w+i] \leq \cdots \leq D[(n/w-1)w+i]$. (Indexing as in Figure 1).*

3. *If for any $(j,k) \in [w] \times [n/w]$ (now indexing as in Figure 2) the following holds, the experiment ends in* abort *(recall that in perfect sorted order, $D[j\ell + k] = j\ell + k$):*

$$j\ell + k \notin \{D[(j-1/2)\ell], \ldots, D[(j+3/2)\ell]\}.$$

That is, the value that should be sorted to the kth word in jth n/w-block is currently located somewhere outside the specified $2n/w$-window spanning this location (see Figure 2).

PROOF. Deferred to full version. (Chernoff bound). □

We now adjust the previous experiment to match that of OASort Steps 3.2-3.2. Namely, we do not assume the items in D begin in sorted order, but rather in arbitrary permuted order π.

Oblivious-Access Sort OASort(D, n)
RandPerm, Transpose, EmulateCircuit, RemRedundant are as described in Remark 3.6.

1. RandPerm(D, n). Perform a random public shuffle of the database items.

2. Sort in parallel w blocks of size n/w (see Figure 1):

   a. Transpose(D, n, w). Reorder data to SIMD form.

   b. EmulateCircuit($D[\times w], C_{\text{sort}}, s(n), n, n$). SIMD emulate boolean circuit C_{sort} on D.

   c. Transpose(D, n, w). Transpose data back to (standard) word form.

Result: w interleaved groups of n/w words, each individually sorted.

3. Merge blocks into 1 sorted list *with overlaps*, by sorting (overlapping) blocks in parallel.

   a. Arrange data to appropriate form (see Figure 2). Namely, let $\ell = n/w$.
   Define $2n$-size database E: For each $i \in \{0, \ldots, w-1\}$ and $j \in \{-\ell/2 + 1, \ldots, 3\ell/2\}$, let $E[2i\ell + \ell/2 + j] \leftarrow D[i\ell + j]$, where $D[i] := -\infty$ (special min elmt) for $i < 1$ and $i > n$.

   b. Sort 2ℓ-size blocks of E in parallel (see Figure 2):

      (i) Reorder words: Define temp array $E'[iw + j + 1] \leftarrow E[2\ell j + i + 1]$ for $i \in \{0, \ldots, 2n/w - 1\}$, $j \in \{0, \ldots, w-1\}$. (Recall $\ell = n/w$).

      (ii) Transpose($E', 2n, w$). Transpose E' bitwise to SIMD form.

      (iii) EmulateCircuit($E', C_{\text{sort}}, s(2n), 2n, 2n$). SIMD emulate boolean circuit C_{sort} on w independent blocks of E'.

      (iv) Transpose($E', 2n, w$). Transpose data back to (standard) word form.

      (v) Reorder words: Return data as $E[2\ell j + i + 1] \leftarrow E'[iw + j + 1]$ for $i \in \{0, \ldots, 2n/w - 1\}$, $j \in \{0, \ldots, w-1\}$. (Recall $\ell = n/w$).

Result: $2n$-size database E contains all n items of D in sorted order, but with overlaps.

4. Remove redundant items (see Figure 2).

   a. RemRedundant($E, 2n$). One-pass to identify redundant items, setting to $-\infty$:

   b. Sort each block again, repeating Step b.

   c. One pass: Compress E back to D, removing $-\infty$ values. Namely, for each $i \in \{0, \ldots, w-1\}$ and $j \in \{1, \ldots, \ell\}$, set $D[i\ell + j] \leftarrow E[2i\ell + j + \ell]$.

Figure 3: Oblivious-access sorting algorithm for *distinct data items.*

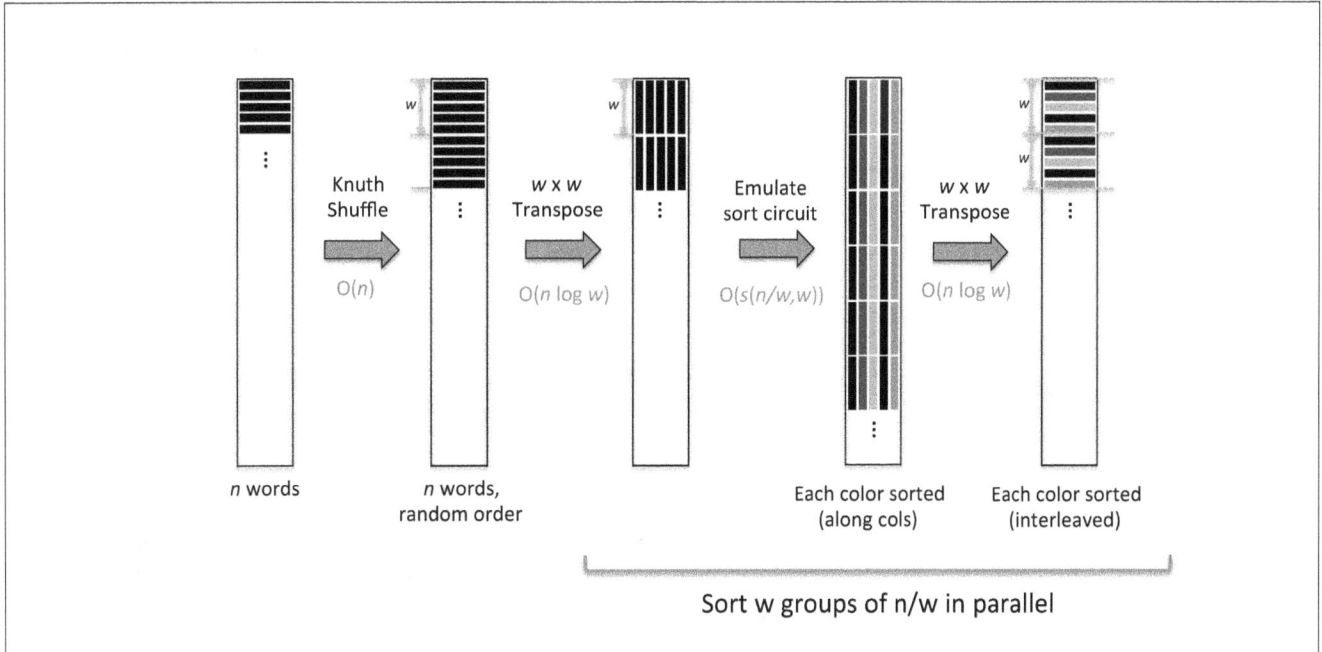

Figure 1: First phases of OASort.

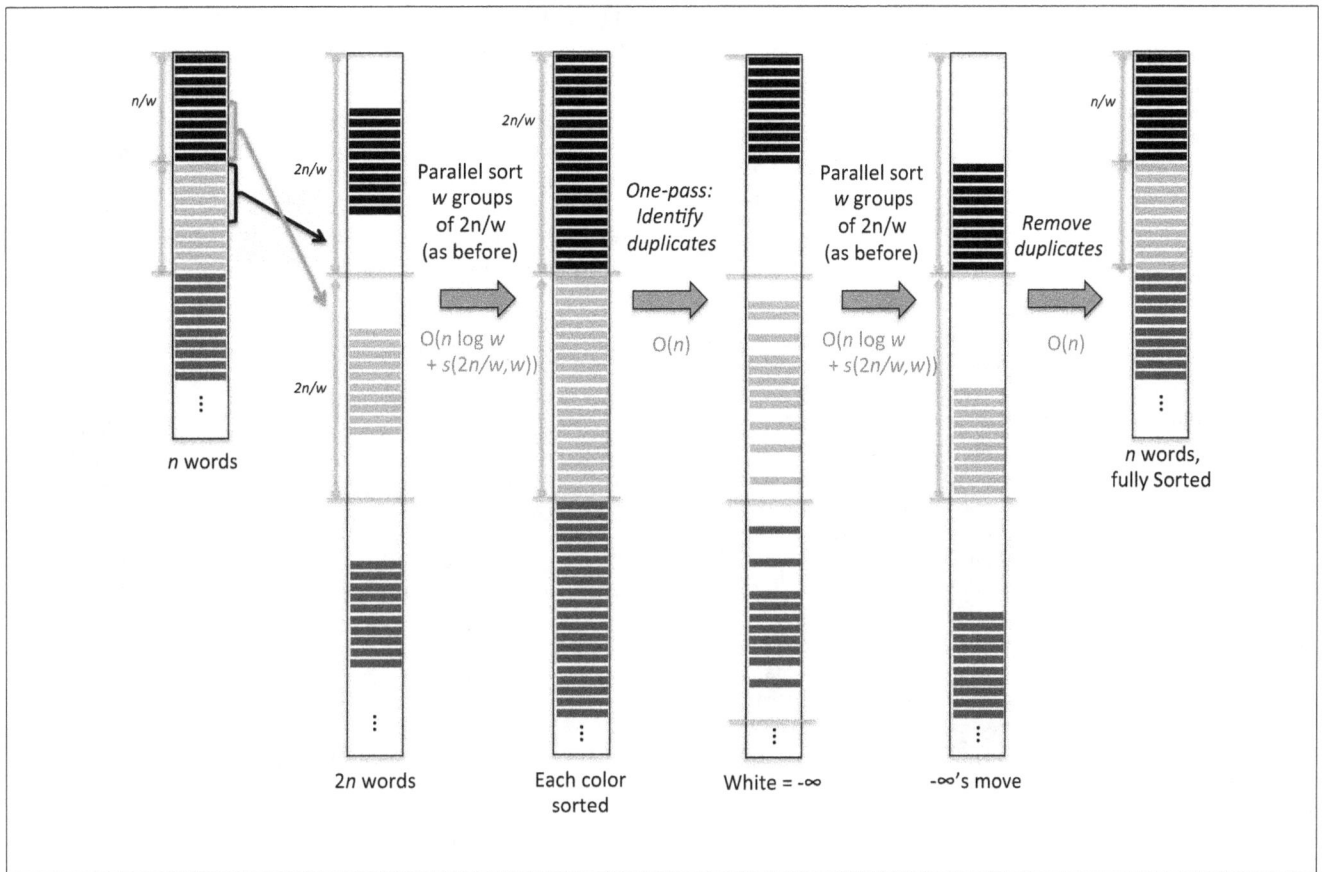

Figure 2: Final phases of OASort.

CLAIM 3.8. *For any fixed $\pi \in S_n$, Claim 3.7 holds also if the assignment in Step 1 is replaced by "Set $D[\sigma(i)] \leftarrow \pi(i)$."*

PROOF. Follows directly: $D[\sigma(i)] \leftarrow \pi(i)$ is equivalent to $D[\sigma(\pi^{-1}(i))] \leftarrow i$, and for fixed π, the uniform distribution $\{\sigma \leftarrow S_n\}$ is identical to $\{\sigma \circ \pi^{-1} : \sigma \leftarrow S_n\}$. $\square$

In the full version, we use the above claims in order to show correctness of OASort:

CLAIM 3.9 (OASort CORRECTNESS). *For any sequence of n distinct initial values $D = (D[1], \ldots, D[n])$, then with probability $1 - e^{-n^{\Omega(1)}}$, OASort(D, n) outputs the values in sorted order $D[1] \leq \cdots \leq D[n]$.*

It now remains to prove obliviousness of OASort.

CLAIM 3.10 (PERFECT OBLIVIOUSNESS). *For any two sequences of n distinct values $D := (D[1], \ldots, D[n])$, $D' := (D'[1], \ldots, D'[n])$, it holds that the distribution of memory access patterns of OASort on input D and D' are identical: $\mathscr{A}ccess[\text{OASort}(D, n)] \equiv \mathscr{A}ccess[\text{OASort}(D', n)]$.*

PROOF. Aside from the initial random shuffle, which induces a fixed input-independent distribution over accesses, all steps of OASort (i.e., Transpose, EmulateCircuit, RemRedundant), in fact have *fixed* access structure. (Note the accesses of EmulateCircuit are determined by the fixed sorting circuit topology). Perfect obliviousness thus follows immediately. $\square$

3.3 Offline ORAM from Oblivious-Access Sort

Now, suppose there exists an oblivious-access sort algorithm OASort, as per Definition 3.3. We now use such an algorithm as a black box in order to construct the desired offline ORAM simulation, with only constant multiplicative cost in bandwidth and computation over the corresponding values for OASort. This procedure is specified in Figure 4. For notational simplicity, we describe the case where the program proceeds in n time steps (this is extended simply by considering longer request sequence arrays S of length $t > n$).

Recall that to obtain an offline ORAM, we must be able to obliviously simulate for programs consisting of data access instructions Access(addr, val) where either val $= \emptyset$ (for read) or a fixed and explicitly specified val (see Definition 2.8).

Our transformation begins by making a single pass through the input $y = (\Pi, x)$, and labeling each item with a triple (index, time, value). Words in the data portion x, denoted by $D[i]$ in Figure 4, will be labeled with: index corresponding to their address i, time $= 0$, and their listed value. Words in the program portion of the input Π, denoted by $S[j]$ in Figure 4 (for request *sequence*), and corresponding to a Read/Write request (addr, command), will be labeled with: index addr, time j (i.e., the jth request in time), and value command. In each execution of OASort on these triples, we will sort only with respect to *two* of the three words, and will carry the third word simply as a "payload."[7]

We next sort the *entire* program-data array (denoted M in Figure 4) with respect to key value (index, time), using an execution of OASort. As a result, the array M is now ordered in blocks of words (of varying sizes), where each block

---

[7]Note that in any case, sorting on words of length $3w$ instead of w incurs only constant complexity overhead.

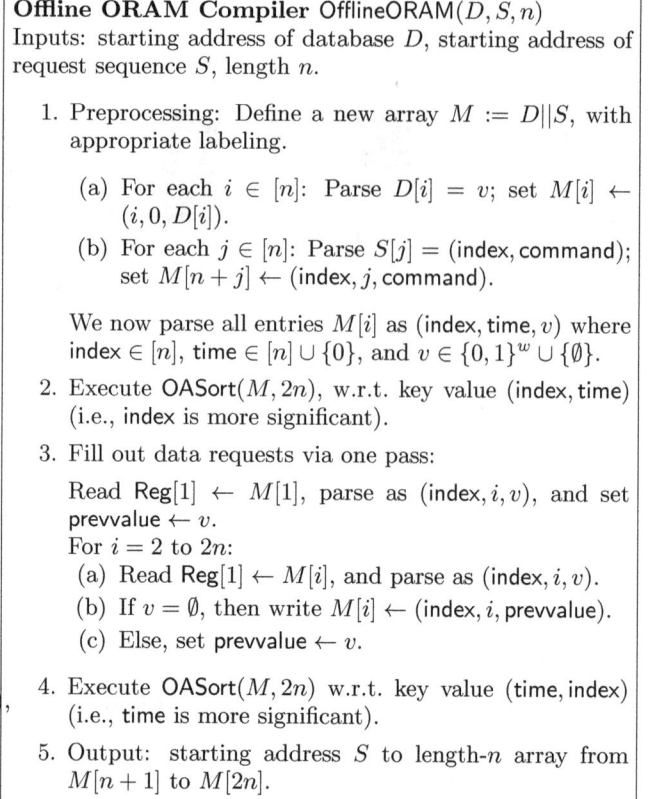

Offline ORAM Compiler OfflineORAM(D, S, n)

Inputs: starting address of database D, starting address of request sequence S, length n.

1. Preprocessing: Define a new array $M := D \| S$, with appropriate labeling.

   (a) For each $i \in [n]$: Parse $D[i] = v$; set $M[i] \leftarrow (i, 0, D[i])$.

   (b) For each $j \in [n]$: Parse $S[j] = (\text{index}, \text{command})$; set $M[n + j] \leftarrow (\text{index}, j, \text{command})$.

   We now parse all entries $M[i]$ as (index, time, v) where index $\in [n]$, time $\in [n] \cup \{0\}$, and $v \in \{0, 1\}^w \cup \{\emptyset\}$.

2. Execute OASort$(M, 2n)$, w.r.t. key value (index, time) (i.e., index is more significant).

3. Fill out data requests via one pass:

   Read Reg$[1] \leftarrow M[1]$, parse as (index, i, v), and set prevvalue $\leftarrow v$.
   For $i = 2$ to $2n$:
   (a) Read Reg$[1] \leftarrow M[i]$, and parse as (index, i, v).
   (b) If $v = \emptyset$, then write $M[i] \leftarrow (\text{index}, i, \text{prevvalue})$.
   (c) Else, set prevvalue $\leftarrow v$.

4. Execute OASort$(M, 2n)$ w.r.t. key value (time, index) (i.e., time is more significant).

5. Output: starting address S to length-n array from $M[n + 1]$ to $M[2n]$.

Figure 4: Offline ORAM, assuming oblivious-access sort procedure OASort.

---

corresponds to a separate index index $\in [n]$. The first item of each block is the data payload itself, word $D[\text{index}]$. Following this, in chronological order, will be the sequence of program requests accessing location index. In the restricted offline setting, we are guaranteed that access requests are limited to either Access(index, val), where val is either $\emptyset$ (for read) or an explicitly specified value. We can thus satisfy each request by making a single pass through M, with a single look-back at each step: Each Access(index, val) is assigned to val, and each Access(index, $\emptyset$) is "filled in" with the value held in the location one previous.

As the final step, we re-sort the elements of M with respect to key (time, index), so as to return them to their original locations. The desired output sequence is now contained within the program portion of memory, S.

PROPOSITION 3.11. *Suppose there exists an Oblivious-Access Sorting algorithm for sorting n words of size $w \in \Omega(\log n) \cap n^{o(1)}$ with computation/bandwidth complexity each comp(n, w). Then there exists an offline ORAM simulating programs of time $t \geq n$ with computation/bandwidth $O(\text{comp}(n + t, 3w))$.*

In particular, if there exists OASort with cost comp$(n, w) \in o(n \log n)$, as is guaranteed by Proposition 3.5 if there exist Boolean sorting circuits of size $o(nw \log n)$, then this yields an offline ORAM with cost $o((n + t) \log(n + t))$: i.e. (for $t \geq n$), with *sub-logarithmic overhead*.

PROOF. The desired offline ORAM compiler OfflineORAM is given in Figure 4. We defer the proof of correctness to the full version of this work.

Consider the complexity of the OfflineORAM steps. Steps 1 and 3 each incur a single pass of the database and simple manipulation, taking $O(n)$ computation. Steps 2 and 4 correspond to executions of OASort on a database of size $n + t$ with word size $3w$ (corresponding to index-time-value triples), requiring time and bandwidth each $\mathsf{comp}(n+t, 3w)$. The claim follows.

Obliviousness of OfflineORAM follows directly from the obliviousness of OASort (Proposition 3.5), since all remaining steps (namely, preprocessing $M := D\|S$ and filling out data requests via one pass over M) have fixed access structure, independent of the values of D and S.

This concludes the proof of Proposition 3.11. $\quad\square$

Simulating a PRAM.

Getting now a PRAM simulation is simple. We assume that the PRAM has n memory cells and n processors (with $O(1)$ registers as internal memory per processor), and at every step each processor can access any cell, perform some computation involving its internal registers, and update any cell. That is, a PRAM program Π is a sequence of the following steps:

1. **Local computation (prepare read):** Each processor performs some local computation on its $O(1)$ registers. At the conclusion of computation, each processor identifies an address $\mathsf{addr} \in [n]$ within memory to read.

2. **Read memory:** Each CPU begins with an address $\mathsf{addr}_i \in [n]$ in memory to read. At the conclusion of this step, each CPU learns the value $\mathsf{Mem}[\mathsf{addr}_i]$.

3. **Local computation (prepare write):** Each processor performs some local computation on its $O(1)$ registers. As the result of computation, each processor identifies an address $\mathsf{addr} \in [n]$ and word $\mathsf{val} \in \{0,1\}^w$ to write to this location in memory.

4. **Write to memory:** Each CPU begins with an address $\mathsf{addr}_i \in [n]$ and an *explicit* value val to write in this location. At the conclusion of this step, each write instruction is implemented within memory. Conflicts in the values written are resolved by priority (say the value of the highest numbered processor; see [26, 39] for a survey).

The observation is that each of these steps itself has the form of a Fixed-Access program. Indeed, consider a (single-CPU) simulation of Π where each PRAM processor's local registers are written in designated portions of memory. Each local computation step can be simulated directly: Namely, for each of the PRAM processors, the simulation will read into memory all $O(1)$ of its local registers, perform the dictated local computation, and write the updated state back to memory, where the resulting Read/Write request information is written in a fixed location. For each Read or Write operation, the simulation will execute the above-described Offline ORAM procedure, where the length-n request sequence is specified in (fixed) locations corresponding to the n processors (instead of n sequential time steps). The priority writing is obtained automatically from the nature of the simulation, which sorts CPU requests chronologically, and assuming that higher numbered processors are later in the program than the lower ones. The computational power required from our simulating CPU is essentially equivalent

to that of the original PRAM CPUs, requiring (in addition) only bitwise logical operations on words and extracting parts of a word.

We thus obtain an oblivious simulation of n-processor PRAM with computation/bandwidth overhead equal to that of our Offline ORAM simulation. In particular, if there exist Boolean sorting circuits of size $o(nw \log n)$, then (combining Propositions 3.5 and 3.11) for any t-step, n-processor PRAM, our simulation requires computation and bandwidth $o(tn \log n)$. Note that this is an asymptotic improvement over any known oblivious PRAM simulation in the standard model [7, 10]. However, we simulate the PRAM by a *sequential* oblivious RAM, in contrast to the Oblivious PRAM setting considered in these works, where a PRAM is simulated on an oblivious PRAM. An interesting question is to what extent our construction may be parallelized to fit within this setting.

4. ACKNOWLEDGEMENTS

We thank Uri Zwick, Peter Bro Miltersen, Emanuele Viola and Ryan Williams for discussing on the state of the art of circuit bounds for sorting.

5. REFERENCES

[1] AJTAI, M. Oblivious RAMs without cryptographic assumptions. In *STOC* (2010), pp. 181–190.

[2] AJTAI, M., KOMLÓS, J., AND SZEMERÉDI, E. An $O(N \log N)$ sorting network. In *Proceedings of the Fifteenth Annual ACM Symposium on Theory of Computing* (New York, NY, USA, 1983), STOC '83, ACM, pp. 1–9.

[3] ANDERSSON, A., HAGERUP, T., NILSSON, S., AND RAMAN, R. Sorting in linear time? In *Proceedings of the Twenty-Seventh Annual ACM Symposium on Theory of Computing, 29 May-1 June 1995, Las Vegas, Nevada, USA* (1995), pp. 427–436.

[4] APON, D., KATZ, J., SHI, E., AND THIRUVENGADAM, A. Verifiable oblivious storage. Cryptology ePrint Archive, Report 2014/153, 2014.

[5] BEAME, P., AND MACHMOUCHI, W. Making branching programs oblivious requires superlogarithmic overhead. In *Proceedings of the 26th Annual IEEE Conference on Computational Complexity, CCC 2011, San Jose, California, June 8-10, 2011* (2011), pp. 12–22.

[6] BIHAM, E. A fast new DES implementation in software. In *Fast Software Encryption, 4th International Workshop, FSE '97, Haifa, Israel, January 20-22, 1997, Proceedings* (1997), pp. 260–272.

[7] BOYLE, E., CHUNG, K., AND PASS, R. Oblivious parallel RAM. *Theory of Cryptography Conference (TCC) 2016A. Available: IACR Cryptology ePrint Archive 2014* (2014), 594.

[8] BOYLE, E., CHUNG, K.-M., AND PASS, R. Large-scale secure computation: Multi-party computation for (parallel) RAM programs. In *CRYPTO* (2015).

[9] CASH, D., KÜPÇÜ, A., AND WICHS, D. Dynamic proofs of retrievability via oblivious ram. In *EUROCRYPT* (2013), pp. 279–295.

[10] CHEN, B., LIN, H., AND TESSARO, S. Oblivious parallel RAM: improved efficiency and generic

constructions. *IACR Cryptology ePrint Archive 2015* (2015), 1053.

[11] CHUNG, K., LIU, Z., AND PASS, R. Statistically-secure ORAM with $\tilde{O}(\log^2 n)$ overhead. In *Advances in Cryptology - ASIACRYPT 2014* (2014), pp. 62–81.

[12] CHUNG, K.-M., AND PASS, R. A simple ORAM. Cryptology ePrint Archive, Report 2013/243, 2013.

[13] DACHMAN-SOLED, D., LIU, C., PAPAMANTHOU, C., SHI, E., AND VISHKIN, U. Oblivious network ram. Cryptology ePrint Archive, Report 2015/073, 2015.

[14] DAMGÅRD, I., MELDGAARD, S., AND NIELSEN, J. B. Perfectly secure oblivious ram without random oracles. In *TCC* (2011), pp. 144–163.

[15] DEVADAS, S., VAN DIJK, M., FLETCHER, C. W., REN, L., SHI, E., AND WICHS, D. Onion oram: A constant bandwidth blowup oblivious RAM. Cryptology ePrint Archive, Report 2015/005, 2015.

[16] FLETCHER, C. W., DIJK, M. V., AND DEVADAS, S. A secure processor architecture for encrypted computation on untrusted programs. In *Proceedings of the Seventh ACM Workshop on Scalable Trusted Computing* (New York, NY, USA, 2012), STC '12, ACM, pp. 3–8.

[17] GENTRY, C., GOLDMAN, K. A., HALEVI, S., JUTLA, C. S., RAYKOVA, M., AND WICHS, D. Optimizing oram and using it efficiently for secure computation. In *Privacy Enhancing Technologies* (2013), pp. 1–18.

[18] GENTRY, C., HALEVI, S., RAYKOVA, M., AND WICHS, D. Outsourcing private RAM computation. In *Symposium on Foundations of Computer Science, FOCS 2014, Philadelphia, PA, USA, October 18-21, 2014* (2014), pp. 404–413.

[19] GOLDREICH, O. Towards a theory of software protection and simulation by oblivious RAMs. In *STOC* (1987), pp. 182–194.

[20] GOLDREICH, O., AND OSTROVSKY, R. Software protection and simulation on oblivious RAMs. *J. ACM 43*, 3 (1996), 431–473.

[21] GOODRICH, M. T. Zig-zag sort: a simple deterministic data-oblivious sorting algorithm running in O(n log n) time. In *Symposium on Theory of Computing, STOC 2014, New York, NY, USA, May 31 - June 03, 2014* (2014), pp. 684–693.

[22] GOODRICH, M. T., AND MITZENMACHER, M. Privacy-preserving access of outsourced data via oblivious RAM simulation. In *Automata, Languages and Programming - 38th International Colloquium, ICALP* (2011), pp. 576–587.

[23] GOODRICH, M. T., MITZENMACHER, M., OHRIMENKO, O., AND TAMASSIA, R. Oblivious ram simulation with efficient worst-case access overhead. In *CCSW* (2011), pp. 95–100.

[24] GORDON, S. D., KATZ, J., KOLESNIKOV, V., KRELL, F., MALKIN, T., RAYKOVA, M., AND VAHLIS, Y. Secure two-party computation in sublinear (amortized) time. In *the ACM Conference on Computer and Communications Security, CCS'12, Raleigh, NC, USA, October 16-18, 2012* (2012), pp. 513–524.

[25] HAN, Y. Deterministic sorting in O($n$loglog$n$) time and linear space. *J. Algorithms 50*, 1 (2004), 96–105.

[26] KARP, R. M., AND RAMACHANDRAN, V. A survey of parallel algorithms for shared-memory machines. University of California, Berkeley Technical Report No. UCB/CSD-88-408 March 1988, 1988. http://www.eecs.berkeley.edu/Pubs/TechRpts/1988/CSD-88-408.pdf.

[27] KNUTH, D. E. *The Art of Computer Programming, Volume 2 (3rd Ed.): Seminumerical Algorithms.* Addison-Wesley Longman Publishing Co., Inc., Boston, MA, USA, 1997.

[28] KUSHILEVITZ, E., LU, S., AND OSTROVSKY, R. On the (in)security of hash-based oblivious ram and a new balancing scheme. In *SODA* (2012), pp. 143–156.

[29] LU, S., AND OSTROVSKY, R. Distributed oblivious RAM for secure two-party computation. In *TCC* (2013), pp. 377–396.

[30] MEDARD, M., AND SPRINTSON., A. *Network Coding: Fundamentals and Applications.* Elsevier, Amsterdam, 2011.

[31] NAOR, M. On recycling encryption schemes or achieving resistance to cache attacks via low bandwidth encryption. Lecture Slides, MIT Workshop on Computing in the Cloud, 2009. people.sail.mit.edu/joanne/recycling_clouds.ppt.

[32] NAOR, M., AND ROTH, R. M. Optimal file sharing in distributed networks. *SIAM J. Comput. 24*, 1 (1995), 158–183.

[33] OSTROVSKY, R., AND SHOUP, V. Private information storage (extended abstract). In *STOC* (1997), pp. 294–303.

[34] PIPPENGER, N., AND FISCHER, M. J. Relations among complexity measures. *J. ACM 26*, 2 (1979), 361–381.

[35] REN, L. Unified RAW path oblivious RAM. Master's thesis, Massachusetts Institute of Technology, 2014.

[36] REN, L., FLETCHER, C. W., KWON, A., STEFANOV, E., SHI, E., VAN DIJK, M., AND DEVADAS, S. Ring ORAM: closing the gap between small and large client storage oblivious RAM. *IACR Cryptology ePrint Archive 2014* (2014), 997.

[37] STEFANOV, E., AND SHI, E. ObliviStore: High performance oblivious cloud storage. In *IEEE Symposium on Security and Privacy* (2013), pp. 253–267.

[38] STEFANOV, E., VAN DIJK, M., SHI, E., FLETCHER, C. W., REN, L., YU, X., AND DEVADAS, S. Path ORAM: an extremely simple oblivious RAM protocol. In *ACM Conference on Computer and Communications Security* (2013), pp. 299–310.

[39] VISHKIN, U. Explicit multi-threading (xmt): A pram-on-chip vision. Online notes. http://www.umiacs.umd.edu/~vishkin/XMT/index.shtml, Visited August 2015.

[40] WANG, X., CHAN, T. H., AND SHI, E. Circuit ORAM: on tightness of the goldreich-ostrovsky lower bound. In *Proceedings of the 22nd ACM SIGSAC Conference on Computer and Communications Security* (2015), pp. 850–861.

[41] WANG, X. S., HUANG, Y., CHAN, T. H., SHELAT, A., AND SHI, E. SCORAM: oblivious RAM for secure computation. In *Proceedings of the 2014 ACM SIGSAC Conference on Computer and Communications Security* (2014), pp. 191–202.

Simultaneous Private Learning of Multiple Concepts

Mark Bun[*]
John A. Paulson School of
Engineering & Applied
Sciences,
Harvard University.
mbun@seas.harvard.edu

Kobbi Nissim[†]
Dept. of Computer Science,
Ben-Gurion University *and*
Center for Research on
Computation & Society,
Harvard University.
kobbi@cs.bgu.ac.il

Uri Stemmer[‡]
Dept. of Computer Science,
Ben-Gurion University.
stemmer@cs.bgu.ac.il

ABSTRACT

We investigate the *direct-sum* problem in the context of differentially private PAC learning: What is the sample complexity of solving k learning tasks *simultaneously* under differential privacy, and how does this cost compare to that of solving k learning tasks without privacy? In our setting, an individual example consists of a domain element x labeled by k unknown concepts $(c_1, \ldots, c_k)$. The goal of a *multi*-learner is to output k hypotheses $(h_1, \ldots, h_k)$ that generalize the input examples.

Without concern for privacy, the sample complexity needed to simultaneously learn k concepts is essentially the same as needed for learning a single concept. Under differential privacy, the basic strategy of learning each hypothesis independently yields sample complexity that grows polynomially with k. For some concept classes, we give multi-learners that require fewer samples than the basic strategy. Unfortunately, however, we also give lower bounds showing that even for very simple concept classes, the sample cost of private multi-learning must grow polynomially in k.

Categories and Subject Descriptors

F.2 [**Theory of Computation**]: Analysis of Algorithms and Problem Complexity

Keywords

differential privacy, PAC learning, agnostic learning, direct-sum

[*]Supported by an NDSEG fellowship and NSF grant CNS-1237235. Part of this work was done while the author was visiting Yale University.

[†]Supported by NSF grant CNS-1237235, a gift from Google, Inc. to Salil Vadhan, a Simons Investigator grant, and ISF grant 276/12.

[‡]Supported by the Ministry of Science and Technology (Israel), and by the Frankel Center for Computer Science.

Permission to make digital or hard copies of all or part of this work for personal or classroom use is granted without fee provided that copies are not made or distributed for profit or commercial advantage and that copies bear this notice and the full citation on the first page. Copyrights for components of this work owned by others than ACM must be honored. Abstracting with credit is permitted. To copy otherwise, or republish, to post on servers or to redistribute to lists, requires prior specific permission and/or a fee. Request permissions from Permissions@acm.org.

ITCS'16, January 14–16, 2016, Cambridge, MA, USA.
© 2016 ACM. ISBN 978-1-4503-4057-1/16/01 ...$15.00.
DOI: http://dx.doi.org/10.1145/2840728.2840747

1. INTRODUCTION

The work on *differential privacy* [14] is aimed at providing useful analyses on privacy-sensitive data while providing strong individual-level privacy protection. One family of such analyses that has received a lot of attention is PAC learning [28]. These tasks abstract many of the computations performed over sensitive information [22].

We address the *direct-sum* problem – what is the cost of solving multiple instances of a computational task simultaneously as compared to solving each of them separately? – in the context of differentially private PAC learning. In our setting, individual examples are drawn from domain X and labeled by k unknown concepts $(c_1, \ldots, c_k)$ taken from a concept class $C = \{c : X \to \{0, 1\}\}$, i.e., each example is of the form $(x, y_1, \ldots, y_k)$, where $x \in X$ and $y_i = c_i(x)$. The goal of a multi-learner is to output k hypotheses $(h_1, \ldots, h_k)$ that generalize the input examples while preserving the privacy of individuals.

The direct-sum problem has its roots in complexity theory, and is a basic problem for many algorithmic tasks. It also has implications for the practical use of differential privacy. Consider, for instance, a hospital that collects information about its patients and wishes to use this information for medical research. The hospital records for each patient a collection of attributes such as age, sex, and the results of various diagnostic tests (for each patient, these attributes make up a point x in some domain X) and, for each of k diseases, whether the patient suffers from the disease (the k labels $(y_1, \ldots, y_k)$). Based on this collection of data, the hospital researchers wish to learn good predictors for the k diseases. One option for the researchers is to perform each of the learning tasks on a fresh sample of patients, hence enlarging the number of patient examples needed (i.e. the *sample complexity*) by a factor of k, which can be very costly.

Without concern for privacy, the sample complexity that is necessary and sufficient for performing the k learning tasks is actually fully characterized by the VC dimension of the concept class C – it is independent of the number of learning tasks k. In this work, we set out to examine if the situation is similar when the learning is performed with differential privacy. Interestingly, we see that with differential privacy the picture is quite different, and in particular, the required number of examples can grow polynomially in k.

Private learning.

A *private learner* is an algorithm that is given an sample of labeled examples $(x, c(x))$ (each representing the information and label pertaining to an individual) and outputs a generalizing hypothesis h that guarantees differential privacy with respect to its examples. The first differentially private learning algorithms were given by Blum et al. [7] and the notion of *private learning* was put forward and formally researched by Kasiviswanathan et al. [22]. Among other results, the latter work presented a generic construction of differentially private learners with sample complexity $O(\log |C|)$.

In contrast, the sample complexity of (non-private) PAC learning is $\Theta(\text{VC}(C))$, which can be much lower than $\log |C|$ for specific concept classes. This gap led to a line of work examining the sample complexity of private learning, which has revealed a significantly more complex picture than there is for non-private learning. In particular, for *pure* differentially private learners, it is known that the sample complexity of proper learning (where the learner returns a hypothesis h taken from C) is sometimes higher than the sample complexity of improper learners (where h comes from an arbitrary hypothesis class H). The latter is characterized by the *representation dimension* of the concept class C, which is generally higher than the VC dimension [3, 2, 12, 4, 18]. By contrast, a sample complexity gap between proper and improper learners does not exist for non-private learning. In the case of *approximate* differential privacy no such combinatorial characterization is currently known. It is however known that the sample complexity of such learners can be significantly lower than that of pure-differentially private learners and yet higher than the VC dimension of C (for proper learning) [4, 18, 10]. Furthermore, there exist (infinite) PAC-learnable concept classes for which no differentially private proper-learner (pure or approximate) exists.

Private multi-learning.

In this work we examine the sample complexity of private multi-learning. Our work is motivated by the recurring research theme of the direct-sum, as well as by the need to understand whether multi-learning remains feasible under differential privacy, as it is without privacy constraints.

At first glance, private multi-learning appears to be similar to the query release problem, the goal of which is to approximate the average values of a large collection of predicates on a dataset. One surprising result in differential privacy is that it is possible to answer an exponential number of such queries on a dataset [8, 25, 20]. For example, Blum, Ligett, and Roth [8] showed that given a dataset D and a concept class C, it is possible to generate with differential privacy a dataset $\hat{D}$ such that the average value of c on $\hat{D}$ approximates the average of c on D for every $c \in C$ *simultaneously*. The sample complexity required, i.e., the size of the database D, to perform this sanitization is only logarithmic in $|C|$. Results of this flavor suggest that we can also learn exponentially many concepts simultaneously. However, we give negative results showing that this is not the case, and that multi-learning can have significantly higher sample complexity than query release.

1.1 Our results

Prior work on privately learning the simple concept classes POINT$_X$ (of functions that evaluate to 1 on exactly one point of their domain X and to 0 otherwise) and THRESH$_X$ (of functions that evaluate to 1 on a prefix of the domain X and to 0 otherwise) has demonstrated a rather complex pic-

ture, depending on whether learners are proper or improper, and whether learning is performed with pure or approximate differential privacy [3, 2, 4, 5, 10]. We analyze the sample complexity of multi-learning of these simple concept classes, as well as general concept classes. We also consider the class PAR$_d$ of parity functions, but in this case we restrict our attention to uniformly selected examples. We examine both proper and improper PAC and agnostic learning under pure and approximate differential privacy. For ease of reference, we include tables with our results in Appendix A, where we omit the dependency on the privacy and accuracy parameters.

Techniques for private k-learning. Composition theorems for differential privacy show that the sample complexity of learning k concepts simultaneously is at most a factor of k larger than the sample complexity of learning one concept (and may be reduced to $\sqrt{k}$ for approximate differential privacy). Unfortunately, privately learning one concept from a concept class C can sometimes be quite costly, requiring much higher sample complexity than $\text{VC}(C)$ which is needed to learn non-privately. Building on techniques of Beimel, Nissim, and Stemmer [6], we show that the multiplicative dependence on k can always be reduced to the VC-dimension of C, at the expense of producing a one-time sanitization of the dataset.

THEOREM 1.1 (INFORMAL). *Let C be a concept class for which there is pure differentially private sanitizer for $C^{\oplus} = \{f \oplus g : f, g \in C\}$ with sample complexity m. Then there is an pure differentially private agnostic k-learner for C with sample complexity $O(m + k \cdot \text{VC}(C))$.*

Similarly, if $C^{\oplus}$ has an approximate differentially private sanitizer with sample complexity m, then there is an approximate differentially private agnostic k-learner for C with sample complexity $O(m + \sqrt{k} \cdot \text{VC}(C))$.

The best known general-purpose sanitizers require sample complexity $m = O(\text{VC}(C) \log |X|)$ for pure differential privacy [8] and $m = O(\log |C| \sqrt{\log |X|})$ for approximate differential privacy [20]. However, for specific concept classes (such as POINT$_X$ and THRESH$_X$), the sample complexity of sanitization can be much lower.

In the case of approximate differential privacy, the sample complexity of k-learning can be even lower than what is achievable with our generic learner. Using stability-based arguments, we show that point functions and parities under the uniform distribution can be PAC k-learned with sample complexity $O(\text{VC}(C))$ – independent of the number of concepts k (see Theorems 3.9 and 3.8).

Lower bounds. In light of the above results, one might hope to be able to reduce the dependence on k further, or to eliminate it entirely (as is possible in the case of non-private learning). We show that this is not possible, even for the simplest of concept classes. In the case of pure differential privacy, a packing argument [17, 21, 3] shows that any non-trivial concept class requires sample complexity $\Omega(k)$ to privately k-learn (Theorem 5.1). For approximate differential privacy, we use fingerprinting codes [9, 11] to show that unlike points and parities, threshold functions require sample complexity $\tilde{\Omega}(k^{1/3})$ to PAC learn privately (Corollary 4.5). Moreover, any non-trivial concept class requires sample complexity $\tilde{\Omega}(\sqrt{k})$ to privately learn in the agnostic model (Theorem 4.6). In the case of point functions, this matches the upper bound achievable by our generic learner.

We highlight a few of the main takeaways from our results:

A complex answer to the direct sum question. Our upper bounds show that solving k learning problems simultaneously can require substantially lower sample complexity than solving the problems individually. On the other hand, our lower bounds show that a significant dependence on k is generally necessary.

Separation between private PAC and private agnostic learning. Non-privately, the sample complexities of PAC and agnostic learning are of the same order (differing only in the dependency in the accuracy parameters). Beimel et al. [6] showed that this is also the case with differentially private learning (of one concept). Our results on learning point functions show that private PAC and agnostic *multi-learning* can be substantially different (even for learning up to constant error). In the case of approximate differential privacy, $O(1)$ sample suffice to PAC-learn multiple point functions. However, $\tilde{\Omega}(\sqrt{k})$ samples are needed to learn k points agnostically.

Separation between improper learning with approximate differential privacy and non-private learning. Recently, Bun et al. [10] showed that the sample complexity of learning one threshold function with approximate differential privacy exceeds the VC dimension, but only in the case of *proper* learning. Thus it remains possible that improper learning with approximate differential privacy can match the sample complexity of non-private learning. While we do not address this question directly, we exhibit a separation for multi-learning. In particular, learning k thresholds with approximate differential privacy requires $\tilde{\Omega}(k^{1/3})$ samples, even improperly, while $O(1)$ samples suffices non-privately.

1.2 Related work

Differential privacy was defined in [14] and the relaxation to approximate differential privacy is from [13]. Most related to our work is the work on private learning and its sample complexity [7, 22, 12, 15, 2, 4, 5, 18, 6, 10] and the early work on sanitization [8]. That many "natural" learning tasks can be performed privately was shown in the early work of Blum et al. [7] and Kasiviswanathan et al. [22]. A characterization for the sample complexity of *pure-private* learners was given in [4], in terms of a new combinatorial measure – the *Representation Dimension*, that is, given a class C, the number of samples needed and sufficient for privately learning C is $\Theta(\mathrm{RepDim}(C))$. Building on [4], Feldman and Xiao [18] showed an equivalence between the representation dimension of a concept C and the randomized one-way communication complexity of the evaluation problem for concepts from C. Using this equivalence they separated the sample complexity of pure-private learners from that of non-private ones.

The problem of learning multiple concepts simultaneously (without privacy) has been considered before. Motivated by the problem of bridging computational learning and reasoning, Valiant [29] also observed that (without privacy) multiple concepts can be learned from a common dataset in a data efficient manner.

2. PRELIMINARIES

We recall and extend standard definitions from learning theory and differential privacy. See the full version of this work for a more detailed account.

2.1 Multi-learners

In the following X is some arbitrary domain. A concept (similarly, hypothesis) over domain X is a predicate defined over X. A concept class (similarly, hypothesis class) is a set of concepts. A k-*labeled* database over a domain X is a database $S \in (X \times \{0,1\}^k)^*$. That is, S contains $|S|$ elements from X, each concatenated with k binary labels.

Let $\mathcal{A} : (X \times \{0,1\}^k)^n \to (2^X)^k$ be an algorithm that operates on a k-labeled database and returns k hypotheses. Let C be a concept class over a domain X and let H be a hypothesis class over X.

DEFINITION 2.1 (PAC MULTI-LEARNER). *Algorithm $\mathcal{A}$ is an (α, β)-PAC k-learner for concept class C using hypothesis class H with sample complexity n if for every distribution $\mathcal{D}$ over X and for every fixture of $(c_1, \ldots, c_k)$ from C, given a k-labeled database $S = ((x_i, c_1(x_i), \ldots, c_k(x_i)))_{i=1}^n$ where each x_i is drawn i.i.d. from $\mathcal{D}$, algorithm $\mathcal{A}$ outputs k hypotheses $(h_1, \ldots, h_k)$ from H satisfying*

$$\Pr\left[\max_{1 \leq j \leq k}\left(\mathrm{error}_{\mathcal{D}}(c_j, h_j)\right) > \alpha\right] \leq \beta.$$

The probability is taken over the random choice of the examples in S according to $\mathcal{D}$ and the coin tosses of the learner $\mathcal{A}$. If $H \subseteq C$ then A is called a proper *learner; otherwise, it is called an* improper *learner.*

An analogous definition for the agnostic setting is given in the full version of this work.

Without privacy considerations, the sample complexities of PAC and agnostic learning are essentially characterized by a combinatorial quantity called the *Vapnik-Chervonenkis (VC) dimension*. Similarly, the sample complexity of non-private multi-learners is characterized by the VC dimension:

COROLLARY 2.2. *Let C be a concept class with VC dimension d. There exists an (α, β)-accurate proper PAC k-learner for C using $O(\frac{1}{\alpha}(d \log(1/\alpha) + \log(1/\beta))$ samples. Moreover, there exists an (α, β)-accurate proper agnostic PAC k-learner for C using $O(\frac{1}{\alpha^2}(d \log(1/\alpha) + \log(k/\beta))$ samples.*

We define a few specific concept classes which will play an important role in this work.

POINT$_X$: Let X be any domain. The class of *point functions* is the set of all concepts that evaluate to 1 on exactly one element of X, i.e. POINT$_X = \{c_x : x \in X\}$ where $c_x(y) = 1$ iff $y = x$. The VC-dimension of POINT$_X$ is 1 for any X.

THRESH$_X$: Let X be any totally ordered domain. The class of *threshold functions* takes the form THRESH$_X = \{c_x : x \in X\}$ where $c_x(y) = 1$ iff $y \leq x$. The VC-dimension of THRESH$_X$ is 1 for any X.

PAR$_d$: Let $X = \{0,1\}^d$. The class of *parity functions* on X is given by PAR$_d = \{c_x : x \in X\}$ where $c_x(y) = \langle x, y \rangle$ (mod 2). The VC-dimension of PAR$_d$ is d.

We focus our study of the concept class PAR$_d$ on the problem of learning parities under the *uniform distribution*. The PAC and agnostic learning problems are defined as before, except we only require a learner to be accurate when the marginal distribution on examples is the uniform distribution U_d over $\{0,1\}^d$. See the full version of this work for the formal definitions.

2.2 Differential privacy

Two *k-labeled* databases $S, S' \in (X \times \{0,1\}^k)^n$ are called *neighboring* if they differ on a single (multi-labeled) entry, i.e., $|\{i : (x_i, y_{1,i}, \ldots, y_{k,i}) \neq (x_i', y_{1,i}', \ldots, y_{k,i}')\}| = 1$.

DEFINITION 2.3 (DIFFERENTIAL PRIVACY [14]). *Let* $\mathcal{A} : (X \times \{0,1\}^k)^n \to (2^X)^k$ *be an algorithm that operates on a k-labeled database and returns k hypotheses. Let* $\epsilon, \delta \geq 0$. *Algorithm* $\mathcal{A}$ *is* (ϵ, δ)-*differentially private if for all neighboring* S, S' *and for all* $T \subseteq (2^X)^k$,

$$\Pr[\mathcal{A}(S) \in T] \leq e^\epsilon \cdot \Pr[\mathcal{A}(S') \in T] + \delta,$$

where the probability is taken over the coin tosses of the algorithm $\mathcal{A}$. *When* $\delta = 0$ *we say that* $\mathcal{A}$ *satisfies* pure *differential privacy, otherwise (i.e., if* $\delta > 0$*) we say that* $\mathcal{A}$ *satisfies* approximate *differential privacy.*

Our algorithms use various tools from the differential privacy literature, detailed in the full version of this work.

2.3 Private learners and multi-learners

Generalizing on private learners [22], we say that an algorithm $\mathcal{A}$ is $(\alpha, \beta, \epsilon, \delta)$-private PAC *k-learner* for C using H if $\mathcal{A}$ is (α, β)-PAC *k-learner* for C using H, and $\mathcal{A}$ is (ϵ, δ)-differentially private (similarly with agnostic private PAC *k-learners*). We omit the parameter k when $k = 1$ and the parameter δ when $\delta = 0$. For the case $k = 1$, we have a generic construction with sample complexity proportional to $\log |C|$:

THEOREM 2.4 ([22]). *Let* C *be a concept class, and let* $\alpha, \beta, \epsilon > 0$. *There exists an* $(\alpha, \beta, \epsilon)$-*private agnostic proper learner for* C *with sample complexity*

$$O\left((\log |C| + \log 1/\beta)(1/(\epsilon\alpha) + 1/\alpha^2)\right).$$

In terms of sample complexity, it is known that private learning (for the case $k = 1$) is an easier task than data sanitization, and several reductions from private learning to data sanitization were given in [19, 5, 6]. For example Beimel, et al. [6] gave a generic transformation from data sanitization to private learning, which generally gives improved sample complexity upper bounds.

A number of works [3, 4, 5, 18, 10] have established sharper upper and lower bounds for learning the specific concept classes POINT$_X$ and THRESH$_X$. In the case of pure differential privacy, POINT$_X$ requires $\Theta(\log |X|)$ samples to learn properly [3], but can be learned improperly with $O(1)$ samples. On the other hand, the class of threshold functions THRESH$_X$ require $\Omega(\log |X|)$ samples to learn, even improperly [18]. In the case of approximate differential privacy, POINT$_X$ and THRESH$_X$ can be learned properly with sample complexities $O(1)$ [5] and $\tilde{O}(2^{\log^* |X|})$ [10], respectively. Moreover, properly learning threshold functions requires sample complexity $\Omega(\log^* |X|)$.

2.4 Private PAC learning vs. Empirical Learning

An *empirical k-learner* is defined similarly to a PAC learner, except its accuracy is measured with respect to a fixed database rather than a distribution on examples. See the full version of this work for a precise definition. When an (agnostic) empirical *k-learner* $\mathcal{A}$ for a concept class C is run on a random sample of size $\Omega(\mathrm{VC}(C))$, it is also a (agnostic) PAC *k-learner*. In particular, if an empirical *k-learner* $\mathcal{A}$ is differentially private, then it also serves as a differentially private (agnostic) PAC *k-learner*.

Generalizing a result of [10], the next theorem shows that the converse is true as well: a differentially private (agnostic) PAC *k-learner* yields a private empirical *k-learner* with only a constant factor increase in the sample complexity. As a consequence, the lower bounds for empirical learning that we present in Sections 4 and 5 apply to PAC learning as well.

THEOREM 2.5. *Let* $\epsilon \leq 1$. *Suppose* $\mathcal{A}$ *is an (agnostic)* $(\alpha, \beta, \epsilon, \delta)$-*PAC k-learner for a concept class* C *with sample complexity* n. *Then there is an* (ϵ, δ)-*differentially private* (α, β)-*accurate (agnostic) empirical k-learner* $\tilde{\mathcal{A}}$ *for* C *with sample complexity* $m = 9n$. *Moreover, if* $\mathcal{A}$ *is proper, then so is the resulting empirical learner* $\tilde{\mathcal{A}}$.

2.5 Fingerprinting Codes

An (n, k)-*fingerprinting code* consists of a pair of randomized algorithms (Gen, Trace). The parameter n is the number of users supported by the fingerprinting code, and k is the length of the code. The codebook generator Gen produces a *codebook* $W \in \{0,1\}^{n \times k}$. Each row $w_i \in \{0,1\}^k$ of W is the *codeword* of user i. For a subset $T \subseteq [n]$, we let W_T denote the set $\{w_i : i \in T\}$ of codewords belonging to users in T. The accusation algorithm Trace takes as input a pirate codeword w' and accuses some $i \in [n]$ (or $\perp$ if it fails to accuse any user).

We define the feasible set of pirate codewords for a coalition T and codebook W by

$$F(W_T) = \{w' \in \{0,1\}^k : \forall j = 1, \ldots, k \; \exists i \in S \text{ s.t. } w_{ij} = w_j'\}.$$

The basic marking assumption is that the pirate codeword $w' \in F(W_T)$. We say column j is *b-marked* if $w_{ij} = b$ for every $i \in [n]$.

DEFINITION 2.6 (FINGERPRINTING CODES). *For* $n, k \in \mathbb{N}$ *and* $\xi \in (0, 1]$, *a pair of algorithms* (Gen, Trace) *is an* (n, k)-*fingerprinting code with security* ξ *if* Gen *outputs a codebook* $W \in \{0,1\}^{n \times k}$ *and for every (possibly randomized) adversary* $\mathcal{A}_{FP}$, *and every coalition* $T \subseteq [n]$, *if we take* $w' \leftarrow_R \mathcal{A}_{FP}(W_T)$, *then the following properties hold.*

Completeness: $\Pr[w' \in F(W_T) \wedge \text{Trace}(w') = \perp] \leq \xi,$

Soundness: $\Pr[\text{Trace}(w') \in [n] \setminus T] \leq \xi,$

Each probability is taken over the coins of Gen, Trace, *and* $\mathcal{A}_{FP}$. *The algorithms* Gen *and* Trace *may share a common state, which is hidden to ease notation.*

3. UPPER BOUNDS ON THE SAMPLE COMPLEXITY OF PRIVATE MULTI-LEARNERS

3.1 Generic Construction

In this section we present the following general upper bounds on the sample complexity of private *k-learners*.

THEOREM 3.1. *Let* C *be a finite concept class, and let* $k \geq 1$. *There exists a proper agnostic* $(\alpha, \beta, \epsilon)$-*private PAC k-learner for* C *with sample complexity*

$$O_{\alpha,\beta,\epsilon}\left(k \cdot \log k + \min\left\{k \cdot \log |C|, (k + \log |X|) \cdot \mathrm{VC}(C)\right\}\right),$$

and there exists a proper agnostic $(\alpha,\beta,\epsilon,\delta)$-private PAC k-learner for C with sample complexity

$$O_{\alpha,\beta,\epsilon,\delta}\left(\sqrt{k}\log k + \min\left\{\begin{array}{l}\sqrt{k}\log|C|,\\(\sqrt{k}+\log|X|)\,\mathrm{VC}(C),\\\sqrt{k}\,\mathrm{VC}(C)+\sqrt{\log|X|}\log|C|\end{array}\right\}\right).$$

The straightforward approach for constructing a private k-learner for a class C is to separately apply a (standard) private learner for C for each of the k target concepts. Using composition theorems to argue the overall privacy guarantee of the resulting learner, we get the following observation.

OBSERVATION 3.2. *Let C be a concept class and let $k \geq 1$. If there is an $(\alpha,\beta,\epsilon,\delta)$-PAC learner for C with sample complexity n, then*

- *There is an $(\alpha,k\beta,k\epsilon,k\delta)$-PAC k-learner for C with sample complexity n.*
- *There is an $(\alpha,k\beta,O(\sqrt{k\log(\frac{1}{\delta})}\epsilon + k\epsilon^2),O(k\delta))$-PAC k-learner for C with sample complexity n.*

Moreover, if the initial learner is proper and/or agnostic, then so is the resulting learner.

In cases where sample efficient private PAC learners exist, it might be useful to apply Observation 3.2 in order to obtain a private k-learner. For example, Beimel et al. [3, 4] gave an improper agnostic (α,β,ϵ)-PAC learner for $\mathtt{POINT}_X$ with sample complexity $O_\alpha(\frac{1}{\epsilon}\log\frac{1}{\beta})$. Using Observation 3.2 yields the following example.

EXAMPLE 3.3. *There is an improper agnostic (α,β,ϵ)-PAC k-learner for $\mathtt{POINT}_X$ with sample complexity $O_{\alpha,\beta,\epsilon}(k\log k)$.*

For a general concept class C, we can use Observation 3.2 with the generic construction of Theorem 2.4, stating that for every concept class C there exists a private agnostic proper learner that uses $O(\log|C|)$ labeled examples.

COROLLARY 3.4. *Let C be a concept class, and $\alpha,\beta,\epsilon > 0$. There exists an (α,β,ϵ)-private agnostic proper k-learner for C with sample complexity $O_{\alpha,\beta,\epsilon}(k \cdot \log|C| + k \cdot \log k)$. Moreover, there exists an $(\alpha,\beta,\epsilon,\delta)$-private agnostic proper k-learner for C with sample complexity $O_{\alpha,\beta,\epsilon,\delta}(\sqrt{k}\cdot\log|C| + \sqrt{k}\cdot\log k)$.*

EXAMPLE 3.5. *There exists a proper agnostic (α,β,ϵ)-PAC k-learner for $\mathtt{PAR}_d$ with sample complexity $O_{\alpha,\beta,\epsilon}(kd + k\log k)$.*

As we will see in Section 5, the bounds of examples 3.3 and 3.5 on the sample complexity of k-learning $\mathtt{POINT}_X$ and $\mathtt{PAR}_d$ are tight (up to logarithmic factors). That is, with pure-differential privacy, the direct sum gives (roughly) optimal bounds for improperly learning $\mathtt{POINT}_X$, and for (properly or improperly) learning $\mathtt{PAR}_d$. This is not the case for learning $\mathtt{THRESH}_X$ or for *properly* learning learning $\mathtt{POINT}_X$.

In order to avoid the factor $k\log|C|$ (or $\sqrt{k}\log|C|$) in Corollary 3.4, we now show how an idea used in [6] (in the context of semi-supervised learning) can be used to construct sample efficient private k-learners. In particular, this construction will achieve tight bounds for learning $\mathtt{THRESH}_X$ and for properly learning learning $\mathtt{POINT}_X$ under pure-differential privacy.

Fix a concept class C, target concepts $c_1,\ldots,c_k \in C$, and a k-labeled database S (we use D to denote the unlabeled

portion of S). For every $1 \leq j \leq k$, the goal is to identify a hypothesis $h_j \in C$ with low $\mathrm{error}_D(c_j,h_j)$ (such a hypothesis also has good generalization). Beimel et al. [6] observed that given a sanitization $\hat{D}$ of D w.r.t. $C^\oplus = \{f\oplus g : f,g \in C\}$, for every $f,g \in C$ it holds that

$$\mathrm{error}_D(f,g) = \frac{1}{|D|}|\{x \in D : (f\oplus g)(x) = 1\}|$$

$$\approx \frac{1}{|\hat{D}|}|\{x \in \hat{D} : (f\oplus g)(x) = 1\}| = \mathrm{error}_{\hat{D}}(f,g).$$

Hence, a hypothesis h with low $\mathrm{error}_{\hat{D}}(h,c_j)$ also has low $\mathrm{error}_D(h,c_j)$ and vice versa. Let H be the set of all dichotomies over $\hat{D}$ realized by C. Note that $\exists f_j^* \in H$ that agrees with c_j on $\hat{D}$, i.e., $\exists f_j^* \in H$ s.t. $\mathrm{error}_{\hat{D}}(f_j^*,c_j) = 0$, and hence $\mathrm{error}_D(f_j^*,c_j)$ is also low. The thing that works in our favor here is that H is small – at most $2^{|\hat{D}|} \leq 2^{\mathrm{VC}(C)}$ – and hence choosing a hypothesis out of H is easy. Therefore, for every j we can use the exponential mechanism to identify a hypothesis $h_j \in H$ with low $\mathrm{error}_D(h_j,c_j)$.

LEMMA 3.6. *Let C be a concept class, and $\alpha,\beta,\epsilon,\delta > 0$. There exists an (α,β,ϵ)-private agnostic k-learner for C with sample complexity $O_{\alpha,\beta,\epsilon}(\mathrm{VC}(C)\cdot\log|X|+k\cdot\mathrm{VC}(C)+k\cdot\log k)$. Moreover, there exists an $(\alpha,\beta,\epsilon,\delta)$-private agnostic k-learner for C with sample complexity $O_{\alpha,\beta,\epsilon,\delta}(\min\{\mathrm{VC}(C)\cdot\log|X|,\log|C|\cdot\sqrt{\log|X|}\} + \sqrt{k}\cdot\mathrm{VC}(C) + \sqrt{k}\cdot\log k)$.*

Lemma 3.6 follows from the following lemma.

LEMMA 3.7. *Let $\epsilon' > 0$ and let $\mathcal{A}$ be an $(\frac{\alpha}{5},\frac{\beta}{5})$-accurate (ϵ,δ)-private sanitizer for $C^\oplus$ with sample complexity m. Then there is an (α,β)-PAC agnostic k-learner for C with sample complexity*

$$O\left(m + \frac{\mathrm{VC}(C)}{\alpha^3\epsilon'}\log(\frac{1}{\alpha}) + \frac{1}{\alpha\epsilon'}\log(\frac{k}{\beta}) + \frac{1}{\alpha^2}\mathrm{VC}(C)\log(\frac{k}{\alpha\beta})\right).$$

Moreover, it is both $(\epsilon + k\epsilon',\delta)$ and $(\epsilon + \sqrt{2k\ln(1/\delta)}\epsilon' + 2k\epsilon'^2,2\delta)$-differentially private.

Using Lemma 3.7 with the generic sanitizer of [8] or [20] results in Lemma 3.6.

PROOF OF LEMMA 3.7. The proof is via the construction of *GenericLearner* (algorithm 1). Note that *GenericLearner* only accesses S via a sanitizer (on Step 2) and using the exponential mechanism (on Step 5). Composition theorems guarantee that *GenericLearner* is both $(\epsilon+k\epsilon',\delta)$-differentially private and $(\epsilon + \sqrt{2k\ln(1/\delta)}\epsilon' + 2k\epsilon'^2,2\delta)$-differentially private. We, thus, only need to prove that with high probability the learner returns α-good hypotheses.

Fix a distribution $\mathcal{P}$ over $X \times \{0,1\}^k$, and let $\mathcal{P}_j$ denote the marginal distribution of $\mathcal{P}$ on the examples and the jth label. Let S consist of examples $(x_i,y_{i,1},\ldots,y_{i,k}) \sim \mathcal{P}$. We use $D = (x_i)_{i=1}^n$ to denote the unlabeled portion of S, and use $S|_j = ((x_i,y_{j,i}))_{i=1}^n$ to denote a database containing the examples in S together with their j^{th} label. Define the following three events:

Algorithm 1 *GenericLearner*

Input: Concept class C, privacy parameters $\epsilon', \epsilon, \delta$, and a k-labeled database $S = (x_i, y_{i,1}, \ldots, y_{i,k})_{i=1}^n$. We use $D = (x_i)_{i=1}^n$ to denote the unlabeled portion of S.
Used Algorithm: An $(\frac{\alpha}{5}, \frac{\beta}{5})$-accurate (ϵ, δ)-private sanitizer for $C^{\oplus}$ with sample complexity m.

1. Initialize $H = \emptyset$.

2. Construct an (ϵ, δ)-private sanitization $\widetilde{D}$ of D w.r.t. $C^{\oplus}$, where $|\widetilde{D}| = O\left(\frac{\mathrm{VC}(C^{\oplus})}{\alpha^2} \log(\frac{1}{\alpha})\right) = O\left(\frac{\mathrm{VC}(C)}{\alpha^2} \log(\frac{1}{\alpha})\right)$.

3. Let $B = \{b_1, \ldots, b_{|B|}\}$ be the set of all points appearing at least once in $\widetilde{D}$.

4. For every $(z_1, \ldots, z_{|B|}) \in \Pi_C(B) = \{(c(b_1), \ldots, c(b_{|B|})) : c \in C\}$, add to H an arbitrary concept $c \in C$ s.t. $c(b_\ell) = z_\ell$ for every $1 \le \ell \le |B|$.

5. For every $1 \le j \le k$, use the exponential mechanism with privacy parameter ϵ' to choose and return a hypothesis $h_j \in H$ with (approximately) minimal error on the examples in S w.r.t. their j^{th} label.

E_1 : For every $f, h \in C$ it holds that $|\mathrm{error}_D(f, h) - \mathrm{error}_{\widetilde{D}}(f, h)| \le \frac{2\alpha}{5}$.

E_2 : For every $f \in C$ and for every $1 \le j \le k$ it holds that $|\mathrm{error}_{S|_j}(f) - \mathrm{error}_{\mathcal{P}_j}(f)| \le \frac{\alpha}{5}$.

E_3 : For every $1 \le j \le k$, the hypothesis h_j chosen by the exponential mechanism is such that $\mathrm{error}_{S|_j}(h_j) \le \frac{\alpha}{5} + \min_{f \in H} \{\mathrm{error}_{S|_j}(f)\}$.

We first argue that when these three events happen algorithm *GenericLearner* returns good hypotheses. Fix $1 \le j \le k$, and let $c_j^* = \mathrm{argmin}_{f \in C}\{\mathrm{error}_{\mathcal{P}_j}(f)\}$. We denote $\Delta = \mathrm{error}_{\mathcal{P}_j}(c_j^*)$. We need to show that if $E_1 \cap E_2 \cap E_3$ occurs, then the hypothesis h_j returned by *GenericLearner* is s.t. $\mathrm{error}_{\mathcal{P}_j}(h_j) \le \alpha + \Delta$.

For every $(y_1, \ldots, y_{|B|}) \in \Pi_C(B)$, algorithm *GenericLearner* adds to H a hypothesis f s.t. $\forall 1 \le \ell \le |B|$, $f(b_\ell) = y_\ell$. In particular, H contains a hypothesis h_j^* s.t. $h_j^*(x) = c_j^*(x)$ for every $x \in B$, that is, a hypothesis h_j^* s.t. $\mathrm{error}_{\widetilde{D}}(h_j^*, c_j^*) = 0$. As event E_1 has occurred we have that this h_j^* satisfies $\mathrm{error}_D(h_j^*, c_j^*) \le \frac{2\alpha}{5}$. Using the triangle inequality (and event E_2) we get that this h_j^* satisfies $\mathrm{error}_{S|_j}(h_j^*) \le \mathrm{error}_D(h_j^*, c_j^*) + \mathrm{error}_{S|_j}(c_j^*) \le \frac{3\alpha}{5} + \Delta$. Thus, event E_3 ensures that algorithm *GenericLearner* chooses (using the exponential mechanism) a hypothesis $h_j \in H$ s.t. $\mathrm{error}_{S|_j}(h_j) \le \frac{4\alpha}{5} + \Delta$. Event E_2 ensures, therefore, that this h_j satisfies $\mathrm{error}_{\mathcal{P}_j}(h_j) \le \alpha + \Delta$. We will now show $E_1 \cap E_2 \cap E_3$ happens with high probability.

Standard arguments in learning theory state that (w.h.p.) the empirical error on a (large enough) random sample is close to the generalization error. Specifically, by setting $n \ge O(\frac{1}{\alpha^2} \mathrm{VC}(C) \log(\frac{k}{\alpha\beta}))$, generalization for agnostic learning ensures that Event E_2 occurs with probability at least $(1 - \frac{2}{5}\beta)$.

Assuming that $n \ge m$ (the sample complexity of the sanitizer used in Step 5), with probability at least $(1 - \frac{\beta}{5})$ for

every $(h \oplus f) \in C^{\oplus}$ (i.e., for every $h, f \in C$) it holds that

$$\frac{\alpha}{5} \ge |Q_{(h\oplus f)}(D) - Q_{(h\oplus f)}(\widetilde{D})|$$
$$= \left| \frac{|\{x \in D : (h\oplus f)(x) = 1\}|}{|D|} - \frac{|\{x \in \widetilde{D} : (h\oplus f)(x) = 1\}|}{|\widetilde{D}|} \right|$$
$$= \left| \frac{|\{x \in D : h(x) \ne f(x)\}|}{|D|} - \frac{|\{x \in \widetilde{D} : h(x) \ne f(x)\}|}{|\widetilde{D}|} \right|$$
$$= \left| \mathrm{error}_D(h, f) - \mathrm{error}_{\widetilde{D}}(h, f) \right|.$$

Event E_1 occurs therefore with probability at least $(1 - \frac{\beta}{5})$.

The exponential mechanism ensures that the probability of event E_3 is at least $1 - k|H| \cdot \exp(-\epsilon'\alpha m/10)$. Note that $\log|H| \le |B| \le |\widetilde{D}| = O\left(\frac{\mathrm{VC}(C)}{\alpha^2} \log(\frac{1}{\alpha})\right)$. Therefore, for $n \ge O\left(\frac{\mathrm{VC}(C)}{\alpha^3 \epsilon'} \log(\frac{1}{\alpha}) + \frac{1}{\alpha\epsilon'} \log(\frac{k}{\beta})\right)$, Event E_3 occurs with probability at least $(1 - \frac{\beta}{5})$.

All in all, setting $n \ge O\left(m + \frac{\mathrm{VC}(C)}{\alpha^3 \epsilon'} \log(\frac{1}{\alpha}) + \frac{1}{\alpha\epsilon'} \log(\frac{k}{\beta}) + \frac{1}{\alpha^2} \mathrm{VC}(C) \log(\frac{k}{\alpha\beta})\right)$, ensures that the probability of *GenericLearner* failing is at most β. $\square$

Theorem 3.1 now follows by combining Lemma 3.6 and Corollary 3.4.

3.2 Upper Bounds for Approximate Private Multi-Learners

In this section we give two examples of cases where the sample complexity of private k-learning is of the same order as that of non-private k-learning (the sample complexity does not depend on k).

THEOREM 3.8. *For every k, d there exists an $(\alpha = 0, \beta, \epsilon, \delta)$-PAC (non-agnostic) k-learner for PAR_d under the uniform distribution with sample complexity $O(\frac{d}{\epsilon} \log(\frac{1}{\beta\delta}))$.*

Recall that (even without privacy constraints) the sample complexity of PAC learning PAR_d under the uniform distribution is $\Omega(d)$. Hence the sample complexity of privately k-learning PAR_d (non-agnostically) under the uniform distribution is of the same order as that of non-private k-learning.

For the intuition behind Theorem 3.8, let $c_1, \ldots, c_k$ denote the k target concepts, and consider the quality function $q(D, (h_1, \ldots, h_k)) = \max_{1 \le j \le k} \{\mathrm{error}_D(h_j, c_j)\}$. On a large enough sample D we expect that $q(D, (h_1, \ldots, h_k)) \approx \frac{1}{2}$ for every $(h_1, \ldots, h_k) \ne (c_1, \ldots, c_k)$, while $q(D, (c_1, \ldots, c_k)) = 0$. The k target concepts can hence be privately identified (exactly) using stability techniques.

In order to make our algorithm computationally efficient, we apply the "subsample and aggregate" idea of Nissim et al. [23]. We divide the input sample into a small number of subsamples, use Gaussian elimination to (non-privately) identify a candidate hypothesis vector on each subsample, and then select from these candidates privately.

PROOF OF THEOREM 3.8. The proof is via the construction of *ParityLearner* (algorithm 2). First note that changing a single input element in S can change (at most) one element of Y. Hence, applying (the (ϵ, δ)-private) algorithm $\mathcal{A}_{\mathrm{dist}}$ on Y preserves privacy (applying *ParityLearner* on neighboring inputs amounts to executing $\mathcal{A}_{\mathrm{dist}}$ on neighboring inputs).

Algorithm 2 *ParityLearner*

Input: Parameters ϵ, δ, and a k-labeled database S of size $n = O(\frac{d}{\epsilon}\log(\frac{1}{\beta\delta}))$.

Output: Hypotheses $h_1, \ldots, h_k$.

1. Split S into $m = O(\frac{1}{\epsilon}\log(\frac{1}{\beta\delta}))$ disjoint samples $S_1, \ldots, S_m$ of size $O(d)$ each. Initiate Y as the empty multiset.

2. For every $1 \le t \le m$:

   (a) For every $1 \le j \le k$ try to use Gaussian elimination to identify a parity function y_j that agrees with the labels of the jth column of S_t.

   (b) If a parity is identified for every j, then set $Y = Y \cup \{(y_1, ..., y_k)\}$. Otherwise set $Y = Y \cup \{\bot\}$.

3. Use algorithm $\mathcal{A}_{\text{dist}}$ with privacy parameters ϵ, δ to choose and return a vector of k parity functions $(h_1, \ldots, h_k) \in (\mathtt{PAR}_d)^k$ with a large number of appearances in Y.

Now fix k target concepts $c_1, \ldots, c_k \in \mathtt{PAR}_d$ and let S be a random k-labeled database containing n i.i.d. elements from the uniform distribution U_d over $X = \{0,1\}^d$, each labeled by $c_1, \ldots, c_k$. Observe that (for every $1 \le t \le m$) we have that S_t contains i.i.d. elements from U_d labeled by $c_1, \ldots, c_k$. We use D_t to denote the unlabeled portion of S_t. Standard arguments in learning theory state that for $|S_t| \ge O(d)$,

$$\Pr\left[\exists h, f \in \mathtt{PAR}_d \text{ s.t. } \begin{array}{l} \text{error}_{U_d}(h, f) \ge \frac{1}{4} \\ \wedge\ \ \text{error}_{D_t}(h, f) \le \frac{1}{40} \end{array}\right] \le \frac{1}{8}.$$

The above inequality holds, in particular, for every hypothesis $h \in \mathtt{PAR}_d$ and every target concept c_j, and hence,

$$\Pr\left[\exists h \in \mathtt{PAR}_d \text{ and } j \text{ s.t. } \begin{array}{l} \text{error}_{U_d}(h, c_j) \ge \frac{1}{4} \\ \wedge\ \ \text{error}_{D_t}(h, c_j) \le \frac{1}{40} \end{array}\right] \le \frac{1}{8}.$$

Recall that under the uniform distribution, the only $h \in \mathtt{PAR}_d$ s.t. $\text{error}_{U_d}(h, c_j) \ne \frac{1}{2}$ is c_j itself, and hence

$$\Pr\left[\exists h \in \mathtt{PAR}_d \text{ and } j \text{ s.t. } h \ne c_j \wedge \text{error}_{D_t}(h, c_j) \le \frac{1}{40}\right] \le \frac{1}{8}.$$

So, for every $1 \le t \le m$, with probability $7/8$ we have that for every label column j the only hypothesis with empirical error less than $\frac{1}{40}$ on S_t is the jth target concept itself (with empirical error 0). In such a case, step 2a (Gaussian elimination) identifies exactly the vector of k target concepts $(c_1, \ldots, c_k)$. Since $m \ge O(\log(\frac{1}{\beta}))$, the Chernoff bound ensures that except with probability $\beta/2$, the vector $(c_1, \ldots, c_k)$ is identified in at least $3/4$ of the iterations of step 2. Assuming that this is the case, the vector $(c_1, \ldots, c_k)$ appears in Y at least $3m/4$ times, while every other vector can appear at most $m/4$ times. Provided that $m \ge O(\frac{1}{\epsilon}\log(\frac{1}{\beta\delta}))$, algorithm $\mathcal{A}_{\text{dist}}$ ensures that the k target concepts are chosen with probability $1 - \beta/2$.

All in all, algorithm *ParityLearner* identifies the k target concepts (exactly) with probability $1 - \beta$, provided that $n \ge O(\frac{d}{\epsilon}\log(\frac{1}{\beta\delta}))$. $\square$

We next show that the class of $\mathtt{POINT}_X$ can be (non-agnostically) k-learned using constant sample complexity, matching the non-private sample complexity.

THEOREM 3.9. *For every domain X and every $k \in \mathbb{N}$ there exists an $(\alpha, \beta, \epsilon, \delta)$-PAC (non-agnostic) k-learner for $\mathtt{POINT}_X$ with sample complexity $O(\frac{1}{\alpha\epsilon}\log(\frac{1}{\alpha\beta\delta}))$.*

The proof is via the construction of Algorithm 3. The algorithm begins by privately identifying (using sanitization) a set of $O(1/\alpha)$ "heavy" elements in the input database, appearing $\Omega(\alpha)$ times. The k labels of such a heavy element can be privately identified using stability arguments (since their duplicity in the database is large). The labels of a "non-heavy" element can be set to 0 since a target concept can evaluate to 1 on at most one such non-heavy element, in which case the error is small.

Notation. We use $\#_S(x)$ to denote the duplicity of a domain element x in a database S. For a distribution μ we denote $\mu(x) = \Pr_{\hat{x}\sim\mu}[\hat{x} = x]$.

Algorithm 3 *PointLearner*

Input: Privacy parameters ϵ, δ, and a k-labeled database $S = (x_i, y_{i,1}, \ldots, y_{i,k})_{i=1}^n$. We use $D = (x_i)_{i=1}^n$ to denote the unlabeled portion of S.

Output: Hypotheses $h_1, \ldots, h_k$.

1. Let $\hat{D} \in X^m$ be an $(\frac{\epsilon}{2}, \frac{\delta}{2})$-private $(\frac{\alpha}{30}, \frac{\beta}{4})$-accurate sanitization of D w.r.t. $\mathtt{POINT}_X$ (see the full version of this work).

2. Let $G = \{x \in X : \frac{1}{m}\#_{\hat{D}}(x) \ge \alpha/15\}$ be the set of all "$\frac{\alpha}{15}$-heavy" domain elements w.r.t. the sanitization $\hat{D}$. Note that $|G| \le 15/\alpha$.

3. Let q be the quality function that on input a k-labeled database S, a domain element x, and a binary vector $\vec{v} \in \{0,1\}^k$, returns the number of appearances of $(x, \vec{v})$ in S. That is, $q(S, x, (v_1, \ldots, v_k)) = |\{i : x_i = x \wedge y_{i,1} = v_1 \wedge \cdots \wedge y_{i,k} = v_k\}|$.

4. Use algorithm $\mathcal{A}_{\text{dist}}$ with privacy parameters $\frac{\epsilon}{2}, \frac{\delta}{2}$ to choose a set of vectors $V = \{\vec{v}_x \in \{0,1\}^k : x \in G\}$ maximizing $Q(S, V) = \min_{\vec{v}_x \in V}\{q(S, x, \vec{v}_x)\}$. That is, we use algorithm $\mathcal{A}_{\text{dist}}$ to choose a set of $|G|$ vectors – a vector $\vec{v}_x$ for every $x \in G$ – such that the minimal number of appearances of an entry $(x, \vec{v}_x)$ in the database S is maximized.

5. For $1 \le j \le k$: If the jth entry of every $\vec{v}_x \in V$ is 0, then set $h_j \equiv 0$. Otherwise, let x be s.t. $\vec{v}_x \in V$ has 1 as its jth entry, and define $h_j : X \to \{0,1\}$ as $h_j(y) = 1$ iff $y = x$.

6. Return $h_1, \ldots, h_k$.

PROOF OF THEOREM 3.9. The proof is via the construction of *PointLearner* (algorithm 3). First note the algorithm only access the input database using sanitization on step 1, and using algorithm $\mathcal{A}_{\text{dist}}$ on step 4. By composition of differential privacy, algorithm *PointLearner* is (ϵ, δ)-differentially private.

Let μ be a distribution over X, and let $c_1, \ldots, c_k \in \mathtt{POINT}_X$ be the fixed target concepts. Consider the execution of *PointLearner* on a database $S = (x_i, y_{i,1}, \ldots, y_{i,k})_{i=1}^n$ sampled from μ and labeled by $c_1, \ldots, c_k$. We use D to denote the unlabeled portion of S, $\hat{D}$ for the sanitization of D constructed on step 1, and write $m = |\hat{D}|$. Define the following good events.

E_1 : For every $x \in X$ s.t. $\mu(x) \geq \alpha$ it holds that $\frac{1}{n}\#_S(x) \geq \alpha/10$.

E_2 : For every $x \in X$ we have that $|\frac{1}{m}\#_{\hat{D}}(x) - \frac{1}{n}\#_S(x)| \leq \alpha/30$.

E_3 : Algorithm $\mathcal{A}_{\text{dist}}$ returns a vector set V s.t. $q(S, x, \vec{v}_x) \geq 1$ for every $x \in G$.

We now argue that when these three events happen algorithm $PointLearner$ returns good hypotheses. First, observe that the set G contains every element x s.t. $\mu(x) \geq \alpha$: Let x be s.t. $\mu(x) \geq \alpha$. As event E_1 has occurred, we have that $\frac{1}{n}\#_S(x) \geq \alpha/10$. As event E_2 has occurred, we have that $\frac{1}{m}\#_{\hat{D}}(x) \geq \alpha/15$, and therefore $x \in G$.

Note that if $q(S, x, \vec{v}) \geq 1$ then the example x is labeled as $\vec{v}$ by the target concepts. Thus, as event E_3 has occurred, for every $\vec{v}_x \in V$ it holds that $\vec{v}_x = (c_1(x), \ldots, c_k(x))$. Now let h_j be the jth returned hypothesis. We next show that h_j is α-good. If $h_j \not\equiv 0$, then let x be the unique element s.t. $h_j(x) = 1$, and note that (according to step 5) the jth entry of $\vec{v}_x$ is 1, and hence, $c_j(x) = 1$. So $h_j = c_j$ (since c_j is a concept in $\texttt{POINT}_X$).

If $h_j \equiv 0$ then the jth entry of every $\vec{v}_x \in V$ is 0. Note that in such a case h_j only errs on the unique element x s.t. $c_j(x) = 1$, and it suffices to show that $\mu(x) < \alpha$. Assume towards contradiction that $\mu(x) \geq \alpha$. As before, event $E_1 \cap E_2$ implies that $x \in G$. As event E_3 has occurred, we also have that $\vec{v}_x \in V$ is s.t. $q(S, x, \vec{v}_x) \geq 1$, and the example x is labeled as $\vec{v}_x$ by the target concepts. This contradicts the assumption that the jth entry of $\vec{v}_x \in V$ is 0.

Thus, whenever $E_1 \cap E_2 \cap E_3$ happens, algorithm $PointLearner$ returns α-good hypotheses. We will now show $E_1 \cap E_2 \cap E_3$ happens with high probability. Provided $n \geq O(\frac{1}{\alpha\epsilon}\log(\frac{1}{\alpha\delta}))$, event E_2 is guaranteed to hold with all but probability $\beta/4$ by the utility properties of the sanitizer used on step 1.

Generalization bounds ensure that event E_1 holds with probability $1 - \beta/4$, provided that $n \geq O(\frac{1}{\alpha}\log(\frac{1}{\alpha\beta}))$. To see this, let $z \equiv 0$ denote the constant 0 hypothesis, and consider the class $C = \texttt{POINT}_X \cup \{z\}$. Note that $\text{VC}(C) = 1$. Hence, with all but probability $1 - \beta/4$, for every $c \in \texttt{POINT}_x$ s.t. $\text{error}_\mu(c, z) \geq \alpha$ it holds that $\text{error}_D(c, z) \geq \alpha/10$. That is, with all but probability $1 - \beta/4$, for every $x \in X$ s.t. $\mu(x) \geq \alpha$ it holds that $\frac{1}{n}\#_D(x) = \frac{1}{n}\#_S(x) \geq \alpha/10$.

Before analyzing event E_3, we show that if E_2 occurs, then every $x \in G$ is s.t. $\#_S(x) \geq \alpha/30$. Let $x \in G$, that is, x s.t. $\frac{1}{m}\#_{\hat{D}}(x) \geq \alpha/15$. Assuming event E_2 has occurred, we therefore have that $\frac{1}{n}\#_S(x) \geq \alpha/30$. So every $x \in G$ appears in S at least $\alpha n/30$ times with the labels $(c_1(x), \ldots, c_k(x)) \triangleq \vec{c}(x)$. Thus, $q(S, x, \vec{c}(x)) \geq \alpha n/30$. In addition, for every $\vec{v} \neq \vec{c}(x)$ it holds that $q(S, x, \vec{v}) = 0$, since $every$ appearance of the example x is labeled by the target concepts. Hence, provided that $n \geq O(\frac{1}{\alpha\epsilon}\log(\frac{1}{\beta\delta}))$, algorithm $\mathcal{A}_{\text{dist}}$ ensures that event E_3 happens with probability at least $1 - \beta/2$.

Overall, $E_1 \cap E_2 \cap E_3$ happens with probability at least $1 - \beta$. $\square$

4. APPROX. PRIVACY LOWER BOUNDS FROM FINGERPRINTING CODES

In this section, we show how fingerprinting codes can be used to obtain $\text{poly}(k)$ lower bounds against privately learning k concepts, even for very simple concept classes. Fingerprinting codes were introduced by Boneh and Shaw [9] to address the problem of watermarking digital content. The connection between fingerprinting codes and differential privacy lower bounds was established by Bun, Ullman, and Vadhan [11] in the context of private query release, and has since been extended to a number of other differentially private analyses [1, 16, 26, 10].

A (fully-collusion-resistant) fingerprinting code is a scheme for distributing codewords $w_1, \ldots, w_n$ to n users that can be uniquely traced back to each user. Moreover, if any group of users combines its codewords into a pirate codeword w', then the pirate codeword can still be traced back to one of the users who contributed to it. Of course, without any assumption on how the pirates can produce their combined codeword, no secure tracing is possible. To this end, the pirates are constrained according to a $marking \ assumption$, which asserts that the combined codeword must agree with at least one of the pirates' codeword in each position. Namely, at an index j where $w_{ij} = b$ for every pirate i, the pirates are constrained to output w' with $w'_j = b$ as well.

To illustrate our technique, we start with an informal discussion of how the original Boneh-Shaw fingerprinting code yields an $\tilde{\Omega}(k^{1/3})$ sample complexity lower bound for multi-learning threshold functions. For parameters n and k, the (n, k)-Boneh-Shaw codebook is a matrix $W \in \{0, 1\}^{n \times k}$, whose rows w_i are the codewords given to users $i = 1, \ldots, n$. The codebook is built from a number of highly structured columns, where a "column of type i" consists of n bits where the first i bits are set to 1 and the last $n - i$ bits are set to 0. For $i = 1, \ldots, n - 1$, each column of type i is repeated a total of $k/(n-1)$ times, and the codebook W is obtained as a random permutation of these k columns. The security of the Boneh-Shaw code is a consequence of the secrecy of this random permutation. If a coalition of pirates is missing the codeword of user i, then it is unable to distinguish columns of type $i - 1$ from columns of type i. Hence, if a pirate codeword is too consistent with a user i's codeword in both the columns of type $i - 1$ and the columns of type i, a tracing algorithm can reasonably conclude that user i contributed to it. Boneh and Shaw showed that such a code is indeed secure for $k = \tilde{O}(n^3)$.

To see how this fingerprinting code gives a lower bound for multi-learning thresholds, consider thresholds over the data universe $X = \{1, \ldots, |X|\}$ for $|X| \geq n$. The key observation is that each column of the Boneh-Shaw codebook can be obtained as a labeling of the examples $1, \ldots, n$ by a threshold concept. Namely, a column of type i is the labeling of $1, \ldots, n$ by the concept c_i. Now suppose a coalition of users $T \subseteq [n]$ constructs a database S where each row is an example $i \in T$ together with the labels $w_{i1}, \ldots, w_{ik}$ coming from the codeword given to user i. Let $(h_1, \ldots, h_k)$ be the hypotheses produced by running a threshold multi-learner on the database. If every user has a bit b at index j of her codeword, then the hypothesis produced by the learner must also evaluate to b on most of the examples. Thus, the empirical averages of the hypotheses $(h_1, \ldots, h_k)$ on the examples can be used to obtain a pirate codeword satisfying the marking assumption. The security of the fingerprinting code, i.e. the fact that this codeword can be traced back to a user $i \in T$, implies that the learner cannot be differentially private. Hence, n samples is insufficient for privately learning $k = \tilde{O}(n^3)$ threshold concepts, giving a sample complexity lower bound of $\tilde{\Omega}(k^{1/3})$.

The lower bounds in this section are stated for empirical learning, but extend to PAC learning by Theorem 2.5. We also remark that they hold against the relaxed privacy notion of *label privacy*, where differential privacy only needs to hold with respect to changing the labels of one example.

4.1 Lower Bound for Improper PAC Learning

Our lower bounds for multi-learning follow from constructions of fingerprinting codes with additional structural properties.

DEFINITION 4.1. *Let C be a concept class over a domain X. An (n, k)-fingerprinting code (Gen, Trace) is compatible with concept class C if there exist $x_1, \ldots, x_n \in X$ such that for every codebook W in the support of Gen, there exist concepts $c_1, \ldots, c_k$ such that $w_{ij} = c_j(x_i)$ for every $i = 1, \ldots, n$ and $j = 1, \ldots, k$.*

THEOREM 4.2. *Suppose there exists an (n, k)-fingerprinting code compatible with a concept class C with security ξ. Let $\alpha \leq 1/3$, $\beta, \epsilon > 0$, and $\delta < \frac{1 - \xi - \beta}{n} - e^{\epsilon}\xi$. Then every (improper) (α, β)-accurate and (ϵ, δ)-differentially private empirical k-learner for C requires sample complexity greater than n.*

The proof of Theorem 4.2 follows the ideas sketched above.

PROOF. Let (Gen, Trace) be an (n, k)-fingerprinting code compatible with the concept class C, and let $x_1, \ldots, x_n \in X$ be its associated universe elements. Let $D = (x_1, \ldots, x_n)$ and let $\mathcal{A}$ be an (α, β)-accurate empirical k-learner for C with sample complexity n. We will use $\mathcal{A}$ to design an adversary $\mathcal{A}_{FP}$ against the fingerprinting code.

Let $T \subseteq [n]$ be a coalition of users, and consider a codebook $W \leftarrow_R$ Gen. The adversary strategy $\mathcal{A}_{FP}(W_T)$ begins by constructing a labeled database $S = (S_i)_{i=1}^n$ by setting $S_i = (x_i, w_{i1}, \ldots, w_{ik})$ for each $i \in T$ and to a nonce row for $i \notin T$. It then runs $\mathcal{A}(S)$ obtaining hypotheses $(h_1, \ldots, h_k)$. Finally, it computes for each $j = 1, \ldots, k$ the averages

$$h_j(D) = \frac{1}{n} \sum_{i=1}^n h_j(x_i)$$

and produces a pirate word w' by setting each w'_j to the value of a_j rounded to 0 or 1.

Now consider the coalition $T = [n]$. Since the fingerprinting code is compatible with C, each column $(w_{1j}, \ldots, w_{nj}) = (c_j(x_1), \ldots, c_j(x_n))$ for some concept $c_j \in C$. Thus, if the hypotheses $(h_1, \ldots, h_k)$ are α-accurate for $(c_1, \ldots, c_k)$ on S, then $w' \in F(W_T) = F(W)$. Therefore, by the completeness property of the code and the (α, β)-accuracy of $\mathcal{A}$, we have

$$\Pr\left[\text{Trace}(\mathcal{A}_{FP}(W)) \neq \perp\right] \geq 1 - \xi - \beta.$$

In particular, there exists an i^* for which

$$\Pr\left[\text{Trace}(\mathcal{A}_{FP}(W)) = i^*\right] \geq \frac{1 - \xi - \beta}{n}.$$

On the other hand, by the soundness property of the code,

$$\Pr\left[\text{Trace}(\mathcal{A}_{FP}(W_{-i^*})) = i^*\right] \leq \xi.$$

Thus, $\mathcal{A}$ cannot be (ϵ, δ)-differentially private whenever

$$\frac{1 - \xi - \beta}{n} > e^{\epsilon} \cdot \xi + \delta.$$

$\square$

REMARK 4.3. *If we additionally assume that there exists an element $x_0 \in X$ with $c_1(x_0) = c_2(x_0) = \cdots = c_k(x_0)$, then we can use a "padding" argument to obtain a stronger lower bound of $n/3\alpha$. More specifically, suppose $c_1(x_0) = \cdots = c_k(x_0) = 0$. We pad the database S constructed above with $(1/3\alpha - 1)n$ copies of the junk row $(x_0, 0, \ldots, 0)$. Now if a hypothesis h is α-accurate for a 0-marked column, it's empirical average will be at most α. On the other hand, an α-accurate hypothesis for a 1-marked column will have empirical average at least 2α. Since there is a gap between these two quantities, a pirate algorithm can still turn an accurate vector of k hypotheses into a feasible codeword.*

As observed earlier, the (n, k)-Boneh-Shaw code is compatible with the concept class THRESH_X for any $|X| \geq n$. Thus, instantiating Theorem 4.2 (and Remark 4.3) with the Boneh-Shaw code yields a lower bound for k-learning thresholds.

LEMMA 4.4 ([9]). *Let X be a totally ordered domain with $|X| \geq n$ for some $n \in \mathbb{N}$. Then there exists an (n, k)-fingerprinting code compatible with the concept class THRESH_X with security ξ as long as $k \geq 2n^3 \log(2n/\xi)$.*

COROLLARY 4.5. *Every improper (α, β)-accurate and $(\epsilon = O(1), \delta = o(1/n))$-differentially private empirical k-learner for THRESH_X requires sample complexity $\min\{|X|, \tilde{\Omega}(k^{1/3}/\alpha)\}$.*

Discussion.

Compatibility with a concept class is an interesting measure of the complexity of a fingerprinting code which warrants further attention. Peikert, shelat, and Smith [24] showed that structural constraints (related to compatibility) on a fingerprinting code give a lower bound on its length beyond the general lower bound of $k = \tilde{\Omega}(n^2)$ for arbitrary fingerprinting codes. In particular, they showed that the length $k = \tilde{O}(n^3)$ of the Boneh-Shaw code is essentially tight for the "multiplicity paradigm", where a codebook is a random permutation of a fixed set of columns, each repeated the same number of times. We take this as evidence that our $\tilde{\Omega}(k^{1/3})$ lower bound for THRESH_X cannot be improved via compatible fingerprinting codes. However, closing the gap between our lower bound and the upper bound of roughly $\sqrt{k}$ remains an intriguing open question.

A natural avenue for obtaining stronger poly(k) lower bounds for private k-learning is to identify compatible fingerprinting codes with shorter length. Tardos [27] showed the existence of an (n, k)-fingerprinting code of optimal length $k = \tilde{O}(n^2)$ (see Proposition 4.8). The construction of his code differs significantly from multiplicity paradigm: for each column j of the Tardos code, a bias $p_j \in (0, 1)$ is sampled from a fixed distribution, and then each bit of the column is sampled i.i.d. with bias p_j. Hence, the columns of the Tardos code are supported on all bit vectors in $\{0, 1\}^n$.

This means that for a concept class C to be compatible with the (n, k)-Tardos code, it must be the case that $\text{VC}(C) \geq n$. Thus, the lower bound one obtains against k-learning C only matches the lower bound for PAC learning C (without privacy). It would be very interesting to construct a fingerprinting code of optimal length $k = \tilde{O}(n^2)$ with substantially fewer than 2^n column types (and hence compatible with a concept class of VC-dimension smaller than n).

4.2 Lower Bound for Agnostic Learning

In the agnostic learning model, a learner has to perform well even when the columns of a multi-labeled database do not correspond to any concept. This allows us to apply the argument of Theorem 4.2 without the constraint of compatibility. The result is that *any* fingerprinting code, in particular one with optimal length, gives an agnostic learning lower bound for any non-trivial concept class.

THEOREM 4.6. *Suppose there exists an (n, k)-fingerprinting code with security ξ. Let C be a concept class with at least two distinct concepts. Let $\alpha \leq 1/3$, $\beta, \epsilon > 0$, and $\delta < \frac{1-\xi-\beta}{n} - e^\epsilon \xi$. Then every (improper) agnostic (α, β)-accurate and (ϵ, δ)-differentially private empirical k-learner for C requires sample complexity greater than n.*

PROOF. The proof follows in much the same way as that of Theorem 4.2. Let (Gen, Trace) be an (n, k)-fingerprinting code, and let $x \in X$ be such that there exist $c_0, c_1 \in C$ with $c_0(x) = 0$ and $c_1(x) = 1$. Let $\mathcal{A}$ be an agnostic (α, β)-accurate empirical k-learner for C with sample complexity n. Define the fingerprinting code adversary $\mathcal{A}_{FP}$ just as in Theorem 4.2. Namely, $\mathcal{A}_{FP}$ constructs examples of the form $(x, w_{i1}, \ldots, w_{ik})$ with the available rows of the fingerprinting code, runs $\mathcal{A}$ on the result, and returns the rounded empirical averages of the k resulting hypotheses.

To show that $\mathcal{A}$ cannot be (ϵ, δ)-differentially private, it suffices to show that if $\mathcal{A}$ produces accurate hypotheses $h_1, \ldots, h_k$, then the pirate codeword produced by $\mathcal{A}_{FP}$ is feasible. To see this, suppose $h_1, \ldots, h_k$ are accurate, i.e.

$$\max_{1 \leq j \leq k} \left(\text{error}_{S|_j}(h_j) - \min_{c \in C} \left(\text{error}_{S|_j}(c) \right) \right) \leq \alpha.$$

Let column j of the codebook W be 0-marked, i.e. $w_{ij} = 0$ for all $i \in [n]$. Recall that $c_0(x) = 0$, and hence $\text{error}_{S|_j}(c_0) = 0$. Therefore, since hypothesis h_j is α-accurate, we have $\text{error}_{S|_j}(h_j) \leq \alpha$. This implies that bit w'_j of the pirate codeword is 0. An identical argument shows that the bits of the pirate codeword in the 1-marked columns are also 1. Thus, if $\mathcal{A}$ produces accurate hypotheses, the pirate codeword produced by $\mathcal{A}_{FP}$ is feasible. The rest of the argument in the proof of Theorem 4.2 completes the proof. □

REMARK 4.7. *Just as in Remark 4.3, a padding argument shows how to obtain a lower bound of $n/3\alpha$ under some additional assumptions on C, e.g. if the distinct concepts also share a common point x' with $c_0(x') = c_1(x')$.*

PROPOSITION 4.8 ([27]). *For $n \in \mathbb{N}$ and $\xi \in (0, 1)$, there exists an (n, k)-fingerprinting code with security ξ as long as $k = O(n^2 \log(n/\xi))$.*

COROLLARY 4.9. *Every improper agnostic (α, β)-accurate and $(\epsilon = O(1), \delta = o(1/n))$-differentially private empirical k-learner for $\text{POINT}_X, \text{THRESH}_X, \text{PAR}_d$ requires sample complexity $\min\{|X|, \tilde{\Omega}(k^{1/2})\}$.*

The same proof yields a lower bound for agnostically learning parities under the uniform distribution.

PROPOSITION 4.10. *Suppose there exists an (n, k)-fingerprinting code with security ξ. Let $\alpha \leq 1/6, \beta > 0$ and $d = \log n$. Then every (improper) agnostic $(\alpha, \beta, \epsilon = O(1), \delta = o(1/n))$-PAC k-learner for PAR_d requires sample complexity $\Omega(n)$.*

PROOF SKETCH. By Lemma 2.5, it is enough to rule out a private empirical learner for a database whose n examples are the distinct binary strings in $\{0, 1\}^d$. To do so, we follow the proof of Theorem 4.6, highlighting the changes that need to be made. First, we let c_0 be the all-zeroes concept, and let c_1 be an arbitrary other parity function. Second, $\mathcal{A}_{FP}$ instead constructs examples of the form $(x_i, w_{i1}, \ldots, w_{ik})$ where x_i is the ith binary string. Finally, when converting the hypotheses $(h_1, \ldots, h_k)$ into a feasible codeword, we instead set w'_j to 0 if $h_j(D) \leq \alpha$, and set w'_j to 1 if $h_j(D) \geq \frac{1}{2} - \alpha$. This works because, while $\text{error}_{S|_j}(c_0) = 0$ with respect to 0-marked columns, any concept (and in particular, c_1) has error $\frac{1}{2}$ with respect to 1-marked columns. □

5. EXAMPLES WHERE DIRECT SUM IS OPTIMAL

In this section we show several examples for cases where the direct sum is (roughly) optimal. As we saw in Section 4, with (ϵ, δ)-differential privacy, every non-trivial *agnostic* k-learner requires sample complexity $\Omega(\sqrt{k})$. We can prove a similar result for ϵ-private learners, that holds even for non-agnostic learners:

THEOREM 5.1. *Let C be any non-trivial concept class over a domain X (i.e., $|C| \geq 2$). Every proper or improper $(\alpha, \beta = \frac{1}{2}, \epsilon)$-private PAC k-learner for C requires sample complexity $\Omega(k/\epsilon)$.*

In [3, 4, 5], Beimel et al. presented an agnostic proper learner for POINT_X with sample complexity $O_{\alpha, \beta, \epsilon, \delta}(1)$ under (ϵ, δ)-privacy, and an agnostic improper learner for POINT_X with sample complexity $O_{\alpha, \beta, \epsilon}(1)$ under ϵ-privacy. Hence, using Observation 3.2 (direct sum) with their results yields an $(\alpha, \beta, \epsilon, \delta)$-PAC agnostic proper k-learner for POINT_X with sample complexity $\tilde{O}_{\alpha, \beta, \epsilon, \delta}(\sqrt{k})$, and an $(\alpha, \beta, \epsilon)$-PAC agnostic improper k-learner for POINT_X with sample complexity $\tilde{O}_{\alpha, \beta, \epsilon}(k)$. As supported by our lower bounds (Corollary 4.9 and Theorem 5.1), those learners have roughly optimal sample complexity (ignoring the dependency in $\alpha, \beta, \epsilon, \delta$ and logarithmic factors in k).

PROOF OF THEOREM 5.1. The proof is based on a packing argument [21, 3]. Let $x \in X$ and $f, g \in C$ be s.t. $f(x) \neq g(x)$. Let μ denote the constant distribution over X giving probability 1 to the point x. Note that $\text{error}_\mu(f, g) = 1$. Moreover, observe that for every concept h, if $\text{error}_\mu(h, f) < 1$ then $h(x) = f(x)$, and similarly with h, g.

Let $\mathcal{A}$ be an $(\alpha, \beta, \epsilon)$-private PAC k-learner for C with sample complexity n. For every choice of k target functions $(c_1, \ldots, c_k) = \vec{c} \in \{f, g\}^k$, let $S_{\vec{c}}$ denote the k-labeled database containing n copies of the point x, each of which is labeled by $c_1, \ldots, c_k$. Without loss of generality, we can assume that on such databases $\mathcal{A}$ returns hypotheses in $\{f, g\}$ (since under μ we can replace an arbitrarily chosen hypothesis h with f if $f(x) = h(x)$ or with g if $g(x) =$

$h(x)$). Therefore, by the utility properties of $\mathcal{A}$, for every $\vec{c} = (c_1, \ldots, c_k) \in \{f, g\}^k$ we have that $\Pr_{\mathcal{A}}[\mathcal{A}(S_{\vec{c}}) = (c_1, \ldots, c_k)] \geq \frac{1}{2}$. By changing the database $S_{\vec{c}}$ to $S_{\vec{c}'}$ one row at a time while applying the differential privacy constraint, we see that

$$\Pr_{\mathcal{A}}[\mathcal{A}(S_{\vec{c}}) = (c_1', \ldots, c_k')] \geq \frac{1}{2} e^{-\epsilon n}.$$

Since the above inequality holds for every two databases $S_{\vec{c}}$ and $S_{\vec{c}'}$, we get

$$\frac{1}{2} \geq \Pr_{\mathcal{A}}[\mathcal{A}(S_{\vec{c}}) \neq (c_1, \ldots, c_k)] \geq (2^k - 1)\frac{1}{2} e^{-\epsilon n}.$$

Solving for n, this yields $n = \Omega(k/\epsilon)$. $\square$

REMARK 5.2. *The above proof could easily be strengthened to show that $n = \Omega(\frac{k}{\alpha \epsilon})$, provided that C contains two concepts f, g s.t. $\exists x, y \in X$ for which $f(x) \neq g(x)$ and $f(y) = g(y)$.*

The following lemma shows that the sample complexities of properly and improperly learning parities under the uniform distribution are the same. Thus, for showing lower bounds, it is without loss of generality to consider proper learners.

LEMMA 5.3. *Let $\alpha < 1/4$. Let $\mathcal{A}$ be a (possibly improper) $(\alpha, \beta, \epsilon, \delta)$-PAC k-learner for PAR_d under the uniform distribution with sample complexity n. Then there exists a proper $(\alpha' = 0, \beta, \epsilon, \delta)$-PAC k-learner $\mathcal{A}'$ for PAR_d (under the uniform distribution) with sample complexity n.*

PROOF. The algorithm $\mathcal{A}'$ runs $\mathcal{A}$ and "rounds" each hypothesis h_j produced to the nearest parity function. That is, it outputs $(h_1', \ldots, h_k')$ where h_j' is a parity function that minimizes $\Pr_{x \sim U_d}[h_j'(x) \neq h_j(x)]$. Since this is just post-processing of the differentially private algorithm $\mathcal{A}$, the proper learner $\mathcal{A}'$ remains (ϵ, δ)-differentially private.

Now suppose $(h_1, \ldots, h_k)$ is α-accurate for parity functions $(c_1, \ldots, c_k)$ on the uniform distribution. Then for each j,

$$\Pr_{x \sim U_d}[h_j'(x) \neq c_j(x)] \leq \Pr_{x \sim U_d}[h_j'(x) \neq h_j(x)] + \Pr_{x \sim U_d}[h_j(x) \neq c_j(x)]$$
$$\leq 2 \Pr_{x \sim U_d}[h_j(x) \neq c_j(x)]$$
$$\leq 2\alpha.$$

Hence, $\mathrm{error}_{U_d}(h_j', c_j) < 1/2$. Since the error of any parity function from c_j (other than c_j itself) is exactly $1/2$ under the uniform distribution, we conclude that $(h_1', \ldots, h_k')$ is in fact 0-accurate for $(c_1, \ldots, c_k)$. $\square$

THEOREM 5.4. *Let $\alpha < \frac{1}{4}$. Every $(\alpha, \beta = \frac{1}{2}, \epsilon)$-PAC k-learner for PAR_d (under the uniform distribution) requires sample complexity $\Omega(kd/\epsilon)$.*

As we saw in Example 3.5, applying direct sum for k-learning parities results in a proper agnostic $(\alpha, \beta, \epsilon)$-PAC k-learner for PAR_d with sample complexity $O_{\alpha, \beta, \epsilon}(kd + k \log k)$. As stated by Theorem 5.4, this is the best possible (ignoring logarithmic factors and the dependency in α, β, ϵ).

PROOF OF THEOREM 5.4. The proof is based on a packing argument [21, 3]. Let $\mathcal{A}$ be an $(\alpha, \beta, \epsilon)$-PAC k-learner for PAR_d with sample complexity n. By Lemma 5.3, we may assume $\mathcal{A}$ is proper and learns the hidden concepts exactly.

For every choice of k parity functions $(c_1, \ldots, c_k) = \vec{c} \in (\mathrm{PAR}_d)^k$, let $S_{\vec{c}}$ denote a random k-labeled database containing n i.i.d. elements from U_d, each labeled by $(c_1, \ldots, c_k)$. By the utility properties of $\mathcal{A}$ we have that $\Pr_{U_d, \mathcal{A}}[\mathcal{A}(S_{\vec{c}}) = \vec{c}] \geq \frac{1}{2}$. In particular, for every $\vec{c} \in (\mathrm{PAR}_d)^k$ there exists a database $D_{\vec{c}}$ labeled by $\vec{c}$ s.t. $\Pr_{\mathcal{A}}[\mathcal{A}(S_{\vec{c}}) = \vec{c}] \geq \frac{1}{2}$. By changing the database $D_{\vec{c}}$ to $D_{\vec{c}'}$ one row at a time while applying the differential privacy constraint, we see that

$$\Pr_{\mathcal{A}}[\mathcal{A}(D_{\vec{c}}) = \vec{c}'] \geq \frac{1}{2} e^{-\epsilon n}.$$

Since the above inequality holds for every two databases $D_{\vec{c}}$ and $D_{\vec{c}'}$, we get

$$\frac{1}{2} \geq \Pr_{\mathcal{A}}[\mathcal{A}(D_{\vec{c}}) \neq \vec{c}] \geq (|\mathrm{PAR}_d|^k - 1)\frac{1}{2} e^{-\epsilon n}.$$

Solving for n, this yields $n = \Omega(kd/\epsilon)$. $\square$

6. REFERENCES

[1] R. Bassily, A. Smith, and A. Thakurta. Private empirical risk minimization: Efficient algorithms and tight error bounds. In *FOCS*, pages 464–473, 2014.

[2] A. Beimel, H. Brenner, S. P. Kasiviswanathan, and K. Nissim. Bounds on the sample complexity for private learning and private data release. *Machine Learning*, 94(3):401–437, 2014.

[3] A. Beimel, S. P. Kasiviswanathan, and K. Nissim. Bounds on the sample complexity for private learning and private data release. In *TCC*, pages 437–454, 2010.

[4] A. Beimel, K. Nissim, and U. Stemmer. Characterizing the sample complexity of private learners. In *ITCS*, pages 97–110, 2013.

[5] A. Beimel, K. Nissim, and U. Stemmer. Private learning and sanitization: Pure vs. approximate differential privacy. In *APPROX-RANDOM*, pages 363–378, 2013.

[6] A. Beimel, K. Nissim, and U. Stemmer. Learning privately with labeled and unlabeled examples. In *SODA*, pages 461–477, 2015.

[7] A. Blum, C. Dwork, F. McSherry, and K. Nissim. Practical privacy: the SuLQ framework. In *PODS*, pages 128–138, 2005.

[8] A. Blum, K. Ligett, and A. Roth. A learning theory approach to noninteractive database privacy. *J. ACM*, 60(2):12, 2013.

[9] D. Boneh and J. Shaw. Collusion-secure fingerprinting for digital data. *IEEE Transactions on Information Theory*, 44(5):1897–1905, 1998.

[10] M. Bun, K. Nissim, U. Stemmer, and S. Vadhan. Differentially private release and learning of threshold functions. In *Proceedings of the 56th Annual IEEE Symposium on Foundations of Computer Science (FOCS 2015)*, pages 634–649, Berkeley, CA, USA, October 18-20, 2015.

[11] M. Bun, J. Ullman, and S. P. Vadhan. Fingerprinting codes and the price of approximate differential privacy. In *STOC*, pages 1–10, 2014.

[12] K. Chaudhuri and D. Hsu. Sample complexity bounds for differentially private learning. In S. M. Kakade and U. von Luxburg, editors, *COLT*, volume 19 of *JMLR Proceedings*, pages 155–186. JMLR.org, 2011.

[13] C. Dwork, K. Kenthapadi, F. McSherry, I. Mironov, and M. Naor. Our data, ourselves: Privacy via distributed noise generation. In *EUROCRYPT*, pages 486–503, 2006.

[14] C. Dwork, F. McSherry, K. Nissim, and A. Smith. Calibrating noise to sensitivity in private data analysis. In *TCC*, pages 265–284, 2006.

[15] C. Dwork, G. N. Rothblum, and S. P. Vadhan. Boosting and differential privacy. In *FOCS*, pages 51–60, 2010.

[16] C. Dwork, K. Talwar, A. Thakurta, and L. Zhang. Analyze gauss: Optimal bounds for privacy-preserving principal component analysis. In *Proceedings of the 46th Annual ACM Symposium on Theory of Computing*, STOC '14, pages 11–20, New York, NY, USA, 2014. ACM.

[17] D. Feldman, A. Fiat, H. Kaplan, and K. Nissim. Private coresets. In M. Mitzenmacher, editor, *Proceedings of the 41st Annual ACM Symposium on Theory of Computing, STOC 2009, Bethesda, MD, USA, May 31 - June 2, 2009*, pages 361–370. ACM, 2009.

[18] V. Feldman and D. Xiao. Sample complexity bounds on differentially private learning via communication complexity. In *COLT*, pages 1000–1019, 2014.

[19] A. Gupta, M. Hardt, A. Roth, and J. Ullman. Privately releasing conjunctions and the statistical query barrier. In *STOC*, pages 803–812, 2011.

[20] M. Hardt and G. N. Rothblum. A multiplicative weights mechanism for privacy-preserving data analysis. In *FOCS*, pages 61–70, 2010.

[21] M. Hardt and K. Talwar. On the geometry of differential privacy. In *STOC*, pages 705–714, 2010.

[22] S. P. Kasiviswanathan, H. K. Lee, K. Nissim, S. Raskhodnikova, and A. Smith. What can we learn privately? *SIAM J. Comput.*, 40(3):793–826, 2011.

[23] K. Nissim, S. Raskhodnikova, and A. Smith. Smooth sensitivity and sampling in private data analysis. In *Proceedings of the 39th Annual ACM Symposium on Theory of Computing, San Diego, California, USA, June 11-13, 2007*, pages 75–84, 2007.

[24] C. Peikert, abhi shelat, and A. Smith. Lower bounds for collusion-secure fingerprinting. In *SODA*, pages 472–479, 2003.

[25] A. Roth and T. Roughgarden. Interactive privacy via the median mechanism. In *STOC*, pages 765–774, 2010.

[26] T. Steinke and J. Ullman. Between pure and approximate differential privacy. In *TPDP 2015*, 2015.

[27] G. Tardos. Optimal probabilistic fingerprint codes. *J. ACM*, 55(2), 2008.

[28] L. G. Valiant. A theory of the learnable. *Commun. ACM*, 27(11):1134–1142, Nov. 1984.

[29] L. G. Valiant. Knowledge infusion. In *Proceedings, The Twenty-First National Conference on Artificial Intelligence and the Eighteenth Innovative Applications of Artificial Intelligence Conference, July 16-20, 2006, Boston, Massachusetts, USA*, pages 1546–1551. AAAI Press, 2006.

APPENDIX

A. TABLES OF RESULTS

The following tables summarize the results of this work. In the tables below C is a class of concepts (i.e., predicates) defined over domain X. Sample complexity upper and lower bounds is given in terms of $|C|$ and $|X|$. Note that for POINT_X, THRESH_X, and PAR_d we have $|C| = \Theta(|X|)$.

Where not explicitly noted, upper bounds hold for the setting of agnostic learning and lower bounds are for the (potentially easier) setting of PAC learning. Similarly, where not explicitly noted, upper bounds are for proper learning and lower bounds are for the (less restrictive) setting of improper learning. For simplicity, these tables hide constant and logarithmic factors, as well as dependencies on the learning and privacy parameters.

Multi-learning with pure differential privacy.

Upper bounds:

C	PAC learning		Agnostic learning	
	proper	improper	proper	improper
POINT_X	$k + \log|C|$	k	$k + \log|C|$	k
THRESH_X	$k + \log|C|$			
General	$\min\{k\log|C|, k\,\mathrm{VC}(C) + \log|X|\,\mathrm{VC}(C)\}$			
PAR_d (unif.)	$k\log|C|$			

Lower bounds:

C	PAC learning		Agnostic learning	
	proper	improper	proper	improper
POINT_X	$k + \log|C|$	k	$k + \log|C|$	k
THRESH_X	$k + \log|C|$			
PAR_d (unif.)	$k\log|C|$			

Multi-learning with approximate differential privacy.

Upper bounds:

C	PAC learning (proper and improper)	Agnostic learning (proper and improper)
POINT_X	1	$\sqrt{k}$
THRESH_X	$2^{\log^* |X|} + \sqrt{k}$	
General C	$\min\left\{\begin{array}{l}\sqrt{k}\log|C|, \\ \sqrt{k}\,\mathrm{VC}(C) + \log|X|\,\mathrm{VC}(C), \\ \sqrt{k}\,\mathrm{VC}(C) + \sqrt{\log|X|}\log|C|\end{array}\right\}$	
PAR_d (unif.)	$\log|C|$	$\sqrt{k}\log|C|$

Lower bounds:

C	PAC learning		Agnostic learning	
	proper	impr.	proper	impr.
POINT_X	1		$\sqrt{k}$	
THRESH_X	$\log^* |X| + k^{1/3}$	$k^{1/3}$	$\log^* |X| + \sqrt{k}$	$\sqrt{k}$
PAR_d (unif.)	$\log|C|$		$\sqrt{k} + \log|C|$	

Information Complexity Density and Simulation of Protocols

[Extended Abstract]*

Himanshu Tyagi
Indian Institute of Science,
Bangalore
htyagi@ece.iisc.ernet.in

Shaileshh Venkatakrishnan
University of Illinois,
Urbana-Champaign
bjjvnkt2@illinois.edu

Pramod Viswanath
University of Illinois,
Urbana-Champaign
pramodv@illinois.edu

Shun Watanabe
Tokyo University of Agriculture
and Technology
shunwata@cc.tuat.ac.jp

ABSTRACT

A simulation of an interactive protocol entails the use of interactive communication to produce the output of the protocol to within a fixed statistical distance ε. Recent works have proposed that the *information complexity* of the protocol plays a central role in characterizing the minimum number of bits that the parties must exchange for a successful simulation, namely the *distributional communication complexity* of simulating the protocol. Several simulation protocols have been proposed with communication complexity depending on the information complexity of the simulated protocol. However, in the absence of any general lower bounds for distributional communication complexity, the conjectured central role of information complexity is far from settled. We fill this gap and show that the distributional communication complexity of ε-simulating a protocol is bounded below by the ε-tail λ_ε of the *information complexity density*, a random variable with information complexity as its expected value. For protocols with bounded number of rounds, we give a simulation protocol that yields a matching upper bound. Thus, it is not information complexity but λ_ε that governs the distributional communication complexity.

As applications of our bounds, in the amortized regime for product protocols, we identify the exact second order term, together with the precise dependence on ε. For general protocols such as a mixture of two product protocols or for the amortized case when the repetitions are not independent, we derive a general formula for the leading asymptotic term. These results sharpen and significantly extend known

results in the amortized regime. In the single-shot regime, our lower bound sheds light on the dependence of communication complexity on ε. We illustrate this with an example that exhibits an arbitrary separation between distributional communication complexity and information complexity for all sufficiently small ε.

Categories and Subject Descriptors

F.2.0 [**Theory of Computation**]: Analysis of algorithms and problem complexity—*General*

Keywords

Information complexity, simulation of protocols, interactive protocols

1. INTRODUCTION

Two parties observing random variables X and Y seek to run an interactive protocol π with inputs X and Y. The parties have access to private as well as shared public randomness. What is the minimum number of bits that they must exchange in order to simulate π to within a fixed statistical distance ε? This question is of importance to the theoretical computer science as well as the information theory communities. On the one hand, it is related closely to the communication complexity problem [44], which in turn is an important tool for deriving lower bounds for computational complexity [24] and for space complexity of streaming algorithms [2]. On the other hand, it is a significant generalization of the classical information theoretic problem of distributed data compression [38], replacing data to be compressed with an interactive protocol and allowing interactive communication as opposed to the usual one-sided communication.

In recent years, it has been argued that the distributional communication complexity for simulating a protocol π is related closely to its *information complexity*[1] $\mathtt{IC}(\pi)$ defined

---

*A full version of this paper is available at http://eccc.hpi-web.de/report/2015/070/.

Permission to make digital or hard copies of all or part of this work for personal or classroom use is granted without fee provided that copies are not made or distributed for profit or commercial advantage and that copies bear this notice and the full citation on the first page. Copyrights for components of this work owned by others than ACM must be honored. Abstracting with credit is permitted. To copy otherwise, or republish, to post on servers or to redistribute to lists, requires prior specific permission and/or a fee. Request permissions from Permissions@acm.org.

ITCS'16, January 14–16, 2016, Cambridge, MA, USA.
ⓒ 2016 ACM. ISBN 978-1-4503-4057-1/16/01 ...$15.00.
DOI: http://dx.doi.org/10.1145/2840728.2840754.

---

[1] For brevity, we do not display the dependence of $\mathtt{IC}(\pi)$ on the (fixed) distribution P_{XY}.

as follows:

$$\mathtt{IC}(\pi) \stackrel{\text{def}}{=} I(\Pi \wedge X|Y) + I(\Pi \wedge Y|X),$$

where $I(X \wedge Y|Z)$ denotes the conditional mutual information between X and Y given Z (*cf.* [37, 12]). For a protocol π with communication complexity $\|\pi\|$ (the depth of the binary protocol tree), a simulation protocol requiring $\tilde{\mathcal{O}}(\sqrt{\mathtt{IC}(\pi)\|\pi\|})$ bits of communication was given in [4] and one requiring $2^{\mathcal{O}(\mathtt{IC}(\pi))}$ bits of communication was given in [7]. A general version of the simulation problem was considered in [46], but only bounded round simulation protocols were considered. Interestingly, it was shown in [8] that the amortized distributional communication complexity of simulating n copies of a protocol π for vanishing simulation error is bounded above by[2] $\mathtt{IC}(\pi)$. While a matching lower bound was also derived in [8], it is not valid in our context – [8] considered function computation and used a coordinate-wise error criterion. Nevertheless, we can readily modify the lower bound argument in [8] and use the continuity of conditional mutual information to formally obtain the required lower bound and thereby a characterization of the amortized distributional communication complexity for vanishing simulation error. Specifically, denoting by $D(\pi^n)$ the distributional communication complexity of simulating n copies of a protocol π with vanishing simulation error, we have

$$\lim_{n \to \infty} \frac{1}{n} D(\pi^n) = \mathtt{IC}(\pi).$$

Perhaps motivated by this characterization, or a folklore version of it, the research in this area has focused on designing simulation protocols for π requiring communication of length depending on $\mathtt{IC}(\pi)$; the results cited above belong to this category as well. However, the central role of $\mathtt{IC}(\pi)$ in the distributional communication complexity of protocol simulation is far from settled and many important questions remain unanswered. For instance, (a) does $\mathtt{IC}(\pi)$ suffice to capture the dependence of distributional communication complexity on the simulation error ε? (b) Does information complexity have an operational role in simulating π^n besides being the leading asymptotic term? (c) How about the simulation of more complicated protocols such as a mixture $\pi_{\mathtt{mix}}$ of two product protocols π_1^n and π_2^n – does $\mathtt{IC}(\pi_{\mathtt{mix}})$ still constitute the leading asymptotic term in the communication complexity of simulating $\pi_{\mathtt{mix}}$?

The quantity $\mathtt{IC}(\pi)$ plays the same role in the simulation of protocols as $H(X)$ in the compression of X^n [37] and $H(X|Y)$ in the transmission of X^n by the first to the second party with access to Y^n [38]. The questions raised above have been addressed for these classical problems (*cf.* [19]). In this paper, we answer these questions for simulation of interactive protocols. In particular, we answer all these questions in the negative by exhibiting another quantity that plays such a fundamental role and can differ from information complexity significantly. To this end, we introduce the notion of *information complexity density* of a protocol π with inputs X and Y generated from a fixed distribution P_{XY}.

Definition 1. **Information complexity density.** The *information complexity density* of a private coin protocol π is given by the function

$$\mathtt{ic}(\tau;x,y) = \log \frac{\mathrm{P}_{\Pi|XY}(\tau|x,y)}{\mathrm{P}_{\Pi|X}(\tau|x)} + \log \frac{\mathrm{P}_{\Pi|XY}(\tau|x,y)}{\mathrm{P}_{\Pi|Y}(\tau|y)},$$

for all observations x and y of the two parties and all transcripts τ, where $\mathrm{P}_{\Pi XY}$ denotes the joint distribution of the observation of the two parties and the random transcript Π generated by π.

Note that $\mathtt{IC}(\pi) = \mathbb{E}[\mathtt{ic}(\Pi;X,Y)]$. We show that it is the ε-*tail of the information complexity density* $\mathtt{ic}(\Pi;X,Y)$, *i.e.*, the supremum[3] over values of λ such that $\Pr(\mathtt{ic}(\Pi;X,Y) > \lambda) > \varepsilon$, which governs the communication complexity of simulating a protocol with simulation error less than ε and not the information complexity of the protocol. The information complexity $\mathtt{IC}(\pi)$ becomes the leading term in communication complexity for simulating π only when roughly

$$\mathtt{IC}(\pi) \gg \sqrt{\mathrm{Var}(\mathtt{ic}(\Pi;X,Y))\log(1/\varepsilon)}.$$

This condition holds, for instance, in the amortized regime considered in [8]. However, the ε-tail of $\mathtt{ic}(\Pi;X,Y)$ can differ significantly from $\mathtt{IC}(\pi)$, the mean of $\mathtt{ic}(\Pi;X,Y)$. In Appendix 5, we provide an example protocol with inputs of size 2^n such that for $\varepsilon = 1/n^3$, the ε-tail of $\mathtt{ic}(\Pi;X,Y)$ is greater than $2n$ while $\mathtt{IC}(\pi)$ is very small, just $\tilde{\mathcal{O}}(n^{-2})$.

1.1 Summary of results

Our main results are bounds for distributional communication complexity $D_\varepsilon(\pi)$ for ε-simulating a protocol π. The key quantity in our bounds is the ε-tail λ_ε of $\mathtt{ic}(\Pi;X,Y)$.

Lower bound. Our main contribution is a general lower bound for $D_\varepsilon(\pi)$. We show that for every private coin protocol π, $D_\varepsilon(\pi) \gtrsim \lambda_\varepsilon$. In fact, this bound does not rely on the structure of random variable Π and is valid for the more general problem of simulating a correlated random variable.

Prior to this work, there was no lower bound that captured both the dependence on simulation error ε as well as the underlying probability distribution. On the one hand, the lower bound above yields many sharp results in the amortized regime. It gives the leading asymptotic term in the communication complexity for simulating any sequence of protocols, and not just product protocols. For product protocols, it yields the precise dependence of communication complexity on ε as well as the exact second-order asymptotic term. On the other hand, it sheds light on the dependence of $D_\varepsilon(\pi)$ on ε even in the single-shot regime. For instance, our lower bound can be used to exhibit an arbitrary separation between $D_\varepsilon(\pi)$ and $\mathtt{IC}(\pi)$ when ε is not fixed. Specifically, consider the example protocol in Appendix 5. On evaluating our lower bound for this protocol, for $\varepsilon = 1/n^3$ we get $D_\varepsilon(\pi) = \Omega(n)$ which is far more than $2^{\mathtt{IC}(\pi)}$ since $\mathtt{IC}(\pi) = \tilde{\mathcal{O}}(n^{-2})$. Remarkably, [18, 17] exhibited exponential separation between the distributional communication complexity of computing a function and the information complexity of that function even for a fixed ε, thereby establishing the optimality of the upper bound $D_\varepsilon(\pi) \leq \mathcal{O}(2^{\mathtt{IC}}(\pi))$ given in [7]. Our simple example shows a much stronger

---

[2] Braverman and Rao actually used their general simulation protocol as a tool for deriving the amortized distributional communication complexity of function computation. This result was obtained independently by Ma and Ishwar in [26] using standard information theoretic techniques.

[3] Formally, our lower bound uses lower ε-tail $\sup\{\lambda : \Pr(\mathtt{ic}(\Pi;X,Y) > \lambda) > \varepsilon\}$ and the upper bound uses upper ε-tail $\inf\{\lambda : \Pr(\mathtt{ic}(\Pi;X,Y) > \lambda) < \varepsilon\}$. For many interesting cases, the two coincide.

separation between $D_\varepsilon(\pi)$ and $\mathtt{IC}(\pi)$, albeit for a vanishing ε.

Upper bound. To establish our asymptotic results, we propose a new simulation protocol, which is of independent interest. For a protocol π with bounded rounds of interaction, using our proposed protocol we can show that $D_\varepsilon(\pi) \lesssim \lambda_\varepsilon$. Much as the protocol of [8], our simulation protocol simulates one round at a time, and thus, the slack in our upper bound does depend on the number of rounds.

Note that while the operative term in the lower bound and the upper bound is the ε-tail of $\mathtt{ic}(\Pi; X, Y)$, the lower bound approaches it from below and the upper bound approaches it from above. It is often the case that these two limits match and the leading term in our bounds coincide. See Figure 1 for an illustration of our bounds.

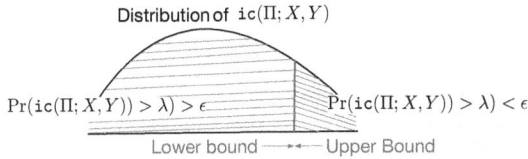
Distribution of $\mathtt{ic}(\Pi; X, Y)$

$\Pr(\mathtt{ic}(\Pi; X, Y)) > \lambda) > \epsilon$ $\Pr(\mathtt{ic}(\Pi; X, Y)) > \lambda) < \epsilon$
Lower bound —•— Upper Bound

Figure 1: Illustration of lower and upper bounds for $D_\varepsilon(\pi)$

Amortized regime: second-order asymptotics. Denote by π^n the n-fold product protocol obtained by applying π to each coordinate (X_i, Y_i) for inputs X^n and Y^n. Consider the communication complexity $D_\varepsilon(\pi^n)$ of ε-simulating π^n for *independent and identically distributed* (IID) (X^n, Y^n) generated from P_{XY}^n. Using the bounds above, we can obtain the following sharpening of the results of [8]: With $\mathtt{V}(\pi)$ denoting the variance of $\mathtt{ic}(\Pi; X, Y)$,

$$D_\varepsilon(\pi^n) = n\mathtt{IC}(\pi) + \sqrt{n\mathtt{V}(\pi)}Q^{-1}(\varepsilon) + o(\sqrt{n}),$$

where $Q(x)$ is equal to the probability that a standard normal random variable exceeds x and $Q^{-1}(\varepsilon) \approx \sqrt{\log(1/\varepsilon)}$. On the other hand, the arguments in[4] [8] or [46] give us

$$D_\varepsilon(\pi^n) \geq n\mathtt{IC}(\pi) - n\varepsilon[\|\pi\| + \log|\mathcal{X}||\mathcal{Y}|] - \varepsilon\log(1/\varepsilon).$$

But the precise communication requirement is not less but $\sqrt{n\mathtt{V}(\pi)\log(1/\varepsilon)}$ *more than* $n\mathtt{IC}(\pi)$.

General formula for amortized communication complexity. The lower and upper bounds above can be used to derive a formula for the first-order asymptotic term, the coefficient of n, in $D_\varepsilon(\pi_n)$ for any sequence of protocols π_n with inputs $X_n \in \mathcal{X}^n$ and $Y_n \in \mathcal{Y}^n$ generated from any sequence of distributions $\mathrm{P}_{X_nY_n}$. We illustrate our result by the following example.

Example 1. **Mixed protocol.** Consider two protocols π_h and π_t with inputs X and Y such that $\mathtt{IC}(\pi_\mathrm{h}) > \mathtt{IC}(\pi_\mathrm{t})$. For n IID observations (X^n, Y^n) drawn from P_{XY}, we seek to simulate the mixed protocol $\pi_{\mathtt{mix,n}}$ defined as follows: Party 1 first flips a (private) coin with probability p of heads and sends the outcome Π_0 to Party 2. Depending on the outcome of the coin, the parties execute π_h or π_t n times, i.e., they use π_h^n if $\Pi_0 = \mathtt{h}$ and π_t^n if $\Pi_0 = \mathtt{t}$. What is the amortized communication complexity of simulating the mixed protocol $\pi_{\mathtt{mix,n}}$? Note that

$$\mathtt{IC}(\pi_{\mathtt{mix,n}}) = n\left[p\mathtt{IC}(\pi_\mathrm{h}) + (1-p)\mathtt{IC}(\pi_\mathrm{t})\right].$$

---

[4]The proof in [8] uses the inequality $\mathtt{IC}(\pi) \leq \|\pi\|$, a multiparty extension of which is available in [13, 27].

Is it true that in the manner of [8] the leading asymptotic term in $D_\varepsilon(\pi_{\mathtt{mix,n}})$ is $\mathtt{IC}(\pi_{\mathtt{mix,n}})$? In fact, it is not so. Our general formula implies that for all $p \in (0, 1)$,

$$D_\varepsilon(\pi_{\mathtt{mix,n}}) = n\mathtt{IC}(\pi_\mathrm{h}) + o(n)$$

This is particularly interesting when p is very small and $\mathtt{IC}(\pi_\mathrm{h}) \gg \mathtt{IC}(\pi_\mathrm{t})$.

1.2 Proof techniques

Proof for the lower bound. We present a new method for deriving lower bounds on distributional communication complexity. Our proof relies on a reduction argument that utilizes an ε-simulation to generate an information theoretically secure secret key for X and Y (for a definition of the latter, see [28, 1]). Heuristically, a protocol can be simulated using fewer bits of communication than its length because of the correlation in the observations X and Y. Due to this correlation, when simulating the protocol, the parties agree on more bits (generate more *common randomness*) than what they communicate. These extra bits can be extracted as an information theoretically secure secret key for the two parties using the *leftover hash lemma* (*cf.* [6, 36]). A lower bound on the number of bits communicated can be derived using an upper bound for the maximum possible length of a secret key that can be generated using interactive communication; the latter was derived recently in [42, 41].

Protocol for the upper bound. We simulate a given protocol one round at a time. Simulation of each round consists of two subroutines: Interactive Slepian-Wolf compression and message reduction by public randomness. The first subroutine is an interactive version of the classical Slepian-Wolf compression [38] for sending X to an observer of Y which is of optimal instantaneous rate. The second subroutine uses an idea that appeared first in [35] (see, also, [30, 45]) and reduces the number of bits communicated in the first by realizing a portion of the required communication by the shared public randomness. This is possible since we are not required to recover a given random variable Π, but only simulate it to within a fixed statistical distance.

The proposed protocol is closely related to that proposed in [8]. However, there are some crucial differences. The protocol in [8], too, uses public randomness to sample each round of the protocol, before transmitting it using an interactive communication of size incremented in steps. However, our information theoretic approach provides a systematic method for choosing this step size. Furthermore, our protocol for sampling the protocol from public randomness is significantly different from that in [8] and relies on randomness extraction techniques. In particular, the protocol in [8] does not attain the asymptotically optimal bounds achieved by our protocol.

Technical approach. While we utilize new, bespoke techniques for deriving our lower and upper bounds, casting our problem in an information theoretic framework allows us to build upon the developments in this classic field. In particular, we rely on the *information spectrum approach* of Han and Verdú, introduced in the seminal paper [20] (see the textbook [19] for a detailed account). In this approach, the classical measures of information such as entropy and mutual information are viewed as expectations of the corresponding *information densities*, and the notion of "typical sets" is replaced by sets where these information densities are bounded uniformly. The set of values taken by an information density (such as $h(x) = -\log P_X(x)$) is called its *spectrum*. Coding theorems of classical information theory consider IID repetitions and rely on the so-called the *asymptotic equipartition property* [11] which essentially corresponds to the concentration of spectrums on small intervals. For *single-shot* problems such concentrations are not available and we have to work with the whole span of the spectrum.

Our main technical contribution in this paper is the extension of the information spectrum method to handle interactive communication. Our results rely on the analysis of appropriately chosen information densities and, in particular, will rely on the spectrum of the information complexity density $\mathrm{ic}(\Pi; X, Y)$. As is usually the case, different components of our analysis require bounds on these information densities in different directions, which in turn renders our bounds loose and incurs a gap equal to the length of the corresponding information spectrum. To overcome this shortcoming, we use the *spectrum slicing* technique of Han [19][5] to divide the information spectrum into small portions with information densities closely bounded from both sides. While in our upper bounds spectrum slicing is used to carefully choose the parameters of the protocol, it is required in our lower bounds to identify a set of inputs where a given simulation will require a large number of bits to be communicated.

1.3 Organization

A formal statement of the problem, along with the necessary preliminaries, is given in the next section. Section 3 contains all our results. While the proofs of our general single-shot results are deferred to the full-version of the paper, proofs of the asymtotic results, derived using our single-shot results, are included in Section 4. The conclusion is stated in Section 5.

1.4 Notations

Random variables are denoted by capital letters such as X, Y, *etc.* realizations by small letters such as x, y, *etc.* and their range sets by corresponding calligraphic letters such as $\mathcal{X}$, $\mathcal{Y}$, *etc.*. Protocols are denoted by appropriate subscripts or superscripts with π, the corresponding random transcripts by the same sub- or superscripts with Π; τ is used as a placeholder for realizations of random transcripts. All the logarithms in this paper are to the base 2.

The following convention, described for the entropy density, shall be used for all information densities used in this paper. We shall abbreviate the entropy density $h_{P_X}(x) = -\log P_X(x)$ by $h(x)$, when there is no confusion about P_X, and the random variable $h(X)$ corresponds to drawing X from the distribution P_X.

Whenever there is no confusion, we will not display the dependence of distributional communication complexity on the underlying distribution. In most of our discussion, the latter remains fixed.

2. PROBLEM STATEMENT

Two parties observe correlated random variables X and Y, with Party 1 observing X and Party 2 observing Y, generated from a fixed distribution P_{XY} and taking values in

finite sets $\mathcal{X}$ and $\mathcal{Y}$, respectively. An *interactive protocol* π (for these two parties) consists of shared public randomness U, private randomness[6] $U_{\mathcal{X}}$ and $U_{\mathcal{Y}}$, and interactive communication $\Pi_1, ..., \Pi_r$. The parties communicate alternatively with Party 1 transmitting in the odd rounds and Party 2 in the even rounds. Specifically, Π_i is a string of bits determined by the previous transmissions $\Pi_1, ..., \Pi_{i-1}$ together with $(X, U_{\mathcal{X}}, U)$ for odd i and $(Y, U_{\mathcal{Y}}, U)$ for even i. For simplicity, we assume that the realizations of Π_i constitute a prefix-free code, *i.e.*, no realizations of Π_i is a prefix of another realization of Π_i. The number of rounds of communication r is a random stopping-time such that the event $\{r = t\}$ is determined by the transcript $\Pi_1, ..., \Pi_t$; we denote the overall transcript of the protocol[7] by Π. The length of a protocol π, $\|\pi\|$, is the maximum number of bits that are communicated in any execution of the protocol.

A random variable F is said to be *recoverable* by π for Party 1 (or Party 2) if F is function of $(X, U, U_{\mathcal{X}}, \Pi)$ (or $(Y, U, U_{\mathcal{Y}}, \Pi)$).

A protocol with a constant U is called a *private coin protocol*, with a constant $(U_{\mathcal{X}}, U_{\mathcal{Y}})$ is called a *public coin protocol*, and with $(U, U_{\mathcal{X}}, U_{\mathcal{Y}})$ constant is called a *deterministic protocol*.

When we execute the protocol π above, the overall *view* of the parties consists of random variables $(XY\Pi\Pi)$, where the two Πs correspond to the transcript of the protocol seen by the two parties. A simulation of the protocol consists of another protocol which generates almost the same view as that of the original protocol. We are interested in the simulation of private coin protocols, using arbitrary[8] protocols; public coin protocols can be simulated by simulating for each fixed value of public randomness the resulting private coin protocol.

Definition 2. ε-**Simulation of a protocol.** Let π be a private coin protocol. Given $0 \leq \varepsilon < 1$, a protocol π_{sim} constitutes an ε-simulation of π if there exist $\Pi_{\mathcal{X}}$ and $\Pi_{\mathcal{Y}}$, respectively, recoverable by π_{sim} for Party 1 and Party 2 such that

$$d_{\mathrm{var}}\left(P_{\Pi\Pi XY}, P_{\Pi_{\mathcal{X}}\Pi_{\mathcal{Y}} XY}\right) \leq \varepsilon, \tag{1}$$

where $d_{\mathrm{var}}(P, Q) = \frac{1}{2} \sum_x |P_x - Q_x|$ denotes the variational or the statistical distance between P and Q.

Definition 3. **Distributional communication complexity.** The ε-error distributional communication complexity $D_{\varepsilon}(\pi|P_{XY})$ of simulating a private coin protocol π is the minimum length of an ε-simulation of π. The distribution P_{XY} remains fixed throughout our analysis; for brevity, we shall abbreviate $D_{\varepsilon}(\pi|P_{XY})$ by $D_{\varepsilon}(\pi)$.

Problem. Given a protocol π and a joint distribution P_{XY} for the observations of the two parties, we seek to characterize $D_{\varepsilon}(\pi)$.

---

[5]The spectrum slicing technique was introduced in [19] to derive the error exponents of various problems for general sources and a rate-distortion function for general sources.

[6]The random variables $U, U_{\mathcal{X}}, U_{\mathcal{Y}}$ are mutually independent and independent jointly of (X, Y).

[7]We allow Π_i to be constant and allow it to depend only on the local observation (and not on the previous communication $\Pi_1, ..., \Pi_{i-1}$). This description of an interactive protocol is very general and is equivalent to the usual protocol-tree based description (*cf.* [4, 8]).

[8]Since we are not interested in minimizing the amount of randomness used in a simulation, and private randomness can always be sampled from public randomness, we can restrict ourselves to public protocols for simulating.

Remark 1. **Deterministic protocols** Note that a deterministic protocol corresponds to an *interactive function*, and for such protocols,

$$d_{\text{var}}\left(P_{\Pi\Pi XY}, P_{\Pi_{\mathcal{X}}\Pi_{\mathcal{Y}} XY}\right) = 1 - \Pr\left(\Pi = \Pi_{\mathcal{X}} = \Pi_{\mathcal{Y}}\right).$$

Therefore, a protocol is an ε-simulation of a deterministic protocol if and only if it computes the corresponding interactive function with probability of error less than ε. Furthermore, randomization does not help in this case, and it suffices to use deterministic simulation protocols. Thus, our results below provide tight bounds for distributional communication complexity of interactive functions and, in fact, of all functions which are *information theoretically securely computable* for the distribution P_{XY}, since computing these functions is tantamount to computing an interactive function [31] (see, also, [5, 25]).

Remark 2. **Compression of protocols** A protocol π_{com} constitutes an ε-compression of a given protocol π if it recovers $\Pi_{\mathcal{X}}$ and $\Pi_{\mathcal{Y}}$ for Party 1 and Party 2 such that

$$\Pr\left(\Pi = \Pi_{\mathcal{X}} = \Pi_{\mathcal{Y}}\right) \geq 1 - \varepsilon.$$

Note that randomization does not help in this case either. In fact, for deterministic protocols simulation and compression coincide. In general, however, compression is a more demanding task than simulation and our results show that in many cases, (such as the amortized regime), compression requires strictly more communication than simulation. Specifically, our results for ε-simulation in this paper can be modified to get corresponding results for ε-compression by replacing the information complexity density $\text{ic}(\tau; x, y)$ by

$$h(\tau|x) + h(\tau|y) = -\log P_{\Pi|X}\left(\tau|x\right) P_{\Pi|Y}\left(\tau|y\right).$$

The proofs remain essentially the same and, in fact, simplify significantly.

3. MAIN RESULTS

We derive a lower bound for $D_{\varepsilon}\left(\pi\right)$ which applies to all private coin protocols π and, in fact, applies to the more general problem of communication complexity of sampling a correlated random variable. For protocols with bounded number of rounds of interaction, *i.e.*, protocols with $r = r(X, Y, U, U_{\mathcal{X}}, U_{\mathcal{Y}}) \leq r_{\max}$ with probability 1, we present a simulation protocol which yields upper bounds for $D_{\varepsilon}\left(\pi\right)$ of similar form as our lower bounds. In particular, in the asymptotic regime our bounds improve over previously known bounds and are tight.

3.1 Lower bound

We prove the following lower bound.

THEOREM 1. *Given* $0 \leq \varepsilon < 1$ *and a protocol* π, *for arbitrary* $0 < \eta < 1/3$

$$D_{\varepsilon}\left(\pi\right) \geq \sup\{\lambda : \Pr\left(\text{ic}(\Pi; X, Y) > \lambda\right) \geq \varepsilon + \varepsilon'\} - \lambda', \quad (2)$$

where the fudge parameters ε' *and* λ' *depend on* η *as well as appropriately chosen information spectrums and will be described below in* (4) *and* (5).

The appearance of fudge parameters such as ε' and λ' in the bound above is not surprising since the techniques to bound the tail probability of random variables invariably entail such parameters, which are tuned based on the specific scenario being studied. For instance, the Chernoff bound has a parameter that is tuned with respect to the moment generating function of the random variable of interest. More relevant to the problem studied here, such fudge parameters also show up in the evaluation of error probability of single-party non-interactive compression problems (*cf.* [20, 19]).

When the fudge parameters ε' and λ' are negligible, the right-side of the bound above is close to ε-tail of $\text{ic}(\Pi; X, Y)$. Indeed, the fudge parameters turn out to be negligible in many cases of interest. For instance, for the amortized case ε' can be chosen to be arbitrarily small. The parameter λ' is related to the length of the interval in which the underlying information densities lie with probability greater than $1 - \varepsilon'$, the essential length of spectrums. For the amortized case with product protocols, by the central limit theorem the related essential spectrums are of length $\Lambda = \mathcal{O}(\sqrt{n})$ and $\lambda' = \log \Lambda$. On the other hand, λ_{ε} is $\mathcal{O}(n)$. Thus, the $\log n$ order fudge parameter λ' is negligible in this case. The same is true also for the example protocol in Appendix 5. Finally, it should be noted that similar fudge parameters are ubiquitous in single-shot bounds; for instance, see [19, Lemma 1.3.2].

Remark 3. The result above does not rely on the interactive nature of Π and is valid for simulation of any random variable Π. Specifically, for any joint distribution $P_{\Pi XY}$, an ε-simulation satisfying (1) must communicate at least as many bits as the right-side of (2), which is roughly equal to the largest value λ_{ε} of λ such that $\Pr\left(\text{ic}(\Pi; X, Y) > \lambda\right) > \varepsilon$.

The fudge parameters. The fudge parameters ε' and λ' in Theorem 1 depend on the spectrums of the following information densities:

(i) *Information complexity density:* This density is described in Definition 1 and will play a pivotal role in our results.

(ii) *Entropy density of* (X, Y): This density, given by $h(X, Y) = -\log P_{XY}\left(X, Y\right)$, captures the randomness in the data and plays a fundamental role in the compression of the collective data of the two parties (*cf.* [19]).

(iii) *Conditional entropy density of* X *given* $Y\Pi$: The conditional entropy density $h(X|Y) = -\log P_{X|Y}\left(X|Y\right)$ plays a fundamental role in the compression of X for an observer of Y [29, 19]. We shall use the conditional entropy density $h(X|Y\Pi)$ in our bounds.

(iv) *Sum conditional entropy density of* $(X\Pi, Y\Pi)$: The sum conditional entropy density is given by $h\left(X \triangle Y\right) = -\log P_{X|Y}\left(X|Y\right) P_{Y|X}\left(Y|X\right)$ has been shown recently to play a fundamental role in the communication complexity of the data exchange problem [40]. We shall use the sum conditional entropy density $h\left(X\Pi \triangle Y\Pi\right)$.

(v) Information density of X and Y is given by $i(X \wedge Y) \overset{\text{def}}{=} h(X) - h(X|Y)$.

Let $[\lambda_{\min}^{(1)}, \lambda_{\max}^{(1)}]$, $[\lambda_{\min}^{(2)}, \lambda_{\max}^{(2)}]$, and $[\lambda_{\min}^{(3)}, \lambda_{\max}^{(3)}]$ denote the "essential" spectrums of information densities $\zeta_1 = h(X, Y)$, $\zeta_2 = h(X|Y\Pi)$, and $\zeta_3 = h(X\Pi \triangle Y\Pi)$, respectively. Concretely, let the tail events $\mathcal{E}_i = \{\zeta_i \notin [\lambda_{\min}^{(i)}, \lambda_{\max}^{(i)}]\}$, $i = 1, 2, 3$, satisfy

$$\Pr\left(\mathcal{E}_1\right) + \Pr\left(\mathcal{E}_2\right) + \Pr\left(\mathcal{E}_3\right) \leq \varepsilon_{\text{tail}}, \quad (3)$$

where $\varepsilon_{\tt tail}$ can be chosen to be appropriately small. Further, let $\Lambda_i = \lambda_{\max}^{(i)} - \lambda_{\min}^{(i)}$, $i = 1, 2, 3$, denote the corresponding effective spectrum lengths. The parameters ε' and λ' in Theorem 1 are given by

$$\varepsilon' = \varepsilon_{\tt tail} + 2\eta \qquad (4)$$

and

$$\lambda' = 2 \log \Lambda_1 \Lambda_3 + \log \Lambda_2 - \log(1 - 3\eta) + 9 \log 1/\eta + 3, \quad (5)$$

where $0 < \eta < 1/3$ is arbitrary. If $\Lambda_i = 0$, $i = 1, 2, 3$, we can replace it with 1 in the bound above. Thus, our spectrum slicing approach allows us to reduce the dependence of λ' on spectrum lengths Λ_i's from linear to logarithmic.

3.2 Upper bound

We prove the following upper bound.

THEOREM 2. *For every $0 \le \varepsilon < 1$ and every protocol π,*

$$D_\varepsilon(\pi) \le \inf \left\{ \lambda : \Pr\left(\mathrm{ic}(\Pi; X, Y) > \lambda\right) \le \varepsilon - \varepsilon' \right\} + \lambda',$$

where the fudge parameters ε' and λ' depend on the maximum number of rounds of interaction in π and on appropriately chosen information spectrums.

Remark 4. In contrast to the lower bound given in the previous section, the upper bound above relies on the interactive nature of π. Furthermore, the fudge parameters ε' and λ' depend on the number of rounds, and the upper bound may not be useful when the number of rounds is not negligible compared to ε-tail of the information complexity density. However, we will see that the above upper bound is tight for the amortized regime, even up to the second-order asymptotic term.

The simulation protocol. Our simulation protocol simulates the given protocol π round-by-round, starting from Π_1 to Π_r. Simulation of each round consists of two subroutines: Interactive Slepian-Wolf compression and message reduction by public randomness.

The first subroutine uses an interactive version of the classical Slepian-Wolf compression [38] (see [29] for a single-shot version) for sending X to an observer of Y. The standard (noninteractive) Slepian-Wolf coding entails hashing X to l values and sending the hash values to the observer of Y. The number of hash values l is chosen to take into account the worst-case performance of the protocol. However, we are not interested in the worst-case performance of each round, but of the overall multiround protocol. As such, we seek to compress X using the least possible instantaneous rate. To that end, we increase the number of hash values gradually, Δ at a time, until the receiver decodes X and sends back an ACK. We apply this subroutine to each round i, say i odd, with Π_i in the role of X and $(Y, \Pi_1 ...., \Pi_{i-1})$ in the role of Y. Similar interactive Slepian-Wolf compression schemes have been considered earlier in different contexts (*cf.* [15, 32, 43, 22, 40]).

The second subroutine reduces the number of bits communicated in the first by realizing a portion of the required communication by the shared public randomness U. Specifically, instead of transmitting hash values of Π_i, we transmit hash values of a random variable $\hat{\Pi}_i$ generated in such a manner that some of its corresponding hash bits can be extracted from U and the overall joint distributions do not change by much. Since U is independent of (X, Y), the number k of

hash bits that can be realized using public randomness is the maximum number of random hash bits of Π_i that can be made almost independent of (X, Y), a good bound for which is given by the leftover hash lemma. The overall simulation protocol for Π_i now communicates $l - k$ instead of l bits. A similar technique for message reduction appears in a different context in [35, 30, 45].

The overall performance of the protocol above is still suboptimal because the saving of k bits is limited by the worst-case performance. To remedy this shortcoming, we once again take recourse to spectrum slicing to ensure that our saving k is close to the best possible for each realization (Π, X, Y).

Note that our protocol above is closely related to that proposed in [8]. However, the information theoretic form here makes it amenable to techniques such as spectrum slicing, which leads to tighter bounds than those established in [8].

The fudge parameters. The fudge parameters ε' and λ' in Theorem 2 depend on the spectrum of various conditional information densities. Our simulation protocol simulates π one round at a time. Simulation of each round consists of two subroutines: Interactive Slepian-Wolf compression and message reduction by public randomness. To optimize the performance of each subroutine, we slice the spectrum of the respective conditional information density involved. Specifically, for odd round t, we slice the spectrum of $h(\Pi_t | Y \Pi^{t-1}) = -\log \mathrm{P}_{\Pi_t | Y \Pi^{t-1}}\left(\Pi_t | Y, \Pi^{t-1}\right)$ for interactive Slepian-Wolf compression and $h(\Pi_t | X \Pi^{t-1}) = -\log \mathrm{P}_{\Pi_t | X \Pi^{t-1}}\left(\Pi_t | X, \Pi^{t-1}\right)$ for the substitution of message by public randomness; for even rounds, the role of X and Y is interchanged. Each round involves some residuals related to the two conditional information densities. Then, the fudge parameters ε' and λ' are accumulations of the residuals of each round.

Specifically, for a protocol π with communication complexity d, for each t, $1 \le t \le d$, we slice the essential spectrums $\left(\lambda_{\mathrm{P}_{\Pi_t | X \Pi^{t-1}}}^{\min}, \lambda_{\mathrm{P}_{\Pi_t | X \Pi^{t-1}}}^{\max} \right]$ and $\left(\lambda_{\mathrm{P}_{\Pi_t | Y \Pi^{t-1}}}^{\min}, \lambda_{\mathrm{P}_{\Pi_t | Y \Pi^{t-1}}}^{\max} \right]$ of $h(\Pi_t | X \Pi^{t-1})$ and $h(\Pi_t | Y \Pi^{t-1})$, respectively, into $N_{\mathrm{P}_{\Pi_t | X \Pi^{t-1}}}$ and $N_{\mathrm{P}_{\Pi_t | Y \Pi^{t-1}}}$ slices of lengths $\Delta_{\mathrm{P}_{\Pi_t | X \Pi^{t-1}}}$ and $\Delta_{\mathrm{P}_{\Pi_t | Y \Pi^{t-1}}}$. Let

$$\varepsilon_t \overset{\text{def}}{=} \Pr\left(h(\Pi_t | X \Pi^{t-1}) \notin \left(\lambda_{\mathrm{P}_{\Pi_t | X \Pi^{t-1}}}^{\min}, \lambda_{\mathrm{P}_{\Pi_t | X \Pi^{t-1}}}^{\max} \right] \right)$$
$$+ \Pr\left(h(\Pi_t | Y \Pi^{t-1}) \notin \left(\lambda_{\mathrm{P}_{\Pi_t | Y \Pi^{t-1}}}^{\min}, \lambda_{\mathrm{P}_{\Pi_t | Y \Pi^{t-1}}}^{\max} \right] \right),$$

and

$$\delta_t = \begin{cases} N_{\mathrm{P}_{\Pi_t | Y \Pi^{t-1}}} + 3 \log N_{\mathrm{P}_{\Pi_t | X \Pi^{t-1}}} + \Delta_{\mathrm{P}_{\Pi_t | Y \Pi^{t-1}}} \\ \qquad + \Delta_{\mathrm{P}_{\Pi_t | X \Pi^{t-1}}} + 3\gamma, \quad \text{odd } t, \\ N_{\mathrm{P}_{\Pi_t | X \Pi^{t-1}}} + 3 \log N_{\mathrm{P}_{\Pi_t | Y \Pi^{t-1}}} + \Delta_{\mathrm{P}_{\Pi_t | X \Pi^{t-1}}} \\ \qquad + \Delta_{\mathrm{P}_{\Pi_t | Y \Pi^{t-1}}} + 3\gamma, \quad \text{even } t. \end{cases}$$
$$(6)$$

Then the fudge parameters ε' and λ' are given by

$$\varepsilon' = \sum_{t=1}^d \left[4\varepsilon_t + 3 \left(N_{\mathrm{P}_{\Pi_t | Y \Pi^{t-1}}} + N_{\mathrm{P}_{\Pi_t | X \Pi^{t-1}}} + 2 \right) 2^{-\gamma} \right.$$
$$\left. + \frac{3}{N_{\mathrm{P}_{\Pi_t | X \Pi^{t-1}}}} + \frac{3}{N_{\mathrm{P}_{\Pi_t | Y \Pi^{t-1}}}} \right],$$

$$\lambda' = \sum_{t=1}^d \delta_t,$$

where δ_t is given by (6). Note that here

$$\Delta_{P_{\Pi_t|X\Pi^{t-1}}} N_{P_{\Pi_t|X\Pi^{t-1}}} = \lambda_{P_{\Pi_t|X\Pi^{t-1}}}^{\max} - \lambda_{P_{\Pi_t|X\Pi^{t-1}}}^{\min},$$

and

$$\Delta_{P_{\Pi_t|Y\Pi^{t-1}}} N_{P_{\Pi_t|Y\Pi^{t-1}}} = \lambda_{P_{\Pi_t|Y\Pi^{t-1}}}^{\max} - \lambda_{P_{\Pi_t|Y\Pi^{t-1}}}^{\min}.$$

Thus, the optimal choice of fudge parameters ε' and δ' is roughly the sum of square roots of the lengths of essential spectrums of $h(\Pi_t|X\Pi^{t-1})$ and $h(\Pi_t|Y\Pi^{t-1})$, summed over $t = 1, ..., d$.

3.3 Amortized regime: second-order asymptotics

It was shown in [8] that information complexity of a protocol equals the amortized communication rate for simulating the protocol, i.e.,

$$\lim_{\varepsilon \to 0} \lim_{n \to \infty} \frac{1}{n} D_\varepsilon(\pi^n | P_{XY}^n) = \text{IC}(\pi),$$

where P_{XY}^n denotes the n-fold product of the distribution P_{XY}, namely the distribution of random variables $(X_i, Y_i)_{i=1}^n$ drawn IID from P_{XY}, and π^n corresponds to running the same protocol π on every coordinate (X_i, Y_i). Thus, $\text{IC}(\pi)$ is the first-order term (coefficient of n) in the communication complexity of simulating the n-fold product of the protocol. However, the analysis in [8] sheds no light on finer asymptotics such as the second-order term or the dependence of $D_\varepsilon(\pi^n | P_{XY}^n)$ on[9] ε. On the one hand, it even remains unclear from [8] if a positive ε reduces the amortized communication rate or not. On the other hand, the amortized communication rate yields only a loose bound for $D_\varepsilon(\pi^n | P_{XY}^n)$ for a finite, fixed n. A better estimate of $D_\varepsilon(\pi^n | P_{XY}^n)$ at a finite n and for a fixed ε can be obtained by identifying the second-order asymptotic term. Such second-order asymptotics were first considered in [39] and have received a lot of attention in information theory in recent years following [21, 33].

Our lower bound in Theorem 1 and upper bound in Theorem 2 show that the leading term in $D_\varepsilon(\pi^n | P_{XY}^n)$ is roughly the ε-tail λ_ε of the random variable

$$\text{ic}(\Pi^n; X^n, Y^n) = \sum_{i=1}^n \text{ic}(\Pi_i; X_i, Y_i),$$

a sum of n IID random variables. By the central limit theorem the first-order asymptotic term in λ_ε equals

$$n\mathbb{E}[\text{ic}(\Pi; X, Y)] = n\text{IC}(\pi),$$

recovering the result of [8]. Furthermore, the second-order asymptotic term depends on the variance $\text{V}(\pi)$ of $\text{ic}(\Pi; X, Y)$, i.e., on

$$\text{V}(\pi) \overset{\text{def}}{=} \text{Var}[\text{ic}(\Pi; X, Y)].$$

We have the following result.

THEOREM 3. *For every $0 < \varepsilon < 1$ and every protocol π with $\text{V}(\pi) > 0$,*

$$D_\varepsilon(\pi^n | P_{XY}^n) = n\text{IC}(\pi) + \sqrt{n\text{V}(\pi)}Q^{-1}(\varepsilon) + o(\sqrt{n}),$$

---

[9] The lower bound in [8] gives only the *weak converse* which holds only when $\varepsilon = \varepsilon_n \to 0$ as $n \to \infty$.

where $Q(x)$ is equal to the probability that a standard normal random variable exceeds x.

As a corollary, we obtain the so-called *strong converse*.

COROLLARY 4. *For every $0 < \varepsilon < 1$, the amortized communication rate*

$$\lim_{n \to \infty} \frac{1}{n} D_\varepsilon(\pi^n | P_{XY}^n) = \text{IC}(\pi).$$

Corollary 4 implies that the amortized communication complexity of simulating protocol π cannot be smaller than its information complexity even if we allow a positive error. Thus, if the length of the simulation protocol π_{sim} is "much smaller" than $n\text{IC}(\pi)$, the corresponding simulation error $\varepsilon = \varepsilon_n$ must approach 1. But how fast does this ε_n converge to 1? Our next result shows that this convergence is exponentially rapid in n.

THEOREM 5. *Given a protocol π and an arbitrary $\delta > 0$, for any simulation protocol π_{sim} with*

$$\|\pi_{\text{sim}}\| \le n[\text{IC}(\pi) - \delta],$$

there exists a constant $E = E(\delta) > 0$ such that for every n sufficiently large, it holds that

$$d_{\text{var}}\left(P_{\Pi^n \Pi^n X^n Y^n}, P_{\Pi_{\mathcal{X}}^n \Pi_{\mathcal{Y}}^n X^n Y^n}\right) \ge 1 - 2^{-En}.$$

A similar converse was first shown for the channel coding problem in information theory by Arimoto [3] (see [14, 34] for further refinements of this result), and has been studied for other classical information theory problems as well. To the best of our knowledge, Corollary 5 is the first instance of an Arimoto converse for a problem involving interactive communication.

In the TCS literature, such converse results have been termed *direct product theorems* and have been considered in the context of the (distributional) communication complexity problem (for computing a given function) [9, 10, 23]. Our lower bound in Theorem 1, too, yields a direct product theorem for the communication complexity problem. We state this simple result in the passing, skipping the details since they closely mimic Theorem 5. Specifically, given a function f on $\mathcal{X} \times \mathcal{Y}$, by slight abuse of notations and terminologies, let $D_\varepsilon(f) = D_\varepsilon(f | P_{XY})$ be the communication complexity of computing f. As noted in Remark 3, Theorem 1 is valid for an arbitrary random variables Π, and not just an interactive protocol. Then, by following the proof of Theorem 5 with $F = f(X, Y)$ replacing Π in the application of Theorem 1, we get the following direct product theorem.

THEOREM 6. *Given a function f and an arbitrary $\delta > 0$, for any function computation protocol π computing estimates $F_{\mathcal{X},n}$ and $F_{\mathcal{Y},n}$ of f^n at the Party 1 and Party 2, respectively, and with length*

$$\|\pi\| \le n[H(F|X) + H(F|Y) - \delta], \tag{7}$$

there exists a constant $E = E(\delta) > 0$ such that for every n sufficiently large, it holds that

$$\Pr(F_{\mathcal{X},n} = F_{\mathcal{Y},n} = F^n) \le 2^{-En},$$

where $F^n = (F_1, ..., F_n)$ and $F_i = f(X_i, Y_i)$, $1 \le i \le n$.

Recall that [8, 26] showed that the first order asymptotic term in the amortized communication complexity for function computation was shown to equal the information complexity $\text{IC}(f)$ of the function, namely the infimum over $\text{IC}(\pi)$

387

for all interactive protocols π that recover f with 0 error. Ideally, we would like to show an Arimoto converse for this problem, *i.e.*, replace the threshold on the right-side of (7) with $n[\mathrm{IC}(f) - \delta]$. The direct product result above is weaker than such an Arimoto converse, and proving the Arimoto converse for the function computation problem is work in progress. Nevertheless, the simple result above is not comparable with the known direct product theorems in [9, 10] and can be stronger in some regimes[10].

3.4 General formula for amortized communication complexity

Consider arbitrary distributions $P_{X_n Y_n}$ on $\mathcal{X}^n \times \mathcal{Y}^n$ and arbitrary protocols π_n with inputs X_n and Y_n taking values in $\mathcal{X}^n$ and $\mathcal{Y}^n$, for each $n \in \mathbb{N}$. For vanishing simulation error ε_n, how does $D_{\varepsilon_n}(\pi_n | P_{X_n Y_n})$ evolve as a function of n?

The previous section, and much of the theoretical computer science literature, has focused on the case when $P_{X_n Y_n} = P_{XY}^n$ and the same protocol π is executed on each coordinate. In this section, we identify the first-order asymptotic term in $D_{\varepsilon_n}(\pi_n | P_{X_n Y_n})$ for a general sequence of distributions[11] $\{P_{X_n Y_n}\}_{n=1}^\infty$ and a general sequence of protocols $\boldsymbol{\pi} = \{\pi_n\}_{n=1}^\infty$. Formally, the amortized (distributional) communication complexity of $\boldsymbol{\pi}$ for $\{P_{X_n Y_n}\}_{n=1}^\infty$ is given by[12]

$$D(\boldsymbol{\pi}) \overset{\text{def}}{=} \lim_{\varepsilon \to 0} \limsup_{n \to \infty} \frac{1}{n} D_\varepsilon(\pi_n | P_{X_n Y_n}).$$

Our goal is to characterize $D(\boldsymbol{\pi})$ for any given sequences P_n and $\boldsymbol{\pi}$. We seek a general formula for $D(\boldsymbol{\pi})$ under minimal assumptions. Since we do not make any assumptions on the underlying distribution, we cannot use any measure concentration results. Instead, we take recourse to probability limits of information spectrums introduced by Han and Verdú in [20] for handling this situation (*cf.* [19]). Specifically, for a sequence of protocols $\boldsymbol{\pi} = \{\pi_n\}_{n=1}^\infty$ and a sequence of observations $(\mathbf{X}, \mathbf{Y}) = \{(X_n, Y_n)\}_{n=1}^\infty$, the *sup information complexity* is defined as

$$\overline{\mathrm{IC}}(\boldsymbol{\pi}) \overset{\text{def}}{=} \inf \left\{ \alpha \mid \lim_{n \to \infty} \Pr \left(\frac{1}{n} \mathrm{ic}(\Pi_n; X_n, Y_n) > \alpha \right) = 0 \right\},$$

where, with a slight abuse of notation, Π_n is the transcript of protocol π_n for observations (X_n, Y_n). The result below shows that it is $n\overline{\mathrm{IC}}(\boldsymbol{\pi})$, and not $\mathrm{IC}(\pi_n)$, that determines the communication complexity in general.

THEOREM 7. *For every sequence of protocols $\boldsymbol{\pi} = \{\pi_n\}_{n=1}^\infty$,*

$$D(\boldsymbol{\pi}) = \overline{\mathrm{IC}}(\boldsymbol{\pi}).$$

The proof uses Theorem 1 and Theorem 2 with carefully chosen spectrum-slice sizes.

For the case when $\pi_n = \pi^n$ and $P_{X_n Y_n} = P_{XY}^n$, it follows from the law of large numbers that $\overline{\mathrm{IC}}(\boldsymbol{\pi}) = \mathrm{IC}(\pi)$ and we recover the result of [8]. However, the utility of the general formula goes far beyond this simple amortized regime. Example 1 provides one such instance. In this case, $\overline{\mathrm{IC}}(\boldsymbol{\pi})$ can be easily shown to equal $\mathrm{IC}(\pi_{\mathrm{h}})$ for any bias of the coin Π_0.

4. ASYMPTOTIC OPTIMALITY

We now present the proofs of Theorem 3, Theorem 7 and Therem 5 using single-shot bounds given in Theorem 1 and Theorem 2. Both the proofs rely on carefully choosing the slice-sizes in the lower and upper bounds.

4.1 Proof of Theorem 3

We start with the upper bound. Note that, for IID random variables (Π^n, X^n, Y^n), the spectrums of $h(\Pi_t^n | Z^n, (\Pi^{t-1})^n)$ for [13] $Z = X$ or Y have width $O(\sqrt{n})$. Therefore, the parameters Δs and Ns that appear in the fudge parameters can be chosen as $O(n^{1/4})$. Specifically, by standard measure concentration bounds (for bounded random variables), for every $\nu > 0$, there exists a constant[14] $c > 0$ such that with

$$\lambda^{\min}_{P_{\Pi_t^n | Z^n (\Pi^{t-1})^n}} = nH(\Pi_t | Z, \Pi^{t-1}) - c\sqrt{n},$$
$$\lambda^{\max}_{P_{\Pi_t^n | Z^n (\Pi^{t-1})^n}} = nH(\Pi_t | Z, \Pi^{t-1}) + c\sqrt{n},$$

the following bound holds:

$$\Pr \left((\Pi_t^n, (Z^n, (\Pi^{t-1})^n)) \in \mathcal{T}^{(0)}_{P_{\Pi_t^n | Z^n (\Pi^{t-1})^n}} \right) \le \nu. \quad (8)$$

Let T denote the third central moment of the random variable $\mathrm{ic}(\Pi; X, Y)$. For

$$\lambda_n = n\mathrm{IC}(\pi) + \sqrt{n\mathrm{V}(\pi)} Q^{-1} \left(\varepsilon - 9d\nu - \frac{T^3}{2\mathrm{V}(\pi)^{3/2}\sqrt{n}} \right),$$

choosing $\Delta_{P_{\Pi_t^n | Z^n (\Pi^{t-1})^n}} = N_{P_{\Pi_t^n | Z^n (\Pi^{t-1})^n}} = \gamma = \sqrt{2c} n^{1/4}$, and $l_{\max} = \lambda_n + \sum_{t=1}^d \delta_t$ in Theorem 2, we get a protocol of length $l_{\max}$ and satisfying

$$d_{\mathrm{var}} \left(P_{\Pi_{\mathcal{X}}^n \Pi_{\mathcal{Y}}^n X^n Y^n}, P_{\Pi^n \Pi^n X^n Y^n} \right)$$
$$\le \Pr \left(\sum_{i=1}^n \mathrm{ic}(\Pi_i; X_i, Y_i) > \lambda_n \right) + 9d\nu$$

for sufficiently large n. By its definition given in (6), $\delta_t = O(n^{1/4})$ for the choice of parameters above. Thus, the Berry-Esséen theorem (*cf.* [16]) and the observation above gives a protocol of length $l_{\max}$ attaining ε-simulation. Therefore, using the Taylor approximation of $Q(\cdot)$ yields the achievability of the claimed protocol length.

For the lower bound, we fix sufficiently small constant $\delta > 0$, and we set

$$\lambda^{(1)}_{\min} = n(H(X,Y) - \delta), \quad \lambda^{(1)}_{\max} = n(H(X,Y) + \delta),$$
$$\lambda^{(2)}_{\min} = n(H(X|Y,\Pi) - \delta), \quad \lambda^{(2)}_{\max} = n(H(X|Y,\Pi) + \delta),$$
$$\lambda^{(3)}_{\min} = n(H(X\Pi \triangle Y\Pi) - \delta), \quad \lambda^{(3)}_{\max} = n(H(X\Pi \triangle Y\Pi) + \delta).$$

Then, by standard measure concentration bounds imply that the tail probability $\varepsilon_{\mathrm{tail}}$ in (3) is bounded above by $\frac{c}{n}$ for some constant $c > 0$. We also set $\eta = \frac{1}{n}$. For these choices of parameters, we note that the fudge parameter is $\lambda' = O(\log n)$. Thus, by setting

$$\lambda = \lambda_n$$

---

[10]The result in [9, 10] shows a direct product theorem when we communicate less than $n\mathrm{IC}(f)/\mathtt{poly}(\log n)$.

[11]We do not require $P_{X_n Y_n}$ to be even consistent.

[12]Although $D(\boldsymbol{\pi})$ also depends on $\{P_{X_n Y_n}\}_{n=1}^\infty$, we omit the dependency in our notation.

[13]We introduce Z as a placeholder for X or Y for brevity.

[14]Although the constant depends on random variables appearing in each round, since the number of rounds is bounded, we take the maximum constant so that (8) holds for every t.

$$= n\mathtt{IC}(\pi) + \sqrt{n\mathtt{V}(\pi)}Q^{-1}\left(\varepsilon + \frac{c+2}{n} + \frac{T^3}{2\mathtt{V}(\pi)^{3/2}\sqrt{n}}\right)$$

$$= n\mathtt{IC}(\pi) + \sqrt{n\mathtt{V}(\pi)}Q^{-1}(\varepsilon) + O(\log n),$$

where the final equality is by the Tailor approximation, an application of the Berry-Esséen theorem to the bound in (2) gives the desired lower bound on the protocol length. $\square$

4.2 Proof of Theorem 5

Theorem 1 implies that if a protocol $\pi_{\mathtt{sim}}$ is such that

$$\log\|\pi_{\mathtt{sim}}\| < \lambda - \lambda', \tag{9}$$

then its simulation error must be larger than

$$\Pr\left(\mathtt{ic}\left(\Pi^n; X^n, Y^n\right) > \lambda\right) - \varepsilon'. \tag{10}$$

To compute fudge parameters, we set

$$\lambda_{\min}^{(1)} = n(H(X,Y) - \delta), \quad \lambda_{\max}^{(1)} = n(H(X,Y) + \delta),$$
$$\lambda_{\min}^{(2)} = n(H(X|Y,\Pi) - \delta), \quad \lambda_{\max}^{(2)} = n(H(X|Y,\Pi) + \delta),$$
$$\lambda_{\min}^{(3)} = n(H(X\Pi\triangle Y\Pi) - \delta), \quad \lambda_{\max}^{(3)} = n(H(X\Pi\triangle Y\Pi) + \delta).$$

By the Chernoff bound, there exists $E_1 > 0$ such that

$$\varepsilon_{\mathtt{tail}} \le 2^{-E_1 n}.$$

Furthermore, $\Lambda_i = O(n)$ for $i = 1, 2, 3$. We set $\eta = 2^{-\frac{\delta}{27}n}$. It follows that

$$\varepsilon' \le 2^{-E_1 n} + 2^{-\frac{\delta}{27}n} \tag{11}$$

and

$$\lambda' \le \frac{\delta}{3}n + O(\log n). \tag{12}$$

Finally, upon setting

$$\lambda = n\mathtt{IC}(\pi) - \frac{\delta}{3} \tag{13}$$

and applying the Chernoff bound once more, we obtain a constant $E_2 > 0$ such that

$$\Pr\left(\mathtt{ic}\left(\Pi^n; X^n, Y^n\right) > \lambda\right) \ge 1 - 2^{-E_2 n}. \tag{14}$$

The result follows upon combining (9)-(14). $\square$

4.3 Proof of Theorem 7

For a sequence of protocols $\boldsymbol{\pi} = \{\pi_n\}_{n=1}^{\infty}$ and a sequence of observations $(\mathbf{X}, \mathbf{Y}) = \{(X_n, Y_n)\}_{n=1}^{\infty}$, let

$$\underline{H}(\boldsymbol{\Pi}_t | \mathbf{Z}, \boldsymbol{\Pi}^{t-1}) \tag{15}$$

$$= \sup\left\{\alpha : \lim_{n\to\infty} \Pr\left(h(\Pi_{n,t}|Z_n \Pi_n^{t-1}) < \alpha\right) = 0\right\}, \tag{16}$$

$$\overline{H}(\boldsymbol{\Pi}_t | \mathbf{Z}, \boldsymbol{\Pi}^{t-1}) \tag{17}$$

$$= \inf\left\{\alpha : \lim_{n\to\infty} \Pr\left(h(\Pi_{n,t}|Z_n \Pi_n^{t-1}) > \alpha\right) = 0\right\}, \tag{18}$$

where $\mathbf{Z} = \mathbf{X}$ or $\mathbf{Y}$, $\boldsymbol{\Pi}_t = \{\Pi_{n,t}\}_{n=1}^{\infty}$ and $\boldsymbol{\Pi}_n^{t-1} = \{\Pi_n^{t-1}\}_{n=1}^{\infty}$ are sequences of transcripts of tth round and up to tth rounds, respectively. For achievability part, we fix arbitrary small $\delta > 0$, and set

$$\lambda_{\mathrm{P}_{\Pi_{n,t}|Z_n \Pi_n^{t-1}}}^{\min} = n\left(\underline{H}(\boldsymbol{\Pi}_t | \mathbf{Z}, \boldsymbol{\Pi}^{t-1}) - \delta\right),$$

$$\lambda_{\mathrm{P}_{\Pi_{n,t}|Z_n \Pi_n^{t-1}}}^{\max} = n\left(\overline{H}(\boldsymbol{\Pi}_t | \mathbf{Z}, \boldsymbol{\Pi}^{t-1}) + \delta\right),$$

$$\Delta_{\mathrm{P}_{\Pi_{n,t}|Z_n \Pi_n^{t-1}}} = N_{\mathrm{P}_{\Pi_{n,t}|Z_n \Pi_n^{t-1}}} = \gamma = \sqrt{2\delta n}. \text{ We set}$$

$$l_{\max} = n\left(\overline{\mathtt{IC}}(\boldsymbol{\pi}) + \delta\right) + \sum_{t=1}^{d} \delta_t$$

$$= n\left(\overline{\mathtt{IC}}(\boldsymbol{\pi}) + \delta\right) + O(\sqrt{n}),$$

where δ_t is given by (6). Then, by Theorem 2, by the definition of $\overline{\mathtt{IC}}(\boldsymbol{\pi})$ and by (16) and (18), there exists a simulation protocol of length $l_{\max}$ with vanishing simulation error. Since $\delta > 0$ is arbitrary, we have the desired achievability bound.

For converse part, we fix arbitrary $\delta > 0$, and set

$$\lambda_{\min}^{(1)} = n(\underline{H}(\mathbf{X}, \mathbf{Y}) - \delta),$$
$$\lambda_{\max}^{(1)} = n(\overline{H}(\mathbf{X}, \mathbf{Y}) + \delta),$$
$$\lambda_{\min}^{(2)} = n(\underline{H}(\mathbf{X}|\mathbf{Y}, \boldsymbol{\Pi}) - \delta),$$
$$\lambda_{\max}^{(2)} = n(\overline{H}(\mathbf{X}|\mathbf{Y}, \boldsymbol{\Pi}) + \delta),$$
$$\lambda_{\min}^{(3)} = n(\underline{H}(\mathbf{X}\boldsymbol{\Pi}\triangle\mathbf{Y}\boldsymbol{\Pi}) - \delta),$$
$$\lambda_{\max}^{(3)} = n(\overline{H}(\mathbf{X}\boldsymbol{\Pi}\triangle\mathbf{Y}\boldsymbol{\Pi}) + \delta),$$

where

$$\underline{H}(\mathbf{X}, \mathbf{Y}) = \sup\left\{\alpha : \lim_{n\to\infty}\Pr\left(h(X_n Y_n) < \alpha\right) = 0\right\},$$
$$\overline{H}(\mathbf{X}, \mathbf{Y}) = \inf\left\{\alpha : \lim_{n\to\infty}\Pr\left(h(X_n Y_n) > \alpha\right) = 0\right\},$$
$$\underline{H}(\mathbf{X}|\mathbf{Y}, \boldsymbol{\Pi}) = \sup\left\{\alpha : \Pr\left(h(X_n|Y_n \Pi_n) < \alpha\right) = 0\right\},$$
$$\overline{H}(\mathbf{X}|\mathbf{Y}, \boldsymbol{\Pi}) = \inf\left\{\alpha : \Pr\left(h(X_n|Y_n \Pi_n) > \alpha\right) = 0\right\},$$
$$\underline{H}(\mathbf{X}\boldsymbol{\Pi}\triangle\mathbf{Y}\boldsymbol{\Pi}) = \sup\left\{\alpha : \Pr\left(-h(X_n\Pi_n\triangle Y_n\Pi_n) < \alpha\right) = 0\right\},$$
$$\overline{H}(\mathbf{X}\boldsymbol{\Pi}\triangle\mathbf{Y}\boldsymbol{\Pi}) = \inf\left\{\alpha : \Pr\left(-h(X_n\Pi_n\triangle Y_n\Pi_n) > \alpha\right) = 0\right\}.$$

Then, by the definitions, we find that the tail probability $\varepsilon_{\mathtt{tail}}$ in (3) converges to 0. We also set $\eta = (1/n)$. For these choices of parameters, we note that the fudge parameter is $\lambda' = O(\log n)$. Thus, by using the bound in (2) for

$$\lambda = \lambda_n = n\left(\overline{\mathtt{IC}}(\boldsymbol{\pi}) + \delta\right), \tag{19}$$

and by taking $\delta \to 0$, we have the desired converse bound. $\square$

5. CONCLUSION

In this work, we have proposed an approach to derive a lower bound on communication complexity of protocol simulation by relating the protocol simulation problem to the secret key agreement. A key step in our approach is identifying the amount of common randomness generated through protocol simulation. Our estimate for the amount of common randomness does not rely on the structure of the function to be computed. This is contrast to most of the existing lower bounds on communication complexity for function computation, such as the partition bound or the discrepancy bound, where the structure of the computed function plays an important role. In particular, a comparison of our approach with other existing approaches for specific functions is not available. An important future research agenda for us is to incorporate the structure of functions in our bound; the case of functions with a small range such as Boolean functions is of particular interest.

Appendix: An example of a mixture protocol

To illustrate the utility of our lower bound, we consider a protocol π which takes very few values most of the time, but with very small probability it can send many different transcripts. The proposed protocol can be ε-simulated using very few bits of communication on average. But in the worst-case it requires as many bits of communication for ε-simulation as needed for data exchange, for all $\varepsilon > 0$ small enough.

Specifically, let $\mathcal{X} = \mathcal{Y} = \{1, \ldots, 2^n\}$ and let π be a deterministic protocol such that the transcript $\tau(x, y)$ for (x, y) is given by

$$\tau(x, y) = \begin{cases} a & \text{if } x > \delta 2^n, y > \delta 2^n \\ b & \text{if } x > \delta 2^n, y \leq \delta 2^n \\ c & \text{if } x \leq \delta 2^n, y > \delta 2^n \\ (x, y) & \text{if } x \leq \delta 2^n, y \leq \delta 2^n \end{cases}$$

for some small $\delta > 0$, which will be specified later. Clearly, this protocol is interactive.

Let (X, Y) be the uniform random variables on $\mathcal{X} \times \mathcal{Y}$. Then,

$$\Pr\left(\Pi \notin \{a, b, c\}\right) = \delta^2.$$

Since

$$\mathsf{P}_{\Pi|X}(\tau(x, y)|x) = \begin{cases} 1 - \delta & \text{if } x > \delta 2^n, y > \delta 2^n \\ \delta & \text{if } x > \delta 2^n, y \leq \delta 2^n \\ 1 - \delta & \text{if } x \leq \delta 2^n, y > \delta 2^n \\ \frac{1}{2^n} & \text{if } x \leq \delta 2^n, y \leq \delta 2^n \end{cases}$$

and similarly for $\mathsf{P}_{\Pi|Y}(\tau(x, y)|y)$, we have

$$\mathtt{ic}(\tau(x, y); x, y)$$
$$= \begin{cases} 2\log(1/(1 - \delta)) & \text{if } x > \delta 2^n, y > \delta 2^n \\ \log(1/\delta) + \log(1/(1 - \delta)) & \text{if } x > \delta 2^n, y \leq \delta 2^n \\ \log(1/\delta) + \log(1/(1 - \delta)) & \text{if } x \leq \delta 2^n, y > \delta 2^n \\ 2n & \text{if } x \leq \delta 2^n, y \leq \delta 2^n \end{cases}.$$

Consider $\delta = \frac{1}{n}$, and $\varepsilon = \frac{1}{n^3}$. Note that for any $\lambda < 2n$,

$$\Pr\left(\mathtt{ic}(\Pi; X, Y) > \lambda\right) \geq \Pr\left(\Pi\{a, b, c\}\right) = \delta^2 = \frac{1}{n^2} > \varepsilon,$$

and

$$\Pr\left(\mathtt{ic}(\Pi; X, Y) > 2n\right) = 0.$$

Thus, the ε-tail λ_ε of information complexity density is given by

$$\lambda_\varepsilon = \sup\{\lambda : \Pr\left(\mathtt{ic}(\Pi; X, Y) > \lambda\right) > \varepsilon\} = 2n. \tag{20}$$

On the other hand, we have

$$\mathtt{IC}(\pi) = H(\Pi|X) + H(\Pi|Y)$$
$$\leq 2\delta[h_b(\delta) + \log n - \log(1/\delta)] + 2(1 - \delta)h_b(\delta)$$
$$\leq \tilde{\mathcal{O}}(\delta^2)$$

where $h_b(\cdot)$ is the binary entropy function.

Also, to evaluate the lower bound of Theorem 1, we bound the fudge parameters in that bound. To that end, we fix $\varepsilon_{\mathtt{tail}} = 0$ and bound the spectrum lengths $\Lambda_1, \Lambda_2, \Lambda_3$. Since (X, Y) is uniform, $h(X, Y) = 2n$ and so, $\Lambda_1 = 0$. Also, note that with probability 1 the conditional entropy density $h(X|\Pi, Y)$ is either 0 or $\log(\delta 2^n)$, which implies $\Lambda_2 = \mathcal{O}(n)$. A similar argument shows that $\Lambda_3 = \mathcal{O}(n)$. Therefore, the fudge parameter

$$\lambda' = \mathcal{O}(\log \Lambda_1 \Lambda_2 \Lambda_3) = \mathcal{O}(\log n),$$

which in view of (20) and Theorem 1 gives $D_\varepsilon(\pi) = \Omega(2n)$.

6. REFERENCES

[1] R. Ahlswede and I. Csiszár. Common randomness in information theory and cryptography–part i: Secret sharing. *IEEE Trans. Inf. Theory*, 39(4):1121–1132, July 1993.

[2] N. Alon, Y. Matias, and M. Szegedy. The space complexity of approximating the frequency moments. In *Proc. ACM Symposium on Theory of Computing (STOC)*, pages 20–29, 1996.

[3] S. Arimoto. On the converse to the coding theorem for discrete memoryless channels. *IEEE Trans. Inf. Theory*, 19(3):357–359, May 1973.

[4] B. Barak, M. Braverman, X. Chen, and A. Rao. How to compress interactive communication. In *Proc. ACM Symposium on Theory of Computing (STOC)*, pages 67–76, 2010.

[5] D. Beaver. Perfect privacy for two party protocols. *Technical Report TR-11-89, Harvard University*, 1989.

[6] C. H. Bennett, G. Brassard, C. Crépeau, and U. M. Maurer. Generalized privacy amplification. *IEEE Trans. Inf. Theory*, 41(6):1915–1923, November 1995.

[7] M. Braverman. Interactive information complexity. In *Proc. ACM Symposium on Theory of Computing Conference (STOC)*, pages 505–524, 2012.

[8] M. Braverman and A. Rao. Information equals amortized communication. In *FOCS*, pages 748–757, 2011.

[9] M. Braverman, A. Rao, O. Weinstein, and A. Yehudayoff. Direct products in communication complexity. In *FOCS*, pages 746–755, 2013.

[10] M. Braverman and O. Weinstein. An interactive information odometer with applications. *ECCC*, page Report No. 47, 2014.

[11] T. M. Cover and J. A. Thomas. *Elements of Information Theory*. Wiley-Interscience, 2006.

[12] I. Csiszár and J. Körner. *Information theory: Coding theorems for discrete memoryless channels. 2nd edition*. Cambridge University Press, 2011.

[13] I. Csiszár and P. Narayan. Secrecy capacities for multiterminal channel models. *IEEE Trans. Inf. Theory*, 54(6):2437–2452, June 2008.

[14] G. Dueck and J. Korner. Reliability function of a discrete memoryless channel at rates above capacity (corresp.). *Information Theory, IEEE Transactions on*, 25(1):82–85, Jan 1979.

[15] M. Feder and N. Shulman. Source broadcasting with unknown amount of receiver side information. In *ITW*, pages 127–130, Oct 2002.

[16] W. Feller. *An Introduction to Probability Theory and its Applications, Volume II. 2nd edition*. John Wiley & Sons Inc., UK, 1971.

[17] A. Ganor, G. Kol, and R. Raz. Exponential separation of information and communication. In *55th IEEE Annual Symposium on Foundations of Computer Science, FOCS 2014, Philadelphia, PA, USA, October 18-21, 2014*, pages 176–185, 2014.

[18] A. Ganor, G. Kol, and R. Raz. Exponential separation of information and communication for boolean functions. *Electronic Colloquium on Computational Complexity (ECCC)*, 21:113, 2014.

[19] T. S. Han. *Information-Spectrum Methods in Information Theory [English Translation]*. Series: Stochastic Modelling and Applied Probability, Vol. 50, Springer, 2003.

[20] T. S. Han and S. Verdú. Approximation theory of output statistics. *IEEE Trans. Inf. Theory*, 39(3):752–772, May 1993.

[21] M. Hayashi. Information spectrum approach to second-order coding rate in channel coding. *IEEE Trans. Inf. Theory*, 55(11):4947–4966, Novemeber 2009.

[22] M. Hayashi, H. Tyagi, and S. Watanabe. Secret key agreement: General capacity and second-order asymptotics. *arXiv:1411.0735*, 2014.

[23] R. Jain, A. Pereszlenyi, and P. Yao. A direct product theorem for the two-party bounded-round public-coin communication complexity. In *FOCS*, pages 167–176, 2012.

[24] M. Karchmer and A. Wigderson. Monotone circuits for connectivity require super-logarithmic depth. In *Proc. Symposium on Theory of Computing (STOC)*, pages 539–550, 1988.

[25] E. Kushilevitz. Privacy and communication complexity. *SIAM Journal on Math*, 5(2):273–284, 1992.

[26] N. Ma and P. Ishwar. Some results on distributed source coding for interactive function computation. *IEEE Trans. Inf. Theory*, 57(9):6180–6195, September 2011.

[27] M. Madiman and P. Tetali. Information inequalities for joint distributions, with interpretations and applications. *IEEE Trans. Inf. Theory*, 56(6):2699–2713, June 2010.

[28] U. M. Maurer. Secret key agreement by public discussion from common information. *IEEE Trans. Inf. Theory*, 39(3):733–742, May 1993.

[29] S. Miyake and F. Kanaya. Coding theorems on correlated general sources. *IIEICE Trans. Fundamental*, E78-A(9):1063–1070, September 1995.

[30] J. Muramatsu. Channel coding and lossy source coding using a generator of constrained random numbers. *IEEE Trans. Inf. Theory*, 60(5):2667–2686, May 2014.

[31] P. Narayan, H. Tyagi, and S. Watanabe. Common randomness for secure computing. *Proc. IEEE International Symposium on Information Theory*, pages 949–953, 2015.

[32] A. Orlitsky. Worst-case interactive communication i: Two messages are almost optimal. *IEEE Trans. Inf. Theory*, 36(5):1111–1126, 1990.

[33] Y. Polyanskiy, H. V. Poor, and S. Verdú. Channel coding rate in the finite blocklength regime. *IEEE Trans. Inf. Theory*, 56(5):2307–2359, May 2010.

[34] Y. Polyanskiy and S. Verdú. Arimoto channel coding converse and Rényi divergence. *Proc. Conference on Communication, Control, and Computing (Allerton)*, pages 1327–1333, 2010.

[35] J. M. Renes and R. Renner. Noisy channel coding via privacy amplification and information reconciliation. *IEEE Trans. Inf. Theory*, 57(11):7377–7385, November 2011.

[36] R. Renner and S. Wolf. Simple and tight bounds for information reconciliation and privacy amplification. In *Proc. ASIACRYPT*, pages 199–216, 2005.

[37] C. E. Shannon. A mathematical theory of communication. *Bell System Technical Journal*, 27:379–423, 1948.

[38] D. Slepian and J. Wolf. Noiseless coding of correlated information source. *IEEE Trans. Inf. Theory*, 19(4):471–480, July 1973.

[39] V. Strassen. Asymptotische abschätzungen in Shannon's informationstheorie. *Third Prague Conf. Inf. Theory*, pages 689–723, 1962.

[40] H. Tyagi, P. Viswanath, and S. Watanabe. Interactive communication for data exchange. *Proc. IEEE International Symposium on Information Theory*, pages 1806–1810, 2015.

[41] H. Tyagi and S. Watanabe. Converses for secret key agreement and secure computing. *IEEE Trans. Inf. Theory*, 61(9):4809–4827, September 1998.

[42] H. Tyagi and S. Watanabe. A bound for multiparty secret key agreement and implications for a problem of secure computing. In *EUROCRYPT*, pages 369–386, 2014.

[43] E.-H. Yang and D.-K. He. Interactive encoding and decoding for one way learning: Near lossless recovery with side information at the decoder. *Information Theory, IEEE Transactions on*, 56(4):1808–1824, April 2010.

[44] A. C. Yao. Some complexity questions related to distributive computing. *Proc. Annual Symposium on Theory of Computing*, pages 209–213, 1979.

[45] M. H. Yassaee, M. R. Aref, and A. Gohari. Achievability proof via output statistics of random binning. *IEEE Trans. Inf. Theory*, 60(11):6760–6786, November 2014.

[46] M. H. Yassaee, A. Gohari, and M. R. Aref. Channel simulation via interactive communications. In *Proc. IEEE Symposium on Information Theory (ISIT)*, pages 1049–1053, 2012.

Satisfiability on Mixed Instances

Ruiwen Chen
School of Informatics, University of Edinburgh
Edinburgh, United Kingdom
rchen2@inf.ed.ac.uk

Rahul Santhanam
School of Informatics, University of Edinburgh
Edinburgh, United Kingdom
rsanthan@inf.ed.ac.uk

ABSTRACT

The study of the worst-case complexity of the Boolean Satisfiability (SAT) problem has seen considerable progress in recent years, for various types of instances including CNFs [16, 15, 20, 21], Boolean formulas [18] and constant-depth circuits [6]. We systematically investigate the complexity of solving *mixed* instances, where different parts of the instance come from different types. Our investigation is motivated partly by practical contexts such as SMT (Satisfiability Modulo Theories) solving, and partly by theoretical issues such as the exact complexity of graph problems and the desire to find a unifying framework for known satisfiability algorithms.

We investigate two kinds of mixing: conjunctive mixing, where the mixed instance is formed by taking the conjunction of pure instances of different types, and compositional mixing, where the mixed instance is formed by the composition of different kinds of circuits. For conjunctive mixing, we show that non-trivial savings over brute force search can be obtained for a number of instance types in a generic way using the paradigm of *subcube partitioning*. We apply this generic result to show a meta-algorithmic result about graph optimisation problems: any optimisation problem that can be formalised in Monadic SNP can be solved exactly with exponential savings over brute-force search. This captures known results about problems such as Clique, Independent Set and Vertex Cover, in a uniform way. For certain kinds of conjunctive mixing, such as mixtures of k-CNFs and CNFs of bounded size, and of k-CNFs and Boolean formulas, we obtain improved savings over subcube partitioning by combining existing algorithmic ideas in a more fine-grained way.

We use the perspective of compositional mixing to show the first non-trivial algorithm for satisfiability of quantified Boolean formulas, where there is no depth restriction on the formula. We show that there is an algorithm which for any such formula with a constant number of quantifier blocks and of size n^c, where $c < 5/4$, solves satisfiability in time $2^{n-n^{\Omega(1)}}$.

Permission to make digital or hard copies of all or part of this work for personal or classroom use is granted without fee provided that copies are not made or distributed for profit or commercial advantage and that copies bear this notice and the full citation on the first page. Copyrights for components of this work owned by others than ACM must be honored. Abstracting with credit is permitted. To copy otherwise, or republish, to post on servers or to redistribute to lists, requires prior specific permission and/or a fee. Request permissions from Permissions@acm.org.

ITCS'16, January 14–16, 2016, Cambridge, MA, USA.
ⓒ 2016 ACM. ISBN 978-1-4503-4057-1/16/01 ...$15.00.
DOI: http://dx.doi.org/10.1145/2840728.2840768.

Categories and Subject Descriptors

F.2 [**Theory of Computation**]: ANALYSIS OF ALGORITHMS AND PROBLEM COMPLEXITY

Keywords

mixed instance; Boolean satisfiability algorithm; quantified Boolean formula

1. INTRODUCTION

Boolean Satisfiability (SAT) is the canonical NP-complete problem. Much effort has gone into designing and analyzing exact algorithms for SAT. Unless NP = P, we cannot hope to find a polynomial-time algorithm for SAT. So we adopt a milder goal: finding algorithms that beat the trivial brute-force search algorithm, which runs in time $2^n \operatorname{poly}(m)$ on Boolean circuits of size m with n variables. There has been significant progress on this over the past couple of decades, motivated by the theoretical significance of the problem and the practical success of SAT solvers [11] in domains such as verification and automated planning.

However, the performance of satisfiability algorithms depends critically on the *type* of the instances. For k-SAT, which is the satisfiability problem on k-CNFs, algorithms running in time $2^{n-n/k}$ are known [16, 20, 15]. Contrastingly, for satisfiability on general Boolean circuits, no upper bound better than the trivial one is known. In general, the more expressive the class of instances on which we are trying to solve SAT, the less we know about how to improve on brute-force search. A partial explanation for this phenomenon is provided by the recent work of Williams [22, 23], which connects progress on SAT algorithms to breakthroughs in circuit lower bounds.

Traditionally, satisfiability is studied for instances of a single fixed type, e.g., k-CNFs, CNFs with a prescribed number of clauses, Boolean formulas of a prescribed size, constant-depth Boolean circuits of a prescribed depth and size etc. We call such instances *pure* instances of the given type. In this paper, we systematically investigate the worst-case complexity of SAT, when the instance is *mixed*, i.e., has different parts of different types. A simple kind of mixing is *conjunctive mixing*, where the instance is formed by the conjunction of pure instances of different types. A more complex kind of mixing which we also study is *compositional mixing*, where the mixed instance is formed by composing circuits corresponding to different types.

Our study of satsifiability of mixed instances is motivated by various considerations. From a practical point of view, there has been a great deal of work recently on SMT (Satisfiability Modulo Theories) solvers [13], which extend SAT solvers by being able to deal with instances which contain not just propositional connectives, but various arithmetic operations, inequalities, etc. Studying the exact complexity of mixed instances is a way of connecting with this work from the theoretical side.

From a theoretical point of view, though we do have many interesting non-trivial satisfiability algorithms now, we do not clearly understand what unifies these algorithms, and what their limits are. Mixed instances provide a test for the flexibility of these algorithms, and analyzing mixed instances gives us a deeper understanding of existing algorithmic ideas.

More compellingly, mixed instances of satisfiability can be used to capture, in a fairly direct way, various NP-hard optimisation problems such as Clique, Vertex Cover, Dominating Set, etc. Upper and lower bounds on the exact complexity of satisfiability for mixed instances translate to these other problems. As a further example, the Max-SAT problem, where we ask for an assignment maximizing the number of satisfied clauses of a CNF formula, can be modelled easily by compositional mixing, where a CNF formula is composed with a threshold gate. The critical thing about these correspondences between different problems is that they preserve the number of variables of the instance, and thus results on exact complexity are easily transferrable from one problem to the other.

Mixed instances also come up fairly naturally in the analysis of important algorithms, such as the Sparsification Lemma of Impagliazzo, Paturi and Zane [7]. More specifically, the question of how best to solve a conjunctive mixture of CNFs with different widths and sizes is still unresolved, and might well play an important role in settling open questions such as deterministic counting of satisfying assignments for k-CNFs.

To state our results, we need some notation. Given classes $\mathcal{C}_1$ and $\mathcal{C}_2$ of instances, we let $(\mathcal{C}_1 \wedge \mathcal{C}_2)$-SAT denote the satisfiability problem for conjunctive mixing of $\mathcal{C}_1$ and $\mathcal{C}_2$. Also, given a function $f : \mathbb{N} \to \mathbb{N}$ and a class $\mathcal{C}$ of instances, we say $\mathcal{C}$-SAT has savings f if it can be solved in time $2^{n-f(n)}$ poly(m) time, where n is the number of variables of the instance, and m its size. We say the savings f is non-trivial if $f = \omega(\log(n))$.

If $\mathcal{C}_1$-SAT has savings f_1 and $\mathcal{C}_2$-SAT has savings f_2, the best savings we can expect for $(\mathcal{C}_1 \wedge \mathcal{C}_2)$-SAT is $\min\{f_1, f_2\}$, without improving on the known algorithms for $\mathcal{C}_1$-SAT or $\mathcal{C}_2$-SAT. An initial question is whether $(\mathcal{C}_1 \wedge \mathcal{C}_2)$-SAT can be shown to have non-trivial savings, given bounds on the savings for $\mathcal{C}_1$-SAT and $\mathcal{C}_2$-SAT.

We give a positive answer to this question for a large number of types of interest, including k-CNFs, Boolean formulas and constant-depth circuits. We critically use the fact that most known algorithms for these problems can be captured by a paradigm called *subcube partitioning*. Algorithms based on subcube partitioning "compose" well with each other, and therefore work well on mixed instances.

As an application of this result, we show a *meta-algorithmic* result for exact complexity of certain NP-hard optimisation problems, which are "expressible" by Monadic SNP formulas. Such problems include Weighted Independent Set, Weighted Clique and Weighted Vertex Cover.

THEOREM 1.1. *Let r be a constant. Any Monadic SNP-expressible weighted optimisation problem on graphs or r-uniform hypergraphs has savings $\Omega(n)$.*

We then show how to get improved savings beyond the bound given by subcube paritioning for mixtures such as conjunctive mixtures of k-CNFS and CNFs with m clauses, for which we get an optimal result by exploiting more carefully the properties of the known algorithms.

In the final section, we move on to compositional mixing. We show how to interpret the satisfiability algorithm of Impagliazzo, Mathews, and Paturi [6] for constant-depth circuits as an algorithm for compositionally mixed instances. Then, we use the perspective of compositional mixing of constant-depth circuits and de Morgan formulas, and show the first non-trivial algorithm for satisfiability of quantified de Morgan formulas, where the formula has unbounded depth. Santhanam and Williams [19] recently showed non-trivial results for the case where the formula is a CNF, but nothing was known about the unbounded-depth case. Our algorithm and its analysis combine various ideas from recent work on satisfiability and lower bounds for Boolean formulas with the approach in [19].

THEOREM 1.2. *For quantified de Morgan formulas with n variables, q quantifier blocks and size at most $n^{5/4-\epsilon}$, where $\epsilon > 0$, there is a zero-error randomized satisfiability algorithm running in time $2^{n-n^{\Omega(\epsilon/(q+1))}}$.*

Our work is not the first to study satisfiability on mixed instances. The literature on satisfiability of random formulas has results [12] on threshold phenomena concerning instances where some of the clauses are 2-clauses and the others are 3-clauses. Patrascu and Williams [14] study the satisfiability problem on mixtures of 2-SAT formulas with two clauses of arbitrary length, and show that under the Strong Exponential Time Hypothesis, such mixed instances cannot be solved in time $O(m^{2-\epsilon})$ for any $\epsilon > 0$, where m is the size of the instance. Porschen and Speckenmeyer [17] study mixtures of Horn clauses and 2-clauses, and show various positive and negative results.

However, as far as we are aware, we are the first to study satisfiability on mixed instances in a systematic way, for various types of instances where polynomial-time algorithms are not known, and indeed do not exist unless NP = P. We believe that our perspective might be useful in unifying results on exact algorithms for various NP-hard problems, as well as in gaining a deeper understanding of known satisfiability algorithms. In particular, the notion of compositional mixing is novel, to the best of our knowledge.

2. PRELIMINARIES

2.1 Circuit Complexity and Satisfiability

Given a circuit class $\mathcal{C}$, $\mathcal{C}$-SAT denotes the satisfiability problem for circuits from $\mathcal{C}$, and $(\wedge \mathcal{C})$-SAT denotes the satisfiability problem for a conjunction of circuits from $\mathcal{C}$. Given circuit classes $\mathcal{C}_1$ and $\mathcal{C}_2$, $(\mathcal{C}_1 \wedge \mathcal{C}_2)$-SAT denotes the satisfiability problem for circuits C where C is the conjunction of C' and C'', for $C' \in \mathcal{C}_1$ and $C'' \in \mathcal{C}_2$. Given circuit classes $\mathcal{C}_1$ and $\mathcal{C}_2$, $(\mathcal{C}_1 \circ \mathcal{C}_2)$-SAT denotes the satisfiability problem for circuits from $\mathcal{C}_1$ each of whose inputs is the output of a circuit from $\mathcal{C}_2$.

There are some standard circuit classes we will use repeatedly. Given a positive integer k, kCNF is the class of CNFs of width k. Given a function $m : \mathbb{N} \to \mathbb{N}$, CNF$[m]$ is the class of CNFs which have n variables and at most $m(n)$ clauses for some n. CNF is the class of CNFs which have n variables, with no restriction on the number of clauses. Similarly, Formula$[m]$ is the class of Boolean formulas (with no depth restriction) which have n variables and at most $m(n)$ literals for some n, with Formula defined as the class of formulas with no restriction on the number of literals. Given a positive integer d and m as before, $\mathsf{AC}^0_d[m]$ is the class of unbounded fan-in Boolean circuits with AND, OR and NOT gates which have n variables, size at most $m(n)$ and depth at most d, for some n. AC^0_d is defined as the class of depth-d circuits with AND, OR and NOT gates, with no restriction on the size. THR is the class of threshold functions, i.e., functions of the form $\Sigma_i a_i x_i \geq b$, where x_i's are input variables, and a_i's and b are arbitrary integers. Given a finite field R, LIN_R is the class of systems of linear equations over R.

We review some known results about satisfiability algorithms. Several of these algorithms exploit a structural property of certain circuit classes, namely the existence of better-than-trivial subcube partitions. We first define this notion.

A *restriction* is a string over the alphabet $\{0, 1, *\}$. A *subcube partition* of size s over $\{0,1\}^n$ is a family of s restrictions in $\{0, 1, *\}^n$ such that for each string in $\{0,1\}^n$, there is precisely one restriction in the family which agrees with the string on all non-$*$ co-ordinates. A circuit C on n variables is said to admit a subcube partition of size s if there is a subcube partition of size s over $\{0,1\}^n$ such that for every restriction in the partition, C is a constant under that restriction. If C admits a subcube partition of size s, a *subcube partition labelling* for C is a list of pairs $(\rho_i, b_i), i = 1, \ldots, s$ such that $\{\rho_i\}_{i=1}^s$ form a subcube partition, and for each ρ_i, C restricted to ρ_i, denoted by $C|_{\rho_i}$, has value b_i.

Given a circuit class $\mathcal{C}$ and a function $f : \mathbb{N} \times \mathbb{N} \to \mathbb{N}$ such that $f(n, \cdot) \leq n$ for all $n \in \mathbb{N}$, $\mathcal{C}$-SAT is said to have *savings* f is there is an algorithm for $\mathcal{C}$-SAT running in time $2^{n-f(n,m)} \mathrm{poly}(m)$ time, where n is the number of variables of the instance from $\mathcal{C}$ and m its size. On occasion, when the parameter m does not appear in the analyzed savings, or is implicit, we model f as a function purely of the number variables. By default, we assume our algorithms to be zero-error randomized algorithms. $\mathcal{C}$-SAT is said to have a *subcube partitioning* algorithm with savings f if there is an algorithm, which for C from $\mathcal{C}$ of size m on n variables, outputs in time $2^{n-f(n,m)} \mathrm{poly}(m)$ a subcube partition labelling for C. Note that the existence of such an algorithm implies in particular that any circuit from $\mathcal{C}$ of size m on n variables admits a subcube partition of size $2^{n-\Omega(f(n,m))} \mathrm{poly}(m)$.

The following is a folklore result, which can be shown by analyzing a natural randomized branching algorithm using Hastad's Switching Lemma [5, 1].

THEOREM 2.1. *For any fixed k, kCNF-SAT has a zero-error randomized subcube partitioning algorithm with savings $\Omega(n/k)$.*

THEOREM 2.2 ([21, 6]). *For a fixed d, $\mathsf{AC}^0_d[m]$-SAT has a zero-error randomized subcube partitioning algorithm with savings $\Omega(n/\log(m/n)^{d-1})$. In particular, the algorithm for CNF$[m]$-SAT has savings $\Omega(n/\log(m/n))$.*

THEOREM 2.3 ([18]). *Formula$[m]$-SAT has a deterministic subcube partitioning algorithm with savings $\Omega(n^3/m^2)$. In particular, for $m = O(n)$, the algorithm has savings $\Omega(n)$.*

2.2 Logical Complexity

We first recall first-order logic on graphs. A graph is represented by the binary edge relation $E(x, y)$, whose arguments range over vertices of the graph. Assume an infinite supply of individual variables ranging over vertices of the graph, denoted by (possibly subscripted) lowercase letters $x, y, z, \ldots$. Formulas of first-order logic over graphs are constructed from atomic formulas $E(x, y)$ and $x = y$ using the propositional connectives $\wedge$ (conjunction), $\vee$ (disjunction) and $\neg$ (negation), as well as existential quantification $\exists$ and universal quantification $\forall$ over individual variables.

Now also assume an infinite supply of set variables ranging over subsets of vertices of the graph, denoted by (possibly subscripted) uppercase letters $X, Y, Z, \ldots$. Formulas of monadic second-order (MSO) logic over graphs are constructed from atomic formulas $E(x, y)$, $x = y$ and $X(x)$ (expressing that vertex x belongs to the set X) using the propositional connectives, universal and existential quantification over individual variables and existential quantification over the set variables. We assume wlog that MSO formulas are in the prenex normal form, with the quantifiers over set variables appearing first. Formulas of monadic second-order logic over graphs (MSNP) are MSO formulas whose first-order part contains only universal quantification over variables.

We will be interested in expressing weighted graph optimisation problems such as Independent Set, Vertex Cover and Dominating Set using these logical formalisms. A weighted graph $G = (V, E, w)$ is a graph (V, E) with a weight function $w : V \to \mathbb{R}^+$. The weight function naturally extends to subsets $S \subset V$ by $w(S) = \sum_{v \in S} w(v)$. Given a MSO formula $\phi = \exists X_1 X_2 \ldots X_k \psi(X_1, X_2 \ldots X_k)$, where ψ is first-order, the max-weighted (resp. min-weighted) optimisation problem $O^{\max}_\phi$ (resp. $O^{\min}_\phi$) corresponding to ϕ takes as input a weighted graph $G = (V, E, w)$ (where the weights are representable in $\mathrm{poly}(|V|)$ bits) and outputs the maximum (resp. minimum) of $\sum_{i=1}^k w(X_i)$ over $X_1 \ldots X_k \subset V$ satisfying $\psi(X_1, X_2 \ldots X_k)$ in G. A weighted graph optimisation problem O is said to be MSO-representable (resp. MSNP-representable) if there is a MSO formula (resp. a MSNP formula) ϕ such that O is either $O^{\max}_\phi$ or $O^{\min}_\phi$.

We are interested in solving MSO-representable and MSNP-representable optimisation problems better than exhaustive search. Note that given an MSO formula ϕ quantifying existentially over q subset variables, the optimisation problems $O^{\max}_\phi$ and $O^{\min}_\phi$ can be solved using exhaustive search in time $2^{qn} \mathrm{poly}(n)$, where n is the number of vertices of the input graph. Given a function $f : \mathbb{N} \to \mathbb{N}$ with $f(n) \leq n$ for all n and a formula ϕ as above, we say that $O^{\max}_\phi$ (resp. $O^{\min}_\phi$) has savings $f(n)$ if there is an algorithm for the problem running in time $2^{qn-f(n)} \mathrm{poly}(n)$.

A number of natural graph optimisation problems can be captured by the formalism above. It is easy to see that Maximum Weight Independent Set, Maximum Weight Clique, Minimum Weight Vertex Cover and Maximum Weight Dominating Set are all MSO-representable. The first three of these problems are also MSNP-representable. In each of these cases, the corresponding MSO formula existentially quantifies over a single subset of vertices.

The framework described above can be extended easily to optimisation problems on r-uniform hypergraphs, with the change that the edge relation E is r-ary rather than binary.

2.3 Random Restrictions

Let $\mathcal{R}_p$ be the random restriction where a subset U of pn variables is chosen uniformly at random, and each variable not in U is assigned 0 or 1 each with probability $1/2$. We give below the shrinkage of formulas under random restrictions; although the parameters here are slightly weaker than those obtained via greedy restrictions (as used in Theorem 2.3 [18] and also in [10]), we can use the results to get satisfiability algorithms for mixed and composed instances. For completeness, we provide proofs in the Appendix.

LEMMA 2.4. *Let F be a de Morgan formula of size cn where each variable appears at most $O(c)$ times. Then, for $p \leq 1/(20c)^2$,*

$$\mathbf{Pr}_{\rho \sim \mathcal{R}_p}[\, F|_\rho \text{ depends on } \geq \tfrac{3}{5}pn \text{ variables} \,]$$
$$< \; 2^{-\Omega(\min\{n/c^4, \, pn\})}.$$

LEMMA 2.5. *Let F be a de Morgan formula of size $L \leq n^{5/4-\epsilon}$ for $\epsilon > 0$, where each variable appears at most $O(L/n)$ times. Then, for $p = n^{\epsilon/2}/n$ and any constant $\epsilon' < \epsilon/2$,*

$$\mathbf{Pr}_{\rho \sim \mathcal{R}_p}[\, F|_\rho \text{ depends on } \geq n^{\epsilon'} \text{ variables} \,] < 2^{-\Omega(n^{\epsilon'})}.$$

Let ϕ be a CNF. We assume clauses and literals in ϕ are in a canonical order. The *canonical decision tree* for ϕ is constructed as follows: If there is no clause left, return 1. If any clause is empty, return 0. Otherwise, query all variables in the first clause; when a literal in a clause is fixed to 0, remove the literal from the clause, and when a literal in a clause is fixed to 1, remove the whole clause; then recurse. We denote by $D(\phi)$ the depth of the canonical decision tree for ϕ. Canonical decision trees for DNFs can be defined analogously.

LEMMA 2.6 (HASTAD'S SWITCHING LEMMA [5, 1]). *Let ϕ be a k-CNF or k-DNF on n variables. Then for any $s \geq 0$ and $p \leq 1/7$,*

$$\mathbf{Pr}_{\rho \sim \mathcal{R}_p}[D(\phi|_\rho) \geq s] < (7pk)^s.$$

3. EXPLOITING SUBCUBE PARTITIONING FOR MIXED INSTANCES

We are interested in designing and analyzing algorithms for $(\mathcal{C}_1 \wedge \mathcal{C}_2)$-SAT which have performance comparable to the best known algorithms for $\mathcal{C}_1$-SAT and $\mathcal{C}_2$-SAT.

First, we show a negative result. There are circuit classes $\mathcal{C}_1$ and $\mathcal{C}_2$ for which the satisfiability problem is in polynomial time, but satisfiability of mixed instances requires exponential time to solve under standard complexity-theoretic hypotheses.

THEOREM 3.1. *(2CNF $\wedge$ THR)-SAT requires time $2^{\Omega(n)}$, assuming the Exponential Time Hypothesis.*

PROOF. Let $\mathcal{C}_1$ be 2-CNF and $\mathcal{C}_2$ be THR. Note that $\mathcal{C}_1$-SAT and $\mathcal{C}_2$-SAT are both polynomial-time solvable. We show that $(\mathcal{C}_1 \wedge \mathcal{C}_2)$-SAT is hard under the Exponential Time Hypothesis, by encoding Independent Set into this problem.

Let (G, k) be an instance of the Independent Set problem, where the question is whether G has an independent set of size at least k. Let n be the number of vertices of G. We reduce such an instance to an instance of (2CNF $\wedge$ THR)-SAT preserving the number of variables as follows. Let $x_1 \ldots x_n$ be propositional variables. The intended interpretation of the variables is that the set of all variables assigned to true should form an independent set in G. To enforce this interpretation, we define clauses as follows: for each edge (i, j) of G, where $i, j \in [n]$, we add a clause $(\neg x_i \vee \neg x_j)$. Note that the collection of clauses of this form is a 2-CNF. We also add a single threshold gate which checks if $\Sigma_i x_i \geq k$. Clearly, the resulting instance ϕ is satisfiable iff (G, k) is a YES instance of Independent Set. It is known [8] that Independent Set requires time $2^{\Omega(n)}$ if the Exponential Time Hypothesis holds, hence the same is true for (2CNF $\wedge$ THR)-SAT. $\square$

Next, we show a positive result when $\mathcal{C}_1$-SAT has a subcube partitioning algorithm with non-trivial savings, and $\mathcal{C}_2$-SAT is polynomial-time solvable. We do assume that $\mathcal{C}_2$ satisfies a certain natural condition. We say that a circuit class $\mathcal{C}$ is closed under restrictions if for any circuit C belonging to the class and for any partial restriction of the variables of C, the resulting circuit C' belongs to the class as well. All commonly studied circuit classes satisfy this condition.

THEOREM 3.2. *Let $f : \mathbb{N} \times \mathbb{N} \to \mathbb{N}$ be a function such that $f(n, \cdot) \leq n$ for all $n \in \mathbb{N}$. Let $\mathcal{C}_1$ and $\mathcal{C}_2$ be circuit classes such that $\mathcal{C}_1$-SAT has a subcube partitioning algorithm with savings $f(\cdot, \cdot)$ and $\mathcal{C}_2$-SAT has a polynomial-time algorithm. Moreover, assume $\mathcal{C}_2$ is closed under restrictions. Then $(\mathcal{C}_1 \wedge \mathcal{C}_2)$-SAT has an algorithm with savings $f(\cdot, \cdot)$.*

PROOF. By assumption, there is an algorithm A_1 which given any $C \in \mathcal{C}_1$ of size m over n variables, outputs a subcube partition labelling for C in time $2^{n-f(n,m)}$ poly(m). We define an algorithm A to solve mixed instances over $\mathcal{C}_1$ and $\mathcal{C}_2$. Let $C \wedge C'$ be an input to algorithm A, where $C \in \mathcal{C}_1$, $C' \in \mathcal{C}_2$ and the total size of the instance is m. Algorithm A first runs A_1 to give a subcube partition labelling for C. For every element of the list which has $b_i = 1$, the algorithm applies the corresponding restriction ρ_i to C' and solves satisfiability on the resulting instance using the polynomial-time algorithm for $\mathcal{C}_2$-SAT. If any of these calls accept, A accepts, otherwise it rejects. Correctness follows from the definition of subcube partition labellings and closure of C' under restrictions. The resulting algorithm has the same savings as for A_1. $\square$

COROLLARY 3.3. *Let R be a finite field. For any fixed k, $(k\mathsf{CNF} \wedge \mathsf{THR})$-SAT and $(k\mathsf{CNF} \wedge \mathsf{LIN}_R)$-SAT have savings $\Omega(n/k)$ using a randomized algorithm.*

PROOF. The result follows from Theorem 3.2 by using Theorem 2.1 and the facts that THR-SAT and LIN_R-SAT have polynomial-time algorithms. $\square$

There are several interesting cases of mixed instances, where there are no polynomial-time algorithms for pure instances of the constituent types unless $\mathsf{NP} = \mathsf{P}$, however there are algorithms with non-trivial savings for the pure instances, and we would like to get non-trivial savings also for the mixed instances. The following result shows generically how to achieve this, in the case that the algorithms exploit subcube partitioning.

THEOREM 3.4. *Let $f_1 : \mathbb{N} \times \mathbb{N}$ and $f_2 : \mathbb{N} \times \mathbb{N}$ be monotone functions such that $f_1(n) \leq n$ and $f_2(n) \leq n$ for all $n \in \mathbb{N}$. Let $\mathcal{C}_1$ and $\mathcal{C}_2$ be circuit classes such that $\mathcal{C}_1$-SAT has a subcube partitioning algorithm with savings f_1 and $\mathcal{C}_2$-SAT has an algorithm with savings f_2. Moreover, assume $\mathcal{C}_2$ is closed under restrictions. Then $(\mathcal{C}_1 \wedge \mathcal{C}_2)$-SAT has an algorithm with savings $f_2(\Omega(f_1))$.*

PROOF. Let the subcube partitioning algorithm for $\mathcal{C}_1$-SAT be A_1 and the algorithm for $\mathcal{C}_2$-SAT be A_2. Given a mixed instance $\phi_1 \wedge \phi_2$, where $\phi_1 \in \mathcal{C}_1$ and $\phi_2 \in \mathcal{C}_2$, we first run A_1 on ϕ_1 to obtain a subcube partition labelling for ϕ_1 of size at most $2^{n - f_1(n)} \operatorname{poly}(m)$, where m is the size of the mixed instance. For each pair (ρ_i, b_i) in the labelling with $b_i = 1$, we run the A_2 on $\phi_2|_{\rho_i}$, where $\phi_2|_{\rho_i}$ denotes ϕ_2 with all values fixed by ρ_i substituted into ϕ_2. We accept iff A_2 accepts for some pair in the labelling with $b_i = 1$.

Correctness of the algorithm follows from correctness of A_1 and A_2, and from the fact that $\mathcal{C}_2$ is closed under restrictions. We now argue the stated bound on the time complexity. Let the subcube partition labelling be $\{(\rho_i, b_i)\}_{i=1}^{s}$, where $s \leq 2^{n - f_1(n)} \operatorname{poly}(m)$. For each restriction ρ_i in the labelling, let n_i be the number of $*$'s in ρ_i and let $V(\rho_i) = 2^{n_i}$. Since the ρ_i's constitute a subcube partition, we have that $\Sigma_i V(\rho_i) = 2^n$.

We consider two types of restrictions in the labelling, based on whether $n_i \geq f_1(n)/2$. If this condition is satisfied, we call the restriction ρ_i *fat*; otherwise, we call it *thin*. Now, the time complexity of the algorithm is at most $\Sigma_i 2^{n_i - f_2(n_i)}$, using the assumption on the savings of A_2. We break up this sum into the corresponding sums for fat and thin restrictions. For thin restrictions, we have that the sum is at most $s 2^{f_1(n)/2} \leq 2^{n - f_1(n)/2} \operatorname{poly}(m)$, as there are at most s terms in the sum, and each term is at most $2^{n_i} \leq 2^{f_1(n)/2}$. For fat restrictions, we have that the sum is at most $\Sigma_i V(\rho_i)/2^{f_2(f_1(n)/2)}$, using monotonicity of f_2. This sum is at most $2^{n - f_2(f_1(n)/2)}$, using the fact that $\Sigma_i V(\rho_i) \leq 2^n$. Thus, the total sum is at most $2^{n - f_2(f_1(n)/2)} \operatorname{poly}(m)$, using the fact that $f_2(n) \leq n$ for all n. This bound corresponds to savings $f_2(\Omega(f_1))$. $\square$

In the case that f_2 grows much smaller than n, we could optimise the parameters in the proof of Theorem 3.4 to achieve savings $f_2(f_1 - f_2(f_1))$. But in most cases of interest, this optimisation does not give us significant benefits. The proof technique of Theorem 3.4 yields some other consequences. If the algorithms for $\mathcal{C}_1$-SAT and $\mathcal{C}_2$-SAT are polynomial-space, the algorithm for mixed instances can be designed to be polynomial-space as well. Moreover, if the algorithms for pure instances count the number of satisfying assignments, a slight modification to the proof yields an algorithm for mixed instances also counting the number of satisfying assignments. This consequence critically uses the subcube partitioning.

Theorem 3.4 yields the following corollaries, using Theorem 2.1, Theorem 2.2 and Theorem 2.3.

COROLLARY 3.5. *There are algorithms achieving:*

- *Savings $\Omega(n/(c^2 k))$ for $(k\mathsf{CNF} \wedge \mathsf{Formula}[cn])$-SAT*

- *Savings $\Omega(n/k \log(m/n))$ for $(k\mathsf{CNF} \wedge \mathsf{CNF}[m])$-SAT*

- *Savings $\Omega(n/(c^2 \log(m/n)))$ for $(\mathsf{Formula}[cn] \wedge \mathsf{CNF}[m])$-SAT*

All of the above algorithms can be modified to count the number of satisfying assignments exactly. We will show in the next section how to get improved savings for items (1) and (2) above. Also note a subtlety here: when there are subcube partitioning algorithms for both $\mathcal{C}_1$-SAT and $\mathcal{C}_2$-SAT, the order in which we run the algorithms might matter in terms of the savings analysis.

We now explain how Theorems 3.2 and 3.4 have interesting consequences for exact algorithms for commonly studied NP-hard graph problems. This involves using the connection in the proof of Theorem 3.1 in the opposite direction, using satisfiability algorithms for mixed instances to get graph algorithms. We are interested particularly here in *meta-algorithmic* results, which show that interesting algorithms exist for a wide class of problems at once. A famous example of such a result is Courcelle's theorem [3], which states that any Monadic Second Order property of graphs can be decided in linear time on graphs of bounded treewidth. Analogously, we wish to have a single result which implies non-trivial exact algorithms for a large number of NP-hard graph optimisation problems. It is natural to use logical formalisms for graph properties to formulate such a result.

THEOREM 3.6. *For any MSO formula ϕ on graphs, the weighted optimisation problems $O_\phi^{\max}$ and $O_\phi^{\min}$ have savings $\Omega(n/\operatorname{polylog}(n))$. For any MSNP formula ϕ on graphs, the weighted optimisation problems $O_\phi^{\max}$ and $O_\phi^{\min}$ have savings $\Omega(n)$.*

PROOF. Let ϕ be a MSO formula. The idea of the proof is to "circuitify" the first-order part of ϕ, converting it into a constant-depth circuit, and then to express the weighted optimisation problem as a satisfiability problem on mixed instances, where one part of the mixed instance is a constant-depth circuit and the other part is a linear inequality. When ϕ is MSNP, the circuitification yields a bounded-width CNF formula rather than a constant-depth circuit, which enables us to get better savings.

Assume without loss of generality that ϕ is of the form $\exists X_1 \exists X_2 \ldots \exists X_q \psi(X_1, \ldots, X_q)$, where ψ is a first-order formula. Suppose we are given a weighted graph $G = (V, E, w)$. We give an inductive procedure to construct a constant-depth circuit C_G corresponding to G, which encodes whether $\psi(X_1, \ldots, X_q)$ holds. Let $|V| = n$. The circuit will have qn variables, denoted by $y_{ij}, i = 1, \ldots, q, j = 1, \ldots, n$. We will use $y_{ij} = 1$ to encode that vertex j of the graph belongs to X_i.

By the definition of first-order formulas, ψ is either of the form $\exists x \psi'(X_1, \ldots X_q, x)$, or of the form $\forall x \psi'(X_1, \ldots X_q, x)$, or a propositional sentence constructed from the atomic formulas. In the first case, we cycle over the n vertices of the graph. For each vertex k, by induction, there is a constant-depth circuit $C'(k)$ in the y variables for ψ' - we define C_G to be the OR over all n of $C'(k)$. Similarly, in the second case, we define C_G to be the AND over all n of $C'(k)$. In the third case, we can express the sentence as a bounded-width CNF in the variables $\{y_{ij}\}$ after substituting occurrences of $E(j, k)$ for vertices $j, k \in V$ by true or false depending on whether $(j, k) \in E$ or not, and similarly substituting occurrences of $j = k$ by true or false, depending on whether $j = k$ or not. Any occurrence of $X_i(j)$ is replaced by the variable y_{ij}.

The circuit C_G has a fixed depth which depends on the quantifier depth of the MSO formula ϕ. Now to solve the weighted optimisation problem $O_\phi^{\max}$, we construct mixed instances of the form $C_G \wedge T$, where T is a linear inequality we choose adaptively. Let $W_{\max} = q\Sigma_{v\in V} w(v)$. We use binary search to find the maximum weight W for which the mixed instance $C_G \wedge T$ is satisfiable, where T is the linear inequality $\Sigma_{i,j} w_j y_{ij} \geq W$. We initialize W to $W_{\max}/2$, using the binary search method to update W depending on the result of our satisfiability query. We will use at most $\log(|W_{\max}|)$ calls to the satisfiability algorithm, and by our assumption that the weights are representable by $\mathrm{poly}(n)$ bits, this will incur at most a polynomial overhead over the running time of a single call to the satisfiability algorithm. For the satisfiability algorithm itself, we apply Theorem 3.2 with Theorem 2.2 and the fact that THR-SAT has a polynomial-time algorithm. This gives us savings $\Omega(n/\mathrm{polylog}(n))$.

Solving $O_\phi^{\min}$ is completely analogous, except that we attempt to find the minimum W for which the mixed instance is satisfiable, where the linear inequality is now that $\Sigma_{i,j} w_j y_{ij} \leq W$.

In the case where ϕ is MSNP, the circuit C_G produced by our procedure is in fact a k-CNF for some fixed k. Hence in this case, we can use Corollary 3.3 to achieve linear savings. □

Algorithms with linear savings are known for a large number of graph optimisation problems, and Theorem 3.6 brings these linear savings results under one umbrella, for problems such as Independent Set, Clique and Vertex Cover.

4. BEATING THE GENERIC SUBCUBE PARTITIONING BOUND

Corollary 3.5 illustrates how Theorem 3.4 can be used to give non-trivial savings for several satisfiability problems with mixed instances. However, the savings obtained in these cases are not the best for which one could hope. In general, if $\mathcal{C}_1$-SAT has savings f_1 and $\mathcal{C}_2$-SAT has savings f_2, we could hope for savings $\min\{f_1, f_2\}$ for $(\mathcal{C}_1 \wedge \mathcal{C}_2)$-SAT. Note that savings asymptotically better than this would imply better algorithms for the pure satisfiability problems $\mathcal{C}_1$-SAT or $\mathcal{C}_2$-SAT. We are able to achieve the optimal savings for mixed instances where one part of the instance is a k-CNF and the other part consists of a prescribed number of clauses of arbitrary length. To achieve these improved savings, we exploit the fact that the best known algorithms for CNF-SAT themselves proceed through reductions to satisfiability of bounded-width formulas.

THEOREM 4.1. *For any positive integer $k \geq 2$ and any function $m : \mathbb{N} \to \mathbb{N}$, $(k\mathsf{CNF} \wedge \mathsf{CNF}[m])$-SAT has savings $\Omega(\min\{n/k, n/\log(m/n)\})$.*

PROOF. Let $\phi = \phi_1 \wedge \phi_2$ be the input formula on n variables, where ϕ_1 is a k-CNF and ϕ_2 is a CNF with $m' \leq m(n)$ clauses. We apply a width reduction procedure due to Schuler [21], and then use a standard algorithm for bounded-width satisfiability [16]. We use the tighter analysis of width-reduction due to [2].

Let $K \geq k$ be a parameter to be fixed later. We apply the following recursive procedure to solve satisfiability on ϕ. If ϕ is a K-CNF, we use the PPZ satisfiability algorithm [16], which runs in time $2^{n-n/K}\mathrm{poly}(n)$, to check if ϕ is satisfiable. If not, then pick the lexicographically first clause

C in ϕ_2 with width greater than K. Assume wlog that the first K literals of C are $x_1, \ldots, x_K$. We construct instances ϕ' and ϕ'' as follows and recursively check satisfiability on these instances. ϕ' is produced by substituting $x_1, \ldots, x_K$ to false in ϕ and simplifying the resulting formula. ϕ'' consists of ϕ, but with the clause C removed. Clearly, ϕ is satisfiable iff at least one of ϕ' and ϕ'' are satisfiable.

This recursive procedure for satisfiability corresponds to a recursion tree where left branches represent substitutions for K literals, and right branches represent removals of a clause. The leaves of this tree are labelled with K-CNFs, corresponding to using the PPZ satisfiability algorithm rather than continuing to use recursion. This tree is highly skewed: there can be at most n/K left branches, as each left branch gets rid of K variables, but there can be as many as m' right branches. The number of paths in the tree with r left branches is at most $\binom{m'+r}{r}$, and each leaf corresponding to such a path is labelled with a formula on at most $n - Kr$ variables.

Let $\alpha = 2^{1-1/K}$. We can estimate the total running time of the satisfiability procedure as at most:

$$
\begin{aligned}
\sum_{r=0}^{n/K} \binom{m'+r}{r}\alpha^{n-Kr} &\leq \sum_{r=0}^{m'+n/K}\binom{m'+n/K}{r}\alpha^{n-Kr} \\
&\leq \alpha^n(1+\alpha^{-K})^{m'+n/K} \\
&\leq \alpha^n e^{\alpha^{-K}(m'+n/K)} \\
&\leq 2^{n-n/K+2(m'+n/K)/2^{K-1}}
\end{aligned}
$$

To fix K, we consider two cases: either $m' \geq 2^k n$, or it is not. In the first case, by setting $K = C\log(m'/n)$ for large enough constant C and using the fact that $k \geq 2$, it can easily be checked that the savings of the satisfiability procedure is $\Omega(n/K)$. In the second case, by setting $K = 3k+1$, it can be checked that the savings of satisfiability procedure is $\Omega(n/K)$. Thus the savings of the procedure is $\Omega(\min\{n/k, n/\log(m'/n)\}) \geq \Omega(\min\{n/k, n/\log(m/n)\})$, as promised, since $m' \leq m$. □

For mixed instances where one part of the instance is a Boolean formula with a prescribed number of literals, and the other part is a k-CNF, we can again use specific properties of known algorithms to combine them more cleverly than in the proof of the generic subcube paritioning bound. However, we aren't quite able to manage optimal savings in this case.

THEOREM 4.2. (Formula$[cn] \wedge k$CNF)-*SAT has (randomized zero-error) savings at least $\Omega(\min\{n/c^4, n/k\})$.*

PROOF. Let $\phi_1 \wedge \phi_2$ be a given instance where ϕ_1 is a de Morgan formula of size cn, and ϕ_2 is a k-CNF formula, We first greedily restrict heavy variables in ϕ_1. Let H be the set of variables appearing at least $2c$ times in ϕ_1. Then $|H| \leq n/2$. We build $2^{|H|}$ branches by restricting variables in H. Let $n' = n - |H| \geq n/2$. For each restriction τ of variables in H, we have that $L(\phi_1|_\tau) \leq cn - 2c|H| \leq cn'$, and each variable in $\phi_1|_\tau$ appears less than $2c$ times.

For each τ, let $\phi_1' = \phi_1|_\tau$ and $\phi_2' = \phi_2|_\tau$; we next apply random restrictions to $\phi_1' \wedge \phi_2'$. Let $p = \min\{1/(20c)^2, 1/28k\}$. Consider the random restriction $\mathcal{R}_p = (U, \sigma)$ where we first choose a random subset U of pn' variables, and then fix variables not in U by a random assignments $\sigma \in \{0,1\}^{n'-|U|}$.

For a random $\rho \sim \mathcal{R}_p$, by Lemma 2.4, the probability that $\phi'_1|_\rho$ depends on at least $\frac{3}{5}pn'$ variables is at most $2^{-\Omega(\min\{n'/c^4,\, pn'\})}$. By Lemma 2.6,

$$\mathbf{Pr}_{\rho \sim (U,\sigma)}[D(\phi'_2|_\rho) \geq s] \leq (7pk)^s \leq 4^{-s}.$$

For each ρ, if $\phi'_1|_\rho$ depends on at least $\frac{3}{5}pn'$ variables, then we enumerate assignments to all remaining pn' variables and check the satisfiability of $\phi'_1|_\rho \wedge \phi'_2|_\rho$. Otherwise, we enumerate assignments to at most $\frac{3}{5}pn'$ variables on which $\phi'_1|_\rho$ depends (this fixes $\phi'_1|_\rho$ to a constant), and then build decision trees for the restricted $\phi'_2|_\rho$.

For a random $\rho \sim \mathcal{R}_p$, the expected number of branches we build for checking the satisfiability of $\phi'_1|_\rho \wedge \phi'_2|_\rho$ is at most

$$M \;=\; 2^{pn'} \cdot 2^{-\Omega(\min\{n'/c^4,\, pn'\})} + 2^{3pn'/5} \cdot \sum_s 2^s 4^{-s}$$

$$\leq\; 2^{pn'-\Omega(\min\{n'/c^4,\, pn'\})}.$$

Finally, the expected total number of branches (and the expected running time of the algorithm) is bounded by

$$2^{|H|+n'-pn'} M \leq 2^{n-\Omega(\min\{n/c^4,\, pn\})} = 2^{n-\Omega(\min\{n/c^4,\, n/k\})}.$$

$\square$

Note that Theorem 4.2 doesn't always yield savings better than Corollary 3.5, however for large k the savings is better, and in general we can achieve savings of the form $\Omega(\max\{n/(c^2 k), \min\{n/c^4, n/k\}\})$ by using either the algorithm of Corollary 3.5 or the algorithm of Theorem 4.2, based on the relationship between c and k.

5. EXPLOITING SUBCUBE PARTITIONING FOR COMPOSED INSTANCES

We now consider composed instances of the form $\mathcal{C} \circ \mathcal{D}$, where each instance has a $\mathcal{C}$-circuit at the top whose inputs are $\mathcal{D}$-circuits. We hope to design efficient algorithms for satisfiability checking or truth-table enumeration, by exploiting existing efficient algorithms for pure instances $\mathcal{C}$ and $\mathcal{D}$.

To start, we describe a simple strategy. Let $C(D_1, \ldots, D_m)$ be an instance of $\mathcal{C} \circ \mathcal{D}$, where D_i's are over the same set of n variables. We first run a partitioning which works for all circuits $D_1, \ldots, D_m$ such that in each part j, each D_i reduces to a $\mathcal{D}'$ instance $D'_{i,j}$, and we get a $\mathcal{C} \circ \mathcal{D}'$ instance $C(D'_{1,j}, \ldots, D'_{m,j})$; then, run an efficient algorithm for $\mathcal{C} \circ \mathcal{D}'$. Obviously, to implement this strategy we need both (1) an efficient partitioning for a collection of $\mathcal{D}$-circuits, and (2) an efficient algorithm for $\mathcal{C} \circ \mathcal{D}'$.

Indeed, the AC^0 satisfiability algorithm of [6] can be viewed as a recursive application of the above strategy. First, an AC^0_d circuit (with OR gates at the bottom) can be viewed as an AC^0_{d-1} circuit fed by clauses. Using Schuler's width reduction [21], clauses of arbitrary length can be reduced to clauses of length at most k; this gives AC^0_d circuits with bottom fan-in at most k, which can be viewed as $\mathsf{AC}^0_{d-2} \circ k\mathsf{CNF}$. By an extension of Hastad's switching lemma [6], there is a (randomized) partitioning for a collection of $k\mathsf{CNF}$'s such that restricted $k\mathsf{CNF}$'s can be written as $k\mathsf{DNF}$'s; by merging into AC^0_{d-2}, this gives $\mathsf{AC}^0_{d-3} \circ k\mathsf{DNF}$ circuits. Then by recursively reducing the depth, we finally get a $k\mathsf{CNF}$ or $k\mathsf{DNF}$ for each part. One subtlety is that, the partitioning

given in [6] there is not a subcube partitioning, but instead each part is defined by a $k\mathsf{CNF}$; however, the $k\mathsf{CNF}$ specifying a part can be combined with the final restricted instance ($k\mathsf{CNF}$ or $k\mathsf{DNF}$), which has a subcube partitioning by the extension of Hastad's switching lemma in [6].

5.1 QBF-SAT

We next apply the strategy to give a non-trivial satisfiability algorithm for quantified de Morgan formulas of superlinear size, by designing an efficient truth-table enumeration algorithm for composed instances $\mathsf{AC}^0 \circ \mathsf{Formula}$.

THEOREM 5.1. *For quantified de Morgan formulas with n variables, q quantifier blocks and size at most $n^{5/4-\epsilon}$ for any $\epsilon > 0$, there is a randomized satisfiability algorithm running in time $2^{n-n^{\Omega(\epsilon/(q+1))}}$.*

Before stating the proof, we outline the main ideas below. Given a QBF, we first use the approach of [19] to "blowup" the instance; that is, enumerate assignments to the innermost n^δ quantified variables and construct an instance of $\mathsf{AC}^0 \circ \mathsf{Formula}$. Following [19], if we can enumerate the truth table of $\mathsf{AC}^0 \circ \mathsf{Formula}$ efficiently, then the original QBF can be evaluated efficiently (with the savings coming from the blowup). To produce the truth table of $\mathsf{AC}^0 \circ \mathsf{Formula}$, we first apply random restrictions to shrink all formulas such that they can be merged into AC^0, and then use fast truth-table enumeration for AC^0 [19].

We first show that the truth table of $\mathsf{AC}^0 \circ \mathsf{Formula}$ (when the formula is small) can be efficiently enumerated. We need the following lemma on AC^0 truth-table enumeration [19].

LEMMA 5.2 ([19]). *There is a randomized zero-error algorithm that, given an AC^0 circuit of depth d and size s, outputs the truth table in time $\mathrm{poly}(n) \cdot (2^n + s 2^{n-\Omega(n/\log^{d-1} s)})$. In particular, there is some small constant $a > 0$ such that when $s \leq 2^{an^{1/d}}$, the algorithm runs in time $2^n \mathrm{poly}(n)$.*

LEMMA 5.3. *There is a randomized zero-error algorithm running in time $2^n \mathrm{poly}(n)$ which outputs truth tables for $\mathsf{AC}^0 \circ \mathsf{Formula}$ instances satisfying the following conditions:*

- *the AC^0 circuit has depth d and size $s \leq 2^{n^\delta}$;*

- *each formula feeding into AC^0 has size $L \leq n^{5/4-\epsilon}$, and each variable appears $O(L/n)$ times in each formula;*

- *$\delta \leq a\epsilon/(d+1)$ for some small constant $a > 0$.*

PROOF. Consider the random restriction $\mathcal{R}_p = (U, \sigma)$, where we first choose a random subset U of pn variables, and then choose a random assignment $\sigma \in \{0,1\}^{n-pn}$ to variables not in U. Let $p = n^{\epsilon/2}/n$. Let $\epsilon' = 2\delta < \epsilon/2$. For a formula G feeding into AC^0, define

$$P_U = \mathbf{Pr}_{\rho \sim (U,\sigma)}[\, G|_\rho \text{ depends on} \geq n^{\epsilon'} \text{ variables}\,].$$

We say U is *good* for G if $P_U < 2^{-\Omega(n^{\epsilon'})}$. Lemma 2.5 gives that, $\mathbf{E}_U[P_U] < 2^{-cn^{\epsilon'}}$, for some constant $c > 0$. Then by Markov's inequality,

$$\mathbf{Pr}_U[P_U \geq 2^{-cn^{\epsilon'}/2}] \leq \frac{\mathbf{E}_U[P_U]}{2^{-cn^{\epsilon'}/2}} < 2^{-cn^{\epsilon'}/2}.$$

That is, a random U is good for G with probability $1 - 2^{-\Omega(n^{\epsilon'})}$.

By a union bound on the $s \leq 2^{n^\delta}$ formulas feeding to AC^0, a random U is good for all formulas with probability $1 - 2^{n^\delta - \Omega(n^{\epsilon'})} \geq 1 - 2^{-\Omega(n^{\epsilon'})}$,

The algorithm runs by choosing U randomly, and then enumerating assignments to variables not in U. For a fixed good U, and a randomly chosen $\sigma \in \{0,1\}^{n-|U|}$, by another union bound on all formulas, the probability that any of the restricted formula depends on more than $n^{\epsilon'}$ variables is at most $2^{n^\delta - \Omega(n^{\epsilon'})} \leq 2^{-\Omega(n^{\epsilon'})}$.

This means, over the $2^{n-|U|}$ assignments to variables not in U, all but $2^{-\Omega(n^{\epsilon'})}$ fraction will give restricted instances with an AC^0 of depth d and size 2^{n^δ} at the top, and formulas each depending on at most $n^{\epsilon'}$ variables at the bottom. For each such instance, we express formulas as CNFs/DNFs (of size $2^{n^{\epsilon'}}$) and merge them into AC^0. This gives an AC^0 circuit of depth $d+1$ and size $2^{n^\delta + n^{\epsilon'}}$. (Note that, it has n^ϵ variables unfixed.) Then we use the truth-table enumeration algorithm for AC^0 by Lemma 5.2 [19]. Since $\epsilon' = 2\delta$ and $\delta = a\epsilon/(d+1)$, for sufficiently small a, by Lemma 5.2, this can be done in time $2^{n^\epsilon} \operatorname{poly}(n)$.

Thus, the running time for branches where all formulas depend on at most $n^{\epsilon'}$ variables is at most $2^{n-n^\epsilon} \cdot 2^{n^\epsilon} \cdot \operatorname{poly}(n) = 2^n \operatorname{poly}(n)$.

For branches where at least one of the formulas depend on more than $n^{\epsilon'}$ variables, we use brute-force enumeration for the remaining n^ϵ variables to evaluate the circuit. Each such branch takes time $2^{n^\epsilon} \cdot 2^{n^\delta} \cdot \operatorname{poly}(n)$. The running time for all such branches is

$$2^{n-n^\epsilon} \cdot 2^{-\Omega(n^{\epsilon'})} \cdot (2^{n^\epsilon} \cdot 2^{n^\delta} \cdot \operatorname{poly}(n)) \leq 2^n \operatorname{poly}(n).$$

$\square$

PROOF PROOF OF THEOREM 5.1. Consider a QBF with n variables and q quantifier blocks. Let F be the de Morgan formula in the QBF, where the size $L(F) \leq n^{5/4-\epsilon}$. Let H be the set of variables appearing at least $2L(F)/n$ times; then $|H| \leq n/2$. Our algorithm has the following stages:

We first enumerate on the innermost n^δ quantified variables, for $\delta = a\epsilon/(d+1)$ for some small constant $a > 0$. Let B be the innermost n^δ quantified variables. Build an AC^0 circuit by enumerating assignments to all variables in B (replacing existential quantifiers by ORs and universal quantifiers by ANDs), and let the bottom layer be fed by F under corresponding restrictions of B. This gives an $\mathsf{AC}^0 \circ \mathsf{Formula}$ instance over $n-n^\delta$ variables, where the top AC^0 circuit has depth q and size 2^{n^δ}, and each formula feeding into AC^0 has size at most $L(F)$.

If we can enumerate the truth table of this composed instance efficiently (in time $2^{n-n^\delta} \operatorname{poly}(n)$), then by the techniques of [19], the original QBF can be evaluated by traversing an AND-OR tree based on the remaining quantified variables, and looking up in the truth table; the running time for QBF-SAT will be $2^{n-n^\delta} \operatorname{poly}(n)$.

In the rest, we focus on enumerating the truth table of the composed $\mathsf{AC}^0 \circ \mathsf{Formula}$ instance. We first enumerate assignments to variables in $H \setminus B$, get at most $2^{|H|}$ branches each with a restricted instance where the formulas have no heavy variables. For each fixing of variables in $H \cup B$, since $|H| \leq n/2$ and $|B| = n^\delta$, the number of unfixed variables is $n' = n - n^\delta - |H \setminus B| = \Theta(n)$. Thus, each restricted

$\mathsf{AC}^0 \circ \mathsf{Formula}$ instance has an AC^0 of depth q and size $2^{O(n'^\delta)}$) at the top, and each formula feeding into AC^0 has size at most $L' = O(n'^{5/4-\epsilon})$, with all variables appear $O(L'/n')$ times. Then by Lemma 5.3, the truth table of each such restricted instance can be enumerated in time $2^{n'} \operatorname{poly}(n)$.

Therefore, we can enumerate the truth table of the constructed $\mathsf{AC}^0 \circ \mathsf{Formula}$ instance in time $2^{|H \setminus B|} \cdot 2^{n'} \operatorname{poly}(n) = 2^{n-n^\delta} \operatorname{poly}(n)$, and thus QBF-SAT is in time $2^{n-n^\delta} \operatorname{poly}(n) = 2^{n-n^{\Omega(\epsilon/(q+1))}} \operatorname{poly}(n)$.

$\square$

6. ACKNOWLEDGMENTS

Supported by the European Research Council under the European Union's Seventh Framework Programme (FP7/2007-2013) / ERC Grant Agreement no. 615075

7. REFERENCES

[1] P. Beame. A switching lemma primer, 1994.
[2] C. Calabro, R. Impagliazzo, and R. Paturi. A duality between clause width and clause density for sat. In *CCC*, 2006.
[3] B. Courcelle. The monadic second-order logic of graphs. i. recognizable sets of finite graphs. *Information and Computation*, 85(1):12–75, 1990.
[4] B. Doerr. Analyzing randomized search heuristics: Tools from probability theory. In A. Auger and B. Doerr, editors, *Theory of Randomized Search Heuristics*, pages 1–20. World Scientific Publishing, 2011.
[5] J. Håstad. Almost optimal lower bounds for small depth circuits. In *STOC*, 1986.
[6] R. Impagliazzo, W. Matthews, and R. Paturi. A satisfiability algorithm for AC^0. In *SODA*, 2012.
[7] R. Impagliazzo, R. Paturi, and F. Zane. Which problems have strongly exponential complexity? In *FOCS*, 1998.
[8] R. Impagliazzo, R. Paturi, and F. Zane. Which problems have strongly exponential complexity? *Journal of Computer and System Sciences*, 63(4):512–530, 2001.
[9] I. Komargodski and R. Raz. Average-case lower bounds for formula size. In *STOC*, 2013.
[10] I. Komargodski, R. Raz, and A. Tal. Improved average-case lower bounds for demorgan formula size. In *FOCS*, 2013.
[11] S. Malik and L. Zhang. Boolean satisfiability from theoretical hardness to practical success. *Communications of the ACM*, 52(8):76–82, 2009.
[12] R. Monasson, R. Zecchina, S. Kirkpatrick, B. Selman, and L. Troyansky. 2+p-SAT: Relation of typical-case complexity to the nature of the phase transition. *Random Structures and Algorithms*, 15:414–440, 1999.
[13] R. Nieuwenhuis, A. Oliveras, and C. Tinelli. Solving SAT and SAT modulo theories: From an abstract davis-putnam-logemann-loveland procedure to DPLL(T). *Journal of the Association for Computing Machinery*, 53(6):937–977, 2006.
[14] M. Patrascu and R. Williams. On the possibility of faster SAT algorithms. In *SODA*, 2010.

[15] R. Paturi, P. Pudlák, M. Saks, and F. Zane. An improved exponential-time algorithm for k-sat. *J. ACM*, 52(3):337–364, 2005.

[16] R. Paturi, P. Pudlák, and F. Zane. Satisfiability coding lemma. *Chicago Journal of Theoretical Computer Science*, 1999.

[17] S. Porschen and E. Speckenmeyer. Satisfiability of mixed horn formulas. *Discrete Applied Mathematics*, 155(11):1408–1419, 2007.

[18] R. Santhanam. Fighting perebor: New and improved algorithms for formula and qbf satisfiability. In *FOCS*, 2010.

[19] R. Santhanam and R. Williams. Beating exhaustive search for quantified boolean formulas and connections to circuit complexity. In *SODA*, 2015.

[20] U. Schöning. A probabilistic algorithm for k-sat and constraint satisfaction problems. In *FOCS*, 1999.

[21] R. Schuler. An algorithm for the satisfiability problem of formulas in conjunctive normal form. *J. Algorithms*, 54(1):40–44, 2005.

[22] R. Williams. Improving exhaustive search implies superpolynomial lower bounds. In *STOC*, 2010.

[23] R. Williams. Non-uniform ACC circuit lower bounds. In *CCC*, 2011.

APPENDIX

A. SHRINKAGE OF FORMULAS UNDER RANDOM RESTRICTIONS

We prove concentrated shrinkage of de Morgan formulas under random restrictions. The results here, in terms of the concentration parameters, are weaker than those obtained via greedy restrictions [18], or mixed greedy and random restrictions [9, 10], but they can be applied to get satisfiability algorithms for mixed and composed instances.

We need the following version of Chernoff bounds on hypergeometric distributions.

THEOREM A.1 (CHERNOFF BOUND [4]). *Let U be a subset of size pn chosen uniformly at random from $\{1, \ldots, n\}$. For $i = 1, \ldots, n$, let $X_i = 1$ if $i \in U$, and $X_i = 0$ otherwise. Let $X = \sum_{i=1}^{n} a_i X_i$ where $a_i \in [0, b]$. Then, $\mathbf{E}[X] = p \sum_{i=1}^{n} a_i$, and, for $t \geq 6\mathbf{E}[X]$,*

$$\mathbf{Pr}[X \geq t] \leq 2^{-t/b}.$$

A sequence of random variables $X_0, X_1, \ldots, X_n$ is called a *supermartingale* with respect to another sequence of random variables $R_1, \ldots, R_n$ if $\mathbf{E}[X_i \mid R_{i-1}, \ldots, R_1] \leq X_{i-1}$, for $1 \leq i \leq n$.

THEOREM A.2 (AZUMA-HOEFFDING INEQUALITY [4]). *If $\{X_i\}_{i=0}^{n}$ is a supermartingale such that $|X_i - X_{i-1}| \leq c_i$ for $i = 1, \ldots, n$, then, for any $\lambda \geq 0$,*

$$\mathbf{Pr}[X_n - X_0 \geq \lambda] \leq \exp\left(-\frac{2\lambda^2}{\sum_{i=1}^{n} c_i^2}\right).$$

Let $\mathcal{R}_p$ be the random restriction where a subset U of pn variables is chosen uniformly at random, and each variable not in U is assigned 0 or 1 each with probability $1/2$.

LEMMA A.3. *Let F be a de Morgan formula of size cn on n variables, where each variable appears at most $O(c)$ times in F. Then for $pn \geq l^2 c^2$,*

$$\mathbf{Pr}_{\rho \sim \mathcal{R}_p}[L(F|_\rho) \geq 2p^{1.5}cn = 2pn/l] \leq 2^{-\Omega(pn/l^2 c^2)}.$$

In particular, for $l = 20$ and $p = 1/(20c)^2$,

$$\mathbf{Pr}_{\rho \sim \mathcal{R}_p}[L(F|_\rho) \geq pn/10] \leq 2^{-\Omega(n/c^4)};$$

for $c = n^{\frac{1}{4}-\epsilon}$, $l = 20n^{\epsilon/2}$ and $p = 1/(400n^{\frac{1}{2}-\epsilon})$,

$$\mathbf{Pr}_{\rho \sim \mathcal{R}_p}[L(F|_\rho) \geq pn/10n^{\epsilon/2}] \leq 2^{-\Omega(n^{2\epsilon})}.$$

PROOF. Consider a step-by-step process where at each step a variable is randomly picked and fixed, and we run this process for $n - pn$ steps. Let $F_0 = F$, and F_i be the restricted formula after the i-th step (which is simplified by eliminating redundant leaves). Note that F_i is over $n - i$ variables. We distinguish two cases based on the size of F_i.

First consider the case that F_i is already small for some $i \leq n - pn$, that is, $L(F_i) \leq (n - i)/3l$. We then apply a random restriction $\mathcal{R}_{p'}$ for $p' = pn/(n - i)$ on F_i; the restricted formula size is at most the number of leaves left. By Theorem A.1,

$$\mathbf{E}_{\rho \sim \mathcal{R}_{p'}}[L(F_i|_\rho)] \leq p'L(F_i) \leq pn/3l,$$

and, since each variable appears at most $O(c)$ times,

$$\mathbf{Pr}_{\rho \sim \mathcal{R}_{p'}}[L(F_i|_\rho) \geq 2pn/l] \leq 2^{-\Omega(pn/lc)}.$$

In the rest, we assume that $L(F_i) > (n - i)/3l$ for $i = 1, \ldots, n - pn$.

At the i-th step, we start with a formula F_{i-1} on $n - (i-1)$ variables. We have $(n - i + 1)/3l < L(F_{i-1}) \leq cn$, and each variable appears $O(c)$ times. For a variable x in F_i, let c_x be the number of times where x appears in the form of $x \wedge G$ or $\overline{x} \vee G$, and let c'_x be the number of times where x appears in the form of $x \vee G$ or $\overline{x} \wedge G$. Note that we can eliminate $2c_x + c'_x$ leaves if we fix $x = 0$, and eliminate $c_x + 2c'_x$ leaves if we fix $x = 1$. We randomly choose x from the remaining variables and randomly fix it; define the random variable

$$Y_i = \begin{cases} 2c_x + c'_x, & \text{if } x \text{ is chosen and assigned } 0 \\ c_x + 2c'_x, & \text{if } x \text{ is chosen and assigned } 1. \end{cases}$$

Since $\sum_x (c_x + c'_x) = L(F_{i-1})$ and $0 \leq \{c_x, c'_x\} \leq O(c)$, we have $\mathbf{E}[Y_i] = 1.5L(F_{i-1})/(n - i + 1)$, and $Y_i \leq O(c)$.

Define $L_i^* = L(F_{i-1}) - Y_i$, then we have $L(F_i) \leq L_i^* \leq L(F_{i-1})$. For a fixed F_{i-1},

$$\begin{aligned} \mathbf{E}[L_i^*] = L(F_{i-1}) - \mathbf{E}[Y_i] &= L(F_{i-1})\left(1 - \frac{1.5}{n - i + 1}\right) \\ &\leq L(F_{i-1})\left(1 - \frac{1}{n - i + 1}\right)^{1.5}. \end{aligned}$$

We wish to compare L_i^* with $L(F_{i-1})\left(1 - \frac{1}{n-i+1}\right)^{1.5}$. Define

$$Z_i = \ln\left(\frac{L_i^*}{L(F_{i-1})\left(1 - \frac{1}{n-i+1}\right)^{1.5}}\right).$$

Then by Jensen inequality, $\mathbf{E}[Z_i] \leq 0$ (conditioning on a fixed F_{i-1}).

Since $L_i^* \leq L(F_{i-1})$, we get

$$Z_i \leq -1.5 \ln\left(1 - \frac{1}{n-i+1}\right) = 1.5 \ln\left(1 + \frac{1}{n-i}\right) \leq \frac{1.5}{n-i},$$

where the last inequality is by the fact that $\ln(1+x) \leq x$.

Since $Y_i \leq O(c)$ and $L(F_{i-1}) > (n-i+1)/3l$,

$$\begin{aligned} L_i^* &= L(F_{i-1}) - Y_i = L(F_{i-1})\left(1 - \frac{Y_i}{L(F_{i-1})}\right) \\ &\geq L(F_{i-1})\left(1 - \frac{blc}{n-i+1}\right), \end{aligned}$$

for some constant b. This gives that,

$$\begin{aligned} Z_i &\geq \ln\left(\frac{L_i^*}{L(F_{i-1})}\right) \geq \ln\left(1 - \frac{blc}{n-i+1}\right) \\ &= -\ln\left(1 + \frac{blc}{n-i+1-blc}\right) \\ &\geq -\frac{blc}{n-i+1-blc} \geq -\frac{2blc}{n-i}, \end{aligned}$$

where the last inequality follows from $n-i \geq pn \gg lc$. Therefore, $|Z_i| \leq \frac{2blc}{n-i}$.

Let $X_0 = 0$ and $X_i = \sum_{j=1}^{i} Z_j$. Then $\{X_i\}$ is a supermartingale with respect to the random choices at each step. By Theorem A.2 (Azuma-Hoeffding inequality), for $\lambda > 0$,

$$\begin{aligned} \mathbf{Pr}[X_i = \sum_{j=1}^{i} Z_i \geq \lambda] &\leq \exp\left(-\frac{2\lambda^2}{\sum_{j=1}^{i}(\frac{2blc}{n-j})^2}\right) \\ &\leq \exp\left(-\frac{2\lambda^2(n-i-1)}{(2blc)^2}\right), \end{aligned}$$

by that $\sum_{j=1}^{i} \frac{1}{(n-j)^2} < \sum_{j=1}^{i} \frac{1}{n-j-1} - \frac{1}{n-j} < \frac{1}{n-i-1}$.

Since that

$$\begin{aligned} e^{X_i} &= \prod_{j=1}^{i} \frac{L_j^*}{L(F_{j-1})\left(1 - \frac{1}{n-j+1}\right)^{1.5}} \\ &\geq \prod_{j=1}^{i} \frac{L(F_j)}{L(F_{j-1})\left(1 - \frac{1}{n-j+1}\right)^{1.5}} = \frac{L(F_i)}{L(F_0)\left(\frac{n-i}{n}\right)^{1.5}}, \end{aligned}$$

we have

$$\mathbf{Pr}\left[L(F_i) \geq e^\lambda L(F_0)\left(\frac{n-i}{n}\right)^{1.5}\right] \leq \exp\left(-\frac{2\lambda^2(n-i-1)}{(2blc)^2}\right).$$

Let $\lambda = \ln 2$ and $i = n - pn$,

$$\mathbf{Pr}\left[L(F_{n-pn}) \geq 2cnp^{1.5}\right] \leq 2^{-\Omega\left(pn/l^2c^2\right)}.$$

□

LEMMA A.4 (LEMMA 2.4 RESTATED). *Let F be a de Morgan formula of size $L = cn$ where each variable appears at most $O(c)$ times. Then, for $p \leq \frac{1}{(20c)^2}$,*

$$\mathbf{Pr}_{\rho \sim \mathcal{R}_p}[\, F|_\rho \text{ depends on } \geq \tfrac{3}{5}pn \text{ variables}\,] < 2^{-\Omega(\min\{n/c^4,\ pn\})}.$$

PROOF. We first apply a random restriction $\mathcal{R}_{p_0}$ for $p_0 = 1/(20c)^2$. By Lemma A.3, with probability $1 - 2^{-\Omega(n/c^4)}$, the restricted formula has size at most $p_0 n/10$, and thus depending on at most $p_0 n/10$ variables (although there are $p_0 n$ variables left).

Then, apply another random restriction $\mathcal{R}_{p_1}$ for $p_1 = p/p_0$, leaving pn variables unfixed. For any restricted formula F' depending on at most $p_0 n/10$ variables, by Chernoff bound (Theorem A.1), in expectation, the restricted formula $F'|_\rho$ depends on at most $p_1 \cdot p_0 n/10 = pn/10$ variables, and

$$\mathbf{Pr}_{\rho \sim \mathcal{R}_{p_1}}[\, F'|_\rho \text{ depends on } \geq \tfrac{3}{5}pn \text{ variables}\,] < 2^{-\Omega(pn)}.$$

Therefore,

$$\begin{aligned} &\mathbf{Pr}_{\rho \sim \mathcal{R}_p}[\, F|_\rho \text{ depends on } \geq \tfrac{3}{5}pn \text{ variables}\,] \\ &< 2^{-\Omega(n/c^4)} + 2^{-\Omega(pn)} < 2^{-\Omega(\min\{n/c^4,\ pn\})}. \end{aligned}$$

□

LEMMA A.5 (LEMMA 2.5 RESTATED). *Let F be a de Morgan formula of size $L \leq n^{5/4 - \epsilon}$ where each variable appears at most $O(L/n)$ times. Then, for $p = n^{\epsilon/2}/n$ and any constant $\epsilon' < \epsilon/2$,*

$$\mathbf{Pr}_{\rho \sim \mathcal{R}_p}[\, F|_\rho \text{ depends on } \geq n^{\epsilon'} \text{ variables}\,] < 2^{-\Omega(n^{\epsilon'})}.$$

PROOF. We first apply a random restriction for $p_0 = 1/400n^{\frac{1}{2} - \epsilon}$. By Lemma A.3, with probability $1 - 2^{-\Omega(n^{2\epsilon})}$, the restricted formula has size at most $p_0 n/10 n^{\epsilon/2}$, and thus depending on at most $p_0 n/10 n^{\epsilon/2}$ variables (although there are $p_0 n$ variables left). For any such "small" restricted formula F', apply another random restriction $\mathcal{R}_{p_1}$ for $p_1 = n^{\epsilon/2}/(p_0 n)$, leaving $n^{\epsilon/2}$ variables unfixed. By Chernoff bound (Theorem A.1), in expectation, the restricted formula depends on at most $p_1 \cdot (p_0 n/10 n^{\epsilon/2}) = 1/10$ variables, and

$$\mathbf{Pr}_{\rho \sim \mathcal{R}_{p_1}}[\, F'|_\rho \text{ depends on } \geq n^{\epsilon'} \text{ variables}\,] < 2^{-\Omega(n^{\epsilon'})}.$$

Therefore,

$$\begin{aligned} &\mathbf{Pr}_{\rho \sim \mathcal{R}_p}[\, F|_\rho \text{ depends on } \geq n^{\epsilon'} \text{ variables}\,] \\ &< 2^{-\Omega(n^{2\epsilon})} + 2^{-\Omega(n^{\epsilon'})} < 2^{-\Omega(n^{\epsilon'})}. \end{aligned}$$

□

On the Computational Complexity of Limit Cycles in Dynamical Systems

Christos H. Papadimitriou
University of California, Berkeley
christos@berkeley.edu

Nisheeth K. Vishnoi
École Polytechnique Fédérale de Lausanne
nisheeth.vishnoi@epfl.ch

ABSTRACT

Dynamical systems are ubiquitous in the study of physical, biological, and social phenomena. A continuous time dynamical system describes the evolution of a process x through a differential equation $\dot{x} = f(x)$, where $f : \mathbb{R}^n \to \mathbb{R}^n$ and $\dot{x} \stackrel{\text{def}}{=} \left(\frac{dx_1}{dt}, \ldots, \frac{dx_n}{dt} \right)$, where n is the dimension. We are particularly interested in dynamical systems in which the domain of f is a compact subset of $\mathbb{R}^n$, such as a simplex.

A dynamical system gives rise to a set of *trajectories*; a set of values of $x(t)$ for $t > 0$ for a given $x(0)$. Under appropriate assumptions, such trajectories are unique given $x(0)$. Understanding a dynamical system entails understanding the limiting behavior of its trajectories. Since trajectories are continuous curves in a compact domain, they may contain *limit sets*, that is, sets of points that are limits of convergent subsequences. Two particularly important, and easy to describe, types of limit sets are *fixpoints* (roots of $f(x)$) and *limit cycles* (closed trajectories that capture periodic behavior). But there are many other kinds of limit behaviors in dynamical systems — including the aptly named *strange attractors*. The study of the *unpredictability* of dynamical systems, also known as *Chaos Theory* is essentially the study of very complex types of limit sets.

However, *there is no chaos in 2-dimensional dynamical systems,* and the intuitive reason is planarity: trajectories cannot cross, and therefore they "confine" one another into benign behavior. The rigorous statement to this effect is an important result dating back to 1900s, first stated by Poincaré and later proved in its generality by Bendixson.

Poincaré–Bendixson Theorem: *In a two-dimensional dynamical system $\dot{x} = f(x)$ on a compact domain where f is continuously differentiable and has no fixpoints, all limit points lie on limit cycles.*

In this paper we consider the Poincaré-Bendixson theorem from the viewpoint of computation. Suppose that we are given a two-dimensional dynamical system over a compact domain, which is guaranteed to not have a fixpoint. How difficult is it to find a point on a limit cycle?

Permission to make digital or hard copies of all or part of this work for personal or classroom use is granted without fee provided that copies are not made or distributed for profit or commercial advantage and that copies bear this notice and the full citation on the first page. Copyrights for components of this work owned by others than the author(s) must be honored. Abstracting with credit is permitted. To copy otherwise, or republish, to post on servers or to redistribute to lists, requires prior specific permission and/or a fee. Request permissions from permissions@acm.org.

ITCS'16, January 14 - 16, 2016, Cambridge, MA, USA

© 2016 Copyright held by the owner/author(s). Publication rights licensed to ACM.
ISBN 978-1-4503-4057-1/16/01...$15.00

DOI: http://dx.doi.org/10.1145/2840728.2840752

We first look at these questions in a discrete planar domain: a grid of points, where the dynamical system is an implicit map from each grid point to one of its eight neighbors (grid points at ℓ_∞ distance one) such that no two edges cross. In such discrete dynamical systems, it is clear that the limit cycles correspond to the "sink cycles" of the directed graph, and hence a discrete version of the Poincaré-Bendixson theorem trivially holds. Computationally, we can show the following:

Discrete Poincaré–Bendixson Theorem: *Given a polynomially computable non-crossing function on a finite subset of the planar grid which has no fixpoints, a cycle always exists, but finding it is* **PSPACE**-*complete.*

Back in the continuous domain, it is not hard to see that, with only black-box access to the function f, *finding a limit cycle has arbitrarily high complexity.* To get around this negative result we could "look inside the black box" that computes f, or settle for approximation. For an appropriate notion of approximate limit cycle we prove the following:

Approximate Poincaré–Bendixson Theorem: *Given a dynamical system $\dot{x} = f(x)$ in a compact domain of any dimension where f is L-Lipschitz continuous and has no ε-fixpoints[1] an $\varepsilon/3L$-cycle exists in the orbit of every point.*

The proof parallels the Poincaré-Bendixson Theorem, except that compactness arguments are replaced by a volume argument. Notice that approximation blunts the distinction between two-dimensional and higher-dimensional systems.

How hard is it then to identify ε-cycles? We study this problem in a framework of *arithmetic circuits*, with arithmetic operations such as real addition, multiplication and sign as gates. We can show:

Complexity of ε-cycle: *Given $\varepsilon, L > 0$, an L-Lipschitz dynamical system through an arithmetic circuit, and a point x, determining whether x lies on an ε/L-cycle, or finding a point that does, is* **PSPACE**-*complete.*

Two challenging and important problems remain open: First, in 2-dimensional systems with no fixpoints, can the true limit cycle guaranteed by the Poincaré- Bendixson Theorem be approached in polynomial space? Naturally, in such systems our above-mentioned result allows us to find in polynomial space ε-cycles for arbitrarily small ε, but these may be very far from a true limit cycle. And second, in the specific multi-dimensional dynamical system that was proposed by Eigen and Schuster in 1979 as a model for the origin of life, can the limit cycle be approached in polynomial time? The paper appears here
http://arxiv.org/abs/1511.07605.

---

[1] An ε-*fixpoint* is a point x such that $\|f(x)\| < \varepsilon$.

Weighted Gate Elimination: Boolean Dispersers for Quadratic Varieties Imply Improved Circuit Lower Bounds

Alexander Golovnev
New York University
251 Mercer St.
New York, NY 10021
alexgolovnev@gmail.com

Alexander S. Kulikov
St. Petersburg Department of
Steklov Institute of Mathematics of
the Russian Academy of Sciences
27, Fontanka
St. Petersburg, Russia 191023
kulikov@logic.pdmi.ras.ru

ABSTRACT

In this paper we motivate the study of Boolean dispersers for quadratic varieties by showing that an explicit construction of such objects gives improved circuit lower bounds. An (n, k, s)-quadratic disperser is a function on n variables that is not constant on any subset of $\mathbb{F}_2^n$ of size at least s that can be defined as the set of common roots of at most k quadratic polynomials. We show that if a Boolean function f is a $\left(n, 1.83n, 2^{g(n)}\right)$-quadratic disperser for any function $g(n) = o(n)$ then the circuit size of f is at least $3.11n$. In order to prove this, we generalize the gate elimination method so that the induction works on the size of the variety rather than on the number of variables as in previously known proofs.

Categories and Subject Descriptors

F.2 [**Analysis of Algorithms and Problem Complexity**]: Miscellaneous

Keywords

Boolean circuits; dispersers; lower bounds

1. INTRODUCTION

1.1 Circuits and the gate elimination method

Denote by $B_{n,m}$ the set of all Boolean functions from $\mathbb{F}_2^n$ to $\mathbb{F}_2^m$, let $B_n = B_{n,1}$ and consider a function $f \in B_n$. A natural question studied in theoretical computer science is the following: what is the minimal number of binary Boolean operations needed to compute f? The corresponding computational model is Boolean circuits. A circuit is a directed acyclic graph with inputs $x_1, \ldots, x_n$, the intermediate vertices have in-degree 2 and are labeled with binary Boolean operations. The size of a circuit is its number of gates. Note that we do not pose any restrictions on the depth or out-

Permission to make digital or hard copies of all or part of this work for personal or classroom use is granted without fee provided that copies are not made or distributed for profit or commercial advantage and that copies bear this notice and the full citation on the first page. Copyrights for components of this work owned by others than the author(s) must be honored. Abstracting with credit is permitted. To copy otherwise, or republish, to post on servers or to redistribute to lists, requires prior specific permission and/or a fee. Request permissions from Permissions@acm.org.

ITCS'16, January 14–16, 2016, Cambridge, MA, USA.

Copyright is held by the owner/author(s). Publication rights licensed to ACM.

ACM 978-1-4503-4057-1/16/01 ...$15.00.

DOI: http://dx.doi.org/10.1145/2840728.2840755 .

degree. By $\mathcal{C}(f)$ we denote the minimum size of a circuit computing f.

Counting shows that the number of small size circuits is much smaller than the total number $|B_n| = 2^{2^n}$ of functions. Using this idea it was shown by Muller [16] that almost all functions from B_n require circuits of size $\Omega(2^n/n)$. This proof is however non-constructive: it does not give an explicit function with high circuit complexity. By saying explicit one usually means that the function is in P or NP. Finding an explicit function with high circuit complexity turned out to be an extremely difficult question. The currently strongest lower bound $3.011n$ was recently presented by Find et al. [10] improving a $3n - o(n)$ lower bound proved by Blum [3] more than 30 years ago.

Essentially, the only known technique for proving lower bounds for circuits with no restrictions on depth and out-degree is the gate elimination method. To illustrate it, we give a proof of a $2n - \Theta(1)$ lower bound given by Schnorr [17]. The $\text{MOD}_{3,r}^n \in B_n$ function outputs 1 if and only if the sum (over integers) of n input bits is congruent to r modulo 3. We prove that $\text{MOD}_{3,r}^n$ requires circuits of size at least $2n - 6$ by induction on n. The base case $n \leq 3$ clearly holds. For the induction step consider an optimal circuit $\mathcal{C}$ computing $\text{MOD}_{3,r}^n$ and its topologically minimal gate A (such a gate exists since for $n \geq 4$, $\text{MOD}_{3,r}^n$ is not constant). Let x and y be input variables to A. The crucial observation is that either x or y must feed at least one other gate. Indeed if both x and y feed only A then the whole circuit depends on x and y only through A. This, in particular, means that by fixing x and y in four possible ways $((x, y) = (0, 0), (0, 1), (1, 0), (1, 1))$ one gets at most two different subfunctions while there must be three different subfunctions under these assignments: $\text{MOD}_{3,0}^{n-2}$, $\text{MOD}_{3,1}^{n-2}$, and $\text{MOD}_{3,2}^{n-2}$ (they are pairwise different for $n \geq 4$). Assume that it is x that feeds at least one other gate and call it B. We then replace x by 0. This eliminates at least two gates from the circuit (A and B): if one of the inputs to a gate computes a constant then this gate computes either a constant or a unary function on the other input and hence can be eliminated from the circuit. The resulting circuit computes the function $\text{MOD}_{3,r}^{n-1}$ so the lower bound follows by induction. The best known lower bound for $\text{MOD}_{3,r}^n$ is $2.5n - \Theta(1)$ by Stockmeyer [20], the best known upper bound is $3n + \Theta(1)$ by Demenkov et al. [6]. Knuth [12, solution to exercise 480] recently conjectured that the circuit size of $\text{MOD}_{3,r}^n$ is equal to $3n - 5 - [(n + r) \mod 3 = 0]$.

In the analysis above, we eliminated two gates by assigning $x \leftarrow 0$. If A computes, say, $xy = x \wedge y$ then we would have eliminated more than two gates since A becomes equal to 0 and hence all its successors are also eliminated. So, the bottleneck case is when both A and B compute parities of their inputs. In this case we cannot make A and B constant just by assigning a constant to x.

1.2 A $3n - o(n)$ lower bound for affine dispersers for sublinear dimension

A natural idea that allows to overcome the bottleneck from the previous subsection is to allow to substitute variables not only by constants but also by sums (over $\mathbb{F}_2$) of other variables. Using this idea one can prove a $3n - o(n)$ lower bound. The proof is due to Demenkov and Kulikov [7], the exposition here is due to Vadhan and Williams [21].

A function we are going to prove a lower bound for is called an affine disperser. Informally, an affine disperser is a function that cannot be made constant by sufficiently many linear substitutions. Formally, a function $f \in B_n$ is called an affine disperser for dimension d if it is not constant on any affine subspace of $\mathbb{F}_2^n$ of dimension at least d.

The notion of dispersers is a relaxation of the notion of extractors — functions that take input from some specific distribution and output a bit that is distributed statistically close to uniform. Unlike extractors, dispersers are only required to output a non-constant bit. To specify the class of input distributions, one defines a class of sources $\mathcal{F}$, where each $X \in \mathcal{F}$ is a distribution over $\mathbb{F}_2^n$. Since dispersers are only required to output a non-constant bit, we identify a distribution X with its support on $\mathbb{F}_2^n$. A function $f \in B_n$ is called a disperser for a class of sources $\mathcal{F}$, if $|f(X)| = 2$ for every $X \in \mathcal{F}$. Since it is impossible to extract even one non-constant bit from an arbitrary source (even if the source has almost full entropy), many special cases of sources are studied (see [19] for an excellent survey). The sources we are focused on in this paper are affine sources and their generalization — sources for polynomial varieties. Affine dispersers have drawn much interest lately. In particular, explicit constructions of affine dispersers for dimension $d = o(n)$ have been constructed [1, 2, 14, 15, 18, 22]. Dispersers for polynomial varieties over large fields were studied by Dvir [8], and dispersers over $\mathbb{F}_2$ were studied by Cohen and Tal [5].

For a $3n - o(n)$ lower bound it is convenient to use xor-layered circuits. In an xor-layered circuit we allow linear sums of variables to be used as inputs to a circuit. Consider the following measure of an xor-layered circuit $\mathcal{C}$: $\mu(\mathcal{C}) = G(\mathcal{C}) + I(\mathcal{C})$ where $G(\mathcal{C})$ is the number of non-input gates and $I(\mathcal{C})$ is the number of inputs of $\mathcal{C}$. Note that a xor-gate that depends on two inputs of an xor-layered circuit $\mathcal{C}$ may be replaced by an input without increasing $\mu(\mathcal{C})$.

A $3n - 4d$ lower bound for an affine disperser $f \in B_n$ for dimension d follows from the following fact: for any affine subspace $S \subseteq \mathbb{F}_2^n$ of dimension D and any xor-layered circuit $\mathcal{C}$ computing f on S, $\mu(\mathcal{C}) \geq 4(D-d-1)$. This can be shown by induction on D. The base case $D \leq d+1$ is clear. For the induction step, assume that $\mathcal{C}$ has the minimal value of μ. Let A be a top gate fed by linear sums x and y (such a gate must exist since f on S cannot compute a linear function as $D > d + 1$). If A computes a sum of x and y then it can be replaced by an input (without increasing μ) so assume that A computes a product, i.e., $(x \oplus c_1)(y \oplus c_2) \oplus c$ where $c_1, c_2, c \in \mathbb{F}_2$ are constants. In the following we assign either

$x = c_1$ or $y = c_2$. This gives us an affine subspace of $\mathbb{F}_2^n$ of dimension at least $D - 1$ (if the dimension of the resulting subspace dropped to 0 this would mean that either x or y was constant on S contradicting to the fact that the considered circuit was optimal). To to proceed by induction we need to show that the substitution reduces μ by at least 4. For this, we consider two cases.

Case 1. Both x and y have out-degree 1.

We then assign $x = c_1$. This trivializes A to c, so all its successors are eliminated too. In total, we eliminate at least two gates (A and its successors) and at least two inputs (x and y). Hence μ is reduced by at least 4. (Note that A must have at least one successor as otherwise it would be an output gate, but this would mean that f was constant on an affine subspace of dimension at least d.)

Case 2. The out-degree of, say, x is at least 2.

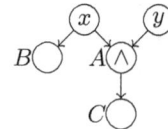

Let B be another successor of x and let C be a successor of A. We assign $x = c_1$. This removes an input x and gates A, B, and C. If $B = C$ then C becomes a constant under the substitution (since both its inputs are constants) so its successors are also eliminated. Thus, in this case we eliminate at least one input and at least three gates implying that μ is reduced by at least 4.

Plugging in an affine disperser for sublinear dimension in this argument gives a $3n - o(n)$ lower bound. It is also interesting to note that the inequality $G(\mathcal{C}) + I(\mathcal{C}) \geq 4(n-d-1)$ is tight. To see this, note that the inner product function is an affine disperser for dimension $n/2 + 1$ (see, e.g., [4, Theorem A.1]) and has circuit size $n - 1$.

1.3 Stronger lower bounds for dispersers for quadratic varieties

The two considered functions, MOD_3^n and an affine disperser, can be viewed as functions that are not constant on any sufficiently large set $S \subseteq \mathbb{F}_2^n$ that can be defined as the set of roots of k polynomials:

$$S = \{x \in \mathbb{F}_2^n : p_1(x) = p_2(x) = \cdots = p_k(x) = 0\}.$$

For MOD_3^n, $k \leq n - 4$ and each p_i is just a variable or its negation while for affine dispersers, $k \leq n - d$ and p_i's are arbitrary linear polynomials. Note that the size of the set S can be easily determined from the number of polynomials in this case:

$$|S| = 2^{n-k}. \tag{1}$$

A natural extension is to allow polynomials to have degree at most 2. The corresponding set S is called a quadratic variety. Formally, a function $f \in B_n$ is called an (n, k, s)-quadratic disperser if it is not constant on any variety of size at least s defined by at most k polynomials of degree at most 2. The main result of this paper is the following.

THEOREM 1. *Let $0 < \alpha \leq 1$ and $0 < \beta$ be constants satisfying*

$$2^{-\frac{2+\alpha}{\beta}} + 2^{-\frac{4+2\alpha}{\beta}} \leq 1, \tag{2}$$

$$2^{-\frac{2}{\beta}} + 2^{-\frac{5+2\alpha}{\beta}} \leq 1, \tag{3}$$

$$2^{-\frac{3+3\alpha}{\beta}} + 2^{-\frac{2+2\alpha}{\beta}} \leq 1, \tag{4}$$

$$2^{-\frac{3}{\beta}} + 2^{-\frac{4+\alpha}{\beta}} \leq 1, \tag{5}$$

and let $f \in B_{n,1}$ be an (n, k, s)-quadratic disperser. Then

$$\mathcal{C}(f) \geq \min\left\{\beta n - \beta \log_2 s - \beta, 2k\right\} - \alpha n.$$

For example, for an $(n, 1.83n, 2^{o(n)})$-quadratic disperser Theorem 1 with $\alpha = 0.535$ and $\beta = 3.6513$ implies a $3.1163n - o(n) > 3.116n$ lower bound. For an $(n, 1.78n, 2^{0.03n})$-quadratic disperser it implies a $3.006n$ lower bound.

Currently, explicit constructions of quadratic dispersers with such parameters are not known while showing their existence non-constructively is easy (see Lemma 1). Theorem 1 can be viewed as an additional motivation for their study.

Cohen and Tal [5] prove that any affine disperser (extractor) is also a disperser (extractor) for polynomial varieties with slightly weaker parameters. In particular, their result, combined with the affine disperser by Shaltiel [18], gives an explicit construction of an $\left(n, \Theta\left(\frac{n}{2^{\log^{0.9} n}}\right), 2^{o(n)}\right)$-quadratic disperser. Two explicit constructions of extractors for varieties over large fields are given by Dvir [8]. For a similar, although different, notion of polynomial sources, explicit constructions of dispersers (extractors) are given by Dvir, Gabizon, Wigderson [9] for large fields, and by Ben-Sasson and Gabizon [1] for constant-size fields.

1.4 Weighted gate elimination

We prove Theorem 1 by extending the gate elimination method. The proof goes by induction on the size of the current quadratic variety S. Note that for quadratic varieties the relation (1) no longer holds: e.g., the set of roots of $n/2$ polynomials $x_1x_2 \oplus 1$, $x_3x_4 \oplus 1$, ..., $x_{n-1}x_n \oplus 1$ contains just one point. For this reason, we proceed as follows. We choose a polynomial p of degree 2 and consider two subvarieties of S: $S_0 = \{x \in S : p(x) = 0\}$ and $S_1 = \{x \in S : p(x) = 1\}$. We then estimate how much the size of the circuit shrinks for each of these varieties and how much the size of the variety shrinks. Roughly, we show that in at least one of these cases the circuit shrinks a lot while the size of the variety does not shrink a lot. That is why we call this method weighted gate elimination.

2. DEFINITIONS

2.1 Circuits

A circuit is a directed acyclic graph with all nodes having in-degree 0 or 2. Nodes of in-degree 0 are labeled with input variables and are called inputs or input gates. Nodes of

in-degree 2 are labeled with binary Boolean functions and are called gates or non-input gates. Some m gates are also marked as outputs. Then such a circuit computes a function from $B_{n,m}$ in a natural way.

For a circuit $\mathcal{C}$, $G(\mathcal{C})$ is the number of non-input gates and is also called the size of the circuit $\mathcal{C}$. By $I(\mathcal{C})$ we denote the number of input gates. For a function $f \in B_{n,m}$, $\mathcal{C}(f)$ is the minimum size of a circuit with n inputs and m outputs that computes f. For a gate A, by $\operatorname{outdeg}(A)$ we denote the out-degree of A.

The 16 binary functions $b(x, y)$ from $B_{2,1}$ are usually classified as follows:

- 2 constant functions: 0, 1;

- 4 degenerate functions: x, $x \oplus 1$, y, $y \oplus 1$;

- 2 xor-type functions: $x \oplus y$, $x \oplus y \oplus 1$;

- 8 and-type functions: $(x \oplus a)(y \oplus b) \oplus c$ where $a, b, c \in \mathbb{F}_2$.

It is not difficult to see that gates computing constant and degenerate functions can be removed from a circuit. Hence an optimal circuit consists of gates computing xor-type functions and and-type functions. We call them xor-gates and and-gates, respectively.

During the gate elimination process, we will make substitutions that make some gates constant. Assume that a gate A becomes constant (in this case, we also say that A is trivialized). Let B be a successor of A (that is, there is a directed edge from A to B), C be the other input of B, D be a successor of B, and E be the other input of D. Since A is now constant, B computes either a constant or a unary function on C so B can be eliminated. This may require also to change the binary function computed at D (that is, negating one of the inputs).

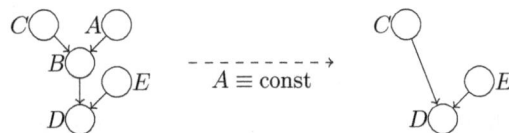

We will also use the following observation. Assume that C is fed by A and B while B is fed by A and D. Then C computes a binary function on A and D. This can be computed directly, without using B so one can rebuild the circuit as shown below. If B has out-degree 1 it can be eliminated from the circuit.

By an xor-layered circuit we mean a circuit whose inputs may be labeled not only by input variables but also by sums of variables. One can get an xor-layered circuit from a regular circuit by replacing xor-gates that depend on two inputs by an input.

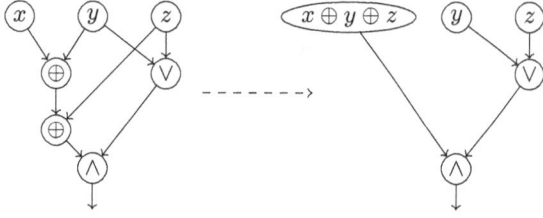

2.2 Quadratic dispersers

DEFINITION 1 (QUADRATIC VARIETY). *A set $S \subseteq \mathbb{F}_2^n$ is called an (n,k)-quadratic variety if it can be defined as the set of common roots of $t \leq k$ polynomials of degree at most 2:*

$$S = \{x \in \mathbb{F}_2^n : p_1(x) = \cdots = p_t(x) = 0\}$$

where p_i is a polynomial of degree at most 2, for each $1 \leq i \leq t$.

DEFINITION 2 (QUADRATIC DISPERSER). *A Boolean function $f \in B_n$ is called an (n,k,s)-quadratic disperser if f is non-constant on any (n,k)-quadratic variety $S \subseteq \mathbb{F}_2^n$ of size at least s.*

The following lemma shows that almost all functions from B_n are $(n, 2^{o(n)}, 2^{o(n)})$-quadratic dispersers.

LEMMA 1. *Let $\omega(1) \leq s \leq 2^{o(n)}$, $k = o\left(\frac{s}{n^2}\right)$. Let $D_n \in B_{n,1}$ be the set of (n,k,s)-quadratic dispersers. Then $\frac{|D_n|}{|B_n|} \to 1$ when $n \to \infty$.*

PROOF. There are $q = \frac{n(n+1)}{2} + 1 = \Theta(n^2)$ monomials of degree at most 2 in $\mathbb{F}_2^n$. Therefore, there are 2^q polynomials of degree at most 2, and at most 2^{qk} (n,k)-quadratic varieties. Each function that is not an (n,k,s)-quadratic disperser can be specified by

1. an (n,k)-quadratic variety, where it takes a constant value,

2. one of two possible constant values that it takes on that variety,

3. values at the remaining at most $2^n - s$ points.

Thus, the number of functions that are not (n,k,s)-quadratic dispersers is bounded from above by

$$2^{qk} \cdot 2 \cdot 2^{2^n - s} = 2^{2^n} 2^{qk+1-s} = 2^{2^n} 2^{-\Theta(s)} = o\left(|B_n|\right).$$

□

3. LOWER BOUND

We will use the following technical lemma.

LEMMA 2. *Let $0 < \alpha \leq 1$ and $0 < \beta$ be constants satisfying inequalities* (5), (2):

$$2^{-\frac{3}{\beta}} + 2^{-\frac{4+\alpha}{\beta}} \leq 1,$$
$$2^{-\frac{2+\alpha}{\beta}} + 2^{-\frac{4+2\alpha}{\beta}} \leq 1.$$

Then

$$2^{-\frac{4}{\beta}} + 2^{-\frac{4}{\beta}} \leq 1, \tag{6}$$
$$2^{-\frac{3+\alpha}{\beta}} + 2^{-\frac{3+2\alpha}{\beta}} \leq 1. \tag{7}$$

PROOF. Since $2 \leq x + \frac{1}{x}$ for positive x,

$$2^{-\frac{4}{\beta}} + 2^{-\frac{4}{\beta}} \leq 2^{-\frac{4}{\beta}} (2^{\frac{1}{\beta}} + 2^{-\frac{1}{\beta}}) =$$
$$2^{-\frac{3}{\beta}} + 2^{-\frac{5}{\beta}} \leq 2^{-\frac{3}{\beta}} + 2^{-\frac{4+\alpha}{\beta}} \leq 1.$$

In order to prove the inequality (7), we use Heinz's inequality [11]:

$$\frac{x^{1-t} y^t + x^t y^{1-t}}{2} \leq \frac{x+y}{2} \text{ for } x, y > 0, 0 \leq t \leq 1.$$

Let us take $x = 2^{-\frac{2+\alpha}{\beta}}, y = 2^{-\frac{4+2\alpha}{\beta}}, t = \frac{1}{2+\alpha}$:

$$2^{-\frac{3+\alpha}{\beta}} + 2^{-\frac{3+2\alpha}{\beta}} = x^{1-t} y^t + x^t y^{1-t} \leq$$
$$x + y = 2^{-\frac{2+\alpha}{\beta}} + 2^{-\frac{4+2\alpha}{\beta}} \leq 1.$$

□

In the following lemma, we use the following circuit complexity measure: $\mu(\mathcal{C}) = G(\mathcal{C}) + \alpha \cdot I(\mathcal{C})$ where $0 < \alpha \leq 1$ is a constant to be determined later. Theorem 1 follows from the lemma with $S = \mathbb{F}_2^n$ which is an $(n,0)$-quadratic variety.

LEMMA 3. *Let $f \in B_n$ be an (n,k,s)-quadratic disperser, $S \subseteq \mathbb{F}_2^n$ be an (n,t)-quadratic variety, $0 < \alpha \leq 1, 0 < \beta$ be constants satisfying inequalities* (2), (3), (4), (5), $\mathcal{C}$ *be an xor-layered circuit that computes f on S. Then*

$$\mu(\mathcal{C}) \geq \min \{\beta(\log_2 |S| - \log_2 s - 1), 2(k-t)\}.$$

PROOF. The proof goes by induction on $|S|$. The base case $|S| \leq 2s$ is trivially true. For the induction step, assume that $|S| > 2s$.

To prove the induction step we proceed as follows. If $t \geq k$ then the right-hand side is non-positive, so assume that $t < k$. Assume that $\mathcal{C}$ is optimal with respect to μ (that is, $\mathcal{C}$ has the minimal value of μ among all circuits computing f on S). We find a gate G in $\mathcal{C}$ that computes a function g of degree at most 2 and consider two $(n, t+1)$-quadratic varieties of S: $S_0 = \{x \in S : g(x) = 0\}$ and $S_0 = \{x \in S : g(x) = 1\}$. Let $|S_0| = p_0|S|$ and $|S_1| = p_1|S|$ where $0 < p_0, p_1 < 1$ and $p_0 + p_1 = 1$ (note that $p_i = 0$ or $p_i = 1$ would mean that G computes a constant on S contradicting to the fact that $\mathcal{C}$ is optimal). By eliminating from the circuit $\mathcal{C}$ all the gates that are either constant or depend on just one of its inputs on S_i, one gets a circuit $\mathcal{C}_i$ that computes f on S_i. Assume that $\mu(\mathcal{C}) - \mu(\mathcal{C}_i) \geq \Delta_i$. Then, by the induction hypothesis,

$$\mu(C) \geq \mu(C_i) + \Delta_i \geq$$
$$\min \{\beta(\log_2 |S_i| - \log_2 s - 1), 2(k - (t+1))\} + \Delta_i =$$
$$\min \left\{ \beta(\log_2 |S| - \log_2 s - 1) + \left(\Delta_i - \beta \log_2 \frac{1}{p_i}\right), \right.$$
$$\left. 2(k-t) + (\Delta_i - 2) \right\}.$$

Hence, if $\Delta_i \geq \beta \log_2 1/p_i$ and $\Delta_i \geq 2$ for either $i = 0$ or $i = 1$ then the required inequality follows by the induction hypothesis. The inequality $\Delta_i \geq \beta \log_2 1/p_i$ is true whenever $p_i \geq 2^{-\frac{\Delta_i}{\beta}}$. Since we want this inequality to hold for at least one of $i = 0$ and $i = 1$ and since $p_0 + p_1 = 1$ we conclude that for the induction step to go through it suffices to have

$$2^{-\frac{\Delta_0}{\beta}} + 2^{-\frac{\Delta_1}{\beta}} \leq 1 \text{ and } \Delta_0, \Delta_1 \geq 2. \tag{8}$$

408

By going through a few cases we show that we can always find a gate G such that the corresponding Δ_0 and Δ_1 satisfy the inequalities (8). For this, we use the inequalities (2)–(7).

We start by showing that the circuit $\mathcal{C}$ must be non-empty. Indeed, if $\mathcal{C}$ is empty then it computes a linear function l. Hence f is constant on both $S_0 = \{x \in S : l(x) = 0\}$ and $S_1 = \{x \in S : l(x) = 1\}$. However $\max\{|S_0|, |S_1|\} \geq |S|/2 > s$ which contradicts to the fact that f is an (n, k, s)-quadratic disperser.

Let A be an and-gate with the maximal number of and-gates on a way to the output of $\mathcal{C}$. That is, for each and-gate we consider all directed paths from this gate to the output gate and select a path with the maximal number of and-gates on it; then we choose an and-gate for which this number is maximal over all and-gates. Since $\mathcal{C}$ is an xor-layered circuit, we may assume that A is a top-gate, that is, it is fed by inputs. Denote by x and y the input-gates that feed A.

Case 1. $\mathrm{outdeg}(x) = \mathrm{outdeg}(y) = 1$.

Case 1.1. $\mathrm{outdeg}(A) = 1$ and A feeds an and-gate B. Let C be the other input of B (it might be an input as well as non-input gate).

Case 1.1.1. $\mathrm{outdeg}(C) = 1$.

We make A constant. Then the gate B is eliminated. Moreover, either $A = 0$ or $A = 1$ trivializes the gate B so all its successors and the gate C are also eliminated (since C is only used to compute B, but B now computes a constant). In both cases x and y are not needed anymore (as the only gate A that was fed by both these inputs is now constant). So, we get $\{\Delta_0, \Delta_1\} = \{2 + 2\alpha, 3 + 3\alpha\}$. The required inequalities (8) follows from (4).

Case 1.1.2. $\mathrm{outdeg}(C) \geq 2$.

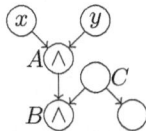

Because of the choice of A, C computes a function of degree at most 2. We make C constant. In both cases we eliminate two successors of C and C itself. This reduces the measure by at least $2 + \alpha$. In one of the cases B is trivialized which causes the removal of the successors of B, the gate A, and inputs x and y. Hence we get $\{\Delta_0, \Delta_1\} = \{2+\alpha, 4+3\alpha\}$ in this case. These Δ_0, Δ_1 satisfy the inequalities (8) because of (2).

Case 1.2. $\mathrm{outdeg}(A) = 1$ and A feeds an xor-gate B.

Since A was chosen as an and-gate with the maximal number of and-gates to the output, the other input of B computes a function of degree at most 2. Hence B itself computes a function of degree at most 2. We make B constant. This eliminates B and its successors. The gate A and its inputs x and y are also not needed. Hence $\Delta_0 = \Delta_1 = 3 + 2\alpha$. The inequalities (8) are satisfied due to (7).

Case 1.3. $\mathrm{outdeg}(A) \geq 2$.

Just by making the gate A constant we get $\Delta_0 = \Delta_1 = 3 + 2\alpha$ since A and all its successors (at least two gates) are eliminated. Similarly to the previous case, the inequality (7) imply that (8) holds.

Case 2. Out-degree of either x or y is at least 2. Say, $\mathrm{outdeg}(x) \geq 2$.

Case 2.1. $\mathrm{outdeg}(A) = 1$ and A feeds an and-gate B. We make A constant. Assume that A computes $(x \oplus c_1)(y \oplus c_2) \oplus c$. Then A can only be equal to $c \oplus 1$ if $x = c_1 \oplus 1$ and $y = c_2 \oplus 1$. That is, when A is equal to $c \oplus 1$ not only its successor is eliminated but also all successors of x and y. In both cases the gate B is eliminated, but in one of them it is trivialized and so all its successors are also eliminated.

Denote by C another gate fed by x. Note that $B \neq C$ (otherwise the circuit would not be optimal).

Case 2.1.1. $\mathrm{outdeg}(y) = 1$.

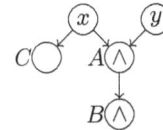

Case 2.1.1.1. B is trivialized when $A = c$. If $A = c$ we eliminate A, B, the successors of B, and y. If $A = c \oplus 1$ we eliminate A, B, C, x, and y. Hence $\{\Delta_0, \Delta_1\} = \{3 + \alpha, 3 + 2\alpha\}$. The inequality (7) guarantees that (8) holds.

Case 2.1.1.2. B is trivialized when $A = c \oplus 1$. If $A = c$ we eliminate A, B, and y. If $A = c \oplus 1$ we eliminate A, B, C, the successors of B, x, and y (if C happens to be the only successor of B then it becomes constant and all its successors are eliminated). Hence $\{\Delta_0, \Delta_1\} = \{2+\alpha, 4+2\alpha\}$. The inequalities (8) are satisfied because of (2).

Case 2.1.2. $\mathrm{outdeg}(y) \geq 2$. Denote by D another successor of y. Note that D might be equal to C, but $D \neq B$.

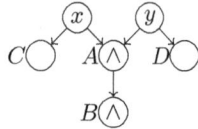

Case 2.1.2.1. B is trivialized when $A = c$. If $A = c$ we eliminate A, B, and the successors of B. If $A = c \oplus 1$ we eliminate A, B, C, D, x, and y. If $C = D$ then this gate becomes constant so all its successors are also eliminated. Hence $\{\Delta_0, \Delta_1\} = \{3, 4 + 2\alpha\}$. The inequalities (8) are satisfied because (5).

Case 2.1.2.2. B is trivialized when $A = c \oplus 1$.

If $A = c$ we eliminate A and B. If $A = c \oplus 1$ we eliminate A, B, C, D, the successors of B, x, and y. In this case we need to take additional care to show that we eliminate five gates even if some of the mentioned five gates coincide. If $C \neq D$ and, say, C is a successor of B then C becomes constant so all its successors are eliminated too. If $C = D$ then C becomes constant so all its successors are eliminated. Hence $\{\Delta_0, \Delta_1\} = \{2, 5 + 2\alpha\}$. The inequality (3) ensures (8).

Case 2.2. $\mathrm{outdeg}(A) = 1$ and A feeds an xor-gate B.

Case 2.2.1. $\mathrm{outdeg}(B) = 1$ and B feeds an xor-gate C.

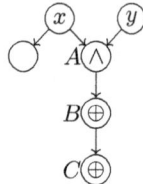

Because of the choice of A, we know that the gate C computes a quadratic function. We make C constant. In both cases we eliminate A, B, C, and the successors of C. Hence $\Delta_0 = \Delta_1 = 4$. The inequalities (8) are satisfied because of (6).

Case 2.2.2. $\mathrm{outdeg}(B) = 1$ and B feeds an and-gate C.

Let D be the other input of C. Note that if $D = A$ then the circuit is not optimal (C depends on A and the other input of B so one can compute C directly without using B).

Case 2.2.2.1. $\mathrm{outdeg}(D) = 1$.

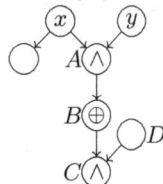

We make B constant. In both cases we eliminate A, B, and C. Moreover, when B is the constant trivializing C we eliminate also D and the successors of C. The gate D contributes (to the complexity decrease) $\alpha \leq 1$ if it is an input gate and

1 if it is not an input. Hence we have $\{\Delta_0, \Delta_1\} = \{3, 4 + \alpha\}$. The inequality (5) guarantees that (8) is satisfied.

Case 2.2.2.2. $\mathrm{outdeg}(D) \geq 2$.

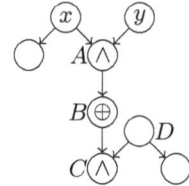

We make D constant (we are allowed to do so because it computes a function of degree at most 2). In both cases we eliminate D and its successors and reduce the measure by at least $2 + \alpha$ (as D might be an input). In the case when C becomes constant we eliminate also the successors of C as well as A and B. Thus, $\{\Delta_0, \Delta_1\} = \{2 + \alpha, 5 + \alpha\}$ (to ensure that all the five gates eliminated in the second case are different one notes that if D feeds B or a successor of C then the circuit is not optimal). The inequalities (8) are satisfied because (2) and $\alpha \leq 1$.

Case 2.2.3. $\mathrm{outdeg}(B) \geq 2$.

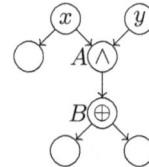

The gate B computes a function of degree at most 2. By making it constant we eliminate B, its successors, and A, so $\Delta_0 = \Delta_1 = 4$. The inequalities (8) are satisfied because of (6).

Case 2.3. $\mathrm{outdeg}(A) \geq 2$.

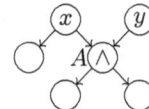

We make A constant. In both cases A and its successors are eliminated. When x and y become constant too (recall that if A computes $(x \oplus c_1)(y \oplus c_2) \oplus c$ then $A = c \oplus 1$ implies that $x = c_1 \oplus 1$ and $y = c_2 \oplus 1$) at least one other successor of x is also eliminated. Thus, $\{\Delta_0, \Delta_1\} = \{3, 4 + 2\alpha\}$. The inequality (5) implies that (8) is satisfied.

$\square$

4. LOWER BOUNDS FOR MULTI-OUTPUT FUNCTIONS

Note that $3.011n + o(n)$ is also the currently strongest lower bound even for functions from $B_{n,o(n)}$ (that is, functions with $o(n)$ outputs). Strongest known lower bounds for multi-output functions from $B_{n,m}$ follow from the following lemma by Lamagne and Savage [13]. It can be read as follows: if instead of one function one needs to compute m functions then at least $m - 1$ additional gates are needed.

LEMMA 4. *Let $f = (f_1, \ldots, f_m) \in B_{n,m}$ such that $f_i \not\equiv f_j$ and $f_i \not\equiv f_j \oplus 1$ for all $1 \leq i \neq j \leq m$. Then*

$$\mathcal{C}(f) \geq \min_{1 \leq i \leq m} \mathcal{C}(f_i) + (m-1).$$

PROOF PROOF SKETCH. Fix a topological ordering of the gates of a circuit and consider the first $\min_{1 \leq i \leq m} \mathcal{C}(f_i) - 1$ gates in this ordering. None of them can compute any of m output functions. Since all the output functions are different, at least m additional gates are needed to compute all of them. $\square$

Thus, it would be interesting to give an explicit construction of a quadratic disperser with good parameters (implying a stronger than $3.011n$ lower bound on circuit complexity) with $o(n)$ outputs. Note that almost all known explicit constructions of dispersers are actually multi-output functions $f \in B_{n,m}$ that output $(1-\varepsilon) \cdot 2^m$ different values on each source. For our purposes, it is enough for a disperser to have at least 2 different values (that is, to be non-constant). Such a disperser is a weaker object than even a single-output disperser, so it might be easier to construct it. For example such a relaxation helps to construct a disperser for polynomial sources (a similar, but still different from polynomial varieties, notion of sources) over smaller fields [1].

5. OPEN PROBLEMS

One can slightly improve the lower bound for quadratics dispersers by a more involved case analysis. Dispersers for varieties of degree 3 allow to get even stronger lower bounds. At the same time we do not see how the presented techniques might lead to, say, a lower bound of $4n$.

The most natural question left open by this study is: to find an explicit construction of an $(n, 1.78n, 2^{0.03n})$-quadratic disperser either with $o(n)$ outputs or with one output. Note that such a construction would automatically imply a new circuit lower bound. It would also be interesting to find explicit constructions of dispersers for polynomial varieties of higher degrees, as well as their applications to circuit lower bounds.

Acknowledgements

The research is partially supported by National Science Foundation under Grant 1319051 and the Government of the Russian Federation under Grant 14.Z50.31.0030.

6. REFERENCES

[1] Eli Ben-Sasson and Ariel Gabizon. Extractors for polynomials sources over constant-size fields of small characteristic. In *Approximation, Randomization, and Combinatorial Optimization. Algorithms and Techniques*, pages 399–410. Springer, 2012.

[2] Eli Ben-Sasson and Swastik Kopparty. Affine dispersers from subspace polynomials. In *Proceedings of the Annual Symposium on Theory of Computing (STOC)*, volume 679, pages 65–74. ACM Press, 2009.

[3] Norbert Blum. A Boolean function requiring $3n$ network size. *Theoretical Computer Science*, 28:337–345, 1984.

[4] Gil Cohen and Igor Shinkar. The complexity of DNF of parities. Technical Report 99, Electronic Colloquium on Computational Complexity, 2014.

[5] Gil Cohen and Avishay Tal. Two structural results for low degree polynomials and applications. *arXiv preprint arXiv:1404.0654*, 2014.

[6] Evgeny Demenkov, Arist Kojevnikov, Alexander S. Kulikov, and Grigory Yaroslavtsev. New upper bounds on the Boolean circuit complexity of symmetric functions. *Information Processing Letters*, 110(7):264–267, 2010.

[7] Evgeny Demenkov and Alexander S. Kulikov. An elementary proof of a $3n - o(n)$ lower bound on the circuit complexity of affine dispersers. In *Proceedings of 36th International Symposium on Mathematical Foundations of Computer Science (MFCS)*, volume 6907 of *Lecture Notes in Computer Science*, pages 256–265. Springer, 2011.

[8] Zeev Dvir. Extractors for varieties. *Computational complexity*, 21(4):515–572, 2012.

[9] Zeev Dvir, Ariel Gabizon, and Avi Wigderson. Extractors and rank extractors for polynomial sources. *Computational Complexity*, 18(1):1–58, 2009.

[10] Magnus Gausdal Find, Alexander Golovnev, Edward A. Hirsch, and Alexander S. Kulikov. A better-than-$3n$ lower bound for the circuit complexity of an explicit function. *Electronic Colloquium on Computational Complexity (ECCC)*, 22:166, 2015.

[11] Erhard Heinz. Beiträge zur störungstheorie der spektralzerleung. *Mathematische Annalen*, 123(1):415–438, 1951.

[12] Donald E. Knuth. *The Art of Computer Programming*, volume 4, pre-fascicle 6a. Addison–Wesley, 2015. Section 7.2.2.2. Satisfiability. Draft available at http://www-cs-faculty.stanford.edu/~uno/fasc6a.ps.gz.

[13] Edward A. Lamagna and John E. Savage. On the logical complexity of symmetric switching functions in monotone and complete bases. Technical report, Brown University, 1973.

[14] Xin Li. A new approach to affine extractors and dispersers. In *Proceedings of 26th Annual Conference on Computational Complexity (CCC)*, pages 137–147. IEEE, 2011.

[15] Xin Li. Extractors for affine sources with polylogarithmic entropy. *Electronic Colloquium on Computational Complexity (ECCC)*, 22:121, 2015.

[16] David E. Muller. Complexity in electronic switching circuits. *IRE Transactions on Electronic Computers*, EC-5:15–19, 1956.

[17] Claus-Peter Schnorr. Zwei lineare untere Schranken für die Komplexität Boolescher Funktionen. *Computing*, 13:155–171, 1974.

[18] Ronen Shaltiel. Dispersers for affine sources with sub-polynomial entropy. In *Proceedings of 52nd Annual Symposium on Foundations of Computer Science (FOCS)*, pages 247–256. IEEE, 2011.

[19] Ronen Shaltiel. An introduction to randomness extractors. In *Proceedings of 38th International Colloquium on Automata, Languages and Programming (ICALP)*, volume 6756 of *Lecture Notes in Computer Science*, pages 21–41. Springer, 2011.

[20] Larry J. Stockmeyer. On the combinational complexity of certain symmetric Boolean functions. *Mathematical Systems Theory*, 10:323–336, 1977.

[21] Salil Vadhan and Ryan Williams. Personal communication, 2013.

[22] Amir Yehudayoff. Affine extractors over prime fields. *Combinatorica*, 31(2):245–256, 2011.

Author Index

www.ingramcontent.com/pod-product-compliance
Lightning Source LLC
Chambersburg PA
CBHW080650220326

41598CB00033B/5158

* 9 7 8 1 4 5 0 3 4 4 1 5 9 *